P9-BHT-426

FOR REFERENCE

Do Not Take From This Room

Contemporary
Literary Criticism

Guide to Gale Literary Criticism Series

For criticism on	Consult these Gale series
Authors now living or who died after December 31, 1959	*CONTEMPORARY LITERARY CRITICISM (CLC)*
Authors who died between 1900 and 1959	*TWENTIETH-CENTURY LITERARY CRITICISM (TCLC)*
Authors who died between 1800 and 1899	*NINETEENTH-CENTURY LITERATURE CRITICISM (NCLC)*
Authors who died between 1400 and 1799	*LITERATURE CRITICISM FROM 1400 TO 1800 (LC) SHAKESPEAREAN CRITICISM (SC)*
Authors who died before 1400	*CLASSICAL AND MEDIEVAL LITERATURE CRITICISM (CMLC)*
Black writers of the past two hundred years	*BLACK LITERATURE CRITICISM (BLC) AND BLACK LITERATURE CRITICISM SUPPLEMENT (BLCS)*
Authors of books for children and young adults	*CHILDREN'S LITERATURE REVIEW (CLR)*
Dramatists	*DRAMA CRITICISM (DC)*
Hispanic writers of the late nineteenth and twentieth centuries	*HISPANIC LITERATURE CRITICISM (HLC)*
Native North American writers and orators of the eighteenth, nineteenth, and twentieth centuries	*NATIVE NORTH AMERICAN LITERATURE (NNAL)*
Poets	*POETRY CRITICISM (PC)*
Short story writers	*SHORT STORY CRITICISM (SSC)*
Major authors from the Renaissance to the present	*WORLD LITERATURE CRITICISM, 1500 TO THE PRESENT (WLC)*
Major authors and works from the Bible to the present	*WORLD LITERATURE CRITICISM SUPPLEMENT (WLCS)*

ISSN 0091-3421

Volume 126

Contemporary Literary Criticism

Criticism of the Works
of Today's Novelists, Poets, Playwrights,
Short Story Writers, Scriptwriters, and
Other Creative Writers

Jeffrey W. Hunter
EDITOR

Jennie Cromie
ASSOCIATE EDITOR

Rebecca J. Blanchard
Vince Cousino
Justin Karr
Linda Pavlovski
ASSISTANT EDITORS

Detroit
New York
San Francisco
London
Boston
Woodbridge, CT

Riverside Community College
Library
4800 Magnolia Avenue
Riverside, CA 92506

REFERENCE
PN771 .C59
Contemporary literary
criticism.

STAFF

Jeffrey W. Hunter, *Editor*

y Cromie, Timothy J. White, *Associate Editors*
Rebecca J. Blanchard, Vince Cousino, Justin Karr, and Linda Pavlovski, *Assistant Editors*

Maria Franklin, *Permissions Manager*
Kimberly F. Smilay, *Permissions Specialist*
Kelly Quin, *Permissions Associate*
Erin Bealmear and Sandy Gore, *Permissions Assistants*

Victoria B. Cariappa, *Research Manager*
Corrine Boland, Wendy Festerling, Tamara Nott, Tracie A. Richardson, *Research Associates*
Tim Lehnerer, Patricia Love, *Research Assistants*

Mary Beth Trimper, *Production Director*
Cindy Range, *Production Assistants*

Barbara J. Yarrow, *Graphic Services Manager*
Sherrell Hobbs, *Macintosh Artist*
Randy Bassett, *Image Database Supervisor*
Robert Duncan and Mikal Ansari, *Scanner Operators*
Pamela Reed, *Imaging Coordinator*

Since this page cannot legibly accommodate all copyright notices, the acknowledgments constitute an extension of the copyright notice.

While every effort has been made to ensure the reliability of the information presented in this publication, Gale Reasearch neither guarantees the accuracy of the data contained herein nor assumes any responsibility for errors, omissions or discrepancies. Gale accepts no payment for listing, and inclusion in the publication of any organization, agency, instituition, publication, service, or individual does not imply endorsement of the editors or publisher. Errors brought to the attention of the publisher and verified to the satisfaction of the publisher will be corrected in future editions.

The paper used in this publication meets the minimum requirements of American National Standard for Information Sciences—Permanence Paper for Printed Library Materials, ANSI Z39.48-1984.

This publication is a creative work fully protected by all applicable copyright laws, as well as by misappropriation, trade secret, unfair competition, and other applicable laws. The authors and editors of this work have added value to the underlying factual material herein through one or more of the following: unique and original selection, coordination, expression, arrangement, and classification of the information.

All rights to this publication will be vigorously defended.

Copyright ©2000
The Gale Group
27500 Drake Rd.
Farmington Hills, MI 48331-3535

All rights reserved including the right of reproduction in whole or in part in any form.

Library of Congress Catalog Card Number 76-46132
ISBN 0-7876-3201-5
ISSN 0091-3421

Printed in the United States of America
10 9 8 7 6 5 4 3 2 1

Riverside Community College
Library
4800 Magnolia Avenue
Riverside, CA 92506

Contents

Preface vii

Acknowledgments xi

Preface

A Comprehensive Information Source
on Contemporary Literature

Named "one of the twenty-five most distinguished reference titles published during the past twenty-five years" by *Reference Quarterly,* the *Contemporary Literary Criticism (CLC)* series provides readers with critical commentary and general information on more than 2,000 authors now living or who died after December 31, 1959. Previous to the publication of the first volume of *CLC* in 1973, there was no ongoing digest monitoring scholarly and popular sources of critical opinion and explication of modern literature. *CLC,* therefore, has fulfilled an essential need, particularly since the complexity and variety of contemporary literature makes the function of criticism especially important to today's reader.

Scope of the Series

CLC presents significant passages from published criticism of works by creative writers. Since many of the authors covered by *CLC* inspire continual critical commentary, writers are often represented in more than one volume. There is, of course, no duplication of reprinted criticism.

Authors are selected for inclusion for a variety of reasons, among them the publication or dramatic production of a critically acclaimed new work, the reception of a major literary award, revival of interest in past writings, or the adaptation of a literary work to film or television.

Attention is also given to several other groups of writers—authors of considerable public interest—about whose work criticism is often difficult to locate. These include mystery and science fiction writers, literary and social critics, foreign writers, and authors who represent particular ethnic groups.

Format of the Book

Each *CLC* volume contains individual essays and reviews taken from hundreds of book review periodicals, general magazines, scholarly journals, monographs, and books. Entries include critical evaluations spanning from the beginning of an author's career to the most current commentary. Interviews, feature articles, and other published writings that offer insight into the author's works are also presented. Students, teachers, librarians, and researchers will find that the generous critical and biographical material in *CLC* provides them with vital information required to write a term paper, analyze a poem, or lead a book discussion group. In addition, complete bibliographical citations note the original source and all of the information necessary for a term paper footnote or bibliography.

Features

A *CLC* author entry consists of the following elements:

■ The **Author Heading** cites the author's name in the form under which the author has most commonly published, followed by birth date, and death date when applicable. Uncertainty as to a birth or death date is indicated by a question mark.

- A **Portrait** of the author is included when available.

- A brief **Biographical and Critical Introduction** to the author and his or her work precedes the criticism. The first line of the introduction provides the author's full name, pseudonyms (if applicable), nationality, and a listing of genres in which the author has written. To provide users with easier access to information, the biographical and critical essay included in each author entry is divided into four categories: "Introduction," "Biographical Information," "Major Works," and "Critical Reception." The introductions to single-work entries—entries that focus on well known and frequently studied books, short stories, and poems—are similarly organized to quickly provide readers with information on the plot and major characters of the work being discussed, its major themes, and its critical reception. Previous volumes of *CLC* in which the author has been featured are also listed in the introduction.

- A list of **Principal Works** notes the most important writings by the author. When foreign-language works have been translated into English, the English-language version of the title follows in brackets.

- The **Criticism** represents various kinds of critical writing, ranging in form from the brief review to the scholarly exegesis. Essays are selected by the editors to reflect the spectrum of opinion about a specific work or about an author's literary career in general. The critical and biographical materials are presented chronologically, adding a useful perspective to the entry. All titles by the author featured in the entry are printed in boldface type, which enables the reader to easily identify the works being discussed. Publication information (such as publisher names and book prices) and parenthetical numerical references (such as footnotes or page and line references to specific editions of a work) have been deleted at the editor's discretion to provide smoother reading of the text.

- Critical essays are prefaced by **Explanatory Notes** as an additional aid to readers. These notes may provide several types of valuable information, including: the reputation of the critic, the importance of the work of criticism, the commentator's approach to the author's work, the purpose of the criticism, and changes in critical trends regarding the author.

- A complete **Bibliographical Citation** designed to help the user find the original essay or book precedes each critical piece.

- Whenever possible, a recent **Author Interview** accompanies each entry.

- A concise **Further Reading** section appears at the end of entries on authors for whom a significant amount of criticism exists in addition to the pieces reprinted in *CLC*. Each citation in this section is accompanied by a descriptive annotation describing the content of that article. Materials included in this section are grouped under various headings (e.g., Biography, Bibliography, Criticism, and Interviews) to aid users in their search for additional information. Cross-references to other useful sources published by The Gale Group in which the author has appeared are also included: *Authors in the News, Black Writers, Children's Literature Review, Contemporary Authors, Dictionary of Literary Biography, DISCovering Authors, Drama Criticism, Hispanic Literature Criticism, Hispanic Writers, Native North American Literature, Poetry Criticism, Something about the Author, Short Story Criticism, Contemporary Authors Autobiography Series,* and *Something about the Author Autobiography Series.*

Other Features

CLC also includes the following features:

- An **Acknowledgments** section lists the copyright holders who have granted permission to reprint material in this volume of *CLC*. It does not, however, list every book or periodical reprinted or consulted during the preparation of the volume.

- Each new volume of *CLC* includes a **Cumulative Topic Index,** which lists all literary topics treated in *CLC, NCLC, TCLC,* and *LC 1400-1800.*

- A **Cumulative Author Index** lists all the authors who have appeared in the various literary criticism series published by The Gale Group, with cross-references to Gale's biographical and autobiographical series. A full listing of the series referenced there appears on the first page of the indexes of this volume. Readers will welcome this cumulated author index as a useful tool for locating an author within the various series. The index, which lists birth and death dates when available, will be particularly valuable for those authors who are identified with a certain period but whose death dates cause them to be placed in another, or for those authors whose careers span two periods. For example, Ernest Hemingway is found in *CLC,* yet F. Scott Fitzgerald, a writer often associated with him, is found in *Twentieth-Century Literary Criticism.*

- A **Cumulative Nationality Index** alphabetically lists all authors featured in *CLC* by nationality, followed by numbers corresponding to the volumes in which the authors appear.

- An alphabetical **Title Index** accompanies each volume of *CLC*. Listings are followed by the author's name and the corresponding page numbers where the titles are discussed. English translations of foreign titles and variations of titles are cross-referenced to the title under which a work was originally published. Titles of novels, novellas, dramas, films, record albums, and poetry, short story, and essay collections are printed in italics, while all individual poems, short stories, essays, and songs are printed in roman type within quotation marks; when published separately (e.g., T. S. Eliot's poem *The Waste Land),* the titles of long poems are printed in italics.

- In response to numerous suggestions from librarians, Gale has also produced a **Special Paperbound Edition** of the *CLC* title index. This annual cumulation, which alphabetically lists all titles reviewed in the series, is available to all customers. Additional copies of the index are available upon request. Librarians and patrons will welcome this separate index: it saves shelf space, is easy to use, and is recyclable upon receipt of the next edition.

Citing *Contemporary Literary Criticism*

When writing papers, students who quote directly from any volume in the Literary Criticism Series may use the following general forms to footnote reprinted criticism. The first example pertains to material drawn from periodicals, the second to material reprinted in books:

[1]Alfred Cismaru, "Making the Best of It," *The New Republic,* 207, No. 24, (December 7, 1992), 30, 32; excerpted and reprinted in *Contemporary Literary Criticism,* Vol. 85, ed. Christopher Giroux (Detroit: Gale, 1995), pp. 73-4.

[2]Yvor Winters, *The Post-Symbolist Methods* (Allen Swallow, 1967); excerpted and reprinted in *Contemporary Literary Criticism,* Vol. 85, ed. Christopher Giroux (Detroit: Gale, 1995), pp. 223-26.

Suggestions Are Welcome

The editors hope that readers will find *CLC* a useful reference tool and welcome comments about the work. Send comments and suggestions to: Editors, *Contemporary Literary Criticism,* The Gale Group, 27500 Drake Rd., Farmington Hills, MI 48333-3535.

Acknowledgments

The editors wish to thank the copyright holders of the excerpted criticism included in this volume and the permissions managers of many book and magazine publishing companies for assisting us in securing reproduction rights. We are also grateful to the staffs of the Detroit Public Library, the Library of Congress, the University of Detroit Mercy Library, Wayne State University Purdy/Kresge Library Complex, and the University of Michigan Libraries for making their resources available to us. Following is a list of the copyright holders who have granted us permission to reproduce material in this volume of *CLC*. Every effort has been made to trace copyright, but if omissions have been made, please let us know.

COPYRIGHTED MATERIALS IN *CLC*, VOLUME 126, WERE REPRODUCED FROM THE FOLLOWING PERIODICALS:

America, December 31, 1983; v. 175, July 6, 1996. © 1983, 1996. All rights reserved. Both reproduced with permission of America Press, Inc., 106 West 56th Street, New York, NY 10019.—*American Quarterly*, v. 34, Fall, 1982. Copyright 1982, Trustees of the University of Pennsylvania. Reproduced by permission of The Johns Hopkins University Press.—*American Record Guide*, January/February 1996; September/October, 1996. Copyright 1996 Record Guide Productions. Both reproduced with permission.—*American Theatre*, v. 13, October, 1996. Reproduced by permission.—*The Americas Review*, v. XIV, Summer, 1986. Copyright © 1986 The Americas Review. Reprinted by permission of the publisher, Arte Publico Press—University of Houston.—*The Atlantic Monthly*, v. 277, February, 1996 for a review of Don't Die Before You're Dead by Phoebe-Lou Adams. Copyright 1996 by The Atlantic Monthly Company, Boston, MA. Reproduced by permission of the author.—*Book World—The Washington Post*, v. XXIII, November 28, 1993 for "Beloved Bloody Country" by Lynn Freed. © 1993, Washington Post Book World Service/Washington Post Writers Group. Reproduced by permission of The Virginia Barber Literary Agency, Inc. All rights reserved./ v. XXVI, May 5, 1996 "Thinking Forbidden Thoughts" by Bruce Bawer. © 1996, Washington Post Book World Service/Washington Post Writers Group. Reproduced by permission of the author.—*Booklist*, March 15, 1993; August, 1995. Copyright © 1993, 1995 by the American Library Association. Both reproduced by permission.—*Boston Review*, v. 19, December, 1994 for "Liliane: Resurrection of the Daughter" in by Laurel Elkind. Copyright © 1994 by the Boston Critic, Inc. Reproduced by permission of the author.—*The Centennial Review*, v. 30, Spring, 1986 for "Breyten Breytenbach's Prison Literature" by Shelia Roberts. © 1986 by The Centennial Review. Reproduced by permission of the publisher and the author.—*Charleston (West Virginia) Gazette*, March 28, 1996. Copyright © 1996 The Charleston Gazette. Reproduced by permission.—*The Christian Science Monitor*, March 10, 1995. © 1995 The Christian Science Publishing Society. All rights reserved. Reproduced by permission from The Christian Science Monitor./ March 8, 1991 for "A Soviet Whitman" by Thomas D'Evelyn. © 1991 The Christian Science Publishing Society. All rights reserved. Reproduced by permission of the author./ March 8, 1991 for "Perestroika Redefines the Poet's Role" by Rushworth M. Kidder. © 1991 Rushworth M. Kidder. All rights reserved. Reproduced by permission of the author.—*Cineaste*, v. VI, 1975; v. XVIII, 1991. Copyright © 1975, 1991 by Cineaste Publishers, Inc. Both reproduced by permission.—*Clues: A Journal of Detection*, v. 3, Fall-Winter, 1992. Copyright 1992 by Pat Browne. Reproduced by permission.—*Commentary*, v. 80, October, 1985 for "Betrayal" by Stephen Schwartz. Copyright © 1985 by the American Jewish Committee. All rights reserved. Reproduced by permission of the publisher and the author.—*Conradiana*, v. XIII, 1981. Reproduced by permission.—*Critique: Studies in Contemporary Fiction*, v. XXX, Summer, 1969; v. XXXI, Winter, 1990. Copyright © 1969, 1990 Helen Dwight Reid Educational Foundation. Both reproduced with permission of the Helen Dwight Reid Educational Foundation, published by Heldref Publications, 119 18th Street, N. W., Washington, DC 20036-1802.—*Denver Rocky Mountain News*, October 19, 1997. Copyright © 1997, Denver Publishing Co. Reproduced by permission of the Denver Rocky Mountain News.—*The Economist*, v. 306, January 30, 1988. Copyright © 1998 Economist Newspaper Group, Inc. Reproduced with permission. Further reproduction prohibited.—*Essays in Literature*, v. 11, Spring, 1984. Copyright 1984 by Western Illinois University. Reproduced by permission.—*Film Comment*, v. 14, January-February, 1978. Copyright © 1978 by Film Comment Publishing Corporation. Reproduced by permission.—*Film Criticism*, v. II, Fall, 1978.

Reproduced by permission.—*Gazette Telegraph*, April 30, 1997. © 1997, The Gazette. Reproduced by permission.—*The Hudson Review*, v. XLIV, Summer, 1991. Copyright © 1991 by The Hudson Review, Inc. Reproduced by permission.—*Indianapolis Star,* April 27, 1997. Reproduced by permission.—*Jerusalem Post*, January 16, 1998. Reproduced by permission.—*Journal of Popular Film*, v. II, Spring, 1973 for "Motifs of Image and Sound in The Godfather" by Judith Vogelsang. Copyright © 1973, 2000 by Judith Vogelsang. Reproduced by permission of the author.—*Kirkus Reviews*, November 15, 1997. Copyright © 1997 The Kirkus Service, Inc. All rights reserved. Reproduced by permission of the publisher, Kirkus Reviews and Kirkus Associates, L.P.—*The Literary Review*, v. 37, Summer, 1994 for "The Poet in the Trenches: The Complete Poems of Anna Akhmatova" by Ervin C. Brody. Copyright © 1984 by Fairleigh Dickinson University. Reproduced by permission of the author.—*The Los Angeles Times Book Review*, August 17, 1986; March 21, 1993; November 9, 1996; November 23, 1997; October 4, 1998. Copyright © 1986, 1993, 1996, 1997, 1998 Los Angeles Times. All reproduced by permission.—*Maclean's Magazine*, v. 108, March 27, 1995; v. 108, June 12, 1995. © 1995 by Maclean's Magazine. Both reproduced by permission.—*Manchester Guardian Weekly*, v. 150, January 9, 1994. Copyright © 1994 by Guardian Publications Ltd. Reproduced by permission of Guardian News Service, LTD.—*The Massachusetts Review*, v. XXVIII, Winter, 1987. © 1987. Reproduced from The Massachusetts Review, Inc. by permission.—*MELUS: Society for the Study of the Multi-Ethnic Literature of the United States*, v. 19, Fall, 1992; v. 23, Spring, 1998. Copyright, MELUS, The Society for the Study of Multi-Ethnic Literature of the United States, 1992,1998. Both reproduced by permission.—*Mester*, vs. XXII and XXIII, Fall 1993 - Spring 1994. Copyright © 1994 by The Regents of the University of California. Reproduced by permission.—*The Nation*, New York, v. 255, November 2, 1992; v. 258, May 9, 1994. © 1992, 1994 The Nation magazine/ The Nation Company, Inc. Both reproduced by permission.—*The National Review*, May 6, 1996 Copyright © 1996 by National Review, Inc, 215 Lexington Avenue. New York, NY 10016. Reproduced by permission.—*The New Criterion*, v. 12, May, 199 for "Anna Akhmatova" by John Simon. Copyright © 1994 by The Foundation for Cultural Review. Reproduced by permission of the author.—*New England Review*, v. 18, Winter, 1997 for "Anna Akhmatova: The Stalin Years" by Roberta Reeder. Copyright © 1997 by Middlebury College. Reproduced by permission of the author.—*The New Republic*, 1985; May 6, 1991. © 1985, 1991 The New Republic, Inc. Both reproduced by permission of The New Republic.—*The New Statesman and Society*, March 15, 1991; v. 6, October 8, 1993. © 1991, 1993 The Statesman & Nation Publishing Co. Ltd. Both reproduced by permission.—*New York*, Magazine, v. 24, January 7, 1991. Copyright © 1991 PRIMEDIA Magazine Corporation. All rights reserved. Reproduced with the permission of New York Magazine.—*The New York Review of Books*, v. 40, May 13, 1993; v. XL, November 23, 1993. Copyright © 1993 Nyrev, Inc. Both reproduced with permission from The New York Review of Books.—*The New York Times Book Review*, December 22, 1974, November 4, 1989; October 17, 1993; January 1, 1995; June 28, 1995; November 12, 1995. Copyright © 1974, 1989, 1993, 1995 by The New York Times Company. All reproduced by permission./ November 30, 1986 for "Conspicuous Exile" by Bruce Robbins; January 1, 1995 for "A Life in Collage" by Valerie Sayers. Copyright © 1986, 1995 by The New York Times Company. Both reproduced by permission of the respective authors.—*Newsday*, April 4, 1997. Newsday, Inc. © 1997. Reproduced with permission.—*Newsweek*, v. CXVI, December 24, 1990. © 1990 Newsweek, Inc. All rights reserved. Reproduced by permission.—*Parnassus: Poetry in Review*, v. 11, Fall-Winter, 1983-84 for "Rimbaud's Nephews" by Terence Des Pres. Copyright © 1983 Poetry in Review Foundation, NY. Reproduced by permission of Georges Borchardt, Inc. on behalf of the author.—*Philadelphia Inquirer*, January 29, 1997. © 1997, The Philadelphia Inquirer. Reproduced by permission.—*Plays and Players*, June, 1985. All rights reserved. Reproduced by permission.—*Publisher's Weekly*, v. 238, April 5, 1991; November 14, 1994; January 22, 1996; September 2, 1996. Copyright © 1991, 1994, 1996 by Xerox Corporation. All reproduced from Publishers Weekly, published by R. R. Bowker Company, a Xerox company, by permission.—*Raritan: A Quarterly Review*, v. X, Spring, 1991. Copyright © 1991 by Raritan: A Quarterly Review. Reproduced by permission.—*Rocky Mountain Review of Language and Literature*, v. 41, 1987. Reproduced by permission.—*The Russian Review*, v. 57, April, 1998. Copyright 1998 The Russian Review. Reproduced by permission.—*The San Diego Union-Tribune*, May 6, 1993. Copyright 1993 Union Tribune Publishing Co. Reproduced by permission.—*Sight and Sound*, v. 47, Spring, 1978. Copyright © 1978 by The British Film Institute. Reproduced by permission.—*Slavic and East European Journal*, v. 36, Spring, 1992; v. 37, Summer, 1993. © 1992, 1993 by AATSEEL of the U.S., Inc. Both reproduced by permission.—*Slavic Review*, v. 52, Fall, 1993; v. 55, Spring, 1996. Copyright © 1993, 1996 by the American Association for the Advancement of Slavic Studies, Inc. Both reproduced by permission.—*St. Louis Post-Dispatch*, April 26, 1998. Copyright © 1998, St. Louis Post-Dispatch. Reproduced by permission.—*St. Paul Pioneer Press*, March 15, 1995. Reproduced by permission.—*Star Tribune*, March 5, 1995 for

"Writer Perry Faces Up to Dark Secret of Murder" by John Darnton. Copyright 1995 Star Tribune. All rights reserved. Reproduced by permission of the author.—*Studies in Short Fiction*, v. 21, Winter, 1984; v. 23, Summer, 1986; v. 26, Fall, 1989; v. 28, Winter, 1991. Copyright 1984, 1986, 1989, 1991 by Newberry College. All reproduced by permission.—*Studies in the Literary Imagination*, v. XVI, Summer, 1983. Copyright 1983 Department of English, Georgia State University. Reproduced by permission.—*Theatre Journal*, v. 44, May, 1992. © 1992, University and College Theatre Association of the American Theatre Association. Reproduced by permission of The Johns Hopkins University Press.—*Time*, October 5, 1987. Copyright Time Inc. 1983. All rights reserved. Reproduced by permission from Time.—*The Times Literary Supplement*, September 19, 1986; January 8, 1993; May 14, 1993; December 24, 1993; November 17, 1995. © The Times Supplements Limited 1986, 1993, 1995. All reproduced from The Times Literary Supplement by permission.—*UNESCO Courier*, v. 43, April, 1990. Reproduced by permission.—*The Vancouver Sun*, May 6, 1995. Reproduced by permission.—*Western American Literature*, v. XX, Summer, 1985. Copyright, 1985, by the Western Literature Association. Reproduced by permission of the publisher.—*The Women's Review of Books*, July, 1984 for "Mujeres en Lucha" by Judith Ortiz Cofer; v. 3, November, 1985 for "Growing Up Black" by Evelyn C. White; v. XI, January, 1994 for "All in the Familia" by Marie-Elise Wheatwind. Copyright © 1984, 1985, 1994. All rights reserved. All reproduced by permission of the respective authors.—*World Literature Today*, v. 60, Summer, 1986; v. 61, Summer, 1987; v. 65, Autumn, 1991; v. 65, Winter, 1991; v. 66, Autumn, 1992; Winter, 1992; v. 67, Summer, 1993; v. 68, Summer, 1994; v. 69, Summer, 1995; v. 71, Winter, 1997. Copyright © 1986, 1987, 1991, 1992, 1993, 1994, 1995, 1997 by the University of Oklahoma Press. All reproduced by permission.

COPYRIGHTED MATERIALS IN *CLC*, VOLUME 126, WERE REPRODUCED FROM THE FOLLOWING BOOKS:

Campbell, Ewing. From *Raymond Carver: A Study of the Short Fiction*. Twayne Publishers, 1992. Copyright © 1992 by Twayne Publishers. All rights reserved. Reproduced by permission.—Cushman, Keith. From "Blind, Intertextual Love: 'The Blind Man' and Raymond Carver's 'Cathedral'" in *D. H. Lawrence's Literary Inheritors*. Edited by Keith Cushman and Dennis Jackson. Macmillan, 1991. © Keith Cushman and Dennis Jackson 1991. All rights reserved. Reproduced by permission of Macmillan, London and Basingstoke.—Ferraro, Thomas J. From "Blood in the Marketplace: The Business of Family in The Godfather Narratives" in *The Invention of Ethnicity*. Edited by Werner Sollors. Oxford University Press, 1989. Copyright © 1989 by Werner Sollors, 1991 by Oxford University Press, Inc. All rights reserved. Used by permission of Oxford University Press, Inc.—Geis, Deborah R. From "Distraught at Laughter: Monologue in Shange's Theatre Pieces" in *Feminine Focus: The New Women Playwrights*. Edited by Enoch Brater. Oxford University Press, 1989. Copyright © 1989 by Oxford University Press, Inc. All rights reserved. Used by permission of Oxford University Press, Inc.—Goodheart, Eugene. From *Pieces of Resistance*. Cambridge University Press, 1987. © Cambridge University Press 1987. Reproduced with the permission of Cambridge University Press and the author.—Jay, Julia de Foor. From "(Re) Claiming the Race of the Mother: Cherríe Moraga's Shadow of a Man, Giving Up the Ghost, and Heroes and Saints" in *Women of Color: Mother-Daughter Relationships in 20th-Century Literature*. Edited by Elizabeth Brown-Guillory. University of Texas Press, 1996. Copyright © 1996 by the University of Texas Press. All rights reserved. Reproduced by permission of the University of Texas Press.—Kunitz, Stanley. From *A Kind of Order, A Kind of Folly*. Little, Brown and Company, 1975. Copyright © 1935, 1937, 1938, 1941, 1942, 1947, 1949, 1957, 1963, 1964, 1965, 1966, 1967, 1970, 1971, 1972, 1973, 1974, 1975 by Stanley Kunitz. All rights reserved. Reproduced by permission of W.W. Norton.—Mitchell, Carolyn. From "'A Laying on of Hands': Transcending the City in Ntozake's Shange's for colored girls who have considered suicide when the rainbow is enuf" in *Women Writers and the City: Essays in Feminist Literary Criticism*. Edited by Susan Merrill Squier. The University of Tennessee Press, 1984.Copyright © 1984 by The University of Tennessee Press. All rights reserved. Reproduced by permission.—Runyon, Randolph Paul. From *Reading Raymond Carver*. Syracuse University Press, 1992. Copyright © 1992 by Syracuse University Press. All rights reserved. Reproduced by permission of the publisher.—Saltzman, Arthur M. From *Understanding Raymond Carver*. University of South Carolina Press, 1988. Copyright © University of South Carolina 1988. Reproduced by permission.—Sternbach, Nancy Saporta. From "'A Deep Racial Memory of Love': The Chicana Feminism of Cherríe Moraga" in *Breaking Boundaries: Latina Writing and Critical Readings*. Edited by Asunción Horno-Delgado, Eliana Ortega, Nina M. Scott, and Nancy Saporta

Sternbach. The University of Massachusetts Press, 1989. Copyright © 1989 by The University of Massachusetts Press. All rights reserved. Reproduced by permission.—Whillock, David Everett. From "Narrative Structure in Apocalypse Now" in *America Rediscovered: Critical Essays on Literature and Film of the Vietnam War*. Edited by Owen W. Gilman, Jr. and Lorrie Smith. Garland Publishing, Inc., 1990. © 1990 Owen W. Gilman, Jr., and Lorrie Smith. All rights reserved. Reproduced by permission.

PHOTOGRAPHS AND ILLUSTRATIONS APPEARING IN *CLC*, VOLUME 126, WERE RECEIVED FROM THE FOLLOWING SOURCES:

Breytenbach, Breyten, photograph by Jerry Bauer. © Jerry Bauer. Reproduced by permission.—Carver, Raymond, photograph by Jerry Bauer. © Jerry Bauer. Reproduced by permission.—Coppola, Francis Ford, photograph. Archive Photos/Hammond. Reproduced by permission.—Perry, Anne, photo by Meg McDonald. MBA Literary Agency. Reproduced by permission.—Shange, Ntozake (touching throat, wearing scarf around head), New York City, 1976, photograph. AP/Wide World Photos. Reproduced by permission.—Yevtushenko, Yegeny (speaking with right hand gesticulation), photograph. The Library of Congress.

Anna Akhmatova
1888-1966

(Pseudonym for Anna Andreyevna Gorenko) Russian poet, translator, and essayist.

The following entry presents an overview of Akhmatova's career. For further information on her life and works, see *CLC,* Volumes 11, 25, and 64.

INTRODUCTION

Anna Akhmatova spent a major part of her career not being able to publish her work in her own country, yet she refused to be silenced. By remaining one of the few artists who did not emigrate during the years of Stalinist oppression in Russia, and by having friends memorize her verse when committing it to paper would have been dangerous, she guaranteed herself and the Russian people a voice. As such she has become one of the most important artistic figures in twentieth-century literature.

Biographical Information

Akhmatova was born Anna Andreyevna Gorenko in Kiev, Russia. Her father was a naval architect and moved the family to the Baltic in 1905. After her father and mother separated, the family settled in Tsarkoe Selo, just outside St. Petersburg. In 1910, Akhmatova married the poet Nikolai Gumilyov, who was at first reluctant for her to pursue poetry. When he saw her talent, however, he encouraged her, and together with poets such as Osip Mandelstam they began the Acmeist movement in Russian poetry. The movement was in opposition to the prevailing Symbolist poetry of the era. At the age of 22, she published her first volume *Vecher* (1912; *Evening*). Her middle-class father had asked her not to dishonor their family name with literary pursuits, so she published under the pseudonym Anna Akhmatova, the Tartar name of her maternal great-grandmother who had descended from Genghis Khan. She developed a cult following in the literary world of St. Petersburg with her second volume, *Chetki* (1914; *Rosary*), and she gained a brilliant reputation in russia where her poetry was widely read. In 1913 she left Gumilev and eventually married Vladimir Shileiko, an Orientalist, whom she divorced in 1921. The Revolution of October 1917 changed both Akhmatova's life and career. In 1921, her first husband Gumilyov was executed after being charged with involvement in a counter-revolutionary conspiracy. She did not emigrate like other artists, and in 1925, there was an unofficial ban on her work. During this period, Akhmatova continued to write poetry, often about the cruel acts being committed in the name of the Revolution and un-

der the rule of Stalin. She memorized her verses and had friends memorize them, fearing arrest if a written copy were found. She married again at this time, to Nikolai Punin, a critic and historian, but this marriage also ended in separation. Many of her friends were arrested and died under Stalin's persecution, and she suffered another great loss in 1935 when her son, Lev Gumilyov, was arrested and subsequently spent fourteen years in prison and in exile in Siberia. The poems in her *Rekviem* (1964; *Requiem*) were inspired by her trips to visit her son in prison in Leningrad and express the sense of loss she felt by the separation. In 1939, Stalin allowed several of her poems to be published, but Akhmatova again fell out of government favor in 1946 when she was denounced by Andrey Zhadanov, Secretary of the Central Committee of the Communist Party. Zhadanov began an ideological campaign against her work, calling it too personal to be relevant to a socialist society. She was expelled from the Union of Soviet Writers and ostracized from the Russian literary world for the next ten years. She was only re-admitted to the Union after the death of Stalin. The ban on Akhmatova's work was not officially lifted until 1988, but interest in her work burgeoned anyway and by the 1960s

Akhmatova was world famous. In 1964 she won the Etna-Taormina international poetry prize, and in 1965 she received an honorary doctorate from Oxford University.

Major Works

A major influence on Akhmatova's work was her relationship to the Acmeists—writers who attempted to restore clarity to poetic language and who utilized the ordinary objects and events of daily life for their subject. Her poems explore her search for identity as a woman, a poet, and a Russian, as they delve into the complexities of human nature. In many of her early volumes the theme of love dominates along with attendant motifs of romantic meetings and separations, togetherness and solitude, and jealousy is often present. The poems in *Evening* paint a portrait of love as long periods of suffering broken up by rare moments of happiness and joy. In *Rosary* she deals with her feelings of guilt and loss over the breakup of her marriage with Gumilev. The poems in this collection contain many religious elements, expressing her strong belief in Christianity. With her third book, *Belaya Staya* (1917; *The White Flock*), Akhmatova turns to more civic-minded themes, including the foreshadowing of World War I in "July 1914." *Requiem* tells the story of a mother separated from her only son and was inspired by Akhmatova's own story and those of the thousands of other Russian women with whom she waited outside prison walls. This cycle of poems chronicles the era of Stalinism and the grief and horror suffered during these years. *Poema Bez Geroya; Triptykh* (1960; *Poem Without a Hero; Triptych*) chronicled her life before and after World War II. The poems described such personal events as love affairs and the suicide of a young cadet who was in love with Akhmatova's friend, but through these autobiographical accounts, she chronicled an epoch time period in world history. In this collection are many veiled statements and complex allusions that are much more opaque than her previous work.

Critical Reception

Critics often discuss Akhmatova's work in its relation to the Acmeist movement. As with other Acmeists, reviewers find Akhmatova's work more straightforward than that of her Symbolist predecessors. Critics often discuss Akhmatova's literary debt to Russian poet Alexander Pushkin, including her unselfconscious impulses, use of allusions, and superb diction and rhythms. Stanley Kunitz states, "[Akhmatova's] poems exist in the purity and exactness of their diction, the authority of their tone, the subtlety of their rhythmic modulations, the integrity of their form." Reviewers praise Akhmatova's unique voice, many arguing that her verse is definitive. John Simon says, "I do see a poet with an original vision and a personal voice who manages to maintain her individual talent within the tradition." Many reviewers discuss the impact the Russian political climate had on

Akhmatova's career and how it helped to infuse a civic element in her work. Many assert that she was the veritable voice of the Russian people during one of its most harrowing periods in history. More specifically, some critics claimed Akhmatova was the mouthpiece for subjugated Russian women and a true feminist leader before Feminism. Ervin C. Brody asserts, "A chronicler of the isolated and intimate psychological events of a woman's emotional and intellectual life as well as the political events in the Soviet Union, Anna Akhmatova is one of Russia's greatest poets and perhaps the greatest woman poet in the history of Western culture."

PRINCIPAL WORKS

Vecher [*Evening*] (poetry) 1912

Chetki [*Rosary*] (poetry) 1914

Belaya Staya [*The White Flock*] (poetry) 1917

Skrizhal: Sbornik [*Ecstasy Collection*] (poetry) 1918

U Samogo Morya [*At the Very Edge of the Sea*] (poetry) 1921

Podorozhnik [*Plantain*] (poetry) 1921

Anno Domini MCMXXI (poetry) 1921

Anno Domini (poetry) 1923

Stikhi [*Poems*] (poetry) 1940

Iz Shesti Knig [*From Six Books*] (poetry) 1940

Izbrannie Stikhi [*Selected Poems*] (poetry) 1943

Tashkentskie Stikhi [Tashkent Poems] (poetry) 1944

Koreiskaya Klassicheskaya Poeziya [*Korean Classical Poetry;* translator] (poetry) 1956

Stikhotvoreniya 1909-1957 [*Poems 1909-1957*] (poetry) 1958

Poema Bez Geroya; Triptykh [*Poem without a Hero; Triptych*] (poetry) 1960

Stikhotvoreniya 1909-1960 [*Poems 1909-1960*] (poetry) 1961

Collected Poems: 1912-1963 (poetry) 1963

Rekviem: Tsikl Stikhotvorenii [*Requiem: A Cycle of Poems*] (poetry) 1964

Beg Vremeni [*Race of Time*] (poetry) 1965

Golosa Poetov [*Voices of the Poets;* translator] (poetry) 1965

Lirika Drevnevo Egipta [*Ancient Egyptian Lyrics;* translator; with Vera Potapova] (poetry) 1965

Stikhotvoreniya 1909-1965 (poetry) 1965

Klassicheskya poeziya Vostoka [*Classical Poetry of the East;* translator] (poetry) 1969

CRITICISM

Stanley Kunitz (essay date 1935)

SOURCE: "On Translating Akhmatova," in his *A Kind of*

Order, A Kind of Folly, Little, Brown and Company, 1935, pp. 39-46.

[*In the following essay, Kunitz discusses the difficulty in translating Akhmatova's poetry from its original Russian.*]

Pasternak was once rebuked by a pedant who came to his door bearing a long list of the poet's mistakes in translating *Hamlet.* The complaint was greeted with laughter and a shrug: "What difference does it make? Shakespeare and I—we're both geniuses, aren't we?" As if to justify his arrogance, Pasternak's *Hamlet* is today considered one of the glories of Russian literature. My Russian friend who passed the anecdote on to me was unable to recall the visiting critic's name.

The poet as translator lives with a paradox. His work must not read like a translation; conversely, it is not an exercise of the free imagination. One voice enjoins him: "Respect the text!" The other simultaneously pleads with him: "Make it new!" He resembles the citizen in Kafka's aphorism who is fettered to two chains, one attached to earth, the other to heaven. If he heads for earth, his heavenly chain throttles him; if he heads for heaven, his earthly chain pulls him back. And yet, as Kafka says, "All the possibilities are his, and he feels it; more, he actually refuses to account for the deadlock by an error in the original fettering." While academicians insist that poetry is untranslatable, poets continue to produce their translations—never in greater proliferation or diversity than now.

The easiest poets to translate are the odd and flashy ones, particularly those who revel in linguistic display. The translator of Akhmatova, like the translator of Pushkin, is presented with no idiosyncrasy of surface or of syntax to simplify his task. Her poems exist in the purity and exactness of their diction, the authority of their tone, the subtlety of their rhythmic modulations, the integrity of their form. These are inherent elements of the poetry itself, not to be confused with readily imitable "effects." The only way to translate Akhmatova is by writing well. A hard practice!

Akhmatova's early poems, like those of most young poets, tend to deal with the vagaries of love, breathtaking now and then for their dramatic point and reckless candor. It has been said that she derived not so much from other poets as from the great Russian novelists of the nineteenth century. She herself enters into her poems like a character in a work of fiction, or in a play. On New Year's Day, 1913, when she was twenty-three, she broke a poem open with an expostulation that the guardians of the State were later to use against her: "We're all drunkards here, and harlots: / how wretched we are together!" On the next New Year's Day she wrote, in bravura novelistic style:

"What do you want?" I asked.
"To be with you in hell," he said.
I laughed: "It's plain you mean
to have us both destroyed."

He lifted his thin hand
and lightly stroked the flowers:
"Tell me how men kiss you,
tell me how you kiss."

This was the period of her brilliant, if disastrous, first marriage, when husband and wife were the toast of the Bohemian set of St. Petersburg, he as Gumi-lev (Gumi-lion) and she as Gumi-lvitsa (Gumi-lioness). Her slender grace and aristocratic aquiline profile were as celebrated as her verses. Though in the post-Revolutionary years that followed she was to meet with terrible misfortunes; endure the indignities of poverty, official contempt, and silence; and suffer the death or exile of those dearest to her, she remained proud and spirited. Even in her last days, after her "rehabilitation"—sleazy bureaucratic euphemism!—she refused to wear the geriatric mask of complacence. In delirium she wrote:

Herewith I solemnly renounce my hoard
of earthly goods, whatever counts as chattel.
The genius and guardian angel of this place
has changed to an old tree-stump in the water.

Tragedy did not wither her: it crowned her with majesty. Her life, in Keats's phrase, became "a continual allegory," its strands interwoven with the story of a people. Indeed, her poems can be read in sequence as a twentieth-century Russian chronicle. The only way to arrange them is in chronological order, while attempting to cover the breadth of her themes and of her expressiveness, which ranges, in Andrei Sinyavsky's words, "from a barely audible whisper to fiery oratory, from modestly lowered eyes to thunder and lightning."

I wish I were a better linguist than I am, but in default of that aptitude I count myself lucky in my partnership with Max Hayward. Akhmatova herself translated with outside help from a number of languages, including Chinese, Korean, Ancient Egyptian, Bengali, Armenian, Georgian, and Yiddish. Translator-poets in the past have consulted linguists as a matter of course, without feeling the need for acknowledging the assistance they received. The modern tendency, reflecting the dynamics of our curiosity about other cultures, is to facilitate and formalize the collaboration between poet and scholar. Largely owing to such combinations of skills, all literatures, however minor or esoteric, are at the point of becoming world literature. If, on occasion, I have rather boldly rendered a line or a phrase, it has always been on aesthetic grounds, never because I felt that my information was unreliable. Intuition is a blessing, but it is better to combine it with clarity of understanding.

In certain quarters the "literal version" of a poem is held sacred, though the term is definitely a misnomer. As Arthur Waley noted: "There are seldom sentences that have word-to-word equivalents in another language. It becomes a question of choosing between various approximations." Translation is a sum of approximations, but not all approximations are equal. Russian word order, for example, says: "As if I my own sobs / out of another's hands were drinking." One has to rearrange the passage to make it sound idiomatic, and one may even have to sharpen the detail to make it work in English, but one is not at liberty to indulge in willful invention. The so-called literal version is already a radical reconstitution of the verbal ingredients of a poem into another linguistic system—at the expense of its secret life, its interconnecting psychic tissue, its complex harmonies.

Here is an early poem of Akhmatova's, written in the year following her marriage to the poet Gumilev—a very simple poem, perhaps the best kind to use for illustration. If you follow the original text word by word, this is how it reads:

> He liked three things in the world:
> at evening mass singing, white peacocks
> and worn-out maps of America.
> Didn't like it when cry children,
> didn't like tea with raspberry jam,
> and female hysterics.
> But I was his wife.

Despite its modesty, the Russian text has its charm and its music, which the slavish transcription forfeits completely. Whatever liberties one takes in translation are determined by the effort to recreate the intrinsic virtues of the source:

> Three things enchanted him:
> white peacocks, evensong,
> and faded maps of America.
> He couldn't stand bawling brats,
> or raspberry jam with his tea,
> or womanish hysteria.
> . . . And he was tied to me.

My deviations from the literal are for the sake of prosodic harmony, naturalness of diction, and brightness of tone. The poem in English is based on the irregular trimeters of the original, and it suggests the rhyming pattern without copying it exactly.

"Lot's Wife" is one of Akhmatova's most celebrated poems, often quoted by Russian poets and often imitated too. The theme seems to fascinate them, for fairly obvious reasons.

> And the just man trailed God's shining agent,
> over a black mountain, in his giant track,
> while a restless voice kept harrying his woman:
> "It's not too late, you can still look back
>
> at the red towers of your native Sodom,
> the square where once you sang, the spinning-shed,
> at the empty windows set in the tall house
> where sons and daughters blessed your
>   marriage-bed."
>
> A single glance: a sudden dart of pain
> stitching her eyes before she made a sound . . .
> Her body flaked into transparent salt,
> and her swift legs rooted to the ground.
>
> Who will grieve for this woman? Does she not seem
> too insignificant for our concern?
> Yet in my heart I never will deny her,
> who suffered death because she chose to turn.

After Richard Wilbur and I discovered that we had been separately struggling with translations of "Lot's Wife," we compared our versions. Both of us acknowledged that it was the last stanza in particular that had given us a bad time. "Literally" it reads:

> Who woman this weep for will?
> Not least does she not seem of losses?
> Only heart my never will forget
> Woman who gave life for one single peep.

The sentiment is noble, but the sound in English is ridiculous. The problem each of us had faced was how to restore the dignity and style that had been lost in transit. Wilbur's fine translation concludes:

> Who would waste tears upon her? Is she not
> The least of our losses, this unhappy wife?
> Yet in my heart she will not be forgot
> Who, for a single glance, gave up her life.

Technically Wilbur's considerable achievement is to duplicate the original ABAB rhyme scheme (not, wife, forgot, life) without wrenching the sense, whereas I have only the second and fourth lines rhyming to suggest the contours of Akhmatova's measured quatrains. My impression, however, is that Wilbur has had to sacrifice, for the sake of his rhymes, more than they are worth. In a poem of his own I doubt that he would say, "Yet in my heart she will not be forgot / Who, for a single glance, gave up her life." Nobody speaks like that, but the constrictions of the pattern did not leave him sufficient room in which to naturalize his diction.

In one of my many discarded versions of the stanza I wrote:

Who will grieve for this woman? Does she not seem
the very least of losses in our book?
Yet in my heart I never will forget her,
who died in payment for a backward look.

Perhaps I felt that the force of "backward look" had already been dissipated in the first stanza, and perhaps my ear resisted the terminal clink of the rhyme, but I can see now that those abandoned lines have the advantage of greater fidelity to the text and ease of movement. I may have made the wrong choice. In any event, I doubt that I have finished tinkering with "Lot's Wife."

The object is to produce an analogous poem in English out of available signs and sounds, a new poem sprung from the matrix of the old, drenched in memories of its former existence, capable of reviving its singular pleasures. The Russian poet Nikolai Zabolotsky had another figure for the process. He said it was like building a new city out of the ruins of the old.

Akhmatova is usually described as a formal poet, but in her later years she wrote more and more freely. Some of her poems, particularly the dramatic lyrics that developed out of her histrionic temperament, are so classically joined that they cannot be translated effectively without a considerable reconstruction of their architecture; others are much more fluid in their making. To insist on a universally rigid duplication of metrical or rhyming patterns is arbitrary and pointless, at any rate, since the effects are embedded in the language of origin and are not mechanically transferable to another language. Instead of rhyme our ear is often better pleased by an instrumentation of off-rhyme, assonance, consonance, and other linkages. Prosody is not founded on law, but on the way we speak, the way we breathe. In this connection Osip Mandelstam's widow offers a pertinent commentary:

> In the period when I lived with Akhmatova, I was able to watch her at work as well, but she was much less "open" about it than M., and I was not always even aware that she was "composing." She was, in general, much more withdrawn and reserved than M. and I was always struck by her self-control as a woman—it was almost a kind of asceticism. She did not even allow her lips to move, as M. did so openly, but rather, I think, pressed them tighter as she composed her poems, and her mouth became set in an even sadder way. M. once said to me before I had met Akhmatova—and repeated to me many times afterward—that looking at these lips you could hear her voice, that her poetry was made of it and was inseparable from it. Her contemporaries—he continued—who had heard this voice were richer

than future generations who would not be able to hear it.

It may be some comfort to reflect that poets are not easily silenced, even in death. As Akhmatova herself wrote, towards the end, "On paths of air I seem to overhear / two friends, two voices, talking in their turn." Despite the passage of time, the ranks of listeners grow, and the names of Akhmatova and Pasternak and Mandelstam are familiar even on foreign tongues. Some of us are moved to record what we have heard, and to try to give it back in the language that we love.

Translation is usually regarded as a secondary act of creation. One has only to cite the King James Bible, Sir Thomas Malory's *Morte d'Arthur,* Chapman's *Homer,* Dryden's *Aeneid,* Fitzgerald's *Rubáiyát,* and for modern instances the poems of Pound and Waley, to demonstrate the fallacy of this view. Poets are attracted to translation because it is a way of paying their debt to the tradition, of restoring life to shades, of widening the company of their peers. It is also a means of self-renewal, of entering the skin and adventuring through the body of another's imagination. In the act of translation one becomes more like that other, and is fortified by that other's power.

Yelena Byelyakova (essay date April 1990)

SOURCE: "Anna Akhmatova: 'Mother Courage' of Poetry," in *Unesco Courier,* Vol. 43, April, 1990, p. 48.

[*In the following essay, Byelyakova provides an overview of Akhmatova's career.*]

The life of Anna Akhmatova was a tragic one. Although she had her moments of glory she also experienced terrible humiliations.

She was born in 1889, and her youth coincided with an extraordinary literary flowering, the silver age of Russian poetry. Her first volume of verses, **Vecher** (**Evening**) was published in 1912. It was followed two years later by **Chyotki** (**Rosary**) which was reprinted eight times and made her name. The themes of most of her early poems are meetings and separations, love and solitude. Their style is rigorous, lucid, laconic.

Her poetry was read throughout Russia, and the critics predicted a brilliant future for this "Russian Sappho". She published regularly—**Belaya staya** (1917; **The White Flock**), **Podorozhnik** (1921; **Plantain**), and **Anno Domini MCMXXI** (1922).

Unlike many intellectuals in her circle, Akhmatova did not

emigrate after the Revolution of October 1917. Yet in 1923 her work ceased to be published. The official view was that her lyrics were alien to the new generation of readers produced by the Revolution. Fame was followed by oblivion: for seventeen years her name vanished from literature.

Life had other trials in store for her. In 1921 her first husband, the poet Nikolay Gumilyov, was executed after being accused of taking part in a counter-revolutionary conspiracy. Her son, the orientalist Lev Gumilyov, was arrested in 1935 and eventually spent fourteen years in prison and exile in Siberia. Her third husband, the art historian Nikolay Punin, died in prison.

Yet Anna Akhmatova continued to write. The anguish she shared with thousands of other women who queued outside the prisons of Leningrad inspired the cycle **Rekviem** (1935-1940; **Requiem**), which tells the tragic story of a mother separated from her only son. She visited her friend the poet Osip Mandelstam, exiled in Voronezh, and wrote poems filled with foreboding about his imminent death. She denounced the illegal and arbitrary acts which were being committed in her country, and exposed the cruelty of Stalin and his entourage. Fearing arrest, she memorized her verses rather than write them down.

In 1940 several poems she had written before the Revolution were published. Later, patriotic lyrics she wrote during the war were published in several newspapers and magazines.

But in 1946 she became the main target of an ideological campaign launched against the artistic and literary intelligentsia by the Central Committee of the Communist Party, which passed a resolution condemning the literary reviews *Zvezda* ("The Star") and *Leningrad* for publishing her poetry, which was branded as "bourgeois and decadent", "devoid of an ideological message" and "alien to the Soviet people".

The entire printrun of her most recent collection of poems was destroyed and she was expelled from the Union of Soviet Writers. For ten years she was again ostracized. Not until the thaw which followed the death of Stalin was she reinstated in the Writers' Union and allowed to publish again. By now the interest in her poetry was immense.

In the 1960s Akhmatova became world famous. Her work was translated into English, French, German, Italian, Czech, Bulgarian and many other languages. Many articles, books and studies were published about her poetry. In 1964 she travelled to Italy where she was awarded the Etna-Taormina international poetry prize, and in the following year she received an honorary doctorate from Oxford University.

Anna Akhmatova died on 5 March 1966. As the years go by the interest in her work continues to grow. Her collections of poems are often reprinted, and unpublished works are coming to light, including some fine patriotic poems which were virtually unknown in the Soviet Union until recently. *Rekviem,* which had appeared in the West in the 1960s, was not published in the Soviet Union until 1987. In 1988, the Communist Party resolution against the reviews *Leningrad* and *Zvezda* was officially rescinded and in 1989 *Zvezda* devoted an entire issue to the centenary of Anna Akhmatova's birth.

The city of Leningrad, which played a major part in her life, was the centre of the centenary celebrations in June 1989. A memorial museum was opened on the Fontanka Embankment, where for over thirty years she had lived and composed some of her most tragic poems. Conferences were organized by the Russian Literature Institute of the USSR Academy of Sciences and the Leningrad Writers' Organization. At literary and musical evenings leading poets read her works and poems dedicated to her by contemporaries including Aleksandr Blok, Marina Tsvetayeva, Osip Mandelstam, and Boris Pasternak. Song cycles of her lyrics set to music by Prokofiev and Slonimsky were also performed.

The anniversary provided the opportunity to pay a fitting tribute to one of the greatest poets of the century.

Susan Salter Reynolds (21 March 1993)

SOURCE: "Shards of Russian History," in *Los Angeles Times Book Review,* March 21, 1993, pp. 3, 9.

[*In the following review, Reynolds discusses the world evoked by the essays in Akhmatova's* My Half Century.]

On the morning of May 13, 1934, Anna Akhmatova and Nadezhda Mandelstam began to clean up the scattered books and papers left by the agents who had arrested Nadezhda's husband, the poet Osip Mandelstam, the night before. While some papers, including the incriminating poem about Stalin ("And every killing is a treat / for the broad-chested Ossete") had already been smuggled out by friends and visitors, one pile still lay by the door. "Don't touch it," said Akhmatova. Nadezhda, trusting the instincts of her friend, left the papers on the floor. "Ah," said the senior police agent, back for a surprise visit, "you still haven't tidied up."

This instinct for survival, what Nadezhda Mandelstam later called her "Russian powers of endurance," kept Akhmatova alive through some of the cruelest decades known to Russian writers. In 1921, her husband, the poet Nikolai Gumilyov, from whom she had been separated for three years, was arrested and executed. Her son Lev Gumilyov was arrested three times, exiled, and spent years of his life in prison for being her son. The great writers of the century, her friends, suffered and died under Stalin. The poet Marina Tsvetaeva hanged herself in 1941; Osip Mandelstam died en route to a labor camp in 1938. Akhmatova herself was "annihilated" in 1919, which meant that she could not publish; resurrected in 1939 by Stalin, only to be annihilated again in 1946 after several visits from Isaiah Berlin in 1945. She was expelled from the Union of Soviet Writers with the enduring epithet: "half nun, half harlot."

This resolution was 'not rescinded until 1988, when Akhmatova, dead for 22 years, was again rehabilitated, making available, for the first time, much of her prose; previously censored studies, essays, and sketches. Ardis Press, long a faithful friend of Russian literature, has now published the most complete collection of her prose in the volume *My Half Century: Selected Prose.*

This is not the relaxed, purgative activity that continental memoir-writing is supposed to be. She was, after all, a lifetime poet, telling Kornei Chukovsky in 1921: "I don't know how to write prose." She believed, as Emma Gershtein writes in the afterword, that "human memory works like a projector, illuminating individual moments, while leaving the rest in impenetrable darkness." What you get is a bit of a difficult read, sustained by curiosity about Akhmatova, and admiration for her. If there is any doubt in your mind about this, or you falter along the way, simply turn to her 1914 collection of poems entitled **Rosary** and consider this quote: "Today I see you," wrote Osip Mandelstam of Akhmatova in 1910, "a black angel in the snow, / and I cannot keep this secret to myself, / God's mark is upon you. . . ."

While Akhmatova's notebooks contain partial outlines and plans for her memoirs, she did not live to complete them. She wrote that she modeled her effort, however, on the autobiographies of Pasternak (*Safe Conduct,* 1931) and Mandelstam (*Noise of Time,* 1922-23), both written in a certain fragmentary style. And fragments are appropriate memorials for lives lived in Russia in the 1920s, '30s and '40s, though Akhmatova describes the frustration of this style in a section called "Random Notes": "I notice that what I'm writing isn't quite right: I have almost ten subjects on two pages and everything is very inconsistent, as they like to put it nowadays."

Indeed, the voice throughout the fragments, many of which were written in the late 1950s and early 1960s, is an ornery old-lady voice. Like a real grande dame, Akhmatova repeats herself, tells stories in which she is admired by individuals and crowds, in which her beauty is mythologized, and in which her detractors are drawn and quartered with downright academic precision.

Writing her memoirs was also a historical burden. "I'm surrounded by the past and it is demanding something from me," she wrote in 1957. What it was demanding of her, it seems, was the need to clarify a period in Russia's literary history that was mercilessly and whimsically perverted by various regimes. Of course she sounds defensive! Of course she sounds petty! Who said what to whom in 1919 or 1945, random comments in journals could mean literal or figurative annihilation. Akhmatova labored, as Olga Carlisle writes in her memoir *Under a New Sky. . . ,* to correct the misperception spread internationally by the Stalin regime that Russia's greatest poets (the ones they'd annihilated) had not been heard from because they had simply "lost their poetic voices in the twenties."

The first two sections of the book, "Pages from a Diary," and "My Half Century" are the most interesting. "Pages from a Diary" includes delightful memories from the author's childhood, and it is in these passages that she is able to abandon herself to the smells of St. Petersburg's staircases, or winters in Tsarskoe Selo, the northern town where she grew up, and whose most famous resident was none other than Pushkin. Born on June 11, 1889, Anna Gorenko took, as her literary name, the Tatar name of her maternal great-grandmother, a descendant of Genghis Khan: hence the resonant Anna Akhmatova.

And she was beautiful; angular, severe, with dark, deep-set eyes, a majestic manner and an ego for drama. But beautiful women, said Shakespeare's Cleopatra, "eat a crazy salad with their meat," and the flirtations, romance, and reshuffling that we associate with a bohemian lifestyle conspired with history to fragment Akhmatova's life and memories. She "gave in," as she put it, at age 21 to the young Symbolist poet Gumilyov, writing in 1907, "I swear by all that is holy to me that this unhappy man will be happy with me." They were married in 1910.

The Symbolists, led by Blok, were dying off, and a new faction, led by Gumilyov and the poet Gorodetsky, sprung up to reject the vagueness of Symbolism. They formed, in 1912, the Poet's Guild, and called themselves Acmeists, proclaiming the poetry of real experience. The most talented among them were Mandelstam, Gumilyov, and Akhmatova; a triumvirate that one detractor called "those Adams and that skinny Eve." They argued and danced and rejected the old at a cabaret in St. Petersburg called the Stray Dog, where, as Akhmatova wrote in her poem of January, 1913, "We are all carousers and loose women . . ."

These days did not last long.

Akhmatova tries, in "Pages," to set aright the misconceptions about Acmeism and Symbolism and her relationship to Gumilyov which dissolved in 1918 (the cover of one of her poetry collections apparently boasted that the author had been "divorced"!), but all this is done more clearly in Judith Hemschemeyer's preface to the second edition, recently out in paperback, of *The Complete Poems of Anna Akhmatova.* In these years, from 1912 to 1922, Akhmatova published five collections of poetry, and "Pages" also contains brief descriptions of their birth and passage through history.

After 1917, debates over Acmeism and Symbolism and evenings at the Stray Dog seem splendid indeed. The second section of *My Half Century* is composed of portraits of writers and friends, many captured by Akhmatova as they are overwhelmed and suffocated by the Revolution. The portraits of Modigliani ("He never spoke about anything mundane") and Mandelstam ("Who can show us the source of this divine new harmony, which we call the poetry of Osip Mandelstam?") are the most affectionate and readable. The others, of Tsvetaeva, Pasternak, etc., are punctuated with brief illuminations from Akhmatova's memory-projector.

Akhmatova died on March 5, 1966. It is clear that in her last years she wanted not only to correct impressions about her life and times but also to breathe again. The trouble for survivors is that they have survived. Akhmatova did not learn of Gumilyov's execution on Aug. 25, 1921, until a week after it had occurred. But on the night of Aug. 27 she wrote a poem called "Terror": "Terror, fingering things in the dark, / leads the moonbeam to an axe. / Behind the wall there's an ominous knock / What's there, a ghost, a thief, rats? . . . I press the smooth cross to my heart: / God, restore peace to my soul."

In this same year, far away, another group of literary friends got depressed, engaged in social quarrels: Virginia Woolf published *To the Lighthouse.* Leonard Woolf published *Hunting the Highbrow.* Akhmatova clutched a cross in her bed at night as her friends' lives were fragmented and scattered to the wind; then rearranged for international consumption. They learned strange skills like how to recognize an agent, and how to write under censorship. "I can't sing," she wrote in **Poem Without a Hero,** "In the midst of this horror." But sing she did.

Perhaps the most beautiful passage in *My Half Century* comes in "Pages from a Diary":

> And if it was destined that poetry should flourish in the twentieth century, namely in my Homeland, I will be so bold as to say that I have always been a cheerful and trustworthy witness. . . . And I am certain that even now we do not truly know what a magical chorus of poets we possess, that the Russian language is young and supple, that

we have only recently begun to write poetry, and that we love and believe in it.—1962

John Bayley (review date 13 May 1993)

SOURCE: "Anna of All the Russias," in *New York Review of Books,* Vol. 40, No. 9, May 13, 1993, pp. 25-7.

[*In the following review, Bayley presents an overview of Akhmatova's life and career in his discussion of three works concerning the poet:* The Complete Poems of Anna Akhmatova, *translated by Judith Hemschemeyer;* Remembering Anna Akhmatova, *by Anatoly Nayman; and* In a Shattered Mirror: The Later Poetry of Anna Akhmatova, *by Susan Amert.*]

Poetry must somehow proclaim its authority. However mysteriously this comes about, its achievement can always be recognized; a great poem continues to assert its magisterial spell in the face of all the tyranny or indifference of passing events. When Yeats wrote in 1919, "The best lack all conviction, while the worst / Are full of passionate intensity," he could not have known that before the end of the century, at a time when convictions of any sort were hard to come by, for both the good and the bad, his words would nonetheless have passed into the language, been stamped on the consciousness of daily speech.

How much more has this authority come to exist in the great poetry of Russia, where it stamped its conviction on the secret speech of the martyrs and the persecuted? A moving photograph in the complete edition of Anna Akhmatova's poems, between the text and the notes, shows a tiny handmade "notebook," formed of a few fragments of paper stitched together, with a poem of hers laboriously copied out in minute handwriting. This had been the treasured possession of a *zek* in one of the gulags, a talisman to strengthen him through years of suffering. Now that particular tyranny has gone, at least for the moment, and poetry of course remains, yet its authority in Russia is perhaps not quite what it was, its "bright name"—in Aleksandr Blok's phrase—not quite so potent. A famous sonnet of Shakespeare's has never enjoyed a moment of such rough magic as when the audience at a hall in Moscow shouted insistently for "Number 66," while Pasternak, with grudging permission from the Soviet authorities, was reading his translations. That sonnet contains the line: "And art made tongue-tied by authority," and goes on to speak of "captive good attending captain ill."

Of course art can always be used for propaganda purposes, and bad art too can sometimes enjoy in a political context the same potency as the good. But since the time of

Pushkin Russian poetry at its best and most venerated has never achieved its force and its popularity by going directly against the state and the establishment. On the contrary: its power has always come from its detachment, its serene confidence in belonging, so to speak, to another and a better world. Not in every case is this true. Nekrasov, writing in the mid-nineteenth century, and in conformity in some degree with the famous critic Belinsky's theory of the social utility of art, is both an excellent poet and a propagandist for social and political reform. For that reason he was one of the few poets, other than the iconic Pushkin, to be thoroughly approved of by the Soviet authorities, who also encouraged another good poet, Mayakovsky, to be their poetic mascot and front man with the Muse. Unable to stand the strain of serving two masters, Mayakovsky committed suicide. Blok, who had earlier shown a wish to serve as a poet the new Bolshevik society, had already died in despair. His well-known poem "The Twelve," for all its undoubted magnificence and impact, in fact falls resoundingly between two stools: it is a poem of wholly personal and symbolic vision which nonetheless tries to be realistic and urgent about historic events and the Reds' seizure of power.

This point against Blok's vision of twelve uncouth Red Guardsmen wandering destructively through St. Petersburg under the leadership of Jesus Christ was made by Pasternak in *Doctor Zhivago,* which contrasts the grim reality of "Russia's terrible years" with Blok's poetically apocalyptic conception of them. Akhmatova, who did not at all care for Blok as a man although she admired some of his poetry, would certainly have agreed with Pasternak's view of the matter. For her, as for Pasternak, the poet indeed had a duty, but it was nothing to do with political principles, or with a regime. It was to stay where you were, in your own country, and write, as a poet, for your own people. For Russian poets to leave Russia and go into emigration was for them to forfeit the mysterious authority which they possessed. It is this knowledge and certainty which fill the four lines at the opening of Akhmatova's tragic poem-cycle *Requiem,* written in memory of the time under the Great Terror when she stood outside the prison in St. Petersburg (then Leningrad) where her son was confined, hoping, like innumerable others, to get a parcel through, or at least a word.

> No, not under the vault of alien
>   skies,
> And not under the shelter of alien
>   wings—
> I was with my people then,
>   There, where my people, unfortu-
>   nately, were.

That is Judith Hemschemeyer's translation, and her versions of Akhmatova's collected poems in the new single-volume Zephyr Press edition—it succeeds the bulky two-volume edition with Russian text and translation on facing pages published three years ago—is in general excellent: accurate, unpretentious, and in the same straightforward and simple key as the original. The usual difficulties and impossibilities remain of course; but Akhmatova was herself a translator, and like all the Russian Acmeist poets she was steeped in the texture and tradition of European and English poetry. She knew the difficulties, and would appreciate how the translator, who learned Russian because of her love for this poetry, has tried to overcome them.

Wendy Rosslyn gives the usual and more elegant version of that stanza's last line "Where my luckless people chanced to be" in her translation of Anatoly Nayman's sensitive and lively memoir of the poet. It is true that the drawback of the word "unfortunately" in English is that it is usually employed in a trivial context—"Unfortunately, she's got another appointment" or something of the sort. "Luckless" is a more obvious poetical word, more rare, more drastic. But it is just because of its commonplaceness that "unfortunately" seems to me to be right in this dire context: the Russian *k neschastiu* is not poetical either. According to Nayman, Akhmatova herself used to get impatient with worshipers of *Requiem,* and its tribute to the "blood and tears" of suffering humanity, pointing out that these are poems, and remain poems. She nonetheless singled out those four lines as the "one good passage," evidently separating the absolutely basic emotion in them from all the artifices of good poetry.

There is a difference, and a vital one, between the inevitable distance of any poetry from what is actually going on, and the deliberate cultivation of a "poetic world" by a Symbolist poet like Blok. Pushkin and Akhmatova are not in the least concerned to be "relevant" to human affairs and responsibilities—sometimes they are and sometimes they aren't—their poetry is in this sense quite unselfconscious, and therefore wholly separate and wholly individual. But it is equally natural that their poetry speaks with its own complete authority, not an assumed or a carefully constructed one.

In this context Nayman makes an unexpected and devastating point. "Strictly speaking, *Requiem* is the ideal embodiment of *Soviet poetry* that all the theorists describe." Its hero is the people, the *narod,* not the people as the regime wanted them to be, and was continually and hypocritically invoking, but the people as they actually were. By upbringing and temperament, and no doubt by conviction too, Akhmatova was instinctively a Christian. So was Pasternak. That is why they had to stay where they were. Not only their instinctive authority as poets depended on it, but their identification with Russia—its past and especially its faith. The great advantage of such a faith against all forms of political idealism, an advantage which would be comical if the human predicament did not make it so inherently tragical, is that it has no trouble in accepting things as they are. Politics and ideology always have to pretend that things could be different, and, in Soviet Russia, that they actually *were* different. Hence the fact that Soviet poetry, so far from identifying like Akhmatova with what was really going on, had no choice but to endorse the Big Lie and to identify with the *narod* as it was ideally supposed to be, not as it was.

Having said that it is necessary also to state—and Nayman too makes this clear—that Akhmatova, like many other poets of her time (like Yeats himself) could seem a tremendous show-off. Her fellow-poet Marina Tsvetaeva used sardonically to refer to her as "Anna of All the Russias." She was regal; she was a queen. Yet she was one absolutely by nature, as if a little girl, a giddy princess, had always known what grave responsibilities ineluctably awaited her, and met them when the moment came without protest or pretension. The showing off was done on her behalf by friends, critics, the hangers-on—devoted or merely sycophantic—which literature attracts, and particularly literature in the Soviet Union, with all the official flim-flam—poets' villages and "Houses of Creativity"—which sought to make the people venerate the chosen bards of the Soviet system as much as the system itself. Ironically all that state-culture worship was transferred by a sort of honorable reversal on the part of their devotees to Pasternak and to Akhmatova herself. They became rival icons to those of the Soviet regime, images of an older and truer faith.

The splendidly refreshing thing about Nayman's memoir—he is himself a poet and was her literary secretary in her old age, when even the post-Stalinist regime did not dare to persecute her more—is that although he reveres Akhmatova as a woman and a great poet his tales about her, and his sparkling critical intelligence about the background and setting of her poems, are not in the least reverential. He assumes her grandeur and her dignity as she assumed them herself; and his accounts of her life in Leningrad, in her small crumbling room on the Fontanka canal and later outside the town in the writers' village of Komarovo, have the homely fascination and humor of Boswell's recollections of Dr. Johnson. When Robert Frost came to Leningrad in the late Fifties a meeting was arranged by a well-known critic and authority on English literature. "Both their names figured in the list of candidates for the Nobel Prize, and the idea of bringing them together seemed an especially felicitous one to the bureaucrats . . ." The Eng. Lit. man was duly impressed—"how grand she was, and how sad she seemed," when she read Frost her poem "The Last Rose." "For some moments we were silent, still."

But Akhmatova later told Nayman with amusement that she had felt like a "Grandma" with a "Grandpa," and moreover that Frost had seriously wanted to know whether it might be profitable to manufacture pencils using the Komarovo pine trees. Entering into the spirit of the thing, she reminded him that anyone felling a tree in the park was fined 500 rubles; but the reader may suspect that Frost was acting the New England farmer, teasing her in his deadpan way and being more playful than either she or her secretary realized. She felt it unfitting and improper for a great poet to have such a "farming streak" in him. In fact two quite different attitudes to Art and the Artist—the Russian one and the American—were misunderstanding each other.

St. Petersburg, as it was in her youth and is now again after the Soviet years of being Leningrad, was at once Akhmatova's court and the kingdom of her poetry. She had been born Anna Gorenko, in far-off Kiev in the Ukraine, but her father being a naval architect the family had moved to the Baltic about the time in 1905 when the Japanese were sinking the Russian fleet at Tsushima. Her mother and father separated, and the family settled at Tsarskoe Selo—"Tsar's Village"—just outside St. Petersburg. She was already being courted by the promising young poet Nikolai Gumilev, who was to fight gallantly as an officer in the 1914 war and to be shot by the Bolsheviks for alleged monarchist conspiracy in 1921. Anna Gorenko was reluctant to marry him, but in the end she did, and they had a son, Lev, mostly looked after as a child by Anna's mother-in-law. Under the Soviet regime he was to be twice imprisoned for long periods for no other reason than that he bore his father's name. The anguish of his arrest and detention with innumerable other victims of the Terror in the Kresty Prison in Leningrad is the subject of Akhmatova's somber and magnificent ***Requiem***.

When she showed signs of being a poet her father begged her not to dishonor the family name by using it in this frivolous context, so she called herself after a Tartar ancestor on her mother's side; the name is cognate with the oriental *Achmet*. Her husband, a difficult, moody man who disliked the routines of domesticity and only cared for "old maps and distant countries," thought it would be ridiculous for one poet to be married to another. Certainly this rare conjunction is not often a success, as was shown in the more recent case of Sylvia Plath and Ted Hughes; yet it is possible for one to inspire the other even as the marital relation deteriorates. Gumilev was a generous man who soon saw that his wife had real talent. On his return from travels in Abyssinia he asked her what she had been writing, and she showed him poems that had been inspired by another Russian poet to whose work he had introduced her. Innokenty Annensky was a withdrawn, scholarly man, who taught classics at the school of Tsarskoe Selo and who had produced a short book of poems called *The Cypress Box*. This had become her Bible, rather as the youthful Pushkin was never without his copy of the poems of the Frenchman Parny.

Gumilev congratulated her warmly on her new poems, and they were a great success when published in the spring of 1912 as her first collection, *Evening*. Her second collection, mostly of love poems, *Rosary*, made even more of a sensation two years later: she became something of a cult figure in the Petersburg literary world. By then her husband had formed round them the circle of poets known as Acmeists or Adamists, of whom Osip Mandelstam was one. Their poetic philosophy was in a sense existential: a precision about things and moments, and a rejection of symbolism and the Ivory Tower.

From the sad majesty of *Requiem* Akhmatova was to look back on herself at this period as the "gay little sinner of Tsarskoe Selo." The events of those years—love affairs, separations, tragedies like the suicide of a young cadet, the lover of her friend Olga Sudeikina—were all to find their way into her strange masterpiece of poetic autobiography, *Poem Without a Hero*, which she wrote in the terrible years before and after the Second World War. Like *The Waste Land* it possesses the mysterious authority, that of Pushkin's *tainstvenni pevets*—the secret-bearing poet—to convey the apocalypse of a whole epoch in the words of a single intimacy. Its uniquely sonorous rhythm, which can only be very imperfectly suggested in English, brings into a liturgical unison past and future, the figures who haunt the threshold of the new century, "the real and not the calendar one," which began for her in 1914, and visitants of quite another kind, doubles from an endless masquerade.

> Since childhood I have feared
>   maskers;
> It always seemed to me
> That some superfluous shadow
> With "neither face nor name"
> Slipped in among them . . .

One of those who slipped into the poem as if by accident was also for her a predestined visitor.

> The guest from the future!—Is it
>   true
> That he really will come to me,
> Turning left at the bridge?

The visitor was Isaiah Berlin, an Oxford professor working in 1945 at the British Embassy, who came to her room over the bridge by the Fontanka canal. His wonderful account of the visit forms one of the introductory pieces to the *Complete Poems,* in which he imparts his sense of reverence and awe at meeting in these circumstances a poet who had become so tranquilly and effortlessly, and as if by natural ordination, a queen, even a goddess: one whose survival and secret life in silence and exile were known only to a few. A

letter to Nayman observed that a friend had found an epigraph for her poetry.

> But I stand on calamity's scaffold
> As if enthroned 'midst the cour-
>   tiers' homage.

And she accepted the homage without either modesty or vanity.

This matter-of-fact acceptance of herself as a vessel of divinity, one chosen to utter mysteries so vital to the human spirit, is often expressed in her poems ("They flow across the blank page / Like a pure stream in a ravine") and in her sense of her intense relation with unknown readers and listeners. Pasternak had the same kind of conviction of himself as poet-savior and redeemer, as in *Doctor Zhivago* and poems like "Gethsemane," but Pasternak did not have her sense of humor and her female down-to-earthness. Clearly she inspired a sense of fun in others, as well as reverence. Comedy was part of the magic.

Isaiah Berlin describes how he met her and was settling down for what turned out to be an all-night conversation, when they were disturbed by his name being shouted in the courtyard below.

It proved to be Randolph Churchill, the son of Winston, who was also on a visit to the British Embassy, and who when looking for Berlin and finding himself in surroundings that reminded him of his old Oxford college, had started hallooing for his colleague as he would once have done in the quad. This was at the beginning of the cold war, and Russian friends and well-wishers were stupefied by the risk and the possible scandal involved. Here clearly—in the eyes of the KGB—were two English spies come to conspire with the great Russian poet, and perhaps even whisk her away to London! The absurdity probably had no ill effects, but it was about this time that the literary establishment resolved once more to denounce Akhmatova for nonfulfillment of the Soviet poetic ideal, while her son was sent into a second term of exile.

Earnest pilgrims from abroad were later to be embarrassed by the squalor in which the distinguished old lady was compelled to live. Nayman recalls a young English university don who was working on the "folk sources" in her poetry. Akhmatova had a drawing of herself by Modigliani over the bed in her small room, and it was suggested he might like to look at it, but the invitation seemed to bother him. Later she said to her secretary with a laugh, "Over there they're not accustomed to seeing old ladies' beds. He looked dreadful when you dragged him to the edge of the abyss. They can't believe that we live like this. Nor can they understand how we write at all in these conditions." The husband of her old friend Punin's daughter, in whose flat she was living (Punin himself had died in a gulag), was a trial to her because of the way he attempted as "a devotee of beauty" to hold literary conversations. When Akhmatova with her secretary and the poet Brodsky was celebrating with some cognac the tenth anniversary of Stalin's death the husband appeared and began to ask her whether "one should not underestimate Voznesensky and Surkov"—both well-known poets during the Soviet regime. Akhmatova maintained a stony silence, but afterward remarked with a laugh about her literary landlord, "I value him highly. In his stead we might have a person who would admonish me with 'Mother, you've left the bathroom light on again.'"

Vivaciously translated, Nayman's memoir makes an ideal companion piece to the wealth of essays and photographs in the volume of collected poems, as it does to Amanda Haight's already classic biography of the poet.* Judith Hemschemeyer and her editor Roberta Reeder have done a superb job, and the latter has been able to include in this translation several poems and fragments discovered in Russia by the scholar M. M. Kralin, and authenticated by Nayman's knowledge of the poet in her last years. Shortly before she died she wrote a couple of final lines:

> Necessity herself has finally sub-
> mitted.
> And has stepped pensively aside.

The delphic utterance might seem to link with that world of shadowy personifications, maskers, and memories in *Poem Without a Hero,* where the poet dryly observed, "There is no death—everyone knows that, / It's insipid to repeat it," taking as her sign the motto of Mary Queen of Scots—"In my end is my beginning"—which she had found in T. S. Eliot's *Four Quartets.*

In another poem she comments, "Without mystery there is no poetry," and she called one series "Secrets of the Craft." Susan Amert takes a further phrase of hers, "In a Shattered Mirror," as the title of an exceptionally learned and elegant study of the technicalities of Akhmatovan poetry, doing the job without any of the contemporary jargon and high-flown theory which the poet herself would have despised. For Akhmatova always maintained there was nothing upstage or recherché in what she wrote, none of the invented world of symbolism. Her mystery, like Pushkin's, was in clarity: in an openness which could appear baffling because it left so much unsaid. Her husband had long before remarked on this, and on the fact that as a poet she did not "invent herself": the point was later elaborated in a study of her poetics by the well-known critic V. Vinogradov.

Susan Amert begins her own book by making a comparison between the early fame of Pushkin and his "Byronic" po-

ems, and the similar success enjoyed by Akhmatova's first two collections. It is a good point, because even Pushkin's friends were baffled by what they considered the homely oddity of his later masterpieces, like *The Little House at Kolomna* and *The Bronze Horseman,* while his enemies claimed he had ceased to be a poet. Though Akhmatova never lost her popularity her devotees were puzzled by the cryptic internal references in *Poem Without a Hero,* while the Soviet literary establishment scurrilously referred to her as the "nun and harlot" whose decadent and frivolous verses were unworthy of the good name of Russian poetry.

Certainly *Poem Without a Hero* is a gift to the critic and commentator, and Susan Amert's chapter on it is illuminating. As with *The Bronze Horseman* this great *poema*'s authority makes its own kind of sense, and has its own impact on the individual reader. Akhmatova herself was a profound Pushkinist, and wrote some fine and subtle essays on his later poetry. Her tastes in the literature of her own country could be sharply arbitrary. She abominated Chekhov: Nayman thinks it was because his "gray" world reminded her too much of her own drab early days at Kiev as Anna Gorenko, before she became the Princess of Tsarskoe Selo. She was not keen on Tolstoy but adored Dostoevsky and reread him continually. She had an almost girlish attachment to Byron's poems; and Isaiah Berlin was a bit bewildered and embarrassed when at the beginning of their long colloquy together she recited to him from memory two cantos of *Don Juan,* in an English stressed so oddly that he could barely recognize it as such.

As her translator emphasizes, "Akhmatova lived in a home constructed not only of Russian literature but world literature." For the Acmeist movement of the early days, as Mandelstam had put it, universal culture was what mattered. And just as Pushkin's poetry seems to resolve itself in the end into a celestial form of fairy tale, coming at once from everywhere and nowhere, so Akhmatova's poems have the same clear, unwondering, unlocalized matter-of-factness about them. She was always sardonic about herself, and impersonally maternal about her creations. Sometimes she saw the muse as a wicked stepmother, drinking her blood "like that evil girl of my youth—love." There was nothing obviously "feminine" about her or her poems, and yet many of the most striking ones show an oblique but profound identity with female impulse—Cleopatra summoning her pride to suicide, Lot's wife giving her life for the sake of a last look back.

She was right also to stress that there was nothing hermeneutic about her poetry, nothing resembling the verbal mysteries of Mallarmé: her mysteries are in the open, as they are in legends. A famous early poem, "The Gray-Eyed King," later set to music by Prokofiev, is an inverted fairy story, with all that form's suggestive intensity, but full of the conviction—so somber in the later postrevolution poems—that magic does not work, that there is no happy ending. Only in the completion of a poem. The gray-eyed king is dead: the peasant mother looks into the eyes of the child she has secretly had by him.

* *Anna Akhmatova: A Poetic Pilgrimage* (Oxford University Press, 1976)

Simon Franklin   (review date 14 May 1993)

SOURCE: "Empress of Poets," in *Times Literary Supplement,* No. 4702, May 14, 1993, p. 26.

[*In the following review, Franklin judges the quality of the discussion and presentation of Akhmatova's work in* In a Shattered Mirror, *by Susan Amert;* My Half Century, *edited by Ronald Meyer; and* The Complete Poems, *translated by Judith Hemschemeyer.*]

Anna Akhmatova, empress of poets, died in 1966. She had grown up in Tsarskoe Selo, the Tsar's Village outside St Petersburg, where Pushkin had been to school. In 1911 in Paris, Modigliani drew her "in the attire of Egyptian queens". With Osip Mandelstam and her husband Nikolai Gumilev she was at the centre of the Guild of Poets professing the creed of Acmeism. Between 1912 and 1922 she published five books of poetry, "lyrical diaries" of precisely evoked fragments of experience, sharp memories of love and guilt and pain. More artists painted her and sculpted her, admirers flocked.

From 1925 she disappeared from public view. *Nobody* would print her. What good were her private insights and precious diction when there was Socialism to be built? During the war she was useful, but in 1946, Andrei Zhdanov, a secretary of the Central Committee of the Communist Party, denounced Akhmatova as "one of the standard-bearers of an empty, aristocratic, drawing-room poetry, which is totally alien to Soviet Literature". Zhdanov's last phrase was, of course, correct.

Her son was arrested, Gumilev had been executed, Mandelstam died in the camps. Akhmatova lived on the margins, migrating from friend's flat to friend's flat, carrying with her the one inviolable possession, her language, into which all was absorbed. She said of her poetry from the late 1930s: "my handwriting had changed and my voice sounded differently".

Akhmatova's "changed handwriting" has attracted many graphologists. In his memoir of his meetings with Akhmatova, Isaiah Berlin expressed concern that some of her later work may be smothered under the "tumulus of learned commentary inexorably rising over it". Susan Amert's admirable study, *In a Shattered Mirror,* shows that erudition can illuminate as well as suffocate.

The early Akhmatova communed with the Muse who "dictated *Inferno* to Dante". Mandelstam once called Acmeism "nostalgia for world culture", and Akhmatova's poems were allusive even when ostensibly direct. They were transparent at a distance but obscure in close-up; openly autobiographical, but notoriously hard to pin to any single event. In much of Akhmatova's later poetry, the inner complexity was brought to the surface. Short poems were combined into cycles, literary echoes merged with pointedly enigmatic semi-references. Here is an adventure-playground for sleuths and intertextualists, but for Akhmatova the multiple resonances were not a game but a mission. A capacious language could overcome time, which blotted out so much of the past and present. When she wrote, she and a very few trusted friends would silently commit the poem to memory and then destroy the writing. Poetry was the concentrated remembrance of words: her own words, words of past poets, words of the women at the prison gates (in **Requiem:** "I have woven a wide mantle / From their meagre, overheard words").

Akhmatova encouraged speculation, but discouraged conclusions. Of her most mysterious cycle, **Poem Without a Hero,** she wrote: "unexpected galleries open up, leading nowhere. . . . The shades pretend to be those who have cast them. . . . Everything doubles and trebles. . . . It is impossible to discern which is the voice and which the echo, which is the shadow of the other".

Sensibly, therefore, Amert does not try to be comprehensive, or to find any single key. Instead she offers selected close readings. She does have a central and plausible thesis—that Akhmatova increasingly meditated on the theme of the Poet rather than recording moments of the Poet's experience—but she does not force her material, and she makes generous use of the observations of other commentators. Indeed, her larger belief is in the "fundamental openendedness and infinite allusiveness of the later poetry". Her role, then, which she plays with delicacy, is to enrich the experience of reading.

The poems in the late cycle, *Sweetbriar in Blossom* (1946—62), for example, frame both a love-story and a series of reproachful evocations on the theme of forgetfulness, the lover's forgetfulness of the poet. The lyrical persona slips in and out of overt and concealed associations with Dido and Aeneas, Keats's Isabella and Lorenzo, Pushkin's Lensky and Olga from *Eugene Onegin,* and of course, Beatrice and Dante, as well as several meetings and partings in Akhmatova's life. The aim is neither to produce a set of erudite footnotes nor to play theoretical games with intertextuality. Amert listens carefully, pursues the echoes to their sources, and arrives at a persuasive interpretation of these enigmatically interlinked fragments, in which "the imagery of death is in every instance counterbalanced by images of transcendence . . . of the poet's triumph over death, oblivion and betrayal through memory and poetry".

These are old-fashioned readings. Amert dismisses "modern-day sophists", and is happy to accept that there is nothing retrogressive in poetic retrospection, in "nostalgia for world culture". She lets Akhmatova set the agenda and the terms.

I suspect that Akhmatova would be rather less pleased at the way she is reflected in Ronald Meyer's volume of her [*My Half Century:*] *Selected Prose.* From a variety of mostly posthumous publications Meyer and a team of translators have put together what they reasonably claim to be "the most complete collection of Akhmatova's prose in any language": autobiographical fragments, memoirs of writers and artists, a set of articles on Pushkin, and about a hundred letters spanning the period from her schooldays in Kiev in 1906 right through to 1965.

In the preface to an edition of her poems, published in the year before she died, Akhmatova stated, with only the faintest motion of tongue towards cheek: "from the very beginning I knew everything about poetry—I never knew anything about prose". Curiously, her list of "three leviathans of the twentieth century" contains only prose-writers: Proust, Joyce and Kafka. But she herself never felt entirely comfortable in prose. She tried a few bits of short fiction, but destroyed them. In her later years she made quite copious autobiographical notes, but with the exception of one brief summary they remained as drafts. Meyer hints that the reason was censorship, but in most cases I doubt it. Akhmatova was well able to finish poems with no immediate prospect of publication. Her narrative cycles of poetry consisted of separate small jewels which reflected one another through their adjacent settings. In prose, the polish was more nervously applied. She lacked the magisterial assurance in her control of the rhythms, in the presence of the Muse at her shoulder.

By far the most resonant of the autobiographical pieces is, not surprisingly, the one which Akhmatova herself passed as finished: "Briefly about Myself", a series of lapidary factual statements in chronological sequence from 1889 to 1965, as taut as a poem. Elsewhere there is a fair amount of parochial polemic, as Akhmatova responded to what she felt were inaccurate accounts of the origins of Acmeism, or of the early influences on her poetry, or of the extent of her early popularity. There are glimpses of gold (the smell of damp leather in the Petersburg cabs; reciting Verlaine with

Modigliani under a Parisian drizzle in 1911), but overall these drafts cannot compare with the best Russian memoirs of the period.

Akhmatova's articles on Pushkin, however, have a special status. All Russians suck in Pushkin with their mothers' milk; Russian writers seem to feel it their occasional duty to meditate publicly on Pushkin's genius (the most famous and fatuous specimen being Dostoevsky's speech at the Pushkin monument in 1880). When she chose, Akhmatova was as capable as any of treating Pushkin as a symbol (of the poet who in time defeated the anti-poets who in his time had destroyed him). But besides communing with Pushkin, Akhmatova also studied him, identified sources, puzzled over documents. She produced a detailed interpretation of the intrigues which led to Pushkin's fatal death in a duel. And her articles on Pushkin's debt to Benjamin Constant, and on his transformation of the Don Juan theme in *The Stone Guest,* have become classics in their field.

For reading Akhmatova's poetry, the non-Russianist now has an "expanded edition" of Judith Hemschemeyer's much-praised labour of massive devotion, *The Complete Poems.* The new edition is a single-volume paperback instead of a two-volume hardback. The parallel Russian texts have been omitted, as has Roberta Reeder's introductory biography of Akhmatova. Hemschemeyer has added translations of some seventy items which first appeared in Russian in 1990, and one spuriously attributed poem has been removed. Seventy pages are allocated to a "Photo Biography". the new paginations throughout will be bibliographically confusing.

The first edition of Hemschemeyer's translations was widely reviewed. Without wishing to dampen her well-earned applause, I hope that her achievement does not discourage others from producing new versions. Hemschemeyer comes close to emulating Akhmatova's precise and restrained diction, but—as she frankly admits in her preface—at the expense of musicality and resonance. Attempts to replicate Akhmatova in rhyme and metre have mostly resulted in wordy doggerel, but translators have to be optimists even if they cannot be perfectionists.

One editorial quibble. Akhmatova *was* a perfectionist. Much of the new material in Hemschemeyer's volume consists of draft fragments. Akhmatova is misrepresented if her deliberately finished poems are merged with her provisionally jotted verses, just as in Meyer's volume drafts mingle with complete pieces under the single label of "prose". Wherever possible, the distinctions should be more clearly signalled.

Sonia I. Ketchian (essay date Summer 1993)

SOURCE: "Axmatova's Civic Poem 'Stansy' and Its Pushkinian Antecedent," in *Slavic and East European Journal,* Vol. 37, No. 2, Summer, 1993, pp. 194-210.

[*In the following essay, Ketchian traces many of the devices and allusions in Akhmatova's poem "Stansy" to Pushkin.*]

The purpose of this paper is to analyze Axmatova's poem **"Stansy"** ("Stances"), first in terms of its obvious Pushkinian predecessor and then in terms of its structure and content. A look into the genre and the distinguishing specifics for each of the two poems involved will precede the discussion of Axmatova's "Stansy." It will be followed by an examination of the poem's evolution through textual variants as it bears on the present discussion. In spite of the obviously close thematic connection between Axmatova's **Requiem 1935-1940** and her cycle "Cerepki" ("Shards"), that comparison must be relegated to a future investigation.

"Stansy" (*stances* or stanzas) is a challenging genre, or subgenre, of poetry to define and classify. In French literature *stances* were usually four-line strophes with unrepeated rhymes and an obligatory pause at the end of the fourth line. The genre's slight role in English literature can be judged by the fleeting mention given to it in the English-language encyclopedias. A case in point is *The Princeton Encyclopedia of Poetry and Poetics,* which states in the last paragraph of the entry on *Stanza:*

> The term "s." is sometimes applied to independent poems of complex metrical pattern, such as the ballade, the sestina, and the sonnet (q.q.v.). Synonymous or analogous terms include the early English batch and stave (q.v.).

All this is of no help for the task at hand. Nor is *The Poetic Dictionary* by A. Kvjatkovskij (*Poeticeskij slovar'*) more enlightening.

The most applicable entry is by Mixail L. Gasparov in *Kratkaja literaturnaja ènciklopedija* (*Concise Literary Encyclopedia*), where he posits the following characteristics for the Russian version of "stansy":

> Once *stances* entered Russian poetry, of the enumerated features only those of genre remained: in Russian poetry of the end of the eighteenth century and the beginning of the nineteenth, the term *stances* was applied to works of elegiac lyrics (most often meditative, less frequently, love lyrics), usually composed in quatrains, most often in iambic tetrameter. The most famous is Pushkin's "Stansy" ("In the hope of glory and

good . . ."). By the second half of the nineteenth century with the gradual disappearance of distinctions between the lyrical genres, the term "*stances*" was no longer used.

Reference is made here to the most famous piece in the genre, Puskin's "Stansy" ("V nadezde slavy i dobra"), which is one of three pieces to bear the Russian version of this word in the title (a fourth uses the French "*Stances*"). The pieces by Puskin include one of the first poems written by Puskin in the Lycée, the French-language "*Stances*" (1814) in five quatrains on the topic of "seize the moment" ("lovi mgnoven'e"); "*Stances*. From Voltaire" ("Stansy (Iz Vol'tera)") in nine quatrains on love ending early and logic taking its place; "*Stances* to Tolstoj" ("Stansy Tolstomu") in six quatrains on "lovi mgnoven'e"; and the one under investigation, "Stansy" ("V nadezde slavy i dobra"), the only Russian one with no explanation in its title. In this poem Puskin probably avoided explanation by giving it a title that in his verse was linked to light moments; his objective was ostensibly to veil its important reflective allusions. The famous poem "Brozu li ia vdol' ulic sumnyx" is called "Stansy" in *Vremennik Puskinskoj komissii. Sbornik naucnyx trudov.*

Although Gasparov states that use of the genre by Russian poets waned noticeably ("vyxodit iz upotreblenija") in the second half of the nineteenth century, yet Esenin, Annenskij, Severjanin, Sologub, Bal'mont, Gumilev and Mandel'stam have such pieces. Their "*Stances*," however, display few similarities to the two under investigation. What is more, Axmatova's "*Stances*," by being an obvious reflection of Puskin's, quietly refers to the general tenor of the master's poem, a fact that allows Axmatova to concentrate much into fewer lines. In many ways, moreover, Axmatova's poem constitutes a contemporary compressed echo of Puskin's text in terms of content and idea.

Puskin's poem titled "Stansy," which opens with "V nadezde slavy i dobra," is the only one of the four poems relevant to the present comparison. This poem seems initially to have been created in Pskov in 1826 and completed upon the poet's release from exile the same year. His objective was to ameliorate the plight of the exiled Decembrists by drawing—with formidable artistic imagination—public and official attention to their treatment, by attempting to soften the attitudes of officials toward them, and, not least, by raising the spirits of the exiles. Moreover, in choosing this named genre with its inherent meditative qualities, Puskin brought to the fore his esthetic deliberations on the role of the aristocracy, on the powers entrusted to an autocrat, as well as on past and present, juxtaposing the new ruler with a great predecessor. Indeed, "the poeticized event is not just *different* from real experience but also more durable, and perhaps more valuable, as well." His [translated] poem reads:

Stances

In the hope of glory and good
I gaze ahead without fear:
The beginning of Peter's glorious days
Was marred by rebellions and executions.

But with truth he captivated hearts,
But with learning he tamed customs,
And from the rebellious Strelets
Before him Dolgorukij was distinguished.
With his autocratic hand
He boldly sowed enlightenment,
He did not scorn his native land:
He was aware of its destiny.

Now an academician, now a hero,
Now a navigator, now a carpenter,
He with his all-encompassing soul
On the throne was an eternal worker.

Take pride in the family resemblance;
In all be like your forebear:
Like him, indefatigable and firm,
And in memory, like him, forgiving.

The history and concept of this poem are treated extensively in D. D. Blagoj's study *Tvorceskij put' Puskina: 1826-1830.* An appeal to the newly enthroned Nicholas I, who in 1826 recalled Puskin from exile in Mixajlovskoe, it illumines the poet's conciliatory expectations and hope for the Decembrists' return under Nicholas' new rule. Puskin's esthetic embodiment of his wish and plan for the return of the Decembrists from Siberia was, regrettably, perceived by his circle more as a form of flattery and a retreat from his convictions. Hence his subsequent reply in verse in 1828, "Druz'jam" ("To My Friends"). Because Nicholas ostensibly fashioned himself after Peter I, Puskin (mostly in anticipation and hope) appears to have portrayed him as striving for the same objectives—a means of appeasing and guiding the tsar in the desired direction. While Puskin's speaker's respect for the tsar *sounds* rather genuine, Axmatova's attempted praise in the abhorred fifteen-poem cycle of 1950, "Slava miru" ("Glory to Peace"), sounds wooden and untypical of her poetry, almost as if the most recent recipient of the Stalin Prize had penned them. Thus, her frantic desire to secure the release from prison of her son Lev Gumilev (1912-1992), who after fighting valiantly in World War Two was arrested for the third time in 1949, was not translated into true art.

To be sure, literary aggrandizement of Peter has a long history. It was practiced in the West by Voltaire in his historical work *Histoire de l'empire de Russie sous Pierre le Grand,* as well as by most eighteenth-century Russian writ-

ers, including Feofan Prokopovic in "Sermon on the Interment of the Most Illustrious, Most Sovereign Peter the Great," Antiox Kantemir in his unfinished heroic epic "Petrida," Mixail Lomonosov in odes and especially in "Slovo poxval'noe Petru Velikomu" ("Eulogy on Peter the Great") and in the two cantos of the heroic epic "Petr Velikij" ("Peter the Great"; twenty-four cantos were planned), as well as by Gavriil Derzavin. A cursory reading of Puskin's "Zametki po russkoj istorii XVIII veka" ("Notes on Eighteenth Century Russian History") suggests admiration for Peter the Great as a great political and historical figure, but Sam Driver notes that "a close reading shows that in fact the poet equates the emperor with tyranny and inhuman despotism" and, what is more, Puskin was concerned about the welfare of the serfs and the nobility alike. Unlike Aleksandr Griboedov, Puskin disapproved of unlimited autocracy, even for Peter, hence the ambiguous depiction of the emperor in *The Bronze Horseman* and elsewhere. Puskin's *"Stances,"* contends Blagoj, is a terse introduction to subsequent works by him connected with the theme of Peter, namely *Arap Petra Velikogo (The Blackamoor of Peter the Great), Poltava,* and *Mednyi vsadnik (The Bronze Horseman).* The example of merciful Peter the Pardoner was grounded in certain facts, among them his pardon of Prince Jakov Dolgorukij's audacities, which was sung by Derzavin in his ode "Vel'moza" ("The Grandee") and by Kondratij Ryleev (one of the executed Decembrists) in the poem "Grazdanskoe muzestvo" ("Civic Valor"). In contrast to the excerpt in "Notes on Eighteenth Century Russian History," Puskin in *"Stances"* mostly underscores Peter's positive traits and achievements, albeit a discordant note resounds in the mention of the Streltsy. Puskin's poetic speaker in *"Stances,"* present through the personal pronoun in line two, fades out thereafter, which lends, as it were, a collective character to the plea. Acknowledging in stanza one the rebellions and executions at the onset of Peter's reign, Puskin then proceeds to highlight the Emperor's positive accomplishments which, to his mind, should be duplicated by Nicholas I, a bold implication for one only recently, and only tenuously, restored to favor. In stanza two the speaker points to a reconciliation between Peter and his subjects.

Stanzas three and four characterize Peter as the highest example of "tsar'-prosvetitel'" (an enlightened monarch)—much in the manner of Lomonosov in the two completed cantos of the epic "Peter the Great" and in his "Eulogy on Peter the Great." Blagoj notes parallels and analogies to virtually every word in Lomonosov—the leitmotif being the glorification of the "sage Teacher and Educator." Lexical echoes can also be observed, particularly in stanza four. Following Lomonosov's lead, Puskin further democratizes Peter. In doing so, his portrait comes close to that of a muzhik through descriptions of the emperor as "plotnik" (Lomonosov, in accordance with his own precepts of distinguishing three styles for appropriate topics, employs the higher-style word "stroitel" in the verse and the prosaic "plotnik" in his prose only) and "rabotnik" (Derzavin used this for the first time) in rhymed position for emphasis. Further, Puskin chooses the versatile word "sejal," which for all its lofty usage recalls also the practical meaning of a peasant sowing seeds in a field. Representing Peter as a reformer, Puskin calls on Nicholas for similar "mercy toward the fallen" ("milost' k padsim")—a plea that will be repeated in various forms to the end of his life. Yet Puskin refrains from spelling out his request in view of its being obvious to all concerned. In this poem Puskin remains hopeful of the realization of his objectives, a fact corroborated by what Blagoj terms "mazornyj jambiceskij stroj, kak u Lomonosova" ("an optimistic iambic arrangement like Lomonosov's"). Puskin's poem "Poslanie v Sibir'" ("Missive to Siberia"; beginning "Vo glubine sibirskix rud" ["In the bowels of Siberian mines"]) was commenced only a few days after the completion of "*Stances*" which, in turn, was written only nine days after "Poslanie k I. I. Puscinu" ("Epistle to I. I. Puscin"). Both "Missive to Siberia" and "*Stances*" were written in the same iambic tetrameter with alternate rhymes and the masculine rhymes placed first, in the odd lines. Indeed, all of Puskin's political lyrics of the second half of the 1820s will assume this form, with lexical echoing among the poems.

In following Puskin's lead for her poem's title, Axmatova alerts the reader to intertextuality without the overt imitation typical of a poem containing the word "imitation" in either the title or subtitle. Yet the indications of intertextuality are closer to the surface, and more easily recognized, than in cases where reference to subtexts does not exist. Axmatova's poem obviously takes Puskin's famous "*Stances*" as a touchstone and a point of reference, while placing it in her own tradition of balladic poems as well. I furnish here the Kralin-Axverdjan version of the [translated] poem as the one I find to be closest, at this level in scholarship, to Axmatova's finished version. Between lines, in fine print, are variant words and phrases from the other versions.

Stances

Moon of the Streltsy. Zamoskvorechye. Night.
Like the procession at Calvary pass the hours of
   Holy Week.
I am having a terrible nightmare. Can it really be
   that
No one, no one, no one can help me?

"It's not possible to live in the Kremlin,"
The Preobrazhensky trooper is right,
There the microbes of ancient atrocities still
   teem:
Boris's wild fear, the malice of all the Ivans,
And the Pretender's arrogance—instead of the

people's rights.

1940, April. Moscow

Axmatova employs Puskin's device of juxtaposing the present ruler with Peter, leaving out the specifics. In her poem the dichotomy is based upon two points of division between the oppressors and the oppressed. First, the Moscow River separates the speaker in Zamoskvorec'e geographically from the other, ruling bank of the Kremlin—"tam." Historically, Zamoskvorec'e was the Streltsy Quarter of Moscow. The speaker seems to unite with the trampled people at the very end and together to stand in opposition to the tyrants. (Puskin attempts to bring Peter closer to the people lexically through "plotnik.") Second, the unmentioned but intimated victims of Stalin are equated to Peter's victims, the Streltsy, who enter the poem by means of the epithet attached to the moon. Allusion to Christ's Passion (and to ***Requiem***) is achieved through "krestnyj xod" and "Strastnaja nedelja." This dimension adds a third element to the comparison, which then counterbalances the three names of tsars and, consequently, the three types of reign that Peter sought to escape. Here, as in her essays on Puskin, Axmatova explains herself through her investigation of his biography and works. She then creates a tacit portrait of Stalin through a montage of his predecessors in the Kremlin using some of Puskin's words, as will be pointed out below. And her speaker's plea for help is rather muted, where her fear is not.

That the portrait is readily recognizable became clear to the poet through Lidija Cukovskaja's reaction to the poem. The incident is recorded by Cukovskaja in her memoirs, *Zapiski ob Anne Axmatovoj* (*Notes on Anna Axmatova*), where she notes that Axmatova wanted to include this piece in a collection she was preparing for publication in June of 1956. Together the friends deleted it, however, for fear the portrait of Stalin was too obvious:

> Anna Axmatova very much wanted to offer [for publication—S. K.] "*Stances*." I, obviously, also wanted to . . . At first all is quiet, elegiac, pensive, and then suddenly in moving to the second quatrain, a blow of violent force. I'm wrong: not "in moving" but without any transition whatsoever, like the lash of a whip: "One mustn't live in the Kremlin."

And in the last two lines—a complete and accurate portrait of Stalin:

> Boris's wild fear and the malice of all the Ivans
> And the Pretender's arrogance instead of the
>   people's rights.

"What do you think, will everyone guess that it is his portrait or have you alone guessed it?" asked Anna Andreevna.

"I think, everyone will."

"In that case, we won't include it," decided Anna Andreevna.

"Only Khrushchev is allowed to assail Stalin."

In a footnote on this page Cukovskaja says: "I quote this poem not in the variant in which it was published in the collection *In Memory of Anna Axmatova* but in the one Axmatova intended to include in *The Course of Time,* no. 61." Strangely, the version is identical to the one in *Pamjati Anny Axmatovoj* with the substitution of "zverstva drevnego" for "drevnej jarosti" in *Pamjati.* Lidija Cukovskaja must have forgotten that she had access to more than one version, for in the summer of 1990 she was incredulous when I pointed out the discrepancies between the two versions she had published. She began reciting the poem by heart as in *Zapiski,* and I pointed out on my sheet with four versions how the other one varied. Because the piece was not published in Axmatova's lifetime, all the several existing versions compete for recognition as final and authoritative. The variant favored by Axmatova, in all likelihood, is the one published by M. Kralin and G. R. Axverdjan alike, quoted above, with the exception of the former's division of lines. The vocabulary is closer to the time of the Ivans, and the punctuation, with the quotation marks in line five, is preferable to that of the other variants. The division of what should be line five into two separate lines—into lines five and six—as opposed to all other variants, is less likely as Axmatova's final version, since to this reader the division not only disrupts the poem's structural unity with Puskin but also the more frequent stanzaic organization into quatrains for Russian poems titled "*Stances.*" Thus, Cukovskaja's entry of June 1, 1956, shows that both Cukovskaja and Axmatova wanted to include "*Stances*" in the collection under preparation.

The two "*Stances,*" iambic in meter and structured in quatrains, differ, however, in other formal aspects. Puskin's five quatrains are composed in a neutral, rather light and optimistic-sounding iambic tetrameter (his other two Russian "*Stances*" are likewise in iambic tetrameter) with alternating masculine and feminine rhymes, closing on the feminine rhymes. This pattern of rhymes, ending with feminine rhymes, softens the poem's manner and conveys to the reader the hope that informs the comparisons and didacticisms. Whether the hope is actual, feigned, or reserved is debatable. Puskin further commends Peter's ability to distinguish between the violent and unruly Streltsy ("bujnyj strelec") of 1698 and the aristocratic dissident Prince Jakov Dolgorukij. The peroration enforces Puskin's mounting unformulated appeal—a pardon for the aristocratic Decembrists, and, if the poem was commenced in Pskov, for the poet himself as well.

Axmatova's two quatrains of weighty and dignified iambic hexameter with enclosing rhymes—less common in Russian verse than rhyming couplets or alternate rhymes—begin and end with forceful, choppy masculine rhymes. While Axmatova obviously aligns her aristocratic son Lev Gumilev with Prince Dolgorukij, who was pardoned by the Emperor, her fear of execution for her son and for others translates Puskin's "bujnyj strelec" into "streleckaja luna," i.e., a moon overlooking nightmarish deaths, which further conflates with the yellow moon in ***Requiem*** and Innokentij Annenskij's frightening yellow moon. Depending on which of the published versions is taken as Axmatova's choice for a final version (Puskin has negligible variations in the Jubilee Edition), the poem appears to have a dual focus—an unspecified, fairly obvious poetic speaker who appears as the twice-repeated personal pronoun "mne" in stanza one, and the vague but recognizable image of Stalin, cleverly montaged from mention of the names and traits of previous occupants of the Kremlin. The fact that Peter moved out of the Kremlin attests, in the speaker's understanding, to his determination to break with the atrocities of the past. In the context of Puskin's poem, Axmatova's metonymical mention of Peter as Preobrazenec (it was the Preobrazenskij Regiment he belonged to) distances Peter's reign, which ultimately had positive results, from Stalin's mass Terror. Peter's necessary harshness for the country's eventual good is thus contrasted to Stalin's unwarranted atrocities. The speaker seems to be urging the current occupant to leave the Kremlin and to follow Peter's lead.

Axmatova's "*Stances,*" published in four different Western imprints until 1989, after which it was included in Soviet collections of Axmatova's works, has five major variants, including the two noted by Cukovskaja. The van der Eng-Liedmeier version seems to be an earlier draft. It even lacks the title and year common to all other versions. The version in Cukovskaja's *Zapiski* and those of Kralin and Axverdjan are nearly identical, save for punctuation marks and some vocabulary distinctions: in line six "zdes'" "—"tam","Ivanov" and the added "i" ("and") for the rhythm as well as for historic color in line seven—"Ioannov," in line five "ne nado"—"ne mozno" and more information on the venue of creation (Moscow) and the time (April, which makes *Strastnaja nedelja* relevant to the time of writing) in Kralin and Axverdjan. I believe that the Kralin and Axverdjan version is the favored one, but that Axmatova wanted to present the Cukovskaja version, as slightly more innocuous, for publication.

Both poems have an equally interesting structure. Puskin's "Stansy" is built on a concept of two's, a structure that can covey a sense of rhetorical balance so long as Nicholas decides to be similar to Peter. Semantically juxtaposed are the two tsars; the poet and the Decembrists; the Strelets and the aristocrat Dolgorukij coupled with the aristocratic poetic speaker. The obvious morphological symmetry in lines one, four, thirteen, fourteen, and eighteen constitutes nothing out of the ordinary: "Slavy i dobra; mjatezi i kazni; akademik—geroj; moreplavatel'—plotnik neutomim i tverd." In proximity, however, to other expressions of doubling the structural symmetry, too, becomes apparent. Anaphorical pairings lend syntactic balance for both contrast and/or juxtaposition as needed. The correspondences are: V—Vo (lines 1, 18); No—No (lines 5, 6); I—I (lines 7, 20); To—To (lines 13, 14); On—On (lines 10, 12). Also similar are: Pred nim—Kak on (lines 8, 19; as being connected with a personal pronoun in the third person which refers to Peter); Nacalo—Na trone (lines 3, 16; not only due to similarity of the two initial sounds but because of contrast/juxtaposition in meaning within the context, since both "Nacalo slavnyx dnej" and "Na trone" refer to Peter's reign). Lines 2 and 4 begin with verbs: Gljazu—Mracili. Further, lines 9 and 17 open with adjectives referring to the royal family: Samoderzavnym—Semejnym. Finally, the third "on" pairs with an implied one: On—[On] Ne preziral (lines 11, 15). Puskin utilizes both sound instrumentation (as will be seen) and structure (morphology and syntax) to further augment his verbal art and to amplify the juxtaposition.

The structure of Axmatova's poem hinges on the pattern of balladic poems, which it follows, hence a sizable collection of epithets: seven in eight lines. In contrast to the traditional ballad, however, all verbs in the poem are in the present tense. The predominance of symbolism based on the number three touches several areas, unusual for the traditional ballad but in keeping with the symbolism of three for the balladic poem, as seen in the three nominative sentences in the very first lines. They provide the time of day twice (the moon, night), the venue (to be contrasted to the Kremlin—it is probably the home of Axmatova's close friend Nina Ol'sevskaja, located in Zamoskvorec'e) and the historical allusion: "Streleckaja luna. Zamoskvorec'e. Noc'." The visual impression of the locus is that of a film frame. In rhythm, sound, and meaning the words simulate the fear of the speaker's pounding heart, further enhanced in the difficult, slow movement of the clock's "krestnyj xod," or rather of the hours of "Strastnaja nedelja." The earlier, van der Eng-Liedmier version stressed ephemeral movement with less of the fear component: "kak legkij dym" ("like light smoke").

The speaker of the poem is difficult to determine. In all likelihood the poem begins with the poet-persona and then changes into the thoughts of the Kremlin despot as reflected through the speaker's mind in her dream (in the version with "zdes" in line six). Ostensibly, in the version with "tam" in line six, the speaker does not change. If the speaker is synchronic to the poet Axmatova and not living in the past, then the word "tam" of the dream could have transposed her not only to the Kremlin but to the past with a view of the future. The speaker, then, is having a nightmare and in

a query with a tripartite reiterative subject she answers her own question through negated emphasis: "Neuzto v samom dele / Nikto, nikto, nikto ne mozet mne pomoc'?" Expecting the worst, the speaker opens the poem with a Streltsy moon as a symbol of torture and death, even when those Streltsy who remained loyal to Peter were exiled to Siberia and their entire property was confiscated. If Peter showed no mercy to the Streltsy, he did, however, pardon the aristocratic Prince Dolgorukij. Conversely, in the years of Stalinist Terror not even a glimmer of hope existed for the aristocratic Gumilev whose persecution was predicated mainly on the fact of his father's execution in 1921.

A jarring prosaism—a distant echo of Puskin's prosaisms—commences the montage of Stalin: "mikroby." The versions with "zverstva" rather than "jarosti drevnej" in line six fit in better here. Where Puskin piles up the various professions Peter engaged in while in Western Europe, Axmatova garners negative characteristics, one for each of the three different namesakes, Boris, Ioann, Samozvanec, to depict one unnamed person, thereby providing a portrait without a portrait, or a metonymical one. Those psychological microbes all begin with sibilants, which create a hissing congregation with other supporting words: for Puskin's "ja bez bojazni"—"strax," for his "nezloben"—"zloby," for Peter working as a common laborer—"spes'." Here Axmatova transfers Puskin's vocabulary to the negative semantic field. These words in Axmatova thus pick up the two "s's" in the poem's title and those in the name Iosif Vissarionovich Stalin. Indeed, in what I consider the ultimate version—"vsex Ioannov zloby"—the older form of the tsars' name begins with two of the same sounds as Iosif, and Axmatova could have changed it for publication from Ioannov to Ivanov in the version presented by Cukovskaja for purposes of camouflage. Moreover, the title "Stansy" contains the first three sounds of Stalin's surname and the opening word repeats the first two sounds: "Streleckaja." More repetition of these sounds comes later: "Strastnoj", "strasnyj." with a proliferation of hissing "s's" and "z's": "snitsja, strasnyj son." Also the word Samozvanec begins with an "s" and contains a "z." Through masterful alliteration Axmatova presents a veritable viper's nest in the Kremlin, which reverberates with hissing and the snake image in the Pretender's lines on Marinea Mnisek in Puskin's *Boris Godunov*. In "*Stances*" Puskin has a delicate network of alliterative "p" sounds for reinforcing Peter's name in Nicholas' mind. Indeed, all the words containing the "p" sound have, or are used in, a positive sense: "vpered, pravdoj, privlek, pred nim, prosvescen'e, ne preziral, preduaznacen'e, moreplavatel', plotnik, prascuru podoben, pamjat'ju." The impact of the alliterated "p" in augmenting Peter's positive image through sound instrumentation is quite effective here. Still, quietly undercutting the overtly glorified image of Peter are the sibilants that Axmatova likewise probably sensed before utilizing them to such advantage in her own poem. In Puskin the sibilants, already signalled in the title, lead from glory and fearlessness and sowing enlightenment to executions, Streltsy, and autocrats, seeming to bind together inextricably the autocrat, country and the Streltsy: samoderzavec, strana, strel'cy, etc. Stanza three has the highest concentration of sibilants (in seven words) with stanzas one and five close behind (five words each).

The only person who can help Axmatova's speaker is the occupant of the Kremlin, but whereas in her poem "Podrazanie armjanskomu" ("Imitation from the Armenian") the ewe's devoured son is beyond help and the mother merely faces the tyrant fearlessly, here, to the speaker's question whether it is true that no one can help her, the focus zooms in on the current man in the Kremlin. Where in real life Axmatova made a desperate appeal to Stalin for her son's life, the poetic speaker's desire for help in **"Stances"** remains an unarticulated wishful attitude shown through the change of focus to the Kremlin.

As in a film, one can visualize the speaker's longing eyes conveying the message. Moreover, there could be here an implied reference through the historical flashback to former occupants of the Kremlin, notably to Stalin's immediate predecessor, Lenin, who in 1921 had Axmatova's first husband, the poet Nikolaj Gumilev (1886-1921), shot, and an indication that she in fact expects no aid now. With mention of "Preobrazenec" Axmatova posits as the instructive ideal Peter I, who in 1703 founded St. Petersburg so as to be able to live away from the Kremlin. By mentioning Peter only metonymically, Axmatova achieves distance and alienation between Peter and the unmentioned and tabooed, as it were, Stalin to show that Peter's "necessary" harshness is not equivalent to Stalin's countless atrocities. Yet some ambivalence may be present here if one considers the fact that most of the tortures and executions of the Streltsy were carried out at Preobrazensk, with Peter present at times. In fact, Puskin's *Boris Godunov* shows an unnamed terror perpetrated by Boris Godunov and that he "interrogated" some victims personally. That the poem is connected to *Requiem* is seen in mention of the Streltsy and the implied victims, her son in particular ("I will howl under the Kremlin towers / Like the Streltsy wives"—"Budu ja, kak streleckie zenki, / Pod Kremlevskimi basnjami vyt' "), as well as the image of the moon (Ketchian, "Moon"). The biblical "Strastnaja nedelja" further corroborates links with *Requiem*, but also hints at the torturing of the Streltsy. Only the inhabitant of the Kremlin can put an end to the terror, a tacit echoing without explicit words of Puskin's own plea. But Stalin remained deaf to these appeals and he lacked the qualities that Puskin sought to bring forth in Nicholas.

A final link to Stalin can be traced through the fact that Axmatova's "Streleckaja luna" literally denotes the Sagittarius moon of the Archer and a southern constellation vis-

ible in late spring (Axmatova's poem is dated April) and summer. It is the ninth sign of the zodiac which the sun enters on November 22 through December 21. In astrology it carries ominous meaning. The question arises as to what Sagittarius moon can exist in April and in the North in Moscow. Again, Axmatova is coding information. It will be recalled that the last day of this sign is December 21 (Capricorn the goat begins on December 22) and Stalin was born on December 21 (new style) in Georgia (construed as the South in Russia), where the constellation is best visible. Thus Axmatova's brilliant, kaleidoscopic image of the Streltsy further intertwines with that of Stalin.

To sum up, it can be noted that, following Puskin's lead, Axmatova expressed artistically, utilizing literary tradition and historical facts as reflected by him, that which was otherwise denied expression in those difficult times—and she moved in her own new direction. Toward this end, she used to advantage devices found in Puskin: allusions, rhetorical devices, structural balance and meaningful sound instrumentation. And in the best tradition of the Russian esthetic imagination she, like Puskin, drew her inspiration from Russia's troubled past and present.

Rosette C. Lamonte (review date Summer 1993)

SOURCE: A review of *My Half Century: Selected Prose,* in *World Literature Today,* Vol. 67, No. 3, Summer, 1993, pp. 628-29.

[*In the following review, Lamonte discusses the ghosts that haunt the pages of Akhmatova's* My Half Century.]

In his preface to *My Half Century,* a splendid selection of the translated prose writings of Anna Akhmatova, Ronald Meyer, the editor of the volume, explains that the author never conceived of composing a chronicle of her life and times. Although, as Meyer points out, it is futile to imagine what the completed work might have been, a model could perhaps be sought in Pasternak and Mandelstam's "autobiographical fragments," as *Safe Conduct* and *The Noise of Time* were defined by their creators. In fact, this form of autobiography is characteristic of the postmodern esthetic, and even of "high modernism." For example, all of Ionesco's published diaries assume this loose, highly suggestive structure (*Notes and Counter Notes: Writings on the Theatre, Fragments of a Journal, Present Past Past Present, Un homme en question, Antidotes, La quête intermittente*). We no longer look for linearity in these accounts, but rather for revealing, allusive, if not elusive traces.

Since Akhmatova did not prepare a final version for publication, Meyer provides his own concise, helpful biographical sketch, in which he includes her in "the magnificent quartet of Russian poets" who were destroyed by the brutally repressive Soviet regime. Osip Mandelstam died on the way to a labor camp, Tsvetaeva hanged herself, and Pasternak was hounded into an early grave after the publication in Italy of *Doctor Zhivago* (1957) and his subsequent selection as the winner of the Nobel Prize in Literature (1958). As to Akhmatova, she was silenced by the August 1946 condemnation of the Central Committee (rescinded only in 1988). This list of victims is also the honor roll of the greatest and purest poetic voices of post-czarist Russia.

My Half Century begins with "Pages from a Diary." Born in Odessa in June 1889, the *velichavaia* (stately, regal) poet glories in the fact that her birth came in "the same year as Charlie Chaplin, Tolstoy's *Kreutzer Sonata,* and the Eiffel Tower." There is humor in this rapprochement between a modern monument, a literary masterpiece, and the greatest clown of our age. This, however, is followed by a reminder that, through her mother, she is a descendant of Genghis Khan. She grew up in Tsarskoe Selo, the czar's summer residence outside St. Petersburg, renamed Pushkin in 1937 in honor of its most illustrious resident. As Meyer declares, "the place held a special importance in her psychological geography." In her own journal the poet evokes the house they occupied, near the station, and which had been in the past a wayside inn. As a child, Akhmatova perused the dwelling's various aspects as she peeled off, layer by layer, the wallpaper in her yellow room until she reached "an unusually bright red." The room becomes a kind of palimpsest. Tsarskoe and nearby Pavlovsk were haunted by history and literature. The poet mentions "the specter of Nastasya Filippovna," the magnificent femme fatale of Dostoevsky's novel *The Idiot.* Looking at the photo in the book, one is struck by the resemblance between these women; Akhmatova could easily have acted the part of Nastasya Filippovna in one of the dramatizations of the novel.

Many ghosts haunt these pages: Nikolai Gumilev (1886-1921), Akhmatova's first husband, whom she met while he was still a student at the Tsarskoe Selo lycée; the symbolist poet Alexander Blok, whose portrait she sketches here; Amadeo Modigliani, who made sixteen drawings of her in Paris for her room in Tsarskoe (they vanished during the first years of the revolution); Osip Mandelstam, who described her in a poem as "a black angel"; Innokenty Annensky, considered by Akhmatova as the master of Gumilev, Mayakovsky, and Pasternak; Marina Tsvetaeva, who took her life in 1941. Akhmatova ponders: "It is frightening to think how Marina would have described these meetings . . . if she had remained alive and I had died on August 31, 1941." When she wrote these lines in 1959, Akhmatova must have felt that she had become the ghost of herself.

The ultimate ghost and teacher is Pushkin, the emblematic poet with whom Akhmatova identifies. She emulated his subtextual way of denouncing the autocratic czars. As Meyer states: "Writing in the 1930s, one of the bleakest decades in Russian history, Akhmatova is the first to identify the source of Pushkin's tale ['The Golden Cockerel'] as Washington Irving 'The Legend of the Arabian Astrologer.' Akhmatova, however, proceeds to interpret Pushkin's use of Irving's tale as a device for political satire, marshaling formidable evidence to prove that the fairy-tale Tsar is based on Nicholas I." She identifies with her predecessor when she speaks of the neglect and disdain he had to suffer. Still, she says, his haughty, stupid contemporaries are now forgotten, recorded by history only as people who somehow came into Pushkin's presence, however marginally. He stands at the center of his century. "People say: the Pushkin era, Pushkin's Petersburg. . . . In the palace halls where they danced and gossiped about the poet, his portraits now hang and his books are on view, while their pale shadows have been banished from there forever."

The essays, vignettes, and letters gathered in *My Half Century* reveal that Akhmatova grew increasingly fascinated with the genre of the memoir. She developed on her own a Proustian attitude toward memory, believing, as he did, that "the human memory works like a projector, illuminating individual moments, while leaving the rest in impenetrable darkness." This is not so different from Proust's privileging of involuntary memory over voluntary remembrance. Some small detail will suddenly recall the whole, re-creating a moment in the past or the essence of a human being. Also like Proust, she realized that the state of childhood is infinitely rich. As an adult one must therefore peel off the layers, just as Akhmatova peeled the wallpaper of her room in Tsarskoe Selo. One must concentrate on recalling a scent, a color, a sensation, a note of music. It is then that something begins to sing inside of one: a poem, a prose sketch, even an intellectual discovery.

From her work on Pushkin we realize that Akhmatova could have been an extraordinary scholar, but fortunately she was not only that. She was a passionate person, and so all she did was infused with feeling. She was luminous because, in her, intelligence went with kindness and kindness with intelligence. Without the combination of the two, each part is unusable. Akhmatova made herself wholly usable, even when a stupid, cruel regime tried to toss her onto the garbage heap. Like Pushkin's contemporaries, the tyrants will be remembered because they lived in the Akhmatova era.

Sonia I. Ketchian (review date Fall 1993)

SOURCE: A review of *The Complete Poems of Anna Akhmatova,* in *Slavic Review,* Vol. 52, No. 3, Fall, 1993, pp. 642-43.

[*In the following review, Ketchian praises that* The Complete Poems of Anna Akhmatova *is an important resource for lovers of Russian poetry, but complains that further editions need better editing to correct mistakes in translation.*]

Judith Hemschemeyer's handsome two-volume verse translation of Anna Akhmatova's poetry with parallel Russian texts and a substantial biographical introduction, "Masks and Mirrors" by Roberta Reeder, was a milestone in 1990 for English-speaking enthusiasts of Russian literature and for admirers of Akhmatova in particular. It drew on the texts and notes of Anna Akhmatova, *Stikhotvoreniia i poemy* (1976) and also A. Akhmatova, *Sochineniia* (Vols. 1-2. 2nd ed., 1967-1968; vol. 3, 1983). Although the first edition was labeled as complete, it is only this new expanded edition that comes closer to being complete by adding some seventy new poems, mainly from the edition, Anna Akhmatova, *Sochineniia v dvukh tomakh* (1990). A fair number of decisions about texts, some arguable, have been influenced by this new imprint.

By omitting the Russian texts, this volume focuses on serving the English-speaking literary community. An indispensable link to the Russian poems is the "Index to Poems by Source"; the "Index of First Lines" includes titles of poems as well. Judith Hemschemeyer's preface is a reworked version of her previous preface, which begins with facts about Akhmatova, discusses the works and continues with the process of translating the present volume. Her careful explanation there of amphibrachs would lead a reader to believe that the book is geared toward high school students or persons with no preparation in poetry. The introduction by Anatolii Naiman is excellent as is the memoir by Sir Isaiah Berlin; the latter, however, veers the volume toward a miscellany; the chronology of Akhmatova's life from the first edition would have been more useful to the book's audience. The index of proper names has been modified to this edition without removing the telling words "covers both volumes." The brief bibliography has several extraneous listings, such as the out-of-print *Life of Mayakovsky* by Wiktor Worosylski but not the ground-breaking, out-of-print *Anna Akhmatova* by Sam Driver.

Over one hundred pages of pictures, some rare, and facsimiles of original title pages, some using Reeder's verbal biography as long captions, overwhelm the intended reader of the poetry but are of interest to scholars and Akhmatova specialists. In fact, no other imprint, even Anna Akhmatova, *Stikhi, perepiska, vospominaniia, ikonografiia* (1977), contains so many pictures, some of which run counter to Akhmatova's practice of controlled moderation—pictures only of trees, a trial of workers, a prison camp, Tashkent, the title page of Annenskii's *Cypress Chest.*

Hemschemeyer's verse translations of the poems, written in collaboration with a bevy of persons providing literal translations, generally keep close to the originals semantically and syntactically. There are a number of excellent renditions ("Rachel," "The visit at night," "Under an oaken slab in the churchyard") and felicitous choices of words ("tawny hand"; "benighted"; "Sweet-smelling April spills"). For anyone conversant with Russian, a major drawback is the general lack of "physical" correspondence between the poems, which the translator addresses in her preface. While the reader missing the aesthetic impact of Akhmatova's meticulously chosen, sophisticated rhymes attributes their absence to current English verse practice, the abrupt departure from Akhmatova's superb rhythm is unsettling. For example, where Akhmatova presents delicately crafted trochaic lines of seven syllables in the poem "V kazhdykh sutkakh est' takoi," the English version "In every twenty-four hours there is one" offers highly uneven lines ranging from three to eleven syllables.

Moreover, the verse translations are marred by a number of errors. In addressing a sampling of these semantic inaccuracies, I allow for poetic license and minor inaccuracies. Errors occur when the translator confuses the short form adjective, used only predicatively in modern Russian, with the long form. The failure to distinguish between homonymic oblique cases of words leads to several instances of rhythmically correct "raven" (and in one case the unambiguous genitive plural form "*voronov*") being mistaken for "crow." In "Veet veter lebedinyi" ("The wind of swans is blowing") "*chary*" is not "goblets," in "Molius' okonnomu luchu" ("I pray to the sunbeam from the window") "*khramina*" is not a "temple," in "Tot avgust, kak zheltoe plamia" ("That August was like a yellow flame") "*smotr*" is not a "vista," and in "Otvet" ("The Reply") "*Strastnaia nedelia*" is Passion Week as indicated by the stress. Finally, in "Novogodniaia ballada" ("New Year's ballad") the entire tenor of the poem changes if the host is not dead; in fact, the first tacit ban on Akhmatova's work may not have occurred in 1925 if this were the case. For this volume's readership "*Piter*" in "Zdravstvui, Piter! Plokho, staryi" ("Hello, Peter. It's bad, old boy") requires annotation as St. Petersburg. Regretfully, this expanded edition, with few exceptions, has made almost no effort to correct mistakes in translation. A careful editing of this useful publication will long render it a dependable staple for lovers of Russian poetry and for scholars with little or no Russian.

John Simon   (essay date May 1994)

SOURCE: "Anna Akhmatova," in *New Criterion,* Vol. 12, No. 9, May, 1994, pp. 29-39.

[*In the following essay, Simon analyzes what Lydia Chukovskaya's* The Akhmatova Journals *reveal about Anna*

Akhmatova, and he also points out what the book is lacking, including better footnotes and better translations of the poet's work.]

"Poetry is what gets lost in translation," observed Robert Frost, and was only partly right. The thrust and sweep of epic poetry translates well enough: there is no dearth of decent translations of Homer, Virgil, Dante. Philosophical poetry also survives quite well: Eliot's *Four Quartets,* for example, has been successfully rendered into a number of languages. Lyric poetry is the one that has the most to lose.

There is, obviously, the problem of rhyme. Unrhymed poetry fares much better in translation: Walt Whitman reads just about as well (or poorly) in French or German. Even as delicate an unrhymed lyric as Leopardi's "L'infinito" has thrived in English. But rhyme is a killer. With elaborate rhyme schemes, tricky rhyming words, and short lines (dimeter, trimeter), the difficulty increases exponentially. Think of Byron's *Don Juan,* or this, from Heine: "Sie sassen und tranken am Teetisch, / Und sprachen von Liebe viel. / Die Herren, die waren ästhetisch, / Die Damen von zartem Gefühl." Verses 2 and 4, with their masculine rhymes, are no problem: "And talked about love and such" and "The ladies who felt so much." But 1 and 3 are impossible: the splendid joke lies in rhyming, femininely at that, *Teetisch* and *ästhetisch*, "tea table" and "aesthetic." Failing this, you've got nothing.

But there are poems untranslatable not because of their intricate rhyme scheme, rich rhymes, or fancy prosody. There exists something even more basic. In my doctoral dissertation,[1] I quote from the journal of Jules Barbey d'Aurevilly for September 19, 1836: "[Maurice de] Guérin est venu. Causé de la poésie des langues, qui est toute autre chose que la poésie des poètes." I commented: "Languages have their intrinsic poetry, a poetry they yield to the proper touch with gracious forthrightness." This is the kind of *objet trouvé* that certain words or sequences of words offer up to the poet, as blocks of marble supposedly suggested to Michelangelo the figures he would hew from them.

Take the last lines of the beautiful "Járkálj csak, halálraitélt" (Keep walking, condemned man) by the great Hungarian poet Miklós Radnóti, which, after giving the contemporary poet various ways to live, concludes with "S oly keményen is, mint a sok / sebtöl vérzö, nagy farkasok." Literally: "And as toughly, too, as the from many / wounds bleeding, great wolves." (The Hungarian "s," by the way, is our "sh.") What is a translator to do, confronted with these darkly resonant sounds? Shoot the poem in the foot, or himself in the head? There is no way "great wolves" can render the mighty rumble of *nagy farkasok. (Nagy,* incidentally, is a monosyllable, not unlike our *nudge.)* This is the *poésie des langues,* the poetry inherent in the sounds of a language's words, and it is

this more than anything that makes a poet such as Anna Akhmatova virtually (virtually? totally!) untranslatable into English.

Consider the opening quatrain of a three-stanza poem of 1921, which the poet dedicated to her friend Natalya Rykova. The "literal" prose translation in Dimitri Obolenski's *Penguin Book of Russian Verse* runs: "All has been looted, betrayed, sold; death's black wing flickered [before us]; all is gnawed by hungry anguish—why then does a light shine for us?" Peter Norman's translation reads: "Everything is ravaged, bartered, betrayed, / The black wing of death has hovered nearby, / Everything is gnawed through by hungry gloom, / Why then did we feel so light of heart?" Stanley Kunitz manages to get one rhyme into his translation: "Everything is plundered, betrayed, sold, / Death's great black wing scrapes the air, / Misery gnaws to the bone. / Why then do we not despair?" With all due respect, Kunitz would never have published such poetry under his own name. Finally, here is the version of Walter Arndt, one of our principal rhyming translators from the Russian: "All is looted, betrayed, past retrieving, / Death's black wing has been flickering near, / All is racked with a ravenous grieving, / How on earth did this splendor appear?"

This seems passable at first glance, but look now at the original: "Vsyo rashishchenyo, predano, prodano, / Chernoy smyerti mel'kalo krilo, / Vsyo golodnoy toskoyu izglodano, / Otchega zhe nam stalo svetlo?" There is no way the sonorities of that very first line can be conveyed in English, especially the play on *predano, prodano.* And not even the supposedly literal version does justice to the simplicity of the last: "Why then did it become light for us?" with *stalo* and *svetlo* again creating an echo effect. Russian poetry is a poetry of sound effects *par excellence,* because Russian is a sonorous, declamatory language; this is what those latter-day stadium-filling poets—the Yevtushenkos, Voznesenskys, and Akhmadulinas—called "pop poets" by Akhmatova, were to exploit to her disgust.

And yet she, too, benefited from big public readings at various times in her life. For Russia is that rare country in which poetry is loved by the masses, a country where simple folk quote poetry at one another and discuss it as people here do a football game. Because they often declaim in huge auditoriums and stadiums, Russian poets have adopted a vatic mode of recitation: part hieratic, part histrionic, loud and singsongy. It was Mandelshtam who reproached one of the most stentorian perpetrators with, "Mayakovsky, stop reading your verse. You sound like a Romanian orchestra." But the vatic mode is still with us, and even such a Westernized poet as Joseph Brodsky, Akhmatova's dearest disciple and protégé, subscribes to it wholeheartedly. This vatic mode, in turn, battens on the "poetry of languages," as the Acmeists, the group of poets to which Akhmatova belonged, certainly did. The Poets' Guild, as the Acmeists called their splinter group from the Symbolists, believed, as Max Hayward puts it, that "language was like any other material, and in fashioning poetic artifacts from it, one had to take account of its natural qualities and limitations."[2]

Anna Andreyevna Gorenko was born in Odessa in 1889, but was moved as a tot to St. Petersburg, living mostly in Tsarskoye Selo, the delightful suburb whose most famous inhabitant had been Pushkin, to whom the future poet was to dedicate many searching critical-historical studies. Her father was a naval engineer; she was the third of five children. One brother was killed in the Revolution, another committed suicide; both beautiful sisters died of tuberculosis, from which only a thyroid condition saved Anna.

When Papa Gorenko bemoaned that the tomboyish girl would become a poet and thus besmirch the family name, the seventeen-year-old changed her name to Akhmatova, as having descended on her mother's side from the Tartar ruler Akhmat, himself a descendant of Genghis Khan, and the last leader of the Golden Horde. As Joseph Brodsky writes in his essay "The Keening Muse" (1982),[3] "the five open a's of Anna Akhmatova had a hypnotic effect and put this name's carrier finally at the top of Russian poetry." In 1905, Anna's parents divorced, and she finished the gymnasium first in Yevpatoria on the Black Sea, then in Kiev. A crush Anna had on a handsome student at St. Petersburg University remained unrequited. She herself quit her law studies and eventually yielded to the persistent and protracted wooing of the poet Nikolay Gumilyov (1886-1921), whom she married, lovelessly, in 1910. The marriage lasted three years, and produced Anna's only child, Lyov.

It was a strange marriage, with infidelity on both sides, but also real love from Gumilyov. Nikolay at first dismissed his wife's verse as insignificant, advising her to become a dancer instead. But upon his return from a lengthy trip to Africa, he was genuinely impressed by Anna's new poems, and told her she must publish a volume. Soon Gumilyov, Akhmatova, and Osip Mandelshtam became the mainstays of a new movement that a hostile critic dubbed "Acmeist." Gumilyov was executed in 1921 for his alleged part in a counterrevolutionary conspiracy, an affair that remains opaque; Mandelshtam died in the gulag in 1937. Akhmatova survived—often precariously—till 1966, and never renounced Acmeism, indeed becoming more Acmeist as she grew older. It was a poetry of the here and now, eschewing both the mysticism of the Symbolists and the radicalism (often, but not always, political) of the Futurists.

When Anna left Gumilyov after three years, it was because she had fallen in love with Vladimir Shileiko, an Orientalist of stature. Being married to him meant becoming his research assistant while also holding down a librarian's job at the Agronomic Institute. Needless to say, this impeded her own writing. Nevertheless, her verse collections, **Evening**, **Rosary**, and **White Flock**, made the young Akhmatova one of the most popular poets of Russia, and this reputation was confirmed by **Plantain** (or *Wayside Herb*, the Russian word carries both meanings), and **Anno Domini MCMXXI**, to say nothing of such later masterpieces as **Requiem** and **Poem Without a Hero**.

What did she look like? There are many likenesses of her by various artists. Too bad that of Modigliani's sixteen drawings (Anna and Amedeo had a touchingly innocent flirtation when she was honeymooning in Paris with Gumilyov) only one survives. The poet Georgy Adamovich writes: "When people recall her today, they sometimes say she was beautiful. She was not, but she was more than beautiful, better than beautiful. I have never seen a woman whose face and entire appearance—whose expressiveness, genuine unworldliness, and inexplicable sudden appeal—set her apart . . . among beautiful women anywhere. Later her appearance would acquire a hint of the tragic: Rachel in *Phèdre*, as Osip Mandelshtam put it. . . ." Or, to quote Ronald Meyer, "Virtually every account refers to the poet's grandeur, regal bearing and stately demeanor. The adjective *velichavaya* (stately, majestic, regal) functions as a code word for Akhmatova." And he quotes an eyewitness, a woman who saw her in 1910 in the poet Vyacheslav Ivanov's literary salon: "Lithe, tall, and svelte, her head wrapped in a floral shawl. The aquiline nose, her dark hair with the short bangs in front and held in place in back with a large Spanish comb. The small, slender mouth that seldom laughed. Dark, stern eyes. [Others call them bright gray.] It was impossible not to notice her."

"A fine, unpretentious woman" Pasternak called Akhmatova in a letter to his cousin Olga Freidenberg. Yet the unpretentious woman was justly proud of her looks, as when she told Natalya Roskina that "sculptors had no desire to sculpt her because she wasn't interesting to them: nature had already done it all." Her nose, by the way, was not aquiline but, even more imposingly, shaped like a big fleshy "S." And consider this tribute from the great satirist Yevgeny Zamyatin, commenting on Annenkov's painting: "The portrait of Akhmatova—or, to be more exact, the portrait of Akhmatova's eyebrows. Like clouds, they throw light and heavy shadows on the face, and in them, so many losses. They are like the key to a piece of music; the key is set, and you hear the speech of the eyes, the mourning hair, the black rosary on the combs."[4]

After the breakup with Shileiko (another three-year marriage) in 1921, Anna moved in with two Petersburg friends, the composer Artur Lurye (or Lourié) and the actress Olga Glebova-Sudeikina, a famous beauty. (A "sex-bomb," Nadezhda Mandelshtam contemptuously called her.) This may well have been a sexual *ménage à trois;* at any rate, it induced a creative outburst in Anna. Years later, her longest and most renowned work, ***Poem Without a Hero***, was to take off from the 1913 suicide of Vladimir Knyazov, a young cadet whom Anna loved, but who loved and was rejected by Olga.

Her fame having peaked around 1921-22, Anna was due for a reaction. Blok died after a painful illness, and Gumilyov was executed for his alleged counterrevolutionary activities, both in 1921. Akhmatova's fifth volume, ***Anno Domini MCMXXI***, appeared in 1922, after which she published no other book till 1940. Attacks on her multiplied, and there was a ban on publishing her. Lurye and Sudeikina emigrated to Paris and, like other friends, urged Anna to follow suit. She refused and, in one of her finest poems, explained why. Instead, she moved back in with Shileiko, from whom she was divorced, but who traveled much, and whose St. Bernard needed looking after.

The poet's health was precarious: tuberculosis plagued her, and, later, heart attacks. While convalescing in a pension in Tsarskoye Selo, she met again Nadezhda Mandelshtam, ten years her junior, with whom she was to be linked in lifelong friendship. She also met Nikolay Punin, the critic and historian, who was to become her third husband, though the marriage was never officially registered. Although she was to stay with him fifteen years ("fifteen granite centuries" she calls it in a poem), the marriage as such probably didn't last longer than the usual three years; but where else was she to go? This despite that a previous Punin wife and, later, a subsequent one inhabited the same house. And as with Shileiko, Anna became an amanuensis to Punin, helping him with translations and lectures. Arrogant and promiscuous, he treated her worse; yet when asked later on which husband she loved most, she implied that it was Punin.

After the Central Committee's unpublished but binding resolution that she was no longer to be printed, Akhmatova worked on her unsubsidized Pushkin studies and on translations, which were allowed her. The Thirties were dominated by Stalin and Yezhov's Great Terror. Anna was staying with the Mandelshtams in 1934 when Osip was first arrested; soon Punin and Lyov, Anna's son, were imprisoned too. They were released upon Akhmatova's petition to Stalin, who liked her poetry, which may eventually have saved her own life. Lyov was to be in and out of prison for much of his life; Mandelshtam, re-arrested, died in the gulag in 1937, as Punin did later on.

Between 1939 and the outbreak of World War II, Akhmatova's fortunes were low, indeed. The critic Korney Chukovsky noted that she didn't even have a warm coat, or, often, enough money for the streetcar. It was at this time that Chukovsky's daughter, the writer Lydia Chukovskaya,

met Akhmatova and became her Boswell. She kept *The Akhmatova Journals,* three volumes in the original, of which we now have the first, 1938-41, as translated by Milena Michalski and Sylva Rubashova, with fifty-four poems—those mentioned in the text—Englished by Peter Norman.[5]

There is something very unsatisfying about having to read these journals on the installment plan. An important character such as Vladimir Garshin, a physician and professor of medicine, and at this time Anna's lover, will appear frequently in these pages, but a footnote on page 21, barely identifying him, concludes: "For more details on him, see *Journals,* vol. 2." Yet the reader should know more. When, like other artists in wartime, Anna was evacuated to Tashkent (whither she traveled clutching the precious manuscript of Shostakovich's Seventh Symphony), she conducted a loving correspondence with Garshin, although he wrote relatively infrequently, and then often about other women. Finally, however, he proposed marriage. Anna not only accepted but even agreed to his request to drop her own proud name and become merely Garshina. When she arrived in, as she put it, "the hungry and cold city of post-blockade Leningrad," Garshin met her at the station and chillingly asked where she wanted to be taken. She named the old Punin apartment. "He took me there, said goodbye at the entrance, and kissed my hand. We never saw each other again. . . . I know very well how relationships are ended, and thank God, I've done it myself a thousand times. But this was simply incomprehensible." Garshin, it turned out, was already married.

There are other problems with Chukovskaya's notes. When a new figure appears, a footnote directs you to an endnote. But it is often not the endnote you expect, which should be, let's say, number 19. Instead, you're directed to look ahead to, say, note 64, where this person is dealt with more extensively. Thus later, when you legitimately get to note 64, you find yourself rereading what you've already read. It is fortunate that the publisher, at the last minute, added a glossary, as it were annotating Chukovskaya's notes. But confusion thrives in other ways, too. The *dramatis personae* appear in three guises: with their full names, i.e., first name, patronymic, and last name; or, thereafter, first name and patronymic; or, often, nickname only—or diminutive of the nickname. So when on a given page a Nikolay Ivanovich (i.e., Khardziev, the poetry specialist and historian) jostles a Nikolay Nikolayevich (i.e., Punin), and then a Nikolay Stepanovich (i.e., Gumilyov) pops up, it's hard to keep them apart. When we next hear the nickname Kolya, it might take even a Russian reader a while to figure out which Nikolay is meant. Of course, it turns out to be yet another: Kolya Demidenko.

Still, one should not be put off. *The Akhmatova Journals*

begins with a moving prologue in which Lydia Chukovskaya tells about how she lost her husband to the gulag; how she, too, might have lost her life but for a friend's warning phone call; and how her having a husband in the camps brought her closer to Akhmatova, who had a son there. The conversations she doesn't dare report in her journal are the many ones about these and other cherished prisoners; instead, there is much talk about writers and writing, and about the trivia of daily life. Especially poignant is the evocation of the way much of Akhmatova's poetry, unsafe to commit to paper, survived:

> Anna Andreyevna,[6] when visiting me, recited parts of "**Requiem**" . . . in a whisper, but at home in Fontanny House did not even dare to whisper it; suddenly, in mid-conversation, she would fall silent and, signaling to me with her eyes at the ceiling and walls, she would get a scrap of paper and a pencil; then she would loudly say something very mundane: "Would you like some tea?" or "You're very tanned," then she would cover the scrap in hurried handwriting and pass it to me. I would read the poems and, having memorized them, would hand them back to her in silence. "How early autumn came this year," Anna Andreyevna would say loudly and, striking a match, would burn the paper over an ashtray.

But already from the outset of the book, in its English translation, we see sloppiness creeping in. Thus the code name the women used for the secret police is given on one page as Pyotr Ivanich; on the next, as Pyotr Ivanovich. Or there'll be a comment such as "Paul was murdered in that room," without any explanation in footnote or endnote. Again, in May 1939, Anna tells us how much she admires Joyce's *Ulysses,* even though it's a mite too pornographic for her; she has read it four times. By October 1940, she tells of reading this "great and wonderful" book six times. Could she have read that difficult work two more times in seventeen months? Was she given to exaggeration? Did her mind wander? Chukovskaya doesn't say.

She walked lightly, this fifty-year-old woman who was often trailed by two secret policemen and who always carried her pocketbook and a shabby suitcase with her writings with her out of fear they might be secretly searched. But she was terrified of crossing wide streets, even when empty, and would cling anxiously to whoever accompanied her. Although she disliked Tolstoy, and mounts a splendid attack on *Anna Karenina,* she concedes that he could be marvelously *zaum.* (*Zaum* or *zaumny yazik* refers to transrational or metalogical discourse, as invented by Khlebnikov and the Futurists, a distant precursor of *poésie concrète.*) Anna herself preferred established languages, reading Dante in Italian and, after six months of mostly self-taught English,

Shakespeare in the original. But for all the various languages she knew, Russian spelling and punctuation were beyond her; she even misspelled the name of her beloved Annensky, the only poet she admitted to being influenced by.

Anna thought poorly of men because there were few to be seen in the prison queues, and perhaps also because none of her husbands ever hung a picture of her over the table. She was unable to judge her own poems until they were old, which is why she avidly recited the new ones to friends, eager for their judgment as well as memorization. She lived in great poverty, often subsisting on potatoes and sauerkraut; sometimes there was no sugar for the tea she'd serve her guests. Here is a characteristic scene, as Anna and her friend, the actress Olga Visotskaya, decide to go queue up in front of the Procurator's office:

> Anna Andreyevna insisted that Olga Nikolayevna should wear her autumn coat (Olga Nikolayevna only had her summer coat here), and she herself would wear her winter coat.
>
> "It will be hard for you to stand in your winter coat," said Olga Nikolayevna. "Better for me to put on the winter coat, and you the autumn coat."
>
> But Anna Andreyevna disagreed.
>
> "No, *I'll* put on the winter coat. You won't be able to handle it. It's tricky. It hasn't had a single button on it for a long time now. And we won't manage to find new ones and sew them on. I know how to wear it even without buttons, whereas you don't. I'll wear the winter coat."

It is piquant to discover Akhmatova admitting to not understanding one of her own poems. She repeatedly declared that she wrote two kinds of poems: those that seemed to come from an external dictation and were easy to write, and those that she willed herself to write and were impossible. She considered Hemingway a great writer, although she hated the cruelty of his fishing. Vyacheslav V. Ivanov, in his "Meetings with Akhmatova," reports that she "approved of observations comparing her early poetry with the prose of Hemingway and describing it as 'novella-like.'" This ties in with something Mandelshtam wrote: "Akhmatova brought into the Russian lyric all the enormous complexity and wealth of the Russian novel . . . Akhmatova's origins lie completely within Russian prose, not poetry. She developed her poetic form, keen and original, with a backward glance at psychological prose."[7] What it all seems to add up to is straightforwardness, lucidity, and narrative progression, apparently considered more appropriate to prose.

Tom Sawyer, for Akhmatova, was "an immortal book. Like

Don Quixote." A bold view in its way, but not unusual for her, who, for example, dared place the *Epic of Gilgamesh* above the *Iliad.* Some of her nonliterary ideas were even stranger: "For some reason, she had got into her head that the steps began right outside her apartment door, and I could not persuade her to cross the landing for anything." Poor Akhmatova! She could no longer even pronounce "sh" and "zh" clearly; some of her front teeth were broken. Nor could she, a pariah in the house of Punin, get a pass to the garden of the House of Entertaining Science (!), where they were all living: "He is someone, a professor, but what am I? Carrion."

Her most cherished poems could not be published; her earlier ones she no longer cared for, and couldn't understand why other people liked them. I myself am more than a little puzzled by her own and other people's judgments on her poetry. In one of her autobiographical sketches, Akhmatova writes that of her entire first book, *Evening* (1912), "I now truly like only the lines: 'Intoxicated by a voice / That sounds exactly like yours . . .'" With all allowances made for what gets lost in translation, it is impossible to understand what could make those two verses special. Even more mysterious, though, is the recollection of the poet Georgy Adamovich about the other great modern Russian poetess, Marina Tsvetayeva: "She [had] just read Akhmatova's 'Lullaby,' and praised it, saying that she would give everything she had written and would write in the future for a single line from that poem: 'I am a bad mother.'" Even if you allow for the context (a father is speaking), how can that line have such value? There is perhaps something even beyond the poetry that gets lost in translations from Akhmatova.

Amusingly, Anna discusses Pasternak's indifference to her work and goes on to comment with wonderful outspokenness: "Haven't you noticed that poets don't like the poetry of their contemporaries? A poet carries with him his own enormous world—why does he need someone else's poetry? When they're young, about 23 or 24, poets like the work of poets in their own group. Later though, they don't like anybody else's—only their own." Vyacheslav V. Ivanov confirms this: "Certainly Akhmatova was not inclined to listen to the praise of other literary figures of the first decade." Her attitude to Tsvetayeva was particularly ambivalent, even though Marina was much more generous: she called her rival "Anna Chrysostom of all the Russians," and her beautiful poem "To Anna Akhmatova" begins "O muza placha, prekrasneyshaya iz muz!" (O muse of weeping, loveliest of muses). This became a metonym for Akhmatova: Muse of Weeping—or, as Brodsky renders it, Keening Muse.[8] Notice, again, the eloquent fanfare of *prekrasneyshaya;* how is an English translator to do justice to that?

Yet there were also times when the Russian language seemed

to thwart Akhmatova. There is a droll page in the *Journals* where Anna agonizes to a couple of friends about something she had written: "One line has been vexing me all my life: 'Gde milomu muzhu detey rodila [Where she bore her dear husband children].' Do you hear: *Mumu*?! Can it be that neither of you, both such lovers of poetry, has noticed this mooing?" Whereupon she proceeds to recite Pushkin's "Monument" to her friends—only, as a footnote tells us, it wasn't that at all, but the epilogue to her own **Requiem;** she was trying to mislead those who, she claimed, were bugging her room. But the greater, metaphysical, risks of her profession haunted her most: "The word is much more difficult material than, for instance, paint. Think about it, really: for the poet works with the very same words that people use to invite each other to tea. . . ."

What is the poetry of Anna Akhmatova really like? Here is how Chukovskaya sees it:

> When you first apprehend it, it does not strike you by the novelty of its form as does, say, the poetry of Mayakovsky. You can hear Baratynsky and Tyutchev and Pushkin—sometimes, more rarely, Blok—in the movement of the poem, in its rhythms, in the fullness of the line, in the precision of the rhymes. At first it seems like a narrow path, going alongside the wide road of Russian classical poetry. Mayakovsky is deafeningly novel, but at the same time he is unfruitful, barren: he brought Russian poetry to the edge of an abyss. . . . Akhmatova's little path turns out to be a wide road in fact; her traditional style is purely external . . . within this she brings about earthquakes and upheavals.

Frankly, in struggling with her poems in Russian—never mind the translations—I cannot find the earthquakes. But I do see a poet with an original vision and a personal voice who manages to maintain her individual talent within the tradition. No wonder she admired T. S. Eliot.

Strange where poets come from! As a child, Anna had no poetry surrounding her: "We didn't have any books in the house, not a single book. Only Nekrasov, a thick, bound volume. My mother used to let me read it on feast days and holidays. This book was a present to Mama from her first husband, who shot himself. . . . I have loved poetry ever since I was a child and I managed to get hold of it somehow. At the age of 13, I already knew Baudelaire, Voltaire and all the *poètes maudits* in French. I started to write poetry early but . . . before I had even written a line, all those around me were convinced that I would become a poetess."

If Chukovskaya were doing her job right, she would answer some troubling questions here. But she never mentions

Nekrasov as one of the influences on Akhmatova's poetry—perhaps because he was greatly concerned with social issues, which Anna, until much later on, was not. But he was a loosener and modernizer of diction, someone from whom Anna may have learned things. The real question, though, is: How did the thirteen-year-old daughter of Russian bourgeois manage to get hold of Baudelaire? (That she knew French is, in Imperial Russia, believable.) And what of this quaint juxtaposition: Baudelaire, Voltaire? Is the sage there merely for the rhyme? As a lyric poet, he is known only for a few poems of love and friendship, and for some terse, biting epigrams. Could Anna's short poems in **Rosary** (or *Beads*) owe something to the latter? Or could something of the former have influenced the manner of the poetic teenager—say this, to Mme du Châtelet: "On meurt deux fois, je le vois bien: / Cesser d'aimer et d'être aimable, / C'est une mort insupportable; / Cesser de vivre, ce n'est rien"? But the most puzzling bit here is "all the *poètes maudits.*" It seems impossible for Anna to have gotten hold of even Rimbaud in 1902, to say nothing of the lesser *maudits.* Lydia should have asked some important questions here, though, to be sure, they were interrupted by the entrance of an old woman—shades of Coleridge and the person from Porlock.

Akhmatova harbors some pretty radical ideas about poetry: "Only through contemporary art can one understand the art of the past. There is no other path. And when something new appears, do you know how a contemporary should feel? As if it is pure chance that it is not he who wrote it, as if . . . somebody had snatched it out of his hands." And what a country for poets, this Russia! As Lydia and a woman friend leave Anna's place, the following happens: "Tusya walked me right up to my house. On the way she recited Tyutchev's 'Spring' to me . . . which, until now, I hadn't given the attention it deserves; and then together we recited Baratynski's 'Autumn,' to which Shura [another friend] had introduced us. . . . I thought: This may be the best poem in Russian literature." None of these women was a poet; what they were is Russians.

From this derives Lydia's worshipful attitude toward Anna, which at times becomes cloying, as when the biographer comments on Anna's refusal to fight for a paid vacation owed to her, which the poet contemptuously rejects as "the communal scuffle." Comments Chukovskaya: "Oh, how grateful I am to her that she understands so well who she is, that in preserving the dignity of Russian literature, which she represents at some invisible tribunal, she never takes part in any communal scuffle!"

The poet's stoicism was indeed heroic, as the state treated her shabbily. "That's my life, my biography," she allows. "Who can renounce his own life?" Much later on, in 1954, she was to formulate it more nobly to Lydia's father, Korney: "I have been very famous and very notorious, and I know now that essentially it's just the same thing." And to Georgy Adamovich: "My lot was to suffer everything it's possible to suffer." So you believe it when Lydia reports, "Anna Andreyevna put the kettle on. We had tea without sugar, with a stale roll." Amid such misery, Anna would prodigally dispense insight: "[Vyacheslav Ivanov] was . . . an outstanding poet, but his poems were often bad. No, no, there is no contradiction here; one can be a remarkable poet, but write bad poems." Or: "The Modernists did a great thing for Russia. . . . They handed back the country in completely different shape from that in which they received it. They taught people to love poetry once again, even the technical standard of book publishing went up."

"I don't know any other country where . . . there is a greater need for [poetry] than here." She was right. In the large, cold, poor, and often lonely spaces of Russia, poetry came to fill a void. If (as it is said) sex was for the French the *cinéma des pauvres,* for average Russians it tended to be poetry. And, of course, gossip. There are delicious pages here of Akhmatova gossiping, for example, about the women in Blok's life, in the midst of which she digresses about Punin: "'But such an accumulation of wives'—once again, she tapped Nikolay Nikolayevich's wall lightly—'is utter nonsense.'" She mocks the pettiness of various literary circles, and concludes, "I am the only one who is indifferent to what people think of my poetry." (But here is Korney Chukovsky: "Akhmatova divided the world into two uneven parts: those who understand her poems and those who don't.")

All her life Akhmatova remained a firm believer in Christianity, Russia being perhaps the premier country for practicing Christians among its artists and intellectuals. A tolerant woman, she was nevertheless repulsed by the homosexual excesses in Mikhail Kuzmin's poetry. She makes shrewd observations about Dostoyevsky: "These are all aspects of his soul. . . . In reality, there never was or will be anything like it." She evokes charmingly her youth as a nervy, unconventional tomboy, and sadly admits to her present discombobulation. I find it regrettable that she so dislikes Chekhov, whose plays, for her, "epitomize the disintegration of theater"; in both his plays and fiction "everybody's situation is hopeless." In Natalya Roskina's memoir, "Good-bye Again," Anna is even blunter: "He was shortsighted in his view of Russia. If one looks too closely, all one sees is cockroaches in the cabbage soup."

In her youth, we learn, Anna was seemingly double-jointed; people thought she should join the circus. (No wonder Gumilyov first suggested she become a dancer!) In maturity, it was her mind that became agile and keen, correctly perceiving, say, the influence of Joyce on Hemingway, Dos Passos, and the rest. She had no delusions about fame: "When you're standing in a courtyard, wet snow falling, queuing for herring, and there is such a pungent smell of herring that your shoes and coat reek of it for ten days, and someone behind you recites: 'On the dish the oysters in ice smelled of the sea, fresh and sharp . . .'—that is something else entirely [from her celebrity in Imperial Russia]. I was gripped with such a fury that I didn't even turn around." Yet this strong, proud woman couldn't finish reading *Uncle Tom's Cabin:* "I felt too sorry for the Negroes."

The Akhmatova Journals, Volume I ends with the 1941 wartime evacuation of Anna, Lydia, and other notables, first to Chistopol, then to Tashkent in Uzbekistan, in Central Asia. It was a difficult sojourn, and there is a fascinating episode (relegated to a footnote) where Chukovskaya gushes to Marina Tsvetayeva about how lucky it was for Akhmatova to have escaped at least Chistopol: "She would certainly have died there. . . . After all, she can't do anything for herself." Tsvetayeva interrupts: "And you think I can?" Soon after, the forty-nine-year-old Tsvetayeva hanged herself. Perhaps the last memorable quotation in this volume has Anna reading her beloved Lewis Carroll again in Tashkent and asking, "Don't you think we too are now through the looking glass?"

There is, of course, much more to even this relatively short first volume. But Peter Norman's translations of some Akhmatova poems are not it. Like all other such translations that I am aware of, they do not begin to convey a true poet. What to do? To reproduce some of her poems in Russian would be redundant for those who know the language, and useless for the rest of us. The best I can do is cite some evaluations of her work.

We have many good descriptions of her personality (I particularly like this from the generally odious Walter Arndt: "Young Roland on his way to the dark tower, crossed with a Beardsley Salome"), but few helpful ones of her verse. Zinaida Gippius (or Hippius), the leading poetess of the preceding generation, rated her and Pasternak highest among their generation.[9] Sidney Monas called her "the supreme mistress of the verbal gesture, poetess of tragic love, who became, in her old age, the poetess, too, of endurance and survival."[10] Aleksandr Blok carped at first: "She writes verses as if standing before a man and it is necessary to write as if standing before God." (Ironically, though, Akhmatova remarked to Vyacheslav V. Ivanov that "there was no humility in Blok's poetry, that humility could only be found in orthodoxy.") Later, Blok considered the truest poets to be Mayakovsky and Akhmatova, "whose muse he saw as 'ascetic' and 'monastic.'"[11]

This is a curious evaluation of someone known as a poet of love, but even more curious is that by Anna's close friend Nadezhda Mandelshtam: "Akhmatova was a poet not of love but of the repudiation of love for the sake of humanity." You might think that this refers to the change in Akhmatova's later poetry, but no: "This woman with a zest for life had rejected all earthly things since her early youth."[12] The gap between such contradictory perceptions is perhaps bridged by Brodsky's view: "It is the finite's nostalgia for the infinite that accounts for the love theme in Akhmatova's verse, not the actual entanglements." Which, in turn, should be balanced against the point of Renato Poggioli in a book that Akhmatova, to be sure, disliked: "The muse of Anna Akhmatova is memory, a memory incredibly near in quality, if not in time, to the incidents she records from the exclusive viewpoint of her 'I.' [Or as Akhmatova put it *contra* Browning in her *Pseudo-Memoirs:* "I speak myself and for myself everything that is possible and that which is not."] Yet in what the poetess reports there is no afterthought or hindsight: one would say that she represents objectively a past which has only a subjective reality."[13]

For what may be the best overview, we must return to Brodsky's "The Keening Muse": "She was, essentially, a poet of human ties: cherished, strained, severed. She showed these evolutions first through the prism of the individual heart, then through the prism of history, such as it was. This is about as much as one gets in the way of optics anyway." But for the effect that Akhmatova had on other people, I go back to Chukovskaya's prologue, entitled "Instead of a Foreword": "Before my very eyes, Akhmatova's fate—something greater even than her own person—was chiseling out of this famous and neglected, strong and helpless woman a statute of grief, loneliness, pride, courage." Short of a reading of her poetry in the original, this will have to do.

And what lay ahead for Anna? It is absurd to summarize so much in a few words, but here goes. After even worse persecution in the Forties under Zhdanov[14] than in the Thirties under Yezhov, expulsion from the Writers' Union and near-starvation (living off the kindness of friends), then ultimate reinstatement, increased economic comfort and various honors, even the power to protect and promulgate others in her profession. Finally trips abroad to receive a major literary prize in Italy, and an honorary doctorate from Oxford—also reunion in Paris with long-lost friends and lovers. It came very late, and was not really enough. But it provides a mellowly bittersweet ending to a life of fantastic ups and downs.

NOTES

1. *The Prose Poem as a Genre in Nineteenth-Century European Literature,* by John Simon (Garland Publishing, 1987), page 139.

2. From the very useful introduction to *Poems of Akhmatova,* selected, translated, and introduced by Stanley Kunitz with Max Hayward (Atlantic Monthly Press, 1973). For my purposes, the two most important collections of source material in English were *Anna Akhmatova: My Half Century, Selected Prose,* edited by Ronald Meyer (Ardis, 1992), and *Anna Akhmatova and Her Circle,* edited by

Konstantin Polivanov and translated by Patricia Beriozkina (University of Arkansas Press, 1994).

3. Collected in *Less Than One: Selected Essays,* by Joseph Brodsky (Farrar, Straus & Giroux, 1986).

4. *A Soviet Heretic: Essays by Yevgeny Zamyatin,* edited and translated by Mirra Ginsburg (University of Chicago Press, 1974), page 90. The "rosary on the combs" refers to the little ornamental spheres on the diadem-like comb, and also alludes to the title of Akhmatova's second volume, *Rosary.*

5. *The Akhmatova Journals, Volume I, 1938-41,* by Lydia Chukovskaya; Farrar, Straus & Giroux, 310 pages.

6. I transliterate the patronymic as "Andreyevna" rather than "Andreevna," as do the translators of the book. Throughout my article, I have silently made such changes in an attempt to achieve consistency, which, even so, may well have eluded me.

7. *In Mandelstam,* by Clarence Brown (Cambridge University Press, 1978), page 97.

8. The poem is handsomely set to music in Shostakovich's *Six Poems of Marina Tsvetayeva.*

9. See *Zinaida Hippius: An Intellectual Profile,* by Temira Pachmuss (Southern Illinois University Press, 1970), page 381: "Although she admired Akhmatova's achievements in poetic expression, Hippius disagreed with her 'typically feminine approach to love,' devoid of all mystery and sublimation."

10. In his introduction to *Selected Works of Nikolai S. Gumilev* (State University of New York Press, 1972), page 17.

11. *The Life of Aleksandr Blok,* Vol. II, by Avril Pyman (Oxford University Press, 1980), pages 141 and 363.

12. For the quotations from Nadezhda Mandelshtam, see Polivanov, *op. cit.,* pages 110 and 114.

13. In *Poets of Russia,* by Renato Poggioli (Harvard University Press, 1960), page 231.

14. The notorious cultural commissar Andrey Zhdanov proscribed Akhmatova in a lengthy execration boiling down to her being "half whore, half nun." In his crude way, Zhdanov was right: she was in fact half glorious love poet and half impassioned religious moralist.

Ervin C. Brody (essay date Summer 1994)

SOURCE: "The Poet in the Trenches: *The Complete Poems of Anna Akhmatova,*" in *Literary Review,* Vol. 37, No. 4, Summer, 1994, pp. 689-704.

[*In the following essay, Brody discusses the poems in* The Complete Poems of Anna Akhmatova, *and Akhmatova's place in Russian literature.*]

Poetry not only occupies a central position in Russian society and plays a primordial role in the life of imagination, it is also a moral force. Russian poets have always been known for their assertion of the free spirit and opposition to tyranny both under the Tsars and the commissars. "When spiritual life is suppressed," Bella Akhmadulina, a contemporary Russian poet, told *The Harvard Advocate,* "people turn to the poet as confessor and priest. When a nation has Russia's difficulties, people seek something lofty, something spiritual" (Quoted by F. D. Reeve in Akhmadulina). In confrontations with the authorities, they fearlessly and consistently manned the intellectual trenches in the never-ending struggle for human rights, and that is why Russia respects and loves her poets.

Few—if any—countries can lay claim to such a distinguished literary tradition as Russia during the last seventy years. In a century riddled by poisonous ideologies and repugnant visions, Russia had been beaten into the ground morally, intellectually, and politically, yet aspirations to freedom and decency were not quite extinct and were nourished by a small group of heroic dissenters. In the shifting political landscape, Anna Akhmatova and her three great contemporaries—Pasternak, Mandelstam, and Tsvetaeva—gave a moving and insightful account of the polarization of society and the discordant intensity of life in the former Soviet Union. To them poetry appeared as a medium of social and spiritual redemption, and their idea of ultimately building a new society was essentially an aesthetic and even mystical process rather than a political one. They offered a basis for sanity and a moderate sort of salvation in a world full of suffering, cruelty, and chaos. It was felt at the time both inside and outside of the Soviet Union that if ever Russia were to be reborn, the poetry of these four great poets would have made a crucial contribution to this renaissance by upholding a national self-awareness that, without them, might have sunk into oblivion. Hence, the poems of Akhmatova and her three friends are essential readings for anyone who wants to understand how Russia succumbed to a brutal dictatorship and how it survived.

A chronicler of the isolated and intimate psychological events of a woman's emotional and intellectual life as well as the political events in the Soviet Union, Anna Akhmatova is one of Russia's greatest poets and perhaps the greatest woman poet in the history of Western culture. When she died in 1966, at the age of 77, the classical Russian literature—"the house that Pushkin built"—which began in the first decades of the nineteenth century, came to its end. She believed that poetry was written to convey the absolute values of people and society. This ideal required considerable courage to sustain in the atmosphere of the utilitarian aesthetics of the day.

In a radical break with the prevailing culture, Akhmatova began her literary career in 1911 as an Acmeist, a rebellious group of young poets fighting against the dominant Symbolists, and wishing to give Russian poetry a new direction. The two groups existed in a state of contention in their attitudes about poetry; it was, despite its inevitable tension, a healthy artistic confrontation concerning intellectual differences. The Acmeists felt that sense is more important than sound and insisted on clarity against the Symbolists' studied vagueness.

Akhmatova's personal life was marked by a long struggle against the domination of exploiting males and, although in the ensuing battle of genders, she occasionally did the dominating, too, in retrospect she can be seen as an early torchbearer for the women's liberation movement. For more than a decade she was the most admired woman in the literary circles, constantly invited to read her poetry before adoring audiences. She was, as Marc Slonim indicates, "one of the most widely read and truly beloved Russian poets. A generation of intellectuals memorized her lines and quoted them in their letters and diaries. She served as their sounding board; they found their own pains, laments and aspirations in her short poems."

Yet, soon the Revolution and Stalin's terror seared her life. Her first husband—the poet Gumilev—was executed, her second husband deported, her son repeatedly imprisoned; and she became routinely persecuted. The authorities banned her from publishing, detesting what she wrote. As they saw it, private yearnings, private joys, and private sorrows were decadent concerns that had no place in the literature of a socialist land. Yet, shattering conventions, she kept her self-respect intact and could not be silenced by fear or sorrow. Art became for her a means of relating morally to the society that she regarded as deeply wounded and indifferent to spiritual values. Her art aspired to a vision of the universe at the same time that it embraced freedom. For many years she had played the foil in the Soviet psychodrama. No matter how terrible her situation had become and how critical her personal traumas, her attachment to her native country was so profound that she refused to leave Russia, and continued to write even if it went unpublished. In her eyes, Russia was greater than her contemporary evils. As she said to Olga Carlisle, "My poetry is my link to our time. When I write, I live with the very pulse of Russian life." To her, the role of the poet was to remember and bear witness.

There was a breathing space in the terror during the Second World War, a significant easing of the ideological straitjacket that had paralyzed intellectual life, when she was able to publish and read her poetry in public. But Stalin changed only tactics for sheer political survival—not strategy—and after the war, she was ostracized again and her son arrested for the third time.

When Stalin died, a new era of tentative rehabilitation began and Akhmatova was invited to publish again. After Pasternak's death in 1960, she had become the sole surviving poet of prerevolutionary Russian literature. In 1964, she went to Italy to receive a high literary prize and next year to Oxford to be awarded an honorary degree. In her old age, she was haunted by the past and visited by the ghosts and legends of her youth, creating "mirrors and masks" (Reeder in *AA*, I, 21-183) for readers and scholars to study. The fusion of her life and poetry in an artistic unity represents a rich cultural heritage for students of art and politics. It reminds us of all the high hopes of the new revolutionary artistic climate that the Bolshevik Revolution initially inspired and of the tragic aftermath, in which in a catastrophic metamorphosis, all traces of such hope were doomed as a crime against the state. In Isaiah Berlin's words, "[Akhmatova's] entire life was what Herzen once described Russian literature as being: one continuous indictment of Russian reality" (*AA* II, 24).

Akhmatova is a lyrical poet, full of melancholy, tenderness, and a great feeling for nature. "Her poems had become classics of Russian literature in her own lifetime. At their best, their simplicity, the perfection of their form, the harmonious balance between sound and meaning can only be compared to Pushkin" (Carlisle, "Woman").

The poems express, above all, the sense of someone tirelessly and painfully searching for her identity, not just her identity as a poet, but also as a woman often ensnared in emotional tangles. They also deal with human nature, people's weaknesses, their hypocrisy, and lack of courage. Their expressiveness ranges, in Andrei Sinyavsky's words, "from a barest whisper to fiery eloquence, from downcast eyes to lightning and thunderbolts" (Akhmatova, *Selected Poems* 18).

The physical world played a major role in shaping her poetry, enabling her to reconstitute the body and texture of particular things. She acquired a precious sense of place and circumstances, and a concern for immediate surroundings. The natural world she creates is, at once, both vibrant and mute as if it were just about to stir again under some powerful impulse. These environmental forces unite with psychological motifs to play on her mind and emotions as her creative process is evolving.

Her poetry draws on many sources, often blending the classical tradition of Pushkin—precision, restraint, concreteness—with such popular elements as the multifaceted Russian folklore with its narrative surprises and symbolic imagery. Yet Mandelstam pointed out that Akhmatova's genesis is in the Russian prose of the nineteenth century. "There never would have been an Akhmatova without Tolstoy and *Anna Karenina,* Turgenev with *Nest of Gentry* and all of Dostoevsky" (157).

Because of the long official harassment, during which she could not publish, Akhmatova was not so well-known abroad as her famous contemporaries, and, until now, only a few selections of her poems came to light in the English-speaking countries.

Thus, it is most welcome news that finally a complete collection of her writings—all of her 725 poems, among them more than 200 poems and fragments never printed before—has been published by the Zephyr Press in an excellent translation by Judith Hemschemeyer, in two magnificent volumes in both Russian and English versions[, entitled *The Complete Poems*]. In addition, the scholarly apparatus includes the translator's preface, a lucid essay on the life and art of Akhmatova by Roberta Reeder, two short sketches by Anatoly Naiman, a young friend and disciple, "A Memoir" by Isaiah Berlin, describing his memorable visit to Akhmatova in 1945, and a veritable mass of useful notes. In its huge quantity of literary material, this edition is a staggering achievement.

To read this marvelous collection may prove irresistible to those who prize the long lost and almost irretrievable world of Russian poetry during and after the Revolution. What makes this publication special is not just its wealth of already familiar and new material, but the deep compassion of the editor and translator for Akhmatova and their passionate involvement in her art and life. While such an intellectual proximity may occasionally rob a translator of an essential detachment and objective distance, Hemschemeyer appears to have overcome the intellectual seduction without losing the freshness, immediacy, and directness of her approach.

"The poet as translator lives with a paradox," says Stanley Kunitz in the notes to his own translation of *Poems of Akhmatova.* "His work must not read like a translation; conversely, it is not an exercise of the free imagination. One voice enjoins him: 'Respect the text!' The other simultaneously pleads with him: 'Make it new!'" and concludes, "The only way to translate Akhmatova is by writing well. A hard prac-

tice!" The translator must also be warned that Akhmatova's words—as those of several other contemporary Russian poets—are not always "innocent" and, in addition to their surface meanings, often carry an extra baggage of veiled political and social implications. This hidden literary minefield might trip up the unwary translator, while in Russia people will immediately perceive the Aesopian ruse and decode the essential message.

Hemschemeyer obviously profited from the work of her predecessors and produced attractive and powerful English versions. It would perhaps be unfair to judge her poetic transplant by the high standard that such superb craftsmen as Kunitz, Walter Arndt (*Anna Akhmatova, **Selected Poems**,* Ardis), D. M. Thomas (*Anna Akhmatova, Way Of All The Earth,* Ohio University Press), and Ronald Hingley (*Nightingale Fever, Russian Poets in Revolution,* Knopf) established but, aside from a certain unevenness which is understandable in view of the huge amount of material, she has made felicitous poetic approximations.

Most of the delicate lyric poems of Akhmatova's first volume, *Evening,* are about aspects of love, personal and emotional, addressed to her present or previous lover or to herself. Her poetry is often one of musing to define the conflict in her own way and face bygone love's shocks and sorrows, such as unhappy encounters (I, 221), confusion (I, 221), suffering (I, 231), jealousy (I, 239, 253), silences (I, 243), desperation after a break (I, 243), yearning for love (I, 247), torment of love (I, 249), sleeplessness (I, 277), quarrels (I, 219, 281), and lack of communication (I, 223). The verses are occasionally suffused with intimations of anxiety (I, 273), doom (I, 239), and death (I, 225, 245). She misses her lover, but often finds differences (I, 261) and indifference (I, 263). Frequently she laments his (I, 263) or her own (I, 265) inability to respond. From time to time there is an uneasy truce between feckless, unlucky lovers who, even when they seem to connect, remain curiously estranged (I, 269, 283). The translator correctly observes: "Poem after poem . . . shows us two people bound together, grappling with their own and their beloved's emotion, struggling to get free and, once free, bewildered and empty" (I, 7). Memory often keeps alive the love that seemed to have died out (I, 257).

Is love a revelation or a catastrophe? There are only rare moments of true happiness and they alternate with long periods of bitterness. Most of the time it is the woman who suffers from indifference or betrayal. The beautiful nature—the sea and the forest—are often there to console her, but even its peace and calm is not quite satisfactory and we sense that it only momentarily stills her passion.

The theme she treats most originally is that of parting (I, 219, 223, 285), which she must have come across several times in her life. In "The Song Of The Last Meeting" (I, 225), even her customary restraint cannot mute the intensity of feeling when in her embarrassment she "pulled the glove for my left hand / Onto my right," as she was leaving him.

In the midst of these highly ambivalent sentiments, she remains attached to her land and people. In a village balled, she identifies herself with a simple peasant woman whose husband "whipped" her "with a woven belt" (I, 239). In a later poem, she speaks enviously of "the quiet, sunburnt peasant women" (I, 338) of the land, reminding us of Levin, Tolstoy's favorite protagonist in *Anna Karenina,* who only felt happy among the humble peasants in the peaceful Russian landscape. In one of his poems, "In Memory of Anna Akhmatova," Yevtushenko asked whether in this high priestess of the old intelligentsia there is a peasant woman. He sees two graves; in one lies Akhmatova, the "beauty, prized highly by a Russia" that had been, and in the other, a peasant woman, but "between them there is not frontier" (214-16). The two Russias—the intellectual and the peasant—are harmonized. Her second book—*Rosary*—gained her a firm place in the literary establishment of the period. While the cycle of love poems continues with its muted, delicate, and fragrant sentiments, this collection is mainly concerned with her anguish over her failed marriage with Gumilev, a growing sense of guilt, a certain awkward resignation, and a repentance for what had happened. She is simultaneously noble and naughty, a refined lady and a courtesan. Religious elements and spiritual zeal dominate many poems. She invokes Christian piety, searching for salvation. Although the male is often indifferent to her—when he touches her, his hand "almost not trembling" (I, 303) and in another, "How unlike a caress / The touch of those hands" (I, 305)—he also suffers, because she does not reciprocate his advances (I, 323, 325).

Her third book—*White Flock*—was published on the eve of the Bolshevik Revolution. An epic tone with classical severity is now added to the lyricism of her love poetry with her civic and war verses. This might have been her reaction to the criticism of her having been too private and solipsistic in her artistic expressions. She now wants to "bestow upon the world / Something more imperishable than love" (I, 379).

The First World War is foretold in "July 1914" when "It smells of burning," "the birds have not even sung today," and a one-legged stranger predicts that "fearful times are drawing near" with "famine, earthquake, widespread death" (I, 427), but she believes that "the enemy will not divide / our land" (I, 429). She is even willing to accept sickness, fever, and give up her child and lover in a poem "Prayer," just to have "the stormcloud over darkened Russia" become "a cloud of glorious rays" (I, 435).

All nature becomes a temple for God's glory, whose help is often invoked. "God is now constantly on her lips . . . One senses in these words, intonations and gestures a nun who makes the sign of the cross as she kisses . . . There is something Old Russian, ancient about her . . . The eternal Russian attraction to self-effacement, humility, martyrdom, meekness, poverty which had such an allure for Tyutchev, Tolstoy and Dostoevsky fascinates her also" (Chukovsky 33).

Plantain—her next volume of poetry—was published just after the Revolution. The most important poem of the collection is devoted to the war, revealing her deep patriotic spirit and rebuking those who wanted to flee the ravaged country at a time when, on the one hand, "The nation awaited its German guests," and, on the other, the guns of the Revolution began to thunder. She hears a voice: "Leave your deaf and sinful land," but she covers her ears, "So that my sorrowing spirit / Would not be stained by those shameful words" (I, 529-31). In a later collection, **Anno Domini MCMXXI**, she reaffirms her commitment to remain in Russia in her desperate hour. "I am not with those who abandoned their land . . . to me the exile is pitiful" (I, 547). There are three poems in the short cycle "Biblical Verses," of which "Lot's Wife" is the most striking. It shows the poet's admiration for those who dare to look back on what they love regardless of the consequences: ". . . my heart will never forget the one / Who gave her life for a single glance" (I, 569). The poem may reflect Akhmatova's skilled use of Aesopian language—a reference to mythology to express her own love of the past and its culture—in order to hide it from the censor. As Reeder points out, ". . . Akhmatova knew when she wrote the poem in 1924 how many simple things she took for granted in her past were lost forever in post-revolutionary Russia" (XX, I, 91). Yet, what she could not say openly in "Lot's Wife," she says in another poem dedicated to Petersburg (I, 607), lamenting the fate of "this city of splendid vistas" which resembles "a savage camp." But she is determined, even if she remains alone, to "preserve / Our sorrows and our joys" of the city. The reader must remember the special spiritual place Petersburg has in the heart of the Russian intellectuals as the cradle of literature, the city of Pushkin and Dostoevsky. The fall of the once mighty Romanov Empire is touched in her poem "Apparition" (I, 609) in which "the horses race" as "if sensing some pursuit" and "the tsar looks around strangely / With light, empty eyes" as if to bemoan the end of his rule.

Written much later—in 1936—and published in a collection, *Reed,* there is a poem, "Dante" (II, 117), which is similar in feeling to "Lot's Wife," but celebrates those who did not look back, that is, did not submit to the authorities. In her poem, Dante—who had been exiled from his native city Florence and when later permitted to return provided he publicly repent, refused—"Even after his death he did not return," but sent the city "curses" from hell and even in paradise "barefoot, in a hairshirt . . . he did not walk / Through his Florence . . ."

The most poignant poem in this group is "Voronezh" (II, 89), dedicated to Akhmatova's good friend, Mandelstam, who, like Dante, was also exiled, but without hope of returning. He died in one of Stalin's gulags in 1938. Akhmatova senses that he will not survive: ". . . in the room of the poet in disgrace, / Fear and the Muse keep watch by turns. / And the night comes on / That knows no dawn." Hemschemeyer's translation of the last line—in Russian "kotoraya ne vedaet rassveta"—is closer in meaning and sound to the original than either Thomas's "when there will be no sunrise" (63) or Kunitz's "which has no hope of dawn" (87).

There are literary works of certain periods which reveal the menace of history with particular force. In such a synthesis of art and history, certain deep-seated emotional motifs may generate an obsessive tendency of haunting the artist's imagination. Memory becomes a moral command.

A cycle of poems, entitled *Requiem,* is the outstanding poetic monument of the era. Hauntingly familiar about the political crossfire in cataloguing the anxieties and depredations of Stalin's despotism, the poems describe what it was to live in a society in which these atrocities were never far away, and in which the ideology behind them destroyed altogether the dignity of daily life. They express Akhmatova's feelings during the three hundred hours when she stood in heat and cold outside the prison walls awaiting news of her son. Both passionate and tender, the cycle is dedicated to the victims of the purges of the late thirties and their families, and records the ordeals endured by her and other women whose fathers, husbands, sons, and brothers were jailed, deported, or executed. The poems were never written down for fear of confiscation and punishment but memorized by herself and others. A cry against the inhumanity of the Soviet regime, *Requiem* reflects on the grief and sorrow of crushed lives, broken families, and the deep, enduring misery that seemed to settle in the very marrow of the streets in Leningrad when ". . . the ones who smiled / Were the dead, glad to be at rest," as Akhmatova grieves in the Prologue (II, 99).

Requiem is more a series of impressionistic sketches than a single long poem. Majestic, bitter, lamenting, the poems are written in classical form with her customary simplicity and intensity. There is no better or more sensitive account of those dramatic historical days. As a chronicle of the worst excesses of a modern police state and, at the same time, as a witness's testament to the enduring power of the individual conscience, this disturbing, enthralling, and extraordinarily moving work is a triumph of moral indignation. As a fascinating psychological document in its diagnosis of the collective illness of the social body, it crystallizes the pain of loss and betrayal of the era. While it is an acknowledgment

of human failure, it also shows a flicker of hope that runs through the experience and "keeps singing from afar" (II, 97). *Requiem* cuts an iconoclastic swath through Soviet literature, stirs the heart, and opens the mind in its interaction between this woman-poet and her society. Rarely have the impoverished and powerless had such an eloquent advocate.

Akhmatova spent the first months of the Second World War in besieged Leningrad before she was evacuated to Tashkent. The war inspired her to write a cycle of poems— *The Winds of War*—calling upon the Russian people to fight against the invaders. The best war poem is "Courage," a festive, grave, and solemn acknowledgment of the seriousness of the situation—"We know what lies in balance at this moment"—and an assurance that ". . . courage will not desert us. / We're not frightened by a hail of lead," and a silent promise to continue the fight. Most touching is her forceful plea for the preservation of the Russian language— "the mighty Russian word!"—which she promises to "transmit" to "our grandchildren / Free and pure and rescued from captivity" (II, 185). The words were her magic kingdom and it was natural for her, as a writer, to protect them. She might have recalled Turgenev, who once said that in the days of doubt about his country, "you alone are my support and prop, Oh great, powerful, truthful, and free Russian language" (Quoted by Haight 125).

It is interesting to note that in 1940, at the time of the short-lived Hitler-Stalin pact, Akhmatova thought of Paris under German occupation and of London bombarded by the Luftwaffe, and recorded those momentous events in two poems. Ilya Ehrenburg recalls that Akhmatova read him her poem about the fall of Paris—"In the Fortieth Year"—and although she was not there, "the epoch floats to the surface like a corpse on the spring flood," adding, "What strikes me in this poem is not only the accurate perception of a scene Anna Akhmatova had not witnessed but also its foresight. I often see the past epoch now as 'a corpse on the spring flood.' I know it beyond error, but for the grandsons it is something like a ghost, a broken mooring or a capsized boat" (494). Ehrenburg later wrote a novel, *The Fall of Paris,* which he personally witnessed. In Hemschemeyer's version, the quote is "And afterwards it floats away / Like a corpse on a thawing river" (II, 173). Both "spring flood" and "thawing river" are close to the original. In the poem, "To the Londoners," (II, 175) she calls the bombardment "The twenty-fourth drama of Shakespeare," and as one of "the celebrants at this terrible feast," she "would rather read *Hamlet, Caesar* or *Lear,*" and "be bearing the dove Juliet to her grave / Would rather peer in at Macbeth's windows," but this new drama she does not "have the strength to read."

Towards the end of the war, she became again the true voice of Russia for many, and her poetry reading in Leningrad was enthusiastically applauded by several thousand listeners. She hoped to be able to punish her poetry again and her essays on Pushkin, but in 1946 she was denounced by Andrey Zhdanov, Secretary of the Central Committee of the Communist Party, and prevented from publishing. Her son was arrested for the third time and she, anticipating arrest, burned her papers, verses, and a play. At this time she wrote several poems under the title "Glory to Peace" praising Stalin with the idea of obtaining clemency for her son. These "forced confessions" have no literary value. As Max Hayward mentions, "The worst punishment Stalin inflicted on poets was not to kill and imprison them but make them praise him" (25).

Akhmatova's most complex work is *Poem Without a Hero*, a record of her literary life. It consists of a number of narrative episodes and lyric digressions in the past and present. Personal and historical destiny, private and public events, are organically linked. The present is illuminated by the past, as events flow from Stalinist Leningrad back to Tsarist Petersburg. Akhmatova succeeds in making the reader live within such vanished moments and to feel for a while that the past is as real and urgent as the present. In this journey of discovery and self-discovery she looks mostly backward, as if listening for echoes of the distant voices of the past and skillfully weaves present and past lives into direct, vivid communication.

The actual action begins in 1913, an age decadent and corrupt but also bright and colorful. The main event is a senseless, romantic suicide. This event shook the intellectual circle to which Akhmatova belonged and, in retrospect, she felt that everybody of that group, herself included, was guilty and should repent. She used this senseless death as a prelude to predict the horrors of the impending war and implied that the catastrophe that visited the land later was a parable for the sins of the world; indeed, it was a collective punishment. The portrayal of succeeding epochs is marked by images of devastation, suffering, and retribution involving both the innocent and the guilty. History's muse has been muffled, her poetic voice stilled, and her capacity to seize the imagination lost.

Poem Without a Hero is soul-searching poetry with a remarkable evocation of a life lived both on a daily level and in the mind, an authentic portrait of a troubled society—yet also—an implied testament to the ongoing vitality and greatness of an entire culture. It is an unforgettable account of human existence in one of the most crucial periods and places in world history. A vanished era is poetically resurrected.

There are many veiled and hidden allusions in the epigrammatic statements of this poem, presenting a labyrinth of complexities and ambiguities. According to Hingley, "the work's difficulties derive from the mystification deliberately cultivated" and "mirrors and boxes with hidden compartments" (244). To Berlin, who asked whether she would ever annotate the poem since the allusions might remain totally unintelligible for future readers, Akhmatova replied that when "those who knew the world about which she spoke were overtaken by senility or death, the poem would die too, it would be buried with her and her century . . . the past alone had significance for the poets . . ." (II, 41).

Poem Without a Hero can be regarded as a summary of Akhmatova's career and a poetic farewell. She made no secret, in her conversation with Berlin, that it was intended as a kind of final memorial to her life as a poet, and to the past of the city—Petersburg—which was part of her being (II, 29-30).

In the last ten years of her life, Akhmatova was contemplating the value of art she had practiced. In rediscovering life's simple miracles, she realized that her poetry was an act of survival. In composing her poems, her mind could leap, twist, adjust itself, and acquire philosophical dimensions involving fundamental issues in life. She knew that while art cannot completely change the future, it still can, in some essential way, lend to it a picture of its own time, and while art cannot fully eliminate our fears either, it also can, by dissecting and analyzing them in a poetic process, diminish their influence and perhaps even provide a temporary escape. She also knew that culture endows people's lives with meaning, although it cannot, finally, be explained but must be simply felt and experienced. Thus, she became convinced that, in a small way, she succeeded in proving the salutary power of art and of the aesthetic experience in a totalitarian age which was determined to eliminate it.

She now went back to her youth as she grew up in Tsarskoe Selo (II, 279) and had long walks in the Summer Garden in Petersburg (II, 283). In an attempt to repossess the broken links with the past, she wrote the lyric "Komarovo Sketches" also known as the "Four of Us" (II, 315), the only poem by any of the four great poet-contemporaries in which all the other three appear, including three epigraphs from the poems that they had dedicated to her. Now that Pasternak, Mandelstam, and Tsvetaeva were all gone, she felt that "We are all a little like guests in life / To live—is only habit." Although she was exhausted by a lifetime of fighting, she still loved beauty over everything else. In "The Last Rose" she wrote, "Lord! You see I am tired / Of living and dying and resurrection. / Take everything but grant that I may feel / The freshness of this crimson rose again" (II, 317).

Deming Brown reviews this period of Akhmatova's life: "In these last years Akhmatova wrote as the conscious representative of an epoch and her personal recollections were designed to embody the historical memory of a whole generation. The subjective impressions in her poetry were now endowed with a generalized cultural and civic intonation. . . . When most Soviet poets were developing 'modern,' 'contemporary' thematics, Akhmatova, in the words of Yevtushenko, 'returned from Leningrad to Petersburg.' But her own maturity and history itself had prevented her from sealing herself in a time capsule so that her poetry was never archaic and always had contemporary relevance" (26).

Much of her later poetry was not allowed to be printed and, had it not been recorded in memory, would have disappeared. In the end, however, what has disappeared is not her poetry, but astonishingly, the seemingly implacable Soviet system which had furnished much of her poetry's subject matter, and then imposed an awful silence. This is truly poetic justice of the first order.

The thousands who came to her funeral on March 10, 1966, were expressing the country's gratitude that she had preserved for them "the great Russian word" pure and intact as she had promised in her wartime poem "Courage." They realized that the corruption of the language, the twisting of words, would have inevitably led to the destruction of common sense and the perversion of thought. But it was not only the language that she had saved.

To a great extent, as a result of the cultural and spiritual labors of Akhmatova and her equally famous friends for the continuity of the free poetic tradition in Russia, the past decades have witnessed a transformation in the consciousness and political thought of the people. According to Andrei Sinyavsky ". . . with their nonconformism they [Pasternak, Mandelstam, Akhmatova, and Tsvetaeva] anticipated the dissidence and paved its way. It is not by chance that today they are the most widely read, most respected writers among the Soviet intelligentsia" (226-27). People learned from their poetry how they had been deceived. The appeal of ideology, the notion of having been led through the wilderness to some utopia, faded out. Over this period people have gradually lost their fear of the omnipotent state and acquired a taste for democracy. Finding the political atmosphere looser and less ominous, both dissidents and ordinary citizens were becoming a little bolder in challenging the authorities. In an intellectual autopsy when a new society is being painfully hammered out in Russia after breaking free from the stranglehold of totalitarianism, who can doubt that these four creative artists and their small liberal group of followers—who, against all odds, restored a mutilated folk memory, a culture that was "occupied territory, occupied by the bureaucrats" (Austin) and brought back the tradition of candor, sensitivity, and free thought in Russian literature—played a cardinal role in the ultimate victory of civilized values, laws of morality and common sense? D. M. Thomas asks: "Can it be by chance that the worst of times found the best of poets to wage war for eternal truth and human dignity?" (23).

There is a danger that now as the new Russia emerges, Akhmatova's poetry may seem less defiant and provocative, the pain muted, and the urgency lost. "The plight is not unfamiliar in cultures emerging from repression in which art often assumed the functions of a moral and political opposition," remarks Serge Schmemann. Yet, as an account of collective behavior in times of social upheavals and of the problem of individual comprehension and choice, her poetry remains vibrant and enduring. Every poem breathes the spirit that made her the authentic spokeswoman of living in truth, of the idea that it is not power that matters but values, reason, sincerity and tolerance: a rare combination of artistic skill and intellectual honesty. Although she has been dead for some twenty-eight years, she has so far confounded the rule that former reputations must fade and memories lose their luster. Her stubborn hostility toward fanaticism and her rejection of the false allure of apocalypse has a universal relevance. Not only Soviet intellectuals but freedom-loving people everywhere owe her a debt of gratitude for what she had written to define the never-changing basics of liberty. Thus, it is no wonder that, despite the relative fortunes of the glasnost and perestroika in Russia, she continues to be a unique aspiration for the younger poets and writers of the land, who, at her death, expressed their sorrow and kept celebrating her artistic achievements.

Yevtushenko asks himself "How could we weep? . . . Alive, / she was beyond belief. / How could she die?" In a reference to her admiration of Dostoevsky he states, "If Pushkin is our sun, surely she is / Our White Night." *White Night* is an early short story by Dostoevsky. He sees the future when "schoolboys, with their hands in fists, / pressing notebooks tight. / And schoolgirls, bearing in their satchels, / surely, notes and diaries . . ." continue to read and study Akhmatova (214).

Twenty-one years after her death, Andrei Voznesensky points to the great attraction Akhmatova's poems still retain for the contemporary reader: "A recent volume of her verses, published in an edition of 200,000 copies, was sold out immediately, and is now obtainable only on the black market." In a poem, "Book Boom," he writes, "Just try to buy Akhmatova. / Sold out. The booksellers say / Her black agate-colored tome / Is worth more than agate today." In an evident *Schadenfreude* he continues, "Those who once attacked her /—as if to atone for their curse— / stand, a reverent honor guard / for a single volume of her verse" (266).

In painting her poetic and physical portrait, Akhmadulina sees her when she was young "with golden eyes" looking—in a reference to her beloved Petersburg—"on two dawns . . . / on fire along the Neva," and when she became old "Like a heavy, gray-haired bell / with prophetic ear and long summons / she speaks with a voice or with ringing / sent out by star after star, / with her indescribable wattle / full of unearthly song." She envies her a "poor captive of hell or heaven" and would gladly give up "the delight of remaining days" for her poetic riches (141).

I can only regret that these three poems by Russia's outstanding contemporary poets were not included in the Zephyr edition. I also miss a contribution by Joseph Brodsky, one of Akhmatova's "orphans" (I, 129), although there are many references to him in the two volumes. He is, unquestionably, the most talented of her many disciples, strongly influenced by her attention and creative criticism. She thought he was the best among the young poets in Russia whom "she had brought up by hand" (Berlin II, 39). Having been inspired by Akhmatova, no doubt, helped him to win the Nobel prize. Czeslaw Milosz remarks that "Brodsky takes over where young Osip Mandelstam and young Anna Akhmatova were stopped."

Russia's unheroic leap into self-destruction reappears as a cautionary tale for all of us, a tale made only bearable by Akhmatova's fundamental compassion and belief in human decency. How she would have enjoyed to see her Petersburg—the city of her great teachers Pushkin and Dostoevsky—shed its Leninist sobriquet and become Peter's city again! Although Russian publishing is still recovering from the combined shock of the disappearance of censorship, the gradual advent of market economy, the emergence of hidden tastes, forbidden themes, mysteries, adventures and pornography, and the intellectual atmosphere of the country is still cloudy as various contenders vie for power in an uncertain and often chaotic contemporary political climate, the lively reception of these two marvelous volumes of poetry is one sure sign of Akhmatova's staying power. She is the authentic touchstone of the second Russian Revolution—the revolution of the intellectuals. Let us hope that this time it will last.

Works Cited

Akhmadulina, Bella. *The Garden: New and Selected Poetry and Prose.*
     New York: Henry Holt, 1990.

Akhmatova, Anna. *The Complete Poems.* Judith Hemschemeyer, trans.,
     Roberta Reeder, ed. Somerville, MA: Zephyr Press, 1992. [Referred
     to as *AA* I and II.]

—. *Anna Akhmatova: Selected Poems.* Richard McKane, trans. New
     York: Penguin Books, 1989.

Austin, Anthony. "For Moscow's Intellectuals, The Night Is Long and
     Cold." *The New York Times* Nov. 30, 1980.

Brown, Deming. *Soviet Russian Literature Since Stalin.* New York:
     Cambridge University Press, 1978.

Carlisle, Olga. *Poets on Street Corners.* New York: Random House,
     1969.
—. "A Woman in Touch with Her Feelings." *Vogue* August, 1979.

Chukovsky, Korney, "Akhmatova and Mayakovsky" in *Major Soviet
     Writers: Essays in Criticism.* New York: Oxford University Press,
     1973.

Ehrenburg, Ilya. *Memoirs 1921-1941* New York: Grosset, 1964.

Haight, Amanda. *Anna Akhmatova*, a *Poetic Pilgrimage.* New York:
     Oxford University Press, 1991.

Kunitz, Stanley and Max Hayward, trans. *Poems of Akhmatova.* Boston:
     Atlantic Monthly Press, 1973.

Mandelstam, Osip. *The Complete Critical Prose and Letters.* Ann
     Arbor: Ardis Publishers, 1990.

Milosz, Czeslaw. "A Struggle Against Suffocation." *The New York
     Review of Books* Aug. 14, 1980.

Schmemman, Serge. "Without Strictures of the Past, Soviet Literature
     Languishes." *The New York Times* Aug. 5, 1991.

Sinyavsky, Andrei. *Soviet Civilization, A Cultural History,* New York:
     Arcade Publishing, 1990.

Slonim, Marc. *From Chekhov to the Revolution, Russian Literature
     1900-1917.* New York: Oxford University Press, 1962.

Thomas, D. M., trans., *Anna Akhmatova, The Way of All the Earth.*
     Athens: Ohio University Press, 1979.

Voznesensky, Andrei, *Arrow in the Wall, Selected Poetry and Prose.*
New York: Henry Holt, 1987.

Yevtushenko, Yevgeny. *The Collected Poems.* New York: Henry Holt, 1991.

John Russell (essay date 1 January 1995)

SOURCE: "The Smallest Museum in Russia: Akhmatova Lived Here (and Lives Here Still)," in *New York Times Book Review,* January 1, 1995, p. 10.

[*Russell is an author and writes for art and culture for the* New York Times. *In the following essay, he describes the museum in St. Petersburg dedicated to Akhmatova.*]

The most moving of all the museums in Russia, right now, is also the smallest and the most unlikely. Niched with no fuss whatever in what was a communal apartment high in the annex of the former Sheremetyev Palace in St. Petersburg, it is devoted to a great Russian poet, Anna Akhmatova (1889-1966). A quiet and almost secret place, it has in it virtually no object of intrinsic value. Its installation is rudimentary. But it is her own room, with her belongings all around, nothing added or subtracted. The linden trees outside the window are the ones whose agitated shadows she remembered in times of trouble. How could her presence not be felt to an almost overwhelming degree?

From 1925 to 1952, it was the nearest thing to a permanent home she had. Here between 1935 and 1940 she composed *Requiem*, a sequence of poems from which posterity will know what it was to be in St. Petersburg during the Stalinist terror and to live in dread from day to day. And in this apartment she later wrote much of the long *Poem Without a Hero*, a phantasmagoric and often cryptic or coded autobiography into which people, places and incidents from her past come crowding.

During much of her life, the Soviet regime did everything in its power to disgrace and discredit Akhmatova and her work. One of her husbands was executed, another died in a prison camp, her only son was repeatedly arrested and then sent to the gulag. After she was expelled from the Union of Soviet Writers in 1946, her room was bugged. The K G B forced the domestic help to report on the company she kept. She was routinely tailed in the street. If she came back home after dark, cameras were trained on her and pictures were taken by the light of magnesium flares.

To find the strait little cabins that make up the museum, we must take the "tricky back staircase" that her friend Lidia Chukovskaya first climbed in 1938. "Each step was as deep as three," she writes in her published diaries. Once arrived, she was led through "a kitchen hung with washing on lines, its wetness slapping one's face."

Today that entrance is bright and clean and dry. And the museum begins with an aspect of Akhmatova that has nothing to do with her status as the conscience of a great city and the spokeswoman for wives, mothers and lovers suffering through the terror. The memorabilia give us an unforgettable notion of Akhmatova's life in St. Petersburg before and just after the Revolution. The pioneer travels of her first husband, Nikolai Gumilev, in Africa on behalf of the Academy of Sciences are mapped and recorded, as are his dandified good looks and his impact as a gifted young poet. Invitations, playbills and vintage photographs document the era in which Akhmatova was free to travel and to publish whatever she pleased. She was hugely admired. In 1911-12 she went to Paris, where every head turned as she walked by and where she made friends with Modigliani and watched an early season of Diaghilev's Ballets Russes. In the museum we get a sense of her living a high-styled life in a great cosmopolitan capital. We see country outings, uproarious evenings in the Stray Dog cabaret, snatched moments *a deux* and the comings and goings of a major dancer, Tamara Karsavina, a major poet, Aleksandr Blok and a major theater director, Vseyolod Meyerhold. Photographed in the likeness of a very young Hamlet, she would have bewitched Shakespeare himself.

Readers who know her for a famous passage or two from *Requiem* think of her primarily as an elegist of genius. But she never lost a gift for candor, concision and a conversational fluency in her poems. What other poet would sum herself up as "the most faithful mate of other women's husbands, / and of many the sorrowing widow"? In seven lines she could sum up a failed marriage with Attic finality

> He loved three things in life
> Evensong: white peacocks
> And old maps of America.
> He hated it when children cried.
> He hated tea with raspberry jam
> And women's hysterics
> . . . And I was his wife

The whole of life was her subject. At 18, she delivered the essence of insomnia in two lines, "Both sides of the pillow / Are already hot." When she was in Paris in 1911 she wrote a short poem beginning, "It's so much fun when you're drunk / And your stories don't make sense."

It is easy to document the Akhmatova of later years in the museum because her room is so minutely re-created. And it is also impossible because there is no way to replicate the generational and matrimonial horror scene set up in 1925 when Akhmatova was taken by her third husband, the art historian Nikolai Punin, to live in the apartment with his former wife and daughter. What became a domestic inferno is now hushed and pristine. Vanished is the primeval phonograph that the neighbors cranked up and played by the hour. Nor does a taped docudrama picture the scene in which Nikolai Punin would glare at his family and say, "Too damn many people get to eat here!"

The place has been cleaned up, not prettied up. Looking at how she lived, we recall that she never learned to cook or sew. She could look very grand, if she wanted to. But often her clothes were torn, top to bottom, unminded for years. It was nothing to her to sleep in a coarse nightshirt under a thick blanket without a sheet. She was content if someone brought her for supper one boiled carrot, long gone cold. Eyeing her few belongings, we remember how the Punins "borrowed" her kettle and went out on the town, locking their door. We also remember how often she was left without, or perhaps did not think of, a knife, a fork or a spoon for guests.

If there are gaps in what we see, and in what she had, that is because this was a communal apartment in which people pilfered. Sometimes a soap dish vanished, sometimes a rare Egyptian brooch. (Modigliani's drawing of Akhmatova, done in Paris, is still there, but in reproduction.) Noting that there is no big desk, we remember how she said that most of what she wrote in the Soviet years was done while sitting on someone else's window ledge. Noting that there are no bookshelves and no books, we remember that she kept her Dante, Pushkin and Shakespeare out of sight in a Florentine chest or credenza.

Through her window, we look down on the garden; it was fenced off in her time. Punin had a key, but she did not. "How is that possible?" someone asked her. "A professor is always a professor," Akhmatova said "But what am I? Carrion."

The offhand use of that disconcerting noun should remind us that no one ever had a finer instinct for the unexpected word that leaves nothing more to be said. When that one word was "no," in relation to the Soviet regime, she never hedged. Her friend Nadezhda Mandelstam says in her memoir *Hope Abandoned* that "Akhmatova's strength lay in her refusal to accept the untruth of the times in which she lived. The manner in which she uttered her 'No' was a real feat of nonacceptance." After she had been married to Punin for 15 years, he brought a mistress to live in the apartment. Akhmatova lost no time. She said simply, "Let's exchange rooms." This was forthwith agreed to.

If there are no manuscripts in the museum, it is because it was so dangerous for her to keep them, she would invite one or two trusted friends to memorize her poems. Then she burned the manuscripts. While her little iron stove crackled ("peacefully and cozily," according to one witness), she sat and talked about the weather.

If there are no marks of esteem from colleagues abroad, it is because Akhmatova was not allowed to receive letters from them. It was a dangerous day for her when in 1945, she was visited by Isaiah Berlin, the Oxford philosopher and historian of ideas. He was only the second foreigner to whom she had spoken since World War I. His visit was undertaken in all innocence. In no way could it have been a threat to the Soviet regime. The many hours that the two spent talking together—he had perfect Russian—could have led to a friendship that would have done honor to our century. Yet what came of this visit, as of the following day, was a long period of heightened harassment of her.

It is therefore, in many ways, a racked and complicated presence that reigns over this museum. Akhmatova the goddess of mourning and the intransigent unbeliever in Soviet ways is a major component. But there was yet another Akhmatova—one who could describe herself in later life as "written by Kafka and acted by Chaplin." She could make her friends laugh till they fell off their chairs. When I met her in London in the 1960's, we were speaking about Shakespeare and she declared firmly that her favorite character was Falstaff—no high heroics for her. Nadezhda Mandelstam did not hand out superlatives easily, but she said of Akhmatova that she had never known "such a wonderful madcap woman, poet and friend."

The annex in which she lived is not at all like the ancestral Sheremetyev Palace to which it is attached. But Akhmatova did not fail to take note of the family motto, "*Deus conservat omnia*," which says that it is the role of God to preserve all things, without exception. In that context, God had a sworn enemy in the Soviet regime. But when we are all through with the Akhmatova museum, and with the feast of reading by or about her that is now available, we may well decide that in respect of Anna Akhmatova God did a very good job.

Michael Specter (essay date 28 June 1995)

SOURCE: "If Poet's Room Could Speak, It Would Tell of Grief," in *New York Times*, June 28, 1995, p. A4.

[*In the following essay, Specter discusses the museum dedicated to Akhmatova.*]

St. Petersburg, Russia—In the diffuse, almost endless light of summer, it is hard to regard this city as a place of suffering. Few people could gaze at the noble mansions and monuments and easily summon thoughts of despair.

In many ways St. Petersburg has, since its creation, always been the spiritual center of the country, the center of science, sophistication, culture and art. But for the last century culture has usually been at war with Russia. Pushkin died here in a foolish duel and Dostoyevsky was taken from the city in chains. Osip Mandelstam, Pushkin's heir, was destroyed by Stalin.

Somehow, though, the poet Anna Akhmatova survived. She lived through the revolution and the Nazi siege, through hunger and disgrace and the murder of her closest friends. She lived through the terror of Stalin, mostly alone in a small room that is now a sad, perpetually empty museum. She lived to tell about it all by carefully committing her poems to memory and then burning the paper they were written on. ("It was like a ritual," her friend the poet Lydiya Chukovskaya wrote. "Hands, matches, an ashtray. A ritual beautiful and bitter.")

Always grand in her restraint, lucid in the agony she was able to convey, Akhmatova was the bard of St. Petersburg. She managed to be everything the city has always been: elegant, expressive and laden with grief. She was, in her disciple Joseph Brodsky's unforgettable phrase, "the keening muse."

But the muse is not in demand these days. Even at the height of the tourist season there are not many visitors to the memorial rooms devoted to her in the Fountain House, a former palace that became a communal residence where she lived during Soviet times. More people visit Dostoyevsky's house in a month than have been to see Akhmatova's rooms this year, even though, in Russia, she is considered one of this century's finest poets.

"She is still loved," said the museum's director, Nina Popova. "But people just don't feel the need to come here. I don't understand it. Maybe the memories are still too strong. Maybe it's too painful for people to be reminded of something so close."

This is a country that cherishes literature like no other. But maybe life in Russia today is moving too fast to waste time on a woman who died 30 years ago and could well have lived in another world. Born in 1889 and raised near here in Tsarskoye Celo (Czar's Village), where Pushkin also once lived, she chose not to emigrate after the revolution. "I am not one of those who left the land to the mercy of its enemies," she wrote. "Their flattery leaves me cold, my songs are not for them to praise."

Her first husband, Nikolai Gumilev, was shot as a subversive in 1921. She was barred from publishing her poetry; she was with Mandelstam when he was arrested. Like most of her friends, he died in the camps.

All this is communicated in the few rooms in which she lived between the years 1922 and 1952. There are silhouettes of her friends, and carefully reworked drafts of some of her shorter poems. There are many drawings of her, for she was tall, lithe, dark and beautiful in an eternally exotic way.

She gained her early fame writing love poems, but history took her in a sharply different direction. She was at her most creative when Russia plunged into the darkest ravine (perhaps proving her friend Mandelstam's comment that great poetry is often a response to total disaster).

When the terror was at its worst, she lived in a single room with a tiny bed, a desk and four books (Pushkin, Shakespeare, Dante and the Bible). Linden trees—beautiful and often mentioned in her poetry—block most of the light even on the sunny days that are now upon the city. There was little heat and less food.

"The souls of all my dears have flown to the stars," she wrote in "The Return." "Thank God there's no one left for me to lose so I can cry."

There is surprisingly little of value or importance in her rooms. Some porcelain; a copy of the one Modigliani line drawing of her that survives (he drew 16); posters that tell the troubled story of modern Russian literature. "Akhmatova or Mayakovsky? Two Russias" was the bill for a lecture on Dec. 16, 1920, at the House of Artists here, when debates between opposing figures like a traditionalist and a futurist were still possible. There are a few short notes for *Requiem*, her great epic of suffering.

Requiem is Akhmatova's story but it is also Russia's. It takes place during the worst years of the purges, between 1935 and 1940, when she stood outside Leningrad's enormous stone prison day after day for 17 months, desperate for some word of her son's fate. Even then she was famous, and a woman, seeing the poet for the first time, timidly approached her. The exchange appears at the beginning of her long story of those terrible years:

> One day somebody in the crowd identified me. Standing behind me was a woman, with lips blue from cold, who had, of course, never heard me called by name before. Now she started out of the torpor common to us all and asked me in a whisper (everyone whispered there):

> "Can you describe this?"

And I said: "I can."

Then something like a smile passed fleetingly over what had once been her face.

Clare Cavanagh (essay date Spring 1996)

SOURCE: "The Death of the Book à la russe: The Acmeists Under Stalin," in *Slavic Review,* Vol. 55, No. 1, Spring, 1996, pp. 125-35.

[*In the following essay, Cavanagh discusses how Akhmatova and fellow Acmeist Osip Mandel'shtam refused to be silenced by Stalinist oppression.*]

In *Of Grammatology* (1967), Jacques Derrida apocalyptically proclaims what he calls "the death of the book," the death, that is, of the self-contained, organically unified, self-explanatory text. The postmodern age, he continues, has replaced the now defunct book with the notions of "writing" (*écriture*) and of a "text" that undermines or explodes any metaphorical bindings that might attempt to confine it within the safely "logocentric" limits of a single, self-sufficient volume. "The destruction of the book, as it is now underway in all domains" is a "necessary violence," Derrida claims; and the rhetorical violence with which he marks the unnatural death of the book finds its counterparts in the famous proclamations of Michel Foucault and Roland Barthes, whose respective essays "What is an Author" (1969) and "The Death of the Author" (1968) commemorate the passing of the autonomous, individual creators of the objects known in less enlightened ages as "books." "[The work] now attains the right to kill, to become the murderer of its author," Foucault announces, and his phrase—indeed, all the phrases I've cited—are bound to give the Slavist pause, not least because such metaphors have had, in recent Russian history, an uncomfortable habit of realizing themselves as they pass from theory into practice.[1]

"There are some countries where men kiss women's hands, and others where they only say 'I kiss your hand.' There are countries where Marxist theory is answered by Leninist practice, and where the madness of the brave, the martyr's stake, and the poet's Golgotha are not just figurative expressions." Roman Jakobson's observation dates from 1931; it is peculiarly apt, though, in the postmodern philosophical context in which Barthes, Foucault and Derrida operate. All three theorists developed their concepts in an environment in which men "only say 'I kiss your hand,'" in which, that is to say, the literal implications of "the death of the author" remain unactivated. They deal explicitly with the development of "literature," the "author" and the "book" in western, "bourgeois capitalist" civilization. The notion of the author, and the concept of the autonomous

human subject that underlies it, are "the epitome and culmination of capitalist ideology," Barthes explains, and "the image of literature" in bourgeois culture is, as a consequence, "tyrannically centered on the author, his person, his life, his tastes, his passions."[2]

What happens, though, when an actual tyrant "tyrannically centers" his attention on the author's person, life and passions? I cannot enter here into all the many ways in which the development of Russian "literature as institution" diverges from its counterparts in the west.[3] The student of Stalinist-era writing, though, is uneasily aware of the cultural specificity of Barthes', Derrida's and Foucault's dead authors and books. All the world's a text, these theorists proclaim; and within this textual kingdom, as Derrida says, "the 'literal' meaning of writing [is] metaphoricity itself."[4] All three theorists are provocateurs or, as Allan Megill puts it, responsive or "reactive" thinkers who seek "to attack received ideas, to demolish previous platitudes."[5] They are practitioners of what their great precursor Friedrich Nietzsche calls "the magic of the extreme."[6] Their dead authors and books trace their lineage back to the God whose death Nietzsche celebrates in *The Gay Science* (1887), and, like Nietzsche, they require a bland backdrop, middle-of-the-road, middle-class, complacent, commonsensical, for their extreme pronouncements to have the desired effect. Like Nietzsche, they demand an audience "made up of us folks here—living in the 'ordinary' world, earning money, raising families, catching buses, experiencing pleasure/leisure of various sorts, and undergoing the vagaries of nature."[7] That is to say, they require a context in which texts are not responsible for the actual deaths of their creators, in which novels may metaphorically bomb in the marketplace or die, in filmed form, at the box office, but are not literally destroyed by anxious writers in their quest for self-preservation or by a state determined to maintain absolute control over its master script of past and present alike. "The twentieth century has given us a most simple touchstone for reality: physical pain," Czeslaw Milosz comments; one might extend his thought and say that the true test of any literary theory must be a dead body.[8] The dead authors and books of Barthes, Foucault and Derrida can retain their purely metaphorical status only in a society that has long since lost the habit of literally destroying writers and texts for their verbal crimes against the state. If the literal meaning, in other words, of phrases like "the death of the author" or "of the book" is the first meaning that comes to mind, as it does for the Slavist, it undermines the very core of these theorists' arguments; it undoes our capacity to conceive of language as mere metaphoricity or of the world as pure interpretation.

The "author" was born, Foucault remarks, "only when [he] became subject to punishment and to the extent that his discourse is considered transgressive . . . an action situated in a bipolar field of sacred and profane, lawful and unlawful, religious and blasphemous."[9] This also describes exactly the kind of situation in which the real-life author (not the "author" in quotation marks) may be called upon to die for his or her transgressive verbal actions, and this is the sort of culture in which Osip Mandel'shtam (1891-1938) and Anna Akhmatova (1889-1966) found themselves living and writing during the period of so-called "high Stalinism," that is, from the early 1930s until the outbreak of World War II and the nazi assault on the Soviet Union. "If they're killing people for poetry," Nadezhda Mandel'shtam recalls her husband saying during their years of exile in the 1930s, "that means they honor and esteem it, they fear it . . . that means poetry is power."[10] What I want to turn to now are the singular poetics and forms of poetic power that Mandel'shtam and Akhmatova derive from writing in a society that paid poets the dubious compliment of taking their persons and their texts with the utmost seriousness.

In her memoirs, Nadezhda Mandel'shtam speaks of writing in the "pre-Gutenberg era" of Russian literature,[11] and her phrase suggests the nature of the "death of the book" as it took shape in Stalinist Russia. By the early 1930s, both Akhmatova and Mandel'shtam had undergone what Akhmatova calls a "civic" or "civil" "death" (*grazhdanskaia smert'*—a more literal translation might read "death as a citizen").[12] They became official non-persons, practitioners of a suspect genre, the lyric, and adherents of an outmoded, "pastist" poetic philosophy, acmeism. ("It does not make new poets of you to write about the philosophy of life of the Seventeenth Century into the language of the Acmeists," Trotskii had warned early on.[13]) Both writers were virtually barred from print. As literature and the arts were transformed into handmaidens of the state, only those writers willing to contribute to what Mandel'shtam calls "the book of Stalin" (*stalinskaia kniga*), the larger text of Soviet letters and life then being scripted by the master artist, Stalin himself, had access to the paper, printers and presses that would guarantee their works a public, "civic" life.[14]

Their poetry continued to live, however, a furtive, underground existence as it was written on scraps of paper and hidden, or circulated in manuscript among friends, or read aloud and hastily memorized. Such a situation would hardly seem conducive to the cultivation of the kind of poetic power Mandel'shtam celebrates in his remarks to his wife. Yet it is precisely at the time that the final nails were being driven into Mandel'shtam's and Akhmatova's civic coffins, the time of the First Congress of Soviet Writers (1934) and the official birth of socialist realism (1932), that Mandel'shtam pronounces his own social command (*sotsial'nyi zakaz*) for himself and his fellow acmeist. "Now we must write civic verse (*Teper' stikhi dolzhny byt' grazhdanskimi*)," Akhmatova recalls him announcing in 1933[15]; and the ironies of his proclamation are manifold. In the first place, he and Akhmatova had been barred from public life precisely

for their failure to write civic poetry, or at least the kind of civic poetry the regime required. They were considered lyric poets par excellence, famed or defamed as the composers of what Soviet critics called "chamber poetry."[16] As such, they were entirely unwelcome in a state that demanded, with increasing insistence, only triumphal marches and collective hymns to accompany the nation's uninterrupted progress towards a glorious future. The dweller in what Mandel'shtam calls "the accidental, personal and catastrophic" realm of the lyric could claim no civil rights in a state dedicated to the eradication of all that is private, personal and unplanned.[17] According to the new work plan for poetry, poets could speak for and to the people only by renouncing their lyric selves as they "dissolve in the official hymn," in Akhmatova's phrase.[18]

Under the Soviet regime, Boris Eikhenbaum notes, "the lyric 'I' became almost taboo."[19] How could practitioners of a forbidden genre, non-citizens barred from public discourse, hope to speak for and to the larger audience that a truly "civic poet" requires? For Akhmatova and Mandel'shtam do indeed produce their most ambitious, audaciously "civic" poetry precisely at the height of Stalin's terror—I have in mind Mandel'shtam's great sequence of *Verses on the Unknown Soldier* (*Stikhi o neizvestnom soldate*, 1937) and Akhmatova's magnificent **Requiem** (**Rekviem**, 1935-1940). Mandel'shtam provides us with a tacit answer to this question by way of the example that he gave Akhmatova of genuine "civic" writing. He followed his social command—"Now we must write civic verse"—with a recitation that was, in effect, his declaration of a sui generis form of civil war (*grazhdanskaia voina*), that is, of war against the state on behalf of its citizenry. The poem he recited to Akhmatova was the famous "Stalin Epigram" (1933), a lyric published only posthumously that proved to be, nonetheless, his death warrant.

> [Translation] We live without feeling the country under us. / Our speeches can't be heard ten steps away. / But whenever there's enough for half a chat— / Talk turns to the Kremlin mountaineer. / His fat fingers are plump as worms, / And his words are as sure as iron weights. / His mighty cockroach moustache laughs, / And his vast boot-tops gleam. / A mob of thin-necked chieftains surrounds him, / He toys with the favors of half-humans. / One whistles, another mews, a third whimpers, / He alone bangs and pokes. / He forges one decree after another, like horseshoes— / One gets it in the groin, another in the head, the brow, the eye. / Every execution is a treat / And the broad breast of the Ossetian.[20]

On hearing the "Stalin Epigram," Boris Pasternak reportedly exclaimed: "This is not a literary fact, but an act of suicide."[21]

It is actually a little of both; it exists on the boundaries between language as metaphor and language as action, and thus incidentally illustrates the problems of speaking, as Barthes and Derrida do, of language as innately, exclusively metaphorical. The poem itself concerns the possibilities, limits and dangers of different kinds of speech. Mandel'shtam contrasts the inaudible "half-conversations" of those who oppose or fear Stalin and the dehumanized mewing and whining of those who support him with the language of the "Great Leader" himself, who demonstrates the real-life consequences of his speech on the bodies of his subjects as he energetically forges new decrees: "One gets it in the groin, another in the head, the brow, the eye." The very energy and efficiency of Mandel'shtam's diction and syntax in these phrases enact the power of the language that he describes.

Mandel'shtam counters this form of language as action with his own verbal deed, the poem itself, and he authorizes the collective "we" he requires for his civic verse precisely by way of his linguistic feat. He proclaims *vo ves' golos,* at the top of his voice, what the Russian people think but dare not say aloud: "But whenever there's enough for half a chat— / Talk turns to the Kremlin mountaineer." Unlike the leader who reserves the powers of speech for himself alone— "He alone bangs and pokes" with his words like "iron weights"—Mandel'shtam derives his verbal authority and force from the multitudes whose innermost thoughts and fears he articulates.

I have been speaking of the "Stalin Epigram" as a form of action, a deed, and I do not mean the terms metaphorically. Mandel'shtam was prepared to take the real-life consequences of his verbal deed—"I'm ready for death," Akhmatova recalls him saying[22]—and the poem precipitated his first arrest, in 1934, which was followed by three years of internal exile, a second arrest in 1937 and finally his death early in 1938 in a transit camp en route to the gulag. Indeed, according to auditors who witnessed his clandestine recitations of the "Stalin Epigram," Mandel'shtam appeared to be staging performance-provocations intended to reach the ears of his epigram's subject; he recited the poem to selected groups of friends and acquaintances, some of whom were almost guaranteed to pass it on to the authorities. The poem in fact existed only in oral form, in performance— Mandel'shtam himself transcribed it for the first time only at his police interrogation in 1934—and it was as oral performance that it precipitated his arrest.[23]

This is, I think, not accidental. In the epigram, Mandel'shtam describes the ominous power of Stalin's spoken words. Through his performance of the epigram, Mandel'shtam demonstrates the equal force of the poet's speech. The poet's voice, condemned to "civic death" in the private domain, may seem inaudible—but it travels far further than "ten steps away." It bypasses the whole elaborate state apparatus designed for the control and repression of the written word to reach the ears of the leader himself, who is compelled to countermand it by his own verbal action in the form of the orders that led to Mandel'shtam's arrest and exile. The "Stalin Epigram," as poem and provocation, thus paradoxically becomes Mandel'shtam's most direct testimony to the power and efficacy of the spoken poetic word.[24]

In Derridian philosophy, western civilization revolves around a misguided, illusory opposition between "fallen," artificial written language and untainted, "natural" speech. We find a similar dichotomy at work in Mandel'shtam's late poetics— and yet, once again, the context in which Mandel'shtam lived and worked gives this opposition a very different coloration than it assumes in Derridian thought. "Writing and speech are incommensurate," Mandel'shtam insists in "Conversation about Dante" (1933), and in "Fourth Prose" (1930) he leaves little doubt about where his own preferences lie. "I have no manuscripts, no notebooks, no archives," he proclaims. "I have no handwriting, for I never write. I alone in Russia work with my voice, while all around me consummate swine are writing." There is an element of truth in Mandel'shtam's characteristic hyperbole; he did indeed compose aloud and on his feet, and he and his wife worked to transcribe his lyrics only after they had been completely composed in the poet's mind and voice.[25]

For the Mandel'shtam of "Fourth Prose" and the revealingly titled "Conversation," however, the idea of a corrupt and fallen written language is based not on western cultural mythologies but on Soviet reality. When all agencies of printing, reproduction and distribution lie in the hands of the government, any author "who first obtains permission and then writes" becomes involved in an act of collaboration with the state whose blessing he has received. He composes his work on what Mandel'shtam calls in one poem "watermarked police stationery" and his "authorized" writings thus take their place in a continuum that begins with state-sponsored poetry and ends with the state's most ominous decrees: "Crude animal fear hammers on the typewriters, crude animal fear proofreads the Chinese gibberish on sheets of toilet paper, scribbles denunciations, strikes those who are down, demands the death penalty for prisoners."[26]

In such a society, only unauthorized speech or, more specifically, oral poetry, can speak a language free of complicity in the state's atrocities; only the poet who works "from the voice" can hope to challenge the state's monopoly on written language. "They have sullied the most pure Word, / They have trampled the sacred Word (*glagol*)," Akhmatova writes in a lyric of the period, and western logocentric mythologies are not what is at stake here, as Akhmatova's own poetry makes clear.[27] In the prose text that opens **Requiem,** Akhmatova derives the authority to compose her tribute to the purges' victims not from any official source but from an unauthorized, oral communiqué from an anonymous fellow sufferer:

> [Translation] In the terrible years of the Ezhov terror, I spent seventeen months in the prison lines of Leningrad. Once somebody "identified" me. Then a blue-lipped woman standing behind me, who had of course, never heard my name, came to from the torpor characteristic of us all and asked me in a whisper [everyone spoke in whispers there], "But can you describe this?" And I said, "I can."
>
> Then something like a smile slipped across what had once been her face.[28]

As in Mandel'shtam's "Stalin Epigram," the poet justifies her civic, collective "we" by virtue of her ability to articulate aloud what other suffering Russians only whisper.

Akhmatova is like Mandel'shtam, too, in her emphasis, here and elsewhere, on the face and mouth that articulate what Mandel'shtam calls "sounds forbidden for Russian lips." "A human, hot, contorted mouth / Is outraged and says 'No,'" Mandel'shtam writes in one fragmentary late poem; and in their late writings both Akhmatova and Mandel'shtam insistently call attention to the mouths, lips and tongues that firmly root speech in the body that may be called upon to account for its verbal crimes against the state. Mandel'shtam makes these lips the basis for a defiant "underground" poetics in the opening lines of one late poem. "Yes, I lie in the earth moving my lips, / But every schoolchild will learn what I say," he announces defiantly from the grave to which he has been confined following his "civic funeral."[29]

Oral poetry is not the only genre that Mandel'shtam and Akhmatova practice in their efforts to avoid signing their names to "Stalin's book," the massive, monstrous, collective text being spun out by the state apparatus with the assistance of the obedient tribe of hired scribes whom Mandel'shtam denounces in "Fourth Prose." Mandel'shtam and Akhmatova were effectively barred from print throughout the 1930s. They could have no hope of seeing their own names and poems printed in anything remotely resembling a conventional book, and the written form that their poems took were handwritten copies scrawled on scraps of paper or laboriously transcribed by hand into unprepossessing school copybooks (I'm thinking now, of course, of Mandel'shtam's "Moscow" and "Voronezh Notebooks"). "It is more honorable to be learned by heart, to be secretly, furtively recopied, to be not a book, but a copybook in one's own lifetime," Maksimilian Voloshin had written shortly after the revolution, and his words proved to be prophetic.[30] Mandel'shtam follows Voloshin's lead as he makes a virtue

of necessity by turning humble, unpublished scraps of paper into a crucial genre of the underground poet. In the "Conversation about Dante," Mandel'shtam inverts the apparent order of things as he condemns "official paper" to oblivion and assigns true permanence only to the rough drafts (*chernoviki*) that cannot be captured on official paper and made to serve official purposes. "Rough drafts," he insists, "are never destroyed . . . The safety of the rough draft is the statute assuring preservation of the power behind the literary work."[31] It is a theory made to order for poets denied access to official paper of any sort, and Akhmatova provides testimony to its efficacy and force in the first dedication to her **Poem without A Hero** (**Poema bez geroia**, 1940-1966). "Since I didn't have enough paper, / I'm writing on your rough draft (*A tak kak mne bumagi ne khvatilo, / Ia na tvoem pishu chernovike*)," Akhmatova explains, and the rough draft she has in mind can only be a page taken from one of Mandel'shtam's perpetually unfinished notebooks.[32] She thus bears witness to the power of the unprinted word and to the indestructibility of the rough draft that has already outlived its less fortunate, more perishable creator.

Akhmatova creates a telling variant on this poetics of the incorruptible rough draft in her late work. "Manuscripts don't burn," Mikhail Bulgakov proclaims in a famous phrase.[33] In Akhmatova's late poetics of the unofficial text, however, manuscripts do burn, and poems do perish—and this is precisely what guarantees their integrity and, finally, their immortality. In her Stalin-era writings, Akhmatova cultivates the genre of the "burnt notebook" and its subsidiary, the "poems written for the ashtray," and the phrases' meanings are both literal and metaphorical.[34] She was in fact forced to burn her private archives more than once, in the hopes of keeping illicit writings out of official hands. Some of the burned texts vanished for good—but others survived, either in her own memory or in the memories and copybooks of friends.

This literal death and resurrection of the poetic text gives rise to the metaphor that enables Akhmatova, the banned, forbidden lyric poet, to take on Stalin himself as she forges her own collective, civic voice to speak for the masses who have been either figuratively or literally obliterated by Stalinist collective rhetoric. The lyric poem can fall victim to Stalinist oppression just as the lyric poet can, and their voices are suppressed for the same reason: they speak for the realm of the personal, the private and the individual that the regime was bent upon destroying. The poem and the poet become arch-victims, then, the best, most fitting representatives of the millions of victims, both living and dead, whose private, individual selves the state had done its best to efface in the name of the collective.

For both Akhmatova and Mandel'shtam, their civic authority is underwritten by their very perishability and the perishability of their works. It is precisely because the poets and their poems are subject to literal, physical death that they are authorized to speak for the dead and dying victims of a nation under siege by its own rulers. In their greatest "civic" poems, Mandel'shtam and Akhmatova are thus able to turn Stalinist rhetoric on its head, as the artificial collective imposed from above meets its match in the genuinely communal voice that rises from below, through the throat of the poet prematurely consigned to civic burial. Thus in "The Verses on the Unknown Soldier," Mandel'shtam employs the militaristic rhetoric of the five-year plans, with their class warfare, enemies of the people, saboteurs, provocateurs and wreckers, to orchestrate a mutiny among the common foot-soldiers who have fallen prey to their generalissimo's grandiose plans. And, as Susan Amert has shown in her wonderful recent study of Akhmatova's late poetry, Akhmatova in her **Requiem** counters the state's inflated rhetoric of the "motherland" with her own "song of the motherland" woven from the wails of the wives and mothers left behind by Stalin's victims.[35] "I renounce neither the living or the dead," Mandel'shtam announced shortly before his own death[36]—and in their civic poetry Mandel'shtam and Akhmatova speak for both the living and the dead by virtue of their faith in the lasting powers of dead authors and dead books.

NOTES

1. Jacques Derrida, *Of Grammatology*, trans. Gayatri Chakravorty Spivak (Baltimore: Johns Hopkins University Press, 1976), 8, 18; Michel Foucault, "What is an Author," in *Language, Countermemory, Practice: Selected Essays and Interviews,* ed. Donald F. Bouchard, trans. Donald F. Bouchard, Sherry Simon (Ithaca: Cornell University Press, 1977), 113-39, esp. 117; Roland Barthes, "The Death of the Author," in *Image—Music—Text,* ed. and trans. Stephen Heath (New York: Hill and Wang, 1977), 142-43.

2. Roman Jakobson, "On a Generation That Squandered Its Poets," trans. Edward J. Brown, in Victor Erlich, ed., *Twentieth-Century Russian Literary Criticism* (New Haven: Yale University Press, 1975), 164; Barthes, "The Death of the Author," 143.

For a provocative discussion of the notion of the "death of the author" in modern French and Russian poetry, see Svetlana Boym, *Death in Quotation Marks: Cultural Myths of the Modern Poet* (Cambridge, Massachusetts: Harvard University Press, 1991).

3. This issue has been ably addressed by other Slavists, both in Russia and the west; one might note here the work of William Mills Todd III, among American Slavists. Among scholars who have followed the lead of Iurii Lotmann and Lydia Ginzburg, one might mention, *inter alia,* Boris Gasparov, Irina Paperno and Aleksandr Zholkovsky, practitioners of a semiotics of culture that might be called the Russian answer to new historicism.

4. *Of Grammatology,* 15.

5. Allan Megill, *Prophets of Extremity: Nietzsche, Heidegger, Foucault, Derrida* (Berkeley: University of California Press, 1985), 340, 347.

6. *The Will to Power,* ed. Walter Kaufmann, trans. Walter Kaufmann, R. G. Hollingdale (New York: Vintage Books, 1968), 396.
7. Megill, *Prophets,* 351.

8. *The Witness of Poetry* (Cambridge, Massachusetts: Harvard University Press, 1983), 66.

9. "What is an Author," 124. For an incisive discussion of the limits of Foucault's theory on Stalinist soil, see Beth Holmgren, *Women's Works in Stalin's Time: On Lidiia Chukovskaia and Nadezhda Mandelstam* (Bloomington: Indiana University Press, 1993), 7-9.

10. *Vospominaniia: kniga pervaia*, 3rd ed. (Paris: YMCA Press, 1982), 178. Elsewhere in the same volume, Nadezhda Mandel'shtam recalls her husband's reproach: "Why are you complaining? . . . Only here do they really respect poetry—they kill because of it. More people die for poetry here than anywhere else" (167). It is easy to mythologize the situations in extremis in which poets are called upon to die for their verse. Whether poetry should ideally be a matter of life and death is a vexed question, to say the least; the fact remains that in certain circumstances, the poetic word has consequences that far outreach the limits of postmodern *écriture.*

11. *Vospominaniia: kniga pervaia,* 200.

12. "Believe me, I've had it up to here / With the triumphs of a civic death," Akhmatova complains in one late lyric ("Torzhestvami grazhdanskoi smerti," *Sochineniia,* v. 3, 502). She explains the nature of her premature burial and "posthumous existence" in her essay on Georgii Ivanov's *Peterburgskie zimy* (1961): "They stopped publishing me altogether from 1925 to 1939 . . . I was witness to my civic death for the first time then. I was thirty-five years old . . ." (*"On Petersburg Winters,"* in Anna Akhmatova, *My Half Century: Selected Prose,* ed. Ronald Meyer (Ann Arbor: Ardis, 1992), 57.

13. Leon Trotskii, *Literature and Revolution,* trans. Rose Strunsky (Ann Arbor: University of Michigan Press, 1960), 171.

14. Mandel'shtam refers to "Stalin's book" in his last lyr-

written in Moscow before his final arrest. The phrase itself is taken from his chilling "Stanzas" (*Stansy*), written in July 1937, as printed in Osip Mandel'shtam, *Sochineniia v dvukh tomakh,* ed. P. M. Nerler (Moscow: Khudozhestvennaia literatura, 1990), v. 1, 316-17. On Stalin as the master artist who fulfills avant-garde dreams of fusing life and art, see Andrei Sinyavsky, *Soviet Civilization: A Cultural History,* trans. Joanne Turnbull (New York: Little, Brown, 1990), 93-113; and Boris Groys, *The Total Art of Stalinism:* Avant-Garde, *Aesthetic Dictatorship, and Beyond,* trans. Charles Rougle (Princeton: Princeton University Press, 1992).

15. Anna Akhmatova, "Mandel'shtam (Listki iz dnevnika),” *Sochineniia,* ed. Boris Filipoff and G. P. Struve (vs. 1-2, Washington, DC: Interlanguage Library Associates, 1967-1968, v. 3, Paris: YMCA Press, 1983), 2: 181.

16. Quoted in Anatoly Naiman, *Remembering Anna Akhmatova,* trans. Wendy Rosslyn (New York: Henry Holt, 1991), 128.

17. Osip Mandel'shtam, "Literary Moscow: The Birth of Plot," *The Complete Critical Prose and Letters,* ed. Jane Gary Harris, trans. Jane Gary Harris, Constance Link (Ann Arbor: Ardis, 1979), 152. All further translations of Mandel'shtam's prose will be taken, with slight modifications, from this edition.

18. "Poema bez geroia," *Sochineniia,* 2: 125.

19. "O Mandel'shtame," *Den' poezii* 1967 (Leningrad, 1967), 167. Eikhenbaum's notes on Mandel'shtam were never completed; although they were written in 1933, they were published for the first time only several decades later.

20. Osip Mandel'shtam, *Sobranie sochinenii,* ed. G. P. Struve, B. A. Filipoff (vs. 1-3, Washington, DC: Interlanguage Library Associates, 1967-1971, v. 4; Paris: YMCA Press, 1981), 1: 202.

21. Quoted in Lazar Fleishman, *Boris Pasternak: The Poet and His Politics* (Cambridge: Harvard University Press, 1990), 176.

22. "Mandel'shtam," *Sochineniia,* 2: 179.

23. On Mandel'shtam's recitations of the epigram, see E. Polianovskii, "Smert' Osipa Mandel'shtama I," *Izvestiia* (23-28 May 1992); and Nadezhda Mandel'shtam, *Vospominaniia: kniga pervaia,* esp. 88, 96-98 165-70. According to both sources, Mandel'shtam's interrogator at the Liubianka Prison denounced the poem as a "provocation" and a "terrorist act."

24. In his notebooks of 1931-1932, Mandel'shtam recognizes the real-life implications of certain kinds of speech: "Only in government decrees, in military orders, in judicial verdicts, in notarial acts and in such documents as the last Will and Testament does the verb [or "word"—the modern Russian for "verb" coincides with the Old Russian term for "word," *glagol*] live a full life" (Complete Critical Prose, 469). By treating his "Stalin Epigram" as a de facto Will and Testament, Mandel'shtam could thus compete with the verdicts and decrees whose "full lives" threatened to deprive him and other Russians of their own more vulnerable lives.

25. *Complete Critical Prose,* 438, 317.

26. *Complete Critical Prose,* 316-17, 314; *Sobranie sochinenii,* 1: 157-158.

27. "Vse ushli i nikto ne vernulsia," *Sochineniia,* 3: 72.

28. *Sochineniia,* 1: 361; translation taken from Susan Amert, *In a Shattered Mirror: The Later Poetry of Anna Akhmatova* (Stanford: Stanford University Press, 1992), 32.

29. "Journey to Armenia" (1933), *Complete Critical Prose,* 372. *Sobranie sochinenii,* 1: 170, 214, 169. On the role of articulation in Akhmatova's late poetry, see Amert, *In a Shattered Mirror,* 32-34.

30. Andrei Sinyavsky quotes Voloshin in *Soviet Civilization,* 233.

31. *Complete Critical Prose,* 415-16.

32. "Poema bez geroia," *Sochineniia,* 2: 101.

33. Bulgakov's phrase is taken from *The Master and Margarita* (*Master i Margarita,* 1940).

34. "And now I'm writing, just as before, without corrections / My verses in a burnt notebook," Akhmatova notes in a poem of 1956 ("Son," *Sochineniia,* 1: 291). I am indebted to Amert's discussions of Akhmatova's "burnt notebooks" and "poems written for the ashtray" in *In a Shattered Mirror,* 143-51.

35. Amert demonstrates that Akhmatova's poem is engaged in a complex, revisionary dialogue with one of the most popular Stalinist-era hymns, "Song of the Motherland" (Pesn' o rodine) (*In a Shattered Mirror,* 30-59).

36. Akhmatova quotes Mandel'shtam in her recollections of the poet (*Sochineniia,* 2: 185).

Roberta Reeder (essay date Winter 1997)

SOURCE: "Anna Akhmatova: The Stalin Years," in *New England Review,* Vol. 18, No. 1, Winter, 1997, pp. 105-20.

[*In the following essay, Reeder analyzes Akhmatova's poetry from the years of Stalinist oppression.*]

> . . . But there is no power more formidable, more terrible in the world, than the poets' prophetic word.
> —Anna Akhmatova

For a long time now Anna Akhmatova has been known in her own country as one of the most gifted Russian poets of the twentieth century. Yet in the West she is still relatively unknown.

For many the only poems by Akhmatova that have been read and recited have been the love poems which she wrote as a young Russian aristocrat at the turn of the century. These poems have always attracted large numbers of enthusiasts, for Akhmatova was able to capture and convey the vast range of evolving emotions experienced in a love affair—from the first thrill of meeting, to a deepening love contending with hatred, and eventually to violent destructive passion or total indifference. But others before her had turned to these themes. What made Akhmatova so revolutionary in 1912, when her first collection, *Evening,* was published, was the particular manner in which she conveyed these emotions. She was writing against the background of the Symbolist movement, and her poetry marks a radical break with the erudite, ornate style and the mystical representation of love so typical of poets like Alexander Blok and Andrey Bely. Her lyrics are composed of short fragments of simple speech that do not form a logical coherent pattern. Instead, they reflect the way we actually think—the links between the images are emotional, and simple everyday objects are charged with psychological associations. Like Alexander Pushkin, who was her model in many ways, Akhmatova was intent on conveying worlds of meaning through precise details.

What is less well understood, however, is that Akhmatova was not only a poet but a prophet. While throughout her life her style remained essentially the same (except in certain works like *Poems Without a Hero* or her verse dramas), over the years themes of political and historical consequence as well as philosophical themes begin to play an increasingly important role in her writings.

Akhmatova often complained about being immured, "walled in," by critics, into a conception of her enterprise which was limited to the very early period of her career. There was good reason for this: except for a trusted few, no one knew of her poems against the Stalinist Terror. These works certainly were not allowed to be published in the Soviet Union, and

only certain examples—a noted one being her famous cycle entitled *Requiem*—were published in the West during her lifetime. Yet many consider these poems to be her greatest. They convey the profound horror as well as the numbness of the average Soviet citizen in response to the vast number of arrests, trials, exiles and deaths of so many innocent sufferers.

Akhmatova could have left Russia after the revolution, as so many of her friends did, but she chose to stay, and in the process took on the burden of speech on behalf of her people. As the poet says in her poem "To the Many," written in 1922:

> I—am your voice, the warmth of your breath,
> I—am the reflection of your face,
> The future trembling of futile wings,
> I am with you to the end, in any case.

In fact, Akhmatova's poetic response to the pressure of historical events began before the revolution. Although until that time her poetry was largely apolitical, when World War I broke out in 1914 she had been moved to write a few extremely powerful poems confronting that development. While her husband, the poet Nicholas Gumilyov, insisted on combining patriotism with a conscious Nietzschean stance of the male seeking situations of utmost danger to prove his Superman status, Akhmatova reacted with a sense of dread and foreboding to the outbreak of the war. In her memoirs, she observes that the real twentieth century began in 1914 when war broke out, for the war brought not only devastation, but revolution and ultimate ruin to the Russian land. The name of the city Petersburg, with its Germanic associations, was altered to Petrograd, a Slavic term, and the name itself became a metonymic symbol for the transformation in the consciousness of the Russian people of its conception of itself and its relation to its sometimes friendly but often hostile neighbor. Of this first year of the war, Akhmatova writes:

> At the beginning of May the Petersburg season began to fade, and everyone left. This time they left Petersburg forever. We returned not to Petersburg but to Petrograd. We fell from the 19th into the 20th century. Everything became different, beginning with the appearance of the city.

Akhmatova interpreted the war as a spiritual event. She viewed it as a portent of things to come, as God's way of showing His displeasure with the Russian people. As she grew older, she became increasingly convinced of this, and later expressed the belief that war and revolution came to Russia as retribution for the indifference shown by the intelligentsia and upper classes toward the suffering of the common people.

The war began on July 19th, Russian Old Calendar (thirteen days behind our calendar). Written the next day, one of Akhmatova's most striking poems about the war is the first in the cycle entitled "July 1914." Unlike the religious imagery in the poems in her earlier collection **Rosary**, where sacred symbolism was often employed to convey a sense of intense passion, here as in the ancient Russian chronicles, religious imagery serves to elevate the historical immediacies of the war to a more philosophical level. In earlier periods the Russian chroniclers would not only relate facts but interpret historical events (such as the incursion of the Mongols) allegorically, as a punishment of the Russian people for their sins. In this poem the themes of retribution and forgiveness through divine intercession are central. Akhmatova remains secure in her belief that Russia would be compelled to live through a terrible period, but that in the end the Madonna would protect them all, spreading her mantle over them as she had in earlier times, playing the ancient role of Woman as Intercessor between the human and the divine, and bringing forgiveness. This image refers here specifically to an Eastern Orthodox holiday, Pokrov or "Intercession," based on the belief that in the tenth century the Madonna appeared in a vision to St. Andrew the Holy Fool at a church in Constantinople and extended her veil over the people as a symbol of her protection. In the poem it is not the poet who acts as prophet, but a one-legged stranger:

> It smells of burning. For four weeks
> The dry peat bog has been burning.
> The birds have not even sung today,
> And the aspen has stopped quaking.
>
> The sun has become God's displeasure,
> Rain has not sprinkled the fields since Easter.
> A one-legged stranger came along
> And all alone in the courtyard said:
>
> "Fearful times are drawing near. Soon
> Fresh graves will be everywhere.
> There will be famine, earthquakes, widespread
>   death,
> And the eclipse of the sun and the moon.
>
> But the enemy will not divide
> Our land at will, for himself:
> The Mother of God will spread her white mantle
> Over this enormous grief."

By 1916 patriotic fervor had been replaced by despair in the minds of most Russians, including Akhmatova. Her poem "In Memoriam, July 19, 1914," written in 1916, depicts the poet as a vessel of God Himself, and now she has evolved from a singer of love songs to a prophet of doom:

> We aged a hundred years, and this
> Happened in a single hour:
> The short summer had already died,
> The body of the ploughed plains soaked.
>
> Suddenly the quiet road burst into color,
> A lament flew up, ringing, silver . . .
> Covering my face, I implored God
> Before the first battle to strike me dead.
>
> Like a burden henceforth unnecessary,
> The shadows of passion and songs vanished
>   from my memory.
> The Most High ordered it—emptied—
> To become a grim book of calamity.

In a poem written in 1915, the poet again takes on the mantel of the prophet:

> No, tsarevitch, I am not the one
> You want me to be.
> And no longer do my lips
> Kiss—they prophesy.

During the course of the war the evolution of Akhmatova from a poet of personal themes to a prophet of historical events was noted by the critic Sergey Rafalovich: "Akhmatova has developed into a great poet. . . . She has not changed the former thread or broken it, she has remained herself, but she has matured. Before, they said hers was a narrow circle but great. . . . She has broadened her range to include more universal themes, but has not perceived them on a lofty scale, but the same scale of themes from ordinary, everyday life."

In February, 1917, the year of revolutions, the country as a whole rose up against the Tsar—workers, merchants, aristocrats. A Provisional Government was declared, but the war continued. Another authority arose parallel to the government—the soviets, or councils of workers and soldiers, which wielded enormous power over the masses. When the Revolution began on February 25, Akhmatova was spending the morning at the dressmaker's, oblivious to what was occurring. When she attempted to go home to the other side of the Neva River, the driver nervously replied that it was too dangerous to go over, so Akhmatova roamed the city alone. She saw the revolutionary manifestoes, the troops, and the fires set by the tsarist secret police in an attempt to keep the masses off the streets. What she captured in recollection, in "Apparition," written in 1919, was the Tsar's inability to comprehend what was happening and why:

> The round, hanging lanterns,
> Lit early, are squeaking,
> Ever more festively, ever brighter,

The flying snowflakes glitter.

And quickening their steady gait,
As if sensing some pursuit,
Through the softly falling snow
Under a dark blue net, the horses race.

And the gilded footman
Stands motionless behind the sleigh,
and the tsar looks around strangely
With light, empty eyes.

Akhmatova spent the summer of 1917 away from the city, on her husband's estate in the province of Tver. But the overall atmosphere of horror and doom hanging over the land continues to assert itself in an evocative poem:

And all day, terrified by its own moans,
The crowd churns in agonized grief,
And across the river, on funeral banners,
Sinister skulls laugh.
And this is why I sang and dreamed,
They have ripped my heart in half,
As after a burst of shots, it became still,
And in the courtyards, death patrols.

Akhmatova was back in Petrograd when the Bolsheviks began the October Revolution. The only record we have of her immediate reaction is a recollection by her intimate friend Boris Anrep, who was saying farewell to her in January, 1918, on his way to London: "For some time we spoke about the meaning of the revolution," he writes. "She was excited and said we must expect more changes in our lives. The same thing's going to happen that occurred in France during the Revolution, but maybe even worse." Her prophecies were beginning to prove true. In verses written in 1917, the poet grieves that her latest poem, which would have been free in the past to take flight, now begs for a hearing:

Now no one will listen to songs.
The prophesied days have begun.
Latest poem of mine, the world has lost its
    wonder,
Don't break my heart, don't ring out.

A while ago, free as a swallow,
You accomplished your morning flight,
But now you've become a hungry beggar,
Knocking in vain at strangers' gates.

Despite the devastation and chaos around her, Akhmatova remained in Russia, at the same time as many of her friends fled. Her reaction to their flight from the homeland figures in her memorable poem titled "When in suicidal anguish," written in 1918. Though the speaker is tempted by the voice calling her to leave her suffering country, she remains, not realizing that the horrors she now faces are small in comparison to those that she and her companions will have to endure in the future. The first few lines may refer to the treaty in which the Bolsheviks capitulated to the Germans, ending their role in the war. (These lines of the poem were not published in Russia until recently.)

When in suicidal anguish
The nation awaited its German guests,
And the stern spirit of Byzantium
Had fled from the Russian Church,
When the capital by the Neva,
Forgetting her greatness,
Like a drunken prostitute
Did not know who would take her next,
A voice came to me. It called out comfortingly.
It said, "Come here,
Leave your deaf and sinful land,
Leave Russia forever,
I will wash the blood from your hands,
Root out the black shame from your heart,
With a new name I will conceal
The pain of defeats and injuries."
But calmly and indifferently,
I covered my ears with my hands,
So that my sorrowing spirit
Would not be stained by those shameful words.

The brutal Civil War began in 1918 and lasted three years. No one thought the Bolsheviks would remain in power for long, but by 1919 Akhmatova was beginning to feel the sense of overwhelming dread that permeated the capital.

Petrograd, 1919

And confined to this savage capital,
We have forgotten forever
The lakes, the steppes, the towns,
And the dawns of our great native land.
Day and night in the bloody circle

A brutal languor overcomes us . . .
No one wants to help us
Because we stayed home,
Because, loving our city
And not winged freedom,
We preserved for ourselves
Its palaces, its fire and water.

A different time is drawing near,
The wind of death already chills the heart,
But the holy city of Peter
Will be our unintended monument.

When her husband Gumilyov returned from the war, Akhmatova asked for a divorce. Their marriage had disintegrated long before, but they had remained friends. After the revolution, Gumilyov had become an important figure in the world of art, helping writers get food and clothing, organizing poetry readings for the masses, and establishing literary circles and workshops for the intelligentsia where he trained new poets and new appreciators of the written word. In August, 1921, however, Gumilyov was arrested on the ostensible charge of involvement in a counterrevolutionary plot. No one thought events would move so quickly—some tried to help, but their efforts were in vain. A possible reason for the arrest of Gumilyov and others was that the Bolsheviks were reacting to the Kronstadt Rebellion that had taken place during the previous March, and that they needed to demonstrate vividly what could happen to those who might have any ideas about resisting the regime. On August 25th, at the age of thirty-five, Nikolay Gumilyov was executed.

Gumilyov's death was shattering to Akhmatova: she felt somehow responsible for it, and she grieved for many years. Her horror was conveyed in a moving poem, "Terror, fingering things in the dark," dated August 27, 1921. In it she personifies the abstract feeling of terror, which leads "the moonbeam to an ax." It would be better, she says, to be executed by rifle or to be hanged on the scaffold than to have to endure the prolonged fear of imminent death, or the pain of someone you love dying. This is a theme that will be developed in Akhmatova's poems about the Stalinist terror—the sense that it is not the actual physical event of exile or execution that is most unendurable, but the anxiety of waiting, waiting for the knock on the door to take you to prison, to the camps, to your death:

> Terror, fingering things in the dark,
> Leads the moonbeam to an ax.
> Behind the wall there's an ominous knock—
> What's there, a ghost, a thief, rats?
>
> In the sweltering kitchen, water drips,
> Counting the rickety floorboards.
> Someone with a glossy black beard
> Flashes by the attic window—
>
> And becomes still. How cunning he is and evil,
> He hid the matches and blew out the candle.
> How much better would be the gleam of the
>   barrels
> Of rifles leveled at my breast.
>
> Better, in the grassy square,
> To be flattened on the raw wood scaffold
> And, amid cries of joy and moans,
> Pour out my life's blood there.

> I press the smooth cross to my heart:
> Go, restore peace to my soul.
> The odor of decay, sickeningly sweet,
> Rises from the clammy sheets.

Never does Akhmatova mention the revolution directly; her attention remains centered on its effects on the life around her. One poem, "Everything has been plundered . . . ," bears a distinct resemblance to Alexander Blok's famous poem "The Twelve," in which despite the pervasiveness of looting, rape, and rout there is an intuitive feeling that this stage of great suffering will lead inevitably to a glorious dawn—symbolized in Blok's work by Christ and in Akhmatova's by "the miraculous," which is drawing near.

> Everything has been plundered, betrayed, sold
>   out,
> The wing of black death has flashed,
> Everything has been devoured by starving
>   anguish,
> Why, then, is it so bright?
>
> The fantastic woods near the town
> Waft the scent of cherry blossoms by day,
> At night new constellations shine
> In the transparent depth of the skies of July—
>
> And how near the miraculous draws
> To the dirty, tumbledown huts . . .
> No one, no one knows what it is,
> But for centuries we have longed for it.

A new society was indeed created in this new Soviet Union, but it was constructed on the basis of a totalitarian state in which the happiness of the many was to be determined and controlled by the few. In this new order, the role of artists and intellectuals was to be a painful one, as became increasingly clear when, in 1922, over a hundred intellectuals, including the philosopher Nicholas Berdyaev, were arrested and exiled. The poet Osip Mandelstam quickly grasped what the new role of the poet was to be in this society: "He [the modern poet] sings of ideas, systems of knowledge and state theories, just as his predecessors sang of nightingales and roses." But Akhmatova did not wish to express in rhyme the accepted theories of the state; as a result, by 1925 she was no longer published and was considered irrelevant. In 1922 the poet Vladimir Mayakovsky, the mighty Futurist and poet laureate of the Soviet State, who before the revolution had often declaimed Akhmatova's love poems, rang the death knell for her verse:

> The chamber intimacy of Anna Akhmatova, the
> mystical verses of Vyacheslav Ivanov and his
> Hellenic motifs—what meaning do they have for
> our harsh, iron age? Of course, as literary mile-

stones, as the last born child of a collapsing structure, they find their place on the pages of literary history; but for us, for our epoch—these are insignificant, pathetic, and laughable anachronisms.

Poets now had to make a choice—to accommodate themselves to the new regime, or to remain consciously on the periphery. Akhmatova chose the latter. She signals this in an unpublished poem of 1921, in which she recalls the ancient name of Russia—the land of Rus:

> A light beer had been brewed,
> On the table a steaming goose . . .
> The tsar and the nobles are recalled
> By festive Rus—
>
> Strong language, facetious remarks,
> Tipsy conversation,
> From one—a risqué joke,
> From the other—drunken tears.
>
> And fueled by revelry and wine,
> The noisy speeches fly . . .
> The smart ones have decided:
> Our job—stay out of the way.

Although on the periphery, in her unpublished works Akhmatova was unambiguous in her negative attitude toward the aftermath of the revolution:

> Here the most beautiful girls fight
> For the honor of marrying executioners.
> Here they torture the righteous at night
> And wear down the untamable with hunger.

In the same year in which those lines were written, 1924, Akhmatova produced one of her most famous poems, "Lot's Wife." Turning to biblical imagery, she takes on the persona of a woman looking back—on the realistic level, to the familiar locales of her native city. But these specific places become metonymic symbols for "the past" that must be let go if one is to make peace with the future, no matter how terrifying it may be. Although Akhmatova's generation at first thought a return to the former way of life might be possible, by 1924 both the émigrés and those remaining in Russia felt compelled to admit that the Bolsheviks were probably going to remain in power indefinitely—perhaps forever—and each individual had to find a way of coming to terms with this recognition.

Lot's Wife

Lot's wife looked back from behind him and became a pillar of salt.

—Book of Genesis

> And the righteous man followed the envoy of
>   God,
> Huge and bright, over the black mountain.
> But anguish spoke loudly to his wife:
> It is not too late, you can still gaze
>
> At the red towers of your native Sodom,
> At the square where you sang, at the courtyard
>   where you spun,
> At the empty windows of the tall house
> Where you bore children to your beloved
>   husband.
>
> She glanced, and, paralyzed by deadly pain,
> Her eyes no longer saw anything;
> And her body became transparent salt
> And her quick feet were rooted to the spot.
>
> Who will weep for this woman?
> Isn't her death the least significant?
> But my heart will never forget the one
> Who gave her life for a single glance.

The suicide of the poet Sergey Yesenin on December 27, 1925, was a shock to Akhmatova, though she had never really liked him as a person or a poet. Of peasant origin, Yesenin hoped one day Russia would become a land of agricultural communes, all committed to sharing the fruits of the earth. But the Social Revolutionaries, who wanted to make this dream come true, lost to the Bolsheviks, who saw the future of the Soviet Union in terms of accelerating industrial progress. Yesenin died a broken, drunken man. In spite of all her criticism of him, however, Akhmatova was upset when she learned the circumstances of his death: "He lived horribly and died horribly," she observed. "How fragile the peasants are when they are unsuccessful in their contact with civilization—each year another poet dies. . . . It is horrible when a poet dies." Although it cannot be proven conclusively, it is possible that her poem, "It would be so easy to abandon this life," written about the death of a poet in 1925, refers specifically to Yesenin:

> It would be so easy to abandon this life,
> To burn down painlessly and unaware,
> But it is not given to the Russian poet
> To die a death so pure.
>
> A bullet more reliably throws open
> Heaven's boundaries to the soul in flight,
> Or hoarse terror with a shaggy paw can,
> As if from a sponge, squeeze out the heart's life.

After her brief time together with Vladimir Shileiko, an

Assyriologist whom she married in 1918 and from whom she separated in 1921, Akhmatova eventually went to live with her lover Nicholas Punin, a famous avant-garde art critic and professor, along with his wife and daughter in a wing of the Sheremetyev Palace. During this time, she began writing less poetry and turned instead to a study of the works of the poet whose example remained central to her own ambitions, Alexander Pushkin. In his work and life she saw parallels to her own situation and to that of other contemporary poets persecuted by the State.

By 1930, in any case, it was becoming increasingly difficult for anyone to publish at all. Stalin was now firmly in power and his control of society extended to the arts. In August 1929 there was a concerted attack against the writers Boris Pilnyak and Yevgeny Zamyatin. The condemnation of their work marked a clear turning point in the relationship between the intelligentsia and the state. Henceforth the Stalinist line would become harder, and any trace of criticism of the state would be forbidden. The increasing storm of abuse against Mayakovsky led to his suicide on April 14, 1930. During this period of collectivization, many Party members lost their jobs for showing leniency toward the peasants. The year 1933 saw another vast purge. Stalin's Terror had begun, but the majority of the population were still unaware of the extent to which it would touch their everyday lives. Nadezhda Mandelstam attempts to explain the feeling at this moment:

> There had been a time when, terrified of chaos, we had all prayed for a strong system, for a powerful hand that would stem the angry human river overflowing its banks. This fear of chaos was perhaps the most permanent of our feelings. . . . What we wanted was for the course of history to be made smooth. . . . This longing prepared us, psychologically, for the appearance of the Wise Leaders who would tell us where we were going. And once they were there, we no longer ventured to act without their guidance. . . . In our blindness we ourselves struggled to impose unanimity—because in every difference of opinion, we saw the beginnings of new anarchy and chaos. . . . So we went on, nursing a sense of our own inadequacy, until the moment came for each of us to discover from bitter experience how precarious was his own state of grace.

In this situation in the early thirties, Akhmatova began translating *Macbeth*, but in the end she only succeeded in working on Act I, Scene iii, the famous witches' scene. She must have seen parallels between the murders committed by *Macbeth* and his wife to gain power and what was occurring in the Soviet Union; Lady Macbeth, the "Scottish queen," appears in Akhmatova's famous poem written in 1933 evoking the blood spilled by the Bolsheviks:

Wild honey smells like freedom,
Dust—like a ray of sun.
Like violets—a young maid's mouth,
And gold—like nothing.
The flowers of the mignonette smell like water,
And like an apple—love.
But we learned once and for all
That blood only smells like blood . . .

And in vain the vice-regent of Rome
Washed his hands before all the people,
Urged on by the ominous shouts of the rabble;
And the Scottish queen
In vain washed the spattered red drops
From her slender palms
In the stifling gloom of the king's home. . . .

One of the first victims of the Stalinist Terror was Osip Mandelstam, who had been her dear and intimate friend from before the Revolution. Akhmatova later called the early 1930s "the vegetarian years," meaning that this would come to be seen as a relatively harmless period in comparison to the "meat-eating" years that followed, but when visiting the Mandelstams in Moscow, she felt that "in spite of the fact that the time was comparatively vegetarian, the shadow of doom lay on this house." She recalls a walk she took with Mandelstam along Prechistenka Street in February, 1934. "We turned onto Gogol Boulevard and Osip said, 'I'm ready for death.'" But when he was finally arrested for the poem in which he portrays Stalin with "cockroach whiskers" and "fingers as fat as worms," the effect on this gentle, sensitive poet was a progressive descent into madness. The secret police came for him when Akhmatova was visiting the Mandelstams in May, 1934. He and his wife were sent away to Voronezh, where in February, 1936, Akhmatova went to visit them.

When her poem reflecting this visit was first published in 1940, the last four lines were omitted. At first glance, the poem seems to be a poetic guided tour of Voronezh, mentioning not only the landscape and townscape, but alluding to the monuments and historical occurrences associated with the place—the statue of Peter the Great, who built his fleet here, and the Battle of Kulikovo, a landmark event in Russian history, which was fought nearby in 1380 (in that encounter, the Grand Prince Dmitry Donskoy defeated the Tatars after many years of domination). As the poem progresses, the mood shifts. At first the images evoke winter stillness, lack of life—crows, ice, a faded dome; but then a sound breaks the stillness—there is a roaring in the poplars, compared in a simile to the sounds of a happy event, to cups clashing together at a wedding feast toasting the joy of the poet and her companions. After the expectation created by this simile—the sense that more happy events are to follow—suddenly in the last four lines anxiety is palpably personified, as in Akhmatova's poem on the death of Gumilyov, "Terror, fingering things in the dark." In the room of the poet in "Voronezh," Fear and the Muse keep watch together:

> And the whole town is encased in ice,
> Trees, walls, snow, as if under glass.
> Timidly, I walk on crystals,
> Gaily painted sleds skid.
> And over the Peter of Voronezh—crows,
> Poplar trees, and the dome, light green,
> Faded, dulled, in sunny haze,
> And the Battle of Kulikovo blows from the
>   slopes
> Of the mighty, victorious land.
> And the poplars, like cups clashed together,
> As if our joy were toasted by
> A thousand guests at a wedding feast.
> But in the room of the poet in disgrace,
> Fear and the Muse keep watch by turns.
> And the night comes on
> That knows no dawn.

Before Mandelstam's death, Nadezhda had experienced what thousands of other women in the Soviet Union endured during those years—hours of standing in endless lines in front of prison windows, waiting for a glimpse of those they loved. Now it was Akhmatova's turn to stand in line. Her son Lev had been arrested in the past and released, but this time, after arresting him on March 10, 1938, he had been tortured. He was sent first to the Leningrad Kresty Prison and condemned to be shot, but then the feared head of the NKVD, Yezhov, was removed, and the beating of prisoners ceased for a time. Lev's sentence was commuted to five years, and he was sent to Siberia. During the period of waiting, Lydia Zhukova, a member of the intelligentsia, had stood in one of those long lines in front of the prison. She remembers seeing Akhmatova. "Wearing something long, dark, and heavy," she recalled, "she appeared to me like a phantom from the past, and it never entered my mind that this old-fashioned lady in an ancient coat and hat would still write so many more brilliant new poems."

Indeed, Akhmatova had begun to throw herself into her work with new energy. Her "mute" period was over, as the impressions of many years of quiet suffering finally rose to the surface. When her creative powers returned, Akhmatova wrote the cycle of poems about the Great Terror that was to capture the attention of the world, *Requiem* (1935-1940). That this work is characterized by a portrayal of intense suffering did not signify, however, that Akhmatova had lost her faith and arrived at unrelieved despair. Inherent in the works of great Russian writers like Dostoyevsky is the Russian Orthodox belief that suffering is at all times an essential aspect of life, a means by which one's faith is continually

tested. Never in any of Akhmatova's writings or conversations with trusted friends did she admit to doubt or lack of faith in the mysterious and often incomprehensible ways of a divine Creator.

A short prose piece, entitled "Instead of a Preface," introduces this memorable cycle:

> In the terrible years of the Yezhov terror, I spent seventeen months in the prison lines of Leningrad. Once, someone "recognized" me. Then a woman with bluish lips standing behind me, who, of course, had never heard me called by name before, woke up from the stupor to which everyone had succumbed and whispered in my ear: "Can you describe this?" And I answered: "Yes, I can." Then something that looked like a smile passed over what had once been her face.

In this great work Akhmatova fulfills her destiny as the voice of her people, taking on the persona of the Mourner in the Russian village, and of the Madonna. This poetic cycle is both universal and specifically Russian in its symbolic implications. On the universal level it depicts the suffering of women in general who, like the Madonna, must stand on the side and witness helplessly the suffering of those who are compelled to meet an incomprehensible destiny. In such circumstances, the woman can only provide comfort and prayer so that the pain and agony may be alleviated somehow. But there are specific Russian references here as well. In the first verse of the cycle the poet compares herself to a peasant woman performing the ancient Russian ritual of *vynos*—the carrying out of the dead from the house to the vehicle that will take the body to the cemetery. Instead of a dead body, however, this time it is a live prisoner, someone beloved. Another specifically Russian cultural allusion is to the icons, the sacred images painted on wood to which the Orthodox pray, and the icon shelf, placed in a special corner of the house where meals and rituals take place. At the end of this work, the poem's speaker compares herself to the wives of the *Streltsy* or Archers, the military corps employed by Peter the Great's sister Sophia, whom they supported in her unsuccessful fight for the throne and who were subsequently executed. Their wives grieved for them under the Kremlin towers, and the event was immortalized in the nineteenth century in a well-known painting by Vasily Súrikov. Through this comparison with women caught up in a famous historical event, the poet elevates the actual situation in which she finds herself, transforming the immediate event into one of universal significance:

> They led you away at dawn.
> I followed you, like a mourner.
> In the dark front room the children were crying,
> By the icon shelf the candle was dying,

On your lips was the icon's chill.
The deathly sweat on your brow . . . Unforgettable!—
I will be like the wives of the Streltsy,
Howling under the Kremlin towers.

In another poem not included in *Requiem,* a poem written in 1939, Akhmatova compares her speaker to another Súrikov painting, one depicting the Boyarina Morozova, a seventeenth-century noblewoman in a sleigh, in chains, being taken into exile for her rebellion against the reforms being introduced into the Orthodox church. The poem also alludes to Viy, the chief of gnomes, whose eyelids reach to the ground (the Gogol story "Viy" contains such a creature):

I know I can't move from this place.
Because of the weight of the eyelids of Viy.
Oh, if only I could suddenly throw myself back
Into some sort of seventeenth century.

On Trinity Eve to stand in church
With a fragrant branch of birch,
To drink of sweet mead
With the Princess Morozova.

And then at twilight in the sleigh,
To sink in the dingy snow.
What mad Súrikov
Will paint my last journey?

In some of the poems in *Requiem,* there are allusions to Tsarskoye Selo, the lovely area near Petersburg where Akhmatova grew up. The town is represented by the poet as symbolic of the womb-like existence of the upper classes before the revolution, a time when they attempted to shut themselves off from the sufferings of the people; reflecting on this milieu, the speaker comes to regard her earlier self as a "gay little sinner":

You should have been shown, you mocker,
Minion of all your friends,
Gay little sinner of Tsarskoye Selo,
What would happen in your life—
How three-hundredth in line, with a parcel,
You would stand by the Kresty prison,
Your fiery tears
Burning through the New Year's ice.
Over there the prison poplar bends,
And there's no sound—and over there how
    many
Innocent lives are ending now. . . .

Other less-known poems written at this time express Akhmatova's pervasive sense of terror and grief. In the simple but powerful quatrain, "And I am not at all a prophet," for example, the simple image of prison keys brings into focus a network of ominous associations linked with the Stalinist terror—associations centered on arrest, exile, and death. Here the poet disowns her claim to be a prophet:

And I am not at all a prophet,
My life is pure as a stream.
I simply don't feel like singing
To the sound of prison keys.

In another unpublished work, "Imitation from the Armenian," Akhmatova pretends merely to be presenting a variation on a theme, reworking a poem by someone else. But the theme of the original (a poem by the Armenian poet H. Tumanjan) has been chosen with great care, and its theme coincides with that of other poems by Akhmatova written during the Terror. Here once again, the vulnerable female, in this case an innocent ewe, witnesses the slaughter of a loved one:

I will appear in your dreams as a black ewe.
On withered, unsteady legs
I will approach you, begin to bleat, to howl:
"Padishah, have you supped daintily?
You hold the universe, like a bead,
You are cherished by Allah's radiant will . . .
And was he tasty, my little son?
Did he please you, please your children?"

One of Akhmatova's most powerful responses to the Terror is her poem "Stanzas" (written in 1940 but not published in the Soviet Union until 1989), in which she indirectly addresses Stalin himself. She enumerates infamous figures in Russian history who have lived in the Kremlin and implies that the leader now in residence there is living up to and even surpassing his predecessors in the enormity of his cruelty. The poem addresses a "Streltsy" or "Archer" moon—which might refer to late winter (associated the astrological sign Sagittarius, the Archer), or to the Streltsy corps rebellion against Peter the Great mentioned earlier, or to both. There are allusions here to tsars like Boris Godunov, the various Ivans, and Dmitry, the Pretender to the Russian throne at the beginning of the seventeenth century who, in attempting to capture Russia with the aid of the Catholic Poles, had alienated the Russian people:

Archer Moon. Beyond the Moscow River. Night.
Like a religious procession the hours of Holy
    Week go by.
I had a terrible dream. Is it possible
That no one, no one, no one can help me?

You had better not live in the Kremlin, the
    Preobrazhensky Guard was right;

The germs of the ancient frenzy are still swarming
   here:
Boris Godunov's wild fear, and all the Ivans' evil
   spite,
And the Pretender's arrogance—instead of the
   people's rights.

In another unpublished poem, "Why did you poison the water?" (1935), the poet complains that instead of being rewarded for staying in her motherland, she is being punished by having her freedom taken away:

Why did you poison the water
And mix dirt with my bread?
Why did you turn the last freedom
Into a den of thieves?
Because I didn't jeer
At the bitter death of friends?
Because I remained true
To my sorrowing motherland?
So be it. Without hangman and scaffold
A poet cannot exist in the world.
Our lot is to wear the hair shirt,
To walk with a candle and to wail.

The implications of the hair shirt and walking with a candle as penance become clearer in Akhmatova's poem on Dante. While Pushkin turned to the Roman poet Ovid as the archetype of the poet in exile, Akhmatova turned to Dante, whom she and Mandelstam were both reading in the thirties. Like the Pushkin poem on Ovid, Akhmatova's work is a thinly disguised reflection on the dignity a poet must retain no matter what external conditions are tormenting him—whether it be the political regime of fourteenth-century Florence or that of twentieth-century Leningrad. After being forced to leave Florence in 1302, Dante was offered the possibility of returning under condition of a humiliating public repentance, which he rejected. He refused to walk "with a lighted candle" in a ritual of repentance:

Dante

Il mio bel San Giovanni

       —Dante

Even after his death he did not return
To his ancient Florence.
To the one who, leaving, did not look back,
To him I sing this song.
A torch, the night, the last embrace,
Beyond the threshold, the wild wail of fate.
From hell he sent her curses
And in paradise he could not forget her—
But barefoot, in a hairshirt,

With a lighted candle he did not walk
Through his Florence—his beloved,
Perfidious, base, longed for. . . .

One of those who had gone into voluntary exile abroad after the revolution was Marina Tsevtayeva. She and Akhmatova had never met, but in the 1910s Tsvetayeva had written a series of adoring poems to Akhmatova, calling her the "Muse of Lament." She had spent many years in Prague and Paris, but in 1937 her husband, Sergey Efron, was implicated in the murder of a Western official by the Soviet secret police and fled to the Soviet Union. Two years later Tsvetayeva and her son followed, joining Efron and her daughter, who had returned earlier. The regime turned on the family, arresting her husband and daughter. Tsvetayeva herself continued to live on a meager sum from a job as a translator which Pasternak had obtained for her. She asked a friend of Akhmatova's to arrange for a meeting between them. The meeting took place in 1940; in March of that year, Akhmatova had written a poem to Tsvetayeva, but she did not read it to her. There is an allusion in the poem to the Marinka Tower—the Kremlin tower in the town of Kolomna near Moscow, a town where Akhmatova sometimes spent the summer during the nineteen-thirties. According to legend, this tower was the site of the incarceration of Marina Mnishek, who had the same first name as Tsvetayeva. She was the aristocratic Polish wife of Dmitry, the seventeenth-century Pretender to the Russian throne:

Belated Reply

   My white-handed one, dark princess.

       —M. Ts.

Invisible, double, jester,
You who are hiding in the depths of the bushes,
The one crouching in a starling house,
The one flitting on the crosses of the dead.
The one crying from the Marinka Tower:
"I have come home today,
Native fields, cherish me
Because of what happened to me.
The abyss swallowed my loved ones,
The family home has been plundered."
We are together today, Marina,
Walking through the midnight capital,
And behind us there are millions like us,
And never was a procession more hushed,
Accompanied by funeral bells
And the wild Moscow moans
Of a snowstorm erasing all traces of us.

No one knows what the two poets discussed at their meeting—two women so very different in their attitudes toward life and their conceptions of poetry: one a product of the muted elegance of Petersburg, expressing her emotion through verse distinguished by restraint, and the other reflecting the noisy bustle of Moscow, declaring her feelings in writings charged with raw emotion. Not having read Akhmatova's unpublished poems from the nineteen-twenties and thirties, Tsvetayeva assumed that Akhmatova had remained fixed in the style and themes of her early period, and in her diary she was critical of Akhmatova's verse. They met behind the closed door of Akhmatova's room in the apartment of the poet's friend Nina Olshanskaya. Later on, during the war, Tsvetayeva was evacuated and ended up in Yelabuga, a town near Kazan, where she could find no work. On the afternoon of August 31, 1941, she was found hanging from a hook inside the entrance of her hut.

Along with many other artistic figures such as Shostakovich, Akhmatova herself was evacuated during the war to Central Asia, where she lived for several years in Tashkent. On the way there she learned about Tsvetayeva's suicide. In "Over Asia—the mists of spring," written on June 24, 1942, Akhmatova included the following lines alluding to her sense of the predicament they shared:

> I've earned this gray crown,
> And my cheeks, scorched by the sun,
> Frighten people with their swarthiness.
> But the end of my pride is near:
> Like that other one—Marina the sufferer,
> I will have to drink of emptiness.

As arrest after arrest intruded on the lives of those around her, around 1940 Akhmatova wrote that she wished emphatically to cast a vote in favor of something positive—not something extraordinary, merely a return to an ordinary situation in which a door could once again be seen as nothing more than a door:

> And here, in defiance of the fact
> That death is staring me in the eye—
> Because of your words
> I am voting *for:*
> For a door to become a door,
> A lock—a lock once more,
> For this morose beast within my breast
> To become a heart. But the thing is,
> That we are all fated to learn
> What it means not to sleep for three years,
> What it means to find out in the morning
> About those who have died in the night.

At the end of the nineteen-forties, when the situation was unchanged, Akhmatova wrote "The Glass Doorbell," in which the glass doorbell performs a function similar to that of the lock as a focus of terror:

> The glass doorbell
> Rings urgently.
> Is today really the date?
> Stop at the door,
> Wait a little longer,
> Don't touch me,
>   For God's sake!

In keeping with this persisting sense of anxiety, on August 14, 1946, the Central Committee of the Communist Party passed a Resolution condemning the journals *Zvezda* and *Leningrad* for publishing the works of Akhmatova and Zoshchenko. As Churchill was to observe, the iron curtain had been rung down earlier that year by Stalin, and the Resolution was a symbolic act confirming this. A few weeks later, on September 4th, Akhmatova and Zoshchenko were expelled from the Union of Writers. In his speech that evening to the Leningrad branch of the Union, Andrey Zhdanov, Secretary of the Central Committee, said: "What positive contribution can Akhmatova's work make to our young people? It can only sow despondency, spiritual depression, pessimism, and the desire to walk away from the questions of public life." After her expulsion, and for many years thereafter, Akhmatova retained a few loyal friends, including Pasternak, who helped her and supported her both spiritually and financially; but most of the people she had known avoided her. She expresses her profound state of alienation in her poem "Prologue," written sometime in the nineteen-fifties, in which she presents herself as a leper:

> Not with the lyre of someone in love
> Do I try to captivate people—
> A leper's rattle
> Sings in my hand.
> You will have ample time to exclaim
> And curse and howl.
> I will teach all the "courageous ones"
> To shy away from me.
> I didn't look for any return,
> And glory I didn't expect,
> I have lived for thirty years
> Under the wing of death.

Akhmatova's son Lev also suffered from the effects of the Resolution. Released from the camps to fight in the war, he had taken part in the capture of Berlin. He was allowed to return to Leningrad after the war had ended, but was arrested again in November, 1949, and sentenced to ten years in a camp in Siberia. It was around this time that Akhmatova wrote a series of short poems as part of a cycle entitled "Shards"—as if to suggest that the individual poems were like fragments of an ancient vessel. She begins the cycle with an epigraph, a phrase taken (and misquoted slightly) from Joyce's *Ulysses:* "You cannot leave your mother an orphan." In the brief quatrain serving as the second poem of the cycle, Akhmatova contrasts the various verbal definitions that may be applied to a single person—in this case, in the biographical subtext, Lev Gumilyov. For the regime he bears the signifier "rebel," but for Akhmatova he is designated by another, more personal, name:

> How well he's succeeded, this fierce debater,
> All the way to the Yenisey plains . . .
> To you he's a vagabond, rebel, conspirator—
> To me he is—an only son.

The West knew little of Akhmatova's life or her works written during the nineteen-forties and fifties. Many thought she had stopped writing verse altogether. By not allowing her to be published for so long—except for a book in 1940 that was immediately confiscated and some poems which were permitted to appear during the war—Stalin had condemned Akhmatova to silence, at least to Western readers. She expresses her sense of this choking silence in part V of "Shards," in which, without mentioning him directly, she compares Stalin to a butcher who had hung her (like Marina Tsvetayeva) "on a bloody hook":

> You raised me up, like a slain beast
> On a bloody hook,
> So that sniggering, and not believing,
> Foreigners wandered in
> And wrote in their respectable papers
> That my incomparable gift had died out,
> That I had been a poet among poets,
> But my thirteenth hour had struck.

Akhmatova's lament for her imprisoned son is heard at the end of one of her greatest works, *Poem without a Hero*. It is a long narrative poem, in a style more reminiscent of the complex opaqueness and erudite allusions of the Symbolists at the beginning of the century than representative of Akhmatova's characteristically direct assertions seizing on metonymic symbols from everyday life. In this work the poet looks back to the period before World War I, to the year 1913, when she and her friends had hidden in the cellars of cabarets, devoting themselves to a life of pleasure while the common people suffered. The Epilogue takes place on a white night of June 24, 1942, with Leningrad left in ruins. The text is chanted in the voice of the author—seven thousand kilometers away from the scene, in evacuation in Tashkent. In this Epilogue, Akhmatova's son is depicted as her double, and death takes the form of a Noseless Slut:

> And from behind barbed wire,
> In the very heart of the taiga—
> I don't know which year—
> Having become a heap of "camp dust,"

Having become a terrifying fairy tale,
> My double goes to the interrogation.
> And then he returns from the interrogation,
> With the two emissaries from the Noseless Slut
> Assigned to stand guard over him.
> And even from here I can hear—
> Isn't it miraculous!—
> The sound of my own voice:
> > I paid for you in cash.
> > For exactly ten years I lived under the gun,
> > Glancing neither to the left nor to the right.
> > And after me came rustling ill repute.

There are several stanzas thought to be conceived for possible inclusion in *Poem Without a Hero* but not included in the text. In one of these the poet identifies herself and other women suffering during the Stalinist Terror with the ancient heroines of Troy—Hecuba, queen of Troy, who looked on helplessly as her dear son, the hero Hektor, died, and the Trojan princess Cassandra, who was condemned to know the future but whose fate it was to have her prophecies ignored:

> Sealing our bluish lips,
> Mad Hecubas
> And Cassandras from Chukloma,
> We roar in silent chorus
> (We, crowned with disgrace):
> "We are already on the other side of hell". . . .

But finally, on March 5, 1953, an event occurred that changed the life of Akhmatova and millions of others in the Soviet Union: Joseph Stalin died. Not long afterward, in a closed session of the Twentieth Party Congress that took place in February, 1956, the new First Secretary of the Communist Party, Nikita Khrushchev, denounced Stalin as a cruel, bloodthirsty tyrant. The "Thaw" had begun. While the Thaw certainly did not fulfill all the hopes of the intelligentsia or the people at large, it did at least mean that the harshest aspects of the reign of Terror were ended, and there was a perceptible loosening of the iron rule of the former regime. Lev Gumilyov, Akhmatova's son, was released in May, 1956, and her own works went into circulation again, though it was not until 1958 that a whole collection of her writings would appear.

In 1957, unsure when—or whether—her works would engage a wide audience again, Akhmatova wrote the poem "They will forget?—How astonishing!" It was her equivalent of Horace's "Exegi monumentum"—a poem imitated by Pushkin—in which the poet asserts that while he may be persecuted and unappreciated in his own time, his spiritual legacy, in the form of his works, will be eternal. In this poem Akhmatova turns to an ancient mythical image of death followed by certain rebirth—the image of the phoenix, symbolic of the everlasting nature of verse:

> They will forget?—How astonishing!
> They forgot me a hundred times,
> A hundred times I lay in the grave,
> Where, perhaps, I am today.
> But the Muse, both deaf and blind,
> Rotted in the ground, like grain,
> Only, like the phoenix from the ashes,
> To rise into the blue ether again.

Although Akhmatova spent the last years of her life under the somewhat looser regime of Khrushchev, she never stopped writing about his feared predecessor, and sometime around 1962 she addressed a poem "To the Defenders of Stalin." These defenders are placed in a long historical line of those who supported the despots, who tormented the innocent:

> There are those who shouted: "Release
> Barabbas for us on this feast,"
> Those who ordered Socrates to drink poison
> In the bare, narrow prison.

> They are the ones who should pour this drink
> Into their own innocently slandering mouths,
> Those sweet lovers of torture,
> Experts in the manufacture of orphans.

A decade earlier, in 1950, hoping to please Stalin so that he would free her son, Akhmatova had written a cycle of poems, "In Praise of Peace," simple poems with a clear message praising the victory of Russia in the war. Despite this effort on her part, her son remained a prisoner in the camps. These poems in this group were written in the officially-sanctioned style of Socialist Realism, and they include the kinds of trite phrases found in hundreds of poems produced during the Stalinist period. The poem entitled "In the Pioneer Camp," for instance, ends with the lines: " . . . There the children marched by with their banners / And the Motherland herself, admiring them, / Inclined her invisible brow toward them." In a poem called "No, we didn't suffer together in vain," written later (in 1961, five years before her death), Akhmatova seems implicitly to refer to this uncomfortable episode in her life. And yet in her own eyes, throughout this grim period when she felt compelled to make some compromises, she retained her inner freedom even as she outwardly groveled before the "bloody puppet-executioner." She had chosen to stay in her country—and she suffered for it, in many ways; but in the end she affirmed her decision to share this appalling epoch with her own people:

> No, we didn't suffer together in vain,
> Without hopes of even drawing a breath.
> We took an oath, we voted—
> And quietly followed our path.
> Not in vain did I remain pure,
> Like a candle before the Lord,
> Groveling with you at the feet
> Of the bloody puppet-executioner.
> No, not under the vault of alien skies
> And not under the shelter of alien wings—
> I was with my people then,
> There, where my people, unfortunately, were.

FURTHER READING

Criticism

Amert, Susan. "Akhmatova's 'Song of the Motherland': Rereading the Opening Texts of *Rekviem.*" *Slavic Review* 49, No. 3 (Fall 1990): 374-89.

> Provides a close analysis of the first two sections of Akhmatova's *Rekviem* and discusses how the poet has put herself in the tradition of Dante and Pushkin.

Cook, Albert. "The Modified Modernism of Anna Akhmatova." In his *Soundings: On Shakespeare, Modern Poetry, Plato, and Other Subjects*, pp. 81-95. Detroit: Wayne State University Press, 1991.

> Analyzes how Akhmatova's poetry differs from the modernism of her contemporaries and asserts that it owes more to the style of Pushkin.

Additional coverage of Akhmatova's life and career is contained on the following sources published by Gale: *Contemporary Authors*, Vols. 19-20, 25-28R; *Contemporary Authors New Revision Series*, Vol. 35; *Contemporary Authors Permanent Series*, Vol. 1; *DISCovering Authors Modules: Poets; Major Twentieth-Century Writers*, Vols. 1-2; and *Poetry Criticism*, Vol. 2.

Breyten Breytenbach
1939-

South African poet, novelist, memoirist, nonfiction writer, and short story writer.

The following entry presents an overview of Breytenbach's career. For further information on his life and works, see *CLC,* Volumes 23 and 37.

INTRODUCTION

Breytenbach is widely regarded as one of the foremost contemporary South African writers, particularly for his poetry, which is written in the traditional white South African language, Afrikaans. As an exile and former political prisoner, Breytenbach conveys in his works his dichotomous role as both a white—and therefore privileged—South African and an outspoken opponent to his country's official policy of apartheid, the system of severe racial segregation, in place until the early 1990s.

Biographical Information

Breytenbach was born in Bonnievale, South Africa, a descendant of the earliest Dutch settlers there who called themselves "Afrikaners." He attended the University of Cape Town until 1959, when he left South Africa and settled in Paris to work as an artist. In Paris he met and married Yolande Ngo Thi Hoang Lien, a fellow artist of Vietnamese descent. Because of South Africa's strict policy at the time against interracial marriage, the couple were not allowed to enter South Africa until 1972, when they were granted special three-month visas. Breytenbach wrote of his contradictory feelings about this return to his homeland in *A Season in Paradise* (1976). In 1975 Breytenbach returned once more to South Africa, on a clandestine mission for the black resistance movement to help organize labor unions. Entering the country under an assumed name, Breytenbach was betrayed by a source in Europe who knew of his true identity. He was quickly arrested and tried for conspiracy and terrorism. Breytenbach is sometimes criticized for his courtroom confession and apology; nevertheless, he served seven years of his nine-year sentence, two of them in solitary confinement. While in prison, Breytenbach gained permission to write, although not to paint. At the end of each day, his writing was collected, examined by authorities, and kept until his release. The work that resulted was *Mouroir: Mirrornotes of a Novel* (1984), a simultaneously surreal and hyper-realistic collection of fragments, impressions, and stories about his experiences in prison, particularly his time in solitary confinement. Since his release from prison,

Breytenbach has maintained his critical stance on events in South Africa, even since the abolishment of the apartheid system.

Major Works

Breytenbach's turbulent and contradictory relationship to his homeland directly informs his work. The poems in *Sinking Ship Blues* (1977), *And Death as White as Words* (1978), *In Africa Even the Flies are Happy: Selected Poems, 1964-1977* (1978), and *Lewendood* (1985) are unconventionally structured. Composed of sentence fragments, isolated images, and dreamlike sequences, they convey brief, intense moments rather than linear narratives. Strongly influenced by the early Surrealists, Breytenbach juxtaposes life and death, growth and destruction, and joy and sorrow, reflecting his own mixed feelings toward South Africa. The isolation and degradation Breytenbach suffered in prison intensified his ideological opposition to the government and gave rise to two works: *Mouroir: Mirrornotes of a Novel* and *The True Confessions of an Albino Terrorist* (1985). The latter is a vivid examination of the South African penal system and Breytenbach's experiences as a political prisoner. Breytenbach chronicled his brief 1972 return to South Africa in *A Season in Paradise,* an ironically titled account of his personal reactions to both the beauty of the African landscape and the horror of apartheid. In 1986 Breytenbach published *End Papers: Essays, Letters, Articles of Faith, Workbook Notes,* a collection of pieces further iterating his political and personal beliefs regarding social injustice. *Memory of Snow and of Dust* (1989) is a novel telling the story of two lovers separated by the man's imprisonment in South Africa; as in earlier writings, Breytenbach used experimental nonlinear narrative. *Return to Paradise* (1993) is considered the third installment (along with *A Season in Paradise* and *The True Confessions of an Albino Terrorist*) in Breytenbach's triptych of works in which he deals autobiographically with South African social and political issues. It is composed of reminiscences, meditations, prose poems, and fragmented observations inspired by another trip he made to his homeland with his wife in 1991. *Memory of Birds in Times of Revolution* (1996) is a collection of essays on Breytenbach's reaction to events in post-apartheid South Africa.

Critical Reception

While Breytenbach is considered South Africa's premier poet to write in Afrikaans, he is not without detractors. His courtroom apologies were widely censured as backtracking, and in fact, the 1975 incognito mission for which he was arrested is sometimes interpreted as having been careless and perhaps arrogant. Some critics have found the publication of *End Papers* in particular as evidence of egotism and self-importance. Additionally, he has at times been accused of exhibiting sexual chauvinism in his work. Nonetheless, Breytenbach's passionate commitment to abolishing apartheid and his continued outspokenness regarding injustice, as well as his lyrical evocation of his beloved African landscape, generally outweigh such criticism.

PRINCIPAL WORKS

Die ysterkoei moet sweet (poetry) 1964
A Season in Paradise (nonfiction) 1976
Sinking Ship Blues (poetry) 1977
And Death as White as Words (poetry) 1978
In Africa Even the Flies are Happy: Selected Poems, 1964-1977 (poetry) 1978
Mouroir: Mirrornotes of a Novel (fiction) 1984
Lewendood (poetry) 1985
The True Confessions of an Albino Terrorist (nonfiction) 1985
End Papers: Essays, Letters, Articles of Faith, Workbook Notes (nonfiction) 1986
Memory of Snow and of Dust (novel) 1989

All One Horse: Fictions and Images (short stories and paintings) 1990
Soos die so (poetry) 1990
Hart-Lam (speeches) 1991
Return to Paradise (nonfiction) 1993
Memory of Birds in Times of Revolution (nonfiction) 1996

CRITICISM

Terence Des Pres (review date Fall-Winter 1983-84)

SOURCE: "Rimbaud's Nephews," in *Parnassus,* Vol. 11, No. 2, Fall-Winter 1983-84, pp. 83-102.

[*In the following review of* In Africa Even the Flies Are Happy: Selected Poems 1964-1977, *Des Pres surveys Breytenbach's works and attempts to assess his importance and success as a political poet.*]

Breyten Breytenbach is not yet a fixed star in rhyme's firmament, but seven years in South African prisons have done wonders for his reputation and a movement championing his life and work is underway. Breytenbach's friends, André Brink among them, have celebrated his cause since the time of his arrest in 1975. An international plea for his release was taken up by PEN, and more recently (May 1, 1983) the *New York Times Book Review* gave over space usually reserved for established heroes and printed an interview-portrait from which Breytenbach emerges like Orpheus back from hell. His work, likewise, is increasingly available in English translation. *A Season in Paradise,* Breytenbach's visionary prose work, made its mildly explosive appearance in America in 1980, and a significant portion of his poetry has been translated from Afrikaans, three volumes so far, one of which may now be got, via London, in the States.

This looks like the rise of yet another poet from elsewhere—not, that is, American—whose art is valued for political reasons. Breytenbach has suffered for his stand against *apartheid* and, being white, he has chosen a fate that he might have evaded. We are right to honor him for this. Unfortunately, some of his behavior prompts embarrassment as much as praise, and so does some of his poetry. His predicament, however, is part of something larger. The kind of poet whose work involves politics is on the increase. And poetry of this kind, it seems to me, is coming to count more and more. We might therefore wish to consider Breytenbach's heroism, if that is what it is, and sort it out.

In the United States we have pretty much agreed that poetry and politics do not mix. Between poetry and life, at least the political aspect of life, no commerce is expected or called for. The New Criticism cemented this separation of powers, and some of our best critics, Helen Vendler for example, continue to uphold the older view. But holding poetry and politics separate cannot mean much to a poet whose native tongue is Afrikaans, and in Breytenbach's case it is less a matter of mixing than of having been violently yoked, historically, culturally, to a condition of language. Both English and Afrikaans, in South Africa, are authorized languages. (Afrikaans comes first politically.) The British won the Boer War, but that has mattered little in the disposition of power, which remains largely in the hands of the Afrikaners, the descendants of seventeenth-century Dutch colonizers. *Apartheid* is their rule and likewise their word. It means, in Afrikaans, apartness. It means 87% of the land given over to whites exclusively, with mass deportation of blacks, 3.5 million so far, 2 million still to go. Under provision of the Terrorism Act, *apartheid* means a state security apparatus that detains whom it pleases, tortures whom it pleases, conducts interrogations in such a way that black men fall to their deaths from high windows. It also means that domination is rooted in a local tongue evolved from Dutch, a language little more than two centuries old, empty of tradition, its historical function to keep a small people, the Boers, the Afrikaners, united and on top. Like any colonial language, Afrikaans isn't innocent, and this is bound to cause trouble for poets, especially a poet like Breytenbach who has stationed himself against his own identity—white, privileged, tribal—as a native Afrikaner.

Almost by definition this poet's plight seems exemplary, but is it? In the long run, maybe, though not without a degree of objection; and because my own view of Breytenbach is critical, I want to avoid unfair irony by stating at once the larger case. Breytenbach has indeed deployed his art against the inhumanity of his country, a land he clearly hates and loves. He has paid, in the flesh, for the principles he holds. He has recently been released from prison (December, 1982) and has gone back to his place of exile in Paris where he aims to take up the double flag of poetry and politics once more—only this time, as he said in the *Times* interview, with stricter care for art. Breytenbach is 44, he is possessed of talent, his career isn't over. At this point neither his literary nor his political import can be judged. He deserves attention and, from people like myself, benefit of the doubt.

The heroism remains to be seen, but thinking of Breytenbach in heroic terms reveals an interesting development within the American literary community. Politics has begun to matter in art, and while some among us see this as stark disaster, others are expecting great things, perhaps the first serious challenge to American poetic practice since the revolt of the modernists. If excellence should thus be compromised, or literary standards relaxed to accommodate some other urgency, then certainly politics in art needs condemning. But that does not have to happen, neither reproof nor tolerance

for slack work. Our poetry at the moment is slack in any case, and not forgetting some wonderful exceptions we behold a state of affairs that can hardly be blamed on politics. Or perhaps it can. Lack of political sense may in fact be the problem—the dilemma of poets who cannot bring their art to touch upon that which touches upon them in grave and unnerving ways. . . .

The circumstances leading up to his arrest need looking into, but my first concern is with his kind of poetry and with the nearly hysterical regard his work has won, not least in South Africa itself. The cardinal question is this: In what manner has Breytenbach's art established his literary identity as a "political poet" and made him a candidate for heroism? The answer, in Breytenbach's case, comes like a shout. His poetry in the main revolts against things as they are, life in general, South Africa in particular, and it proceeds in a surrealist mode that from poem to poem is more or less savage, more or less shrill and enraged. There is little calm or tenderness, and this goes deeper than moral revulsion merely. Writing in Afrikaans means, for this poet, that he writes against himself. He is trapped in radical ambiguity and the problem is language itself. In consequence, there is much guilt and self-doubt and hyperbolic attempt at resolution. Exceptions occur—moments of peace, of absolving rather than hostile humor—when he is able to identify with the black condition or when he manages to become one with the land itself apart from those who have defiled it. I have seen some of Breytenbach's ink drawings (in *Sinking Ship Blues,* Toronto, 1977), which are remarkably consonant with the larger spirit of his poetry and which offer further evidence that Breytenbach's vision is notable for three things: surrealist dismemberment, especially of biological forms; humor and a kind of raucous play that is deep-seated and usually quite dark; and, finally, a prevailing sense of woundedness, sometimes muted, sometimes grimly festering.

A country that keeps its flies happy is a place, as Hamlet might say, far gone with rot. And more than a little, Breytenbach reminds me of Hamlet, vexed and melancholic, darkly playful and given to antic fits. In **"Goodbye, Cape Town,"** a poem from *And Death White as Words,* the poet is on his way back into exile, and he addresses the city of his departure this way:

> if someone would grant it me I'd search beyond
>   your walls
> for a Jonah tree
> if you were a woman I'd elaborate on the smells
> of your pocked skin and gurgling glands
> lovely arch-whore
> slut flirt hell-cat bitch
> but you're not even a mother
> you're an abortive suicide

gushing wounds of water between the quay and
    the flanks of this boat
my cape, man's cape, capelove, heart's cape
I wanted to breathe you into a full blown rose
but you stayed just a mouth and a tongue[.]

Mere name-calling, we might say; and it is, although not merely. Breytenbach is not a namer in Whitman's manner, but rather a compulsive giver of names, a re-namer, in surges of metonymic flow. This is a standard surrealist device, part of the poet's stock in trade. But in Breytenbach's usage it is an odd device, because while everything stays in motion nothing really moves. We see the metamorphic vigor of his vision, but also its stuckness—an imagination steadily inventive but unable to surmount its occasion. The poet's ambiguous relation to his subject—in this case outright love and hate—is also visible, and perhaps likewise a certain unwillingness to accept his ties to the world. In an early section of *A Season in Paradise,* Breytenbach introduces his wife through five different names, none of them *her* name. At best this is a mode of playful blessing, but metonymy is also, as we see above, the rhetorical basis of cursing. Incantation, curse, a language of infliction, these are tools of Breytenbach's art. We might wonder upon whom the injury falls.

Breytenbach's attitude toward things female is seldom as abusive as the Cape Town poem suggests. His sexual chauvinism is rampant, but usually in a manner quieter, more naive and taken for granted, and I suspect that it stems from another, deeper chauvinism, the Boer-ish kind, not entirely cast out despite the fact that this poet has set himself against that nation and all its ways. Some of its ways are still with him. That Breytenbach has not escaped his roots is surely partial cause of his furious bursting forth. There is an obsessional character to such poetry; and metonymy, the need to re-name, is one way obsession asserts itself. The love-hate relation to South Africa runs in alternating current through Breytenbach's work, shifting on the instant from plaint to endearment, as in the lines above. The passage also suggests that we are with a poet for whom peace, if it comes at all, is momentary in the image of an isolated tree. Trees with their small zones of saving shade appear often in these poems, and the reference to Jonah is especially revealing: this poet's prophetic appointment remains unsure. His mission is urgent but its success is doubtful—success in this case being the poet's capacity to breathe rich life into a language that, as he receives it, seems no more than a mouth.

Much of Breytenbach's harshness, his fitful intensity, arises from his fight with the language in which he finds himself trapped. The political hegemony of Afrikaans must somehow be subverted, its authority over the soul subdued. But in what manner and at what cost? The task is formidable, it provokes distrust toward poetry itself, and often the out-

come is devalued by a willful margin of discount. There are moments, I suspect, when writing in Afrikaans feels like going over to the enemy—in which case, what is poetry? In a poem called **"Constipation,"** Breytenbach offers one of his several answers:

Not that Coleridge doesn't belong to the school
    of damned poets
      he says
the outcasts capable of ejecting at a given
    moment
a waxy fart of hideous pain
through the tunnel and turnstile of blood
    and there I agree
for what is a poem
other than a black wind?

The image is not felicitous, but, for a poet stuck in the role of *poète maudit,* not inaccurate either. That Breytenbach aims to insult seems clear, and if—to use Bakhtin's distinction—an "official" Afrikaans exists, strict in decorum, then the poet's "unofficial" imagery and diction constitutes an attack. We are again in the presence of a curse, and the sad thing about Breytenbach is that for all his desire to bless and to pray, the curse too often prevails. The poem just quoted begins: "For all true poetry is cruel." That we may doubt, although the governing spirit in this case is Artaud, from whom Breytenbach takes the poem's epigraph: "No one has ever written or painted, sculpted, modelled, built, invented except to get out of Hell." We can doubt that too, but as a commentary on Breytenbach's work it goes a long way. Hell, for this particular poet, is the moral torment of being white in South Africa. And hell is language itself, which belongs to the oppressors and does not afford, as for example English does, the alternative support of an adversary tradition—Swift's savage indignation—as part of the poet's inherited power. He writes, then, to escape an infernal predicament that his poetry keeps him locked into, and Breytenbach has come to see this himself. In the *Times* interview he told Donald Woods that henceforth he would write no more in Afrikaans: "I've long felt there was hope for it only if it were used in resistance to apartheid, but I think it is now too late."

That decision may cost him more than he thinks. Too late it might be for the white supremacists of South Africa to stop a racist *Götterdämmerung.* But dispossessed poets tend to stick to their mother tongue no matter what. Joseph Brodsky, for example, can feel that his poetry is Russian but not Soviet. That is a valid distinction, but Breytenbach does not have a similar option. Even so, critics who know Afrikaans point to his command of Afrikaner idioms as one of his especial strengths. And from the poetry available in translation we can see that Breytenbach further undermines his parent tongue by stabbing it with lines from languages of the oppressed—Swahili in particular. He also uses place-names, Dimbaza, Limehill, Stinkwater, which dramatize the particular evil of *apartheid*, places not unlike concentration camps to which the black population is being deported to rid the Afrikaner paradise of its "black spots."

Breytenbach's situation, in other words, has not been without *some* resources, but not without agony either, and in any case a hard ambiguity remains. By ambiguity I do not mean the American kind that plays hide and seek and declines to take a stand, but the white African search for a purchase nowhere in sight. The cost, as I have suggested, is guilt and frustration. There are the fathers, whom Breytenbach rejects. And then there are the brothers, with whom, he knows, he is not one. His dislocation is extreme, and perhaps he is right to feel that in his earlier poetry he reached a dead end. He did not always feel that way, however, and that he began by appealing his case to the high court of French surrealism seems, in retrospect, inevitable.

"Reality," he says in one poem, is "just a boundary a rumour." But having conferred that sort of potency upon his art, he goes on, in another poem, to take it back: his "poems are just day trips." Searching for bedrock, Breytenbach's imagery settles at the biological level, and while there is much stench and rot, there are also moments when life is sweet, a mothering plenitude that blesses and protects. In **"Fiesta for an eye"** he defines his place of reprieve:

> you know no other fig tree which stands
> as this one stands cleaved by the butchering
>   sun
> bleeding over its litter of coolness
> stuffing its figs full of palates so that later it can
>   taunt the sun
> no tree rivals this mother of coolness
> where wedlock is celebrated
> where the firm root is fitted
> to the red-mouthed orifice in the ground
> flesh rouses flesh
> and the figs are full of milk[.]

That is life under the aspect of the Mother, fruitful, erotic, a good in itself. Under the aspect of the Father, on the other hand, life is empty, caged, at best a shabby affair or even a kind of death. The following lines are from a poem called **"I will die and go to my father"**:

> friends, fellow mortals,
> don't tremble; life still hangs
> like flesh from our bodies
> but death has no shame—
> we come and we go

> like water from a tap
> like sounds from the mouth
> like our comings and goings:
> it's our bones which will know freedom
> come with me
>   bound in my death, to my father
> in Wellington where the angels
> use worms to fish fat stars from heaven;
> let us die and decompose and be merry:
> my father has a large boarding-house[.]

Blasphemy and biblical parody are constants in Breytenbach's work, and his easy reference to both the Old and the New Testaments, in the lines just quoted, suggests that he might have had a fairly stern religious upbringing. In any case he presumes that Afrikaners take their Christian National Education seriously. Their version of Christian belief has provided a patriarchal discourse useful to white supremacy, and Breytenbach attacks it as false doctrine and as an especially repugnant kind of hypocrisy. His assault is sometimes dancing, sometimes heavy-handed, and when he unmasks the virtues of the fathers by putting himself within the Afrikaner voice, his irony verges on straight hatred. The following stanza is from a poem called **"The struggle for the Taal,"** Taal being a local name for the Afrikaner language itself:

> From the structure of our conscience
> from the stores of our charity
> we had black contraptions built for you, you
>   bastards—
> schools, clinics, post-offices, police-stations—
> and now the plumes blow black smoke
> throbbing and flowing like a heart.

So much for righteousness and love-thy-neighbor sentiment. So much, too, for Breytenbach's attempt to attack from within. Not that poetry can't handle such tactics. Brecht was a master at just this sort of satire, but he had giants to back him up, Marx and Luther among them, and could feel that his Nazi adversaries were the destroyers rather than the guardians of the German he deployed with such sting. Breytenbach, on the other hand, must fall back on his heart and its furies, and cannot afford to move too close to a target that, in some vestigial sense, is himself. His saving grace is humor, humor as a liberation, as an irreverent aside that keeps him safely to the side, or as a playfulness turning grimness to whimsy. Breytenbach's zaniness is one of his strengths and it is almost always active. But often he allows his sense of political urgency to hobble what might otherwise impress us as true wit. We are left to guess how much is laughter, how much grimace. In a poem called **"icon"** he surveys the gory world depicted in a Bosch-like painting and then concludes:

above all this a spiky jesus stands out on a cross
with no more hope of decomposing
than a butcher bird's prey on a barbed wire fence,
with a sneer along his beard;

further behind for ever out of reach (like marilyn
    monroe)
rises an empty cool grave[.]

Much of Breytenbach's verse reads like that, and at first it struck me as arbitrary, in search of scandal, not unlike a good deal of surrealist poetry in general. Too often this poet seems fierce in his focus and yet reckless in his connections, slapdash, in some sense callow. To get beyond these first impressions has been my task, and I would now suggest that the passage quoted above contains much that is Breytenbach's hallmark and the ground of genuine poetic authority. Of those six lines, each in turn surprises; none could be predicted, yet they add up to a complex image of considerable power. Who is this sneering Jesus if not the poet himself, a savior who cannot save nor remove himself from the horror he beholds. And seen through the barbed wire of *apartheid*, who is Monroe but the white goddess promising a bliss not to be had, neither in life nor in death nor in art, certainly not in South Africa. We might still wonder at the exact balance of humor and pain, but the passage itself is a strong emblem of impotence, of anger venting itself in bitter play. And the religious reference counts. In this land, the poet says, redemption does not come.

I want to go on to the larger implications of Breytenbach's art, but having looked mainly at the difficulties of his poetry I have perhaps given the idea that this poet always writes with clenched fist and curled lip, a black wind of rage and disgust. There is no denying his hyperbolic tendency, his deliberate unpleasantness, his penchant for insult. But this basic disposition arrives at different temperatures, hot and cold, warm and cool, the barometer sometimes dropping toward storm, sometimes rising to a wispy sky. By way of a last look at Breytenbach's poetry I would therefore like to cite one of my favorites, a small poem that—possibly because it *is* small—comes to us quietly, with kindness and unusual lyricism, a poem I quote entire for the craft it reveals and for the political vision it embodies. It is called **"First prayer for the hottentotsgod,"** and we need to know two items of background information: first, that the Afrikaans word *hottentotsgot* means praying mantis; next, that in Bushman or Hottentot myth, this small insect is thought to be a god. Here is Breytenbach's prayer:

they say, little beast, little creator, the elders say
that the fields of stars, the earth-dwellers and all
    things
that turn and rise up and sigh and crumble

were brought forth by you, that you planted an
    ostrich-feather
in the darkness and behold!   the moon!
o most ancient one,
                  you who fired by love
consume your lover, what led you to forsake
the children of those—the human stuff—
remember?   summoned by you
from the mud?
there are fires in the sky, mother, and the moon
cold as a shoe, and a black cry like smoke
mixed with dust—for your black people, people
    maker, work
like the dust of knives in the earth that the
    money
might pile up elsewhere
for others—
grassyyellow lady of prayer,
          hear our smoke and our dust—
chastise those who debased your people to
    slavery[.]

Empowered by prayer and a myth not his own, Breytenbach transforms an Afrikaner saying ("plant a feather and a chicken will sprout up"), goes on with humor to make serious use of rhetorical stuttering, then moves from myth into history, from the high sorrow of The Human Condition to a particular plight, in the course of which a second diction intrudes, to end where a poem of this kind must end, not with the consolations of *lacrimae rerum*, but with the black cry rising from its definite pain. Breytenbach's surrealist tilt, in this instance, rests lightly in his appeal for an insect's intervention in human affairs, a joke not altogether joke when we consider the likely efficacy of any black appeal to any South African deity, be it God or god or little beast. The poem successfully identifies with the voice of the victims, and the interdictions of the white fathers give way to the wisdom of the black elders. As befits a creation myth in Breytenbach's erotic cosmology, we are here within the governance of the Mother, she who in her ardor devours the Father. In every way but one—the prayer won't be answered—the poem works to appease and absolve the poet's own sources of torment. He does not expect peace, but guilt dissolves and rage no longer consumes him.

Especially cunning is Breytenbach's use of repetition. Midway the poem starts renaming itself. The first half culminates in the stammer of its big question, and then the poem goes on in a way that demystifies myth and allows history to show through—a fall, if you prefer, from eternity into the specific anguish of time. The little creator becomes a people-maker, the starry fields turn to fire. The magical moon, now a cold shoe, loses its consoling splendor. And life rising, sighing, falling, becomes a particular people being worked, as we might say, to death, ground down like the blade of a knife after hard use. Humankind's muddy genesis ends up concretely with blacks enslaved. And a second diction intrudes upon the first, clashes, takes over. The result is a minor infraction of poetic statute, not unlike the marriage of white and "non-white" which, in some places, is deemed unlawful.

My metaphor may seem indecorous, but I use it to suggest the way this poem, by permitting the language of politics to intervene, becomes itself a little allegory of political intrusion—life broken and debased by injustice politically imposed. The poem's subject is not *only* the spectacle of Creation and the Fall, but also the reality behind the myth, in this case the millions of human beings enslaved and brutalized, working *in* the diamond mines, the asbestos mines, working *for* the more than 1,000 American corporations using these people and using them up; and plainly, through this kind of labor the money does pile up elsewhere, for example in the endowments of American universities. I do not mean to indict American ways and means, but only to open *our* connection to Breytenbach's world. No doubt, though, remarks like these will meet with the same objections as the poem's last lines—neither, it might be argued, belongs to true poetry or correct criticism. The test of the poem's last lines, however, is not received taste or purity of diction. The test is how false and trivial the poem would be without those lines. If the political references were absent, or veiled in metaphor, no doubt the poem would be more pleasant, but it would also be inconsequent, a snippet of doubtful comfort got by retreat into myth. History would then appear as we prefer it to appear, under the aspect of eternity—in other words *necessary*, as if slavery were in the nature of things, which it isn't.

Breytenbach's debt to surrealism is fundamental. It defines his art as much as his problematic relation to Afrikaans. We might suppose that the psychic rending his language forced upon him predisposed him to surrealist solutions, but timing is also a factor. The young poet-painter arrived in Paris in 1961, just as the surrealist upsurge of the Sixties was getting underway; and that was a time of zany politics and tactics truly bizarre. Surrealism itself, as the brainchild of Breton and his friends, was still much in evidence, indeed established and respectable, almost, in fact, a tradition. That is an irony I leave to others, but in any case exhibitions and journals devoted to surrealist art and poetry had become part of the literary environment, and the movement's basic techniques—summed up by Picasso as "a horde of destructions"—had become the property of poets everywhere. The principle of radical freedom in the arts had been legitimized and any poet, nowadays, will employ surrealist techniques now and then, if not centrally then as one resource among many.

But on the evidence of his work I would judge that for a poet like Breytenbach back in the Sixties, angry at the world and newly arrived in art's sacred city, surrealism meant more than taking liberties. The movement's originating impulse—antisocial, politically wild, bent on cultural ruin—seems very much alive in Breytenbach's usage. No doubt the attention early surrealists paid to revolution in Russia, their respect for Trotsky and their Mexican connection, endorsed Breytenbach's need to oppose and dismantle official versions of reality. And no doubt the weapons of ridicule and dark humor appealed to a poet whose job was to condemn much in himself. Humor is essential to the surrealist spirit; its ludic energies are central to its character. At the same time, we should not allow surrealism's playfulness, its lighthearted delight in causing cultural havoc, to obscure its more ferocious intent. To fire a pistol randomly into the crowd was the surrealist program expressed metaphorically. The surrealist game of chaotic sentence construction produced, in its first and most famous session, *le cadavre exquis boira le vin nouveau*—new wine to be drunk by an exquisite corpse. The image of the slashed eye in *Un Chien Andalou* means more now than it did in 1928 when Buñuel haphazardly made the film. In retrospect the surrealist assault on the human image seems clear, and in his recent memoir Buñuel says of himself and the band of exterminating angels to which he belonged: ". . . we all felt a certain destructive impulse, a feeling that for me has been even stronger than the creative urge." Much of this can be written off as *épater les bourgeois*, but not all. The logic of assault, once let loose, cannot easily be reined in. And the distance between the pen and the gun, we have come to see, isn't far. Camus had this in mind when he warned us that, in our time, to create is to create dangerously.

It may be that all art harbors delight in destruction; that the motive for metaphor is as much transgression as transformation; that visionary faith in a new world is fuelled by a fury of disgust for what is—and certainly the guardians of the *status quo* do their best to keep things disgusting. Taking their lead from Lautréamont and especially Rimbaud, the French surrealists were the first poets and painters of our time to proceed as a group, with manifestos and programs and tribal rites, into the soul's darker energies. These they hoped to put at art's disposal—and in some cases, notably for Eluard and Aragon, at the disposal of the Communist party. Breytenbach himself hasn't a Marxist bone in his body, nor does ideology in general interest him. The situation in South Africa hardly calls for dialectical analysis. But the *spirit* of surrealist attack, its hard-bitten political mode in particular, must surely have spoken to Breytenbach's need. The surrealist archive holds plenty of examples that sound straight from Breytenbach's pen, for example (and keeping in mind that Monsieur Thiers was the man whose military forces slaughtered the Communards of 1871), here is Benjamin Perét's *Pour que M. Thiers ne crève pas tout à fait*, written in 1929, from which I quote a translation of the first and last lines:

> Belly full of shit pigs feet
> poisonous head
> it's me Monsieur Thiers.
> I freed our country
> planted onions in Versailles
> and combed Paris with my machine gun....
> and if my belly swells
> it's because I've danced
> with the ants in the
> breadbasket of the Republic[.]

That something of this spirit lodged itself in Breytenbach's art is clear at first glance. And that he has seen his own identity in this fracturing light is apparent from his private myth of Rimbaud. In *A Season in Paradise* he rewrites Rimbaud's *Season in Hell* and at the heart of it locates Rimbaud as his especial precursor. In this version of the Rimbaud myth, the earlier poet dies several deaths (much as Breytenbach claims he himself died more than once—accident, dismemberment, funeral—in his childhood), and then returns a second time to Africa. "What is clear," Breytenbach says, "is that the track of his single foot was later noticed in the desert. He vanished without trace, gloriously, like a white line on a sheet of white paper. Africa is reality. And in Africa you cannot die." From there the mythical Rimbaud begins "to migrate southward," turning up in Namibia, in the mines of Kimberley, a hunter, a bartender, a mercenary. In one of these appearances Rimbaud causes the death of Eugene Marais, the poet often called the father of serious poetry in Afrikaans. And if, as Breytenbach observes, "there's arms smuggling again these days off the Skeleton Coast," this too is Rimbaud's doing. The point of Breytenbach's sketch of Rimbaud, as I read it, is that the true history of the surrealist spirit began in France and passed to Africa where it now continues in South Africa's back of beyond. Its foremost carrier, we may guess, is Breytenbach.

Every writer constructs his or her own prehistory, and for an Afrikaner the task is doubly pressing. With no illustrious tradition to take in and cast out, the bearers of Afrikaans must look elsewhere. Escape from parochial constraint becomes paramount, and the regard South Africans have for Breytenbach's achievement has much to do with the measure of international fame he managed to bestow upon his nation's poetry—never mind how. He went to Paris, received the confirmation of Rimbaud, created a voice. This, as much as the poetry itself, is the source of his heroism. It has been his strength, and it has been his downfall. For like the mythical Rimbaud, Breytenbach travelled from France to Africa with revolutionary intentions. "Everyone," he wrote in *Season,* "should be an arms-smuggler at least once in his life."

And so it was, in 1975, when Breytenbach returned to make contact with underground elements, that he got himself arrested and slapped into jail.

If this is heroism it is also a sad story. Nowhere can I find a straightforward account of Breytenbach's activities while on his revolutionary errand. "It would seem," says André Brink, "that his aim was to contact some of the people he had met on his previous visit, in order to evaluate the situation and to devise a programme of future action." That sounds innocent enough. Donald Woods is a bit more specific. Breytenbach's mission, as Woods sees it, was "to contact anti-apartheid white and some black spokesmen, such as Steve Biko, in order to channel money from European church groups to the black trade unionists in South Africa," the hoped-for outcome being to "develop a political infrastructure among anti-apartheid whites." That sounds laudable and at least makes sense. Other views have been less positive. Writing for *London Magazine,* Christopher Hope derides Breytenbach for being foolish and perhaps disingenuous: "He crept about the country in a manner most likely to attract attention, visiting friends, arranging secret meetings on the rooftops of blocks of flats, passing messages to his fellow conspirators in hollowed-out books and gathering in his wake a motley assembly of the credulous, the earnest, the well-meaning and the lost and lonely." That sounds more than a little like surrealist theater, a point to keep in mind. In any case, Denis Hirson (translator of the volume under review) tells us that Breytenbach was "charged under the Terrorism Act with being instrumental in the formation of Okhela (Zulu for 'spark'), a white wing of the African National Congress. The aim of the organization was allegedly to bring about revolutionary change in South Africa under leadership of the black liberation movement by various means, including armed struggle." What that might entail isn't said, nor exactly why Breytenbach pleaded guilty at his trial. It seems possible, however, that Breytenbach was clumsy, even stupid, about what he was doing. And the Bureau of State Security—known as the BOSS—swept him up like a fly.

Paradise passed into hell, and a literary conceit became grimly real. Breytenbach thereby emerges as a dramatic example of the *literary* revolutionary. I do not mean the writer who puts forth radical ideas in his work only, but one who like Byron begins to take his own literary identity seriously and comes to believe that what he is in his poems he must also be in the world. Breytenbach's deliberate misreading of Rimbaud's life—abandonment of poetry for African gun-running—suggests the logic of his own career as he must have envisioned it himself. And the *style* of his return, if it was as silly as Christopher Hope claims, is the surrealist style—impulsive, bizarre, a sort of childlike earnest play. Except that whereas the French surrealists had been satisfied to barge into halls and theaters to cause scandal and break up cultural events, Breytenbach aimed to crack the BOSS, one of the most efficient organs of government terror in the world. What followed could only be a debacle. At best, we can say that at least this poet took poetry seriously. But then, we might also say that he did not take it seriously enough.

The situation suggests that Breytenbach had grown dissatisfied with the kind of power to be had from words alone. He was sick of his impotence as *mere* writer, and wanted literary commitment to be more, or different, than it can be. During his 1973 visit he joined a symposium at the University of Cape Town and there delivered what can only be called a diatribe, aimed point-blank at himself and his South African colleagues. His remarks, and even more the tone of his address, throw light on his poetry and reveal the state of mind that would shortly land him in prison. He began by saying that "all talk in this sad bitter motley-funeral-land is politics—whether it is whispered talk, talking shit, spitting into the wind or speaking in his master's voice." His categories are telling, especially the agony implicit in "speaking in his master's voice." Presumably, Breytenbach's own category would be "spitting into the wind." He went on to ask: "Are we nothing, then, as writers, but the shock-absorbers of this white establishment, its watchdogs?" He attacked not only *apartheid* but also American policy in Vietnam, and he advocated "taking a stand." By way of conclusion he put the problem of his art this way: "I want to come as close as I can in my work to the temporal—not the infinite; that has always been around. And infinity says nothing. What hurts is the ephemeral, the local."

Breytenbach's Cape Town manifesto is not without point, but it brims with pain and recrimination and what it tells us, finally, is that this poet's burden had gotten to be more than he could bear. Art and life crossed, poetry and politics collided, and the larger truth of Breytenbach's predicament is that politics drags eternity down into time. What hurts is indeed the temporal—conditions which do not have to exist but do, to the detriment of many and the benefit of some few, so long as men and women support or do not seek to change the *status quo*. The BOSS exists to keep things as they are, and the response of someone like Breytenbach suggests that the situation in South Africa maims not only bodies but also the spirit. For those who think that poetry's proper realm is the human condition minus its political torment, Breytenbach's run-in with politics might seem to prove their point. But for those in search of a poetry strong enough to confront the worst we do behold and can imagine, his example is valuable for the chances he has taken and the mistakes he has made.

Impossible to say what will happen to his art if Breytenbach gives up writing in Afrikaans. Almost by accident he has created, in his native tongue, the precedent he needed but could not find when he began. Perhaps his despair is premature. Perhaps even now there are others for whom his achievement *and* his excesses have opened a way. Breytenbach has been lucky in that his brief flare as a literary revolutionary cost no terminal damage. In the long run, the harm might be less than the gain. In the *Times* profile, Donald Woods reports that imprisonment, for Breytenbach, "helped him to square accounts with himself as a part of what he regards as a necessary process for white South Africans opposed to apartheid—the need to pay an expiative price for it." That is extreme, like something out of Dostoevsky, except of course that it happened. The man was there, he suffered, and he now views his ordeal as a kind of redemption. The old rage is gone, and with it, we may hope, the violence of a voice grounded in guilt. What happens next will be worth attending. The question of heroism, meanwhile, can stay in solution.

Stephen Schwartz   (review date October 1985)

SOURCE: "Betrayal," in *Commentary,* Vol. 80, No. 4, October 1985, pp. 71-74.

[*In the following review, Schwartz examines revelations made in Breytenbach's* The True Confessions of an Albino Terrorist *and reflects on his own involvement in the political movement to support Breytenbach.*]

Breyten Breytenbach, considered the best modern poet in the Afrikaans language, first received substantial publicity in the English-speaking world in 1977. At that time, he had been imprisoned in his native South Africa for some two years. A further legal proceeding, based on charges of terrorist activity while in prison, brought him to the attention of the liberal and Left communities of Britain and the U.S. In 1982, thanks to efforts by French president François Mitterrand, Breytenbach was released. *The True Confessions* is a semi-poetic account of his trials and imprisonment. It has been widely reviewed here, with Joseph Lelyveld, in the *New York Times Book Review*, typically comparing Breytenbach's martyrdom with that of the Russian poet Osip Mandelstam, who was imprisoned and eventually consigned to an anonymous death in the Siberian labor camps for writing a poem attacking Stalin. The South African poet has even made it onto the American talk-show circuit.

Let us begin with Breytenbach himself, his origins and his literary work. Breyten Breytenbach was born in 1937 in the heart of Afrikaner society. His two brothers are, today, active supporters of the South African establishment, with one serving as a commanding officer in the South African forces in Namibia, the other affiliated with the state security agencies. Breytenbach became a prominent member of the group of nonconformist Afrikaans writers known as the *sestigers*, or 60's generation, a group which also includes the novelist André Brink.

Breytenbach's poetic style is a distinctively affecting mixture of surrealism and philosophical pessimism: his wit, and his austere figures, come across rather invitingly in English translation. He is also a talented painter, and when he left South Africa in the mid-1960's he went to live in Paris. There he met a Vietnamese artist, Yolande Ngo Thi Hoang Lien, and married her. Yolande became the central subject of his creative work, which developed into an extended erotic meditation drawing on Buddhist and other Asian sources. Unfortunately, Yolande's Asian ethnicity also barred Breytenbach from returning to South Africa in her company: their case clearly contravened the country's then-standing laws concerning racially mixed marriages.

The conflict between Breytenbach's love for his wife and his identification both with the South African landscape and with the Afrikaans language drove him, in the years that followed, into an extreme position on the apartheid regime. By 1975 he had formed an organization at first called Atlas and then Okhela ("Spark" in Zulu), made up of South African whites living in European exile and collaborating with the black-led African National Congress (ANC). Like the ANC, Okhela saw its future in armed struggle.

In the mid-70's Breytenbach chose to return to South Africa, utilizing a false passport in the name of Christian Galaska, a French citizen. His mission was to set up a network of Okhela supporters and black activists, including the ill-fated leader Steve Biko (who died in detention in 1978); the practical aim was support for black trade unions. As *The True Confessions* hauntingly recounts, in South Africa Breytenbach was tracked down and arrested as he was preparing to fly back to Europe.

At this point the story becomes complicated. When he appeared in court Breytenbach presented himself as a contrite, erring son of the Afrikaner nation, pleading for forgiveness. Even more curiously, the Left, in South Africa and elsewhere, which had done little enough to help him after his arrest, altogether backed off from any further association, denouncing him as a virtual renegade and stool pigeon. He was sentenced to nine years' imprisonment, and had served two (entirely in solitary confinement) when the charge of terrorism from within prison walls returned him to court in 1977.

During the second trial, while the pro-ANC Left continued to hold him at arm's length, an informal network of artists in Europe and North America began working to organize and express some form of solidarity with him. It was then that I myself became involved. I had been active in a related matter concerning Argentina, and through a literary acquain-

tance in Holland was asked to participate in the Breytenbach effort. I did so, becoming the head of the Committee on the Breytenbach Case, based in San Francisco but circulating materials throughout the United States. Until the middle of 1978 I received a continuous flow of documentation on the affair from Europe. We published bulletins describing the poet's progress through the second trial, which ended in a minor fine; we then concentrated on demands for his release.

In May 1978, a new item was introduced into the mosaic. I received from my European contact a clipping from a South African newspaper, reporting the assassination in Paris of Henri Curiel, an Egyptian Jew who had been a close acquaintance of Breytenbach during the latter's European exile. Curiel had been identified in the French press as a "mastermind of terrorism," and was described by the South Africans as "the mystery man who sent Breytenbach to South Africa clandestinely." An accompanying note from my European correspondent stated that Curiel had indeed maintained an "underground organization for training [in] guerrilla warfare, counterfeiting passports, instructing in coded information methods." Furthermore, that the passport given by Curiel to Breytenbach before the latter's flight to South Africa "probably was in fact a trap," and that Breytenbach had been "set up by some Stalinists (or, say, Moscow-oriented . . . activists), who . . . subsequently tipped off the . . . South African secret police."

It would be hard for someone not in my situation at that moment to imagine the impact this letter had on me. My European friend was unchallengeable as a source of information. The very possibility that a man of Breytenbach's talent as a writer and painter could have been so offhandedly sacrificed by Soviet political agents called to mind the queasiest moments of Stalin's own reign. Too, the idea was not reassuring that our little group of pro-Breytenbach activists might have been simply victims of our own enthusiasm. We had committed resources and time, attracting a certain degree of harassment from defenders of South Africa while also working in a kind of moral quarantine, regarded with ill-concealed hostility by the rest of the anti-apartheid movement in the U.S. We had thought the coolness of our pro-ANC contacts was a product of racial suspicion that could be overcome considering the human-rights aspects of the case and its potential for embarrassing the Pretoria regime. We were wrong. The Breytenbach affair was, and is, much more of a potential scandal for the South African Left than for the country's political rulers.

For the plain truth, as Breytenbach's book confirms at numerous points, is that he was betrayed. "I was betrayed even before I arrived [in South Africa]," he declares flatly. "It was not my idea to go down there but I had to submit myself to the majority decision. . . . Stupidly vain, when told there were certain things which only I could do, it touched me, and I fell for it." And who, then, was responsible for this? "My dear, ineffective, fat, institutionalized friends in the liberation movement . . . those professional diplomats, those living off the fat of the suffering of our people back home and who've done so for years and will do so until they die." And why did this sleazy drama transpire? Because Breytenbach had begun to question the Stalinist tendencies dominating the South African Left. "To my shame as a South African I have to admit" that the Communist party of South Africa "was among the first organizations lauding the Soviet Union for its invasion of Hungary and again later of Czechoslovakia." As for Curiel, that he "was a KGB operative had crossed" Breytenbach's mind. "It's really not so farfetched . . . some of his oldest friends quit . . . because, they say, he was using [them] as a vehicle to serve the Soviets. . . . He never made any bones about his total commitment to orthodox Soviet Communism, call it Stalinism."

The full betrayal involved in the Breytenbach case is only comprehensible through a further digression on the Curiel case, a strange matter in its own right. Although I dropped out of touch with the Breytenbach enthusiasts in Europe soon after receiving the clipping and letter on Curiel's assassination—I was simply too demoralized to continue—I remained interested in learning more about Curiel. In 1981, Claire Sterling devoted a full chapter of her book *The Terror Network* to Curiel, in which she claims that the process ending in the latter's assassination in Paris had begun when Breytenbach, disillusioned and abandoned in prison, divulged information on the Curiel network to the South African secret police. She notes that, presumably on the basis of Breytenbach's information, Curiel's terrorist support network had been exposed in the French magazine *Le Point* in 1976. In a highly interesting tidbit she also points out that Curiel was the cousin of the famous British subordinate of Kim Philby, George (Bihar) Blake, who has been described as the most effective of all Soviet spies.

Late last year Jean-François Revel became involved in the Curiel controversy when, writing in *Encounter*, he defended *Le Point*, for which he now writes, against a pro-Communist French author, Gilles Perrault, who had produced a massive apologia for Curiel titled *Un Homme à Part* ("A Man Apart"). Perrault's opus, an incredibly prolix exercise in revolutionary "hagiography" (to use Revel's term), depicts Curiel as a hero of Third World solidarity and peace, more concerned with arranging meetings between Israelis and moderate Palestinians than with his admittedly "fanatical" attachment to the Soviet Union. Perrault fails to address the charges in Claire Sterling's book, which appeared three years before his, or to deal with the association between Curiel and Blake. He does, however, directly state that those who sent Breytenbach to South Africa knew he was headed for disaster.

During the Breytenbach solidarity campaign of 1977, we tried to portray him as a victim of a kind of treason on the part of his Afrikaner parents and brothers. But as his memoirs show, his Afrikaner family stood by him with greater loyalty than was shown by his adopted "family of the revolution." This brings us to the real tragedy of Breyten Breytenbach. It is not that a talented artist was temporarily locked up by a repressive regime against which he had plotted violent resistance, but rather that such an individual should accept his betrayal, as he seems to do in his memoirs, and place the blame on his own "weaknesses" as an intellectual. Breytenbach has as yet done virtually nothing to subject his leftist mentors and betrayers to the kind of searching moral inquiry one takes for granted must be addressed to his Afrikaner compatriots, including his own relatives. In this he resembles no one so much as the character Rubashov in Arthur Koestler's great novel about Stalinist betrayal, *Darkness at Noon*.

By now it should be obvious to all that the world is a curious and cruel place, in which the sentiments of a poet and painter are easily perverted by such paradoxes as the need to find a new family relationship where one's own has been unsatisfying. Breytenbach seems to have learned a bitter lesson from this experience: he has declared that from now on he will concentrate only on his poetry and painting. Yet this, I believe, is the wrong lesson. Breytenbach is no Mandelstam, and the comparison is specious: Mandelstam lost his life for writing a single poem, whereas Breytenbach, after participating in a revolutionary conspiracy, came out of prison safely. But neither should Breytenbach allow himself to become a Rubashov, one who accepts his degradation at the hands of his putative comrades. At least the person on whom the fictional Rubashov was based, Nikolai Bukharin, attempted to subvert the 1938 Moscow trial in which he was judged and condemned. In this respect Breyten Breytenbach still has much to learn; one can be thankful that now he has the opportunity to learn it.

Sheila Roberts   (essay date Spring 1986)

SOURCE: "Breyten Breytenbach's Prison Literature," in *The Centennial Review*, Vol. 30, No. 2, Spring 1986, pp. 304-13.

[*In the following essay, Roberts discusses* Mouroir *and* The True Confessions of an Albino Terrorist, *both of which Breytenbach wrote during his prison term in South Africa.*]

It has been said that each of us can remain mentally faithful to only one landscape, usually that of our childhood and youth. This fidelity is strongly evident in writers-in-exile, many of whom seem compelled to recreate endlessly the lost loved land—however hostile their feelings might be to the regimes of their native countries. We think immediately of Joyce, Solsenitzyn, or Milan Kundera, and of South Africans like Dan Jacobson and Breyten Breytenbach.

Breytenbach has experienced several kinds or degrees of exile. He left South Africa voluntarily in 1961 and established himself in Paris as a painter and poet with his Vietnamese-born wife Yolande. Under the racial classification then in force in South Africa, Yolande was not regarded as white and Breytenbach's marriage to her was therefore considered illegal. However, they were allowed visas to enter South Africa in 1973 to attend a writers' conference. For the duration of their stay they were dogged by reporters and cameramen, treated partly like prodigal children but mostly like celebrities. In my opinion the experience was disastrous for a long-abroad and homesick Breytenbach. The fawning and attention he had received had been in such large doses that he became an addict, one who had to contrive a return; not any return, however, but one with some attendant glamor and panache. My theory explains for me the inexplicable elements of his subsequent behavior.

Breytenbach joined Okhela, a splinter group of the South African Communist Party, and accepted an assignment to enter South Africa clandestinely for the purpose of recruiting membership. The following year, 1975, he returned to South Africa under a false name, with a French passport, his appearance very thinly disguised. Breytenbach, a poet and a painter, was an ill-trained secret agent. In an article in *The London Magazine*, Christopher Hope describes his activities:

> . . . He crept about the country in a manner most likely to attract attention, visiting friends, arranging secret meetings on the rooftops of blocks of flats, passing messages to his fellow conspirators in hollowed-out books, and gathering in his wake a motley assembly of the credulous, the earnest, the well-meaning and the lost and lonely. There were as well several shrewd, hard-bitten activists who should have known better, all drawn to Breytenbach's self-inflated and noisy passage like fluff to a demented vacuum cleaner. To say he left a trail does not do him justice: he positively blazed one. The police let him run and arrested him as he was about to leave the country. (January 1981)

Breytenbach served seven years of a nine-year sentence for treason. He was released in 1982 and immediately returned to France. Within two years his Johannesburg publisher had released four volumes of poetry in Afrikaans, a work of fiction in both English and Afrikaans titled *Mouroir,* and an autobiographic work, ***The True Confessions of an Albino Terrorist,*** written only in English.[1] According to published interviews, Breytenbach now completely rejects his Afrikaner heritage and declares his intention of never again writing in Afrikaans.[2]

Imprisonment is a kind of exile, one that locks the prisoner away from and yet holds him trapped at the center or core of his country. For Breytenbach the experience had this extra dimension of cruelty: he was locked in the "heart" of the only landscape he could be mentally loyal to while everything in his conscious mind called out for him to reject the country and its structures. Also, while in police custody he experienced, as he says, "the terrible destruction" of his love for his brother Jan, a Brigadier-general in the South African equivalent of the Green Berets, then later the death of his mother (whose funeral he was not allowed to attend), and the news that his father had suffered a stroke.

Since this second, prison-exile, Breytenbach has created for himself two further kinds of exile—a mental one in that he has allowed the South African landscape to die for him, and a verbal one in that he has discarded Afrikaans as a medium, refusing to use the language in which most of his earlier memories must reside and in which his dreams must play themselves out. But thus he has felt the need to pare himself down.

While the "essence" of Breytenbach's novel *Mouroir* (a title that conflates the two French words mourir and miroir) "is the prison and thus the prison experience of the author,"[3] it is also essentially a portrayal of the South African earth. Many of the thirty-eight sections that make up *Mouroir* seem to me to arise out of not unpleasant waking dreams. Causality, linearity, and the identifiability of character, as in rational narrative, are flouted, and yet not all of the tones and moods, the lights that move over the surface of the pieces, are despairing or even gloomy. For instance, **"Wiederholen"** opens with a carefully considered and realistically detailed celebration of the Cape dune landscape; **"The Double Dying of an Ordinary Criminal"** begins with an evocative and brilliantly recognizable depiction of the Natal South Coast; and **"The Self-Death"** has a description of Cape Town on a hot summer's night. For me it is as if, wide-awake and remembering, Breytenbach recorded with deep intimacy areas of South Africa. Then, the pleasure of that specific and perhaps (for him) easy creation dissipating (and sometimes the pleasure begins to dissipate before the end of the description), his awareness of his incarceration with all its complexities of guilt, shame, and terror would overwhelm him. His mind would then construct surreal and nightmarish events—always interpretable in terms of the author's own condition—and spin them out against the realistic backdrop of vibrant memory and desire.

Derek Cohen has pointed out that "*Mouroir* . . . is a work which powerfully and uniquely challenges assumptions about the nature of fiction."[4] It can be seen as a post-modernist work, one that Nadine Gordimer praises for bypassing the useless and overused vehicle of narrative and plot.[5] I should like to come back to a consideration of these aspects of the novel, but for the moment add that for me the book presents the random movement of consciousness as well as the force of the appalled imagination of the prisoner captured not only in time but in space, brooding on the hidden presence of the landscape surrounding him and tortured by recollections of his absurd and cowardly behavior. In solitary confinement, Breytenbach had a great deal of time to recollect (hardly in tranquility) that immediately on his arrest he dropped his bravura pose as secret agent and confessed all, having no hesitation in implicating all those he had contacted. During his trial he was abject: he apologized to the judge, to Prime Minister Vorster, and even to the policemen who had arrested him. *Mouroir* is at times dense with shame and guilt as well as with the author's conviction that all those on the "outside" had rejected him. For instance, in **"The Other Ship"** the narrator comes upon people seated at table aboard ship. He is horribly uneasy,

> . . . he does not sit down with the others, he is not correctly dressed, his heart is fluttering too painfully in his throat, and judging by the way they are looking or not looking at him, it is evident that his presence is unwelcome. He was absent already. People are raising crooked smiles at him. People have mouths full of toothlike reflections.[6]

That the South African landscape was a crucial part of Breytenbach's inner life at that time is made touchingly clear in his account of his great joy when the authorities transferred him from prison in Pretoria to one in the Cape, the province of his birth. He writes, addressing his reader as Mr. Investigator:

> Light caught us somewhere in the Karoo. . . . The expanse of the land all around, Mr. Investigator. The beauty of it, Mr. Investigator. the glory, yes. It was building up in me. We were going South. I was going to see the mountains, sir, and I now saw the Karoo unfolding. . . . I was singing anything that came into my head, Mr. Investigator: it was pouring out of me, all the broken filth of Pretoria. I sang of rock and hill and bush and lizard and moon. . . . Of the breathtaking prehistoric beauty of the desert: and of the madness of conquerors and the humiliation of the oppressed. . . . It was home—a home that would never be home again, which I had become alienated from forever—but the alienation was not from the earth that I still recognized, with which I still felt at peace.[7]

Breytenbach had come from an old respected Cape Afrikaner family. During his trial his father drove north to be with him, even though it made the old man physically ill to cross the Vaal River and enter the Transvaal. Breytenbach's father, affectionately called "Oubaas"—the Old Boss—by his wife and children, "used to be among the audience, day after day, sitting halfway towards the back, very straight, his face entirely closed. How he must have suffered", so Breytenbach muses.[8] This figure of the suffering closed-faced father appears and reappears in *Mouroir,* sometimes specifically named "Oubaas", as does the figure of the dying mother, and the robust army officer, mockingly renamed "John Wayne". Other images that repeat themselves are those of (predictably) birds, trapped butterflies and moths, ships at sea, the moon, and slaughtered horses; images suggesting freedom, wildness, magnificence—sometimes roaming at large and sometimes destroyed.

Breytenbach was initially jailed in Pretoria, in the significantly named Pretoria Central Prison. He was housed in solitary, close to the death cells which were themselves close enough to the gallows to tremble and resound when an execution took place. Breytenbach found himself "in the heart of the labyrinth",[9] in the heart of the heart of the heart of a country that had many times already been referred to by others as a vast prison camp but whose landscapes he was compulsively loyal to, whether he liked it or not. **"The Double Dying of an Ordinary Criminal"**, to a certain extent the central piece of *Mouroir,* records with starkly realistic details, stylistically incongruous perhaps in a work like *Mouroir,* the process and legislated rituals of a hanging. Thus a piece which begins with an evocative physical landscape goes on to embody a violently contrived legal killing.

Mouroir was composed in prison. The manuscript was examined minutely by detectives as it was in progress, and the entire work stored away by the authorities until Breytenbach's release. I cannot help but feel that his strong impulse to record the complex emotional truth of his prison experiences was modified, distorted perhaps, by a desire to confuse this initial police readership and their threatened censorship. The fragmentariness of the novel can also partly be explained by the day-to-day removal of the sections, a condition that led to "Writing" taking on "its pure shape, since it had no echo, no feedback, no evaluation, and perhaps ultimately no existence."[10]

The psychologically central section of *Mouroir* is the realistically detailed death by hanging. These details are repeated in *The True Confessions of an Albino Terrorist,* Breytenbach's autobiographic work prepared after his release in 1982. The details are more poignant and terrifying now because Breytenbach presents them in a very direct yet personal manner, there being no narrator or persona—no distance—between author and reader. Of hanging, he writes:

It must be like a wall. Very often—no, all the time, really—I relive those years of horror and corruption, and try to imagine, as I did then with the heart an impediment to breathing, what it must be like to be executed. What it must be like to be. Executed. Hanged by the passage of breath and of words . . . the indecency of man to man of handcuff and hood and rope and trapdoor—the earth falling for ever away; we are the wind and we are the birds, and the singing, singing of the weighted ropes. . . .[11]

He adds, again addressing Mr. Investigator, the representative of his captors, his critics, his readers, and all who judge him, "You have made of my mind a misery of images which I shall never be able to express."

I am convinced that because he was writing *Mouroir* in prison, Breytenbach availed himself of greater subterfuges of form and style than he might have found congenial had he been a free man, "anomaly and mental leapfrog" being the self-conscious devices in construction of the text.[12] Breytenbach obscured the real-life identities of some of his characters, sending critics on a "spot-the-symbol" hunt in their reviews. He also disguised his own identity, or rather, the onionlike layers of his own as author/narrator/personae/ prisoners. He spells his name in several different ways, and at times refers to himself as Jan Blom or Don Espejuelo. At the end of the book he signs himself off as Juan T. Bird. Jaunty (Jail)bird?

Yet if it would seem to the reader of *Mouroir* that all the named entities refer to aspects of the author's own shifting identity, Breytenbach takes pains to dispel this impression in *The True Confessions* while still insisting on the unfixed nature of the human character. In *The True Confessions* he reveals the real-life characters behind such strange names as Galgenvogel, Nefesj, and Tuchverderber. The author now out of prison, the narrative spoken into a tape-recorder in safety, *The True Confessions* has no need to treat delicately or metaphorically with Breytenbach's captors, from the lowliest prison warden to the judge who ignored pleas for clemency (even from the prosecution itself) and gave Breytenbach nine years. Now Breytenbach lashes out at these people, sometimes by name, sometimes by means of insulting, invented names such as Jiems Kont (James Cunt, for a detective), Judge Silly, Colonel Witnerf (Colonel Whitenerves), and Warrant-officer Donkey. He mocks their faces and bodies, their moustaches and haircuts, their vanities, their vulgarity, stupidity, and puritanically perverted obsessions with the sex-lives of their prisoners. Breytenbach takes revenge in the only way he can.

Breytenbach's revulsion with secret policemen and the work

they do comes out in certain poems. For instance, in **"La Pucelle"** he writes:

the little streets dark and wet and empty
except for the vast metal turd
a motor-in-state full of Secret Police
fat and gleaming like sterile semen
in the tiny barren tunnels of a wound—

and there in the powerful motor, in the heart of
    the cancer
the almighty Leader has on his arsehole
calluses from hemorrhoids full of secrets
and a telephone cupshaped in his mouth[13]
(my translation)

What the various works arising from Breytenbach's prison experiences all do is evoke strongly, at times with a visceral immediacy, the daily horrors of life in prison. However, many of the poems take time off, as it were, to celebrate the wondrousness of life on the outside, the joy the poet derived from being with his wife Yolande, and the firmly-established warmth of childhood memories. The prose works repeatedly emphasize the mutability of the human personality. For example, *The True Confessions* opens with the insistence that

. . . if there is one thing that has become amply clear to me over the years, it is exactly that there is no one person that can be named and in the process of naming be fixed for all eternity.[14]

This idea of the unfixed personality, an interesting philosophic stance, did not originate with Breytenbach, but is understandably crucial to a man with his experiences. *One man named Breytenbach* found himself in the position of being charged with and admitting to treason. Now, another Breytenbach invents or reinvents his confessions for us and, that done, a new Breytenbach goes forward into life like a creature that has sloughed off a couple of skins.

In *The True Confessions* he burns the last bridges linking him to South Africa. He records the final destruction in him of the power of the South African landscape, its death as an imaginative source. He writes that on the day of his release

. . . that same afternoon we left Cape Town in the Alfa Romeo of [Professor Kharon's] son. This was the start of the death journey. I was a mummy sitting there looking at the horrendously beautiful country rushing at us.[15]

The landscape no longer has the ability to uplift and delight him: this time he does not sing. He is insulated against it and will in time peel off that layer of himself forever.

In this autobiography he spits out his hatred and derision of almost everyone he has ever known in South Africa, not only secret policemen. He harshly criticizes his own brothers, his fellow writers, friends and academics, and also people like Christian Barnard (who visited him in prison) who live and work within the South African system. He states flatly that one should never trust any South African because "the 'system' is historically defined and conditioned, and the people come like words from the belly of the system."[16] He claims that Afrikaans is a creole language (while at the same time, in very Breytenbach-like fashion producing four volumes of intricate, dense poetry in that very language). He sees those who are trying to preserve Afrikaans as "objectively strengthening the ideology of the White rulers" and declares that it is of very little importance to him "whether the language dies of shame."[17]

Breytenbach's rejection of Afrikaans as a medium of expression for his future work is, again, a sloughing off of an identity, this time a cultural one. Thus he throws out various aspects of himself, those that are attached to landscape, language, family, and history. We will have to await the new Breytenbach, expressing himself in French or English or Italian. Unless he is about to discard the poet in himself as well and rely only on the painter to express a perception of the world that must for some time to come be colored with bitterness.

NOTES

1. The volumes of poetry are titled *Driftpoint, Eklips, Yk,* and *Buffalo Bill.* All Breytenbach's work initially brought out by Taurus, Box 85218, Emmarentia, Johannesburg 2029, before being released to European and American publishers.

2. *Index on Censorship.* London, 3/83.

3. Derek Cohen, "Radical Dislocations: *Mouroir* and the 'Prison of Fiction'," a paper delivered at the African Studies Association Conference, Los Angeles, October 1984.

4. Derek Cohen, op. cit.

5. Review in *The Atlantic Monthly*, April 1984, pp. 114-116. It is a little surprising to find an author like Gordimer, who always avails herself of the vehicle of narrative and plot, praising its absence in Breytenbach's work.

6. *Mouroir.* New York: Farrar Straus and Giroux, 1984, p. 46.

7. *The True Confessions of an Albino Terrorist.* Johannesburg: Taurus, 1984, p. 232.

8. *The True Confessions*, op. cit., p. 53.

9. *The True Confessions*, op. cit., p. 55.

10. *The True Confessions*, op. cit., p. 142.

11. *The True Confessions*, op. cit., pp. 194-5.

12. Derek Cohen, op. cit.

13. *Buffalo Bill.* Johannesburg: Taurus, 1984, p. 96.

14. Op. cit., p. 3.

15. Op. cit., p. 297.

16. Op. cit., p. 216.

17. Op. cit., pp. 321-322.

Barend J. Toerien (review date Summer 1986)

SOURCE: Review of *Lewendood*, in *World Literature Today,* Vol. 60, No. 3, Summer 1986, p. 511.

[*In the following review, Toerien calls Breytenbach's* Lewendood *both "rich and generous" in its poetic intentions.*]

Breytenbach's fourth published volume of poems written while he was held in South African prisons bears the cryptic title [**Lewendood**] **Life and Death,** which can also be read as "Living Death." It is the first part of the overall prison series **The Undanced Dance** and consists of poems written shortly after his incarceration and while in solitary confinement in the Pretoria jail. Surprisingly, the poems are in no way sad or despondent; on the contrary, they pulsate with vitality and an inner joy. There is a dispassionate look at his condition, a Dantesque descent into lower circles as he makes poems of graffiti found on the prison walls, of prison routines, the warders' activities, the rare sight of the moon, and so on. The writing of poetry is a way of keeping sane, and quite a few poems deal with the art of writing poetry. The man is so full of ideas and insights and "visions" that they spill wastefully out and over the bounds of his verse at times.

In a few longer poems Breytenbach converses with his alter ego, "Don Espejuelo." These are more prosy letters in which he is able to talk forthrightly about his situation and the world in general. The most constant presence in the volume, however, is that of his Vietnamese wife Yolande, waiting for him in Paris. Other poets are also present, as he quotes or twists their words: many older Afrikaans poets, but also Sylvia Plath, Descartes, Saint Paul, and doubtless quite a few more.

It must be stated that some of the selections are dull and flat, much too voluble and without the inner tension that one expects (wrongly?) in a poem. Not that this detracts from the book as a whole; it is too rich and generous for that. Breytenbach is only too fully aware of the qualities of poetry. In a remarkable piece which has only the numeral 3.13 as its title (all the poems are arranged numerically) and is tightly constructed of long lines with hidden and unobtrusive rhymes, he ponders on the art of poetry in an extended metaphor, finishing as follows (*vers* means "verse" but also "heifer"):

> . . . for the verse must be able to calve, even if
> it's often a messy and noisy abortion—the angel
>   leads—
> when the day's tolling yet clappers like bird seed
> but the vanguard of stars each already swelling
> a squash in the garden of night, when blood
> besmears the grass and shadows long and limp
>   and blue
> lie waiting for the stirring of the water—
> you by the hand through the orchard to the
>   sweet
> uncertainty of a specific moment
> where something sooner or later
> must happen, and you can hold your breath
> for joy, forgetfulness or for fright.

Vincent Crapanzano (review date 17 August 1986)

SOURCE: Review of *End Papers*, in *Los Angeles Times Book Review*, August 17, 1986, pp. 1, 9.

[*In the following review, Crapanzano finds* End Papers *disturbing and somewhat indulgent of Breytenbach's rage against South African apartheid but otherwise worthy of praise.*]

Breyten Breytenbach is a South African poet, painter and political activist. An Afrikaner by birth (though he refuses to be identified with the Afrikaners because of the political implications of such an identification), Breytenbach committed, in *his* people's eyes, the unpardonable crime. He sought to overthrow, violently if necessary, the South African government and the monstrous edifice of apartheid it had constructed. Breytenbach was arrested, tried, and imprisoned for seven years—two in solitary confinement—before he was released in 1982. (He has described these years of imprisonment in two books, *Mouroir* and *The Confessions of*

an Albino Terrorist.) The miscellaneous writings collected in *End Papers* were written before and after his imprisonment. They address dissidence, exile, imprisonment, the responsibility of the writer, political commitment, the artifice of culture, and above all South Africa and its apartheid. Although some essays are about travel (Palermo, Los Angeles and Berlin), and others about writers (Jorge Luis Borges) and cultural events (Pina Bausch's Wuppertal Tanztheater), they are also confined by Breytenbach's experience of South Africa. "For the White man," he tells us, "apartheid is a distance of mind, a state of being, the state of apartness."

"South Africa is a symbol. South Africa is a reality," Breytenbach writes. "These two truths are intimately linked, as are the mirror and memory, and both operate simultaneously." Like other white South Africans, those who think, at any rate, Breytenbach is caught between the symbol and reality, between the mirror and memory. Writing is a form of combat, he says. He is morally outraged. He decries the inhumanity of apartheid. He demands *real* change—majority rule—and envisions, sometimes naively, especially in his pre-prison writings, some sort of socialist society. But these positions do not give him a secure vantage point. His vision is fractured. "Can any of us see South Africa whole?," he asks, and he answers no. "We are institutionally (historically?) incapacitated. And we have to accept the maiming, the limitation." He refuses the easy—the European—vantage point, adopted, despite their anguish, by such writers as Nadine Gordimer and John Coetzee. He writes letters to, and converses with, figures who seem to be his critical alter ego. He asks: What happens if the Other—the Odder—is the I?

This question cannot be answered—certainly not in a society as divided as South Africa. Given the existential and political separation legislated by apartheid, the self's other remains always wooden, opaque, mechanical, of mythological proportion. In such a world, Breytenbach never tires of telling us, there can be no real cultural creativity. "Nearly all South African writing reflects varying stages of exile and alienation." (Breytenbach's own exile in France becomes a metaphor for the South African writer's condition.) Exile cuts the writer from that close and continuous contact with his people that keeps him alert and his language alive.

> The real *language* of the writer
> consists of two components:
>   the sounds that disturb him from
> within, that push from in-
>   side—and the *people* who speak
> his language. Language is
>   people. When you are deprived of
> one of these it is as if
>   you have only one leg, which keeps
> getting weaker because

you use it too much.

Such a position is particularly painful for a writer like Breytenbach who considers the distance we create between the writer and his public an artifact of Western culture.

The exile is marginal. He is lonely and awkward. Like the prisoner, he has to depend upon his own resources, and he risks inventing a self which can have no contact with those with whom he wishes to communicate.

> In the slammer you invented a
> you in order to make life bearable,
>   to breastplate yourself with a
> certain dignity. Outside you will
>   invent yourself as a re-creation, a
> reincarnation. The invention
>   will no longer be a go-between but
> an aperture, a cycle of hope,
>   a verse embodied with stresses.

Transitions are particularly difficult.

After seven years in prison, Breytenbach finds the world he returns to "becoming greyer, smoother, less textured." All over the world, he observes in a grand cliche, you can stay in identical, air-conditioned rooms, eating the same "continental" breakfast and finding on the same concave screen "not a glimmer of difference between the ad and assassination." All is image. You have to go to the Third World, he says, forgetting that the same hotels exist there (or are longed for) "to meet stench and crying and colour and the laughter of people laughing in the pre-air-conditioned-period way."

> With bodyshakes. To experience
> the deadline and the death of your
>   adaptation. The deafness of your
> glib skin. Also the vague unease,
>   the raspy breath and the guilty
> gut.

Would not such a visit be tourism for the alienated?

There is something deeply troubling about Breytenbach's writing. There is a bit too much of him in it all. One is tempted to read **End Papers** as symptom rather than as message. Maimed by his people, by his imprisonment, his exile, by all the injustices he sees around him, he indulges his pain. He gives way to an intolerance, an impatience, a rebelliousness, a violence, that lacks humanity. He reminds us: "There is a broken mirror, the wooden object with shards of sun-spewing and image-scattering glass, used to lure larks down to earth, to kill them." Such is one use of the mirror, but need it be the South Africans?

James Campbell (review date 19 September 1986)

SOURCE: "Learning to Walk by Walking," in *Times Literary Supplement*, No. 4355, September 19, 1986, p. 1028.

[*In the following review, Campbell praises* Mouroir *and* The True Confessions of an Albino Terrorist *but finds* End Papers *somewhat self-satisfied and unworthy of publication.*]

Seven years' imprisonment in South African gaols split the Afrikaner writer Breyten Breytenbach into three. He first avenged himself on his captors with the almost impenetrable prose of **Mouroir: Mirrornotes of a Novel,** the basis of which he wrote in confinement. This was followed by the pained lucidity of **The True Confessions of an Albino Terrorist,** composed immediately after his release. And now comes **End Papers,** a collection of speeches, letters, pseudo-interviews, poems and other bits and pieces, full of good intentions but also well stocked with banality and platitude, dating from immediately before and after his period of incarceration.

As is now well known, Breytenbach was arrested at Jan Smuts Airport in 1975 while attempting to leave South Africa to return to France, where he had lived since 1961. Under a false name, he entered the country on an underground mission on behalf of the ANC-affiliated group, Okhela, to which he belonged. He was tried and sentenced to nine years' imprisonment, of which he served seven, much of it in solitary confinement. Once arrested, he seemed to lose his stomach for the struggle, and while he did not betray his comrades, Breytenbach admits that the experience of interrogation, trial and imprisonment broke him—an admission which contributes to the impression of reliability and authenticity emanating from **The True Confessions.**

It is unusual, though not unknown, for a white man to go to prison for his political beliefs in South Africa, and since his release coincided with the increasing volume of lowkey civil war in that country, Breytenbach found himself, in 1982, a celebrity. From having been just a writer, not a very prominent one, he was now a "prison writer"—and, what's more, one who had served his time in the world's most conspicuous trouble spot. Publishers like this sort of thing: Breytenbach's predict that **The True Confessions** "will rank among the classic writings from prison"; a claim that I am not about to argue with. **The True Confessions** is a monumental work: one which gives full expression to a man's moment by moment struggle to rescue himself from hell. But Breytenbach seems to have taken his achievement as a licence to publish, now, whatever he writes, in the faith that it will be edified by his distinctive experience. **End Papers** is touted as completing "the publication of Breytenbach's prison writings", which is altogether misleading unless one accepts that everything an ex-convict writes constitutes "prison writings".

For all his having sought, and discovered, a verbal equivalent for pain, for all his intelligent alertness to the twists and turns of morality in an immoral State, Breytenbach is frequently an untidy writer, addicted to diversions, unable to resist puerile jokes and puns. "It is bad manners to talk with your mouth full of words", he remarks, and one is often tempted to use his witticism against him. All three books of "prison writings" would have benefited from firmer editing. The original draft of *The True Confessions* was typed up from tape-recordings ("talk talk talk") and although it was conscientiously worked over later, the finished product retains a good deal of the speaker's natural loquaciousness.

The tale of Breytenbach's arrest and imprisonment is told in the form of a confession to "Mr Investigator", the cruel incarcerator, with whom the prisoner forms a perverse intimacy, and in the face of whom he experiences not only terror and hatred but respect and even a horrified liking. Mr Investigator, after all, knows more about the wretch behind this account than anyone else does. Mr Investigator specializes in destroying personality, and Breytenbach is quick to admit to him that he has succeeded in destroying his. Some pictures of him taken during his interrogation later appeared in the press:

> And then, maybe they weren't of me. Those were the pictures taken of the hulk that they were excavating at that point, or of that man who was alive in that web at that time.

What *The True Confessions* does so brilliantly is relate how a character disappears under multiple layers of exile in prison: exiled from society at large, from his family, from his former life in Paris where he was already an exile, exiled in solitary confinement from his fellow inmates, and even exiled, like a pariah, from the Afrikaners, his own people, who are holding him. In addition, though, the tale provides a chart, as it were, of the process of reconstruction. In this, the act of writing itself is paramount. "It is by walking that you learn to walk." *The True Confessions* is the story of the search for the identity of its own narrator.

After much bargaining, with the help of pleas lodged by the Afrikaner literary establishment, Breytenbach was finally allowed to write in prison (his other request, that he be permitted to paint, was refused), on condition that he hand in the fruits of his labours at the end of each day and keep no notes. In return, the "Greys" promised that his pages would be given back on release, and the promise was kept.

This placed the writer in a bizarre situation, having to practise his essentially private activity "knowing that the enemy is reading over your shoulder . . . knowing also that you are laying bare the most intimate and the most personal nerves and pulsebeats in yourself to the barbarians". The result of this endeavour was *Mouroir*, a collection of stories written in a prose deliberately refracted in order to elude the philistine scrutiny of Mr Investigator and his cohorts (who, incidentally, included Breytenbach's brothers).

Every prisoner, in whatever society—even those who have to cope only with letter censors—learns the art of literary evasion, some becoming expert in making themselves understood only by those they wish to understand them. The thought of a novel whose form and content are determined by such constraints is an intriguing one, but perhaps Breytenbach has succeeded too well in being elusive. While parts of the intensely lyrical *Mouroir* are pleasing when read sentence by sentence, a collection of these sentences yields little. In *The True Confessions* he describes writing in the dark, suggesting that this "wording" is perhaps "akin to the experiments that the surrealists used to make in earlier years", and Breytenbach's kaleidoscopic prose does have a similarly random feel about it. Obsessed on the one hand by the necessity to confess, and, on the other, by the omniscience of his totalitarian captors (experts in "washing brains"), Breytenbach has produced in *Mouroir* a poetic muddle.

One backs away from these "mirrornotes" relieved, at first, to find the solid, recognizable prose of *End Papers*. The earliest of its thirty-eight items dates from 1967; the latest from June of this year. That Breytenbach treats them most earnestly is attested by the fact that they are furnished with forty pages of "End Notes". But for the most part they are remarkably ordinary: **"Dear David"**, for example, solemnly dated like all the others, is a letter to a passing acquaintance in New York; it includes its own false starts, plus simple observations on Parisian life and American women, with the announcement that the author is a happy male chauvinist ("Never rape a lady against her wishes" is one of his earlier jokes).

There are intelligent responses to South Africa's unique "conscious banalization of humanity", to the call for a cultural boycott, and to the axiom that "time . . . is Black", but the most striking impression *End Papers* gives is that Breytenbach now supposes the world is keen to hang on his every word. What he has to say on the nature of the South African State, on apartheid, on repression, on the role of the writer faced by one or more of these, he said to much greater effect in the context of the particularity forced on him by the subject matter of *The True Confessions*. At this best, he is an explorer of both self and form (and frequently claims that they are inseparable); at worst, he is unable to recognize a jotting when he makes one.

Bruce Robbins (review date 30 November 1986)

SOURCE: "Conspicuous Exile," in *New York Times Book Review,* Vol. XCI, No. 48, November 30, 1986, p. 21.

[*In the following review, Robbins finds* End Papers *interesting from the point of view of literary and political history but less compelling than Breytenbach's earlier works.*]

In 1975, after more than a decade of exile in Paris, the "whitish" (his term) Afrikaans-speaking poet and painter Breyten Breytenbach returned to South Africa incognito in order to help organize white resistance to apartheid. Arrested and convicted, he spent seven years in prison, two of them in solitary confinement. It is probably thanks to this involuntary sojourn—a story told with freshness and modesty in *The True Confessions of an Albino Terrorist* (1985)—that we now have *End Papers,* a collection of 50-odd addresses, analyses, poetico-political fragments and essays by Mr. Breytenbach, together with extensive notes on their occasions.

International publicity helped get the author out of prison, and since his release and return to France in December 1982 he has stayed in the spotlight. For obvious reasons, he has been a fixture at PEN, Unesco and anti-apartheid conferences around the world, where on the evidence of this book he has acquitted himself stylishly, and with more political acumen that one might have predicted from his verse.

Even the most legitimate outrage has its ruts, but Mr. Breytenbach avoids most of them. He is drawn to uncomfortable topics: the likelihood that "reform" measures will only reinforce apartheid, and the relations between black and white resistance writers (white writers must choose "absolute solidarity with their Black colleagues, *even without any recognition from the latter*").

In his reports on the conference circuit, Mr. Breytenbach drops some names (he describes to the blind Borges the latter's new medal, eats spaghetti with Sophia Loren and Ugo Tognazzi, shares prison anecdotes with Lev Kopelev, the original of Solzhenitsyn's character Rubin in *The First Circle*). And his excursions into travel writing, which go with the same territory, are not always worth the detour ("Berlin the scarred . . . Rome eternally seductive"). To his credit, however, Mr. Breytenbach tends to be self-conscious about such lapses, as about the other ironies of being a prison-produced celebrity whose least word on sundry matters is suddenly publishable.

One of these ironies is that although he became newsworthy by virtue of having physically "been there," his chosen subject is often the meaning of *not* being there, of feeling displaced from the revolutionary center as a white, and even

more as an exile and an artist. Mr. Breytenbach strikes the same chord again and again, making the book resound with his ambivalence. Fearing that his location and vocation make him irrelevant to, or even a betrayer of, the South African blacks who are "chucking the stones they cannot eat," he makes an eloquent appeal for solidarity.

Less explicitly, however, he also glorifies that same treacherous irrelevance as a precondition of poetic lucidity and an antidote to tyrannies old and new. For a poet to be in exile, he says, is to be cast off from his people and language; an Afrikaans-speaking writer in an English-speaking world knows the disadvantages of being cut adrift. Yet he also has special reasons for arguing that literature demands detachment from the language (and values) of the tribe. Thus certain questions remain, vexing the prose into nervous animation. Is his marginality a sign of artistic sterility or vitality? Is it a model of proper, permanent opposition to authority or a mark of political impotence?

Mr. Breytenbach's problem may be simply his definition of art, or rather the (conference-induced?) urge to define it. In sections like "Poetry Is" and "I Write," he scrolls slowly through mutually contradictory concepts: communication, silence, memory, forgetting, propaganda, pollution, survival, rape. The listing is a subversive act, for it suggests that all answers to Sartre's question "What is literature?" have become equally possible and equally meaningless—even if Sartre's call to engagement remains. At any rate, what is most interesting in Mr. Breytenbach's own writing is not the familiar celebration of art as a bastion of individual autonomy against the state, but his timely experiments with cultural interaction, bastardization, mutation. The mixing of cultures answers apartheid in its own terms.

Breyten Breytenbach recently returned to South Africa on the occasion of an award for *YK,* one of the volumes of poetry he wrote while in prison. It is tempting but premature to interpret this gesture as a judgment on his own attraction to the esthetics of exile. In any event, his act can only add to the interest of *End Papers,* whose drama lies in literature's scramble after history at its most dramatic.

Henry Kratz (review date Summer 1987)

SOURCE: Review of *End Papers,* in *World Literature Today,* Vol. 61, No. 3, Summer 1987, pp. 482-83.

[*In the following review, Kratz offers high praise for* End Papers.]

Breyten Breytenbach spent seven years (1975-82) in a South African prison, two of them in solitary confinement, for "treason" because of his outspoken criticism of the apartheid government. He is best known here for his account of this incarceration, *The True Confessions of an Albino Terrorist* (1984), but in South Africa he is regarded as one of their foremost poets (he writes his verse in Afrikaans) and even won the prestigious Hertzog Prize in 1984, although he felt compelled to refuse it. On top of that, he is a painter of some distinction (in fact, the dust jacket of *End Papers* bears his own illustration). Breytenbach resides in Paris, having become a naturalized French citizen.

End Papers consists of miscellaneous "essays, letters, articles of faith, workbook notes," and even some poetry, written at various times between 1968 and 1985. The materials are presented in chronological order following a preface called "Pretext" and fall naturally into two groups: those written before his incarceration (**"Blind Bird"**) and those written afterward (**"Burnt Bird"**), with an appendix giving background and supplementary information on the individual items. Many of the articles were written originally in French, Afrikaans, or Dutch, and most were published before in some form.

The malevolent nature of apartheid is the major theme of the volume's writings. Perhaps the most sweeping indictment is contained in the essay **"Vulture Culture,"** written in 1971: "Apartheid is . . . the artificially created distance necessary to attenuate, for the practitioners, the very raw reality of racial, economic, social and cultural discrimination and exploitation. . . . Apartheid is the White man's night, the darkness which blurs his consciousness and his conscience. . . . Apartheid is at the same time the implement of exploitation and the implementation thereof. . . . It is Fascist. . . . It is totalitarian. . . . It is paranoic." "Believe me," he says at another point, "South Africa is a fine example of how Apartheid . . . has corrupted masters and oppressed ones equally."

Many of the essays are devoted to the role of the writer in society. The author points out that in Third World countries the writer "is practically without exception a member of the so-called élite," so that he is often an "outsider to his own people." He believes that the writer has the responsibility "to resist by all means the foisting on society of clichés and lies; . . . to be technician of the conscience—not in a moralist way, but to the extent that the only 'sin' is that of ignorance."

Breytenbach, though convinced that ultimate majority rule in South Africa is inevitable, sees little hope for much progress in the immediate future. The Botha regime, he contends, while making a few minor concessions to give the impression of increased liberalization, is actually doing its best to strengthen the bastion of majority rule. Breytenbach severely criticizes Britain, West Germany, and the United States for their support of the South African government.

A collection such as *End Papers* does not lend itself well to a summary review. There is much more of interest between the covers than I have indicated. The talented, dedicated, and courageous author gives us many insights and much to ruminate over. It is a book that everyone should read.

Herbert Mitgang   (review date 4 November 1989)

SOURCE: "A Poet's Obsession with Apartheid," in *New York Times Book Review,* November 4, 1989, p. 15.

[*In the following review, Mitgang finds universal relevance in the themes relating to injustice in* Memory of Snow and of Dust.]

In *Memory of Snow and of Dust,* a follow-up to his searing memoir of his seven years in a South African prison on a trumped-up charge of terrorism, *The True Confessions of an Albino Terrorist,* Breyten Breytenbach continues his campaign of conscience against apartheid. This time Mr. Breytenbach puts a novelistic stamp on his work. Using the freedom made possible by fiction, the self-exiled Afrikaner poet, painter and translator reaches still deeper into his past, recalling aspects of his torture, trial and imprisonment. And he reminds the reader that apartness can be a fact of life even in Paris, that city of light and enlightenment where he now makes his home.

In *Memory of Snow and of Dust,* Mr. Breytenbach writes in a meditative manner that eventually builds to reveal the raw reality of apartheid. The author uses a variety of weapons—poetry, drama, biography, philosophical dialogue, fragments of plays and films, letters and vignettes and midnight recollections. Sections of the novel are set in the future, enabling him to develop symbols and to project hopes onto unborn generations.

Mr. Breytenbach assumes that we know a good deal about the diamond-cold heart of South Africa. In fact, readers have long been aware of Alan Paton's *Cry, the Beloved Country* and, more recently, the novels of Nadine Gordimer, André Brink and J. M. Coetzee; in theater, the plays of Athol Fugard; in journalism, the books and lectures of Donald Woods, the banned South African newspaper editor now living in London, whose personal story about his friendship with Steve Biko, the murdered black leader, was made into the film *Cry Freedom.*

A reader who pays close attention to *Memory of Snow and of Dust* is rewarded with opinionated interior monologues that supplement the daily flow of information about the conflict between the races. Scenes and time frames shift as if they were in a kaleidoscope. As one of his country's leading white commentators—who has experienced the meaning of life in solitary confinement—Mr. Breytenbach has knowledge that comes from the inside. One of the impressions his novel leaves is that apartheid is a two-edged weapon: not only does it keep the black majority apart, but it also separates the white minority from contact with black life.

The novel is divided into two unequal sections. The longer first part, which is set in Europe and different parts of Africa, is called Utéropia—meaning the innocent, idealized world of the unborn. It chronicles the lives of Meheret, an Ethiopian journalist, and her lover, Mano, a South African writer of mixed blood who can pass for white. Meheret discloses the history of her family and sends fantasy messages to their unborn child. Mano, meanwhile, has formed a film production company and returns to his country to research a movie about the life of an exiled writer. What begins almost as a meditation soon develops into a nightmare.

In the second part, "On the Noble Art of Walking in No Man's Land," reality comes down hard on Mano. He is lured back to South Africa, trapped by men with concealed weapons, arrested and sentenced to death for a purported murder. Here, the author expands his *True Confessions of an Albino Terrorist.*

Memory of Snow and of Dust is a poetic novel. Here is how the author describes the arrest of Mano after a betrayal within the ranks of the anti-apartheid underground: "Two other men stepped forward from the shadows of the hall— the one with the raincoat must have been waiting on the stairs, the other near the street exit. They didn't say a word but their eyes never left my face. The butterfly in my stomach had become a stone. It is miraculous the way flight can turn into dead falling. It all went very quickly and yet as if in slow motion, with each action precisely defined and senseless, dislocated."

There are light touches in the novel as well. Mr. Breytenbach has fun ridiculing "an international congress of writers." "The meeting turns out to be a crashing non-event," he writes. "Delegates with angry cheeks debate heatedly behind closed doors on policies which cannot in any way impinge upon the real world. . . . It is probably good for such a congregation to exist. The fuddled-minded ones, the charitable hearts, the never-never authors also need their own whacky club."

Mr. Breytenbach's characters do not confine themselves to observations about South Africa. "What could be said about Paris at present?" Mano asks himself, and answers that it is a city "accessible only to stressed joggers and their feminist spouses. That the poor are railroaded out to the sub-

urbs where they will give birth to marginals and the permanently unemployable."

In *Memory of Snow and of Dust,* Mr. Breytenbach has written a novel that is obsessed with injustice anywhere, whether it is called apartheid or another name.

J. M. Coetzee   (essay date Spring 1991)

SOURCE: "Breytenbach and the Censor," in *Raritan,* Vol. X, No. 4, Spring 1991, pp. 58-84.

[*In the following essay, Coetzee examines Breytenbach's notions of self and other in his writings during and after his prison sentence.*]

One of the major poems in Breyten Breytenbach's collection *Skryt* is entitled **"Brief uit die vreemde aan slagter"** (**"Letter from Foreign Parts to Butcher"**), subtitled "for Balthazar." *Skryt* did not appear in South Africa. First published in the Netherlands in 1972, it was banned for distribution in South Africa by the Publications Control Board. In banning it, the responsible committee singled out **"Brief uit die vreemde"** and the list of the names of dead persons following it, reading the poem in terms of "very strict reference" to then Prime Minister Balthazar John Vorster and interpreting its ending as an accusation against the white man and particularly the Afrikaner. Numerous poems from *Skryt* were incorporated into the 1977 collection *Blomskryf,* but **"Brief uit die vreemde"** was not one of them. It is this poem for which Breytenbach apologized at his trial in 1975: "I would specifically like to apologize to the Prime Minister for a crass and insulting poem addressed to him. There was no justification for it. I am sorry."

Since the first half of the poem is obscure to the point of being cryptic, it is likely that the committee came to its decision on the basis of the second half of the poem alone, where the torture and killing of detainees by the Security Police is referred to in unmistakable terms and B. J. Vorster is directly addressed as the butcher/obstetrician presiding over their deaths (the list appended to the poem of detainees who had by that date died at the hands of the Security Police is an extra-poetic gesture whose significance will emerge below). However, we should not for that reason ignore the first half of the poem: it is one of Breytenbach's most intensely worked out treatments of death and resurrection and belongs intimately with the accusations of the second half.

Since his first verse collection, the figure of Lazarus has been part of Breytenbach's poetic mythology. The first half of the *butcher* poem, without naming Lazarus, is an account of a resurrection from the grave/cell. In thus making the speaker a transworldly traveler, it seeks to entitle him to a knowledge of dying (in this case under torture) and death and so to a right to accuse Vorster in the name of "the rearisen prisoners of Africa." By its own power, but also by gathering about it the context of Breytenbach's earlier figuration of the Lazarus-poet, it attempts to establish poetic authority to speak in the name of the martyred/tortured *gemarteldes* of John Vorster Square (Security Police headquarters), who (as the appended list makes clear) did not at the time include a white. In its I-address the poem therefore implies two different readers: a reader directly addressed, "jy" (you), Balthazar, *butcher*, but also an invisible third person, a reader over the shoulder, a "prisoner" ready to question Breytenbach's authority to speak as I for him.

As I have mentioned, the word-play, imagery, and symbolism of the first half of the poem make it difficult of access, whereas the language of the second half, without being simple, is plain in its meaning. This is not only because the poem is designed to grow more and more naked as it builds up towards an historic accusation (the poet in the person of a history yet to be written pointing a finger at the oppressor) but because it takes over the language of the Security Police at its most shameless and cynical when it presents lies *as* lies in the arrogant certainty that, while no one will believe them, no one dare repudiate them. (I refer, of course, to official accounts of detainees jumping out of windows in fits of remorse, slipping on bars of soap and killing themselves, hanging themselves by their own clothing, and so forth.)

> I stand on bricks before my fellow-man
> I am the statue of liberation
> who with electrodes on the balls
> tries to scream light in the dusk
> I write slogans in a crimson urine
> over my skin and over the floor
> I stay awake
> suffocating on the ropes of my entrails
> slip on soap and break my skeleton
> murder myself with the evening newspaper
> tumble out of the tenth floor of heaven
> to salvation on a street among people

When the police explain a prisoner's death by saying that he slipped on a bar of soap, the unstated continuation is: and we defy any court in the land to reject that explanation. It is one of the linguistic practices of totalitarianism to send out coded messages whose meaning is known to all parties, but to enforce (by censorship) a literal interpretation of them, at least in the public arena. Thus "slipped on a bar of soap" is known by all parties to mean "died under torture," but its public interpretation is nevertheless forced to remain "slipped on a bar of soap." When Breytenbach parodies the codes, as here, his unstated continuation is: here I create an arena

in which the codes are unmasked and denounced. His challenge therefore takes place on the grounds of power itself: on the one hand, police power protected from denunciation and reprisal; on the other hand, the power of a rhetoric (a skill with words) employed for the purpose of mockery on a public stage. It goes without saying that the motive for banning the poem was, by denying it a public stage, by reasserting control over public staging, to deny it the power of its superior rhetoric to unmask the codes.

But this is where the position of a speaker speaking "uit die vreemde" raises difficulties of a moral as well as of a practical order. Both the speaker and the poem (publishable and indeed published abroad) are operating outside the jurisdiction of the rival power (the police, the censors), as they are operating outside the speech community and political community they address. Is the challenge therefore not morally empty? The question is not answered by, for example, André Brink when he explains "die vreemde" as "a space or experience strange to the butcher. In brief: *all that is foreign to the butcher. . . .* [Thus] nothing that the one [i.e., butcher or prisoner] says can make sense to the other." It is not far-fetched to understand Breytenbach's return to South Africa in 1975 as an existential response to the question, that is, as placing himself on the same footing as the enemy, as acting out the myth of humiliation, incarceration, and rebirth into the authority of the reborn—a myth not solely Christian in its currency—on which the poem draws.

The attack on B. J. Vorster himself is twofold. On the one hand Vorster is attacked as the chief of the security forces and hence as the one who will ultimately stand on the dock of history:

> say it to me now, butcher
> before the thing becomes a curse
> before it is left to you to plead only by mouth
> of graves
> before the rearisen prisoners of Africa

Insofar as the Lazarus-prophet-poet writes his prophetic-apocalyptic history of the future here, he is prophesying again the reversal of jurisdiction, the inevitability of the judge-executioner becoming the accused. But insofar as the poem itself places Vorster on the dock, it attempts to bring that future about. Thus the claim Breytenbach makes is a claim of power (the power to make the future happen) which Vorster even as self-claimed steersman of the state lacks.

The second prong of the attack is more interesting and in a way more radical. Picturing the scream of pain issuing from the dying prisoner as a bloody birth in the hands of the butcher-obstetrician, Breytenbach asks:

does your heart also tighten in the throat
when you grasp the extinguished limbs
with the same hands that will stroke your wife's
    secrets?

Secrets: Breytenbach might as well have written *secret parts.* The exposure to public gaze is not just of the forbidden secrets of the torture chamber, not just of the (putative) private revulsions of B. J. Vorster himself (the irony is complex here: Breytenbach asserts that Vorster has a conscience and challenges him to deny it), but of the mysteries (forbidden to the public gaze by decency itself) of the Vorster marriage bed. The poem is a low blow, a dig at the private parts not of the man but of his defenseless wife, an insult to male honor, more rather than less offensive when one considers the age of its targets (Balthazar and Tini were in their midfifties in 1972). The excess of the poem is an excess of intimacy.

What does it mean to say that **"Brief uit die vreemde"** is "crass and insulting"? Insultingness is not a property internal to the poetic text. An insult is an act, a speech act. After insult, what happens next? What does the transgressive act set in train?

Without implying that "Brief uit die vreemdè" gave rise to the animosity against Breytenbach that led to a nine-year (rather than a seven-year or a five-year) sentence, one can say that, as an insult to Vorster, to the security police, to the community whose interests they protected, the poem had its consequences. But it was not Breytenbach's first transgression. In the poems before **"Brief uit die vreemde"** and the subsequent apology for **"Brief uit die vreemde"** (which provides one kind of answer to the question: what happens next?), Breytenbach had made one attempt after another to turn transgressive speech into transgressive act.

In Breytenbach's first collection, which appeared in 1964, the poem that comes closest to naming the forbidden is **"Breyten Prays for Himself."** But the strategy of this poem is one of irony: the poet pretends to identify himself with the white bourgeois who wants no more than to slide through life without trouble:

So that others may bear it
May be arrested, Shattered
       Stoned
       Hanged
       Scourged
       Used
       Tortured
       Crucified
       Interrogated
Placed under house arrest

Banned to dim islands to the end of their days
Languish in dank holes
....
But not *Me*
But us never give Pain or lament

In the 1969 **Cold Fire** the insulted figure of authority is the emperor Tiberius, who retreats from the summer heat into "halls chopped out of the mountain" while outside his subjects "sit and stink / small and brown like turds." Breytenbach's Tiberius casts an eye (an "imprisoned" eye) over his aquaria and, beyond them, over the seas where his ships sail "an ordered world,"

so that in the evenings—when the red god
behind the headland leaves a red toga in the
    breakers—
in company and pretension of fat-arse senators
he could blessedly wade
the volumes of his white body
in the standing fresh water of his marble swimming
    pool

The whiteness of Tiberius alerts us that we are reading an allegory of South African overlordship. But the poem settles for a mixture of tepid fascination with and revulsion for the stillness of imperial power. If the poem intends a barb, it is hard to see where the point of the barb lies, except in the demotic "vetgat" (fat-arse).

"Evening People" prophesies the inheriting of the earth by the poor. Its terms are not specific to South Africa, but since the epigraph is taken from the Afrikaans poet Totius, South Africa must be taken as its implied referent. "Die wêreld is ons woning nie" ("The world is not our dwelling-place"), says Totius; but from its first line the poem sets out to contradict this father-figure of Afrikaans letters: "The world is not God's . . . / The world belongs to mankind."

listen Richman Possessor Investor Fascist
listen Church and State rotten Politician
listen to mankind sick to death with hope
one of these days you will drown in your piss
for the world is no God's
nor does the world belong to the Devil
look the world has grown fast to Man
and each will get his hole full of earth

The poem strikes at Totius. Is one fanciful to feel that, in its lack of specificity—a specificity displaced onto its cloacal imagery—it hesitates to finger its living targets?

To Fly, Breytenbach's first extended prose piece, published in 1971, is surrealistic in the manner of his artwork of the period. Therefore, as if to make its denunciatory intent clear, it concludes by explaining itself.

> Although this essay does not wish to be symbolic, it is to me a representation of our specific cancer and leprosy, our highly civilized refinement and putrefaction that can motivate and explain away murder and mass murder, imprisonment and torture procedures. Daily we passed Auschwitz by train but we did not see the smoke, we looked across the bay at Robben Island but thought it was a leper colony.

In the allegory of *To Fly* white South Africa is a huge institution for the mentally ill, of whom the narrator is one. The garden is patrolled by a "park official, . . . caretaker in . . . butcher's jacket," who shoots patients for misbehaving. An obsessive, murderous regime of law and order is set in an apocalyptic landscape of mass extinction.

This vision is presented not through the eyes of a prophetic outsider but of a narrator confined inside his blind "white" vision. "God is on the side of prison guards, butchers and male nurses," he tells himself piously. His greatest pleasure is a private one, defecating. But even that has dangers: using old papers to wipe his backside, he has to be careful not to read them, for they may be "forbidden fruit, . . . subversive propaganda, . . . books of poetry and other declarations of superfluous freedoms." As trouble mounts in the world outside him, he cuts off his penis, cuts out his tongue, puts out his eyes with irons. "Now I can hide away undisturbed in my blind body. . . . All I have left to get to grips with is my brain (organization) and my ego (commissioner)."

Thus the repudiation of the South African order is achieved by splitting and casting off a self-confessing, storytelling self who is at home in it. The potential for ambivalence in this ironistic procedure (who/what is the real target, the regime of mutilation and death or the self who is at home in it?) seems to be felt all too keenly by Breytenbach. In his own person—that is, as a new I—he addresses the narrator-I:

> That is why I am so grateful to you . . . because I could kick you and I could spit on you, I could get rid of my bad temper. Because I am a moralist. White is dead. That is the one level.

This concluding authorial statement subverts the transgressive force of the work by in effect repudiating the narrator, denying him an identity, and then gesturing vaguely toward a "level" on which he can be recuperated.

In the companion piece *The Ant-Nest Swells Up*, the concluding move is again to claim to cast off all masks:

It ought to be crystal clear that I am asking you for Rebellion. The duty of the artist is to overthrow his government. . . . Can't you see that the poem is a curse of protest, that it must reflect the smell of spilled blood, of inhumanity, the bestiality of suppression; that it cannot and may not be an aesthetic cocoon, a watered-down and scented European-derived dribble of piss!

Besides **"Brief uit die vreemde,"** *Skryt* contains several poems of straightforward denunciatory content. One is **"The Promised Land."**

> [Johannesburg] a glittering image: hell with God
>
> God the Bureau of State Security
> God wearing his helmet,
> in one hand an attaché case full of shares and gold
> in the other a whip,
> God erect in all His shining majesty
> on the shoulders of blacks buried to the waist in
>   the earth's
> . kingdom

The problem that poetry like this raises for Breytenbach is the same that is raised by the Totius poem: it is transgressive, but all that it transgresses in the end is a certain decorum of address. It cannot be said to be an *act* as the poem on Vorster is. Relying solely on a rhetoric of abjuration, it remains within the rhetorical realm and so is always vulnerable to being trumped by a yet more violent rhetoric.

The alternative to frontal rhetorical assault is an ironistic manoeuvre of identifying with, parodying, and mocking the enemy. It is not too much of a generalization to say that, as transgressor, Breytenbach shuttles between these two manoeuvres, as, for example, in **"Life in the Earth."**

> blessed are the children of Dimbaza,
> of Welcome Valley, Limehill and Stinkwater
>   dead
> of sicknesses, undernourishment, poverty—
> for they make clean the *baas*'s field of vision,
> for they escape hell,
> for they vacate the territory of the Boer
>   —the Boer and his God—
>   —the hand of the God— . . .
> . . . .
> twice-blessed and holy are the moles
> and the worms and the ants
> in the land of sunshine
> in the land of the Boer
> in the land that the Lord gave him.

In ironic manoeuvres such as this, conventional critical wisdom has it, the less visible the line of difference between speaker and enemy, the more potentially powerful the effect. On the other hand, if the line of difference becomes too nearly invisible, the reader may be left bewildered (the early history of the reception of Swift's "Modest Proposal" provides a case in point). Plotting one's distance from the enemy seems to be merely a technical matter. Yet, in the end, seeming to identify with the enemy, to speak the enemy's language, raises an unsettling ethical question: is the ironic poem merely a second-best substitute for the private diaries of the tyrant (who ought then to be able to trump anything the poet can come up with) or does the tyrant truly not know what he intends as well as the poet does? If the latter, how does the secret sympathy of poet for tyrant arise? It is in the face of this latter question, perhaps, that Breytenbach takes the defensive steps he does at the conclusions of **To Fly** and **The Ant-Nest Swells Up.**

The dilemma can be restated in the form of two questions. If the passion behind my denunciation is not the passion of a pure (idealistic) moralism, whose target may as well be universal tyranny, Roman or South African, what does it stem from? And if there is any risk I take in denouncing tyranny, what is it? The answer to the first question is: my passion stems from the fact that I am implicated (historically, emotionally) in South Africa; insofar as the present-day South African order is, and rests upon, a crime, that crime is part of me and I wish to purge myself of it. The answer to the second question is: I take the risk of reidentifying myself with what I could leave behind. I risk the European identity I have half-adopted by resuming a white South African identity I detest. Thus the paradox clarifies itself: to repudiate white South Africa I have to be a white South African; or: to repudiate evil I have to embody evil.

The paradox is lived out by Breytenbach in the act of writing in Afrikaans, "a bastard language" or, to be more specific, the language of a split self. **"Brief uit die vreemde"** has to be written in the language of the tyrant, spoken nowhere but in the land of the tyrant, but also in the mother-language:

> I write poetry in afrikaans language of
>   bodyspasms: brew-
>   smell
> of my first milk, grain of my father's fingertips

The movement *back* holds terrible regressive perils. *Lewendood* (*Life-and-death, Living-death*) is the title of one of Breytenbach's prison volumes. But the paradox of that title is already announced in the first poem of the first volume, with its instructions for the funeral of one Breyten Breytenbach. Poetry and death, love and death:

> my heart is in the Boland and nothing

> can desecrate it it is stored
> in a little coffin in white Wellington

Exile and death too. Looking out on Paris through the rain-streaked windowpane of his apartment, the poet sees "forbidden death's-herald water-images" of his parents and of the Boland where he was born. There is no doubt that the paradox of being and not being an Afrikaner has been lived out personally by Breytenbach in the most intense terms.

A Season in Paradise dates, in censored form, from 1976. Before the book could appear in Afrikaans, Breytenbach had to accept the excision of passages that alarmed or offended the publisher. Bowing to that veto, he thereby entered the realm of the enemy's discourse and power. Thus when denunciation of the enemy comes, Breytenbach is able to implicate himself in it as both subject and object:

> We South Africans, we will go on haunting the
> world forever. We are, all of us, slightly nuts, there
> is a bleeding crack running through each of
> us. . . . We are mad, all of us, with rigid faces. . . .
> We are maimed, we are only half human, but we
> know it, we are mad and realize that we are mad.

Do we notice the Cretan liar lurking here? Even if what we hear is supposed to be mad speech, the words with which the address ends are clearly intended to cast aside the cloak of madness: "By taking cognizance of the nature of the struggle we are involved in and share . . . we expand our humanity and our language." The madness is not really Breytenbach's: it belongs to *other* people. What runs through Breytenbach may be a scar (like a birthmark) left by a mad formation and a scar (like a whiplash) left by the mad behavior around him ("I too . . . have . . . been placed in the humiliating position of being subjected to the discriminating system I despise"), but not madness itself. If Breytenbach is seeking the nature of his own implication, it continues to elude him.

Hence his resort to a deus ex machina, a savior who will end the reign of madness and institute a new age. Messianic thinking is all too common and all too understandable in South Africa; but the savior Breytenbach announces allows the poet a special role as visionary John the Baptist:

> I say unto you, from the heart of the country
> he will come to you, one of you,
> strung on blood
>   he will be of your making
> and where he goes a way will be paved
> and women will drop their stitches
> and fire will emerge barking from the barrels of
>   guns
> houses will grow black

fig trees will wither
he will command armies
he will avenge injustice
and settle old scores
for all those years of existing without a decent
    living wage
when you [sic] laborers had to sleep on cement,
content with porridge

some of you will of course—it's in a man's
    nature—
lie down on your stomachs like bloated worms . . .
offering . . .
anything, "anything, master Kaffir, no
matter what, anything but death, oh, my own
mashter Kaffir"
    and he will be wearing a gorgeous smile
and a halo and a Sten and he will
not harm the sparrows of the veld
neither will he rip up the choppers
from the locusts

I have pointed earlier to a movement (a shuttling? a lurching?) between poems of rhetorical denunciation with a certain emptiness at their heart, and poems of ironic identification with the enemy. The poem I have quoted, loose and occasional though it is, responds to the unsettled position of a poet to whom both speaking from outside and speaking from inside are sources of unease. It is essentially a poem of *settling scores*. The slave becomes master, the arrogant master embraces the self-abasing, sickening language of the powerless, a language beneath language, baby-speech (the translation above is Breytenbach's own). It envisions and revels in apocalypse, salvation, the end of all division. Invoking a magical violence so overwhelming that it does not even entail force, it is a poem that by its nature belongs to an epoch, the end of an age: settling scores, it seeks by its own excess to close the book on the restlessness and division running through the earlier poetry.

"Imagine a dialogue of two persons," writes Mikhail Bakhtin,

in which the statements of the second speaker are omitted, but in such a way that the general sense is not at all violated. The second speaker is present invisibly, his words are not there, but deep traces left by these words have a determining influence on all the present and visible words of the first speaker. We sense that this . . . is a conversation of the most intense kind, for each present, uttered word responds and reacts with its every fibre to the invisible speaker, points to something outside itself, beyond its own limits, to the unspoken words of another person. . . . The other's discourse . . . is merely implied, but the entire structure of speech would be completely different if there were not this reaction to another person's implied words.

Such *hidden polemic* and *hidden dialogue* Bakhtin identifies in all Dostoevski's mature novels. He goes on:

By no means all historical situations permit the ultimate semantic authority of the creator to be expressed without mediation in direct, unrefracted, unconditional authorial discourse. When there is no access to one's own personal "ultimate" word, then every thought, feeling, experience must be refracted through the medium of someone else's discourse, someone else's style, someone else's manner.

It would be as naive in Dostoevski's case as in Breytenbach's to argue that a change in "historical situation," specifically the removal of external censorship, would have resulted in "direct, unrefracted, unconditional authorial discourse" from which hidden dialogue would have been absent. Censorship, or at least the office of the censor, is not the sole "semantic authority" at which Bakhtin hints. But the work Breytenbach did in the period from 1975 to 1982 was written under extraordinarily restricted circumstances, and, even though there was opportunity afterwards for revision, it bears traces, not always in the most obvious way, of a censored origin. As the concept of hidden contestatory dialogue opens up hidden areas of Dostoevskian discourse, it also alerts us to the possibility of a hidden contestation in Breytenbach. In the following discussion of Breytenbach's prison writings, I will be concentrating on hidden voices *against* which Breytenbach speaks.

Even in detention, before his trial, Breytenbach was allowed to write. The poems that emerged were published as **Voetskrif** (*Footwriting*), dedicated to his principal interrogator, Colonel Broodryk, at the latter's insistence: "You dedicate this to me and I allow you to have it published," as Breytenbach reported it. One poem had to be omitted.

In prison, writing was permitted on four conditions: that it would be shown to no other prisoner or warder, that it would not be smuggled out, that each piece would be handed in for safekeeping when completed, that all notes would be destroyed. Four volumes of poetry from the prison period, making up Parts I-IV of **The Undanced Dance,** were eventually published.

In **True Confessions** Breytenbach addresses his position as a prisoner vis-à-vis the censor: "A bizarre situation . . . when you write knowing that the enemy is reading over your shoulder . . . , knowing also that you are laying bare the most intimate and the most personal nerves and pulsebeats in yourself to the barbarians, to the cynical ones who will gloat over this." Besides this testimony, there is textual evidence that at least some of the poems of **The Undanced Dance,** even as published, are, in the most obvious sense, censored. For instance, an untitled poem in **Lewendood,** a rather inconsequential two-stanza lullaby, appears in translation in *Judas Eye* in what one must conclude was the originally intended form: with a third stanza in which a litany of South African relocation camps and razed settlements ("night-hooded names / I'm not yet allowed to say") is added to the litanies of sacked cities and death camps in the earlier stanzas.

Before turning to poems in which a hidden dialogue can be read, I would like to point to the contrasting phenomenon of the monologic poem. The most extreme example is the poem entitled **"Place of Refuge,"** from which I quote at length.

> there were insects in your beards
> a slipperiness around the supple kernels of your
>   eyes
> and soft saliva threads plaited about the red
>   tongue
> but the soft laughter and taunting were worse than
>   a dog
>   barking
> high priests of prejudice
> the further you persecute us the more brutal you
>   become
> unthinking retrogression to more primitive,
>   archetypal
>   behavior
> a joint grubbing for psycho-amnesia
> buried beneath mud is the pigs' god-idea . . .
>
> and on our trail your sniggers degenerated
> with battle-axes bringing light and smoldering
>   torches
> the dim sign of your heads with bruises for
>   features
> and the mouths slackened in an idiot babble
> and you have no knowledge any more of who
>   you were
> no laws any more to join freedom to responsibility
> no conscience any more belonging to a field of
>   reference—
> just that we must be exterminated

With its catalogue of images from horror films, this poem carries out a demonization, a bestialization of the enemy; perhaps also an exorcism, an anathematization. Insofar as the speech of the enemy is "an idiot babble," insofar as he is without self-awareness or conscience, no dialogue, open or hidden, is possible with him. The poem is itself, in fact, not only monologue but the most violent repudiation of dialogue.

"(Language Struggle)" exemplifies an intermediate form. It speaks in the tired, lifeless voice of a "grey reservist of over a hundred years" addressing "you" who are young, black, and rebellious:

> we will recite the ABC to you from the beginning
> we will tell you what's what
> with the guidelines of our Christian National
>   Education . . .
>
> You will learn to be obedient,
> obedient and subservient.
> And you will learn to use the Language [Afri
>   kaans],
> you will use it subserviently

In Bakhtin's system, this is "double-voiced discourse," not yet truly dialogic, in which the writer takes possession of another's discourse for his own purpose—in this case, one presumes, a satiric one. I have already pointed to the ambivalence of this procedure, an ambivalence of which Breytenbach seems to be aware: "taking possession of" always raises the question, who is taking possession of whom?

Side by side with this poem we can set **"The Conquerors"**:

> because we would not acknowledge them as
>   human beings
> everything human in us dried up
> and we cannot grieve over our dying
>   because we wanted nothing more than fear
>   and hatred
> we did not recognize the human uprising of
>   humanity
> and tried to find rough solutions but too late
> the flowers in the fire
>
> no one is interested in our solutions—
>
> we are past understanding
> we are of another kind
> we are the children of Cain

Again the voice is lifeless. Though it shifts from past to present tense, it speaks from beyond the grave, epitaph more than elegy. But this time a dialogue of sorts is occurring, carried on more by the voice of the past (which uses the language of the living, of *menslikheid*, humanity) rather than the voice of the present. **"(Language Struggle)"** and **"The Conquerors"** speak for two moments in the history of white domination: a moment of self-ignorance and a moment of fatalistic self-knowledge. The voice is the same in both cases: the voice of a sleepwalker in the corridors of history, the voice of unregenerate, doomed colonialism.

The obvious question is: why does Breytenbach say "we" in both poems when he means "you"? What is achieved in disguising accusation as self-accusation, or in assuming the voice of someone one repudiates? Can these people not speak for themselves in their own voices, issue their own grim ukases, their own despairing epitaphs? Why must Breytenbach speak for *both* sides? Why surrogate monologue, but also, why hidden dialogue, why even a hidden polemic with an enemy who belongs to the realm of the dead?

The answer is as obvious as the question. As a matter of brute fact, the speech of the enemy against which Breytenbach directs himself is never as open, naked, brutal as he would wish it to be. It is, on the contrary, evasive, circuitous, self-censored. Locating the murderous and/or self-destructive heart of Afrikaner nationalism is like grappling with Proteus. Or, to put it in another way, the Afrikaner puts up a more expert case for himself in the dock of history than Breytenbach's two speakers do. What Breytenbach performs in these poems is ventriloquism in two different forms; but it is also in both cases a preemption of the enemy's speech, and, to that extent, censorship: a presentation of the enemy's case in heightened or parodic but finally self-damaging form in a medium to which the enemy does not have access (for in the reality of present-day politics, white South African nationalism has access to the reader's ear only as accused, never as prosecutor).

Therefore, although there is indeed a dialogue, or a dialogization, relating to these two poems and others like them, it is not a dialogue *in* them so much as a dialogue *around* them, a dialogue "in the air," so to speak, concerning the right and the power to speak. It is a dialogue in which Breytenbach has the enemy in a double bind. As long as you speak the language of naked colonial domination, he says, no one will listen to you. They will listen only to those who speak *of* you, or to whose who, like myself, pretending to speak for you from within you, speak a message that confirms what everyone already knows about you. And as long as we speak for you, we will give you the voice of naked colonial domination. Thus speaks Breytenbach in what we can think of as the frame around the poems.

Perhaps because the confrontations they play out are so onesided, it is hard to detect in these two poems any real engagement of energy. In contrast, consider **"—'n Spieëlvars—"**:

> you! you! you!
> it's you I want to talk to cunt

> you ride around without saddle or driver's
>   license
> in the gutters and yards of my verses
> my death
> you dig around with your lance in the white
>   acres
> where I wanted to multiply
> for nation and fatherland
> (but soon there will be nothing left of either)
> my death
> . . . .
> you with your yellow eyes you with the left hand
> you with the missing beard you with the sand
> over the tongue
> with your nine-year sentence like a pregnancy
> I'll make you a widower chop-chop

> for you make me shiver
> you make plaints
> of pleasure
> you lay the cold caress of your lips
> here upon my life
> and *here* and *here*
> come kiss me in my mouth
> you hand-picked dog
> come and draw lines through my young thoughts
> and pack stones over my slack wings

> must I wait still longer?
> o my snow-white shadow Death
> my own secret police
> I will be yours forever
> and you are
> mine mine mine

The imprint of Sylvia Plath lies heavily on this poem, not least in its jagged rhythms and wild swings of mood. But from Plath Breytenbach has learned something deeper too: that I and You need not stand for fixed positions. The I here is the vindictive, death-ridden jailer and killer, but he is also the self that longs for liberation despite seeing no other form of liberation looming but death (his own death, not that of others, one hastens to add). *You* is clearly Breytenbach the prisoner, in comic form; but he is also the persecuting figure of the oppressed slave, the lover death whose perverse embrace ("*here* and *here*") he craves, the ever-watchful other in the mirror, and, finally, a figure with wings that answer to his own (unused?) wings. In fact, many of the avatars of the I—censor, secret policeman, winged guardian-persecutor—are shared by the You. What we have is a true mirror-poem, *spieëlvers*, in which it is not clear what is self, what image. The end of the poem thus looks (eagerly) forward to a moment not only when the self is possessed by death but when death is possessed by the self. It is a poem of accelerating dialogical frenzy in which it is no longer possible to say what the *position* of the self is: the interchange between self and other is, in effect, continuous. Insofar as the poem *reflects* on the process of gathering frenzy, it is a poem *about* the process of imitative violence, a poem that reveals that violence by enacting it.

> Looking into South Africa is like looking into the mirror at midnight when one has pulled a face and a train blew its whistle and one's image stayed there, fixed for all eternity. A horrible face, but one's own.

So wrote Breytenbach in 1971. This figure of a man looking into a mirror dominates Breytenbach's retrospective postprison writings. Out of the transaction between the watcher and the figure in the mirror, spy and persecutor watching him back, come glimpses of the truth of himself. The surface of the mirror and the surface of the blank page touched by the pen become indistinguishable: moving the pen, the self both creates and calls up on that surface a sardonic counterself mocking his effort to see himself transparently, telling him to try again. The figure in the mirror behaves, in fact, just like the security policemen who, at the time of Breytenbach's first interrogation, put two blank pages in front of him and told him to write down the story of his life; then, when he was finished, read them, tore them up, and told him to try again.

What has changed in the decade since 1971 is the attitude to the face in the mirror. In 1971 Breytenbach was still reacting with horrified fascination, disgust, and a certain dark glee: a complex but essentially reactive response. After prison, in *True Confessions, Mouroir,* and *Book: Part One,* the relationship has become more purposeful, as though, realizing that he is manacled/married to the mirror-self for life, Breytenbach has settled down to make the most of the relationship.

Breytenbach drafted *True Confessions* by talking into a microphone, a process that he calls "this jumbletalk, this trial." What truth will emerge from the trial? Whatever it is, it cannot be predicted: only in the process of dialogue between self and mirror/page will it reveal itself. If there were to be a new interrogation, a new trial, the truth would come out differently: "I'd be somebody else—as sincere, as keen to help, as obsessed by the necessity to confess." Thus the posture of the writer before the mirror/page is assimilated with the attitude of the cooperative prisoner under interrogation. And who is the interrogator? In a sense, the reader who wants to read what Breytenbach has to say; but also the self that writes itself. "Mr. Investigator[:] *you* know that we're always inventing our lives. . . . You and I entwined and related, parasite and prey[,] image and image-mirror."

Thus far we have only another ingenious poststructuralist

figure of textual self-production, writing as a looking in a mirror and construction of the self, without any particularity. But the African connection has not been elided. Coming to the end of his long confession, Breytenbach can write:

> Mr. Investigator. . . . I see you now as my dark mirror-brother. We need to talk, brother I. I must tell you what it was like to be an albino in a white land. We are forever united by the intimate knowledge of the depravity man will stoop to. Son of Africa. Azanians.

Who is the interrogator here? Not (or not only) the persecuting white brother who polices the psyche but a black mirror-brother, just as haunting and persecutory, an accomplice in a crime (an historical crime?) in which there have been two parties, not one. Simone Weil is helpful. In every act of destruction, she writes, the I leaves behind its trace. "A hurtful act is the transference to others of the degradation which we bear in ourselves." Since the victim is no longer single, but shares the degradation of the oppressor, the I becomes double, multiply double: interrogator and revolutionary, criminal and victim, colonizer and colonized, even censor and writer. The black in the mirror is not Other but other/self, "brother I."

The long talking in the empty room with which *True Confessions* began thus culminates not in dialogue with the dark brother but in the discovery that for true knowledge to come about, dialogue must take place with the mirror. So when Breytenbach writes, in retrospect, that he does not regret having gone through the "underground" experience, the word is rich in significance, referring not only to his history as a secret agent and a prisoner but to a history of blind burrowing that has led not to the light but instead to the illumination, the insight that light-seeking is a process of blind burrowing. "What one has gone through becomes a new corridor outlining the innards of the labyrinth; it is a continuation of the looking for the Minotaur, that dark centre which is the I (eye), that Mister I [mystery]."

The white policeman, the black revolutionary, enemies brought together in the mirror. Is the mirror the place, then, where history is transcended? Does the dialogue with the mirror-self extend to dialogue between the selves in the mirror? Can dialogue with the mirror be trusted to proceed peaceably, or will it degenerate into hysterical confrontation such as we saw in **"Place of Refuge"** and see again in the 1986 "Pretext" to *End Papers,* where control of dialogue is allowed to break down (in a controlled experiment) and an exhibition is given of hysterical self-accusation, a spiraling descent into "the bottomless pit of deprecation and disgust"? Can the twins be reconciled?

These questions are beyond the scope of *True Confessions.*

It is in *Mouroir* that Breytenbach tries to put into practice—
the practice of writing—the theory outlined in *True Confessions*. *Mouroir* is an assemblage of stories, parables,
meditations, and fragments linked by the coupled symbol-
isms of mirror and labyrinth. The text is a kind of Ariadne's
thread that Breytenbach spins behind himself as he advances through the labyrinth of his fictionalizing toward a
meeting with something that is both the self beckoning from
the mirror—Mister I—and the monstrous other who will not
be recuperated into amity: Death.

Of course a merging of self with mirror-self is not achieved,
the surface of the mirror/page does not melt away, the heart
of the labyrinth is not attained. Instead, a new surface re-
curs at every turn, becoming a point of entry into yet another branch of the labyrinth. The text moves forward by a
process of metamorphosis of images, as in dreams. Text becomes coextensive with life: text will not end till writing ends;
writing will not end till breath ends.

What has Breytenbach done? By seeing or claiming to see
through the hostile identity in the mirror, by making the surface of the mirror something that one goes *through*, that is
merely an opening to an infinite progress, he has deferred
the confrontation with his twin, and further has turned this
deferring into a model of textual production. On the basis
of the moment of genesis he describes in *True Confessions*—the moment when the police interrogator returns his
life-story to him with the comment "Try again"—he has constructed a program of writing which is indistinguishable from
the theoretical justification for that program.

But the moment of "Try again" is not the only moment that
the writing again and again rehearses. Out of the repertoire
of memory, the writing repeats even more crucially the moment of Breytenbach's confession to the court when pride
had to be swallowed and humiliating apologies uttered—
when the role of a child repenting its naughtiness had to be
embraced—*and* when this self-humbling was refused as not
good enough to deflect a punitive sentence.

How does Breytenbach account for that calamitous turn of
events? "Without being political it was an attempt to explain
how I got to be standing where I was, without rejecting my
convictions," he writes of the statement he made in his defense. "Read it—you will also hear the insidious voice of
the [security police] controller in it. It was in [his] hands a
week before the trial commenced, and Vorster himself had it
on his desk before it was read in court."

It is hard to know quite how to read this account. Nowhere
does Breytenbach accuse the police, or B. J. Vorster, of trying to influence the trial magistrate. Nevertheless, the implication seems to be that a deal was made (apologies,
self-abasement, public acceptance of the authority of the fa-

ther in return for a lighter sentence) and that the deal was
reneged on. Cryptically, Breytenbach writes: "It [is] not my
intention [in this book] to take revenge on a system or on
certain people—at least, I don't think it [is]." And he goes
on: "We are too closely linked for that."

We are too closely linked for that? Have family ties ever been
a barrier to revenge? The motives behind *True Confessions*
and *Mouroir*—the main texts of Breytenbach's mirror-
phase—are extraordinarily complex. They include, yes, a
primitive desire to get back at the people who shut him up:
the torrents of infantile name-calling, in which people's
names are turned into, precisely, cacophony (B. J. Vorster
as Chief Sitting Bull, for instance), testify to that. They also
include a more cautious project—instigated, perhaps, by a
realization of how infantile it is to throw excrement at those
figures of power who reject his stories of himself—to incorporate the censor-figure into himself (calling it the figure in
the mirror, calling it the I) and *manage* it in that way. How
successful this incorporation is, is doubtful: the test, I have
suggested, is *Mouroir*, and *Mouroir* is, finally, an inconsequential work, a doodling with Ariadne's thread rather than
a search for the Minotaur. Breytenbach is not without moments of clarity about how essentially magical his plan is
for mastering the voice that says No. Writing is a way of
survival, he writes. "But . . . at the same time it becomes the
exteriorization of my imprisonment, . . . the walls of my confinement."

The hysteria of a consciousness that encounters wherever
it looks nothing but reflections of itself had already received
extreme embodiment in Dostoevski's 1864 *Notes from Underground*. Like Dostoevski's narrator, Breytenbach shuttles
between self-accusation and accusation of the reader; like
him, he takes up the pen in order to get a grip on himself, to
try to control a sterile multiplication of selves (Breytenbach
describes *Book: Part One* as "the journal of an attempt to
stay clear or gain clarity"). One of the fates of confession—
of secular confession at least—since Rousseau has been to
spin itself out endlessly in an effort to reach beyond self-
reflection to truth. In both Breytenbach and Dostoevski the
task of taking charge of the process of self-reflection at first
seems to the narrating self no more than a preliminary task
to be performed (a sentry to be passed) before the real work,
the real storytelling, can begin: in Dostoevski's case, Part II
of *Notes*, in Breytenbach's case the story of life underground. Only later does the realization dawn that getting to
the real self (finding the Mystery I) is a life's task, like cleaning the Augean stables.

In his public, political person, Breytenbach expresses attitudes towards the censorship of literature typical of most
cosmopolitan, progressive intellectuals. "Censorship is an
act of shame. Censorship is a motion of no confidence in
your fellow and in yourself. It has to do with manipulation,

with power, with . . . repression." For the writer to give his consent to being censored is fatal. "It takes root inside you as a kind of interiorized paternalism. . . . You become your own castrator." There can be no compromise. "Once you submit to the thought restrictions of the power managers, enter their game, . . . they have already won the day."

There is no hint in these utterances that the policeman/censor of the imagination is already in place in Breytenbach as his mirror-self, or that writing, as in *Mouroir,* is, if not playing at the censor's game, at least playing a game with the censor.

There may be a certain appeal in thinking that, despite all the years of being tracked in the labyrinth of the self, the policeman/censor has at this crucial public moment rendered himself invisible, censored himself out of Breytenbach's awareness. But it is more fruitful to introduce here the distinction between esoteric and exoteric doctrine. No writer can without ambivalence welcome or invite censorship. Nevertheless, every writer knows that he or she writes against a manifold of internalized resistances which are in essence no different to the internalized censor. Breytenbach goes further than an acknowledgment of the fact of inner censorship, and therefore further than most writers, when he turns the confrontation with the censor into not only a subject of rumination but a textually productive dialogue. *True Confessions,* like the first part of *Notes from Underground,* is *about* being confronted by a self-knowledge which is also a form of blockage or deflection; *Mouroir* whatever its weakness, is, like the second part of *Notes from Underground,* a way of turning the deflections, if not the blockages, into narrative.

The reason why the mirror-couple of writer and censor must remain part of the writer's esoteric doctrine (which is by no means to say that it is secret) is that, as a theory of the vicissitudes of blockage and deflection, it is inherently incompatible with political practice. Insofar as there is a political discourse about the censor, it is a discourse of *control*: either of taking control of the censor or of evading his control.

In the general run of events, writers have confronted the censor in the genre of polemic, where dialogue, such as it has been, has followed a course of accelerating violence and loss of difference. Certainly in Breytenbach's writings before the mirror-phase we find violence of language and crudity of thought whenever the figure of the censor is evoked: the polemic is simply incorporated into the text. The question raised by the post-1980 poetry is: does the incorporation (at least esoterically) of the censor/persecutor/policeman into the process of composition itself provide him with a way out of the automatism of imitative violence? Can we go so far as to say that Breytenbach has found a way out of imitative violence *tout court*?

The answer must remain suspended. But if we consider the fate of the literature of self-reflexiveness from Rousseau's *Confessions* to Beckett's *The Unnamable*, it seems all too likely to be No. Turning the gaze from the window to the mirror has never been a *way out* or a *way past*: it has always proved to be what Breytenbach in *Mouroir* discovers it to be: a diversion.

Barend J. Toerien   (review date Autumn 1991)

SOURCE: Review of *Soos die so* and *All One Horse: Fictions and Images,* in *World Literature Today,* Vol. 65, No. 4, Autumn 1991, p. 756.

[*In the following review, Toerien offers a generally positive assessment of* Soos die so *and finds the writing in* All One Horse *luminous and reminiscent of South American magical realism.*]

Breyten Breytenbach's new collection of poems with the enigmatic title *Such As* or *As Is* marks his return to the Afrikaans language after a series of prose works in English. In the foreword, written in Paris as a 1974 New Year's resolution, he undertakes to write a poem each day for the rest of the year. This he manages to do for more than half a year before faltering; but in September 1988 he takes up the project again and finishes off the year. His incarceration in jail intervened, of course, and what is remarkable is that the later entries do not differ much in style from those of 1974, presumably because they are all diary jottings, spontaneous and free of fixed meter or rhyme. It must be kept in mind that the writer's prison volumes such as *Eklips, (yk), Lewendood,* and *Buffalo Bill* were carefully wrought poems, mostly in standard forms, a fact perhaps attributable to the time available and to the lack of distractions?

Breytenbach has lost none of his poetic mastery, and he ranges widely with effortless ease. Included here are tender love poems to his wife, irritations expressed at the agony of the writing act and the uselessness of poetry, nostalgia for South Africa mixed with scorn for his country's political doctrines, meditations on Africa ("He repulses you, pulls you closer / holds you tight, strikes you lame / with love in the magical circle / of sand and poverty / and fire that lives under the scorching: / you stand shivering, exile of Africa"), and outrage at such injustices as the killing of Tiro by a letter bomb, to name but a few of the themes. There is again, as in his earlier books, the tendency to "milk" multiple meanings from words through accentuation, hyphenation, or shifts in spelling ("manieskrifte" for "manuskripte"); this tends to be irritating. Fixed idioms are given playful twists ("I pull my dream till daybreak"), and there are willful echoes of other poets (Yeats in "When you are old and small and dressed in black"), but more so of Afrikaans poets. Time and time again the verse is lit up by sharp, evocative flashes ("at night you shrink / your shadow seeks shelter in you"; "light has a white voice").

The poems are direct, like untouched first drafts, and at times have the joyous simplicity of a Cat Stevens. It must be stated, however, that the volume as a whole would have had a greater impact if some of the chaff had been left out. Still, when good, Breytenbach is very very good, as my translation of **"12 April 1974"** may indicate.

> he got up and raised both arms
> and a day fell away, a gray one
> that never would be repeated just that way
> and he revealed in his night miner's voice:
> I carry my pain alone
> it is ingrown in me
> quite like a toenail
> it is the carapaced being
> which is no one's fault
> I am the flesh, my pain the bone
> when a dog someday
> buries it in the garden
> I will be altogether gone.

All One Horse is a volume of twenty-seven short prose pieces and a like number of reproductions of watercolors by the poet and painter. The texts are surrealistic to the extreme, phantasmagorical even, yet based on clear, everyday realities. The title is explained in the introduction as taken from Chuang Tzu: "Heaven and earth are one finger, all things are one horse"—not that this clarifies much. The image of the horse does recur in the pieces time and again as a symbol for freedom, the imagination, for life itself.

The texts have the clear, nightmarish quality of dreams or at times of childlike visions, and though no place or character or incident can be pinned down or recognized (as with the magic realism of the South Americans), they all are recognizable only too well. Statements that occur in the text itself characterize the book very aptly: "Some dreams have the contours and cavities of skulls," and "Memory is imagination." Breytenbach has turned out to be a master of English. The language is rich, exact, and never far from exuberance, as in the line "It was his wish to be happy, like a radio playing all to itself on the beach."

Robert L. Berner (review date Winter 1991)

SOURCE: Review of *Memory of Snow and of Dust*, in *World Literature Today*, Vol. 65, No. 1, Winter 1991, pp. 175-76.

[*In the following review, Berner calls* Memory of Snow and of Dust *a "remarkable development" in Breytenbach's literary canon.*]

Since his release from prison, Breyten Breytenbach has returned to Paris, resumed his career as a distinguished Afrikaans poet, and begun to write in English. An introductory poem in **Memory of Snow and Dust** says that "the biography I am . . . writing is always [a] book of myself." We are tempted, therefore, to look for autobiographical analogies in the novel, which deals with a South African in Paris who is arrested when he returns to South Africa on behalf of his political party and also with a South African writer who has exiled himself to Paris after serving a prison term. Such an approach, however, does not begin to take account of the novel's extraordinary richness.

In the first of two sections Meheret, an Ethiopian journalist in Paris, meets Mano, a "Cape Coloured" actor, and is pregnant when he returns to South Africa, where he is arrested, charged with a murder he did not commit, and condemned to death. Her story, addressed to her unborn child and telling of her life in Ethiopia, her parents and ancestry, and her affair with Mano, is often interrupted by Barnum, who is called "the ghost writer," and this section seems to be his account of the relationship of Meheret and Mano. The second section is Mano's description of his final experiences in South Africa, which he imagines Barnum is writing but which is also, he says, his own screenplay. The result is a remarkable display of intellectual fireworks with many cross-references, a number of them autobiographical, a multivoiced work that balances the various truths about the complexities of South Africa. To cite just one example, Barnum introduces Ka'afir as a cynic who describes South Africa as a place where all the tribes, including the whites, hate one another—"How wonderful it is to be able to kill in the name of Freedom!"—and later he defends the building of prisons as a means of reducing unemployment. In a screenplay with which Barnum interrupts Meheret's story, however, a black woman is tortured to reveal the whereabouts of her terrorist brother, also named Ka'afir. Later Mano encounters another Ka'afir in an adjoining cell awaiting execution. Finally, to complicate matters further, in one of the essays in **End Papers** Breytenbach identifies Ka'afir as "an African poet, my friend." We are left wondering whether Ka'afir is an actual friend inserted into the novel or a fictitious character in the essay.

In another essay Breytenbach attributes to Denise Levertov a sentiment that illuminates his intentions: "In the end only language can be my home." Permanently exiled, cut off from his origins, writing in a second language or in a first for an inevitably minor audience, Breytenbach has taken refuge in the greater, if lonelier, country of language. In **Memory of Snow and Dust** he has produced a deeply personal work which is also a rich display of artistry. Much of it, particularly in the latter section, is so obscure as to be almost incomprehensible, but it will repay study by those who have followed Breytenbach's remarkable career, in which it is a major development.

J. M. Coetzee   (essay date 1992)

SOURCE: "Breyten Breytenbach: *True Confessions of an Albino Terrorist* and *Mouroir*," in *Doubling the Point: Essays and Interviews,* 1992, pp. 375-81.

[*In the following essay, Coetzee provides overviews of* True Confessions of an Albino Terrorist *and* Mouroir.]

South of the city of Cape Town lies a tranquil, almost rural, suburb named (after the wine) Tokai, and zoned for white occupation only. Driving through Tokai you pass, on your right, forest and vineyard, on your left comfortable houses with spacious lawns and gardens. Then at a certain point the suburban idyll ends, giving way to a monotonous gray wall ten feet high, behind which you can glimpse watchtowers and blank-faced buildings. This is Pollsmoor, a maximum-security prison, the home at one time of ·Breyten Breytenbach, poet, painter, and convicted "terrorist." **The True Confessions of an Albino Terrorist** is the story of how Breytenbach came to be in Pollsmoor, what he did there, and how he departed.[1]

Breyten Breytenbach was born in 1939 into an ordinary small-town Afrikaner family. One of his brothers became an officer in the South African armed forces, another a well-known journalist. Breytenbach's comments on his brothers give an idea of how far he has moved from his origins. The first he calls "a trained (and enthusiastic) killer," the other "a fellow traveller of the [security police], with decidedly fascist sympathies." Breyten, the maverick of the family, early made a name for himself in literary circles, and came to be seen as the leading poetic talent of his generation. Even after he left South Africa, took up residence in Paris, married a woman who would be called in Afrikaans *anderskleurig*, "of another color" (meaning of a color other than white), and involved himself in the antiapartheid movement, he remained the idol of much of the Afrikaans literary world. In 1973 he obtained official dispensation to visit his homeland. Audiences at poetry readings gave him and his wife a rapturous welcome. The word in the air was "reconciliation." The prodigal son would yet return, the breach would be healed, and all would be well.

The next time Breytenbach visited South Africa, circumstances were different. He had shaved off his beard, and he carried a passport identifying him as Christian Galaska, citizen of France. His mission was to recruit members to Okhela, a resistance organization that had already embarrassed the West German government by stealing classified documents and revealing details of military cooperation between Bonn and Pretoria. Tipped off by an informer in Europe, the South African security police kept "Galaska" under surveillance for a while, then closed in and arrested him. At the end of a trial conducted in surprisingly subdued terms, Breytenbach was given a stiff nine-year sentence. (In **True Confessions** he claims that the authorities reneged on a deal to let him off lightly in return for not conducting a political defense.) He spent two years in isolation in Pretoria Central Prison, a spell from which he emerged with his sanity miraculously unimpaired, followed by five years in Pollsmoor. In 1982 he was released and flown off to France.

The Breytenbach case has troubled and continues to trouble Afrikaners. Breytenbach took the position from the beginning that he had gone into exile, that the reasons for his exile were political, and that only changes that would bring all political exiles home would bring him home. Afrikaner public opinion, on the other hand, particularly liberal opinion, preferred to see his defection as a family matter, a generational quarrel within the greater Afrikaner family, to be sorted out within the family. To those who hold this view it remains possible for Breytenbach to be a great Afrikaans writer while still adopting the stance of a rebel. But in **True Confessions** Breytenbach spells out his position anew. He is not a rebel but a revolutionary, in will if not in deed. And he is no longer one of the family.

> To be an Afrikaner is a political definition. It is a blight and a provocation to humanity . . . I do not consider myself to be an Afrikaner. To be an Afrikaner in the way they define it is to be a living insult to whatever better instincts we human beings may possess.

Given his unequivocal rejection of his Afrikaner birthright, why should Breytenbach have received from the police and prison authorities the odd touches of indulgence, mixed in with the usual harshness and cruelty, that we find described in this book? Breytenbach suggests that Red Cross and other international observers exerted a cautionary influence on his jailers. His own deliberately unheroic attitude ("Be pliant and weak when you have to. Cry if you must") may have contributed, too.

But I think there is a deeper reason. Prisoners in South Africa are not permitted to conduct economic activities from within jail. Breytenbach is a professional painter and writer. The letter of the law would have been on the side of the authorities if they had prohibited him from painting or writing in prison. In fact he was given permission to write, though not to paint. The works he wrote in prison, *Mouroir* among them, were taken into custody as they were completed and returned to him on his release. The censors have allowed the publication of these works in South Africa. The public buys and reads them. They are honored with literary prizes. Why? Breytenbach writes:

> People who absolutely rejected me and my ideas and what my life stood for but who, perhaps from an obscure sense of uncomfortableness, if not guilt, and also, surely, because of a true concern for my work, applied to the minister to allow me to continue writing. "For the sake of Afrikaans literature." Was it a way for some of them to establish in their own minds their evenhandedness?

Perhaps. The fact is that, by the standards of the Afrikaans literary tradition, Breytenbach is a great poet. He is a poet, moreover, whose emotional makeup includes feelings of passionate intimacy with the South African landscape that, Afrikaners like to think, can be expressed only in Afrikaans, and therefore (here comes the sinister turn in the reasoning) can be experienced only by the Afrikaner. Closeness of fit between land and language is—so the reasoning goes—proof of the Afrikaner's *natural* ownership of the land. (Ideas like these are not new: *natural* congruence between a people, a language, and an ancestral landscape is a commonplace of German Romanticism.) There is a considerable communal investment in presenting the Afrikaans literary tradition—a tradition, let it not be forgotten, that is the occasion for a vast echoing ideological discourse in classrooms and cultural organs—as speaking with a single voice on the subject of the land. There is a certain interest, even for official, establishment Afrikaans culture, in seeing Breytenbach as the bearer of a talent that he cannot, despite himself, betray; and to view his politics as an aberration that does not touch his poetic soul. There is an interest in not acknowledging that there can coexist in a single breast both a belief in a unitary democratic South Africa and a profound Afrikaans *digterskap*, poetness.

Hence the notion that the "terrorist" in Breytenbach can be incarcerated and punished while the poet in him can be left free. By acting as though Breytenbach must be a radically divided personality, one self a poet to be saved, the other self a traitor to be condemned, the greater Afrikaner family preserves its belief (and perhaps does so sincerely and in good faith) that the language, the mystical nation-essence, is greater than the fallible vessels who bear it.

The embrace of the Afrikaner, stony yet loving, finds its expression in the insufferable intimacy forced on Breytenbach by his security police interrogators, in which compassion and cruelty seem at times pathologically intertwined ("I am convinced that some of the people they have killed in detention probably died when the interrogator was in a paroxysm of unresolved frustrations, even that the interrogator killed in an awkward expression of love and sympathy"). The interrogators feed upon, and therefore depend upon, their prisoners. But Breytenbach extends the scope of the Hegelian master-slave dyad. What is the difference, he asks himself, between the "true confession" he utters into a microphone in Palermo in 1983 (eventually to become this book) and the "true confession" his interrogators demanded in Pretoria in 1975? Are not both of them answers to the question "What is the truth of your mission to South Africa?"? Before the interrogator, before the microphone, before the blank page, Breytenbach finds himself in the same position, staring at himself. So he develops the mirror as the master metaphor of his book; and the most interesting passages are the dialogues he conducts with the figure in the mirror, which is variously the cruel interrogator, the "true" Breytenbach, and the dark brother-African: "I see you now as my dark mirror-brother. We need to talk, brother I. I must tell you what it was like to be an albino in a white land. We are forever united by the ultimate knowledge of the depravity man will stoop to. Son of Africa. Azanians."

To his "dark mirror-brother" Breytenbach expresses his misgivings about the postrevolutionary South Africa of the future, which he foresees will fall under a no less totalitarian regime than the present one, and his bitterness against the "fat, institutionalized friends in the liberation movement" who sent him off on his fool-hardy mission in the first place. Bitterness emerges even more strongly in his judgments on white South Africa: "Let that bloated village of civil servants and barbarians [Pretoria] be erased from the face of the earth." As he observes, one of the effects of prolonged isolation is to kill off parts of you, "and these parts will never again be revived."

What will survive of Breytenbach's *True Confessions*, I think, is not the narrative of capture, interrogation, and imprisonment, absorbing enough though that is, nor the apologia he gives for his quixotic foray into the fortress of the enemy, valuable though that is for its analysis of the appeal of direct political action to the intellectual. A feature of Breytenbach's poetry is that it *stops at nothing*: there is no limit that cannot be exceeded, no obstacle that cannot be leaped, no commandment that cannot be questioned. His writing characteristically *goes beyond*, in more senses than one, what one had thought could be said in Afrikaans. The pages of *True Confessions* that stand out, that could have been written by no one else, are those in which he tries to feel his way into the experience of the condemned man, into the experience of death itself, and then into the moral world of the men who order deaths, build prisons, carry out tortures, and then into the very interior of the mad thinking of "security" itself.

Mouroir was written during Breytenbach's prison years. It is a more substantial work than *True Confessions*, but more difficult, and probably of less general appeal. In quality it is variable. Subtitled "Mirrornotes of a Novel," it consists of thirty-eight pieces, some short, some long. Some are no more than jottings. Others are profoundly impressive in their evocation of a terminal landscape, a landscape from beyond the war, where children go about giving birdcalls to lure the fled birds back to the earth. Though certain fragments are linked closely enough for us to follow an erratic, dreamlike narrative line through them, we would be hard put to form the pieces into the skeleton of any conceivable novel. We are better advised to read the book as an assemblage of stories, parables, meditations, and fragments, some of them centering on the themes of imprisonment, death, and freedom, others linked by the recurrent figures of the mirror and the labyrinth (the title of course plays on *mourir*, to die, and *miroir*, mirror). It is not too fanciful to conceive of the text that Breytenbach has left us as a kind of Ariadne's thread that he spins behind him as he advances through the labyrinth of his fictions (and his dreams) toward a meeting with the monstrous Other who is also both the self in the mirror and death.

But a merging with the mirror-self is not achieved, the heart of the labyrinth is not attained. Instead, as in Jean Cocteau's Orpheus films, the surface of the mirror becomes a hole of entry into another world, into yet another branch of the labyrinth. Thus we find Breytenbach's text moving forward by a continual process of metamorphosis, particularly a metamorphosis of landscape. Though the process seems dreamlike, the forward movement is purposeful, the motivations are not obscure, the connections are present on the surface or not too far beneath it. It is a form of writing that pays its respects to Kafka and Nabokov (one of Breytenbach's alter egos is called Gregor Samsa). In technique it owes much to the *nouveau roman*, though its focus is less on surfaces, as in Robbe-Grillet and Claude Simon, more on interiors and the properties of interiors: darkness, softness, wetness. Nevertheless, Breytenbach's voice is clearly his own.

The weakest sections are those in which Breytenbach works in the mode of the parable. When he deprives himself of the generative, metamorphosing powers of language and follows the more linear path of irony, the end results are thin. His irony gains bite only when he turns it on himself, as in his story about the radical writer who gives a press conference at the Rome airport before flying off to join the liberation struggle in South Africa: "Not in salons and ivory towers will revolutions be made. Purification in the struggle. Self-sacrifice. Freedom! (*Liberté!*) . . . Fierce fire in the pupils before the lashes are lowered."

How to write a revolutionary literature is a question to which *Mouroir* returns several times. One story deals with a writer who gives in to the pleas of friends and commences a conventional bourgeois tale of suburban adultery. Soon he discovers how hard it is to carry on writing when one's pants are soaked in horse blood. Nevertheless he plods on, in gathering darkness, till the fictional world he has created turns nasty, takes on a life of its own, and rends him.

The bloody horse alluded to here becomes a complex, ambivalent, and recurrent symbol in *Mouroir* as a whole. In the richly meaningful cover Breytenbach designed for the Afrikaans edition, a naked pink (albino?) figure (the artist?) passes by a barred window, his head covered (replaced?) by the huge eyeless severed head of a horse: stalking horse, Trojan horse; also Minotaur, mirror-taurus, figure of death from the dead center of the labyrinth; also the ludicrous counterimage of the warlike, passionate centaur.

A word must be said about the translation. There exists no Afrikaans edition of *True Confessions*. The edition we have must be accepted as a work written in English by Breytenbach. However, tell-tale solecisms indicate that Breytenbach is translating, and sometimes mistranslating, from an Afrikaans original. *Mouroir*, on the other hand, appeared in South Africa in 1983 in an edition partly in English but mainly in Afrikaans. Since no translator is named in the preliminaries to the American edition, we are justified in inferring that Breytenbach again did some or all of the translation; and the recurrence of idiosyncratic mistranslations tends to confirm this conclusion.

While the translation of parts of *Mouroir* is little short of masterly, in other parts it is nothing short of inept. Examples: "And then he went away with the cancer" (instead of "And then he died of cancer"); "wire obstacle" (instead of "barbed-wire entanglement"); "sucking black" (instead of "pitch-black"); "a sentence of grass" (instead of "a strip of grass"). These mistranslations emerge from a cursory check of a few odd-sounding passages. A careful check would, I am sure, produce hundreds more. Should the author's response be that what I call mistranslations are in fact creative reworkings, I would have to reply that what we have been given to read remains a poor substitute for the original.

NOTES

[1] Breyten Breytenbach, *The True Confessions of an Albino Terrorist* (New York: Farrar, Straus and Giroux, 1985) and *Mouroir* (New York: Farrar, Straus and Giroux, 1984).

Helize van Vuuren   (review date Autumn 1992)

SOURCE: Review of *Hart-lam,* in *World Literature Today,* Vol. 66, No. 4, Autumn 1992, pp. 763-64.

[In the following review, van Vuuren finds Hart-lam *valuable to an understanding of Breytenbach's political and artistic vision.]*

Breyten Breytenbach is a complex phenomenon: painter, poet, prose writer, exile, ex-convict, and "terrorist," as well as public figure in the South African political and literary arena. He publishes creative work both in Afrikaans and in English, and these works span many genres. Between 1964 and 1991 he produced fourteen collections of poetry—all of them in Afrikaans, with English translations of some of his prison poetry (of which there are five collections) published in *Judas Eye, and Self Portrait/Deathwatch*. Apart from three books containing short prose pieces, he has also published two novels in Afrikaans, one in English (*Memory of Snow and of Dust,* 1988), a poetic manifesto, a travel journal (*A Season in Paradise,* 1976), and a collection of political pieces (*End Papers,* 1986), as well as the seminal South African prison autobiography, *The True Confessions of an Albino Terrorist* (1984).

Breytenbach's most recent publication is *Hart-Lam,* a slim volume of collected speeches (one in Afrikaans and three in English), given at various occasions in Stellenbosch, Cape Town, New York, and Stockholm. The first two speeches, **"Fragments of a Growing Awareness"** and **"A Dog at Dinner,"** were written for South African audiences and deal with the place of cultural activity within the political arena. Of more importance for the reader of South African literature and specifically for an understanding of Breytenbach's work are the two papers dealing variously with exile and with his view of his own work, **"The Long March from Hearth to Heart"** (New York, 25 October 1990) and **"Painting and Writing for Africa"** (Stockholm, 27 January 1991). In the New York speech Breytenbach deals incisively and extensively with the phenomenon of exile, with special reference to how it manifests itself in his own oeuvre: "Exile . . . showed me . . . the mechanisms of survival. It made my mother tongue into a 'homeland', a movable feast, indeed a dancing of the bones." Because of the oppressive regime of apartheid, South African literature is characterized, as is Russian literature, by an extensive corpus of writings on and from exile. **"The Long March from Hearth to Heart"** is a valuable addition to the greater understanding of this human condition and to how it influences creative writers and their work.

In the Stockholm paper Breytenbach comes to terms with his role in the political arena and with public expectations of him. Since his release from prison in South Africa (where he served almost eight years under the Act on Terrorism) Breytenbach seems to have become increasingly disen-

chanted with politics and the struggle for liberation, seeing his role as less of a political activist and more of a committed writer. In **"Painting and Writing for Africa"** he describes the way that people expect him to behave:

> I have the impression that people are waving their fists and shouting: "Tell us about exile! Give us, again and again, the juice extracted from your years in prison! Confirm for us that Afrikaans is a racist language and that the Boers are all fascist! Make us feel sorry for you! . . . Give us politics, none of your confusing and ambiguous artistic prattling!

Still, he refuses to fit into this prescribed role. Breytenbach states categorically: "I'm through with politics." *Hart-Lam* serves as a valuable introduction to one of the most important South African writers of today.

Lynn Freed (review date 28 November 1993)

SOURCE: "Beloved Bloody Country," in *Washington Post Book World,* Vol. XXIII, No. 48, November 28, 1993, p. 4.

[In the following review, Freed praises Breytenbach's ability in Return to Paradise *to be both evocative and satiric of South Africa and its people.]*

This wonderful book [*Return to Paradise*], the third in Breyten Breytenbach's trilogy of exile, incarceration and return, centers around a three-month visit he made to South Africa in 1991. The book is written with a wild heart and an unrelenting eye, and is fueled by the sort of rage that produces great literature.

After more than half a lifetime spent in exile—with the exception of a few visits home, and seven years in a South African prison for "terrorism"—Breytenbach opens *Return to Paradise* with the statement of statements for South African exiles and expatriates: "There is such a thing as an incurable nostalgia." And yet, so saying, he goes on to examine, to expose, to deride—sometimes gently, often savagely—the root and branch of the nostalgia, the nature of "the beloved bloody country."

"To my mind," he writes in the preface, "only a fool would pretend to understand comprehensively what South Africa is really about, or be objective and farsighted enough to glimpse its future course . . . It has been my pleasure to disagree with the living and the dead."

For the reader, it is sheer pleasure to go along for the journey. Breytenbach's writing reveals the eye of a painter, the ear of a poet. There is the keenest sense of immediacy in his writing, as if one were standing just behind him, moving with him through the thicket towards what passes for truth.

En route, no one is spared, certainly not Breytenbach himself. He talks of his own "white-sight," his own failure to see. Doubling back on an ecstatic description of a garden, a landscape, a mountain, he will remind himself and his reader that "along the edges of the well-to-do estates a disorderly metropolis of poverty is gnawing its way through."

"South Africa," he says in one of his characteristic litanies, "is the photographer's paradise: undefiled desert, landscapes, cloud-towers of fancy in the electric heavens, rubbish dumps where women and children scratch for sustenance; the sombre shifting shapes of galloping buffalo . . . white joggers with pink fat-rolls shuffling along to burn off the excess, hungry blacks trotting to work . . . the upper lip and the inflamed neck veins of the suburban housewife . . . the worried blind look of the writer."

And then, suddenly, in true South African style, he will roll into a textbook guide of class and race stereotypes, which, because they carry sufficient truth in them, can be hilarious. "Television presenters have weak eyes and they emit a language of their own—the Afrikaans a fulsome Germanic strain of throat-terrorism." "South African Jews have a sort of superior sympathy for the Boers." And, "it is habitual for youngish Afrikaners to wipe out their entire immediate families in one go, usually with a firearm."

Breytenbach's portraits themselves are extraordinary, resonant. Here, for instance, is Mandela. "Only the lips in repose betrayed him—severe, dark, aloof, bitter. It is the mouth which sometimes says more, and more eloquently, than the voice can; lips close over the unsayable: *This cannot be spoken about, so why bother?*"

And here is Jesse Jackson at an early Mandela rally "with shiny hair and shiny moustache and a camel hair coat and a nose for the television-lens like a fly for s—. Each time the camera looked his way he was on his feet with clenched fist held high and a pious tear in the combative eye . . ."

There are flashbacks to anti-apartheid meetings in other African countries, many of them engineered by Breytenbach himself, hilarious vignettes, diatribes against places, against people. White liberals, his friends included, "starry-eyed recent converts," white fascists, the ANC, "the new hegemony," blacks, browns, academics of course, other writers—all come under Breytenbach's passionate, furious, ironic eye. His reactions are not predictable, but they are always true, with a wonderful absence of heartfelt horror, never the shocked liberal gasp. "'Aren't you *ever* happy?'"

asks Albie Sachs, fellow ex-exile. "'Now that we've won, can't you *rejoice*?'"

But how can Breytenbach rejoice? He has the obstinate insight of the artist, the perspective of the philosopher, the remove of an old warrior in exile. Again and again, he returns to the subject of exile. It is, he says, "coming face to face with the self as mirror (or mirror as self?), and it strikes me that exiles often put pipes in their mouths to lift their hats jauntily to an imaginary mirror. Maybe the mirror is home." The writer himself, he says, "flies through language as wide and as unique as his wings. Like all birds he sings in French when in France, Afrikaans in Africa, English in London . . . It's the only way to be indigenous."

Finally, when the visit is over, this indigenous Afrikaner leaves his country with a question.

"Why did I come back?" he asks. "Nostalgia, unfinished business, loose ends, to complete the incomplete, for annihilation, death-wish. Why will I not return to stay? Too late now. Foreigner here. Painted monkey. Bitter dreams. No roots. Attachment too painful. Deathwish. . . ."

J. M. Coetzee (review date 2 December 1993)

SOURCE: "Resisters," in *New York Review of Books*, Vol. XL, No. 20, December 2, 1993, pp. 3-6.

[*In the following review, Coetzee offers praise for* Return to Paradise.]

In 1960 Breyten Breytenbach left his native South Africa to live in Paris, where he wrote poetry and painted. There he fell in love with and married a woman of Vietnamese descent. Interracial marriages being illegal in the South Africa of those days, he could not return home with his wife; he refused to return without her.

In 1972, in a gesture of conciliation toward the Afrikaans intellectual community, which was troubled by such treatment of a man who had in the meantime become widely acknowledged as the leading poet of his generation, the South African government granted Breytenbach and his wife visas for a brief visit. During this visit Breytenbach gave an uncompromising address at a writers' conference: it is because Afrikaners are a bastard people, he said, that they are obsessed with racial purity; apartheid is the law of the bastard. As for the future of South Africa, that lay in the hands of black South Africans; the task of white intellectuals could only be to work for the transformation of their own community.

In furtherance of this goal, Breytenbach returned to South Africa on a forged French passport to recruit sympathizers to an organization dedicated to sabotaging military and industrial targets. Because of incompetence and perhaps even treachery among his ANC associates, he was picked up by the security police, put on trial, and given a long sentence, of which he served seven years.

In 1980, while he was still in prison, his book *A Season in Paradise* appeared, first in the Netherlands, then in the English-speaking world—a memoir of the 1972-1973 visit interspersed with poems, reminiscences, and reflections on the South African situation (it includes the text of the address mentioned above). The title *A Season in Paradise* casts an ironical glance at Rimbaud's *Une Saison en enfer*; Breytenbach's new book, *Return to Paradise,* carries the echoes further ("this region of damnation," he calls the country now)—in fact, as he explains in a preface, the two *Paradise* books are meant to be read together with his prison memoir, *The True Confessions of an Albino Terrorist,* as an autobiographical triptych addressing a chapter of his life now closed, a chapter during which he struggled to grasp the nature of his links to the landscape and history of the continent on which he was born.

Return to Paradise is casually organized, as was the earlier book. It is a loose narrative of the journey he made in 1991, again accompanied by his wife, through F. W. De Klerk's "reformed" South Africa, intercut with horror stories from South African newspapers and with flashbacks to visits to other parts of Africa.

Breytenbach—who is now a French citizen—had visited South Africa several times in the 1980s—visits hemmed in by official obstructionism—so what he sees in 1991 does not come as a complete surprise to him. Nevertheless, as he remarks after a tour through the killing fields of Natal province, where, in a landscape of unsurpassed beauty, ANC and Inkatha adherents daily slaughter each other with gun and spear, "I am looking at the future and it chills me to the bone. . . . The land is awash in blood."

If the future holds not interracial harmony but interethnic and internecine warfare without end, then where did it all go wrong? At whose door does the fault lie?

In part Breytenbach blames the present state of affairs on the ANC's policy of "making the townships ingovernable," in part on the Zulu leader Gatsha Buthelezi, waging a stubborn, clandestine war for his share of the spoils; but he identifies the ultimate source of evil as elements in the white state that have decided, "If we have to be brought down we shall topple the pillars of Babylon with us." These elements, "niched within the shadowy reaches of occult structures and operations and secret funds," pull the strings that control

the daily may-hem, "like mad dogs who go on biting even without orders to do so."

This is not an original analysis. Whoever it may have been who fired the first shot, the bloodletting today is being carried out by ANC-affiliated youth beyond the control of family or party leadership, by Buthelezi's irregulars battling against what they see as the marginalizing of the Aulu people, and by agents, some from ultra-right organizations, some within the state security forces, operating directly or through proxies to create as much chaos as they can. Nor can Breytenbach offer an account of what is happening on the ground any more vivid—or more appalling—than what he quotes from the daily newspapers.

If there is anything surprising about Breytenbach's views, therefore, it is that he seems to regard the spectacle of cliques of middle-aged men negotitating their slice of the cake while their followers fight it out as a betrayal of the promise of the revolution. "We are too pusillanimous to make the Revolution, to abort it, then to use the corpses as stepping-stones to the masters' table of shared power." "This is the new [South Africa] . . . more broadly based hegemony but [the] same mechanisms and same sadness." One is tempted to ask: What does Breytenbach expect from politicians? Is politics not about making deals?

In a preface to the English-language edition dated 1993, Breytenbach grudgingly moderates his lament that the revolution has been betrayed. "In order to sleep soundly the dream must be devoured," he concedes in a sinister metaphor, hinting that the state selects the best children, the revolutionary dreamers, to sacrifice first.

He moderates his lament but does not withdraw it: the new order he sees emerging is not the order he fought for. While he is not so naive as not to recognize that his "small whimpers for an impossible revolution" are utopian, he refuses to yield up the right of the poet to imagine a future beyond the capacity of politicians and so to have a prophetic say in the future—even the right to bite the hand that has fed him.

What, besides the wasted prison years, has Breytenbach given up to the revolution? He has been dragged into the factionalism, intrigue, and backstabbing of exile politics. He has also been part of the anti-apartheid circuit, attending conferences, making speeches, giving readings. *Return to Paradise* allows only glimpses of what this circuit entailed: among other things, holding his tongue when he saw funds from Western philanthropists being cynically ripped off; not antagonizing venal African dictatorships' where to have the most elementary freedom of movement he had to pay off the thugs assigned to guard him.

We get a fuller picture of the poet's life on the 1991 visit to South Africa, also paid for by a foundation: readings in noisy lecture halls where the audience doesn't understand the language and comes only to inspect the oddity named Breytenbach; perplexed responses ("But aren't you *ever* happy? Now that we've won, can't you *rejoice*?" asks an ANC comrade). His hosts react with incomprehension and hostility when he asserts that his role in the future will be as it was in the past: "To be against the norm, orthodoxy, the canon, hegemony, politics, the State, power. . . . Man is the enemy of the machine"—sentiments which do not go down well in a country that has, as he observes dryly, slid straight from pre-humanity to post-humanity.

The message Breytenbach brings with him on his tour is that the world is losing interest in Africa the Beggar Continent. "To Europe Africa is only a mass of human matter making a mass sport of dying." South Africans, spoiled by decades in the international spotlight, will have to learn to be self-sufficient. What he does not add, but might have, is that American and European foundations are no longer going to pay for South African intellectuals to congregate in exotic locales and talk about their visions of the future. In more ways than one, **Return to Paradise** signals the end of a certain road, not for Breytenbach alone but for left-leaning South African intellectuals in general: unless they are able to find a role for themselves that gives them critical (and economic) independence from a government they will have helped to bring to power, they will be absorbed into an establishment, become part of an orthodoxy.

So the spirit in which Breytenbach concludes his autobiographical triptych is by no means one of tranquility. On the contrary, he uses **Return to Paradise** to lash out, in anguish and bitterness, in all directions: against white liberals, against the South African Communist Party and "more-doctrinaire-than-thou" bourgeois leftists, against former associates like Wole Soyinka ("whenever a head of state beckons he will comply") and Jesse Jackson ("each time the camera looked his way he was on his feet with clenched fist held high and a pious tear in the combative eye; when the camera swung away he was back to supercilious boredom"), and particularly, for its leaders' treatment of him when he was in jail, against the ANC itself:

> Not only did the ANC withhold assistance from my dependants, not only did they disavow me, but the London clique of bitter exiles intervened to stop any manifestation of international or local support for my cause. They black-balled and maligned me, abetted by well-meaning "old friends" inside the country. Even Amnesty International was prevailed upon not to "adopt" me as a prisoner of conscience.

Of the ANC leadership, only Nelson Mandela is singled out for praise. To Mandela, as seen on a ceremonial visit to France, Breytenbach devotes several pages of close and even affectionate attention:

> His mind seemed totally unshackled, freed from fear and small considerations, so that he could speak it directly (in contrast to Mitterrand's, which is infinitely devious, or that of De Klerk—maimed by apartheid—which has to juggle with the unsaid and the need to emit double messages). . . . Only the lips in repose betrayed him—severe, dark, aloof, bitter. It is the mouth which sometimes says more, and more eloquently, than the voice can; lips close over the unsayable: *This cannot be spoken about, so why bother?*

But the plague that Breytenbach pronounces upon all the parties to the South African conflict—a judgment in which, despite the pungency of the language, there remains something wild and out of control—makes up the less interesting half of the book. His best pages address a more intimate and more fundamental concern: what it means to him to be rooted in a landscape, to be African-born. For though Breytenbach has spent almost all his adult life in Europe, he is not a European:

> To be an African is not a choice, it is a condition. . . . To be [an African] is not through lack of being integrated in Europe; . . . neither is it from regret of the crimes perpetrated by "my people". . . . No, it is simply the only opening I have for making use of all my senses and capabilities. . . . The [African] earth was the first to speak. I have been pronounced once and for all.

What he means by saying that Africa allows him to use his senses and his capabilities fully is revealed in page after magical page as he responds to the sights and sounds of "the primordial continent." An immensely gifted writer, he is able to descend effortlessly into the Africa of the poetic unconscious and return with the rhythm and the words, the words in the rhythm, that give life. This faculty of his is not individual, he insists, but is inherited from his Afrikaner ancestors, "forebears with the deep eyes of injured baboons," whose lives had been spent in intimate relation with their native landscape, so that when he brings forth that landscape in words he is speaking in their voices as much as his own.

It is this very traditional, very African realization—that his deepest creative being is not his own but belongs to an ancestral consciousness—that gives rise to some of the pain and confusion of **Return to Paradise.** For though Breytenbach may recognize how marginal he is in what is nowadays on all sides, and with equal irony, called "the new South Africa," and may even enjoy dramatizing himself as the one without a self, the bastard, the "nomadic nobody," or, in his favorite postmodern figure, the face in the mirror, a textual shadow without substance, he knows that exile blunts feeling and that ultimately he owes his strength to the earth and the ancestors. Thus the most moving passages in the book tell of visiting his father's deathbed, renewing friendships, making peace with his brothers, taking his wife— the good angel who has watched over him through so many tribulations—to the old places of Africa.

Adam Kruper (review date 24 December 1993)

SOURCE: "Maltreated Angel," in *Times Literary Supplement,* December 24, 1993, p. 22.

[*In the following review, Kruper finds the political writing in* Return to Paradise *somewhat heavy-handed and incoherent but admires Breytenbach's descriptive abilities when he does not discuss politics.*]

For a long time during his Parisian exile, Breyten Breytenbach was better known as an artist than as a poet or revolutionary; and he painted the picture reproduced on the cover of this book [*Return to Paradise*] himself. It depicts a tall blond prisoner, with wings, followed by his saturnine, small captor. Both figures are wearing red shoes. Red shoes feature from time to time in his text as well, and seem to have some special meaning for Breytenbach. Since I do not know what their meaning is, I cannot be at all sure that I understand the artist's intention, but Breytenbach seems to see himself as a misunderstood and maltreated angel, brought back to Paradise under constraint; and that, indeed, is pretty much the message contained in the book under review.

"I'm aware of the superficiality", Breytenbach admits when his wife reads his notes for this book; he then sums up, very fairly, its plot: "from airport to dinner table to lecture room". It is, moreover, his third return to Paradise. Perhaps the outstanding Afrikaans poet of his generation, he left South Africa as a young man in 1960, emigrating to Paris where he married his Vietnamese wife. In 1973, he made his first return visit, which he wrote about in the ironically titled *A Season in Paradise.* In 1975, he went back again, this time in disguise, a conspirator; he was swiftly apprehended and spent seven years in prison. While imprisoned, he published a book of poems dedicated to his warder. Later, he wrote a second memoir, *The True Confessions of an Albino Terrorist* (this title is heavily ironic; he had already confessed very fully in court). *Return to Paradise* is the record of his most recent visit, in 1991, when he wandered, bewildered and disillusioned, through post-apartheid South Africa.

As one of the most famous Afrikaans victims of South African censorship and repression, Breytenbach spent many years on the international goodwill circuit which supported opponents of the South African regime, in particular the African National Congress (ANC). Gadaffi, Sankara and Mitterand were assiduous hosts. Accounts of these junkets are scattered throughout the book, apparently in order to establish the author's credentials as a serious political figure; there are hints of power-worship, though descriptions of the great are carefully counterpointed by accounts of meetings with impecunious poets.

Breytenbach sees himself as something of a politician—and this visit to South Africa seems to have been connected with various, vaguely defined, political meetings. And evidently he did play a part in setting up the symbolically important meeting of ANC exiles and white business and political leaders from South Africa, in Dakar, in 1987. He has, too, plans for a think-tank on African democratic reform, which is to be established on a small island off the West African coast. But he is now an ex-revolutionary, without ideological bearings; "I've run out of convictions", he claims. At times he presents himself as a disreputable but honest man, without illusions, a sort of Rick, the Humphrey Bogart character in *Casablanca*; but then he gets overexcited and needs his wife "to comfort me, to cool my fevered imagination and the narcissistic deathwish, to bring a modicum of equilibrium". He has not, though, got Bogart's way with women, or with ideas. In fact, Breytenbach is more of a Walter Mitty character. He is distrusted by the Afrikaners and by the ANC, and he cannot express his ideas coherently. His one-liners are limp. "It is not a revolution, and for the time being it has little to do with democracy", he remarks of the South African interregnum. (A piece of graffiti which he copies from a Cape Town wall is more interesting: "We have moved from the interregnum to the intrarectum".) Periodically, he lectures in apocalyptic vein to groups of intellectuals. "I waded in making very clear my disdain for starry-eyed recent converts in general and Stellenbosch political yuppies in particular. I said it would be disastrous to leave the past with hands poking out above ground; I warned against the new hegemony. . . ." This may have gone down well in Stellenbosch, but it falls flat on the page. Then, too, he employs a more mystical idiom. "No, there is no dream. Revolution is a small white dog hunting a ghostly elephant. I am a gadfly." On balance, perhaps the one-liners are preferable.

The best parts of this book have nothing to do with politics. They are the occasional descriptions of landscapes, rendered with the intensity of a painter, and the portraits of his Afrikaner friends: the politician, Van Zyl Slabbert, organizing civil rights groups, managing committees—and slipping away from a meeting to watch an inter-provincial cricket game at Newlands; the poets, Uys Krige and Jan Rabie; the novelist André Brink; and his brother, who was a South African war hero in Angola and is now also a mystic concerned about elephants. These are his true points of reference.

"One day", he writes at the end, "I should write a book about exile, about what it is like to have turned in upon oneself, and give a description of the blunting caused by estrangement from the intimate and the familiar." If that book is about a South African artist in Paris, rather than a Left-Bank Parisian in South Africa, then it should be worth reading.

Breyten Breytenbach with James Wood (interview date 9 January 1994)

SOURCE: "An Afrikaner Trapped in No Man's Land," in *Manchester Guardian Weekly,* Vol. 150, No. 2, January 9, 1994, p. 28.

[*In the following review, Wood and Breytenbach discuss major themes in* Return to Paradise.]

In 1975, the South African poet and painter Breyten Breytenbach was arrested at the airport at Johannesburg, on his way back to his home in France. Working under a false identity, he had been recruiting agents for an underground movement in exile called Okhela. For an hour he attempted to convince his captors that, far from understanding Afrikaans, he was in fact an Italian professor. But he had been trailing secret policeman behind him like a shoelace since his arrival. They knew exactly who he was: he was the famous Afrikaner poet Breyten Breytenbach, and brother of the even more famous war hero and patriot, Jan. They had probably read his poetry.

Breytenbach was sentenced to nine years' imprisonment. He served seven of them, two in solitary confinement in a cell six by nine feet, and 13 feet high. He has written superbly about these years in his memoir, *The True Confessions of An Albino Terrorist* (1984). It is one of the sublime vulgarities of literature that nothing makes for literary interest—nothing is more useful technically to the writer—like the presentation of a life stripped to nothing and forced to rebuild itself.

Breytenbach's account of his struggle—nothing less than a struggle for meaning—in solitary confinement makes *The True Confessions* horribly gripping. Reading it is like waking up to hear an intruder in the next room: every movement, every detail is murderously important, haloed with presence. With a dry bureaucratic relish, Breytenbach tells us about every brick in his cell, every change of the seasons glimpsed through his high window, every fact about the Pretoria jail (at that time, white prisoners got more meat than black prisoners; coloureds got more bread). He was sen-

tenced on November 25, 1975; he sees the moon again for the first time, he writes with grim pleasure, on April 19, 1976 when, "at about twenty-three minutes to four in the afternoon, I am in the largest of the three exercise yards. . . ."

These data are compelling; but *The True Confessions* is also a book of beauty, for it is about the blooming of a new selfhood, strengthened, shriven, sacrificed. What Breytenbach discovers in prison is the negative rhapsody, the Biblical inversion of riches-in-poverty: ". . . by being forced to turn in upon yourself you discover, paradoxically, openings to the outside in yourself . . . You grow rich with the richness of the very poor; the smallest sign of life from outside becomes a gift from heaven to be cherished. You really see things for what they are, stripped of your own overbearing presence. A blanket really is a blanket, and though it is grey, it has a million colours in it . . . No king was ever as blessed as you are."

In person, Breytenbach has the terrible dignity that accompanies those who have suffered privations, but, as it were, suffered them on their own terms. Calm, controlled, quiet, he seems temperamentally lean. There is no wastage: it is as if every superfluity, every excess, has been used up in the combustion of a perfect self-knowledge. Physically, he embodies this deep equilibrium: he is wiry; his beard is severely cropped; lucid eyes stare out of a strong, deeply grooved face.

But there is a suppleness too, the slyness and internal jubilation of the psychological victor. For he is a kind of victor—it is the victory of the martyr. He says: "Prison, in some ways, strengthened what were already my deepest psychological tendencies—a desire to please and at the same time a need to lash out, to say 'dammit, I'm going to be and do exactly what I want'."

This self-division—wanting to please and needing to rebel—flows from Breytenbach's strange relationship with the Afrikaner establishment. By the time he was arrested he was the most famous Afrikaner poet, cherished for his revitalisation of the language, anthologised, read in schools. As he knows, his political fierceness against his own people flatters them. It is a kind of maternal scourging which the establishment understands even if it despises its message, for it places Afrikanerdom at the heart of the South African problem. In this sense, Breytenbach honours Afrikanerdom even as he murders it.

Over the years, he has returned again and again to his fatherland from his home in Paris, now a scourging parent and now a sulky child. And in the end, it always lets him come. This dialectic of longing and disappointment, acceptance and rejection is the deep current of his writing, and of his new book *Return To Paradise* (an account of a recent visit in 1990). "One had been building up to the big return to the New South Africa," he says, "and then one discovers that one is redundant after all, and perhaps this book is a rather devious way of coming to terms with my redundancy. I want to be accepted. But no one from any of the movements was coming over to me to say, 'Hey brother come in, don't sit out there in the cold, we need you.'"

The new book is a meeting with ghosts; some of them glow with a kind of sad and noble after-life, like Nelson Mandela or the courageous Harry Gwala, regional ANC leader, paralysed from the shoulders down by a government poison attempt. But most disappoint, like the priest ("a seasoned pharisee") who welcomes him back, saying: "Now there's a future for everybody", and some terrify, like Paul Gough, one of his old interrogators from prison days, whom he bumps into in a restaurant. None is family, none is home. The country is now a place of fervent lies: "Everybody who wants to be somebody in the country now lays claim to having been in the resistance movement; we are all of the ANC. Rumours of heroic feats abound." (Breytenbach is supportive of the ANC, but suspicious of its centralising tendencies.)

A sense of locatedness only comes from the land itself, rising from it like heatwaves. It glimmers: "How we love Africa! In the dark we are all Africans," he writes. And then it boils into the air and disappears: "I am of a people who are the truly mortification of Africa, a people of colonists without a metropolis, with whom nobody wants a shared history. . . ."

On whose side am I anyway? he asks at one point. And the answer must be: on his only. Of course, he is also on the side of right, and he speaks eloquently of the engine of revolution that powered him in the late 1960s towards political action, "a longing for metamorphosis, for making the world change. Writing goes utterly with this, for writing is always rewriting the world. And writing is revolution not politics. Politics is the maintenance of power, the administration of power even when it's done by good people." (It is this he fears about the ANC and its future course.) "But", he continues, "the stench of politics tends to drive away the perfume of revolution, and we must be perpetually fighting this. Not to stand still in power, but to keep on moving in revolution, challenging existing structures."

He is on the side of right, but the model for this notion of perpetual revolution, perpetual movement, is not Marx or Mao but the self, his self. He has always questioned his right to fight on behalf of the black majority; on the contrary, he must fight because of what apartheid does also to whites, what it does to him. Behind the noble, sad, preposterous suffering of his life, behind the adventure of sacrifice, the eternal scrutiny of revolution, the familial bounce

of acceptance and dismissal—behind all of this is the revolution of the self.

So Breyten Breytenbach is never truly an exile, because he always has this self, and the cunning of its survival; or if you prefer, he is the truest exile ever, lost in the endless difficulty of Afrikaner selfhood. His dilemma reminds me of the marvelous passage from Camus's *The Plague,* and I read it to him. The plague-ridden inhabitants of an Algerian town have been quarantined, the gates locked. "Thus too they came to know the incorrigible sorrow of all prisoners and exiles, which is to live in company with a memory that serves no purpose . . . Hostile to the past, impatient of the present and cheated of the future, we were much like those whom men's justice, or hatred, forces to live behind prison doors." As I read this, his eyes water a little, he rocks back and forward. "Ah, it's incredible, you know! Camus has it absolutely. That's what it's like."

Perhaps only the African landscape, for Breytenbach, is not electrified with rejection. Whenever he writes about it he rhapsodises. For the African landscape seems to him gloriously simple, free of history and time, free (rather than deprived) of memory, "The magic of Africa is its rhythm of timelessness . . . its clarity, its bareness, its horizons burned clean of history and time. It is so clear, so natural, that it becomes incomprehensible."

In a way, the political South Africa he longs for is this forlorn impossibility, a place burned free of history and time and memory; a place, like the endlessly renewing self, waking up each day to make itself anew. But he knows, of course, that the South Africa of politics, even the comparatively sweet stench of ANC politics, cannot forget history, will not, and perhaps, must not. And so the sadness begins all over again.

Barend J. Toerien (review date Summer 1994)

SOURCE: Review of *nege landskappe van ons tye bemaak aan 'n beminde,* in *World Literature Today,* Vol. 68, No. 3, Summer 1994, pp. 622-23.

[*In the following review, Toerien admires Breytenbach's breadth of scope and spontaneity in* nege landskappe.]

In spite of—understandably—bitter renouncements of his people and country and the resultant switch to English for his prose works, Breyten Breytenbach, like many other exiled and transposed poets before him, seemingly finds it difficult to write poetry in a language other than his mother tongue. So we have in ***nege landskappe van ons tye bemaak aan 'n beminde*** (nine landscapes of our time dedicated to a loved one) a hefty volume containing a rich harvest of poems in Afrikaans and an exultant celebration of words and language.

Dedicated to the poet's Vietnamese wife, the collection is in nine sections (the Buddhist holy number of wholeness) and displays a richness of themes in a wealth, almost an extravagance, of words. There is a delight in language, as in the lines "to travel / through dictionaries and other scapes / where R's roll and stars jell and hisses / at times unexpectedly ripple like water over suffixes." The language is colloquial and would be hard to understand by nonspeakers of Afrikaans; Breytenbach's poetic mastery can therefore scarcely be appreciated internationally.

The poems are life-affirming, even though death is celebrated—death as the rich fulfillment of life—and are largely looser in construction than were the prison poems of the series *The Undanced Dance—Voetskrif, Eklips, 'yk', Buffalo Bill,* **and** *Lewendood*—probably because he then had more time on his hands. Not that the poems of *nege landskappe* are not sculpted or polished, but the forms are less obvious and have grown spontaneously, often enriched with unobtrusive rhyme patterns. There is also an astonishing exploration of the words themselves, revealing new and hidden meanings. The poetry has a strong visual element, often surrealistic and even bizarre, as also highlighted in the recent exhibition of Breytenbach's paintings in South Africa, works which showed an affinity with Max Ernst, Magritte, and Bruegel.

Throughout, the reader is made aware of Breytenbach's obsession with words and the act of writing poetry. There is a negative side to this, as some of the central sections seem prolix, especially when coupled with arguments that are none too easy to follow; but we are always conscious of the wholeness of the poet's vision. As one of his titles states, he "seeks refuge in words," as for instance: "chickens with rubber gloves sometimes / come to scratch after ants small like letters / that will strip all meaning / from dead words slavishly dragged into poetry"; or "to commit love together / was to climb up a tree / when first buds with eyes shut / start enticing the bees / and to chisel words / with shiny blind hands in a dark living room."

The second section or "landscape" deals with concrete actions on the poet's property in Catalonia, where he finds ease in a peaceful environment. Political poems of protest against injustices in South Africa form the third section; it fits in well with the book's overall wide and wise vision of oneness, a summing up through peaceful acceptance. The line "the true landscape is one of peace" occurs several times. Other "landscapes" deal with the concept of love, with space, with the past, immortality, time, and death. And always there is Breytenbach's amused and ironic stance, un-derlined by a quote from Mozart used as a colophon: "und dessentwegen / Je faisois un piccolo quodlibet."

Bruce Bawer   (review date 5 May 1996)

SOURCE: "Thinking Forbidden Thoughts," in *Washington Post Book World,* Vol. XXVI, May 5, 1996, p. 5.

[*In the following review, Bawer finds Breytenbach's search for truth and justice in* The Memory of Birds in Times of Revolution *admirable despite the book's flaws.*]

In 1991, before the fall of the white deKlerk regime in South Africa, the Afrikaans writer and anti-apartheid revolutionary Breyten Breytenbach—who had spent seven years as a political prisoner and several more years as an exile in Paris—published an open letter to his friend Nelson Mandela, complaining that Mandela's African National Congress should "stop being the victims" and instead assume its proper role as "actors for change and construction." The letter, which appears in his new book, *The Memory of Birds in Times of Revolution,* was typical of Breytenbach (*A Season in Paradise, The True Confessions of an Albino Terrorist*). Refusing to play the martyr or to idealize his fellow activists, Breytenbach has frustrated the expectations of Europeans who, bathing him in a pity that he angrily rejected, wanted from him the angels-vs.- demons clarity of politics and not the ambiguities of art.

Soon after Breytenbach released his letter, apartheid collapsed—the fulfillment of his lifelong dream. Yet he was devastated. He returned home from exile, but felt out of place. "I find myself nowhere," he wrote. Dismayed to see Mandela, now president, install "a new hegemony of mediocrity," he drafted another open letter, asking, "Did you have to include quite that many crooks and demagogues and dogmatists?" He was irked at his former comrades-in-arms who, "tongue-tied by guilt or a false sense of solidarity," believed "that repeating the mumbo-jumbo of slogans constitutes revolutionary literature," and who, calling him "a bird of doom" and a "smug moral magistrate," asked him, "Why can't you be happy now we've won?"

The essays in this book seek, in large part, to answer that question. With apartheid's fall, South Africa seems to Breytenbach a place of chaos and contradiction. Moral clarity is more elusive than ever, and Breytenbach is perplexed not only about his proper relationship to the new regime but about the meaning and purpose of just about everything. Repeatedly, he asks: Can humans really learn, grow, change, improve? Is there any ultimate meaning to war, suffering, exile, peace, freedom, triumph? Each essay constitutes a new attempt to define himself, to solve the riddle of Africa, to figure out how the pieces of his world fit together, to decide what he should think and do—and what he should say to us about what we should think and do.

Ultimately, for Breytenbach, these questions all lead to a consideration of the writer's vocation. Having lost his role as an insurrectionist, he strives to recover his identity as a creative artist. Noting that Marx, Freud, Nietzsche, Jung, Trotsky and Darwin were all "writers first and foremost," he perceives that though the antiapartheid struggle is over, the writer's fight for revolution (truth, fairness, humanity) against politics (selfishness, expediency, dishonesty) never ends. Even with Mandela in charge, Breytenbach and other writers who recognize that "aesthetics and ethics cannot be separated" still need to "subvert . . . the hegemony," to fight "for revolution against politics."

Though his solipsism can be exasperating (he seems unable to write about South Africa without focusing on himself), and though he is not above the political cliches and moral posturing for which he criticizes others, Breytenbach's passionate desire to know and serve the truth, whatever it may be and whoever it may offend, is deeply admirable.

Barend J. Toerien (review date Witner 1997)

SOURCE: Review of *Die hand vol vere: 'n bloemlesing van die poësie, met twee briewe,* in *World Literature Today,* Vol. 71, No. 1, Winter 1997, p. 210.

[*In the following review, Toerien offers a positive assessment of* Die hand vol vere.]

A selection of Breyten Breytenbach's poetry made by his friend and academic Ampie Coetzee has the disarming title *A Hand Full of Feathers,* an Afrikaans idiom for empty-handedness and one which the author has used on several occasions in earlier poems. The selection also contains some new poems as well as two letters between the two friends.

It is a generous selection, but it can never be generous enough. Breytenbach's output is so large and of such a consistently high standard, that only a *complete* collection of his poetry can satisfy: that will no doubt come some day. Meanwhile, here is Coetzee's choice. He has also included poems from relatively obscure Dutch literary magazines as well.

Breytenbach's poetry is difficult to define; in general "surrealistic," but at the same time grounded in the simple, natural folklore of his people and culture. With irony he hints at traces, but he also quotes from Afrikaans poets, forcing one to look anew at accepted Afrikaans tenets. These effects are lost on the overseas and non-Afrikaans reader, unfortunately, but nevertheless his poetry has an immediate universal appeal when translated by himself, as in *Judas Eye.* His range is wide, his linguistic reach unlimited.

As selected editions go, one can easily criticize *Die hand vol vere.* To my mind there could have been more poems from his prison volumes, his so-called *Undanced Dance* books, and definitely more from *Voetskrif.* Absent also is the direct accusation leveled at the then prime minister, calling him a butcher, which caused the banning—in South Africa—of the volume in which it appeared in the Netherlands, *Skryt.* But Breytenbach's full, rich range, is shown here, from the tender love poems to his Vietnamese wife through scathing denunciations of the apartheid government of South Africa. And the lasting impression left, apart from his evident zest in his wizardry with language, is one of life-affirming joy.

Additional coverage of Breytenbach's life and career is available in the following sources published by Gale: *Contemporary Authors,* **Vols. 113, and 129;** *Contemporary Authors New Revision Series,* **Vol. 61; and** *DISCovering Authors Modules: Poets.*

Cathedral
Raymond Carver

American short story writer, poet, and scriptwriter.

The following entry presents criticism on Carver's short story collection *Cathedral* (1983). For further information on his life and works, see *CLC*, Volumes 22, 36, 53, and 55.

INTRODUCTION

Carver's 1983 short story collection *Cathedral* contains much of the author's most popular and highly respected work. The twelve stories in *Cathedral* build on Carver's earlier work, exhibiting characteristics such as inarticulate characters isolated by their inability to relate to one another; an unsentimental treatment of joblessness, alcoholism, and estrangement; and a prevailing mood of despair and hopelessness. However, in *Cathedral*, Carver departs from the intensely minimalist style that characterized much of his earlier work. These stories are longer and more inclusive, providing greater insight into the emotions and perceptions of his characters. In addition, in such stories as "A Small, Good Thing," "Cathedral," and "Where I'm Calling From," Carver allows his characters to experience a sense of hopefulness and the opportunity to commune with one another—circumstances largely absent from his previous work. When asked about the collection in an interview, Carver said: "the first story I wrote was 'Cathedral,' which I feel is totally different in conception and execution from any stories that have come before. I suppose it reflects a change in my life as much as it does in my way of writing."

Plot and Major Characters

In many of the stories from *Cathedral,* Carver focuses on daily events, common occurrences in the lives of his characters. Couples and families are his main subjects, and frequently experience some type of epiphany during the course of the story. In "Careful" a man struggles to clear his ears from deafening wax. "Bridle" is about the downward spiral of a farm family losing their farm, requiring them to relocate. The family is forced to move a second time when the father suffers a head injury, leaving him unable to support his wife and four children. In "Feathers," Carver recounts a defining moment in the lives of Jack and Fran, a couple who visit their friends Bud and Olla one evening. Confronted with their hosts' peacock, a model of preorthodontics teeth, and an ugly baby, the couple is transformed. Fran believes the evening has destroyed their happiness, but Jack views it as the pinnacle of their contentment and success. "Chef's

House" focuses on a defining moment in the life of another couple. Edna agrees to reunite with her alcoholic husband, Wes, for one summer to share a friend's beach house. During the summer Wes refrains from drinking, allowing the pair to enjoy an idyllic holiday. When Chef returns, requiring Edna and Wes to leave, Wes again succumbs to his despondency.

Major Themes

Carver's work in *Cathedral* falls roughly into two categories. Stories such as "Feathers," "Careful," and "Compartment" illustrate a sense of futility and hopelessness that pervades the characters' lives. The protagonists are isolated by their inability to relate to one another and to articulate their feelings. Denied the ability to express themselves they become frustrated, losing hope that their lives will improve. For instance, in "Preservation" the husband and wife cannot express to one another how they believe their lives have come to ruin. The wife watches her husband retreat after he loses his job, but she is unable to reach him or help him regain his optimism. Carver's characters are doing the best they can in difficult circumstances, but often lack traits that allow them to triumph over their problems. However, while "A Small, Good Thing," "Where I'm Calling From," and "Cathedral" deal with dark subjects, Carver's tone in these stories is different. His protagonists are able to communicate with one another and to improve their situations. In "A Small, Good Thing," for instance, the confrontation between parents and a baker results in solace for both parties. The baker confronts his antisocial behavior and the parents acknowledge their grief.

Critical Reception

Critics responded positively when *Cathedral* was published in 1983. Carver was nominated for the National Book Critics Circle Award and the Pulitzer Prize for fiction in 1984. He also received the 1983 Mildred and Harold Strauss Living Award from the American Academy and Institute of Arts and Letters. The collection continues to garner praise, and such stories as "A Small, Good Thing," "Cathedral," and "Where I'm Calling From" remain among his best-known and most highly regarded works. Most scholarship about *Cathedral* has focused on Carver's shift from a minimalist style evident in earlier collections such as *What We Talk About When We Talk About Love* (1981) and *Will You Please Be Quiet, Please?* (1976) to the longer, more developed stories in *Cathedral*. As one critic noted, the length of the stories seemed to increase as the length of the collection's titles decreased. Reviewers also noted Carver's more hopeful tone. While a few commentators felt betrayed by Carver's new attitude, arguing that it bordered on sentimentality, most critics cited it as evidence of Carver's growing range and skill. In a review of *Cathedral*, Irving Howe wrote: "A few of Carver's stories . . . can already be counted among the masterpieces of American fiction."

PRINCIPAL WORKS

Near Klamath (poetry) 1968
Winter Insomnia (poetry) 1970
Put Yourself in My Shoes (short stories) 1974
At Night the Salmon Move (poetry) 1976
Will You Please Be Quiet, Please? (short stories) 1976
Furious Seasons and Other Stories (short stories) 1977
What We Talk about When We Talk about Love (short stories) 1981
The Pheasant (short stories) 1982
Two Poems (poetry) 1982
Cathedral (short stories) 1983
Fires: Essays, Poems, Stories (essays, poetry, and short stories) 1983
If It Please You (short stories) 1984
The Short Stories of Raymond Carver (short stories) 1985
The Water (poetry) 1985

*Where Water Comes Together with Other Water (poetry) 1985
*Ultramarine (poetry) 1986
Those Days: Early Writings (short stories and poetry) 1987
†*Where I'm Calling From: New and Selected Stories* (short stories) 1988
A New Path to the Waterfall (poetry) 1989

*These works were published together in England as *In a Marine Light* in 1987.
†The new short stories from this volume were published in England as *Elephant, and Other Stories* in 1988.

CRITICISM

Paul Gray (review date 19 September 1983)

SOURCE: A review of *Cathedral*, in *Time*, Vol. 122, September 19, 1983, p. 95.

[*In the following review, Gray suggests that* Cathedral *contains hidden depths of meaning.*]

For years now, the demographics of the American short story have been moving up-scale. The line of Hemingway drifters and Flannery O'Connor grotesques seems to be dying out. Characters rarely worry any more about finding God or their next meal. They are likely instead to be well educated, sensitive to a fault, politically liberal, and affluent enough to feel pleasurable guilt in their possessions. They tend, in short, to resemble the stereotypical reader of *The New Yorker*, which is where the luckiest of these fictional people are chosen to appear. The rejected ones must troop off to the quarterlies and go through their paces (at greatly reduced rates) for smaller audiences composed of people with whom they can feel equally at home. These days a good many characters in short stories are also quarterly readers.

Author Raymond Carver, 45, has successfully bucked this trend toward the gentrification of short fiction. Furthermore, he has done so in part in *The New Yorker*, where three of the twelve stories in *Cathedral* originally appeared.

Carver's art masquerades as accident, scraps of information that might have been overheard at the supermarket checkout counter or the local beer joint. His most memorable people live on the edge: of poverty, alcoholic self-destruction, loneliness. Something in their lives denies them a sense of community. They feel this lack intensely, yet are too wary of intimacy to touch other people, even with language. "What's to says?" wonders one man. Another, traveling to meet the son he has not seen in many years, dreads the moment of greeting: "He really didn't know what he was going to say."

Such uncertainty leads to eruptions of inappropriate behavior. In **"Feathers,"** a man named Jack and his wife Fran are invited to dinner at the home of one of Jack's co-workers. They arrive and find a peacock strutting about the front yard, a wife happily domesticated in the kitchen and their host offering them drinks in a room where a TV set is carrying a stockcar race. All of this is too much for Fran, who did not want to come in the first place. She eyes the screen: "Maybe one of those damn cars will explode right in front of us. Or else maybe one'll run up into the grandstand and smash the guy selling the crummy hot dogs." Her aggressive remark is double-honed: it registers Fran's contempt for her enforced surroundings and the notion that there is nothing like violence to break up tedium.

Carver's stories radiate a sense of laconic menace. The worse the fates of his people, the more elliptically they seem to be telegraphed. In **"Chef's House,"** Edna is persuaded to rejoin her husband Wes. He tells her he has stopped drinking and is living in a rented house with a view of the ocean. Together, they happily pass a summer. But then the landlord says his daughter needs the house, and Wes and Edna will have to leave. Edna realizes that his news will send West back to booze and her away from him: "Wes got up and pulled the drapes and the ocean was gone just like that. I went in to start supper. We still had some fish in the icebox. There wasn't much else. We'll clean it up tonight, I thought, and that will be the end of it."

Not all of Carver's surprises are unhappy ones. Much of the vibrancy of his fiction stems from the sense, achieved in offhand cadences, that blessings can fall as unexpectedly and undeservedly as damnations. In **"Cathedral,"** the title story, a husband grudgingly awaits the arrival of a house guest: "This blind man, an old friend to my wife's, he was on his way to spend the night. His wife had died." The narrator's sympathy is initially in short supply: "A blind man in my house was not something I looked forward to."

As the evening wears on, though, the husband reflects on changes that he had not intended to undergo. Robert, the visitor, is a hearty eater and drinker; when marijuana is offered, he tries that too. The television is on, flickering out a documentary on cathedrals. The host feels the urge to explain cathedrals to the blind man, but finds that he lacks both the words and the inspiration: "The truth is, cathedrals don't mean anything special to me," he tells his guest. "Nothing. Cathedrals. They're something to look at on late-night TV. That's all they are." The speaker proves himself wrong; he is able not only to draw a passable version of a cathedral on a grocery bag, but also allows himself to be guided by Robert in doing so. Ignorance communes with sightlessness to give, temporarily, a shape to the unknown.

Such transcendent moments glimmer sporadically throughout Carver's spare fiction. To describe him as a minimalist seems fair but misleading. His stories appear much slighter than they really are. They exist, no matter how, casual or slangy their surfaces, in exactly the same spot as the best of their predecessors: the point of the fulcrum where inference tips toward importance.

Joseph G. Knapp (review date 31 December 1983)

SOURCE: A review of *Cathedral*, in *America*, December 31, 1983, p. 438.

[*In the following review, Knapp praises Carver's poignancy and emotional depth in* Cathedral.]

Rarely, and at unpredictable intervals, a writer of genius appears on the literary scene, who waves a wand over the relentlessly banal events of everyday life and transforms them. Such a master of the short story form is Raymond Carver. His first two collections of stories, ***Will You Please Be Quiet, Please?*** and ***What We Talk About When We Talk About Love***, announced to critics that an extraordinary talent had emerged from the obscure town of Clatskanie, Ore. In this latest collection of stories the author takes to its ultimate fruition Emerson's dictum that "all matter is emblematic of spirit." For Carver, all material events are evocative of the spirit, and each is crafted from a surprising perspective.

Hawthorne had found that "moonlight in a familiar room" was the requisite blending of reality and fantasy that short story writers needed. Carver does not need the moonlight, nor even dusk; he performs his sleight of hand even under the glare of the strongest sun. The objects can be as grotesque as false teeth enshrined above a television set or as tentative as the artificial community of motel dwellers living around a communal pool. Each story takes the humdrum and distills from it a poignant human emotion, a feeling that something horrible is about to happen.

Cathedral is a collection of 12 stories, each with a different voice and vision. **"A Small, Good Thing,"** which was this year's first-place winner in *Prize Stories: The O. Henry Awards*, is a subtle combination of human tragedy and human banality. Scotty's mother has arranged for her son's birthday cake on Monday afternoon, but on Monday morning Scotty is struck by a hit-and-run driver on his way to school. The baker is unaware of this tragic event and calls at night about the boy. The parents, physically and emotionally exhausted from their vigils at their son's bedside, think the caller is a crank and are enraged at these obscene calls. This painful babble is echoed on the professional level with the doctor's false assurance that the boy is surely not in a coma; he simply cannot wake up. What ultimately happens to Scotty, his parents and the baker, however, must be left for the reader to discover.

The tour de force of the entire collection is the title story. The narrator's wife has invited a blind man to dinner. The narrator notes that his blind guest smokes, drinks and even "watches" television; he wonders how the blind can fall in love without seeing the beloved. Eventually it becomes so late that the only program on television is a documentary on cathedrals. The blind man suggests that his host draw a picture of what he is seeing, and his hand will ride his host's hand as he draws. The narrator puts in windows with arches, draws flying buttresses and great doors.

> "I kept at it. I'm no artist. But I kept drawing just the same. 'Close your eyes now,' the blind man said to me. 'Are they closed?' he said. 'Don't fudge. Keep them that way,' he said. He said, 'Don't stop now. Draw.' So we kept on with it. His fingers rode my fingers as my hand went over the paper. It was like nothing else in my life up to now. Then he said, 'I think that's it. I think you got it,' he said. 'Take a look. What do you think?' But I had my eyes closed. I thought I'd keep them that way for a little longer. I thought it was something I ought to do. 'Well?' he said. 'Are you looking?' My eyes were still closed. I was in my house. I knew that. But I didn't feel like I was inside anything. 'It's really something,' I said."

In Carver's craft and vision, even the blind see and even the most obtuse of us are "trembling emblems of immortality."

James W. Grinnell (review date Winter 1984)

SOURCE: A review of *Cathedral*, in *Studies in Short Fiction*, Vol. 21, No. 1, Winter, 1984, pp. 71-2.

[*In the review below, Grinnell praises Carver's writing, arguing that he has improved on his old style and added new elements.*]

Things are finally looking up for Raymond Carver. In a way it is entirely fitting that this, his third volume of short stories is entitled *Cathedral* and that the collection ends with the title story, for in both Carver's life and writing, as in a Gothic cathedral, all signs are pointing upward.

Such was not always the case. Married at eighteen and burdened at that early age not only with the responsibility of a wife and children but also with a succession of dreary jobs, it is a wonder that he wrote at all. Raised in poor neighborhoods in Yakima, Washington, he somehow was able to attend college, to graduate with a B.A. from Chico State in California, to find his way to the University of Iowa's Writers' Workshop where he spent a year just barely surviving financially. He then took to drinking, wasting most of his thirties. He makes no excuses; he did not drink to escape nor for inspiration—he "was into the drinking itself."

Prior to 1983, he produced two books of stories, *Will You Please Be Quiet, Please?* and *What We Talk About When We Talk About Love*. Only the titles of the collections are long; the stories themselves are short, averaging fewer than ten pages each. Despite his poverty, which sometimes forced him from an overcrowded apartment to write while sitting in his car, and despite his drinking, he was a careful craftsman. The stories of the first two books are hard, austere little vignettes restricted to the viewpoints of their hard, austere and not-very-articulate characters. It is to these qualities that the stories owe their appeal and to which Carver owes the considerable reputation that they won for him.

And now comes *Cathedral* a book with a one-word title and a dozen, more fully fleshed-out stories. They are still hard little gems of fiction but they are a few carats heavier than those of the earlier books. Six of the twelve are first person narrations; all are restricted to their characters' stunted perspectives, which is to say, to Carver's tight control. He does not mock his people nor does he suggest that their lives would be improved if they examined them, if they were to expect, inspect and introspect more. A kind of literary minimalist, Carver simply presents his people and their stark lives as if there were nothing richer out there, no American milieu of affluence, of new horizons, of hope. We readers have to carry our own emotional baggage to and from these stories because Carver will not porter for us.

For example, in the opening story, **"Feathers,"** the lethargic routine of the narrator and his wife is broken when a co-worker invites them home for dinner. And a strange home it is, furnished with a T.V. upon which sits a plaster of Paris cast of crooked teeth, and before the television a La-Z-Boy chair for the host. This host has an odd little wife, plump and retiring, to whom the crooked teeth once belonged, and together they have a pet peacock and a fat ugly baby. Says the narrator, "Bar none, it was the ugliest baby I'd ever seen. It was so ugly I couldn't say anything. No words would come out of my mouth."

This was not the only time words failed him. As the evening wore on, it became very special for him despite the almost grotesque assemblage. Because he could not quite articulate that special quality, he closed his eyes to freeze a picture of it forever in his memory. It worked but ironically, because that evening was the beginning of an even drabber life for the narrator and his wife. They went home and conceived a child who later developed "a conniving streak in him." They never return the invitation and now "mostly it's just the TV."

So it goes with Carver's characters. Often they experience a special moment which almost affords them a glimpse of something elusive—a better life perhaps. But they cannot quite fathom the experience and so they retreat to drink or to dull routines made somehow even duller by the missed chance.

One of the stories, **"The Compartment"** is set entirely on a train in Europe and concerns a failed father-son reunion. Another, dedicated to one of Carver's former drinking partners, John Cheever, is entitled **"The Train"** and is set entirely in a suburban New York train station. In this story Carver seems to be paying tribute to Cheever by using Cheeveresque elements in a way not entirely unlike what John Updike did in the "Bech Wed" section of *Bech Is Back*.

But for the most part, Raymond Carver sticks with and refines familiar territory and people. Using these familiar elements, he reaches new heights in a story called **"The Bridle"** and peaks in the title story, **"Cathedral."** This little masterpiece concludes with its first person narrator trying to describe to a blind man a cathedral that he sees on television. When words fail, he tries to express the experience by holding the man's hand while sketching a cathedral. The blind man, really more perceptive than he, has the narrator close his eyes. He achieves a new dimension of perception. He tells us, "My eyes were still closed. I was in my house. I knew that. But I didn't feel like I was inside anything! 'It's really something,' I said."

Raymond Carver's life is coming together and his art is blooming. He recently received a grant from the American Academy and Institute of Arts and Letters that will provide a tax-free income for five years. He also won a 1983 O. Henry Prize Story Award. It is more than coincidental that he gave up alcohol in 1977. It would seem that much of what was is no more. It would also appear that much of what was not is now beginning. *Cathedral*, I think, is a major part of that beginning.

Patricia Schnapp (review date Summer 1985)

SOURCE: A review of *Cathedral*, in *Western American Literature*, Vol. XX, No. 2, Summer, 1985, pp. 168-69.

[*In the review below, Schnapp, who is a professor at Bowling Green State University, discusses the significance of the inability to articulate essential truths and beliefs in Carver's characters.*]

A red-eyed peacock startles a couple visiting acquaintances who have an extraordinarily ugly baby. A man tells his estranged wife that he's about to go crazy because of his plugged-up ear. A wife comes home to find her unemployed husband unaware that the refrigerator has quit working and the food is thawing out. In Raymond Carver's *Cathedral*, his third collection of short fiction, stories are pared down to the banal details that compose most of our lives. And yet these very banal details explode in the mind with reverberating and ominous innuendo.

Frank Kermode has declared that Carver is a master of the short form, and Carver's **"A Small, Good Thing,"** which is included in this collection, was this year's first place winner in William Abraham's distinguished annual "Prize Stories: The O. Henry Awards."

There is no melodrama in Carver's spare, laconic, but brilliantly evocative fiction. **"Vitamins,"** for instance, begins: "I had a job and Patti didn't. I worked a few hours a night for the hospital." Patti does get herself a job, however, "for her self-respect." She sells vitamins door to door. Eventually the narrator attempts to have an affair with one of his wife's co-workers, but it is aborted by the advances of a black man at a "spade club" the couple goes to. The frustrated narrator returns home. His wife hears him and, thinking she has over-slept, gets up and dresses. The story concludes:

> I couldn't take any more tonight. "Go back to sleep, honey. I'm looking for something," I said. I knocked some stuff out of the medicine chest. Things rolled into the sink. "Where's the aspirin?" I said. I knocked down some more things. I didn't care. Things kept falling.

Things do keep falling in Carver's fictional world. With just a few exceptions, he suggests throughout his stories that we are victims of the continuous collapse of our hopes. In **"The Bridle,"** one of the characters says significantly, "Dreams, you know, are what you wake up from."

At times in his fiction adultery or alcoholism or estrangement afflicts a marital relationship, but always there is the problem of communication, for Carver's characters are essentially inarticulate. But it is precisely their inarticulateness that haunts us. It is what they do not say, what the author refuses to divulge, that is nuanced with menace, tinged with sinister suggestion. Under the quiet surfaces of his stories throb foreboding hints of disintegration and disaster.

Carver's characters, of course, reflect our own inarticulateness, our inability to tell others of our anxieties and expectations, of the random and confused impulses which determine our behavior. He writes of our silences.

But these silences in Carver are like the ominous silence before a storm. They portend danger. And we read his stories with increasing alertness and mounting apprehension, waiting for and expecting the worst. Only rarely, as in the title story, do we see, and through a most unlikely agent—in this case, a blind man—the towering cathedral of our possibilities.

Mark A. R. Facknitz (essay date Summer 1986)

SOURCE: "'The Calm,' 'A Small Good Thing,' and 'Cathedral': Raymond Carver and the Rediscovery of Human Worth," in *Studies in Short Fiction*, Vol. 23, No. 3, Summer, 1986, pp. 287-96.

[*In the following essay, Facknitz compares "The Calm," "A Small Good Thing," and "Cathedral," arguing that these stories represent unique attempts by Carver to create acceptance, closure, and connection among his characters.*]

Raymond Carver is as successful as a short story writer in America can be. The signs of his success are many: prestigious and ample grants, publication in the best literary quarterlies and national magazines, and, from all appearances, an unperturbed ability to write the kind of stories he wishes to write. By contrast, the causes of his success are ambiguous. Carver's writing is often facile, and one might argue that he has chanced upon a voice that matches a jaded audience's lust for irony and superficial realism. Whatever the proclivities of his readers, Carver knows their passions and perversions well. In story after story, in language that babbles from wise lunatics, Carver's penetration of characters is honest and fast. But they compose a diminished race—alcoholics, obsessives, drifters, and other losers who are thoroughly thrashed by life in the first round. Only recently have his characters begun to achieve a measure of roundness, and as they have, the message of his work has shifted considerably. Once all one could draw from Carver's work was the moral that when life wasn't cruel it was silly. In several key stories since 1980, he has revealed to readers and characters alike that though they have long suffered the conviction that life is irredeemably trivial, in truth it is as profound as their wounds, and their substance is as large as the loss they suffer.

In their essay on *Will You Please Be Quiet, Please?* (1977), Carver's first major collection of stories, David Boxer and Cassandra Phillips call Carver's world one of "unarticulated longing, a world verging on silence"[1] in which people speak with the "directionless quality, the silliness, the halting rhythm among people under the influence of marijuana," (80-81) and they rightly call such speech "realistic language of a different sort—a probe stuck beneath the skin of disassociation itself" (81). Indeed, it is hard for Carver's characters to say what they mean under any circumstances. Often they try to rephrase their ideas for inattentive listeners, who are as likely as they to be dulled by drugs, alcohol, and overeating. Thus speech is stuporous and communication far from perfect. However, for Boxer and Phillips "passivity is the strength of this language: little seems to be said, yet much is conveyed" (81) and they compare the simplicity of Carver's dialogue to Pinter's and write of "emotional violence lurking beneath the neutral surfaces." One could go further and assert that in his early stories Carver's obsessive subject is the failure of human dialogue, for talking fails in all but the title story of *Will You Please Be Quiet, Please?*, and that story's message is that sometimes the best thing we can say is nothing.

The theme of failed speech is only slightly less domineering in *What We Talk About When We Talk About Love* (1981). An important exception is **"The Calm."**[2] In the story, the narrator watches and listens from a barber chair while a drama unfolds. Its cast is composed of two pairs. In the first pair is Charles, a bank guard, who tells the men in the shop of having wounded a buck the day before, and old Albert, dying of emphysema, who is offended by Charles's brutality. Opposite them is a pair of men without names, the barber and the man with the newspaper. As the owner of the shop, the barber represents order and tranquility, while the other man is a nervous type who exacerbates the tension that develops between Charles and Albert. In allegorical terms the story combines Cruelty (Charles) and Disruption (the man with the newspaper) and makes them the antagonists of Humanity (Albert) and Order (the barber). The plot, then, is very simple: Disruption meddles in the inevitable conflict between Cruelty and Humanity and then step by step Order re-asserts itself. Thus calm is bestowed upon Order's client, the narrator in the barber chair, the witness or internal audience who has played no part in the drama but for whom the moral comes clear.

This primary narrator at moments gives way to a secondary narrator, the guard Charles, as he tells the story of the hunt which he undertook with his hang over son, a young man with a weak stomach and a worse aim. Scarcely a nimrod, Charles is defined by his doltishness and vulgarity. He tells of wounding the buck:

> It was a gut shot. It just like stuns him. So he drops his head and begins this trembling. He trembles all over. The kid's still shooting. Me, I felt like I was back in Korea. So I shot again but

missed. Then old Mr. Buck moves back into the bush. But now, by God, he doesn't have any oomph left in him. The kid has emptied his goddamn gun all to no purpose. But I hit solid. I rammed one right in his guts. That's what I meant by stunned him. (117)

In fact, the hemorrhaging animal has plenty of oomph left in him. Though father and vomiting son follow a gory track, by nightfall they haven't caught up with the wounded deer and abandon him to slow death and scavengers. Inept and immoral, the two renounce an obligation, one that a man of Albert's fiber would likely call sacred. Charles confuses hunting with war, and in doing so he travesties the deepest symbolism of the hunt and idiotically confuses the archetypes of violence and necessity. Yet one sees a measure of perverse respect in his assumption that a bullet in the intestines amounts to nothing more than stunning. This offends Albert, and he tells Charles "You ought to be out there right now looking for that deer instead of in here getting a haircut" (119). In other words, Albert asserts a principle that ought to be self-evident to an American man: hunting is not war; the animal is not an enemy to be loathed and tortured. Albert reminds him of his duty to administer a *coup de grace* and then, by butchering and eating the animal, justify the creature's fear and death.

That such a message is implied by Albert's straightforward statement is clear from Charles's retort: "You can't talk like that. You old fart. I've seen you someplace" (119). In a way his indignation is appropriate. Albert breaks a cultural rule as surely as the guard did in letting the wounded buck wander off. Moreover, in an American barbershop an egalitarian law inheres, and on entering one accepts a kind of truce similar to the set of restraints entering a church entails as one puts aside particulars of class and values. American males in their unspoken codes have reserved parking lots, alleys, bars, committee rooms, and the margins of athletic fields for physical and verbal violence, and they are likely to find arguments in barbershops as unsociable as spitting in a funeral parlor. Thus, the greatest deviant is the stranger with the newspaper, for his motive is malicious delight in causing trouble, in particular the disruption of the conventions of order. He is an "outside agitator" who brings out the worst in Charles and Albert, makes them breech the truce implied by the setting, and finally is more culpable than they for theirs are crimes of passion rather than malice. Albert is overpowered by righteous indignation, and Charles by the humiliation of being accused of breaking the masculine code of the hunt. The stranger defends nothing; rather, he seeks pleasure by provoking others.

The argument ends very soon, for once the barber asserts himself he easily vanquishes the man with the newspaper. First Charles leaves, complaining of the company, and then

Albert goes, tossing off the comment that his hair can go without cutting for a few more days. Left with no one on whom to work his irascibility, the man with the newspaper fidgets. He gets up and looks around the shop, finds nothing to hold his attention, and then announces that he is going and disappears out the door. What has happened is not clear but the barber is nonplused. Although he sides with Albert, allowing that after all Albert had provocation, the barber was forced to keep the peace and has lost a line-up of clients. Temporarily in a bad humor, he says to the narrator, who has said and done nothing all along, "Well, do you want me to finish this barbering or not?" (121) in a tone that suggests to the narrator that the barber blames him for what has occurred.

The ill-feeling does not last. The barber holds the narrator's head and bends close and looks at him in the mirror while the narrator looks at himself. Then the barber stands and begins to rub his fingers through his hair, "slowly, as if thinking about something else," and "tenderly, as a lover would." The story is close to its end, and suddenly the reader has material before him that in no manner impinges on the events of the story and which, at first glance, appears irrelevant:

> That was in Crescent City, California, up near the Oregon border. I left soon after. But today I was thinking of that place, of Crescent City, and of how I was trying out a new life there with my wife, and how, in the barber's chair that morning, I had made up my mind to go. I was thinking today about the calm I felt when I closed my eyes and let the barber's fingers move through my hair, the sweetness of those fingers, and the hair already starting to grow. (121)

Much was transpiring in the heart and mind of the narrator—who is also the internal audience—but in the long run only the general fact that he was coming to an important decision matters. Revealing the particulars of his life that bear upon the decision would shift the focus of **"The Calm"** from how we receive blessings from others to the use such blessings are to us. This would trivialize and demystify the story, for Carver means to imply that while important gifts can only be given to those ready to take them, we cannot give them to ourselves. They come from outside of us from barbers whose names we never learn, or, as **"A Small, Good Thing"** and **"Cathedral"**[3] will show, from bakers and blind men whom coincidence brings into our lives. Once we read the final paragraph of **"The Calm,"** we assume that the narrator was in a turbulent state of mind while making an ostensibly objective record, and though we see nothing of the process except the external sequence, we guess that what he witnesses makes him better able to bring order into his life. Hair grows out, and calm does not last, but the barber proves to the narrator that he cannot create order by himself, though, like Albert, who has developed a sour temper and has trouble breathing in old age, he can always let the matter go a few more days.

Procrastination is occasionally impossible. In **"A Small, Good Thing,"** one of the best stories in the most recent collection, *Cathedral* (1984), Ann and Howard Weiss confront the destruction of well-being. Because they dare to confront the catastrophe of their son's death, they are rescued, in this case by their principal malefactor.

One Saturday Ann orders a birthday cake for a party for her son which will take place Monday afternoon. Monday morning the boy is struck by a car while walking to school. At first he appears little hurt, and walks home, but suddenly he loses consciousness and over several days his condition worsens as sleep subsides into coma and at last he dies. Meanwhile doctors, nurses, and technicians come and go, offering encouragement to the parents and looking for clues to why the boy won't wake. Each time the doctor revises his opinion of the boy's condition, Ann guesses the truth, and the discrepancy between what she is told and what actually happens broadens as the story advances. Yet the doctors are not lying. Their reason and their tests are deceiving them, and all the hypotheses, diagnoses, X-rays, and scans fail to reveal "a hidden occlusion," a "one-in-a-million circumstance," (80) that kills the child. Thus, while all the rational and objective ways of making sense are defeated, the truth persists in the mother's worst intuitions. When the boy dies, the doctors need an autopsy because things need explaining, and they must satisfy the need to know why their minds and machines failed. The parents must make sense in another way. They must voice an unspeakable grief, and they accomplish this by listening to someone else's suffering.

Early in the story Ann goes to the baker, a man who will torment her more than he can guess. Carver develops the scene:

> She gave the baker her name, Ann Weiss, and her telephone number. The cake would be ready on Monday morning, just out of the oven, in plenty of time for the child's party that afternoon. The baker was not jolly. There were no pleasantries between them, just the minimum exchange of words, the necessary information. He made her feel uncomfortable, and she didn't like that. While he was bent over the counter with the pencil in his hand, she studied his coarse features and wondered if he'd ever done anything else with his life besides be a baker. (60)

Much later in the story, while Ann sits by the phone after having called relatives to tell them of the boy's death, the baker phones. He has made several calls in the last few days—it was impossible to say precisely how many—and Howard and Ann have taken the calls as perverse jokes on the part of the hit-and-run driver. Through misapprehension, the cake and the boy come to have the same name, and the baker speaks in malicious metaphor when he says to the desperate woman, "Your Scotty, I got him ready for you. Did you forget him?" (83) This is language of an extraordinary kind. No longer "minimum exchange, or the necessary information," such an utterance is a linguistic perversion for it means most when misunderstood.

When it occurs to Ann that the baker is her tormentor, she and her husband rush down to the shopping center and beat on the back door in the middle of the night until the baker lets them in. There she lights into him:

> "My son's dead," she said with a cold, even finality. "He was hit by a car Monday morning. We've been waiting with him until he died. But, of course, you couldn't be expected to know that, could you? Bakers can't know everything can they, Mr. Baker? But he's dead. He's dead, you bastard!" Just as suddenly as it had welled in her, the anger dwindled, gave way to something else, a dizzy feeling of nausea. She leaned against the wooden table that was sprinkled with flour, put her hands over her face, and began to cry, her shoulders rocking back and forth. "It isn't fair," she said. (86-87)

Nothing here can be misunderstood. The facts are plain, and the steps in her understanding of what bakers can and cannot know are clear and logical. Her anger is pure, and purifying: it is as physical and overpowering as the nausea that succeeds it, and the emotion and the sensation are as honest and undeniable as her recognition that her son's death was not fair.

Her speech abolishes the social conventions, suspicions, and errors that brought them to the point of confrontation. Ann, Howard, and the baker are tangled in a subtle set of causes, and Carver suggests again, as he has in many stories (e.g. **"The Train," "Feathers"**), that through imperceptible and trivial dishonesties we create large lies that can only be removed by superhuman acts of self-assertion. In response to Ann's overwhelming honesty, the menaced baker puts down his rolling pin, clears places for them at the table, and makes them sit. He tells them that he is sorry, but they have little to say about their loss. Instead they take the coffee and rolls he serves them and listen while he tells them about his loneliness and doubt, and about the ovens, "endlessly empty and endlessly full" (89). They accept his life story as consolation, and while eating and listening achieve communion. Carver ends the story at dawn, with hope, and pushes forward symbols of sanctified space and the eucharist:

> "Smell this," the baker said, breaking open a dark loaf. "It's a heavy bread, but rich." They smelled it, then he had them taste it. It had the taste of molasses and coarse grains. They listened to him. They ate what they could. They swallowed the dark bread. It was like daylight under the fluorescent trays of lights. They talked on into the early morning, the high, pale cast of light in the windows, and they did not think of leaving. (89)

Carver's characters rarely achieve a transcendent acceptance of their condition as does Ann Weiss. Indeed, more commonly they resign themselves without struggle or thought. They are rarely attractive people, and often readers must work against a narrator's tendency to sound cretinous or Carver's propensity to reveal characters as bigots and dunces. As the story opens, the first-person narrator of **"Cathedral"** appears to be another in this series of unattractive types. He worries about the approaching visit of a friend of his wife, a blind man named Robert who was once the wife's employer. He has little experience with the blind and faces the visit anxiously. His summary of the wife's association with Robert is derisive, its syntax blunt and its humor fatiguing:

> She'd worked with this blind man all summer. She read stuff to him, case studies, reports, that sort of thing. She helped him organize his little office in the county social service department. They'd become good friends my wife and the blind man. How do I know these things? She told me. And she told me something else. On her last day in the office, the blind man asked if he could touch her face. She agreed to this. She told me he ran his fingers over every part of her face, her nose—even her neck! She never forgot it. She even tried to write a poem about it. She was always writing a poem. She wrote a poem or two every year, usually after something really important happened to her. (210)

Clearly he is jealous, and so emphasizes the eroticism of the blind man's touch. But she was leaving the blind man's office to marry her childhood sweetheart, an officer in the Air Force whom the narrator refers to as "this man who'd first enjoyed her favors" (210), and much of his jealousy toward the first husband transfers to the blind man Robert. Thus Robert sexually threatens the narrator, with his blindness, and by virtue of being a representative of a past that is meaningful to the wife. The narrator is selfish and callous; however, he is one of Carver's heavy drinkers and no reader could be drawn through **"Cathedral"** because he cares for

him, and perhaps what pushes one into the story is a fear of the harm he may do to his wife and her blind friend. Yet Carver redeems the narrator by releasing him from the figurative blindness that results in a lack of insight into his own condition and which leads him to trivialize human feelings and needs. Indeed, so complete is his misperception that the blind man gives him a faculty of sight that he is not even aware that he lacks.

The wife and blind man have kept in touch over the years, a period of change and grief for each, by sending tape recordings back and forth. The life of a military wife depressed the young woman and led to her divorce from her first husband, but the narrator's view of her suffering is flat and without compassion:

> She told the blind man she'd written a poem and he was in it. She told him that she was writing a poem about what it was like to be an Air Force officer's wife in the Deep South. The poem wasn't finished yet. She was still writing it. The blind man made a tape. He sent her the tape. She made a tape. This went on for years. My wife's officer was posted to one base and then another. She sent tapes from Moody AFB, McGuire, McConnell, and finally Travis, near Sacramento, where one night she got to feeling lonely and cut off from people she kept losing in that moving-around life. She balked, couldn't go it another step. She went in and swallowed all the pills and capsules in the medicine cabinet and washed them down with a bottle of gin. Then she got in a hot bath and passed out.
>
> But instead of dying she got sick. She threw up. (211)

Suicide is mundane, for him merely a question of balking at life, and dying is roughly the equivalent to throwing up, something one might do *instead*, much as the narrator stays up nights drunk and stoned in front of the television as an antidote to the "crazy" dreams that trouble his sleep. To his credit, he does not claim moral superiority to his wife, and sees the waste of his drinking and the cowardice of staying in a job he can neither leave nor enjoy. He is numb and isolated, a modern man for whom integration with the human race would be so difficult that it is futile. Consequently he hides by failing to try, anesthetizes himself with booze, and explains away the world with sarcasm. He does nothing to better his lot. Rather he invents strategies for keeping things as they are and will back off from even the most important issues. When he wisecracks that he might take the blind man bowling, his wife rebukes him: "If you love me, you can do this for me. If you don't love me, okay. But if you had a friend, any friend, and the friend came to visit, I'd make him feel comfortable" (212). Each ignores that she says *him*, not her, and the emotional blackmail of "if you don't love me, okay" appears not to register. He responds that he hasn't any blind friends, and when she reminds him that he hasn't any friends at all, much less blind ones, he becomes sullen and withdraws from the conversation. What she has said is aggressive and true and to respond to it would imply recognition of the many and large insufficiencies of his life. Instead, he works away at a drink and listens while she tells him about Beulah, the blind man's wife who has recently died of cancer. There's no facing this subject. He listens for a while as she talks about Beulah:

> "Was his wife a Negro?" I asked.
>
> "Are you crazy?" my wife said. "Have you just flipped or something?"
>
> She picked up a potato. I saw it hit the floor, then roll under the stove.
>
> "What's wrong with you?" she said. "Are you drunk?"
>
> "I'm just asking," I said.
>
> Right then my wife filled me in with more detail than I cared to know. I made a drink and sat at the kitchen table to listen. Pieces of the story began to fall into place. (212-213)

Death is a subject they touch on often but never pursue, and they go on as married couples do in Carver's stories, never forcing a point because each hurt touches on another hurt. Thus, because each serious effort risks the destruction of a stuporous status quo that he maintains by various strategies of denial, they never touch each other.

The narrator inadvertently makes a friend of the blind man. At the end of an evening of whiskey and conversation that bewilder him and leave him sitting alone in his resentment, he is left with Robert when his wife goes upstairs to change into her robe. Together they sit, the narrator watching the late news, Robert listening, his ear turned toward the television, his unseeing eyes turned disconcertingly on the narrator. After the news there is a program about cathedral architecture and the narrator tries to explain to Robert what a cathedral looks like. They smoke some marijuana and he blunders on, failing to express the visual effect of a cathedral's soaring space to a man who, as far as the narrator can tell, has no analogues for spatial dimension. When Robert asks what a fresco is, the narrator is at a complete loss. The blind man proposes a solution, and on a heavy paper bag the narrator draws a cathedral while Robert's hand rides his. He begins with a box and pointed roof that could

be his own house, and adds spires, buttresses, windows, and doors, and at last he has elaborated a gothic cathedral in lines pressed hard into the paper. When Robert takes his hand and makes him close his eyes to touch the cathedral, he "sees." Even when he is told that he can open his eyes, he chooses not to, for he is learning what he has long been incapable of perceiving and even now can not articulate:

> I thought I'd keep them that way a little longer. I thought it was something I ought not to forget.
>
> "Well?" he said. "Are you looking?"
>
> My eyes were still closed. I was in my house and I knew that. But I didn't feel inside anything.
>
> "It's really something," I said. (228)

The cathedral, of course, is the space that does not limit, and his perception of *something*—objective, substantial, meaningful—that cannot be seen with ordinary sight depends on his having to perceive as another perceives. In fictional terms, he learns to shift point of view. In emotional terms, he learns to feel empathy. In the moment when the blind man and the narrator share an identical perception of spiritual space, the narrator's sense of enclosure—of being confined by his own house and circumstances—vanishes as if by an act of grace, or a very large spiritual reward for a virtually insignificant gesture. Following the metaphor of the story, the narrator learns to see with eyes other than that insufficient set that keeps him a friendless drunk and a meager husband.

In a reminiscence on John Gardner, his late teacher, Carver pauses to reflect that at some point in late youth or early middle age we all face the inevitability of our failure and we suffer "the suspicion that we're taking on water, and that things are not working out in our lives the way we'd planned."[4] For a time there is nothing anyone can do against the debilitating effect of such a recognition. But in **"The Calm," "A Small, Good Thing,"** and **"Cathedral,"** protagonists are taken from behind by understanding. When it occurs, understanding comes as the result of an unearned and unexpected gift, a kind of grace constituted in human contact that a fortunate few experience. Of course, Carver does not imply a visitation of the Holy Ghost, nor does he argue that salvation is apt to fall on the lowliest of creatures in the moment of their greatest need as it does, say, in Flannery O'Connor, whose benighted Ruby Turpin in "Revelation" is saved in spite of herself when shown the equality of all souls in the sight of God. Grace, Carver says, is bestowed upon us by other mortals, and it comes suddenly, arising in circumstances as mundane as a visit to the barber shop, and in the midst of feelings as ignoble or quotidian as jealousy, anger, loneliness, and grief. It can be represented in incidental physical contact, and the deliverer is not necessarily aware of his role. Not Grace in the Christian sense at all, it is what grace becomes in a godless world—a deep and creative connection between humans that reveals to Carver's alienated and diminished creatures that there can be contact in a world they supposed was empty of sense or love. Calm is given in a touch, a small, good thing is the food we get from others, and in the cathedrals we draw together, we create large spaces for the spirit.

1. David Boxer and Cassandra Phillips, "*Will You Please Be Quiet, Please?*: Voyeurism, Dissociation, and the Art of Raymond Carver," *The Iowa Review*, 10 (1979), 84.

2. "The Calm" is collected in *What We Talk About When We Talk About Love* (New York: Alfred A. Knopf, 1981).

3. Both stories appear in Carver's most recent collection of fiction, *Cathedral* (New York: Alfred A. Knopf, 1983).

4. "John Gardner," *The Georgia Review*, 37 (1983), 418.

Eugene Goodheart (essay date 1987)

SOURCE: "Raymond Carver's *Cathedral*," in *Pieces of Resistance*, Cambridge University Press, 1987, pp. 162-66.

[*In the following essay, Goodheart analyzes Carver's moral code, arguing that he is at his best when his characters adhere to it.*]

The affectless narrative voice of a Raymond Carver story defends itself against surprise or shock or pain. The most banal situations propose inexplicable signs of menace that require, in response, a discipline of unemotional terseness. Nothing much happens at the dinner party in **"Feathers,"** the first of the stories in Carver's latest collection, except for the weird appearance of a vulture-sized peacock, which stares at the guests and to which Jack, the narrator, responds at intervals with three "god damns," as if the word were a talisman for preserving equanimity. The peacock, the plaster cast of misshapen teeth on top of the TV, the very ugly baby of the hosts give the story a quality of surreal menace that never quite materializes. Though nothing of consequence happens at the dinner, the friendship between the men (the wives have just been introduced to each other) is significantly altered. "We're still friends. That hasn't changed any. But I've gotten careful with what I say to him. And I know he feels that and wishes it could be different. I wish it could be too." Every detail conspires to estrange the friends from each other, whatever else they might wish.

The threat to Carver's characters lies within. They are vulnerable to their own weakness. Informed by his landlord that he must vacate a house he has rented, Wes of **"The Chef's House"** refuses to be consoled by his estranged wife. "'Suppose,' [she asks him to imagine], 'nothing had ever happened.'" But Wes, a half-reformed alcoholic, can imagine no such power and freedom for himself. "'I don't have that kind of supposing left in me. We were born who we are.'" Here the narrator is the wife who has imagined such freedom, a freedom that would make it possible for them to get back together, but who at the end acknowledges her husband's incapacity for it. "We'll clean it up tonight, I thought, and that will be the end of it."

Carver's characters are alcoholic, unemployed, occasionally violent to their spouses and children, victims of passion or circumstance. They are characters on the margins of middle-class life with the values and occupations of the middle class: sales people, teachers, business people, who nevertheless seem always on the brink of *lumpen* existence. They do not quite fall out of the middle class, but the threat of catastrophic failure seems always imminent. They live transient lives in rooms, apartments, and houses which either do not belong to them or to which they do not belong. Neither the utilities nor the furniture can ever be depended on—as if the external world had taken on the emotional uncertainty or inertia of the inner lives of the characters.

Carver writes of a time (the present) when everything seems to have gone wrong. In **"Preservation,"** the breakdown of a refrigerator plunges the husband into despair because he remembers that his folks had one that lasted twenty-three years. Carver, with perhaps a bit too much contrivance, makes the fridge and the thawing packages of frozen food an objective correlative for the moral desolation of the time. Yet he also suggests that it may be an illusion that things have changed for the worse. The wife's parents, after all, were divorced, the father had disappeared from her life, and he had died in a car that leaked carbon monoxide.

Have things changed, or is change an illusion? Carver's answer to such a question is a double perspective, true to our experience of both past and present. The past seems better than the present until we recall the actual events of the past; but such recollection cannot alter our sense of *present* hopelessness or meaninglessness. Right now, whatever the past was and meant to the people who lived it, there is a general sense that things have not only gone wrong, but that they'll never be right again. America, the land of the future, suddenly seems at the end of its tether. Carver's fiction doesn't explicitly encompass conditions of structural unemployment, incorrigible violence in our cities, the closed frontier, and our sense of baffled manifest destiny, but he has superbly caught the mood generated by these conditions.

Even some of Carver's admirers have found the sad passivity of his characters a limitation of his art. In his review of *Cathedral*, Irving Howe mentions the judgment of a friend who finds the work "cold" and then goes on to construe the judgment as referring to "a note of disdain toward the people he creates," an impatience with "the resignation of his characters." Howe even hears in this note a wish that "they would rebel against the constrictions of their lives." I for one hear neither the note of disdain nor the note of impatience. The story **"Chef's House"** knows that Wes's inability to suppose is more authentic than the wife's desire not "to hear him talk like this." He is sorry, but he can't help it. "'I can't talk like somebody I'm not. If I was somebody else, I wouldn't be me. But I'm who I am.'" His wife in effect acknowledges Wes's truth with an economical sympathy that is characteristic of the narrative voice in most of the stories. "Wes, it's all right, I said. I brought his hand to my cheek."

Wes could be speaking of the moral aspect of Carver's art as well as of his own character. In his first collection of stories, *In Our Time*, Hemingway presented characters, not unlike Carver's in their terseness, who refused to act up to feelings that they didn't have. The false note for Carver, as for Hemingway, is supposing yourself to be other than you are.

Like Hemingway's characters, Carver's characters possess a code (there is even the code of the alcoholic) which dictates their behavior. There is a right way and a wrong way to be despairing, or ineffectual, or lost. Carver actually gives us an aesthetic of failure. This is why I find Carver's prize-winning **"A Small, Good Thing"** flawed in its attempt to redeem the "evil" baker, who unknowingly intrudes upon the lives of the grief-stricken parents of a dead child, continually phoning them to remind them of the birthday cake they had ordered and forgotten to pick up. The baker, sullen and dimly conceived through most of the story, suddenly becomes a figure of compassion, who asks forgiveness for the kind of man he has become. "I was a different kind of human being," he says. Perhaps. But the concluding episode in which he tries to console the parents with coffee and freshly baked bread strikes me as a bit of willed Dickensian sentimentality.

There is, of course, the danger that the very limitations of these characters and the medium in which they live will produce monotonous art. The danger is reduced, however, by Carver's resourcefulness in creating a variety of events and effects. How different and yet alike are the two stories of ineffectual husbands, **"The Chef's House"** and **"Preservation."** Only on rare occasions does the weirdness of a Carver story fail to emerge "organically" from the situation and seem contrived, an unnecessary turn of the screw. In an early story, **"Mr. Coffee and Mr. Fixit,"** the hero's mother is a sixty-five

year old swinger, whom her son discovers kissing a man on the sofa of her house, an unusual but plausible scene of our time. But when the son remembers one of her former lovers, "an unemployed aerospace engineer," who walked with "a limp from a gunshot wound his first wife gave him," we seem to have entered the zone of jokiness. The integrity of **"The Student's Wife"** (a story in an earlier collection, *Will You Please Be Quiet, Please?*) is also slightly compromised because it introduces the main character as an admirer of Rilke, whose poems he reads to his wife in bed. The rest of the story beautifully unfolds the insomnia and despair of the wife, who loses her husband every night to a heavy "jaws clenched" sleep. Rilke is an irrelevance. Carver's tact, his instinct for the right detail, is usually so sure that the rare failure jars.

One can see in the title story, **"Cathedral,"** which appropriately concludes the present volume, an effort on Carver's part to transcend his medium, or rather to find within the medium the gestures of fancy or imagination that will reduce its poverty. **"Cathedral"** is told like many Carver stories in a somewhat disconsolate voice, that of a husband bemused by his wife, who has invited home a blind man for whom she had worked as a reader and helper many years before. The disconsolateness disappears, however, in the extraordinary relationship that develops between the two men, in which the husband teaches the blind man to visualize a cathedral by having him hold his hand as he draws it. As in D. H. Lawrence's story, "The Blind Man," blindness becomes a metaphor for imagination: the power of the mind to ascend to the spires. Carver's story risks pretentiousness, but wholly avoids it, for he preserves in the telling the simplicity and authenticity of language that characterize all his stories.

Carver's minimal art achieves maximal effects. Frank Kermode, I think, is right to speak as he did of Carver's capacity to evoke "a whole moral condition" in a seemingly slight sketch. One wonders where Carver will go from here. He is a lyric poet, who writes verse as well as stories. It is hard to imagine him working in the more extended form of the novel. In a revealing autobiographical essay (see *In Praise of What Persist*, edited by Stephen Berg), Carver describes his career as a short-story writer as a response to the baleful influence of his children, who did not allow him time for the longer effort of the novel. The circumstances of his life produced a "discovery" about the novel.

> To write a novel, it seemed to me, a writer should be living in a world that makes sense, a world that the writer can believe in, draw a bead on, and then write about accurately. A world that will, for a time anyway, stay fixed in one place. Along with this there has to be a belief in the essential *correctness* of that world. A belief that the known

world has reasons for existing, and is worth writing about—is not likely to go up in smoke in the process. This wasn't the case with the world I knew and was living in. My world was one that seemed to change gears and directions, along with its rules, every day. Time and again I reached the point where I couldn't see or plan any further ahead than the first of next month and gathering together enough money, by hook or by crook, to meet rent and provide the children's school clothes.

Although Carver's is not the only possible world, it is one in which many people live, and one he writes very accurately about. In the paradoxically lyric way of the minimalist writer, Carver has not only made sense of this world, he has given it value.

Keith Cushman (essay date 1988)

SOURCE: "Blind, Intertextual Love: 'The Blind Man' and Raymond Carver's 'Cathedral'," in *D. H. Lawrence's Literary Inheritors*, edited by Keith Cushman and Dennis Jackson, Macmillan, 1991, pp. 155-66.

[*In the following essay, which was originally published in Études lawrenciennes in 1988, Cushman states that although Carver was not influenced by D. H. Lawrence's short story "The Blind Man" when Carver wrote "Cathedral," the stories are very similar.*]

Anyone who reads Raymond Carver's **'Cathedral'**, the title-story of his 1983 collection, with a knowledge of D. H. Lawrence's short stories might easily conclude that **'Cathedral'** is a shrewd, intriguing rewriting of 'The Blind Man'. Carver's tale presents a scrambled reprise of the crucial elements of Lawrence's great story. Lawrence's triangle of characters consists of a blind husband (Maurice Pervin), his wife (Isabel), and the wife's sighted friend (Bertie Reid). In **'Cathedral'**, the unnamed husband and wife are sighted, but the wife's visiting friend (Robert) is blind. The interplay of husband, wife, and visitor comprises the slight action of both stories. Both 'The Blind Man' and **'Cathedral'** conclude with a potentially transforming act of ritual communion between the two men. The husband in **'Cathedral'** genuinely enters Robert's world of blindness; Maurice Pervin does not realize how badly his attempted communion with Bertie has failed. The evidence seems clear: Carver uses Lawrence's story as the scaffolding for his own.

'Cathedral' is typical of Carver's stories in presenting trapped characters leading lives at once banal and nightmarish. As in W. H. Auden's 'As I Walked Out One

Evening', 'the crack in the teacup opens / A lane to the land of the dead'. Carver is a master at presenting what Gary L. Fisketjon has called the 'terrifying implications of Normal Life' (qtd. in Stull 237). As Joe David Bellamy has put it, '[b]eneath the surface conventionality of [Carver's] salesmen, waitresses, bookkeepers, or hopeless middle-class "occupants" lies a morass of unarticulated [sic] yearnings and unexamined horrors; repressed violence, the creeping certainty that nothing matters, perverse sexual wishes, the inadmissible evidence of inadequacy' (qtd. in Stull 239). With failed communication and missed connections so ubiquitous in Carver's stories, the mysterious but unmistakable oneness experienced by the husband and Robert at the end of **'Cathedral'** has a powerful impact, especially since the story concludes the collection. Indeed, beginning with **'Cathedral'**, Carver's work became somewhat less bleak and chilly.

In **'Cathedral'**, Carver enigmatically dramatizes the possibility of human change and redemption. This element of **'Cathedral'** is made all the more compelling by the awareness that Carver is rewriting the end of Lawrence's story, where no real communion takes place. One story resonates against the other. **'Cathedral'** offers a complex critique of 'The Blind Man' even as it draws upon it. Chalk up one more striking example of Lawrence's influence on contemporary fiction writers.

This argument is vitiated by one major flaw. Raymond Carver wrote me in autumn 1987 that though he 'had read those three or four stories of [Lawrence's] that are always anthologized—"The Horse Dealer's Daughter" and "Tickets, Please" and one or two others', he had not read 'The Blind Man' when he wrote **'Cathedral'**. Carver does acknowledge that when he read 'The Blind Man', not long after writing **'Cathedral'**, he liked Lawrence's story 'a good deal'. He even had his students at Syracuse read 'The Blind Man' 'in the fall term of 1982 (when [he] first read the story)'. Still, he does not '*recall* noticing any, or many, similarities' to his own story when he read 'The Blind Man'. He also supplies a fascinating account of the genesis of **'Cathedral'**:

> The thing that sparked the story was the visit of a blind man to our house! It's true. Well, stories have to come from someplace, yes? Anyway, this blind man did pay us a visit and even spent the night. But there all similarities end. The rest of the story was cobbled up from this and that, naturally.

Thus, the Lawrentian scaffolding of **'Cathedral'** collapses.[1]

Though my study of the influence of 'The Blind Man' on **'Cathedral'** has abruptly ended, you will note that my essay continues. The very existence of Lawrence's strong text about three characters—wife, blind man, visiting old friend of the wife—creates a powerful intertextual relationship between the stories. To Julia Kristeva, intertextuality 'has nothing to do with matters of influence by one writer upon another, or with the sources of a literary work'. Rather, it is defined 'as the transposition of one or more *systems* of signs into another' (qtd. in Roudiez 15). Roland Barthes expands upon this definition in noting that

> any text is an intertext; other texts are present in it, at varying levels, in more or less recognisable forms: the texts of the previous and surrounding culture. Any text is a new tissue of past citations. Bits of codes, formulae, rhythmic models, fragments of social languages, etc. pass into the text and are redistributed within it, for there is always language before and around the text. Intertextuality, the condition of any text whatsoever, cannot . . . be reduced to a problem of sources or influences. . . . (Barthes 39)

Though Carver had not read 'The Blind Man' when he wrote **'Cathedral'**, he nevertheless produced a story that resides within the intertextual orbit of 'The Blind Man'. The stories speak to and illuminate one another. Fredric Jameson, commenting on Lawrence Kazdan's movie *Body Heat* (which he sees as a new version of James M. Cain's *The Postman Always Rings Twice*), notes that 'our awareness of the preexistence of other versions, previous films of the novel as well as the novel itself, is now a constitutive and essential part of the film's structure' (67). 'The Blind Man' is similarly present in our response to **'Cathedral'**—and vice versa.

Both 'The Blind Man' and **'Cathedral'** associate blindness with a greater depth of being than is possible in the rational, limited sighted world. Over the centuries, the blindness trope has importantly signified the distinction between sight and insight. In classical mythology, the blind seer Tiresias perfectly embodies this tradition. When Oedipus gouges out his eyes, he is violently dramatizing his hard-won knowledge that all along he had been 'blind'. His decision literally to blind himself contains a triumphant element, for the deeper understanding associated with blindness is to be preferred to the superficial grasp of reality associated with sight. The blinding of Gloucester in *King Lear* follows the same paradigm: paradoxically, Gloucester can 'see' only after being blinded. Mr. Rochester is temporarily blinded at the end of *Jane Eyre* while selflessly trying to rescue his mad wife from the burning Thornfield Hall. Again blindness is associated with greater insight.

'The Blind Man' and **'Cathedral'**, each in its own way, draw on this blindness trope, for Lawrence's blind Maurice and Carver's blind Robert see more deeply than their sighted counterparts. In 'The Blind Man', blindness is associated with instinct and the unconscious; in **'Cathedral'**, it finally

represents an experience of self-abnegation and shared transcendence. Both tales rewrite a story central to the Western tradition. Both are rooted in the same cultural and literary heritage.

'The Blind Man', written in 1918 just after the Armistice, was first collected in *England, My England and Other Stories* (1922). World War I provides the background for many of these stories. Maurice Pervin, blinded and disfigured in Flanders has lived at the Grange with his wife Isabel for a year. He does menial work around the farm and discovers that his life seems 'peaceful with the almost incomprehensible peace of immediate contact in darkness'. He and the pregnant Isabel spend time talking, singing, and reading together 'in a wonderful and unspeakable intimacy'. She also reviews books for a Scottish newspaper, carrying on an 'old interest' (347).

The Pervins share a 'whole world, rich and real and invisible', but sometimes Isabel suffers from a 'weariness, a terrible ennui', and Maurice is overcome by 'devastating fits of depression, which seemed to lay waste his whole being' (347). Though Isabel believes that 'husband and wife should be so important to one another, that the rest of the world simply did not count' (349), the strain of her difficult, complex marriage makes her yearn for 'connection with the outer world' (348). When her old friend Bertie Reid, barrister, Scotsman, and minor literary man, writes, she invites him to visit.

Maurice has encouraged Isabel to invite Bertie, for, isolated in his blindness, he yearns to make contact with his wife's old friend. Like Birkin in *Women in Love*, he seems to feel that an intimate relationship with a woman is not enough. But the visit is not a success. The high tea prepared by Isabel for the two men makes Maurice restless, and he retreats to the barn, where he sits pulping turnips. Isabel sends Bertie out through the wind and rain to fetch her husband. In the barn, 'filled with hot, poignant love, the passion of friendship', Maurice is eager that he and his wife's friend should 'know each other'. He runs his hand over Bertie's skull and face and then grasps the 'shoulder, the arm, the hand of the other man'. When Maurice asks his visitor to touch his eyes, Bertie, trying unsuccessfully 'by any means to escape', lays 'his fingers on the scarred eyes'. Maurice covers Bertie's fingers 'with his own hand, [pressing] the fingers of the other man upon his disfigured eye-sockets, trembling in every fibre' (364). Maurice proclaims that he and Bertie have 'become friends', but Bertie cannot bear it 'that he had been touched by the blind man, his insane reserve broken in'. He is 'like a mollusc whose shell is broken' (365). No wonder Lawrence described the end of 'The Blind Man' as 'queer and ironical' (*Letters III* 303).

A Lawrentian schema can be discerned beneath the surface of 'The Blind Man'. Maurice and Bertie represent two

Lawrentian poles of being. Maurice does not 'think much or trouble much' but lives in the 'sheer immediacy of blood-contact with the substantial world' (355). With his 'slow' mind and 'quick and acute' feelings, he is 'just the opposite to Bertie, whose mind was much quicker than his emotions'. The brittle Bertie is a 'man of letters, a Scotsman of the intellectual type, quick, ironical, sentimental' (349). He cannot 'approach women physically' (359). Maurice and his world of darkness are too much for him. At tea, Bertie, both fascinated and repulsed by the blind man, looks away from him and, 'without knowing what he did', picks up a 'little crystal bowl of violets from the table, and held them to his nose' (358), retreating to the safe world of polite civilization and refinement.

Isabel is caught between the extremes embodied in these antithetical men. Bertie is essentially neuter, and Isabel is devoted to Maurice. Nevertheless, the Maurice-Isabel-Bertie triangle includes a submerged erotic element. Isabel feels fulfilled by the 'blood-prescience' (355) she experiences through Maurice; she 'couldn't do without' his 'presence—indefinable—.' But she also feels isolated and incomplete and longs for Bertie's intellect. Of course, Bertie is unable to rise to the occasion. He observes to Isabel that there is '[s]omething lacking all the time' in her relationship with her husband but suggests lamely—and self-reflexively—that everyone is 'deficient somewhere' (361). The erotic tension is most visible in the scene in which Bertie and Isabel chat shortly after his arrival while 'helpless desolation' (356) comes over the shut-out Maurice.

The uninitiated reader of Lawrence is apt to conclude that 'The Blind Man' offers a simple lesson in the value of living in the darkness. The 'sheer immediacy of blood-contact with the substantial world' creates for Maurice a 'certain rich positivity, bordering sometimes on rapture'. We too should learn Maurice's 'new way of consciousness' (355) and should discover the 'peace of immediate contact in darkness' (347).

But as Janice Harris reminds us, 'Lawrence is not an advocate of any one way of knowing, blood prescience included' (278). The 'rich suffusion' (355) of Maurice's state sometimes becomes swamp-like and overwhelming. 'The Blind Man' is actually a parable of unintegrated being, of the impossibility of bringing together body and mind, darkness and light.

Carver's 'Cathedral' lacks such allegorical resonances, but it reads like a dream-image of Lawrence's story. As in 'The Blind Man', the intrusion of a visiting outsider breaks an imperfect marital equilibrium. As in Lawrence's story, Carver's characters eat together and talk inconsequentially while the husband grows jealous and uneasy. The husband is insecure; the wife feels that something is lacking in her marriage. The tension generated by 'Cathedral', like that in 'The Blind Man', is resolved by a surprising ending. Carver's story is also like Lawrence's in developing a fundamental dialectic between sight and blindness.

The husband narrates 'Cathedral', providing the story with the off-hand, colloquial texture characteristic of Carver's fiction. Robert, the blind man who is an old friend of the narrator's wife, does not conform to stereotypes of blindness. He has a beard and a booming voice, his clothes are 'spiffy' (216); he does not use a cane or wear dark glasses; he owns two television sets. Like Bertie Reid, the husband is uncomfortable with the other man's blindness: 'his being blind bothered me' (209). The narrator perceives the visitor as a threat.

The three people drink lots of scotch, they eat dinner, they smoke marijuana, they watch television (though of course the blind man cannot see). The wife falls asleep on the sofa as her husband and the blind man watch a late-night television program about medieval cathedrals. Robert asks the narrator to describe a cathedral to him—not an easy task. The narrator soon gives up, remarking that 'cathedrals don't mean anything special to me. Nothing'. Robert then suggests that they 'draw [a cathedral] together': 'He found my hand, the hand with the pen. He closed his hand over my hand. "Go ahead, bub, draw," he said'. Though the narrator is 'no artist', he starts drawing and can't stop. 'You got it, bub', encourages the blind man (226-7). The wife awakens, but the husband continues to draw. Robert asks him to close his eyes, and he does. The blind man's 'fingers rode my fingers as my hand went over the paper. It was like nothing else in my life up to now' (228). The story ends enigmatically:

> I was in my house. I knew that. But I didn't feel like I was inside anything.
>
> 'It's really something,' I said. (228)

The submerged erotic tension of Lawrence's story is closer to the surface in 'Cathedral'. The narrator, emotionally estranged from his wife, is unable to make human contact with anyone. He conceals his self-pity behind cynical humor, meanwhile keeping everyone at a distance. Jealous of his wife's first husband, the 'man who'd first enjoyed her favors', he is also jealous of her blind friend, who years ago had said goodbye to her by touching 'his fingers to every part of her face, her nose—even her neck!' (210). The husband's jealous feelings are probably not misplaced: 'My wife finally took her eyes off the blind man and looked at me. I had the feeling she didn't like what she saw' (215).

The husband attempts to deaden his inner pain by pursuing various forms of sensory oblivion with his wife: the heavy drinking, marijuana smoking, and 'serious eating': 'We ate everything there was to eat on the table. We ate like there was no tomorrow. We didn't talk. We ate. We scarfed. We grazed that table' (217). Bertie Reid is effete and intellectual, the husband in **'Cathedral'** is crude and unintellectual, but both reveal the limitations of sightedness.

The wife also seeks oblivion, for she too finds herself in a bad way emotionally. Like Isabel in 'The Blind Man', she is an in-between character. This different woman suffers from aimlessness and anomie. Her suicide attempt at the breakup of her first marriage tells us that, unlike her husband, she at least does not hide from her emotions. She also writes poetry in order to confront and examine her life. (In contrast, the husband remarks sourly that poetry is not 'the first thing I reach for when I pick up something to read' [210].) Her happiness over her old friend's visit also demonstrates her openness to human contact. The husband notices that she is 'wearing a smile' when she returns from the train depot with the blind man. 'Just amazing' (214), he says. She is one of the walking wounded, whereas her husband is one of the living dead.

In 'The Blind Man', Lawrence revisits, rethinks, and in some ways parodies important themes and ideas in *Women in Love*, which he had essentially completed by November 1917. Like the novel but in miniature, the story dramatizes and questions the possibility of significant relationship, man to woman and man to man (and man and woman to the cosmos). 'The Blind Man' also resembles *Women in Love* in its central fascination with wholeness of being. The butterflies Ursula looks at and the 'fleshy' water-plants in the 'soft, oozy, watery mud' both represent principles of life. How can a person incorporate both principles—the light and the darkness, the 'silver river of life' and the 'black river' (19, 172)—into his being?

In *Women in Love*, Lawrence explores these difficult questions with high seriousness and great intensity. The novel leaves the questions unresolved, for Lawrence is too great an artist to force resolutions where no real resolutions are to be found. Nevertheless, the novel's rawness and turbulence express his urgent effort to discover the dynamic unifying principle that would bring man and woman together, man and man together, body and soul together. 'The Crown' and the late additions to *Twilight in Italy* are characterized by the same restless quest after the absolute. Though he offers no clear answers in any of these works, he genuinely seeks such answers. *The Rainbow* had pointed hopefully toward the possibility of personal integration, but *Women in Love* is more troubled, problematic, and open-ended.

Any truths offered by *Women in Love*—if truths there be—are at best fragile and provisional. If in *Women in Love* Lawrence pursues ultimates, in 'The Blind Man' and most

of the other *England, My England* stories, he seems content (or even pleased) to acknowledge that no such ultimates are available. *Women in Love* is urgent and impassioned; 'The Blind Man' is detached and sardonic. 'The Blind Man' revisits the notions of *Blutbrüderschaft* and wholeness of being, so crucial to *Women in Love*, but almost by way of playing artistic games with them. As brilliant as the story is, it has something of the *jeu d'esprit* about it.

Both 'The Blind Man' and **'Cathedral'** explore the possibility of male bonding. Isabel is not present in the final scene of 'The Blind Man'. The wife in **'Cathedral'** is awake at the end of the story, but is excluded from the two men's experience. She does not join them in their darkness. **'Cathedral'** is most powerfully like 'The Blind Man' in the attempted ritual communion between blind and sighted male characters with which both stories end.

Maurice's attempt to make contact with Bertie is both abortive and destructive. The conclusion of the story rewrites the naked wrestling match in the 'Gladiatorial' chapter of *Women in Love*. Birkin and Gerald almost seem to obliterate the boundaries separating them: 'Often, in the white, interlaced knot of violent living being that swayed silently, there was no head to be seen, only the swift, tight limbs, the solid white backs, the physical junction of two bodies clinched into oneness' (270). But if Birkin and Gerald come close to achieving oneness, Maurice's reaching out toward Bertie only accentuates the terrible gulf of separateness.

It is not often observed that the laying on of hands at the end of 'The Blind Man' is in part comic. Bertie agrees—'in a small voice'—to let Maurice touch him out of fear and 'very philanthropy'. When Maurice stretches out his 'strong, naked hand to him' (363), he accidentally knocks Bertie's hat off—a detail worthy of Samuel Beckett. Just as in 'Gladiatorial', Maurice's concerted laying on of hands includes a covertly sexual element. Maurice 'seemed to take him, in the soft, traveling grasp', and Bertie stands 'as if in a swoon'. Bertie is 'mute and terror-struck', afraid 'lest the other man should suddenly destroy him'. The final irony is that for all of his blood-prescience and instinctual connection with the dark forces of nature, Maurice Pervin does not know what he is doing in the final scene because—simply and comically—he is blind. Though Bertie is broken by the experience in the barn, the deluded Maurice feels triumphant: 'The new delicate fulfilment of mortal friendship had come as a revelation and surprise to him, something exquisite and unhoped-for' (364).

Bertie's eyes are closed when Maurice runs his hand over his face. At the end of the story, Bertie is 'haggard, with sunken eyes'; his eyes are 'as if glazed with misery' (364, 365). But, unlike the narrator of **'Cathedral'**, he has never entered Maurice's rich realm of darkness. Darkness and light, body and mind, all the familiar Lawrentian dualisms are doomed to remain forever apart. Lawrence's sardonic joke at the end of the story is at his own expense.

Raymond Carver has said that **'Cathedral'** is 'totally different in conception and execution from any stories that have come before'. When he wrote the story, he 'experienced this rush and I felt, "This is what it's all about, this is the reason we do this"' (**'Art'** 210). The 'opening up' Carver experienced in writing the story is most strikingly reflected in the conclusion, which, as I have shown, powerfully rewrites the communion scene in 'The Blind Man'.

The details of touch in the two stories are similar. Maurice Pervin covers Bertie Reid's hand with his own, pressing the 'fingers of the other man upon his disfigured eye-sockets', and Bertie stands 'as if in a swoon, unconscious, imprisoned' (364). In contrast, in **'Cathedral'** when Robert's fingers 'rode my fingers as my hand went over the paper', '[i]t was like nothing else in my life up to now' (228). Though the end of Carver's story is cryptic, there is no denying the oneness experienced by the two men in their community of touch and darkness.

It is no accident that the narrator and Robert draw a cathedral—a fact beautifully underscored by Carver's choice of title—for the implications of the story are somehow religious. Tellingly, the blind man asks if the husband is 'in any way religious'. He responds, 'I guess I don't believe in it. In anything. Sometimes it's hard' (225). Yet the shared experience at the end of the story offers a glimpse of religious belief. When the two men draw together, making physical contact, one blind and the other with his eyes closed, the narrator experiences transcendence, an experience 'like nothing else in my life', an experience in which he does not 'feel like I was inside anything' (228). The story even conjures up a vision of lost religious community when the blind man tells the narrator: 'Put some people in there now. What's a cathedral without people?' (227).

Lawrence's world of darkness is sacred but insufficient, for the darkness cannot be reconciled with its necessary antithesis. When Maurice forces the sighted Bertie to enter his all-encompassing darkness, he destroys him. In contrast, the narrator of **'Cathedral'** truly enters Robert's darkness, and that darkness is redemptive.

'The Blind Man' communicates the unavoidable separateness between people. Sixty-five years later, Carver reimagines the story and finds a way to dramatize the possibility of renewed, revitalized human contact, to suggest that the barriers between self and self can be broken down. The story perfectly embodies Carver's remark that though he was not religious, he had to 'believe in miracles and the possibility of resurrection' (**'Art'** 212). At the end of **'Cathedral'**, the

bruised, strung-out, cynical narrator has reentered the human community. Lawrence may have considered himself a 'passionately religious man' (*Letters II* 165), but he believed in struggle and commitment, not miracles. Resurrection never comes easily in Lawrence's works.

No doubt **'Cathedral'** had a personal dimension for Raymond Carver. He had much to overcome en route to becoming one of America's best, most influential short story writers: estrangement from wife and children, long years of dreary jobs, difficulty in getting established as a writer, a terrible history of alcoholism, before lung cancer finally killed him at the age of 50. The haunting affirmations of **'Cathedral'** reflect the hopeful upswing in the last decade of Carver's life as much as the change in his way of writing. These affirmations connect with the sense of moral certitude he articulated in 1981, proclaiming that 'in the best novels and short stories, goodness is recognized as such. Loyalty, love, fortitude, courage, integrity may not always be rewarded, but they are recognized as good or noble. . . . There *are* a few absolutes in this life, some verities, if you will, and we would do well not to forget them' (qtd. in Stull 242). Such absolutes and verities were unavailable to the author of 'The Blind Man' two generations earlier, no matter how strenuously he sought them. **'Cathedral'**, which yearns for absolutes, contains 'The Blind Man', which denies that absolutes are possible.

Both 'The Blind Man' and **'Cathedral'** are spun out of one of the hoariest clichés of our culture: love is blind. In 'The Blind Man', Maurice Pervin's blindness finally convinces us of our irredeemable loneliness. But to love in **'Cathedral'** is to become blind: to enter the darkness, to respond instinctively, to abnegate self. Though Carver had not read 'The Blind Man' when he composed **'Cathedral'**, how brilliantly he has rewritten Lawrence's story.

NOTES

1. One former student of Carver's remembers 'only two occasions on which he spoke with any heat. On the first he said that D.H. Lawrence was one of the best writers in the language and one of the worst, and sometimes in the same story' (Naughton C1).

WORKS CITED

Barthes, Roland, 'Theory of the Text', *Untying the Text: A Post-Structuralist Reader*, ed. Robert Young (Boston: Routledge & Kegan Paul, 1981), 31-47.

Carver, Raymond, 'The Art of Fiction LXXVI' (interview with Mona Simpson), *Paris Review* 25.88 (1983): 192-221.

Carver, Raymond, *Cathedral: Stories* (New York: Knopf, 1983).

Carver, Raymond, Letters to Keith Cushman, 17 November and 8 December 1987.

Harris, Janice Hubbard, *The Short Fiction of D.H. Lawrence* (New Brunswick, NJ: Rutgers UP, 1984).

Jameson, Fredric, 'Postmodernism, or The Cultural Logic of Late Capitalism', *New Left Review* 146 (July-August 1984): 53-92.

Lawrence, D.H., 'The Blind Man', *The Complete Short Stories*, Vol. 2 (New York: Viking, 1969), 347-65.

Lawrence, D.H., *The Letters of D.H. Lawrence: Volume II: June 1913-October 1916*, ed. George J. Zytaruk and James T. Boulton (Cambridge: Cambridge UP, 1981).

Lawrence, D.H., *The Letters of D.H. Lawrence: Volume III: October 1916-June 1921*, ed. James T. Boulton and Andrew Robertson (Cambridge: Cambridge UP, 1984).

Lawrence, D.H., *Women in Love*, ed. David Farmer, Lindeth Vasey, and John Worthen (Cambridge: Cambridge UP, 1987).

Naughton, Jim, 'Carver: The Master's Touch', *Washington Post*, 4 August 1988: C1, C6.

Roudiez, Leon S., Introduction, *Desire in Language: A Semiotic Approach to Literature and Art*, by Julia Kristeva; ed. Leon S. Roudiez; trans. Thomas Gora, Alice Jardine, and Leon S. Roudiez (New York: Columbia UP, 1980), 1-20.

Stull, William L., 'Raymond Carver', *Dictionary of Literary Biography Yearbook: 1984*, ed. Jean W. Ross (Detroit: Gale, 1985), 233-45.

Arthur M. Saltzman (essay date 1988)

SOURCE: "*Cathedral*," in *Understanding Raymond Carver*, University of South Carolina Press, 1988, pp. 124-56.

[*In the following excerpt, Saltzman compares such stories as "Feathers," "Chef's House," and "The Compartment"—which reflect hopelessness and despair—with "A Small, Good Thing" and "Where I'm Calling From" in which Carver allows his characters more compassion and choice.*]

"I knew I'd gone as far the other way as I could or wanted to go, cutting everything down to the marrow, not just to the bone.[1] In this way Carver announces a deliberate de-

parture from the relentless austerity of *What We Talk About When We Talk About Love* in favor of the "fleshed out" fictions of *Cathedral*. "Generous" is the term of approval employed by several reviewers to recognize the ventilation of the claustrophobic method and attitude that heretofore had dominated Carver's work. Perhaps befitting the increased stability and ease in Carver's personal life, the strapped constituents of Carver country breathe a bit more freely in this volume.[2]

Nevertheless, the majority of the stories dispute any claim to a fundamental break from the tenor of the three preceding collections. While there is impressive evidence in *Cathedral* of his having begun to transcend the haplessness and brittle restraint that commonly besets his characters, Carver by no means forsakes the "down to the marrow" aesthetic that governed his earlier collection. It may prove instructive, then, to contrast those stories in *Cathedral* that adhere to the established style with those that signal an opening out into what could be termed a postminimalist direction.

"**Feathers**" teases the reader with the prospect of meaningful repair in the lives of Jack and Fran only to capitulate to the pervading despair of previous volumes. Jack's first-person narrative turns out to be a prolonged complaint about the irredeemable leakage of time, which is temporarily disguised by the comic conditions of a dinner party at Bud and Olla's. The invitation by his friend at work had originally seemed to Jack to be little more than an opportunity to break the boredom, but in retrospect it stands forth in his mind as the final incident commemorating the halcyon days of his marriage:

> That evening at Bud and Olla's was special. I knew it was special. That evening I felt good about almost everything in my life. I couldn't wait to be alone with Fran to talk to her about what I was feeling. I made a wish that evening. Sitting there at the table, I closed my eyes for a minute and thought hard. What I wished for was that I'd never forget or otherwise let go of that evening. That's one wish of mine that came true. And it was bad luck that for me that it did. But, of course, I couldn't know that then.[3]

Jack recalls, or revises, that early period of his marriage as a time when innocence was a kind of enclave for him and Fran; they felt complete unto themselves and believed they needed neither children nor outside acquaintances to complicate their love. Looking back over the narrative, however, as the fast-forward conclusion of "**Feathers**" requires the reader to do, exposes intimations of the impending estrangement of Jack and Fran.[4] Their insistence upon self-sufficiency, for example, appears to be a shield against incursions that would expose the fragility of their relationship, while their routine discussions of things they wish for but never expect to have—a new car, a vacation in Canada, a place in the country—come to suggest more profound deficiencies.

Having declared her reluctance to accept the dinner invitation, Fran is openly contemptuous of Bud and Olla's lower-class home in "the sticks." To be sure, Bud and Olla are unrefined to say the least: their furnishings are vulgar, their conversation coarse, and their life style utterly unfettered by pretension or taste. Still, they are friendly and as hospitable as their means and manners allow; moreover, the unselfconscious happiness they share makes them invulnerable to disdain.

Jack and Fran, on the other hand, are helpless in the face of confusion or crisis. When upon their arrival Bud and Olla's pet peacock, a huge, ungainly bird, lands in front of their car, their mutual ineptitude shows through:

> "My God," Fran said quietly. She moved her hand over to my knee.
> "Goddamn," I said. There was nothing else to say (8).

> Awe, anger, and bewilderment constitute the full store of their reactions.

The evening is marked by the contrast between the pinched behavior of Jack and Fran, and the natural, if uncultivated, good will of their hosts. While Jack worries that he is over-dressed for the occasion, Fran barely manages to hide her contempt, which is revealed most markedly as she watches a televised stock car race with the men: "maybe one of those damn cars will explode right in front of us," Fran said. "Or else maybe one'll run up into the grandstand and smash the guy selling crummy hot dog's" (11). At first Jack attributes her attitude to the fact that "the day was shot" in the weird company of Bud and Olla, but upon reflection at the end of **"Feathers,"** it appears to have been a sign of a more comprehensive impatience that Jack failed to interpret fully.

However, nothing fazes Bud and Olla; even potentially uncomfortable subjects they themselves introduce (about their money problems or her father's death) are smoothly incorporated into the fabric of their abiding love for one another. The plaster cast of Olla's twisted teeth commemorating the eventual miracle of orthodontia, and which sits on top of the television set like a prized relic, is a source of shared enthusiasm over their progress: "That's one of the things I'm thankful for. I keep them around to remind me how much I owe Bud" (13). The stalking peacock, which has free reign over their roof and yard and which is welcome inside the house to play with the baby, may strike their guests as forbidding, but "Joey" is one more member of the family. If Joey

does not possess the transfiguring divinity of Flannery O'Connor's bird of paradise in "The Displaced Person," his scaled-down majesty earns no less devotion from Bud and Olla; meanwhile, for Fran and Jack the aggressive peacock symbolizes their harassment.

In short, Bud and Olla do not depend on the meager gestures of charity that their guests can muster. Even the astonishing ugliness of their squalling baby— "Even calling it ugly does it credit," Jack confides (20)— cannot affect Bud and Olla's domestic pride. Indeed, the child makes Fran feel deprived; she grows wistful about seeing her niece in Denver. Holding and playing with him triggers her plea to Jack later that night, which is reminiscent of Mary's urgent desire to be "diverted" at the close of **"What's in Alaska?"**: "Honey, fill me up with your seed!" (25).

But the child they ultimately produce does not avail them, and the marriage tenses, then unravels. Fran quits her job, puts on weight, cuts her luxurious hair that Jack had adored. She habitually curses the episode at Bud and Olla's as though they had caused the downfall of Fran and Jack's last stand of innocence. Jack becomes sullen and uncommunicative—"We don't talk about it. What's to say?" (26)—and increases his distance from Bud at the plant. Whereas Bud brags about his son, Jack merely says that everyone at home is fine and broods about the fact that his boy "has a conniving streak in him" (26). The unexpected detour that **"Feathers"** takes preempts the story's apparent development toward the verge of reconstituted love; as a result, every detail of the dinner party becomes an ironic portent of present desolation.

Seduction by hope intensifies marital vulnerability. In **"Chef's House,"** as in **"Feathers,"** futility surfaces like some awful genetic code. Wes convinces his estranged wife to relinquish the life she has been building apart from him in favor of rejoining him as he struggles to recover from alcoholism. Currently living in a rented house with an ocean view, Wes tells Edna that he needs her to complete his self-reclamation project. Although their children keep their distance, Wes and Edna spend a good summer together, and Edna, who narrates the story, confides that she has begun to believe in their solidarity again. The inevitable crisis comes in the form of Chef, who returns to ask them to vacate the premises. (He wants the house back for his daughter, who has lost her husband.) Immediately they sense that whatever they have been restoring is counterfeit, that defeat has rooted them out of hiding.

Baffled by the injustice of it all, Wes also feels oddly confirmed in his original definition of his limited expectations, and he suddenly finds himself beyond the reach of his wife's consoling:

Then I said something. I said, Suppose, just suppose, nothing had ever happened. Suppose this was for the first time, Just suppose. It doesn't hurt to suppose. Say none of the other had ever happened. You know what I mean? Then what? I said.

Wes fixed his eyes on me. He said, Then I suppose we'd have to be somebody else if that was the case. Somebody we're not. I don't have that kind of supposing left in me. We were born who we are. Don't you see what I'm saying?(31-32).

It *does* hurt to suppose, for supposing deludes Carver's characters into fantasies that burst at the slightest instigation; such is the pathology of surrender. Edna cannot hold out for long against her husband's logic, and she ends up absorbing his attitude. The same sort of "I should have known better" tonal quality rules both **"Feathers"** and **"Chef's House"**; in both cases reform is too demanding to imagine into existence. For Carver to bother to extend **"Chef's House"** to include verification of Wes's relapse and Edna's final renunciation would be redundant.

Uncontrollable circumstances claim two more victims in **"Preservation."** Three months of unemployment has steeped Sandy's husband in the same funk as Wes. He has essentially given up the fight, so he spends his days lazing on the sofa, an emblem of his surrender: "That goddamn sofa! As far as she was concerned, she didn't even want to sit on it again. She couldn't imagine them ever having lain down there in the past to make love" (37). His unstated justification may be that because man cannot prevail, he must learn how to endure; therefore, he adopts a posture of equanimity that Sandy finds maddening. When she happens upon his book *Mysteries of the Past*, and reads about a man discovered in a peat bog after two thousand years, her husband's petrified figure comes readily to mind.

When their freezer gives out, they are surrounded with perishables on all sides—a precise image of their own domestic entropy. Sandy frantically prepares to cook up as much as possible before everything spoils, but her husband is not up to any exertion and drops off to sleep on the sofa. She considers the prospects for finding a decent used freezer at an auction, but she can only sustain enthusiasm on her own for so long. The sight of her barefoot husband standing in the water puddling from the useless freezer once again recalls the preserved corpse from *Mysteries of the Past*: "She knew she'd never in her life see anything so unusual. But she didn't know what to make of it yet" (46). In predictable Carver fashion, Sandy's inarticulateness completes her bondage.[5]

The expense of psychological and verbal repression is evidenced in the airless interior monologue of **"The Compartment,"** whose title metaphor connotes the main character's predicament of self-containment without self-sufficiency. Myers is traveling by train to visit his son at the university in Strasbourg. It has been eight years since their last contact. A letter from his son, whose signature included "love," has initiated the flicker of optimism that has enabled Myers to subdue, for the moment, his suspicion that the boy had been guilty of "malign interference" between his parents, thereby hastening their violent separation.

Myers's unease about the impending meeting fills him with ambivalence, for the clutch of past irritations and blame continues to oppress him. Furthermore, in the intervening eight years Myers has not changed for the better. His aloofness, which is intimated to be one of the principal reasons behind his failed relationships, has intensified, as suggested by the fact that in planning his vacation he could barely imagine anyone whom he might have informed of his absence. His insularity is also documented by the meagerness of his leisure—he reads books on waterfowl decoys—as well as by his aspiration to live "in an old house surrounded by a wall" (48). He envies the man who shares his railcar because his inability to speak English and his talent for sleep combine to ensure his inviolability. Meanwhile, Myers passes the time by perusing guidebooks about places he has already visited and regretting that he had not gotten to reading them before—a situation that precisely parallels his belatedness in familial affairs.

Briefly put, Myers is a man trapped in the conditional tense. His European vacation has been contaminated from the beginning by his self-imposed segregation. He feels isolated and maladaptive in the most exotic cities, and about as spontaneous as a spider. The prospect of encountering his son at the train station sets off a prolonged series of calculations, as though he were a foreign ambassador uncertain of the local amenities: "Maybe the boy would say a few words—*I'm glad to see you—how was your trip*? And Myers would say—something. He really didn't know what he was going to say" (50).

Because he cannot envision the future, Myers is mired in his troubled past. The climax of **"The Compartment"** comes when he discovers that the gift he had bought for his son, the watch he was keeping in his coat pocket, has been stolen. He ludicrously tries to intuit who the thief is, but this only increases his humiliation and anger. He is helpless among foreigners; the invasion of his privacy confirms for him that the entire adventure has been a mistake. He realizes that he had not wanted to see his son, that somehow their true enmity had been obscured.

Myers does not get off the train at the Strasbourg station. He watches a romantic parting at the platform, but is careful to avoid being seen by his son, who is probably waiting there for him. Nor does he have the courage to ask the conductor if the train's next destination is Paris. Indeed, Myers is a man for whom *any* contact seems like "malign interference." Lost in regret, he wanders onto the wrong railcar while his own is uncoupled. Even Myers himself recognizes this last embarrassment as representative of the dissociation that defines him. His belongings gone, surrounded by strangers whose appearance, language, and joviality exclude him, Myers wanders down the maze of tracks: "For a moment, Myers had the impression of the landscape shooting away from him. He was going somewhere, he knew that. And if it was the wrong direction, sooner or later he'd find it out" (58). Sleep finally arrives like a benediction.

The husband in **"Vitamins"** is just as exasperating as Sandy's. In response to his wife's ranting about how she detests her job coordinating a group of young women who sell vitamins door to door—even her dreams are infected by vitamins, she bitterly complains—he recoils into muteness. He has a "nothing job" of his own as a hospital janitor; however, instead of commiserating with Patti about her misery, he rationalizes making passes at her employees during a drunken party and, later compelling one of them, Donna, to meet him on the sly.

This is familiar territory—trying to lose one's guilt in tawdriness, to court oblivion like a lover. He takes Donna to a "spade bar" he has frequented in the past, and once settled, they begin to grope one another with impunity. But their tryst is interrupted by the arrival of two black men who insinuate themselves at their booth. One of the men, Nelson, who has just returned home from Viet Nam, brags about the tactics of psychological warfare he had learned there and begins to practice them. He offers to display the prized shriveled ear he had cut from a corpse and startles them with sudden threats of violence. Most disturbing are his lewd offers to Donna to pay for her company, which he fortifies with suggestions that the man's wife is probably involved in some obscene relationship of her own even as they speak. In this way Nelson serves as a kind of vile conscience for the would-be lovers. They feel exposed, out of their depth; even though they manage to extricate themselves from the bar, Nelson's last remarks follow them: "He yelled, 'It ain't going to do no good! Whatever you do, it ain't going to help none!'" (107).

Sentenced to failure by this vulgar prophet, the unnamed husband and Donna recoil from one another into their respective justifications. He asks perfunctorily about her plans, but "right then she could have died of a heart attack and it wouldn't have meant anything" (108). She makes a clumsy effort at building a faith in a new beginning in Portland: "There must be something in Portland. Portland's on everybody's mind these days. Portland's a drawing card.

Portland this, Portland that. Portland's as good a place as any. 'It's all the same'" (108).

It is all the same for him as well when he comes home to Patti's rantings over yet another bad dream. Once again Carver demonstrates how attempts to escape confining routines merely reveal, their viciousness and resiliency:

> I couldn't take any more tonight. "Go back to sleep, honey. I'm looking for something." I said. I knocked some stuff out of the medicine chest. Things rolled into the sink. "Where's the aspirin?" I said. I knocked down some more things. I didn't care. Things kept falling (109).

He is assailed by gravity. From aimless anger, to furtiveness, to apathy and resignation—so runs the course of private ruin.

In **"Careful,"** Lloyd's cramped accommodations in Mrs. Matthews's boardinghouse are similar to Mr. Slater's "vacuumed" dwelling in **"Collectors."** Lloyd has neither clock nor telephone to trouble his womb-like limbo; out of work and alcoholic—his attempt to wean himself from hard liquor with cheap champagne now has him downing it by the bottle—he has diminished to a blur. In fact, he has grown so incurious about affairs outside his attic apartment that when one afternoon he passes his landlady's door and notices her collapsed on the floor, he "chooses" to assume she is asleep instead of injured or dead and hustles back to his quarters. Nor can he muster the energy to reflect about his "mildly crazy" habits for very long. "Then, the more he thought about it, the more he could see didn't matter much one way or the other. He'd had doughnuts and champagne for breakfast. So what?" (112-13).

On the day his wife, Inez, shows up for a serious discussion about their future, Lloyd is suffering from a blocked right ear. Their separation, a result of what Inez had termed an "assessment," has apparently been a tonic for her, for she arrives with new clothes and new vitality; she is set to thrive. For his part Lloyd is at the low point of his postpartum depression. As in **"Chef's House,"** a wife's departure signals the imminence of collapse. With symbolic aptness his ear condition has upset his equilibrium and made it difficult to hear his wife. His head feels like a barrel in which his own solipsistic, self-pitying voice endlessly reverberates, which is a far cry from that time "long ago, when they used to feel they had ESP when it came to what the other was thinking. They could finish sentences that the other had started" (117). Now her cares and consolations spatter uselessly against him.

After failing with assorted and potentially hazardous implements to dislodge the buildup of wax, Inez seeks out Mrs.

Matthews for help. She returns with baby oil, which she warms to pour into Lloyd's ear. Clearly her apprehensive husband is in need of supervision, and Inez's attentions are of necessity more maternal than wifely. ("Careful" sounds like the plea of a nervous child or a parent's gentle patronage.) Lying on his side to let the oil do its work, Lloyd feels helpless; his whole apartment seems out of whack.

Lloyd's ear finally opens, first to his delight, then to his dismay as he realizes that there is little he can do to stave off another such episode. Meanwhile, Inez consults with Mrs. Matthews in the hall; perhaps she is finalizing the transfer of the nursemaid role to the landlady. Due to the time lost to the crisis, she does not have the time to go into the subject that brought her here in the first place. In the end Inez escapes to other commitments, leaving Lloyd to contend with his inertia. But with his impacted condition—plugged up and mired in irresponsibility—Lloyd is not going anywhere at all.

"The Train" is Carver's sequel to John Cheever's story "The Five-Forty-Eight" (1958).[6] Cheever's story concerns the revenge of a secretary against her rather vile boss, Blake, who used her sexually only to fire her in order to escape further complications. She has exhibited signs of mental instability, and she now tracks her culprit to the train, where she accosts him, showing him that she is carrying a gun in her purse. Blake cannot elicit aid from the other passengers; with nightmarish poetic justice it turns out that the only other passengers around him are also people he has mistreated in the past. When he and his secretary are finally alone at the station, she makes him submit to a symbolic act of repentance and self-excoriation: he must drop to his knees and smother his face in the dirt. Nevertheless, his recriminations extend only so far as his fear of death; the woman's departure leaves no lesson or epiphany in its wake. Although he does seem to be more intensely aware of the tenuousness of what had always been the secure surroundings of Shady Hill, "he got to his feet and picked up his hat from the ground where it had fallen and walked home."[7]

Carver picks up the forgotten thread of Miss Dent, who is preparing for her trip back into the city. The model story is reimagined according to the spartan specifications of the Carver style: Miss Dent's complexities are contracted to a motiveless menace, and the thoughts of the woman who still carries the gun with which she has recently threatened a man are suspended by a matter-of-fact style that also inhibits the "gift for dreams" she had been credited as having in Cheever's rendition. Moreover, her plot is displayed by the indecipherable conversation of an old man and middle-aged woman who are sitting near Miss Dent in the station waiting room. Their absurd agitations invoke Miss Dent's sense of irony and she considers what their reaction would be were she to inform them that she has a gun in her bag.

All of a sudden the couple converges on her with bizarre accusations:

> "You don't say much," the woman said to Miss Dent. "But I'll wager you could say a lot if someone got you started. Couldn't you? But you're a sly boots. You'd rather just sit with your prim little mouth while other people talk their heads off. Am I right? Still waters. Is that your name?" (153).

Apparently Miss Dent is hardly manifested by her outrageous episode; every Carver character, after all, is the hero of some tragedy so supremely important that he cannot lend himself to another's.

As the anonymous passengers watch these three people board the train, "they felt sure that whatever these people's business had been that night, it had not come to a happy conclusion. But the passengers had seen things more various than this in their lifetime" (155). Everyone is a closet mystery, but the rampant preoccupation and self-interment of Carver's characters prohibit them from experiencing any more substantial intersection than this. It appears that Cheever's Blake, who only enters **"The Train"** by implication, is unremarkable in his immunity to reflection. Furthermore, since they are obsessed by their own stories, they "are only lethargically aware that the world is diverse and 'filled with business of every sort,'" and they "cling to the prejudice that they do not care to know more. They can't be shouted at."[8] Its plot potential squandered, **"The Train"** speeds off into the darkness.

The interest the narrator takes in the newly arrived Minnesota family in **"The Bridle"** results from her suspicion that their bankruptcy mirrors her own sense of a foreclosed future. Holits, his wife, Betty, and their two sons have come to Arizona in search of better luck. As co-manager (with her husband, Harley) of the apartment building, the narrator is concerned at first about whether or not the new tenants will be responsible about paying their rent, but she feels for their predicament; bad luck can come to anyone, and "no disgrace can be attached to that" (191). Holits pays his rent and damage deposit with fifty-dollar bills, and she is moved to wonder about the "exotic" fates of the bills themselves as they pass from place to place and hand to hand. Indeed, even her unfortunate tenants have the advantage of *movement*; meanwhile, she is rooted to a claustrophobic role, her life assigned to a gruff husband who spends the day addicted to television and who sleeps at night "like a grindstone" beside her (201).

Both as building manager and as a stylist (she abjures the term "beautician" as too old-fashioned), the narrator presides over the sad little dramas that are played out on the premises. These range from the pedestrian—bouts with alcohol, disaffection, and loneliness—to the wickedly cynical, as seen in the building party that features a drawing for an attorney's free divorce services. When Betty gets a split-shift waitressing job, she comes to the narrator for a dye job on her roots, and under the soothing influence of the hair stylist's care (paralleling the consequences of the barber's "sweet" art in **"The Calm"**), Betty confesses the history of her tribulations. She is Holits's second wife—his first wife ran out on him and the children. Holits bought a racehorse, which he named for Betty, and which he believed would be the instrument of their salvation. However, Fast Betty has proven to be a perennial loser, and mounting gambling losses as well as the cost of upkeep itself has sundered their dreams of "working toward something" (199). The narrator compliments Betty's cuticles, but it is meager solace for someone who is convinced that she is a long shot who will never finish in the money; she does not even bother to dream anymore. Cosmetic improvements—the dye job on her hair, the new job, the new residence—cannot change her essential entrapment.

After this episode Betty keeps away from the narrator for some time, and Holits also appears to have found employment, for he is seldom seen. The climax of the story occurs when during a drunken party with some of the other renters at pool side after closing hours, Holits tries to dive into the water from atop the cabana. He hits the deck, gashing his forehead. The narrator, incensed by the display (and probably by her exclusion from the group as well) rushes to the scene. The scene concludes with a blundering rush to the hospital, with Holits deliriously repeating his complaint: "I can't go it" (204). Significantly, Harley sleeps through the entire crisis.

"I can't go it": the phrase is an apt motto for Holits, for whom the crash to the deck is but one more in a line of downfalls. Betty quits her job to nurse him and Holits grows sullen and standoffish. Soon they are seen packing up for another move. Forever at a loss, they must believe in luck because, presumably, luck can change. Meanwhile, Harley has no compassion to waste on that "crazy Swede" and his family, and he settles back in front of the television as though "nothing has happened or ever will happen" (207). In a surprisingly rebellious exhibition, his wife inserts herself between Harley and his television screen, but she finds she has nothing whatsoever to say to him.

When she goes up to clean the vacated apartment, the narrator discovers Holits's bridle. Perhaps he forgot it. Perhaps he left it behind as part of a ceremony of divestiture in hopes of preparing the way for a different life. For the narrator the bridle is a clear symbol of restraint, of being controlled from without: "The bit's heavy and cold. If you had to wear this thing between your teeth, I guess you'd catch on in a hurry"

(208). She knows what it is to be cruelly reined in, to be perpetually at the mercy of someone, or something, beyond the reach of reason.

The stories discussed above follow the general tone established in Carver's three previous collections. The absence of recourse and the unnourished hopes shrunken to a grudge; the misfired social synapses and the implied ellipses like breadcrumb trails leading from breakdown to breakdown; the "preseismic" endings that "are inflected rather than inflicted upon us"[9]; the speechless gaps where intimacies are supposed to go—these characteristics persist. On the other hand, some of the stories in *Cathedral* do suggest an opening out that indicates, however subtly, an ongoing evolution in Carver's art.

The reformulation of **"The Bath"** in *What We Talk About When We Talk About Love*) as **"A Small, Good Thing"** in *Cathedral* is an obvious place to begin to examine this contrast. Carver himself has indicated that the enhancement of the original story's "unfinished business" is so fundamental that they now seem to him to be two entirely different stories.[10] Certainly the structure of his sentences has been changed in several instances to be less fragmentary, less constrained. For example, while she is waiting for the arrival of the doctor in **"The Bath,"** the mother's dread is nearly wordless, and absolutely privatized: "She was talking to herself like this. We're into something now, something hard."[11] In **"A Small, Good Thing,"** however, Ann (she has been granted a name and a fuller identity, as have the other characters in the story) is presented as having a more extensively characterized consciousness, which is thus more sympathetic and accessible:

> She stood at the window with her hands gripping the sill, and knew in her heart that they were into something now, something hard. She was afraid, and her teeth began to chatter until she tightened her jaws. She saw a big car stop in front of the hospital and someone, a woman in a long coat, get into the car. She wished she were that woman and somebody, anybody, was driving her away from here to somewhere else, a place where she would find Scotty waiting for her when she stepped out of the car, ready to say *Mom* and let her gather him in her arms.

> In a little while, Howard woke up. He looked at the boy again. Then he got up form the chair, stretched, and went over to stand beside her at the window. They both stared at the parking lot. They didn't say anything. *But they seemed to feel each other's insides now, as though the worry had made them transparent in a perfectly natural way* (70-71; my italics)

With the expansion of the original version comes a development of the spiritual cost of the crisis. The result of every extension of detail in **"A Small, Good Thing"**—from the increased dimension of the baker when he is first introduced, to the transcendence of merely symbolic function of the black family at the hospital—is to decrease the distances that separate Carver's characters from one another and Carver's narrator from the story he relates. For one critic the expansion represents a movement away from "existential realism" toward a comparatively coherent, more dramatic, and more personal "humanistic realism."[12]

Carver's most profound revision is to carry the plot beyond the state of abeyance of Scotty's coma. (**"The Bath"** concludes in the middle of the phone call, just before the "death sentence" is actually pronounced.) In **"A Small, Good Thing,"** Scotty's death spasm occurs even as the doctor is discussing with the parents the surgery that he will perform to save the boy. Having been assured only the previous day that Scotty would recover, Ann and Howard are absolutely overwhelmed, and they dazedly prepare to withstand the autopsy, to call relatives. Under these more developed circumstances the baker's call is no longer just the ironic plot gimmickry it had been in **"The Bath"**; instead, his interruption of and ultimate participation in the family's loss in **"A Small, Good Thing"** precipitates the cycle of "dramatic recognition, reversal, confrontation, and catharsis" that finally gives the story the finished contours of tragedy—the "low-rent" tragic pattern fleshed out to classic dimensions.[13] Replacing the blank, dazed reaction of the anxious mother in the former version is her wild anger at the "evil bastard" who has blundered into their grief; when translated to the context of their open wound, his message about the birthday cake sounds ominous and malicious: "Your Scotty, I got him ready for you,' the man's voice said. 'Did you forget him?'" (83).

He hangs up, and only after a second call and hangup does Ann realize that it must have been the baker. Blazing with outrage, desperate to strike out against their defeat, Ann and Howard drive to the shopping center bakery for a showdown. The baker, menacingly tapping a rolling pin against his palm, is prepared for trouble, but Ann breaks down as she tells him of the death of her son. Her debasement is complete, but Carver rescues her from the isolated defeat in which so many of his previous protagonists have been immured. The baker apologizes, and in that instant's compassion is moved to confess his misgivings and his loneliness, and the cold remove he has kept to: "I'm not an evil man, I don't think. Not evil, like you said on the phone. You got to understand what it comes down to is I don't know how to act anymore, it would seem" (88). Their shared bond is inadequacy in the face of loss, joined by a need to be forgiven for that inadequacy. Consequently, whereas in previous stories people clutched themselves in isolated corners against their respective devastations, here they manage to come together in the communal ceremony of eating warm rolls and drinking coffee: "You have to eat and keep going. Eating is a small, good thing in a time like this" (88).

The availability of nourishment discloses their common "hunger." Ann Howard, and the baker begin a quiet convalescence, eating what they can, talking until morning. Unlike **"The Bath,"** whose focus is the title's solitary baptism, a purgative reflex meant to ward off catastrophe, **"A Small, Good Thing"** affirms the consolations of mutual acceptance. Ann and Howard had refused food throughout the story, which suggested their desperate denial. The closing scene "exteriorizes" their misery so as to make available to them the healing impulses of the baker and the small, but significant, brand of grace that human sympathy can provide.

In **"Where I'm Calling From,"** too, commiseration instigates recuperation. In a drying-out facility where the inhabitants are identified and exiled by alcoholism, the narrator is at first unwilling or unable to relate his own story. Everyone at the facility is seized by the same trembling; everyone gauges his relative distance from everyone else's latest stage of collapse, trying to navigate through the mirrorings of his own disease.

Instead of confessing, the narrator persuades a fellow drunk, J.P., to tell his story. By recalling how conditions decayed, J.P. demonstrates a "talking cure" for impacted personalities. Whereas ritualized blandishments about willpower and self-esteem are barely sustaining to people who best recognize themselves in defeat, J.P.'s tale of how he met and married Roxy, a chimney sweep, increases the man's vigor as it frees his voice. It also clears a path for the narrator to follow out of his own eviscerated grimness.

J.P. characterizes Roxy as arrestingly natural and unselfconscious; their courtship started when J.P. was at a friend's house where she had just finished cleaning the chimney. Upon receiving payment, Roxy offered the friend a kiss for good luck, at which point J.P. decided to request the same gift. As J.P. proceeds with his story, Roxy is revealed to be neither maudlin nor promiscuous, just resilient—someone whose capacity for love derives from substantial resources of self-respect. Certainly their relationship had been the best thing to come along in J.P.'s life, until the booze preempted everything.

But Carver does not let **"Where I'm Calling From"** wither at this familiar impasse. Roxy arrives at the facility to visit J.P., for whom her embrace is an immediate tonic. The narrator marvels at her strength and self-assurance, which sharply contrasts with all the lurking, stalking, and shame that he has been witnessing every day: "Her hands are broad and the fingers have these big knuckles. This is a woman who can make fists if she has to" (142-143). He asks for a kiss, and she gives it easily, taking him by the shoulders as if to brace him for the treatment.

When he was twelve years old, J.P. tells the narrator, he fell down a dry well, and "everything about his life was different for him at the bottom of the well. But nothing fell on him and nothing closed off that little circle of blue. Then his dad came along with the rope, and it wasn't long before J.P. was back in the world he'd always lived in" (130). Salvation is possible, but it requires patience—the one-day-at-a-time creed of the recovering alcoholic—and the belief that "that little circle of blue" is as substantial and reliable as one's entrapment. **"Where I'm Calling From"** concludes with the narrator's memories of tranquility and his ultimate resolve. Whereas in **"The Compartment,"** Myers lamented his having no idea what he might say to his son, here the narrator figures that saying "It's me" on the telephone is a way to begin again. Obviously he is in the early stage of therapy, but as he determines how to talk to his wife without argument or sarcasm and how to reconnect with his girlfriend again, it appears that where he is calling from need not diminish nor disqualify the fact, that, finally, he is *calling*.

In like fashion the protagonist of **"Fever"** finds his anxieties mitigated by the basic inducements of human contact. One of the practical crises Carlyle must face in trying to deal with his abandonment by his wife, Eileen, for his colleague—a mutual friend and fellow high school art teacher "who'd apparently turned his grades in on time" (158)—is locating a dependable babysitter now that fall classes have begun again. His hurried choices, which include a careless teenager and a gruff, ghoulish woman with hairy arms, are disappointing and encourage his fear that Eileen's leaving has left unpluggable cracks everywhere.

Eileen telephones to solicit his understanding in "this matter" (recalling the plastic connotations of Inez's marital "assessment" in **"Careful"**) and to verify her happiness, as though it might be of some indefinable consolation to him. Her unctuous earnestness exasperates him, especially because it is conveyed by the jargon of pop psychology: they are still "bonded," she is "going for it," they need to keep the "lines of communication open," he needs to adopt a "positive mental attitude," . . . and say, how's your karma? But despite what Carlyle deems her "insanity," Eileen is prescient enough to have realized that he needs a sitter for the children and a housekeeper. She provides the name of Mrs. Webster, an older woman who had once worked for Eileen's lover's mother (how civil! how sophisticated they are!) and whom she promises he can count on (in contrast, presumably, to her own inconstancy).

Whatever his doubts toward Eileen, Carlyle discovers in Mrs. Webster the kind of quiet dignity and supportiveness, particularly in her intimacies with her husband, that Holly had dreamed of in **"Gazebo"** as being the special province of the elderly, and indeed, that Carlyle had hoped would represent his future with Eileen. As a result of Mrs. Webster's taking over the household, Carlyle is suffused with calm; he becomes more intrepid in his relationship with his girlfriend (whom he had previously admired for her ability to equate understanding him with not pressuring him), and the family begins to thrive to the extent that Carlyle can face the truth about his wife's permanent decision not to return. When he falls ill, Mrs. Webster easily expands her ministrations to incorporate him as well as his children, and not even fever can deter his prospects for renewal, which have been due in large measure to Mrs. Webster's indiscriminate love.

When Mrs. Webster arrives one day with the news that she and her husband are leaving for Oregon to work on a mink ranch, Carlyle's initial response is panic; to be sure, the sudden shattering of one's delicate composure is common enough throughout Carver's stories, and it would not be surprising for **"Fever"** to conclude with Carlyle dangling over the pit of his own disarray. Eileen calls again. She has intuited her husband's distress, for which she prescribes journal writing in order to translate and extinguish his problems. But once again Carlyle figures that her craziness contaminates the communication she extols.

Nevertheless, Carlyle is spared a final breakdown. He relates the history of his relationship with Eileen to the eternally patient Mrs. Webster, who bestows her acceptance and predicts his restoration: "'Good. Good for you,' Mrs. Webster said when she saw he had finished. 'You're made out of good stuff. And so is she—so is Mrs. Carlyle. And don't you forget it. You're both going to be okay after this is over'" (185). Consequently, Carlyle learns that he is ready to come to terms with life in the wake of loss. In fact, "loss" is a misnomer for the abiding legacy of his past, in that it "would become a part of him now, too, as surely as anything else he'd left behind" (186). Subdued, yet resolute, Carlyle turns away from the departing Websters and toward his children. This closing gesture implies his emergence from fever and vulnerability, if only to the degree that he is able to offer himself, which is the surest sign of health Carver ever provides.

"There are a few absolutes in this life, some verities, if you will," writes the author, "and we would do well not to forget them."[14] Beyond the slow wash of hopelessness throughout Carver's fiction, the stiff coil of the common run that blocks all aspiration, are those moments of fortitude and affirmation that surface in *Cathedral* and provide some positive, even sentimental, texturing that counters the savage attenuation of character, description, and outlook. Carver specifically heralds the volume's title story on these grounds: "When I Wrote **'Cathedral'** I experienced this rush and I felt, 'This is what it's all about, this is the reason we do this.'"[15]

The story opens with the narrator explaining his consternation at learning that, following the death of his wife, a blind man is coming to stay at his home. His resistance to the idea is partly due to the awkwardness he anticipates—he has never known a blind person, and "in the movies, the blind moved slowly and never laughed" (209)—and partly due to the fact that the man, an old friend of the narrator's wife and with whom she has conducted a longstanding relationship of mailed tape recordings, represents a part of his wife's life that excludes him. She had been a reader for the blind man during the time of her relationship with her childhood sweetheart, a United States Air Force officer-in-training, which ended in his departure and her bungled suicide attempt. Both her lover and Robert, the blind man, were incorporated into poems that her husband cannot appreciate. Now the narrator is reluctant to endure the intrusion of a man who represents a competitive part of his own wife's life—a man who "took liberties" with her by reading her face with his hands! The awakening of his own selfishness makes the narrator sullen. He tries in vain to imagine how Robert's wife could have stood living with a man who could never see her, and in doing so exposes his own rather repellant insularity and lack of compassion.

However, Robert turns out to be a natural-born confounder of stereotypes. He is a robust, broad-gestured man who easily gets his bearings in new surroundings: he ravages his dinner, readily accepts his host's offer to smoke some pot, and even proves quite comfortable "watching" television. The combined influence of these activities inspires unaccustomed ease in the narrator; when his wife's robe falls open after she falls asleep, he cavalierly reasons that the blind man is unaware, of course, and does not bother to cover her up again.

As the two men turn their attention to a television documentary about cathedrals, the narrator tries to approximate what they are like for the sake of his guest, but "It just isn't in me to do it. I can't do any more than I've done. . . . The truth is, cathedrals don't mean anything special to me. Nothing. Cathedrals. They're something to look at on late-night TV" (226). At Robert's suggestion the narrator gets pen and paper and together, and with Robert's hand riding on top of the narrator's, they begin drawing a cathedral. In this way the amenities of keeping company evolve into a communal ceremony comparable to that which closes **"A Small, Good Thing."** With Robert's encouragement—"Never thought anything like this could happen in your lifetime, did you, bub? Well, it's a strange life, we all know that. Go on now. Keep it up" (227)—the narrator is able to let go of his inhibitions and collaborate in an expressive vision. "It was like

nothing else in my life up to now," he confesses to himself (228).

Eyes closed now, the narrator surrenders himself to Robert's gentle guidance, much as Carlyle gave himself over to Mrs. Webster's care in **"Fever."** Both stories, along with **"A Small, Good Thing"** and **"Where I'm Calling From,"** emphasize the abundant compensations of shared experience. The protagonists of these stories are not necessarily more articulate than their precursors—the narrator of **"Cathedral"** can only come up with "'It's really something'" to appreciate the spiritual climax of the story—but they are available to depths of feeling they need not name to justify. If the images that conclude the richest stories in *Cathedral* are gestures by heavy hands—the breaking of bread against suffering or the unblinding of the blind—they begin to establish a basis for conduct beyond the limits set by stylistic austerity or introversion clung to like some ethical stance. A blind man whose wife has died and a man who admits that he does not believe in anything join together to create a cathedral. It is neither perfect nor complete, but the process is encouraging and adequate for now. Robert's belief in the concluding story is known throughout the volume: it *is* a strange life. The most sympathetic, most human of Carver's characters "keep it up" anyway.

NOTES

1. Quoted in William L. Stull, "Raymond Carver," *Dictionary of Literary Biography: 1984*, ed. Jean W. Ross (Detroit: Gale, 1985) 242.

2. Carver notes that the stories in *Cathedral* reflect what has been the most "composed" period of his life: "I feel more comfortable with myself, able to give more. Maybe it's getting older and getting smarter. I don't know. Or getting older and more stupid. But I feel closer to this book than to anything I've ever done." Ray Anello and Rebecca Boren, interview, *Time* 5 Sept. 1983: 67.

3. Raymond Carver, "Feathers," *Cathedral* (New York: Knopf, 1983) 25. Further references to stories in this collection are noted parenthetically in the text.

4. Michael J. Bugeja views this as a crucial structural flaw in the story. See "Tarnish and Silver: An Analysis of Carver's *Cathedral*," *South Dakota Review* 24 (1986): 77-80.

5. Citing this story, Michael Gorra complains that Carver's style actually "dictates rather then embodies his characters' predicament" ("Laughter and Bloodshed," *Hudson Review* 37 [1984]: 156). A similar dissent is registered by T. Coraghessan Boyle against the formulaic tedium of the "Catatonic Realists": "You know the story, you've read it a thousand times: Three characters are sitting around the

kitchen of a trailer, saying folksy things to one another. Finally one of them gets up to go to the bathroom and the author steps in to end it with a line like, 'It was all feathers'" ("A Symposium on Contemporary American Fiction," *Michigan Quarterly Review* 26 [1987]: 707).

6. John Cheever, "The Five-Forty-Eight," *The Housebreaker of Shady Hill and Other Stories* (New York: Harper, 1958). "The Five-Forty-Eight" earned the Benjamin Franklin Short Story Award in 1955.

7. Cheever, 134.

8. Mark A. R. Facknitz, "Missing the Train: Raymond Carver's Sequel to John Cheever's 'The Five-Forty-Eight,'" *Studies in Short Fiction* 22 (1985): 347.

9. Marc Chenetier, "Living On/Off the 'Reserve': Performance, Interrogation, and Negativity in the Works of Raymond Carver," *Critical Angles: European Views of Contemporary American Literature,* ed. Marc Chenetier (Carbondale: Southern Illinois University Press, 1986) 173. Chenetier maintains that Carver's method "bludgeons presence upon the reader" through his "violent economy"; however, "past the opening lines the text proceeds to unravel into misdirection" (166).

10. Quoted in Larry McCaffery and Sinda Gregory, "An Interview with Raymond Carver" *Mississippi Review* 40/41 (Winter 1985); 66.

11. 'The Bath," *What We Talk About When We Talk About Love* (New York: Knopf, 1981) 54.

12. William L. Stull, "Beyond Hopelessville: Another Side of Raymond Carver," *Philological Quarterly* 64 (1985): 7-9.

13. Stull, "Beyond Hopelessville" 10.

14. Quoted in Stull, "Raymond Carver" 242.

15. Quoted in Mona Simpson, interview, "The Art of Fiction LXXVI," *Paris Review* 25 (1983): 207.

Adam Meyer (essay date Summer 1989)

SOURCE: "Now You See Him, Now You Don't, Now You Do Again: The Evolution of Raymond Carver's Minimalism," in Critique, Vol. XXX, No. 4, Summer, 1989, pp. 239-51.

[*In the following essay, Meyer, a professor at Vanderbilt University, traces Carver's use of minimalist style through-out his career, arguing that Carver returns to his previous, more expansive style in* Cathedral.]

At this point in his career, there can be little doubt that Raymond Carver is "as successful as a short story writer in America can be,"[1] that "he is becoming an Influence."[2] Still, despite (or perhaps because of) this position, Carver remains a controversial figure. Much of the debate about Carver's merits centers around a similar debate about minimalism, a style that a few years ago was very hot and very hotly criticized, and that, now that it is cooling off, is under even more fervent attack. Much of the controversy is sparked by a confusion of terminology. As hard as it is accurately to define minimalism, for the same reasons we cannot entirely pin down such terms as realism, modernism, or post-modernism. It is even harder to say who is or is not a minimalist, as demonstrated by Donald Barthelme's being called a minimalist as often as he is called one of the post-modernists against whom the minimalists are rebelling.[3] Nevertheless, Carver is generally acknowledged to be "the chief practitioner of what's been called 'American minimalism.'"[4] Now that this has become a pejorative appellation, however, his admirers are quickly trying "to abduct [him] from the camp of the minimalists."[5] If he is to be successfully "abducted," however, it will not be because the label is no longer popular, but because it no longer fits.

The fact of Carver's membership in the minimalist fraternity has never been fully established. Many critics, as well as Carver himself, noted that his latest volume of new stories; *Cathedral*, seemed to be moving away from minimalist writing, that it showed a widening of perception and style.[6] This is certainly true, but it is not the whole story. If we look back over Carver's entire output, an overview encouraged by the recent publication of his "selected" stories, *Where I'm Calling From*, we see that his career, rather than following an inverted pyramid pattern, has actually taken on the shape of an hourglass, beginning wide, then narrowing, and then widening out again. In other words, to answer the question "Is Raymond Carver a minimalist?" we must also consider the question "Which Raymond Carver are we talking about?," for he did not start out as a minimalist, and he is one no longer, although he was one for a period of time in between.

This hourglass pattern emerges when we read all of Carver's stories chronologically, or, to a lesser extent, when we read *Where I'm Calling From* from cover to cover. Carver's evolution can perhaps be best understood when we examine several stories that have been published at different times in different versions. Carver, an inveterate rewriter, has stated that he would "rather tinker with a story after writing it, and then tinker some more, changing this, changing that, than have to write the story in the first place."[7] Sometimes this tinkering results in only minor changes, as Carver makes clear when he cites admiration for Evan Connell's statement, "he knew he was finished with a short story when he found himself going through it and taking out commas and then going through the story again and putting commas back in the same places" (*F* 15). At other times, however, the result is an almost entirely different work. While the rewriting process is not unusual in itself, Carver's unwillingness to stop even after a piece has been published is not typical. One significantly revised publication that has elicited much critical commentary is **"A Small, Good Thing,"** which appears in *Cathedral*. It is a retelling of **"The Bath,"** a story from Carver's most minimalistic volume, *What We Talk About When We Talk About Love*, that transforms the piece into something far removed from that style. In fact, this change was responsible for alerting many readers and critics to the "new" Carver presented in *Cathedral* as a whole.[8]

The basic situation in both stories is the same. A woman goes to a baker to order a special cake for her son Scotty's birthday party. The morning of his birthday, however, he is struck by a hit-and-run driver and becomes comatose. The baker, knowing only that the cake has not been picked up, calls the house and leaves threatening messages. The presentation of these events is very different in the two works, so by comparing them we can come to understand some of the salient features of minimalism. Most obviously, **"The Bath,"** ten pages long, is approximately one-third the length of **"A Small, Good Thing,"** an indication of the further development of the rewritten version. The characters in both stories are usually referred to by nouns or pronouns (the boy, the mother, he, she), but in **"The Bath"** we do not learn the mother's full name, Ann Weiss, until the last page, whereas she announces it to the baker in the second paragraph of **"A Small, Good Thing."** This might seem like a small thing, but it is indicative of a larger change. If we juxtapose the two versions of this early encounter between Mrs. Weiss and the baker, we clearly see a fundamental change in Carver's narrative strategy. In **"The Bath,"** Carver writes:

> The mother decided on the spaceship cake, and then she gave the baker her name and her telephone number. The cake would be ready Monday morning, in plenty of time for the party Monday afternoon. This was all the baker was willing to say. No pleasantries, just this small exchange, the barest information, nothing that was not necessary.[9]

In **"A Small, Good Thing,"** Carver rewrites:

> She gave the baker her name, Ann Weiss, and her telephone number. The cake would be ready on Monday morning, just out of the oven, in plenty of time for the child's party that afternoon.

> The baker was not jolly. There were no pleasantries between them, just the minimum exchange of words, the necessary information. He made her feel uncomfortable, and she didn't like that. While he was bent over the counter with the pencil in his hand, she studied his coarse features and wondered if he'd ever done anything else with his life besides be a baker. She was a mother and thirty-three years old, and it seemed to her that everyone, especially someone the baker's age—a man old enough to be her father—must have children who'd gone through this special time of cakes and birthday parties. There must be that between them, she thought. But he was abrupt with her—not rude, just abrupt. She gave up trying to make friends with him. She looked into the back of the bakery and could see a long, heavy wooden table with aluminum pie pans stacked at one end; and beside the table a metal container filled with empty racks. There was an enormous oven. A radio was playing country-Western music.[10]

The first version is sparse and elliptical, giving the reader only "the barest information, nothing that [is] not necessary," while the second offers a more expansive view, providing physical details of the characters and the bakery, as well as exploring the mother's thoughts. The revision also hints more fully at the conflict that will be developed later in the story. Kim Herzinger's definition of minimalism, "equanimity of surface, 'ordinary' subjects, recalcitrant narrators and deadpan narratives, slightness of story, and characters who don't think out loud,"[11] clearly fits the first paragraph, but it does not entirely account for the second, particularly in its exploration of the character's inner thoughts.

The most significant change from **"The Bath"** to **"A Small, Good Thing,"** however, is in their endings. Minimalist stories have been heavily criticized for their tendency to end "with a sententious ambiguity that leaves the reader holding the bag,"[12] and **"The Bath"** certainly follows this pattern. It ends literally in the middle of one of the baker's telephone calls: "'Scotty,' the voice said. 'It is about Scotty,' the voice said. 'It has to do with Scotty, yes.'" (*What* 56). At this point in the story, Scotty's medical condition is still uncertain, and, although the reader has figured it out, the parents still do not know who is making the horrible calls. This ending, then, is very much up in the air, and the reader leaves the story with a feeling of uneasiness and fear. **"A Small, Good Thing,"** however, goes beyond this point in time. Scotty dies. The parents come to realize that the baker has been making the harassing calls, and they confront him. Once they explain the situation, the baker, feeling deep remorse for having bothered them, offers them some fresh rolls, telling them that "[e]ating is a small, good thing in a time like this" *C* 88). The story now ends on a note of communion, of shared understanding and grief: "They talked on into the early morning, the high, pale cast of light in the windows, and they did not think of leaving" *C* 89). The result is a story that has moved far beyond its minimalistic origins. Carver said in an interview that

> [t]he story hadn't been told originally, it had been messed around with, condensed and compressed in **"The Bath"** to highlight the qualities of menace that I wanted to emphasize. . . . But I still felt there was unfinished business, so in the midst of writing these other stories for *Cathedral* I went back to **"The Bath"** and tried to see what aspects of it needed to be enhanced, re-drawn, re-imagined. When I was done, I was amazed because it seemed so much better.[13]

Most critics agree with this evaluation of **"A Small, Good Thing,"** which won the O. Henry award as the best short story of 1983.[14] "The revision completes the original by turning the sum of its fragmentary parts into a coherent whole that has a powerful dramatic structure, a beginning, middle, and end," writes William Stull,[15] and Marc Chenetier feels that it signals "a movement away from threatening ambiguity, a working towards hope rather than horror, and the abandonment of features Carver may have come to consider akin to the narrative 'gimmicks' he has always denounced."[16] Indeed, as indicated earlier, nearly all of the stories in *Cathedral* show this movement away from the "gimmicks" of minimalism.

By looking at a story that has been published in three different versions, we get a fuller picture of the whole of Carver's evolution, his movement at first toward and then away from minimalism. **"So Much Water So Close to Home"** first appeared (in book form) in Carver's second volume, the small press book *Furious Seasons* (1977). It was reprinted in his second "major" volume, *What We Talk About When We Talk About Love* (1981) and appeared a third time in another small press book, *Fires: Essays, Poems, Stories* (1983). Most recently, it appeared as one of the selected stories in *Where I'm Calling From* (1988). The basic plot is the same in each publication. Stuart Kane and his buddies go fishing. As soon as they arrive at their campsite, they find a dead girl floating in the river. They decide to tie her to a tree so that she will not be lost downstream and then proceed to fish and drink for the remainder of the weekend. The story is told from the point of view of Stuart's wife, Claire, and is largely concerned with the strain that this event puts on their marriage, as she, empathizing with the dead girl, feels that her husband should have abandoned his trip and reported the body immediately.

A comparison of the way this material is treated in the first and second versions shows the several ways in which, according to John Barth, a story can be minimalistic. First, Barth says, "there are minimalisms of unit, form and scale: short . . . paragraphs, super-short stories";[17] Carver's story is reduced by half in the revision, and long paragraphs, such as the one in which Claire explains the circumstances of the body's discovery, are broken up into many smaller ones (in this case, five). Second, "there are minimalisms of style: a stripped-down vocabulary; a stripped-down syntax that avoids periodic sentences";[18] this can be seen in Carver's alteration of "They fish together every spring and summer, the first two or three months of the season, before family vacations, little league baseball and visiting relatives can intrude"[19] to "They fish together every spring and early summer before visiting relatives can get in the way" (*What* 80). Third, and most important, "there are minimalisms of material: minimal characters, minimal exposition . . . , minimal *mises en scene*, minimal action, minimal plot";[20] this third of Barth's observations is the one on which I wish to concentrate and illustrate here, for it is the key to seeing the change in Carver's aesthetic.

In the first version (*FS*, 1977), we are given long descriptions of the fishing trip, of Claire's reactions to her husband's behavior, of her thoughts about their past relationship, of the physical separation she imposes upon him, of the identification and subsequent funeral of the dead girl, and of many other actions and thoughts on several characters' parts. In the second version (*What*, 1981), however, these passages are either considerably reduced or eliminated altogether. As a result, this second version, since it stays on the surface of events and does not really allow us to get inside of the characters, seems to confirm the criticism that Carver's work is cold or unfeeling, that he lacks sympathy for his characters. For example, the last line of the opening paragraph in the first version—Claire's "Something has come between us though he would like to believe otherwise" (*FS* 41)—sets up, even sums up, much of the emotional conflict that is to be examined in the story. Its elimination in the second version leaves us unsure of the real motivations of the characters, thus diminishing our understanding of what is actually going on and, consequently, our concern for the people involved.

There are many more examples of such revisions, excisions that require more inference on the reader's part rather than providing him with more information. Consider, for instance, a long passage from the first version in which Claire thinks back on her previous life:

> The past is unclear. It is as if there is a film over those early years. I cannot be sure that the things I remember happening really happened to me. There was a girl who had a mother and father— the father ran a small café where the mother acted

as waitress and cashier—who moved as if in a dream through grade school and high school and then, in a year or two, into secretarial school. Later, much later—what happened to the time in between?—she is in another town working as a receptionist for an electronic parts firm and becomes acquainted with one of the engineers who asks her for a date. Eventually, seeing that's his aim, she lets him seduce her. . . . After a short while they decide to get married, but already the past, her past, is slipping away. The future is something she can't imagine. (*FS* 49-50)

This passage, continuing in much the same vein for the rest of the page, provides us with valuable information about the character, her background, and her feelings about herself and her marriage. Therefore, when this is replaced by "I sit for a long time holding the newspaper and thinking" (*What* 84), we are obviously missing out on a key to understanding the actions within the story. We also miss out on fully comprehending the developing relationship between Stuart and Claire when several scenes showing her physical revulsion toward her husband, the way "his fingers burn" (*FS* 51) when he touches her, are reduced or eliminated. A long argument about her refusing to sleep in the same bed with him (*FS* 53), for example, becomes "That night I make my bed on the sofa" (*What* 85), again making it harder for the reader to grasp what is going on in the story. Unlike the first version, these elliptical revisions result in a minimalistic story whose "prose [is] so attenuated that it can't support the weight of a past or a future, but only a bare notation of what happens, now; a slice of life in which the characters are seen without the benefit of antecedents or social context."[21.]

Not only does the first version provide a fuller understanding of the main characters, it also presents important and detailed pictures of some of the minor characters who are all but eliminated in the revision. We have already seen how the baker's transformation from a mere voice on the other end of the telephone in **"The Bath"** to a fully realized person with his own history and concerns in **"A Small, Good Thing"** adds a whole new dimension, a fuller sense of humanity to that story, and the same is true here. For example, Carver's revision of **"So Much Water So Close to Home"** eliminates an important scene in which the couple's son, Dean, questions his father, only to be told to be quiet by his mother (*FS* 51). More significantly, Carver dramatically redraws his portrait of the victim. Although it seems like a minor detail, there is a world of difference in the reader's perception when a character is called "Susan Miller" rather than "the body." The *Furious Seasons* version of **"So Much Water So Close to Home"** contains the following scene, a description of a television news report in which the dead girl's parents go into the funeral home to identify the body:

Bewildered, sad, they shuffle slowly up the sidewalk to the front steps to where a man in a dark suit stands waiting and holding the door. Then, it seems as if only a second has passed, as if they have merely gone inside the door and turned around and come out again, the same couple is shown leaving the mortuary, the woman in tears, covering her face with a handkerchief, the man stopping long enough to say to a reporter, "It's her, it's Susan." (*FS* 52)

There is also a description of what she looked like, her high school graduation picture flashed on the screen, and what she did for a living. In this way, she and her family become alive for the reader, who is now able to identify with them just as Claire does. When all we are told is that "the body has been identified, claimed" (*What* 84), however, we fail to reach this sort of understanding. We also therefore fail to understand fully Claire's motivation in attending her funeral.

Once again, the ending has been radically changed in the rewrite. In the first version, Claire returns from the funeral. Stuart attempts to initiate physical contact with her, but she rebuffs him, even stomping on his foot. He throws her down, makes an obscene remark, and goes away for the night. He sends her flowers the next morning, attempting to make up, but she "move[s her] things into the extra bedroom" (*FS* 60). At the end of the story, still not understanding his actions, she says to him, "'For God's sake, Stuart, she was only a child'" (*FS* 61). Her sense of continued sympathy for Susan and incomprehension of Stuart's behavior, her further separation from him, is perfectly in keeping with the previous actions and motivations of the characters. She had said earlier that her real fear was that "one day something [would] happen that should change something, but then you see nothing is going to change after all" (*FS* 49), yet it is clear at the end of the story that a fundamental alteration of her marital relationship has occurred. In the second version of the story, however, when Stuart attempts to initiate sexual activity with her, she allows herself to be symbolically raped; the sentence "I can't hear a thing with so much water going" (*What* 88) clearly recalls the rape and murder of the other girl. She even goes so far as to participate actively in the violation. "'That's right,' I say, finishing the buttons myself. 'Before Dean comes. Hurry'" (*What* 88). Her motivation here is unclear, made even more so by its having been so understated in the earlier parts of the story. We do not understand what has caused her to change her mind about Stuart, nor why she is seemingly willing to return to the status quo. The ending is not ambiguous, like the ending of **"The Bath,"** but it is rather illogical and unconvincingly forced.

As we have seen, then, the revision of this story makes it more minimal than it had been, reduces it rather than enlarges it. When Carver assembled the stories for *Fires*, however, he decided to republish the first version (with some minor changes) rather than the second. As he explains in the afterword to the volume, "I decided to stay fairly close to the versions as they first appeared . . ., which is more in accord with the way I am writing stories these days [i.e., the stories in *Cathedral*]" (*F* 189).[22] Elsewhere Carver has stated that *What We Talk About When We Talk About Love* is a very "self-conscious book in the sense of how intentional every move was, how calculated. I pushed and pulled and worked with those stories before they went into the book to an extent I'd never done with any other stories."[23] The end result, however, was not entirely satisfactory. "I knew I'd gone as far the other way as I could or wanted to go," he said, "cutting everything down to the marrow, not just to the bone,"[24] so he began to move in the other direction, first in *Fires* and then in *Cathedral*. Carver's movement away from minimalism is also apparent in his selection of the stories to be included in *Where I'm Calling From*. Only seven of the seventeen stories in *What We Talk About When We Talk About Love* are included, compared with eight of the twelve in *Cathedral*. Even more tellingly, Carver chooses four stories that appear "minimalized" in *What We Talk About When We Talk About Love* but reprints them in their other, fuller forms—for example, **"A Small, Good Thing"** rather than **"The Bath"** and the third **"So Much Water So Close to Home"** rather than the second.

This movement at first toward but then away from minimalism can also be traced in **"Distance,"** otherwise known as **"Everything Stuck to Him"** (in *What*), another story that is printed in all four volumes (*FS, What, F, Where*). While the changes here are much less dramatic than those in the three versions of **"So Much Water So Close to Home,"** the pattern is similar. The location of the story, for instance, is given in the first version as "Milan . . . in his apartment in the Via Fabroni near the Cascina Gardens" (*FS* 27), in the second as simply "Milan" (*What* 127), and in the third as "Milan . . . in his apartment on the Via Fabroni near the Cascina Gardens" (*F* 113). The lack of specificity in the second version indicates that it has been "minimalized," but Carver ultimately rejects this in favor of the fuller, more detailed description.[25] The story is selected for *Where I'm Calling From* in this third version.

An even better example of these changes in Carver's aesthetic, however, is the story **"Where Is Everyone?,"** which was first published in the journal *TriQuarterly* in the spring of 1980. It reappeared, under the title **"Mr. Coffee and Mr. Fixit,"** in *What We Talk About When We Talk About Love* (1981). In the transition it was reduced by a third, Carver having cut from it the same sort of material that he excised in the second publication of **"So Much Water So Close to Home."** The story does not have much of a plot in either case. It is rather unusual among Carver's stories in that it is

almost entirely composed of the narrator's reminiscences of past events, such as his wife's affair with an unemployed aerospace worker, his children and their actions, his father's death, and his widowed mother's sexual activities. The story is difficult to follow both chronologically and emotionally in both versions, but in the earlier, fuller version we are given many more clues. As Marc Chenetier points out:

> In its much longer version as **"Where Is Everyone?,"** it makes plain a number of details that remain quite puzzling in the shortened text. . . . The barest skeleton necessary for suggestion remains and a number of incidents that can be read as explanation in **"Where Is Everyone?"** are left as mere questions or unclear allusions in **"Mr. Coffee and Mr. Fixit."** . . . All of the details that made for "understanding" or "answering" a story in the interrogative mode have been toned down and have lodged the interrogations dismissed from the title at the heart of the story itself.[26]

The two stories begin similarly, but they diverge sharply in a passage in which the narrator recalls his relationship with his children. "I hated my kids during this time," he says. "One afternoon I got into a scuffle with my son. . . . I said I would kill him."[27] He goes on to explain the way the children, Katy and Mike, tried to take advantage of the situation, but he indicates that they were also deeply hurt by it, as seen by Mike's locking his mother out of the house one morning after she had spent the night at her lover's house and then beating her up when he does let her in. Not only is this passage missing from the revised version, but the son has been eliminated from the story altogether, and the daughter, whose name has been changed from Katy to Melody, just as the wife's has gone from Cynthia to Myrna, is little more than a stick figure who only appears in one brief paragraph. The result again is to provide the reader with less information about the state of the family; we get hints, but that is all. The narrator is also more reticent about himself. His comparing the situation to a scene in a novel by Italo Svevo (*TQ* 206), for instance, provides some insight into his personality and sets him apart from the standard, even stereotypical, Carver character. Not only does he read, a rarity in itself, but he reads novels by obscure Italian writers. This reference is eliminated in the revision, once more depriving us of a fact that might help us to make sense of the character's actions. The same is true of the sentence "'No one's evil,' I said once to Cynthia when we were discussing my own affair" (*TQ* 210). This fact, as well as the way it seems to slip out without the narrator's being fully aware of having divulged it, opens up a whole new level of interest and awareness, one that remains blocked off when the line is deleted, as it is in the second version.

This obscuring of the central characters and their relationships continues throughout **"Mr. Coffee and Mr. Fixit."** In **"Where Is Everyone?,"** although the narrator says that "conversations touching on love or the past were rare" (*TQ* 208), they do exist and are presented to us. At one point, for example, Cynthia says to the narrator, "When I was pregnant with Mike you carried me into the bathroom when I was so sick and pregnant I couldn't get out of bed. You carried me. No one else will ever do that, no one else could ever love me in that way, that much. We have that, no matter what. We've loved each other like nobody else could or ever will love the other again" (*TQ* 207). This glimpse of the past, besides being touching, appearing as it does in the midst of anger and violence, explains the tie that binds the couple together despite their problems. Ironically, the other important interpersonal relationship in the story exists between the narrator and his wife's lover, Ross, even though they have never met. In **"Mr. Coffee and Mr. Fixit,"** there are a few elliptical references to this feeling of connection on the narrator's part: "But we had things in common, Ross and me, which was more than just the same woman" (**What** 19); or "I used to make fun of him when I had the chance. But I don't make fun of him anymore. God bless you and keep you, Mr. Fixit" (**What** 19-20). The rationale behind these statements is obscure. Here is another example of a peculiar bind that Carver can get himself into; when he "omit[s] what other writers might regard as essential information, it is often hard to know what has precipitated a given situation."[28.] In **"Where Is Everyone?,"** these passages are expanded, and the connection becomes easier to see. For example, the narrator had once suggested that Mike join the Army. Cynthia disagreed, but Ross spoke in favor of the idea. "I was pleased to hear this," the narrator says, "and to find out that Ross and I were in agreement on the matter. Ross went up a peg in my estimation. . . . He [had] told her this even after there'd been a pushing and shoving match out in his drive in the early morning hours when Mike had thrown him down on the pavement" (*TQ* 208). The narrator was more than willing to admit to his wife that Ross was "[o]ne of *us*" (*TQ* 210) at the time, and now he realizes that his anger toward Ross was really only jealousy because "he was something of a fallen hero to my kids and to Cynthia, too, I suppose, because he'd helped put men on the moon" (*TQ* 209). In the longer version, then, Ross, like the minor characters we have examined in the other stories, emerges as a person in his own right, more than just the lover of the narrator's wife. We can now see how the narrator comes to identify with him (they are, after all, two men in similar positions) and eventually to forgive him. When all we see is the forgiveness, though, we do not understand how it came to be.

Once again the endings are significantly different from one version to the other. In **"Where Is Everyone?,"** the narrator returns to his mother's house to spend the night. She reluctantly informs him of his wife's affair. He tells her, "I know

that. . . . His name is Ross and he's an alcoholic. He's like me" (*TQ* 212). She responds, "Honey, you're going to have to do something for yourself" (*TQ* 212) and wishes him good night. The story ends with the following description:

> I lay there staring at the TV. There were images of uniformed men on the screen, a low murmur, then tanks and a man using a flame thrower. I couldn't hear it, but I didn't want to get up. I kept staring until I felt my eyes close. But I woke up with a start, the pajamas damp with sweat. A snowy light filled the room. There was a roaring coming at me. The room clamored. I lay there. I didn't move. (*TQ* 213)

This ending is somewhat ambiguous, but it does point to an apocalyptic change in the narrator's life, the sort that has resulted in his having reached the level of understanding he possesses at the time, about three years later, when he is narrating these events. **"Mr. Coffee and Mr. Fixit,"** however, ends in this manner:

> "Honey," I said to Myrna the night she came home. "Let's hug awhile and then you fix us a real nice supper."
>
> Myrna said, "Wash your hands." (**What** 20)

This ending so lacks any kind of summation, let alone consummation, that it baffles the reader. We do not even know when "the night she came home" is—Is it at the time of the events or at the time of their narration? What will be the effect of the things of which we have been told on the lives of those involved? We simply have to guess, with little to go on. Once asked about his endings, Carver stated, "I want to make sure my readers aren't left feeling cheated in one way or another when they've finished my stories. It's important for writers to provide enough to satisfy readers, even if they don't provide 'the' answers, or clear resolution."[29.] The ending of **"Mr. Coffee and Mr. Fixit,"** however, far from being satisfying, is the sort that, "rather than suggest[ing] depth . . . only signal[s] authorial cop out."[30.] This is undoubtedly one of the reasons that, as in the case of **"So Much Water So Close to Home,"** when Carver compiled the material for *Fires*, he returned, nearly word for word, to the original fuller version. Still one of his less successful pieces, as he tacitly admits by not selecting it for *Where I'm Calling From*, **"Where Is Everyone?"** is certainly better in that less minimal form.

John Biguenet finds **"Mr. Coffee and Mr. Fixit"** to be such a good example of everything he dislikes about minimalism that he uses it as the principal illustration in his satirical article "Notes of a Disaffected Reader: The Origins of

Minimalism." After providing a summary of the story that is almost as long as the story itself, he writes:

> It sounds like parody, doesn't it? Fifteen years ago it would have been parody. But it's not parody; it's paraphrase. If paraphrase is literature purged of style, then paraphrase is a kind of minimalism, and since the absence of style is a style itself, a disaffected reader might argue that paraphrase is an apt description of minimalist style. The reader, like a child with crayons hunched over a coloring book, authors the story.[31]

In **"Where Is Everyone?,"** however, Carver has already colored in the story for us, and we must keep in mind that it is this fuller, more expansive, more "authorly" version that he ultimately chooses to stand by. As we have seen by comparing the three versions of this story, as well as the various versions of other stories we have examined, Carver has undergone an aesthetic evolution, at first moving toward minimalism but then turning sharply away from it. The stories in **What We Talk About When We Talk About Love**, including **"The Bath,"** the second **"So Much Water So Close to Home,"** and **"Mr. Coffee and Mr. Fixit,"** do indeed follow Barth's definition of the "minimalist esthetic, of which a cardinal principle is that artistic effect may be enhanced by a radical economy of artistic means, even where such parsimony compromises other values: completeness, for example, or richness or precision of statement."[32] In the final analysis, however, Carver rejects this minimalist aesthetic. In **Fires** and **Cathedral**, and in the selected (and, incidentally, the new) stories in **Where I'm Calling From**, he is clearly opting for "completeness, richness, and precision." Therefore, if "most readers [take] their measure of him from his second collection of stories [i.e., **What**],"[33] they get a distorted picture of the actual scope and direction of his writings, which "both before and since" that volume are quite different.[34] Carver has said that he does not consider himself a minimalist, that "there's something about minimalist that smacks of smallness of vision and execution that I don't like,"[35] but this statement alone is not enough to remove the label. What should be enough, however, is the content of the work itself; rather than simply expressing his dissatisfaction with those stories he felt "were becoming too attenuated,"[36] he rewrote them or returned to an earlier version of them, so that they were more in keeping with his real style. It is no coincidence that, as he has moved away from his arch-minimalist phase to a more natural form, he has no longer felt this need to rewrite. "I feel that the stories in **Cathedral** are finished in a way I rarely felt about my stories previously," he told an interviewer shortly after the publication of that volume,[37] and in a profile written at the time of the publication of **Where I'm Calling From**, he expresses regret at having "mutilated" some of his earlier stories when

he says, "I used to revise even after a story was printed. I guess now I have a little more confidence."[38] As this most recent collection makes abundantly clear, Raymond Carver may have been a minimalist, but he used to be and has once again become much more.

NOTES

1. Mark A. R. Facknitz, "'The Calm,' 'A Small, Good Thing,' and 'Cathedral': Raymond Carver and the Rediscovery of Human Worth," *Studies in Short Fiction* 23 (1986): 287.

2. Robert Houston, "A Stunning Inarticulateness," *The Nation* 233 (4 July 1981): 23.

3. The best discussion of these issues is found in the special "Minimalism" edition of *Mississippi Review* (#40-41, 1985). The essays are edited by Kim A. Herzinger, who also contributes a fine introduction setting forth the problems of definition and inclusion. Several of the other essays are quite useful (and often humorous), and an important interview with Carver is included. Nor should one miss John Barth's excellent "A Few Words About Minimalism," *Weber Studies* 4 (Fall 1987): 5-14, the most succinct and enlightening view of the controversy yet to appear.

4. Michael Gorra, "Laughter and Bloodshed," *Hudson Review* 37 (Spring 1984): 155.

5. Marilynne Robinson, "Marriage and Other Astonishing Bonds," *New York Times Book Review*, 15 May 1988: 1. It is interesting to note that Robinson herself is often grouped with the minimalists.

6. Carver's comments can be found in his interviews with: Mona Simpson and Lewis Buzbee, *Writers at Work: The Paris Review Interviews*, Seventh Series, ed. George Plimpton (New York: Viking, 1986) 317-18; Larry McCaffery and Sinda Gregory, *Mississippi Review* 40-41 (1985): 65; and Kay Bonetti, *Saturday Review* 9 (Sept./Oct. 1983): 22. Critics who have made remarks along these lines include: Anatole Broyard, "Diffuse Regrets," *New York Times*, 5 Sept. 1983: 27; Irving Howe, "Stories of Our Loneliness," *New York Times Book Review*, 11 Sept. 1983: 1, 43; Laurie Stone, "Feeling No Pain," *Voice Literary Supplement* 20 (Oct. 1983): 55; Bruce Allen, "MacArthur Award Winners Produce Two of Season's Best," *The Christian Science Monitor*, 4 Nov. 1983: B4; Dorothy Wickendon, "Old Darkness, New Light," *The New Republic*, 21 Nov. 1983: 38; Josh Rubins, "Small Expectations," *New York Review of Books*, 24 Nov. 1983: 42; and Michael J. Bugeja, "Tarnish and Silver: An Analysis of *Carver's Cathedral*," *South Dakota Review* 24 (Autumn 1986): 73, 82-83, 87.

7. Raymond Carver, *Fires: Essays, Poems, Stories* (Santa Bar-

bara, CA: Capra Press, 1983) 188; further references will be parenthetical (*F*).

8. The most useful account of these two stories is in the best single article on Carver, William L. Stull's "Beyond Hopelessville: Another Side of Raymond Carver," *Philological Quarterly* 64 (Winter 1985): 1-15; I have kept my comments about them brief here largely because of his excellent explication. Other critics who touch on "The Bath" and "A Small, Good Thing" include: Howe 43; Allen B4; Rubins 41-42; Jonathan Yardley, "Ordinary People from an Extraordinary Writer," *Washington Post Book World*, 4 Sept. 1983: 3; and Marc Chenetier, "Living On/Off the 'Reserve': Performance, Interrogation, and Negativity in the Works of Raymond Carver," *Critical Angles: European Views of Contemporary American Literature*, ed. Marc Chenetier (Carbondale and Evansville: Southern Illinois U P, 1986) 170. Carver himself remarks on these two stories in his interview with McCaffery and Gregory, 66.

9. Raymond Carver, *What We Talk About When We Talk About Love* (New York: Alfred A. Knopf, 1981) 48; further references will be parenthetical (*What*).

10. Raymond Carver, *Cathedral* (New York: Alfred A. Knopf, 1983) 80; further references will be parenthetical (*C*).

11. Kim A. Herzinger, "Introduction: On the New Fiction," *Mississippi Review* 40-41 (1985): 7.

12. Anatole Broyard, "Books of the Times," *New York Times*, 15 Apr. 1981: C29. For other criticisms of Carver's minimalist endings see: Gorra 156; Stull 2, 5; and Adam Mars-Jones, "Words for the Walking Wounded," *Times Literary Supplement*, 22 Jan. 1982: 76.

13. McCaffery and Gregory 66.

14. William Abrahams, ed., *Prize Stories 1983: The O. Henry Awards* (Garden City, NY: Doubleday, 1983). Abrahams has a brief paragraph in his introduction explaining why he so much prefers "A Small, Good Thing" to "The Bath." A dissenting view, however, can be seen in Rubins, 41-42, who finds the new ending too sentimental.

15. Stull 7.

16. Chenetier 170.

17. Barth 8.

18. Barth 8-9.

19. Raymond Carver, *Furious Seasons* (Santa Barbara, CA:

Capra Press, 1977) 43; further references will be parenthetical (*FS*).

20. Barth 9.

21. Gorra 155.

22. Carver also comments on the different versions of this story in his interview with Kay Bonetti, which is available on cassette through the American Audio Prose Library (CV III 1083). The excerpt from the interview that appears in *Saturday Review* does not include this portion.

23. Simpson and Buzbee 316.

24. Simpson and Buzbee 317.

25. Chenetier briefly discusses the story's three versions, but he misses this all-important point when he states that "Distance" is "retitled 'Everything Stuck To Him' in its passage from *Fires* and *Furious Seasons* to *What We Talk About*" (176). The correct chronology is from *Furious Seasons* to *What We Talk About* and then back to *Fires*, thus conforming to the hourglass pattern I have been stressing.

26. Chenetier 179.

27. Raymond Carver, "Where Is Everyone?," *TriQuarterly* 48 (Spring 1980): 203; further references will be parenthetical (*TQ*).

28. Robert Towers, "Low Rent Tragedies," *New York Review of Books*, 14 May 1981: 37.

29. McCaffery and Gregory 77.

30. Peter LaSalle, untitled review, *America*, 30 Jan. 1982: 80.

31. John Biguenet, "Notes of a Disaffected Reader: The Origins of Minimalism," *Mississippi Review* 40-41 (1985): 44.

32. Barth 5.

33. Stull 1.

34. Stull 2; see also 6, 14n. Stull is the only critic to have remarked on this "before and since" pattern that I have been exploring, but he does so only in passing.

35. Simpson and Buzbee 317.

36. McCaffery and Gregory 65.

37. McCaffery and Gregory 67.

38. David Gates, "Carver: To Make a Long Story Short," *Newsweek*, 6 June 1988: 70.

Michael Wm. Gearhart (essay date Fall 1989)

SOURCE: "Breaking the Ties That Bind: Inarticulation in the Fiction of Raymond Carver," in *Studies in Short Fiction*, Vol. 26, No. 4, Fall, 1989, pp. 439-46.

[*In the essay below, Gearhart traces the differences between the original story, "The Bath," and Carver's revision of the same story, "A Small, Good Thing."*]

Raymond Carver has been widely acknowledged as a short story writer whose glimpses into the lives of "everyday" people have made him a master of the genre. The typical Carver character is a down-and-out blue-collar type familiar with the trauma of marital infidelity, alcoholism, and financial hardship. As critics have thoroughly noted, these characters share an inability to articulate their frustrations in words which causes their social, moral, and spiritual paralysis: "each new moment can bewilder a character, freeze him or her into a confusion of inaction. Carver . . . is famous for the passivity with which his characters confront, or fail to confront, their experience."[1]

Carver's first two collections of stories, *Will You Please Be Quiet, Please?* and *What We Talk About When We Talk About Love*, are relentless portraits of human despair and futility. But with the publication of *Cathedral* in 1984, critics acknowledged an unmistakable loosening of Carver's stark "minimalist" prose style, and noted the development of human potential in his characters. Carver's premature death in 1989 precludes a definitive answer concerning whether this movement in his work was an aberration or the beginning of a trend, and Carver's recent retrospective, *Where I'm Calling From*, which includes little previously unpublished material, adds no insight into this question. However, a close re-reading and comparison of two key stories, **"The Bath"** and a revision of that story, **"A Small, Good Thing,"** raise a more essential question: how do the characters in **"A Small, Good Thing"** escape the inarticulation that suffocates the typical Carver character?

In both stories, Howard and Ann Weiss's uncomplicated lives are upset when their only son Scotty is struck by a car and hospitalized on his eighth birthday. The baker, from whom the birthday cake has been ordered, begins to make threatening telephone calls to the parents when the cake is not picked up. (The parents, of course, have forgotten about the cake, and receive these calls as they individually slip away from the hospital to check on things at home.) **"The Bath"** closes on a note of existential terror with the mother answering the phone, assuming the hospital is calling, only to hear the baker respond to her question "Is it about Scotty?" with the cryptic, "It has to do with Scotty, yes."[2]

Conversely, **"A Small, Good Thing"** is three times longer than **"The Bath,"** and introduces a completely opposite conclusion—one of healing and forgiveness. In this story the mother finally realizes that it is the baker who is calling, and she and her husband confront him with the news of Scotty's death (his condition is left undecided in the first version). This confrontation leads to the baker's examination of his own pitiful existence and to the subsequent scene of forgiveness and reconciliation.

Laurie Stone makes an important observation when she states that "Carver steers the story [**"A Small, Good Thing"**] with his distinctive descriptive wizardry, *conveying how the parents feel through their actions*."[3] Carver generally eschews authorial comment in his stories in favor of brief, emotive descriptions, and continues to do so in **"A Small, Good Thing."** What, then, accounts for the fullness of style and for the final scene of resolution and reconciliation in this story so absent in his previous work? It is this: Carver's focus on the implicit communication between the characters through unspoken language and, moreover, the fact that this substitution of implicit communication for verbal inarticulation becomes a self-conscious act on the part of the characters.

Some differences between **"The Bath"** and **"A Small, Good Thing"** are immediately apparent. In the former, descriptions of the characters are brief, when they occur at all. The father is never given a name. In **"A Small, Good Thing,"** even minor characters are described, and scenes in which they appear are developed. The effect is that a sense of humanity emerges between the characters that is wholly absent in the first story. The best example of this is a passage in both stories in which Ann Weiss's (the mother) interaction with a black family, who are awaiting the outcome of their son/brother Nelson's accident, is described. In simple terms, the passage is lengthened in the second story from approximately 250 to 650 words, most of them devoted to a physical description of the black family. But significantly, in the expanded version the characters share their pain and experience. Much of this occurs through verbal interaction, but not without some key nonverbal prompting.

In the first version, Ann explains to Nelson's father why she is at the hospital, giving the details of Scotty's accident and condition. The man's reply to her closes the scene: "The man shifted in his chair. He shook his head. He said, 'Our Nelson'" (56). Thus ends the interaction between the two. But in the second version, a slight nonverbal clue leads to the verbal interaction of the grieving parents: "'That's too bad,' the man said and shifted in his chair. He shook his head. He looked down at the table, and then he looked at Ann. She was still standing there."[4] The man then proceeds to give the details of how his son was knifed, an innocent bystander at a fight. The paragraph that follows his description makes two things clear: verbal communication is disturbingly inadequate, but the nonverbal signals that trigger the attempt are sufficient to induce the desire for shared humanity:

> Ann looked at the girl again, who was still watching her, and at the older woman, who kept her head down, but whose eyes were now closed. Ann saw the lips moving silently, making words. She had an urge to ask what those words were. She wanted to talk more with these people who were in the same kind of waiting she was in. She was afraid, and they were afraid. They had that in common. She would have liked to have said something else about the accident, told them more about Scotty.... Yet she didn't know how to begin. She stood looking at them without saying anything more. (74)

This passage contains an unusual amount of authorial direction to the reader, for the rewrite incorporates a crucial change. In the first version, when the man shifts in his chair, shakes his head, and looks down at the table, he is utilizing what Stephen R. Portch calls a "regulator": an action that involves "both speaker and listener."[5] A regulator can "provide a pause . . . or tell the speaker to continue, repeat, elaborate" (9). In this case, the man's regulator says, in essence, "I don't want to talk about it." But in the revision, Ann utilizes a regulator of her own—her insistent stare—which causes him to continue. This minute difference allows for the possibility that these two people will communicate, and foreshadows the final exchange between the Weisses and the baker in **"A Small, Good Thing."**

Regulators are mostly subconscious, and perhaps this fact accounts for the tentativeness and ultimate inadequacy of the conversation between Ann and Nelson's father in **"The Bath."** But as the characters in **"A Small, Good Thing"** (particularly Ann Weiss) become increasingly self-conscious in regard to body language, their ability to use it as a substitute for verbal shortcomings increases accordingly.

Early in **"A Small, Good Thing,"** the reader witnesses the deterioration of language and the subsequent dependence upon implicit communication. The inefficiency of words is obvious when Howard Weiss, the father, first returns home to clean up after being with Scotty at the hospital. The phone rings, and Howard assumes that the hospital is calling:

"There's a cake here that wasn't picked up," the voice on the other end of the line said.

"What are you saying?" Howard asked

"A cake," the voice said. "A sixteen-dollar cake."

Howard held the receiver against his ear, trying to understand.

"I don't know anything about a cake," he said.

". . . what are you talking about?"

"Don't hand me that," the voice said. (62-63)

The reader knows that the voice is the baker's, but Howard does not. Language clearly works for the reader, while it baffles the character. But the inherent ambiguity of language is not always one of perspective. When Howard returns to the hospital, the doctor is attempting to explain Scotty's condition without causing alarm in the parents. The word "coma" is bounced back and forth between them, highlighting the concurrent imprecision and importance of language. The doctor begins by proclaiming that "it is not a coma," then changes to "I don't want to call it a coma," and finally relents with "It's not a coma yet, not exactly." Ann says, "It's a coma" (66).

While language breaks down, body communication becomes more significant. When Dr. Francis is unable to express himself adequately in words, he resorts to more physical and formal displays. Each time he enters the room, he "shook hands with Howard, though they'd just seen each other a few hours before" (65). When he leaves the room, he pats the parents on the shoulders; as their son's condition worsens, the physical displays become increasingly compassionate. When Scotty dies, Dr. Francis embraces Ann, and "He seemed full of some goodness she didn't understand" (82).

The doctor's unconscious use of regulators to augment his speech is a nonverbal device that becomes immediately evident to the reader, if not to the Weisses. He constantly resorts to "looking at the boy" as a way of buying time when he cannot offer verbal encouragement to the parents. It would seem that this lack of words might be disconcerting to the parents, but they find solace in the doctor's very appearance: "The doctor was a handsome, big-shouldered man with a tanned face. He wore a three-piece blue suit, a striped tie, and ivory cufflinks. His gray hair was combed along the sides of his head, and he looked as if he had just come from a concert" (65-66). Contrast his appearance with that of the radiologist, who later comes to take more x-rays of Scotty: "He had a bushy mustache. He was wearing loafers, a Western shirt, and a pair of jeans" (68). Ann's reaction to him is markedly different from her unquestioning faith in Dr. Francis: "She stood between this new doctor and the bed" (68). The radiologist is straightforward in his speech compared to Dr. Francis, yet Ann distrusts him. But when speech is inadequate, nonverbal signs gain added significance, and physical appearance is no exception. As Stephen Portch points out, "Physical appearance usually has an immediate—and often lasting—impact" (11). And judgment of a stranger based on physical appearance is to be expected. It is more significant that during this period of crisis in the parents' lives, their own verbal communication gives way to implicit communication.

After Dr. Francis has provided his less-than-satisfactory explanation of Scotty's condition, the parents attempt to verbalize their fears: "Ann put her hand on the child's forehead. 'At least he doesn't have a fever,' she said. Then she said, 'My God, he feels so cold, though. Howard? Is he supposed to feel like this?'" "'I think he's supposed to feel this way right now,' he said"(67). But both Howard and Ann realize that their words are empty, and although at this point the action is mostly subconscious, body language substitutes for their inability to fully articulate their fears. Howard "felt a genuine fear starting in his limbs," and Ann "knew now they were into something hard," but neither is capable of expression:

> Howard sat in the chair next to her. They looked at each other. He wanted to say something else to reassure her, but he was afraid, too. He took her hand and put it in his lap, and this made him feel better, her hand being there. He picked up her hand and squeezed it. Then he just held her hand. They sat like that for a while, watching the boy and not talking. (67)

Although the process is a gradual one, the movement toward self-consciousness has begun, and soon these characters will make a discovery that no Carver character before them has made: they need not be the hapless victims of verbal inarticulation.

Scotty's condition remains unchanged for the next several hours, and both the doctor and the parents are increasingly alarmed that he is not waking. As his condition becomes less explicable, language is less adequate, and body language more important. Now the Weisses reveal their first spark of self-consciousness in regard to implicit communication. As Howard and Ann stare out the window, the narrator makes a rare intrusion: "They didn't say anything. But they seemed to feel each other's insides now, as though the worry had made them transparent in a perfectly natural way" (70-71). Then Dr. Francis returns and again personifies the ambiguous nature of language. He is reticent about Scotty's tests until Ann asserts, "It is a coma, then?" (71). The doc-

tor rubs his cheek (another regulator to stall for time) and answers, "We'll call it that for the time being, until he wakes up" (71). This, of course, is like calling a person dead until resurrected. But the parents cling to whatever hope is offered, and the doctor shakes Howard's hand and leaves.

The Weisses decide to check on things at home, and Howard suggests that Ann go, to freshen up and eat something. She objects at first, but when she looks at Howard, she makes a discovery: "She understood he wanted to be by himself for a while, not have to talk or share his worry for a time" (72). This ability of one character to empathize with another's inarticulation is a rarity in Carver's fiction. Ann has reached beyond her own personal situation to consider someone else's, and in so doing, she confronts her own inability to communicate. As she prepares to leave the hospital, her self-conscious awareness of the process is revealed:

> She stood in her coat for a minute trying to recall the doctor's exact words, looking for any nuances, any hint of something behind his words other than what he said. She tried to remember if his expression had changed any when he bent over to examine the child. She remembered the way his features had composed themselves as he rolled back the child's eyelids and then listed to his breathing. (72-73)

Ann's cognizance of the significance of body language is even more evident when she returns to the hospital. Her husband's posture convinces her that something is wrong: "She looked at him closely and thought that his shoulders were bunched a little" (79). This information is repeated four lines later: "His shoulders were bunching, she could see that" (79).

Howard's body language is the result of his initial inability to tell his wife that the doctors have decided that surgery is necessary. But before the full impact of this information can set in, they notice that Scotty has opened his eyes. They run to his bedside, but Scotty's "eyes scrunched closed, and he howled until he had no more air in his lungs. His face seemed to relax and soften then. His lips parted as his last breath was puffed through his throat and exhaled gently through the clenched teeth" (80).

A shaken Dr. Francis escorts the Weisses to the doctor's lounge, and once more the shortcomings of language are highlighted as Ann gropes to find the words to express her grief: "She . . . though how unfair it was that the only words that came out were the sort of words used on TV shows where people were stunned by violent or sudden deaths. She wanted her words to be her own" (81). Her desire is to confront her situation rather than be controlled by it. But Dr. Francis is yet unable to express himself directly: "There are still some things that have to be done, things that have to be cleared up to our satisfaction. Some things that need explaining" (81). This time it is Howard who clarifies the ambiguity: "'An autopsy,' Howard said. Dr. Francis nodded" (81).

After returning home, the bereaved couple receives two more phone calls from the baker. Finally, Ann realizes that the baker is calling to harass them about the cake. Although it is midnight, she tells Howard to drive her to the bakery, and the stage is set for the story's final scene.

The closing action can be divided into two phases: before and after the baker is told of Scotty's death. In the first phase, almost all of the important communication is implicitly expressed through body language. When the baker explains tersely that he works sixteen hours a day just to make ends meet, Ann's response is entirely nonverbal, but it is clear that her point has been made: "A look crossed Ann's face that made the baker move back and add 'No trouble, now'" (86). The baker then responds with a less-than-subtle physical threat of his own: "He reached to the counter and picked up a rolling pin with his right hand and began to tap it against the palm of his other hand" (86).

This type of body movement substitutes for more than words—it also replaces socially unacceptable acts of violence. Portch refers to this type of implicit communication as an "adaptor," or actions that "originated for practical purposes and have become assimilated into behavioral patterns . . . the clenching of a fist in anger has the practical purpose of preparing the hand to administer a blow. But more often than not, the fist is clenched to signal anger without a blow being struck" (10).

When the Weisses first entered the bakery, Ann "clenched her fists. She stared at him [the baker] fiercely. There was a deep burning inside her, an anger that made her feel larger than herself, larger than either of these men" (85). She has effectively communicated to the baker through this adaptor what she later admits to him (and perhaps to herself) in words: "I wanted to kill you . . . I wanted you dead" (87). Similarly, the baker's manipulation of the rolling pin suggests that he will do what is necessary to defend himself if physical violence occurs, but these nonverbal signals serve to preclude that violence. The spoken messages delivered in the first half of this to preclude that violence. The spoken messages delivered in the first half of this passage amount to little more than childish verbal jabs, while the nonverbal signals are loud and clear. The Weisses and the baker are sizing up each other, waiting to see what will happen.

Things change when Ann reveals to the baker the details of Scotty's death. After a final admonishment to him, she breaks into tears, and Howard and she are notably silent

for the final two pages of the story. The baker's initial reaction to the news of Scotty's death is nonverbal—"he shook his head slowly"—but then an outpouring of words that are the baker's healing takes place:

> Then he began to talk. They listened carefully. Although they were tired and in anguish, they listened to what the baker had to say. They nodded when the baker began to speak of loneliness, and of the sense of doubt and limitation that had come to him in his middle years. He told them what it was like to be childless all these years. To repeat the days with the ovens endlessly full and endlessly empty. (88-89)

The baker's ability to articulate his meaningless existence makes him unique among Carver's characters; he is the first to use language in a cathartic sense, the first to confront the nature of his own existence. His philosophical self-examination is a turning point in his life, for he takes the initiative of asking for forgiveness: "I'm not an evil man, I don't think. Not evil like you said on the phone. You got to understand what it comes down to is I don't know how to act anymore, it would seem. Please,' the man said, 'let me ask you if you can find it in your hearts to forgive me?'" (88). The baker finds his forgiveness through the words that have for so long eluded him.

But more significant, perhaps, is the salvation of Ann and Howard Weiss, for they win a self-conscious battle with inarticulation and, in so doing, provide for the redemption of the baker. Had the embittered man not been confronted by the Weisses, he would never have faced his unresolved conflicts. But unlike the baker, the Weisses do not gain their epiphany through words, but through their ability to empathize with another's pain in the time of their own sorrow: "Although they were in grief, they listened to what the baker had to say." They do not speak; they listen. And they nod. In the absence of words, healing is the literal and figurative act of silent communion with the baker, who prepares hot rolls and coffee for the Weisses, reminding them that "Eating is a small, good thing in a time like this" (88). The concluding passage in the story serves as a final restatement of the double theme of verbal inarticulation and the ability of implicit communication to function admirably as its substitute:

> "Smell this," the baker said, breaking open a dark loaf. "It's heavy bread, but rich." They smelled it, then he had them taste it. It had the taste of molasses and coarse grains. They listened to him. They ate what they could. They swallowed the dark bread. It was like daylight under the fluorescent trays of light. They talked on into the

early morning, the high, pale cast of light in the windows, and they did not think of leaving. (89)

Perhaps the most significant aspect of this reconciliation is revealed in the concluding sentence, which suggests that if a self-conscious understanding of nonverbal communication is gained, then human communication—not just implicit, but verbal—is possible. It is not until the Weisses have partaken of silent communion with the baker that they are able to talk "on into the early morning." Their willingness to allow the baker's actions to facilitate their healing is the culmination of their growing capacity throughout the story to understand implicit communication. In the absence of this ability, it is doubtful that they, much less the baker, could have avoided the fate of the typical Carver character—paralysis.

NOTES

1. Michael Gorra, "Laughter and Bloodshed," *Hudson Review*, 37 (1984), 151-64.

2. "The Bath," in *What We Talk About When We Talk About Love* (New York: Random House, 1982), p. 56. Subsequent references are cited in the text.

3. Laurie Stone, "Feeling No Pain," *Village Voice Literary Supplement*, No. 20 (Oct. 1983), 54-55; emphasis mine.

4. "A Small, Good Thing," in *Cathedral* (New York: Random House, 1984), p. 74. Subsequent references are cited in the text.

5. *Literature's Silent Language* (New York: Lang, 1985), p. 11; subsequent references are cited in the text. This work is an excellent introduction to the occurrence of nonverbal signals in literature, and focuses on the work of specific writers, including Hemingway, with whose style of writing Carver's stories have been compared.

Arthur A. Brown (essay date Winter 1990)

SOURCE: "Raymond Carver and Postmodern Humanism," in *Critique*, Vol. XXXI, No. 2, pp. 125-36.

[*In the following essay, Brown—a professor at the University of California, Davis—argues that* Cathedral *is not a radical departure from Carver's style, but an example of his postmodern humanist writing.*]

When Raymond Carver wrote **"Cathedral,"** he recognized that it was "totally different in conception and execution from any stories that [had] come before." He goes on to say, "There was an opening up when I wrote the story. I knew I'd gone as far the other way as I could or wanted to go, cutting everything down to the marrow, not just to the bone. Any farther in that direction and I'd be at a dead end" (*Fires* 204). He began to write longer stories, and his characters started to see things more clearly. Perhaps Carver was exaggerating, however, when he said that **"Cathedral"** was "totally" different.

Carver's writing has remained postmodern, a distinction as apparent as it is challenging to describe. The teacher of a drawing class once said as my class worked on contour drawings of a tree, "Don't lift your pencil from the page. Keep your eyes on the tree. Concentrate until you get a headache, until your pencil is on the branch of the tree." The contour drawing seems an apt metaphor for postmodern fiction, with its attention to surface detail, its resistance to depth, and its aspect of self-consciousness, where the medium merges with the subject—the creation of the fiction is the subject of the fiction. The pencil is on the tree. What can happen in postmodern fiction is what happened in that drawing class—when we looked down at the page, finally, we saw a good deal of contour drawing and little tree. What makes Carver's postmodern fiction so remarkable is that the tree is still there. He never loses sight of his subject, which is real life, even while his subject is also the creation of fiction.

"Cathedral" is the final story in the collection of stories by the same name; it is the first Carver wrote in this collection. William Stull characterizes the change the story represents in Carver's writing as a movement away from the "existential realism" of his earlier stories toward a "humanist realism."

> Existential realism . . . treats reality phenomenologically, agnostically, and objectively. Whether dead or in occultation, God—the archetype of the author—is absent from the world, which is discontinuous, banal, and, by definition, mundane. . . . The style of existential realism is, therefore, studiously objective, impersonal, and neutral. . . . Humanist realism, in contrast, takes a more expressive, more "painterly" approach to its subjects. . . . Such realism treats reality metaphysically, theologically, and subjectively. (7-8)

Stull thoroughly examines the revision of a story entitled **"The Bath,"** which first appeared in *What We Talk About When We Talk About Love*. In *Cathedral*, **"The Bath"** has become **"A Small, Good Thing,"** and the most obvious difference is that it continues where the first story left off. The characters move from a serious miscommunication to a very real kind of communion. "Eating is a small, good thing in a time like this" (*Cathedral* 88), says the baker to the couple whose son was killed by a hit-and-run driver and whom he had senselessly tormented, and he shares bread with them. It is a very different kind of eating from that found in many of Carver's earlier stories. In **"The Idea,"** for example, eating—like the television, like language itself—substitutes for communion and is used by his characters to block out the realization that they are dissociated from themselves and from others, especially those with whom they should be the most intimate. **"A Small, Good Thing"** ends: "They talked on into the early morning, the high, pale cast of light in the windows, and they did not think of leaving" (89). Thus, **"The Bath,"** which, according to Stull, had been "an existential tale of crass casualty," has become "a story of spiritual rebirth, a minor masterpiece of humanist realism" (13).

Stull refers to existential realism as postmodern, while he associates humanist realism with the classic realism of Balzac, Henry James, and the early James Joyce. Stull says, "Humanist realism . . . differs from its postmodern counterpart in both philosophical orientation and fictive techniques" (7). But Carver is as postmodern in **"Cathedral"** as he was in the existential stories in *Will You Please Be Quiet, Please?*, particularly **"Neighbors,"** **"Collectors,"** and **"Put Yourself in My Shoes."** Rather than characterize Carver's work in *Cathedral* as humanist realism, let us call it humanist postmodernism. The central action in **"Cathedral"** is itself a kind of contour drawing, where not one but two hands hold the pencil.

Most important, Carver does not need to revert to classic realism to express themes of brotherly and spiritual love. In today's world, these themes are more effectively realized in postmodern fiction. Carver's first accomplishment was to join realism with the resistance to depth and the self-consciousness peculiar to postmodern fiction. His second accomplishment has been to leave behind the themes of dissociation and alienation, which post-modern writers inherited from the modernists, and show that reassociation is possible. He has done this because his own theory of fiction never lets him leave real life.

Concerning the difference in the conception and the execution of **"Cathedral,"** Carver said that he supposes "it reflects a change in [his] life as much as it does in [his] way of writing" (*Fires* 204). Mona Simpson and Lewis Buzbee once asked Carver, "Are your characters trying to do what matters?" He responded:

> I think they are trying. But trying and succeeding are two different matters. In some lives, people always succeed. . . . In other lives, people don't succeed at what they are trying to do. . . . These lives are, of course, valid to write about, the lives of the people who don't succeed. Most of my own experience has to do with the latter situation. . . . It's their lives they've become uncomfortable with, lives they see breaking down. They'd like to set things right, but they can't. And usually they do know it, I think, and after that they just do the best they can. (*Fires* 201)

Thus it is Carver's personal experience that caused him to write about waitresses and salesmen, millworkers, the unemployed, would-be actors and writers, and people whose marriages had failed. His personal experience dealt with both a life he perceived as not succeeding and also with that perception. "And suddenly everything became clear to him" is a quote from a short story by Chekhov that Carver kept on a card near his desk. He explains:

> I find these words filled with wonder and possibility. I love their simple clarity, and the hint of revelation that's implied. There is mystery, too. What has been unclear before? Why is it just now becoming clear? What's happened? Most of all—what now? (*Fires* 24)

Seeing is intricately related to being. The writer's art is not separate from existence but is part of it, not merely because it is the writer's task to see clearly and to show what he sees to others, but because seeing is a part of all of our lives. Without it we do not exist. In **"Fires,"** Carver talks about the biggest influence on his life and writing—the fact that he had two children—and about a moment in a laundromat when it became clear to him that the things he had hoped for, the things he thought were possible in his life, simply were not going to happen. "But like that it came to me," Carver says. "Like a sharp breeze when the window is thrown open" (*Fires* 24). Moments of sudden clarity are moments of seeing, and these moments are dangerous and mysterious, like the wind. Our very identities are changing.

"The Pheasant" is a story about a young actor who has been living with an older woman for her money and her connections. "He could call himself an actor at long last" (*Fires* 150), says the omniscient narrator. What one can call oneself, the nature of one's identity, and the fact that identity is dependent upon watching others and being watched, as is the case in the acting profession, are ever-present themes in Carver's stories, and an element of self-consciousness is usually present during the moments in which everything becomes clear to his characters. These are moments of self-realization for the characters, but, in addition, an element of self-consciousness enters the story itself—the story seems aware of its own existence.

In **"The Pheasant,"** the young man's identity as an actor is tenuous. One night just before his thirtieth birthday, he and his older woman-friend drive three hundred miles up the coast from Los Angeles to her beach house. On the way, as she dozes, he speeds up to hit a pheasant that crosses the path of the car. Driving again, after having stopped to look at the dead bird, the young man asks his companion, "How well do you really know me?" (149). She has no idea what he means. This is the point at which the exposition occurs and the character's brief biography is presented; in other words, it is here that the reader begins to know the young man. He asks, "Do you think I'd act, that I'd ever do something against my own best interest?" (150). She says she thinks he would. The young man remarks that the countryside is "[s]omething out of Steinbeck" (151), recalling the trucker in *Grapes of Wrath* who swerved to hit the turtle crossing the road. Finally, the young man tells his companion that he killed the pheasant intentionally:

> She gazed at him for a minute without interest. She didn't say anything. Something became clear to him then. . . . [He] suddenly understood that he no longer had any values. No frame of reference, was the phrase that ran through his mind. (151)

"The phrase that ran through his mind": it is as though we hear the actor-character, as well as the narrator-writer, reflexively making life into fiction. The story continues: "'Is it true?' she said. He nodded. 'It could have been dangerous. It could have gone through the windshield'" (151). As soon as we are conscious, then, of the fiction, the question is asked: "Is it true?" Truth and danger go hand-in-hand, through the windshield.

Windows and breezes, or rushes of wind, figure heavily in Carver's fiction, especially at moments of sudden clarity. The word "window" comes from the Old Norse "vindauga," which means literally "wind eye." The window might be a symbol of fiction itself. Truth comes through it. We see ourselves by watching others, and in this revelation is mystery: "What has been unclear before? Why is it just now becoming clear? What's happened? Most of all—what now?" There is danger, for it is dangerous to consider that we might not know ourselves, that we might "act . . . against [our] own best interests." Here the young actor avoids danger to himself by killing the pheasant instead; he uses the pheasant's death to discover his own identity. Is that not the way we use fiction—both in the writing and the reading of it—to take us through crises we would rather not experience firsthand?

The most self-conscious of Carver's stories is probably **"Put Yourself in My Shoes."** He says in **"Fires"**:

> I once sat down to write what turned out to be a pretty good story, though only the first sentence of the story had offered itself to me when I began it. For several days I'd been going around with this sentence in my head: "He was running

the vacuum cleaner when the telephone rang.". . . Pretty soon I could see a story, and I knew it was my story, the one I'd been wanting to write. (*Fires* 17)

It is not surprising that the sentence suggested a story to Carver; in fact, it might have suggested more than one. **"Collectors"** is about a vacuum cleaner salesman named Bell—as though Carver cannot help connecting the vacuum cleaner to the telephone—who essentially collects another man's identity. More to the point, in **"Put Yourself in My Shoes"** the main character is a writer. It is Carver's story, and it is Myers's. Perhaps there is a play on this character's name as well, with the words "my" and "yours." Perhaps it is also the reader's story.

One of postmodern fiction's assumed roles is to remind the reader not only of how he reads the text but, by extension, of how he reads the world. In reading we are creating a reflection of ourselves, as there is no perception without a perceiver. The world, like the text, is a fictional construct—although, unlike the text, it is also real. We identify our own search for identity with the writer's, and vice versa. By reminding us of this, the writer is doubly (or infinitely) identified, and so is the reader. This is the reason mirrors are so prevalent a sign in postmodern fiction, as they are in Carver's stories, for they represent the text itself. If windows are a symbol of fiction, mirrors are a symbol of postmodern fiction. Looking into them is no small matter, for the character's, the writer's, and the reader's existences are affirmed—and perhaps altered—in them.

"The telephone rang while he was running the vacuum cleaner" (*Will You Please* 130) is the first sentence in the story. Myers's girlfriend Paula is calling from the Christmas office party at the firm Myers quit in order to write a novel. The first thing she tells him is that a fellow worker committed suicide. This is the first of several incidences of violent deaths that are related by one or another character in this story that is so concerned with storytelling. It is no accident that violence and death should be immediately under the surface. Carver says, "I like it when there is some feeling of threat or sense of menace in short stories. . . .There has to be tension, a sense that something is imminent . . . or else, most often, there simply won't be a story" (*Fires* 17). There are more than artistic or technical reasons for the danger, however, for what is usually at stake is a character's identity, a character on the brink of being and not being. And yet, can we place the concerns of a character ahead of "artistic or technical" concerns? The story, too, is struggling to exist. Analogous to danger and the fear of death for a character is the possibility of a story not being written, or not being read, and that very fear and possibility make the story.

Paula wants Myers to come to the party, but Myers says no. He watches the snowflakes fall outside the window, rubs his fingers across the glass, then writes his name on the glass. Myers's writing his name on the window suggests, almost too clearly, that, like all writers, he obtains his identity from watching. Myers and Paula decide to meet at a bar, and on the way Myers looks at the people, the sky, and the buildings: "He tried to save it all for later. He was between stories, and he felt despicable" (132). They decide to leave the bar and visit the Morgans, in whose house they had lived when the Morgans were in Europe. As they start up the walk to the front porch, a dog runs out from the back of the house, heads straight for Myers, and knocks him over. Inside the house, Morgan, who is not too pleased with the unexpected visitors, asks Myers if he is all right. "I saw it," Morgan says. "I was looking out the window when it happened" (135). The narrator tells us that "this remark seemed odd to Myers." The idea of somebody watching him is what Myers finds odd, and he immediately turns this around and studies the man. At this point, Morgan is described, as though Carver, or the narrator, and Myers are working together. When Paula or the Morgans talk about what Myers does, which they do repeatedly, they say "he writes" rather than "he is a writer." He is still "between stories" and without an identity. "What did you write today?" Morgan asks, and Myers replies, "Nothing" (137).

Then the storytelling begins. The Morgans are eager to provide Myers with some material, and, after Morgan tells the first story, Mrs. Morgan, Paula, and Morgan himself offer different opinions as to which character's point of view would hold the most interesting possibilities for the story Myers should write. Morgan's remark reminds us of the title of the story we are reading when he says, "Put yourself in the shoes of that eighteen-year-old coed who fell in love with a married man. Think about *her* for a moment, and then you see the possibilities for your story" (139). Morgan adds, "It would take a Tolstoy to tell it and tell it *right*" (140).

Carver uses the stuffy, professorial Morgan to remind us of literature and its great traditions in order to make the point that those traditions are of the past—they will no longer work for today's stories or storytelling. In **"Fat,"** the story that begins *Will You Please Be Quiet, Please?*, the waitress-narrator has been telling a story to her friend. "What else? Rita says, lighting one of my cigarets and pulling her chair closer to the table. This story's getting interesting now." As if responding to both Rita and the reader, the waitress-narrator continues, "That's it. Nothing else" (5). At the point where the traditional story would have begun, today's story ends. There are no conclusions, no judgments.

After Morgan has finished his tale about the eighteen-year-old coed, the two couples hear singing. They go to the window to watch Christmas carolers across the street, and Mrs.

Morgan says sadly, "They won't come here" (140). In fact, the singers do not come to the Morgans' house. Mrs. Morgan then decides to tell Myers a story she hopes he can use. It is a fairly long story, and it ends: "Fate sent her to die on the couch in our living room." The line sends Myers into a fit of laughter. The Morgans' idea of storytelling—of stories controlled by a universal, larger-than-life force that orders them and defines their meanings—is too much for Myers, and his laughter destroys the surface calm of the visit. "If you were a real writer," says Morgan, ". . .you would not laugh. . . .You would plumb the depths of that poor soul's heart and try to understand" (147).

"Plumbing the depths" is precisely what Carver and Myers will not presume to do. Says Carver:

> What creates tension in a piece of fiction is partly the way the concrete words are linked together to make up the visible action of the story. But it's also the things that are left out, that are implied, the landscape just under the smooth (but sometimes broken and unsettled) surface of things. (*Fires* 17)

By keeping us on the surface, Carver is adding force to whatever is beneath it, or to the terrible sense that nothing is there at all. Dean Flower contrasts Carver's approach with Hemingway's theory that "you could omit anything if you knew that you omitted, and the omitted part would strengthen the story and make people feel something more than they understood" (Baker 143). Flower writes of the stories in *Will You Please Be Quiet, Please?*:

> In their terse objectivity as well as subject matter . . . these episodes suggest Carver as a descendent of Hemingway, relocated in the Pacific Northwest. But where Hemingway's purified style was meant to imply volumes of unspoken knowledge, like the seven-eighths of an iceberg underwater, Carver's method suggests that the other seven-eighths either isn't there or isn't knowable. (281)

Hemingway never loses sight of his frame of reference, his values. If he leaves something out, it is only because he is so sure of what it is and he believes that, by leaving it out, he can make it felt more strongly. Carver has less choice about what he leaves out. There is no universal referent, no code of ethics or incontestable values, no resource of significant events to draw from in postmodern fiction. There may be no real reason, no cause, for the breaking down of our lives. There is no choice but to stay on the surface.

On the surface we find more than enough for real stories, and the real feelings of the characters in **"Put Yourself in My Shoes"** are evident from the beginning of the narrative in the observable surface details. "The real story lies right here, in this house, in this very living room, and it's time it was told!" Morgan cries (147). He does not realize that the story *is* being told. He accuses Myers of stealing from him, which is precisely what Myers is doing, whether or not he took Morgan's "two-volume set of 'Jazz at the Philharmonic'" (149), as Morgan accuses him of having done. Myers is stealing Morgan's identity for a story he is already writing in his head, just as it has been written by the narrator and just as we are reading it. In stealing Morgan's identity, Myers's own is reestablished, as are the narrator's and the reader's. As Myers and Paula leave the house, the dog yelps in fear and jumps to the side. Myers exists again. The story ends:

> Myers patted her hand. . . .Her voice seemed to come to him from a great distance. He kept driving. Snow rushed at the windshield. He was silent and watched the road. He was at the very end of a story. (150)

In this story about storytelling, about itself, Myers, like the young actor in **"The Pheasant,"** is protected from the wind by a windshield. Like Myers and Carver, we are protected from the real danger of not existing by the story itself. Myers and Carver seem happy, at least for the moment, and we are happy for them—and for ourselves.

Alongside the quote by Chekhov on Carver's wall was a quote by Ezra Pound: "Fundamental accuracy of statement is the ONE sole morality of writing" (**Fires** 14). Citing this quote, William Stull states that, prior to writing **Cathedral**, Carver "embraced an aesthetic of accuracy, objectivity, and authorial neutrality" (4) and that "this moral and aesthetic orientation suggests a subject as well as a style" (5). The question is whether the moral and aesthetic orientation suggests the subject, or the subject suggests the moral and aesthetic orientation. We have discussed the importance of subject and of real life to Carver, as well as the more humble reasons he might write about "the lives of the people who don't succeed." In any case, Carver qualifies Pound's quote by adding that "[fundamental accuracy of statement] is not everything by ANY means" (**Fires** 14). Carver uses "fundamental accuracy of statement" in order to make real life, as he sees it, vivid.

In **"On Writing,"** Carver quotes V. S. Pritchet's definition of a short story: "something glimpsed from the corner of the eye, in passing."

> Notice the "glimpse" part of this [Carver continues]. First the glimpse. Then the glimpse given life, turned into something that illuminates the moment and may, if we're lucky . . . have even further-ranging consequences and meaning. The

short story writer's task is to invest the glimpse with all that is in his power. He'll bring his intelligence and literary skill to bear (his talent), his sense of proportion and sense of the fitness of things: of how things out there really are and how he sees those things—like no one else sees them. And this is done through the use of clear and specific language, language used so as to bring to life the details that will light up the story for the reader. For the details to be concrete and convey meaning, the language must be accurate and precisely given. (**Fires** 17-18)

Four things come together here: subject ("how things out there really are"), seeing ("how he sees those things—like no one else sees them"), language ("the use of clear and specific language"), and, inseparable from the others, meaning.

In an essay entitled "Will You Please Be Quiet, Please?: Voyeurism, Dissociation, and the Art of Raymond Carver," David Boxer and Cassandra Phillips write: "In Carver's works, the gulf between the seer and the seen—that is, between writer and subject—is very small indeed. His voice barely impinges upon the story being told" (79). We are again reminded of the contour drawing, in which ideally the pencil seems to be on the tree itself. Boxer and Phillips continue:

> [Carver] seems to have appropriated what he's writing about and to have kept the stolen thing closely intact out of fascination or respect. And so, as we read his stories, we feel we're accomplices in this faintly stealthy act of appropriation. Like the writer, we're voyeurs, peering into the disturbed lives of these unsuspecting characters. This is what is unique about Carver, his thorough but subtle manipulation of the metaphor of the voyeur at every level of his writing. (79-80)

Boxer and Phillips briefly examine the role of the voyeur in literature.

> [Whitman] used voyeurism as a way of resolving the paradox of the One and the Many, the individual and the other. Whitman's omniscient self plays at being invisibly present at the events described by the poet . . . "I am the man, I suffer'd, I was there." Thus, voyeurism becomes emblematic of an ultimate form of identification and empathy. But in our century a strong bond has been forged between voyeurism and alienation, disconnectedness rather than connectedness. (78)

They point to examples of this alienated voyeur in the work of Eliot, Fitzgerald, and Hemingway and of contemporary writers such as Fowls, Panchen, Barth, Walker Percy, and Leonard Michaels, among others. If Carver makes us—the readers—feel like accomplices in voyeurism, then a kind of collaboration is implied, a connection at least between writer and reader, even if this is achieved at the characters' expense. Furthermore, have we not suggested that seeing, rather than being separate from life, is at the very heart of it, that it is a necessary part of being? What the writer does is intensify this phenomenon, both for himself and for his readers. Carver's art, rather than being one of dissociation, is an art of association, of participation. As though his success at writing has brought this home to him, Carver is ready, at the time he writes **"Cathedral,"** to share this success with his characters.

A blind man comes to spend the night with the narrator of the story and his wife. The blind man, whose wife has just died of cancer, is an old friend of the narrator's wife. She had worked for him, reading case studies to him in his office in the county social-service department, while her first husband was in officer's training school. That her job was reading and her work with the blind man was performing a kind of social service are details that show that Carver wants us to be aware of reading and of its humanist possibilities. Moreover, the narrator's wife had written a poem about the blind man touching her face. The narrator seems uneasy about all this.

> How do I know these things? She told me. And she told me something else. On her last day in the office, the blind man asked if he could touch her face. She agreed to this. She told me he touched his fingers to every part of her face, her nose—even her neck! She never forgot it. She even tried to write a poem about it. She was always trying to write a poem. She wrote a poem or two every year, usually after something really important had happened to her. (*Cathedral* 210)

His wife having written a poem about the blind man touching her face connects human intimacy to reading and writing in an obvious way. The narrator dwells on the poem, which his wife had showed to him when they first started seeing each other.

> In the poem, she talked about what she had felt at the time, about what went through her mind when the blind man touched her nose and lips. I can remember I didn't think much of the poem. . . . Maybe I just don't understand poetry. (210)

By the end of the story, thanks to the blind man, it is clear that this seemingly insensitive narrator is perfectly capable of understanding poetry.

More subtly, the blind man's touching the face of the narrator's wife is almost itself an act of reading and writing, as though one human being is reading and writing another. As with the contour drawing, the blind touching can be seen as a metaphor for postmodern fiction. Again the attention is on the surface, but here the surface is human. The blind man's touching the face of the narrator's wife is a very different way of seeing and establishing another's—or one's own—identity from Myers's rubbing his fingers and writing his name on the cold glass. Here the knowledge of others and of ourselves is a more intimate knowledge, although we cannot forget that the knowledge is blind, appearing not in the light of some controlling order but in darkness. It is a human knowledge, simply a human connection.

The narrator is jealous of the blind man, especially since his wife's friendship with the man dates back to the time of her first husband, "the man who'd first enjoyed her favors" (210). But there seem to be other reasons the narrator does not want the blind man to stay with them. Blindness is strange to him. Not only has the blind man known his wife longer than he has, and in ways that he has not known her, but from tape recordings his wife has exchanged with the blind man over the years, the man even seems to know him. He had heard the blind man say on one of the tapes, "From all you've said about [your husband], I can only conclude . . ." And then the tape had been interrupted.

After dinner, the three drink, smoke marijuana, and watch television. The narrator tells us, "Every night I smoked dope and stayed up as long as I could before I fell asleep. My wife and I hardly ever went to bed together at the same time. When I did go to sleep, I had these dreams. Sometimes I'd wake up from one of them, my heart going crazy" (222). It is significant that he puts this in the past tense. Presumably, the events he is narrating have changed his domestic life. Furthermore, the loss of marital intimacy he describes recalls Carver's earlier stories—again **"The Idea"** is a good example—in which any intimacy, sexual or even conversational, either no longer exists or was never there. In his foreword to William Kittredge's *We Are Not in This Together*, Carver writes, "There's God's plenty of 'disease' in these stories, a phrase Camus used to describe a certain terrible kind of domesticity" (ix). In **"The Idea,"** an almost hyper real symbol of this "dis-ease" is the ants the woman finds after her husband has gone to bed; in **"Cathedral,"** it seems to reveal itself surrealistically in the narrator's dreams. In **"Cathedral,"** however, we are not left with the bad dreams, and Carver may be pointing to a way out of this "dis-ease."

After his wife has fallen asleep, her robe having slipped open as she sits back on the sofa between the narrator and the blind man, the narrator asks the blind man if he is ready to go to sleep. The blind man responds, "Not yet. . . . No, I'll stay up with you, bub. If that's all right. I'll stay up until you're ready to turn in" (222). There is a program on the television about cathedrals, and it occurs to the narrator that the blind man might have no idea what a cathedral looks like. He asks him, and the blind man says he does not have a good idea and asks the narrator to describe one. The narrator tries but has a difficult time.

> They're massive. They're built of stone. Marble, too, sometimes. In those olden days, when they built cathedrals, men wanted to be close to God. In those olden days, God was an important part of everyone's life. (225)

God was also an important part of fiction, and fiction now must find its way without him. The blind man asks the narrator whether he is in any way religious. The narrator shakes his head and says he guesses he does not believe in anything. He ends his description of cathedrals by saying, "The truth is, cathedrals don't mean anything special to me. Nothing. Cathedrals. They're something to look at on late-night TV. That's all they are" (226).

The blind man asks the narrator to get a pen and some heavy paper. The narrator gets a ball point pen from his wife's room upstairs and a shopping bag from the kitchen, items that remind us of his domestic life. The blind man puts his hand over the narrator's hand and tells him to draw. He tells the narrator to close his eyes. The television station goes off the air. Together, they draw a cathedral. "His fingers rode my fingers as my hand went over the paper," the narrator says. Thus the blind man is feeling not the finished drawing of the cathedral, not the paper or the cathedral itself, but the making of it—he is participating in the drawing of the cathedral. The blind man says, "I think that's it. I think you got it. . . . Take a look. What do you think?" (228). The narrator has almost become the blind man, and the blind man the narrator. Who is drawing for whom? Reader and writer have merged. The narrator does not want to open his eyes.

> "Well?" [the blind man] said. "Are you looking?"

> My eyes were still closed. I was in my house. I knew that. But I didn't feel like I was inside anything.

> "It's really something," I said. (228)

If the contour drawing is a metaphor for postmodernism, then this contour drawing, of one hand upon another's, is a metaphor for humanist postmodernism. Through the making of a fiction together, the narrator and the blind man come to communicate; even more, they become aware not merely of their physical but of their spiritual being. The narrator shows the blind man a cathedral, and the blind man shows the narrator how to see. He shows him what a cathedral means. He shows him something larger than himself. And the narrator is good enough to show us.

WORKS CITED

Baker, Carlos. *Ernest Hemingway: A Life Story*. New York: Avon Books, 1980.

Boxer, David, and Cassandra Phillips. "Will You Please Be Quiet, Please?: Voyeurism, Dissociation, and the Art of Raymond Carver." *Iowa Review* 10.3 (1979): 75-90.

Carver, Raymond. *Cathedral*. New York: Vintage, 1984.

———. *Fires*. New York: Vintage, 1984.

———. Foreword. *We Are Not in This Together*. By William Kittredge. Washington: Graywolf Press, 1984.

———. *Will You Please Be Quiet, Please?*. New York: McGraw-Hill, 1978.

Flower, Dean. "Fiction Chronicles." *The Hudson Review* 29 (1976): 270-82.

Stull, William, "Beyond Hopelessville: Another Side of Raymond Carver." *Philological Quarterly* 64 (1985): 1-15.

Nelson Hathcock (essay date Winter 1991)

SOURCE: "'The Possibility of Resurrection': Re-vision in Carver's 'Feathers' and 'Cathedral'," in *Studies in Short Fiction*, Vol. 28, No. 1, Winter, 1991, pp. 31-9.

[*In the essay below, Hathcock compares "Feathers" and "Cathedral" to illustrate the ways in which Carver allows his characters greater freedom and ability to redeem their lives.*]

In two of his late stories—**"Feathers"** and **"Cathedral"**—Raymond Carver appears to have changed his estimation of the potential power in his characters, the power to reconstruct their lives through language and, in the process, arrive at some understanding or intuitive accord. Unlike earlier Carver protagonists, the inhabitants of what one critic has called "Hopelessville," (Newlove 77) these narrators show an uncommon interest in the way they tell their stories. The stories themselves dramatize the characters' incipient awareness of their own authority: the control of their own language. This act of assertion reveals their ability to read, at last, the texts of their own lives. They "read" in the sense that Barthes defines the activity—an erotic interaction with the fabric of their memories, fears, and desires—and the "text" resulting from this practice resists the characters' tendency to fall passively silent (Barthes 31-47). The nihilism that many readers have faulted Carver for espousing is successfully deflected by these two narrators; through language, through the engaged imaginative act of "telling," they are granted a new vision of their lives and, in the process, a re-vision of meaning.

Many critics of Carver's early work have been concerned with the extreme economy to which he submits both himself and his imagined world. This restrictive aesthetic seems either to impress or discourage, according to how the reader interprets the implied struggle for power. James Atlas notes that for all the "talk" in the stories, it "is groping, rudimentary. [These characters] have no wisdom to purvey. . . . Language becomes just another misfortune, without our ever quite knowing why" (Atlas 96). Such a notion of language is, another critic maintains, precisely the point: "In his early stories [the] obsessive subject is the failure of human dialogue" (Facknitz 288). Emphasizing this failure, both responses call attention to the control of language.

In his essay **"On Writing"** Carver himself dwells upon the necessary element of control:

> If the words are heavy with the writer's own unbridled emotions, or if they are imprecise and inaccurate for some other reason—if the words are in any way blurred—the reader's eyes will slide right over them and nothing will be achieved. The reader's own artistic sense will simply not be engaged. (*Fires 16*)

Language, Carver tells us, is both an obstacle and the means of confronting that obstacle. Even this passage is marked with the evidence of conflict: its indeterminacy gives evidence of the same malleability that Carver warns against. We cannot know how a word is "heavy" or "imprecise" or "inaccurate" or "blurred" without knowing *a priori* something of the author's intent. But such assumptions seem unnecessary if a corresponding "artistic sense" is brought into play because it is the re-written text—one produced by the reader—that is vital. Carver acknowledges the duplicity of words while asserting in the same breath that the writer fights against this liability, that emotions must be "bridled." He fights *for*, the implication seems to be, the vision of the reader. If the reader's eyes "slide right over" the "blurred" language, the reader does not in reality see it and so cannot re-*vise* it through his/her "artistic sense." For Carver then writing is reading and reading, writing. Both must be creative practices; in fact, both are the same practice. This observation is noteworthy because in **"Feathers"** and **"Cathedral,"** the author allows characters to discover this "artistic sense" within themselves, and they begin to "read" for the first time.

An earlier story might serve as a counterpoint. **"What We Talk About When We Talk About Love"** speaks less of love than of the inadequacy of language to convey those monumental abstractions that spring from "unbridled emotions." Even the title suggests a practice of displacement. The attempt to talk about love results in story, but the stories in this case are struggles that fail to elicit their audience's "artistic sense." As Mel the cardiologist says, "I'll tell you what real love is . . . I mean, I'll give you a good example. And you can draw your own conclusions" (*What We Talk About 144*). Like the writer posited by Carver above, Mel assumes that language must catalyze a process, but, as the story illustrates, he senses also the inadequacy of his role in that process. All his efforts to explain the meaning of his parables end in questions, *non sequitur*, or just inconclusive silence. We see the breakdown of response in Nick's final utterance: "I could hear my heart beating. I could hear everyone's heart. I could hear the human noise we sat there making, not one of us moving, not even when the room went dark" (154). This scene *could* be read as a moment of communion in which the story culminates, but for the presence of that "human noise." What better description of "blurred" language could Carver have settled upon? What more apt rendition of a scene in which "nothing will be achieved" than the stasis and darkness that blot out this story at its end, leaving literally nothing for the "eye" to rest upon?

In speaking of the self-conscious labor that went into the stories of *What We Talk About When We Talk About Love*, Carver resorts to the terminology of struggle:

> I pushed and pulled and worked with those stories before they went into the book to an extent I'd never done with any other stories. When the book was put together and in the hands of my publisher, I didn't write anything at all for six months. And then the first story I wrote was **"Cathedral,"** which I feel is totally different in conception and execution from any stories that have come before. . . . There was an opening up when I wrote that story. (*Fires 204*)

Such language is significant, as the pushing, pulling, and working result in an "opening up." The trope of escape into freedom mirrors the writer's paradigm that Carver proposes in the passage cited earlier. A condition of being "bridled" will result in words that engage, or open up to, the reader's artistic sense." If this metaphor encompasses the artistic process, then **"Feathers"** and **"Cathedral,"** both results of Carver's changed practice, could also manifest that practice as he now conceives it. A rare enough phenomenon for characters in the Carver world before now, the liberation of creativity becomes the redemptive act in these later stories. Creation is the only act with meaning because it generates its own, and in these two narrators we find characters concerned to an unprecedented degree with reading and drawing accurately from the texts of their lives. As of yet, both are but nascent artists, and neither story affords any guarantees that the evolution begun will continue, but possibility is verified as each consciousness shows itself ready to grasp and wrest interpretation from the world rather than simply process it.

In a review of **What We Talk About,** Michael Koepf points to one agency of isolation that has generally been neglected by critics: "Raymond Carver is the consummate master of Now. There are no getaways of hope allowed into the future or back into the past" (Koepf 16). The characters of the early Carver are quarantined not only in their physical and emotional selves, but in time as well (one might note the number of stories set in the present tense). Narrative, however, means that the past is recoverable. It acts as a "getaway of hope" into the future by re-vising the past. In this regard, **"Feathers"** provides an interesting example. While Jack, the narrator, recalls an evening spent with a friend from work and his wife, it is the backward and forward motion through time that grants his memory its significance. He faces the past by imposing upon it his imaginative reconstruction, and by means of this re-vision finds some solace for the future. Borrowing from Harold Bloom's theory of tropes as psychic defenses, we might posit the narrative drawn from memory as a defense against ignorance; Jack's story—his troping of the past—becomes a weapon to combat feelings of powerlessness (Bloom 8). In the process Jack encounters the limits of his expressive resources, but the value in his story lies in his struggle with those limits. He acts, rather than accept the confusion that has shrouded his failed marriage. The recurring question "What's to say?" is answered by the story itself.

Jack's approach to his text is emotional, structured by a stream of associations. The opening paragraph—with its seemingly random collocations, advanced by the choppy cadences of speech—reveals a consciousness gradually challenging itself:

> This friend of mine from work, Bud, he asked Fran and me to supper. I didn't know his wife and he didn't know Fran. That made us even. But Bud and I were friends. And I knew there was a little baby at Bud's house. That baby must have been eight months old when Bud asked us to supper. Where'd those eight months go? Hell, where's the time gone since? I remember the day Bud came to work with a box of cigars. Dutch Masters. But each cigar had a red sticker on it and a wrapper that said IT'S A BOY! I didn't smoke cigars, but I took one anyway. "Take a couple," Bud said. He shook the box. "I don't like cigars either. This

is her idea." He was talking about his wife, Olla. (**Cathedral** 3)

This passage proceeds by associative strands, broken by a pair of questions. But these questions are not merely interrupters; they spark the telling of the story altogether, challenging Jack's attempts to recover time and redeem the present by reading his past accurately. The aggregate of details must be sorted through for Jack to arrive at, or select, his significant moments. He has trouble remembering Bud's wife's name, even as he recalls their baby, but by an inductive sequence, returning to the day the child was born, he triggers the memory of her name, the last word of the paragraph: Olla. This psychological process is the "opening up" Carver speaks of in connection with these stories. The freedom and assertiveness of this passage, something we take for granted in fiction, is new in the realm of Carver's own work.

However, as the narrative progresses, clearly it is less a series of challenges to Jack's power of recall than to his powers of rendition. Throughout the visit to Bud and Olla's, Jack and Fran encounter sights that surprise, dismay, and enthrall them. In his memory the patina of a strange beauty settles over all of these things so that his recollection then demands embellishment and honing, even the crude sort of which Jack is capable. He is faced with spanning that gap between experience and re-vision, as in this passage describing the couple's arrival and their greeting by Bud's peacock, Joey:

> The bird moved forward a little. Then it turned its head to the side and braced itself. It kept its bright, wild eye right on us. Its tail was raised, and it was like a big fan folding in and out. There was every color in the rainbow shining from that tail.
>
> "My God," Fran said quietly. She moved her hand over to my knee.
>
> "Goddamn," I said. There was nothing more to say.
>
> The bird made this strange wailing sound once more. "*May-awe, May-awe!*" it went. If it'd been something I was hearing late at night and for the first time, I'd have thought it was somebody dying or else something wild and dangerous. (8)

Initially, nothing in Jack's description seems other than mundane, his lack of verbal resources revealed in the cliches he resorts to—"like a big fan" and "every color of the rainbow." He can only curse because "there was nothing more to say." But this statement reports his reaction *then*. To Fran he said nothing more, but as he tells his story later, he can say more, something less hackneyed, more truthful, suggesting both fear and attraction.

Further challenges lie in store, as when Olla finally brings baby Harold into the gathering. The appearance of Harold leaves both Fran and Jack gasping. The moment is humorous, but primarily because Jack again confronts a sight defying description, and his attempts to encompass Harold's ugliness quickly blossom into awkward, hyperbolic repetition:

> Bar none, it was the ugliest baby I'd ever seen. It was so ugly I couldn't say anything. No words would come out of my mouth. I don't mean it was diseased or disfigured. Nothing like that. It was just ugly. It had a big red face, pop eyes, a broad forehead, and these big fat lips. It had no neck to speak of, and it had three or four fat chins. Its chins rolled right up under its ears, and its ears stuck out from its bald head. Fat hung over its wrists. Its arms and fingers were fat. Even calling it ugly does it credit.

Aside from Jack's persistence in denying the child a sex, part of the comedy lies in his realization that "no words would come out of [his] mouth." *Then* Jack was struck dumb, but *now* the memory calls forth a flood of words that—while repetitive and monosyllabic—still indicate that in his present attempt to convey the "specialness" about that night, Jack will consciously push himself to speak, to re-vise his experience in order to speak. He is resisting the temptation to fall silent.

After the meal, Harold's debut, and Joey's entrance, Jack sits at the table appreciating the ineffable warmth that the night has generated. He knows that the night is "special" and wants to be alone with Fran to tell her what he is feeling: "I made a wish that evening. Sitting there at the table, I closed my eyes for a minute and thought hard. What I wished for was that I'd never forget or otherwise let go of that evening" (25). That night, upon returning home, Jack and Fran conceive their own child, in spite of never having wanted children before. Their son's coming signals a deterioration in their marriage, and in the present from which the story is told they "don't talk about it. What's to say?" If the story ended here, in the disconsolate silence that overcomes so many others, it would surely qualify as more deadend than "opening-up." But Jack continues, and the final passage seems a testimony to memory—re-vision—as a sanctifying power:

> But I remember that night. I recall the way the peacock picked up its gray feet and inched around the table. And then my friend and his wife saying goodnight to us on the porch. Olla giv-
> ing Fran some peacock feathers to take home. I remember all of us shaking hands, hugging each other, saying things. In the car, Fran sat close to me as we drove away. She kept her hand on my leg. We drove home like that from my friend's house.(26)

Jack's wish has come true because he has held on to the night in memory and has committed it to language. The final scene suggests that this is not "bad luck" but rather the part of the past that redeems the present. It consoles by reminding Jack that his and Fran's "mistake" had its real inception in love. He realizes that "the change came later," and his re-vision of the past has led him to that knowledge. With the close of his narrative stressing the promise of that night, Jack defeats the stasis of despair.

This passage from stasis into possibility is recorded even more clearly in **"Cathedral,"** the story Carver felt to be a breakthrough. Much against his wishes, the unnamed narrator must confront a part of his wife's past when she is visited by a blind man who was once her employer. The narrator's prejudices and cynicism comprise limitations from which he has been too boorish or lazy to free himself. However, his confrontation with Robert, the blind man, has astounding effects on his own vision. His wife tells him the story of Robert's marriage to Beulah, that ends eight years later with her death by cancer. The narrator's version reveals a consciousness ripe for change. He is impressed, almost in spite of himself, by the fact that a woman could marry, live with a man, and die without his ever knowing what she looked like.

> It was beyond my understanding. Hearing this, I felt sorry for the blind man for a little bit. And then I found myself thinking what a pitiful life this woman must have led. Imagine a woman who could never see herself as she was seen in the eyes of her loved one.... Someone who could wear makeup or not—what difference to him? She could, if she wanted, wear green eyeshadow around one eye, a straight pin in her nostril, yellow slacks and purple shoes, no matter. And then to slip off into death, the blind man's hand on her hand, his blind eyes streaming tears—I'm imagining now—her last thought may be this: that he never even knew what she looked like, and she on an express to the grave. (*Cathedral* 213)

In the dynamic of the passage, the narrator contradicts his admission that "It was beyond my understanding"; in fact, "understanding" and "imagining" become identical. By revising the story provided by his wife, the speaker manages his own comprehension and through it feels the pangs of sympathy, none of which pervade his earlier account of his wife's attempted suicide. The act of the imagination becomes the first stage of genuine human contact.

Another example of such an energetic transfer occurs when the trio sits down to dinner:

> We dug in. We ate everything there was to eat on the table.
>
> We ate like there was no tomorrow. We didn't talk. We ate.
>
> We scarfed. We grazed that table. We were into serious eating. The blind man had right away located his foods, he knew just where everything was on his plate. I watched with admiration as he used his knife and fork on the meat. (217)

A simple colloquialism gives way to pleonastic variations on a theme, much like Jack's description of Harold in **"Feathers."** Significantly, though, as soon as the narrator reveals an awareness of his medium, troping in his own clumsy way, he also begins to notice the blind man, and that recognition is tinged with "admiration." the story thus far has shown that sympathy and admiration for others are novel feelings for this speaker. He is beginning, as Mark Facknitz observes, "to see with eyes other than that insufficient set that keep him a friendless drunk and a meager husband" (Facknitz 295). He is, in fact, learning to read, which is learning to revise.

In the crucial passage, the narrator and Robert sit watching "something about the church and the Middle Ages" on television; that is, Robert listens, and our speaker watches and tries to describe what is depicted. When he attempts to convey a cathedral to his blind guest, he faces the bounds of his experience because of the limits of his language: "I'm just no good at it." Robert's solution is to have the narrator draw a cathedral on heavy paper while he rests his hand on the drawing hand. Caught up in the imaginative transfer, the speaker closes his eyes as Robert suggests and continues to draw, thinking, "It was like nothing in my life up to now."

> But I had my eyes closed. I thought I'd keep them that way for a little longer. I thought it was something I ought to do.
> "Well?" he said. "Are you looking?"
> My eyes were still closed. I was in my house. I knew that. But I didn't feel like I was inside anything.
> "It's really something," I said.(228)

The narrator experiences the same freedom that Carver himself describes above when he mentions an "opening up." He does this as a culmination of his pushing, pulling, and working with his language, in the process learning to do more than empathize or shift point of view. Point of view implies a metaphoric enclosure, a role, a situation. He has transcended that kind of specification, and, in so doing, has escaped the bonds of his experience that trapped him. He is no longer "inside" anything. The confrontation with language has led him into the realm of an ineffable "something" beyond a linguistic register, beyond the power of words to inhibit, to the point at which they shatter. This confrontation and the attempt to achieve it, Carver implies, is the struggle that will result in "something," not "human noise" and darkness.

In a *Paris Review* interview in 1983, Carver answered Mona Simpson's question "Are you religious?" by saying, "No, but I have to believe in miracles and the possibility of resurrection" (*Fires* 206). In these two stories we see Carver directing "miracles" of the type he believed possible. In the effort to transform actions into words or words into actions, these characters arrive at a language that is ultimately a means of freedom and enfranchisement, of vision and revision.

WORKS CITED

Atlas, James. "Less is Less." *The Atlantic Monthly* June, 1981:98.

Barthes, Roland. "Theory of the Text." *Untying the Text: A Post-Structuralist Reader.* Ed. Robert Young. Boston: Routledge, 1981.31-47.

Bloom, Harold. *Poetry and Repression: Revisionism from Blake to Stevens.* New Haven: Yale UP, 1976.

Carver, Raymond. *Cathedral* New York: Vintage, 1984.

———. *Fires* New York: Vintage, 1984.

———. *What We Talk About When We Talk About Love.* New York: Vintage, 1972.

Facknitz, Mark. "The Calm,' 'A Small, Good Thing,' and 'Cathedral': Raymond Carver and the Rediscovery of Human Worth." *Studies in Short Fiction* 3 (1986): 287-96.

Koepf, Michael. "The Collapse of Love: *What We Talk About When We Talk About Love.*" *San Francisco Review of Books* May-June 1984:16.

Newlove, Donald. "Fiction Briefs." Saturday Review April 1981:77.

Ewing Campbell (essay date 1992)

SOURCE: "Maturity: *Cathedral*," in *Raymond Carver: A Study of the Short Fiction*, Twayne, 1992, pp. 48-66.

[*In the following excerpt, Campbell, a professor at Texas A&M University, traces the changes in Carver's writing, noting that in* Cathedral *he exhibits great skill in adopting a softer, more hopeful tone.*]

If a great number of critics hailed the publication of *What We Talk About When We Talk About Love* in 1981 as the establishing event of Carver's career, it is the arrival of *Cathedral* three years later that confirms his place among short-story writers of the first rank. The confirmation results in part, however, not from a continuation of what established him, but from his manifest growth and the more generous spirit visible in his work.

The defining features of Carver's fiction alter during the period between the two books. The voice remains the same, but the vision becomes less grounded in despair. The fictional framework is enlarged and reinforced by traditional structures. Empty spaces fill with beginnings, middles, ends. Truncations vanish; where once the narrative halted in emotional tumult, the story continues and equilibrium is restored. Despair becomes redemption; the alienated are reconciled. Hardboiled realism turns out to be allegory with a soft center.

The techniques, situations, and effects of popular forms become the tools, material, and goals of his fiction. He exploits the melodrama of what was once the exclusive province of daytime television (now also under primetime lights and cameras), the thrills of detective fiction, and the convictions of a culture's assimilated lessons.

It is a sign of Carver's maturity that he makes these adjustments skillfully, with a power and quiet confidence seldom seen in the toilers of such genres. The sureness of a writer at case with himself is felt in his willingness to develop complete narratives that shun the old poetics of withholding, in his willingness to permit affirmative resolutions, and in his opening up of the narrative to include aspects (sentimentality, for example) traditionally dismissed by literary critics as unsuitable for serious fiction.

Aside from being exemplars of maturity in a fine craftsman who has enlarged his reach and grasp, certain stories in *Cathedral* provide excellent opportunities to note the retrieval of sentimentality and religious melodrama from the storehouse of cultural assumptions and the restoration of their aesthetic value during the 1980s. When literary historians look back, they will wonder what so modified tastes that melodrama could move from radio to the hot klieg lights of daytime television, from afternoon to primetime drama, and finally from the electronic medium to award-winning serious fiction. "But in a knowledge of authors and their times," as Paul Valéry observes, "a study of the succession of literary phenomena can only excite us to conjecture what may have happened in the minds of those who have done what is necessary to get themselves inscribed in the annals of the History of Letters":

> If they succeeded in doing so, it was through the concurrence of two conditions which may always be considered as independent: one is necessarily the production of the work itself, the other is the production of a certain *value* in the work by those who have known and liked it once it is produced, those who have enforced its reputation and assured its transmission, its conservation, its ulterior life.

That value bestowed by others—editors who like and select a work for publication, critics who transmit its reputation, and members of grants and awards panels who determine material and symbolic stamps of value—was denied for most of the twentieth century, as Jane Tompkins has pointed out, to works that were accused of trading in "false stereotypes, dishing out weak-minded pap to nourish the prejudices of an ill-educated and underemployed female readership."[16] However, with the major institutional changes of the 1980s, a visible shift in literary criteria took place, and no story better illustrates this shift than **"A Small, Good Thing."**

"A Small, Good Thing"

"A Small, Good Thing" provides a clear contrast between the quintessential Carveresque, as represented by **"The Bath"** in *What We Talk About When We Talk About Love*, and the new fiction of *Cathedral*. Certain therapeutic themes highly charged with iconographic intensity make their appearance in the story, reinforcing convictions so deeply held that we are often unaware of their presence or force. Moreover, the story's record of awards and reprintings testifies to the cultural shift toward sentimentality that characterizes the decade of the eighties and expresses the degree to which devalued elements appreciated during this shift.

Unlike numerous stories by Carver in more than one version, **"The Bath"** and **"A Small, Good Thing"** are not variations of the same story, although the characters, initiating situation, and crisis remain the same. In the McCaffery-Gregory interview, Larry McCaffery identifies them as two versions of a story taking radically distinct courses. Carver amends his interviewer's definition, calling the narratives "two entirely different stories" that he found difficult to think of "as coming from the same source" (McCaffery, 66). On this point, the author can be trusted, for certain parallels between Vladimir Nabokov's "Signs and Symbols" and Carver's **"The Bath"** insist that the former exercised an influence on Carver as he composed the latter. To that extent "Signs and Symbols" was a source for the **"The Bath,"** but not for **"A Small, Good Thing."**

In both omniscient narratives, parents of a hospitalized son spend his birthday worrying about his life in the care of medical people. In the Nabokov story, the son is grown, suffering from insanity, and in danger of killing himself in the asylum; in the Carver story, the son has been struck by a car, is in a coma, and in danger of dying from the trauma. In both stories three telephone calls function as menacing signs. The falling back on signs and symbols in **"The Bath"** underscores Carver's fondness for a sense of threat, which he confesses to in **"On Writing"**: "I like it when there is some feeling of threat or sense of menace in short stories. I think a little menace is fine" (*Fires*, 17).

"The Bath" opens with Ann Weiss's visit to a baker and an order for a birthday cake. On Monday, the day of Scotty's birthday party, the boy is struck by a hit-and-run driver: "He fell on his side, his head in the gutter, his legs in the road moving as if he were climbing a wall" (*What*, 48). Here Scotty resembles Nabokov's image in "Signs and Symbols" of an unfledged bird knocked from its nest and twitching in a puddle.

Scotty picks himself up and returns home where, before slipping into a coma, he tells his mother what happened. At the hospital, the parents begin their vigil, watching for signs of recovery, dealing with medical people as they search for signs of the problem and taking turns going home for a bath. During the father's trip home the baker, without identifying himself, calls twice, making cryptic remarks about the cake that was not picked up. Disoriented in his fear for Scotty's life, the father does not make the connection or mention the calls to Ann upon his return to the hospital.

Finally persuaded to go home and freshen up, Ann encounters an African-American family waiting at the hospital for news about their son Nelson. A moment of mistaken identity and a disconnected exchange underscore the emotional states of the respective individuals. In the last brief scene, Ann reaches home, and the story closes with the third and final telephone call from the baker: "'Scotty,' the voice said. 'It is about Scotty,' the voice said. 'It has to do with Scotty, yes'" (*What*, 56).

The effect of this closure is powerful in the context of Ann's emotional state, even to the reader who knows the caller is the baker. She is terrified. Her only child is in a coma at the hospital. She has just encountered another mother waiting for word about her hospitalized son. She has not slept for a long while and is disoriented. The last thing she needs to hear at this moment is the jarring ring of a telephone with a sinister voice from the other end of the line encouraging her worst fears with ambiguous words.

Unlike many of Carver's stories that end in overt loss of control, this one provides clear motivation for a breakdown. However, because Carver has made the provision this time, an actual breakdown becomes unnecessary, and he leaves it out. In the empty space following the last full stop, the reader involuntarily experiences the powerful emotions that Ann would feel. The result is a story that exemplifies the Carveresque as well as any story Carver ever wrote.

And yet, he rewrote **"The Bath"** as **"A Small, Good Thing,"** expanding it to three times its original length, giving it a fully developed structure with a beginning, middle, and end, and a resolution of reconciliation, effectively removing both the Nabokovian influences and its distinctly Carveresque qualities, while at the same time creating for it a much wider appeal than his stories usually enjoy.

As a truncated, indirect work of fiction, **"The Bath"** remains consistent with the other stories of *What We Talk About When We Talk About Love*. Along with the title story of the collection, **"So Much Water So Close to Home,"** and **"Why Don't You Dance?"** it is one of the most memorable fictions in the book, but the synergetic force of the whole collection is what makes itself felt among those readers and critics who respond favorably to the work.

Readers without patience to seek out the hidden complexities of indirect or elliptical narration tend to reject Carver's fiction on grounds that the stories are incomplete. They fail to find a sense of development or proper closure. Accustomed to overt conflict and its clear resolution, they believe the stories are devoid of significance, of events that would explain the characters' motivation and retarded emotional states, and of consequences when explanatory events do occur, as in **"The Bath."** Even when taken together as a coherent mosaic of scaled-down narratives, the stories portray unpleasant realities without relief. All too often, these readers complain, Carver chooses to eliminate character-shaping relations and to give only the result of the character's static confusion.

Such objections ought not to be dismissed without consideration, yet a little reflection reveals that they fail to take into account the method of indirection, which has become the technique of choice in this century. This method, in conjunction with Carver's desire to focus on a limited time or action for the sake of realism, has contributed to his minimalist reputation, a designation that irritated him. It also helps to form what I call his defining signature. Granted, the technique derives in part from an obsessive desire to avoid great glares and had evolved in Carver by the time of this collection to the point that even the epiphany—which might have created a sense of closure, dynamism, and meaning— had been trimmed of all devices that would render its meaning immediately clear. And yet, the patterns of Carver's fiction—repetition, parallelism, opposition, shared elements—have the power to reveal missing scenes, relations, explanations, the past, and the future. The lesson of these truncated narratives is that much of their merit can be found in the omitted parts, which patience and care can flesh out.

However, no such claim can be made about **"A Small, Good Thing,"** for neither its structure nor its theme owes anything to truncation or the signs and symbols of Nabokovian menace. Instead, it depends on sentimentality and a different category of characterization, on cultural myth and a therapeutics of passion for its effect.

Howard and Ann Weiss, their child Scotty, and the unregenerate baker appear in both stories, but compare the two Howards:

> It had been a good life till now. There had been work, fatherhood, family. The man had been lucky and happy. (*What*, 49)

> Until now, his life had gone smoothly and to his satisfaction—college, marriage, another year of college for the advanced degree in business, a junior partnership in an investment firm. Fatherhood. He was happy and, so far, lucky—he knew that. (*Where*, 282)

College, an MBA, a junior partnership in an investment firm. This Howard is like no previous character in Carver's fiction, and the family doctor is a stereotype that viewers of soap opera will recognize immediately: "The doctor was a handsome, big-shouldered man with a tanned face. He wore a three-piece blue suit, a striped tie, and ivory cuff links. His gray hair was combed along the sides of his head, and he looked as if he had just come from a concert" (*Where*, 284-85). The only stock items missing are the overcoat and silk scarf these doctors are usually wearing when they come from the symphony to take pulses and lift eyelids. There is, furthermore, the melodramatic scene of Ann and Howard performing their vigil while Scotty lies in a coma:

> "I've been praying," she said.

> He nodded.

> She said, "I almost thought I'd forgotten how, but it came back to me. All I had to do was close my eyes and say, 'Please God, help us—help Scotty,'

and then the rest was easy. The words were right there. Maybe if you prayed, too," she said to him.

> "I've already prayed," he said. "I prayed this afternoon—yesterday afternoon, I mean—after you called, while I was driving to the hospital. I've been praying," he said.

> "That's good," she said. For the first time, she felt they were together in it, this trouble. She realized with a start that, until now, it had only been happening to her and to Scotty. She hadn't let Howard into it, though he was there and needed all along. She felt glad to be his wife. (*Where*, 286)

Whether Scotty will live in **"The Bath"** is an open matter— he is alive when the story ends with the baker's telephone call underscoring the menace—but he must die in **"A Small, Good Thing"** in order to fulfill the thematic requirements of sacrifice and redemption. As Tompkins argues, "Stories like the death of little Eva [in *Uncle Tom's Cabin*] are compelling for the same reason that the story of Christ's death is compelling" (Tompkins, 127). The pure die to redeem the unregenerate, and through Scotty's death, the baker will be brought back into the world, where people know how to behave.

In *Madness and Civilization*, Michel Foucault notes the moral tenor of water treatments and travel for disturbed behavior and emphasizes the correlation between salvation and a return to the world: "If it is true that the techniques of immersion always concealed the ethical, almost religious memories of ablution, of a second birth, in these cures by movement we can also recognize a symmetrical moral theme, but one that is the converse of the first: to return to the world, to entrust oneself to its wisdom by returning to one's place in the general order of things, thus forgetting madness."[17]

Along with a therapeutics of movement and immersion, Foucault devotes attention to beliefs in cures by passion: "By subjecting the nervous fibers to a stronger tension, anger gives them more vigor, thus restoring their lost elasticity and permitting fear to disappear" (Foucault, 181). Foucault's emphasis on the necessity of the immediate, on cures by passion, and on cures by regulation of movement wonderfully parallel the conceits of Hemingway's anachronistic hunter in "The Short Happy Life of Francis Macomber." Here are the white hunter Wilson's explanations of Macomber's newfound courage: "Hadn't had time to be afraid with the buff. That and being angry too. Motor car too. Motor cars made it familiar. Be a damn fire eater now. He'd seen it in the war work the same way. More of a change than any loss of virginity. Fear gone like an operation. Something else grew in its place. Main thing a man had. Made him into a man.

Women knew it too. No bloody fear."[18] It is Macomber's need to react without thinking, what Foucault calls the necessity of the immediate, that forestalls his fear. When he had time to think about the wounded lion earlier, he became frightened, and in Wilson's world, cowardice is a sign of disturbed behavior. Having been a car racer, Macomber's reaction in the moving car is nothing more than a familiar reaction brought on by the regulation of movement. And of course he is angry about his wife's infidelity—Foucault's cure by passion. Along with other eighteenth-century notions and cultural traces, a therapeutics of passion has leached down to us through the centuries and is still with us in the fiction of Hemingway and Carver.

Elaborating his morality play and perhaps taking his cue from Hemingway's example, Carver resorts to cures by passion, giving Ann Weiss an angry vigor as she realizes the telephone calls have come from the baker. She insists on their going to the shopping center. Confronting the man, "She clenched her fists. She stared at him fiercely. There was a deep burning inside her, an anger that made her feel larger than herself, larger than either of these men" (**Where**, 299). This correlation of Foucault's curative anger purifies Ann's condition, concentrating her thinking, fortifying her resolve, leaving her, as Wilson might say, with "no bloody fear."

For the baker's anger and consequent behavior, Carver administers a prescription of fear, curing his patient, according to Foucault, just as eighteenth-century doctors would have done: "Fear, in the eighteenth century, was regarded as one of the passions most advisable to arouse in madmen. It was considered the natural complement of the constraints imposed upon maniacs and lunatics" (Foucault, 180). Confronted by the infuriated Ann Weiss, the baker loses his bluster, which is replaced by a constraining fear. "A look crossed Ann's face that made the baker move back and say, 'No trouble, now'" (**Where**, 299).

A conversion follows. He confesses, repents, and asks forgiveness. Bread and coffee are brought out, and the three of them commune until dawn. A sense of redemption is everywhere felt in the atmosphere of this resolution. What we have here is religious allegory, for the iconography of this reconciliation belongs, not to the neorealist phase of Carver's earlier fiction, but to the tradition of typological narrative with its doctrine of theological types, what Tompkins calls "a narrative aimed at demonstrating that human history is a continual reenactment of the sacred drama of redemption" (Tompkins, 134).

The popularity of a work is certainly indicative of the values of its time, but not necessarily of literary values. In the twentieth century, at least, there has been a clear line between popular literature and serious literature. However, when popularity and critical opinion agree, the convergence speaks with authority about the aesthetics of the period, expressing something profound about the culture that produces such a convergence.

"A Small, Good Thing" was published in *Ploughshares*, honored in *Prize Stories 1983: The O. Henry Awards* and *The Pushcart Prize* (1983—84), and reprinted in the *Ploughshares Reader: New Fiction for the Eighties* (1985). And yet, there has been some dissent, noted by Carver when he told McCaffery and Gregory, "I've had people tell me they much prefer **'The Bath,'** which is fine, but **'A Small, Good Thing'** seems to me to be a better story" (McCaffery, 66).

If the author's judgment can withstand the passage of time, a radical shift in literary values must be seen to have occurred in the 1980s, a shift that may seem perplexing to future critics. However, Jane Tompkins, asserting the power of nineteenth-century sentimental narratives, may have located the source of that shift. In **"A Small, Good Thing,"** Carver creates the illusion of realistic fiction, but, as Tompkins explains about *Uncle Tom's Cabin*, "what pass for realistic details . . . are in fact performing a rhetorical function dictated" by the story's ruling religious paradigm of sacrifice and redemption (Tompkins, 136).

A set of governing beliefs, organizing and sustaining a pervasive cultural myth, "invests the suffering and death of an innocent victim with just the kind of power that critics" have traditionally withheld from such literature (Tompkins, 130), but critics are not free-floating entities unaffected by powerful social currents. When a cultural shift occurs, they react to prevailing attitudes just as others do, adjusting literary criteria to meet cultural pressures. It may be that this need to adjust best explains the critical reception of **"A Small, Good Thing."** It may be that, at the deepest levels, even tough-minded critics are governed by our most persistent cultural myths.

"Vitamins"

Although evidence of the melodramatic stands demonstrably present in **"A Small, Good Thing,"** the story is just one of several in *Cathedral* that rely on emotional effects and materials drawn from popular forms. The fictional situation of **"Vitamins,"** which exploits the thrills of risky sex, personal danger, and racial fears found in much detective fiction, is another. It develops in the following manner: Patti sells vitamins door-to-door and supervises other women doing the same. The characters forming the core of the group—Patti, Sheila, Donna—are experiencing bad times. Vitamins aren't selling well, and their personal lives are falling apart. Sheila is the first to forsake the business, taking off for Portland when she finds Patti unresponsive to her advances: "One night this Sheila said to Patti that she loved her more than anything on earth. Patti told me these were her words. Patti had driven Sheila home and they were sitting in front of Sheila's place. . . . Then Sheila touched Patti's breast. Patti said she took Sheila's hand and held it. She said she told her she didn't swing that way" (**Where**, 184). Sheila's sexual advance is the first of three such events in the story, Patti's rebuff the first of three such rejections. Together, they shape the informing patterns of the story.

The second occurs at a Christmas party thrown by Patti to cheer up the group. Attached to Patti, but attracted to Donna and finding himself with her in the kitchen, the narrator embraces her, receives a warm response, but is told, "Don't. Not now" (**Where**, 186).

This refusal is clearly more deferral than rejection, a conclusion that is confirmed when Donna shows up later as the narrator is leaving the hospital, where he works nights on the cleaning crew. They begin their night together by going to an after-hours jazz bar owned and frequented by African-Americans. They are joined in their booth by Khaki, Benny, and Nelson, the latter just back from Vietnam with a human ear in his silver cigarette case and $500 in his wallet.

The central event of the story occurs in the booth. It is also in this crucial scene that we discover significant parallels with popular detective fiction. Indeed, we encounter specific parallels with a chapter from Timothy Harris's detective novel *Good Night and Good-bye* (1979).

Like Donna and Carver's narrator, Harris's detective, Thomas Kyd, finds himself in a bar booth threatened by hostile blacks. At one juncture, "Mojo's hand snaked out and grabbed my collar while the guy next to me leaned his weight against me and took hold of my ear. . . . 'He got two, Mojo. He don't need this ear. Let's take him in the back.'"[19] Then later, Mojo tells the detective, "You thought Baltimore was jiving you when he talk about cutting off your ear. The dude's bad, man. How many ears you cut in Nam, Baltimore?" (Harris, 149).

We might also compare two other passages, the first from Harris's novel: "I stood up, and this time Moth and Baltimore moved quickly to let me out of the booth. 'I haven't got the stomach for the work. I was in Nam. I've seen guys cut ears off stiffs. It never did anything for me except make me sick.' I smiled into Baltimore's watchful ill-humored face. 'That's strictly an animal act you got there, friend. That shit belongs in a cage'" (Harris, 150). And the second from Carver's story:

> He looked around the booth. He looked at Nelson's wallet on the table and at the open cigarette case next to the wallet. He saw the ear.

"That a real ear?" Khaki said.

Benny said, "It is. Show him that ear, Nelson. Nelson just stepped off the plane from Nam with this ear. This ear has traveled halfway around the world to be on this table tonight. Nelson, show him," Benny said.

Nelson picked up the case and handed it to Khaki.

Khaki examined the ear. He took up the chain and dangled the ear in front of his face. He looked at it. He let it swing back and forth on the chain. "I heard about these dried-up ears and dicks and such."

"I took it off one of them gooks," Nelson said. "He couldn't hear nothing with it no more. I wanted me a keepsake." (**Where**, 194)

Carver's handling of the situation seems mythic in its use of a blind character (metaphorically blind in this instance) as intervening agent, clairvoyant in perceptions, oracular in pronouncements. Nelson looks at the couple with his alcohol-reddened eyes as if trying to place the narrator and sees that they are betraying Patti. "What I want to know is, do you know where your wife is? . . . while you setting [*sic*] here big as life with your good friend" (**Where**, 192). He suggests that Patti is also out with someone and makes the third sexual advance of the story, offering Donna $200 to perform fellatio on him.

Donna's rejection of this offer is the final refusal of the story, but like her protestation at the party, it is not sincere. She confesses to the narrator as they return to the hospital parking lot, having made their escape, that she needs the money and is sorry she did not accept the $200. Now, she too will leave for Portland. "I'm not going in. I'm leaving town. I take what happened back there as a sign" (**Where**, 195).

It takes a particular state of mind—as Isak Dinesen simply, but convincingly demonstrates in *Out of Africa*—to find a sign in an event. The state is brought on by a maelstrom of disasters. What seems at first a mere coincidence of circumstances becomes the dominant factor of one's life, evolves into an obsession, and eventually is seen as having a necessary central principle, which if only known could bring the chaos into a coherence that can be dealt with. In that final stage, the individual is prepared to find a sign in anything that lends itself to the situation.

For Dinesen it was the confrontation between a white cock and a chameleon. In an attempt to save himself, the chameleon opened his mouth and shot out his clublike tongue, which the cock plucked out. The gruesome event struck her profoundly and left her shaken. In her state of mind, it was irrefutable testimony to danger: "I looked down on the stones and dared not look up, such a dangerous place did the world seem to me."[20] Donna has also seen the cock pluck out the chameleon's tongue, so to speak, in her willingness to take money for sex, and she has taken it for a sign, which makes up her mind for her.

When the narrator reveals that he has also been thoroughly shaken by the event, we are left with but one conclusion. Although not admitting it, he has had a sign, as well, and the experience has altered him. He returns home and starts looking through the medicine cabinet, spilling pills in the sink, making a racket, and disturbing the fully dressed but sleeping Patti, who wakes and blames him for letting her oversleep.

It is true that the narrator reacts to Nelson's threats in a way similar to Mr. Harrold's reaction in **"Pastoral"** to having a gun on him, and were it not for the pattern of sexual advances and rejections in the story, suggesting human relations as the theme, we might suspect **"Vitamins"** of being a variation on the theme of mortality. However, there can be no dismissal of the pattern.

First, the narrator is *told* by Patti that Sheila made a pass and was gently rebuffed. Then he makes a pass at Donna and is put off. Finally, Nelson makes a pass at Donna. She refuses him while actually wanting to accept. Such a pattern strongly suggests that saying *no* is not final for these characters. In two out of three instances the narrator can be certain of that.

And what about Nelson? Is he an avenging angel or oracle? Whatever he is, the narrator cannot dismiss his words. His judgment must be reckoned with, for he takes one look at the couple and says to the narrator, "You with somebody else, ain't you? This beautiful woman, she ain't your wife. I know that" (**Where**, 192). Then he says that Patti is out with another man. He also reads Donna correctly. She would, admittedly, have taken the money for the sex.

And finally, he yells after the couple, "It ain't going to do no good! Whatever you do, it ain't going to help none!" (**Where**, 195). That too is true. Like a spirit, Nelson's presence seems to follow them. In three out of four instances, the narrator can be certain that Nelson's reading is accurate. Perhaps he is also accurate about the fourth. Perhaps Patti is with another person.

Badly shaken by his encounter with Nelson, the narrator cannot be certain of much, least of all that Patti has not betrayed him with Sheila or someone else. Like Wyman in **"Will You Please Be Quiet, Please?"** he may have failed to see

Patti's potential for passion—or seen it and refused to acknowledge it. In either case, he must confront the possibility, and that makes him an altered person.

Recalling Carver's past use of the themes of mortality and human relations, we might be justified in asking if he is merely repeating himself or contributing something new to his old preoccupations. After a moment's thought, we can observe one difference immediately: the two themes, treated separately in earlier stories, are rendered complex in **"Vitamins"** by combining them in a narrative pattern that subordinates the mortality issue to the question of human relations, although the threat of death or harm is the catalyst that directs our attention to the characters' relations.

All of the events—the drinking, the sexual disruptions and disappointments, the futile attempts to escape their dismal plights by fleeing to Portland or Arizona, as Patti and the narrator speak of doing—underscore the narrator's recognition of what their lives have become: empty, meaningless, oppressed by poverty and the pressures of trying to make ends meet. As Patti says early in the story, "I don't have any relief. There's no relief!" (**Where**, 187), then later, "Middle of winter, people sick all over the state, people dying, and nobody thinks they need vitamins. I'm sick as hell myself" (**Where** 188). And it's true. These characters are spiritually sick, beaten down by a life over which they have no control. Things are falling apart, and there are no vitamins that will help. In this condition, they are typical Carveresque characters confronting a depressing nihilism.

Typical they may be, but Nelson is another matter altogether. Like Scotty in **"A Small, Good Thing,"** he possesses mythic qualities; Scotty is a Christ figure, and Nelson both the blind seer and avenging angel. Both are representations of the symbolic in someone real. Carver's essays **"On Writing"** and **"Fires"** offer helpful information about Nelson's function. The first essay underscores Carver's fondness for creating a feeling of threat, the "sense that something is imminent" (**Fires**, 17), that certain forces are relentlessly set in motion. The second essay reveals the origin of Nelson, who changes the direction of **"Vitamins."** In **"Fires,"** Carver recounts how he was once interrupted by a telephone caller seeking someone named Nelson. Noting the inflections of black English in the caller's speech, Carver imagines his characters in a situation that demands the Nelson we encounter: threatening, the sole custodian of judgment and prophecy, perceiving the scene and foretelling the outcome, able to transcend everyday realism. Nelson is a character, in essence, much closer to Sophocles' Tiresias than to the powerless, inarticulate people we are accustomed to seeing in Carver's fiction.

Carver's exploitation of white America's fear of the black male and other persistent myths separates the fiction of *Cathe-*

dral from earlier Carveresque fiction while, at the same time, linking it with detective and sentimental genres. Even when Carver returns to his old form, as he does in **"The Bridle,"** capturing the colloquial diction and syntax of his narrator, there is something different about the work. It is fleshed out, no longer without resolution, and there is a felt sympathy, a pathos not always present in the early stories and almost always missing from stories in *What We Talk About When We Talk About Love*.

"The Bridle"

Sympathy emanates from Carver's enterprising narrator-apartment manager, Marge, who has installed a professional chair with sink and turned the front room of her living quarters into a beauty parlor, where she collects the rents, writes receipts and, most important, talks to interested parties. As up-to-date as any current member of the National Hairdressers and Cosmetologists Association, she disdains the title of *beautician* and calls herself a *stylist*.

In charge of a corporate-owned apartment complex in Arizona, Marge and her husband, Harley, observe the arrival of a family of four in flight from the chaos of their life in Minnesota. Marge rents them an apartment, but it is not until later, when she gets the new tenant into her beautician's chair and relaxed by a manicure, that Betty starts talking.

Back in Minnesota after his first wife left him, Holits met and married Betty. Their life together began well enough, but then something happened. Holits bought a horse, took to betting on it, and gambled away the farm. Although Carver does not include the scene in this story, one need not imagine what passed between the travelers before their departure; Carver provides the prototype in **"Vitamins"**:

> Then we got to talking about how we'd be better off if we moved to Arizona, someplace like that.
>
> I fixed us another one. I looked out the window. Arizona wasn't a bad idea. (*Where*, 187)

The idea occurs, distilled in the alembic of a mind beholding nothing. The character contemplates the prospect of departure, its unfulfilled promise, and symbolic escape. It is a familiar scene in Carver's fiction, and Carver leaves it out in **"The Bridle."**

Now in Arizona, their possessions reduced to an old station wagon, clothes, and a bridle, they are hoping for a change of luck and a new life. However, once again, something happens. Under the influence of drink and at the urging of others, Holits attempts to leap from the roof of the pool cabana into the water, misses, splits his head open, and is left permanently addled. Before long, the fam-

ily gives up the apartment and moves on, leaving the bridle behind.

No doubt Holits had retained the tackle to flatter himself about his knowledge of horses, but by the time it is overlooked or left intentionally, the harness, reins, and bit have come to be, not an instrument Holits's uses to control and guide brute force, but rather the symbol of Holits's condition, controlled rather than controlling. As Marge puts it at the end of the story, "If you had to wear this thing between your teeth, I guess you'd catch on in a hurry. When you felt it pull, you'd know it was time. You'd know you were going somewhere."[21]

One feels the power of that image, a negative force that life exercises on individuals, especially those on whom Carver focuses his attention. More often than not, they are incapable of stating with any precision what they sense. Consequently, we must interpret their strange physical reactions or indirect comments that say important things in commonplace utterances.

Still under Marge's spell in the chair, Betty remembers that her school counselor once asked what her dreams were. It was a question without an answer then, but asked the same question now, she would reply, "Dreams, you know, are what you wake up from," adding to Marge, "You don't know what it's like" (*Cathedral*, 200).

But Marge knows. She is on the point of revealing just how clearly she knows when Carver deftly restrains her by guiding Harley into the room. She never finishes, but the reader sees the affinity between these two wives, sees as well the similarity between Holits and Harley. Betty's burden is Marge's too. As Marge expresses it, "Sometimes I lie awake, Harley sleeping like a grindstone beside me, and try to picture myself in Betty's shoes. I wonder what I'd do then" (*Cathedral*, 201). Her curiosity is rhetorical, for she must know that she would continue her life as it is, exchanging one stonelike husband who sees and understands nothing of the drama she is witnessing for another.

After the family leaves, Marge inspects the apartment and finds it clean: "The blinds are raised, the bed is stripped. The floor shines. 'Thanks,' I say out loud. Wherever she's going, I wish her luck. 'Good luck, Betty'" (*Cathedral*, 208). With this sympathetic farewell expressed across an unknown space, Marge once again acknowledges her affinity with Betty. She may not be able to articulate the significance of what she has experienced, but she can hardly fail to detect the presence of forces that control people against their will and damage them. She expresses as much by thinking of the bridle.

"Cathedral"

To weave sympathy, sentimentality, and melodrama into the fictional fabric of *Cathedral* with the assurance of an artist unburdened by lingering doubts and have the mature quality of the writing widely acclaimed by critics and readers alike—these are notable accomplishments perhaps best explained by the originality of the title story, which first appeared in *Atlantic Monthly* and was reprinted in *Best American Short Stories*, 1982. Carver's imaginative invention may find its explanation in something as simple as his use of the rarely seen opposite of an archetypal pattern.

"Cathedral," more than any other story, is the emblem of the new Carver. The disillusioned first-person narrator, often but not always a child, is one of literature's most familiar structures and a chief example of dynamic characterization. In the paradigm, the protagonist discovers a profound truth that is necessary in order to take one's place in mature society. The structure goes back as far as Oedipus, and individuals who have read Turgenev's "First Love," Joyce's "Araby," and Sherwood Anderson's "I Want to Know Why" will recognize this paradigm immediately. "Cathedral," however, provides the rare opposite of this familiar type: a narrator who discovers a life-affirming truth without the pain. While it is true that such a story runs a risk of sinking into the sentimentality of "A Small, Good Thing," Carver contrives to avoid the hazard in an instructive manner.

Robert, a blind friend of the narrator's wife, who comes for a visit, is the catalyst of the story, serving as the Tiresias figure. His reception is mixed: enthusiastically welcomed by the wife, grudgingly received by the narrator. Bub, as Robert calls the narrator, is mean spirited, asocial, and governed by questionable assumptions about the blind and members of ethnic groups. To his remark that he has no blind friends, his wife responds,

> "You don't have *any* friends."...
>
> I didn't answer. She'd told me a little about the blind man's wife.
>
> Her name was Beulah. Beulah! That's a name for a colored woman.
>
> "Was his wife a Negro?" I asked. (*Where*, 268)

Although a grown man, Bub is no better informed than the adolescent narrator who must be disabused of a mistaken notion about the world. Carver's way of setting up the theme on the first page is to show how little Bub understands about blindness, then to anticipate the final and central event of the story: "She told me he touched his fingers to every part of her face, her nose—even her neck! She never forgot it. She even tried to write a poem about it. . . . She

wrote a poem or two every year, usually after something really important had happened to her. . . . In the poem, she talked about what she had felt at the time, about what went through her mind when the blind man touched her nose and lips" (*Where*, 266-67). This will eventually form one of the harmonious parts of the story, but here, Bub can no more see the point than Oedipus could. He goes on to compound his folly by revealing his contempt for the blind: "Imagine a woman who could never see herself as she was seen in the eyes of her loved one. A woman who could go on day after day and never receive the smallest compliment from her beloved. A woman whose husband could never read the expression on her face, be it misery or something better" (*Where*, 269). One need only recall Oedipus's taunt to Tiresias in order to compare the contempt shared by the two protagonists: "for thee that strength is not, since thou art maimed in ear, and in wit, and in eye."[22] Oedipus and Bub possess full sight, but are blind, while Tiresias and Robert are blind, but can see clearly. As Tiresias warns, "And I tell thee—since thou hast taunted me even with blindness—that thou hast sight, yet seest not" (Sophocles, 380). Ultimately, both will be instructed by the blind.

After dinner, the three of them settle down comfortably in the living room so that Robert and Bub's wife can talk about the past 10 years. When Bub thinks they are about through discussing old times and the intervening years, he turns the television on. She leaves to change into her robe, and Bub invites the blind, middle-aged man to smoke marijuana with him. Returning to find them smoking, Bub's wife joins them, but soon falls asleep.

The two men give their attention to a program about the church in the Middle Ages, Bub watching, Robert listening, one ear turned toward the set, as Bub attempts to explain what a cathedral is, but discovers he cannot express what he sees. Undaunted, Robert suggests some heavy paper to draw on. As Bub draws, Robert places his hand over Bub's drawing hand. When the picture is finished, he runs his fingers over the lines. Then he has Bub close his eyes and continue drawing:

> So we kept on with it. His fingers rode my fingers as my hand went over the paper. It was like nothing else in my life up to now.
>
> Then he said, "I think that's it. I think you got it," he said. "Take a look. What do you think?"
>
> But I had my eyes closed. I thought I'd keep them that way for a little longer. I thought it was something I ought to do.
>
> "Well?" he said. "Are you looking?"

My eyes were still closed. I was in my house. I knew that. But I didn't feel like I was inside anything.

"It's really something," I said. (**Where**, 279)

Thus, in a replication of his wife's much earlier experience, the narrator discovers the refutation of his assumptions about the blind and seeing. We can imagine the shape of the cathedral materializing before his inner eye as he learns that conventional vision is not the only way to see things and that the eyes are not the only organs with which one can view the world. We can also see that he has not quite grasped the meaning of his experience, but he has acknowledged that special quality his wife experienced and tried to recapture in a poem when he says, "It's really something."

To express such a lesson would be didactic and the worst possible way of developing the theme, not only sentimentalizing the story, but also rendering Bub more articulate than he is. Bub never seems to notice that his experience is identical to his wife's; the discovery is left to our powers of inference. Moreover, in the context of the smoking, Carver allows for a belief on Bub's part that the *something* he experiences is an effect of the marijuana. And therein lies Carver's success.

Although Bub, like his wife 10 years before when she let Robert feel her face, receives a profound, perhaps a character-altering, experience, it would be too much to conclude from what has passed that he experiences a conversion like the baker's in **"A Small, Good Thing."** Nothing suggests that he will have any more friends from this point on or be governed any less by such spurious notions as, for example, blind people don't smoke because they can't see the smoke. What we can conclude, though, is that he will view from now on his wife's experience in a manner different from his initial attitude, that his attitude toward Robert will be wholly different also, and that he has experienced an event that has the power to trigger the imagination.

With all of his imperfections, Bub remains thoroughly realistic, not a symbol in a modern allegory. We can believe him when he says, "My wife finally took her eyes off the blind man and looked at me. I had the feeling she didn't like what she saw" (**Where**, 270). However, there is the indisputable sense that she may well like what she sees after Robert departs, for in a single event her husband has moved considerably closer to sharing her values—intuitively perhaps, unconsciously, but also convincingly.

Randolph Paul Runyon (essay date 1992)

SOURCE: "*Cathedral*," in *Reading Raymond Carver*, Syracuse University Press, 1992, pp. 137-85.

[*In the excerpt below, Runyon examines the connecting elements and recurring themes in the short stories from Cathedral.*]

"Feathers"

"Before and after" (14), Bud said, holding up an "old plaster-of-Paris cast of the most crooked, jaggedy teeth in the world" (12) next to his wife Olla's orthodontically straightened ones. It is one of several sights Jack and Fran have to endure on their visit to Bud and Olla's house. Another is the pet peacock that wanders into the house during dinner, is "smelly" (25), and lets out blood-curdling screams. Still another is their hosts' offspring, "the ugliest baby" Jack has "ever seen," with "no neck to speak of" and "three or four fat chins" (20).

Yet Jack, who narrates the story, is able to say that "that evening at Bud and Olla's was special. . . . That evening I felt good about almost everything in my life. . . . I wished . . . that I'd never forget or otherwise let go of that evening" (25). Fran was of a different opinion. "Fran would look back on that evening at Bud's place as the beginning of the change. . . . 'Goddamn those people and their ugly baby,' Fran will say, for no apparent reason." It was a change for the worse: Fran has since cut her lovely long hair and has "gotten fat on me, too" (26), Jack says. They have a child now, but he "has a conniving streak." And Fran and Jack no longer talk to each other very much. Jack's wish that he would never forget that evening was "one wish of mine that came true. And it was bad luck for me that it did. But, of course, I couldn't know that then" (25).

We are thus presented with two differing interpretations of the meaning of the visit. For Fran it was a disagreeable experience, and the beginning of what went wrong in their lives. But for Jack it had been a glimpse of paradise—though a paradise that in retrospect he realized he'd never see again—symbolized by the peacock: "'They don't call them birds of paradise for nothing,' Bud said" (23). The baby may have been ugly, but to Bud and Olla, Jack imagines, "It's our baby" (24). He remembers "Olla giving Fran some peacock feathers to take home . . . all us shaking hands, hugging each other, saying things" (26).

But is a third interpretation possible? Is **"Feathers"** about anything else, too?

From our somewhat different vantage point as nonparticipants in the story, we can make some observations that may have escaped Jack and Fran. One of them is that this story of an evening they will both always remember began with an anecdote about the difficulty of remembering. Jack had telephoned Bud once

> to see if he wanted to do anything. This woman picked up the phone and said. "Hello." I blanked and couldn't remember her name. Bud's wife. Bud had said her name to me any number of times. But it went in one ear and out the other. "Hello!" the woman said again. . . . I still couldn't remember her name. So I hung up. The next time I saw Bud at work I sure as hell didn't tell him I'd called. But I made a point of getting him to mention his wife's name. "Olla," he said. Olla, I said to myself. *Olla*. (4)

The strange thing about this is the resemblance between "Olla" and "Hello," between what Jack heard her say and what he couldn't remember. The voice on the other end of the line is practically telling him the name he is racking his memory to find. "Olla" and "Hello" are almost the same, yet not quite: close enough for their similarity to be noticed—by us, if not by Jack—yet not enough alike for one to be taken for the other. We might remember that in **"Are You a Doctor?"** a story whose plot arises out of a telephone call made to a wrong number, which was what Jack's abortive call must have appeared to Olla to have been, Arnold Breit had made a similar transposition of syllables when he thought Cheryl's name was Shirley.

A number of other things in **"Feathers"** present themselves in pairs, of which one can be taken to stand for the other. When Fran and Jack first arrived, they saw a baby's swing set in the front yard and some toys on the porch. "It was then that we heard this awful squall. There was a baby in the house, right, but this cry was too loud for a baby. . . . Then something as big as a vulture flapped heavily down from one of the trees and landed just in front of the car" (7). It was the peacock, which occupies the stage long before they get to see the baby.

Then there are the teeth, the "before" and "after" Bud is so proud to exhibit (he had paid for the orthodontic work that Olla's parents had not been able to afford). The more closely we examine these teeth, however, the more slippery the notion of before and after becomes. The mold, of course, is just a copy of a prior original: Olla's teeth as they were before the treatment began. So the "before" is a copy, while the "after" is the (revised) original. But there is another copy: "That orthodontist wanted to keep this," Olla announces as she holds the mold in her lap. "I said nothing doing. I pointed out to him they were *my* teeth. So he took pictures of the mold instead. He told me he was going to put the pictures in a magazine." Bud wonders "what kind of magazine that'd be. Not much call for that kind of publication, I don't think" (14).

Yet there still is another copy, another version of this "picture in a magazine." For a few pages later, when Fran asks why Olla decided to get a peacock in the first place, she answers, "I always dreamed of having me a peacock. Since I was a girl and found a *picture* of one *in a magazine*. I thought it was the most beautiful thing I ever saw. . . . I kept that picture for the longest time" (18; emphasis added). So the peacock in their house is the copy of the original magazine picture, which in turn is an echo of the magazine picture mentioned earlier of the mold of Olla's teeth, which in turn . . . : not an *infinite* regression by any means, yet one of significant length.

It is fitting that the first story in Carver's new collection of stories should begin with this evocation of a chain of befores and afters, of originals and copies, of forerunners (the peacock that, in its initial appearance, could be taken for the baby) and avatars (the baby as the later version of the peacock, which had occupied the house, and Olla's affections, first). That, as we have been accustomed to discover by now, is the way his short story sequences appear to be put together: a chain of befores and afters bearing a strange resemblance to each other.

"Chef's House"

In this chain of resemblances the second story in *Cathedral*, like the first, is also about a house that affords a glimpse of paradise lost. This time it is told from the point of view of the wife. Edna had been separated from Wes but accepted his invitation to join him in a place with an ocean view he was renting for next to nothing from a recovered alcoholic named Chef. Wes was on the wagon too. "He said, We'll start over. I said, If I come up there, I want you to do something for me. . . . I want you to try and be the Wes I used to know. The old Wes. The Wes I married" (27).

Things went very well in that idyllic spot. Edna found herself wishing the summer would never end. She put her wedding ring back on. They drank no alcohol. Wes would pick flowers for her, and they'd go fishing. Their children, grown up now, "kept their distance" (29). But one afternoon Chef came by with the sad news that they had to leave. "Chef said his daughter, Linda, the woman Wes used to call Fat Linda from the time of his drinking days, needed a place to live and this place was it." Her husband had disappeared, she had a baby and couldn't afford to live anywhere else.

Wes is devastated. "This has been a happy house up to now, he said. We'll get another house, I said. Not like this one, Wes said. It wouldn't be the same, anyway. This house has been a good house for us. This house has good memories to it" (30). Edna tries in vain to keep Wes from giving up. "I said, Suppose, just suppose, nothing had ever happened. Suppose this was for the first time. . . . Say none of the other had ever happened" (31). But Wes replies "Then I suppose we'd have to be somebody else if that was the case. Somebody we're not. I don't have that kind of supposing left in me" (32). He can see no future, no more room to continue the fresh start they had been able to make as long as they could live in Chef's house.

And that's about where the story ends. "He seemed to have made up his mind. But having made up his mind, he was in no hurry. He leaned back on the sofa, folded his hands in his lap, and closed his eyes. He didn't say anything else. He didn't have to" (32).

For both Jack and Wes, the house they visit—Jack and Fran for an evening, Wes and Edna for a summer cut short—is an almost magical place where they can see a vision of how life ought to be lived. "This house has been a *good* place for us. This house has *good* memories to it," according to Wes. "That evening I felt *good* about almost everything in my life," Jack had said. Wes speaks of "good *memories*," and Jack made the wish "that I'd *never forget* or otherwise let go of that evening." Though they are at opposite moments in their lives—Jack and Fran at the beginning of their marriage, the child they will have not yet born, and Wes's children already grown—the future for both men is evidently bleak. It's just that Jack didn't know it yet.

Two smaller details from **"Feathers"** reappear here. The fatness of Bud and Olla's child—"big fat lips . . . three or four fat chins. . . . Fat hung over its wrists. Its arms and fingers were fat" (21)—returns in the name Wes gave its counterpart, Fat Linda, who is the baby's counterpart because both are the off-spring of the owner of the house that afforded that glimpse of paradise. The other recurrence concerns what happens to Jack's attempt to engrave on his memory the name he was so embarrassed at having forgot: "Olla, I said to myself. *Olla*" (4). Now when Wes lies back on the sofa and lapses into silence, Edna tells us that "*I said his name to myself. It was an easy name to say, and I'd been used to saying it for a long time*" (32; emphasis added)—unlike Jack, of course, who was saying that name to himself for precisely the opposite reason: to get so used to saying it that he wouldn't forget. This echo emblematizes the essentially complementary nature of these two opening stories, the first looking toward the future, the second backward to the past, because their living at Chef's house was apparently a condition of their living together at all, and this may be one of the last times Edna will ever pronounce Jack's name.

"Preservation"

What happens near the conclusion of **"Chef's House"**—the way Wes demonstrated his abject surrender to bad luck when he "leaned back on the sofa, folded his hands in his lap, and closed his eyes" (32)—is what happens at the be-

ginning of **"Preservation"**: "Sandy's husband had been on the sofa ever since he'd been terminated three months ago" (35). "He made his bed on the sofa that night, and that's where he'd slept every night since it happened" (35-36). After a discouraging visit to the unemployment office "he got back on the sofa. He began spending all of his time there, as if, she thought, it was the thing he was supposed to do now that he no longer had any work. . . . It's like he *lives* there, Sandy thought" (36; Carver's emphasis).

The title of the story, which for once does not actually appear in the text itself, is doubly evoked (1) by the story Sandy's husband kept rereading as he lay on the sofa of "a man who had been discovered after spending two thousand years in a peat bog" (36)—in a state, that is, of almost perfect preservation—and (2) by the sudden demise of the refrigerator, that is by its inability to *preserve* their food any longer. "I have to cook everything tonight" (40), Sandy says, and proceeds to clean out the fridge. She "started taking things off the shelves and putting stuff on the table." Wes "took the meat out of the freezer and put the packages on the table. . . . He took everything out and then found the paper towels and the dishcloth and started wiping up inside" (41). Strangely, Sandy and her husband's cleaning out the refrigerator and cleaning up the mess inside repeats what happened on the last page of the preceding story. The refrigerator in Chef's house had not broken down, but since he had informed Edna and Wes that they had to leave they did feel obliged to clean it out—to eat up, that is, what was left inside: "I went in to start supper. We still had some fish in the icebox. There wasn't much else. We'll clean it up tonight, I thought, and that will be the end of it" (33). The idea is not to waste the food they have. Sandy and her husband have a lot more they'll have to eat, way too much, in fact: "'I've got to fry pork chops tonight,' she said. 'And I have to cook up that hamburger. And those sandwich steaks and the fish sticks. Don't forget the TV dinners, either'" (42).

The refrigerator had given out, Sandy's husband determines, because "we lost our Freon. . . . The Freon leaked out" (41). It's not the only time that gas leaks out in this story. Sandy has decided that they should go to the Auction Barn that evening because they were advertising new and used appliances. Her husband does not share her eagerness: "Whoever said anything about us buying an icebox at an auction?" (44), he asks. Sandy, however, remembers what "fun" (43) it was to go to auctions with her father when she was a child, although her father died in a car he had bought at one of those auctions. It "leaked carbon monoxide up through the floorboards and caused him to pass out behind the wheel. . . . The motor went on running until there was no more gas in the tank. He stayed in the car until somebody found him a few days later" (45).

Her father's death and the icebox's demise respond to each

other in interesting ways. A leaking gas caused both events. The faulty car had been an auction bargain—"he said he'd bought a peach of a car at this auction for two hundred dollars. If she'd been there, he said, he'd have bought one for her, too" (45)—while the faulty refrigerator is to be replaced by one bought at auction. Her father's undiscovered body had doubtless begun to deteriorate in those few days as had the food in her fridge: "She opened the door to the freezer compartment. An awful smell puffed out at her that made her want to gag" (39). Sandy doesn't say so, but the association of these two events is surely powerful enough that she could have smelled the memory of her father's corpse when she opened that door and the "warm, boxed-in air came out at her."

"The Compartment"

Sandy's father in the icebox, and especially in the "freezer *compartment*," is answered, too, in an interesting way by the story that follows, in which a *father* has "decided he wasn't going to leave the *compartment*. He was going to sit where he was until the train pulled away" (55; emphasis added). Carver's choice of a title for this story draws attention to this connection to its predecessor. This decision to stay put echoes as well, of course, Sandy's husband's decision to spend the rest of his life on the living room sofa reading about the corpse discovered in a Netherlands bog.

Myers, on vacation, was touring Europe alone. His son, whom he hadn't seen since the divorce eight years before, had written him a letter from Strasbourg, France, where he was studying. Myers had decided to visit him for a few days on his way from Milan to Paris. Myers had always believed that the breakup of his marriage had been "hastened along . . . by the boy's malign interference in their personal affairs" (47). The last time he had seen him they had actually come to blows—the son, thinking he had to defend his mother from his father's anger, "charged him. Myers sidestepped and got him in a headlock while the boy wept and pummeled Myers on the back and kidneys." Myers "slammed him into the wall and threatened to kill him. He meant it. 'I gave you life,' Myers remembered himself shouting, 'and I can take it back!'" (47—48).

In the train compartment, Myers "looked at guidebooks. He read things he wished he'd read before he'd been to the place they were about . . . he was sorry to be finding out certain things about the country now, just as he was leaving Italy behind" (48). But he is tired of trying to make himself understood to foreigners and probably will not spend his whole six weeks of vacation in Europe after all. When he returns from the WC Myers discovers that the expensive Japanese watch he has bought as a gift for his son is missing from the coat he had left behind in the compartment. Through sign language, he tries to ask the other passenger

in the compartment if he saw anyone take it, but the man shrugs in incomprehension. Myers stalks out into the corridor but sees no chance of making anyone else understand either.

When he returns to his seat, it comes to him that "he really had no desire to see this boy whose behavior had long ago isolated him from Myers's affections. . . . This boy had devoured Myers's youth, had turned the young girl he had courted and wed into a nervous, alcoholic woman whom the boy alternately pitied and bullied" (54). So when the train pulled into Strasbourg Myers "decided he wasn't going to leave the compartment. He was going to sit where he was until the train pulled away" (55).

As he looks through his compartment window Myers doesn't see his son on the platform. While the train is still in the station, he gets up and opens the compartment door. "He went to the end of the corridor, where the cars were coupled together. He didn't know why they had stopped. Maybe something was wrong. He moved to the window. But all he could see was an intricate system of tracks where trains were being made up, cars taken off or switched from one train to another" (57). What happens at this point is that Myers becomes caught up in that intricate system switching and coupling. He wanders into the second-class car next to his first-class one. The train begins to move. He returns to his car and compartment—but his suitcase is gone. "It was not his compartment after all. He realized with a start they must have uncoupled his car while the train was in the yard and attached another second-class car to the train. . . . He was going somewhere, he knew that. And if it was the wrong direction, sooner or later he'd find it out" (58).

"A Small, Good Thing"

What has happened to Myers is what has also happened to his story, for Carver's sequences are part of an intricate system of switching, coupling, and decoupling too, and while Myers's journey started out in a car coupled at one end to **"Preservation,"** it ended in a car coupled to **"A Small, Good Thing,"** which, as it turns out, is a car from another train: a revised version of **"The Bath,"** from *What We Talk About When We Talk About Love*.

We know that story. We know how it too, like **"The Compartment,"** concerns a missed appointment: Myers's missed rendezvous with his son at the Strasbourg station is thus echoed by the one Mrs. Weiss had made with the baker to pick up her son's birthday cake. We recall as well how, like the story to which it is coupled here, this one concerns a gift for the son that does not get delivered: the expensive Japanese wristwatch that disappears from Myers's pocket, and all the gifts that Scotty would not get to open for his birthday. We recall that just before he was struck by the car, "the birthday boy was trying to find out what his friend intended to give him for his birthday that afternoon" (60).

What we didn't know when we read **"The Bath"**—the identity of the mysterious telephone caller and whether the boy would survive—is what **"A Small, Good Thing"** goes to some lengths to tell us. The caller is the baker whose cake was not picked up, and after the boy's death, the Weisses go to his bakery for a confrontation that turns into a reconciliation. The "small, good thing" the contrite baker offers them is bread.

It is now quite a different story from **"The Bath."** This version is in a way more comforting—the scene in the bakery becomes almost heartwarming—but in another perhaps more troubling. Coming as it does just after **"The Compartment"** the son's death now comes dangerously close to fulfilling the filicidal wish Myers had made when "he slammed him into the wall and threatened to kill him. He meant it. 'I gave you life . . . and I can take it back!'" Tess Gallagher, in her Introduction to *A New Path to the Waterfall*, speaks of the persistent image of the "son as an oppressive figure" (xxiv) in Carver's poetry (she mentions **"The Compartment"** as well), with particular reference to **"On an Old Photograph of My Son,"** which appears in that collection. The son, a "petty tyrant," bullies his mother in that poem—as had Myers's son ("This boy had . . . turned [his mother] into a nervous, alcoholic woman whom the boy alternately pitied and bullied"): "Hey, old lady, jump, why don't you? Speak / when spoken to. I think I'll put you in / a headlock to see how you like it. I like / it" (86). The poet writes, apparently speaking out of Carver's own ambivalent feelings towards his son, "I want to forget that boy / in the picture—that jerk, that bully! / . . . Oh, son, in those days I wanted you dead / a hundred—no, a thousand—different times." What Carver confesses in **"Fires,"** an essay on what had influenced his writing over the years, gives us some understanding of how he could have felt, as Myers did, that "this boy had devoured [his] youth." In the mid-1960s he was in a busy laundromat keeping a keen eye out for the next available dryer. He also had to worry about his children, who were at a birthday party but whom he would have to pick up as soon as he could get the laundry done.[1] His wife was working that afternoon as a waitress. Every time he thought he had a dryer someone else beat him to it.

> In a daze I moved away with my shopping cart and went back to waiting. But I remember thinking at that moment, amid the feelings of helpless frustration that had me close to tears, that nothing—and, brother, I mean nothing—that ever happened to me on this earth could come anywhere close, could possibly be as important to me, could make as much difference, as the fact that I had

> two children. And that I would always have them and always find myself in this position of unrelieved responsibility and permanent distraction. . . . At that moment I felt—I knew—that the life I was in was vastly different from the lives of the writers I most admired. I understood writers to be people who didn't spend their Saturdays at the laundromat and every waking hour subject to the needs and caprices of their children. (*Fires,* 32—33)

He did get published—**"Neighbors"** appeared in *Esquire*—"But my kids were in full cry then . . . and they were eating me alive" (39)—as the son in **"The Compartment"** "had *devoured* Myers's youth." And then Carver uses a railroad metaphor that puts him in very nearly the same situation as Myers at the end of **"The Compartment"** (the difference being that though Myers found himself on the wrong track he was still going somewhere): "My life soon took another veering, a sharp turn, and then it came to a dead stop off on a siding." He is evidently alluding to his descent into alcoholism, but it is clear that part of what drove him there was his despair at not having the time to write, time his children consumed.

How close Myers may be to Carver himself is suggested by the fact that the protagonist of **"Put Yourself in My Shoes,"** whom we saw to bear some remarkable resemblances to the author, had the same name.

What consolation the baker can offer Ann and Howard Weiss for the loss of their son as they accept the bread he offers them at midnight in his bakery and talk on with him into the early morning hours brings them to about the same point that Myers's decision to forego meeting his son had brought him. "He decided he wasn't going to leave the compartment"; "they did not think of leaving" (89).

Such a dark reading of the story, influenced by Carver's decision to place it immediately after **"The Compartment,"** with its tale of a father's enmity toward his son, contrasts with William Stull's sunnier interpretation. In "Beyond Hopelessville: Another Side of Raymond Carver," Stull is right, of course, to say that **"A Small, Good Thing"** is more hopeful than **"The Bath,"** as Carver himself has indicated in several interviews, but I think he goes too far when he says that here "Carver goes farther still . . . toward a final vision of forgiveness and community rooted in religious faith" (11). Quite correctly calling our attention to the manner in which the Weisses" and the baker's breaking of bread recalls the Last Supper, Stull nevertheless presumes more than I am willing to accept when he argues that "a subtle but pervasive pattern or religious symbols" in the story "suggests the presence of a third kind of love in Carver's work" in addition to erotic and brotherly love; "Christian love." Stull sees the rite of Christian baptism in the baths the parents take: "While their innocent child (a Christlike figure, to be sure) lies suspended between life and death, each of the parents bathes. Carver calls attention to this seemingly incidental action by making it the title of the original story" (12)—as if forgetting his argument that the second story is the Christianized version of the hopeless, secular first.

Stull, who has not only written widely on Carver but has even resurrected some of his early work (in *Those Days*) and certainly done more than anyone else to promote Carver's academic reputation, is the foremost Carver scholar we have, and "Beyond Hopelessville" is probably the most influential article yet to appear on Carver's work. Its principal thesis that the distance between *Will You Please Be Quiet, Please?* and *Cathedral* encompasses a significant movement "beyond Hopelessville" is undeniably correct in general terms, but precisely because of the article's special significance in Carver studies I'd like to take the opportunity to quarrel with its theological conclusion—as well as to indicate that Stull and I do agree on one very crucial point, though we interpret it differently: The slain son *is* a sacrificial victim. In my reading, he is slain by the father, the same father (the father behind the scenes in a number of Carver's stories and poems who is to a starting degree Carver himself, who can become a writer only by sacrificing his son) who in the immediately preceding story, **"The Compartment,"** wishes his son were dead. In Stull's reading, Scotty is a sacrificial son because he is the Son of God: "The child Scotty dies—painfully, irrationally, unjustly—in a sacrifice that recalls not only the crucifixion but also Christ's teaching. As Jesus makes clear again and again in the Gospels, the child is the emblem of perfect faith: "Whosoever shall not receive the kingdom of God as a little child, he shall not enter therein' (Mark 10:15). . . . With unwitting cruelty, [the baker] torments the Weisses, taunting them and taking the name of the Christlike child in vain" (12). Stull then cites Matthew 18:6: "But whoso shall offend one of these little ones which believe in me, it were better for him that a millstone were hanged about his neck." The problem here is that Scotty is nowhere depicted in the story as "one of these little ones which believe in me." At most he believes in his birthday, and the likelihood of presents. Nor can the baker be blamed for taking Scotty's name in vain if he was unaware (not having read Stull's article) that the child was "Christlike."

Where Stull, using the King James Version, cites "whoso shall *offend*," the Revised Standard Version gives "whoever *causes* one of these little ones who believe in me *to sin*," a more accurate translation of the original Greek "causes . . . to stumble" (*an skandalisé*)—which resonates intriguingly with what really did happen to Scotty: "the birthday boy stepped off the curb at an intersection and was immediately knocked down by a car . . . the boy got unsteadily to his feet. The boy wobbled a little. . . . He walked home" (60—61). If anyone causes the boy to stumble, it's not the baker but the driver of the car.

Stull is of course right to say that Carver's story recycles elements of the Christian Gospels, but I think it is risky to conclude from that that the story buys into the Christian message itself. "In breaking bread together," Stull writes, "the characters reenact the central rite of Christianity, the Lord's Supper. 'It's a heavy bread, but rich,' the baker says—an apt description of the Eucharist" (12—13). It may be more accurate to say that Carver's characters here achieve, on their own, without divine intervention, a genuine but purely human communion. They don't need God to do it, and Carver doesn't need a Christian conversion to write it. Stull, having brought Carver back into the fold of the "humanist realism" of a James Joyce or a Henry James by arguing that *Cathedral*, in contrast to his earlier stories, is "more expressive, more 'painterly'" (8), seems to want to bring him back into the church as well: "A study of Carver's revisions reveals not only another side of his realism, the humanist side, but also another spirit in his work, a spirit of empathy, forgiveness, and community tacitly founded on Judeo-Christian faith" (6). The way Carver recycles his own stories, particularly in their sequential resonance, allows us to see how he can incorporate elements of a prior narrative into a new one without having to "found" the new one on the old. What I'm criticizing in Stull—that he "reads into" Carver's story the haunting presence of a prior narrative (by another Hand, in this instance)—could be turned against my own reading of Carver were it not for the preponderance of evidence. More importantly, I am *not* suggesting that the second story (of two sequentially linked ones) actually retells the first or is dependent on the first for anything more than the raw material it gives such a strong impression (or illusion) of borrowing. What essential relation it may have with the story it echoes or recycles is likely to be an ironic one, each playing off the other for a greater effect. What's missing from Stull's reading is the very real possibility of irony in Carver's recycling here of the Christian foundation myth.

"Vitamins"

Before Mrs. Weiss told the baker her son was dead, when the atmosphere was still tense with anger—the Weisses' for the baker's sinister phone calls, the baker's for their sticking him with an unbought cake—he had said: "You want to pick up your three-day-old cake? . . . There it sits over there, getting stale. I'll give it to you for half of what I quoted you. No. You want it? You can have it. It's no good to me, no good to anyone now" (85—86). The vitamins in **"Vitamins"** are a product no one wants either. The narrator's wife tries to sell them door to door but business is terrible. "Nobody's buying vitamins. . . . Middle of winter, people sick all over the state, people dying, and nobody thinks they need vitamins" (98). The narrator concurs: "Vitamins were on the skids, vitamins had taken a nose-dive. The bottom had fallen out of the vitamin market" (100).

The vitamins are not the only thing in **"Vitamins"** into which the cake of the immediately preceding story is transformed, as if it had passed through the distorting process of dream. Dreams are in fact thematic in the story, as the narrator's wife is plagued by nightmares: "Everybody dreams," she tells her husband. "If you didn't dream, you'd go crazy. I read about it. It's an outlet. People dream when they're asleep. Or else they'd go nuts. But when I dream, I dream of vitamins. Do you see what I'm saying?" (97) "A dream," Freud wrote in *The Interpretation of Dreams*, "is a (disguised) fulfilment of a (suppressed or repressed) wish" (194; the parentheses are Freud's). It is inevitably distorted into a disguise in order to get past the dream censor of the conscious part of the brain. The raw material for the disguise in which the unconscious clothes its wish is the "day residue"—the events of the immediately preceding day. "In every dream it is possible to find a point of contact with the experiences of the previous day," but dreams "make their selection" from those immediately previous events "upon different principles from our waking memory, since they do not recall what is essential and important but what is subsidiary and unnoticed" (197). Carver's sequential stories behave in similar fashion: each successive one functioning like a dream, picking up details left over from the immediately preceding story—details that are generally of quite minor significance there—and using them as raw material for its own narrative. We earlier saw Freud's dream analysis emerge as a model for understanding how these stories work when we found that the protagonist of **"Night School"** was caught up in the analysis of a dream that repeated an event that seemed to have come from the immediately preceding story.

The birthday cake, as I was saying, returns in **"Vitamins"** as the vitamins themselves. Or rather, the relatively unimportant detail of the baker's halfhearted attempt to sell Mrs. Weiss the cake at half price, together with his frustration at being unable to sell it at all, returns in the form of Patti's inability to unload her vitamins. Two details about that cake, its having dried out after three days ("There it sits . . . getting stale") and it's having almost become the body of the boy whose name is on it ("Your Scotty, I got him ready for you" [83], the taunting voice on the phone said to the grieving mother *after* her son had died, as if he had his corpse ready for burial), also recur, in the form of something that resembles a piece of stale food: "It looked like a dried mushroom" (106). It is the "dried-up" (107) severed ear of an enemy soldier, brought back from Vietnam by Nelson, a sinister black vet the narrator encounters in the back room of Khaki's Off-Broadway Bar. The narrator was there with Donna, one of his wife's vitamin salespeople, and he had been confi-

dent of scoring with her until Nelson sat down at their table and spoiled things by showing them the ear and by proposing to purchase Donna's sexual services.

Other minor details from the immediately preceding story emerge again here. When Ann Weiss realized whom the calls were coming from, she and her husband drove to the shopping center where the bakery was located.

> The sky was *clear and stars were out.* . . . They parked in front of the bakery. All of the shops and stores were closed. . . . The bakery windows were dark, but when they looked through the glass they could see a light in the *back room.* . . . They drove around behind the bakery and parked. . . . She knocked on the door and waited. . . . "I'm closed for business," he said. "What do you want at this hour? It's midnight. Are you drunk or something?" (85; emphasis added)

It was the same hour of night when the narrator of **"Vitamins"** left work and went with Donna to Khaki's bar: "I'd walked out of the hospital just after *midnight*" (100; emphasis added). The baker complained that he was "closed for business . . . at this hour," while the narrator was in the habit of frequenting the Off-Broadway "because I could get a drink there *after closing hours*" (99; emphasis added). The weather was precisely the same: "It'd *cleared* up *and stars were out.*" The baker's accusation that the Weisses were "drunk or something" was genuinely true in the narrator's case: "I still had this buzz on from the Scotch I'd had." The Weisses had to go to the back room of the bakery, as the narrator goes to the back room of the bar: "The front half of the Off-Broadway was like a regular café and bar. . . . We went through the café and into the big *room in back*" (101; emphasis added).

The recurrence of details is naturally puzzling. Why should the scene in Khaki's bar come this close to repeating the scene in the bakery? What does the confrontation with the black Vietnam vet have to do with the confrontation with the baker? To the extent that Carver's stories recycle residual details from their immediate predecessors as dreams recycle day residue, this question might not really have an answer, because what dreams are devised to express is not the hidden meaning of what happened the day before but the repressed wishes of the unconscious. The day residue is just the clothing of the disguise. With these stories, however, the situation is a little more complicated, for each preceding one is not only a fund of leftover residue to be mined for raw material for the next, but is itself—but virtue of its relation to *its* immediate predecessor, if for no other reason—something like a dream. And of course there are other reasons for saying Carver's stories are like dreams, as **"A**

Small, Good Thing" for instance reveals when it shows itself, as does **"The Compartment,"** to be a dream about the death of his son.

Perhaps it would be more accurate to say a *daydream*. In "The Relation of the Poet to Day-Dreaming" Freud suggests that the imaginative writer is a daydreamer, and that a daydreamer is like a child at play: "Every child at play behaves like an imaginative writer, in that he creates a world of his own or, more truly, he rearranges the things of his world and orders it in a new way that pleases him better. . . . Now the writer does the same as the child at play; he creates a world of phantasy which he takes very seriously" (35). Freud also maintains that daydreams and night dreams are really the same. "Language, in its unrivaled wisdom, long ago decided the question of the essential nature of dreams by giving the name of 'day-dreams' to the airy creations of phantasy. If the meaning of our dreams usually remains obscure in spite of this clue, it is because of the circumstance that at night wishes of which we are ashamed also become active in us. . . . Such repressed wishes . . . can therefore achieve expression only when almost completely disguised" (39). Normally, he writes, we would find other persons' daydreams boring, if not in fact repellent. "But when a man of literary talent . . . relates what we take to be his personal day-dreams, we experience great pleasure. . . . The writer softens the egotistical character of the day-dream by changes and disguises, and he bribes us by the offer of a purely formal, that is, aesthetic, pleasure in the presentation of his phantasies" (42—43). So the writer's ability to disguise his daydreams to make them more palatable to the reader performs the same task as the dream work of the unconscious, which disguises its repressed wishes in order to express them without the conscious realizing what they mean. Carver's stories, I believe, are day-dreams to the extent that through his art he has made his fantasies palatable to the reader; yet they resemble night dreams to the degree that they treat their immediate predecessor in his short story sequences as day residue to be transformed into the fabric of its disguises. Freud does not say whether the "changes and disguises" the successful writer exerts on his daydreams are consciously or unconsciously done; it is quite probable they are a mixture of both. Certainly what happens in nocturnal dreams is an unconscious phenomenon. We have seen in Carver some evidence of conscious change in the alterations he has made in his stories so that they will "couple" (in the railroad sense) better in sequence. Yet surely much of what we are uncovering here is unconscious as well, and thus all the more intriguing.

But if we are going to try to tackle the question of the reason for the resemblance between the back room of the bakery and the back room of Khaki's bar we must first be sure we are in command of all the details of that resemblance. One parallel that needs to be made more explicit is the one between Nelson and the baker. Both are sinister, in fact downright mean, and both threaten violence. Nelson had "*little* red *eyes*" (102; emphasis added); while Ann Weiss found, when she first set eyes on the baker, that his "*eyes* were *small*, mean-looking" (86; emphasis added). Nelson threatens violence by attributing the thought of it to the narrator: "I bet you thinking, 'Now here a big drunk nigger and what am I going to do with him? Maybe I have to whip his ass for him!' That what you thinking?" (104—5). Likewise the baker had made a show of warning against violence at the very moment he was brandishing a weapon: "A look crossed Ann's face that made the baker move back and say, 'No trouble, now.' He reached to the counter and picked up a rolling pin with his right hand and began to tap it against the palm of his other hand. . . . The baker continued to tap the rolling pin against his hand. He glanced at Howard, 'Careful, careful,' he said to Howard" (86).

Yet at this point the resemblance surely ends, for the encounter with Nelson ends on an angry note while the meeting with the baker is suddenly transformed, when Ann Weiss tells him what happened to her son, into a reconciliation. Benny, who was a friend of the narrator's, had brought Nelson over to be introduced. Unfortunately, they decided to join the narrator at his table. What begins as a friendly gesture, at least on Benny's part, will soon turn into something much uglier, as Nelson becomes increasingly aggressive. What began, however, as a hostile confrontation turned into something much more amiable in the other story when the baker, in sudden contrition, "cleared a space for them at the table. . . . Howard and Ann sat down and pulled their chairs up to the table. The baker sat down, too. 'Let me say how sorry I am,' the baker said" (87). "Although they were tired and in anguish, they listened to what the baker had to say. They nodded when the baker began to speak of loneliness, and of the sense of doubt and limitation that had come to him in his middle years. He told them what it was like to be childless all these years" (88—89).

Why is it that these two back-room scenes should bear so many ties of resemblance and yet turn out so differently? Have we overlooked something that could resolve this discrepancy?

Well, yes—in one small detail that was added to **"The Bath"** when it became **"A Small, Good Thing."** The family that Ann Weiss had met in the hospital when she was looking for the elevator in **"The Bath"**—"she turned and saw a little waiting room, a family in there, all sitting in wicker chairs, a man in a khaki shirt, a baseball cap pushed back on his head, a large woman wearing a housedress, slippers, a girl in jeans, hair in dozens of kinky braids" (55)—has been transformed into a *black* family: "she turned to her right and entered a little waiting room where a Negro family sat in wicker chairs. There was a middle-aged man in a khaki shirt and pants. . . .

A large woman wearing a housedress and slippers. . . . A teenaged girl in jeans, hair done in dozens of little braids" (73). One could argue that they were black already because of the "kinky braids" (since changed to "little" ones). But Carver's greater explicitness now makes it possible to see this family as a middle term between the baker and Nelson. Like Nelson, they are black—and the fact that these two consecutive stories should both feature black characters is itself worthy of comment, since there are otherwise so few in Carver's white working-class world. Like the baker, they are in a position to sympathize with Ann Weiss's plight, and to receive her sympathy in return. This was not particularly evident in **"The Bath,"** where the only response Ann elicits when she tells them about her son's accident (he is not yet dead in either story) is that the father shakes his head and repeats his own son's name (56). In the revised version, the father responds to Ann's recital of her plight with an account of what happened to his son. "Our Franklin, he's on the operating table. Somebody cut him. . . . We're just hoping and praying, that's all we can do now" (74).

Not only does Carver strengthen the connection between the two stories by explicitly naming the family as black, but he goes on to give a name to the proprietor of the bar where the narrator encounters the sinister Nelson that comes directly from the description of the black father who commiserated with Ann Weiss. He was "a middle-aged man in a *khaki* shirt and pants," while the Off-Broadway Bar "was run by a spade named *Khaki*" (99; emphasis added). Khaki was a reassuring presence: the narrator might have had reason to fear for his safety when he frequented this all-black establishment were it not for Khaki's devotion to preserving the peace, and for his friendly attitude toward him.

> A story went around once that somebody had followed somebody into the Gents and cut the man's throat while he had his hands down pissing. But I never saw any trouble. Nothing that Khaki couldn't handle. . . . If somebody started to get out of line, Khaki would go over to where it was beginning. He'd rest his big hand on the party's shoulder and say a few words and that was that. I'd been going there off and on for months. I was pleased that he'd say things to me, things like, "How're you doing tonight, friend?" Or, "Friend, I haven't seen you for a spell." (99—100)

Khaki came over at the right moment, when things were getting especially tense with Nelson. "Khaki had a hand on my shoulder and the other one on Benny's shoulder. He leaned over the table. . . . 'How you folks? You all having fun?'" (106) Benny assures him that they are, but the narrator takes advantage of Khaki's presence to make his exit. "Khaki was watching Nelson now. I stood beside the booth with Donna's coat. My legs were crazy. Nelson raised his voice. He said, 'You go with this mother here, you let him put his face in your sweets, you both going to have to deal with me.' We started to move away from the booth. . . . We didn't look back. We kept going" (107).

Khaki's name gives us the clue we need. The amiable proprietor of the Off-Broadway Bar is the reincarnation of the khaki-clad father who commiserates in as friendly a way as their circumstances permit with Ann Weiss, while Nelson is that of the baker in his menacing mode. The black father anticipates the baker's other mode by offering sympathy to Ann Weiss and receiving hers in return, as does the baker in the final scene. The bakery and the bar can with appropriateness resemble each other so much (the clear night sky, the stars, the midnight hour, the back rooms in both instances) because the baker's two personae—his sinister side and his commiserating side—are represented, alternately, by Nelson and Khaki together at the narrator's table.

In **"Fires,"** Carver tells a curious anecdote that tells us significantly more about just how it was that Nelson came to stand for that menacing baker.

> Not so long ago in Syracuse, where I live, I was in the middle of writing a short story when my telephone rang. I answered it. On the other end of the line was the voice of a man who was obviously a black man, someone asking for a party named Nelson. It was a wrong number and I said so and hung up. I went back to my short story. But pretty soon I found myself writing a black character into my story, a somewhat sinister character whose name was Nelson. At that moment the story took a different turn. But happily it was, I see now, and somehow knew at the time, the right turn for the story. (**Fires**, 29—30)

Nelson's name, as well as his presence in the story at all, was thus due to the purest chance: "This character found his way into my story with a coincidental rightness I had the good sense to trust" (30). But it is a coincidence on top of a coincidence, for his name is the same as that of the son over whom the father in khaki was in anguish in **"The Bath"**: "'Nelson,' the woman said. 'Is it about Nelson?' . . . The man shifted in his chair. He shook his head. He said, 'Our Nelson'" (55—56). Carver changed the name to Franklin in **"A Small, Good Thing"**: was he covering his tracks? Was the anecdote about the telephone call a ruse? Surely not, yet that phone call itself seems to come right out of this story about the effects of a mysteriously sinister voice on the phone. By comparing in detail the scene in the back room of the bakery with the one in the back room of Khaki's bar we explored the remarkable extent to which the baker who made those calls resembles that "somewhat sinister character whose name was Nelson." Carver's anecdote about the fortuitous event that interrupted, yet influenced the writing of **"Vitamins,"** while appearing to stress how much Nelson's presence in that story is the product of chance, actually reveals how much that story grows out of the one that immediately precedes it in *Cathedral*'s unfolding sequence.

One more incident in **"Vitamins"** deserves our attention, for its strange resemblance to something that happened in **"A Small, Good Thing"** can, I think, be interpreted. It takes place early in **"Vitamins,"** quite possibly before Carver's phone rang with the wrong number, because it would appear not to have much to do with Nelson. Yet it has a lot to do with the death of the Weisses' son. Sheila, one of the vitamin sellers working under the narrator's wife, Patti, "passed out on her feet, fell over, and didn't wake up for hours" (93). It happened at a Christmas party Patti gave for her employees. Sheila had had too much to drink. "One minute she was standing in the middle of the living room, then her eyes closed, the legs buckled, and she went down with a glass in her hand. . . . Patti and I and somebody else lugged her out to the back porch and put her down on a cot and did what we could to forget about her" (93). Sheila's sudden collapse into unconsciousness uncannily repeats Scotty's: "he suddenly lay back on the sofa, closed his eyes, and went limp" (61). Why should this be so? What does Sheila have in common with the Weisses' son?

The answer draws us back to our reading of **"A Small, Good Thing"** as it coupled with **"The Compartment"**—to the father's daydream of the death of his son. Myers, we recall, had been locked in Oedipal conflict with his son. Although he accused him of turning "the young girl [Myers] had courted and wed into a nervous, alcoholic woman whom the boy alternately pitied and bullied," the son on another occasion had sought to come to his mother's rescue, to show her he loved her more than his father did. It had happened in a family dispute when she began angrily breaking china plates, and Myers uttered what the son interpreted as a threat: "That's enough,' Myers had said, and at that instant the boy charged him" (47). Now in the eyes of the narrator of **"Vitamins"** Sheila, like Myers's son, was a rival for his wife's affections. "One night this Sheila said to Patti that she loved her more than anything on earth. Patti told me these were the words. . . . Then Sheila touched Patti's breast. Patti . . . told her she didn't swing that way" (92—93). Sheila's sudden collapse into unconsciousness, by recalling Scotty's, shows the extent to which a father's jealousy, already invoked in **"The Compartment,"** presides in secret over the events of **"A Small, Good Thing."** There is absolutely no evidence of this in **"A Small, Good Thing"** considered by itself—Howard Weiss's expressions of grief are genuine, and heart-rending to read. But when we consider the larger underlying narrative that extends to the stories on either side (not to mention such a text as **"On an Old**

Photograph of My Son") we can see a father's jealousy at work. Sheila, as the rival for his wife's affections, stands—or rather, falls—for the hated son. In our reading of **"The Bath"** in the context of the stories that accompanied it in *What We Talk About When We Talk About Love*, we found what lay behind the apparently innocent image of a son sitting on the sofa with his mother, which was what Scotty was doing just before he lapsed into the coma from which he never recovered. It is reason enough to justify a father's jealous rage.

When Sheila fell her hand had struck the coffee table, and when she woke the next morning "she was sure her little finger was broken. She showed it to me. It looked purple" (93). Later it grew "as big as a pocket flashlight" (94). "But she'd made a serious pass at Patti, a declaration of love, and I didn't have any sympathy." We have seen before, in "Fat," how phallic fingers can be. This tumescent digit, which though it belongs to a woman in fact belongs to an Oedipal son, has received a symbolically castrating blow.

"Careful"

The next story begins, too, with a woman having apparently fallen into unconsciousness on the living room floor. "Once . . . he stopped on the landing and looked into his landlady's living room. He saw the old woman lying on her back on the carpet. She seemed to be asleep. Then it occurred to him she might be dead. But the TV was going, so he chose to think she was asleep. He didn't know what to make of it" (111—12). It's hard for us to know what to make of it either, for nothing happens later in **"Careful"** to integrate it into the story, which concerns not the old woman but her lodger, Lloyd, who stumbles across the sight of her deathlike slumber. It's almost as if this woman dead asleep on the living room carpet were something left over from the previous story—a kind of day residue, to use the term from Freud's dream analysis that has, as I have indicated, a certain relevance to how Carver puts his story collections together. Indeed, in the Alton interview Carver said that the germ of a story or poem is for him often, quite literally, residue: "I never start with an idea. I always *see* something. I start with an image, a cigarette being put out in a jar of mustard, for instance, or the remains, the wreckage, of a dinner left on the table. Pop cans in the fireplace, that sort of thing" (*Conversations*, 154).[2] Carver's point of course is that his stories begin with an image. But the choice of images he provides tells us something more, for they are all images of debris, of remnants left over from a previous event.

Two of the remarks the observant Lloyd makes, however, do serve a purpose beyond his awareness, thanks to Carver's practice of planting resemblances in his sequentially occurring stories. That "it occurred to him she might be dead" confirms the suspicion that Sheila's similarly unconscious state was likewise a semblance of death—not hers of course but Scotty's. And that "he chose to think she was asleep" echoes the doctor's words with which the Weisses tried to comfort themselves in the hospital: "Now he simply seemed to be in a very deep sleep—but no coma, Dr. Francis had emphasized" (61). "Howard gazed at his son. . . . Scotty was fine, but instead of sleeping at home in his own bed, he was in a hospital bed" (65). The landlady was evidently not dead, for the lodger later "saw the old woman down in the yard, wearing a straw hat and holding her hand against her side" (112). That something might be wrong with her hand recalls the injury Sheila's hand received in her descent: "The hand holding the drink smacked the coffee table when she fell" (93). As residue from the immediately preceding story, the scene of the woman asleep on the living room floor persists, even though it seems to have no immediate relevance to the story it finds itself in now. On the other hand, we can see that it has a great deal of relevance to the sequence in which the story appears, confirming the interpretation to which Sheila's collapse gave rise—that she was a figure for the son as rival for the wife's affections.

Sheila's—and Scotty's—reappearance in the form of the woman on the floor is not, however, the residue from which Carver has fashioned his story. That role belongs to another piece of detritus—a classic case perhaps of one man's trash being another's treasure—left over from the story just before: the object of disgust Nelson showed off in the Off-Broadway Bar, the body part retrieved from the corpse of a Viet Cong soldier. "I looked at the ear inside. It sat on a bed of cotton. It looked like a dried mushroom. But it was a real ear, and it was hooked up to a key chain. . . . 'I took it off one of them gooks,' Nelson said. 'He couldn't hear nothing with it no more. I wanted me a keepsake'" (106—7). The whole story recounted in **"Careful"** turns upon the problem Lloyd is having with his ear: "He'd awakened that morning and found that his ear had stopped up with wax. He couldn't hear anything clearly, and he seemed to have lost his sense of balance, his equilibrium, in the process. For the last hour, he'd been on the sofa, working frustratedly on his ear, now and again slamming his head with his fist" (113). A problem, as it happens, of too much residue.

Lloyd, an alcoholic who has taken up drinking champagne, is living apart from his wife. But Inez does pay a visit to his third-floor apartment that morning, just as he has worried himself into a helpless state over his ear. As he tells her his tale of woe the chain to which Nelson had attached his keepsake (Nelson "took up the chain and dangled the ear. . . . He let it swing back and forth on the chain" [107]) returns here too, in the chain attached to Lloyd's memory of the last time he had this problem. "My ear's plugged up. You remember that other time it happened? We were living in that place near the Chinese take-out joint. Where the kids found that bulldog dragging its chain? I had to go to the doctor

then and have my ears flushed out" (114—15). Inez is willing to do what she can to help but unfortunately her nail-file technique (she couldn't find a hairpin) is neither safe nor effective. But she does have the bright idea of going downstairs to ask his landlady if she "has any Wesson oil, or anything like that. She might even have some Q-tips. I don't know why I didn't think of that before. Of asking her" (119).

She returns with baby oil, and some good advice on how to use it: warm the oil, pour it in the ear, and massage gently. "She said it used to happen to her husband. . . . She said try this. And she didn't have any Q-tips. I can't understand that, her not having any Q-tips. That part really surprises me" (120). Inez still doesn't understand that putting any solid object into the ear, whether hairpin or Q-tip, is only going to push the wax deeper in, though her stubborn insistence on procuring cotton swabs does serve the purpose of recalling the "bed of *cotton*" on which Nelson's ear was displayed. However, by following Mrs. Matthews's instructions to the letter, success is achieved. "He heard a car pass on the street outside the house and, at the back of the house, down below his kitchen window, the clear *snick-snick* of pruning shears. . . . 'I'm all right! I mean, I can *hear*. It doesn't sound like you're talking underwater anymore'" (121—22).

So the old woman whose supine state resembled death did have an important part to play after all. It's just that her unconsciousness, whether from having blacked out or simply from sleep, still seems a naggingly irrelevant episode, troubling because of its apparent lack of purpose. We went some distance toward making sense of its presence in the story when we found how it served to confirm our sense of what was going on in the sequence at this point. But I think I can now show that that opening scene has more to do in the story—and not just in the sequence—than that.

Let us look once more at Lloyd's behavior the day the principal events of the story take place: "He was on the sofa, in his pajamas, hitting his fist against the right side of his head. Just before he could hit himself again, he heard voices downstairs on the landing. . . . He gave his head another jolt with his fist, then got to his feet" (113). At that moment we had no idea *why* he was hitting his head with his fist. We would learn the reason in the next paragraph—that it was because his ear is stopped up—but before we did his self-inflicted blows had the stage to themselves, and they were incomprehensible. And they continue: "Now and again slamming his head with his fist" (113). "He pounded his head a good one" (114). "He whacked his head once more" (116).

All that we have seen up to now of the way the stories in **Cathedral** and in the two earlier collections retain echoes of prior events, words, and gestures should justify my making the following hypothesis. In slamming his fist against his head Lloyd was not only trying to clear the obstruction in his ear, but as a figure for the father in the ongoing narrative hidden in the sequence of these stories he was also trying to inflict on himself the injury his son had suffered—the son whose death he had wished for in **"The Compartment,"** the son who died in **"A Small, Good Thing."** For the father in **"The Compartment"** had in fact *slammed* him into the wall" as Lloyd kept "slamming his head with his fist," while Scotty suffered a "hairline fracture of the skull" (66) that was caused by his head hitting the pavement ("He fell on his side with his head in the gutter" [61]) and died from "a hidden occlusion" (80). An occlusion is the stopping up, the closing, the obstruction of a passage—in Scotty's case something like a blood vessel in the brain, in Lloyd's the auditory canal of his ear.

Something really does *happen* in the buried narrative hidden between Carver's stories: one event succeeds another. The father desires the son's death, then the son dies, and then the father, chastened by the fulfillment of his wish, repents of his desire and tries in his anguish to turn the suffering inflicted on the child upon himself. But then something else takes place, and that is the reason the old woman downstairs who provides the remedy for Lloyd's suffering was first glimpsed passed out on the living room floor as if she were dead, repeating Sheila's collapse that itself repeats the son's. For by her recreation of Scotty's coma she becomes, in the buried narrative the sequence tells, the son (as Sheila had when she took on the son's Oedipal role of rival for the wife's affections). And by providing the cure for Lloyd's head pounding and for his auricular occlusion, she delivers the son's forgiveness. (It is not perhaps by accident that it should appear in the form of "*baby* oil," instead of the cooking oil Inez had originally requested.) That reconciliation, of course, is this father's deepest desire. For the same poem where Carver confesses "Oh, son, in those days I wanted you dead" ends with these words: "But don't / worry, my boy—the pages turn, my son. We all / do better in the future" (**"On an Old Photograph of My Son"**).

These stories tell this story by recycling each other's details (for example, the ear) as dreams do the residue of the immediately preceding day, so it is fitting that Lloyd should doubt the permanence of the cure just effected and fear his malady might return *as he slept*: "He began to feel afraid of the night that was coming. . . . What if, in the middle of the night he accidentally turned on his right side, and the weight of his head pressing into the pillow were to seal the wax again in the dark canals of his ear? . . . 'Good God,' he said. . . . 'I just had something like a terrible nightmare'" (122—23). It is fitting, too, that this fear of falling asleep should invoke not only the fate that befell the son (who fell into a sleep from which he never awoke) but also the dread Patti evidently had of falling asleep and having dreams that

offered her no solace, just the same worries that had fatigued her throughout the day. "I even dream of vitamins when I'm asleep. I don't have any relief. There's no relief! At least you can walk away from your job and leave it behind. I'll bet you haven't had one dream about it. I'll bet you don't dream about waxing floors or whatever you do down there" (97). Her husband performs janitorial duties in a hospital. It's a remarkable coincidence that she should complain that her husband doesn't dream of *wax*.

"Where I'm Calling From"

After Inez's departure, even though his ear is, at least for the moment, cleared of its obstruction, Lloyd still must face his other problem—his addiction to champagne. "In the beginning, he'd really thought he could continue drinking if he limited himself to champagne. But in no time he found he was drinking three or four bottles a day" (119). On the next to last page of the story we find him taking a fresh bottle out of the fridge. "He *worked* the plastic cork out of the bottle as *carefully* as he could, but there was still the festive *pop* of champagne being opened" (124; first two emphases added). These words form some resonant echoes. When his ear was stopped up, Lloyd thought that "it felt like it had when he used to swim near the bottom of the municipal pool" (115) and "his ears would *pop*" (116; emphasis added) when he cleared the water out of them by blowing with his mouth and nose closed tight. Before Inez arrived he had been "*working* frustratedly on his ear" (113; emphasis added). And of course the title, already repeated in Lloyd's plea to "Be *careful*" (118; emphasis added), reappears in the adverb that describes how he worked the cork out of the bottle. Not surprisingly, that cork bears a close resemblance to what the landlady once saw emerge from her husband's ear: "this one time she saw a piece of wax fall out of his ear, and it was like a big plug of something" (120).

This conclusion to **"Careful"** not only recalls the events that had preceded it but anticipates the subject of the story to follow, which takes place at a "drying-out facility" for confirmed alcoholics. Lloyd's favorite drink is what the narrator consumed en route to the sanitarium: "We drank champagne all the way" (138). Early in the story the narrator witnesses the same kind of event that Lloyd had glimpsed as he mounted the stairs to his apartment. Tiny, one of the inmates at Frank Martin's farm, "was *on his back on the floor* with his eyes closed" (128; emphasis added), as Mrs. Matthews had been "lying *on her back on the carpet*" (111; emphasis added) with her eyes closed as if she were asleep. We never find out why she was doing that; Tiny was having a quasi-epileptic seizure, apparently brought on by alcoholism. The narrator spends most of the story listening, primarily to fellow drunk J.P., who first tells him how he fell into a well when he was twelve, and then how he met his wife. Both episodes repeat significant elements of what Lloyd went through in the story before.

> It was a dry well, lucky for him. . . . But he told me that being at the bottom of that well had made a lasting impression. He'd sat there and looked up at the well mouth. Way up at the top, he could see a circle of blue sky. . . . A flock of birds flew across, and it seemed to J.P. their wingbeats set up this odd commotion. He heard other things. He heard tiny rustlings above him in the well, which made him wonder if things might fall down into his hair. . . . He heard wind blow over the well mouth, and that sound made an impression on him, too. In short, everything about his life was different for him at the bottom of the well. But nothing fell on him and nothing closed off that little circle of blue. Then his dad came along with the rope, and it wasn't long before J.P. was back in the world he'd always lived in. (130)

Lloyd described what it felt like to have his ear stopped up in ways that anticipate J.P.'s experience both of being trapped in a cylinder and of hearing how cylinders distort sounds. "When I talk, I feel like I'm talking inside a barrel. My head rumbles. . . . When *you* talk, it sounds like you're talking through a lead pipe" (115). J.P.'s being "at the bottom of that well" recalls Lloyd's memory of being "near the bottom of the municipal pool" (115) when he had had the same sensation in his ears. When the wax was removed, he could hear things like the "rustlings" and the wind blowing over the mouth of the well: "Lloyd heard the sound her breath made as it came and went . . . the clear *snick-snack* of pruning shears" (121-22). J.P.'s terror of something falling on him from above parallels the claustrophobia induced by the sharply slanting ceiling of Lloyd's top-floor apartment. "He had to stoop to look from his windows and be careful getting in and out of bed" (111). That too-low ceiling contributed to the terror he felt at the thought of his ear problem returning: "What if he woke up then, unable to hear, the ceiling inches from his head?" (122-23). J.P. was rescued by clinging to his father's rope; Lloyd had been at the end of his: "he'd tried everything he could think of, and he was nearing the end of his rope" (114).

Lloyd's rescue is evoked in the most remarkable way by the other story J.P. tells. It was Lloyd's wife (with help from the landlady downstairs) who managed to clean out his occluded canal, while what made J.P. fall in love with the woman who became his wife was the fact that she cleaned out obstructed passages for a living.[3] Roxy was a professional chimney sweep with all the traditional regalia of the trade and had shown up to clean the chimney at the house of a friend J.P. was visiting. "She's wearing a top hat, the sight of which knocked J.P. for a loop. . . . She spreads a blanket on the hearth and lays out her gear" (131)—as, with much less aplomb, Inez had "emptied the purse out onto the sofa. 'No hairpins,' she said. 'Damn'" (117). The sexy chimney sweep is "wearing these black pants, black shirt, black shoes and socks. . . . J.P. says it nearly drove him nuts to look at her. She does the work, she cleans the chimney. . . . J.P. and his friend . . . raise their eyebrows when the upper half of the young woman disappears into the chimney" (131).

What are we to make of these two particular bits of recycling: Lloyd's ear blockage transformed into J.P.'s falling into a well and one wife's ear cleaning become another wife's chimney sweeping? Their effect, I believe, is to justify my hypothesis about the sleeping Mrs. Matthews. I had suggested that the person really responsible for curing Lloyd's malady was the landlady, that his wife was only the medium through which her cure was effected, and furthermore that the old lady passed out on the carpet really represented the son, who was symbolically saving his father from his self-inflicted pain. What happens in the first of these two episodes in **"Where I'm Calling From"** is that the father-son relationship that I had said was behind Lloyd's aural occlusion has now been brought out into the open: here a father rescues a son; in **"Careful"** it was the other way around. Each story is a complement to the other, as so many story pairs have shown themselves to be. And the wife still has a part to play, but her contribution has been separated out and re-presented in a totally *different* story.

Near the end of **"Where I'm Calling From"** a scene takes place that both repeats the scene near the beginning of **"Careful"** in which Lloyd spied on his landlady stretched out on her living room rug and does so in terms of a father-son connection. Lloyd had glanced into his landlady's apartment on his way up the stairs; here, the narrator, in bed with his wife on a Sunday morning, thinks he can hear something outside the window. His wife suddenly remembers who it must be: the landlord, who was going to paint the exterior of the house.

> I push the curtain away from the window. . . . It's the landlord, all right—this old guy in coveralls. But his coveralls are too big for him. . . . And a wave of happiness comes over me that I'm not him—that I'm me and that I'm inside this bedroom with my wife. . . . The old fart breaks into a grin. It's then I realize I'm naked. . . . I can see the old fellow nod to himself like he's saying, "Go on, sonny, go back to bed. I understand." He tugs on the bill of his cap. Then he sets about his business. He picks up his bucket. He starts climbing the ladder. (145)

Everything is reversed. The landlady has become a landlord. The protagonist has changed from voyeur into someone whose nakedness is the object of someone else's gaze—while in both cases the person doing the viewing is climbing up, (the stairs, a ladder) at the time. That the landlady represented the son (not Lloyd's son, of course, but the son of the father whose presence haunts these stories from **"The Compartment"** on) is evidenced by the fact that in this reversal the landlord addresses the narrator—"Go on, sonny, go back to bed"—as if he were a father speaking to his son. It is the reversal, that is, of the landlady as son and the lodger as father. And the forgiveness that I contended the son was extending to his father by offering the remedy that would make him stop slamming his fist against his skull—that filial forgiveness has now become a paternal blessing: "Go on, sonny. . . . I understand."

"The Train"

"The Train," which is inscribed "for John Cheever," begins where Cheever's "The Five-Forty-Eight" leaves off, with Miss Dent holding a gun on the man who had seduced her and then fired her from her job.[4] She had followed him into his train home to Shady Hill, sat next to him, and explained that she had a pistol in her purse. In the darkness past the station parking lot, as Carver picks up the story, "She'd made him get down in the dirt and plead for his life. While the man's eyes welled with tears and his fingers picked at leaves, she pointed the revolver at him and told him things about himself. . . . 'Be still!' she'd said, although the man was only digging his fingers into the dirt and moving his legs a little out of fear" (147). Blake's terror, and especially the way his eyes "*welled* with tears," evokes J.P.'s terrifying experience at the bottom of the well, though it was J.P. who said that "being at the bottom of that well *had made a lasting impression*" (130) on him, and Miss Dent who "knew she *would remember for a long time* the sound he made through his nose as he got down on his knees" (148; emphasis added). This persistent memory of the sound of his nose is an even more precise recycling of J.P.'s recollection of a similarly breathy noise: "He heard wind blow over the well mouth, and that sound made an impression on him, too" (130).

How is it that the scene of a son trapped and then rescued from deep in the ground by his *father* gets transformed into one of a *woman* trapping a man and forcing him to "get down in the dirt"? It is that what had been separated into two stories in **"Where I'm Calling From"**—the plot of **"Careful"** divided into the episode at the well and J.P.'s courtship of his chimney-sweep wife—has been put together again into one. For Miss Dent, while putting her victim through an experience that recalls J.P.'s in the well, at the same time bears a significant resemblance to J.P.'s wife: both are women extraordinarily capable of violence. Miss Dent had "held a gun on a man . . . she put her foot on the back of his head and pushed his face into the dirt" (147), and Roxy "is a woman who can make fists if she has to" (143). "Her hands are broad and the fingers have these big knuckles. This woman broke a man's nose once" (142).[5]

In **"The Train"** Miss Dent leaves the man groveling in the dirt and goes into the station to wait for the next train back to the city. An odd couple enter, an elderly man wearing stockings but no shoes and a middle-aged woman who speaks to him in a mixture of Italian and English. They seem to be discussing a cocktail party they have just left, and what they say to each other is as opaque to the reader as it must have been to Miss Dent, something about a girl "alone in a house filled with simps and vipers," an "imbecile they call Captain Nick" (150), "*café au lait* and cigarettes, their precious Swiss chocolate and those goddamned macaws" (151), and having to sit through "home movies about Point Barrow, Alaska" (152).[6] There is nothing I can think of in any other Carver story to compare to this barrage of pointless information, pointless, that is, until we realize that it does serve at least one function: it puts Miss Dent in the same situation in which **"The Train"** puts the reader who does not know Cheever's story. Carver after all does not tell us exactly how his story is an homage to Cheever; he doesn't tell us which Cheever story this is the sequel of, or even that this is one. Carver's story in fact can stand alone, just like all the others in *Cathedral* (which is to say that it can also be part of a larger whole, as they are); we don't need to have read Cheever's story to understand Carver's. Yet while all that is true, Carver evidently still felt the need to put in his story some telltale sign that would make the reader feel that he or she has arrived on the scene too late, that a lot must have already happened before the story began.

What happens at the end of the story points in the same direction. As Miss Dent and the man and woman get on the train, "The passengers naturally assumed that the three people boarding were together; and they felt sure that whatever these people's business had been that night, it had not come to a happy conclusion" (155). As the old man had held the waiting room door for the middle-aged woman and then for Miss Dent, so that they emerged onto the platform with Miss Dent between them, this was not an unreasonable assumption. But in fact they were not together; neither had they transacted any business. The extent of their interaction in the waiting room had been: the man and Miss Dent exchanged a "Good evening" (148—49); Miss Dent silently shook her head when the woman said to her companion, "If you really must smoke, *she* may have a match" (149); the woman once referred to Miss Dent in the third person in the midst of an argument with the man (151); the woman eventually did address her directly: "'You don't say much. But I'll wager you could say a lot if someone got you started. . . . What *do* they call you?' 'Miss Dent. But I don't know you'" (153); later, Miss Dent almost began to open a conversation, but just then the train pulled into the station.

The three people boarding the train were just as much a closed book to the passengers already on the train as the couple's bizarre conversation had been to Miss Dent; more than that, by assuming they were together the passengers raise the same issue that the story itself raises by being an unannounced sequel to Cheever's "The Five-Forty-Eight"; are the *stories* together or not?

It is of course the same question that Carver's stories always raise: are they to be read intertextually—in conjunction with the story just finished—or not? Are they all, in this sense, sequels?

"Fever"

Arthur Saltzman accurately observes that the narrator of **"Where I'm Calling From"** "is at first unwilling or unable to relate his own story. . . . Instead of confessing, the narrator persuades a fellow drunk, J.P., to tell his" (147). The woman in **"The Train"** makes the same observation about Miss Dent: "You don't say much. But I'll wager you could say a lot if someone got you started. Couldn't you? But you're a sly boots. You'd rather just sit with your prim little mouth while other people talk their heads off" (153). The wife in **"Fever"** likewise urges the husband she has left to talk it out: "Tell me about yourself," she said on the phone. "He told her the kids were fine. But before he could say anything else, she interrupted him to say, 'I know *they're* fine. What about *you?*'" (165).

"Fever" is the account of Carlyle's eventually successful effort to accept his wife's not coming back. He teaches art at a high school; Eileen ran away with the drama teacher, leaving Carlyle to cope with his two young children alone. After some bad experiences with babysitters, his luck changes dramatically when his wife puts him in touch with the grandmotherly Mrs. Webster. For six weeks things go beautifully, until Carlyle comes down with a severe bout of the flu. His fever and headaches keep him in bed for several days, while Mrs. Webster takes care of both him and the children.

During this time Eileen occasionally telephones to ask how he is and to say that her life has significantly improved since she left him, all in a trendy psychobabble about her "karma" and his that convinces Carlyle she is going crazy. "Eileen must be losing her mind to talk like that" (164). Her perceived insanity is mentioned at least a half-dozen times in the story. On one occasion even Eileen shows that she realizes how strange she must sound: "'You may think I'm crazy or something,' she said. 'But just remember.' *Remember what?* Carlyle wondered in alarm, thinking he must have missed something she'd said" (168). On another Carlyle tells his girlfriend Carol why he's not going to answer the phone. "It's my wife. I know it's her. She's losing her mind. She's going crazy. I'm not going to answer it" (175). When he falls ill, Eileen advises him to keep a journal of his illness, just like Colette.[7] "She wrote a little book about what it was like, about what she was thinking and feeling the whole time she had this fever. . . . Right now you've just got this discomfort. You've got to translate that into something usable" (181). Carlyle can make no sense of what seemed like pointless advice. "It was clear to him that she was insane" (182).

Miss Dent was crazy too, in fact certifiably insane—had even been institutionalized for it—not in **"The Train"** but in Cheever's "The Five-Forty-Eight." "Oh, I know what you're thinking," she said as she sat next to Blake on the train, aiming the pistol in his direction from inside her purse.

> You're thinking that I'm crazy, and I have been very sick again but I'm going to be better. It's going to make me better to talk with you. I was in the hospital all the time before I came to work for you but they never tried to cure me, they only wanted to take away my self-respect. . . . Even if I did have to kill you, they wouldn't be able to do anything to me except put me back in the hospital. (289)

She was evidently insane even before she came to work for him and did not become so because he seduced her. In Cheever's story, her vengeance is thus not so much the act of a woman taking a stand against male injustice as it is the irrational act of a poor demented soul. We can read Carver's **"The Train"** and not realize this about her, as long as we do not follow the hint his dedicatory lines to Cheever make and track down "The Five-Forty-Eight." But if we do read Cheever's story and appreciate the extent to which Carver's **"Train"** is a sequel to it, then we are also in a position to appreciate the extent to which **"Fever"** is a sequel to both, and Eileen's craziness a distant echo of Miss Dent's. This is particularly evident when we compare Miss Dent's words: "You're thinking that I'm crazy" (289) to Eileen's: "You may think I'm crazy" (168). More than this unites Eileen to Cheever's heroine, for they both also share a firm belief in the efficacy of the talking cure. "It's going to make me better to talk with you," Miss Dent had said. And later: "I won't harm you if you'll let me talk" (290). Eileen's insistence that Carlyle articulate his thoughts during his illness finally bears fruit when, in the midst of a splitting headache, he begins to talk to Mrs. Webster, not about his fever but about what Eileen's leaving means. "Mrs. Webster, there's something I want you to know. For a long time, my wife and I loved each other more than anything or anybody in the world" (184). And he goes on at considerable length, spilling out all the thoughts that had been pent up for so long and that had surely contributed, psychosomatically, to his having fallen sick. "There, it's all right,' Mrs. Webster said. She patted his hand. He sat forward and began to talk again." The children came into the room. "Carlyle looked at them and went on talking." They kept quiet but started to giggle. "Carlyle went on talking. At first, his head still ached. . . . But then his headache went away." He had started "in the middle," after the birth of the children, but now he went back to the very beginning, when he and Eileen had first met. "You just keep talking, Mr. Carlyle," Mrs. Webster said. "Sometimes it's good to talk about it" (185). He talked so much more that the children had time to fall asleep and wake up again.

When he was finally all talked out, not only had his headache disappeared, but at last "he understood [the marriage] was over, and he felt able to let her go . . . it was something that had passed. And that passing . . . would become a part of him now, too, as surely as anything else he'd left behind" (186). Eileen, crazy as she may have seemed to him to be, was right about one thing. "Remember," she had said, "sickness is a message about your health and your well-being. It's telling you things" (181). His fever was trying to tell him something: it was telling him he had something to tell.

In the end it's Carlyle who begins to resemble Miss Dent. It did both of them good to talk it out. And it turns out they had almost the same dreams: earlier in the story, "when the alarm went off, he wanted to keep his eyes closed and keep on with the dream he was having. Something about a farmhouse. . . . Someone . . . was walking along the road carrying something. Maybe it was a picnic hamper. . . . In the dream, there seemed to exist a sense of well-being" (169). "I dream about picnics and heaven and the brotherhood of man," Miss Dent had told Blake (293).

Carlyle has at least one thing in common with Miss Dent's victim, too. Blake's eyes, we recall, had "*welled* with tears and his fingers picked at leaves" (147) (in a passage that recalled J.P.'s terror in the well). Carlyle "felt a *welling* in his chest as he kissed each of his children goodbye" (171).[8.]

"The Bridle"

Like Carlyle, and like the Miss Dent of Cheever's story, Betty Holits too finds it helps to talk it out. "And that's fine with me," Marge tells us in **"The Bridle."** Marge is a hairstylist, and Betty is her customer. "They like to talk when they're in the chair" (198). Marge at the same time manages, with her husband, Harley, an apartment complex where the Holitses have rented a suite. But the more Betty talks the more it appears that the character in this story to which the protagonist of **"Fever"** bears the most resemblance is her husband, who like Carlyle is referred to by his last name as if it were his first. Holits, like Carlyle, had a wife (before Betty) who "lit out on them" (198), leaving him with two children to raise.

Holits, an unemployed farmer from Minnesota who has moved west with his family to look for work, had earlier developed a passionate interest in horses and bought a racehorse on which he pinned all his hopes. He named it Fast Betty, after his wife, but it didn't exactly live up to its name. When they moved into the apartment complex and were unloading their possessions from the car, Marge had seen him carry in "something [with] straps hanging from it" that she recognized as a horse's bridle (191-92). At the end of the story, after Holits sustains a head injury from a drunken leap one night from the roof of a cabana onto the deck of the pool and the family moves out a week later, Marge goes to clean the vacated apartment. Betty had left the rooms in unexpectedly tidy condition, but there was one thing left behind. "One of the bureau drawers is open and I go to close it. Back in a corner of the drawer I see the bridle he was carrying in when he first came. It must have been passed over in their hurry. But maybe it wasn't. Maybe the man *left* it on purpose" (208; emphasis added). At the end of **"Fever"** too we had seen Carlyle leaving something behind, the marriage his wife had walked out on: "their life together . . . was something that had passed. And that passing . . . would become a part of him now, too, as surely as anything else he'd *left behind*" (186; emphasis added).

The parallel is even greater if we can place any faith in the possible pun between the *bridle* Holits left and the *bride* (or *bridal* hopes) Carlyle left behind—or in Holits having named the horse after his wife, so that its bridle, by evoking the horse, evokes his bride. Betty recognizes the incongruity of the horse bearing her name: "The Betty part is a joke. But he says it can't help but be a winner if he names it after me. A big winner, all right. The fact is, wherever it ran, it lost" (199).

The duplication of Betty's name is itself duplicated by the odd way Marge duplicates *her* name on the fifty-dollar bills with which the Holitses paid their first installment of rent: "I write my name in ink across Grant's broad old forehead: MARGE. I print it. I do it on every one. Right over his thick brows. People will stop in the midst of their spending and wonder. Who's this Marge?" (192) Marge is like Carver in this regard—not that he keeps writing his name everywhere, but he does keep writing the same words in different places, both between and within his stories.[9.] The activity in which Marge is here engaged offers an intriguing case in point, for her disfiguration of U. S. Grant's forehead is echoed in the climactic later scene of Holits's fall from the cabana roof:

> He dragged up one of the tables and climbed onto that. Then . . . he lifted up onto the roof of the cabana. . . . They're egging him on. They're saying, "Go on, you can do it." "Don't belly-flop, now." "I double-dare you." Things like that.

Then I hear Betty's voice. "Holits, think what you're doing." But Holits just stands there at the edge. He looks down at the water. He seems to be figuring how much of a run he's going to have to make to get out there. He backs up to the far side. He spits in his palm and rubs his hands together. . . . I see him hit the deck. . . . Holits has this gash on his forehead. (203)

Forehead, that is, is written into both scenes. Now is this done haphazardly, promiscuously, as are Marge's MARGEs? Or is there an underlying reason for this echo?

There are actually two.

Holits was trying to make a leap into the swimming pool from the cabana roof, but he failed because he couldn't run fast enough: "He seems to be figuring how much of a *run* he's going to have to make to get out there." He thus came to resemble his beloved Fast Betty, the horse that could never run fast enough, that, "wherever it *ran*, it lost." His drunken and foolish behavior would brand him for life with a scar on his forehead in which one can read his identification with the horse whose name is also the name of his wife. Thus does Marge's gesture of inscribing her name on a man's forehead find its echo in the trace of another wife's name.

His head injury at the same time recalls the headache and fever Carlyle suffered in the immediately preceding story, for as Holits's wound was self-inflicted so too, in the final analysis, was Carlyle's psychosomatic illness. He fell sick because he couldn't cope with his wife's having left him (and once he had talked out all his feelings on that subject, he was suddenly cured of his headache). Now while Holits's first wife did leave him in apparently similar circumstances (left him, that is, with two children to take care of by himself), his second wife Betty didn't. Yet apparently it was despair that brought him to make his near-suicidal leap, a despair that we may be able to understand by paying attention to Marge's meditation on the meaning of the bridle he left behind, in the concluding words of the story:

"Bridle," I say. I hold it up to the window and look at it in the light. . . . I don't know much about them. But I know that one part of it fits in the mouth. . . . Reins go over the head and up to where they're held on the neck between the fingers. The rider pulls the reins this way and that, and the horse turns. It's simple. The bit's heavy and cold. If you had to wear this thing between your teeth, I guess you'd catch on in a hurry. When you felt it pull, you'd know it was time. You'd know you were going somewhere.

Clearly, *bridle* here takes on a *bridal* connotation. Holits may

have had the bridal bit between his teeth, but he had apparently lost the ability, and more importantly the will, to go where it was telling him to go: "I can't *go* it" (104; emphasis added), he had mysteriously said after he fell. "'What'd he say?' . . . 'He said he can't go it. . . . ' 'Go what? What's he talking about?'" It's understandable, after the failure of his farm and his long period of unemployment. He may have started working again, Marge thinks, just before the accident. But if so his injury and subsequent hospitalization have put an end to that; he no longer seems in full control of his faculties—when their friends wave at his departure he doesn't at first respond but then raises his hand and then "keeps waving at them, even after they've stopped" (207).[10.]

Yet he has to keep on *going* all the same, as the conversation between Marge and Harley reveals, with its repeated emphasis on that word: "He asks me where they're going. But I don't have any idea where they're going. Maybe they're going back to Minnesota. How do I know where they're going? But I don't think they're going back to Minnesota. I think they're going someplace else to try their luck" (206).

"Cathedral"

Marge's fascination with the idea of her name cropping up in strange places, in the mouths of strangers—"People will stop in the midst of their spending and wonder. Who's this Marge?"—finds a precise counterpart in the wonderment the narrator of **"Cathedral"** feels when his wife plays for him a tape from her blind correspondent. Before her marriage to the narrator, she had worked as a reader to Robert, and they had continued to exchange tapes in the years since. "I was on the tape, she said. . . . After a few minutes of harmless chitchat, I heard my own name in the mouth of this stranger, this blind man I didn't even know! And then this: 'From all you've said about him, I can only conclude—' But we were interrupted, a knock at the door, something, and we didn't ever get back to the tape" (212). Marge's heart-to-heart talk with Betty Holits had suffered a similar interruption: "I'm starting to tell how it was before we moved here, and how it's still like that. But Harley picks right then to come out of the bedroom" (201). And Betty "for some reason . . . doesn't come back to get her hair done" any more so the conversation is never resumed. The architecture of Raymond Carver's *Cathedral*, its ongoing sequence of contiguous repetitions, is about to be broken off too, since **"Cathedral"** is the last story in the collection. It is therefore fitting that one of the last of these repetitions should be about the sudden interruption of discourse.

The narrator is at first annoyed by the news that Robert is coming to visit. He has never had much to do with blind people and knows he is going to feel uncomfortable. But Robert is a jolly sort, who clearly enjoys good food, good whiskey, and good dope, though it was his first time for the latter. "We thought we'd have us some cannabis" (220), the narrator tells his wife when she came back downstairs and encountered the smell. High on pot, the blind man and the narrator sit up until late into the evening, listening to a TV program about "the church and the Middle Ages" (222) for which the narrator gives Robert a running commentary. He does his best to depict the spires, the gargoyles, and the flying buttresses. But realizing the difficulty of describing a cathedral to someone who has never seen one, he asks, "If somebody says cathedral to you, do you have any notion what they're talking about?" (223-24) Robert responds that he knows, since the man on the television had just said as much, that "they took hundreds of workers fifty or a hundred years to build," that "the men who began their life's work on them, they never lived to see the completion of their work. In that wise, bub, they're no different from the rest of us, right?" (224) If Carver's *Cathedral* is self-naming, then the kind of cathedral it is is one of these unfinished ones, for the nature of its architecture is forever open-ended, each last word always open to the possibility of being succeeded by another.

The last word in this case is the final scene of the story, which finds the narrator trying to draw a cathedral on the "heavy paper" (226) the blind man had asked him to look for (an empty shopping bag served the purpose), pressing down very firmly with the pen so that Robert would be able to follow the tracings with his fingers. "So I began. First I drew a box that looked like a house. . . . Then I put a roof on it. At either end of the roof, I drew spires. Crazy" (227)—then windows, arches, gargoyles, people, and all. The blind man now tells him to close his eyes. "'Keep them that way. . . . Don't stop now. Draw.' So we kept on with it. His fingers rode my fingers as my hand went over the paper. It was like nothing else in my life up to now" (228). But it *was* like something else, two stories before, in **"Fever"**: "'Like this, like this,' he said, guiding their hands. . . . '*Suggestion* is what it's all about,' he said, holding lightly to Sue Colvin's fingers as he guided her brush. 'You've got to work with your mistakes until they look intended. Understand?'" (172) Carlyle, we recall, was a high school art teacher. Should we take his advice? Should we work with the products of chance—what in his context are pupils' mistakes but in ours such possibly chance occurrences as the way this passage so strikingly anticipates the one that concludes the book—until they look intended?

Or *are* they intended? I think they are intended to make us think, to feel a sense of wonder as we linger in Carver's *Cathedral* to explore some of its more obscure passages, to realize how—as at Chartres, for example—one image in stained glass or statuary responds to another somewhere else in the fabric (Joseph's coat of many colors to Jesus' seamless robe, his fall into the pit to Christ's descent into

hell, or the silver cup hidden in the sack of grain to the chalice of the Eucharist). "*Suggestion*," to adopt another piece of Carlyle's pedagogical advice, "is what it's all about."

Though distributed at different places in **"Fever,"** two other moments anticipate what happens at the end of the title story. "At school, they were just leaving the medieval period and about to enter the Gothic" (176)—as were the narrator and Robert as they kept pace with the television broadcast. The "heavy paper" that Robert asked the narrator to procure, and that was indispensable for the effect he wanted him to create, had already appeared in a drawing "on heavy paper" Eileen had sent him "of a woman on a riverbank in a filmy gown, her hands covering her eyes, her shoulders slumped. It was, Carlyle assumed, Eileen showing her heartbreak over the situation" (164).

Yet the concluding scene where the blind man's fingers "rode" the narrator's as he drew the cathedral while both were high on cannabis recalls as well the conclusion of **"The Bridle"** when Holits was high on the cabana roof. For in his loser's run he was, as we have seen, acting the part of the horse wearing the bridle with reins that "go over the head and up to where they're held on the neck between the *fingers*. The *rider* pulls the reins this way and that, and the horse turns." And in a significant reversal, while at first it was the narrator who was in charge, drawing the cathedral on the heavy paper so that Robert could then move "the tips of his fingers over the paper" (227) to get some idea of what it looked like, by the time the story ends it's the blind man who is guiding the narrator, riding him with his fingers. He is showing him what it is like to be blind. He tells him to shut his eyes and then to keep on drawing. "His fingers rode my fingers as my hand went over the paper. It was like nothing else in my life up to now. Then he said, 'I think that's it. I think you got it'" (228), as if he were an art instructor congratulating his student. "'Take a look. What do you think?' But I had my eyes closed. I thought I'd keep them that way for a little longer. . . . 'It's really something,' I said."

In a question-and-answer session at the University of Akron in 1982 Carver said that in his view to build a cathedral was to engage in a collaborative endeavor. "This is a far-fetched analogy, but it's in a way like building a fantastic cathedral. The main thing is to get the work of art together. You don't know who built those cathedrals, but they're there" (*Conversations*, 23). He was referring to the collaboration between writer and editor, though surely the kind of joint effort in which the blind man and the narrator are engaged in **"Cathedral,"** which he was then writing or had recently completed, was on his mind. But this uncertainty as to authorship extends to the uncertainty into which *Cathedral*'s stories lead us: to which of these two stories can the origin of the image of the riding fingers be traced—**"Cathedral,"** which was written first, or **"The Bridle,"** which the stories' order places before the other in the total fabric of the work?[11] "*Cathedral*, in other words, is a cathedral in the Carverian sense: like the protagonists of its title story, its stories ride each other, depend on each other, collaborate with each other to create together what they could not have done by themselves.

NOTES

1. That is, he thinks he remembers it was a birthday party, but he isn't entirely sure: "They were with some other kids that afternoon, a birthday party maybe. Something.... As I say, I'm not sure where our kids were that afternoon. Maybe I had to pick them up from someplace, and it was getting late, and that contributed to my state of mind" (32). In light of the fact that in "The Bath" (and later in "A Small, Good Thing") the son dies on his birthday and that the cake was an elaborately iced birthday cake makes the uncertainty of his recollection all the more interesting. Concealed beneath it may be a kind of birthday wish that could be expressed only in a fiction: that his children had never been born.

2. When Alton later asks Carver about the role of the unconscious in his work, he acknowledges its relevance: "JA: You have a dream motif in many stories [he mentions "The Student's Wife," "Elephant," and "Whoever Was Using This Bed"]. There are several more that involved dreams occurring, and I wonder what importance you place on the unconscious mind and its relation to the kind of surface reality you record. You get at the unconscious only in an indirect way.... I wonder if you think about it much. RC: I don't think about it very much. It may be one of those things you don't think about but that's sometimes relevant to your work" (*Conversations*, 164).

3. In her short story "Turpentine," Tess Gallagher has her narrator tell practically the same tale and make the same connection between the shape of a well and the shape of a chimney: "A chimney sweep had come to our house not long ago. He'd learned his trade in Germany, where the sweeps go to weddings and kiss all the women on the cheeks for luck. He'd told an incredible story about falling into a well at the age of twelve. He'd had to be rescued by his father.... His affection for chimneys, he thought, was entirely due to the excitement and danger of his falling into a well when he was twelve" (*The Lover of Horses*, 12). Ginny Skoyles, who tells this story, found that people were always telling her their life stories and confesses that "sometimes I told them back one of the stories someone else had told me. And once in a while I told it back as though it had happened to me. It was harmless enough and it gave me something to say" (60). Gallagher's narrator, in other words, is a thief of stories. In an oddly self-referential way, so too is the author of the story—or Carver, depending on who told it first.

4. More precisely, it begins just before Cheever's story ends. Miss Dent walks away, leaving Blake in the dirt. When it was safe to do so, he gets up and makes his way home.

5. The man was J.P., with whom she would trade blows in the troubled years of their marriage (134).

6. Mark Facknitz was also struck by the incoherence of the scene: "We eavesdrop, but learn little. In fact, the more they say, the less we know. Why is this man in his socks? What is all this about a trip to the North Pole? ... The growing, inchoate set of questions suggests many meaningful and intriguing stories, none of which can cohere unless Miss Dent asks for elaborations, for sense" (346).

7. Which makes "Fever" the third story in a row to allude to other writers—John Cheever in the dedication to "The Train," and in "Where I'm Calling From" the author of *The Call of the Wild*: "Jack London used to have a big place on the other side of this valley," Frank Martin told his guests. "Right over there behind that green hill you're looking at. But alcohol killed him. Let that be a lesson to you. He was a better man than any of us. But he couldn't handle the stuff, either" (137).

8. Cheever's story may provide the origin, too, for those almost unbearably troubling words the woman's son utters in Carver's story "Why, Honey?" (in *Will You Please Be Quiet, Please?*): "Kneel is what I say, kneel down is what I say, he said, that's the first reason why" (173). For they are what Miss Dent said to Blake: "When the train had passed beyond the bridge, the noise grew distant, and he heard her screaming at him, '*Kneel down! Kneel down! Do what I say. Kneel down!*'" (293). Note that not only is the command the same, but the accompanying phrase "what I say" appears in both passages. Could the son be speaking the torment of a seduced and abandoned lover?

9. Of which this is, among those published in the three collections studied here, the fiftieth. This would exclude *Furious Seasons*, which stands apart from the rest of Carver's fiction because of the wholly untypical title story ("unusual among Carver's stories for its disruption of linear progression, its conflation of dream and reality, and a surprising lushness of style" [Saltzman, 96]) and its not having been published by a major press. It would exclude the stories in *Fires*, too, which unlike the other collections consists of poetry and essays as well as stories. I do not think the stories in *Fires* or *Furious Seasons* exhibit the sequential echoing structure of those considered here.

10. Holits has become a strange parody of the man in "Viewfinder" who climbed up on the roof of his garage, as Holits did on the roof of the cabana, and waved.

11. After *What We Talk About* "the first story I wrote was 'Cathedral'" (*Conversations*, 44).

Kirk Nesset (essay date Spring 1994)

SOURCE: "Insularity and Self-Enlargement in Raymond Carver's *Cathedral*," in *Essays in Literature*, Vol. 21, No. 1, Spring, 1994, pp. 116-28.

[*In the essay below, Nesset, a professor at Whittier college, argues that the stories in* Cathedral *differ from Carver's earlier work in that some of the characters are able to escape their self-imposed insularity.*]

In **"The Compartment,"** one of Raymond Carver's bleakest stories, a man passes through the French countryside in a train, en route to a rendevous with a son he has not seen for many years. "Now and then," the narrator says of the man, "Meyers saw a farmhouse and its outbuildings, everything surrounded by a wall. He thought this might be a good way to live—in an old house surrounded by a wall" (**Cathedral** 48). Due to a last minute change of heart, however, Meyers chooses to stay insulated in his "compartment" and, remaining on the train, reneges on his promise to the boy, walling out everything external to his selfish world, paternal obligation included.

Meyers's tendency toward insularity is not, of course, unique among the characters in *Cathedral* or among the characters of earlier volumes. In *Will You Be Quiet, Please?* there is the paranoid self-cloistering of Slater and Arnold Breit, and in *What We Talk About When We Talk About Love* we read of James Packer's cantankerous, self-absorbed disgruntlement about life's injustices. In *Cathedral* appear other, more extreme versions of insularity, from a husband's self-imposed confinement to a living room in **"Preservation"** to another's pathetic reluctance to leave an attic garret in **"Careful."** More strikingly in *Cathedral* than before, Carver's figures seal themselves off from their worlds, walling out the threatening forces in their lives even as they wall themselves in, retreating destructively into the claustrophobic inner enclosures of self. But corresponding to this new extreme of insularity, there are in several stories equally striking instances where—pushing insularity the other way—characters attempt to throw off their entrapping nets and, in a few instances, appear to succeed. In *Cathedral*, and in *Cathedral* only, we witness the rare moments of their comings out, a process of opening up in closed-down lives that comes across in both the subjects and events of the stories and in the process of their telling, where self-disenfranchisement is reflected even on the level of discourse, rhetorically or structurally, or both.

As one might expect, "de-insulation" of this kind necessarily involves the intervention of others: the coming out of a self-enclosed figure depends upon the influence of another being—a baker or a babysitter or blind man, or even a fellow drunk on the road to recovery, who, entering unexpectedly into a character's life, affords new perspective or awareness and guides him along, if not toward insight then at least away from the destructively confining strictures of self. As one might expect further, such interventions and influences are mobilized in the stories through the communal gestures of language—through the exchanging of tales and through communicative transactions, particularly, where separate identities blend and collaborate rather than collide. Thus even as "Carver's task," as Paul Skenazy writes, is to depict the "tiny, damning confinements of the spirit," in *Cathedral* it is also to go beyond depicting the suffocations and wilted spirits of characters in chains (78). Engaging in what he calls a kind of writerly "opening up" of his own, Carver draws out in various uplifting moments the momentary gratifications and near-joys characters experience when, however temporarily, the enclosing walls come down—when their self-preoccupations lift and they sense new freedom, a freedom they may or may not ever truly participate in at all (Interview 21).

But since outright freedom is for many of Carver's lot as terrifying as total lack of mobility (think of Arnold Breit in **"Are You a Doctor?"** or Lloyd in **"Careful"**), the freedoms Carver's newly-liberated characters experience manifest themselves ironically as forms of enclosure, ample and humane as those enclosures may be. Be they a comforting memory of one's old bedroom, or the warm, fragrant reality of a bakery, or a vision of the awesome interior of a cathedral, they are enclosures nevertheless. Trying to free themselves of the fetters of insecurity and addiction, Carver's characters expand both inwardly and outwardly and, thanks to the beneficial incursion of other lives and other stories, imagine larger, more spacious enclosures—places big enough and light enough to allow the spirit room to breathe. In *Cathedral*, by and large, characters are more insulated than ever, cut off from their worlds and from themselves; but a few of them, like J.P. in **"Where I'm Calling From,"** trying patiently and steadfastly "to figure out how to get his life back on the track" (135), demonstrate through shared stories and through overtures toward human connection new and unprecedented awareness. It is an awareness of collective confinement, a sense that we can and often do help each other set aright our derailed lives, that by opening up to others and to ourselves, we do indeed occasionally get those lives back on track.

"Where I'm Calling From" is the story of a man coming to grips with addiction within the security of an alcohol treatment home. Contrary to the situations of **"The Compartment," "Preservation,"** and **"Careful"**—situations in which men blockade themselves in ways as offensive to others as they are self-destructive—this narrator's confinement is both positive and necessary. Locking himself up voluntarily in "Frank Martin's drying out facility" (127), he is a stronger version of Wes in **"Chefs House,"** a wavering recoveree who lapses back into alcoholism when his summer retreat—the sanctuary of his fragile recovery—falls out from under him. Up until now, this narrator (like many of Carver's narrators, he goes unnamed) has insulated himself with drink, with the buffering torpor alcohol can provide, his addiction being both a reaction to and the cause of his failing marriage. Arriving at Frank Martin's dead drunk, exchanging one extreme state of insularity for another, he takes refuge from a prior refuge—one that was killing him. Sitting on the porch with another recovering drunk, J.P., he takes further refuge in the story his new friend has to tell.[1]

It is significant that throughout most of the story Carver leaves his characters sitting where they are. Protected yet still exposed to the chill of the outer world, the porch is that liminal space existing between the internal security of a cure-in-progress and the lure, if not the danger, of the outer world. On the porch, the narrator and J.P. are at once sheltered and vulnerable, their physical surroundings an objective correlative to the transitional state of their minds and wills. Beyond the "green hill" they see from the porch, as Frank Martin tells them, is Jack London's house—the place where the famous author lived until "alcohol killed him" (137). Beyond that—much farther north—is the "Yukon," the fictive *topos* of London's "To Build a Fire," a place where, as the narrator recalls later, a man will "actually . . . freeze to death if he can't get a fire going" (146). With his wet clothes, tragically enough, London's figure is hardly insulated from the chill, even though, ironically, he's bundled up in the manner of the two strongest figures in Carver's story: J.P.'s wife, Roxy, whose "big knuckles" have broken her husband's nose, wears both a "coat" and "a heavy sweater" (142); Frank Martin, hard-edged and tough and looking like a "prize-fighter," keeps his "sweater buttoned all the way up" (137).

By the end of the story, sitting alone and enjoying the transitional comforts of the porch, Carver's narrator fails to recall, or subconsciously omits, the tale's sad conclusion—the fact that, at the mercy of the elements, London's man eventually freezes to death, his life extinguished along with his fire. Still upset perhaps about Tiny's "seizure," the narrator chooses not to think of the extreme consequences of ill-prepared exposure to the outer world. Nor does he remind himself that death entered the heart of the sanctuary only days before, this time without claiming its prize. Subject also to bodily complaints, J.P. suffers from the "shakes" and the narrator from an occasional "jerk in [his] shoulder"; like Tiny, the fat electrician from Santa Rosa, J.P. and his friend are each in their own way overpowered by biology, by nature. Their bodies—like their minds—are adjusting and compen-

sating in the process of recovery. Just as love was once upon a time "something that was out of [J.P.'s] hands"—something that set his "legs atremble" and filled him "with sensations that were carrying him every which way" (132)—the aftermath of drinking is for both men superseded in intensity only by death, the ultimate spasm, which proceeds from both within and without, insulate themselves however they may.

Before "going inside," Frank Martin suggests a bit of recommended reading, namely *The Call of the Wild*. "We have it inside if you want to read something," he says. "It's about this animal that's half dog and half wolf" (137). Like London's "animal," we learn, the narrator is similarly divided, torn by inner impulses. At the outset of his first visit, Frank Martin had taken the narrator aside, saying, "We can help you. If you want help and want to listen to what we say" (138). Thinking now in retrospect, the narrator says, "I didn't know if they could help me or not. Part of me wanted help. But there was another part" (138). Partly civilized, partly wild, the narrator is in one sense interested in protecting himself from *himself*, his retreat at Frank Martin's a gesture of attempted self-domestication that, considering present circumstances, unfortunately did not come off the first time. "We're not out of the woods yet," he says, describing the second aftermath of addiction, the physical extremity of which leaves him and his friend trembling in their chairs, still caught up in the war of selves. "In-between women," Skenazy writes of this story, "in-between homes, in-between drinks, the narrator locates himself in his disintegration" (83). And yet it is between selves, we should hasten to add, where he begins to come to terms with disintegration, and begins imagining ways to reintegrate, rebuild.

Above all he wants "to listen," as Frank Martin says, though it is not Frank he listens to chiefly but to J.P. "Keep talking, J.P.," he says early on (130), interjecting this and like phrases throughout the story in the manner of a refrain: "You better keep talking," he says (136). The coming out of hardened insularity involves intensive listening, as necessary for him as telling is for J.P., and for Carlyle in **"Fever,"** who comes out of a psychological and physical ordeal by spilling his pent-up turmoils to a babysitter. For this narrator, significantly, the process of coming out involves *going into* the narrative of another, involves entering imaginatively into a discourse which, arising of the communal act of storytelling, is at once familiar and unfamiliar. Since "commiseration instigates recuperation," as Arthur Saltzman observes of this story, J.P.'s story initiates through both comradery and displacement the continuation of the narrator's own story—and, if all goes well, the reassembly of the fragments of his life (147). Which is not to say, of course, that there are not perils as well as benefits in transactions of discourse, the sharing of stories. In **"Will You Please Be Quiet, Please,"** a secure, seemingly happy man comes unglued at hearing the tale of his wife's infidelity, a story she tells him herself; in **"Sacks,"** a son enclosed by his own world and concerns meets his father briefly in an airport, and upon hearing the story of his father's adultery (and his parents' ruined marriage), he seals himself off completely from his father, more alienated and embittered than ever by the old man's confession. Before *Cathedral*, generally, narrative transactions—if transaction has taken place at all—constitute perilous intercourse indeed.

But in **"Where I'm Calling From,"** as in other stories in *Cathedral*, Carver would have us believe otherwise. "I'm listening," the narrator says, waiting for J.P. to go on with his tale. "It's helping me to relax, for one thing. It's taking me away from my own situation" (134). Still, J.P.'s story helps him do more than merely "relax." Listening, and the imagination required of close listening, takes him away from his "own situation" even as it brings him closer to the heart of his problems. His inner crisis is externalized in J.P.'s story, both in the pairing of their present circumstances and in the details of his friend's narration—in such odd details, in fact, as the "well" J.P. fell into as a boy. Like the chimneys from which J.P. ends up making his livelihood later in life—narrow, tubular enclosures associated with the family to whom he becomes attached (they run the chimney-sweeping business)—the well is a trap, a darkly insulating prison; it represents the extent to which J.P. senses, enclosed until very recently in a bottle, he has hit "the bottom" in the present trajectory of his life.[2] For both the narrator and J.P., the well represents literally the pitfalls of experience, the dark refuges in which they find themselves (voluntarily or involuntarily) existing, places they are extricated from ultimately only through the intervening efforts of others. Like J.P. "hollering" at the bottom of the well, the narrator is waiting for a drop-line of his own, his "line out" being (along with his willingness to reform) the telephone. By the end of the story he has tried calling his wife twice, and is about to call his "girlfriend," hoping to make contact with the women in his life. Not by any means out of the woods yet, though, he is still wavering in his resolve. In one of the story's last lines, he says, thinking of his girlfriend, "Maybe I'll call her first"—suggesting, given what we know about her drinking habits, that that line out may send him tumbling back into the hole. Torn between the warmth of stability and the chill of the outer world, between civilization and wilderness, he is, we assume, still at war with himself.

With two layers of female protection, in a sense, buffering him from the world, he is mildly obsessed with the women in his life, so it is not surprising that his life and J.P.'s story intersect finally in a woman's kiss. Far more hopeful than the peacock in **"Feathers"**—one man's token of a kind of radiant bliss he'll never know—Roxy's kiss is for the narrator a token of "luck," emphasizing more than his need for help from without, a rope down the well of his life. As a

gesture, Roxy's kiss underscores the degree to which women provide security in his life; he has depended on them, certainly, as much as he has in the past on drink, or as he has recently on the captivating flow of J.P.'s narrative. Our sense of his greatest personal security comes with his description of the time his landlord, coming around one morning to paint the house, awakened him and his wife in their bedroom:

> I push the curtain away from the window. Outside, this old guy in white coveralls is standing next to his ladder. The sun is just starting to break over the mountains. The old guy and I look each other over. It's the landlord, all right—this old guy in coveralls. But his coveralls are too big for him. He needs a shave, too. And he's wearing this baseball cap to cover his bald head. Goddamn it, I think, if he isn't a weird old fellow. And a wave of happiness comes over me that I'm not him— that I'm me and that I'm inside this bedroom with my wife. (145)

Seated on "the front steps" in the chill air beyond the porch, the narrator warms himself with this memory of the past— triggered, seemingly, by the kiss he gets from Roxy (before she and J.P. "go in," leaving him outside alone). He associates his "happiness" then, in his memory, with being "inside" the bedroom with his wife, suggesting not only how much women are integral to his well-being but also how beneficial certain walls and enclosures have been to him at times. "Outside," in the form of a strange, skinny old man, are reminders of toil and old age, and, as before, of what lies beyond that—illness and decrepitude and death; "inside," on the contrary, there is security and leisure, embodied by a laughing wife and the enveloping comforts of a warm bed, and by a recognition of his circumstances as being as secure then as they were.

Thus the contact the narrator makes with an old man one morning is recapitulated by his contact with a younger man years later, though contact is closer now since both men are "outside" and are working communally in their efforts to find ways back in. Epitomized in the gesture of Roxy's kiss, the intersection of their lives and stories has initiated a recuperation that may get them, as J.P. says, "back on the track." So crucial is this intersection, ultimately, that it is manifested even on the level of the story's structure, in the way the story unfolds. With its disruptions in time and narrative continuity, the story mirrors the psychic energies of the narrator, wavering from man to man in its focus, intertwining the individual threads of their stories and lives in a manner that makes them come to seem oddly inseparable, fused in a brotherly textual knit. Promoting such healthy complicity, **"Where I'm Calling From"** embodies and dramatizes our collective tendencies to discover ourselves in the stories of others, and to complicate other lives with our own as we collaborate toward understanding, toward liberation from the confinements that kill.

In **"A Small, Good Thing"** we find a similar coming together of lives—rather more disparate lives, but with problems no less serious. It is the story of a couple dealing with the loss of a child, and of the consolation they find eventually, haphazardly, in the company of a baker; it is a story about the way fear and worry and grief can cause people to break out of the habitual, insulating, self-preoccupations of their lives, and about how the narratives of others can cushion the violent unsettling such break-outs bring on. As in **"Where I'm Calling From,"** recovery entails "listening," as characters enter briefly into the lives of others through channels of verbal interaction. In this story, however—perhaps because Ann and Howard Weiss, its central figures, are simultaneously more stable and more emotionally vulnerable than J.P. and his friend, and because the story evokes a greater sense of affirmation overall, despite its subject—the liberating aspects of attentive listening are rather more noticeable. With a fullness and optimism unequaled in any other story, Carver dramatizes here what William Stull calls "talk that works" (11). Carver provides here in essence an answer to the failures his characters have been subject to all along, failures of characters who, in stories in all of his books, talk and listen with characteristically poor results. Corresponding to this new fullness of possibility, the shape of the story itself swells out to new proportions (revised from its original form as **"The Bath"**), reflecting on the level of narrative the kind of psychological and spiritual expansion taking place within.

"So far," the unnamed narrator says of Howard Weiss, "he had kept away from any real harm, from those forces he knew existed and that could cripple or bring down a man if the luck went bad, if things suddenly turned" (62). As for J.P.'s friend, "luck" is important to Howard; its capriciousness, he knows, dictates somehow over the details of his world—has in fact allowed "forces" to insinuate themselves into the placid interior of his life, forces manifesting themselves after the initial blow in the ominous calls of the baker. His insular bubble of security now on the point of bursting, Howard remains sealed in his "car for a minute" in the driveway, his leg beginning to "tremble" as he considers the gravity of his circumstances. Trying to "deal with the present situation in a rational manner" (62), his motor control is suddenly as erratic as that of Frank Martin's clients. Similarly affected, Ann's teeth begin to "chatter" as fear takes her over, and as she realizes that she and her husband are "into something now, something hard" (70). Both Howard and his wife—like recovering alcoholics—are afflicted by the physical consequences of their dealings with an irrational, overpowering problem, in the face of which rationality is useless. Thanks to a bit of bad luck, their secure and self-enclosed familial world is turned inside out.

As the focal figure of the story, Ann seems both more preoccupied and more sensitive than her husband, not necessarily because her parental (maternal) attachment to the boy is greater than Howard's, but because she is afforded more interior space in the story throughout. Thus, despite the intensity of her preoccupation in their days-long vigil, she momentarily glimpses the walls around her, walls erected in the tide of catastrophe. "For the first time," the narrator says, describing Ann's realization after many hours in the hospital, "she felt they were together in it, this trouble" (68). Realizing she has shut herself off to everything but her son and his condition, she acknowledges that she "hadn't let Howard into it, though he was there and needed all along. She felt glad to be his wife." If in a sense the disruptive force of calamity clarifies, it also causes both Ann and her husband, hemmed in now by fear and dread, to project outward as they seek respite from confinement. Worry insulating them as security had before, they stand staring "out at the parking lot." They don't "say anything. But they seem . . . to feel each other's insides now, as though the worry had made them transparent in a perfectly natural way" (71). Their interior state of affairs is "natural," of course, because it is *nature*—and their powerlessness in the face of it—that makes them transparent, that prompts them, fire-distilled now by mutual concern, to gaze out the window the way J.P. and his friend stare from the porch. After Scotty's death, however, they will have to "get used to . . . being alone" (82); soon they will have to readjust tensions in the marital bond that have been for years filtered by their son's presence. What was once a common refuge is suddenly no longer available to them.

As in **"Where I'm Calling From,"** the act of exchanging stories is also a kind of refuge, though here it becomes an even more compensatory one. Ann and Howard end up in a bakery, giving up the oppressive environment of the hospital—and a house full of painful mementoes—for a warmer, more spacious setting. The narrative transaction occurring in the bakery is for husband and wife the "restorative measure" the doctor mistakenly diagnoses in discussing Scotty's "very deep sleep"; at the hands of the baker the Weisses are doctored as their son could not be. Contrary to the situation of J.P. and his friend, recovery is administered to them by a speaker who cannot empathize with his listeners, a man as ironically unlike them as anybody could be. "I don't have any children myself," the baker tells Ann and Howard, "so I can only imagine what you must be feeling" (87). Still, sparked by his power to "imagine" their grief, he begins his tale of "loneliness, and of . . . what it was like to be childless all these years," offering them if nothing else at least the consolation of knowing that they know what they are going to miss. Thus husband and wife listen, and listening, enter the baker's world—his story—to temporarily escape their own. "They listened carefully," the narrator says, drawing through repetition special attention to the act, "they listened to what the baker had to say" (88).

Elsewhere in *Cathedral*, remarkably, hearing and listening are treated in less optimistic terms: in **"Careful,"** a man's metaphorical deafness to the world is figured in the literal blockage of his ear with wax; in **"Vitamins,"** a similar if more general kind of deafness finds its emblem in a dismembered, dried-out human ear. But in other stories—in **"Fever"** and **"Where I'm Calling From,"** for instance—characters indeed turn their ears to others, and come away better for it. "I got ears," the blind man says in **"Cathedral,"** affirming, in spite of his handicap, that "Learning never ends" (222). In **"Intimacy,"** one of Carver's last stories, a fiction-writing narrator calls himself "all ears," exploring both the idea of the writer as plunderer of experience (as earlier, in **"Put Yourself in My Shoes"**) and of the writer as listener, as someone who, by listening carefully, reconstructs memory and experience in order to reorder the disorder of his past. In **"A Small, Good Thing,"** more strikingly than ever, telling and listening are beneficial, recuperative activities. And yet what is crucial is not so much the substance of the stories as it is the process of the telling. "I was interested," J.P.'s friend says of J.P.'s tale. "But I would have listened if he'd been going on about how one day he'd decided to start pitching horseshoes" (132). Enveloped similarly in the baker's tale, Ann and Howard listen, escaping the still unthinkable reality of their present circumstances by entering the far more stifling, insulated life of their host, and thus they begin a slow journey out of the darkness of grief. Though it is still dark outside, it is "like daylight" inside the bakery; warmed by the light and the ovens and the sweet rolls they eat, and revived by shared compassion, Ann and Howard do "not think of leaving."

The welcome light of possibility, finally, along with hopes if not promises of self-regeneration, is reflected in the shape of the story overall, which we have here in its revised form; **"A Small, Good Thing"** is two-thirds again as long as the original published version, **"The Bath,"** and is the longest story Carver ever collected. Like many stories in *Cathedral*, which Carver describes as "fuller and more interesting somehow" as well as "more generous," the revised version of this story reflects part of an "opening up in this book" which, as Carver says, is absent in "any other of the books" (Interview 22). From the shadowy, overdetermined world of **"The Bath,"** where the tiny enclosure of a bathtub provides a sole comfort for characters ("Fear made him want to take a bath," the original narrator says of Howard), we traverse to the indoor daylight of the bakery, where food and talk and commiseration actually do make a difference, if not redeeming characters of their miseries then consoling them at least, allowing them to understand that loneliness and hardship and death are part of the natural order of things, and that as people they are not in it alone. Embodied in this

"fuller" version of the story, Carver's "opening up" suggests further the very real extent to which style can wall an artist in—suggests how as an artist Carver, like a few of his more fortunate characters, is capable of breaking free of enclosing environments, exchanging them not only for greater capaciousness but, we must assume, for a new understanding of himself and his craft as well.

In the title story, **"Cathedral,"** the coming out of a self-insulated figure is more dramatic than ever before, not simply because he is more fully shut off than some but because, like Meyers riding away from his son on a train to nowhere, he is ignorant of the serious nature of his insularity. Walled in by his own insecurities and prejudices, this narrator is sadly out of touch with his world and with himself, buffered by drink and pot and by the sad reality, as his wife puts it, that he has no "friends." As are the figures in **"A Small, Good Thing"** and **"Where I'm Calling From,"** however, he too is given an opportunity to emerge from the strictures of self-enclosure, though here it is not a story that opens him up but a more subtle nonverbal transaction—an odd, unspoken communication between him and his blind guest, Robert. And as is often the case in the conversations of Carver's characters, talk fails him, and yet his failure is more than made up for by the connection he finally succeeds in making, by the self-liberating results of his attempt.

Not surprisingly, this narrator lives in a narrow, sheltered world. Like Howard and Ann, he is threatened abruptly from without; the appearance of his wife's friend constitutes—at the outset, at least—an invasion of his enclosed existence. "A blind man in my house was not something I looked forward to," he admits (209), and later adds, "Now this same blind man was coming to sleep in my house" (212). His territorial impulses, spurred on certainly by insecurity, make for what Skenazy calls an "evening of polite antagonism between the two men" (82). The narrator's buried hostility, we suppose, is rooted in the blind man's association with aspects of his wife's past and of her independent nature in general—aspects that are intimidating to him, not the least of which is her former marriage, a subject with which he is obsessed. Simultaneously fascinated by and reluctant to hear the blind man's story ("my wife filled me in with more details than I cared to know," he says; "I made a drink and sat at the kitchen table to listen" [213]) he searches for himself indirectly in his wife's relationship with Robert. Like J.P.'s friend, this man's sense of a secure identity depends upon his bond with a female, a bond he seems to need to see perpetually reinforced—though, perturbed by his insensitivity, his wife isn't about to give him the reinforcement he craves. Referring to his wife's conversation with Robert in the living room, he says, "I waited in vain to hear my name on my wife's sweet lips" (218). His muddled search for self, we guess, involves a continual gauging and protecting of the autocratic status of his name. A year earlier, listening to Robert's half of a taped conversation, he'd been startled to hear his "own name in the mouth of [a] stranger, this blind man" he did not know (212). Insistent upon asserting his identity over his wife, therefore, he blankets her past the way he has lately blanketed his present—with insulating self-absorbency. Summing up her prior life, he refers to his wife's ex-husband only as her "officer," adding, "Why should he have a name?" (211). He is no ideal listener, having predicated the names and stories of others under the subject of his own tyrannical yet precarious identity: he listens for purposes of self-validation, relegating the rest of experience—like Robert's marriage—to a place "beyond [his] understanding" (213).

It is fitting that Robert, the invader in the house, is insulated only physically, left in the dark only by his handicap. Extremely outgoing—not to mention friendly—he has done "a little of everything," from running a sales distributorship to traveling in Mexico to broadcasting "ham radio." His activities, unlike those of his host, bring him out into the world, his booming voice having extended as far as Alaska and Tahiti before making its way into the narrator's home. Unlike the baker and J.P.—relatively restrained men—Robert is characterized by the strength of his personality, and he serves accordingly as the extra-durable guide needed to pull his host out of his shell (though like the Weisses, Robert, too, is dealing with grief, having just lost his wife; "I know about skeletons," he says [223], responding to the narrator's query regarding the TV). As the narrator fails to describe the image he sees on television, Robert listens, and having "listened" to failure, takes charge of the situation. "Hey, listen to me," he says, activated suddenly by his host's admission of verbal impotence. "Will you do me a favor? I got an idea. Why don't you find us some heavy paper. And a pen. We'll do something. We'll draw one together. Get us a pen and some heavy paper. Go on, bub, get the stuff' (226). Robert's initiative in the matter of the narrator's failings, not to mention the remedy he employs in general, suggests that verbal handicaps—and the larger problems they are symptoms of—are debilitating as blindness (stemming as they do from the willed blindness of ignorance, oversight). Robert's handling of the situation, finally, suggests that handicaps are first and foremost challenges to overcome.

"[M]ost of the communication in this story," writes Michael Vander Weel, in reference to the joint project of the drawing, "comes through shared non-verbal work, as expression that stops short of the effort and commonality of speech" (120). Indeed, as Irving Howe observes, the drawing of the cathedral is a "gesture of fraternity" that, like the meal preceding it, establishes solid contact between the men and in turn nudges the narrator temporarily out of his self-contained world (43). The subject of their mutual efforts—the cathedral—as a symbol represents a kind of common hu-

manity and benevolence, and of human patience and fortitude, in the process of "a-spiring."[3] Curiously enough, it is within the walls of the cathedral that the narrator ultimately ends up. "I was in my house," he says at the end of the story, his eyes still tightly closed—bringing to mind the "box" he drew when he and Robert began, something that "could have been the house [he] lived in" (227). What begins as an enclosing spatial configuration of his home—and present level of awareness, we assume—gradually swells in proportion to become something far more spacious than what he started with, something with interior depths as enlightening to him as bakeries and bedrooms are comforting to others.

"I didn't feel like I was inside anything," he says (228), unwilling still to open his eyes. While Meyers "close[s] his eyes," alternately, to whatever encroaches on his personal life—his voluntary blindness as bad as Lloyd's deafness in its turn—the narrator of **"Cathedral"** finds not escape but sanctuary within self-confinement, his sanctuary existing, by virtue of his closed eyes, within that inner vestibule of self, where selfishness gives way at last to self-awareness. A man obsessed with the faculty of vision ("Imagine," he says earlier of Robert's wife, "a woman who could never see herself as she was seen in the eyes of her loved one" [213]), he clings to a miraculous glimpse of a world beyond the borders of his insular life, blinding himself voluntarily to the distracting reality of his former world. The profundity of his new awareness staggers him; "It was like nothing else in my life up to now," he says, and adds, in the story's final sentence, "It's really something." The indefiniteness of his language—he is usually a little more glib than he is here—expresses the sheer incomprehensibility of his revelation, and the fact that he registers it as such. He experiences "depths of feeling," as Saltzman calls them, that only a few enlightened characters in *Cathedral* experience, feelings that he "need not name to justify" (154). The changes working in him are not unlike those "impossible changes" Ralph Wyman undergoes in **"Will You Please Be Quiet, Please?,"** where even more pronounced tensions of jealousy, possessiveness, and self-preoccupation are vented finally in human contact. Just as Ann Weiss wants "her words to be her own" after the death of her child, seeking out a personal vocabulary of grief, this narrator reaches for words weighty enough to fit his experience, and, failing gloriously in that, settles for indefinites. Impossibly changed, reduced to semi-inarticulateness, he keeps his eyes fastened shut, wavering between self-awareness and habitual existence in a new and newly-spacious enclosure; he is "no longer inside himself," as Skenazy writes, "if not quite outside, no longer alone, if not quite intimate" (83).

Naturally, this coming out is mirrored by rhetoric of the story. Early on in the story, the narrator feels momentarily "sorry for the blind man," his insulated hardness beginning to to soften. As the walls of his resentment noticeably crack, he watches with "admiration" as Robert eats, recognizing Robert's handicap to be no impairment to his performance at the dinner table. The tonal shift in the final sequence of the story-marked by a kind of mild ethereality flooding the last lines—illustrates on the rhetorical level the opening up the narrator has undergone, and, certainly, is yet to undergo. Like Robert, who is on a journey by train, dropping in on friends and relatives, trying to get over the loss of his wife, the narrator is also on a journey, one signaled by signposts in his language and played out by the events of the story he tells. His destination—as are the destinations for all of Carver's travelers, whether they leave home or not—is necessarily a confining one. But it is also a destination where one's sense of shared confinement makes for heretofore-unknown freedoms. "What's a cathedral without people?" Robert asks, bidding his host to add a touch of humanity to the drawing, to "put some people in there" (227). Approaching his destination, the narrator begins to realize just how exhilarating confinement can be, once one sees beyond the narrow enclosure of self that larger, more expansive enclosure of society. He begins to sense, as did perhaps the builders who toiled for years to raise the cathedrals they would never see—people who were, as Robert says, "no different than the rest of us" (224)—he begins to sense, the warmth of the blind man's touch still vibrating in his hand, that we are all in this together, and that that really *is* something.

Carver wrote **"Cathedral"** on a train, writing in his cabin during a transcontinental journey from Seattle to New York.[4] Enclosed in tight quarters, rubbing shoulders with all kinds of people, heading somewhere in a hurry: the writing environment seems an appropriate one, considering the story—and the volume of stories—which was to come of that ride. "It was a different kind of story for me, no question," he explains in his preface to *Where I'm Calling From*. "Somehow I had found another direction I wanted to move toward. And I moved. And quickly" (*i*). Reflecting the process of his "opening up," Carver is in this collection definitely going somewhere in a hurry; in *Cathedral*, as in no other volume of his stories, characters *connect* with one another, however briefly, and as a result of their connections come away changed. Such momentary connections, of course, do not reflect the tone of the book as a whole. Most of the stories—**"The Compartment"** or **"The Train,"** say, ironically stories about people on trains—are slightly fuller explorations, or re-explorations, of Carver's old familiar territory, reimmersions into tableaux where human proximity not only provides no real connection but also alienates, with disconnectedness and alienation coming hand-in-hand as end-products of insularity, terminal self-enclosure. In these stories, as well as in the lighter ones, Carver suggests that life hemmed in rigidly by walls is a hard life indeed—suggests, contrary to Meyers's observation, that this is perhaps not "a

good way to live," this having a ticket to ride and no idea where one is going, no connection with one's fellow travelers.

As Irving Howe notes, the stories of this volume "draw upon the American voice of loneliness and stoicism, the native soul locked in this continent's space" (42). While in rare moments we find characters transcending the fettered states of soul by means of smaller, personal unfetterings of self, such moments do not deny the "locked" status of the characters in general, or the darker implications of Carver's vision overall. Still, Carver implies, it is through our collaboration with others that we free ourselves from the slavery of self-absorption. We see in these stories that compassion, as well as stoicism, is a prerequisite not just of happiness but of survival, and that while confinement may be the precondition of many lives there is still a good deal of freedom available within it—freedom which becomes tangible only when it is recognized for what it is. In this sense the stories of *Cathedral* are on a par with those that Carver and Jenks praise as editors of *American Short Story Masterpieces*, stories which have, as they say, "the ambition of enlarging our view of ourselves and the world" (xiii)—enlarging us as readers, that is, both in the sense of expanding and setting us free.

NOTES

1. For a brilliant narratological and stylistic analysis of this story see Verley.

2. See also Carver's later story "Elephant" (*Where I'm Calling From*), in which a reformed alcoholic refers to his drinking days, and his vision of an alcoholic relapse, as "rock bottom."

3. For this coinage I am indebted to Lonnquist.

4. This bit information I gleaned in a conversation with Tess Gallagher, who refutes Carver's assertion in his preface to *Where I'm Calling From* that "[a]fter a good night's sleep, [he] went to his desk and wrote the story 'Cathedral.'"

Works Cited

Carver, Raymond, *Cathedral*, New York: Random House, 1984.

———, Interview, *Saturday Review.* Sep-Oct 1983: 21-22.

——— and Tom Jenks. *Introduction. American Short Story Masterpieces.* New York: Delacorte, 1987.

————, *What We Talk About When We Talk About Love*, New York: Random House 1981.

————, *Where I'm Calling From*, 1st edition, Franklin Center, PA: Franklin Library, 1988.

————, *Will You Be Quiet, Please?* New York: McGraw-Hill, 1977.

Howe, Irving, "Stories of Our Loneliness." *New York Times Book Review*, 11 Sep 1983: 42-43.

Lonnquist Barbara C. "Narrative Displacement and Literary Faith: Raymond Carver's Inheritance form Flannery O'Connor."*Since Flannery O'Connor: Essays on the Contemporary American Short Story*. Ed. Loren Logsdon and Charles W. Mayer, Macomb,
IL: Western Illinois University, 1987, 142-50.

Saltzman, Arthur, *Understanding Raymond Carver*, Columbia: U of South Carolina P, 1988.

Skenazy, Paul, "Life in Limbo: Raymond Carver's Fiction." *Enclitic* 11 (0000): 00-00.

Stull, William. "Beyond Hopelessville: Another Side of Raymond Carver," *Philological Quarterly* 64 (1985): 1-15.

Verley, Claudine, "Narration and Interiority in Raymond Carver's 'Where I'm Calling From.'"
Journal of the Short Story in English 13 (1989): 91-102.

Weele, Michael Vander. "Raymond Carver and the Language of Desire." *Denver Quarterly* 22 (1987): 00-000.

FURTHER READING

Criticism

Gallagher, Tess. Introduction to *Carver Country: The World of Raymond Carver*, by Bob Adelman and Tess Gallagher, pp. 8-19. New York: Charles Scribner's Sons, 1990.
    Provides an account of Carver's life, along with insight into influences on his writing.

Lehman, David. "Tales of Ordinary Madness." *Newsweek* (5 September 1983): 66.
    Reviews *Cathedral*, claiming that while Carver was successful illustrating misery and hopelessness, his stories are too limited.

Meyer, Adam. "The Masterpiece: *Cathedral*." In *Raymond Carver*, pp. 124-47. New York: Twayne Publishers, 1995.
    Analyzes several stories from *Cathedral*, tracing changes in Carver's tone and style.

Weber, Bruce. "Raymond Carver: A Chronicler of Blue-Collar Despair." *New York Times Magazine* (24 June 1984): 36-51.
    Surveys Carver's life, placing his work within the context of changes in the literary world.

Interviews

Bonetti, Kay. "Ray Carver: Keeping It Short." *Saturday Review* (September-October 1983): 21-3.
    Remarks on the Mildred and Harold Strauss Living Award Carver won and compares *Cathedral* to his earlier work.

Simpson, Mona. "The Art of Fiction LXXVI: Raymond Carver." *The Paris Review* 25, No. 88 (Summer 1983): 192-221.
    Discusses alcoholism, why Carver wrote, and how *Cathedral* marked a transition for him.

Additional coverage of Carver's life and career is contained in the following sources published by Gale: *Contemporary Authors*, Vols. 33-36, rev. ed., 126; *Contemporary Authors New Revision Series*, Vols. 17, 34, 61; *Dictionary of Literary Biography*, Vol. 130; *Dictionary of Literary Biography Yearbook*, Vols. 84, 88; *DISCovering Authors Modules: Novelists*; *Major 20th-Century Writers*, Vols. 1, 2; and *Short Story Criticism*, Vol. 8.

Francis Ford Coppola
1939-

American filmmaker, producer, and screenwriter.

The following entry presents an overview of Coppola's career. For further information on his life and works, see *CLC,* Volume 16.

INTRODUCTION

Francis Ford Coppola is both an acclaimed and a controversial director. His adaptation of Mario Puzo's novel, *The Godfather* (1972), made him a powerful Hollywood force and also a magnet for criticism. In addition to directing, Coppola is a producer and the head of Omni Zoetrope (formerly American Zoetrope), a studio he started in 1969 to help young filmmakers produce their work.

Biographical Information

Trained in film at the University of California at Los Angeles, Coppola worked with Roger Corman as an assistant director and writer. Corman offered him his first opportunity to direct on *Dementia 13* (1963). The film was not well received, however, and his next film, *You're a Big Boy Now* (1966), was overshadowed by Mike Nichols's *The Graduate,* released at the same time. In retrospect, many critics find *You're a Big Boy Now* a fresh, zany look at the disillusionment and joys of growing up. In 1968, Coppola directed his first—and perhaps his last—musical. His version of *Finian's Rainbow* (1968) was released amidst a barrage of negative reviews. All during production, Coppola was plagued by the problems of an inexperienced filmmaker attempting to create a large-scale musical. Warner Brothers, however, dealt the death blow. The studio, sure of the film's success, expanded the 35mm print to 70mm to give it the aura of a grandiose musical. In the process, however, Fred Astaire's feet were cut off the bottom of the screen. When his next film, *The Rain People* (1969), received a lukewarm critical reception, Coppola's future looked questionable. When first asked to direct the film version of Mario Puzo's novel *The Godfather* (1972), Coppola turned it down. He only reluctantly agreed the second time because he needed the money. While *Part I* was in production, Coppola fought for three things: Marlon Brando for the part of Don Corleone, Al Pacino for the part of Michael Corleone, and the adaptation of the film as a period piece rather than setting it in the present. Because of these aspects of the film, among others, Coppola transformed what some considered a strictly sensational novel into an epic of family loyalty within the world of organized crime. The film ended up propelling

Coppola to the top of Hollywood's elite directors. Several of Coppola's productions have been plagued with problems and controversy. The filming of *Apocalypse Now* (1979) became infamous for its difficult production and skyrocketing costs. The collapse of one of its stars, Martin Sheen, made reworking several of the scenes impossible and caused Coppola to add the last-minute voice-over narration. The filming of *The Godfather, Part III* (1990), also went well over budget due to time restrictions and obligations to deliver to the studio for a Christmas release. The last-minute replacement of the ill Winona Ryder with Coppola's daughter Sophia drew criticism and the usual difficulties on the set due to an inexperienced actress. Coppola has won numerous awards, including the Golden Palm Award at the Cannes Film Festival for *The Conversation* in 1974, Director's Guild Awards as best director in 1972 and 1974, and several Academy Awards.

Major Works

Coppola's groundbreaking *The Godfather,* traces the fortunes and misfortunes of the Corleone family, prominent members of the Italian mafia in New York City. The story's main focus is on Michael Corleone as his American and Italian ideals conflict and he changes from a peripheral figure to the head of the family business. *The Godfather, Part II* (1974) takes up Michael's story again as he heads the family during its declining years. His story is juxtaposed to flashbacks of his father Vito Corleone, the original don, as he leads the family into its ascendancy. Vito represents the old values of family and loyalty while Michael has taken the family away from these traditional values to pursue a more corporate, capitalistic success. In the end, Michael's attempts are unsuccessful and the family is left in a shambles. *The Godfather, Part III* goes beyond the world of organized crime and American capitalism to include international finance and intrigue at the Vatican. Michael begins to regret his life and goes looking for redemption through the Catholic Church. Among Coppola's more personal, lower budget films is *The Conversation* (1974), which traces the mental breakdown of a professional wiretapper who loses his professional detachment and becomes overcome with paranoia. *Apocalypse Now* uses the novella *Heart of Darkness*, by Joseph Conrad, as the organizing principle through which Coppola looks at the Vietnam War. Captain Willard is sent by the American generals to assassinate the renegade Colonel Kurtz, who has led a group of soldiers into the jungle and begun to wage his own kind of war. The major conflict between the generals and Kurtz is the role of morality in the fighting of a war. Willard represents the mediating principle in the film between these two opposing sides. Coppola's *Bram Stoker's Dracula* (1992) represents his vision of the vampire myth and is characterized by elaborate, stylized costumes and a beautiful, youthful Hollywood cast.

Critical Reception

Several critics complained that Coppola's *The Godfather* glorified and romanticized the mob in America and violence in general. Although Coppola tried to address this concern with less violence and a more pessimistic ending in *The Godfather, Part II*, critics still found his portrayal of Vito Corleone as too sympathetic and idealized. There is much disagreement about which of the *Godfather* films is superior, some claiming *Part I*, others *Part II* and most agreeing that *Part III* was one part too many. There is general agreement, however, that Coppola forever changed the gangster genre and that his *Godfather* saga left a permanent mark on the American psyche. Jack Kroll summed up the first two films' success saying, "*Godfather I* and its sequel were that rarity, a tremendous critical and box-office success that earned its studio, Paramount, a total of $800 million, plus nine Oscars and a permanent place in American culture." Many reviewers complain that Coppola does not live up to his stated message in his films, especially in *Apocalypse Now*, which some reviewers said left Coppola's view of America's involvement in Vietnam unclear. Leonard Quart and Albert

Auster asserted, "Coppola's strength as a director is not psychological revelation or personal intimacy. It's the pictorial and metaphoric, the strong narrative and the ambitious conception which distinguish his work." Some reviewers have concluded that Coppola strives too hard for box-office success and feel it compromises his artistic vision, but Stephen Farber takes a different view. He stated, ". . . Coppola is the rare movie tycoon who is also a serious artist, and his best work compares with the best being done anywhere in the world."

PRINCIPAL WORKS

Dementia 13 [director] (screenplay) 1963

Is Paris Burning? [with Gore Vidal, Jean Aurenche, Pierre Bost, and Claude Brulé] (screenplay) 1966

You're a Big Boy Now [adapted from the novel by David Benedictus; also director] (screenplay) 1966

Finian's Rainbow [director] (screenplay) 1968

The Rain People [also director] (screenplay) 1969

Patton [with Edmund H. North] (screenplay) 1970

The Godfather [with Mario Puzo; also director] (screenplay) 1972

The Conversation [also director] (screenplay) 1974

The Godfather, Part II [with Puzo; also director] (screenplay) 1974

The Great Gatsby [adapted from the novel by F. Scott Fitzgerald] (screenplay) 1974

Apocalypse Now [with John Milius; also director] (screenplay) 1979

One from the Heart [with Armyan Bernstein; also director] (screenplay) 1982

The Outsiders [director] (film) 1983

Rumble Fish [with S. E. Hinton; also director] (screenplay) 1983

The Cotton Club [with William Kennedy; based on a story by Coppola, Kennedy, and Puzo; also director] (screenplay) 1984

Peggy Sue Got Married [director] (film) 1986

Gardens of Stone [director] (film) 1987

Tucker: The Man and His Dream [director] (film) 1988

New York Stories [co-director with Woody Allen and Martin Scorsese] (film) 1989

The Godfather, Part III [with Puzo; also director] (film) 1990

Bram Stoker's Dracula [director] (film) 1992

CRITICISM

Judith Vogelsang (essay date Spring 1973)

SOURCE: "Motifs of Image and Sound in *The Godfather*," in *Journal of Popular Film*, Vol. II, No. 2, Spring, 1973, pp. 115-35.

[*In the following essay, Vogelsang analyzes the importance of visual and aural clues in foreshadowing the transformation of Michael Corleone's values in* The Godfather.]

Introduction

Out of the darkness, the blacks and whites of Sicilian gangster society (the black screen, the black and white credits, the fade-up from black to the undertaker), we have a three-hour glimpse of the Corleone family, fictional creations, a vision of Italian underworld life in America.

The first line of **The Godfather,** "I believe in America," is spoken by a man for whom the American system of justice did not work. The story he tells Don Corleone, and the visual and aural components of the opening scene, incorporates most of the film's major themes. This scene foreshadows and details in miniature the conversion of the godfather's son, Michael Corleone, from a believer in America (war hero, college boy) to his final position as the Don and godfather, leader of the most powerful gangland family in America.

Even the film's beginning blackness and its closing blackness, interrupted by those vivid years of soft color—decisive years for Michael—are thematic ingredients and capable of multiple interpretation. Put one way, Michael changes his American-good vs. Corleone-evil perspective of the family business and colors it with emotional meaning and personal importance so that he's capable of seeing the reasons behind the family's actions and no longer sees only a black and white picture of the world. By the end of the film, the return to black and white coincides with Michael's new Corleone-good vs. American-evil point of view—a complete reversal of values which results in a similar visual effect.

Put another way, the original blackness yields to illumination—the film itself—of the Corleone lifestyle. When the conflicts are resolved, the darkness returns. The final image is of a door closing on Kay's (and the viewer's) face. There are, of course, other ways of interpreting the cycle of the monochrome titles, color movie, and return to monochrome. My purpose here is not to detail all the possibilities, but rather to show a consistent and remarkable directorial intelligence guiding the progress of the film—evidence that **The Godfather** is a significant artistic achievement and not the mere "entertainment" it has been labelled so far.

As conceived and written by the screenwriter, Mario Puzo, what happens to the godfather affects not only him and his immediate family, but the members, employees, and loyal supporters of all the branches of the Corleone empire. The godfather's life also affects the Corleone enemies, and even the careers of those senators, congressmen, police officers, informers, and newspapermen on the Corleone payroll.

Consequently, the circumstances surrounding significant events in the godfather's experience permeate with special meaning the lives of all those connected to him. These circumstances—objects, motives, and attitudes—provide the impetus and are the source for the image and sound motifs which dominate and guide the film. They are for Francis Ford Coppola, the film's director, the real substance and structure of the film, the form and the content of the art object he shapes.

The visual and aural motifs are weaved by Coppola into the structure of the film, either as recurring reminders or as foreshadowing devices and connecting bridges from scene to scene. The motifs combine to create a rich and moving experience for the viewer. Like all aesthetic objects, **The Godfather** is an experience rather than an idea. It succeeds or fails on an experiential level, just as the fortunes of the Corleones depend largely on the experiences of the godfather.

The central action of the film is foreshadowed in the first scene. The undertaker relates the story of his daughter's attempted rape by some non-Italians after she flaunted tradition by going to the movies unchaperoned with an American boy. She stayed out, drank whiskey, and eventually had her nose and jaw broken in a struggle with the Americans she so innocently trusted. When the camera pulls back from the storyteller's face, we see in the foreground the godfather's crooked jaw. Next we hear his voice and immediately encounter him as a prosperous, gruff, slightly beaten-up patriarch. At this point we don't know these images are foreshadowings but we perceive all of them—broken jaw, beatings, wealth, black and white merging to soft colors—as realistic recreations. It is only gradually as the film progresses that we are struck by the recurring images. In particular, we see in the hospital scene, a turning point for Michael and the film, that Michael's nose and jaw are broken by an American police captain. This event contributes significantly to Michael's dedication toward the aims and methods of his gangster family. The disfiguring of his face also creates an obvious parallel to his father's face. The undertaker's opening story comments on the godfather's appearance and foreshadows the breaking of Michael's jaw later in the film.

In addition, the undertaker's daughter meets her fate in a car. Automobiles are the literal and figurative vehicle for much of the Corleone activity and become a major theme in the film. At first cars are generically representative of American culture and they work against the Italians. As events can culture and they work against the Italians. As events unfold and circumstances change, the car becomes a vital and indispensable gangland tool.

The godfather offers wine to the undertaker during this scene to compensate for the detrimental American influence suffered by the undertaker. The theme of liquids, especially wine vs. water, Italian vs. American, is also a part of the thematic structure of the film.

These themes and others will be discussed separately and traced from scene to scene throughout the film in the following pages.

Coppola's attention to vital detail and his continuing insistence on these details may appear to the casual viewer as random recreations of realism. But these are not just "atmosphere" or details; these are events and objects which take on emotional, social, political, and philosophical importance as the godfather, the old Don and the new Don, encounter them and interact with them.

Oranges and Fish

Oranges, either the fruit or the color, appear in shots involving traitors to the Corleone family, or in scenes depicting misfortune or death in the family. Oranges, an essential factor preceding Don Corleone's wounding and his later death, color irrevocably certain scenes indicating character tendencies and truths in an exclusively visual way. The pivotal orange scene, and the logical motivation for the choice of orange, is the attempted assassination of the godfather.

The first appearance of the orange motif comes in the wedding feast of Connie and Carlo at the beginning of the movie. The main characters are introduced to the viewer much like musical statements are introduced in a symphonic overture. We see or hear the characters we will be learning more about as the symphony unfolds and the themes mix together to create major movements or sequences. Tessio, who betrays Michael Corleone years later at the very end of the film, is introduced to us as he tosses and toys with a large orange.

Proceeding chronologically: when Tom Hagen flies to Hollywood to convince producer Jack Woltz that the Don's favorite godson, Johnny Fontane, should star in Woltz' next picture, oranges are part of the centerpiece on the dinner table. Woltz has worked against the family by deliberately barring Johnny from appearing in his movie. The scene ends with the death of Woltz' valuable racehorse.

When Don Corleone stops in Chinatown to buy fruit, the first one he picks out is an orange. The regular driver and bodyguard, Paulie, didn't show up for work that day and the not-so-bright and ineffectual son, Fredo Corleone, fails to guard Don Corleone against the gunmen who shoot five bullets into him, wounding the godfather gravely. As he falls, a bucket of oranges overturns and spills out over the street. Fredo can only fumble his own gun, drop it, and weep uncontrollably over his father's body. Shortly afterward when the godfather is recovering at home, we discover that Fredo is being sent to Las Vegas to learn the casino business— banishment for his mistakes. Later, in Las Vegas, Fredo (now Freddy) takes sides against the family in an argument Michael is having with casino boss Moe Green. Freddy's actions are more than stupid, they are considered traitorous by Michael, the rising Don. This betrayal of the family is visually foreshadowed earlier in the film by Fredo placing himself quite obviously next to a huge basket of oranges in the godfather's recovery room at home.

In the shot where the godfather realizes he is about to be gunned-down, we see behind him an orange-colored poster advertising a championship boxing match. A few scenes later Michael Corleone waits for the narcotics dealer Sallozzo and his bodyguard Police Captain McClusky in front of famous fighter Jack Dempsey's Restaurant in Manhattan. By the end of the scene, Michael murders them.

When Connie calls her brother Sonny, the interim Don, for help after her husband Carlo beat her up, Sonny goes after Carlo and finds him on the street, acting like a neighborhood boss and dressed entirely in an orange suit. Later, Michael reveals Carlo as a pernicious traitor to the family, the one who betrayed Sonny to Barzini's people and who set-up Sonny to be assassinated.

At the meeting of the five families called by the aging Don to make a truce, we learn who the real traitor is by the placement of oranges in bowls in front of each Corleone enemy, before the Don later reveals it to Tom Hagen. Not only does Phillip Tattaglia have oranges in the frame with him, but the powerful man influencing Tattaglia, Barzini, is also photographed with a conspicuous orange in the foreground. These men will later be disposed of in a multiple, nearly choreographed assassination ordered by Michael.

The death of Don Corleone is visually foreshadowed by his attention to some (orange) goldfish in an aquarium as we fade up on the scene in which Michael is establishing himself as the new Don and talks about the impending move to Nevada.

We have already learned through Luca Brasi's murder that fishes convey the message of death in Sicilian tradition. In a previous scene, Luca enters the Tattaglia territory—a cocktail lounge—on a mission for the Corleone family. We see him in the background talking with Bruno Tattaglia. In the foreground are two large bronze (gold) fish on a glass partition, visual foreshadowings of Luca's and eventually the

Don's death. Sonny later receives Luca's bullet-proof vest wrapped around fish, explained in the film as a Sicilian message signifying Luca's death.

And finally, the last traitor to the progress and success of the Corleone family is the old Don himself. We see him with Michael and Kay's little boy sitting in the garden. Years have passed since we first met the Don and he is now an old, useless man dressed in baggy pants, a wrinkled shirt and a cap to shade the sun. He is mopping his brow and teaching his grandson (unsuccessfully) how to use an outsized, antique, pesticide flit-gun. He is also cutting up an orange. He cuts a piece of the orange and puts it in his mouth to scare the boy. The boy cries, horrified by his grandfather's trick. The old Don gets up with the orange still in his mouth and pretends to be a monster. His grandson chases him through the tomato patch trying to squirt him with the flit gun (a clear liquid spills out). The godfather suffers a heart attack and dies. The passing of the old Corleone guard is completed in this scene. The child, the future Don, is betrayed by the old man with the orange-monster trick. The old man has become a useless monster to the family. He no longer makes the decisions or conducts family business. He is in Michael's way because there can be only one Don to a family and the presence of the old man brings up a question of Michael's authority.

Thunder and Screech

Most of the significant violent acts in the film are prefaced with sounds like thunder, loud echoes, and noises like screams. This aural motif can be traced throughout the film and is a pattern that once again has a specifically "realistic" origin in the dramatic moments when Michael murders the men who plotted to kill his father, discussed in further detail below.

The first screeches we encounter are the adoring cries of Johnny Fontane's fans at Connie Corleone's wedding. The godfather hears the screams, and instinctively asks in a concerned way, what is going on outside. While Johnny sings a lovesong, Michael reveals that the Corleone family has committed violence on Johnny's behalf in the past. We soon learn they will again in the future. When the plane that Tom Hagen takes to Hollywood arrives to make Johnny's producer an offer he can't refuse, we hear the wheels screech to a stop on the runway. Brief thunder can be heard outside producer Woltz' estate as the camera dollies in to Woltz' bedroom and Woltz and viewers discover the decapitated head of Khartoum, the producer's prize thoroughbred. Woltz responds with a series of terrified screams. There is a direct cut to a close-up of the godfather's head as he listens intently to Tom, now back in New York.

There are several instances of thunder-and-screech-like noises in the crucial hospital scene when Michael visits his wounded father. It is in this scene, at the Don's bedside, that Michael decides to adopt the family business as his business. The sound structure intensifies the plot structure and parallels it. The viewer's experience of fear and suspense in this scene is largely due to the sound track which reveals more than the story does about Michael's fate.

Michael's experience visiting his father in the hospital is the turning point or critical action in the movie in many ways. As he enters the empty hospital there is a recurring, echoing noise which is eventually distinguished as a record playing over and over the word "tonight." The second instance comes with the loud footsteps of Enzo, the baker's helper—in squeaky shoes—who Michael at first believes to be an assassin come to kill his father. Near the close of the scene when corrupt Captain McCluskey and the police arrive, there is the rumble of thunder and the squeal of patrol car brakes.

Some other instances of this motif in the hospital scene are the echoing front door as it bangs shut, the creak of the bed being moved, and the squeal of tires on a passing enemy car.

Before tracing the thunderbolt motif any further, it is interesting to discuss the hospital scene in terms of its significance to Michael's career in gangster life.

Michael still remains uncommitted to the family business at this point in the film. In the opening wedding scene when he is dressed in a brown Army uniform we hear him explain to his American girlfriend, "That's my family, Kay, not me." Gradually Michael becomes more and more involved with the family so that by the end of the film when he is the new Don he dresses in black and gray, rides in a black, chauffeur-driven limousine, and wears a black fedora. These are the monochromes we began with and the ones to which Michael must return before striking a median. From the beginning of the movie through the hospital scene he still dresses like an ordinary American—Army uniform, brown corduroy jacket, brown overcoat, no hat—and he rides in cabs. Midway in the film when he is in Sicily and experiencing an enforced return to his heritage, he dresses all in gray—a softer, more chromatic version of black.

The selection of Enzo as the other visitor to the Don's hospital room is a significant one. Enzo, we remember from the first scene of *The Godfather,* is the Italian national, here only on a visa "for the war effort." He is helping in a bakery and wants to avoid being deported back to Italy, preferring to stay in the United States and marry the baker's daughter. The baker comes to Don Corleone to arrange for Enzo's remaining in the U.S. Enzo has one foot in Italy and one foot in America. He can barely speak English, but he will marry the baker's daughter. When Michael murders Sallozzo and

McClusky, he must leave the U.S. and go to Sicily. He misses home very much but finally tries to opt wholly for his Italian heritage. He visits the town of his name—Corleone—and marries a Sicilian girl.

In the hospital, there is a shot of Michael watching for the supposed killers in which we see only half his face, the other half hidden behind a wall. He is half-decided to become a true Corleone and is on the look-out for someone who turns out to be the official half-Italian, half-American character. Enzo is the parallel to what Michael will shortly be in Sicily. This double theme is supported in the scene by the two intravenous bottles flowing into the old Don—one white (realistic glucose, metaphoric water), the other dark (realistic blood, metaphoric wine)—by Michael's repetition of "I'm with you now," and by Enzo and him teamed as bodyguards outside the hospital in a pretense that works.

Michael learns to turn another pretense to his advantage in this scene. He realizes, as he lights a cigarette for the shaking Enzo, that he has a steady hand in moments of intense crisis. His physical appearance does not convey his psychological state. Since he discovered this attribute through the means of lighting a cigarette, he continues to use this device for the rest of the film whenever he is deceitful on behalf of the family—when he bluffs Moe Green and when he lies to his sister as she accuses him of murdering her husband. At the very last of the movie, when Michael tells the final critical lie to his wife about not killing Carlo, he is able to put out the two cigarettes he has lit in preparation for the lie. He no longer needs the crutch of even this small action to aid him in the deceit needed in carrying out the family business.

The film ends with Clemenza, loyal *capo* in the Corleone empire and embodiment of the unconscious solutions to the contradictions between Sicilian culture and American culture (Michael's foil), kissing Michael's hand in respect—acknowledging and joining the new Don.

Returning to the motif of thunder and screech, we come to Michael's first act of murder, the assassination of Sallozzo and McClusky in Louis' Italian-American Restaurant. (A logical setting for Michael's dual loyalties.) When he goes into the men's room to locate the gun that has been placed there for him, and he finds it, we hear the rumbling, thunderous noise of the subway below. He stops, recovers from emotion, and the subway (underworld) thunder dissolves into the screech of subway brakes. Michael walks out to the dinner table and does not immediately follow his instructions to shoot them. He sits down. The subway noises repeat. The sound imagery is committed to the inevitable structure of the film. Because Michael has committed himself to the family, he must go through with the plan. He stands up and shoots them both as Clemenza instructed—

twice in the head. The subway sounds from this scene, then, are the *integral, realistic* source for the use of the thunder and screech motif in **The Godfather.** The motifs in the film are not random or contrived. They flow naturally out of and into the structure of the work.

In Sicily the appearance of Apollonia hits Michael "like a thunderbolt." Apollonia, the name suggesting a potential balance between the two cultures warring in Michael, will never be able to make the adjustment to America. We see that she takes little interest in learning English and seems unable to extricate herself from her Sicilian heritage. The image-motif appropriate for conveying and intensifying these facts in the viewer's experience of Apollonia follows quickly: she is driving their car, recurring symbol of American culture throughout the film when the bomb planned for Michael explodes, killing her instantly. This scene comes just after Michael learns about Sonny's death and incorporates the thunder, screech and car motifs successfully in a moving and revealing segment of the film.

She was the wrong wife for Michael, just as Sonny was the wrong Don for the family.

The next scream is Connie Corleone's as she is beaten by Carlo. She crashes all of her dishes to the floor in a violent scene with her husband. He beats her and her scream turns into the cry of the baby in her mother's arms as she calls home for help. Sonny talks to her and predictably flies out of the house in a rage of revenge and drives to his death at the tollgate.

The gunning down of Santino seems like a tribute to another very American movie, *Bonnie and Clyde.* In fact, the character of Sonny may have been modeled by James Caan partially on Warren Beatty's Clyde Barrow. Both characters took things "too personally" for successful completion of their careers in crime. Each could not concern himself only with "business." Emotionalism and an incomplete understanding of what America is all about (when combined with legend or foreign cultures) cannot sustain an outlaw very long. He will be murdered by those who delete sentiment from their business conduct. The true myth of the 20th-century anti-hero is not embodied in the character of Sonny, but in the more rational Michael. Michael understands how to separate feelings from the essential logic of family business and winds up cold-blooded and unflinching, very much like another famous 20th-century movie hero involved in a similar myth, Humphrey Bogart. In the café scene in Sicily, Al Pacino does a brief Bogart imitation with the inflection in his line, "I'm an American, hiding in Sicily."

The final reference to the thunder and screech murder motif comes at the meeting of the five families called by the old Don to end the gangland war. Vito Corleone promises a truce—no more killing—so long as his son Michael can return home to America unharmed and free from any "accidents," such as the bullet of a police officer, a faked jail-cell suicide, or covering all other possible deaths—"if he should be struck by a bolt of lightning." This is an interesting verbal statement of what has been up to now (except for the meeting with Apollonia) a strictly aural motif.

Cars

In the opening wedding scene, the cars parked outside the Corleone residence are scrutinized and the license plate numbers recorded by the FBI (federal police). Sonny and several family members and henchmen rush out to chase the FBI away. They don't succeed. The American automobiles adopted by the Sicilian families work against the family at the beginning of the story. In the undertaker's narrative, his daughter was attacked in a car, reinforcing the initial position of automobiles as hostile American devices. By the end of the film, however, with Michael's take-over, the Corleone family has learned how to use the American policeman and the American automobile to family advantage. In the final baptism/murder scene, one of the Corleone killers dresses like a New York City policeman and motions Barzini's chauffeur to move his illegally parked car. The chauffeur refuses and the fake cop writes out a ticket for the car, taking down its license number. The car doesn't move and awaits Barzini's return. As Barzini approaches, the fake officer pulls out his gun and shoots Barzini. Instantly, a Corleone car pulls up in the foreground and picks up the cop, driving off safely. Michael has had his irony as well as his revenge in this scene.

Cars are a very American symbol in *The Godfather.* It takes the course of the film for cars to become totally integrated with the Corleone purpose. The history and meaning of the automobile in the film parallels the change and integration of Michael as head of the family. Cars are the literal and figurative vehicle for much gangster activity in the film. When Sallozzo kidnaps Tom Hagen he has only to say, "Get in the car, Tom."

The godfather's chauffeur/bodyguard doesn't show up for work the day the godfather is shot. Don Corleone is wounded when he gets out of the car to buy fruit. His inept son Fredo rests unawares on the running board of the auto moments before his father is wounded. Don Corleone falls onto and bleeds onto the car before rolling off and dropping to the street.

When Michael learns about his father's shooting he is walking down the street with his American girlfriend, Kay, who spots the head line in a newspaper and points out the bad news to Michael. As he crosses the street to phone home, one black car intersects his path.

Paulie, the traitorous bodyguard who failed to show up the morning Don Corleone was shot is himself killed in a car while at the wheel. This is an interesting scene on several counts. Paulie picks up Clemenza at his house out in Queens. Clemenza, as will be discussed later, is the character who plays out in microcosm the concerns of the cosmos of the film. He is the successful embodiment of Sicilian and American culture. He recognizes no contradictions in his life and no hypocrisy. He knows how to cook Italian food, knows how to use American weapons, teaches Michael how to shoot and kill, can at once see the usefulness and danger of cars, and is able to say with no irony, "Leave the gun, take the canolis."

As Paulie pulls out of the driveway on their way to the city, Clemenza admonishes him to "watch out for the kids" as he backs up. Meanwhile, he has arranged for Paulie's death to take place later that afternoon. On their return from the city, Clemenza asks Paulie to "Pullover, I gotta take a leak." As Clemenza steps out of the car and walks over to the weeds to relieve himself (a purifying water runs throughout the film) Paulie is shot in the back of the head and slumps over the wheel. The car is abandoned. Clemenza has effectively used it. He has toured the west side for good hiding places, picked up dessert, and disposed of a traitor all in the vehicle.

When Michael wants to go to the city to see Kay and to visit his father in the hospital, Sonny insists that bodyguards drive him. Michael says no, he'll take a cab, but Sonny prevails. Michael sits in the backseat of a black Corleone car as the bodyguards sit in front and drive. The camera pulls back and lets the car drive ahead. It travels down a ramp and into a dark tunnel, just as Michael is travelling deeper into involvement with his family.

At the confrontation outside the hospital, the turning point in Michael's career, police cars arrive from the right side of the screen, Corleone cars from the opposite side. At this point, cars are used by both sides equally well.

In Sicily, Michael refuses to ride with his benefactor, Don Tommasino, preferring to walk to the town of Corleone. The contact with America is through Don Tommasino, a man who needs an auto, a wheelchair, or at least a cane to get around in Sicily (American crutches). Don Tommasino's presence is foreshadowed in the scene where Michael plots the murders that result in his trip to Sicily. In that scene, set in the Corleone house, Sonny enters the frame on the right and inexplicably fondles a walking cane. Like so many significant details in *The Godfather,* this seemingly random action may go unnoticed as a superficial piece of business. Actually it is a carefully planned preview of something to come, another interconnection.

Michael eschews Americanisms as much as he can in his

family and heritage. As he and his two bodyguards walk along the road, jeeploads of American soldiers pass them by. Michael ignores them while his Sicilian translator and bodyguard (and later traitor) tries to hail a ride.

When Michael goes to call on the Vitelli family in an effort to court the Sicilian girl who struck him "like a thunderbolt," he drives there in his car. Next to a true Sicilian, Michael is an American.

Simultaneous with this scene in Italy, back in America Kay arrives at the Corleone residence in a cab. She is very much an outsider in her bright red, square-shouldered outfit and yellow taxi. Kay asks Tom to deliver a letter to Michael and while she is there she asks about a badly damaged car in the driveway. Tom claims it was just an accident in which nobody got hurt. But later in the film brother-in-law Carlo is strangled in a car in the Corleone driveway and in his struggle smashes the windshield very much like this car's windshield is smashed, many scenes preceding.

Santino stops his car at the causeway tollgate and pays for his sentimental rages and for speaking out against the family in front of an outsider by being killed in a flurry of machine gun fire. He dies as he gets out of the car and tumbles to the ground. He would not have been a successful Don.

Back in Sicily, Michael is teaching Apollonia to drive. She is not learning driving or English very well. She cannot be Americanized. Don Tommasino arrives in his car with bad news from America—Sonny is dead. In the next few shots, Apollonia is blown-up in Michael's car by a bomb we suppose is meant for him. She is the wrong wife for the future Don, not adjustable to a working combination of two cultures.

There is an immediate dissolve from Apollonia's burning car-tomb to the cars parked outside the meeting of the five families. Family business goes on and the American automobile becomes an integral, significant tool in that business.

Clemenza's Microcosmos

The character of Clemenza, loyal *capo* of the Corleone family, as stated earlier, successfully incorporates most of the major contradictory themes of the film. Clemenza, a character without irony, is perhaps not smart enough to see the contradictions he epitomizes. For Michael Corleone, the transcendence of the conflicts between his Italian and his American sides is a long and difficult struggle of the personality. For Clemenza, it comes naturally.

Fat Clemenza is introduced in the overture-like wedding sequence as he dances gaily with Mrs. Corleone and the other guests and then turns abruptly aside to ask for wine. "Paulie,

bring more wine. Paulie, more wine," he says as he sweats profusely. As Paulie brings the wine, Clemenza reminds him to do his job—circulate, keep watching for trouble. A family wedding and the possibility of attack are on Clemenza's mind at the same time.

Clemenza is the man Don Corleone recommends to punish the attempted rapists of the undertaker's daughter. Vito Corleone says, "We need someone who won't get carried away." Clemenza's only excesses are his pounds of fat. He has no extra-marital sexual entanglements (like Michael, unlike Sonny). He knows that the family is all-important. He doesn't lose his head.

When Sonny is home with his wife and infant child awaiting news of his seriously wounded father, a loud noise is heard—gunshot? slam of a door? clap of thunder?—the baby screeches and Clemenza appears at the door. He tells Sonny a fact: the word is out on the street that the Don is already dead. Sonny reacts as foolishly as the ancients who killed the messenger bearing bad news. Clemenza calms him and asks how he can help.

Later, at the Corleone house, Clemenza is making Italian dinner for the men while Michael talks to Kay on the telephone. When Michael gets off the phone after not being able to tell Kay he loves her (there were many people around and Clemenza was listening), Michael goes immediately to the sink and pours himself a glass of water. He drinks the water to purify himself from the call and from the ensuing lesson from Clemenza in Italian cooking—excesses on both ends of the scale for Michael. Significantly, Clemenza's secret to the sauce is the addition of wine. Italian wine purifies Clemenza of the reason he is doing all the cooking. The Corleone family, under Sonny's leadership, has begun hitting their enemies and the men of the family are about to go into hiding.

Clemenza tells Sonny at the end of this scene, "Oh Paulie, you won't see him no more." A few scenes earlier we saw Clemenza executing the order to kill Paulie. While Paulie is shot in the head, Clemenza is out of the car purifying himself by "taking a leak." Again, his instructions to the assassin show he knows all the things important to being a successful Mafia man in America, "Leave the gun, take the cannoli."

Besides the cooking lesson, Clemenza is the one who instructs Michael how to murder. A gunshot begins the target practice scene in Clemenza's basement. Behind them are two photos on the wall. One is the Pope and the other is a 1940's pinup girl. Michael makes light of Clemenza's repeated instructions to drop the gun after the killing and walk out of the restaurant. For a brief instant, Clemenza believes that Michael will sit down and finish his dinner at a table with

Michael will sit down and finish his dinner at a table with two corpses, but then he recovers and says, "Don't fool around, kid." Clemenza sees no humor in the act or in the possibility of alternate action. There is only one way to commit a successful murder. As he finishes the shooting lesson Clemenza remarks to Michael how proud the whole family was of his being a war hero. He then makes the comment, as he holds the gun in his hand, "They should have stopped Hitler at Munich. They never should've let him get so far." Again, there is no contradiction for Clemenza between condemning a mass murderer in another country and preparing to murder for the family in the U.S.

In the spectacular baptism scene Clemenza is seen racing up several flights of stairs in order to beat an elevator and be there waiting when the doors open. As he runs up the stairs, he sweats an enormous amount and constantly wipes his brow with a handkerchief. As he reaches the landing, he presses the button for the elevator to stop, the doors open and he shotguns the unsuspecting rival gangsters to death. This act required a great deal of personal purification and the director has once again provided a literal, realistic motivation for the metaphorically necessary water at this point. There is also some comfort in the knowledge that we know this is one of the last violent acts Clemenza will perform for the Corleone family. He has asked to form a family of his own.

The use of a handkerchief to wipe the excess water away is a bit of business used throughout the movie by most of the characters—Sonny (after sex with the girl at the wedding), Luca Brasi (before he attempts to deceive the Tattaglias), Michael (before he murders Sallozzo and McClusky) and by Don Corleone (in the last scene, to compensate for the orange trick). Water compensates for the overly Sicilian act and wine for the excessively American act. The water and the wine are joined significantly in the crucial hospital sequence—the two colors of liquid going into the Don intravenously—and in the final baptismal sequence where both water and blood are made holy.

Baptism

The culmination of the major themes of the film comes with the baptism of Connie Corleone's baby and the reciting of the baptismal vows by the child's godfather, Michael Corleone, the new Don. While Michael has the legitimate alibi of attending his godson's baptism, the murders he has masterminded—of all the heads of the other gangster families—takes place. Church music plays throughout the long sequence, sanctifying both baptism and murder.

As Michael repeats the vows for the child, he is undergoing his own spiritual union into the community not of Christ, but of the underworld. Intercut with his words, said once by the priest and repeated by Michael, are the ingeniously choreographed killings of all the Corleone enemies.

Each enemy of the Corleone family is killed in a way we are prepared for. Moe Green is shot while he gets a massage. When Michael visited Las Vegas to buy out Moe Green's casino, Freddy denies any disagreement between him and Moe by going over to Moe in front of Michael and squeezing Moe several times on the shoulders in a massage-like gesture.

Philip Tattaglia, called a pimp by Don Corleone and by Sonny, is killed in bed with a girl young enough to be his daughter.

The other, less significant heads of families are killed by Clemenza in the rising elevator. They will no longer rise at the expense of the Corleone family.

Barzini, the master enemy, the man really behind Sallozzo and his bodyguard Police Captain McClusky, is killed on the courthouse steps by a man impersonating a police officer. McClusky was not a true police officer in the traditional sense because, as the Corleone family made sure to reveal in the newspapers, he was all mixed up in the rackets. That kind of policeman is a fake and deserves to be killed. And Barzini gets his justice on the courthouse steps from another sort of fake policeman, a Corleone killer dressed like a cop.

The child is baptized with holy water as Michael is baptized by the blood of his victims. The circle is complete, his American and Italian, water and wine elements are integrated into the new godfather.

All that remains are a few loose ends. He must dispose of the traitor Carlo who set-up Sonny to be murdered. In a clever postponing of Carlo's inevitable death, Michael forces him to confess that Barzini was the man who approached him. Carlo steps into the car to be driven to the airport and Clemenza strangles him from the backseat. Almost all the outstanding debts are paid.

But Tessio, the other formerly loyal Corleone *capo*, has tried to set Michael up to be assassinated. Tessio must be dealt with. Instead of being true to the Corleone family, Tessio has sold out to Barzini in what Michael describes as a smart move. But Tessio loses his gamble, realizes the Corleones know, and tells Tom Hagen that Michael shouldn't take it personally. It was only a betrayal for business reasons. Tessio is taken away in a car and killed.

Individual deceits, the first of a lifetime to come, must now be committed by Michael. First he must deny to his sister that he had Carlo killed because it was a necessary move to continue the family business. Carlo would not have been trustworthy since he had betrayed Sonny for personal reasons. Michael lies to his sister and has a doctor sent for to calm her. She will recover.

Now to Kay, Michael tries lighting two cigarettes in an attempt to use his old ploy of outward calmness when he is about to use deceit for the good of the family. Kay may know him too well for this to succeed with her. He must put out the last vestige of a crutch for his behavior. He puts out the cigarette, puts down the lighter and faces her squarely. In another of the film's chillingly beautiful moments, he denies the killing to her. It is a triumphal deceit. She leaves to fix them a drink. Once outside the room, she looks back. The new loyal family members and Clemenza surround Michael. Clemenza kisses the new Don's hand in respect. We hear the title spoken, "Don Corleone." One of the men closes the door, shutting Kay out. The last shot is of her face, the knowledge of her husband's real business is in her face, and then the door closes.

Once more we return to the blackness of the opening titles. The closing credits are in black and white. It's a return to mystery in the underworld and for Michael a full acceptance of the family vs. the society in good and evil terms. The film's director has brought us around magnificently to the resolution of conflicting motifs into a final unity even of colors. The glimpse is over.

Vincent Canby (review date 22 December 1974)

SOURCE: "*The Godfather, Part II:* One Godfather Too Many," in *New York Times,* December 22, 1974, p. D19.

[*In the following review, Canby complains that "Much of the time it's next to impossible to figure out who's doing what to whom* [in The Godfather, Part II], *not, I suspect, because its mode is ambiguity, but because it's been cut and edited in what looks to have been desperation. . . ."*]

If Francis Ford Coppola were a less intelligent and less talented filmmaker, one might indulge the failed aspirations of *The Godfather, Part II*—if not the thick fog of boredom that settles in before the film is even one hour old. Clumsy directors may not be entitled but because their gaffs are not exactly unexpected, they are more easily accommodated. We snicker and laugh at multi-million-dollar dreadfuls like *The Valachi Papers* and *Crazy Joe*. Our good spirits remain intact since there's no particular surprise or sorrow. The earnest confusions of *The Godfather, Part II* are something else again. They look like the solemn attempts to rip-off one of the best, most successful commercial American movies

ever made, Coppola's original screen adaptation of Mario Puzo's *The Godfather.*

Rip-off is an unkind word and, in this case, not really accurate since it implies a willingness to take the easy way, to exploit in the most obvious, cheapest manner an earlier success. Now I hardly think that Coppola, Puzo (who collaborated with him on the new screenplay) and Paramount Pictures did not hope to make a bundle on *Part II,* but it's apparent in the physical scope (New York, Las Vegas, Sicily, the Caribbean), expense and shape of the new film that this was meant to be something more than a sequel, something more than a revisit to a planet of murderous, vengeful apes.

Well it is and it isn't.

It's actually two films cross-cut into each other. The first is the story of young Vito Corleone (who grew up to be the Mafia don played by Marlon Brando in *The Godfather*), from his early days in Sicily when his father was murdered by the Black Hand to his first rather nobly motivated criminal triumphs in New York's Little Italy in 1917. The second is the story of Michael Corleone (Al Pacino), who inherited the Corleone Family control from old Vito at the end of *The Godfather* and here goes on to win a Las Vegas gambling empire, with time out for an aborted attempt to take over the rackets in Cuba just before the Castro revolution.

Part II is as stuffed with material as a Christmas goose. It's a mass (sometimes mess) of plots, subplots, characters, alliances, betrayals, ambushes, renunciations, kisses of death, you name it. Much of the time it's next to impossible to figure out who's doing what to whom, not, I suspect, because its mode is ambiguity, but because it's been cut and edited in what looks to have been desperation, a quality that *Part II* shares with another Coppola film, *The Conversation.*

There are dozens of narratives going on more or less simultaneously in *Part II,* a couple of which give every sign of being material enough for an interesting, self-sustaining individual film if lifted out of this fractured epic. One has to do with the first forays into crime by young Vito, played with a fascinating, reserved passion by Robert De Niro until the shadow of Brando's earlier performance falls over it and turns it into what amounts to an impersonation.

Another promising sequence has to do with Michael's uneasy alliance with a Jewish mob king, Hyman Roth (played by Lee Strasberg, the head of the Actors Studio, in what becomes the dominant performance of the picture), and the efforts of the pair to seize control of Havana with Battista's cooperation.

"We're bigger than U.S. Steel," Hyman says genially to

Michael as they sit sunning themselves on the terrace of a Havana (actually Santo Domingo) hotel. The most chilling moment of the film has nothing to do with mob vengeance, with family betrayals or with virtue corrupted. It is a street scene in Havana when Michael watches impassively as Battista's police round up some revolutionaries, one of whom blows himself up with a hand grenade. You suddenly realize not only how isolated from the real world Michael has become, but also how isolated are the concerns of the rest of the film.

One of the most remarkable qualities of the original *The Godfather* was the manner in which it suggested all sorts of sad truths about American life, business, manners, goals, entirely within a headlong narrative in which character was defined almost entirely in terms of action. The relentless forward motion of the film was as much the content of the film as the gang wars it seemed to be about. The ending was inevitable and tragic.

The cross-cutting in the new film gives it a contemplative air, but the truths it contemplates about fate, family and feuds seem hardly worth all the fuss and time (three hours and 20 minutes).

I've been told that one of Coppola's intentions in *Part II* was to de-romanticize *The Godfather,* which some critics had accused (wrongly, I think) of glorifying crime. At the end of *The Godfather,* Michael Corleone, the once sensitive Ivy League student who has become the new don, is left lonely in his new authority. At the end of *Part II* he is still lonely, though we are asked to believe that he is now a more ruthless, more wracked man who suspects enemies everywhere around him and as easily orders the execution of a brother as he cooperated in the execution of a brother-in-law in the first film. The difference between Michael in the first film and *Part II* is not one of real substance but of degree.

Coppola also seems intent on contrasting the comparatively noble criminality of Michael's father Vito, in his early days in Little Italy, with Michael's use of power for its own sake later on. The idea that old-time criminals were somehow less vicious and venal than today's is, however, as romantic as any notion that turned up in the original film. *Part II* doesn't illuminate or enrich the original film. It simply brackets it with additional information that may not make too much sense unless you've seen the first one.

It also seems to have been written by writers wearing wooly mittens—the dialogue is that clumsy. You get the idea when Kay, Michael's middle-class, WASP wife, admits that what Michael thought was a miscarriage wasn't. "It was an abortion, Michael," says Kay who, though grieving, has a way with words, "just like our marriage is an abortion."

Leonard Quart and Albert Auster (review date 1975)

SOURCE: A review of *Godfather, Part II*, in *Cineaste*, Vol. VI, No. 4, 1975, pp. 38-9.

[*In the following review, Quart and Auster assert that despite operating within the commercial form in* The Godfather, Part II, *Coppola has created "an epic about immigrants which begins to take hold of the whole saga of Americanization and the spiritual dissolution that resulted from it."*]

The Hollywood epic has usually meant Charlton Heston in beard, toga, or armor, spectacular effects and battle sequences, an inflated budget, and an adulteration of history and myth. In fact, Hollywood has rarely even bothered to vulgarize American history and myth, preferring to mine less controversial properties like the Old and New Testaments, the Crusades, and the Greeks and Romans.

There have, of course, been a number of puerile and a few brilliant epic films about the American Experience: *Birth of a Nation, Gone with the Wind* and *Citizen Kane,* to name three of the best. Even in these films, however, with their formal virtuosity, grandeur of conception, and moments of revelation, the historical process is usually romanticized, distorted or personalized—reinforcing our mythology, not illuminating it. *Gone with the Wind* romanticizes slavery, the plantation and the Southern planter; *Birth of a Nation* romanticizes the Ku Klux Klan, is patently racist, and promotes the most stereotypical versions of Reconstruction; and *Citizen Kane* eschews the historical and social for the psychological, aesthetic and expressive. The latest effort in the tradition of epics which seriously try to evoke the American Experience is Francis Ford Coppola's *The Godfather, Part II.* Though possibly less artistically complete than the three above films, *Godfather II* attempts to confront the historical process in a manner the other failed to do.

Godfather II is a sequel to a film whose narrative drive and choreographed violence made it one of the better genre films of recent years. It is colder, more severe, less violent and much more ambitious than the original *The Godfather.* Coppola still operates within a commercial context, often using epic compositions and local color as a substitute for real explanation and exploration. But there is more here than beautiful long shots and interesting lighting; there are moments when the epic and tragic elements are fused and something is revealed about how the dream in America distorted and destroyed immigrants' lives.

It is true that serious objections can and will be raised to the use of the gangster as an archetype of the immigrant experience—especially by those whose success was achieved outside of criminal avenues. Nevertheless, the linking of Horatio Alger and criminality is as old as the epithet "Robber Baron", and the events of the last decades in Southeast Asia, Chile, Watergate, with their plots and laundered bank accounts smack of nothing less and possibly more than the gangster ethos. The gangster and politician may well be the last frontier of the Horatio Alger myth.

Coppola and his co-writer Mario Puzo seek to do more than expose and demythologize the Mafia. They use the character of Michael Corleone (Al Pacino) to dramatize the tragic dilemma that dominates the film. In the traditional epic style (Kane's mysterious "rosebud", Scarlett O'Hara's idyllic Tara), there is a flashback to an idealized moment in Michael's life. He remembers his father's birthday party in 1941 and his decision to break from father and tribe, to go to war and choose his "country over his blood." He has made a commitment to strangers, and left the passionate, amoral, but roughly just world of his father, Don Vito Corleone behind.

In *The Godfather* we see the Don in his old age, a benevolent and moral murderer, mythologized and personalized without a historical setting in which to place him. In *Godfather II* Coppola has provided us with the early years of Don Vito, taking us operatic vendettas of Sicily, to the nostalgic archetypal scenes of emigration and settlement. Here the future Don moves casually from the life of a stoical, taciturn worker to a role of criminality and power. This part of the film is shot by Coppola thru soft-focus lens and in light, golden-toned colors. Images of the Statue of Liberty, Castle Gardens, tenements, music halls, pushcarts, processions and festivals are reproduced, sometimes looking like the photos of Jacob Riis and Lewis Hines.

The detail is rich, vital and aesthetic and Robert De Niro's young Don Vito emanates quiet authority and intelligence, his gravelly voice making a distinct link with Brando's older Don in *The Godfather.* And though the whole immigrant epic of confrontation with an alien world and the tensions of acculturation are left untouched, the traditional codes of honor, obligation, familial responsibility that bound the first Don come alive. It is this strong tribal world that the young Michael seeks to escape, and though he ultimately becomes an integral part of the mob, he ironically sways it in directions which subvert its basic traditions.

He opts for corporate respectability through a partnership with Hyman Roth—who represents only betrayal and death. Roth is beautifully played by Lee Strasberg, him a facade of lower middle class homilies and tastes; obsessive talk about health and an avuncular manner barely hide his murderous calculations and imperial plans. Roth's life, unlike Don Vito's, is devoid of family and friendship—his sole commitment is to making profits. His vision is not of a tribal chieftain who

wishes to sustain and protect his brood while making war with and profit from strangers, but of an ITT executive who desires a Latin American empire and a president of his own choosing in the White House. It's a vision in which flesh and blood don't matter, and all people are mere commodities to be traded, sold and replaced. This world view is shared by a U.S. Senator, Pat Geary (G. D. Spradlin), whose venality and racism are excelled only by his pomposity and hypocrisy. These men make natural partners for Fulgencio Batista, the decadent and corrupt dictator of Cuba whose only ideology is a commitment to a share of the profits of international corporations.

Michael's decision to have the family go "legit in five or six years" is his ultimately futile attempt to bridge the gap between the tribal universe of Don Vito's and the corporate one of Hyman Roth. It is also a way to extend his earlier decision, seemingly undermined by the death of his father, older brother and first wife in *The Godfather,* to make a life in the wider world. Michael's decision is undermined by the world into which he seeks entry. The old Mafia of Don Vito's Genco Olive Oil Company, with its numbers, juke boxes and prostitutes, is nearing its end, to be replaced by a Mafia which is just one more multi-national corporation whose legitimacy is mere appearance. So the old tribal traditions no longer work, but for Coppola their abandonment has only tragic consequences.

The center of Michael's new legitimate empire is a Xanadu upon the shores of Lake Tahoe. The family lives in a beautiful armed fortress, and there Michael tries to bind up its fragments. But the cheerless dancers, the unctuous speeches, and the strains of "Mr. Wonderful" performed at his son's communion are empty echoes of the earthy Tarantella and the bawdy folk songs that opened the wedding sequence in *The Godfather.* There ethnic and family feeling are authentic and intense, as Don Vito accepts warm congratulations, provides advice and metes out justice to friends and relations. The Lake Tahoe celebration is a cold spectacular, acculturated and alienated, with Senator Geary's hypocritical eulogy to Michael serving as a metaphor for the event.

The family has also gone through changes. Michael's sister Connie, in a self-destructive rage towards Michael, has begun to drift from man to man, and has committed the most heinous of sins, neglect of her children. Fredo, Michael's weak, hapless older brother, cannot control his wife, and feels only rage towards Michael for his younger brother's having assumed the role that by rights should be his. He breaks the familial code by conspiring with Roth in an attempt to murder Michael. The tribal world enters jarringly in the person of Frankie Pentangeli (Michael V. Gazzo), an old line Mafia captain, who in melancholy and anger demands a Tarantella at the communion party and the right from

Michael to make war on Roth's New York allies. Pentangeli is crude, feeling, colloquial, loyal; he lives in Don Vito's old house in the Bronx and maintains his roots. He is also a murderer, of course. Coppola doesn't romanticize him, but he makes his presence an implicit judgment on Michael and his way of life.

Coppola continually intercuts the Little Italy of the young Don Vito with the affluent world of Roth and Michael's byzantine plots. Much of the plotting and betraying take place in Cuba at the point of Castro's victory. This provides epic material for Coppola's camera, though he sometimes augments the spectacular with a bit of insight into the decadence and destructiveness of pre-Revolutionary Cuba. He also avoids the taint of reflex anti-communism of movies like *Che.* But though Coppola does wisely recognize the significance of history, the film primarily remains on a pictorial plane—an epic frame for the actions of·the family. It is not the history of immigrants or the Cuban revolution which are prime, it's the family's movement through the two films from simple loyalties and unity to complex relationships and dissolution which are at its heart. For Coppola there is history and there are individuals, but he never quite dramatizes the relationship between them. What he does convey is the rapacity of capitalists without ever getting to the root of capitalism. Thus, he includes scenes where the heads of multi-national corporations, including the Mafioso chieftains, gather to divide up the Cuban spoils, but there is no indication that these capitalists have anything to do with the crisis of Cuban society except to cash in on it. Coppola's and Puzo's historical treatment lacks a certain resonance not aided by repeated references to the metaphor of a declining empire. It's an analysis which might have benefited by more Marx than Gibbon, more historical dialectics and less of a belief in historical inevitability. .

Though Coppola may not have a profound sense of history, he is entirely capable of illuminating the breakdown of the traditional codes and values, and its tragic impact on Michael and the Corleone family. The decline of the family is filmed in dark, chiaroscuro interiors, in sterile affluent rooms where people are often blurred or seen as silhouettes against lighted windows. It is joyless and alienating and its darkness contrasts vividly with the epic light that suffuses Little Italy and the world of the young Don Vito. In the same way, Michael's ghostly, affectless and near dead countenance contrasts sharply with the quiet grace and warmth of the young Don Vito. Coppola is truly gifted at eliciting the striking image and metaphor.

Coppola, in a profound understanding of the code's decline, comprehends that it doesn't just disappear—there are aspects of it that continue to live, though in adulterated and distorted ways. In what seems like one last gesture for the old ways, Frankie Pentangeli's testimony before a senate

crime committee is stilled by invoking the code of silence (*omerta*). Frankie also commits suicide, following the old imperial tradition of defeated tribal chiefs. But he is an anachronism, and it is Fredo's betrayal of brother Michael, Kay's abortion and her and Michael's separation which are more characteristic of the new world. Kay is a WASP outsider who belongs to the non-racket past of the Michael of *The Godfather.* Coppola doesn't do much with Kay except use her to illustrate Michael's double-edged relationship to the tradition. When learning that she's aborted his expected child, Michael literally closes the door on her, as he had done in a different situation at the end of *The Godfather.* She has transgressed the most sacred and fundamental familial and machismo codes—a clear sign of the family dissolution. It is ironic, though, that Michael's connection to this aspect of the code seems ritualistic rather than deeply felt. He obviously wants a son and believes in the sacredness of the family, but it's an abstract ideal for him; he never demonstrates the feeling for his children which the young and old Don Vito radiate and bask in. In fact, it's Fredo who acts as surrogate father for Michael's unhappy son, Anthony.

The death of Michael's loving but submerged mother severs the last link to the Corleone tradition. And even her haunting but ineffectual affirmation of the code, "you can never lose your family", can only be viewed ironically. The family lies in fragments and even the loyal stepbrother and consigliore, Tom Hagen (Robert Duvall), is baited by Michael, and seems to want out of the whole operation. Michael's alienation is only accentuated by his senseless vendetta against already weakened enemies like Fredo, Roth and Pentangeli—adhering to the forms of the code while losing its substance. Coppola views the violence with a more critical eye than on previous occasions. It's more detached and impersonal than the stern justice that Don Vito deals to personal enemies like Don Fanucci and Don Ciccio, or even the politically meaningful slaughter of the five families at the end of *The Godfather.* Still, one sometimes feels that Coppola's demystification of the Mafia doesn't go far enough, that the young Don Vito is viewed in too heroic a mold, and that the virtues of the tribal Mafia of De Niro (young Don Vito) and Brando (old Don Vito) absolve it from judgment, and that for Coppola their sense of roots and familial feeling make their criminality less vicious.

But Michael is another story and—like Welles' Kane, dying alone in his vacant baroque palace or, like Scarlett, setting off alone to Tara—Coppola's last shot is of Michael sitting in somber isolation, tragically contemplating his empire. Why is Michael as alienated as he is? Is the tragedy based on his being forced into his father's world without ever having a choice—as is implied by the final flashback at the end? Is it the breaking from his father's tradition, and its consequences which brings on the tragic mask? Coppola never does say. Michael's alienation and emotional deadness are apparent throughout *The Godfather* as well as here, but never subjected to real analysis. Coppola's strength as a director is not psychological revelation or personal intimacy. It's the pictorial and metaphoric, the strong narrative and the ambitious conception which distinguish his work.

Coppola has worked through the conventions of the crime genre movie to make an epic film about America. The film has its violence, shootouts and murders, but it also comes close to capturing part of America's tragedy and nightmare—one which goes far beyond the parochial world of the Mafia.

From *The Godfather* through *The Godfather, Part II,* the Corleones, like most immigrants to America, experienced the transformation of the claustrophobic and sometimes destructive love and loyalty of family and tribe into a fragmented, rootless and materially comfortable form of the capitalist success story. For Coppola to have gone further—to have looked more deeply into the structure of capitalism and its ethos—would have been to risk commercial failure.

But what Coppola has done is weighty and grand. He has made a visually beautiful film, containing strong, distinctive performances by De Niro and Pacino, while operating within a commercial form. And he has taken a giant step from the more accessible, coherent and action-filled *The Godfather,* to create an epic about immigrants which begins to take hold of the whole saga of Americanization and the spiritual dissolution that resulted from it.

Carlos Clarens (review date January-February 1978)

SOURCE: "The Godfather Saga," in *Film Comment,* Vol. 14, No. 1, January-February, 1978, pp. 21-3.

[*In the following review, Clarens asserts that Coppola's* The Godfather *epic does not translate well to television, and complains that the film's restructuring does not add much to the film, except in its early sequences.*]

Long before the success of *Roots* in January, 1977, Francis Ford Coppola had envisioned combining the two parts of *The Godfather* into one seven-hour film for theatrical release. Few directors have been that ambitious, and none from Hollywood. Their work is mainly to be seen in art houses and colleges all over the nation: Mark Donskoi, and the Gorky trilogy; the three films based on the Marcel Pagnol plays, *Fanny, Marius,* and *Cesar,* and Satyajit Ray's three-part Story of Apu. But the sudden popularity of the novelistic form on television, as attested by *Rich Man Poor Man, Captain and the Kings,* and the British *Upstairs Downstairs*

series made it a natural for the TV audience. NBC paid Paramount and American Zoetrope, Coppola's company, a reputed $12 million for both pictures; then Barry Malkin, a friend and ex-classmate of Coppola's, re-edited both films, plus some cutting-room-floor footage, into the shape of a dynastic novel—a dance to the music of violent times in which the one unchanging partner is Death.

Let it be remembered for the record that any hint of ethnicity had disappeared from Hollywood crime movies since the early Thirties, right after *Scarface* and the vigorous campaign of the Sons of Italy in America. Only averted moviegoers could be sensitive to the modified discrimination that took over the screen. With the pressure groups putting on the pressure, Hollywood retreated further into a flavorless no-man's land where the melting pot had overcooked. Films dealing with Italian gangsters can be counted with the fingers of Mickey Mouse's glove. Prior to *The Godfather* there were *The Black Hand* (1950), *Pay or Die* (1961), and *The Brotherhood* (1968). The one claim to fame in director Richard Thorpe's long career, *The Black Hand* starred Gene Kelly as a fictional Italo-American who destroys the hold of the Black Hand criminal society on Little Italy around the turn of the century; there is a real, ancestral dread of betrayal buried beneath the MGM all-is-well complacency. Richard Wilson's *Pay or Die* told the same basic story, with Ernest Borgnine enacting the historical role of a New York detective who laid down his life in the service of his fellow Italo-Americans. *The Brotherhood* pitted small-time racketeers against the big honchos of crime, and it starred Kirk Douglas and Alex Cord as Italian brothers-in-crime; the director was Martin Ritt. Three films in nearly forty years, if we exclude Raoul Walsh's *The Enforcer* (1950) and Stuart Rosenberg's *Murder Inc.* (1960) which played down the ethnic element. Enter Francis Coppola in 1971, with the courage of his convictions and a best-seller in his hands.

There were cuts to be made when the Corleones came to TV. Luca Brasi is pinned down to a bar counter with an ice-pick prior to being garroted; but we don't see the hand being stabbed, which renders the scene unlikely. A U.S. senator is caught *in flagrante delicto* with a dead prostitute; but we get only a late, momentary glimpse of the blood-drenched woman, which makes the scene unintelligible. Still, it's a wonder that so much violence remained (I had just seen *The Wild Bunch* mutilated on the tube beyond sense or continuity), and, to compensate for lost footage, many a scene cut for the final release print was weaved back into the narrative. Since the film's structure was episodic to begin with, this posed no technical problem; inserts could be accommodated without the film's losing its continuity. The time element, however, was altered whenever contiguous scenes were separated by new footage.

The new footage works best in the first televised segment

which carries Vito Andolini (later Corleone) from 1901 to the mid-Twenties; it provides enriching footnotes to a chapter told perhaps too succinctly in the theatrical release version. In Sicily, two gunmen in the service of Don Ciccio, the rich landowner who has the town of Corleone in his grasp, come to the Andolini home and ask for the child, Vito; his mother tells them she'll bring him in herself. Years later, already a grown man in Little Italy, Vito watches two street kids attacking Don Fanucci (Gastone Moschin) and slashing his throat; Vito (Robert DeNiro) recoils into a shadowy doorstep to avoid any intervention, as Fanucci collects his own blood in his hat so as not to stain his impeccable white suit, a brilliant illustration of a paragraph in Puzo's original. Vito's home life in New York is enriched with a few short scenes. The tooth-for-a-tooth character of the grown man is conveyed in the return to his homeland as a rich, influential merchant. In the release version, Vito knifes the now-decrepit Don Ciccio; on television he also executes his aging underlings.

DeNiro gains the most from the additions, if only because he operates within the flashback-to-the-roots principle on which the saga thrives. But also in this segment is a personal gesture of the film director to establish his own position in the genealogy of the Corleones. In New York, an ex-gunsmith in the Italian army fashions a gun for young Vito, while the gunsmith's small son, named Carmine, plays the flute in a dimly-lit backroom. The child, we are to assume, is Coppola's father, Carmine, who scored the music for *The Godfather, Part II.* It's a charming novelistic device that later will parallel Michael Corleone's reminiscence of his own family; it suggests an atavistic memory, a continuity that doesn't depend on actual experience. It's also boldly carried over in the structure of *Part II.* Whose flashbacks are we witnessing when Michael Corleone (Al Pacino), born 1921, reminisces about the turn of the century? The director's, of course.

Afterward, the added footage doesn't really contribute much that is important to the saga, and the strict chronology of events even diminishes some of the power of *Part I.* In the novel as in the original screenplay, Puzo and Coppola set up the almost demi-urgical aura of Vito Corleone (now played by Marlon Brando) with the Hollywood episode dealing with Jack Woltz (John Marley). Don Corleone demonstrates his power to penetrate the fief of someone as powerful as himself, and play an almost impossible (and impossibly bloody) trick on the man. The grotesque physique that Brando adopted—somewhere between the mask of grief and the traits of an acromegalic: can this be the same character played earlier by Robert DeNiro as a limpid-eyed Bronzino?—and his restraint of voice and gesture function better when the omniscience of Don Corleone has been established. On television, with DeNiro lingering in the mind, we respond much more to the character's humanity.

What becomes a legend most? Not television, for certain. Film passes more quickly through the tube than through the gate of a projector, and concentration suffers from the familiar surroundings; some strategies are therefore exposed a bit nakedly. In *Part I,* Coppola was following Puzo's best-selling text; in *Part II* he is largely on his own, if one excepts the Sicilian and Little Italy flashbacks (which are less important to Puzo). But whatever seemed to work in the first is repeated almost identically in the second. This calculated arrangement of episodes that recall each other has been disturbed by the new format. There were precise correspondences: Woltz has to be taught a lesson in humility (*Part I*) and so does the arrogant WASP senator (*Part II*); both men are guilty of kinky sexual tastes ("*Infamia!*", exclaims the Godfather, a family man, upon hearing that Woltz keeps a child star in his home for sexual purposes); both lessons are bitterly learned in blood-soaked beds. Luca Brasi's garroting in a bar rates an encore with Pentangeli in the sequel. The traitor Fabrizio, responsible for the killing of Michael's first wife, dies in exactly the same manner, as his car blows up. (It seems an alternate death for Fabrizio was shot—at the hands of Michael himself in his own Buffalo store—but it was discarded in favor of another mirror image.) Family events like weddings and christenings introduce relationships between the Corleones and the larger "family." And, as in films directed by Chabrol and Bertolucci, communal eating and dancing define tribal customs here. The massacre that seals Michael's takeover is repeated at the end of the saga, both versions, in the cross-cut disposal of brother, associate, and enemy.

It's one of the surprises of the season that *The Godfather* on television failed to live up to expectations. The series were billed as The Complete Novel for Television, but even with a carefully worded foreword to the effect "it does not represent any ethnic group" and that it was "a fictional account of a small group of criminals," much of the TV audience hesitated before inviting the Corleones to spend a long weekend in their living-room. *The Godfather* is hardly *Roots,* nor is it *Rich Man Poor Man.*

The Godfather, especially as televised, was something of a downer. It chronicled the moral deterioration of a family, the loss of a tradition, the death of the dream; and it accomplishes all this through the metaphor of the criminal organization. Each age has its pleasures, its style of wit, and its own ways of killing (with apologies to Boileau), but even within Mafia generations there is a downward graph. When young Vito Corleone commits his first murder, the killing of Fanucci takes on the aspect of ritual blood-spilling, down to the *coup de grace.* Vito is dispensing retribution; Michael, his son, will dispense merely death. In the larger sense which the picture strives for—Coppola fashioning a lyrical poem from Puzo's one sentence about the boy Vito arriving in America—the romance of immigration hardens into a power play behind lowered blinds, and the mystical francmasonry of crime deteriorates into utilitarian carnage.

The ending of *The Godfather* tries for the desolate grandeur of *Richard the Third;* alas, without the benefit of a few exalting speeches, it comes across differently. What can a man gain in saving his soul if he loses his power? And Al Pacino's not-so-gradual transformation into a lizard is so opaque a performance that it calls for, at the very least, some of the Sam Shepherd bravura vested on a similar case, in the play *Angel City.*

Viewers could play the guessing game after watching *The Godfather* on the tube—a game that Puzo eschewed in the novel by having a factual background and naming names like Maranzano, Anastasia, and Lucchese, which reverberate in the mind like pistol shots. The one real gangster actually named in all seven hours of *The Godfather* is not an Italian, but the legendary Arnold Rothstein. Bugsy Siegel is given the pseudonym of Moe Green, Meyer Lansky that of Hyman Roth. (Yes, Shirl, there is a Jewish mafia, so why isn't Hadassa picketing?) Coppola must have reasoned that to allow the outside world, the honest world which must exist for contrast, to take on any relief would have imperiled his airtight universe. There is a terrifying, unforgettable scene in *The Roaring Twenties,* the gangster film directed by Raoul Walsh in 1939, where a couple of innocent bystanders are hopelessly caught between warring factions in a restaurant. There are no innocent bystanders in *The Godfather*—no bystanders period.

The one character who could possibly fulfill the function gives Coppola the worst trouble: Michael's second wife, Kay, who's a New Englander. A film about a society where women are subservient need not follow suit in the dramatic sense. Kay could have given us an insight, as a surrogate of the outside, non-criminal, non-Italian world; instead she is made to nag, to act dumb, to have an abortion, which is nothing but legalized sin. But worst of all, she is a wraith, and Diane Keaton's performance cannot be blamed on anyone; there *is* no performance when each shot seems to cancel the preceding.

Since the Syndicate has gone legit in so many activities, most of the drama is played nowadays in conference rooms and courtrooms; and it doesn't play too well. The congressional hearing is the least dramatic sequence in *The Godfather,* also the only one where you'll hear the word *mafia* on the soundtrack, uttered by a dopey chairman who's no match for Michael's guile. So *Part II,* if only for the sake of drama, was forced to go after bigger fish abroad. To show that entire nations can be corrupted and that crime can be organized on an international scale, Coppola takes Michael Corleone to Havana and sits him at Batista's table next to the ITT imperialists so that the American mafioso can scoop

Herbert Mathews in forecasting the fall of the regime and pull out stakes. Since the Cuba sequences were photographed in the Dominican Republic, where Gulf + Western has vast holdings, and since Paramount backed both *Godfathers*, is one to infer that Coppola is pursuing his metaphor into the actual making of the film?

In 1972, *The Godfather* became more than a box-office hit; it became a syndrome, an ethnic rallying point, a source of imitation, here and especially abroad. (Francesco Rosi's *Lucky Luciano,* 1973, was a Left-wing riposte to *The Godfather:* it showed *mafiosi* manipulated by the system, both victims and executioners.) There was an upsurge of mafioso pride with a made-to-order gang war, followed by a refocusing of attention from the part of crime commissions, which made it all a mixed blessing for the mafia. It's always risky to try to account for any one movie's popularity, at least until a certain time of reflection has elapsed and we can see the past in sharp detail. Can we honestly believe that America was in the throes of a Catholic revival when *The Sound of Music* topped the charts in 1965? Or that we were afraid of flying when *Airport* became the box-office hit of 1970?

The temptation to indulge in instant sociology is irresistible. In 1972 we were all looking for alternate systems; it was the height of the Nixon administration; in 1974, New York audiences cheered when Michael Corleone slammed the door on Kay's questioning face near the end of *Part II.* In all her feeble inadequacy, Kay represented doubt and lack of acceptance: she was out of place in the world of the Godfather, where blind allegiance was the price to pay for having our problems solved. There are, in fact, no scenes (other than a family-picture scene) between Brando and Keaton.

But most of us in the audience responded to Don Corleone, consciously or no. If we ever came to him with a real problem or an imagined slight he would right things for us; we'd be in good hands, face to face; and our case would not be lost in the intricacies of the system. America was getting too complicated and, who knows, such a father figure could even take on Con Edison single-handed! In the pages of *The New York Review of Books* (where some of our most rational fears materialize), Luigi Barzini fears that the New World hungers after myth and transcendence, and fashions it from our shoddiest weaknesses.

David Thompson (essay date Spring 1978)

SOURCE: "The Discreet Charm of *The Godfather,*" in *Sight and Sound,* Vol. 47, No. 2, Spring, 1978, pp. 76-80.

[*In the following essay, Thompson asserts, "The Godfather*

is so weighed down with the wish to be classy, dramatically precise and socially significant, that it is empty of creative passion."]

How does one convey outrage these days without sounding pedantic or shrill? We have bypassed that tone in the effort to elevate films with goodwill. The role of active dislike is nearly in abeyance. At any event, this is a discriminating attack, and I will be as calm as possible with it, even if outrage is upsetting. But to talk about movies is a matter of considering life.

The public is a pill able to reject any germination. Its members regularly perish, but the body maintains its stumbling, life-like progress. The crowd has had to cultivate an impassivity greater than the dismay of its individuals. We absorb trash, the humdrum and masterpieces with sturdy indifference: the critical labels are no more penetrating than the warnings on cigarette packets. TV, the medium that reaches so many more people in a common instant, mocks connections. It has suppressed the individual with its ratings. It has cancelled the prospect of works of the imagination enriching the masses. We know now that the process merely impacts us, dissolving the strenuous duties of personality and responsibility.

The wonderful and the abominable have collapsed together in mutual resemblance. They measure our time and permit the buying of time that sustains TV, a medium in which the chance of enlightenment has passed beyond the disappointment of half-baked information and dispiriting entertainment to become a household monotone, switched on like a light. TV is a domestic service, a distraction from concentration, solitude and company. It removes burdens we hardly recall: to be troubled or pleased, to be ourselves.

I am trying to deal with *The Godfather.* It is no longer necessary to specify which of the two parts. TV has amalgamated them, just as it does the volumes of *The Forsyte Saga,* the tableaux of *Civilization* and its own daily ingredients— news, drama, comedy, sport, movie, commercial—until they are all chiefly things seen on the box, different complexions of the screen's haze. TV is a liquid in which the sediment of cell life is in perpetual motion, tormenting earlier cultural expectations, such as narrative, understanding and moral sensibility.

I am talking about the two films made by Francis Ford Coppola, which seemed to me on the larger screen a landmark of personal work emerging from the industrial context. *Part I* had everything except the Buñuel who might have intertwined baptism and gangland *coup d'état* with barbed-wire ribbons. Coppola regarded that compromise with a pained, straight-faced acceptance which now seems fundamental to the entire work. Perhaps he hoped that his inabil-

ity to take a stance at the end would be read as irony or ambiguity; perhaps he never realised his own predicament. For all his sophistication, there is something guileless in the work and glib pleasure at the smooth machinery of slaughtering rivals intercut with the baptism liturgy. Francis enjoys the sardonic timing as much as Michael does, and may be as unable to see the human consequences that it veils.

Still, *The Godfather* had the apparent virtue of the best American films: it did not cheat its own compulsive melodramatic energy. Paramount required a wholehearted climax, and Coppola's straight face was too intent on mechanics to handle disintegration. Coppola is misled by expressive perfection; he thinks it alters or places the human situation being treated. The American movie has never dealt with doubt, without the nullifying excuse of self-pity or madness. Its dramas work like trustworthy engines: the gravest flaw of *Citizen Kane* is that Welles cannot abandon his immature satisfaction with neatness—everything fits, works and hums. The director has fallen for Kane's debilitating ambition: to have the people think the way he tells them to think. American heroes are as convinced as scripts, schedules and release patterns imply. They accomplish and achieve; even the alienated, dying Kane initiates an elegant riddle.

Just as Michael Corleone ended that first part secure, so Coppola had a brimming hit. I doubt if anyone in America, let alone Hollywood, hated or disapproved of him—that is a measure of his negligible risk; it also reflects the sweet poison of the product. In its brief time, *The Godfather* was the biggest grosser ever, and that easily overlooked the grossness of its own pusillanimous ending. *The Godfather* was filled with a kind of superficial dynamism that *Kane* first identified, and which has been the beacon for the intelligent pic trade ever since: it is sensational narrative powered by the hush and detail of gravity and consequence that are never explored because the show must go on.

It is the rhetoric of marketable impact, and it is like a good aircraft, the manufacture of the atom bomb, aerosol deodorants or guaranteed pills. Such things teach our senses inertia (it is necessary to be very cool to fly in a 747 without frenzies of delight or fear, and pills take risk away from actions that ought to be felt as perilous). Such toys and conveniences have a cute efficiency, as detached from any creative personality as *The Godfather.* Of course, cameras must be included among these glamorous, dead machines, so that it is not surprising if the camera's product suffers from the same lustrous suppression of vitality.

From a full-page ad in *The New York Times,* November 11, 1977—Pacino's blank saint's face and the massive headline: 'The Godfather as you've never seen it!': 'Starting tomorrow—and continuing for the next three nights—NBC will broadcast one of the major presentations of this or any season. It is called "Mario Puzo's The Godfather: The Complete Novel for Television". For the first time viewers will have the opportunity to see the Godfather story told in chronological order. The keynote of the nine-hour presentation will be the first television showing of **The Godfather, Part II** plus important film never-before-seen on any screen! . . . The entire production has been personally—and masterfully—reshaped for television by the man who directed . . . both **Godfather** movies, Francis Ford Coppola. He has been able in this new form to achieve a sense of continuity and scope that simply could not be realised in a theatrical presentation.'

Then, in far smaller type, at the foot of the page, this grim waiver couched as solicitude: 'PARENTAL DISCRETION ADVISED'. Has anyone adding the phrase ever wondered about the actual processes comprising parental judgment? Does anything else in TV help nourish it? Or is it simply the slick escape of the medium from the implications of offence and distress, as opposed to the reckless envy that will go out and buy? Did anyone pause to reflect how far **The Godfather** is a devout study of the efficacy of cruel parental discretion? Or is the skirting of real parental care only part of the pessimism that supports the inhumane patriarchy of **The Godfather**?

The network hype has the language of critical judgment, no matter how inflated, but parental discretion so advised is the cowardly side-stepping of any fixed attitudes towards TV's own materials, part of the irresponsible orthodoxy: 'We just carry these programmes . . . you can always turn off . . . the views expressed in this programme are those of the contributors, not the station.' 'Parental discretion' is usually invoked to excuse acts of violence, sexual passages and what is called profane language. No one ever advises it in the total matter of watching TV or not, or of submitting to the systematic fragmentation of all programmes, with the aromatic, expansive glue of commercials: **The Godfather,** say, interrupted and sticky with the unambiguous lyricism of pizza, spaghetti sauce, tomato paste and olive oil—the staples that made a legitimate business for the Corleone family. Perhaps they also perfected a competitively priced paste that could be sold to the movies for a trouble-free and non-cancer-causing blood?

Francis Ford Coppola is an American success story. Everyone loved him for his very rapid transit from film school. Corman quickies and off-the-cuff nudies to the prestige, epic panorama and box-office green ones of **The Godfather.** It was tactful of him to fill that jumbo sandwich with the poised paranoia of so 'difficult' and 'unconventional' a film as **The Conversation,** in which blood gushes back from the toilet in a traumatic plumbing malfunction. As he finished **Godfather II,** Coppola spoke to *Film Comment.* It is a statement of dreamy contentment, decorated with all the ways of stick-

ing kindly arrows in Jack Clayton's fudging of Coppola's script for **Gatsby**—which is easy to credit, even if so many fond mentions of Clayton and humble deprecations of how little a writer does smack of a mafia kiss.

But in that interview Coppola rejoiced in the big bucks of **Part I,** the freedom he had won for **Part II** and the limitless vistas that confronted the movie world's new Don: 'I'm not *that* rich, but I'm gettin'. I had to go through a lot of agonising decisions because I can always say why don't I just go and make money. I could sit down and write the most commercial movie ever made. I feel I could pull it off. Just make a hundred million dollars and spend the rest of my life . . . I'm now thirty-five and that's what I thought I was doing with **The Godfather** and then with **Godfather II,** I was making a film that would also appeal to an audience. At some time you've got to cut off and say, "O.K. I've made enough money."'

By 1976 Coppola was no longer so relaxed. The project that he eventually moved on to, **Apocalypse Now,** was proving as much of a white man's grave as its subject, the Vietnam war. Immense difficulties of scripting, casting, finding locations and military assistance and of violent weather were hindering the picture. *Apocalypse When?* it has been called in the past year, during which George Lucas and Steven Spielberg slipped past Coppola in the championship for best bankable movie-maker. Way behind schedule, the picture will not open now until the autumn of 1978, and only then if Coppola can fashion something commercially coherent out of 1.5 million feet of film. Perhaps it will prove as glib and catchy as *Star Wars,* but it may be a Xanadu—sprawling, untidy and housing a monstrous study of human nature too awkward to swallow. That might turn Coppola into something more than a smart student; nothing as yet indicates that he knows the feelings of loss or failure.

Whatever that outcome, it was in the time of **Apocalypse** that Coppola was called on—personally and masterfully— to reshape **The Godfather** for TV. It was the first time that a director had an opportunity to reassess a released film. **Part I** was televised in 1974, to the largest audience ever for a movie—since surpassed by *Gone With the Wind.* NBC and Paramount immediately worked out a financial deal (reportedly $15 million) for an eventual amalgamation of both parts that used a chronological format, 'laundered' the violence and language and restored some footage cut from the theatrical release versions.

By the time the work came to be done, Coppola was marooned in the Philippines, so that no one can or will say how 'personally' he worked on the TV **Godfather.** Still, who could doubt that this unique opportunity would have appealed to him? No American director could be blasé about the size of the audience, the thrill of national unity—as tempting to film-makers as to presidents—the chronological clarification and, perhaps best of all, the originality of a venture for a man tempted by the trend-setting lead as young entrepreneur of ideas and imagination. Coppola's editor, Barry Malkin, made an assembly of all the possible material, some of which had to be retrieved from the Paramount vaults. In three months, Malkin compiled a 9 ½-hour version. This was put on videotape so that Coppola could examine and approve it from the jungle.

Much more had still to be done: two hours were cut from Malkin's assembly, and the whole had to be broken into well-formed episodes that would fit the four-night showing. Great care was taken to anticipate the commercial breaks so that they would do the least damage to a structure of self-contained acts. The two men used telephone and telex, and they met on several occasions. In addition, they had to find a framework for all four nights—an aura for the Godfather Show—that would bind the series. (It is in the nature of such series that they describe events in which the centre does hold and neither ideas nor principles fall apart—again, the commercial glue acts as DNA.) The TV version testified to the ingenuity and thoroughness of the work, even if Malkin did most of it under Coppola's distracted guidance. By March 1977, 'a version edited to our ideas' was put before NBC.

And so it rolled, stopping and starting, on the nights 12-15 November, in three 2-hour episodes and a 3-hour conclusion. What can be said about it in the way of regular criticism, as opposed to this diatribe rigmarole?

NOTES

1. There was an air of well-being in the land. The press admired the emphatic coherence of its new form. Ordinary viewers congratulated one another on having seen it. The ratings were good, if not colossal. It was an event as widely appreciated as *Roots,* the running of *Gone With the Wind, Star Wars* or the live coverage of any celebrity's funeral.

2. Only a fool would confirm the extra 'continuity and scope' of the TV version, yet hardly anyone complained at, or seemed to notice, the wearying shortcomings in those very areas. Chronological sequence on TV was obtained at the cost of having to see 6 ½—7 hours of film over a span of 75 hours with some thirty interruptions in the film-stream for commercials, introductions and wrap-ups. Of course, no one debated the innate merit of chronology as a structure. The theatrical tension of two distinct approaches to the family, the second framing and reflecting on the first, was mutely sacrificed. Yet again the orthodoxy was heeded that films should have a beginning, a middle and an end, in that order. Eighty years old, the American movie is as pledged as ever to the naturalness of story as a way of taming time and alleviating the critical interpretation of history. What does

that do to even apocalypse if there is a beginning, a middle, an end, and a rating, for the end? The screen size (on average) was reduced from about 240 square feet to 1 ½ square feet. An electronic patterning of lines was substituted for Gordon Willis' photography, and the film's haunting contrast of interior gloom and exterior sunshine was more than a TV set could accommodate. By turns, the movie was glaring or obscure; throughout, it was stippled and miniature—a film on a dusty horizon. This was scarcely remarked on: one might reasonably conclude that TV is not watched. It is endured or countenanced, like a climatic medium.

3. The devices used to bind the film were very revealing. There were persistent voice-overs that the film should not be interpreted as a slur upon Italians. On the first night, Talia Shire, Coppola's and Michael Corleone's sister, appeared on camera—reportedly Coppola himself had declined this chore—to say that it would be 'grossly unfair' to let the Corleones represent all Italians. (It would have been wittier if the real, hardworking and conscientious mafia had been cleared, too.) Titles also announced that, despite bloodiness and the ostensibly favourable portrait of the gangsters, this was actually a study of 'the self-destructive effects of crime and violence.' The film was framed every night with a tragically composed close-up of the brooding Michael Corleone, sitting by the ruffled lake where his last brother had been executed, looking into the past and embodying the lonely travails of presidential retreat—Sunset at Lake Tahoe? The TV film was shaped as Michael's testament, the family history seen through his eyes. No matter the listless decadence of Pacino's presence, it became the tragedy of a man who had become malignant trying to preserve his royal line. Every execution and betrayal is justified by his Nixonian urge to keep the thing together. We now expect and trust an Attila of principles, if he struggles with change, breakdown and the indistinct anxieties of our paranoia.

4. The amalgamated work is a saddened but respectful portrait of Michael. It is dark proof of the attractiveness of the villain in the American movie, so long as he is photographed in repose, seen to think before he destroys, and so long as sincerity persuades him to trample on principle. On TV, this was accentuated by the small screen finding close-ups in what once were fuller, theatrical compositions; where sheer space or another person competed with Michael's head; the TV image closed in on his pensive face. When Michael assures Kay that he did not know, we respond to the necessary damage our hero has had to do to honour and himself for the good reason that the film respects poker-faced deceit and is anchored in Michael's insolent look. It never mocks him—there is no humour anywhere in the film—it only shows him. And whatever such balanced film-making shows it implicitly glorifies. That is why Coppola asserts that he has analysed wickedness while the audience of *The Godfather* has aspired to its inner basis of noble sacrifice. The public watches in a spirit of wanting to belong to this fam-

ily, wanting to share its heroic purpose and its embattled unity.

If Coppola sought irony, it has been smothered by the romanticism of the American movie: unflawed melodramatic progress and undimmed glamour bestowed on the people. Together, they promote our dominant response: identification, not any sort of detachment. None of the characters has the all-round raggedness of people in Renoir or Rossellini films, for they are all slyly turned towards us for inspection—they have only that one facet. They are sensibilities aware of being seen, and calculating the effect they make upon the spectator. It is a film tradition flanked by politicians and the grinding charm of people in commercials. The politician has been taught by the American movie, and there is a natural association between *The Godfather* and recent political manners in America. Michael is a grasping vote-seeker; he campaigns with people, instead of mixing with them. Business, the family, stability and development are discreet cloaks for his one ambition: maintained authority.

5. Al Pacino devours the opportunities offered by the role of Michael and makes him the most baleful, depleted father-figure in American pictures. Nevertheless, the figure outweighs the drabness of the man. There has never been a study of such reticent iniquity, and no clearer proof of the way presentational style disarms any intention in the characterisation. Perhaps Coppola deplores and fears Michael, but he cannot find a way of communicating that. The process of showing and seeing a central character, without ridicule, passion or dangerous critical rebuke, is insurmountable. Michael is Satan, but he impresses as a wounded angel; the self-destructive criminality turns into the self-abuse of a lapsed saint. The film is inspired by Michael's self-pity.

Let me mention two things in Pacino's performance, one a moment, the other a motif that lasts three hours. When Michael arrives at the hospital to visit his father he finds the police guards gone. He smells a plot, and with the timid baker, Enzio, he mounts guard on the hospital steps to warn off the coming assassins. A black car loiters and then drives away in frustration. Enzio's nerves are in tatters and he fumbles a cigarette into his mouth. Michael's own steady hand lights it for him. The new-found Medici, revealed by ordeal, notices his own calm with a faraway satisfaction that promises the most cold-blooded of the Corleones. He mentions his nervelessness to no one else in the picture, but we see it: it is one of those privileged moments of communion between a lonely character and the anonymous crowd—as when Kane whispers his enticing clue, knowing that there is a link between our attention and curiosity and his hope to explain himself.

Moments later, the fragile Pacino is beaten by Sterling

Hayden's crooked cop (a character of nearly amiable viciousness who is made so much more hateful and coarse than Michael's shy Iago). Michael's face swells immediately and a dark bruising stays there for months. Equally, Pacino's childlike speech lisps all the more with the intimation of a broken face, and his fretting hands are often up to guard or cushion it. The bruising never fades. It spreads through the whole face, like the fatigue of someone too suspicious to sleep. The moment of establishing himself also sets off the gradual degradation of his character: as a creative design it is brilliant, but not enough to rise above the passive, beseeching pain that Pacino projects. Even at the end he is a morbidly sentimentalised version of the pathetic waif Vito who came to America with a shipload of immigrants.

6. There is an undeniable pleasure with the TV version in collecting those moments reclaimed from the out-takes. Our family loyalty treasures every incident in the scrapbook: the discovery that the young Hyman Roth was once employed by Vito Corleone; a glimpse of that girl, ruined by Johnny Fontane, and cherished by the movie mogul; vengeance on the Sicilian guard who caused the death of Apollonia; a moment when Michael and his guards stop during their Sicilian ramble, and the guards beg him to tell them stories about America; Frankie Pentangeli remembering the old ways at the first communion of Michael's son, and surreptitiously teaching the boy to drink wine; and Kay and Michael in bed together when Michael might have been with the family. This last detail lays the subtlest hint of his guilt being associated with Kay. She will be his wife, and the instrument he uses to provide a dynasty, but she presents a challenge to his single-minded family loyalty. She is the only outsider in the film not treated with contempt, killed or ignored—and it is a very perilous status.

7. She is also the figure around whom a greater film might have been made; she is the only person who questions the Corleone ethics and who stands for an alternative, if sketchy faith in people. Diane Keaton was quoted amid the fuss of *Looking for Mr. Goodbar* as saying that in *The Godfather* she had felt a kind of stooge, helpless witness to all the scenes enjoyed by the men. How wrong that it only shows the career pressures on an actress of uncontrived benevolence. It also accounts for her feeling bound to try the callous novelty of *Goodbar.* Keaton fits few American stereotypes. Her presence is alive with uncompromising kindness. She is capable of playing a decent person in any film honestly committed to human values. The comparison I think of is with Ingrid Bergman in the Rossellini films.

As it is, in *The Godfather* she has wonderful moments of pain, crushed innocence and humiliation that her dignity endures: Tom Hayden turns her away without Michael's address; the black beetle Michael returns from Sicily and claims her for a street walk, with a chaperoning car of bodyguards prowling behind, reminding us of the village women who attended his courting of Apollonia—a marriage he never mentions to Kay. She is excluded from the inner chamber at the end of *Part I* and heartbroken at leaving her children. This is the one act of moral courage in the film, and if illusionist realism was the only mode open to Coppola then it should have been expanded and Kay made central.

Imagine our perception of the Corleones if it came through her eyes—not remarkably intelligent or refined, but capable of being appalled, dependent on a man yet loathing his acts. Kay's dissent could be crucial, but it would have sent the audience away in their millions. Imagine, too, a possible development of her part: suppose that she cut across the half-hearted antagonism of police law and mafia order and uttered a cry of abused nature—of life itself, rather than the methodical business of Murder Inc. That might leave Keaton's Kay as vulnerable and moving as Bergman in *Europa 51.* Then it would no longer be possible to feel such reverence for the Corleones.

Could Coppola have conceived and tolerated an ending in which Kay informs and is ordered dead by Michael, or would that have infringed on the property of Puzo and Paramount, as well as the comfort of the audience? The Corleones require a quite contrary opponent, not rival hoodlums. They are the body and spirit-snatchers of American cinema; only the mechanisms of impersonal style in movie-making have made them admirable. But that hypothetical film would be as disturbing as *Europa 51,* and much less 'viable' than *The Godfather.*

Perhaps it is forlorn criticism to wish that Rossellini had directed *The Godfather*—though he would have called it 'The Age of the American Mafia', moving attention and questions from the genteel spider to the web of circumstances that form him. Nor does the juxtaposition of things written and spoken by Coppola deny that he is a respectable ringmaster, a Hollywood ideal. *The Godfather* is the work of a deft engineer at putting a dreadnought together, but a man unaware how the process of that film works. Paradoxically, that is only possible in a system brought up on the simpleminded notion of pure film, detached from meaning, life, society and the thoroughly impure personality of an author.

The Godfather is a supreme American film, but it is not good enough. Worse than that, it resists the potential that makes all imaginative work hopeful: that the public may pursue a more searching sense of themselves and their lives. Coppola's film is a fantasy that urges us to be less concerned with our real experience. It is part of the American movies' mythology that experience is as private as fantasy. The loss of individual integrity allowed by this leads to the blurred mass of millions that constitutes both the success and the meaning of *The Godfather:* the reassured audience—con-

firmed in its dreadful nihilism—is the model for a public placid about its own powerlessness to resist authorities.

One must be harsh with Coppola because of his lack of vulgarity. Tastefulness is easily mistaken for worth. He is thoughtful, clean and pretentious; he wants to make a righteous critique of the mafia, not a gangster movie. If he could settle for a simpler target, the film might be wilder, more personal, more touched by poetry—*White Heat,* say, or *Baby Face Nelson,* pulp works glowing with energy and vitality, and as funny as they are fearsome. *The Godfather* is so weighed down with the wish to be classy, dramatically precise and socially significant, that it is empty of creative passion. It has only entrepreneurial force and reliability—like the bombs, the aircraft and the aerosols. Its most prominent personality is the narcissistic and anal Satanism permitted in the moodiness of Al Pacino; not even its villainy is generous or outgoing—discretion is everything.

But this respectability is as much a cultural failure as it is in Buñuel's bourgeoisie. It is the blind eye of the American film, condoning the starriness of its central figures and turning the subject into a monstrous fantasising melodrama. We long to be with the Corleones: they are samurai or Arthurian knights standing on watch for threatened values and defending them to the death, including the death of value. The blind eye is like the face of every Hollywood star who pretends to be unaware of the camera taking the close-ups that will win the hearts of the audience. The realism required for the proper treatment is not photographic or a test of art direction. It hangs upon the attitude of the film-maker—it could be the humane scrutiny of Rossellini or the scorn of Buñuel. It cannot be Coppola's meek complicity. He does not appreciate how far the approach of a skilled mechanic honours the Godfather's code.

As for the public, we have abided by *The Godfather*'s Stalinist implications, without knowing if there is really a mafia. Perhaps no one credits those sinister figures more than the people who make and see films. Movie mafia are the creatures of our insecurity and paranoia—we wish for resolute fathers and comprehensive organizations in what often seems a chronically scattered, undesigned world. To admire the Corleones, to digest their melodrama and the commercials in the same meal, is part of our cultural breakdown, and a symptom of our longing for some domineering conspiracy. It is a movie for those who prefer to live in darkness.

Anthony Ambrogio (essay date Fall 1978)

SOURCE: *"The Godfather, I* and *II:* Patterns of Corruption," in *Film Criticism,* Vol. III, No. 1, Fall, 1978, pp. 35-44.

[In the following essay, Ambrogio traces the imperfect repetitions between The Godfather Part I *and* II *and asserts that they demonstrate the breakdown of the Corleone family and its criminal organization.]*

NBC's 12-15 November 1977 telecast of *Godfather I* and *II* in reedited, almost strictly chronological form, padded by the addition of scenes previously cut, provided some insights into and confirmations of elements in the original films but didn't improve upon the initial structure of the pictures, particularly the point-counterpoint of *Godfather II.* The "complete novel for television" received disappointing ratings and even provoked some unfavorable critical reassessment of the original films.[1] This lukewarm reception contrasts sharply to the rave reviews *Godfather I* and *II* received when first released in 1972 and 1974, respectively. In fact in 1974, many critics proclaimed *II* even better than its predecessor.[2] No doubt, *II*'s dual-plot structure contributed to this preference; in *II,* the early history of Vito Corleone (née Andolini), the Godfather, adapted (and considerably embellished) from the unfilmed portions of the book, alternates with the continuing story of his son Michael (Al Pacino), the new Godfather, taken up from where *I* left it. Together these two sections of *II* provide a fascinating framework, backward and forward in time, for the original film. TV disrupted this framework; the Godfather saga lost its epic quality by no longer beginning *in medias res,* with *I.*

Despite the flashbacks, which comprise almost half of its running time, *Godfather II* was advertised as "Michael's story," and most critics were quick to see it as such, since it completes Michael's degeneration, begun in *I,* from a nice ex-college boy, ex-war hero to a ruthless criminal. (For that matter, *I,* is "Michael's story," too.) What critics failed to see was the artful way in which this transformation is accomplished.[3]

For *II*'s modern section, director Francis Ford Coppola and his co-scenarist, *Godfather* novelist Mario Puzo, the architects of *Godfather I,* simply went back to their drawing board, unrolled their old blueprints, and remade *The Godfather* with, however, several significant differences. They repeated the pattern they established in *I* while playing upon it numerous subtle, clever variations in order to underline the further and complete corruption of the Corleone family: every important incident in the first film has a parallel in the second. Carlos Clarens was the first critic to catalogue in print several of the many parallel sequences between *I* and *II,* but he doesn't realize or stress the reason for these repetitions or note that they're *imperfect* repetitions—by design.[4] A complete catalogue—and comparison—of these inexact parallels will reveal that reason and design.

Godfather I begins with a large, outdoor celebration—the wedding of the Godfather's daughter—while the Godfather holds court inside, taking care of business and personal matters (e.g. undertaker Bonasera's request that the Godfather avenge *his* daughter; godson Johnny Fontane's request for a part in a movie); *Godfather II* begins the same way—the new Godfather throws a gala outdoor party in honor of his son's first communion and also attends to business and personal matters (e.g. Frankie Pentangeli's trouble with the Guzzardo brothers; his sister's parade of boyfriends and neglect of her children). In each movie, we see that these initial matters are later acted upon; the most notable—and most parallel—of them are the intimidation of movie producer Jack Woltz (John Marley) in *I* and of Senator Pat Geary (G. D. Spradlin) in *II.* Both the producer and the Senator—after refusing to accede to a Corleone request—undergo ordeals which persuade them to change their minds (the proverbial "offer they can't refuse"): they wake up stunned and bloody in bed. Woltz finds his Arabian stud horse's severed head under the covers and Geary finds his favorite s & m prostitute cut up and dead under the covers. (Clarens also mentions these parallels.)

Early in *I,* there is an unsuccessful attempt on the Godfather's life; even earlier in *II,* there is an attempt on the new Godfather's life. Both films proceed from these points to tell tales of gang warfare and betrayal within the organization and the family. Barzini (Richard Conte) surreptitiously leads the Five Families in opposition to the Godfather's organization in *I;* Hyman Roth (Lee Strasberg) duplicitously threatens Michael's operations in *II.* (In both films, the factions ostensibly reconcile. In *I,* Vito Corleone (Marlon Brando) calls a meeting of the Five Families; they sit around a conference table while the Godfather makes an impassioned plea for peace. This plea is apparently heeded, and everybody becomes "business" partners again, planning to go into dope dealing together. In *II,* Michael Corleone and Hyman Roth seem to form an uneasy alliance; they also become business partners and sit around a conference table with others, planning to divide up Cuba together. Of course, reconciliation in both films is only a smoke screen; violence between the two factions erupts again before each film ends. Just as his father balked at becoming involved with drug dealing, so Michael balks at investing money in Roth's Cuban scheme—a smart move, since Castro's guerrillas take over the country shortly afterward. However, in a reversal inspired by *I*—wherein Michael prevents his father's attempted murder while Don Vito is recovering in the hospital—Michael is prevented in *II,* from having Roth murdered while Roth is recovering in the hospital. Michael becomes the unscrupulous criminal his father's opponents were.

Trusted Corleone lieutenant Tessio (Abe Vigoda) betrays the family to Barzini in *I;* in *II,* another trusted lieutenant, Frankie Pentangeli (Michael V. Gazzo), Clemenza's successor, betrays the family to the government. Each pays the price for his treachery. Similarly, brother-in-law Carlo Rizzi

(Gianni Russo) betrays the family and sets up Sonny (James Caan) in *I;* in *II,* brother Fredo (John Cazale) betrays the family and sets up Michael. In each case the delinquent family member is given a grace period (no one touches Carlo while Don Vito is alive, nor Fredo while Mama Corleone is alive) before he, like Tessio and Pentangeli, is eliminated. Both movies have as their climax a blood bath, a series of multiple murders carried out under Michael's orders; he uses these executions to consolidate his organization's power, ruthlessly wiping out "business" opponents (Barzini, the heads of the Five Families, and Moe Green [Alex Rocco] in *I;* Hyman Roth in *II*), traitors to the group (Tessio in *I;* Pentangeli in *II*), and the traitors to the family (Carlo in *I;* Fredo in *II*). Clarens also notes this parallel slaughter.

But the parallels do not stop there. In *I,* Michael convincingly lies to his wife, Kay (Diane Keaton), assuring her he had nothing to do with Carlo's death, then ushers her out of his office and closes the door on her, effectively shutting her out of his life as he goes back to business. In *II,* the latent problems in their relationship (re)surface, and her resentment over his refusal to go legitimate causes her to leave him. Exerting his Godfatherly authority, Michael retains custody of their children. On one of her clandestine visits to see them, Kay tarries too long trying to get her son to kiss her goodbye. He is on the verge, about to come embrace her, when Michael returns to find Kay on the threshold. He goes to the door and quietly, firmly, shuts it in her face. This gesture is a repetition of his closing her out in *I,* but it takes on added weight here because of the different circumstances and has a note of finality to it. Indeed, we do not see Kay again in *II.*

As is obvious, Coppola and Puzo clothe their retelling of *I* in different terms, disguising the similarities between the two films by using different locales (Florida, Cuba, and more of Nevada than in *I*) and the later-model cars, hair styles, and fashions of the fifties in *II,* and by adding to *II* a variety of contemporary detail (the Cuban revolution, the Kefauver-like Senate sub-committee investigation)—all to obscure its thematic and narrative duplication of *I.* Besides returning to *I* for their inspiration, Coppola and Puzo also return to the book, incorporating flashbacks of the early life and career of Vito Corleone (here played by Robert DeNiro), which helps to contribute to the deceptive "new look" of *II.* However, Coppola and Puzo's talent and integrity save *II* from being a mere copy of *I:* they use its repetitions to expand upon ideas put forth in *I,* and they use its Vito Corleone flashbacks to counterpoint Michael's contemporary story; they develop possibilities which are only suggested in the hastily and sketchily written (but admittedly fascinating) pages of Puzo's novel.

Godfather II's repetition of key incidents in *Godfather I* shows the perpetuation of crime and the criminal empire in the second generation of Corleones. At the same time, *II's* imperfect repetitions show the expansion of evil, the degeneration of crime and of that criminal empire. Coppola and Puzo subtly illustrate the loss of any kind of tradition or honor in this dirty business and the gradual and complete corruption of Michael Corleone, a process which begins in *I*—when he avenges himself upon Captain McClusky (Sterling Hayden), the crooked cop who broke his jaw, and Sollozzo, the "Turk" (Al Lettieri), who had his father shot—but which reaches completion here.

Godfather II may begin with a big celebration, as does *I,* but the latter celebration is inferior to the former. There is none of the ethnic verve of *I*'s wedding in *II*'s expensive, homogenized communion party, situated in the alien land of Lake Tahoe. Don Vito's suburban New York estate, though somewhat removed from the city, is still close to his roots and to the heart of the Italian community, of which he and his family remain very much a part. In Nevada, the Corleones are strangers in a strange land, where people cannot even pronounce their name correctly.[5] In Nevada, there is no Italian community: in *I,* Italian-American singing sensation Johnny Fontane (Al Martino) croons a love song at Connie Corleone's wedding; in *II,* a local boys' choir—practically all blue-eyed blonds—sings some innocuous "inspirational" piece at Anthony Corleone's communion party. In *I,* everybody dances to sprightly or romantic Italian music—Tessio with a little girl, Clemenza with a Corleone soldier, the Godfather with his daughter; in *II,* all the party guests sit around while two heavily made-up performers do a theatrically torrid tango on stage. In *I,* an old man leads the wedding guests in a bawdy Sicilian rendition of "C'e la luna 'n mezzo mare," to which everybody—even Mama Corleone (Morgana a King)—adds a verse or sings the chorus; in *II,* Frankie Pentangeli (a New Yorker, in Nevada to see Michael) tries to get the WASPish band to play something Italian, something as familiar as "La Tarantella," and all it can come up with is "Pop Goes The Weasel"! All the guests laugh, and Pentangeli is ridiculed off the stage; the old ways are shown to be inoperative in modern-American Nevada. This action sets the tone for the rest of the modern segment of *II.*

Central to *Godfather I* is the Corleone family structure; that family structure completely collapses in *II.* No family portrait is taken on this day, as one is at Connie's wedding. Of course, when *II* begins, the family is no longer complete anyway: some of the Corleones (Don Vito, Sonny) are already gone—and, by the film's end, only one (Michael) will remain. Also, when *II* begins, several surviving Corleones' present conditions reveal the family's further degeneration: Fredo is married to a non-Italian "broad" over whom he has no control, and twice-divorced Connie (Talia Shire) neglects her children and flits around the world and from man to man, still making the same mistakes in her choice of mates. (Her latest is Merle Johnson [Troy Donahue]—another somewhat beefy pretty-boy in her first husband Carlo's image.) These two are a far cry here from the naive innocents they were at the beginning of *I,* where Connie was in her virginal wedding white and Fredo—still ineffectual and awkward in his tux—was unattached and unharmed by marital and other entanglements.

The attempt on Michael's life comes much sooner in *II* than does the attempt on Don Vito in *I.* Although Michael escapes injury whereas the Don does not, the attack on him is much closer to home than the one on Don Vito: his bedroom is riddled with bullets and his wife's life is endangered along with his. Later, Michael violently decries this *infamita,* bitterly complaining to Frankie Pentangeli about this breach in the unwritten code: "In my home! In my bedroom, where my wife sleeps, where my children come and play with their toys." The assassination attempt (like Senator Geary's earlier insulting remark about Michael's "fucking family") is not kept on a business level, as is the attempt on Don Vito; Michael's family is indiscriminately threatened.

The attack on Michael is just one example of how much more corrupt everything is in *II.* The Corleone organization destroys a race horse to get its way with Jack Woltz in *I;* in *II,* it murders a woman to get its way with Pat Geary.[6] Treachery in *II* penetrates nearer to the inner circle: brother-in-law Carlo—the outsider—betrays the family in *I;* brother Fredo—an insider, a blood relative—betrays it in *II.*[7] Likewise, Tessio—the lesser of the two Corleone lieutenants (and not Clemenza, the more favored *caporegime*)[8]—betrays the organization in *I,* but Frankie Pentangeli—Clemenza's successor, to whom the family entrusted its original New York territory, who now lives in the Corleones' former home—betrays it in *II.*[9]

Though less extensive than *Godfather I*'s blood bath, *II*'s is more brutal: *I*'s murders are all "necessary," their vengeance "legitimate"; *II*'s murders are gratuitous—they represent an extreme form of vindictiveness on Michael's part. He has to eliminate Moe Green, Barzini, and the heads of the Five Families as a matter of "business" in *I*—in order to solidify his family's position, and because Barzini is out to get him first—but, in *II,* he doesn't need to murder Hyman Roth because the old man is no longer a threat to him or his business. Roth's empire, power, and influence are no more; Roth himself is no more than an exile from his adopted country, Israel—a walking corpse because of the disease that will terminate his life in a matter of months—about to be imprisoned by the authorities as soon as he sets foot on American soil. In fact, the hardest part about killing Roth, Michael's henchmen tell him, is getting a clear shot at him: from the moment Roth gets off his plane, he'll be surrounded by reporters and police and F.B.I. agents, ready to take him to jail. But Michael insists the job be done anyway. In *I,* Carlo—a despicable person anyway—is actually responsible

for Sonny's death and deserves to die, but, in *II,* Fredo—a poor, misguided fool—only bumblingly and unwittingly helps Michael's enemies, never dreaming Michael might come to any bodily harm because of it, so Michael's insistence on Fredo's execution (especially since he knows Fredo's mental limitations and has escaped injury anyway) is utterly unnecessary.

Similarly, Pentangeli's betrayal in *II* is not as damaging nor as personally dangerous to Michael as Tessio's is in *I.* Fear, not selfish reasons of gain, motivates Pentangeli: the Guzzardo brothers have tried to kill him (their abortive attempt here parallels the Tattaglia's successful one on Luca Brasi in *I*—both Pentangeli and Brasi are lured to a bar and strangled from behind); he mistakenly believes Michael is responsible for this attack and only turns to the authorities out of self-preservation. Therefore, his betrayal is not as calculated nor as deadly as Tessio's: it only involves turning state's evidence, not being party to murder.

The Corleone organization neutralizes both Tessio's and Pentangeli's threats, but it neutralizes Pentangeli's before any real damage is done: the Corleones fly in Frankie's brother from Italy and prominently display him next to Michael when Pentangeli appears before the Senate subcommittee. The sight of his brother in the company of his former boss grimly reminds Pentangeli of the Corleones' power, and he tells the committee nothing. Thus, he never goes as far as Tessio, who has already arranged a meeting between Michael and Barzini in *I,* at which time Michael is to be killed. His actual betrayal of Michael prevented, Pentangeli—convicted of numerous crimes—is doomed to spend the rest of his life in prison; however, that is not revenge enough for Michael, and he persuades Tom Hagen to go to Pentangeli and make him an offer he can't refuse: his life in exchange for the complete monetary and physical security of his family. So, we next find Pentangeli dead in his bath, his wrists slit.[10]

There is some reason for Michael's cold and calculating behavior in *I:* he must regain the family's lost position in the underworld and hold his family together. In light of this "necessity," his elimination of his enemies, his lies to his wife, and his other actions are all understandable—even justifiable from his point of view. However, his behavior becomes more of a habit in *II,* the means become an end in themselves. This change in Michael, along with and as part of the many parallels to *I,* best illustrates the altered, harsher tone of *II.* Michael becomes less and less human as *II* progresses until, like Paul Newman's Hud, he is left with nothing but his empire and his wealth.

One by one, Michael cuts himself off or is cut off from his family. He banishes his brother Fredo when he discovers Fredo has been disloyal to him and only reconciles with

Fredo after their mother's death so that Fredo will be conveniently close by when Michael gives the order to have him murdered. Michael has already demoted Tom Hagen from *consigliore* to the family's Las Vegas lawyer in *I;* in *II,* he shunts him aside and distrusts him more and more.[11] He loses his mother to illness. Before her death, he has a heart-to-heart talk with her, just as he has with his father in *I.* However, while Don Vito gives him vital advice, telling him that whoever approaches him with a deal to meet Barzini will be the traitor, his mother's advice about how to be strong like his father and keep the family together in his time of crisis is useless. He loses his wife because of his adamant refusal to give up crime and make the Corleone family legitimate. She tells him she aborted their last baby because she wants to stop this process—which we can see from film to film—of the continuation and perpetuation of one Corleone generation to the next of crime and violence and revenge, these "recessive traits" growing more dominant in each succeeding Corleone. He slaps her when he hears about the abortion, when she calls their marriage an abortion, and thus commits another crime against his family, against his own wife—a crime which only the uncouth Carlo, who constantly beat his wife, Connie, is guilty of in *I.* And, although he keeps his sister and his children with him, it is only through power and not through love. Connie has been through the mill; after her broken marriages and countless affairs, she has nowhere to go and no one to turn to but Michael, who needs her because he needs someone to take care of his children. (The final irony/indignity for neglectful mother Connie is that she ends up entirely domesticated, chaperoning a brood of kids, her own and Michael's.) He keeps his children to spite Kay and because he must *possess* them—not because he wants them. He is hardly with them; he merely orders subordinates, such as Tom Hagen, to buy expensive presents for them (especially for his son) because he's usually away for their birthdays and the holidays.[12]

Michael Corleone's saga is contrasted to his father's through the parallels to *Godfather I* and by counterpoint to the interspersed flashbacks of young Vito's life. In 1901, nine-year-old Vito loses his family to one of those insane Sicilian vendettas: local Mafia chieftain Ciccio has his father and older brother—and his mother—killed. Friends help Vito escape to America. There, he is shunted around on Ellis Island, given the wrong name, and quarantined for small pox. A pathetic scene shows the boy alone in a bare room, singing to himself (an important image to compare to later shots of Michael). His window affords him a clear view of the back of the Statue of Liberty.

Later (1917), we see Vito the young man now integrated into American society—or at least into Italian-American society: he has a job and friends and has begun a family of his own. When local Black Hand bigwig Fanucci (Gastone Moschin) threatens his job and friends and family, he eliminates that threat by eliminating Fanucci. Soon, he and friends Clemenza and Tessio are prospering in the "olive-oil importing" business, and they gain and command the respect of the community. Now that circumstances permit it, Vito takes his family back to his homeland, where he evens up his score with the now-ancient Don of Corleone.

Vito's vengeance is extra-legal and reprehensible, but it is justified—if no way else—in the manner of Greek tragedy, where only more bloodshed erases a crime of bloodshed. However, like Michael's trio of killings at the end of *II,* young Vito's two murders are excessive. For example, after shooting Fanucci twice and killing him, Vito shoves his revolver in the dead man's mouth and blows Fanucci's brains out. And Vito feels compelled to plunge his knife into Ciccio even though the old Mafia Don is on his last legs—in worse shape than Hyman Roth—when Vito confronts him. (Nearly blind and practically deaf, he doesn't recognize Vito and can't even hear the name of the person Vito has come to avenge. The added TV footage here underscores Vito's excesses by showing him brutally murdering Ciccio's old henchmen, too—as Clarens also notes.)

Middle age mellows Vito Corleone, as *I* shows. He operates his organization like a business; there is a civilizing influence upon it and him. He avoids open bloodshed whenever possible and conducts his affairs on a business level, keeping all personal reasons out of them. Just the opposite happens to Michael Corleone. Starting off at a fairly civilized level, he gradually degenerates. The policies of Vito Corleone's heirs become increasingly immoral, beginning in *I* with hot-headed Sonny's murderous, manic campaign against the Five Families when his father is hospitalized. Michael deceptively "normalizes" conditions when he takes over—until *II,* when his policies become totally immoral, divorced from any kind of code of ethics.

The last shot of the contemporary sequence of *II*—a revealing one of Michael, alone—comes in for a close-up of his face, a face which has taken on certain sinister aspects ever since McClusky broke his jaw in *I,* but which looks colder and harder than ever now. This scene shows clearly what Michael has become and gains even more force by comparison with the final sequence of *II,* into which it dissolves—another flashback, but to Michael's past, not Vito's. This segment surprises (and delights) the viewer because it seems to be some unshown portion of *I.* Actually, its date is 7 December 1941, almost five years before the beginning of that film. The place is the Corleone dining room, where the family is preparing for a birthday. Sonny brings his friend Carlo home for dinner and practically pushes his sister onto Carlo's lap throughout the scene (a perhaps too easy irony, but revealing nonetheless: the seeds of Sonny's, Carlo's, and Connie's destruction are planted early, here). All the brothers—Sonny, Tom Hagen, Fredo, and Michael—

sit around the table discussing Japan's attack on Pearl Harbor; Sonny dominates the conversation, complaining about the nerve of those Japs to start a war on his father's birthday (another, more subtle irony: it is significant—fitting—that Don Vito's birthday should be on Pearl Harbor Day, since the Corleone birthright is one of war and slaughter, as the two pictures make clear). Tessio, who brought in the birthday cake, mentions that 30,000 men have rushed to enlist. Sonny sneers, wondering who'd be stupid enough to do a thing like that; Michael quietly says that he would: he enlisted in the Marines that morning. Sonny immediately greets this news with a belligerent attack, Tom with an attempt at logical argument against Michael's position, and everybody else with shock.

Sonny can't understand how Michael could do such a stupid thing, especially on their father's birthday; he tells him that the only group ever worth fighting for is one's own flesh and blood. Their argument is interrupted by the arrival of Don Vito, and everybody rushes off to wish him happy birthday, leaving Michael sitting alone at the table, contemplating, while they sing "For He's a Jolly Good Fellow" off-screen. (Michael's loneliness here contrasts to his father's isolation when he first comes to the U.S. Then, Vito's isolation was societally ordained; now, Michael's is self-made.)

In both the contemporary and the flashback sections of *II,* then, Michael is left alone at the end, in an isolation he has created against his own family. And, while on December 7 his isolation may be based on a nobler principle, allegiance to a cause or ideal larger than that of Family, his present isolation—after he has succeeded to his father's position and is now supposedly dedicated to his father's principles and the concept of Family—is due to no high ideal at all, not even that of blood being thicker than water, since his family no longer exists—since he has destroyed it. The movie ends with the image of the earlier Michael, sitting by himself at the table, but this shot—this entire flashback segment—has been superimposed over, has evolved from, the final shot in the contemporary segment and everything that has preceded it: we are made to see how far Michael has fallen. (The importance of this scene coming where it does is evident: the otherwise chronologically presented TV version does not tamper with its original position.)

The wheel has come full circle—and then some. The last surviving member of his vendetta-depleted family, Don Vito had come to America and established a new family, had moved from personal vendetta to businesslike behavior, to rationality and respectability. College student and war hero Michael, at one time not part of the family business, had been the prime example of that new rationality and respectability, his family's best and brightest hope. In *I,* when it is already too late and Michael has become inextricably in-

volved in the family business, his father tells him during their heart-to-heart talk about those former high hopes. He thought Michael might have become "Senator Corleone . . . Governor Corleone . . ." Michael waves away the never-to-be-fulfilled dream. Then, for the rest of *I* and throughout *II,* he slides steadily downward from business to personal vendetta to senseless killing.

The two films never specifically deal with the motivation for Michael's degeneration, but the audience never really questions that motivation, either. A viewer takes Michael's actions for granted because he senses that *I* and *II* deal with larger issues in which personalities are submerged and subject to manipulation by greater forces: they are a working-out of the age old notion about the sins of the father and the more recent notion about the souring of the American dream.

We don't expect Michael to escape from his heritage, and he doesn't. Ironically, when he finally, wholeheartedly embraces that heritage, he cannot cope with it. He is the victim of his own wrong choices and the fact that the younger generation is not equal to the older. Faced with a set of circumstances similar to those his father surmounted, he tries to but cannot solve them in as satisfactory a fashion (because everything—including Michael—is worse than it was in his father's time). Like father, like son, but—as much as he would like to be—Michael can no more be Don Vito than hot-headed Sonny or feeble Fredo can. His love for his father eventually involves him in the family organization he sought to avoid: his quick thinking at the hospital, which saves Don Vito's life, earns him a broken jaw from McClusky and triggers in him his father's streak of revenge (though he insists to his brothers that his murder of Sollozzo and McClusky is "just business"). Hiding out in Corleone, Michael relives his father's Sicilian experience and loses a loved one (his Italian wife) to a vendetta. After this episode, Michael—unlike his father—can never escape from the cycle of murder and retribution bred in him. He remains the Sicilian killer his father outgrew. Don Vito, during the conciliatory meeting he convenes in *I,* voluntarily ends the violence: both he and Tattaglia have lost a son; he says they must call it quits—there can be no more killing.

Michael can never call it quits. He is incapable of adopting and still preserving his roots. He displaces his family from the East to the West, and is then bewildered when it falls apart in this incompatible environment. He clings to inappropriate customs, not making allowances for new conditions, and ignores the more important traditions. Always out of step with his family, when he thinks he is acting most like his father, he is actually most unlike him; he tries too hard, and destroys his family while trying to preserve it.

Other directors have sometimes re-made their own films, often to rethink and expand upon themes set forth, to expose flaws inherent but not apparent in their originals (e.g. Ford in *The Searchers* [1956] and *Two Rode Together* [1961], Hawks in *Rio Bravo* [1959] and *El Dorado* [1967] and again in *Rio Lobo* [1970]), but none have succeeded quite so artfully as Coppola and Puzo in the two *Godfathers.* By telling the tale of the Godfather and then essentially retelling it in order to show the deterioration in the second generation of Corleones, they masterfully make the same thing different and the same theme more far-reaching.

NOTES

1. See especially Carlos Clarens, "The Godfather Saga," *Film Comment,* 14, no. 1 (Jan.-Feb., 1978), pp. 21-23.

2. For two prominent examples, see Judith Crist, "All in the Family," *New York,* 23 Dec. 1974, pp. 70-71, and Pauline Kael, "Fathers and Sons," *The New Yorker,* 23 Dec. 1974, pp. 63-66.

3. I partially except Richard Schickel who, in "The Final Act of a Family Epic," *Time,* 16 Dec. 1974, pp. 70 and 73, notes the repetition-alteration technique used in the wedding-communion party celebrations of *I* and *II.*

4. "Whatever seemed to work in the first is repeated almost identically in the second" ("The Godfather Saga," p. 22). "*Almost* identically" is the key here. Clarens continues: "This calculated arrangement of episodes that recall each other has been disturbed by the new TV format." True, but the arrangement is so much a part of the two films' inherent structures that it carries over anyway. For example, TV segments 1 and 3 end at the same parallel point—in the middle of the wedding and communion celebrations, which then begin the next days' episodes.

5. Senator Geary mangles the name "Corleone" when he speaks it publicly. However, in private he has no trouble saying it right. His "real American" contempt for the Corleones expresses what must be the prevailing attitude toward Michael and his "kind." Geary—who doesn't like these displaced, ethnic Easterners with their "greasy hair"—even stoops so low as to make a disparaging remark about Michael's family: he says he doesn't care for his "whole fucking family"—a comment which understandably angers Michael. In New York, in *I,* people don't make such personal slurs—they leave their families out of business. Even Californian Jack Woltz, Geary's parallel in *I,* who makes a number of ethnic slurs when he is approached by Tom Hagen about Johnny Fontane, never resorts to the kind of familial insult the Senator does in *II.*

6. The significant look which passes between Tom Hagen, kneeling by the dazed Senator's bed, and a Corleone tor-

pedo, standing and wiping his hands just inside the bathroom, makes it obvious to the audience—if such confirmation is necessary—that the Senator is being framed for the killing which the hit-man performed. However, an alert observer of this scene may note—in the last shot of the bed, just before the cut—that the victim's stomach does move. This suggests either that the "victim" is in on the frame up or—more likely—that the actress playing the part of the corpse is not a complete adept in the art of shallow breathing.

7. *Godfather I* foreshadows Fredo's treachery in *II.* When Fredo tries to defend Moe Green in *I,* Michael tells him, "You're my brother and I love you. But don't ever take sides with anyone against the family again." Unfortunately, Fredo does not heed these words.

8. Richard Castellano's Clemenza is given far more screen time and is shown to be more intimate with the family than Tessio is. For example, it is Clemenza who makes spaghetti for the group and gives Michael, whom he addresses familiarly as "Mikie," advice about cooking, about love, and—later, when they're setting up Sollozzo and McClusky—about killing.

9. Clemenza himself was supposed to be the betrayer in *II.* However since Richard Castellano considered his services too valuable and played hard-to-get, he remained ungotten for *II.* Coppola, figuring that public identification of Castellano with Clemenza was too great to permit him to substitute some other actor for the part, hit upon the expedient of writing Clemenza out of the script (it's mentioned that he died of natural causes) and writing a new character in, one who supposedly got the nod from Clemenza before he passed on. Besides Pentangeli's overall Clemenza-like demeanor, the clearest indication that he was meant to be Clemenza comes when he tries to explain to Michael why he should get better treatment from the Corleones in New York: he says he deserves it because he was with Don Vito in the old days. However, *I* makes no mention of and never shows Pentangeli, whereas all other characters in *II* (except Hyman Roth—a necessary afterthought on the part of the scriptwriters, since they'd eliminated all of the Corleones' other enemies in *I*) can be found in *I.* Obviously, Pentangeli's speech was originally written for Clemenza. Thus, Pentangeli is meant to represent someone closer to the Corleones than Tessio was.

10. With all of this excess, Michael proves himself to be far less scrupulous than his father, who always only allowed an eye for an eye. When undertaker Bonasera, in *I,* asks the Godfather to have the two boys who brutally beat his daughter put to death, Don Vito tells him, "That would not be justice; your daughter is still alive." Once Bonasera accordingly alters his request—"Then make them suffer, as she has suf-

fered"—the Don readily complies and orders that the guilty duo be brutally beaten.

11. Michael's demotion of Hagen is all the more telling in *II* because it follows on the heels of a promotion: at the beginning of *II,* Michael leaves Tom in charge as acting Don while he goes to Florida, New York, and Cuba on Hyman Roth-Frankie Pentangeli business. When he confers this post upon Hagen, Michael tells him that he always regarded him as a brother. Hagen is choked with emotion. "I always wanted to be thought of as a brother by you, Mikie," he says. However, as *II* progresses, Michael steadily moves away from this early growing-together; he later makes Tom wait outside while he discusses business with some associates. This belies Michael's action at the beginning of *II* when he lets Hagen sit in on his meeting with the Senator and others, telling Geary that he trusts Tom implicitly. In the end, he becomes so suspicious of his step-brother that he accuses him of duplicity and disloyalty.

12. When Michael returns from his months-long trip away from his family, he sees his present-by-proxy to his son, the toy car Tom Hagen sent for him, unused and snow-covered on the lawn. When Michael goes inside his home, no one is there to greet him. He wanders through the house and sees Kay at work in front of her sewing machine. She is engrossed and does not notice him. He stands there and says nothing to her. Through these wordless scenes, Coppola visually conveys Michael's estrangement from his family.

William M. Hagen   (essay date 1981)

SOURCE: "*Heart of Darkness* and the Process of *Apocalypse Now,*" in *Conradiana,* Vol. XIII, No. 1, 1981, pp. 45-53.

[*In the following essay, Hagen analyzes the relationship between Coppola's* Apocalypse Now *and Joseph Conrad's* Heart of Darkness *and concludes, "I tend to see* Apocalypse Now *as a failed masterpiece, another instance of the fact that the production-editing process cannot bear too much of the conceptual load in a feature film."*]

Toward the end of *Apocalypse Now* we reach that supremely Conradian moment when Willard, the Marlow figure, confronts the object of his journey, Colonel Kurtz. Does he come to rescue Kurtz and, in so doing, test himself? If Francis Ford Coppola had chosen to follow Joseph Conrad here, he might have gotten some desperately needed U.S. military assistance. But that was not the kind of script conclusion the director of *The Godfather* and *Godfather II* had planned for his war epic.

Still, Coppola underscores the significance of the meeting by altering his style. When Willard is taken into the temple for the first time, the whole pace of the film slows down, as if in imitation of the ponderous immensity of Brando. Brando-Kurtz slowly emerges into the light and pats water on his gleaming bald head, in a kind of ritual cleansing. The camera holds the shots for a much longer period than usual, allowing movement to be dictated by the actors rather than by focusing in or editing. Dialogue too proceeds at a much slower pace, with pauses occurring within sentences as well as between them. Questions are left hanging for a few extra beats, even when there is nothing particularly threatening about them. Of course, the pace has been slackening ever since the Do Lung Bridge sequence, but this scene is so slow it borders on worship. Brando is meant to by mythic, the still center of darkness, worshipped and self-worshipping, capable of every atrocity including self-annihilation through his double. Willard is so affected by the atmosphere of disorder and stasis, that he has to force himself to kill Kurtz. Through lighting, camera angles, and cross-cutting, the murder itself is transformed into a kind of dance in and out of darkness, creating a visual-aesthetic experience quite as isolated as the slow-motion destruction of a Sam Peckinpah film. The acquiescence of Kurtz and the preliminary appearance of Willard out of black water make the whole affair a kind of rite of rebirth-initiation into the world of Kurtz through slaying of the king.

With the exception of the rather abrupt thematic cross-cuts between the murder and the ritual killing of a caribou, the encounters are quite stunning and organic . . . visually. We could perhaps accept the deliberate departure from Conrad's novel if the director did not also seek to build in the psychological-moral dimensions of *Heart of Darkness*. His characters may be caught in a ritual of death and rebirth, but he wants them to have depth all the same. He wants viewers to confront the immensity of this war one more time. Above all, he wants to explain everything through Kurtz. So Coppola picks up Kurtz' last words and tries to build a structural theme for the last portion of the film. By the time we hear "The horror!" for the last time, in a memory replay, we are likely to have worked up that fine wrath normally reserved for all those who quote outrageously out of context.

Conrad's Kurtz mouths his last words as a message to himself and, through Marlow, to the world. He has not really explained himself to Marlow before this final exclamation. Through Marlow's summary and moral reactions, we come to a sense of the possibilities of meaning rather than definite meaning. The message is more Marlow's and the reader's than it is Kurtz'. By contrast, Coppola's Kurtz precisely defines "horror"; the only way we can make his definition our message is to see his horror and enact his definition with Willard. The way to judgment lies through vicarious violence. Judgment is self-judgment.

The problem with even this transaction is that Willard seems almost unmoved by his experience. He certainly expresses no moral judgment. The worst he says is that he sees "no method" in Kurtz' operations. This statement may strike the reader of Conrad as uncomfortably similar to the Station Manager's amoral judgment of Kurtz' atrocities as merely "unsound" or bad for company business. The separation of reason from civilized morality, the fragmentation of the self so typical of the technocrat, causes Marlow to prefer the nightmare of Kurtz. Better to commit atrocities passionately than to account them wrong on grounds of efficiency. Like Dante—whose traditional moral hierarchy he reflects—Marlow can summon up a measure of sympathy for those who succumb to their emotions or appetites and reserve unmeasured scorn for those who pervert reason. Within the film, only the general at the briefing and Chef show the rational or emotional repugnance toward Kurtz; Willard, the professional soldier, is more than halfway friendly with this horror. After Chef joins the heads and Willard becomes part of the horror, we may realize that the whole point of the scenes at the Kurtz compound is to make the audience confront Kurtz' horror without moral mediation. From the very beginning, the shots of the compound were carefully filled with more separate images and actions, especially around the edges of the frame, than the eye could integrate. The eye was always kept moving and focusing on different parts of the screen. We did not have Marlow's field glasses or his sensibility to distance us or focus in sympathetically; we were entrapped and overwhelmed in an amoral medium range. Thus, instead of judgment or self-judgment, we are likely to come away from this perceptual overdose with the feeling that it has been a bad trip, and nothing more.

Other contributors to this symposium will undoubtedly analyze this and other portions of the film to show the many differences and similarities to Conrad's text. Hopefully, they will pay homage to the cinematic power of the film. After all of the analyses, however, one may be moved to wonder just what the director-writer and the other contributors had in mind, with regard to *Heart of Darkness,* or what process led from the novel to such a mixture of visual spectacle and moral-intellectual vacuity.

The program handed out at the screenings of the 70-mm print of *Apocalypse Now* gives the following script credits: "Written by John Milius and Francis Coppola; Narration by Michael Herr." Nowhere in the formal credits is Joseph Conrad or *Heart of Darkness* mentioned. The novel is briefly referred to in the program's log: "September 3, 1976. Marlon Brando arrives. He reads *Heart of Darkness* and shaves his head for the Col. Kurtz role." Within the film itself, the novel is not accorded reference equal to *The Golden Bough* or T. S. Eliot's poetry; it is not recited as quotation or included among the books in the bibliographic pan toward the end of the film. Of course, for the cognizant, there are plenty of lines, or echoes of lines, as well as the unmentioned epigraph to Kurtz' favorite poem, "The Hollow Men."

In point of fact, Conrad's name originally appeared in the screen credits, but was removed after one of the listed writers protested through the Screen Writer's Guild. Coppola is quite candid about the three texts that contributed to the final script: the novel, Michael Herr's *Dispatches*—originally published as a series of *Esquire* articles—, and John Milius' script, entitled *Apocalypse Now,* which built some of its passages from Herr's book and *Heart of Darkness.* The script itself went through several phases: the original 1969 script by Milius, collaborative revisions during preproduction period (1975-76), Coppola's revisions during production, and Herr's narration, added after shooting was completed in 1977.

To read the statements regarding *Heart of Darkness* by the two main architects of the script, Milius and Coppola, is to confront a tangle of high intentions, self-delusion, and probably self-protection. It is harder to verify what Milius says about his original script or its collaborative revision because, apart from two fragments in *Film Comment* (July-August 1976), nothing has been published. In an interview included with the script fragments, he claims to have used *Heart of Darkness* "in an allegorical sense." Kurtz went up the river with a military mission and a moral mission: he was to turn the tribesmen into a fighting force and bring them "democracy and Western civilization." He succeeds admirably in the first mission at the cost of the second mission and his own civilized sanity. Milius depicts him as having made sense of the war by embracing tribal values:

> [To Willard] We revel in our own blood; we fight for glory, for land that's under our feet, gold that's in our hands, women that worship the power in our loins. I summon fire from the sky. Do you know what it is to be a white man who can summon fire from the sky?

Milius meant for the audience to confront the tribalization of Americans in the very first scene of the original script. That scene depicts the colonel's team members ambushing a column of Viet Cong. G. I.s emerge from the jungle, one by one, dressed and painted like savages. The camera records the scene from the point of view of the victims: the audience is variously blasted by a shotgun, incinerated by a flame-thrower, and scalped by an American wearing a peace sign on his helmet. Quite apart from the Kurtz behind the spooky voice on the tape recording and the ghostlike images of the photos, then, this was to be the reality Willard moved toward. As opposed to the film, this was madness with enough method for a professional soldier to admire. Willard's journey was to be an odyssey, with adventures that threatened to delay or divert him from his mission, while revealing the purposelessness of our war effort. Encounters with a surfing colonel (Cyclops), Playboy bunnies in a downed helicopter (Sirens), the Do Lung Bridge sequence (visit to underworld for further instruction?), and a meal at an old French plantation (Circe? Lotus-eaters?) would make grand scenes and trigger an analysis of his own role in the war.

The jungle was to have the force of the environment in *Bridge on the River Kwai,* becoming more powerful and primeval as Willard approached the Kurtz compound. Willard's line in the film—"Even the jungle wanted him dead"—picks up a theme enunciated by Kurtz in Milius' script. He shows Willard a rotting hole in his side and points to the insects swarming around him: "The beast of the jungle did the rest. I haven't long to go. . . . the only justice will be had by the beasts. . . . Theirs will be final, and we will have made no more mark on this jungle than a stone thrown into an ocean." Even though this may sound like Conrad merged with *Lord of the Flies* one assumes that the Milius script would have stressed the surroundings as a means of initiation to Kurtz' world rather than as a green backdrop out of which pop tigers, banners, tracer bullets, and arrows. Certainly the above-mentioned opening establishes the jungle and swamp first; the ambushers emerge from underwater and behind foliage.

Given the opening view of savage Americans, the inefficiency of the official war effort, and the power of the jungle, the conversion of Willard to Kurtz' side in Milius' script would seem inevitable. They would join forces and die together. Coppola apparently agreed that some conversion to Kurtz' position was the more logical conclusion, but bowed to audience surveys which indicated a preference for Willard alive and faithful to his original mission. One speculates some problems, however, since Willard was to have undergone psychological change during his journey. Was this change to be represented only by a change of allegiance? His late assertion that he kills because "it feels so good," delivered to Kurtz in the Milius script, would seem appropriate at any point in the script for a man "who exists only because of the war." Perhaps he merely joins the more efficient war. At any rate, the self-doubting, guilt-ridden Willard, established in the first scene of the film, is Coppola's creation.

On the other hand, Milius' Kurtz definitely seems more of a piece than Brando-Coppola's Kurtz. If the jungle environment were actually established as a force, if Kurtz' other lines were as strong as those in the published fragment, if we can imaginatively fill out Kurtz by using the comparison Milius makes to the Paul Newman character in Milius' previous film, *The Life and Times of Judge Roy Bean,* then Milius' Kurtz would have gone down (with Willard) in a blaze of apocalyptic glory. We would probably have been spared Kurtz'

unearned realization of "The horror! The horror!" whispered to us in stereo or sexophonic (70-mm version) sound.

One must be careful, however, not to use a speculated script to construct "the film that might have been." It is quite evident that Milius established much of the plot and most of the lavish scenes in the first half of the film, all of which constitute a major variance from the method of *Heart of Darkness.* Milius says he wanted the spectator "to see the exhilaration of it all . . . the horror of it all: you're going right into the war with no holds barred." Certainly his first scene preserves no Conradian mental and moral distance from the action. The direct approach to the war, as a series of perceptual traumas that threaten to reduce the mind to passivity owe as much to the acid journalism of Michael Herr's *Dispatches* filtered through a sensibility fascinated with war as to what Stanley Kauffmann calls Coppola's "apparent sense that the world is seen most truthfully when it is seen as spectacle." If Milius' Kurtz was more of a piece, he was more a piece of this action, living in splendor with wives, babies, and few doubts.

Coppola was quite dissatisfied with the conception of Willard in the original script. Although Milius claims that his script was not political, Coppola saw the whole thing as "a political comic strip" up to and including the end.

> Attila the Hun [i.e., Kurtz] with two bands of machine-gun bullets around him, taking the hero Willard by the hand. . . . Willard converts to Kurtz' side; in the end, he's firing up at the helicopters that are coming to get him, crying out crazily.

He decided to "take the script much more strongly in the direction of *Heart of Darkness*—which was, I know, opening a Pandora's box." In particular, one can see problems in his conception of Willard, whom he felt was "literally zero" in Milius' script. He wanted to "psychologize" Willard, following Conrad's lead, but "In no way could he get in the way of the audience's view of what was happening, of Vietnam." The latter statement certainly reveals that Coppola never understood the role of Marlow in the novel. By the same token, I think his instincts were right: one cannot have a spectacle vicariously experienced and an experience filtered through a narrator who has changed mentally and morally as a result of that experience. Scenes which enlarge our sense of a real world, as in the picaresque novel, usually do so at some expense to character; scenes which enlarge or create a crisis for the character who is our vantage point are often not fully objectified. Would the helicopter assault have been as effective if the camera had been restricted to Willard's vantage point? Would Conrad's Kurtz have seemed as powerful if Marlow had faithfully recorded all that he said? Some film theorists would add that Coppola's instincts were right even if he *had* understood the role of Marlow because film redeems material reality or its immediate perception more naturally than consciousness. Critics who bemoan the medium's tendency to reduce Conrad to large scenes and large characters, to present his work as primarily romantic, might be tempted to agree. At any rate, Coppola's problem was that he wanted it both ways: he wanted the exhilarating episodes of Milius and he wanted the psychological dimension of Conrad's Marlow. Michael Herr's method of grabbing all the experience one can get in the great trip of life would not help him achieve a balance. So he went into production with this problem, hoping that a good actor might help him resolve it. He had hopes that "the part would play the person." The role of Willard was offered to Steve McQueen, Al Pacino, James Caan, Jack Nicholson, Robert Redford. Since the problem of Willard was also the problem of Kurtz, many of the same actors were offered the Kurtz role. Apparently, only in the editing room would Coppola realize the results of such contrary impulses—a film with radically different styles in different parts.

During the shooting of **Apocalypse Now,** Eleanor Coppola, the director's wife, began keeping a journal which was to help her make a documentary film of the production. So far as I know, that documentary was either not completed or not released. She drops all mention of it about mid-way through the journal, where personal and family problems increasingly enter. The journal itself, published by Simon and Schuster under the title of *Notes,* unfortunately, is too fragmentary and begins too late in the process to offer much information on specific script decisions that moved the film closer to or farther away from *Heart of Darkness.*

What it does reveal is just how many script decisions were deferred till production was actually underway. Coppola the director shot scenes by day, while Coppola the writer rewrote scenes by night. Throughout, he hoped that important elements of plot, character, and theme could achieve conceptual clarity during the process of production. For instance, although he was sure enough about the Willard part to fire Harvey Keitel because he projected too strongly, he apparently did not realize that Sheen's Willard was verging toward nonentity till late in the picture. At that point, probably after Sheen's physical breakdown rendered him unable to reshoot extensively, Coppola made the decision to have Michael Herr work up the voice-over narration to fill out the character. Even if Conrad's Marlow suggested this method, it was not part of the original script. For another more extreme instance, *Notes* presents Brando as having virtual veto power over his lines and character. "Francis hadn't been able to write a scene that Marlon thought was really right." He arrived without having read *Heart of Darkness:* he and Coppola had to work out the character, almost in front of the cameras. Coppola rescripted some scenes after viewing the footage of those very scenes. The isolation of Brando-

Kurtz from his men, enshrined in his temple compound, is as much due to the problems of working out character on a two-week time schedule as it is to any thematic intention. In the original Milius script and in Coppola's mind he might have been integrated into that part of the film fashioned by "*Heart of Darkness* and me," but *Notes* and the interview make it clear that the anxious director and his overweight, opinionated star conceived and filmed the character at almost the same time. "As soon as Brando started to improvise, Frances could begin to direct, that is, see the direction the scene should go." It is not surprising that the character has more physical and visual presence than psychological power. The cinematographer, Storaro, more deliberately planned his effects.

Some critics have suggested that *Notes* itself should be regarded as a kind of publicity release. (Did husband, who suggested the journal become a book, also suggest changes? Certainly he filled out some details.) Throughout the journal, the director displays self-doubts about his product, while maintaining the highest esteem for his sources, Conrad's novel and our corporate Vietnam experience. The self-doubt, later displayed in the test showings of different versions of the film, rather artfully becomes Coppola's own journey into darkness during the process of filmmaking. The open-ended approach to script fits right in, of course. Almost two months into production, early in the journal, the director's wife sets up a thematic connection that becomes prevalent in the book:

> Willard and Kurtz are not resolved. . . . Now he [Frances Coppola] is struggling with the themes of Willard's journey into self and Kurtz' truths that are in a way themes he has not resolved within himself, so he is really going through the most intense struggle to write his way to the end of the script and understand himself on the way.

> More and more it seems like there are parallels between the character of Kurtz and Francis. There is the exhilaration of power in the face of losing everything.

Later, as Sheen settles into his muted Willard and Brando is due to arrive, the resolution of Kurtz becomes the primary problem. Rereading Conrad does not help Coppola: "The ideas of what Kurtz represents are so big that when you try to get a handle on them they are almost undefinable." Unfortunately, his decision to use a star for the Kurtz role and his own realistic proclivities push him in the direction of defining, whereas Conrad is careful to suggest. Where specific outlines are not credible, the character, like his compound, is presented as too large to be contained in the frame. Isolated bigness and hollowness are the result: a huge temple honeycombed with small barren rooms, a large body with a shining oval head, a rhetoric that echoes more than it means.

The director's journey becomes a personal journey for the whole crew, for his family, especially for this wife, who wants to create something herself. Still later, when Sheen collapses, Coppola seems to collapse too and begins talking about divorce. Finally, the creative journey is connected to the war: "there was no simple solution to the script. Just as there was no simple right answer as to why we were in Vietnam." In the program notes, Coppola ties it all together, projecting the journey as an audience catharsis as well:

> Over the period of shooting, this film gradually made itself; and curiously, the process of making the film became very much like the story of the film. . . .
>
> I, like Captain Willard, was moving up a river. . . .
>
> It was my thought that if the American audience could look at the heart of what Vietnam was really like . . . they would be only one small step away from putting it behind them.

Coppola's statements here may strike us as pretentious and self-serving, but I tend to think that he has made the common mistake of artists who imagine that the experience of the audience and the stature of the artwork can somehow be predicted by the anguish of the creative process. In wanting to improve the Milius script, especially after the Do Lung Bridge sequence, he turned to *Heart of Darkness* and the somewhat improvisatory method itself. However, by not working out the precise relation of *Heart of Darkness* to the conception of the film in script form, Coppola insured a less faithful adaptation. In a process of conceptualization *and* production, different script considerations externalize as physical factors and personalities. Without a firm script or a director with a firm conception, group spontaneity can all-to-easily give way to anxiety and competition. Costly sets, actors, sound engineers, a tribe of extras, stocks of explosives, a meticulous cinematographer (who wants to organize by shot frames rather than by scenes) directly or indirectly pressure the director to help fill in the blank places of the script. In such a situation, the medium may have more voices than the message.

Ironically, although Coppola wanted to draw the greatness of the film from the greatness of the novel, the section of the film most like *Heart of Darkness* is the weakest because he makes the rather romantic assumption—which is, in fact, a misreading of the novel—that experience itself will immediately dictate certain discoveries. He forgets the years of reflection Marlow has given to his experience, the "recollection in tranquility" that Wordsworth argued must follow

"the spontaneous overflow of powerful emotions" if they are to be shaped into art. Although one may shuffle the scenes around like cards, although sound or narration may be added, the scenes themselves cannot be done again; celluloid is much less tractable than words.

I tend to see *Apocalypse Now* as a failed masterpiece, another instance of the fact that the production-editing process cannot bear too much of the conceptual load in a feature film. Coppola needed something definite to improvise *against.* I would reluctantly speculate that his film would have achieved greater unity if he had relied more on Milius' scripted version of *Heart of Darkness* than the novel itself.

John Hellmann   (essay date Fall 1982)

SOURCE: "Vietnam and the Hollywood Genre Film: Inversions of American Mythology in *The Deer Hunter* and *Apocalypse Now,*" in *American Quarterly,* Vol. 34, No. 4, Fall, 1982, pp. 418-39.

[*In the following essay, Hellmann traces how Michael Cimino's* The Deer Hunter *and Coppola's* Apocalypse Now *use different American genres—the western and the hard-boiled detective, respectively—to portray two different interpretations of the Vietnam War.*]

Since their respective releases in 1978 and 1979, Michael Cimino's *Deer Hunter* and Francis Coppola's *Apocalypse Now* have enjoyed remarkable popular and critical success. But their wide recognition as contemporary cinematic masterpieces has been accompanied by a corresponding controversy regarding their thematic significance and coherence. In addition, none of the commentaries on either of these two epic-scale films about the Vietnam War has searched for possible connections between them. My first purpose in this essay is to show that each film draws its design from a popular American narrative formula, with the separate formulas providing the basis for the differences between *The Deer Hunter* and *Apocalypse Now* as interpretations of the Vietnam War. I further wish to demonstrate that a link between those formulas establishes an underlying relation between the two films, embodying their essential aesthetic strategy. The allusion of *The Deer Hunter* to *The Deerslayer* signals the presentation of the Vietnam War through the popular genre for which Cooper's Leatherstocking Tales are the prototype: the western. Similarly, the opening scenes of *Apocalypse Now* establish the presentation of the symbolic journey of *Heart of Darkness,* itself an adventure/mystery tale, through the specific conventions of the hard-boiled detective formula. This use of popular genres that are related as central American myths of the nineteenth and twentieth centuries connects the two films.

A popular genre, as Stanley Solomon succinctly defines it, is "a certain mythic structure, formed on a core of narrative meaning found in those works that are readily discernible as related and belonging to a group."[1] As the two most enduring genres of American pulp literature, Hollywood movies, and television series up to the time of the Vietnam War, the western and hard-boiled detective formulas provide *The Deer Hunter* and *Apocalypse Now* with a culturally resonant means for interpreting a national experience. And because both formulas are genres of romance, they provide the directors with the "mythic, allegorical, and symbolistic forms"[2] that Richard Chase has traced as the main strategy of the American literary tradition for encountering the contradictions and extreme ranges of American culture and experience, of which Vietnam is a recent and particularly traumatic example.

Despite its decline in recent years, the western has been the major formula story of American popular culture over the last century and a half, establishing its central significance as American myth. Rather than a single pattern of action, the western is defined instead by the influence of its symbolic landscape, a frontier between civilization and wilderness, upon a lonely hero.[3] The confrontation of these basic forces creates a sharply delineated conflict resulting in a variety of stock characters and plot configurations. With its emphasis on the relation of the hero to a frontier landscape, the western deals with the conflict created by the dominant direction of American experience, the flight from community (Europe, the East, restraint, the conscious) into a wilderness (America, the West, freedom, the unconscious).

With *The Deer Hunter,* Cimino, who in the subsequent *Heaven's Gate* turned with notorious ambition directly to the genre, presents America's experience in Vietnam through the conventions of the western. While virtually every commentary on the film has pointed out the connection between the protagonists of *The Deerslayer* and *The Deer Hunter,* to my knowledge only David Axeen and Colin Westerbeck, in separate articles, have gone beyond this to the perception that the film is presented in the terms of the form Cooper invented. But instead of exploring the specific elements involved, both use the observation to dismiss the film for being, as Axeen phrases it, "fatally oversimplified":

> The problem with the Cooper-Cimino Western is that it asks us to suspend our knowledge of history, and ignore the realities of social structure. . . . Neither Cooper nor Cimino wants to consider the people and forces really in control. They want us to identify with their heroes as natural aristocrats in still unspoiled wilderness domains.[4]

This familiar criticism leveled at the romantic tradition of

American literature identifies the link between that tradition and Cimino's use of the western in *The Deer Hunter.* As Leslie Fiedler has shown, the "low" forms of fantasy literature, particularly those emphasizing violence and terror, have provided symbolic vehicles for the exploration of basic conflicts within the American consciousness.[5] Although the function of the popular western, as John Cawelti has observed, is "to resolve some of the unresolvable contradictions of American values that our major writers have laid bare,"[6] the genre has, in the hands of literary practitioners such as Owen Wister and filmmakers such as John Ford, served as a vehicle for sophisticated popular art. In addition, it has also provided an important influence and impetus for the more disturbing explorations of American culture found in Hawthorne, Melville, Twain, Hemingway, and Faulkner. The western formula affords Cimino the strengths of the central national myth in dealing with Vietnam as a collective American trauma. At the same time, *The Deer Hunter* achieves more than a perpetuation of past myth by its understanding of the essence of the myth and its critical examination of it. Unlike *The Green Berets*, an unthinking use of the western formula, *The Deer Hunter* is a western affected by the shift in landscape. *The Deer Hunter* is an important artistic interpretation of the war precisely because it so fully comprehends the essence of its source and self-consciously explores its meaning in reference to recent American experience.

In *The Deer Hunter* the actions and character of a lonely hero, Michael Vronsky (Robert De Niro), are closely associated with wilderness landscapes, the basis for a structure of violent conflicts and sharp oppositions. The film turns on such characteristic devices of the western as male bonding, the repressed love of the hero for a "good woman," the terror of confrontation with savage denizens of a hostile landscape, dancehall girls, even a "shoot-out" across a table in a crowded gambling room. But even as Cimino thus sets the Vietnam experience squarely in the context of the dominant American historical/mythic tradition, he stands the genre on its head. Assimilating the Vietnam experience into the American consciousness by embodying it in the western formula, Cimino substitutes for its traditional plot motifs (implying the inevitable triumph of white consciousness) a story of traumatic captivity. The accusations of racism made against *The Deer Hunter* are not correct in a political or social sense; Vietnamese are shown among the victims of the Viet Cong in the Russian roulette captivity scenes, a black American soldier without arms in the military hospital is one of the most vivid statements against war in the film, and white Americans are prominently shown placing bets in the final Russian roulette scene. But the film does employ the imagery that has obsessed the romantic tradition of American literature from its beginnings with a violent confrontation between the conscious and unconscious, civilization and wilderness, played out in the white imagination as a struggle between light and dark. *The Deer Hunter*, through the western formula, presents Vietnam as yet another historic projection of an internal struggle of white American consciousness, but one where the dream of mastery over nature and the unconscious, or alternatively of benign communion with them, is turned upside-down into a nightmare of captivity.

The defining elements of the western are first presented in *The Deer Hunter* in a timelessly mythic configuration: the hero, Michael, lives on an edge between civilization and nature. The Pennsylvania steel town named Clairton where he was raised represents both European tradition and modern industrialization, and the surrounding mountain forest embodies the original American wilderness. Cimino has written that he explained to his director of photography "at the beginning my feelings about location, my feelings about the importance of size and presence of landscape in a film—and the statement that landscape makes, without anyone realizing it."[7] His mythic intentions are asserted by his representation of a Pennsylvania steel town with a composite of eight separate locations from Cleveland to Pittsburgh, of the Alleghenies with the Cascade Mountains of Washington state, and of the deer with a stag imported from a wildlife preserve in New Jersey—representations that sacrifice authentic setting for a more powerfully symbolic landscape.[8]

The deer hunter himself has the salient traits embodied in his Cooper prototype and in virtually every western hero to follow. Living on the outer edge of the town in a trailer, he is a part of the community, and yet is clearly separated from it by his alienation from its corruption and by his strict adherence to a personal code closely associated with the uncorrupted wilderness and its original inhabitants. For example, he despises all of his friends except Nick (Christopher Walken) for their inability to understand the ritualistic importance of killing a deer with "one shot." And at the wedding reception he responds to whispers from Stanley (John Cazale) about the actual father of the pregnant bride's unborn child by running down the street stripping off his clothes, a compulsive flight from social corruption. Finding little relevance in the old European traditions of the community, Michael has, like his literary ancestor, turned to nature. In the opening sequence he perplexes his companions by insisting that they go on a hunt that night because the "sun dogs" he sees in the sky are an old Indian sign of "a blessing on the hunters sent by the Great Wolf to his children."[9] And in strong contrast to his detachment from the elaborate rituals of the Russian Orthodox wedding, which he knows are mocked by the pregnancy of the bride, he is intensely involved in the proper preparation, practice, and culmination of the hunt. Finally, the taunts of Stanley that Michael does not take advantage of opportunities with women clearly set Michael in the tradition of the celibate western hero.

Michael is also characterized as separated from his community by the more disturbing traits of the western hero. Suggestively, the characters regard Michael with both respectful awe and uneasy perplexity, finding his omen-reading crazy and his hunting prowess extraordinary. From the viewer's perspective also, Michael's characteristics have contradictory significance. His need to prove self-reliant results in reckless activity, as in the scene in which he risks his own and his friends' lives by passing a truck on the inside merely on a casual bet. And his deer hunting, attractive for its skill and sense of value, results in the image of a gutted deer sprawled across his old Cadillac's hood as it speeds down the mountain road to drunken singing. Even Michael's distaste for the practice and consequences of sexual promiscuity is set off against his repressed passion for Nick's girlfriend (Meryl Streep), revealed in his chivalrous courting of her during the wedding reception. Indeed, the narcissistic, promiscuous, and pistol-flashing Stanley, who is Michael's antagonist, is also the dark reflection of Michael's repressed self, just as the outlaw is the mirror image of the western hero. When Michael derides Stanley's obsession with womanizing and carrying a pistol by holding up a bullet and saying "*this* is *this*, this isn't something else," his insistence on the bullet's lack of symbolic significance, while he himself cradles his deer-slaying rifle, must be ironic for the viewer. Michael, like the western hero, is a man of extraordinary virtues and resources, which are dangerous unless properly channeled into a role protective of the community.

While the defining elements of the western, the influence of a frontier landscape upon the character and actions of a lonely hero, are those of *The Deer Hunter*, they are conceived in more complex psycho-symbolic terms. The western has conventionally projected the conflicts of the American consciousness in black-and-white characters representing good and evil (hero versus outlaw, lawmen versus rustlers, cavalry versus Indians, noble Indian tribes versus threatening tribes) in a single landscape. Cimino uses the same psycho-symbolic method and terms, but dramatizes the conflicts within the consciousness of the hero and projects them in a division of both characters *and* landscape. The film develops through the stock oppositions and melodramatic confrontations of the western, but they are presented more explicitly as external images of the protagonist's consciousness, projections of his impulses and thus of the national consciousness he represents as mythic hero. As a result, Vietnam functions in the film as a mirror image of America, a dark landscape turning upside-down the benign landscape of Cimino's mythic Alleghenies.

This relation of Michael as western hero to the landscapes and secondary characters of *The Deer Hunter* is brilliantly embodied in the remarkable cut with which Cimino abruptly moves the film from America to Vietnam. One moment

Michael, after returning to the bar from the mountain hunt, is in a quiet reverie as he listens with his male friends to melodic piano; the next, surrounded by dead American soldiers, he lies unconscious amid the exploding horrors of Vietnam. The effect of the cut is to have Michael wake up from his dream of the deer hunt to a nightmare inversion of the landscape and its relation to the hero and community. The first third of the film shows Michael in flight to nature and away from a strained, corrupt, but strongly bonded community. But, as Michael recovers consciousness, that flight has taken the viewer into hell. The camera shoots Michael from a downward-looking angle showing him struggling to lift himself from the jungle grass, a sharp contrast to the upward-looking angles of Michael against the sky during the deer hunt. The community, a small Vietnamese village, is surrounded not by snow-capped, pine-forested mountain peaks but by dark jungle foliage. In contrast to the opening shots of the film showing Michael and his friends at the mill harnessing fire to make steel, now helicopters destroy the village with incendiary bombs. Steven's pregnant bride metaphorically and his mother literally dragged him from the male haven of the bar; now a grinning North Vietnamese cadre tosses a grenade into a shelter full of women and children. Michael and his friends found satisfaction in hunting and gutting a deer; now pigs fight over the entrails of dead American soldiers. Nature and civilization are the dominant terms of both the American and Vietnamese settings, but in Vietnam the asylum of nature has become an invading hell.

Yet Michael is revealed as in his element here, for his influence and impulses have been unleashed in this frontier landscape. His countenance immediately verifies this, for the hunter who guided himself by Indian lore now wears a cloth headband about his head and has war paint (for camouflage) streaked on his face. He is, in fact, an airborne ranger, and both his appearance and the term "ranger" link him to the tradition of Indian fighters who used Indian skills, became like Indians, to protect the community from Indians. Michael, who like the Deerslayer and other western heroes could only flee the internal threat of corruption inherent in social relations, responds to the external threat of a darker-skinned man firing on a woman and child by literally purging him from the earth with fire. Michael's intense compulsions in the first third of the film were manifested in reckless driving, excessive drinking, flight from women, and a hunt resulting in the image of a gutted deer. Michael, like the western hero, finds a place for his violent impulses only in a threatened community. This scene classically parallels the image of the frontier hero protecting innocent settlers by killing the savage Indian. But Michaels' method, a furious blast from a flamethrower, visually asserts the deeper ambiguity of the scene—it opened with the village being blown apart by American napalm. The North Vietnamese soldier is only an undisguised version of the evil that Michael's "good" forces bring to the community. And both the "evil"

North Vietnamese and "good" American helicopters act out the repressed hatreds against community found in the male culture of Clairton's bars and hunts.

This ambiguity, based in a visual presentation of the "good" and "evil" elements of the western in clear mirror relation to each other, is brought to its fullest implications in the central sequence of the film, the forced Russian roulette scenes. This scene has been the focus of the most outraged attacks on the film, for it has to many critics seemed to present white America as innocent victim of the savage Viet Cong.[10] And, indeed, it is a portrayal of America's experience in Vietnam out of that earliest source of the western, the Indian captivity narrative in which innocent whites are subjected to hideous tortures. But there are deep ambiguities within this apparent confrontation between innocent whites and dark savages. The Viet Cong, as they grin, drink beer, and bet money while forcing their captives to play Russian roulette, display the same impulse and even the same iconography as did Michael and his friends in the bar in Clairton when they drank and bet on televised football. And the one-shot nature of Russian roulette is a parallel to the one-shot value of Michael's hunt. Finally, just as Michael has been the restrained, intense leader of loutish companions, the Viet Cong have the look of grinning, stupid brutes except for the impassive, controlled visage of the leader.

The effect is that the Viet Cong function as demonic images of the latent impulses of the American culture, particularly as embodied in the western hero, Michael. The Indians and other darker races, closely associated with the wilderness landscape in which the white culture confronts them, have functioned in the myth and literature of American culture as symbols of forces in the unconscious. The larger symbolic design and implications of the film are a continuation of those elements of the western: the Vietnam jungle and its savage Viet Cong denizens are the nightmare inversion of the American forests and beautiful deer. Nightmare and dream, both landscapes and their inhabitants are projected aspects of the unconscious, a region beyond the confines, restraints, and limits of the conscious mind embodied in the community. The captivity scene, as did the Puritan narratives of Indian captivity, embodies a nightmare journey into the darker implications of wilderness. If the wilderness landscape (the unconscious) is a place to which the hero goes in order to dominate his passions without external restraints, it can also be the place where he may find himself captive to those same passions. The hunter becomes the hunted, the one shot of complete control an emblem of self-destruction.

By making a captivity narrative the central episode of the film, Cimino inverts the terms of the western formula. While the captivity narrative was a major nonfiction genre of early American writing, the western employs its horrors only to set the revenge/quest plot in motion; in effect, the western substitutes a fantasy emphasizing the eventual assertion of white power and value for a genre of historical narrative that had emphasized the dilemma posed by the experience of complete passivity before an alien culture. Conceiving of the Vietnam War as a western in which the captivity experience is the pivotal episode, Cimino makes *The Deer Hunter* deeply disturbing on the most resonant level of cultural myth.

The final third of the film develops the consequences of the captivity experience. *The Deer Hunter* presents Vietnam as a frontier landscape so hostile that America, having come as hunter with dreams of omnipotence, is held captive in it and forced to confront the full implications of its own impulses. There is no revenge/quest in *The Deer Hunter* because it would be beside the point; the point is to determine how a culture proceeds once it has experienced the inversion of its central assumptions about itself. Michael's resourcefulness as western hero enables him and Nick to kill their captors, but not before they have suffered the experience of being held captive to unrestrained violence. Nick, who called Michael a "control freak" and resisted his obsession with killing the deer with "one shot" in favor of "thinking about the deer" and "the way the trees are in the mountains," is psychologically destroyed. In the Puritan narratives of Indian captivity, as Richard Slotkin has pointed out, "captivity psychology left only two responses open to the Puritans, passive submission or violent retribution."[11] Nick in effect follows both courses. He first has to be restrained by Michael from repeatedly beating a Viet Cong corpse, but then turns the unleashed impulse to destroy back upon himself. Unable to call Linda, then lured into the Russian roulette of Saigon, fading into dope and finally death, Nick embodies an innocent acceptance of nature that cannot survive the dark revelations of Vietnam. Michael, the hunter who dominates nature (his unconscious) through controlled violence (repression), discovers in captivity that he cannot be omnipotent.

For both of these Adamic characters Vietnam is a "fall," but for Michael it is a fortunate one. In the second deer hunt of the film, which follows the Vietnam captivity experience, he does not shoot the deer despite his increasingly frantic pursuit of it. Instead, when the deer faces him, he shoots into the air and says "okay," then sits by a stream and angrily shouts the word, which is this time echoed back by the mountains. "Okay" is of course an expression of acceptance, and Leo Marx identifies the echo as a standard device of pastoral literature representing the establishment of a reciprocal relationship with nature, the "pastoral ideal" of locating a "middle ground somewhere 'between,' yet in a transcendent relation to, the opposing forces of civilization and [primitive] nature."[12] When at the climax of the film Michael once again faces Nick across a table at a Russian

roulette game, he is desperately attempting to bring Nick back from his captivity in the violent compulsions once latent but "controlled" in Michael and subsequently transferred to Nick in the first Russian roulette scene. While Michael has responded to the trauma by moving toward a cautious version of the acceptance of nature that Nick had, Nick has become the alienated nihilist Michael had seemed potentially. Nick had abandoned the "one-shot" obsession of Michael for simple primitivist communion with his benign ideal of nature, but the traumatic experience of captivity has turned his innocence into the opposite extreme of an obsession with a "one-shot" submission to passivity. The same experience has led Michael to abandon his "one-shot" obsession with control, instead accepting a balance, or "middle ground," between the conscious and unconscious.

A common device in such Hollywood westerns as *The Searchers* and *The Magnificent Seven*, perhaps originating in Cooper's use of Natty Bumppo and Duncan Heyward in *The Last of the Mohicans*,[13] is the "doubling" of the hero. Typically, the experienced hero rides off at the end, free but alone, and the "novice hero" settles down with a woman, domesticated but "happy." This gives both forces of American consciousness mythic affirmation and thus avoids a cultural choice. Cimino has reversed the usual fates of the two heroes, with the experienced hero giving up his freedom in order to "settle down" in the community and the novice hero now finding himself unable to return to it. In addition, he has substituted for the ambiguous image of riding off into the sunset a clear image of self-destruction in an alien landscape.

In settling down, Michael does not abandon the personal code of the western hero based on the hunter myth.[14] He instead brings it to the preservation of the community. After accepting the freedom of the deer, a recurring symbol for the feminine principle of the unconscious,[15] he returns to his male companions that night to find Stanley, in response to sexual taunts, pointing his pistol at their friend Axel. In a rage at this mirror image of the compulsion he has just thrown off, Michael purges Stanley through Russian roulette of his dark obsession with male sexual power. With this purgation of his darker self, Michael is able to overcome his initial confusion and passivity upon his return to go back down into town and join Linda, who embodies the feminine values of love and compassion and the possibility of a stable relationship. He also brings the crippled Steven home from the machine-like institution at the veterans hospital, and then returns to Vietnam in an attempt to bring back Nick. Michael's return is set against the background of America's flight from Vietnam during the fall of Saigon. His agonized failure is nevertheless a crucial journey *The Deer Hunter* suggests America must make, a return to its Vietnam experience to face the fact of its destroyed innocence. When he holds Nick's blood-soaked head Michael faces, and thus can fully recognize, the result of his prior obsession.

The controversial ending of the film is thus neither jingoistic absolution for America's Vietnam involvement nor an ironic commentary. All the surviving characters, male and female, have been brought together by the hero to a table in the former male haven of the bar. Close shots of the table being set, chairs lifted, and characters squeezing in around the table emphasize the daily heroism involved in preserving a community. Accepting loss and trauma, the western hero has taken a place in the community. In joining in the spontaneous singing of a tearful "God Bless America," finished by a smiling toast to Nick, Michael also joins it in asserting the continuing value of the ideal embodied in a simple love for America, for the dream of a benignly magnificent landscape, but with a full awareness both of the dangers of chaotic nature and of a person's, or society's, obsession with control. The basic impulse of the western has been the concept of regeneration through violence. In *The Deer Hunter* this concept is stood on its head, for the regeneration results from the response of the hero to violence turned back on him. Purgation is replaced by shock, and then acceptance. Vietnam is viewed as the self-projected historical nightmare through which America can awaken from its dream of innocence into a mature consciousness.

The opening scenes of **Apocalypse Now** quickly disabuse the viewer of any expectations that the film will attempt a faithful adaptation of *Heart of Darkness*. Instead, they signal the development of the broad symbolic outline of Conrad's classic novella through the specific ethos, imagery, and pattern of the hard-boiled detective formula. Many commentators have noted a similarity between the voice-over narration spoken by Captain Willard (Martin Sheen) and the narration of Raymond Chandler's detective Philip Marlowe, but Veronica Geng, while not perceiving the full use of the formula, has identified the most explicit particulars of this source in the film:

> Willard talks in the easy ironies, the sin-city similes, the weary, laconic, why-am-I-even-bothering-to-tell-you language of the pulp private eye. . . . Our first look at Willard is the classic opening of the private-eye movie: his face seen upside down, a cigarette stuck to his lip, under a rotating ceiling fan . . . , and then the camera moving in a tight closeup over his books, snapshots, bottle of brandy, cigarettes, Zippo, and, finally, obligatory revolver on the rumpled bedsheets. This guy is not Marlow. He is a parody—maybe a self-created one—of Philip Marlowe, Raymond Chandler's L. A. private eye.[16]

Geng sees these private-eye elements as vaguely function-

ing to transform the film into a black comedy with overtones of pulp literature and comic books, but they more specifically signal the use of the hard-boiled detective formula as the structural, stylistic, and thematic center of the film, the specific source by which Coppola presents the Vietnam subject through the broad symbolic vision of *Heart of Darkness*. Once this is perceived, elements of **Apocalypse Now** that formerly appeared confused or at least puzzling and gratuitous become apparent as aspects of a complex presentation of one source in the terms of another.

The hard-boiled detective genre, originating in the *Black Mask* pulp magazine in the 1920s, is a distinctly American version of the classic detective story, raised to a high artistic level by Dashiell Hammett and Raymond Chandler in fiction, and by John Huston and Howard Hawks in film. The private eye, rather than the brilliant mind of the classic detective, is a twentieth-century urban, and thus more sophisticated and cynical, descendant of the western hero, combining the tough attributes necessary for survival in his environment with a strict integrity based on a personal code of ethics. The setting is a modern American city, most often in southern California, embodying an urban wilderness or "neon jungle" that is geographically, historically, and mythically correct for the genre, because the hard-boiled detective moves through a corrupt society that has replaced the frontier.

There are important similarities, reflecting their common source in quest/myths, between *Heart of Darkness* and the hard-boiled detective formula. Both have isolated protagonists on a mystery/adventure who are in the employ of others while actually preserving their personal autonomy of judgment. In both works the protagonist encounters revelatory scenes of the depravity of his society in the course of his journey. And the final apprehension of the criminal, while on the surface restoring moral order, actually ends in dissolution, with the protagonist more cynical about his world than before. Thematically, both Conrad's novella and the hard-boiled detective genre are generally understood to be journeys through a symbolic underworld, or hell, with an ultimate horror at the end providing a terrible illumination. In method both combine the classic quest motif of a search for a grail with a modern, geographically recognizable locale. And while the clipped, slangy style of the hard-boiled genre has on the surface little in common with the obscure, evocative style of *Heart of Darkness,* they pursue similar purposes in the dreamlike (or nightmarish) effect with which they render reportorial detail. The one crucial distinction between *Heart of Darkness* and the hard-boiled genre lies in the relation of the protagonist to the criminal. The detective, despite his similarity to the underworld in speech and appearance, remains sharply distinct from the murderer, for in not only exposing but also judging the murderer he embodies the moral order of the ideals of his society not found in its reality; Marlow, in contrast, comes to identify with Kurtz, finally admiring him as much as he is repelled by him, thus making *Heart of Darkness* ultimately a psycho-symbolic journey within to the unconscious. As a result, while the hard-boiled formula posits an individual integrity as an alternative to a corrupt society, Conrad's novella implies a universal darkness in man.

In *Apocalypse Now* Coppola uses the hard-boiled detective formula as a means for transforming the river journey of *Heart of Darkness* into an investigation of both American society (represented by the army) and American idealism (represented by Colonel Kurtz [Marlon Brando]) in Vietnam. The river journey in *Apocalypse Now* is full of allusions to southern California, the usual setting of the hard-boiled genre, with the major episodes of this trip through Vietnam centering around the surfing, rock music, go-go dancing, and drug-taking associated with the west coast culture of the time. As a result, the river journey drawn from *Heart of Darkness* takes the detective and viewer, not through Vietnam as a separate culture, but through Vietnam as the resisting object of a hallucinatory self-projection of the American culture. Captain Willard's river journey is both external investigation of that culture and internal pursuit of his idealism. Willard is a hard-boiled detective hero who in the Vietnam setting becomes traumatized by the apparent decadence of his society and so searches for the grail of its lost purposeful idealism. Kurtz represents that idealism and finally the horrific self-awareness of its hollowness. If the hard-boiled detective, denied by his pervasive society even the refuges of nature and friendship with a "natural man" available to the western hero, is forced by his investigation of a corrupt society to retreat into his own ruthlessly strict moral idealism, *Apocalypse Now* forces the detective into a quest for that idealism itself.

From the beginning of the film it is clear that Willard lacks the genre detective's certainty of his own moral position. Willard has already been to Vietnam, and upon leaving has found that home "just didn't exist anymore." Further, his return to Vietnam is without clear purpose: "When I was here I wanted to be there, when I was there all I could think of was getting back into the jungle." While the opening imagery establishes Willard's identity as hard-boiled detective, it also asserts his diminished version of that figure. The close-up shots of a photograph of his ex-wife and of letters from home represent what he has had to abandon. His drunken practice of Oriental martial arts, as opposed to the controlled drinking and solitary chess-playing of Philip Marlowe, represents a shift from tormented purpose to self-destruction. And Sheen's taut characterization generally embodies this deterioration of the detective's cynical armor for his personal idealism into the explosive alienation of a James Dean. Similarly, the narration written by *Dispatches* author Michael Herr and spoken by Sheen in voice-over,

widely derided as a banal parody of Raymond Chandler, evokes the sardonic perspective of a Philip Marlowe without the strong sense of personal identity conveyed by Marlowe's penetrating wit. Willard takes the mission to assassinate Kurtz as a murderer despite his feeling that "charging a man with murder in this place was like handing out speeding tickets at the Indy 500." Willard could also be called a murderer, for he has a record of unofficial assassinations. When the soldiers come with his orders he responds drunkenly with "What are the charges?" And in the voice-over narration he says of Kurtz, "There is no way to tell his story without telling my own, and if his story is really a confession, then so is mine." Willard's quest, as that of a hero figure of a central American mythic formula, becomes an investigation of not just corrupted American reality but of the American view of its ideal self.

In melding *Heart of Darkness* and the hard-boiled detective formula, *Apocalypse Now* owes more of its particulars to the latter. Willard, having been summoned from his Saigon quarters, an equivalent to the private eye's seedy downtown office, receives his assignment from a general who clearly evokes the manager in *Heart of Darkness* by speaking of "unsound" methods while engaging in the brutal exploitation of a country. The specific development of the scene, however (as the general tells Willard that Kurtz disappeared with his Montagnard army into Cambodia when he "was about to be arrested for murder"), is made in the terms of a conventional episode of the hard-boiled formula. Sitting over an elegant lunch in the elaborately furnished trailer serving as his headquarters, and with a melancholy expression listening to Willard's record as an assassin before having him assigned to "terminate" Kurtz, the general is, in the context of the Vietnam War, a military version of the powerful client who receives the detective with palpable distaste in his impressive mansion. Marlow's private aloofness from his employers in *Heart of Darkness* is portrayed in *Apocalypse Now* as the hard-boiled detective's retention of his self-reliance and judgment while ostensibly working for his client: "I took the mission. What the hell else was I gonna do? But I really didn't know what I'd do when I found him."

Likewise, while the journey downriver in *Apocalypse Now* adopts the parallel development in *Heart of Darkness* of the protagonist's growing repulsion from his society and increasing attraction to Kurtz, this pattern is once again specifically presented according to the hard-boiled formula. In that formula the detective, while pursuing the murderer, uncovers such pervasive corruption in the society that his final isolation and judgment of the criminal is undercut. George Grella identifies the portrayal of the official representatives of society, the police, in the detective genre as "brutal, corrupt and incompetent."[17] These traits are consecutively the point of the three major discoveries Willard makes on his journey about how the army is "legitimately" fighting the war. Witnessing Colonel Kilgore's use of over-powering technology to decimate a Viet Cong village full of women and children in order to capture briefly a surfing beach, Willard is shown with expressions of puzzlement and disgust, saying: "If that's how Kilgore fought the war, I began to wonder what they really had against Kurtz. It wasn't just insanity and murder. There was enough of that to go around for everyone." After leaving the USO show where he has seen profiteering and dehumanized sex, the glamorous corruption typical of the detective novel, he comments in voice-over: "The war was being run by a bunch of four-star clowns who were going to end up giving the whole circus away." And his reaction to the futile and apparently endless battle of the Do Lung bridge, fought merely so the generals can say the bridge is open, is a disgusted, "There's no fuckin' CO here." These scenes develop vague parallels from *Heart of Darkness* through the specific terms of the detective formula.

Similarly, Marlow's attraction in *Heart of Darkness* to the hearsay he encounters concerning Kurtz is developed in *Apocalypse Now* through a stock device of thrillers: a dossier full of fragments of evidence that the detective must study and interpret. Willard, repelled like Marlow and the hard-boiled detective by the depravity of his society, recognizes in his "investigation" of Kurtz that this "murderer" is the embodiment, in vastly larger scale of his own inner ideals. Kurtz has openly asserted the purposeful action, unhypocritical ruthlessness, autonomy from considerations of personal gain, and adherence to a personal code that are the hard-boiled characteristics of Willard. As a result Willard, like Marlow, finds himself attracted to the murderer. In the voice-over narration, as he looks through Kurtz's dossier, Willard speaks of how the more he learns of Kurtz the "more I admired him," how Kurtz made a report to the Joint Chiefs and Lyndon Johnson that was kept classified because he apparently saw the developing failure of the American approach to the war, and how Kurtz ignored his lack of official clearance to order effective operations and assassinations. Here again Coppola follows the hard-boiled formula while altering its plane to the symbolic investigation of the self adapted from *Heart of Darkness*. The detective often has a friend or is attracted to a woman who turns out to be the murderer, but he discovers this later and is only then confronted with the dilemma; Willard is attracted to Kurtz *after* society has identified him as a murderer. Like Marlow, he consciously moves away from a corrupt, inefficient society toward an idealistic, efficient outlaw. By the time he approaches Kurtz's compound Willard has made Marlow's "choice of nightmares":[18] "Kurtz was turning from a target into a goal."

This identification of the detective figure with the murderer, never allowed in the hard-boiled formula, is brought to its disorienting climax in the scene that Coppola has called the most important in the film,[19] the shooting by Willard of the wounded Vietnamese woman, followed with Willard's explicit explanation: "We'd cut 'em in half with a machine gun and give 'em a Band-Aid. It was a lie. And the more I saw of them, the more I hated lies." Just before Willard later kills Kurtz, Kurtz says that there is nothing he "detests more than the stench of lies." By developing *Apocalypse Now* according to the defining elements of the hard-boiled formula, but extending the investigation into the self, Coppola shocks the audience from a moral witnessing through the detective figure of the external horror of his society into a questioning of the formula's normal source of order; the moral idealism, the uncorrupted honesty, the purposeful efficiency of the detective himself. This scene prepares the viewer to experience the confrontation between Willard and Kurtz as a meeting of the detective figure with the final implications of his moral idealism. Thus *Apocalypse Now* shows Vietnam forcing the hard-boiled detective hero into the investigation of his unconscious provided by the symbolic motif of *Heart of Darkness*.

The final scenes of the film, set at Kurtz's compound in Cambodia, represent the most visible use in the film of Conrad's novella. Here again, however, the particulars owe considerably more to the hard-boiled detective formula. In many works of the genre the murderer turns out to be what Grella calls a "magical quack," a charlatan doctor or mystic presiding over a cult or temple.[20] Free of social restraint, Colonel Kurtz has, like his literary namesake, set himself up as a god among primitive tribesmen, becoming a ghastly figure of evil. The Russian "fool" in *Heart of Darkness,* now a countercultural American photo-journalist (Dennis Hopper), still praises Kurtz mindlessly in mystical terms. But these elements are presented within a more detailed portrayal of Kurtz as the "magical quack" the hard-boiled detective tracks down to his southern California headquarters, a significance first suggested by allusions to Charles Manson in a newspaper story about the Sharon Tate slayings and in the similarity of the "Apocalypse Now" graffiti to the "Helter Skelter" scrawled at the LaBianca home. This portrayal is even clearer in the plot development, for whereas Marlow confronts a pathetic Kurtz crawling away in the grass, this Kurtz, if psychologically "ripped apart," is nevertheless still a powerful, controlling figure who has Willard brought to him. Like the magical quack in the hard-boiled detective formula, he sneeringly taunts, tempts, and intimidates Willard. The murderer often scorns the detective for his low socio-economic position and quixotic quest (Kurtz tells Willard, "you're an errand boy sent by grocery clerks to collect the bill"), has him held captive and drugged or beaten (Kurtz has Willard caged, brutalizes him by leaving him exposed to the elements and drives him into hysteria by dropping the severed head of a boat crewman into his lap). Grella identifies one function of the "magical quack" device in the hard-boiled formula to be an emblem of the desperate search of the faithless for significance in a dispirited world (the wor-shipping photo-journalist and Willard's converted predeces-sor on the assassination mission, the zombie-like Captain Colby, embody this trait). Even more important in Grella's view is that

> the bizarre cults and temples lend a quasi-magi-cal element of the Grail romance to the hard-boiled thriller—the detective-knight must journey to a Perilous Chapel where an ambivalent Merlin fig-ure, a mad or evil priest, presides. His eventual triumph over the charlatan becomes a ritual feat, a besting of the powers of the darkness.[21]

The explicit use of Weston's *From Ritual to Romance* (shown by the camera as one of Kurtz's books) in the final confrontation between Willard and Kurtz involves precisely the ritualistic pattern described above, though once again with the implications of a confrontation with the self brought from *Heart of Darkness.*

While the hard-boiled formula is completed by Willard's re-jection of his attraction to Kurtz when he sees that Kurtz is indeed a murderer without "any method at all," and by his resistance to Kurtz's intimidation and brainwashing in or-der to fulfill his mission, he himself knows that his slaying of Kurtz is at the latter's direction: "Everyone wanted me to do it, him most of all." The ritualized confrontation further suggests that the detective figure is in fact killing not an external evil, but his unconscious self.[22] Willard's discov-ery of the moral chaos that has resulted from Kurtz's pur-suit of a moral ideal has led him to see the darkness that pervades not only the hypocrisy of the army, but also the darkness at the heart of his own pursuit of an honest war. The indulgence in death and depravity, of total power, that Willard finds in Colonel Kurtz's display of severed heads, his reading of selected lines from Eliot, and his parable of a Viet Cong atrocity is a devastating illumination of the same hollowness, the darkness, that in *Heart of Darkness* Marlow finds in the figure of Kurtz. Here the Vietnam context and hard-boiled detective persona of the protagonist give it a specific commentary on the American identity: not just the corrupted American reality, but the American self-concept of a unique national idealism is itself a fraud, a cover for the brute drives for power that dominate Americans as much as any people. Just as Marlow discovers in Kurtz the essential lie of European imperialism, Willard as hard-boiled detective finds in Colonel Kurtz the essential lie of his own and his nation's Vietnam venture.

Both Willard and Kurtz, discovering the inherent weakness and corruption of their society, have turned mentally to the enemy. Willard speaks admiringly during the film of "Charlie's" purity and strength, observing that the Viet Cong soldier "squats in the bush" and doesn't "get much USO."

Kurtz tells Willard that his illumination came when he real-ized "like I was shot with a diamond . . . bullet right through my forehead" that the Viet Cong's cutting off the children's arms he had inoculated was a stronger act: "If I had ten di-visions of those men then our problems here would be over very quickly." This motif has been mistakenly interpreted as the film's view that America was defeated by its reliance on technology and by its conscience.[23] Viewed in the con-text of the detective formula, it is properly understood as a critique of the hollowness of a "mission" that is based on an illusory abstraction as much as is the redeeming "idea" of Conrad's imperialism. The pure pursuit of an ideal, the obsession with efficient method, becomes the lack of "any method at all," the moral chaos Willard finds at Kurtz's com-pound, and that dark illumination causes him to draw back from his grail.

In the river journey Willard uncovered the corruption of the actual American mission; in Kurtz Willard finds the empti-ness even of the ideal. This is the significance, a virtually explicit reference to the role of the genre detective, of Kurtz's telling Willard "you have a right to kill me . . . but you have no right to judge me." Willard acts out the reassuring ac-tion of an agent of moral order, but in doing so realizes that he is judging himself, taking a moral stance towards his own unconscious self. When Willard leaves with Kurtz's book (a report on which Kurtz has scrawled "Drop the bomb" and "Exterminate them all!") and Lance, the surfing innocent trau-matized into acid-dropping acceptance of the surrounding madness, he duplicates Marlow's lie to Kurtz's "Intended." Willard at last sees, like Marlow, that the only possible re-sponse to the utter dissolution of his moral assumptions is to preserve innocence and the false ideal. Willard departs a hard-boiled detective who has made an investigation down the ultimate mean streets, his soul: "I wanted a mission, and for my sins they gave me one. Brought it up to me like room service. It was a real choice mission, and when it was over, I'd never want another."

The different interpretations of the Vietnam War provided by *The Deer Hunter* and *Apocalypse Now* result logically from the different meanings of the western and hard-boiled detective genres. Since the western is a nineteenth-century myth looking forward to a new civilization, and the detec-tive formula a twentieth-century myth looking around at a failed society, the visions that *The Deer Hunter* and *Apoca-lypse Now* bring to the Vietnam experience are literally a cen-tury apart. In *The Deer Hunter* Cimino transforms Vietnam into a regenerative myth that makes the traumatic experience a conceivably fortunate fall for the American Adam; in *Apocalypse Now* Coppola presents Vietnam as a nightmare extension of American society where only a marginal indi-vidual may preserve the American ideal. Beyond the impli-cations of the separate use of the two formulas is the different relation of each film to its formula. *The Deer Hunter* stands the western myth on its head, retaining its central elements while showing that the Vietnam landscape inverts its meaning; *Apocalypse Now* follows the pattern of action of the detective formula but extends the area of investigation to the self, merging the genre with the theme of *Heart of Darkness*. The result is that *The Deer Hunter* insists that Vietnam can be encountered in strictly American terms, while *Apocalypse Now* undermines the one dependable source of American order, the idealistic self-concept embodied in the "pure" motivation of the formula hero. Cimino sees the Vietnam involvement as a projected mirror where Americans can recognize their darkest impulses, but in response return once again to the original promise Cooper had recognized in the precolonial days of the young Deerslayer. Coppola views Vietnam as the projection of southern California into an alien landscape where even American idealism stands at last exposed.

The Deer Hunter and *Apocalypse Now,* while presenting distinctly different interpretations of the Vietnam War based on the separate formulas shaping their structures, also have an underlying relation resulting from their common use of major formulas of American popular romance that are themselves linked by the relation between their central heroes. The major criticisms leveled at the two films, their implausibility and ambiguity, are essential aspects of the romance mode by which the major American narrative tradition has dealt with extreme experience revealing basic cultural contradictions and conflicts. Both *The Deer Hunter* and *Apocalypse Now* avoid the limits of naturalistic, fragmented, or personal approaches to the war (found respectively in James Webb's novel, *Fields of Fire,* Michael Herr's memoir, *Dispatches,* and the film, *Coming Home*) by couching the terror of Vietnam in American myths. Each of these two films takes a hero who is a version of the national archetype, thus embodying the essential longings and anxieties of the American psyche, and sends him on a quest conveying the aberrant, fragmented, hallucinatory Vietnam experience while giving it a familiar, meaningful structure. Within the generic confines of the western and hard-boiled detective formulas, Vietnam may be contemplated, the terror reenacted, and the meaning probed. These formulaic genres, comprising central moral fantasies of American culture, provide collective dreams through which the trauma of the Vietnam War may be reexperienced, assimilated, and interpreted. Further, since these films significantly invert or undercut the implications of their mythic sources, they suggest the significance of Vietnam as a pivotal experience for American consciousness.

1. Stanley Solomon, *Beyond Formula: American Film Genres* (New York: Harcourt, 1976), 3.

2. Richard Chase, *The American Novel and Its Tradition* (Baltimore: Johns Hopkins Univ. Press, 1957), 13.

3. For my definitions and discussions of the characteristic elements of the western and hard-boiled detective genres, I draw largely on Solomon's *Beyond Formula* and John G. Cawelti's *Adventure, Mystery, and Romance: Formula Stories as Art and Popular Culture* (Chicago: Univ. of Chicago Press, 1976). My discussion of the hard-boiled detective genre also draws on George Grella's fine essay, "Murder and the Mean Streets: The Hard-Boiled Detective Novel," in *Detective Fiction: Crime and Compromise,* ed. Richard Stanley Allen and David Chacko (New York: Harcourt, 1974), 411-29.

4. David Axeen, "Eastern Western," *Film Quarterly,* 32 (1979), 17. Westerbeck calls the film a western, but only to attack it as a simplistic and "sickening," cowboys-and-Indians melodrama. See his "Peace with Honor: Cowboys and Viet Cong," *Commonweal,* 2 March 1979, 115-17.

5. Leslie Fiedler, *Love and Death in the American Novel,* rev. ed. (New York: Stein and Day, 1975), 142-82.

6. Cawelti, *Adventure, Mystery, and Romance,* 194.

7. Michael Cimino, "Ordeal by Fire and Ice," *American Cinematographer,* Oct. 1978, 1031.

8. Ibid., 965, 1006-07.

9. Dialogue has been transcribed from the films.

10. See, for instance, Marsha Kinder's "Political Game," *Film Quarterly,* 32 (1979), 13-17, and comments in "Vietnam Comes Home," *Time,* 23 April 1979, 23.

11. Richard Slotkin, *Regeneration Through Violence: The Mythology of the American Frontier, 1600-1860* (Middletown, Conn.: Wesleyan Univ. Press, 1973), 145.

12. Leo Marx, *The Machine in the Garden: Technology and the Pastoral Ideal in America* (New York: Oxford Univ. Press, 1964), 23.

13. See Michael D. Butler's "Narrative Structure and Historical Process in *The Last of the Mohicans,*" *American Literature,* 48 (1976), 117-39.

14. For a discussion of the relation of the hunter myth to the code of the western hero see "Book Two: The Sons of Leatherstocking" in Henry Nash Smith's *Virgin Land: The American West as Symbol and Myth,* 49-120, and Slotkin's chapter "Man Without a Cross: The Leatherstocking Myth (1823-1841)" in *Regeneration Through Violence,* 466-516.

15. See Slotkin, *Regeneration Through Violence,* 429, 490.

16. Veronica Geng, "Mistuh Kurtz—He Dead," *New Yorker,* 3 Sept. 1979, 70.

17. Grella, "Murder and the Mean Streets," 414.

18. Joseph Conrad, *Heart of Darkness,* ed. Robert Kimbrough, rev. ed. (New York: Norton, 1971), 63.

19. Greil Marcus, "Journey Up the River: An Interview with Francis Coppola," *Rolling Stone,* 1 Nov. 1979, 55.

20. Grella, "Murder and the Mean Streets," 422-23.

21. Ibid, 423.

22. See Garrett Stewart, "Coppola's Conrad: The Repetitions of Complicity," *Critical Inquiry,* 7 (1981), 455-74.

23. See David Bromwich, "Bad Faith of *Apocalypse Now,*" *Dissent,* 27 (1980), 207-10, 213.

William Simon (essay date Spring 1983)

SOURCE: "An Analysis of the Structure of *The Godfather, Part One,*" in *Studies in the Literary Imagination,* Vol. XVI, No. 1, Summer, 1983, pp. 75-90.

[*In the following essay, Simon provides a close analysis of the narrative structure of Coppola's* The Godfather, Part One.]

This essay attempts to perform several critical tasks. It is primarily an analysis of the narrative structure of *The Godfather, Part One,* directed in 1972 by Francis Ford Coppola. In these terms, my aim is to explain how meaning is created in that film through an understanding of its narrative structuring and the significance of its cultural codes.

At the same time the essay is involved with the application to film of critical methods derived from several important contemporary texts in narrative theory and aesthetics. In these terms, the following constitutes a test of the efficacy and validity in applying such analyses and methods to the study of film narrative. The purpose here is not to apply any one methodology or model of analysis in a rigid fashion. Rather, several central ideas from a number of texts are absorbed into the critical analysis. Perhaps the most important notions to be tested here are derived from Wolfgang Iser's works on reader response theory, *The Implied Reader* and *The Act of Reading.*[1] I shall attempt to apply Iser's concept of the "narrative gap" and the ways in which this gap causes the spectator to retroactively reread narrative information. As well, I shall rely on the concepts of the hermeneutic and cul-

tural codes from Roland Barthes' *S/Z.*[2] Iser's "narrative gap" and Barthes' hermeneutic code will together provide us with the tools to understand Coppola's ordering of narrative information. I shall also briefly refer to the concepts developed under the notion of "duration" by Gérard Genette in *Narrative Discourse.*[3] The relations of narrative time to story time and the function of ellipses will prove relevant.

This essay can also be viewed as a contribution to the continuing evaluation of American narrative film in the period roughly between 1965 and 1975.[4] In this respect, I proceed from the view that this period constitutes one of the richest and least understood and appreciated periods in American film history. The collective work of Altman, Coppola, Kubrick, Scorsese, Penn and Peckinpah, and such major individual achievements as Lester's *Petulia,* Polanski's *Chinatown* and Malick's *Badlands* are marked by an important overarching theme, the insistence that psychological and/or physical violence are at the core of American life. In addition, the films of this period are characterized by major developments in narrative form and structure, by the highly successful absorption into a mainstream popular narrative form of the characteristics of "open structure" associated with modernist narrative. This analysis of *The Godfather, Part One* treats the film as one of the key works of the period and as emblematic of many of its most basic characteristics and qualities.

Coppola's *The Godfather, Part One* is distinguished among other things by the number of scales or levels upon which it operates. In its combination of epic structure and highly individuated family melodrama, it is perhaps the American film which most closely approximates the nineteenth-century realist historical novel.

Three levels can be distinguished in the film's story-line. The film concentrates on the members of a single Italian-American family, the Corleones, in the period from approximately 1945 to 1955. At the same time, because the head of the family is the Don of one of the Mafia's Five Families, the film portrays the history of the Mafia during this period. On another level the life of the Corleones as an individual family and its significance as that of a Mafia Family are intimately related over the course of the film, creating an image of the Mafia Family's operations as being dialectically related to the mores and social ethos of the specific Italian-American family. A third level of meaning, one perhaps not as thoroughly interrelated to these first two levels, attempts to have the experiences of the Corleones correspond to an image of America during the decade depicted in the film. Coppola describes this large-scale ambition of the film in the following way: "The film always was a loose metaphor: Michael as America." Also, "I always wanted to use the Mafia as a metaphor for America."[5] This metaphor presumably suggests that the experiences of

Michael over the course of *Part One,* emerging from World War II as an innocent hero, becoming progressively corrupted as he becomes involved in the Family's "business," are to be understood as a representation of America's postwar history. Certainly the large contours of the Family's "progress" from first generation immigrants in New York's Little Italy to a home in the Long Island suburbs to total respectability on the West Coast (in this case, Nevada) corresponds to a quintessential American success story.

Aesthetically, *The Godfather* also operates on at least two levels. In its representation of the Corleone family, it is a deeply realistic work emphasizing highly individuated characterizations and the detailed observation of family mores and behavior. At the same time, the film is conceived on an epic, even operatic scale. It is divided roughly into four "acts," each building slowly to a heightened climax. Many scenes are set within family religious rituals and/or holidays (two weddings, a baptism, Christmas), thus expanding the meaning of these scenes in an epic direction as well.

There is another way of understanding the multiple levels upon which *The Godfather, Part One* operates. This has to do with what might be considered authorial attitude towards the characters and their actions. Like most gangster films, *The Godfather* treads a delicate line between valorization of its criminal characters and criticism of them. Certainly the characters in *The Godfather* conform to two of the central myths of violence described by John Cawelti in his valuable essay "Myths of Violence in American Popular Culture."[6] They conform to the "vigilante" myth in that they are positively shown as protecting the weak in the absence of an efficacious law enforcement system. And they conform to the "myth of equality through violence" in the ways in which they use their skills at violence and crime to rise from poverty to a position of wealth and power. In the rhetoric achieved by comparative characterization in the film, the principal members of the Corleone family, Don Vito Corleone and his son Michael, are infinitely more intelligent and less obviously corrupt than any of the other characters.

What is perhaps not so obvious about the film is how a critique of the Mafia and especially the central character, Michael Corleone (and accepting Coppola's intended metaphor, America), is constructed in the film. This critique can be considered an argument which is formulated through the film's narrative structure and its treatment of certain key characters. In the following analysis I shall pay special attention to the unfolding of this critical argument since it provides the ultimate key to the meaning of the film.

One other aspect of the following analysis should be introduced. In discussing American narrative films of the late 60's and early 70's earlier, I suggested that the representation of violence at the core of American society was the central theme of these films. The representation of violence is always a contentious issue but one way to understand its function and significance is to try to understand its narrative and moral contexts in individual works, as Cawelti suggests in his essay.[7] Consequently, a large part of the analysis is concentrated on those violent sequences that so often constitute the dramatic climaxes in *The Godfather.* Special attention is paid to the cultural codes surrounding this violence and the specific and very complex treatment of it.

The opening sequence of *The Godfather, Part One* portrays the marriage of Don Vito Corleone's only daughter Connie to one Carlo Rizzi. The sequence lasts some 26 minutes of the film's 175 minute running time and is by far the longest sequence in the film.[8] While obviously contracting the story time through ellipses, the sequence creates the effect of a linear continuous whole, encompassing the duration of the wedding celebration.

Despite this sense of continuity, the sequence is structured on a strong set of oppositions created by cutting alternatively between Don Vito's study and the celebration in the garden outdoors. The oppositions revolve around the cultural codes that interpenetrate both the Corleone and the Mafia levels of the family. The laying out of these codes helps set in motion the critical argument of the film. The oppositions run something like the following. The interior study is very darkly lit, the characters sitting in dark shadow. The garden is bathed in sunlight. The action in the study consists of Mafia business: a series of men pay their respects to Don Corleone and ask for a service. Contracts are assigned in response to these requests. The study is an exclusive private sanctuary; only males have access to it. It is a space where men report violent violations of their families and arrange for violent reprisal.

The garden provides strong contrasts. The basic activity is the celebration of a marriage, defined as a perpetuation of the family. (References are made to the forthcoming children of the bride and groom.) The activity is open, social and inclusive, embracing not only men, women and children, but even rival Mafia Families. The dancing, singing, joking, and picture-taking are celebratory, privileging the family as a unifying totality.

While the activities of the two spaces contrast sharply, there are also indications that they are inextricably related. For instance, it is made clear that the head of the household cannot deny a request on his daughter's wedding day. Thus, the criminal contracts being established in the study are a direct product of a particular social code of the family. Also, while at this point in the film, the violent stories related in the study seem antithetical to the celebratory spirit of the wedding, as the film unfolds and the marriage of Connie and Carlo turns increasingly violent, it is understood that the violence suggested in this first scene is a dialectical component of that marriage. What appears initially as opposition is progressively understood as dialectical. Violence on different levels is exposed as the inescapable underside of the marriage in the film. Framed by this marriage and the subsequent baptism, the film relates the violence of organized Mafia criminality to family rituals and ethos.

The setting up of the oppositions in the interior and exterior segments of the wedding sequence establishes certain implications. The exclusiveness of the study and inclusiveness of the garden create a system by which certain characters can be understood as "insiders" and others as "outsiders." Obviously, male members of the Mafia Family are insiders while women and children are defined as outsiders. Michael, the youngest son, just returned from the war, still in uniform, educated at an Ivy League college, accompanied by a non-Italian girl-friend, is the most important outsider. He dissociates himself from the family business ("That's my family, Kay, it's not me.") and unlike his older brothers, is seen only in the garden. The overarching plot of **The Godfather, Part One** traces the shift in Michael's position from outsider to insider and the changes such a shift produces.

The other significant outsider is Kay, Michael's girl-friend. She is an outsider by virtue of being a woman, a non-Italian and a total newcomer to such rituals as an Italian wedding. The degree to which she is an outsider is especially suggested in her dialogue with Michael. She is constantly asking questions about family customs, the wedding celebration and Don Corleone's "business," about which she is especially dismayed.

Kay's position at the beginning of the film as someone who is alien to the values and activities depicted in the opening sequence is especially important in establishing her as the character through whom the critical argument of the film will be formulated. In order to appreciate how Kay functions in this respect, it is useful to observe how she is placed in relation to one of the central cultural codes of the Italian-American ethos of the film, namely the assumption that marriage exists for the purposes of procreation, preferably of male offspring. In different ways, Kay is systematically juxtaposed to manifestations of this code. For example, in this opening sequence, the first close-shots of her are immediately preceded by shots of Luca Brazzi, a brutal and almost retarded enforcer for Don Corleone, rehearsing the salutation with which he is about to greet Don Corleone: "May your first child be a masculine child." Kay's first dialogue is to ask Michael in a dismayed way who this strange creature is. In other words, she is immediately juxtaposed as alienated from this character and his statement of the absolutely central theme of the operative ethos of the film. In the next section of the film, in a scene in which she and

Michael emerge from Radio City Music Hall during the Christmas season, she is juxtaposed with the words "The Nativity" on the marquee. Much later in the film during a period when she and Michael have been separated, it is revealed that she is working as a school teacher, that is as a kind of surrogate mother. Much later in the film, when she is married to Michael and has learned something of the family culture, it is she who asks Michael to stand as godfather for Connie and Carlo's son. Her partial assimilation into the family is conveyed through her newfound understanding of this code.[9]

One last point about the wedding sequence has to do with the patterns it establishes in terms of the representation of violence in the film. In several important senses, the wedding sequence functions as an introduction to the workings of the Mafia, an almost instructional exposition carried out entirely in words. The scenes of petitioners to Don Corleone establish how contracts are made and imply that violence will be part of the execution of the contract. A story that Michael tells Kay about how Don Corleone freed the singer Johnny Fontaine from his contract with a band-leader specifies how violence functions as a central aspect of the Don's "business." However, these references are all verbal; violent action is either described or related, or implied by euphemisms.

The film's next sequence is both a continuation of the series of illustrations on how the Mafia operates and the culmination of the first act of the film. It also alters in complex ways the representation of violence, concluding with the film's first violent climax. Its organization merits special attention.

The action of this sequence grows out of the wedding sequence in that it shows how Tom Hagen, Don Corleone's adopted son and "consigliore," obtains a role in a film for Johnny Fontaine, the Don's god-son and one of the petitioners at the wedding. Unlike the first sequence with its strong sense of linear continuity over a protracted period, this sequence consists of three brief scenes, totalling 7 ½ minutes of film time and covering 12-15 hours of story time. Prominent ellipses create important narrative gaps from scene to scene.

In the first scene, Hagen confronts Jack Woltz, the studio head, demanding that Johnny be given the part. Woltz violently refuses, asks Hagen to leave, and tells a henchman to find out who Hagen works for. After the first ellipsis, we now see Woltz entertaining Hagen at his mansion later that evening. Woltz is clearly more deferential towards Hagen because, we soon learn, he now understands that Hagen works for Don Corleone. The narrative gap, created through the elision, activates the spectator to fill in missing narrative information. Presumably, in the interim, Woltz's henchman had discovered that Hagen worked for Don Corleone, a fact important enough to cause Woltz to invite Hagen for dinner.

The level of narrative information omitted in this ellipsis is not very significant. The importance of it has to do with the way in which Coppola introduces the procedure of the narrative gap as a way of structuring the spectator's apprehension of narrative information. This gap, in effect, sets the groundwork for the next one which is infinitely more significant and dramatic.

In the dinner scene between Woltz and Hagen, despite Woltz's initial deference, he concludes by stating that Johnny Fontaine will never work for his studio. After another ellipsis, the next scene commences with an exterior shot of Woltz's mansion. Suspenseful music accompanies the series of shots which bring us into Woltz's bedroom where he is sleeping later that night. As the music reaches a climax, Woltz stirs in his bed. He lifts the sheet and discovers the bloody, severed head of his prize racehorse which he had proudly showed off to Hagen during the evening. Woltz screams in horror, a scream which continues over the exterior shot of his mansion which ends the sequence and the first major act of *The Godfather.*

The narrative gap between the second and third scenes of the Hollywood sequence sets the stage for the sensational effect of the violence in the third scene. The audience has in no way been prepared for the action; no causation has been established. We are put in the position of retrospectively inferring that after Woltz's second refusal, Hagen had commanded someone to sever the horse's head and place it in Woltz's bed as he slept. Beyond the violence of the image itself, the power of this infamous scene derives from the fact that we have not been prepared for it, that we discover the horse's head at the same time as the victim of the violent act does. Furthermore, the mode of narrative information is virtually the opposite of all previous manifestations of violence in the film. For the first time, violence or the horrifying result of it is dramatized and visualized directly. The violent power of Don Corleone and his agents is demonstrated to us directly as we experience it through the victim.

The hermeneutic pattern of withholding narrative information and then gradually revealing enough information for the spectator to fill in the narrative gap operates on a visual as well as a narrative level. In this final scene of the Hollywood sequence, the music signals that something dramatic is to happen but the initial distance of the camera in the exterior and interior shots withholds the information. The camera's slow movements suggest an intentionality, that it is moving toward something, but it is only after some time that the camera draws close enough to reveal the crucial information and its suggestion as to the nature of the elided narrative action. The handling of the camera in relation to narrative information in the space of action in this scene is a complement to the opening shots of the film. Here, the film's action starts on a tight close-up of the first petitioner addressing an unseen and unheard character. A very gradual pulling out of the camera reveals Don Corleone as the addressee of the petition. Only subsequent shots reveal that other members of the Family are in the study. This type of visual patterning activates the sense that the spectator is not always in full possession of the necessary narrative information. It suggests that things are sometimes hidden or obscured. And more often than not, as we have seen and shall continue to see, the missing information attests to the violent power of the Corleone Family or their antagonists.

While the "horse's head" sequence is the culmination of the first act of the film, the next scenes which properly speaking initiate the second section contain two interesting additional revelations about the previous section. The first scene (which consists of the Corleone Family strategy meeting about the attempts of a rival Family to engage them in the drug business) starts with a dissolve from the end of the "horse's head" scene to a close shot of Don Corleone, presiding over the meeting. While it quickly becomes clear that the meeting concerns totally new business, the dissolve acts as a certification of agency. That is, the dissolve strongly suggests that Don Corleone is to be understood as the agent/cause of the severed horse's head. The chain of causality is suggested only after the effect has been seen.

Further, in the next scene, brief reference is made to a garland of flowers standing in the Don's office. We are told that they were sent by Johnny Fontaine on the occasion of his assuming the role in the film. We are to read in that Woltz's discovery of his prized horse's severed head led him to offer Johnny the role. Narrative closure for this episode is achieved slowly and retroactively, activating the spectator to tie together its meaning.

One of the most striking features of *The Godfather, Part One* is the way in which its four acts are arranged in strikingly different systems of structuring the narrative information, a process already observed in the differences between the wedding and Hollywood scenes in the first act. The second act is also structured according to a quite different system; this quickly becomes clear as it begins to unfold. This section deals with the conflict over the drug business between the Corleone Family and the Tattaglia Family and its partner, Virgil Salozzo. The first part of the act deals with the Tattaglias' attacks on the Corleone Family, culminating in the attempted assassination of Don Corleone. The second part deals with Michael's gradual involvement in the family business as a response to the attack on his father.

Its climax is the shooting of Salozzo and the Police Captain McCloskey by Michael.

The first part of the act proceeds as a series of brief quickly edited scenes—none of them more than three minutes or so in length. Several of the scenes are parallel edited in contrast to the continuity of action in the first section. Beyond the contrast in the duration and temporal arrangement of the scenes, several other contrasting patterns operate during this section. Perhaps the most important involves the shift in terms of who is exercising violent power in the film. In the first half of this second act, the Corleones become victims to Salozzo and the Tattaglias. While the attacks on the Corleones are not presented as elaborately or dramatically as the "horse's head" scene, they share with that scene that characteristic of being totally unexpected; they are not prepared for through expository information. Only after Luca Brazzi is strangled, Tom Hagen kidnapped and the Don shot in quick successive scenes do the characters reflect that a large-scale "war" has been initiated by Salozzo and the Tattaglias. Thus, the pattern of unexpected violence continues though directed now at the Corleones.

The reversal of this pattern in the second act of this section commences with the scene of Michael's visit to his father in the hospital. This is the longest uninterrupted scene in a long time, lasting approximately 9 minutes after 13 scenes, none of which exceeds 3 1/4 minutes. In this scene, Michael with the help of one other man, succeeds brilliantly in foiling a second attempt on his father's life. The scene is structured very largely around Michael's aural and visual point of view, one of the few scenes in the film which is so strongly focalized by the perspective of a single character. Through its duration and emphasis on point of view, the structure privileges Michael as he takes the first steps towards total involvement in the family affairs.

This section of the film culminates with another dramatic act of violence, Michael's shooting of Salozzo and McCluskey, his policeman protector. From the first, the structure is radically altered in terms of how the narrative information is revealed. Instead of creating a narrative gap through elision and presenting the violence as an unexpected outburst, this incident is set up with great care. We hear the Family members discuss Michael's suggestion that he shoot the two. When they finally decide to go along with the plan, we see Michael being tutored on how to shoot. Painstaking detail surrounds the plan. Instead of elision, detailed linear causal suspense becomes the operative narrative mode. The function of the continuity at this point is to concentrate attention on Michael's developing character, his intelligence and courage as he establishes himself as the heir apparent. The violence of Michael's shooting Salozzo and McCluskey gains its impact from the detailed concentration on his actions, rather than from its unexpectedness.

The third act of *The Godfather, Part One* is a transitional one, preparing the way for Michael's final ascendance as Godfather. This section is occupied largely with Michael's experiences in Sicily where he is waiting out the aftermath of his killing of Salozzo and McCluskey and with the elimination of Sonny, the oldest Corleone son, from contention as heir apparent.

While it is a transitional section of the film, Coppola structures it in a very interesting way in order to foreground certain aspects of the cultural ethos underlying the action of the film.[10] The section is largely organized around an alternation of scenes in Sicily and scenes in New York. In Sicily, Michael meets and marries a beautiful peasant woman. The atmosphere of the courtship and wedding is idyllic, pastoral, and old-worldly with the threat of Mafia violence hovering for the most part at the edges of the action.

By contrast, the New York scenes trace the increasing violence in Connie and Carlo's marriage and Sonny's even more violent protectiveness of his sister. The Corleone family's enemies use this violence on the family level to eliminate Sonny, murdering him as he drives to gain revenge on Carlo for beating Connie.

In effect, the contrastive editing from Sicily to New York can be understood as being based on the comparison of marriages, of male/female relationships, of domestic situations, all within the pervasive ethos and cultural codes of this film. The specific editing of scenes in relation to each other intensifies the contrasts. From a lyrical treatment of old-worldly Sicilian courtship ritual, we cut to Sonny, hurriedly leaving his illicit mistress in order to beat Carlo to a pulp. The cut back to Sicily is to wedding bells and a romantic old world ceremony, an ironic reminder of the film's opening scene.

The New York scenes fill in details of the cultural ethos. That Mafia business is the province of males only is clearly stated in a family dinner scene when Sonny admonishes Carlo with the words "We don't discuss business at the table." Ironically, Sonny himself had earlier violated this code. This breech by both men links them and suggests that Sonny's inability to live up to the domestic family ethos disqualifies him as the potential Don. His violent overreactions in his brotherly protectiveness lead directly to his death.

If Sonny is negatively criticized according to the family ethos, it should be added that while Michael's situation seems idyllic, the double standard of his situation is also sharply and ironically underlined by the edited juxtaposition of certain scenes. Immediately after the lyrical erotic scene of Michael and his new bride's wedding night, Kay, who has been patiently waiting for Michael's return, comes to the Corleone compound to inquire of him. This juxtaposition emphasizes the degree to which Michael ignores his relationship to Kay. His hypocrisy in relation to her establishes the cultural grounds upon which the critical appraisal of Michael will be carried out in the film's final scenes.

Two manifestations of violence in this third act require attention. The murder of Sonny as he drives to Connie's is another outbreak of violence that is totally unprepared for in the narrative. It is only over the course of the film's final hour that a detailed explanation of the murder is provided. Similarly, the Sicilian section ends with Michael's new wife killed by a bomb exploding in their car, a bomb intended for Michael. Minimal preparation is given for this sudden outburst. Only after the two murders is it clarified that they are the antagonists' response to the murders of Salozzo and McCluskey. Again, the pendulum has swung so that the Corleones are victims of unexpected attacks. The final act of the film deals with the restoration of the Corleones' power.

This final act begins with a series of scenes covering the transition in power from Don Corleone to Michael over an approximately seven year period. Don Corleone arranges for the meeting of the Five Families in which a peace is arranged and Michael is guaranteed safe return from Sicily. Vito tutors Michael and warns him of danger from Don Barzini, a family head who was behind the Salozzo-Tattaglia opposition. The Corleone Family begins a move into Las Vegas gambling. Michael finds Kay and marries her, never telling her about his Sicilian wife. Finally, Don Corleone dies and the stage is set for Michael's ascendance to power.

The climactic scenes of this act of the film revolve around two rituals, Don Corleone's funeral and the baptism of Connie and Carlo's son with Michael as the child's godfather. The funeral is related to the film's opening scene in that the ritual becomes a "front" for conducting Mafia business. As Don Corleone had warned, one of the family confidantes, Tessio, attempts to arrange a meeting between Michael and Don Barzini.

The baptism scene follows immediately after the funeral and is structured in a very complex way, making it the climactic scene of violence. In effect, what happens in this scene is that Michael's elimination by assassination of his five most important rivals (including Don Barzini) is intercut with the actual baptism ritual in a very elaborate montage.

The most basic notion suggested by this intercutting is that the shooting of the rivals and the baptism are happening simultaneously. However, the complexity of the structuring goes far beyond the parallel editing principle.

First it should be noted that the baptism scene is related to the opening wedding scene in that it involves the product of Connie and Carlo's marriage. Superficially, both the wedding and the baptism are positive procreative celebrations but both are represented as having a dialectically related underside. They are situations for violent Mafia activity. Like the wedding scene, the baptism scene is structured on edited oppositions, the baptism ritual ceremony on the one hand and the murders of the five rivals on the other.

Beyond the similarity, there are also several significant differences. Unlike the Mafia business during the Wedding and unlike the treatment of Michael's killing of Salozzo and McCluskey but like so many of the other violent actions, there is no narrative preparation, no causal explanation of what is about to happen. The shots of men readying themselves and the shootings themselves take place in a narrative void; only after the scene is complete do the characters gradually verbalize the significance of the action, that Michael has successfully eliminated his most serious rivals.

The preparations for the killings are shown in very brief shots cut into the early stages of the baptism. We see one man cleaning a gun, another putting on a policeman's uniform, another walking to an undisclosed location. Several of the victims are seen in everyday activities, oblivious to the impending threats. Because none of these activities have been narratively prepared for, these isolated shots remain on the level of hermeneutic enigma. Only as the sequence develops and we see the actual shooting do we understand that the first group of men was preparing to shoot the rivals. At points, the editing of the very brief shots of different activities seems to match or compare the activities. For example, at one point the movement of an assassin cleaning a machine gun is matched by similarity of movement to the priest's hand anointing the baby. The obvious reading is to see the two activities as contrasting but the intent of the montage in its entirety is to suggest the inextricable relations between the activities, that the series of shootings are related to the baptism. The fact that the sound from the baptism ceremony continues over shots taking place in diverse locations in New York and Las Vegas reinforces this sense of identity of the actions.

The brief shots of the actual killings of the rivals are intercut with the crucial phase of the baptism ritual when Michael affirms his faith and renounces Satan. This editing produces an extremely strong effect. Once again, interpreting the juxtaposition as highlighting the contrast between the holy ritual and the brutal violence constitutes the most obvious response to the sequence of shots. However, because we recognize the victim as Michael's enemies, it is also possible to read the shots of Michael intercut with the murders as editing on agency, as declaring that Michael is responsible for these murders. In these terms, the sacrilegious profanation of the baptism ceremony is especially striking; Michael's violent actions totally negate any serious meaning of the vows he is proclaiming.

Ultimately, this extremely complex montage can be seen as positing a double meaning of Michael's experience as Godfather. He is not simply standing as Godfather for Connie and Carlo's son. He is also being initiated as the new Mafia-level Godfather of the Corleone Family. The successful slaughter of his enemies in an elaborately orchestrated plot, represented in the context of his baptism vows, testifies to his power and right to become Mafia Godfather. And the inextricable ties between family and Mafia activities are powerfully demonstrated. The profanation of family ritual and values is established as a necessary condition or attribute of the Mafia Godfather. The horrible double standard of the cultural ethos is exposed in this grand operatic scene.

Some of the implications of this great climactic scene are underlined in the film's few remaining scenes, culminating in the critical portrait of Michael with which the film ends. First, Tessio, the old family friend who had betrayed the Corleones to Barzini is led off presumably to his death. Then, Michael for the first time confronts Carlo with the accusation that he had betrayed Sonny to his enemies. Two points are noteworthy about this brief scene. First, it continues the profanation of the baptism. Michael exclaims to Carlo while trying to make him confess, "Do you think I'd make my sister a widow? I'm godfather to your son." This reassurance leads Carlo to confess and Michael immediately has him strangled to death. In short, the brief invocation of family values is immediately negated by Mafia vengeance.

The other interesting factor is that the accusation of Carlo's perfidy in Sonny's assassination is mentioned in this scene for the first time, approximately 45 minutes of film time and some 7 or 8 years of story time after Sonny's death. This is one of the most extreme cases of the operation of a narrative gap in the film. It causes the spectator to think back to Carlo's actions in relation to Connie and Sonny and to reinterpret them as purposeful baiting of Sonny to leave him isolated for the assassination.

The final statement on the meaning of Michael's new status as Godfather is played out in a scene with his wife Kay. The scene begins with Connie invading the male sanctum of the study hysterically accusing Michael of killing her husband. She is led off, but Kay remains to confront Michael about Carlo. Michael, as the modern Godfather, agrees to break the code that he had previously insisted upon, namely that Kay never ask him about his business affairs. For one of the very few times in the film, Coppola employs a direct shot-counter-shot editing pattern between Michael and Kay during the ensuing dialogue. The directness with which the two look into each other's eyes, reinforced by the editing pattern, establishes a code of privileged honesty and respect between them. Kay asks him if he had Carlo killed. Michael stares into her eyes and answers "No." Kay smiles in relief and goes to the next room to pour them drinks. In a brilliant

series of shots, she pours the drinks as in the background, several of Michael's henchmen kiss his hand and address him for the first time as Don Corleone, in effect saluting him for his day's brilliant success. In a shot from inside Michael's study, Kay is seen observing this action. Then, as the door to the study is closed, she is eliminated from view. The screen goes to black and the film ends.

This final shot constitutes a gesture of utter exclusion, virtually a negation of her existence from Michael's point of view as Godfather. He has invoked their marital bond by agreeing to break the male code just this one time, then profaned that bond by lying to her. The exclusion and negation of her performed by closing the door, amounts to the psychological murder of Kay. As such, it comments on Michael's situation as Godfather, negates his position at the beginning of the film. It suggests the denial of human contact and positive social ethos that he is required to assume in his new position. It shows him stone-hearted and isolated, alone with his agents of violence.

Interestingly, in discussing why he decided to film *Part Two* of *The Godfather* Coppola stated that he wanted to make clear what he felt had been stated about Michael in *Part One* but not sufficiently understood. "I wanted to take Michael to what I felt was the logical conclusion. He wins every battle; his brilliance and his resources enable him to defeat all his enemies. I didn't want Michael to die. I didn't want Michael to be put into prison. I didn't want him to be assassinated by his rivals. But, in a bigger sense, I wanted to destroy Michael. There's no doubt that by the end of this picture, Michael Corleone, having beaten everyone, is sitting there alone, a living corpse . . . Michael is doomed."[11]

It is my contention that a careful reading of *Part One* makes it clear that this critical image of Michael and the values by which he lives has already been fully achieved.

1. Wolfgang Iser, *The Implied Reader: Patterns of Communication in Prose and Fiction from Bunyan to Beckett* (Baltimore: Johns Hopkins Univ. Press, 1974); and *The Act of Reading: A Theory of Aesthetic Response* (Baltimore: Johns Hopkins Univ. Press, 1978).

2. Roland Barthes, *S/Z*, trans. Richard Miller (New York: Hill and Wang, 1974).

3. Gérard Genette, *Narrative Discourse: An Essay in Method,* trans. Jane E. Lewin (Ithaca, N. Y.: Cornell Univ. Press, 1980).

4. The key work in this evaluation is Robert Phillip Kolker, *A Cinema of Loneliness: Penn, Kubrick, Coppola, Scorsese, Altman* (New York: Oxford Univ. Press, 1980).

5. Coppola in Stephen Farber, "Coppola and *The Godfather*," *Sight and Sound,* 41:4 (Autumn 1972), p. 223.

6. John Cawelti, "Myths of Violence in American Popular Culture," *Critical Inquiry,* 1:3 (March 1975).

7. Cawelti, pp. 523-24.

8. I am indebted to the students in my course, "Seminar in Film Analysis," in New York University's Department of Cinema Studies in Spring 1981 for the timing of scenes.

9. It is very significant that in **The Godfather, Part Two,** when Kay's and Michael's marriage is shattered, she takes her most dramatic stand against Michael by having an abortion. She purposefully chooses to violate the codes surrounding procreation.

10. It is important to note that the complex structuring of scenes in this section of the film, as well as the cross-cutting of the baptism scene and the elimination of the rivals in the last act, are not handled in this fashion in Mario Puzo's novel. The creation of the complex juxtapositions seems clearly to be Coppola's accomplishment, given the unimaginative linearity of the novel.

11. Coppola, quoted in Robert K. Johnson, *Francis Ford Coppola* (Boston: Twayne Publishers, 1977), p. 148.

Thomas J. Ferraro   (essay date 1989)

SOURCE: "Blood in the Marketplace: The Business of Family in *The Godfather* Narratives," in *The Invention of Ethnicity,* edited by Werner Sollors, Oxford University Press, 1989, pp. 176-208.

[*In the following essay, Ferraro analyzes the relationship between family and business in Puzo's* The Godfather, *and how Coppola's* The Godfather II *and Richard Condon's* Prizzi's Honor *build upon the original* Godfather *narrative.*]

> Giorgio introduces me to his friend Piero Paco, hero of the Italo-American breach into American literature. He looks like a massive gangster but turns out to be a plain, nice guy with a lot of folksy stories and no complexes. He doesn't feel guilty about blacks, doesn't care about elevating Italo-American prestige. He's no missionary for wops. No gripes about the Establishment. He just decided in the best American way to write a book that would make half a million bucks because he was tired of being ignored.

> "You don't think struggling Italo-Americans should stick together and give each other a push up from the bottom of the pile where they've always been?" I ask him. But he's no struggling half-breed anymore. He's made his pile; he's all-American now.

> "I'm not going to push that crap," he says engagingly.

—Helen Barolini, *Umbertina* (1979)

> What, after all, could be more American than the success stories of penniless immigrant boys clawing their way to wealth and respectability by private enterprise? What legitimate American business tycoon ever objected to being called "ruthless," to being credited (like the good boxer) with the "killer instinct". . . ?

> What is more, *The Godfather* could be seen to represent not only some of the continuing principles of the American way of life, but the ancestral ideals it had somehow inexplicably lost on the way. In Don Corleone's world bosses were respected and loved by their subordinates as surrogate fathers. Men were men and women were glad of it. Morality ruled unchallenged, and crime, for the most part, was kept off the streets. Families stuck together under patriarchal control. Children obeyed—fathers, and virtuous wives were not afraid of losing their status to mistresses. . . . No wonder *New York* magazine exclaimed (according to the paperback edition's blurb): "You'll find it hard to stop dreaming about it."

—E. J. Hobsbawm, *"Robin Hoodo"*

In his 1969 blockbuster, *The Godfather,* Mario Puzo presented an image of the Mafia that has become commonplace in American popular culture. Since Puzo, it has been taken for granted that the Mafia operates as a consortium of illegitimate businesses, structured along family lines, with a familial patriarch or "godfather" as the chief executive officer of each syndicate.[1] Puzo's version of the Mafia fuses into one icon the realms of family and economy, of southern Italian ethnicity and big-time American capitalism, of *blood* and the *marketplace.* "Blood" refers to the violence of organized crime. "Blood" also refers to the familial clan, and its extension through the fictive system of the *compare,* or "co-godparenthood." In *The Godfather,* the representation of the Mafia fuses ethnic tribalism with the all-American pursuit of wealth and power. Since its publication, we have regarded this business of family in *The Godfather* as a figment of Puzo's opportunistic imagination, which it remains in part.

But the business of family in Puzo's Mafia is also a provocative revision of accepted notions of what ethnicity is and how it works—the new ethnic sociology in popular literary form.

During the late seventies and early eighties, there was a short outburst of scholarly interest in *The Godfather* and its myriad offspring. A consensus about the meaning of the saga's popularity emerges from the books and essays of Fredric Jameson, Eric Hobsbawm, John Cawelti, and John Sutherland. The portrayal of the Corleone family collective allows Americans, in the post-Vietnam era, to fantasize about the glory days of "closely knit traditional authority." The portrayal of the power and destructive greed of the Mafia chieftains permits Americans to vent their rage at "the managerial elite who hold the reins of corporate power and use it for their own benefit."[2] The family and business thematics are, in each instance, disengaged from one another. As Jameson puts it: on the one hand, the ethnic family imagery satisfies "a Utopian longing" for collectivity; on the other hand, "the substitution of crime for big business" is the narrative's "ideological function."[3] In standard treatments like these, Puzo's narrative is regarded as a brilliant (or brilliantly lucky) instance of satisfying two disparate appetites with a single symbol. This perspective, formulated in the late seventies, seems to have settled the issue of the novel's popularity.

I want to reopen that issue. We need to return to *The Godfather* because we have too easily dismissed its representation of the Mafia as a two-part fantasy. Of course, *The Godfather* is not reliable as a roman a clef or as a historical novel: Puzo's details are fuzzy, mixed-up, and much exaggerated.[4] "There was things he stretched," as Huck would put it, and everyone knows it. But critics have been too ready to accept his major sociological premise—family and business working in tandem—as pure mythology. The importance of *The Godfather* lies not in a double mythology, I would argue, but in its taking of the fusion of kinship and capitalist enterprise *seriously.* Its cultural significance lies not in the simultaneous appeals of "family" and "business" imagery but rather in the appeal of an actual structural simultaneity: *the business of family.* By failing to pause long enough to consider its surface narrative, critics have underestimated not only the strategies of the novel but the insights and intuitions of its huge audience as well.

Readers have underestimated the business of family because little in traditional theories of the family, ethnicity, and advanced capitalism has prepared them to recognize it. In both scholarly and popular treatments, ethnic culture and extended kinship are interpreted as barriers to the successful negotiation of the mobility ladder, particularly its upper ranks. Southern Italian immigrants and their descendants have long been thought to exemplify the principle that the more clannish an ethnic group, the slower its assimilation and economic advancement.[5] Herbert Gans's *Urban Villagers*, Virginia Yans-McLaughlin's *Family and Community*, Thomas Kessner's *The Golden Door*, and Thomas Sowell's *Ethnic America* essentially update the social-work perspectives of writers such as Phyllis H. Williams and Leonard Covello.[6] In 1944, Covello wrote,

> Any social consciousness of Italo-Americans within "Little Italies" appertains primarily to sharing and adhering to the family tradition as the main motif of their philosophy of life.... The retention of this cultural "basis" is essentially the source of their retarded adjustment.[7]

This long-standing tradition of identifying the Italian family structure as a dysfunctional survival runs aground on the Mafia.

Historians and sociologists attest to the difficulty of interpreting the Mafia in terms of a linear model of assimilation and upward mobility. All commentators recognize that the Mafia was not simply transported here; that it grew up from the multiethnic immigrant streets, rather than being passed on from father to son; and that Prohibition was the major factor in shaping its growth. In *A Family Business*, the sociologist Francis A. J. Ianni concedes these points, only to stress the family structure of the syndicates and the origin of this familialism in southern Italy:

> [The Lupullo crime organization] *feels* like a kinship-structured group; familialism founded it and is still its stock in trade. One senses immediately not only the strength of the bond, but the inability of members to see any morality or social order larger than their own.

Ianni's research tempts him into abandoning the tradition of placing ethnic phenomena on a linear continuum running from Old World marginality to New World centrality.[8] His research supports and his analysis anticipates (if it does not quite articulate) the cutting edge of ethnic theory. It is time for the criticism of ethnic literature generally, and of *The Godfather* in particular, to take advantage of such theory.

Scholars in a number of fields are working to change the way we think about ethnicity, ethnic groups, and ethnic culture. In identifying the social bases of ethnicity, theorists are shifting emphasis from intergenerational transmission to arenas of conflict in complex societies. They argue that we need to examine ethnic cultures not as Old World survivals (whatever their roots) but as strategies to deal with the unequal distribution of wealth, power, and status. In this light, ethnic groups are seen to include not only socially marginal peoples but any groups who use symbols of common descent and tradition to create or maintain power. From a historian's perspective, European family structures and traditions do not necessarily dissolve in the face of capitalism but rather, as they have always done, evolve to meet its changing needs.[9] Herbert Gans has spoken of "cost-free" ethnicity among the middle classes, but ethnicity is often *profitable* as well.[10]

In his work, the anthropologist Abner Cohen conceives of ethnic groups as "interest groups," in which ethnic symbols function in lieu of more formal structures such as the law. By the symbolic apparatus of ethnicity, he means the emphasis on common history and tradition, endogamy and social boundary maintenance, religion and ritual, and everyday encoded behavior, including "accent, manner of speech, etiquette, style of joking, play," and so forth: the rhetoric and codes of "blood."[11] As Cohen explains, the symbolic apparatus of "ethnicity" incites genuine loyalty and emotion, whose power and idiosyncrasy should not be underestimated. But the apparatus also serves utilitarian purposes within society at large, including the economic marketplace. In many of our most familiar examples, the function of ethnic ritual is primarily defensive, organizing a group on the margins of society: but the uses of ethnicity can be quite aggressive as well. The Italian-American Mafia is a case in point. As Ianni and others have demonstrated, it is the ethos of ethnic solidarity that puts the *organization* into Italian-American organized crime.

In her discussion of *The Godfather*, Rose Basile Green comes the closest of any critic, I think, to unpacking in Cohen's fashion what she herself calls the "socioeconomic ethnic image" of the Corleone crime syndicate. Unlike almost everyone else, Green takes seriously Puzo's portrayal of the syndicates not as a historical novel about actual gangsters but as a treatise (however romanticized) "dealing with the contemporary strategy of gaining and securing power." Yet her analysis splits into typical parallel paths: crime as a means for social mobility versus the family as a locus of traditional southern Italian responsibility. Although Green identifies "a subtle line between personal interest and structural power," she too fails to make the strongest connection between the private family life ascribed to Don Corleone and the illegitimate enterprise he heads. When Green says that *The Godfather* explores "the contemporary strategy of gaining and securing power," she means by "strategy" the tactics of bribery, intimidation, the brokerage of votes, intergang warfare, and so forth, with which Don Corleone conducts business outside the confines of his own organization. But the most noteworthy device for gaining and securing power in Puzo's depiction is internal to the Corleone syndicate. The device is not a gun or payola but, quite simply and obviously, that mystified entity the "southern Italian family."[12]

"Tell the old man I learned it all from him and that

I'm glad I had this chance to pay him back for all he did for me. He was a good father."
—Michael Corleone

As narrator in *The Godfather*, Puzo adopts the familiar role of cultural interpreter, mediating between outside readers and an ethnic secret society. Puzo's agenda, implicit yet universally understood, is to explain why Sicilian-Americans have made such good criminals. The answer, generally speaking, is their cult of family honor. The Corleones believe, with a kind of feudal fervor, in patriarchy, patronage, and protection. *The Godfather* is saturated with the imagery of paternity, family, and intimate friendship; with the rhetoric of respect, loyalty, and the code of silence; with references to Sicilian blood and the machismo attributed to it; with the social events—weddings, christenings, funerals, meals, and so forth—that embody the culture of family honor. Always the business of crime is interlaced with the responsibilities of family. In the film, for instance, Clemenza frets over a request from his wife even as he presides over the execution of Paulie Gatto: "Don't forget the cannolis!" Don Vito himself is a true believer. He believes in the mutual obligation of kinfolk. He seeks to expand his wealth and power to protect his dependents and to make his protection available to more and more people. He recruits from within his family to keep the business "all in the family" for the family's sake. "It was at this time that the Don got the idea that he ran his world far better than his enemies ran the greater world which continually obstructed his path."[13] At the same time, "not his best friends would have called Don Corleone a saint from heaven"; there is always "some self-interest" in his generosity (*G*, 215). For everyone recognizes the wisdom of family honor—Corleone's honor—given the special exigencies of operating in a big way in an outlawed underground economy.

In his analysis of the ethnic group as an interest group, Abner Cohen stresses the growth potential wherever there is a sector of an economy that has not been organized formally:

> Even in the advanced liberal industrial societies there are some structural conditions under which an interest group cannot organize itself on formal lines. Its formal organization may be opposed by the state or by other groups within the state, or may be incompatible with some important principles in the society; or the interests it represents may be newly developed and not yet articulated in terms of a formal organization and accommodated with the formal structure of the society. Under these conditions the group will articulate its organization on informal lines, making use of the kinship, friendship, ritual, ceremonial, and

other symbolic activities that are implicit in what is known as style of life.[14]

The ethnic ethos means sticking together, respecting the authority of the group rather than that of outsiders, defending the group's turf, and abiding by tradition. The reasoning comes full circle, for tradition is equated with group solidarity. The family is the core element of the group and its most powerful symbol. Under the appropriate conditions the ethos of "ethnicity" is by no means anachronistic in the advanced stages of capitalism, no matter how rooted such values might be to the past of particular groups. Wherever ethnicity can facilitate enterprise, capitalism as a system can be said to be one of ethnicity's primary motors, not its antithesis. Focusing on the old moneyed elite of London, Cohen has argued that ethnicity functions among the privileged as well as the impoverished and among "core" castes as well as racial and national minorities. In another case study, the historian Peter Dobkin Hall implicates family and tradition in the mercantilism of Massachusetts elites, 1700-1900.[15] As both Cohen and Hall contend, a precondition for capitalized ethnicity is a legal vacuum. Here I wish to add a corollary based on the history of the Mafia: the desire to engage in enterprise, not simply in a vacuum (where there is no law or formal arrangements) but in an economic zone outside the law and *against* formal arrangements, makes some form of family and ethnic organization a necessity.

The seemingly "feudal" ethos of family honor, deeply internalized, cements individuals together in American crime, structuring syndicates and giving them their aggrandizing momentum. Loyalty and devotion to group honor are the values around which individuals are motivated, recruited, judged, and policed in the Mafia. These values are especially good in binding criminals together and in making criminals out of those otherwise not drawn to the outlaw life. They came into the forefront in America when Prohibition created an enormous unorganized sector of the national economy, legally proscribed, but promoted by immense appetites and the willingness of the actual legal structure to play along, especially "for a price." They are also especially needed to hold together the large-scale enterprises, not structured or protected by law, that prohibition creates but that survive after it: rackets devoted to gambling, loansharking, prostitution, various forms of extortion, and eventually drugs. In legitimate business, a prized executive who sells himself and perhaps a secret or two to another company is regarded as an unexpected operating loss. A *capo-regime* who becomes a stool pigeon can bring the whole system down. The ideology of tradition and of group solidarity, principally of the family, is ideal for rationalizing crime syndicates, in both senses of the term "rationalize": ideal for organizing them because it is ideal for justifying their existence and their hold over their members.

Scholars report that actual mafiosi crime syndicates are family based. In *A Family Business*, Ianni analyzes the structure of a major American Mafia clan—the "Lupullo" family—abstracting four general rules of organization:

> the merging of social and business functions into one kin-centered enterprise; the assignment of leadership positions on the basis of kinship; the correlation between closeness of kin relationship and the hierarchy of positions; and the requirement of close consanguineal or affinal relationship for inclusion in the core group. . . .[16]

Ianni produces several diagrams to illustrate his thesis: a genealogical table of actual and fictive (godparent-godchild) relations; a flowchart of the subdivisions and their operations within the crime syndicate; and a third table, which combines the preceding two.[17] The third table diagrams what Ianni calls the "power alliances" (relations of respect and deference) between leaders within the Lupullo crime hierarchy. The pattern of authority within the syndicate mimics the pattern within the patriarchal clan.

In *The Godfather*, Mario Puzo provides a narrative equivalent of the Lupullos' power chart. During the wedding scene, Puzo introduces the Corleones in terms of their dual roles as family members and company executives. Vito Corleone is president and chief executive officer, as well as father or godfather to everyone within the organization. Genco Abbandando, *consigliori* (right-hand man), has been his best friend during his American childhood, his honorary brother, the son of the man who took him in and gave him his first job. But Genco is dying, and it is suspected that Tom Hagen, Vito Corleone's "adopted" son, will be taking over as counselor. Vito's eldest, Sonny, operates one of the principal three divisions or *regimes* of the family. The other two division leaders (*capo-regimes*), Tessio and Clemenza, are *comari* of Vito, godparents to each other's children. Fredo, the second son, serves his father as bodyguard and executive secretary. Michael, the youngest son, is the black sheep of the family and has nothing to do with its business. By tradition, the women are "civilians." But Connie's groom, Carlo Rizzi (an old boyhood chum of Sonny), expects, through this marriage, to rise quickly in the syndicate.

The network of nuclear family, extended kin by blood or marriage, and honorary kinship is not simply a structural convenience. The ideology of family operates neither as false consciousness in the vulgar sense nor as rhetoric that is entirely and self-consciously hypocritical. The rhetoric of solidarity works to organize the Corleone syndicate *because* of its hold over the imaginations and passions of leaders and those in the common ranks alike. As Cohen explains it, ethnic symbols function in lieu of formal structures precisely because of their transutilitarian, emotional appeal. This "dual" nature of symbolization is illustrated especially well in Puzo's depiction of Tom Hagen's admission into the Corleone syndicate.

Sonny Corleone had brought Tom Hagen, an orphaned waif of German-Irish extraction, into the Corleone household, where he was allowed to remain. "In all this the Don acted not as a father but rather as a guardian." Only after Hagen goes to work for Don Corleone is he treated as a fourth son:

> After he passed the bar exam, Hagen married to start his own family. The bride was a young Italian girl from New Jersey, rare at that time for being a college graduate. After the wedding, which was of course held in the home of Don Corleone, the Don offered to support Hagen in any undertaking he desired, to send him law clients, furnish his office, start him in real estate.
>
> Tom Hagen had bowed his head and said to the Don, "I would like to work for you."
>
> The Don was surprised, yet pleased. "You know who I am?" he asked.
>
> Hagen nodded. . . . "I would work for you like your sons," Hagen said, meaning with complete loyalty, with complete acceptance of the Don's parental divinity. The Don, with that understanding which was even then building the legend of his greatness, showed the young man the first mark of fatherly affection since he had come into his household. He took Hagen into his arms for a quick embrace and afterward treated him more like a true son, though he would sometimes say, "Tom, never forget your parents," as if he were reminding himself as well as Hagen. (*G*, 51-52)

In the scene above, Hagen moves into the Don's inner circle. It is a *dual* movement, enacted simultaneously, into the inner realm of Don Vito's familial affections and into the ranks of his crime organization. Tom touches the Don's heart by volunteering, despite his origins, to submit himself to the Don's will and risk his life and freedom in the company. By the same token, the Don rewards Hagen's voluntary show of respect with a symbolic "adoption" that signifies the bond of loyalty upon which their futures as gangsters will depend. The symbol of paternity here works emotionally and pragmatically at the same time. Indeed, the father-son bonding is all the more powerful because of its economic component, while its utility depends, in the absence of biological paternity, quite precisely upon the psychological density of the tie.[18]

So far I have been juxtaposing the sociology of ethnic and familial interest groups with various elements of *The Godfather*, treating the latter as if it were merely an illustration of the former—as if *The Godfather* were a kind of sociological tract or social-work guide to the Mafia. Of course, *The Godfather* is not exposition, but a novel; not sociology, but story. Yet the populist, fictional composition of *The Godfather* does not mean it is any less effective than the scholarship of Cohen or Ianni as a medium for implicating the ethnic family in capitalism. Puzo uses the resources of fiction—imagery and rhetoric, characterization, and, most of all, narrative—to make a case for the interpenetration of family and business. In the instance of Tom Hagen's admission to the Corleone family, Puzo rigs a set of circumstances and unfolds an event in such a fashion that the strands of father-son emotion and corporate personnel management are not phenomenologically separable. Hagen's recruitment/initiation functions as a microcosm for the interpenetration of family and business in the narrative as a whole. Through melodrama, Puzo undermines the still common assumption that family and business operate as separate spheres. Puzo combines family and business within the same narrative site. He also subverts the reader's desire, in keeping with a purified notion of the family and a vilified notion of the economy, to subordinate one phenomenon to the other, as cause and effect, in any given instance. In *The Godfather* the syndicate never, or almost never, uses family imagery *merely* to structure itself in lieu of better alternatives, thereby "corrupting" the forms and values of an otherwise sacrosanct ethnic tribe. On the other hand, the family never engages in business *simply* to support itself, dirtying its hands to keep head and heart clean. Always the two phenomena are causally intermingled. By the deviousness of situation and event, Puzo contextualizes the ethnic family within the capitalist economy while excavating the contribution of ethnic culture and the rhetoric of ethnicity to illegitimate enterprise.

To a greater extent perhaps than we have become used to in analyzing modernist, high-brow literature, the story line is crucial to *The Godfather*. Even the critics most hostile to Puzo admit that his great gift is storytelling, including the creation of memorable characters, but especially the creation and maintenance of suspense—of beginnings that captivate, middles the keep you going, and endings that satisfy. In *The Godfather*, Puzo narrates two plots that lock together into a single, resounding conclusion.[19] When the novel opens, a breakdown in filial obedience exposes the Corleone syndicate to "a hostile take-over bid" from the Barzini-Tattaglia group. At the same time, business matters threaten the lives of Corleone family members and precipitate dissent among them. This double crisis is the hook that captures our attention: a business in trouble, a family in trouble. We cheer for a solution to both crises—nothing less will satisfy—and Puzo contrives brilliantly to give it to us. Both crises, potentially disastrous, are solved when Don Vito's youngest son, Michael, ascends to his father's place and successfully squelches the Barzini-Tattaglia threat. It is a stunning illustration of the structural logic of family business in narrative terms. The return of the prodigal son alleviates the problem of managerial succession, while the resurrection of the syndicate's power base restores the primacy of family values and commitments. Puzo's story is "dual" in the sense that the ethnic symbols of the Mafia are dual and that Tom Hagen's adoption as a Corleone is dual. So tightly constructed is Puzo's plot around the theme of duality that the novel's denouement seems inevitable. To save the business, you must regroup the family; to save the family, you must regroup the business.

In *The Godfather,* Puzo uses Connie Corleone's wedding to illustrate the overlapping structures of family and business in the American Mafia of the 1940s. In the ***Godfather*** film (the lens of which constantly obscures our view of the novel), Coppola plays with a contrast between the beneficent private life of the Corleones (the sunlit wedding feast) and their business escapades (inside the darkened house, inside their hearts of darkness).[20] Yet, Coppola's moral allegory reifies a distinction between the private and the corporate, home and work, explicitly undermined by the novel. In Puzo's design, business associates *are* the proper wedding guests, because one's family and friends are one's proper coworkers and retainers. The specter of communal solidarity, embodied in the wedding, marks a plateau of harmonious unity from which the Corleones are about to fall. As Puzo introduces the members of the Corleone family at Connie's wedding and their environment, he not only unpacks the functional interdependence of family and business. He explicates and foreshadows a disturbance in family-business equilibrium, reciprocally engendered, mutually threatening, that is the medium for the *Godfather* narrative. As Puzo imagines it, the incipient threat to the Corleone empire is analytically inseparable from the breakdown in the familial solidarity of the syndicate—including Genco's death, the Don's creeping senility, Sonny's disobedience, the disloyalty of Carlo and Tessio, Hagen's intransigent foreignness, Michael's rebellion. At the same time, tensions in the family arise directly out of the involvement in the business of crime.

At the opening of the novel, Don Corleone is nearing retirement, which has him justifiably worried about the leadership of the syndicate. In standard corporate management, such a problem can be handled either by promotion of the best available personnel from within company ranks or by recruitment from outside the company (intercorporate "raiding"). But for the Corleones, of course, the problem of the company executive is strictly a family matter, and that makes it a problem indeed. The right-hand man, Genco Abbandando, dies on the day of the wedding, leaving Don Corleone no choice but to promote Tom Hagen, an adopted son whose German-Irish descent precludes consideration for

the top post of don. Both Clemenza and Tessio, the two *capo-regimes,* are nearing retirement themselves; moreover, they are not quite family enough. Of the don's own sons, neither Sonny nor Fredo seems finally to have the mettle to be don, while Michael, once favored to head the family, is now an outcast:

> [Sonny] did not have his father's humility but instead a quick, hot temper that led him into errors of judgment. Though he was a great help in his father's business, there were many who doubted that he would become the heir to it. . . . The second son, Fredrico . . . did not have that personal magnetism, that animal force, so necessary for a leader of men, and he too was not expected to inherit the family business. . . . The third son, Michael, did not stand with his father and his two brothers but sat at a table in the most secluded corner of the garden. (*G,* 17)

The leadership vacuum, familially engendered, is the weak link that tempts the Barzini-Tattaglia consortium (fronted by Sollozzo, the drug dealer) to take over the Corleone rackets. Weaknesses in the character of family members and in their relations with one another expose the Corleone family to, quite literally, a hostile takeover bid.

Concomitantly, and inseparably, business tensions have precipitated disputes within the intimate family circle. Michael has fallen out with his family because he objects to the way its members make a living, committing himself instead to the defense of his country and the "straight arrow" mobility of a Dartmouth education. Connie's old-fashioned Sicilian wedding seems to symbolize the unity of the Corleone generations. Yet the garden celebration actually screens dissent between Connie and her father, traceable to Corleone involvement in the rackets. "Connie had consented to a 'guinea' wedding to please her father because she had so displeasured him in her choice of a husband" (*G,* 20). The persistence of the Corleone syndicate means that one of the qualifications for a Corleone son-in-law is potential for criminal leadership. Don Corleone objects to Carlo Rizzi as his daughter's husband not because he doubts Carlo's qualities as a mate but because he questions Carlo's ability and trustworthiness as a gangster. For his own part, Carlo marries Connie not only out of love but also because he hopes to rise in the Corleone syndicate. When Don Corleone violates the principle of familial promotion, providing Carlo with a living but not an executive role, Carlo seeks revenge on his father-in-law and the family. Carlo sets up the assassination of Sonny, bringing the syndicate to the brink of disaster. By Puzo's design, as demonstrated in this instance, any analysis of family-business disrepair comes full circle: we trace family problems to business questions, only to find the intrusion of business into family life returning to haunt the business.

Carlo's betrayal, like that of Paulie Gatto and ultimately of Tessio himself, illustrates the point of vulnerability in a family business within a competitive market. The principles of maximizing profits and employing insiders are not always compatible. Syndicate leaders are tempted, for the sake of performance, to slight certain inept family members. Syndicate members are tempted, for personal gain, to betray their organizations. As long as a doctrine of familial loyalty is obeyed to the letter, neither temptation wins the day. But when family principles break down, the company is in danger.

The leadership vacuum in the Corleone syndicate is filled by the reestablishment of order in the Corleone patriarchy, when Michael returns to his family, his descent culture, and his filial "destiny." In *The Godfather,* the crisis of managerial succession is a crisis, as Cawelti notes, of "family succession" which can be solved only *familially*.[21] Puzo resolves the dual crisis by having Michael grow a familial conscience and an ethnic consciousness, mandating his ascent to his father's position as patriarch. At the novel's opening, Michael is a family pariah—*scomunicato,* excommunicated.[22] Before the war, Michael was the chosen heir to his father's regime, but later he refuses to have anything to do with the business and barely anything to do with the members of his family. He courts an "Adams" for a wife. Puzo's narrative counteracts the seeming decline of the Corleone syndicate by charting Michael's rebirth as a Corleone family member and a businessman of crime.

Michael's return as a once prodigal son is enacted in a steplike progression that mirrors the rhythms of religious initiation—baptism, confirmation, the sacrament of marriage or the priesthood. Killing Sollozzo and the police captain, Michael commits himself to his father's honor and a life of crime, *simultaneously*. In Sicily, he is symbolically rebaptized a Sicilian, learning the history of the Italian Mafia, converting to the old traditions, even taking a local wife (subsequently killed). Back in America, he is apprenticed to his father. When Don Corleone dies, Michael takes over the business and the family, becoming godfather to Connie's firstborn and "Don Michael" to his business associates. During the actual christening of his godson (as Coppola depicts it), Michael's henchmen execute a series of murders that restore the internal solidarity of the Corleone syndicate and enlarge its boundaries and standing. When he acts his father's part, even Michael's face begins to resemble Don Vito's in his prime. Puzo's drama of monarchical, Oedipal succession reverses the familiar convention of second-generation "orphanhood" with which the novel begins.[23]

Any analytic attempt to separate what Michael does out of an emotional recommitment to his father or his ethnic past from what Michael accomplishes out of a pragmatic enlistment in his father's company is doomed to echo in the wilderness. Readers even vaguely familiar with the *Godfather* narrative know that the brutal simultaneous killings at the end of the novel reestablish and indeed improve the Corleones' standing in the American Mafia. But it is less well recognized, and the film underplays, how the ending reintegrates the Corleone household. Critics argue that Puzo deploys family imagery to win sympathy for Michael's otherwise morally egregious plans. Critics misconstrue the strategies of the novel, however, when they subordinate the familial pleadings of the narrative to its capitalist melodrama, as if the reintegration of the family were merely an ideological cover for the reincorporation of the syndicate. The two structures are interrelated; neither can rightly be subordinated to the other.

Standing godfather to his nephew, Michael accepts family leadership and embodies family unity, literalizing his newly won title as patriarch of an extended family, crowned "Don" Michael Corleone. Michael tightens the family circle around him. Hagen returns from Nevada. Traitors to family honor—Gatto, Rizzi, Tessio—are weeded out. Michael's success in restoring the Corleone empire is as much the act of a truly obedient son as his godfatherhood is a basis for taking over the syndicate, for the crime organization becomes a structure on which the Corleones are reunited. Coppola's film version leaves us with a trace of dissent in the air, ending with Kay's recognition of Michael's ruthless criminality. In the novel, Puzo restores the equanimity of husband and wife and, by symbolic extension, of the Corleone family at large. Tom Hagen explains to Kay why it was necessary, from the standpoint of their ethos, for Michael to order the executions of Carlo Rizzi, Tessio, and the others. Kay acquiesces to Hagen's explanation and Michael's desire that she come home. She undergoes a rite of cultural self-transformation, to make herself into the kind of Italian-American woman the criminal environment expects. Whereas the film ends with Kay's anguish, the novel ends with Kay's conversion to Catholicism. Every morning she goes to mass with her mother-in-law, there to say, in the final words of the novel, "the necessary prayers for the soul of Michael Corleone" (*G,* 446). The peace of the Corleones is thereby restored. Michael does not mend matters with Kay simply to make the company perform better, any more than he restores the power of the syndicate simply to win his wife back and reintegrate his family; as Puzo has rigged the plot, the two go hand in hand.

> The single aspect of *The Godfather* that seems to have made the deepest impact on the American public is Puzo's use of the central symbol of "the family." This symbol's influence has virtu-

ally changed overnight the American public's favorite term for a criminal organization.

—John Cawelti

For its depiction of an ethnic subculture that functions as an interest group, *The Godfather* would warrant attention from scholars—even if, like *The Fortunate Pilgrim,* the novel had disappeared into obscurity upon publication. But the novel has had a major impact on popular culture. The figure of "the godfather" outstrips all but the most ubiquitous cultural symbols, falling somewhere between Huckleberry Finn and Superman, perhaps better known than Uncle Sam himself.[24] The novel has possibly been the best-seller of all time. By 1971, when the first film was released, there were over one million hardcover copies in circulation—multiple copies in every library in every town in America—with at least ten million more paperbacks.[25] Historically, the reading of the novel framed the film—not, as in academic criticism, the other way around. The novel still sells, another five or ten million to date, in a $1.95 paperback series of "classic bestsellers." The most immediate spin-offs were the two films; versions of those films rearranged for television; and the video format, which frequently offers both films on a single cassette. By 1975, 260 more books on the Mafia theme had been released, principally of the hard-boiled variety.[26] In 1984, Puzo himself tried again with *The Sicilian,* his fictional account of Salvatore Giuliano. Ethnicity in crime has figured in several major films, including **The Cotton Club** (coscripted by Coppola, Puzo, and William Kennedy), *The Gang Who Couldn't Shoot Straight, Mean Streets, Broadway Danny Rose, Heart of the Dragon, Scarface,* and *Once upon a Time in America.* The popularity of the family "dynasty" sagas, especially in their many ethnic varieties, can be traced in part to Puzo's model. More telling still has been the ceaseless production of *Godfather* clones, emphasizing the fusion of family and crime. Practically a genre of their own, they include (auto)biographical works like Gay Talese's *Honor Thy Father,* Joseph Bonanno's *Man of Honor,* and Antoinette Giancana's *Mafia Princess;* novels like Vincent Patrick's *Family Business* and Richard Condon's *Prizzi's Honor;* academic studies like Francis A. J. Ianni's *A Family Business;* and films and teleplays, including "Our Family Honor," ABC's ill-fated attempt to combine Italian-American gangsters with Irish-American cops.

What are we to make of the lasting fascination with *The Godfather?* Since its appearance, scholars have recognized *The Godfather* as an artifact of what is called, perhaps misleadingly, the "new ethnicity." The timing of the novel and its immediate offspring, from the book's publication in 1969 to the television series in the late seventies, corresponds to the rise of a celebratory attitude toward ethnic identity. This celebration encompassed not only groups by and large still marginal—blacks, Indians, newcomers from Asia and the Hispanic Americas—but also the descendants of European immigrants, including the Italians, who were increasingly well established in the middle classes. Necessarily, the connections drawn between the increased salience of ethnicity and *The Godfather's* popularity have been premised on the prevailing interpretation of *The Godfather* as a two-part fantasy, in which family sanctuary and successful corporate enterprise are polar opposites. My reading of *The Godfather,* emphasizing the complicity of family and business, calls for a reexamination of the novel's role in the new ethnic self-consciousness. Both the popularity of *The Godfather* and the celebration of ethnicity are complex phenomena, reflecting a myriad of attitudes toward race, class, and gender as well as toward ethnicity—attitudes often in conflict with one another. By claiming that *The Godfather* articulates the business of family, I do not wish to mute these other voices. My ambition is to point the way toward evaluating the voice of family business within the larger cacophony of debate.

Scholars like Jameson and Cawelti, working within the frame of traditional *Godfather* interpretation, seek to locate in the novel an anticapitalist energy—not an overt critique so much as an impulse, the energy of a potential critique partially veiled and misdirected. Both critics argue that Puzo portrays the Mafia as the center of a capitalist conspiracy and, simultaneously and irreconcilably, as a refuge from the conspiracy of capitalism. Because Puzo's Mafia functions as "the mirror-image of big-business," its brutality provides a focus for anticapitalist anxiety and an outlet for anticapitalist anger.[27] Similarly, the juxtaposed, equally powerful image of the family reflects, in Jameson's terms, a "Utopian longing" for escape from the prison house of capitalism. "The 'family' is a fantasy of tribal belongingness," echoes Cawelti, "that protects and supports the individual as opposed to the coldness and indifference of the modern business or government bureaucracy."[28]

In the standard view, *The Godfather's* putative double fantasy reflects the misdirected energies of the new ethnicity; the new ethnicity arises from frustration with capitalism yet mutes its resistance in clamor about the decline of the family and traditional values.[29] My analysis of *The Godfather* suggests we might hesitate, however, before accepting the majority opinion, that the family in the novel embodies a refuge from capitalism. We need especially to question whether a case for the subversive nature of *The Godfather* can rest on the myth of the Italian-American family as a precapitalist collectivity, when Puzo mounts all his forces to undermine this false dichotomy. The representation of the southern Italian family in *The Godfather* is not the kind of saccharine portrayal of innocent harmony—the haven in a heartless world—that scholars take as the benchmark of ethnic nostalgia. In *The Godfather,* capitalism is shown to accommodate, absorb, and indeed accentuate the structures of family and ethnicity. Americans respond to *The Godfather* because it presents the ethnic family not as a sacrosanct European institution, reproduced on the margins of America, but as a central American structure of power, successful *and* bloodied.

The desire of scholars to identify ethnic pietism as a locus of anticapitalist energy has blinded them to an alliance between the new ethnicity and procapitalist celebration of the family. This alliance is an insufficiently recognized strain in recent popular culture. At least until World War II, and perhaps into the 1970s, the dominant attitude toward the ethnic family in the United States assumed its incompatibility with capitalism, whether ethnicity was favored or not. The rabid Americanizers of the early decades attempted to strip immigrant workers of their familial and cultural loyalties. Among immigrants themselves, many feared that the price of upward mobility might be family solidarity, even as most in their midst deployed the family as a basis for group enterprise and mutual financial support. And intellectuals who were skeptical of capitalism, whether partly or wholly, based one strand of their critique on the damage that capitalism supposedly inflicted upon traditional family cultures. These family doomsayers tend less and less to be nativist Americanizers and guardians of ethnic tradition, but the nostalgia among scholars remains loud and clear. While the myth of the natural ethnic family still holds sway among intellectuals, the general public has come increasingly to accept and indeed welcome the idea of compatibility between ethnicity and capitalism. To accent the Italian example, for instance, public figures ranging from Lee Iacocca to Geraldine Ferraro and Mario Cuomo emphasize the contribution of family values to their own success stories, occasionally stretching our imaginations.[30] Similar rhetoric appears in the reemergence of the critique of the black family, in the widespread lauding of Asian- and Caribbean-American merchants and their schoolchildren, and in the general appeal for a new American work ethic. In this light, *The Godfather* feeds upon a strain of American rhetoric and expectation that has reached full salience only in the last decade.

Perhaps no artifact of American culture, popular or serious, has made the case for the business of family with quite the force of *The Godfather*. At no time in United States history has ethnicity enjoyed the vogue that it first achieved in the years of *The Godfather*'s greatest popularity and, in large measure, now maintains. The congruence is no coincidence. *The Godfather* does indeed participate in the new ethnicity by celebrating the ethnic family. But the Mafia achieves its romantic luster not because Puzo portrays the Italian-American family as a separate sphere, lying outside of capitalism, but because the Italian-American family emerges as a potent structure within it. The ethnic family in *The Godfather* feeds off a market sensibility rather than undermining it.[31] The Corleones can provide protection from the market only because they have mastered it. Indeed, the height of romance is reached in *The Godfather* with Puzo's choice of the Mafia as a model for family enterprise, for illegal family enterprises are capable of growing and expanding to an extent that the structure and regulation of legitimate capitalism will ultimately not support.

If *The Godfather* does indeed harbor anticapitalist energies, as a thorough reading of the novel might suggest, then perhaps scholars have been looking for that energy in the wrong places. Jameson concludes,

> When indeed we reflect on an organized conspiracy against the public, one which reaches into every corner of our daily lives and our political structures to exercise a wanton and genocidal violence at the behest of distant decision-makers and in the name of an abstract conception of profit— surely it is not about the Mafia, but rather about American business itself that we are thinking. American capitalism in its most systematized and computerized, dehumanized, "multi-national" and corporate form.[32]

Jameson and the others may be correct in insisting that fascination with *The Godfather* is motivated, at a deeper level, by anticapitalist anxiety. But the real scare occasioned by *The Godfather,* however much suppressed, is about capitalism not in its "most systematized and computerized, dehumanized" form, but rather in its more "intimate" varieties—ethnic, familial, personal. My reading of *The Godfather* suggests that if we wish to press charges against capitalism, we press charges against family and ethnicity, too. One strand of rhetoric in twentieth-century America, familiar to us from Howell's *Hazard of New Fortunes* and sources pervasive in our culture, suggests that Americans can go home to escape the specter of capitalism. Professionals often complain about taking work home with them, mentally if not literally. How much more frightening, then, is the alternative represented by Puzo: when some Americans go home to papa, they end up confronting the boss. Critics have been quick to interpret the brutality of the Mafia as a symbol for the violence to the individual inherent in capitalism, and to assume that the family represents an escape from that violence. Yet the melodrama of *The Godfather* implicates the family not only in the success of the Corleone empire but in its cycle of self-destructive violence as well. Michael reintegrates the family business only *after* burying a brother, murdering a brother-in-law, alienating a sister, and betraying the trust of his wife. For Americans who experience family and economy as interwoven pressures (if not actual combined enterprises), the Mafia genre may allow a focusing of resentments, even if, inevitably, a Mafia analogy overstates them. For the cost of employing blood in the marketplace is finding the company at home.

My speculations notwithstanding, there is no direct way to study popular opinion and pinpoint the popular interpretation of *The Godfather.* Indeed, it would be a mistake to assume there is any single interpretation (any more than there is a single "mind of the masses"). The great strength of popular literature may be its ability to entertain different, even contrary readings. But we can at least consider how other American artists catering to mass audiences have read the message of Puzo's novel. Two of the novel's best offspring—the film *Godfather II* (1974) and *Prizzi's Honor* (1982) by Richard Condon—illuminate the novel's reception. Although Puzo receives credit for the **Godfather II** screenplay, along with Coppola, the film offers a perspective on the Corleones very different from either that of the novel or that of its reasonable facsimile, the first film. Pauline Kael actually throws almost all the credit for **Godfather II** to Coppola: "This second film . . . doesn't appear to derive from the book as much as from what Coppola learned while he was making the first."[33] For our purposes, however, it is not essential to distribute praise or blame, but simply to note that the film differs significantly enough from the original narrative to constitute a "rereading" of it (even if it is, in part, Puzo's own). Whereas the original *Godfather* narrative winds the fates of the Corleone family and the Corleone business together, Coppola's **Godfather II** separates the two strands. In *Prizzi's Honor,* on the other hand, Richard Condon uses all the devices in Puzo's novel, plus some of his own, to bond family and business tighter than ever. *Prizzi's Honor* surgically extracts Puzo's theme from underneath his excesses and Coppola's sermonizing and exposes it to a scintillating parody. The greatest testament to *The Godfather* has been paid not by critics or scholars but by Condon and John Huston, who directed the 1985 film version from Condon's own screenplay. Together, **Godfather II** and *Prizzi's Honor* can be construed as leading voices in a debate about the meaning of Puzo's novel and the future of the genre in which all three works participate.

> This time I really set out to destroy the family. And I wanted to punish Michael.
>
> —Francis Coppola[34]

Among scholars and film critics, **Godfather II** is commonly regarded as a greater work of art than the first movie, and infinitely preferable to the novel. In the standard interpretation, the second film sheds the Mafia of its sentimentally familial wrappings and reveals it for what it is and perhaps has always been: capitalistic enterprise in its most vicious form. Pauline Kael interprets this revelation moralistically. **Godfather II** is to be praised for eliminating the illusion that there might be anything desirable about the Corleone crime family.[35] Fredric Jameson stresses the historicity of **Godfather II**. For him, **Godfather II** explodes the illusion of the Mafia's "ethnicity" by attributing its origins to social ar-

rangements in "backward and feudal" Sicily and its growth in America to the advanced stages of capitalism. The second film, according to Jameson, submits the themes of the first "to a patient deconstruction that will in the end leave its ideological content undisguised and its displacements visible to the naked eye."[36] For both Kael and Jameson, the deconstruction of the family and the ethnic group is a precondition for truth. But to my mind, it is they along with Coppola himself, not Puzo, who run the greatest risk of romanticizing the Sicilian-American family.

Godfather II narrates the further adventures of Michael Corleone, interspersed with flashbacks to the early days of his gangster father, Don Vito Corleone. The film is a political morality tale with a vengeance. In the original narrative, as Don Vito's business goes, so goes his family: their fates are intertwined. But in **Godfather II** Michael promotes his criminal enterprise at the expense of his personal family, group solidarity, and the Italian-American heritage. The central plot is a Byzantine series of maneuvers between Michael Corleone and the Jewish gangster Hyman Roth (modeled on Meyer Lansky). In their struggles, both Michael and Roth use a Corleone *capo-regime,* Pantangele, now living in the old Corleone house on Long Island, as a pawn. To counter Roth, Michael manipulates the imagery of the criminal "family"—Roth as Michael's "father," Pantangele as his "godson"—with complete cynicism. He succeeds by deliberately evacuating the idioms of family and ethnic solidarity of all meaning *except* as short-term (and short-sighted) instruments in a (transethnic, transfamilial) quest for power.

In the process, Michael's multinational crime outfit is reduced to merely a conglomerate of illegal enterprises. The network of ties with his father's retainers back in New York City unravels; Michael's nuclear family falls completely apart; and the southern Italian ethos that structured his father's world is vanquished entirely. Michael's evil is measured on a scale marked out in emphatically familial and ethnic units. The detail is endless. At the novel's end, Michael arranges the deaths not only of Roth (his "father") and Pantangele (his "son") but of his natural brother Fredo. Fredo has traded information with Roth; but he has also served as the only real father that Michael's children have ever known. Michael wins the trust of his partners and underlings only by blackmail, bribery, and the promise of mutual profit; such trust lasts only as long as convenient for all parties; and such relations frequently end in death as well as dissolution. Family and community have disintegrated among the Corleones. In the opening scene, the band at his son's first-communion party cannot play a tarantella but at Pantangele's frustrated urgings, comes up with "Three Blind Mice." In his portrayal of Michael, Coppola draws upon one of the most familiar of ethnic themes—second-generation infidelity—chastising him accordingly.

The loss of family/ethnicity, coupled with the consummation of Michael's business deals, spell one thing: Michael has *Americanized*. The Corleone empire has become, in Hyman Roth's phrase, "bigger than General Motors and AT&T." But it has cost Michael and his people their inheritance. It is an old story. By the film's end, Coppola has used Michael to update Abraham Cahan's *The Rise of David Levinsky*, outfitting the Russian-Jewish merchant as a 1970s CEO in Sicilian garb. Like Levinsky, Michael trades his roots for rubles. The film exploits that peculiarly American paranoia of cultural and social orphanhood amid fortune and fame. Isaac Rosenfeld called Cahan's novel "an exemplary treatment of one of the dominant myths of American capitalism—that the millionaire finds nothing but emptiness at the top of the heap."[37] Reviewing *Godfather II* in *Commentary*, William Pechter concluded that Michael was "another instance of that unrevivably exhausted cliché: it's lonely at the top."[38]

By comparison, Michael's father had found the top of his heap quite rewarding:

> And even Don Corleone, that most modest of men, could not help feeling a sense of pride. He was taking care of his world, his people. He had not failed those who depended on him and gave him the sweat of their brows, risked their freedom and their lives in his service. (*G*, 215)

At the end of the original narrative, Michael has lost his brother Sonny and the enforcer Luca Brasi to the five-family war; his *capo-regime* Tessio and brother-in-law Carlo Rizzi to treachery; and, possibly, his sister Connie, because of Carlo. But around him coalesces a new family regime: his mother, new wife Kay, Fredo, Tom Hagen, Clemenza and his men, the new capo Rocco Lampone and his men, and Albert Neri. In Puzo's *Godfather*, family and business work in tandem, although with no guarantee of perfect profits or perfect harmony. *Godfather II* rends them asunder once again.

Ironically, *Godfather II* would seem to have been more hospitable than the original narrative to the twin appetites identified by Cawelti, Jameson, and other critics. Formal analysis suggests that if Americans in the seventies needed to vent rage at capitalism or fantasize about ethnic solidarity, then *Godfather II* would be the better vehicle for doing it. In the original story, the "mirror-image corporate capitalism" thesis is compromised, as Stanley Kauffmann has noted, by the unconventional "blood-bonds of loyalty" in the Mafia.[39] In *Godfather II*, those bonds are broken and Michael Corleone's operations are identified as mainstream big-time capitalism. In the original story, nostalgia about the Italian-American family is compromised by the Corleones' criminal enterprise. In *Godfather II*, the linear narrative of assimilation (Levinsky-style) feeds a yearning for a time when the Sicilian family withstood the ravages of individualism, personal greed, and the capitalist dynamic. For the television special (a mini-series first broadcast in 1977), Coppola rearranged films *I* and *II* into chronological order, neatly literalizing this romantic revision.

From directors to actors and critics, the professional film community bestowed raves upon *Godfather II*, hailing it as a sign that Hollywood could still produce art and rewarding it with the "Best Picture" Oscar for 1974. Yet the public reacted with an indifference that was more than a little surprising, given the unparalleled success of the novel and first film as well as the usual appetite for sequels. William Pechter accurately noted at the time, "I know of no one except movie critics who likes *Part II* as much as part one."[40] Public coldness to *Godfather II* has, if anything, deepened over the years. Curiosity brought millions into the theaters to see *Godfather II* the first time around, but most viewers told their friends afterward not to bother, nor did they return for a second showing. America's notorious disdain for unhappy endings may account for the film's unpopularity. Yet, having said so, we need to specify what, after all, makes Michael's triumph over his enemies, both Hyman Roth and the Senate Investigation Commission, so unsatisfying for so many.

As I have argued, *Godfather II* reasserts in unmistakable terms an antithesis between ethnic familial solidarity and success in capitalist enterprise. Perhaps the unpopularity of the film signals in part a resistance to this delusive dichotomy. Many intellectuals favor the film because they cling to the idea of a naturalistic, precapitalistic family. Most Americans, on the other hand, increasingly believe in the compatibility between family values (which ethnics are now thought to epitomize) and the capitalist system. The original narrative promotes changing expectations; the sequel disappoints them. Certainly, the general audience resents the condescension in *Godfather II*, in which Coppola assumes he must strip the Corleones of all redeeming value in order to communicate the social costs of their megalomania. Moviegoers are unhappy less with the villainy of Michael's empire, which they acknowledge, than with the film's underlying, regressive sociology: that the breakup of family life is a necessary precondition for syndicate expansion. The tendency in our own era is no longer to underestimate the compatibility of the ethnic family and capitalism. The desire is now to overestimate, and hence romanticize, the growth potential and structural flexibility of the ethnic family business. In the final analysis, *Godfather II* strips the original narrative of its populist sociology, returning to the well-worn conventions of "up from the ghetto" novels. In *Prizzi's Honor*, on the other hand, Richard Condon restores the Mafia genre to its original source of strength—the icon of family business—generating a parody of Puzo's novel that is, at the same time, an interrogation of the business of family.

> They had to have at least two minds: the group mind that made them need to be a part of a family, and a separate individual mind that let them survive inside the grinding, double-crossing mass of their families, betraying their own people for money again and again, fifty thousand times. She was sure that it was the *macho* disease that made the Sicilians so fucking dumb. The family lived only for power—and money, because it meant more power.... Money, beyond a point that they had left behind long before, was only grease for the chariot. All those who followed behind the chariot gained money but, in appropriate measures, they were following the chariot because of the prodigious power on the chariot.

—Irene Walker

Prizzi's Honor, like *The Godfather,* begins with a wedding as an occasion to bring the Prizzis together and explain the structure of their syndicate and their relations with other families:

> Corrado Prizzi's granddaughter was married before the baroque altar of Santa Grazia de Traghetto, the lucky church of the Prizzi family.... Don Corrado Prizzi, eighty-four, sat on the aisle in the from pew, right side of the church.... Beside Don Corrado sat his eldest son, Vincent, father of the bride, a cubically heavy man.... Beside Vincent was his brother, Eduardo, and his third "natural" wife. Baby.... Directly behind Don Corrado sat Angelo Partanna, his oldest friend and the family's counselor.... Behind the first two rows on the right side of the church, captured like pheromones in the thickening smell of hundreds of burning beeswax candles, in serried ranks, row upon row, were lesser Prizzis, one more Partanna [Charley], and many, many Sesteros and Garrones.[41]

Men from these four families—Prizzis, Partannas, Sesteros, and Garrones—constitute the upper levels of the Prizzi organization. The central character of the novel, Charley Partanna, bears a surname that is the name of a town in Sicily (destroyed by earthquake in 1969), like Vito Corleone. On the internal cover of the hardcover (immediately following the epigraph page of the Berkley paperback), the web of command is diagrammed in a chart reminiscent of Francis A. J. Ianni's breakdown of the Lupollo family.... This structural diagram combines genealogy with company organization, suggesting that not only corporate leadership but also the

relation between the units themselves is familial. A web of marriage unites the Prizzis with other Mafia families. "Heavily larded among them were relatives from most of the principal families of the *fratellanza* in the United States. Sal Prizzi had married Virgi Licamarito, sister of Augie 'Angles' Licamarito, Boss of the Detroit Family . . ." (*PH,* 12). Condon explains the system of "profitable repair" operating between the Prizzis and the noncriminal sector of society—"the New York City Police Department . . . the multinational conglomerates, the Papal Nuncio, the national union leaders, . . . the best and brightest minds of the media, the district attorney's office, the attorney general's office, and the White House staff"—all of whom are represented at the wedding (*PH,* 12-13). To an even greater degree than Puzo, with more irony yet more telling detail, Condon explicates the mechanisms of power, responsibility, cash flow, and production: precisely how the semiretired don, counselor Angelo Partanna, boss Vincent (chief operating officer), and underboss Charley, who is in disfavor with Vincent but not with the don, are related; how Eduardo heads the legitimate side of their operations, which does the laundering for the rackets, in what ways the Prizzis differ from other Mafia crime outfits; and so forth. "They took a poll and sixty-seven percent of the American people think that what they all call the Mafia is the most efficiently run business organization in the whole country," quips one of Condon's characters (*PH,* 122).

At times in *The Godfather,* Puzo's narrative commentary suggests a tongue-in-cheek guide to the manners and mores of the Mafia. *Prizzi's Honor* serves the Mafia as Lisa Birnbach's *Preppy Handbook* serves the old-boy, old-money networks of the Northeast. The Prizzis call themselves a brotherhood—*fratellanza*—but they mean by that not a coterie of equals but a male hierarchy: "you must obey your superiors, to death if necessary, without question," swears the initiate, "for it will be for the good of the brotherhood" (*PH,* 43). The Prizzis operate as a unit in both their personal and their business lives, decisions being controlled from the top and always with a mind to "Prizzi's Honor." The main protagonist, Charley Partanna (Jack Nicholson's role) personifies the system. In the opening scenes of the film, we see, in quick succession, the birth/baptism of Charley Partanna, the brass knuckles he is given for a birthday present, and his blood-rite initiation into the Prizzis. Charley's father is Don Corrado's *consigliere.*[42] Charley is the don's godson. Charley calls Don Corrado "padrino" ("little father"), a diminutive meaning "godfather." At seventeen, Charley becomes a made man in the family; in his thirties, he becomes the enforcer and underboss; now, in his mid-forties, he is the heir apparent to the family, after the don's son Vincent ("Domenic" in the film) and the don himself. "As we protect you, so you must protect Prizzi Honor" is the Mafia creed (*PH,* 42). There is no functional distinction, as the Prizzis understand it, between Charley's "birth" into the Prizzi family and his "initiation" into it. From birth, he has been destined to be, in turn, a dependent of this clan, a soldier, its chief executive in charge of security, and, ultimately, boss and don. "Both men, father and son, had been bred to serve their feudal lords" (*PH*, 53). There is no more distinction between Charley's biological descent and cultural election that between the familial and professional nature of the Prizzi organization.

Condon focuses throughout the novel on the interdependence of family and business, the personal and professional, playing his comedy on the tensions between them. No pretense of separation is maintained. Boss Vincent resents underboss Charley, for a scandal caused by his own daughter, Maerose; so Vincent deals not through Charley, as custom dictates, but through his father, Angelo. The personal penetrates the professional, and vice versa. Business is conducted in homes as well as in offices, and frequently over meals. Don Corrado lives in a grand old city mansion, "as befitted a business executive," but owns neither the home nor any of its contents, out of respect for both "the rules of humility and austerity" and the diligence of the Internal Revenue Service. Don Corrado's house, literally, is his business quarters. The lack of private lives is underscored by the virtual absence of women in the inner sanctum of the Prizzi family, a literalization of both Mafia mythology and Puzo's narrative precedent.[43]

The structural hierarchy, male bonding, and Sicilian cult of honor constitute the context for the action of the novel. Like that of *The Godfather,* the plot in *Prizzi's Honor* involves a botched caper that exposes the Prizzis to hostile maneuvers by the other New York families and leads to a crisis of managerial/familial succession: familial double-crosses, with Charley acting Michael's role as the prodigal son, who temporarily turns against the family; and a murderous resolution that brings the appointed heir to power, restores the primacy of the crime organization, and resolidifies the nuclear and extended family of the new don. The details in Condon's novel and in Huston's film echo those in Puzo's and Coppola's works in an amusing game of one-upmanship. A wedding initiates both works, but Puzo/Coppola produce an adman's fantasy of a Sicilian garden party. Condon and Huston, on the other hand, produce a credible representation of an actual Brooklyn wedding: the women dressed in black, not white; a VFW hall, rather than a garden; Sinatra tunes as well as old folk songs; and so forth. The closer attention one pays, from first phrase to last, the funnier and more pointed the connections. More important than the refinement of *The Godfather*'s cultural milieu is Condon's brilliant plot conceit, which highlights and at the same time satirizes the family-business mentality of the Prizzis.

Prizzi's Honor is, in the words of a *Playboy* reviewer, "the best episode of *As the Underworld Turns* since Puzo's *Fools Die*."[44] The reference to the soap opera is not gratuitous,

since the action of *Prizzi's Honor* involves a problem marriage between its central characters, Charley and Irene (née Maida Walcewicz) Walker, who is a free-lance assassin, or "contractor," in the occasional employ of the Prizzis. The marriage between Charley and Irene violates the sanctity of the Prizzis' family business. Irene is a Catholic Pole, whose former husband (murdered by Charley on orders from the don) is a Russian Jew. "How come you aren't a wop and I meet you at Teresa Prizzi's wedding?" asks Charley, who falls in love and marries her against that logic (*PH*, 33). Irene's foreign background is merely a symbol for her real outsiderhood. "You and this woman see everything with the same kind of eyes," Maerose tells Charley, knowing better and setting Charley up for a fall (*PH*, 96). True, both Charley and Irene kill people for the mob; otherwise, though, their operations are like night and day. "Let's see how it goes," warns Angelo. "A mixed marriage" (*PH*, 144).

The film plays up the comedy of middle-class manners between Charley, an Italian chauvinist, and his wife, Irene, who wants to keep on working after marriage. In the novel, Irene's sexual autonomy is, quite explicitly, a corollary of her independence in the marketplace of crime. Irene is a loner, a one-woman company, an entrepreneur whose approach to business exemplifies the norms of a free market:

> The fantastic thing about Charley was that he *was* a Boy Scout. Charley paid his dues to his life. Charley believed.... Charley knew he was serving a purpose, not a buck.... It was different for [Irene].... She wasn't locked into any family, she was a straight, commercial freelance who couldn't expect any protection from anybody if she didn't do the job right.... (*PH,* 117-18)

While Charley is a *sottocapo*, Irene is a *contractor.* The idiom is perfect. Irene makes deals independently, strictly on a cash basis, accepting no retainer and maintaining no ties to any particular outfit. As a cover, Irene is a tax consultant. To her the world operates simply as the circulation of dollars; loyalty is just a matter of the origin of the next paycheck. She is therefore the perfect foil to a family-business mentality.

Just prior to the novel's denouement, the Prizzis appear to be in shambles. No money is coming in, the Filargi caper has soured, and the other families are maneuvering to take over the entire business. Vincent has been assassinated, and Charley is turning traitor. The Prizzis suffer as the Corleones suffer after Sonny's death. Condon resolves the crisis by duplicating one strand of *The Godfather*'s narrative logic, turning the family over to the rightful heir—in this case, Charley. Don Corrado offers Charley the position of boss, second-in-command, with the promise of that of don after

Don Corrado's death. The Prizzis need Charley, yet Charley needs to earn that promotion. Charley must repair the family's relations with the other syndicates and with the police; and, in the dual logic that organizes these narratives, Charley must prove his fidelity. The price is steep: he must deliver Irene to the cops himself—dead. "Zotz her? Clip Irene?" (*PH*, 294). The borderline in Charley's decision is clearly demarcated. Will he honor his contract with Irene or the Prizzis' ethic of familial loyalty?

"The family were what he had been since Sicily started breeding people. They were his food. They had been with him forever. There were hundreds of thousands of them, most of them ghosts, some of them bodies. They were all staring at him, waiting to know what he would do" (*PH*, 296). The weight of all the Prizzi tradition, his respect for his *padrino* and father, who are waiting for his decision, and Charley's training and dreams overdetermine the decision:

> He thought of becoming Boss of the Prizzi family. His entire life had pointed him toward that. He had trained for that since he was thirteen years old and now it could happen. He could feel the power as if it were the texture of fine, strong cloth between his fingers. He could taste it as if his mother had come back to cook one more glorious meal for him. He thought of the money . . . eight million dollars a year, every dime tax free, every dime safe in Switzerland. . . . (*PH*, 269)

Becoming boss means filling his father's shoes, his mother's expectations: family is money is destiny when you are born into the Prizzis. Eight million dollars and Mom's home cooking, too! In *Prizzi's Honor*, as in *The Godfather*, the working out of the Oedipal crisis prompts the return of the prodigal son and the reintegration of the crime family. Charley's quest for power runs along pathways of filial obedience; the strength of the Prizzis depends on Charley's urgency to obey. Being asked to become don is for Charley, as for Michael, an offer he can't refuse.

Charley sets Irene up for the kill, by telling her that the don accepted her terms of settlement, paying all she asked. Irene knows that Charley is lying, because the don would never settle the Las Vegas score by returning the money she stole from the Prizzis.[45] She considers the love-match canceled. In accordance with her own methods, Irene prepares to kill Charley, transmuting the marriage contract into a murder contract in her mind: "She didn't feel the grief anymore. Charley was a contract she had put out herself, and had given to herself; full fee" (*PH*, 305). In contrast to Irene's cold-bloodedness, Charley feels the righteous conviction of Praise duty:

> [Irene] had a different and much paler, thinner

meaning when he judged her beside the total meaning he got from his family. He was now Boss of that family. He had to set an example that would be remembered as long as the family stood. He saw dimly that it was right to sacrifice the woman he loved so that the family could go on and on fulfilling its honor, which was its meaning. He suddenly saw clearly that Irene had stepped so far out of line that there was nothing left to do but to whack her. (*PH*, 300)

Charley kills Irene before Irene is able to kill him. Charley wins not because he is technically more proficient or luckier but because he has the *emotion* of Praise honor motivating him and the full force of the Praise clan backing him up. However much the business of family causes friction (the "grinding, double-crossing mass of their families"), still there is a corporate front (*PH*, 103). Irene dies because she stands alone, without a family, without protection.[46] The structural equivalent in *The Godfather* is the death of Carlo Rizzi, kin by marriage, but an outsider, a traitor. In the ending of each novel, the integrity of the crime family is reinstated by sacrificing a "family" member whose membership was suspect in the first place and compromised by that member's activities. The murder of Irene is also an ironic footnote, highlighted in the film, on the conventions of romantic love so favored in American popular culture.

"The surprise ending will knock your reading glasses off!" runs a blurb on the paperback, credited to the *New York Times*. Yet the eliminating of Irene, and Charley's having to do it, is a perfect culmination for the novel's strategy of playing feudal capitalism off against free-market independence. Alternatively, Charley and Irene could flee the Prizzis and go together to Hong Kong, where they would be outfitted with new identities. (Irene's past misdeeds to the Prizzis, and the current difficulties with the police, preclude Irene's remaining with the family.) This alternative ending would require a conversion in Charley's character, to the point where he could see himself turning his back on history for autonomy and romantic love. But at least such an ending would remain consonant with the hypothesis of the narrative—namely, that feudal capitalism, which dominates the American underworld, operates by sacrificing individualism to the group. Readers and film viewers are surprised because they expect a dreamy ending, in which Charley gets his family and Irene, too. Such an ending, however, violates the business of family in the world of the Prizzis. The principle of family honor precludes romantic love because romance presumes a free-market logic of one-to-one relationships. In the film, the overlay of sappy music and the casting of Nicholson as Charley, who acts superbly but is mistaken for Nicholson the loner, tips expectations in the direction of a romanticized ending. To conclude with Charley as the don, while still happily married to Irene, would be to entertain a fantasy of irreconcilables (of the sort that scholars characteristically misattribute to *The Godfather*). In the final chapter, Charley calls up Maerose, initiating their reconciliation. Maerose and Charley are now both outcasts who have returned to the family. Maerose's claim on Charley is ethnic. She reminds him in the film. "We grew up together, Charley. We are the same people." By marrying Maerose, Charley reunites the Prizzis and Partannas in the incestuous bond that maintains the power of their family.

What are the implications of *Praise's Honor* as a revision of *The Godfather*? Like Puzo, Condon makes it clear from start to finish that *the* theme to be pursued in a Mafia narrative is the question of business and family. Condon's comedy is effective because we, as readers, already understand the structural interdependence of business and family in the Mafia and accept it basically as truth. Condon does not mean, of course, to celebrate the business of family. Whereas Puzo provides a thin coat of narrative irony, Condon paints in layers and layers of satire, usually comic, but occasionally courting a grimmer dimension. From start to finish, Puzo eliminates no more than a dozen or so mobsters, who deserve it anyway. Condon burns down the Palermo Gardens nightclub, with 89 people dead, 217 severely burned, and 4 blinded, most of them innocent guests and "civilians." Condon also corners his main character into killing his wife. Both **Godfather II** and *Praise's Honor* submit the Mafia to moral scrutiny. **Godfather II** depends on a romanticized ideology of family for its critique, so that Coppola, in the final analysis, is caught within a family-business hermeneutic circle. *Praise's Honor* adopts a position truly contrary to that of the family-business mentality; it assumes, in the figure of Irene, the possibility of a free marketplace, in which individuals function independently of one another and the realm of the personal is uncluttered by the operations of business. In so doing, Condon is able (like Puzo in the first novel) to question the naïveté of free-market spokesmen and ethnic romanticizers, who think that the domains of "family" and the "group" are extra-economic. But Condon accomplishes something far more emphatically than does either Puzo in *The Godfather* or Coppola in **Godfather II:** that is, to chart the special costs of doing business familially.

In *Praise's Honor,* the family business grows beyond its members' need for wealth, annexing their freedom to its own dynamic, the growth of the syndicate. "Money, beyond a point that they had left long before, was only grease for the chariot" (*PH,* 103). The Praise organization empowers its members, but it also imprisons them, psychologically and literally. Other, more legitimate forms of family business may not police their boundaries with quite the brutality of the Prizzis, but they may not prosper as much either. In *The Godfather,* the loss of individual liberty among the Corleones, however implicit, is buried under the glorification of familial

loyalty, whereas Richard Condon's carefully developed "surprise" ending etches in the popular consciousness an image of familial tyranny to give nightmares: Charley knifing Irene, in the throat, from the marriage bed.

As an analysis of the mechanics of family capitalism and a critique of its appeal, *Praise's Honor* supersedes *The Godfather.* Let us not forget, however, that Puzo made the way for Condon's accomplishment. Puzo is often maligned for exploiting the stereotype of Italian-American criminality, which has long been used to discriminate against the general Italian-American population. But, in the final analysis, *The Godfather* does not so much rehash an old tale, whatever its strands of inheritance, as tell a new one. In *The Godfather,* Puzo refashions the gangster genre into a vehicle for reversing the traditional antithesis between ties of blood and the American marketplace. In so doing, he transforms the stock character of the Italian-American outlaw into the representative super(business)man; and he transforms the lingering image of immigrant huddled masses into the first family of American capitalism.

1. It is not unreasonable to assume that Puzo derived his emphasis on the familial aspect of the Mafia from the reports of Joseph Valachi, whose Senate hearings were in 1963 and whose book came out in 1967. In *The Italians,* itself a nonfiction leading seller of 1964, Luigi Barzini summarized how Valachi's testimony reshaped common American ideas about organized crime:

> The convicted American gangster, Joseph Valachi . . . explained the facts of life of the Sicilian village, probably as old as Mediterranean civilization, the principles guiding Homeric kings and heroes in their decisions, to a Senate committee and an awestruck twentieth-century television audience. He patiently pointed out that an isolated man was a dead duck in the American underworld; that he had to belong to a family, his own, or one which accepted him; that families were gathered in alliances, and the alliances in a loose federation called *Cosa Nostra,* governed by an unwritten code.

Luigi Barzini, *The Italians* (New York: Bantam, 1965), 284.

Puzo may have derived his view of the Mafia, then, not only from his Hell's Kitchen experience but from Valachi, either directly or through Barzini's explication (Don Corleone's biggest competitor is named Barzini). But if Valachi first introduced the notion of family crime, and Barzini explicated it, it was Puzo who made the symbol ubiquitous.

2. The preceding two quotations are from John G. Cawelti, *Adventure, Mystery, Romance: Formula Stories as Art and*

Popular Culture (Chicago: Univ. of Chicago Press, 1976), 78. The tandem reappears in John Sutherland's *Bestsellers* and in essays by Fredric Jameson and Eric Hobsbawm. E. J. Hobsbawm, "Robin Hoodo: A Review of Mario Puzo's *The Sicilian*," *New York Review of Books*, Feb. 14, 1985, 12-17; Fredric Jameson, "Reification and Utopia in Mass Culture," *Social Text* I (1979). 130-48; John Sutherland, *Bestsellers: Popular Fiction of the 1970s* (London: Routledge & Kegan Paul, 1981), chap. 3.

3. Jameson, "Reification and Utopia," 146.

4. Puzo's own, scattered comments on the social realities behind *The Godfather* reveal little. In an interview, he emphasizes that the novel was meant to be not realistic but romantic: "To me *The Godfather* isn't an exposé; it's a romantic novel." As quoted by Tom Buckley, "The Mafia Tries a New Tune," *Harper's,* Aug. 1971, 54. In *The Godfather Papers,* Puzo claims to have written the novel "entirely from research," then testifies that actual mafiosi found his fictional depictions very true to life. Mario Puzo, *The Godfather Papers and Other Confessions* (New York: Putman, 1972), 35.

5. Puzo's autobiographical novel, *The Fortunate Pilgrim* (1964), seems on its surface to exemplify the long-standing tradition of interpreting Italian-American familialism as a barrier to mobility. One reviewer wrote, "The writer renders with fidelity the life-style of an Italian-American community in which Old Country values of propriety, order and obedience to established authority collide with New World ambition, initiative, and disdain for tradition." Sheldon Grebstein, "Mama Remembered the Old Country," *Saturday Review,* Jan. 23, 1965, 44. Yet, I would argue, the novel harbors a countervailing analysis, demonstrating how the Puzo family used traditional values to ensure a steadily progressive mobility, culminating in Mario's freedom to become a writer.

6. Herbert J. Gans, *Urban Villagers: Group and Class in the Life of Italian-Americans* (New York: Free Press, 1962); Virginia Yans-McLaughlin, *Family and Community: Italian Immigrants in Buffalo, 1880-1930* (Ithaca: Cornell Univ. Press, 1977); Thomas Kessner, *The Golden Door: Italian and Jewish Immigrant Mobility in New York City, 1880-1915* (New York: Oxford Univ. Press, 1977); Thomas Sowell, *Ethnic America* (New York: Basic, 1981).

Most Italian immigrants to the United States originated from the *Mezzogiorno,* the regions of Italy south and east of Naples, including Sicily. The traditional view of Italian-American ethnicity is extrapolated from several very well known, mid- to late-twentieth-century studies of southern Italy: Phyllis H. Williams, *South Italian Folkways in Europe and America: A Handbook for Social Workers, Visiting Nurses, Schoolteachers, and Physicians* (New Haven: Yale Univ. Press, 1938); Carlo Levi, *Christ Stopped at Eboli,* trans.

Frances Frenaye (New York: Farrar, Straus & Giroux, 1947); Edward Banfield, *Moral Basis of a Backward Society* (New York: Free Press, 1958): and Ann Cornelisen, *Women of the Shadows* (New York: Dell. 1976). These essays prompted American social workers like Leonard Covello and scholars like Herbert Gans, Rudolph Vecoli, Thomas Sowell, Thomas Kessner, and Virginia Yans-McLaughlin to adopt a variant on the "culture of poverty" argument for blue-collar Italian Americans, although Cornelisen, for one, warns against approaches based on "residual vestiges of peasant mentality." Cornelisen, *Women of the Shadows,* 220.

For an overview of traditional scholarship on Italian Americans, including an analysis of its limitations, see Micaela di Leonardo, *The Varities of Ethnic Experience: Kinship, Class, and Gender among California Italian-Americans* (Ithaca: Cornell Univ. Press, 1984), 17-25, 96-108.

7. Leonard Covello, "The Influence of Southern Italian Family Mores upon the School Situation in America," in Francesco Cordasco and Eugene Bucchioni, eds., *The Italians: Social Backgrounds of an American Group* (Clifton, N.J.: Kelley, 1974), 516. Covello's extremely influential essay was originally written as a dissertation in 1944 and finally published as *The Social Background of the Italo-American School Child: A Study of the Southern Italian Family Mores and Their Effect on the School Situation in Italy and America* (Totowa, N.J.: Rowman & Littlefield, 1972).

8. Francis A. J. Ianni, with Elizabeth Reuss-Ianni, *A Family Business: Kinship and Social Control in Organized Crime* (New York: Russell Sage Foundation, 1972), 55. Ianni notes that "the acculturation process works in crime as elsewhere" (61), but nonetheless traces the familial structure of the Luppollo syndicate back to Italy: "The origins of this familialism are Italian and not American" (155).

The urgency to place the Mafia along an Old World-New World continuum resurfaces in the work of the historian Humbert S. Nelli, who adopts the opposite position from Ianni's. Nelli concedes the "group unity" and "cooperative effort" of Italian-American mobs, but stresses almost entirely the individualism and "American way of life" of the gang leaders. See Humbert S. Nelli, *The Business of Crime: Italians and Syndicate Crime in the United States* (Chicago: Univ. of Chicago Press, 1976), 255-57.

Scholars of the Mafia in southern Italy also insist on the evolving interdependence of familial and/or fraternal organization and capitalist enterprise. The Italian Mafia in recent years is thought to have been restructured in imitation of the Italian-American Mafia. See Pino Arlacchi, *Mafia Business: The Mafia Ethic and the Spirit of Capitalism,* trans., Martin Ryle (New York: Schocken, 1986); Anton Blok, *The Mafia of a Sicilian Village, 1860-1960: A Study of Violent*

Peasant Entrepreneurs, with a foreword by Charles Tilly (New York: Harper & Row, 1975); and E. J. Hobsbawm, *Primitive Rebels: Studies in Archaic Forms of Social Movement in the 19th and 20th Centuries,* 2d ed. (New York: Praeger, 1963), chap. 3.

9. Eli Zaretsky, *Capitalism, the Family, and Personal Life* (New York: Harper & Row, 1976). Zaretsky's small book, little known, is an extraordinarily lucid reappraisal, spanning several centuries, of the relation between Western family structure and capitalism.

10. For a review essay on what I am calling the new ethnic theory, consult Werner Sollors, "Theory of American Ethnicity, or: "? S ETHNIC?/TI AND AMERICAN/TI, DE OR UNITED (W) STATES S SI AND THEOR?" *American Quarterly* 33 (Bibliography, 1981), 257-83. I am myself indebted to this article for bringing Abner Cohen, among others, to my attention.

The rise of the new ethnicity, as represented in the work of Michael Novak, Peter Schrag, Richard Gambino, even Glazer and Moynihan, has prompted severely critical responses, primarily from the political Left. Typically, the work of the ethnic demythologizers challenges the romance of ethnicity either by dismissing ethnic cultural difference altogether or by reducing difference to a variable entirely dependent upon *class.* In Stephen Steinberg's *The Ethnic Myth,* ethnicity is, for all explanatory purposes, entirely discounted. In Herbert Gans's very influential work, family values are interpreted as the product of working-class status and are hence "pan-ethnic," shared by blue-collar folk of all backgrounds, whereas the ethnicity of the middle class is what Gans calls "symbolic," meaning that it is private, a matter of individual identity and friendship without socioeconomic significance. Tellingly, Gans says middle-class ethnicity is "cost-free" without inquiring into its profitability; the middle-class family is implicated in capitalism, once again, only as a buffer or safety valve for the system. See Steinberg, *The Ethnic Myth: Race, Ethnicity, and Class in America* (New York: Atheneum, 1981); Gans, "Symbolic Ethnicity: The Future of Ethnic Groups and Cultures in America," in Herbert J. Gans et al., eds., *On the Making of Americans: Essays in Honor of David Riesman* (Philadelphia: Univ. of Pennsylvania Press, 1979); Gans, foreword to Neil C. Sandberg, *Ethnic Identity and Assimilation* (New York: Praeger, 1974).

11. The quote is from Abner Cohen, *Two-Dimensional Man: An Essay on the Anthropology of Power and Symbolism in Complex Society* (Berkeley: Univ. of California Press, 1974), 99. See also Abner Cohen, "Introduction" to *Urban Ethnicity,* ed. A. Cohen (London: Tavistock, 1974), ix-xxiv.

Major critical efforts to reconceive ethnic literature in the light of new ideas about ethnicity include William Boelhower,

Through a Glass Darkly: Ethnic Semiosis in American Literature (Venice: Edizioni Helvetia, 1984); Jules Chametzky, *Our Decentralized Literature: Cultural Mediations in Selected Jewish and Southern Writers* (Amherst: Univ. of Massachusetts Press, 1986); Mary V. Dearborn, *Pocahontas's Daughters: Gender and Ethnicity in American Culture* (New York: Oxford Univ. Press, 1986); and Werner Sollors, *Beyond Ethnicity: Consent and Descent in American Culture* (New York: Oxford Univ. Press, 1986).

12. Rose Basile Green, *The Italian-American Novel: A Document of the Interaction of Two Cultures* (Rutherford, N.J.: Fairleigh Dickinson Univ. Press, 1974), 355, 357, 364.

For a brief yet elegant discussion of *The Godfather,* in the context of an overview of Italian-American literature, see Robert Viscusi, "*De Vulgari Eloquentia*: An Approach to the Language of Italian American Fiction," *Yale Italian Studies* I (Winter 1981), 21-38. Implicitly challenging traditional accounts of ethnic literature, Viscusi acknowledges the inventive role of the imagination in the creation of a post-European ethnic culture. His language-oriented approach is itself calculated to invent terms in which we might appreciate a previously ignored literature. By emphasizing the linguistic savvy of Italian-American writing, Viscusi means to present this literature in the strongest possible light, given the bias toward language of the journal sponsoring his essay and, more important, of the critical community it represents. Whereas Viscusi's highly "literary" approach seems to have nothing whatsoever to do with business, is it a coincidence that the most important property he attributes to Italian-American literature is its ability to "be *diplomatic,* to *negotiate* the terms on which Italian America can exist" (emphasis mine)?

13. Mario Puzo, *The Godfather* (New York: Putnam, 1969), 216. Further references to this edition are given in parentheses in the text.

14. Cohen, "Introduction," xvii.

15. Peter Dobkin Hall, "Marital Selection and Business in Massachusetts Merchant Families, 1700-1900," in Michael Gordon, ed., *The American Family in Social-Historical Perspective,* 2d ed. (New York: St. Martin's, 1978), 101-14.

For other discussions of ethnicity, economics, and ethnic businesses, see Ivan H. Light, *Ethnic Enterprise in America: Business and Welfare among Chinese, Japanese, and Blacks* (Berkeley: Univ. of California Press, 1972); John Bodnar, Roger Simon, and Michael P. Weber, *Lives of Their Own: Blacks, Italians, and Poles in Pittsburgh, 1900-1960;* Thomas Sowell, *Race and Economics* (New York: McKay, 1975).

16. Ianni, *A Family Business,* 157.

17. Ibid., 64-65, 92, 116-18.

18. The don reminds Tom of his real background, less to take away from the meaning or Tom's initiation into the don's nuclear family than to highlight, by contrast, that meaning. Tom's marriage to an Italian-American, like his adoption by Don Corleone, constitutes a rebirth as an Italian-American on his wedding day.

19. There is much excess baggage in this sprawling, desperately populist novel: great detail on postures of war between the families, which Sutherland deviously and persuasively attributes to Puzo's reaction to World War II (*Bestsellers,* 45); well-stroked portrayals of the making of the Corleone soldiers, including Rocco Lampone, Luca Brasi, and the ex-cop Albert Neri; speculations in the *National Enquirer* vein into the activities, both private and public, of Frank Sinatra and friends; painfully unnecessary excursions into the sexual lives of Sonny, his mistress Lucy Mancini, and Dr. Jules Segal. In my experience teaching the novel, the reactions to these tangents vary. Sinatra merits a passing interest, the sex lives of Sonny and the doctor hardly any at all. The passages that chronicle the making of McCluskey the bad cop and Neri the enforcer are avidly read; similar chronicles become hallmarks of the Mafia genre subsequently. In *The Godfather,* the tangents do not so much detract from the main narrative as fill it out during its middle stretches, sustaining interest while holding final revelations in abeyance.

20. "The visual scheme is based on the most obvious life-and-death contrasts; the men meet and conduct their business in deep-toned, shuttered rooms, lighted by lamps even in the daytime, and the story moves back and forth between the hidden, nocturnal world and the sunshine that they share with the women and children." Pauline Kael, "Alchemy: A Review of Francis Ford Coppola's *The Godfather.*" *New Yorker,* March 18, 1972, 132.

21. "The novel is a tale of family succession, showing the rise of the true son and heir and reaching a climax with his acceptance of the power and responsibilities of Godfather. It tells how Michael Corleone comes to understand his father's character and destiny and then allows himself to be shaped by that same destiny." Cawelti, *Adventure, Mystery, Romance* 52-53.

In his review of the first *Godfather* film for *Commentary,* William S. Pechter was perhaps the first critic to emphasize that while the icon of "the Godfather" meant Don Vito Corleone, the narrative belonged to Michael:

What is the family whose claims override all others in *The Godfather*? It is, for one thing, a patriarchy, and the story the film has to tell is basically not Don Corleone's but Michael's: a story of his initiation into the family by an act of murder, of the succession of the youngest, most assimilated son to the patriarchal powers and responsibilities and the ethnic mystique of his father.

Pechter, "Keeping Up with the Corleones," *Commentary* 54 (July 1972), 89.

22. "[The southern Italian peasant] despised as a *scomunicato* (pariah) anyone in any family who broke the *ordine della famiglia* or otherwise violated the *onore* (honor, solidarity, tradition, 'face') of the family." Richard Gambino, *Blood of My Blood: The Dilemma of the Italian-Americans* (Garden City, N.Y.: Doubleday, 1974), 4.

23. Mary Antin wrote in 1912, "I was born, I have lived, and I have been made over. . . . Did I not become the parent and they [her parents] the children, in those relations of teacher and learner?" Antin, *The Promised Land* (Boston: Houghton Mifflin, 1912), xii. In 1981, Richard Rodriguez echoed Antin's Emersonian image of self-birth, in an aside to "my parents—who are no longer my parents, in a cultural sense." Rodriguez, *Hunger of Memory: The Education of Richard Rodriguez* (Boston: Godine, 1981), 4.

24. Claude Brown reports that "godfather" ranks among the most popular handles, or nicknames, of black inner-city America. *New York Times Magazine,* Sept. 16, 1984, 38. I have a suspicion that *The Godfather* is also a secret vice for very different segments of American society. More than one professor of English has confessed that Puzo may, after all, have some considerable gifts. A black woman, also an English professor, told me she had read the novel five times and once saw the film at a theater three days in a row! I hope, by explaining my own fascination with the text, I do not deprive others of the mystique of a favorite vice.

It is also a wonderful fact, without being a coincidence, that Puzo's major project after *The Godfather* screenplays was scripting *Superman: The Movie* and *Superman II.* For what is the story of Superman if not a meta-narrative of immigration, about a refugee whose power derives from his dislocation, whose secret identity is hidden under a disabling Anglo-conformity (as Clark Kent), but whose true promise is revealed in his fight "for truth, justice, and the American way"? And who, conversely, is Don Corleone if not the latest in a continuing series of ethnic supermen? For a discussion of superman imagery in the context of American ethnicity, consult Sollors, *Beyond Ethnicity,* chap. 3.

25. "The Making of *The Godfather,*" *Time,* March 13, 1972,

61. By 1980, reports John Sutherland, *The Godfather's* publishers were claiming worldwide sales of fifteen million. The title Sutherland gives the novel, "the bestseller of bestsellers," echoes nicely the Sicilian phrase for the boss of bosses, *capo di tutti capi.* Certainly, no other contemporary work has sold as well. How one compares a present-day popular novel with, say, *Gone with the Wind* or *Uncle Tom's Cabin* is no easy matter. Sutherland, *Bestsellers,* 38, 46.

26. For a review of the Mafia literature from 1969 to 1975, see Dwight C. Smith, Jr., "Sons of the Godfather: 'Mafia' in Contemporary Fiction," *Italian Americana* 2 (Spring 1976), 191-207; the statistical reference is from p. 192. A shorter bibliography appears in Cawelti, *Adventure, Mystery, Romance,* 304n.

27. In Jameson's view ("Reification and Utopia," 145), the butchery of the Corleones symbolizes the "wanton ecocidal and genocidal violence" of capitalism in America. Cawelti adds (*Adventure, Mystery, Romance,* 78). "I suspect there is a definite relation between the fascination with limitless criminal power . . . and the public's reluctant awareness of the uncontrollable power of violence in the hands of the government."

28. Jameson, "Reification and Utopia," 146; Cawelti, *Adventure, Mystery, Romance,* 78.

29. "At a time when the disintegration of the dominant communities is persistently 'explained' in the (profoundly ideological) terms of the deterioration of the family, the growth of permissiveness and the loss of authority of the father, the ethnic group can seem to project an image of social reintegration by way of the patriarchal and authoritarian family of the past," Jameson, "Reification and Utopia," 146-47.

30. Well into the seventies, even after the rise of the new ethnicity, it was conventional to attribute the poor performance of Italian-Americans in the professions, the arts, the American Catholic church, politics, and big business to the tenacity of familial values and southern Italian culture. In the last few years, however, the conspicuous rise of Italian-Americans has reversed the age-old formula. Stephen S. Hall wrote in a 1983 cover story for the Sunday *New York Times Magazine:*

> Is there a single thread that runs through all these [stories of successful Italian-Americans]? If anything, it is the unusual propensity to merge, rather than separate, the professional and the personal. Borrowing from a culture in which the extended family can easily include 30 to 40 "close" relatives, Italians thrive on community. They are accustomed to large numbers of people, and they

seem to have developed an emotional facility in dealing with them. Even in large companies, they have a knack for keeping things on a human scale. "The professional community," explains one Italian-American psychotherapist, "becomes the next family."

Hall, "Italian-Americans: Coming Into Their Own," *New York Times Magazine,* May 15, 1983, 29.

31. It is amusing to speculate how Puzo's usage of ethnicity in his career as a writer parallels, broadly speaking, the usage of ethnicity depicted in his novels. Puzo began his career in the now venerable fashion of aspiring American literati, with a novelistic account of his years as an expatriate (in postwar Germany), *The Dark Arena* (1955). Only subsequently did he specialize in ethnic narrative and become known as a specifically Italian-American writer. With *The Fortunate Pilgrim* (1964), Puzo was able to promote himself as an earnest realist, little known but "serious," as if Italian-American writers toiled honestly on the margins of the American literary community just as their characters worked on the margins of the American economy. With *The Godfather* (1969) and its offspring, Puzo launched himself on a career as both a popular novelist and a Hollywood screenwriter, exploiting ethnic materials for power and profit, as if in faint imitation of the exploitation of family and ethnicity by his Mafia characters.

32. Jameson, "Reification and Utopia," 145.

33. Pauline Kael, "Fathers and Sons," *New Yorker,* Dec. 23, 1974, 64.

34. Francis Coppola, as quoted by William S. Pechter, "Godfather II," *Commentary* 59 (March 1975), 79.

35. "Many people who saw 'The Godfather' developed a romantic identification with the Corleones; they longed for the feeling of protection that Don Vito conferred on his loving family. Now that the full story has been told, you'd have to have an insensitivity bordering on moral idiocy to think that the Corleones have a wonderful life, which you'd like to be part of." Pauline Kael, "Fathers and Sons," 64. See also her review of the first film: Kael, "Alchemy," 132-44.

36. Jameson, "Reification and Utopia," 147.

37. Isaac Rosenfeld, "David Levinsky: The Jew as American Millionaire," in Abraham Chapman, ed., *Jewish-American Literature: An Anthology* (New York: New American Library, 1974), 619.

38. Pechter, "Godfather II," 79.

39. Stanley Kauffmann, "On Films," *New Republic*, April 1, 1972, 26.

40. Pechter, "Godfather II," 80. Pechter, furthermore, is the only critic I know who prefers the first film to the second, and the only one to recognize the retrospective romanticization of *Godfather II*. He emphasizes how "the schematic ironies of *Part II*—that Michael's fall should parallel his father's rise—dictate that the young Vito Corleone be glorified (as a pre-organization-man gallant bandit) far beyond any such romanticization in part one." I would stress less the explicit romance of Vito as bandit than the implicit romance of the more mature Vito's family. The precondition to Michael's fall is a state of grace, represented not by young Vito but by the Corleone family of his youth.

41. Richard Condon, *Praise's Honor* (New York: Coward, McCann & Geoghegan, 1982), 11-12. Further references to this edition are given in parentheses in the text.

42. [Puzo uses the term *consigliori,* with an "o" and an "i," throughout *The Godfather;* Condon spells it *"consigliere,"* with the "e"s, in the Italian fashion. Condon's spelling seems to be much the more common usage.] Both authors liberally spray italicized words throughout their novels, in a long-standing tradition of ethnic representation. Condon uses even more Italian terms than Puzo (Charley is always cooking up something) and takes care to spell correctly in (western) Sicilian dialect. This is another instance of Condon's fine-tuning of Puzo's detail.

43. Don Corrado, Angelo Partanna, and Vincent Praise are all widowers (exceedingly strange, in a world in which men kill men, that these three have outlived their womenfolk). Eduardo takes mistresses but does not marry. And Charley, who lost his mother as a child, is a bachelor pressing fifty. These men "mother" each other, incorporating the female realm into the male, the personal into the professional. "[Angelo] swore to God he didn't know how Charley did it. 'I'm telling you, Charley, I close my eyes and I think your mother cooked this.'" Appropriately enough, the one significant Praise female, Maerose (the only Praise who cooks better than Charley), is an outcast. Exiled, Maerose spends the course of the novel conniving to be forgiven for her sins and readmitted to the family.

44. I am quoting the blurb from the 1985 movie tie-in paperback edition: Richard Condon, *Praise's Honor* (New York: Bantam. 1986).

45. It is preposterous that Irene could keep the money from the Las Vegas scam, not to mention her life. It is also preposterous that Charley would not imagine Irene's participation, especially after learning the nature of her profession. The novel assumes that Charley is willing to cover for Irene;

the film supposes that Irene lies to Charley and that Charley is so in love that he is willing to take her word.

46. Operating within the mob's sphere of influence, never mind subcontracts, is tricky business. As Barzini paraphrases Valachi, "An isolated man was a dead duck in the American underworld; . . . he had to belong to a family, his own, or one which accepted him." Barzini, *The Italians*, 284. Henry Hill's autobiography, written with Nicholas Pileggi and entitled *Wiseguy,* could restore the image of the mob outlaw to respectability.

David Everett Whillock (essay date 1990)

SOURCE: "Narrative Structure in *Apocalypse Now,*" in *America Rediscovered: Critical Essays on Literature and Film of the Vietnam War,* edited by Owen W. Gilman, Jr. and Lorrie Smith, Garland Publishing, 1990, pp. 225-37.

[*In the following essay, Whillock explores how Coppola set up oppositions in environment, characters, and story-motifs, and used mediators to bridge the opposites.*]

I love the smell of napalm in the morning.

It smells like victory.

Major Kilgore in *Apocalypse Now*

When Francis Ford Coppola made public his decision to produce and direct *Apocalypse Now* in 1975, there were only a few films that depicted the Vietnam conflict in any direct way. While *The Boys of Company C* and *Go Tell the Spartans* were released before *Apocalypse Now, The Green Berets* was the only film in release that directly treated America's involvement in combat during the Vietnam conflict. Because of Coppola's past cinematic success in *The Godfather* (1972) and *The Godfather Part II* (1974), anticipation for a definitive film about the Vietnam war was high in both cinematic and historical circles. However, because of the film's lengthy production process (four years), *Apocalypse Now* was the last of several films released in the middle and late 1970's.

Films that focused on Vietnam in the 1970's for the most part investigated how the conflict affected the returning veteran and his placement or displacement in American society. Only two films released in the 1970's, *Go Tell the Spartans* and *The Boys of Company C,* placed their characters in combat situations. Gilbert Adair in his book *Vietnam on Film* considers these two films as opportunistic in the wake of the pre-release publicity of *Apocalypse Now:*

While neither *The Boys of Company C* nor *Go Tell the Spartans* is absolutely devoid of interest, they are what one might call "quickies"; if not B movies then resolutely A minus, whose existence seem motivated solely by opportunism . . . inspired by the hope of cashing in on the much delayed *Apocalypse Now.*[1]

Apocalypse Now made its public debut at the 1979 International Cannes Film Festival in France. The film entered as a "work in progress," and shared the top picture honor, the *Palme d'Or,* with the West German film *The Tin Drum.* John Simon wrote in the *National Review* that one reason Coppola's film was so long in production was that an ending to the film was not easily conceived.[2] At Cannes, Coppola had hoped to resolve the indecision which had led him to film three different endings. Yet Coppola presented an ending at Cannes that he later dropped for the American release.[3] On October 3, 1979, the decision was made by United Artists to release the film nationwide after a two-month marketing trial in Los Angeles, Toronto, and New York. *Apocalypse Now* met with mixed critical response but was nominated for eight Academy Awards including best picture, direction, adapted screenplay, supporting actor, cinematography, art direction, and sound. The film won two Oscars: sound and cinematography. *Apocalypse Now* remains a controversial film in two regards: its adaptation of Joseph Conrad's novella *Heart of Darkness* and its surrealistic depiction of the Vietnam war.

THREE POINTS OF ANALYSIS

Methodological foundations for critical analysis have become commonplace in contemporary academic criticism. The importance of any method is underscored by film scholar Bill Nichols when he writes that "methodologies are a tool to aid the writer and reader in understanding the world: [that is] how things relate, or better, how relationships function."[4] In the following investigation of *Apocalypse Now,* a narrative structural analysis based on the theories of Lévi-Strauss will focus on these functional relationships.[5] This analysis will be developed through three narrative elements: 1) the environment portrayed in the film; 2) the characters; and 3) the story motifs. The environment of the film consists of the physical setting and the cultural background of the opposing societies caught in the conflict: Vietnam and the United States. The analysis of the characters is concerned with both major and minor characters and their relationships to each other as well as their function(s) within the story. In contrast, the story-motifs will investigate those elements of the plot that underscore binary demarcations that are found not only in dialogue and narration, but in action as well.

The analysis of each element is achieved through the identification and discussion of each "constituent unit" (which Lévi-Strauss has termed "binary bundles of relations") and how such binary opposition within the story are resolved. The resolution, according to Lévi-Strauss, is dependent upon a mediator.[6] A mediator is any element within the story that facilitates the resolution of the binary opposition.

The resolution, achieved through the mediating device, is the transformation of the opposing binary units into a closer relationship. As the mediating device "permutates" (transforms) the binary opposition toward a more middle position, the characteristics of each binary unit will become less distinctive. The resolution of the narrative takes place once the transformation of opposition is complete.

Using this method Lévi-Strauss allows the film scholar to view the Vietnam war film as an entity in itself and separate from the American war films of the past. The justification and method of war found in World War II films, for example, are clearly seen as righteous. However, the Vietnam war film does not present these elements in such a biased manner. In fact, the justification for the war is at issue in these films. By using Lévi-Strauss we are compelled to explore both sides of the equation. By resolving the contradictions found in the narratives through the mediator, the viewer comes closer to his/her own resolution of the war.

ENVIRONMENT

In *Apocalypse Now,* the basic constituent unit found in the environment is that of the binary opposition between controlled/uncontrolled. Lévi-Strauss defines such binary opposition as Culture/Nature. By extension of Lévi-Strauss' formula for the structure of myth, the relationship of the oppositions would thus be: nature is to culture as uncontrolled environment is to controlled environment. The opposition between the uncontrolled environment and controlled environment in *Apocalypse Now* is more specifically exemplified as city/jungle.

The environmental conflict is introduced in the first sequence of *Apocalypse Now.* Willard's alcoholic opening nightmare is of a peaceful lush green jungle immediately bursting into an apocalyptic red explosion of napalm as an air attack is in progress. He awakes from this nightmare only to be confronted with the realization that he is "only in Saigon." As he approaches the window, the camera reveals Saigon as an ordered and modern city. Concrete buildings, modern domestic vehicles, and paved streets assure Willard that he is not in the jungles of Vietnam. Willard laments his position by expressing his knowledge that every day he remains in the city he gets "weaker," while every day that "Charlie squats in the jungle," Charlie gets stronger. (This strong/weak opposition becomes a significant point later with the confrontation between Kurtz and Willard.)

There are five separate physical settings that deserve attention in this analysis. They are: 1) the combination of Saigon and intelligence headquarters at Nha Trang; 2) the battle for the Vietcong village at Vin Drin Drop; 3) the episodic experiences of the journey up the Nung River; 4) the last American outpost at Do Lung Bridge; and 5) Kurtz's fortress near Nu Mong Ba in Cambodia.

These environments represent permutations (transformations) between the binary oppositions of controlled and uncontrolled. As Willard's mission up the Nung River takes him through these environments, the opposition between controlled and uncontrolled moves closer to resolution. An analysis of each environment will clarify their function in the transformation.

Saigon and Nha Trang. Saigon and intelligence headquarters at Nha Trang are the most controlled environments in *Apocalypse Now.* The Mayor's request over the radio that off-base American soldiers not hang their laundry in the street windows informs the audience that the city government of Saigon has a strong control of the city's internal affairs while there exists a force of United States soldiers to control "outside" problems that might come into the city from the jungle. The COMSAC headquarters at Nha Trang is also a highly controlled environment because of its need for security from "outside" intruders. As Willard enters the perimeter of the headquarters, he is carefully checked and signs a security sheet to be allowed to enter. Once inside the headquarters, the controlled environment is maintained through Army regularity as he is met by a Major who informs Willard that he may "stand at ease." (This maintenance of discipline within the Army system begins to dissolve as Willard moves further away from Saigon and Nha Trang.)

Battle for Vin Drin Drop. Once Willard receives his mission, he is taken to Major Kilgore who is currently involved with "mopping up" an attack on a Vietcong strong hold. The contrast between the ordered life of both Saigon and Nha Trang, and the chaos of battle is evident in this sequence. (The oppositions between Culture and Nature are particularly exemplified by buildings: a burned-out French church standing among the bamboo structures of the village huts.)

The next morning Kilgore and his Air Ninth Cavalry attack the village at Vin Drin Drop. This Vietcong village also underscores the differences between the controlled environment of a "hot" society (culture) as compared to a "cold" society (nature). The village is physically in opposition to Saigon. There are no concrete buildings in this village and the streets are dirt paths into the surrounding jungle. However, there is an internal order in this village. As the attack begins, a grade school is in session. The guard on duty sounds the alarm and the children are removed in an orderly fashion. The soldiers that defend this village are trying to protect themselves against "outsiders" from the air, not the jungle. Indeed, the jungle for this village is friendly as its density protects the defending soldiers.

The war machines in these separate environments are also indicative of the binary oppositions between the film's presentation of nature and culture. The American war machine, which depends upon the notion of "replaceable parts," is in direct opposition to the village war machine, which is made up of old machine guns and vehicles that are for the most part not replaceable. In light of such a differential, the Vietcong village is quickly destroyed, as the village war machine is no match for the American. The Vietcong run into the jungle to be protected by its dense cover, while Major Kilgore radios in a napalm strike from Air Force jets. Militarily, there is no equality within the binary opposition of modern war machines/antiquated war machines.

Nung River. The Nung River is the mediating environment between the opposition of controlled/uncontrolled environment. The importance of the river as a linking device is echoed by Willard when he states that the Nung River "snaked through the war like a main circuit cable plugged straight into Kurtz." The river touches both the controlled environment of the city (culture) and the uncontrolled environment of the jungle (nature). The river remains a kind of fulcrum that balances the extremes of culture and nature (controlled/uncontrolled environments). This is exemplified when Chef, one of the characters in the boat, wants to go ashore into the jungle to gather mangos. While in the jungle, he and Willard are surprised by a tiger. After the incident Chef exerts his preference for a more controlled environment by expressing that he must remember never to "get off the boat." This preference is echoed by Willard who suggests that one should never get off the boat unless he is willing to go "all of the way." In fact, he reminds us that Kurtz got off the boat and is now fully indoctrinated into the uncontrolled environment of the nature opposition. Willard's point becomes important to the narrative when he leaves the boat to assassinate Kurtz.

The river as mediator can be illustrated by comparing the city (culture) to the jungle (nature). As discussed earlier, the opposition found in the environments of *Apocalypse Now* is Saigon (city) and Kurtz's compound (jungle). The Nung River, because of its relation between that of Saigon and Kurtz's compound, is a mediator between the two. The Nung River carries Willard's boat from Saigon, yet it also carries the boat back. Thus the river is both of Saigon (culture) and of Kurtz's compound (nature). As a result, the river's function in *Apocalypse Now* is that of a mediating device.

Aptly, the closer the river gets to Kurtz and the further from Saigon, the less control there is over the environment. While Willard is on the river, the opposition between nature and culture becomes pronounced when a Vietnamese sampan is stopped by the American boat to search for smuggled weapons. The orderly search is suddenly ripped apart by an over-anxious crew member who kills the family on board because of a sudden movement by one of the family members to protect a hidden puppy. The death of the members aboard the junk is a turning point on the river. From that point on, the river is no longer a symbol for safety. This is underscored by the events at Do Lung Bridge on the Nung River.

Do Lung Bridge. This bridge, we are told, is the last American outpost before Cambodia. Willard and his crew arrive during a phantasmagoric night battle to destroy the bridge. A controlled environment does not exist here. As the boat arrives, American soldiers at the bridge jump into the river begging the crew to take them back to civilization. Willard is met by a dispatcher who is also anxious to leave, telling Willard he is in the "armpit of the world." When Willard tries to locate the commanding officer at the outpost, he is met with remarkably unstructured methods of warfare. There is neither order nor a commanding officer; there is only chaos and death.

As the crew leaves the bridge and gets closer to Kurtz, the environment has transformed from culture to nature. The boat passes burned villages and wrecked war machines as they move upstream. Half of a fuselage and stabilizer of a crashed B-52 stick out of the river, symbolizing the loss of control that the American war machine has over the jungle. In fact, the symbolic fulcrum represented by the river slowly dissolves as the boat goes deeper into the jungle. With the death of two crew members (one by a Vietcong bullet, and one by a native spear), the boat itself is no longer safe.

Kurtz's fortress. Willard and the remaining two crew members arrive at Kurtz's fortress to find that the Colonel has gone insane. The bodies of dead North Vietnamese, Vietcong, and Cambodians are left decaying in the jungle heat. In contrast to the environment in Saigon, cultural control is missing. There is no rank among Kurtz's army, no distinction between the native Montagnards and the invading Americans with Kurtz. In the fortress there are no streets nor buildings. Only the Buddhist temple serves as a protection from the jungle. Kurtz's army sleeps in the open leaving the jungle to control the outer perimeters of the compound.

The resolution between controlled environment and uncontrolled environment is represented by the Nung River. The "balance" of the story begins to shift toward the jungle and its uncontrolled environment after the Do Lung Bridge. Equilibrium is restored only after the death of Kurtz when Willard leaves the uncontrolled environment and makes his way back down the river toward Saigon.

In this fashion, the river connects both the controlled and uncontrolled environments of the narrative. Willard uses the river to travel to and from both environments. The extreme end of the uncontrolled environment in the binary relationship no longer exists at the end of the film; however, neither does the controlled environment. Willard's experience has led him (and the audience) to conclude that there is no controlled environment. Recall how the battle of Vin Drin Drop revealed a madness of a distinct method without real control. At the Do Lung Bridge, both method and control are absent.

The resolution of the binary environments is one of several within the story. Lévi-Strauss argued that to analyze a myth all such bundles of relations must be investigated before stating whether there is a resolution within the myth (narrative) or not. The oppositions between characters may give further insight into the question of resolution within *Apocalypse Now.*

CHARACTERS

While there are several constituent units found among the characters of *Apocalypse Now,* two units in particular deserve attention in this analysis: first, the binary opposition between the Generals of the United States Army and Colonel Kurtz, and second, the binary opposition between two minor characters, Lance and Chef.

Generals/Kurtz. The central binary opposition in *Apocalypse Now* is that between the Generals of the United States Army and Colonel Kurtz. The generals have decided that Kurtz's methods are unsound and his command must be terminated. In an intercepted taped message, Kurtz says that the Vietcong are animals that are not threatened by the orderly, methodical form of combat orchestrated by the controlled environment of the generals. Thus, Kurtz must be annihilated. The Generals tell Willard that Kurtz has taken the war into his own hands and is operating in an unorderly, non-methodical war "without any human decency at all."

Kurtz is full of contradictions himself. He views the war through the binary oppositions of purity of will versus corruption of will. The answer for Kurtz lies in the dialectic existence of life and death (also to be discussed as a thematic opposition under story-motif). Kurtz's view of the war is in direct contrast with the Generals' view. The Generals want a war with rules and moral decency, while Kurtz feels that the war cannot be fought without the strength of the primordial instincts of survival, no matter what the moral cost. The opposition between the Generals and Kurtz is placed in the dichotomy of method/no method of war. Willard is sent by the Generals to resolve the conflict that exists between them. The conflict is resolved for the Generals by the assassination of Kurtz.

Willard serves as a distinct function in this conflict. Like the Nung River in the constituent unit of controlled/uncontrolled environment, Willard plays a mediator in the opposition between the characters of Kurtz and the Generals. The character of Willard is the mediator because of his centered position in the continuum between the Generals and Kurtz. Lévi-Strauss would see Willard as mediator because of his "position halfway between two polar terms, he must retain something of that duality—namely an ambiguous and equivocal character." This is exemplified by Willard's indecision about the mission. While he agrees to take the mission, Willard describes his concern over killing an American and fellow officer. However, Willard also recalls killing "six people close enough to blow their last breath in [his] face." The audience realizes that he is not necessarily of the "orderly decent humanitarian world" that was described by the General at Nha Trang. The experience of the Vietnam war has changed him. He is no longer a cultural being, yet his resistance to killing Kurtz implies that he is equally not of the "evil" world that the Generals have proclaimed Kurtz to be a part of. Thus, Willard is ideologically in the middle, binding the two points of view together.

As a true mediator, Willard resolves the conflict between the Generals and Kurtz. He solves the Generals' problem by killing Kurtz. However, he also resolves a problem for Kurtz. Kurtz wanted his view of the war presented to his son. After killing Kurtz, Willard takes the position paper written by Kurtz to give to Kurtz's son. With the paper in hand, Willard exits the compound leaving both Kurtz and the Generals behind. After his mission is complete, his orders are to call in an air strike to destroy Kurtz's headquarters. Instead, he shuts off the radio, the only representative of culture left in the film, and begins his journey back down the river. Even in one ending of the film when an airstrike does destroy the compound, the viewer is left with the impression that it was not Willard who called it in.

Chef/Lance. A particular relationship between two crew members of the boat is also indicative of the binary oppositions between nature and culture in **Apocalypse Now.** The crew members Chef and Lance are representatives of culture and nature respectively. Chef is a New Orleans Saucier who represents, through his profession, a high cultural role. Chef was raised to become a professional chef. He has, in essence, a pedigree. He was trained through his early life to become a specialist in sauces and was preparing to study in France when he was drafted. The cultural side of Chef is also underscored by his desire not to kill. This is illustrated when the boat detains the Sampan on the river to search for weapons. When a sudden move on board the junk begins the carnage, it is Chef who does not shoot his weapon even though he is directly in danger.

At the other end of the continuum is Lance, a secondary character who represents nature. He is a professional surfer. Instead of transforming a raw material into something for use, as Chef does, Lance becomes part of that which he uses. The natural wave of the ocean is his tool and it remains untransformed for Lance's use. His name alone underscores a natural image (a lance is a native weapon used by Kurtz's warriors). Another strong indication of Lance's function in this opposition is found in Lance's behavior going up the river. The closer the boat gets to Kurtz's compound the more Lance takes on the look of a native. By the time the crew reaches the compound, Lance has adopted their dress. Because Lance has accepted this existence, he is spared the cruel death that awaits Chef.

The function for Willard as secondary-character mediator is a simple one. He is neither a part of Lance's nature nor of Chef's culture. Willard's mediating role between Lance and Chef is developed early in the journey up the river. It is Willard who goes with Chef to gather mangos, and it is Lance who accompanies Willard at Do Lung Bridge. More important, after the other crew members are killed, the three remaining characters become representatives of the binary oppositions that exist in the narrative. The boat thus becomes a microcosm for the larger conflict.

In this structural analysis, the binary oppositions of the characters as represented by the Generals and Kurtz exemplify the extreme binary opposition of the continuum between nature and culture, and other characters (Chef and Lance) represent a closer relationship between nature and culture. The permutation between the binary characters occurs through the continuum of relations between other "closer" characters. With Willard as mediator, the two extreme oppositions between Nature and Culture come closer together. Resolution occurs when Willard kills Kurtz and takes Kurtz's position paper back with him. Neither extreme triumphs over the other as Willard mediates a compromise in this element of the narrative.

The resolution of character and environmental conflicts has, overall, a direct influence on the outcome of the story. However, more subtle conflicts also give the story a depth of meaning. These subtle recurrences of binary oppositions, the story-motifs, give the narrative an internal structure which allows the more obvious conflicts of characters and environment a progression toward resolution through their mediating devices. It is these subtle conflicts within the story that support the major "spine" or focus of the story.

STORY-MOTIFS

One binary opposition is foremost between two elements of the story-motif that supports the characters and environment of **Apocalypse Now.** This conflict is found in the story-motif of method of war/no method of war.

The underlying theme of *Apocalypse Now* is Kurtz's unsound method of warfare versus the General's sound method of war. Kurtz finds war an immoral event that should be fought without judgment and with moral terror. Kurtz's method has in essence become unsound because the war for Kurtz is not the "conventional war" fought by the Generals of a cultured nation.

Kurtz emphasizes this lack of morality in the Vietnam war when he tells Willard of his experience in the Special Forces. Kurtz was assigned to inoculate the children of a village for polio. After the forces inoculated the children and left, the Vietcong chopped the inoculated arms off of the children to stop the infestation of the American serum (cultural medicine). What Kurtz found so ingenious is the purity of will that it took to achieve such an act. He says, "it was as though a diamond bullet went into the center of my forehead and I realized that it was this kind of purity of will that would win the war. If I had ten divisions of men with that kind of will, I knew I could win." For Kurtz, an Army of men without human compassion would win the war. To the Generals this was no method for fighting a "humanitarian war." While *Apocalypse Now* does not exemplify the type of war the generals or Kurtz embrace, a permutation (transformation) of the story-motif between the binary oppositions of the General's method of war and Kurtz's no-method of war is represented in the film's presentation of the battles of Vin Drin Drop and Do Lung Bridge.

The battle of Vin Drin Drop and the Do Lung Bridge are permutations that are indicative of the developing resolution between the two extremes of Culture (method) and Nature (no-method). In *Apocalypse Now* the permutations of the story-motif, represented as method/no-method of war, resolve the conflict between binary oppositions. By bringing together both binary oppositions in the two battles (Vin Drin Drop and Do Lung Bridge) the extreme oppositions are placed closer together in the continuum. Thus, resolution takes place between the two extremes in the story-motif of *Apocalypse Now.*

CONCLUSIONS

To discuss the resolutions found in *Apocalypse Now,* we must break the narrative into three specific elements: transformation, opposition, and mediation. The transformation that occurs in *Apocalypse Now* is Willard's decision to bring Kurtz's story back with him after he has killed Kurtz. Willard's decision metaphorically offers the audience a way out of Vietnam. Through the process of the film the audience has an opportunity to view the war as a confusing conflict between the General's ideal method of war and Kurtz's non-method. Through Willard's mission up the Nung River, the horror of war is presented as the insanity of both methods. The audience becomes a witness to war and will hopefully understand its futility.

The binary opposition between the Generals and Kurtz is one of many in *Apocalypse Now.* While that particular constituent unit is the focus of the narrative, there are other binary units that have an indirect relationship to the General's/Kurtz opposition and which affect the outcome of the resolution that occurs between the central characters. Using the three levels of analysis (environment, characters, and story-motif) and the major binary opposition of nature/culture, we can chart several examples of constituent units found in the narrative within each level. These binary demarcations can be illustrated through the following series of antinomies.

CULTURE	NATURE
ENVIRONMENT	
The United States	Vietnam
"Hot Society"	"Cold Society"
Saigon	Kurtz's Compound
CHARACTERS	
Generals	Kurtz
Chef	Lance
STORY-MOTIF	
Method of War	No-method of war
Humanity	Savagery
Modern Machinery of War	Antiquated Machinery of War
Corruption of Will	Purity of Will

With this list there is evidence that *Apocalypse Now* is structured by binary oppositions. However, according to Lévi-Strauss the function of the narrative is to resolve the binary oppositions. In *Apocalypse Now* there are several oppositions resolved through the permutations achieved by the mediators. As developed through the preceding analysis of environment, characters, and story motifs, the constituent units of Saigon/Kurtz's compound, the Generals/Kurtz, and method of war/no-method of war are transformed and resolved through mediating devices. The binary opposition between the major characters of the Generals/Kurtz is resolved through Willard; the environment opposition is resolved by the Nung River; and through the mediating device of the events on the Nung River (battles of Vin Drin Drop and Do Lung Bridge), the binary opposition in the story motif of method/no method of war is resolved.

The permutations leading to the resolution of method/no

method of the war and between that of culture/nature in the analysis of environment are dependent upon Vin Drin Drop and Do Lung Bridge. As battles, these locations are a midpoint between the General's idealistic viewpoint of the war and Kurtz's lack of "sound method" for waging war. As geographical locations they are of special importance in the transformation from the ordered city of Saigon and the unordered jungles of Kurtz's compound. Whereas the permutations and resolution between culture/nature in the analysis of characters is developed through the mediating device of Willard, Willard remains a fulcrum between the major character opposition of Chef/Lance.

One of the most important underlying story-motifs, as expressed by method/no method, is exemplified as corruption of will/purity of will. This "theme" in **Apocalypse Now** is the "unpronounced" conflict in the method/no method opposition. This binary opposition is finally resolved through Willard's assassination of Kurtz.

What special insights, then, does this analysis give us? The development of the Vietnam war in our culture has taken on mythic proportions. Media representations of the Vietnam war give us an opportunity to investigate our social fabric and help understand the war and its effects on our culture. These representations also allow our culture to articulate interpretations of a historical event through narrative forms to new members of our society. Through the narrative structure of **Apocalypse Now** our cultural contradictions may be played out on the screen and through a cinematic resolution we may come to terms with our own doubts and confusion about the war America lost.

NOTES

1. Gilbert Adair, *Vietnam on Film* (London: Proteus Publishers, 1981): 114.

2. John Simon, "Apocalypse Without End," in *Mass Media and the Popular Arts,* Fredric Rissover and David Birch, eds., (New York: McGraw-Hill, 1981): p. 444. There were three separate versions of the ending in *Apocalypse Now.* For this analysis the ending used in the theatrical release 35 millimeter version will be used. This ending portrays Willard leaving Kurtz's headquarters safely with a subsequent airstrike on the headquarters after Willard departs.

3. Eleanor Coppola chronicles the development and the production of *Apocalypse Now* in her book *Notes* (New York: Simon and Schuster, 1979).

4. Bill Nichols, ed., *Movies and Methods: An Anthology* (Berkeley: University of California Press, 1976): 1.

5. Using Lévi-Strauss' formula, the application of the oppo-

sition between nature/culture and uncontrolled environment/controlled environment is possible. Claude Lévi-Strauss, *Structural Anthropology, Volume I,* Trans. Claire Jacobson and Brooke Schoepf (New York: Basic Books, 1963): 228.

6. Lévi-Strauss, *Structural Anthropology, Volume I:* 226-228.

Jack Kroll (review date 24 December 1990)

SOURCE: "The Corleones Return," in *Newsweek,* Vol. CXVI, No. 26, December 24, 1990, pp. 58-9, 61.

[*In the following review, Kroll describes the problems which plagued Coppola during the filming of* The Godfather Part III.]

The pressure is unbelievable," says Francis Ford Coppola. "This is just another movie. It's a *Godfather* movie. But it's become a big sporting event. It's about Francis—is he going to die or live?" In the last frantic days before the release of *The Godfather Part III* on Christmas Day, Coppola feels like a bull facing an army of matadors—the public that's been waiting for the next chapter in the *Godfather* saga for 16 years, since the release of the second *Godfather* in 1974. It's doubtful whether a movie director has ever felt this much pressure. *Godfather I* (1972) and its sequel were that rarity, a tremendous critical and box-office success that earned its studio, Paramount, a total of $800 million, plus nine Oscars and a permanent place in American culture.

For 15 years Coppola was besieged by successive regimes at Paramount, begging him to do a third Godfather. Always he refused, cracking that the only way he'd ever do it was as a farce, "Abbott and Costello Meet the Godfather." It was Paramount's current chairman, Frank Mancuso, who finally broke down Coppola's resolve. After a succession of classically inane ideas of how to do a Coppola-less *Godfather,* involving directors like Soviet expatriate Andrei Konchalovsky and actors like Sylvester Stallion and Eddie Murphy, fate came to Mancuso's aid in the form of financial catastrophe that overwhelmed Coppola. A slew of box-office disappointments like *One from the Heart, Rumble Fish, Gardens of Stone* and *Tucker* forced the director into an apocalypse now of debts; litigation and bankruptcy. Mancuso ambushed Coppola as neatly as Don Corleone waylaid his victims. A rat-tat-tat of dollars—$3 million to direct, $1 million to write the script, 15 percent of the box-office gross—and the deed was done.

Problems, problems: What followed was nearly a year of filming, in Rome, Sicily and New York, that made the problems of the first two "Godfathers" look like a makeup fix on a Pee-wee Herman movie. Budget Problems, starring a rise from the projected $44 million to $54 million. Casting Problems, starring the last-minute drafting of Coppola's inexperienced, 18-year-old daughter, Sofia, to replace an ill Winona Ryder. Most of all Coppola Problems, starring a brilliant American director who couldn't understand why the gods kept singling him out for troubles and torments. "What is there about me that invites this controversy?" asks Coppola. "Why do I have to be an oddball on the edge of extinction? Why do people enjoy that?"

Between daily self-questionings in this Jobean vein, Coppola managed to finish his movie in time for the Christmas 1990 release that Paramount had desperately beseeched. Coppola points out that meeting this deadline caused the kind of financial hemorrhaging that escalates budgets. Working with an "army of editors," he says, means that "we're paying maybe 50 times what it would cost if we could just mix with one editor." Plaintively he adds, "I started out saying 'I'm going to be a good boy. I'm going to do everything perfect. I'm going to work day and night.' And unavoidably I got tagged with my budgets going over. It's impossible to be a good boy." Mancuso bears out Coppola's self-defense. "No one was more responsible about the budget than Francis himself," he says. "He did everything possible to live up to it. I'm upset with the perception that he's irresponsible. It's absolutely untrue."

Now, as technicians are whizzing out 1,800 prints for a wide national release (Coppola is rightly concerned about the quality control that could affect Gordon Willis's lusciously somber, Renaissance-hued cinematography), reactions are coming in from professionals, critics and cinema sneaks who have seen the early screenings. These range, perhaps inevitably, from thumbs turned downward with dislocating force to huzzahs for the best *Godfather* of them all. While the nation prepares for an orgy of Godfolderol, let's pan-and-scan through one of the most dramatic production stories in movie history.

First, Coppola and Mario Puzo (whose 1969 best-selling novel was the cause of it all) meet in the spring of 1989 to bat out a screenplay. They do this in the inspiring ambience of a gambling hell in Reno, Nev. "We'd work for hours and when we ran out of ideas, we'd go down to the casino," says Coppola. "Mario would play roulette and I'd play craps or 21. After a while we'd be embarrassed about losing so we'd go upstairs and work on the script."

Pooping out: Coppola needs six or eight months to write the script. He and Puzo get six weeks. This means that when shooting starts in Rome he spends every night plus weekends making revisions. When Robert Duvall angrily rejects Paramount's cheapskate offer of $1.5 million to reprise his role of Tom Hagen, the Corleone family *consigliere* (Al Pacino gets $5 million as mob scion Michael Corleone, Diane Keaton $2 million as Kay, his ex-wife), Coppola has to write Duvall out of the script and beef up George Hamilton's role of B. J. Harrison, Michael's smooth WASP lawyer. Paramount doesn't want Hamilton (a pale reflection of the studio's recalcitrance on G1, when they didn't want Marlon Brando, Pacino, Keaton and just about everyone who made the movie a classic. But those were *autres temps* and *autres schmoes*).

The Duvall matter is soon eclipsed when Winona Ryder, who has been making one film after another, poops out. The time-squeezed Coppola calls on his daughter, Sofia, a Mills College freshman on holiday, to play the role of Michael's daughter, Mary. Sofia, fresh from the shower, is whisked to the studio to do a scene immediately. Everyone, from Paramount officials to Coppola's wife, Eleanor, is aghast. The director is accused of "child abuse" and warned that nice-kid Sofia, who had only played walk-on bits in her father's films, would be "scarred for life" by vicious reviews. But Coppola, who has in fact written Mary with Sofia in mind, accepts the trade-off of an unfledged actress for "the real thing." "Mary is this kind of idealized, innocent daughter," says Sofia, "and he definitely sees me as his innocent daughter." Once again fate has linked the mythic Corleones with the real Coppolas. Sofia, who joins Coppola's sister, Talia Shire (as Michael's sister, Connie), Coppola's 80-year-old father, Carmine (composer), and sundry other relatives in what the director calls "the biggest home movie in history," is clearly answering an inner need of her father. "I knew the only way I could come through with this film was to make it as personal as I could," says Coppola. Assigning Sofia a place in the fateful Corleone saga clearly helps Coppola to exorcise the grief that still clings to him over the loss of his 23-year-old son Gian-Carlo, who died in a boating accident in 1986 during the filming of *Gardens of Stone*.

The gutsy Sofia breaks down and cries several times under the pressure, but she gets stronger. She is aided by a dialogue coach who takes her through "psycho-relaxation" exercises, and by the entire cast, especially Andy Garcia as Vincent, the sexy killer who falls for first-cousin Mary. Whatever the fate of the film, it's clear to everyone that G3 is going to make Garcia a big star, as G1 did for Pacino and G2 did for Robert De Niro. The darkly handsome 34-year-old (*The Untouchables, Internal Affairs*) can smolder, explode, charm and, best of all, act. In his scenes Garcia loves to improvise, land unexpected punches, which delights Coppola but drives the meticulous Gordon Willis nuts. As Coppola puts it: "Andy is an exciting and essential part of the story; without him it would be rich old guys brooding about their sins."

While Garcia is heating up the film, Pacino discusses Shakespeare with Bardo-philiac Coppola, who sees elements of Lear, Hamlet and Coriolanus in the character of Michael.

Coppola creates a diabetic seizure for Michael inspired by the mad scenes of Lear and Hamlet. But the Method-trained Pacino says: "As much as I love Shakespeare, I couldn't really connect it to my role. I was busy figuring out how to get from one side of the room to another." Coppola, says Pacino, is "an amazing asset. He fills you up with the world of the movie."

It's a tough world. Coppola's problems range from a financial lawsuit that crops up in the middle of shooting, to worrying about Diane Keaton, who is going through a real-life romantic crisis with Pacino. "She didn't really want to do it," he says. "It's tough to come back 16 years later and still be in the thankless job of a supporting player. You could tell it was tough for both Diane and Al, especially when they were both in Rome but not living together."

Another problem is the violence that Paramount, and *Godfather* fans, expect Coppola to cook up not as fast-food action with gore sauce but as haute cuisine. "Everyone's seen everything," he says. "The trick is to stage it so that some detail or odd thing makes it stick in your mind and renew its horror." Despite his stated aversion, Coppola comes up with some recipes for carnage in G3 that are classics of shock, worthy of Kurosawa, whom he calls "the great father of screen violence."

Bedeviled: The real violence is the disruption and anxiety that buffet Coppola as he wills together these huge, exhausting *Godfather* movies, his recognized masterpieces toward which he has ambivalent feelings. They are *their* movies," he says, meaning they really belong to the system, not to the artist. He says he prefers his small, intimate films like *The Rain People* (1969) and *The Conversation* (1974). Of course he is wrong and he surely knows it. There is more poetry, more inspired invention, more fun and wit and vision and power in the G-movies than in any but a few American films. The fear and terror that bedevil Coppola on his globe-trotting, money-gobbling, deadline-crushing Godfathering may really be the fear that this is his true work, work he has been dragooned, cajoled and forced into by the failure of his more cherished projects. "It's not as though we were walking around in the *Godfather* movies thinking we were making art," he says. "We were just trying to get through it." Not to force a comparison, but Coppola's favorite, Shakespeare, probably said the same thing. Necessity is the Godmother of invention.

Karen Jaehne (review date 1991)

SOURCE: A review of *The Godfather Part III*, in *Cineaste*, Vol. XVIII, No. 2, 1991, pp. 41-3.

[In the following review, Jaehne lists several of the faults of Coppola's Godfather III *and concludes, "Maybe it's time for Coppola to give up sequels and create some original sins."]*

A baroque vision of life at the top of the criminal ladder in the rusty hues of blood and dried blood, *The Godfather Part III* is about the cost of redeeming one's soul, especially when that soul has been so neglected it looks like the dilapidated house at Lake Tahoe where *Godfather II* stopped and *Part III* begins. Michael Corleone's life is redeemed, apparently, during the flashforward to his death in the garden, when he falls off his chair. Straight but stiff.

"The only wealth," sighs the Godfather (Al Pacino) in the first of dozens of epigrammatic lines of dialog, "is children. More than power or money." Aha! So a child is what he will have to pay for his soul! But which child? Anthony (Franc D'Ambrosio), who's given up capos for opera capes? Nah, he's abandoned the Family for Art. But here comes Mary (Sofia Coppola), with a madonna's resemblance to Michael's first wife, whom he married during exile in Sicily. She died for his sins, when she got behind the wheel of his car.

When the crimes of the fathers are visited on the sons, there's nothing like a female sacrifice to elevate the tragedy. It reeks of ancient blood ritual, recalling the *Oresteia,* that Greek trilogy in which Aeschylus immortalized the horrors of the House of Atreus—child sacrifice, fratricide, patricide, matricide, even genocide at Troy, but also a new order of justice ushered in by a democratically-inclined Athena to cleanse Orestes from the terrible traditions of blood revenge.

Godfather III needed to present such a transition to a new and higher form of justice, but in the by now apocryphal six weeks in a Reno casino that it took to write the script, clearly nobody thought of anything new or lofty. This tale of decadence only hints at a dark past seeping into a dark present with some properly Viscontian touches—opera, incest and seething Sicily.

The political engagement of *Godfather III* is equally tiresome and second hand. While it may have been shocking in the Seventies to assert that one could make a business out of crime or that Mafia "businessmen" could wield substantial political clout, the last twenty years of indictments against public officials and financiers, along with the utter collapse of integrity in American leadership makes mincemeat of many of the film's brave assertions. "I don't need tough guys. I need more lawyers!'," says the Godfather. Tell it to Ed Meese. "The higher I go, the crookeder it gets." Tell it to the Iranscam Special Prosecutor.

"Politics and crime—they are the same thing." That one is emblazoned across the screen in subtitles, indicating that the Italians knew long ago the lessons of the S&L scandals. And when a Cardinal "contemplates eternity," he's playing for time. The dialog recapitulates the cynical lessons of two decades, adding nothing and merely recalling that several of the Watergate engineers also found God somewhere between the White House and their publishing houses. Wouldn't be it great to read *The Memoirs of Michael Corleone: Doin' the Vatican Rag*?

Our disappointment in the film goes beyond the customary stupidity of sequels rushed through production to satisfy studio release patterns. After creating one of the great mythic characters of American cinema, Coppola shows the effects on his own life of the last two decades by taking a dive for Paramount Pictures. But beyond sheer need or avarice (reportedly $5 million if he could get the film out in 1990), most annoying is his failure to cap the theme running through the previous *Godfathers*—the transfer of power from one generation to the next.

The previous films showed us the decline of power from a father in the old Mafia to a son who must carry on in a modern mob. In part III, however, we see the decline of power from God—he who made and rules the very universe—to his children who purport to carry on his works on earth, the Vatican fathers. The sons of God upstage the sons of Sicily.

The script of Mario Puzo and Coppola retains the structural framework of the other two films: the opening scene at a family ritual celebration; the family's position within the Mafia being challenged; the intrafamily disputes calling for a new Godfather; the unsuitability of the 'crown prince'; the perception of their 'business' as the cutting edge of the American way and the concomitant search for new 'markets,' culminating with a challenge to the family's supremacy that exacts an act of violence from the wannabe Godfather even against his will, leading to a spectacular series of killings, as a newly designated heir seizes control of the clan and discovers in his power only splendid isolation. The old don succumbs in his garden like those Roman Emperors who, after the savagery of Ancient Rome, retired to contemplation and cabbages.

The grandeur of the conception is not diminished by using a formula, but the formula serves both the content and style to make of it a kind of 'spaghetti Bertolucci' movie. The frame is too ornate for the picture, and the plot fails to carry us beyond melodrama. The affectation of style becomes the content, as in Sergio Leone's spaghetti westerns. This Family doesn't feud: it squabbles. Their business is not the crime intrinsic to the American Way of Life. They just have nasty colleagues.

Like the "just say no" culture of the Eighties, they want to get clean and sober and into an international conglomerate. That is presented as an abstraction by the name of Immobiliare (the word means real estate and has a cognate in every European language). Once beyond the confines of Little Italy, the Corleones are tiresomely amorphous and have the occasional glamour of folks promoted by *Vanity Fair*. They wear designer clothes and act elusive. They may found Mobsters Anonymous!

When we first rejoin *la Famiglia* Corleone, Michael is being celebrated at a mass as he receives the Order of San Sebastian for his benevolence. Anyone daring to express surprise at his newfound stature is silenced with a rude "Shaddup! Ya tink ya know beduh dan da Pope?!" Infallibility has never been the Pope's *forte*: now come the Corleones to reinforce it.

Still, the key to this ***Godfather*** is nothing less than theological, forcing us to ask if an old mobster's soul can be saved according to the doctrine of the Church (none of this weird fundamentalist stuff). Michael himself asks, "What is the use of confession, if I don't repent?" Damned good question—but keep your eye on the business implications of following the letter of the law: a confession usually prompts absolution (in the movies it always does). Indeed, Michael's confession of his sins to the man who would be Pope is the linchpin of the film (even if the scene seems to lack the creative force we expect of such a moment). He admits to having killed his brother and the confessor blesses him. He's not even sent off with his rosary for a Hail Mary!

Because the priest to whom he entrusts all this becomes Pope, that Pope can then permit Michael to join the worthy board of Immobiliare. We are forced to ask ourselves if this is the reason for the poisoning of that Pope; it is only suggested, but we do get a clear picture of foul play with the Pontiff. Do not make the mistake of thinking that the Pope's knowledge of Michael's crimes implicates the Pope himself in any intrigue. On the contrary, Michael has been forgiven, and his confessor is the only one who knows for sure. Michael can repent later, once he's seen his daughter die in his place on the steps of the opera house.

It has been difficult to get two or more critics to agree on the financial details of the plot, depending on the need to acknowledge the international banking and business conflict that constitutes the motor of the storyline. Archbishop Gilday (Donal Donnelly) approaches Michael to help him out of the embarrassing situation of accounting for a $750 million deficit in the Vatican coffers (betrayed by an unscrupulous or atheist accountant). Michael says, "Let's make a deal."

Their negotiation culminates in Michael giving $600 million to the Vatican directly or making it an investment into the business (this is unclear) in exchange for a sizable chunk of Immobiliare Internationale, twenty-five percent of which is controlled by the Vatican. But the upright European businessmen on the board of Immobiliare hesitate to permit this known criminal into their midst.

They apprise Corleone of ancient, gnarly rules that bind their decisions, which may even require the consent of the Pope himself. (About financial matters? Could Michael Milken be Pope?!) As a kind of option. Michael contributes $200 million to a church fund through the new $100 million endowment of the Corleone Foundation, headed up by the virginal Mary Corleone.

When the Pope falls ill (as happened in 1978 when two popes died in suspiciously quick succession), the Vatican bells toll and the byzantine process of electing a new pope stops all business. Michael hangs out in Sicily waiting to be let in back in Rome. And here we pick up the developing relationship between Michael and Vincent Mancini (Andy Garcia).

Vincent is the illegitimate (everything else is illegitimate; why not the next Godfather?) son of Michael's brother Sonny (James Caan). He is also a hood who has been creating havoc among the New York mob because he staunchly defends Uncle Michael against upstart mobster Joey Zasa (Joe Mantegna), his employer. Even if Vinnie's methods are those of a blabbermouth street kid who has crashed Michael's all-too-legitimate party, he brashly gets what he seeks in an audience with the Godfather.

He's like a mutt from the pound about to be trained like a German Shepherd. Most important, he is the protégé of the now murderous Aunt Connie (Talia Shire), who warns Michael, "They fear you!" To which he cannily replies, "They ought to fear *you.*" Yes, the women have become as monstrous as the men. The only ironic comment comes from ex-wife Kay (Diane Keaton), now a socialite who shows up to tell Michael, "Now that you're respectable, you're more dangerous than ever."

If the movie has a message, that's it. Watching the refining process of Vincent, we rather regret his transition from a volatile street fighter into a manipulative mobster. He is the life of the film, this leather-clad, fast-talking stud, the only one with enough charisma to interest either Michael or us for an entire three-plus hours or into another sequel. It is inevitable that we compare Vincent to Michael. Garcia to Pacino. And to Marlon Brando and Robert de Niro as the original.

Andy Garcia plays the gangster as a man with the strong family loyalties of someone trying to get under an umbrella he really needs. But he also has a keen intelligence honed

by the martial arts rather than The Method. He can't throw away lines, as did Brando and de Niro; nor can he reproduce Pacino's dormant volcano persona. Garcia is like a cat prowling and pouncing, nothing escaping his youthful predatory instincts. He is only dull when he preys upon Goddaughter Mary. Here, we should see the crackle and spark of sin: instead, she is so flummoxed in his presence that he can only coax her through her lines with eyes that widen in patience rather than desire. A taboo requires recognition: poor Sofia Coppola plays the role as a maiden gently awakening to love not lust.

This relationship needs to feed into the Corleone family's increasing resemblance to the mythic Borgias of the Renaissance, a theme underlined by dialog like "What's this with the Borgias? Those days are over." At the Minetta Lane Tavern, an infamous Greenwich Village pub frequented by gangsters, Vincent and Mary rendezvous. She asks if her father killed Vincent's father Sonny, and Vincent tells her reassuring stories. The children propagating family legend dare not face the family history.

If the past has shaped these characters, it's hard to know why. Even their Sicilian roots have been spruced up; when did the Sicilian wing of the family move from the traditional square stucco villa outside Agrigento to the elegant Santo Domingo Hotel in Taormina (a seventeenth century baroque monastery renovated to five-star status)? Stolid Tom Hagen replaced by day-glo George Hamilton?

For a film decrying excess and corruption, its own departure from verisimilitude and credible characters allows for no moral or esthetic yardstick: you are forced to go back and see the first two films to figure out why Michael is nattering on about the legitimate world. We got glimpses of legitimacy and commonplace expectations in those films; we knew just how abnormal each family member was. *Godfather III,* however, breathes the thin air of the thoroughly idle rich. The muscular ambition of Andy Garcia as Vincent provides some foil to what often feels like a Robin Leach tour of lifestyles of the rich and *famoso.* The token violence, isolated as set pieces, makes this "mob manqué."

It attains grand guignol when Aunt Connie gives a neat package of poisoned cannoli to poor old Don Altobello (Eli Wallach) an old Sicilian family friend who turned on Michael. Under the gaze of her opera glasses, he devours his gift during the opera's *canzone.* Which returns us to the original dilemma of making this film in a society where law and order have ceased to command respect! The Borgia ethic is the rule rather than the exception. A casino full of capos gets strafed in Atlantic City—that's hoary news compared to the corruption of Pete Rose or the plagiarism of Martin Luther King, Jr.

Perhaps it's a harbinger of things to come that the Godfather is worried about his soul. Michael's search for redemption could have made a formidable foundation for this unwieldy plot construction, even as his old gang lined up behind him, hoping the cleansing affects of the Immobiliare deal could stretch to purify their money too. The business deal with the Vatican, however, is a Hydra-headed problem of the plotline that distracts us from the Godfather's spiritual struggle.

"The power to absolve debt," says the worldly archbishop, "is greater than the power of forgiveness." Lines like this seem to speak to Coppola's reasons for making the film, from publicized bankruptcy in 1990 to the tragic death of his son Gio in 1986. But absolution, as any Hollywood Catholic knows, cannot be had from Paramount. Maybe it's time for Coppola to give up sequels and create some original sins.

David Denby (review date 7 January 1991)

SOURCE: "The Grandfather," in *New York*, Vol. 24, No. 1, January 7, 1991, pp. 57, 64-5.

[*In the following review, Denby complains, "The Godfather* III *has its moments, but I think one can state as a principle that a man's desire to withdraw from life cannot serve as the center of an epic drama (not, that is, without Shakespeare's poetry)."*]

For much of its two-hour-and-forty-minute length, I waited for *The Godfather Part III* to explode, and for a long time it only wheezed. The movie certainly isn't boring, but much of it is heavy-spirited and glum, as if the Mafia and the *Godfather* movies themselves had become unspeakably important facts of American life, permitting neither levity nor excitement. Michael Corleone (Al Pacino), only about 60 but old in body and spirit, sets the tone. The hollow-eyed Pacino performs brilliantly, but he appears to be sinking within himself, and for a long time the movie sinks with him. Fortunately, *Godfather III* finally does come to life: The last half-hour will become legendary.

In the original *Godfather* (1972), the twin elements of family piety and hair-raising violence nourished and enlarged each other in ways that were unsettling and funny. The intensity of the Corleones' love for one another drew us in, yet as soon as we began to think that they weren't quite monsters, that they were vital and attractive, they would kill someone. The bullets slamming into bodies, the feet kicking through windshields, rebuffed our weak sentimentality. Francis Coppola's story moved ahead fiercely yet with just enough space for texture and detail—for the interweaving of major and minor characters, foreground and background, mob and

America. The narrative possessed a fullness and decisiveness without equal in American movie history.

Part II (1974) extended the Corleone family saga forward into Michael Corleone's unhappy maturity and the period of the family's control over Las Vegas in the fifties and sixties, and backward to Vito Corleone's youth in Sicily and Little Italy early in the century. Though perhaps not as exciting or as emotionally involving as the first film, *Godfather II* was a work of aggressive high intelligence, a bitter and sardonic view of the corruption of America and a frightening embodiment of paranoia as a way of life.

Godfather III renews the emotions established at the end of *Part II*—those moments in which Michael, desolated by the enormity of his responsibilities and the horror of his crimes, grows increasingly lonely and motionless in his lakeside Nevada house. By 1979, a shrewd but self-disgusted man, he's become sick of gangster life. He has moved back to New York—a large apartment on Fifth Avenue—and has taken the Corleone family out of the rackets altogether. A financier, he buys himself respectability by contributing millions to the Catholic church. *Part III* opens with a huge party, which matches the wedding scene at the beginning of *The Godfather,* though without the bounding, sunshiny happiness. The party has the grayness of Michael's face. Pacino's hair is combed up, bristling; his brow is deeply furrowed. Hunched inside his rich man's business suit, he looks smaller, as if lifetime habits of calculation had shrunk his body.

Michael tries to buy a controlling interest (with Vatican approval) in an international conglomerate and runs afoul of an Italian Mr. Big, a corrupt financier misusing church funds. Set in the Vatican Bank and the Vatican itself, much of this intrigue, resounding hollowly in the gloomy, magnificent rooms, is grand yet muffled, distant from us and from the first two films. Coppola and Mario Puzo (who again collaborated on the screenplay), seizing on fresh real-life scandals and rumors (not just the Sindona Affair but the surprising early death of John Paul I), seem to have forgotten that the first two films were about crime as the American way of business, about a powerful family preying on the corruptibility of the country. Suddenly, the American theme is lost, and Coppola and Puzo are off in Rome remaking *The Shoes of the Fisherman.* A lot of the screenplay is overexplicit and stiff—lazy—and the hushed solemnity gets a little thick. The movie needs someone like manic Joe Pesci from *GoodFellas* scampering across the marbled floors of its self-esteem.

Nothing quite commands us emotionally. Michael's sister, Connie (Talia Shire), slinks in and out, a fierce witch in black plotting murders. Kay (Diane Keaton), though remarried, experiences a mild return of affection for Michael. (So what?) His son, Anthony (Franc D'Ambrosio), wants to become an opera singer and rejects his dad, but he's no more than a sweet-faced cipher. In a catastrophic decision, Coppola, ever his own Godfather, cast his daughter Sofia as Michael's daughter Mary (the talented Winona Ryder had dropped out). Miss Coppola has a thick, curled upper lip that she doesn't have the training and technique to use as an actress. She appears raw and unprotected, naked almost, and since she has a flat, uninflected voice as well, the exposure is complete. When the rising young hood Vincenzo (Andy Garcia), the bastard son of Michael's brother Sonny, and a dangerously attractive man, falls in love with her, we are baffled. His semi-incestuous desire for her is meant to be the mainspring of the plot, but the spring isn't wound.

Michael seeks redemption. But like all movie gangsters, he's pulled back into feuds and revenge—the knife in the stomach, the blood on the floor. *The Godfather III* has its moments, but I think one can state as a principle that a man's desire to withdraw from life cannot serve as the center of an epic drama (not, that is, without Shakespeare's poetry). Anguished and saturnine and at times deeply funny, Pacino gives a detailed, moving performance. But the emotions that he's playing—self-abnegation, despair—don't fuel a large film. If the talented Garcia, as the young Mafioso, had been allowed to take over the movie, just as Pacino took over *The Godfather* when Brando's Don Vito withdrew, *Godfather III* might have worked. But Garcia's character, a hothead who suddenly matures, doesn't develop in an interesting way.

Gordon Willis is on hand again as cinematographer, and the interiors have his usual dark splendor, the Sicilian scenes a golden lushness that is both enchanting and heartbreaking. The level of craft is very high, but until the end there's only one sequence that flows with Coppola's old mastery—the assassination of a New York hood (Joe Mantegna) during a Mulberry Street festival. Mantegna is the latest in a series of *Godfather* actors with tremendous presence. Playing gangsters, these actors must feel they *are* someone in the world. That, of course, was always part of the comedy of the films—the elaborate punctilio among thugs, which eventually collapses into shooting.

In the final sequence, an obvious parallel to the climax of the first movie (with elements of Hitchcock's *The Man Who Knew Too Much* thrown in), Michael's son makes his debut in *Cavalleria Rusticana* in Palermo, and Coppola cuts together the action onstage, assassination attempts in the opera house, the settling of scores in the Vatican and elsewhere. Passion, sacrifice, murder—an overwhelmingly rich Italian diet. The sequence, both darkly voluptuous and lurid, is obvious in the way that *Cavalleria Rusticana* is obvious, but it's also thrilling and great. The tragedy of Michael Corleone is complete at last. No movie lover could truly wish it to go on any longer.

Elaine Showalter (review date 8 January 1993)

SOURCE: "Blood Sell," in *Times Literary Supplement*, January 8, 1993, p. 14.

[*In the following review, Showalter discusses the vampire genre and Coppola's version, concluding, "More about coffers than coffins, this* Dracula *will neither join the canon of vampire classics nor enrich Coppola's artistic reputation."*]

"There is not a theatre in Paris without its Vampire!" a French critic exclaimed in 1820; and London and New York might say the same today. From Francis Ford Coppola's new **Dracula** to John Landis's sexy *Innocent Blood*, from Nigel Finch's stylish updating of a nineteenth-century German opera by Heinrich August Marschner for BBC2, and Shimako Seto's melancholy *Tale of a Vampire* (shot in Deptford library, Chiswick and Rotherhithe), to Mark Morris's startling ballet, everybody's doing that Transylvanian rag. *Vlad the Impaler*, an adaptation of Marin Sorescu's play, *The Third Stake*, was broadcast on Radio 3 in November 1992, and the latest title in Anne Rice's "Vampire Chronicles", *The Tale of the Body Thief . . .* is on the American bestseller lists, as is Bram Stoker's original *Dracula* (1897). In the breathless words of a BBC press release, "the world is poised on the brink of vampire fever".

In his history of the horror film, *Dreadful Pleasures* (1985), James B. Twitchell suggests that epidemics of vampire fever strike in twenty-year cycles, but there is always a reason why a country has vampire trouble, and each era has offered its own rationale for the children of the night. The vampire's Romantic resurrection in 1819, in a novel by Byron's friend, Dr John Polidori, which became the source of Marschner's opera, came from metaphysical scepticism and fantasies of foreign threats to the stable British family. If Stoker's *Dracula* has been filmed over 150 times, it is because it offers a potent cultural mythology as well as a series of erotic and horrific images. Not only the most aesthetic but also some of the campiest Draculas have succeeded on the screen because directors from F. W. Murnau to Andy Warhol so clearly put the stamp of their own moment on the story. Whether out of German post-war expressionist malaise (Murnau's *Nosferatu*, 1921); English Cold War longing for new cultural blood (Hammer Studio's *Horror of Dracula*, 1958); American racism (William Marshall's *Blacula*, 1972); bisexual decadence (Tony Scott's *The Hunger*, 1985); or teenage homosexual panic (Joel Schumacher's *The Lost Boys*, 1985), directors have found a way to use the vampire legend to illuminate issues and styles of their own time. Even Batman, who is to Dracula as Jekyll is to Hyde, has been revamped as a contemporary neurotic.

In the 1990s, the Dracula legend has taken on new political

and cultural meanings. The weekly New York digest of the Romanian TV news begins with a montage of national heroes including the original Dracula, Vlad the Impaler, who defended the country against the Turks in the fifteenth century, although one might think his habit of staking his enemies in the rectum and arranging them artistically about the landscape would be somewhat off-putting. In *Mad Forest*, Caryl Churchill's play about the Romanian revolution of 1989, Dracula is one of the characters, a sleek aristocrat desperately courted by a starving dog, in an allegory of a poor country's cringing susceptibility to tyrants. Since vampirism is a sexually transmitted disease of the blood, parallels to AIDS must resonate in every contemporary version, whether or not the director intends them, and Coppola's shots of blood cells and transfusions led the *New York Times* critic, Frank Rich, to see the film as an allegory of AIDS.

One of the most consistent interpretations of *Dracula* has been to see it as the projection of Jonathan Harker's unconscious. On the eve of his marriage, this rigid, buttoned-up, obsessively punctual young solicitor goes on a journey to the east, where he meets his double, the lascivious Count Dracula, who will act out his repressed desires. In the German "Nosferatu" versions of the story, Harker is actually bitten and turns into a vampire, despite his wife's effort to save him by spending the night with Dracula so that he will be surprised and killed by the rays of the rising sun. Indeed, although no director has noticed it, in the Stoker novel Harker recognizes one of the female vampires who come to seduce him in the castle; he "seemed somehow to know her face and know it in connection with some dreamy fear". Stoker hints that this "fair girl", who bends over him with scarlet lips as he closes his eyes "in a languorous ecstasy", is Lucy Westenra, the best friend of Harker's fiancée, Mina, and a Victorian vamp who receives marriage proposals from all the other men in the novel. Because Harker, too, secretly desires her, Dracula fixates on her even before he gets to England, and she is his first victim.

Coppola saw the Harker role as relatively unimportant, and cast the wooden Keanu Reeves, whom he has quaintly called "a matinée idol", in the part, in a misguided effort to pull teenage girls into the audience for the film. But his *Dracula* has other attractions: weird and interesting performances by Anthony Hopkins and Gary Oldman; surprisingly active heroines played by Sadie Frost and Winona Ryder; beautiful operatic costumes by the Japanese designer, Eiko Ishioka, drawing on exotic fauna such as the Australian frilled lizard and *fin-de-siècle* artists including Mucha, Beardsley, Klimt, Leighton and Moreau; clever use of retro cinema techniques by Coppola's son, Roman Coppola; and buckets and buckets of blood. From beginning to end, the film is a series of allusions and homages to cinematic classics. The script by James V. Hart (fleshed out into a book as the curiously-titled *Bram Stoker's Dracula: The novel of the film*) echoes the historical framing-device of a vampire seeking his lost bride through the centuries from *Blacula;* the opening battle-scene of impaled bodies against a red sky follows Kurosawa's *Kagemusha;* the blue flames around the wolves come from Murnau's *Faust;* the setting of Dracula's castle pays homage to Cocteau's *La Belle et La Bête;* the plot ending suggests Disney's *Beauty and the Beast,* and, as Coppola himself notes (in his introduction to *Bram Stoker's Dracula: the film and the legend,* the "only official companion book"), "the whole thing climaxes in an enormous John Ford shootout—no one had ever portrayed that".

What Coppola's **Dracula** lacks, however, is a coherent aesthetic and ideas of its own. Victorian vampire trouble came from the sexual repression of women, but Coppola's heroines do not need any help from a vampire to express their pent-up sexuality. Mina hotly embraces the prudish Harker, lets Dracula pick her up in the street, and take her to dinner with absinthe. Lucy, in a series of low-cut orange chiffon dresses out of *Flaming June*, flings herself at her suitors with all the finesse of a Mae West, reaching for the Texan's Bowie knife while pleading "Quincey—let me touch it. It's so big." The girls giggle over pornography, and writhe in masturbatory pleasure in their beds.

The sharp contrasts between British empiricism, research and domestic decorum, and "Transylvanian" superstition, timelessness and polymorphous perversity, which make Stoker's novel so delectable, break down in Coppola's sloppy goulash. Anthony Hopkins's Van Helsing is as batty and incestuous as Dracula, a raving replay of Hannibal Lecter. The "Victorian young guns" who court Lucy and hunt Dracula are half-crazy themselves; Dr. Seward, who runs a lunatic asylum that looks more like Bedlam than the sedate retreats of the 1890s, is a drug addict. Most problematic, despite his frequent metamorphoses into beasts, Gary Oldman's Dracula is a loving and uxorious fellow at heart who seems much happier in London (where, hippie sunglasses apart, he dresses like a normal Victorian gentleman) than at home in Transylvania, where he is weighed down by Kabuki robes and a haircut that resembles the frontal lobes of the brain. Coppola, whose masterpieces (**Apocalypse Now,** the **Godfather** saga) and disasters (**The Cotton Club, Tucker**) have tended to be over budget and over time, has been disarmingly honest about his hopes to make a lot of money with this film, in order to finance more experimental projects for his studio. American Zoetrope; but, after grossing $32 million in its first weekend in the United States, **Dracula** dropped 49 per cent at the box office.

Coppola calls the vampire's reincarnation in London "Young Dracula", but Gary Oldman does not convey a sense of youth. In the BBC2 series, *The Vampyr,* however, Omar Ebrahim's Ripley is youthful, sexy and frightening. Marschner's original opera played to full houses at London's

Lyceum Theatre for sixty performances in 1829, and the modern version directed by Nigel Finch, should also be a hit, for, unlike Coppola's *Dracula,* it succeeds in bringing a distinctive contemporary vision to the vampire myth. *The Vampyr* mixes Polidori, *Faust* and Jack the Ripper in the story of a vampire who, disinterred by real-estate developers, rises to power in the ruthless world of London high finance and must kill young women in order to stay alive. Combining British suspicion of the foreign entrepreneur with women's fear of serial killers, *The Vampyr* successfully taps some of the major urban anxieties of the 1990s. Handsomely filmed in locations around London, and magnificently sung by an attractive cast including Fiona O'Neill, Philip Salmon and Richard Van Allen, this "soap opera" could reach the wide audience Coppola aimed at. Finch, who directed *The Lost Language of Cranes,* does not shy away from the homoerotic subtexts of the vampire story, and both the slangy contemporary libretto (by Charles Hart, who wrote *The Phantom of the Opera*) and the generous use of nudity and violence, are intended to bring new life to a neglected work and broaden the television viewers' appreciation for a serious art form.

In contrast, Coppola's cinematic decisions and Columbia Pictures' manic mega-marketing of *Dracula* tie-ins seem to have no purpose beyond the cash register. More about coffers than coffins, this *Dracula* will neither join the canon of vampire classics nor enrich Coppola's artistic reputation.

FURTHER READING

Criticism

Bogue, Ronald L. "The Heartless Darkness of *Apocalypse Now.*" *Georgia Review* XXXV, No. 3 (Fall 1981): 611-26.

> Interprets the ending of Coppola's *Apocalypse Now* based on the assertion that the film is an imitation of Conrad's *The Heart of Darkness,* as opposed to an adaptation.

Calhoun, John. Review of *Coppola and Eiko on "Bram Stoker's Dracula,"* by Francis Ford Coppola and Eiko

Ishioka. *TCI: Theatre Crafts International* 27, No. 2 (February 1993): 56.

> Discusses the importance of the costumes in Coppola's *Bram Stoker's Dracula,* as exhibited in the director's book with designer Eiko Ishioka.

Chown, Jeffrey. "What's in a Name?" *Hollywood Auteur: Francis Coppola,* pp. 217-23. New York: Praeger, 1988.

> Discusses Coppola as a Hollywood auteur.

Cowie, Peter. "Coppola Remarried to the Mob." *Variety* (3 January 1990): 1, 10-1.

> Discusses how Coppola became involved in the making of *The Godfather Part III.*

Crist, Judith. "All in the Family." *New York* 7, No. 51 (23 December 1974): 70-1.

> Praises Coppola's *The Godfather Part II* as being even better than the original.

Gow, Gordon. Review of *The Godfather Part II,* by Francis Ford Coppola. *Films and Filming* 21, No. 10 (July 1975): 42-3.

> Complains that "*The Godfather, Part Two* is remorselessly protracted, dwelling lugubriously upon the central figure of Michael, for whom Al Pacino, so fine in *The Godfather, Part One,* can in the present circumstances arouse very little of my interest."

Haskell, Molly. "*The Godfather Part II:* The Corleone Saga Sags." *Village Voice* (19 March 1989): 88-9.

> Complains of the lack of dialogue and active thought in Coppola's *The Godfather Part II.*

Rosenbaum, Jonathan. Review of *The Godfather Part II,* by Francis Ford Coppola. *Sight and Sound* 44, No. 3 (Summer 1975): 187-88.

> Asserts that while in many ways *The Godfather Part II* is superior to the original, the film actually adds nothing new to the Corleone saga.

Sarris, Andrew. Review of *The Godfather,* by Francis Ford Coppola. *Village Voice* (16 March 1972): 63.

> Discusses the secrecy surrounding Marlon Brando's performance in *The Godfather,* and notes other fine performances in the film.

Additional coverage of Coppola's life and career is contained in the following sources published by Gale: *Contemporary Authors,* **Vol. 77-80;** *Contemporary Authors New Revision Series,* **Vol. 40; and** *Dictionary of Literary Biography,* **Vol. 44.**

Cherríe Moraga

1952-

American poet, essayist, dramatist, and editor.

INTRODUCTION

Moraga's publications are noted for their honest exploration of taboo subjects within American Chicano culture, particularly issues related to female power and sexuality. Moraga writes about her own experiences as a feminist lesbian and minority woman, as well as the common experience of Latinas in America. She is also a highly regarded editor of compilations of writings by minority women and is a co-founder of Kitchen Table/Women of Color Press.

Biographical Information

Moraga was born in Whittier, California, to a Chicana mother and an Anglo-American father. This disparity in her parents' backgrounds allowed Moraga first-hand knowledge of the tensions between Latinos and those in the dominant American culture. When she was nine, her family settled in the San Gabriel Valley, near Los Angeles, where Moraga felt the strong influence of her mother's extended family. Listening to stories related orally by female relatives afforded Moraga the opportunity to experience a uniquely feminine mode of story-telling that she would later employ in her own writing. Moraga, along with her brother and sister, was of the first generation in her family to graduate from college, attending a small private college for her undergraduate work and then San Francisco State University for her graduate degree. After receiving her bachelor's degree in 1974, Moraga taught English for two years at a private high school in Los Angeles. During that time she made two decisions that would significantly affect her future: she joined a writing group and she came out as a lesbian. Moraga has said that, in the writing group, she for the first time began to take her writing seriously; but at the same time she was told by the group that her vocabulary was too limited and that she could not write poems to women because that would confuse readers. Discouraged but more self-confident, Moraga decided to take a year off to concentrate on writing and reading. At this time she moved to San Francisco and became immersed in the city's highly charged political atmosphere; she also became aware of the political implications of her own minority ethnic and sexual status. For her master's thesis in 1980, Moraga co-edited a collection of writings by minority women, titled *This Bridge Called My Back: Writings by Radical Women of Color* (1981). Moraga moved to Boston and then New York City to find a publisher for the book. Finally, she co-founded Kitchen Table/Women of Color

Press to publish the book, which won the Before Columbus Foundation American Book Award in 1986. While living in New York, Moraga became intrigued with the idea of writing for the theatre. She began writing plays and earned a residency at INTAR (Hispanic-American Arts Center), directed by María Irene Fornes. Since then she has returned to the San Francisco area as a writing instructor at the University of California at Berkeley and continues her activities in feminism and the movement to expand and give voice to Chicano culture.

Major Works

This Bridge Called My Back, co-edited with Gloria Anzaldúa, is an anthology of writings by women of color that includes poetry, fiction, essays, letters, and other genres exploring sexual, ethnic, and class identity from a feminist viewpoint. Moraga contributed two poems ("For the Color of My Mother" and "The Welder") and one essay ("La Güera") to the collection. In 1983 Kitchen Table/Women of Color Press published *Cuentos: Stories by Latinas,* again edited by Moraga with Alma Gómez and Mariana Romo-Carmona which included two stories by Moraga. The anthology is the first published collection of fiction by Latina feminists, as well as the first to focus on Latina sexuality, particularly lesbianism, a taboo topic in Latino culture, and language, freely mixing Spanish and English. Also in 1983, Moraga published the first collection of her own poetry and essays, *Loving in the War Years: Lo que nunca paso por sus labios.* Again focusing on female sexuality, race, and class, although from a considerably more personal perspective, *Loving in the War Years* contains one of Moraga's most important concerns: reclaiming and revising the image of La Malinche, the figure from Spanish mythology who represents the threatening female betrayer and who, according to Moraga, contributes to the subordinate and passive position of women in Latino culture. In 1984 Moraga's first play, *Giving Up the Ghost,* was given its first staged reading by a Minneapolis feminist theatre group called At the Foot of the Mountain. A non-traditional drama consisting of poetic monologues in Spanish and English spoken by two women at different points in their lives, *Giving Up the Ghost* explores the oppressive forces that have damaged the women's perceptions of themselves. Moraga's next play, *Shadow of a Man* (1988), concerns a family's reaction to the father's self-destruction through alcoholism and the keeping of sexual secrets. *Heroes and Saints* (1989) is a surrealistic and political drama of a family of farm workers in the San Joaquin Valley suffering from pesticide poisoning. In *The Last Gen-*

eration (1993) Moraga returned to the themes of her earlier poetry and prose works, mainly the rapid disappearance of Mexican-American heritage due to the demands of assimilation, and the desire to create a "queer Aztlán," her own lesbian interpretation of the ultimate Chicano community. In *Waiting in the Wings: Portrait of a Queer Motherhood* (1998) Moraga recorded her experience of becoming a mother, including her baby's premature birth and her relationships with the father and her own partner.

Critical Reception

Moraga's work is considered groundbreaking in several ways. Because of the anthologies she has edited, she is credited with paving the way for Latina writers to create their own tradition of story-telling, and she is the first openly lesbian Latina to have published her work. Additionally, Moraga's trademark style of mixing Spanish with English in her writing serves to highlight both the tension and the harmony between the two cultures, and her dramatic writings are acknowledged as a successful continuation of the revolutionary Chicano *theatro* of the 1960s and 1970s.

PRINCIPAL WORKS

This Bridge Called My Back: Writings by Radical Women of Color [editor, with Gloria Anzaldúa, and contributor] (anthology) 1981

Cuentos: Stories by Latinas [editor, with Alma Gómez and Mariana Romo-Carmona] (anthology) 1983

Loving in the War Years: Lo que nunca paso por sus labios (poetry and essays) 1983

Giving Up the Ghost: Teatro in Two Acts (drama) 1984; published in 1986

Shadow of a Man (drama) 1988

Heroes and Saints (drama) 1989

The Last Generation (poetry and essays) 1993

Heroes and Saints and Other Plays (drama) 1994

Waiting in the Wings: Portrait of a Queer Motherhood (memoir) 1998

CRITICISM

Judith Ortiz Cofer (review date July 1984)

SOURCE: "Mujeres en Lucha," in *Women's Review of Books,* July 1984, p. 5.

[*In the following review, Cofer praises the stories in* Cuentos—*of which Moraga is an editor and contributor—and the poems and prose in* Loving in the War Years *for their focus on the Latina's search for identity and individuality.*]

"We are New York and Island Puerto Rican, Los Angeles Chicana, and Chilena. We are Latina writers and activists who identify as U.S. Third World women." So proclaim the editors of *Cuentos,* an eclectic collection of fiction by and about Latinas in the U.S. The stories cover such a wide spectrum of style, language and technical proficiency that the issues confronted in the individual stories become the best handle for a discussion of the collection. The editors are the first to admit that the framework of the book is thematic, the Latin-American woman writer being still in search of an identifiable voice in the literary world. As "heirs to a culture of silence" they have been excluded from the mainstream not only by their sex, but also by class, race and education. Latin American women writers in the U.S. must *develop* a literary tradition of their own because, even though there have been great Latin American women writers, "from Sor Juana Inez de la Cruz in the seventeenth century to Julia de Burgos in the twentieth century," their work cannot reflect the historical-political experiences of Latin American women in the U.S.A. The introduction to *Cuentos* points out:

> Unlike the Latin American writer in Latin America, the U.S. Latino writer is considered a "non-white" person and as such a "minority writer". Writing is so dependent upon education that most people of color, because they are poor, are deprived of access to recorded history or written artistic expression. This is further complicated for Latinos by the fact that we are largely born not speaking English.

Cuentos is the result of the struggle to create a context for the diversity of Latina writing. Within its pages women of backgrounds that range from the New York Puerto Rican to the Los Angeles Chicana to the South American in self-imposed exile find their individual voices and try to blend them into a clear, loud chorus of protest and disillusionment, as well as victory and joy. Their stories speak of labyrinthine boundaries and their ability to develop the strength to climb out of their personal, familial, professional prisons through self-definition. They take justifiable pride in being the first women in their families to dare break away: "Most of the writers in *Cuentos* are first generation writers. This means that your mother couldn't have written the story—or even helped you write it."

Though the women writers in this collection define themselves under the general labels of Latin American and feminist, their backgrounds, traditions, education, politics, and sexuality are as multitudinous and individual as their styles. Some of the stories are in standard American English, some in Spanish (ranging in dialect from the Puerto Rican to the South American) and others are in a combination of both (a practice linguists call code-switching). It is evident that the varied voices, styles and languages form an attempt at self-affirmation, and a joining together of a group of individuals within a framework of meaning and permanence.

In a working illustration of their philosophy of an all-embracing bi-culturalism the editors of **Cuentos** state:

> In este libro, we wish to stretch la imaginacion— help the reader become accustomed to seeing two languages in a book, learning to make sense of a thing by picking up snatches here, phrases there, listening and reading differently. **Cuentos** validates the use of "spanglish" and "tex-mex". Mixing English and Spanish in our writing and talking is a legitimate and creative response to acculturation.

Through all the differences of language and specific background details the writers represented in this anthology are bound by the fact that the hispanic tradition mandates passivity through cultural indoctrination starting at birth, and that to break her predetermined vows of silence, chastity and obedience is considered betrayal by the Latina of her race, her family and God. This is why the Latin American women writers consider themselves *mujeres en lucha*; women forever struggling against the forces that would silence them.

"Cuentos" are the stories heard from our mothers and grandmothers, the only way they had, on a stormy night, or a quiet afternoon setting in the patio over a cup of *café con leche*, to tell us of the domestic wars and victories, the private and silent acts of heroism, courage and self-denial conducted by the women; bits of wisdom, warnings, about men, babies and other women passed down from mother to daughter.

These "cuentos" served their purpose when one could rely on the permanence of family networks and their continuance. In the great diaspora of the twentieth century, recording our legacy in written form has become imperative.

Cuentos is divided into three sections, each prefaced by an editorial-philosophical statement. (This, perhaps, is a weakness in that it focuses the reader's expectations in one direction and thus somewhat limits the scope of the stories.) The stories in "Uno" are headed by a rather impassioned editorial statement:

> Feeling like we were born with too much inside of us and that we decide to express ourselves in any deeply felt way, they will think us crazy, sick, or senile. The characters in these stories are "possessed"—possessed in opposition to the forces that deny their humanity.

The first story, by Gloria Lieberman of Chile, is "La Confesion," a nightmare-like internal monologue of a woman who has been committed to an insane asylum for political reasons. There she is alternately ignored and tortured, silenced and forced to talk, and finally declared unfit. It is an extreme situation but one with which we all identify: the rage and grief of powerlessness. In "Dona Marciana Garcia" by Rocky Gomez we are made to feel the impact of a culture clash between two women of the same community: one, an old "curandera," and the other a young woman from Dona Marciana's own barrio, "who had recently graduated from nursing school and for the past year or so had been talking bad about Marciana's practice to the village women, trying to discredit her vast knowledge of herbal medicine, midwifery and occasional witchcraft." The fear of the new ways represented by Esperanza (Hope) is symbolic of the double threat that the Latin American woman faces as she emerges from her barrio and tries to join the mainstream of American life: she is distrusted by the white community for her color and language while also subject to suspicion by her own community. Old Dona Marciana concludes: "Esperanza entered the university an innocent and honest Mexican and emerged totally Americanized, casting away her old customs, traditions and beliefs, betraying not only herself but also everything la Raza held sacred."

These writers do not content themselves with denouncing the white, male-oriented society in which they conduct their varied lives; they also point out the injustices perpetrated by woman upon woman, as in the Spanish-language "Como el cristal al romperse," in which Sonia Vasquez describes the fragmented world of a Puerto Rican woman in an American hospital for the mentally ill. Her inability to express herself and her nurses' unwillingness to look beyond the surface of her needs becomes a scathing indictment of the annihilating effects of tokenism.

"Dos" presents stories about the battle for identity: the painful and continuing search for a framework of existence that will integrate their history as oppressed people, and provide them with viable alternatives to the inauthentic values imposed by societal expectations.

Many of the stories in "Dos" deal with the confusing stage between childhood's innocent acceptance and the painful discovery of being "different" in a world that rewards conformity and sameness. One of the most moving accounts of such an experience occurs in "Hunger's Scent" by the Afro-Puerto Rican, Cenen. The scene it describes is easily identified: a migrant camp site after a storm. Extreme poverty accompanied by natural disaster. The cosmic irony of "things could be worse"; but mainly it is about the humiliation of having your need exposed to the world like an open sore, and worse, having "them" pity you:

Tents had been leveled to the muddy ground and dragged off by the wind. Suddenly seeing their tent homes crumpled or spread out in puddles like untidy sheets, the kids screamed to the bus driver to stop at the entrance to the clearing they camped in. It was too late. None of us could take the pain caused by this white woman seeing our poverty. It hurt.

The loss of innocence and freedom is common to us all, whatever background we come from; for the Latin American woman, the end of childhood usually means the beginning of sex-linked alienation, of subjugation to male-oriented rules. The identity given to her is based on her willingness to comply: she must choose to be a *virgen* or a *puta*: virgin or whore. As the editors point out in "Tres": "The most severe restriction placed on the Latina is in relation to sexuality." Historical constraints inhibit the Latin American woman from freely expressing her sexuality: to be openly sexual is to be ostracized; to be different in your sexual preference, as in choosing lesbianism, may be interpreted as outright betrayal of family, nation and God.

The stories in "Tres" deal frankly with sexual choice and its consequences. They range from the poetical descriptions of Cherríe Moraga: "Then she let her mind wander and drawing the cool evening air into her mouth, holding it inside her, she imagined it like a pin of light, penetrating her rib cage, piercing her heart where the love would begin, enflaming her belly where the baby would grow," to the hilarious misadventure of Gloria, in Rocky Gomez' selection, who wants only one thing in life—to be a man. To attain this unlikely goal, Gloria sports a butch haircut and dark powder on the sides of her face to imitate a beard. She is even willing to marry a girl who claims Gloria has impregnated her.

All of the Latina's experience of love and rejection, birth, death and of coming home to find herself, are in this collection. There is anger at both sides of the two worlds they straddle, but there is also hope and reconciliation. The protagonist of Aurora Levins Morales' story says it best, returning to her hometown in Puerto Rico after self-imposed exile in San Francisco:

> When I came back, I expected to be foreign. To have to introduce myself, explain. I found I was familiar, expected to show up sometimes, as all the immigrant children of the barrio are expected. The barrio nodded its head to me, asked after my family, called me by my name.

Cuentos proves that the Latin American woman in the U.S. is learning to speak for herself, not just as camp-follower for the political campaigns of others, but for herself, in her own voice, about her own experiences and dreams.

Ever since Dona Marina, also known by her Indian name Malintzin or Malinche, joined forces with Cortes in the conquest of Mexico as his translator, advisor and mistress, any Mexicana/Chicana who sells out to the white race automatically joins her ranks of betrayers of La Raza. For centuries Malintzin has played the double role of Mother of the mestizo people and patroness to "Las Vendidas."

In her collage of poems, journal entries, essays, and short stories [*Loving in the War Years*] Cherríe Moraga makes a strong case for the defense of Malinche, the demeaned muse of the Chicana writer, whose reputation has suffered at the hands of sexist history. Through her exploration of the personal and political drama of her own life, Moraga promotes Malinche from violated female to spiritual mother. But the road to self-discovery and empowerment is long, narrow and slick with the tears of the women who have preceded her. Her mother: "How slow and hard change is to come. How although this book has taken me from Berkeley to San Francisco to Boston, Brooklyn, Mexico, and back again, sigo siendo la hija de mi mama. My mother's daughter." Her grandmother: "She shows me her leg which has been operated on. The wound is like a huge crater in her calf—crusted open, a gaping wound. I feel her pain so critically." And her women lovers: "My first poems were love poems. That's the source—el amor, el desco—that first brought me into politics."

Despite calling herself "the eternal well of pathos," Moraga does not wallow in self-pity. Boldly, she examines the meaning of being a Chicana and a lesbian in the United States today. This requires no little sacrifice. She admits that her public self-analysis, her writing, has alienated her from her family. *La familia*. The one constant in a Latina's life. Yet her work has also brought her new friends, new loves and a deeper understanding of the complexity of human relationships.

Loving in the War Years reflects the author's sense of her divided self:

> Some days I feel my writing wants to break itself open. Speak in a language that maybe no "readership" can follow. What does it mean that the Chicana writer, if she truly follows her own voice, may depict a world so specific, so privately ours, so full of "foreign" language to the anglo reader, there will be no publisher. The people who can understand it, don't/won't/can't read it. How can I be a writer in this? I have been translating my experience out of fear of an aloneness too great to bear. I have learned analysis as a mode to com-

municate what I feel the experience already speaks for. The combining of poetry and essays in this book is the compromise I make in the effort to be understood. In Spanish, "Compromiso" is also used to mean obligation or commitment. And I guess, in fact, I write as I do because *I am committed* to communicating with both sides of myself.

The divided self communicating with both sides of itself may be the elusive answer to the question of self-identity that confronts the Latina in the U.S. today.

Moraga recounts the anguish of being the one who breaks away from tradition, the link that outweighs the chain—the procession of suffering women: "Dolores my grandmother, Dolores her daughter, Dolores her daughter's daughter." It is in her poetry that Moraga allows herself to speak the words that set her free. But it is sometimes as if she were the vulnerable animal caught in the steel trap of her own loyalty, as if she were having to chew away at her own flesh in order to set herself free.

> there is a very old wound in me
> between my legs
> where I have bled, not to birth
> pueblos or revolutionary
> concepts or simple
> sucking children
>
> > but a memory
> > of some ancient
> > betrayal.

The "ancient betrayal" is of course the haunting echo of Malinche coming down through the centuries, her restless spirit longing to be expiated by the blood of her heirs. Through Moraga's words, she defends her right to choose. "I did not move away from other Chicanos because I did not love my people. I gradually became anglicized because I thought it was the only option available to me toward gaining autonomy as a person without being sexually stigmatized."

The prose and poems construct a visual panorama of a life in which history and fiction are integrated. It is a personal integration that she seeks through her work. The process of self-analysis and self-revelation is a painful one, but Moraga does not shirk from what she has determined to be her mission, to complete the empowerment of the Chicana woman by having her realize that sexual repression is also political repression. "The extent to which our sexuality and identity as Chicanas have been distorted both within our culture and by the dominant culture is the measure of how great a source of our potential power it holds." To cast off the persistent demands of her culture, her "familia," the Chicana must be willing to take control of her own sexual destiny. The result of her defiance will be the "shunning" by her own people as a traitor to her race, Moraga argues: "even if the defiant woman is *not* a lesbian, she is purported to be one: for, like the lesbian in the Chicano imagination, she is una *Malinchista*. Like the Malinche of Mexican history, she is corrupted by foreign influences which threaten her people."

The Chicana political consciousness is so deeply involved with the "Movimiento," so used is the Chicana to fighting alongside her men for equality, that what Moraga is suggesting involves a complicated break with the chain of historical events that have formed the prescribed norms of her culture: that she will be a good, loyal daughter, then a good, loyal wife. Her bonds to her women friends, her "companeras," were to be strictly secondary, Moraga suggests that the time has come to recognize "what being a Chicana feminist means—making bold and political the love of the women of our race."

With *Loving in the War Years* she has established a line of communication; without hiding her vulnerability she has claimed the right of every Chicana to love herself and other women because "no one else can or will speak for us. We must be the ones to define the parameters of what it means to be female and mestiza."

Cherríe Moraga with Luz María Umpierre (interview date Summer 1986)

SOURCE: "Luz María Umpierre with Cherríe Moraga," in *The Americas Review,* Vol. XIV, No. 2, Summer 1986, pp. 54-67.

[*In the following interview, Moraga discusses her writing and her position as a Latina writer in the United States.*]

I interviewed Cherríe Moraga during the summer of 1985 at her home in Brooklyn. By then her book *Loving in the War Years* had been published and I was particularly interested in the essays included in the collection. I was also interested in having Cherríe Moraga herself do a self-portrait of her life as a Chicana and a Lesbian.

[*Umpierre:*] *Artists should be allowed to do self-portraits of themselves; so, in that spirit, who is Cherríe Moraga?*

[Moraga:] First of all, I am originally from Los Angeles and I am Chicana. All of my family are Chicanos. My father is Anglo, so I basically grew up in the cultural experience of Chicanos because *toda la familia era chicana*, but with the presence of my father throughout. I was born in 1952; I am going to be 33. I am living in New York City, where I am trying to make a living as a writer. I have lived in New York for four or four and a half years. But before that I was in California. I spent about four years living in the San Francisco Bay area. I have been seriously writing for about ten years. I wrote somewhat in college, but primarily my experience in college, in terms of writing, was terrible. I mean, they did plenty to convince me that I could not write.

Do you come from a large or a small family? What kind of environment did you grow up in?

Well, in my immediate family, I have a brother and a sister, so my immediate family was five people, but my grandmother, who just died last year, left maybe like ninety something people from her, and the majority of them live in the Los Angeles area, and many of them live in the same town. My family was basically a family of cousins and aunts and uncles, and people *que siempre está ahí en la casa.* And also, sometimes we had people taking care of my grandmother, you know, like mejicanas, who were also living with us, who took care of my grandmother. My grandmother lived next door for many, many years, and for a short time lived with the family. So it was like a huge family.

So it was like an extended family.

Yes, definitely, that's how you would describe it, like an extended family. Everybody in everybody's business.

Where did you go to college?

I went to college in a private school in Hollywood. Real small, it used to be like a Catholic college, and then when I went there it looked like it was very progressive. It was in the late sixties, so I went there because it was very liberal, you know, policies, etc., and I began to take some writing there, and I wrote some terrible short stories.

Why were they terrible?

Well, actually, one of the reasons why they were so terrible is because I felt very much that I was writing with secrets. I saved them to remind me of who I am and where I came from. I remember one story in particular which was about this woman who was losing her mind, and there was this homosexual seduction scene in it, and the woman, you know, the protagonist, freaks out, and it was the most homophobic thing you would ever want to read in your life. It was actually when I came out as a lesbian, which was also ten years ago, that I really felt my writing took a real major shift because it was like something had been lifted in me. If I could reveal that secret to myself, then there was very little else that was going to be more scary than that, because that was

very traumatic. That made a major change in my writing and I primarily began writing as a poet.

What books have you published up to now or what books do you consider your major works?

In 1981 I published *This Bridge Called My Back: Writings by Radical Women of Color,* which is a collection of writings by women of color here in the United States, so it has contributions by Native American women, Latinas here, African-American and Asian women. I started working on that in 1979 with Gloria Anzaldúa, who is a Chicana writer, and that work is primarily a collection of essays. Many of us have been working, doing a lot of work very isolated, sort of the token women of color in a predominantly white women's movement. So that book was an effort to really bring together the voices of women of color in the same position as me and Gloria, but all across the nation, and to some extent to begin to define a kind of feminist politics that included our own race and identities as well. That was published through The Feminist Press and soon after that I got involved with Kitchen Table, Women of Color Press. We began to work on trying to build a press for women of color. In 1983 one of our first projects was to put together a collection of writings by Latinas in the U.S. Basically the Press' dedication has always been to try to publish the works that would not be published elsewhere or would not traditionally have visibility and one of the things that struck me was that, particularly for Latinas here in the U.S., there is a huge amount of censorship and very little space left in which to put our work because we either write in Spanish and they want it in English or we write in English and they want it in Spanish or we write in both and nobody wants it. And we did a book too that came from a perspective that really took very seriously the conditions of Latinas, and which wanted to create an interest in fiction in this case. So that book is called *Cuentos/Short Stories* by Latinas and that was published in 1983. I edited that with Alma Gómez, who is Puerto Rican, and Mariana Romo Carmona, who is *chilena.*

In that same year I also published my last book which is called *Loving in the War Years* (*Lo que nunca pasó por sus labios*). That book is basically one that I had been working on for over seven years. I mean, the work covers that span of time, but the very last work in that book was an essay called **"A long line of vendidas."** I had originally considered the book as all being poetry because that was my major form, but there seemed to be certain things that needed to be expressed, that necessitated the form of essay, so that's like fifty pages in the book. That's a lot! What happened after doing *Bridge* which, as I explained, was a lot of different voices of women of color here, I found that that opened me up very much to wanting to be even more specific about my identity. It was not enough to say that I was a Third World Woman or a woman of color, that my particular experience as a Latina and even more as a Chicana was very different from that of an Asian woman or a Black woman; so that, from the first secret being revealed, it was necessary to go on. And *Loving in the War Years* is very much to me about being specifically Chicana and a lesbian together. That book freed me up a lot. It is very much an autobiography, but with different forms. It was the kind of book that allowed me to finally put on paper some things that needed to be down, and opened me up to being able to write things that were less specifically centered on my actual biographical experience and more about identifying with the lives of others. From then I basically started working in the theater. This form has allowed me to give voice to a lot. There have been numerous plays about Chicanos, but none particularly about Chicanas, and giving voice to all these women that I know from that very extended family gives me a greater enjoyment in writing; more than I have ever had in my life.

What in particular are you writing now? You were talking to me about the theater, do you have something already written down?

Since *Loving in the War Years* came out, I have three theater pieces by now, none of them are finished. They are in various stages of work. The first one I began is called *Giving up the Ghost.* This may end up being fiction. There are so many monologues that it's just like an oral history but with fictional characters. It's very much about the life of a character named Gorki, a girl growing up in East Los Angeles. I didn't grow up in the *barrio.* Everybody thinks I did. Being a Chicana, you had to grow up in East Los Angeles or in *el barrio.* But that was very much the world that I observed, that I was close to, and the kids I grew up with and things like that. About this little girl, Gorki, I think the whole point of this particular work is that I really need to get into the forces that form any young Chicana, in terms of sexuality and identity, and how much sexuality is so fundamental in us, seeing ourselves both as women of color and as Third World people. This girl's story starts at puberty, that's when a lot of trouble starts for us; it focuses on that and goes all the way up into her adulthood and, at this point, all happens through monologues. So that's one thing, and this tentatively may be published in the spring by Western Press, who are now in Los Angeles.

The other work is called *The Shadow of a Man,* which is not the title that it's going to eventually have. This play is about a Chicano family and very much about the mother of that family, and I *love* this. It's only in its first draft form but it's really a play. And I think at the heart of it, it's really very much about how women protect men, that the women and the daughters really have the pulse on the family, and how the men are protected and mothered by the mother, and even by the daughters and that the relationships are really much more, from what I see, in the family among Chicanos. That there can be great love between husband and wife, but the real relationships are between mother and son, and mother and daughter and father and son. There is a way in which husband and wife are often very strange to each other. I am very excited about that work because I think that there is enough outside of me that is really a pleasure to go into.

And on the last piece, I actually finished the first draft yesterday, it's called *La extranjera.* This is a musical, which I have never done in my life, so it's a lot about playing. It's about a relationship between a man and a woman that are married, Chicanos. The woman actually transports refugees, and deals with issues of bi-culturalism. The husband being more assimilated, and the woman being more attached to Mexico and a political refugee, a Salvadorian woman, an old lady, who arrives and moves into their home and what happens to them.

From what you are saying, what I see then is a progression.

Oh, the critic on the spot!

No, I'm just trying to pull the strings together. You are trying to deal with themes that are very much inside of you because you have lived through them and in this last description of this play, in particular, what I see is still very much the issue of the family, its importance and the divisions in the family, which of course, you experienced as a child being torn between two different parents as well as two different cultures. Is that correct?

Yes, that's correct. You know, I can't make a living just writing. I always feel that writing is so isolating that I need to be doing also work that involves me with various communities of people. In the last couple of years I have been doing work around violence against women of color, specifically rape and incest, and I never in my life thought that I would ever be involved with those issues. But there is always a connection, and somehow, organically, your writing gets involved in this kind of stuff too. Although my particular focus is the theme of the Chicano family, the Latino family, what happens in families, *punto,* is the heart of everything. The family is this private place, so anything is allowed to happen there, any kind of power exchanges, any kind of control; it's like the place you first learn to suffer. To me, since it's the heart of everything, it's like its own little drama, and for theater this is wonderful, because the dynamics of the family are endless. I think too, as a writer, you are very focused on your private voice, the voice inside you, so I have always gone back to where does that voice get formed? When did I first hear this little voice that separates me from all these crazy things happening around me? And that's the voice you end up writing from, and, if you don't go back to the source, you are going to be a bad writer.

Since we are talking about voice and speaking, we can certainly step to something that I want to bring out, which is the subtitle of your book **Loving in the War Years,** *which to me is more important than the title,* Lo que nunca pasó por sus labios. *How did you come up with that subtitle?*

The first title was the original title of the book, and that was very much when the majority of the poems dealt a lot with being a lesbian, so literally it was about your love being in battles, that nobody is letting you do this. So you got to love in opposition. But towards the latter half of the book, both the poems and the essays were dealing much more with family issues, since that's the first place where you learn to suffer and also the first place where you learn to love. So how can you talk about whether you are heterosexual or gay or whatever, about loving, unless you talk about your home? My reason for writing that book was the overpowering sense that what I was writing was valuable, and specially in the last few years, to see that I had never read what I was writing about in any place. So that I was writing about things that I perceived in my family or violence that I experienced against me or people I loved. I knew the whole thing was completely taboo, and I experienced that when I was writing it because everything I began to write I never thought I would publish. And I had to tell myself that I wasn't going to publish it so I could write it. And afterwards, I would put it away, thinking that it was possible, that maybe it could be published. If I didn't read it to myself after being written, then I thought that it wasn't appropriate to be *read* by others.

Or it wasn't appropriate to be said.

Or it hasn't *been* said. That's what I'm saying, if it hasn't been said, it's not supposed to exist, so you're making it up anyway. So *lo que nunca pasó por sus labios* is like trying to make it *be* said, to come out of your mouth because it has never been said, that was the major thrust of the line; that's how I felt.

So if I were to tell you that writing to you is a vicarious experience, that it comes from the experiences that you have lived in the past, and that that's what your writing is about, would that be correct?

Well, I'm only 33 years old, what I'm seeing happening now is that I feel that there are certain chronological limitations. I'll be writing something when I'm 60, that I could never conceive of now, so in some level I don't feel that is just because it happened to me. I felt that that's what **Loving in the War Years** was, but that's not what my writing is now,

because what I'm finding is that I believe in racial memory. Like for instance, when I go to Mexico, there are certain things that come up for me that I think I'm not supposed to feel because I was born in L.A.; I am Chicana. Why do I feel like I know how to act in Mexico? And it comes from someplace else.

Like a collective memory.

Exactly, so I believe in that and I believe that what I need to do as a writer is to continue opening my heart bigger and bigger, and bigger, so that my capacity to identify increases; so everything is possible to be written. That makes you a better writer because you then know that on some level you should be able to empathize with your enemies in order to write that conflict as the conflicts experienced in life. You don't have to like them or even agree with them, but if you are going to show what really happened, then you need to do that. I feel that for me it has been expanding and expanding what I'm capable of experiencing in my writing.

Do you consider yourself part of a tradition, a literary tradition or a non-literary tradition?

That's a very hard question to answer. Norma Alarcón asked me that question before, but she was asking more in terms of literary tradition. I think in this country, in the U.S., the tradition with which I feel most affinity—it's funny, because it really doesn't exist now—is the tradition of writers from the 30's who were largely from the working class, and they wrote out of the Depression. That's the only time in this country in which Blacks and Chicanos had a cultural movement of writing. But the thing that was very particular about this group was that it occurred at a time when lots and lots of people were nationally mobilized and that there was this literature that was coming out of it that was really not necessarily from educated people. It came out a lot from telling stories. But it was done with the consciousness that the way things were was not the way things should be. They were outside writers. I think it's really weird to be a U.S. writer. I can't identify with a U.S. writer, because that picture doesn't describe me.

When you go to Mexico and they ask about North American writers, they are thinking of white people. They are not thinking of Chicanos, they are not thinking of Black people, so on some level I can't identify with that tradition at all, neither in content or form. And I am not a Latin American writer, the main reason being that I write predominantly in English, but also because it's not my world. And yet, I can see elements in my writing, particularly in my last production of **La extranjera,** which are Latin American. There was a certain sensibility in it that had a lot to do with indigenous influences and also a kind of emotional sensibility that is *puro latino.* So in some level, that's part of the tradition I grew up from, and I think it's also somewhat like different levels of reality; there being an internal reality, and an external reality. So I see that as being very latino, very Latin American, and I have it.

There was this woman that looked like a real theater person, this white woman, that saw this production of **Giving up the Ghost,** and she came after me and said to me, "Have you ever read," its name slipped out of my mind, but it was a play by García Lorca. And I said no, and I had only read then *Bodas de sangre*; that was a couple of years ago, and since she told me, I started reading more of Lorca's. To a large degree as a writer, I am not that well read, do you know what I mean? She found it very hard to believe that I had not read Lorca because then she said: "This is the first time that it really occurs to me that it's true, that there is a cultural sensibility, it's not just that you copied it, but that in fact it's in your blood, that you experienced it." I think too that saying that I'm not well read, also makes me not know if I come from a literary tradition. I am very literate in English and I am not as literate in Spanish, and I refuse to read translations any more, so for me, like right now I'm reading Rosario Castellanos; for me to read a novel in Spanish, is like being in the fourth grade. It's very hard to see that your mind is already in one place of development and the language barrier slows you down. It occurs to me that I have things in common with some Latin American writers. Like the first time I read *Pedro Páramo* [Juan Rulfo], it blew my mind because there was a sort of *sabor* that was in it that was very familiar to me, that in fact even reading that novel, I felt like it kind of went into some place inside me that won't come up.

So you are talking about having read Rosario Castellanos, Pedro Páramo; so you are not as illiterate in Spanish as you are trying to convince me.

No, but what I'm telling you is that this is a very late development, and it is hard to explain, because I feel too like, for a lot of it, I had to study. You know, I went to school, and I graduated from college, but that's not the issue. But it is a fact that when I went to high school, I never read a book. I like to read, but I could never read a book from front to cover. I wasn't a reader, which a lot of writers are. I was like a doer. Our family was the first generation to go to college. So I am sitting in the classroom and all these kids have read everything; it seemed to me that they had read everything and I had read nothing. In my first year of college I read 30 books. I just sat down, like work, and read them. I don't even know what I got, but it was just that kind of thing, and there has always been that sense of catching up.

I already told you my reasons for not writing well in college. But it also had to do with not really being seen as the type of person to be a writer, because I was a woman, Chicana, and you know, I wasn't their type. The people who were writers were the white males, and some of the white women, and then when I got involved in Feminism, the same thing happened. I went into these women writers' workshops, and I started writing in the voice of the people that I knew, and I was told that I needed to read because I didn't have a big enough vocabulary. This totally beat my spirit. It was very ironic. And also I had written a love poem to a woman and in the middle of the poem I said "she" and the women at the workshop told me that wasn't right, because you are a woman writer, and the readers think that you are writing to a man and so you can't do that. You have to prepare your reader and not use "she" in the middle of the poem. So in both of those counts, what I remember was: one, that I didn't have enough words, which was the class thing; and two, that I couldn't write a poem to a woman. So I packed my bags and I moved to San Francisco, to the Bay area, and started collecting unemployment. And I decided that I was going to give it a year, and I was going to read my ass off. I was just going to read and read and I was going to write.

What did you read?

I read all white literature.

From what you read, what things did you like?

I read a lot of lesbian literature, because I had never read any lesbian literature, so I did a lot of investigation on that—because that was going to take care of both things, you could be a lesbian and a writer—and also I was reading. I also read a lot of Adrienne Rich, and I wrote. That was the year in which, at the end of it, I came up with that poem that is in **Loving in the War Years, "For the Color of My Mother."** I basically decided that I would give it a year and make these readings and, if by the end of the year I was shit, I would never write again, which I think has a lot to do with class stuff. Because I basically felt that if I was no good, I was not going to spend my life doing this. You have to make a living; you have to have a life, and if you are not going to make it, you can't be bullshitting around. So everything kind of rode on that. I did these readings and it was great. There were at least two poems in all the things that I wrote that I knew were good poems. And they ended up being things like **"For the Color of My Mother"** that had everything to do with the seeds of other things that I'll be writing later. So what I am finding is again the same kind of problem: that as a Latina writer, I am being exposed to people who are Latinos, but for one thing, very well educated in the language that I basically know on a familiar level.

It seems that you have a great deal of anguish over the problem of language, and I want you to talk about that.

Well, that's what I was going to say, that when that woman told me that I didn't have enough words, the irony of it all was that I was right from the jump, but I didn't know it. You have to go through your journeys to find that out. What gets me is that I feel that there are a lot of potentially good writers along the way who are burnt so bad, they don't get it out. What I am finding, particularly doing theater, is that my ability to remember *verbatim* how people talk, to remember the poetry in using Spanglish, to really know those voices is not a question of having more words. It was a question of deepening into the words that exist. So in the theater it comes out because I have a lot of characters doing one line in English and one in Spanish and there is really a lot of switching back and forth. In the theater that I have been involved with, nobody else does it; it's all a Latin American group of people that I'm working with and basically everybody, for the purposes of the theater, needs to write predominantly in English and so everybody writes completely in English with a few exceptions.

When I first started coming out with this English and Spanish, people started saying, "Wait a minute, what is this?" and it kind of became an issue, not a controversy, but it brought up a lot of discussion among us. I felt very defensive about it because I could not have, for example, this character, Hortensia, talking completely in English. It would not have worked. In this last play I did that more and I think it was less effective. It takes all this conviction to believe that the emotional comprehension will be there, even if somebody misses a line because they don't understand English, or they miss a line because they don't understand Spanish. So in terms of the issue about language being important is that to me that's the only way of refining, of having a fine tune, to what is close and what I know. It's like even in the essays that I write, like knowing *that* is all right to put in a journal entry. If that journal entry had the heart of whatever it is that you needed to say. I am not anti-intellectual, I've never been anti-intellectual, but it's that that kind of language is not necessarily the only language to use to talk about an idea.

That's very important because I think that the problem that some people are having in dealing with your work and the works of other women writers, especially of Hispanic origin in this country, is that you don't fit boundaries of genres. That you cannot be pinpointed and they cannot say this is totally a poem, because a poem of yours may be an essay, and an essay may turn into poetry. Therefore genre boundaries are broken here. I think that's an important issue that has to be dealt with.

Yes, but then you think, who invented the genres anyway? and what really gets me is that it would be different if I had a choice, but I don't have a choice. Anytime I have attempted to write at those other ways, I am a lousy writer.

That's the way it comes out. Just because I'm mixing genres, it doesn't mean that it's not right. It's a different criteria about what should be omitted in the editing process, and since I've worked so much as an editor too, particularly for women of color, I have a different set of criteria. What is important for me is how to get the best part of the voice alive and keep it alive.

That's an important point that you are bringing out, the question of who determines what is artistic and what isn't. That is at the core of this issue of genre that we were talking about. In regard to the essays in **Loving in the War Years** *that you have mentioned before as having been more difficult to write than the poetry—even though, in my opinion, the essays in that collection are a cornerstone and the closest we have been to having a political voice in writing as Hispanic lesbians in the U.S.—why were they difficult to write?*

Well, I think some of it is actually a very practical problem, because I feel that when you are working in creative writing, like poetry or theater, there is an organic kind of organization of materials that happens. But when you are also trying to combine ideas and particularly when you are not just keeping with ideas, but you are also involved with poetic combining, like the journals, I have a real hard time. I think that has something to do with training. I know that somehow not having the training has helped me because then I value kinds of writings that may have gotten x'd out. But not having the training also hurts me in the sense that I always feel that I have more to say than I'm ready to deal with. What happens is that in that particular essay, which is only 50 pages, when you think about all the ideas that are in there, it could have been much longer, and emotionally what it took me to do that was so immense that I had to say: I am not willing to. The way I look at it now is that I think that in many ways it's like an outline. An outline which the only way in which it is going to be developed is through the other writings that I am doing.

One of the things that really hit me, that came to me as a revelation when I was writing **"A long line of vendidas"** was that I understand oppression; I understand what homophobia is. I know the kinds of oppressions people go through, I have gone through as a lesbian, but the answers to what it means to me to be a Latina lesbian, I would not find out unless I understand the sexuality of heterosexual women as well as lesbians who are Latinas. We came from the same family. It does not serve me to be isolated from them, either theoretically or politically. They would not want me as a sister, but the fact of the matter is that I am their clue. Lesbians are their clue to who they are as heterosexual women, or as simply sexual women who have put their attachments to men, and I put mine to women, but we are like the same breed, whether we want to see or not. That to me was a great revelation. One which can be analyzed or explained on paper, but doesn't move me to the degree that having Hortensia living it in the play does. I change through that, I am relieved, I can go on. I needed to write that essay out of a political necessity, but it did not bring me the joy or the relief of finally having Hortensia in the play.

The man in Latino culture comes and goes; he puts his thing inside, but that doesn't make him a father. And the mother, her sexuality and independence are so apparent. Even though they think we are submissive, we are incredibly independent. Inside our private lives, we were never voiced. It's like Hortensia is not someone who is going to, by any stretch of the imagination, consider herself a Feminist. She lies constantly, gives the man his little things, puts him up. She lives her life, but she is not full. And to write her talking, I love it, I am completely relieved, I feel very vindicated on some level. It's like saying yes, these women exist, I wasn't nuts. But to analyze that is different. I could not have given Hortensia voice until some of those things were put on paper in the form of an essay. And there are times always for that form to come up again, it will come up again, but it's not a form that I feel comfortable with, that I enjoy. It's very drenching.

Well, it may be drenching, but it's incredibly important. When you write, do you think of an ideal audience? Do you think of someone that you want to communicate with, some particular audience, some particular reader, or is it more a writer trying to simply get things out of her system?

I think it depends on what I am writing. I think primarily the basis of it is my relationship to myself. If it works for me, if it moves me, or it reflects back something that seems true, I mean, I discover my writing, I don't plan it. If I discover it, then I know it's true. So I am the audience. The other thing is that depending on the form, like for instance with **"A long line of vendidas,"** there were definitely times when I had a certain audience in mind, and you can almost see it from section to section. There was one point, when I talked about *la Malinche* that I am definitely talking to a Chicano audience, heterosexual male. I'm still keeping my own voice, but clearly they are the people that I am trying to explain it to. There is another section where I feel that the audience is white Feminists.

Speaking of Feminists, what kind of feminism do you purport?

That is also hard to answer because I think I have been very discouraged by the Feminist Movement, so, you get me on one of my bad days and I'll say "those feminists." I remember what Feminism meant to me when it occurred to me that there was an analysis on sexual oppression. I would never

say I was not a Feminist. I thought feminism made visible a lot of very invisible kinds of oppressions that happened indoors. The kind of feminism that I believe in, I guess, is one that is almost so integrated into other struggles that it almost threatens to become invisible again, but it can't. What I mean by that is that just me, as a person, for instance, if I'm working in a Latino situation that's dominated by men, it's like you are bringing in the missing element, your consciousness as a Feminist. If I'm working with white women, it's like feminism isn't the issue to me there. I'm bringing other elements like racism, etc.

The thing that I value about feminism is that it is hooked up with the personal life and most of the movements have never done that, so I feel that I have to hold fast to that, and I don't care where I go, nobody is going to tell me that what happens in our personal private lives is not a political issue. I think feminism on some level has beat that to death and it has made a lot of excuses around that, made trivial lies of very powerful notions. I am concerned about, in any given situation, who has the power and who doesn't, and to examine that with a political analysis and how does that affect us personally. My enemy might look just like me, if for some reason or another, he or she has the power. Feminism is the only movement that has allowed the so called "invisible oppression" to become visible. The analysis and the practical implications of that have to be integrated into all struggles: imperialism, etc.

Do you have much contact with other Latina writers?

Mostly friendship networks, more than anything else. It depends on the projects, when I was writing **Cuentos,** I had a lot of involvement with other Latina writers.

What I am trying to get at is do you consider yourself a part of a group of writers or a generation of writers?

No, not yet. I feel very isolated as a Latina and a writer. I feel that it really is about writing in resistance, trying to go into places, like for instance, working in the theater, which is a Latin American theater, and to go in there to learn skills that other people might have, but to try to keep my own voice and my own vision. I feel that I am a part of a movement of women of color writers. I feel that I have gotten a lot of inspiration from Black women writers in this country. I think that in English they are really writing the hottest thing around, and I admire their kind of bravery for the issues that they bring up. I get a lot of courage from their work, but we are culturally *very* different, so it's not like I can turn to them, particularly the more Spanish I use, and say "Can you give me support for this?" I am in a writing group that has two working class white women, two black women and myself, and they are wonderful people and they support my work very much, but there is definitely this place where I am not going to get the feedback and the push I need, and the only place I get that is from friends. But even the Latina writers I know who are writing are suffering under the same thing, so we even have this sort of self imposed isolation as well. You feel so bad about what you are doing, or it's so hard for you to feel that you have a right to write it that you would not even be telling your friend that you need her to read it.

There is another question which is something that I normally ask, at least to the writers that I talk to, either formally or informally, because sometimes I feel that I live a double life in which, on the one hand, I have to speak like a critic because, if not, I will not be able to live in an academic world and gain food for my own subsistence; but, on the other hand, I have my heart where it really is, which is in writing, so sometimes I think that that's one of the things some critics lose track of, that we should be asking writers to tell us what can we do in order to let them be more visible, what are we doing that is wrong. This is something that I feel, that, as a Feminist critic, it is important for us to get feedback from the writers.

Well, I thought a lot about reviews and criticism ever since *Loving in the War Years* came out, because the book has gotten very little visibility, which has made me then kind of aware of what the problem is with criticism. I feel that mine is not a book that can easily be played back, and that it also involves some kind of involvement from the critic to deal with the issues that the book brings up. I feel for the most part that's not what most critics are willing to do. When I read a review, I look to the critic to give me kind of like a sign pulse, also to be sometimes like this bridge between me as a writer and the audience because criticism has worked that way for me. If I like a work, then I go and I read a review about it. It sometimes helps me understand it and gives the book more depth, so I feel that in the scholarly sense, in the sense of studying, in the sense of the criticism, it really is taking the book to heart and then being able to say to some people, "Look at this," and "You see this?" Like for instance, Mirta Quintanales has done a study in which she was saying how many times I mentioned the word "mouth" in *Loving in the War Years*. She has made this connection with what that meant, and I am so excited, because I am not consciously putting in "mouth" every so often. But it also teaches me about what it was I was after. And when that is played back to me, it makes me realize that my expression has some kind of organic cohesiveness, and that's very exciting and also very helpful. What it does to me is that it gives me a lot of confidence, that if I stay close to the bone of my work, that it will have an organic whole, that it will make sense, my conscious makes sense, and that's all that really matters.

So it's that, and also, I'll like to see, and occasionally it has

happened, somebody saying what's missing, and not just "The writer should have done this," but "This is where we need to go from here," "This is what is missing here," and "Why is this missing?" "Is the writer chickening out?" Writing is such an isolated thing, and I have always had this fantasy of writing in a community, and that seldom happens, but the critic can be a part of that. So it's not incumbent upon me to answer everything, but the critic's role is to say "This is not an answer."

Raymund A. Paredes (review date 1987)

SOURCE: Review of *Giving Up the Ghost*, in *Rocky Mountain Review of Language and Literature*, Vol. 41, No. 1-2, 1987, p. 127.

[*In the following review, Paredes notes that* Giving Up the Ghost *"represents the most radical element of contemporary Chicana writing" because of Moraga's portrayal of sexual relationships and Roman Catholic culture in the Mexican-American community.*]

A self-described "Chicana lesbian," [Cherríe] Moraga earlier published *Loving in the War Years,* a collection of stories, poems, and essays notable for their passion and intelligence. In her latest work, a two-act play entitled *Giving Up the Ghost,* Moraga develops explicitly Chicano contexts and characters: the play is set in the East Los Angeles *barrio* and her characters speak authentically in the English-Spanish patois associated with the *pachuco* culture of urban teenagers. The two main characters, Marisa and Amalia, come to accept the superiority of homosexual love after Marisa endures a brutal rape as a schoolgirl in a Catholic school and Amalia experiences the death of her male lover. At several points in the play, Marisa appears as her "younger self," the *pachuca* Corky who recognizes, after her rape, that her pretended toughness not only cannot protect her against predatory men but violates her instinctive tenderness. Only in their lesbian relationship can Marisa and Amalia realize their full potentialities as loving human beings.

Giving Up the Ghost represents the most radical element of contemporary Chicana writing. Moraga portrays heterosexual love as inherently abusive, an act of violent penetration which in the context of the excessively masculine culture of Mexican Americans becomes more brutal still. Her location of Marisa's rape in a Catholic school suggests her distrust of the Church's traditional patriarchy and its promise of protection to innocent and virtuous women. What is perhaps most remarkable about Moraga is her unwillingness to abandon Mexican American culture as hopelessly misogynistic; she clings to her ethnic identity fiercely, demanding in her work that the culture transform itself in behalf of women's rights of self-determination.

Nancy Saporta Sternbach (essay date 1989)

SOURCE: "'A Deep Racial Memory of Love': The Chicana Feminism of Cherríe Moraga," in *Breaking Boundaries: Latina Writing and Critical Readings,* edited by Asunción Horno-Delgado, Eliana Ortega, Nina M. Scott, and Nancy Saporta Sternbach, 1989, pp. 48-61.

[*In the following essay, Sternbach examines Moraga's attempts to return to the pre-Malinche Latino notion of womanhood in her feminism.*]

One of the most pressing and current feminist debates in the U.S. is the long-standing complaint that U.S. Third World women have lodged in regard to the continued racism within Anglo-American feminist circles; the accusations tend to focus on the latter's failure to acknowledge, take into account, or address the issues of women of color. Even the most well-intentioned feminists find themselves being asked about, and thus responding to, the questionability of women's liberation when an entire population is oppressed. During the seventies, a new genre of Chicana poetry emerged that began to address some of those issues; in them, the Chicana speaker rails against the Anglo-American women's liberationist for her condescension, her lack of sensitivity, and her choosing of the agenda for all women. Such is the context for Marcela Lucero's poem, "No More Cookies, Please":

> WASP liberationist
> you invited me
> token minority
> but your abortion idealogy
> failed to integrate me.
> Over cookies and tea
> you sidled up to me and said
> 'Sisterhood is powerful.'[1]

Certainly Chicanas were not alone in their evaluation of the Anglo-American feminist movement. In Black activist and academic circles, to mention only a few, open debates with some of the most widely respected feminist theorists in the Anglo-American world took place; again, the accusations focused on white women having co-opted, generalized, condescended to, or ignored the perspective of women of color. These debates were public, as we can appreciate from Audre Lorde's "Open Letter to Mary Daly" and Barbara Smith's "Towards a black feminist criticism,"[2] and served as a springboard to openly raising the questioning that remains controversial today. Because of these and many other initiatives,

some Anglo-American feminists began to appreciate that their presumptuousness about the "liberation" of "minority women" was actually preventing any meaningful dialogue from taking place between white and Third World women. Likewise we learned that our own problematized definition of liberation was not a model to be imposed on others. Nothing could be clearer than Chicana poet Bernice Zamora's recent affirmation: "I'm not a feminist because I wish not to imitate the North American white woman."[3]

Those of us who are bilingual (and many of us who are not) have noticed one of the few Spanish words that fully and completely integrates itself into everyday English is "machismo." More dramatically, we have begun to hear a feminine form, *macha*, a tough, patriarchally-defined woman who is not necessarily of Latina heritage. We are familiar, too, with the complaints of Anglo-American women traveling in Latin American countries, about what they have called "the rampant machismo," and their testimonies that read like diatribes against a culture they claim to love. They wonder aloud how their Latin American counterparts can tolerate it. Likewise, we hear the defenses of these cultures; machismo is just as prevalent in the U.S., but with greater degrees of subtleties; a far higher percentage of women are doctors and lawyers in Latin America than in the U.S., a fact that has been true for most of the century and is not simply the result of the liberation movements of the seventies. There is a respect for the older woman in the Latin American culture that the U.S. would do well to learn and practice as well.[4]

A further complication of the question was incorporated into a Chicana's response to the machismo from which she personally suffered. Such has been the case in poems like "Machismo Is Part of Our Culture":

> Hey Chicano bossman
> don't tell me that machismo is part of our culture
>   if you sleep
> and marry W.A.S.P.
>   You constantly remind me,
>   me, your Chicana employee
> that machi-machi-machismo
> is part of our culture.
>   I'm conditioned, you say,
> to bearing machismo
> which you only learned
> day before yesterday.
>   At home you're no patrón
>   your liberated gabacha
>   has gotcha where
>   she wants ya,
>   y a mi me ves cara
>   de steppin' stone.
> Your culture emanates

from Raza poster on your walls
from bulletin boards in the halls
and from the batos who hang out at the barrio bar.
Chicanismo through osmosis
acquired in good doses
remind you
to remind me
that machi-machi-machismo
is part of our culture.[5]

In Lorna Dee Cervantes' poem, "Para un revolucionario," the speaker must remind her "carnal" that she, too, is Raza and would like to share in the dream of the revolution that, up until that time, he had only offered to his *hermanos*:

Pero your voice is lost to me, *carnal*,
in the wail of *tus hijos*
in the clatter of dishes
and the pucker of beans on the stove.
Your conversations come to me
de la sala where you sit,
spreading your dream to brothers,
where you spread that dream like damp clover
for them to trod upon,
when I stand here reaching
para ti con manos bronces that spring
from *mi espíritu*
(for I too am Raza).[6]

We also learned that sexuality and its free choice and practice—a major component of white feminism—was simply not a unilateral agenda for women of color, or not always prioritized as it was with white feminists. Rather, we began to see that it had to be viewed concurrently with other issues such as class, ethnicity, cultural norms, traditions, and the paramount position of the family. This issue alone resulted in difficult lessons for white women who had not yet begun to perceive the complexities of being a Latina woman in the U.S., let alone a Latina feminist.

For all of these reasons, Cherríe Moraga's *Loving in the War Years: Lo que nunca pasó por sus labios* is a timely and important work.[7] It is a compendium of nearly a decade of Moraga's works that includes short fiction, poetry, and testimonial essay. Two of those essays, whose length comprise the majority of that book, contain the essence of Moraga's thinking, incorporating dreams, journal entries, and poetry as part of her testimonial discourse. One of the essays in particular, a work she has entitled **"A Long Line of Vendidas,"** addresses some of the issues I have just mentioned and will be the focus of this essay.

The naming of this essay (a title appropriated, whose meaning is then reassigned, an ironic and contemporary use of the term "vendida") not only connects Moraga to a mestiza

Chicana past but also questions, reevaluates, and finally takes issue with it. As we shall see, the customary uses of the *vendida* myth are restructured in Moraga's analysis in order to forge a reevaluation of the Malinche legend from which it derives.

The entire collection begins with the words: "Este libro covers a span of seven years." From the outset, the speaker prepares the reader for the bilingual text that ensues: the trajectory of the light-skinned Chicana whose paternal Anglo surname[8] helps her pass for white in a culture that demands conformity from her. Submerged into this dominant culture, alien to her maternal Chicana heritage, Moraga uses the act of writing as a process of *concientización* in order to reclaim her Chicanismo. The writer's relationship with her text, as a medium by which to define and articulate herself, parallels a process of withdrawal and then renewal; that is, her separation from both family and culture lasts until she is eventually led back to these heritages as the *política* (radical political woman) of the last essay whose feminist, lesbian consciousness offers us a theoretical basis for some of the above-mentioned issues.

Her purpose, she tells us in the introduction, is not merely artistic or literary, but rather political "because we are losing ourselves to the gavacho" (p. iii). In this sense, the book itself becomes a kind of sacrificial offering, thereby aligning it with other Latin American testimonial texts whose purposes are to counteract or give voice to a certain historical circumstance by the act of writing or converting oneself into what René Jara has called, "testigo, actor y juez."[9] That which Moraga witnesses, acts upon, and judges is the confluence of the two social movements that inform her discourse: the women's movement and the Chicano movement.

In an act that places her within her historic and literary moment, Cherríe Moraga (like so many Chicana/o writers) draws upon, conjures, reinvents, and reinterprets Mexican myth and pre-Hispanic heritage. Like other Chicana writers of her generation (and certain Mexican writers of the previous one), Moraga begins her own analysis by a contemporary Chicana feminist application of the Malinche myth and its personal significance to her. While Moraga is not original in her desire to reassess Malinche, her view of the myth does offer a sharp departure from contemporary Chicana re-evaluations. In both literature and criticism, Malinche's mythical presence has affirmed the fact that neither Mexicans or Chicanos (although for different reasons in each case) have made their peace with her. When Chicana writers began their re-assessment, almost all of them spoke in counterpoint to Octavio Paz' landmark essay, "Los hijas de la Malinche," calling themselves instead "las hijas de la Malinche."

Paz' work underscores the need for Mexicans to examine their history in order to elucidate answers to their questions of identity. Paz sees Malinche as the ultimate Mother figure, but neither the Great Mother embodied in the female deities of the Aztec empire nor the Virgin Mother as represented by Guadalupe. Rather, she is the mythical, even metaphorical mother, her flesh serving as a symbol of the Conquest, the rape of Mexico.[10]

The well-known story is as follows: Malinche's mother, in an act of respect or fear toward her new husband, sold her daughter into slavery so that the son born of the new marriage would inherit both the title and the crown due the young Malintzín Tenepal (Malinche). When Hernán Cortés arrived in Tabasco, Malintzín was among the group of young women presented to him. Because Malinche grew up in the Valley of Mexico, she spoke Nahuatl; her residence with the Tabasco Indians made her bilingual. Soon thereafter she also learned Spanish and with this, the Spaniards renamed her doña Marina. Thus, by the time she set off with Cortés (actually to return home), she had already been offered twice as an object of exchange by the weaker of two parties in order to assuage any possible violence by the stronger.

This act, inspiring countless poems by both Mexican and Chicana writers, has offered as many points of view. Perhaps because Malinche is associated with the Aztec past, mestizaje, and violence of the Conquest, she may also be read as a metaphor for the silencing of the Indian voice that encased this act. Thus, in Rosario Castellanos' poem "La Malinche," for example, the poet puts words into Malinche's mouth, making her the speaker who now protests her use as an object of exchange, a currency traded for coffee beans, a colonized object who berates the woman responsible for the transaction—her mother. Although sympathetic to her plight, by such a characterization Castellanos simultaneously allows the reader to imagine Malinche's voice while still casting her as a victim.[11] Thus, the victimization of Malinche does not represent a contrary view to many male writers of her generation.[12]

Chicana poet Lucha Corpi also writes about her as a victim in her series, "Marina Poems." In the one entitled "Marina Mother," the speaker sums up Malinche's dilemma by addressing herself to Malinche's mother:

>　　Tú no la querías ya y él la negaba
>　　y aquel que cuando niño ¡mamá! le gritaba
>　　cuando creció le puso por nombre "la chingada."[13]

If these poets seem to indicate a Malinche vindication (and they are seconded by what can now be called a Chicana tradition of writers, critics, and historians such as Norma Alarcón, Cordelia Candelaria, Adelaida del Castillo, and Marcela Lucero-Trujillo),[14] others have written about how painful it is to be Malinche or her daughter ("como duele

ser Malinche"),[15] or how they long for her to redeem them, or to finally speak in her own voice, as in Sylvia Gonzales' "I Am Chicana":

>　　I am Chicana
>　　Waiting for the return
>　　of la Malinche,
>　　to negate her guilt,
>　　and cleanse her flesh
>　　of a confused Mexican wrath
>　　which seeks reason
>　　to the displaced power of Indian deities.
>　　I am Chicana
>　　Waiting for the coming of a Malinche
>　　to sacrifice herself
>　　on an Aztec altar
>　　and Catholic cross
>　　in redemption of all her forsaken daughters.[16]

In a later Chicana rendition of Malinche, the speaker is Malinche herself, Malinche the feminist, Malinche who addresses herself to Cortés after his refusal to marry her, even after she bears his child:

>　　Huhn-y para eso te di
>　　mi sangre y mi pueblo!
>　　Sí, ya lo veo, gringo desabrido,
>　　tanto así me quieres
>　　que me casarás con tu subordinado Don Juan,
>　　sin más ni más
>　　como si fuera yo
>　　un kilo de carne
>　　—pos ni que fueras mi padre
>　　pa' venderme a tu antojo
>　　güero infeliz . . .
>　　　　　　　　　　!!!
>　　Etcétera
>　　　　etcétera.[17]

For Moraga, then, beginning to write, that is, an articulation of her Chicana identity, must include a re-evaluation of the problematic "role-model" Malintzín, the "traitor" and "chingada" she was taught to hate, mistrust, and never, under any circumstances, emulate. Even the Chicana who is unaware of Malinche's historical role "suffers under her name," Moraga claims. By underscoring the inherent contradiction in Malinche's dilemma (and, by association, all Mexican and Chicana women's), Moraga also confronts her own problem and resultant pain: the daughter betrayed by a mother who showed preference for her male children. What makes Moraga's assessment different is that in this case the daughter, in turn, is accused of betraying her race by choosing the sex of her mother as the object of her love. On the one hand, the importance of family and the closeness and attachment of the mother/daughter relationship is "paramount and essential in our lives" because the daughter can always be relied upon to "remain faithful a la madre" (p. 139). But the converse is not always the case; while the fidelity of the daughter is expected, the mother, who is also socialized by the culture, does not always reciprocate. It is here that Moraga parts company with other Chicana writers.

While other writers focus on Malinche herself as if they were her actual daughters, Moraga prefers to direct her analysis toward Malinche's mother, likening her to her own. A case in point is that, for both Malinche and Moraga, brothers were their mothers' choice. In order to show her "respect [for] her mother" (p. 90), the young Moraga was required not only to wait on her adolescent brother and his friends, but also to do so graciously.

The legacy of Malinche also lingers for any woman with the audacity to consider her own needs before those of the men of her family. By placing herself (or any woman, including her daughter) first, she is accused of being a traitor to her race (p. 103). By fulfilling her daughter's desire and need for love, the mother is also labeled la chingada. Her "Mexican wifely duty" means that sons are favored, husbands revered. "Traitor begets traitor," Moraga warns: like mother, like daughter. Malinche's mother, then, was the first traitor (mother) who begot the second one (daughter).

While Moraga stresses the daughter's inevitable pain with the discovery of this truth, she equates that pain with Malinche's: "What I wanted from my mother was impossible" (p. 103). In this respect, she focuses on Malinche's relationship with her mother: a daughter betrayed. All of these factors contribute to the cultural messages the young Chicana learns about herself and ultimately internalizes: that is, the "inherent unreliability of women" and female "natural propensity for treachery" (pp. 99-101).

Moraga continues the Malinche analogy by stressing her own identity as the product of a bicultural relationship: the daughter of a white father and a brown mother. "To be a woman," a brown woman, and a Chicana entailed reclaiming the "race of my mother." It meant loving the Chicana in herself and in other women; it meant departing from her mother and Malinche's model and "embrac[ing] no white man" (p. 94). It meant finally returning to the race of her mother through her love for other women—her Chicana lesbianism. Although Moraga acknowledges that her mother may be a "modern-day Chicana Malinche" (p. 117) by marrying a white man, she herself, the "half-breed Chicana," in a departure from both these predecessors and a transgression of all standards and norms, chooses a sexuality "which excludes all men, and therefore, most dangerously Chicano men" (p. 117). It is an act that labels her as the worst traitor of all, a "malinchista," one who is swayed by foreign influences. Her conclusion, paradoxically, brings her back to her

people, the people of her mother: "I come from a long line of vendidas" (p. 117), she confesses, although she is obviously giving a new and perhaps reclaimed meaning, if such a thing is possible, to the word *vendida*.

In this new vocabulary, *vendida* refers to how Moraga is perceived rather than how she perceives herself. Similarly, it allows its author to poke fun at such labels. The term, like "bruja" and "loca," used specifically to trivialize women's experience, can now be seen as an act of female empowerment. Such appears to be the case for Moraga. In order to avoid being classified in this manner, she must be servile to one man and she must denounce her sexual love for women. In order to be the socially accepted Chicana, even if she is a politically active radical, she must not question the foundational basis of her loyalty and commitment to la causa, a commitment that, in Moraga's view, also entails an unswerving heterosexuality, a sexual loyalty to the Chicano male (p. 105).

Moraga reports that the current debate among Chicana women focuses on how to "get their men right" (p. 105) rather than on questioning the premises of what Adrienne Rich has called "compulsory heterosexuality."[18] The Chicana feminist who critiques sexism in the Chicano community finds herself in a personal, political, and racial bind. She will be called *vendida* if she finds the "male-defined and often anti-feminist" values of the Chicano community difficult to accept. She will be accused of selling out to white women, of abandoning her race, of having absorbed the struggle of the middle class, of being malinchista, "puta," or "jota" (p. 98), even if she is heterosexual; it is greatly exacerbated if she is not. Thus, her role is not only the gender-neutral one of joining her man in earning a living and struggling against racism, but is also the gender-specific one as cultural nurturer, responsible, among other tasks, for the socialization of children. If she then cares to "challenge sexism," she will undergo this particular struggle single-handedly because this juggling act will also require that she "retain . . . her femininity so as not to offend or threaten *her man*" (p. 107). In this sense, Moraga sees her in the same light as the "Black Super-woman," the myth that only black women themselves were able to dispel.

In order to be a Chicana feminist, then, it is not enough for Moraga to examine the lost pages of history in order to reclaim female heroes, though this is one of its essential ingredients. Too often, these female luminaries are presented in relation to their men instead of in their own right. Calling this the "alongside-our-man-knee-jerk-phenomenon,"[19] Moraga asserts that the most valuable work being done in Chicana scholarship is that which puts "the female first, even when it means criticizing el hombre" (p. 107). She finally concludes that learning to do a self-study of one's culture, learning to read it critically, is not analogous to betrayal of that culture (p. 108).

In that vein, she takes issue with Chicana historians, guilty of the "knee-jerk phenomenon," who have attempted to trivialize the white women's movement as having nothing to offer them. Perhaps, because it was precisely within this movement that Moraga herself sought refuge and found it, she is particularly sensitive to this charge. Although her essay does not reveal this personal information, and the entire book could hardly be read as an apology to white feminism, it does contain a list of activities in which feminist women of color have been working at the grass-roots level for a decade: sterilization abuse, battered women's shelters, rape crisis centers, health care, and more (p. 106). Thus, she is quick to note that the use of white male theoreticians, such as Marx and Engels, is perfectly acceptable within the Chicano community but, paradoxically, the use of white female theoreticians is not, either within the Chicana or Chicano community. "It is far easier for the Chicana to criticize white women who . . . could never be familia, than to take issue with or complain . . . to a brother, uncle, father" (pp. 106-7).

The heterosexual Chicana who criticizes her male counterpart or relatives will jeopardize her chances of receiving male approval, be it through her son or her lover: an approval necessary to being a *política*, an approval that allows access to, or a taste of, male privilege, an approval that will procure her a husband. She is what Evangelina Enríquez and Alfredo Mirandé have identified as the "contemporary vendida."[20] This situation is further exacerbated if she is not heterosexual, although these authors do not discuss this point. Moraga explains that only the woman intent on the approval can be affected by the disapproval (p. 103). The lesbian, on the other hand, not subject to male sanctions and out of his control, will often serve as an easy scapegoat; weaknesses in the movement can be blamed on her, the model she sets for other women being a dangerous example. Her decision to take control of her own sexuality, as well as her independence, likens her to the Malinche model we discussed earlier. She is a "traitor" who "succumbs" to the foreign influences that have corrupted her people (p. 113).

In a study of the cultural stereotypes typically available to Chicana women, Shirlene Soto, for example, has noted that the figures most often used—Malinche, La Llorona and the Virgin of Guadalupe—have historically been models to control women, a point with which Moraga concurs. Soto, like Enríquez and Mirandé, also fails to address the issue of how much more poignant and true all those statements are when there is a clear sexual rejection of the male, as in Moraga's case. Nevertheless, sexual rejection does not necessarily signify a cultural one.

Viewed as an agent of the Anglos, the Chicana lesbian is seen as an aberration, someone who has unfortunately caught *his* disease. For these reasons, perhaps, Moraga believes that control of and over women cannot be based or blamed entirely on these so-called inherited cultural stereotypes but rather on the institution of obligatory heterosexuality. Nowhere in print had any Chicano or Chicana addressed lesbianism or homosexuality in their theoretical analyses of liberation. For this, Moraga would have to turn to the Black feminists, the same women, she asserts, who had served as role models for the Chicana feminist movement in its formation. "If any direct 'borrowing' was done, it was from Black feminists" (p. 132) and not from the white feminists normally blamed for infiltrating the Chicana feminist movement. Until she had this example, then, her sexuality had isolated and estranged her from her race: "It seemed to me to be a Chicana lesbian put me far beyond the hope of salvation" (p. 125). Yet she recognizes now that because one aspect of a culture is oppressive, it does not mean "throwing out the entire business of racial/ethnic culture" that is essential to identity (p. 127).

Such a questioning brings us to the ambiguous title and subtitle of her book, ***Loving in the War Years: Lo que nunca pasó por sus labios.*** By choosing to represent the book bilingually, she again likens herself to Malinche, her bilingual and trilingual forebear. "Lo que nunca pasó por sus labios" suggests that a silence is about to be broken, though the multiple possibilities of "sus" (her, his, their, your) do not reveal exactly who will break it: Moraga? Malinche? Chicana lesbians? All of them? In this way, her essay approximates the titles of Latin American women's testimonial discourse: "Let me speak!" "They Won't Take Me Alive," "Tales of Disappearance and Survival." All of these indicate a strength, a fortitude, and a resolve to break silences and assert one's voice. In the case of so many of Moraga's Latin American counterparts, a lack of education has impeded their single-handed publishing of their own testimonies; thus, many will contain a "co-producer" to actually write their discourse. For Moraga, the education is not a problem; in her case, bilingualism is the impediment.

Having learned what has mockingly been called "kitchen Spanish" or "Spanglish," yet also needing to be fluent in English in order to operate within the dominant culture and obtain the education that her mother encouraged her to pursue, Moraga confesses to her anglicization; it was a means to achieve her much-desired independence. In this sense, there is also a linkage; her reacquaintance with her Chicano roots required a return to Spanish, required a knowledge of it, implied an attitude on the part of the speaker who refused to be humiliated any longer by her bilingualism/biculturalism with such terms as "nolingual."[7]

When Moraga discovers a bicultural group whose most

comfortable language is what I prefer to call "bilingual" (bilingual as a noun as well as an adjective), she finally is in a position of not feeling shame for "shabby" English or "incorrect" Spanish. Having come from a home where English was spoken, Moraga acknowledges that this claim on, and longing for, her Spanish "mothertongue" had no rational explanation. After all, she did not have her language stripped from her, as had so many children of the Southwest. Here, it is more appropriate to consider it the ancient language of her heart. In this sense, language is not simply a means of communicating ideas, passions, feelings, and theories, but is also symbolic, representing, among other emotions, love for one's culture. As it becomes a touch-stone for that culture, especially in circumstances of exile, one must also relearn its nuances as one learns to accept the entirety of one's culture, both its positive and its negative. "I know this language in my bones . . . and then it escapes me" (p. 141). Humiliated and mortified, Moraga must call the Berlitz language school in New York City in order to return to her Spanish, to her love of her mothertongue, to a love for her mother, to her love for her culture, to her love for her raza, to her "deep racial memory of love." "I am a different woman in Spanish. A different kind of passion. I think, *soy mujer en español. No macha. Pero mujer. Soy Chicana*—open to all kinds of attack" (p. 142). One of these attacks, no doubt, is the accusation that she does not belong and does not speak the language of her mother, even if she feels it in her bones. She articulates the contradiction she faces with one of her journal entries after the Berlitz episode: "*Paying for culture. When I was born between the legs of the best teacher I could have had*" (p. 141). The painful journey she embarks upon in order to discover this truth allows her a return to her mother, to her people, to "la mujer mestiza," to a new awareness of what it means to be Malinche's daughter.

NOTES

1. Marcelo Christine Lucero-Trujillo, "No More Cookies, Please," in *The Third Woman: Minority Women Writers of the United States*, ed. Dexter Fisher (Boston: Houghton Mifflin, 1980), 402-3.

2. Lorde's "Open Letter to Mary Daly," in *Sister Outsider*, in which she discusses the "history of white women who are unable to hear Black women's words, or to maintain dialogue with us" (Trumansburg, N.Y.: The Crossing Press, 1984), 66, and Smith's not knowing "where to begin," in "Toward a black feminist criticism," in *Feminist Criticism and Social Change: Sex, Class and Race in Literature and Culture*, ed. Judith Newton and Deborah Rosenfelt (New York, London: Methuen, 1986), 3.

3. Parul Desai, "Interview with Bernice Zamora, a Chicana Poet," *Imagine: International Chicano Poetry Journal* 2, no. 1 (Summer 1985): 29.

4. Olivia Espin, "Cultural and Historical Influences on Sexuality in Hispanic/Latin women: Implications for Psychotherapy," in *Pleasure and Danger: Exploring Female Sexuality*, ed. Carol Vance (Boston: Routledge and Kegan Paul, 1984), 155.

5. Marcela Christine Lucero-Trujillo, "Machismo is Part of Our Culture," in *The Third Woman*, 401-2. The fact that the same author exemplifies both positions, that is, the turning away from both the Anglo-American feminist and the Chicano macho, indicates her articulation of a new voice that will incorporate a feminism specific and appropriate to her Chicana reality.

6. Lorna Dee Cervantes, "Para un revolucionario," in *The Third Woman*, 381-83 (for you with bronze hands).

7. Cherríe Moraga, "A Long Line of Vendidas," in *Loving in the War Years: Lo que nunca pasó por sus labios* (Boston: South End Press, 1983). All subsequent passages will be from this edition and the page numbers will be contained within parentheses after each passage.

8. Moraga offers no example of what this surname was but leads us to imagine that in discovering her Chicana roots, she also molts the paternal name in favor of the maternal one.

9. René Jara, "Testimonio y literatura," in *Testimonio y Literatura: Monographic Series of the Society for the Study of Contemporary Hispanic and Lusophone Revolutionary Literatures*, no. 3, ed. René Jara and Hernán Vidal (Minneapolis: Institute for the Study of Ideologies and Literature, 1986), 1.

10. Octavio Paz, "Los hijos de la Malinche," in *El laberinto de la soledad* (México: Fondo de Cultura Económica, 1973), 59-80.

11. Rosario Castellanos, "La Malinche," in *Poesía no eres tú* (México: Fondo de Cultura Económica, 1972), 295-97.

12. Most notable are the views of Carlos Fuentes and Octavio Paz.

13. Lucha Corpi, "Marina Madre," in *Palabras de Mediodía/Noon Words*, trans. Catherine Rodríguez-Nieto (Berkeley: El Fuego de Aztlán Publications, 1980), 119. I prefer my own translation of these verses: "You no longer loved her and your husband denied her / When the child that used to call her 'Mamá' / grew up, he called her 'whore.'"

14. Norma Alcarcón, "Chicana's Feminist Literature: A Revision through Malintzín/or Malinche: Putting Flesh Back on the Object," in *This Bridge Called My Back: Writings*

by Radical Women of Color, 2nd ed., ed. Cherríe Moraga and Gloria Anzaldúa (New York: Kitchen Table Women of Color Press, 1983), 182-90; Aledaida del Castillo, "Malintzín Tenepal: A Preliminary Look into a New Perspective," in *Essays on La Mujer*, part 1, ed. Rosaura Sánchez (Los Angeles: UCLA Chicano Studies Center Publications, 1977), 124-49; Marcela Christine Lucero-Trujillo, "The Dilemma of the Modern Chicana Artist and Critic," in *The Third Woman*, 324-31; Cordelia Candelaria, "La Malinche: Feminist Prototype," *Frontiers* 5, no. 2 (1980); Rachel Phillips, "Marina/Malinche: Masks and Shadows," in *Women in Hispanic Literature: Icons and Fallen Idols*, ed. Beth Miller (Berkeley: University of California Press, 1983), 97-114; Shirlene Soto, "Tres modelos culturales: La Virgen de Guadalupe, la Malinche y la Llorona," *fem*, 10 no. 48 (Octubre-Noviembre 1986): 13-16.

15. These exact words appear in two early Chicana poems, "Como duele," by Lorenza Calvillo Schmidt, and an untitled poem by Adaljiza Sosa Riddell, both in *Chicanas en la literatura y el arte*, ed. Herminio Ríos-C. and Octavio Romano-V. (Berkeley: Quinto Sol, 1973).

16. Sylvia Gonzales, "I Am Chicana," in *The Third Woman*, 422.

17. Angela de Hoyos, "La Malinche a Cortez y Vice Versa (o sea, 'El Amor No Perdona, Ni Siquiera Por Amor')," in *Woman, Woman* (Houston: Arte Público Press, 1985), 54. (Hmph, and that's why I gave you / my blood and my people! / Yes, now I see it, you uncouth gringo / you love me so much / that you'll marry me off to your subordinate, Don Juan / without a second thought / as if I were a piece of meat / Well, even if you were my father / to go selling me at your whim / you stupid gringo . . . / !!! / Etcetera / Etcetera).

18. Adrienne Rich, "Compulsory Heterosexuality and Lesbian Existence," in *Women: Sex and Sexuality*, ed. Catharine R. Stimpson and Ethel Spector Person (Chicago and London: University of Chicago Press, 1980), 62-91.

19. Cherríe Moraga is perhaps one of the best known Chicana writers outside the Chicana community. She is widely anthologized and the one who most white women quote as a representative Chicana voice. The "alongside-our-man-knee-jerk-phenomenon" appears in Cheris Kramarae and Paula A. Treichler's *A Feminist Dictionary* (Boston: Pandora Press, 1985), 41. On the other hand, she is hardly ever anthologized by Chicano critics, which may have been one of the reasons for an essay such as this one. The Mexican feminist magazine, *fem*, however, has regularly published her poetry. See their issue on Chicanas (10, no. 48 [Octubre-Noviembre 1986]).

20. Evangelina Enríquez and Alfredo Mirandé, "Liberation, Chicana Style: Colonial Roots of Feministas Chicanas," *De Colores: A Bilingual Quarterly Journal of Chicano Expression and Thought* 4, no. 3 (1978): 15.

21. Juan Bruce-Novoa, "Una cuestión de identidad: ¿Qué significa un nombre?" in *Imagenes e identidades: El puertorriqueño en la literatura*, ed. Asela Rodríguez de Laguna (Río Piedras, P.R.: Huracán, 1985), 283-88.

Hal Gelb (review date 2 November 1992)

SOURCE: Review of *Heroes and Saints*, in *The Nation*, Vol. 255, No. 14, November 2, 1992, pp. 518-20.

[*In the following review, Gelb notes that in* Heroes and Saints *Moraga "has written with compassion and intelligence about the difficulties of change," although she fails to fully explore some of her principal characters.*]

As one of several Bay Area feminists who made their reputations in other genres but are now (or again) writing for the theater, Cherríe Moraga has expressed a desire to create plays that inspire a new vision while they challenge political correctness.

And in many respects her new work, **Heroes and Saints,** produced by Brava! For Women in the Arts at San Francisco's Mission Cultural Center, does just that. An unusual blend of realism, surrealism and political theater, it is written partly in English, partly in Spanish. Moraga sets the play in a San Joaquin Valley town where growers threaten to shoot farm-workers who are protesting pesticide-related deaths by hanging their dead children from the grapevines crucifixion-style. But rather than proceed by making a frontal attack on toxic sprays, Moraga chooses to emphasize the human drama of a Latina family suffering the effects of the poisons. One daughter, Yolanda, loses a baby to them (a performance by Jennifer Proctor that calls up excruciating depths of pain). Another, Cerezita (Jaime Lujan), herself suffering from a birth defect, is—in what could have been fierce poetry had it been realized less awkwardly—simply a head poised on a wheeled cart. The mother (Juanita Estrada), protecting this daughter, tries to keep her from the world. But following one of a number of extraordinarily powerful moments in Albert Takazauckas's production, this one a highly erotic love scene between the head and a sympathetic priest in which the young woman tries and fails to recover a sense of her body, Cerezita carries the corpse of her sister's baby to the fields and is shot.

Ultimately, it's clear that this is not only not agitprop but that the fight against pesticides is not even the central conflict. The real action of the play is the daughter's rebellion against the mother and what she stands for, which is framed as a social and political fight, not a psychological one. The mother is reactionary, a sexually and otherwise repressive, fatalistic figure who must be overthrown. And it's here that *Heroes and Saints* fails in its aspirations. When Moraga contrasts the mother with an older woman activist based on Dolores Huerta, we know we are seeing the acceptable role model. Moraga isn't able or doesn't wish to get inside the way the mother has internalized her oppression as she gets inside Cerezita's yearning or Yolanda's agony, although elsewhere she has written with compassion and intelligence about the difficulties of change.

Cherríe Moraga with Mary Pat Brady and Juanita Heredia (interview date Fall 1993-Spring 1994)

SOURCE: "Coming Home: Interview with Cherríe Moraga," in *Mester,* Vols. XXII and XXIII, Nos. 2 and 1, Fall 1993-Spring 1994, pp. 149-64.

[*In the following interview, Moraga discusses her career, creative influences, and her notion of feminism.*]

In 1981, Cherríe Moraga and Gloria Anzaldúa redefined the feminist movement in the United States. The publication of *This Bridge Called My Back: Writings by Radical Women of Color* challenged the feminist movement to rethink the privileged term "woman." *Bridge,* by providing a combination of *testimonios,* poetry, short fiction, and essays, suggests the multiplicity of experiences and the various diasporas filling the streets of the United States. But until *Bridge*'s publication, these experiences were largely hidden from literary and academic sight. *Bridge* put pressure on both the terms "woman" and "feminist" and initiated a rethinking of Anglo-American feminism which had until then largely ignored its Anglo middle-class biases.

Shortly after the publication of *This Bridge Called My Back,* Moraga began working on her ground-breaking autobiography, *Loving in the War Years: Lo que nunca pasó por sus labios* (1983). In this cross-genre collection, Moraga explores the experience of writing with "your *familia* on one shoulder and the *movimiento* on the other." She discusses the seemingly contradictory experience of being a Chicana and a lesbian, and she critiques *familia,* the Chicano Movement, white racism, and sexism. The style of the text, in combining poetry, prose, and fiction, reinforces the content's challenges to existing hierarchies, institutionalized racism, homophobia, and patriarchy. The concluding essay, **"A Long Line of Vendidas"** is one of the most anthologized Chicana feminist essays. Moraga next turned to writing theater. Her three plays, *Giving Up the Ghost, Shadow of a Man,* and

Heroes and Saints, argue for the intimate link between political and economic realities and daily family culture. *Giving Up the Ghost* (1986), written largely in poetic monologues, describes the experiences of a young woman coming to terms with her sexuality, her past, and the puzzles of heterosexuality. *Shadow of a Man* (1990) examines family dynamics built around keeping a threatening secret. Set in the deadly pesticide fields of California's agribusiness, *Heroes and Saints* (1992) depicts a Chicano community's attempt to confront genocide, racist apathy, and family loss. While each of Moraga's plays tackles serious subjects, she infuses all of her work with humor and poetry, with Chicanidad.

Most recently, Moraga has published *The Last Generation* (1993), a collection of essays and poems. In this volume she addresses the post-Quincentennary *movimiento,* the state of Chicano/a activism, the siege upon gays and lesbians of color, and her own identity as a woman turning forty. Her poetry and essays are less autobiographical in this collection, but they continue to draw on family memories and experiences.

As we sat in a small café down the street from Arroyo Books in Highland Park on April 24, 1994, Moraga reflected on her artistic production to date, commenting on issues of representation, reception, and literary production. Before we started the interview, Moraga and her sister JoAnn noted the surrounding barrio. They had lived there in the first years of their lives before moving to South Pasadena and then to San Gabriel. So the reading that Moraga was to give later that Sunday afternoon to a packed audience at Arroyo Books was something of a homecoming.

[*Mary Pat Brady and Juanita Heredia*:] *There is no doubt that both your fiction and essays, for example,* **This Bridge Called My Back: Writings by Radical Women of Color,** *has had a profound impact on mainstream literary criticism in academia. How do you feel about the teaching of this text by mainstream feminists? Do you think there is any misappropriation? Do you think that they dismiss it as a sociological piece of work? How can we reach a better understanding of this text?*

[Cherríe Moraga:] I think initially what happened with the book was what Gloria [Anzaldúa] and I had envisioned or hoped which is that it be used by Chicano Studies, Women Studies, community centers and all of that. It has been used on all those levels. In that sense I feel like it has fulfilled its mandate. What feminist theorists have done with it is mixed. One of the ways in which it has been misappropriated is that sometimes they look no further than *Bridge.* They do all this Anglo material and then only do *Bridge,* which somehow covers everything they think they need to know about other women of color. *Bridge* is thirteen years old. It came out in 1981. A lot has changed since then; there is a certain way in which some of the material is generic, women of color. I think that white feminists as a whole feel more comfortable working with the generic notion of women of color and try to put everyone under that rubric as opposed to the specificity of each of the ethnic/racial groups. The book has a lot of things missing. It is not at all international in perspective. If I were to do a *Bridge* now, it would have to be much more international. To be talking about women of color feminism in the United States and not connect with all the diasporas is ridiculous. On the one hand, some white women use it as a way to cover themselves. On the other, in terms of the criticism that has come out about *Bridge* I do not know. Norma Alarcón has written extensively about how *Bridge* has been misappropriated, I think she articulates that fine. That is her job. Frankly I stopped reading the criticism. It is not just about *Bridge,* but it happens with my own individual work. For the most part, I don't really mind very much as long as it keeps generating ideas and discussion. On an individual level, I would wonder what really are the motives of each of the individuals involved in teaching this book. Do they have a broad perspective or serious anti-racist politics or are they just appropriating the book? I have no control over that so I try not to worry about that because there is nothing I can do. Once the work is out, it has its own life. It is not yours anymore which is fine with me. I just try not to pay too much attention and I let the critics battle it out with each other.

That's the next move if you were going to do another anthology, a broader one, more inclusive of various diasporas?

No, I would not do that. I have been teaching a class called "Indígena Scribe" for about three years now which is a group of Native-American, Chicana, and Latina writers. The material that is coming out of that group of people is very specific using *indigenismo* as a kind of base root which is fascinating to me. I would be interested in doing a collection possibly of their creative work which is very original in trying to show why that indigenous root connection is significant in the creative imagination. But, that is very, very specific. I think my tendency is to aim to get more and more specific as opposed to producing another generic work. Of course, it was not generic at the time. But I don't think that I would put myself in the position of doing another collection of people outside my own ethnic/racial background because the time is not right for that. The reason we did *Bridge* was because the time was right. It was more out of the virtue of the invisibility that women of color had in the women's movement. That is no longer the case. Every single writer in *Bridge* has her own book now. Those are all established writers. Now there is a body of indigenous literature. There is a body of Latina literature. There is a body of Asian-American literature. It is a different time and place. It would have to be reconceptualized in a totally different manner. There is not a need for another *Bridge,* but there is a need for other kinds of more specific writings. Also, editing is a lot of work. One has to be really driven by a particular vision and that's what *Bridge* was. We were driven by a particular vision in 1979 out of virtual isolation and invisibility.

One element I liked about **Esta puente, mi espalda** *(the Spanish version of* **Bridge***) is your inclusion of the interview that Ana Castillo did with the Watsonville workers whereas most literary anthologies would exclude that kind of voice. Was it a way to bridge the gap between community and academia?*

Well it was an attempt to do that. Most of those women were already going to college. They were community-based women, but they were not *obreras*. There is a lot more that could have been done around that. In doing another collection, I certainly would not limit it to writers only. If I were not going to do a creative writing anthology and focus on feminism of a certain type, I think now I would work much harder to record oral histories and interviews from people who were really working-class, *campesina* women. I think that was a nice gesture in the right direction. I agree with you. That is what is needed as opposed to this academic separation.

What was the experience of making **Cuentos: Stories by Latinas** *like? How did you meet the other two editors, Alma Gómez and Mariana Romo-Carmona? What was it like forming the networks?*

Alma was part of the collective, Kitchen Table Press. When we started Kitchen Table Press, the first book we did was *Bridge* because it had been published by a white feminist press and it went bankrupt. We had to get lawyers to try to get the book back. Actually, a lot of the motivation for Kitchen Table Press came about because of those kinds of situations where women of color did not have control over their own production. In essence we never intended to do *Bridge.* We also never intended to do *Home-girls* because *Home-girls* was going to be done by the same press. Then suddenly the press dropped both projects leaving it up to us to save them. The first two projects were to rescue those books.

The third project *Cuentos: Stories by Latinas* was kind of conceived among the collective which mostly consisted of black women. There had been collections of black women writers. At that time in 1983, there were very few by Latinas that were not simply Latin American women in translation. We were trying to connect U.S. Latinas with Latin American women and cover all the classes too that a lot of bourgeoisie Latin American women had ignored. Also we wished to include material that was unequivocally feminist which other collections had not done up to that point. Alma was Nuyorican and we wanted someone who was Latin American and that's how we met Mariana so that we could cover those three areas. A fourth person who essentially wrote the introduction with me was Myrtha Chabrán who was *puertorriqueña* born on the island, a good generation older than me. She was very critical in the development of that book as well.

Your movement around cities from Los Angeles to New York to San Francisco has converted you into an urban traveler. How have these experiences affected your writing? Have community activities influenced you in any way?

Well, I was told by a psychic many years ago and I can't forget it because I don't want it to be true. She said, "Forget your house on the ocean. You are never going to be a writer who can escape and have a nice contemplative life." That's probably true. I think about that, which is why I always end up in the cities all the time. I still think about leaving the cities. Now that I have a child even more so. But I am always drawn to cities because I think one of the reasons is just survival. Being both Chicana and lesbian, major cities are the only safe place where one can be both of these identities visible at once and find a cultural community to cultivate all of those identities. It has always been that more than anything else; the bottom line is that one has to feel that one can be all those parts of yourself wherever you are living. I think that is why I have always gravitated to cities. Even when I left San Gabriel to move to Hollywood, it was easier to be all those things in Hollywood or Silver Lake than San Gabriel which was the suburbs.

In terms of political or community activism, I always feel that I have known some hard core organizers and I am not one of them. I have not been on the front line of organizing. I have always been community based though. As an artist, I have always felt that I wrote out of a political and community point of reference and I have also done political organizing. But there has always been this trade-off between how much time I had to write and how much time I had to be an organizer. I always ended up choosing more myself as an artist and say, "Well, that's the work. That's my work, but at the same time trying to keep links and connections with the kinds of activism going on in a community so that I had something to write about." I had a base from which to write.

I think teaching for me has always been an element of that community. I see teaching as a way to raise consciousness, to advocate, to agitate, to cultivate a new generation of people who will be challenging agendas. Particularly now that I am not teaching in academia, but that I am teaching in a community base in the Mission District in San Francisco, that I am teaching queer youth, many of whom are very high risk, who live on the streets. Those kinds of things always keep me sharper, less complacent, more challenged, to deal with young people. My concepts are constantly challenged. But I am not doing what my sister does for example. There are a lot of differences. As a principal of a bilingual school in La Puente, she talks about having to be social worker, cop, keeping youth out of the house when parents are drug addicts, this one is threatening to kill that one. It is very first hand, direct contact with Raza who are in need. For the most part as a writer, it keeps you a little bit removed, not to say that I don't experience this, but I deal with the kids I teach. I say that I am not front-line out of respect for the people who have direct contact with these situations. People need to know that there is a difference between being an organizer and being an artist. Both of them have absolutely appropriate roles in the world. I am thinking of my friend Barbara García in Watsonville who began *La clínica para la salud de la gente*. When the earthquake hit in Watsonville back in 1989, she was there in a tent city 24 hours a day basically organizing the damned city better than the Fire Department by making sure everybody was fed, clothed, with a roof over their head. That is front-line work. She is a sister. She needs my work the same way I need hers. It is mutual, but it is not the same thing. I reiterate that because people in academia have this notion that because you live in the barrio, you are a writer, that is somehow front-line work. Yet, it is not. I really think that is an academic perspective. It is very convenient for me to think that too, but there is a difference.

Do you see yourself as part of a generation of U.S. Latina writers?

Yes, I see myself as part of the first generation of U.S. Latina writers. In terms of volume and production of Latina/Chicana writing in the United States, we are a very young group of writers. I mean I did not have a generation to read. By virtue of that, most of us that are producing now are really writing the literature that a generation younger than us is capable of reading. There is something for them to read. But I still feel we are very young. We are not even writing close to what I hope we can be writing in twenty years.

When you don't have that history, when you don't have that literary tradition, it is very liberating and exciting because it has a kind of political significance and the writing that follows will never quite be that same kind of ground-breaking phenomenon. But by the same token, I think we are cultivating our voice: we have not had a lot of role models and practice. I feel like all of us are still learning how to do it. People seem to be getting better at it.

Who do you include in this generation?

In terms of Chicana writers, I think of Sandra Cisneros, Ana Castillo, Gloria Anzaldúa. I consider these women to be the primary ones. Also, Lorna Dee Cervantes is the top for me as a poet. She is fabulous. I would also include Denise Chávez, Helena María Viramontes and others still. But I think that Sandra, Ana, Gloria and Lorna Dee are probably the most significant in terms of the impact they are having at the national level, a national readership. In some cases, the ground that they are breaking in terms of theme and subject.

It is an interesting border literary position to be in because the works of these authors can be used in both American and Latin American literary traditions.

Well I think that will happen more with the translations. Also, Elena Poniatowska has done a lot to expose Chicana writers in Mexico because there is such prejudice against us, basically elitism and class, that they did not take us seriously. In that respect, she has been very significant in making our works known. Also, I think there is cross-fertilization that is happening because of lesbian connections that happen among Latinas in Latin American and in the United States.

In **Loving in the War Years,** *one of the ways you represent the female body is through the historical figure of the Malinche, who strives for self-empowerment as a resistance against patriarchal domination. How do you see women redefining their sexual roles and "putting flesh back on the object" as critic Norma Alarcón says?*

This is what I like about Gloria and Ana's work. I do feel like they are trying to examine what is WOMAN. What is Mexican woman which is not what all the writers are trying to do. Not all Chicana writers are about that, just because they are writing about women. Everybody has different levels of skill, talent and concerns. When I think about *Borderlands* and *The Mixquiahuala Letters*, those are two books that really did try to unravel what is la mujer mexicana/chicana. It is incredibly painful to look at that. It is not pretty how we have been distorted as a people, as a consciousness, a collective notion of what la mujer mexicana/chicana is. It is not nice. It is not a pretty picture. I think a lot of people deal with it in different ways. Some people create positive images while others dress her differently. Those are all ways that they create her.

But the work that I gravitate towards is a work that tries to tear it apart. Even then if all you see is the raw guts and it does not smell or look good, at least you are starting from somewhere. That is what moves me as a writer, what I need to read and I will read anybody who does it even if she is not Latina.

I think of a book like, *Thereafter Johnny*, by Carolivia Herron,

a black woman. It is a crazy book where this woman writes about incest, but in a very taboo way. What you can see there is an artist trying to unravel a theme. It goes back into slave history trying to figure out what slavery did to black men and women and how it destroyed their relationship with each other. What she comes up with is devastating. Again, it is not a pleasant work but I ate that book up because I feel like I am trying to do that for better or for worse. As lousy as I do it or as good as I do it, that is what I want to do. If there is anything I knew being raised as a Mexican daughter, it is the beauty in it and the horror in it. I want to give to that and recreate her. But I may never recreate her. I may write until I am ninety and just be taking it apart.

So for me the best Chicana literature is about that. Malinche is part of that. The reason we have been so drawn to her figure over and over again is because how a woman can go from being Malintzin to *la Chingada* says everything. Right? Look at what Chingada means. She is our paradigm. How you change from being an Aztec princess to the fucked one and culpable for everything that ever happened to Mexican society tells you something about what Mexican culture is about in relation to women. Of course, everything is written out of an act of love. If I didn't give a damn about my culture and did not love it so much, I would have escaped it and done something else.

In your writings, you seem to be dialoguing with a variety of authors—Octavio Paz in El laberinto de la soledad, *Carlos Fuentes in* La muerte de Artemio Cruz *and more.*

I am dialoguing with many people. I dialogue with García Lorca because I write theater. As a gay man or a homosexual, his passion, his desire, his revolutionary vision, writing in a time as an act of resistance, I feel a lot of affinity with him and he also wrote extensively on women. Yet, he is not a woman, so there are places in his works that are twisted about women and yet, I am drawn to some of his revelations about women. I am connected with the Spanish and the Indian. You end up being in dialogue with everything.

I remember the first time I read the Egyptian writer Nawal El-Sadaawi I thought I would lose my mind because I thought she was a Mexican. In terms of sensibility, I felt there was something in this novel that made me start thinking about the broader connection. In the end we are all related. I just think that I do look a lot at what Arabic women write. I don't know if that is just an accident that I just start finding myself drawn to it, even southern Italian women writers or others.

Maybe you could talk more about that aspect. Who are your influences? Who do you read? For example, I have seen articles comparing you to John Rechy.

Also there have been many articles that have compared me and Richard Rodríguez which I understand. It is not because we both have the same political perspective. The truth of the matter is that I feel like what Richard writes about are the same things that preoccupy me. All that stuff—his complexion, his desire, church, education and more. Yet, his conclusions are totally confused, but his writing is beautiful, though, and he writes about the right subjects. I think he is one of the few Chicano male writers who is writing about the issues we need to hear. Unfortunately, his conclusions are off. In a sort of perverted way, I have always felt a kind of kinship with him.

The writers who have had an impact on me are Rosario Castellanos, García-Lorca and James Baldwin by virtue of the fact that he is colored and queer. Also, he wrote about it when I could not read anybody else who was colored and queer. He was also someone who was deeply committed politically and also deeply committed to the description of desire. He refused to compromise desire for politics. That was very rare when everybody else was telling me I had to do that.

In recent years I read works by Native American women. I love the works of Leslie Marmon Silko, especially *Ceremony*; she is a visionary, not being afraid to envision. In fact her visions come true. She is very important. As a poet, Jo Harjo. I have always read black women since the beginning. Recently as a playwright, I have read all of August Wilson's work. It really depends. You go through different periods of your life.

Would you like to discuss the impact of your mother's role on your writing?

I felt like *Loving in the War Years* was a love letter to my mother far more than anything else. There is a line about family—for better or for worse it is a place you learn to love.

I think that the specific role of my mother is important in terms of my writing in that she is the storyteller in the family. I learned more about storytelling than through reading. Unlike Gloria Anzaldúa who was one of those kids who hid under the covers hiding trying to read with the flashlights, I was a worker. I liked to work. I did things.

[JoAnn:] Someone asked me what was she like when she (Cherríe) was little. Was she very outgoing? I said no. She was very private. It was only when we pretended together that her imagination came about. Other than that, my mother and I told the stories to her. We were the storytellers. She was the storer of the stories who eventually ended up being the spokesperson of the stories.

[Cherríe:] I think part of it too was that my sister JoAnn and I are so close in age, about eighteen months apart, a companion constantly in childhood. She said to me in moments of great significance, "This is very important. Remember this. Five years from now let's talk about this." A record was being kept. We were conscious as children of significant facts that were happening. Memories were very important. My mother and my aunts were always passing stories down so that it became important to talk about what was happening around us.

Certainly there were all kinds of secrets and silences in the family, but passion was acceptable in a certain degree except when it became my own at sixteen. Desire for life. Between JoAnn and my mom everything was coming to me as the youngest. In *Shadow of a Man*, I identify a lot with the youngest child Lupe because she is also the emotional sponge of the family. JoAnn was much more *rebelde* than I was. I took everything in, particularly my mother's pain. When one does that, it cultivates a listener and a sense that other people have lives, a compassion for others. As a writer, you have to be a listener and have a compassion about other people's lives. As a child my mother cultivated that for me for better or for worse because there are many negative aspects about taking in this emotional strength too. It is also too much to burden a kid. Yet, if there is anything I drew on it would be my understanding; at seven years old I had all the complexity of an adult. It was a complex life because my mother was two generations older than me. At the age of seven I thought I understood her whole life. Life was not simple. Everything had multi-leveled layers to it. The world was something I had to unravel and come to terms with. It was not safe, necessarily but you had to be able to deal with it. So it was like drama, right? And I think more than anything that's how she affected my sense that I use now as a writer. Essentially anybody's life is worthy of literature.

When you talk about a writer's block, you said it is because you have a secret. Could you talk a little more about the connections you see between secrets and writing?

Well I think the danger about writing is that it anticipates you. If you are open and fluid enough with your work, the writing can sometimes leak information into you, like dreams. If you are plugging into the same unconscious place, you may not be able to live up to what you see. Yet, that is the kind of writing that is the best kind of writing, the place that touches our unconscious. As you are keeping the secret, you are going to work very hard to repress your unconscious. The writing will not be as good because the unconscious is much smarter than the ego, one level of writing. If a writer can tap into her unconscious, the writing is going to be much richer with other voices and memories. If a writer cannot tap into her unconscious, the writing is going to be flatter work.

Is there a connection between indigenismo *and the indigenous imagination and secrets?*

I don't know for sure. If we have Indian blood in us, it has been buried in the family. I could not tell you. As a Mexican, I am drawing from indigenous influences. In looking more closely at that *raíz* one begins to draw from those unconscious places, the *indigenismo* is the one where I end up going. That is part of the terrain of my unconscious for whatever reason—if it is racial memory, biological, DNA, I don't know. I have no control over this process. It is happening of its own accord. I do it with reservation too by virtue of the fact that I do not want to claim what is not mine. By the same token, what is there is there. Just let it come to you as opposed to pushing it.

Could you talk about how you started writing teatro *and what brought you to it?*

I started writing theater by accident when I finished **Loving in the War Years** which is essentially an autobiography, essays, and poems. When I finished it in 1983, I felt like I had finished my own story, not to say I would not write from my own perspective but in a certain way I thought a burden had been lifted from me. So I continued to write in my journals but suddenly it was not autobiography. It was other people talking to me and that is how **Giving Up the Ghost** came about which is a kind of transition because it is more *teatropoesía* with monologues and poetic voices. That is the transition from poet to playwright. Then I just fell in love with theater. I had been in New York at the time and I submitted **Giving Up the Ghost** to apply for María Irene Fornes' "Hispanic Playwriting Lab," in New York City, at Inter Theater. Once I started working with her, I was connected with others. I began to write dialogue for the first time in my life.

Had she been a big influence on you?

I would say just in that period. People credit her with having more influence on me than she does. There are a lot of Chicano playwrights who continued to work with her. She has a style of playwriting that deals more with character than plot development which is the same thing with me. She does really approach it as a poet. On that level, she had a strong influence on me in the sense that had I worked with a traditional playwright, I never would have written plays. But she let me approach it as a poet and encouraged that.

But the difference lies in the fact that María Irene is not as focused on language in her work as I am. As a poet, I feel that is the main thing for me. In theater, that element is not as important—to be able to write visual images in language

and yet, that is what I still aim to do in theater. For example, August Wilson does that, but it is not a priority for most playwrights. In that sense, I take a departure from her. And she really supported that in my own writing. Also, politically we had different perspectives.

The reason I continue to write theater is because I feel it is the one place that I can expose the *poesía* in the common tongue. Traditionally, people do not put those two things together. Yet, the way we grew up, basically anyone bilingual, people learned to speak English in a beautiful combination—the spoken Spanish with the written English. To me this is very poetic particularly when I grew up among *cuentistas*. The theater is then one way that allows me to contribute to that.

After that I only worked with her for a year and then she directed a play of mine **Shadow of a Man** in New York City in 1990.

I think it is interesting that you talk about the pleasures of writing as well as the frustrations. Could you expand on that and the problems of getting produced in Los Angeles? What does it mean to be a playwright in Los Angeles?

Well, UCLA was very interested in doing **Heroes and Saints**. It is ironic to me that Los Angeles, which has the biggest Mexicano/Chicano population outside of Mexico City, is the one place where it seems that it is the most difficult for me to get my plays produced. On a certain level the frustration is that I am barred (censored) from my own audience, the reason for that being that the caliber of Latino actors that I would like to work with are here in Los Angeles. Although there are also many good ones in San Francisco, most of them end up moving here to Los Angeles to work. Those are actors I would like to work with. It is a mutual feeling that I know many actors who would like to do my work. The places that they can afford to work, which pay them well enough, are places like "South Coast Repertory," "The Mark Taper Forum," "San Diego Repertory," all of which are mainstream houses. Although my plays receive readings and serious considerations, they have yet to be produced in L.A. The plays are of the size and of the caliber that to do them on a community level is fine for smaller towns. That is fine for me because I always want the work to get out, but the level of acting that I would like to have and the quality of production that I would like to have means that I have to work at those larger theaters. For the most part when they decide to do the work, they know two names, Culture Clash and Luis Valdez. If they know other names, they will pick other plays usually if they find them not threatening in any way. If you attempt to be a playwright who writes about themes that are more confrontational, a mainstream theater is very nervous about taking a risk with their largely Anglo-dominated audiences because they feel it could be a financial failure. So people like Valdez are shoe-ins because his name will bring an initial audience to them regardless of the quality of the work. That has not changed. There are other fine playwrights in my situation who are encountering those same obstacles. I find that my hands are tied. I find it very lucky that I work with a resident theater company, BRAVA for women in the arts. With them I can cultivate the work and receive high quality openings so I could see the work to fruition. But after that . . . But the politics of it are very frustrating.

I think it would be frustrating as you are writing.

Well, I think I am lucky in the sense that I have a place to produce my work. That is a big deal since most playwrights do not even have that. I feel very fortunate that I have a home base company that will support my work. Other places like "Berkeley Repertory" have commissioned me. So things are beginning to loosen up. But if I did not have a company where the work would be produced, then I think it is hard to envision the work. The material conditions affect what you are capable of envisioning. The fact that I feel safe to envision because I have a chance of acquiring a good production through BRAVA has helped the work continue to develop. Otherwise why do it if your work is going to stay on the page.

What kind of political work do you think teatro *does versus say poetry or short stories? Do you think it has different political possibilities?*

Well, there are but it is problematic because technically it is a great form because you do not have to be literate to go to the theater. It can reach bodies of people that it would not normally reach, but unfortunately the way most theater is set up now the audiences tend to be exclusive. The good thing now about the *teatro* BRAVA where I work is that it always spends an equal amount of time, money and energy trying to cultivate the audiences. If it is a Latino play, they cultivate Latino audiences. An Asian-American play cultivates that respective audience. On one level, theater is very exclusive. The play runs for five weeks and nobody sees it. On another it has the possibility of being more accessible than anything on the printed page. My family is a good example. My parents' generation never read any of my work, but when I started writing plays all of them wanted to come and be there because it is something that is available to them.

What inspired you to write your first play **Giving Up the Ghost** *after the poetry and essay form in* **Loving in the War Years***?*

The Corky character [the main protagonist] came to me. I did not do anything. I was really excited about her because she was not me. She was someone else that I admired. As I said at UCLA, much of it is related to my own biography in the sense that I had been involved with a woman who was ostensibly heterosexual. That was the first time it had ever happened to me and I could not understand heterosexual desire. Yet, somehow by touching this person I knew it was true. I had to understand that. As a lesbian writer, I felt as if I was not going to be able to go any further as a Chicana lesbian writer. I was not going to be able to reach other Chicanas if I could not understand heterosexual Chicanas. If I could not write for heterosexual Chicanas, I was going to be a very limited writer. I had to understand all female desire, not just lesbian desire. In fact I started to understand that lesbian desire is so influenced by heterosexual desire that I also needed that heterosexual understanding in order to understand my own lesbianism. In writing the character of Amalia, I became conscious of the fact that I needed to write this so I could understand all women. After that, the experience did help me because the transition to **Shadow of a Man** became easy. I could write about the mother, the aunt and everyone else. Whereas when I started writing in the first ten years, my lesbianism was so embattled, having to write and speak its name was so embattled that there was no room for anything else. When I finished **Loving in the War Years,** there became room. Then the voice broadened. It is interesting that you can be accused that you are betraying lesbianism because you write about heterosexual concerns without realizing that I should be able to write about a white heterosexual man. My job is to write it all well and to expand what I am capable of doing so that when I write the Chicana lesbian experience, it is informed.

In **Giving Up the Ghost** *one of the last lines is "making familia from scratch." What does that mean to you?*

When the character says it, it means that you cannot make peace with your biological family when your queerness makes it impossible for you to fit. As a Chicana lesbian, the character Marisa has a love for family that is so profound because she was Corky as a child. Her love of family, her loyalty to her sister, her mother, her race and everything betray her. She is betrayed by her mother, her cousin, her first lover, the man who rapes her and more. She is betrayed by all these so-called family members who betray her love. As an adult Marisa says, "OK. I am not giving up family. I need family. But if I have to make family from scratch, that is what I will do." What that means is that she will create her own queer family. That is why Amalia plays the mother role too because Marisa is young enough that she is still looking for her mother in her lovers which I think is typical. In that last monologue she says, "If I have to, I will." But if you notice the last gesture of the play where she is making love to herself, she says, "If I put my fingers to my own forgotten places," it means where you begin to make family from scratch is the love of yourself and then you begin to reconstruct.

I was also very moved by the reading you did of a selection in **The Last Generation***, your latest book, at UCLA. You implied that the Chicano culture is disappearing. Could you expand on this issue?*

Well I am talking about my own family that is not necessarily representative of all Chicanos. There are plenty of Chicanos who are cultivating themselves fine. Witnessing that loss in my own family was very personal. However, I know that I am not alone. Many Chicanos are experiencing that phenomenon. What keeps the culture cultivated is contact with new generations of mexicanos coming into the country. But if you don't have that what keeps it cultivated is a political movement that affirms the culture. That is the reason my niece who is quarter-breed is now taking Chicano studies classes. There is no reason for her to do that. She can get along perfectly well in life without ever recognizing the quarter Mexican she is. It is just that somewhere along the course of history, she might perceive something valuable in that culture. Why does my nephew wish suddenly that he were darker? It is very confusing since society works hard to get everyone "whitified." What was once denigrated is suddenly given value which makes you attracted to it. The way you make it attractive is by having available to young people the culture—literature and the arts.

That is why the arts are so important. My frustrations about most Chicano Studies Programs are that they only cultivate the social sciences. Nobody is encouraging artists, writers and dreamers. Nobody is cultivating dreamers. What exactly is the new generation supposed to be drawn to? Are they supposed to be drawn to being social workers and sociologists? Every single one of them? What people are drawn to is what moves them! What they remember is a song! What they remember is a painting! What they remember is some crazy poet one day!

That is the reason the sixties and the seventies were such an active time too. It is not just because there was a political movement happening, but there was a cultural movement to enhance that political movement. It is very important. I feel that when the activism may not be there the reason they keep the arts alive until the activism kicks in again.

Is that what you mean by cultural nationalism—the arts and literature?

No, I am talking about a land-based movement in organizing our communities.

When you say that you had to come out of the closet as a cultural nationalist, is that because so much Chicana feminism has defined itself as critiquing nationalism?

Yeah, and I do too. I'm a bit tongue and cheek. I like to mess that way because people take it all so seriously. The cultural nationals expect that myself as a lesbian feminist would not have strong feelings about Aztlán, connections about a land-based movement, indigenous rights or sovereignty. They assume that, as a lesbian feminist, I am excluded from those kinds of concerns. Chicana feminists question how I could be attracted to that race politics.

How do you reconcile your different views in the essay entitled "*Queer Aztlán*" *of* **The Last Generation***?*

It is supposed to be a breeding ground for ideas and to agitate. There is one person who likes a little bit of this or a little bit of that. Why can't we have it all? Even though on a pragmatic level, this may be very difficult to realize. Yet, I wanted to put between the pages of one essay a whole range of issues of which I believe in which most people may find contradictory. For example, I may share a politics with José Montoya, but then does he share my lesbian feminism? No he does not. Still that is something that he should know that I share with him. What does it mean that a lesbian feminist shares that politics? It is asking, "Hey, come along with this part." The same experience occurs with the lesbian feminists. They think I must think X, Y, Z, but then I say that I thought Aztlán had some really good ideas. I don't want to lose both aspects. I think there is something really important about the unabashed radicalism of that nationalist period—uncompromising, because I always feel that one ends up compromising. There is something about being that cutting edge.

Also there is an indigenous internationalist movement happening at this moment in which Chicanos can have a place in that if they are willing to carry that responsibility.

Is an international movement one of the things that gives you the most hope?

Yes, it is. I feel that it is also an alternative way of living from the most simple level to the most global. That gives me hope. Changes can actually happen on an immediate basis on how people construct their own communities from the local to the global. When I look around that does inspire me.

In that movement, who are you thinking of?

All of the material from **The Last Generation** was written during the Quincentennial. There were many international indigenous tribunals that were happening at the time. I know of individuals—Native women in Canada, in the United

States and Latin America who are building coalitions with each other. They are also creating self-sustaining cottage industries, for example, in Texas, indigenous women are working for water and land rights in a legal context from the national to the local level. Much of the work is geared by and for women. To me these are very inspiring examples to everyone.

Of course there is always that big rip-off that happens to Native culture which to me is only a reflection of the kind of power it has, the fact that people want to steal it.

Have you read the testimonio *by Rigoberta Menchú? What impact did it have on you?*

Yeah, that book changed my life just by virtue of the fact that you had a testimony like that on a very concrete, very real-life level that really made explicit the complicity the United States had in the particular conditions of people who are ostensibly related to you. The element that really drew me was that I always taught it at U.C. Berkeley. Every semester, this book turned the students into radicals overnight. I had a student whose parents were *Somocistaso* but then he was turned around by this book. You cannot ignore it. It is impossible to conceive of anyone suffering to that extent and to know what a cushy life one has. There is no way to read that and not feel that you are somehow complicit in that woman's suffering or her family's suffering. But that little seed of realization never leaves you in a very important way. It is wonderful to teach it.

Marie-Elise Wheatwind (review date January 1994)

SOURCE: "All in the Familia," in *Women's Review of Books,* Vol. XI, No. 4, January 1994, p. 22.

[*In the following review, Wheatwind praises Moraga's commitment to Chicano culture and feminist ideals as reflected in* The Last Generation.]

The Last Generation, a comprehensive new collection of prose and poetry by Cherríe Moraga, embraces a myriad forms and audiences. It includes personal narratives, insightful dreams, poetic forays into the author's past, political visions of her community's future, and prose transliterations of talks and presentations given at various conferences and symposia.

Just as the themes interweave like common threads in the five different sections of the book—**"New Mexican Confession," "War Cry," "La Fuerza Feminina," "The Breakdown of the Bicultural Mind"** and **"The Last Generation"**—each

section contains a mix of the writing styles that intimate the personal (poetry, letters and personal narrative) and demand the political (essays which call us to change ourselves and our world). Those familiar with Moraga's earlier books will recognize the dissolution of the boundaries between creative and academic writing. *The Last Generation* further dissolves these boundaries by "talking breed talk" to a culture whose "Third and Fourth and First Worlds are collapsing into one another."

This book, Moraga explains in the introduction, emerges from the ashes of "disregard, censure, and erasure." She writes "out of a sense of urgency that Chicanos are a disappearing tribe, out of a sense of this disappearance in my own familia." A "mixed-blood," a mestiza of Anglo and Mexican American heritage, she has written previously about the contradictions of being a light-skinned Chicana activist in the dominant culture of "Amerika." She now mourns the fact that the younger generation of her family and community have been taught not to be Mexicans, but Americans. Moraga's refusal to accept this prompts her to write "as I always have, but," she adds, "now I write for a much larger familia." Her "familia" encompasses not only Chicanos but the ancient Aztecs and Mayans, as well as the broad range of Latinos in our country who are refugees, immigrants and first-generation citizens.

In the essay **"The Breakdown of the Bicultural Mind,"** Moraga writes that she knows that her "breedblood . . . is the catalyst" of her activism and art, but she also recognizes the cause of her mixed heritage "within the larger framework of a white supremacist society" and proclaims her fierce, undivided loyalty to "the products of rape and the creators of a new breed":

> I am not that rare breed of mixed-blood person, a Jean Toomer, who writes, as Alice Walker said of *Cane,* "to memorialize a culture he thought was dying." I am that raging breed of mixed-blood person who writes to defend a culture that I know is being killed. I am of that endangered culture and of that murderous race, but I am loyal only to one. My mother culture, my mother land, my mother tongue . . . (p.129)

But what exactly is the "mother tongue" of a Chicana who has grown up hearing Spanish while being taught to speak (read, write, learn) only in English? Moraga resolves this literary oppression as many Chicana/os writing today have, by including words and phrases in Spanish throughout her book to emphasize not only where she's coming from but who she's speaking to.

Throughout *The Last Generation* Moraga examines the colonization, patriarchal authority and homophobia that stifle the world we inhabit, and makes direct comparisons between these forms of oppression and the ecological destruction of the planet. She offers her world view as an admonition—and incitement to collective activism—entreating "a resurrection of the ancient in order to construct the modern":

> We are speaking of bottom-line considerations. I can't understand when in 1992 with 100 acres of rainforest disappearing every minute, with global warming, with babies being born without brains in South Tejas, with street kids in Río sniffing glue to stifle their hunger, with Mohawk women's breast milk being contaminated by the poisoned waters of the Great Lakes Basin, how we as people of color, as people of Indian blood, as people with the same last names as our Latin American counterparts, are not alarmed by the destruction of Indigenous and mestizo peoples. How is it Chicanos cannot see ourselves as victims of the same destruction, already in its advanced stages? Why do we not collectively experience the urgency for alternatives based not on what our oppressors advise, but on the advice of elders and ancestors who may now speak to us only in dreams? (pp. 170-171)

Obviously, these are not questions for which there are easy answers. What Moraga points to, again and again, is the potential power of women, "la fuerza feminina," and to our special relationship as women to the earth: "Whether myth, metaphor, or memory, she is called 'Mother' by all peoples of all times." If women remain the chief caretakers, nurturers and providers for our children and our elders, and as we make up half of the (underpaid) agricultural and urban workforce, clearly the solution lies in having control over the lands on which we live and depend. Moraga feels it is especially incumbent upon women, as inhabitants and female relatives of mother earth, to act responsibly toward the earth and each other, to protect and defend that which is being defiled and destroyed.

> Land remains the common ground for all radical action. But land is more than the rocks and trees, the animal and plant life that make up the territory of Aztlán or Navajo Nation or Maya Mesoamerica. For immigrant and native alike, land is also the factories where we work, the water our children drink, and the housing project where we live. For women, lesbians, and gay men, land is that physical mass called our bodies. (p. 173)

Ultimately, it is the physical and emotional landscape of the body—Moraga's body and those whom she loves or struggles to reconcile with—that is the focus of *The Last Generation*. Sometimes Moraga politicizes the body, as in

"**The War Continues,**" a poem of startling simplicity that speaks as much for those persecuted and abused in this country as it does for anybody on earth who has experienced the violence of racism, apartheid and "ethnic cleansing." The poem conveys, with a minimum of words and lines, the vulnerability of humans:

> Flesh is full
> of holes.
>
> It is made
> to breathe
> secrete
> receive.
>
> It is nothing
> against
> bombs
> and
> bullets.
>
> It is not meant
> to be a barrier
> against
> anything. (p. 46)

Moraga insists in a final stanza that she "will resist you flee / you who believe / you are not made / of the same / skin / and / bones," but we are made painfully aware that the war continues for others who, despite resistance, are defeated.

Other poems and essays evoke bodily intimacy, giving us glimpses of love between women that are complicated by the boundaries and restrictions of our society and our slowly evolving roles as sisters, daughters and lovers. Sometimes these glimpses are poignant images of past relationships tinged with a sense of loss, as in "**La Despedida.**"

> In Indian tongue, the word for lonely
> is not knowing who you are.
> You no longer call my name
> and I am no longer
> you whom you sought to know. (p.50)

Moraga makes real for us the myriad dimensions of lesbian relationships. This means exploring the emotional dimensions of sexual attraction, as she does in the short, humorous prose piece "**Indian Summer,**" which sasses the seriousness of commitment:

> "You can't stay here." That's the first thing out of her mouth as she puts one muddy paw inside the front door. I like living like this, always on the edge of her throwing me out.

"Why now?"

"Cuz I'm getting too attached, that's why."

(p. 108)

The problem of commitment in relationships and the urgency of committing ourselves to changing the world are inspiring and continuing themes in Moraga's work, and no less so in her newest book. I was hoping, however, that she would also reflect more here on her vital work as a teacher, both in the academies of America and in the theatres where her plays have been produced. Perhaps Moraga is too modest to believe writing about herself on the front lines is as important as mobilizing "a global community." This is suggested by her demoting the fact that she is one of only a few Chicana playwrights whose work has been produced to a brief footnote in one essay. Her work at the University of California, Berkeley, and with Latino immigrants in a community program, mentioned briefly in another essay, focuses on the travails of her students, not on the trials and triumphs of her own work as an instructor. I think there are many of us who would benefit from Moraga's musings on her struggles and successes as a teacher.

As a Chicana writer and educator whose schooling was completely devoid of Chicano poetry, fiction, or drama, I want to believe that I am of "the last generation" to have experienced that void. Cherríe Moraga was one of the first to fill that emptiness by helping to establish a canon of Chicana literature, and the prose and poetry of her newest book show she intends to keep those political and intellectual fires burning bright for us all.

Jan Clausen (review date 9 May 1994)

SOURCE: "The Axis of Herstory," in *The Nation,* Vol. 258, No. 18, May 9, 1994, pp. 634-37.

[*In the following review, Clausen finds* The Last Generation *prophetic of racial, class, and gender clashes to come in the twenty-first century.*]

In *The Last Generation: Prose and Poetry,* Cherríe Moraga records this wrenching break from a Chicana perspective:

I write this on the one-week anniversary of the death of the Nicaraguan Revolution.

We are told not to think of it as a death, but I am in mourning. . . . There is a protest. We, my camarada and I, get off the subway. I can already hear the voices chanting from a distance. We can't make out what they're saying, but they are Latinos and my heart races, seeing so many brown faces. . . . as I come closer to the circle of my people, I am stunned. "¡Viva la paz en Nicaragua!" it states. "¡Viva George Bush!" "¡Viva UNO!" And my heart drops. Across the street, the "resistance" has congregated—less organized, white, young, middle-class students. *¿Dónde 'stá mi pueblo?*

The irony is characteristic; Moraga has always had an unflinching instinct for the significant contradiction. One thinks of a key passage in her classic 1983 essay **"A Long Line of Vendidas"**:

Oppression. Let's be clear about this.
Oppression does not make for hearts as big as all outdoors. Oppression makes us big and small. Expressive and silenced. Deep and Dead.

Like that piece, *The Last Generation* is much concerned with an accurate reckoning of damage—but one always in the service of hope. "*And our liberation won't happen by some man leading the way and parting the Red Sea for us. We are the Red Sea, we women,*" Moraga concludes. Her femaleness is insistently inflected by culture, class, sexuality and the imperatives of a stubborn home-grown anti-colonialism: "I am the result of the dissolution of blood lines and the theft of language; and yet, I am a testimony to the failure of the United States to totally anglicize its mestizo citizens." Looking south, she sees herself in an inescapably *international* feminist context—but the "discussion" she seeks is primarily one among *indígenas* and Latinas.

Her "insistent cultural nationalism," as she calls it, differs in interesting ways from her work of a decade ago, when she emerged as an eloquent voice in the U.S. feminist/lesbian of color movement. Her anthology *This Bridge Called My Back: Writings by Radical Women of Color,* co-edited with Gloria Anzaldúa, is a feminist classic whose relevance has only increased in the dozen years since its initial publication. Both it and her previous mixed-genre collection, *Loving in the War Years,* emphasized a coalitional politics and awareness. Now she charts her return to Aztlán, the Chicano "imagined community" that she proposes to reinvent from a feminist, lesbian perspective—a project clearly made possible by the recent broadening of Chicano and Latino cultural politics from the patriarchal and heterosexist sixties ideology that she critically reviews in her essay **"Queer Aztlán: The Re-formation of Chicano Tribe."**

All the while, she's lost none of her hallmark sensitivity to historical complications that mock a simple nationalist quest for purity. She writes searchingly of her own mixed background: "My white family was kept distant from me, not because of its conquests, but because of its failures." Repeatedly if obliquely she laments the wound of failed coalitions and dissolved relationships:

> I had a Black family once and what happened to that? Like my Mexican childhood, my Puerto Rican dreams, my white forgetfulness. What happened to all those women I laid and made history with?

Among the many boundaries she refuses are those among conventionally construed literary genres. She's a poet whose surreal imagination is at its most convincing in some of the "prose" passages: for instance, the unnerving dream image of half-human, half-animal "calf-children," "goat-people," in whom she recognizes herself, "the hope of the future, these mixed beings." **"La Ofrenda,"** a favorite, is a short story/prose poem about two Chicanas who "weren't meant to be lovers, only sisters. But being a sister ain't no part-time occupation." It ends with a line in which cadence and imagery work flawlessly together ("I, who have only given my breast to the women"); the preceding dialogue between teenage lesbians is sad and harsh and hilarious:

> "Fuck fuck chinga'o, man, fuck!"

> "Tina . . ." I can barely hear myself.

> "Tiny. The name's Tiny."

> "What're you doin' in there?"

> "I'm crying, you faggot. That's what you want, isn't it? To see the big bad bitch cry? Well, go get your rocks off somewhere else."

> "I don't have rocks."

> "In your head!"

Moraga's romanticism can occasionally be cloying, her language obvious and labored. ("Mirrored in her huge deer eyes / I have neither vagina / nor pigment politicized.") More often, her risks and rawness pay off, form and content blending in "enough poetic and visionary suggestions to make the case for liberation as a *process* and not as a goal," to borrow Edward Said's recent praise of Frantz Fanon. In the strength of her longing, the outlines of the not-yet-visible begin to form: "I am not the church-goer that my mother is, but the same faithfulness drives me to write: the search for [the Aztec female deity] Coyolxauhqui amid all the disfigured female characters and the broken men that surround them in my plays and poems."

Indeed, she's no churchgoer; it's a compliment to say that this is a *very* queer book. From its insouciant gender-bending to a bilingualism that may present a mild obstacle to English-only readers (get used to it, it's the wave of the future), and from its images of dykes who fuck—or want to be—boys to its naming of the "mongrel" status of biracial and binational identity, this book is all about not fitting into *any* accepted categories. One wonders how the seemingly sedate Nicaraguan opponents of Article 204 will respond—for in the context of a shared Latino "identity that dissolves borders," as Moraga puts it, clearly the echoes of this *rebeldía* will reverberate in Managua.

As for the reverse effect, she notes that within the decade "our whole concept of 'America' will be dramatically altered; most significantly by a growing Latino population whose strong cultural ties, economic disenfranchisement, racial visibility, and geographical proximity to Latin America [discourage] any facile assimilation." [*The Last Generation* charts] a world in which the axis of herstory starts in São Paulo, goes over to Lima, then up to Managua, San Cristóbal and East Los. The reassuringly fixed evil of the color line has become a labyrinth. The twenty-first century, already under way, will have as its central problem the race/class/gender grid.

Catherine Wiley (review date October 1995)

SOURCE: Review of *Shadow of a Man*, in *Theatre Journal*, Vol. 47, No. 3, October 1995, pp. 412-14.

[*In the following review, Wiley finds Denver's Su Teatro production of* Shadow of a Man *"triumphant" for women, particularly Latinas.*]

Denver, capital of the only state to pass legislation forbidding the inclusion of sexual orientation in official anti-discrimination language, seems an unlikely place to stage a play by lesbian writer Cherríe Moraga, but theatre about AIDS, coming out stories, and plays written by openly gay authors have never been so popular here.

Denver's El Centro Su Teatro, one of the oldest amateur bilingual *teatro Chicanos* in the United States, is Poor Theater at its best. In a partially remodelled school flanked by a Purina Dog Chow factory and Interstate 70 located in one of Denver's oldest and poorest barrios, Su Teatro has served its community for over twenty years.

Moraga's play [*Shadow of a Man*] is in many ways a radical revision of Arthur Miller's *Death of a Salesman* with the sexual tension of Miller's subtext placed in the foreground. Moraga's Willy Loman is Manuel, an alcoholic on the verge of losing his job as he watches his familial authority disintegrate. The disintegration is catalyzed by the emergence into the present of sexual secrets, shadows, from his past. The repository of these secrets is his youngest daughter, Lupe. As a twelve-year-old girl on the eve of her confirmation, Lupe discovers that she "wants to be in the skin" of her friend Frances Pacheco. Having asked the question at the play's opening of why the Church makes having secrets a sin, she decides that her sexual feelings are not a sin because they are part of her. Manuel's self-destruction as *his* secret becomes known is thus echoed optimistically by his daughter, who may, the play implies, someday affirm her secret without any shadows.

Sexual revolt motivates every member of this family. The eldest son flees home by marrying an Anglo. The eldest daughter gives away her virginity in an effort to subvert traditional expectations of nice Chicana girls. Lupe's biological father, Conrado, is discovered to be the man her mother, Hortensia, truly loves but could not marry. Manuel loved his *compadre* Conrado so much that he gave him his wife for one night. The prohibition against homosexuality demands that Manuel use his wife as a stand-in for himself, but he despises her for frustrating his desire.

Like Willy Loman, Manuel is the weak center around which his family orbits, but Hortensia refuses to let him defeat her and the play's focus on the interaction of Hortensia, her sister, and her two teenage daughters makes *Shadow of a Man* a woman's play. Lupe is often paired with her aunt Rosario, a woman who has defied convention by divorcing and choosing to live alone. Lupe too may escape the confines of traditional Mexican American expectations for women.

For Lupe, the most devastating aspect of these expectations is her primary role as caretaker for her father, a role which may extend to an incestuous relationship with him. As the offspring of Manuel's inexpressible love for Conrado, Lupe is the child/woman from whom Manuel seeks comfort at night. When he approaches the stage area representing Lupe's bedroom, backlighting throws his menacing distorted shadow over her.

Like *Salesman*, *Shadow* paints the American dream as a sexual fantasy of unrequited love and both Willy and Manuel see in their love objects (Biff and Conrado), the embodiment of what the American male should be. But their sexual transgressions—Willy's affair(s) on the road and Manuel's exploitation of his wife and daughter—point to the disease behind the dream. Conventionally successful or not, a life constructed on lies is only a shadow.

While both *Salesman* and *Shadow* end with the father's funerals, Hortensia does not echo Linda's "We're free," but she admits that a husband "stays a stranger in his own home." With no men left in the house, it is finally free of strangers and their shadows. Manuel is not mourned: Hortensia even tells Lupe to cover her mirror so that Manuel's spirit will not return to carry the family away. Two generations of women have survived men's violence and Lupe's desire to be with women leaves the audience with hope for her future.

While in the script, Lupe's budding attraction to women is no less subtle than the hints that her relationship with Manuel is incestuous, this production mutes Lupe's sexuality and gravitates around Hortensia and Rosario: Hortensia's weakness contrasting Rosario's fortitude. Debra Gallegos and Yolanda Ortega-Erikson who have performed together for years, are outstanding as the two sisters. Rudy Bustos who says that he was inspired to direct the play by taking a women's studies class, describes *Shadow* as "a micro-view of a Latino family" which offers "a starting point for discussion about where and what Latinos are today." *Shadow of a Man* is much more than this, and like the playwright, Su Teatro's rich production leaves the women triumphant in their survival.

David J. DeRose (essay date October 1996)

SOURCE: "Cherríe Moraga: Mapping Aztlan," in *American Theatre,* Vol. 13, No. 8, October 1996, pp. 76-78.

[*In the following essay, DeRose discusses Moraga's involvement with the Brava Theater Center in San Francisco's Mission District.*]

Cherríe Moraga and I are sitting at the kitchen table in her San Francisco home, swapping stories about growing up in California. It is a badge we both wear proudly, and it has deep spiritual meaning for both of us—particularly for Moraga, who senses in the California landscape racial memories of *Aztlan*, the ancient North American homeland of the Chicano. She tells me a story about driving through the Southern California desert near San Diego.

"I'm driving along in this van listening to music. Looking at the desert landscape. I start thinking a lot about Aztlan: that this land was originally Mexico, and before that, Mexican Indian territory. And I know this land has memory, and that this whole Anglo experiment is very recent. It's obvious the terrain is Mexican. It's a deep, deep feeling." Suddenly, Moraga's van rounds a bend and she finds herself staring at a sunlit mountainside upon which someone has painted giant letters spelling out AZTLAN. "For a moment I don't know if it is an apparition or what. I stop and look at it. Somebody has written these letters—somebody else has had my same experience. And you start believing in collective unconscious, and racial memory, and the importance of being indigenous to this land."

The land and its spirit

That sense of heritage, one's spiritual link to the land, is a common theme of Moraga's three best-known plays: *Heroes and Saints* (1992), *Circle in the Dirt* (1995) and, most recently, *Watsonville: Some Place Not Here,* which opened in June as the inaugural production of San Francisco's new Brava Theater Center. Through interviews, videotaped oral histories and research into current events, Moraga has been creating a cultural and political map of the California landscape—particularly Chicano territory—resulting in a series of plays set in real California working-class communities.

Heroes and Saints takes place in "McLaughlin," Moraga's pseudonym for McFarland, a small San Joaquin Valley town in which abuse of the once-fertile land—in the form of pesticide-drenched crops, farmland and water—has led to a generation of cancer-bearing farm workers and deformed offspring. Moraga embodies the poisoned fruit of this landscape in the startling character of Cerezita, a young woman born without a body—she subsists as only a head, which her family has kept hidden from the world—who has a powerfully empathetic relationship to the land and its spirit. Like the land, Cerezita's Chicano farm worker family and neighbors are seen not in terms of their natural beauty and bounty, but as exploitable, even disposable resources. The outcome of this treatment, in Cerezita's visionary language, is a martyred landscape: "a thousand minicrucifixions," with the trunk of each grape vine, staked to its wooden cross, "a little gnarled body of Christ writhing in agony . . . intertwined with the other little crucified Christs next to it."

The land's commercial value is again weighed against its natural bounty in *Circle in the Dirt,* a collection of oral histories examining life in East Palo Alto, a tiny, impoverished community in the heart of Northern California's wealthy Silicon Valley. *Circle* was commissioned as a community arts project by Stanford University and the East Palo Alto Task Force to chronicle the life of a neighborhood about to be invaded by a major real estate development. East Palo Alto was dubbed "murder capital of the U.S." in 1992 and has subsequently been treated by politicians and developers as an ongoing crime scene worthy of being plowed under or covered in shopping malls and waterfront condos. But in Moraga's play, East Palo Alto's diverse immigrant population sees, behind the social and commercial turmoil, the area's natural fertility: "They all talk about gardens, or the breeze, the late afternoon, what grows well in that soil," Moraga notes.

Many of her characters see the fate of the Chicano people as intrinsically tied to the fate of *la tierra*, the land. Nowhere is this more evident than in *Watsonville,* in which the land (rather than serving as a passive object of exploitation or symbol of oppression) becomes an agent in the play's dramatic action. When the circumstances of a cannery workers' strike in the small shoreline town that gives the play its name go from bad to worse, the women strikers rally around a miraculous apparition: the image of Our Lady of Guadalupe—linked in Mexican folklore to Tonantzin, the Aztec goddess of the earth and fertility—which appears in the weathered trunk of an ancient California oak. Later, "la tierra" itself speaks when a major earthquake destroys the town, killing thousands but sparing the cannery workers who have gathered near the tree to pray for guidance and assistance.

Pray and the earth responds

While it might seem easy to dismiss this sequence of events as religious sanctimony or a contrived "deus ex machina" (as some reviewers did), the events of the play are neither right-wing bible-thumping nor overly convenient dramaturgy. Instead, Moraga turns these seeming miracles (both based on actual events of the late 1980s) into a litmus test of race and class discrimination by daring her audience to accept and validate the belief in ancient Indian animism— what Moraga calls the "indigenism"—of her uneducated, unsophisticated Chicana cannery-workers. For Moraga's characters, "If you pray long and hard enough, then the earth responds. There is a spirit there."

The spiritual relationship of Moraga's characters to the earth is constantly complicated by their relationship to another terrain: the social environment of contemporary California. As a Chicana theatre artist, a feminist, a lesbian and the product of a devout upbringing in what she calls "the Mexican Catholic Church," Moraga sees her plays as a kind of ongoing conversation—"even," she jokes, "if it is a one-way conversation"—a dialogue between herself and the various communities or institutions with which her heritage, her lifestyle and her work as a writer place her in contact or opposition.

But Moraga's plays take place within an even more diverse social and domestic landscape—they are peopled predominantly by women (in contrast to the early *actos* of Luis Valdez in the 1960s, where women were merely supporting cast) and so empower a wider and more representative cross-section of voices within the Chicano community. In *Watsonville,* a street-tough single mother must learn to understand a co-worker's lesbianism; a pious old woman must come to terms with a young priest who has abandoned the church; that young ex-priest must, in turn, put aside his cynicism and accept the old woman's embrace of a miraculous apparition in a tree. One of Moraga's gifts is her ability to pair up characters of opposing views and let us hear their voices, their perspectives, in an open dialogue that favors neither.

The audiences attending *Watsonville* demonstrate how Moraga's dialogue spills off the stage and into the community. On any given night one might see a lesbian couple sitting next to an old Chicano husband and wife, who are in turn sitting next to members of the affluent white "arts crowd," sitting next to some tough young barrio *cholos.* Considering these audience dynamics, it seems fitting that Moraga's *Watsonville* should be the inaugural production of Brava's newly acquired Theater Center (housed in a former vaudeville theatre) in the heart of San Francisco's famous barrio, the Mission District.

A women's arts organization under the artistic directorship of Ellen Gavin, Brava has been carving out a space for itself in the Mission since 1986 with arts workshops, full-scale theatre productions, and youth and community activities. Moraga, a playwright-in-residence at Brava (through the National Theatre Artist Residency Program, jointly developed by the Pew Charitable Trusts and TCG, with major funding from the Trusts), wants to "build within the barrio," not import or gentrify from without. She hopes the new theatre center will "bring good art to and develop good art out of the barrio and its inhabitants"—and echo with seldom-heard voices from the landscape of Aztlan in the '90s.

Julia de Foor Jay (essay date 1996)

SOURCE: "(Re)Claiming the Race of the Mother: Cherríe Moraga's *Shadow of a Man, Giving Up the Ghost,* and *Heroes and Saints,*" in *Women of Color: Mother-Daughter Relationships in Twentieth-Century Literature,* edited by Elizabeth Brown-Guillory, 1996, pp. 95-116.

[*In the following essay, de Foor Jay examines mother-daughter relationships in* Shadow of a Man, Giving Up the Ghost, *and* Heroes and Saints.]

Cherríe Moraga's courageous voice first emerged in the 1980s and has since become a significant one for Chicana, feminist, and lesbian studies. It has been heard in several genres: poems, fiction, essays, and plays,[1] sounding the theme of betrayal, informed by various myths and legends in the Chicano/Chicana culture. She focuses, in particular, on the myth of La Malinche. In the pattern of Malinche, a woman who does not conform to prescribed roles is labeled La Vendida, the "sell-out," or La Chingada, the "traitor" (also slang for "the violated one"). Moraga attacks this encoding, arguing that women have been socialized by male-cen-

tered, heterosexual-centered ideologies into "selling out" or betraying their own daughters, apprenticing them for submission and servitude. In her plays *Shadow of a Man, Giving Up the Ghost,* and *Heroes and Saints,* Moraga explores this process of socialization and its effects on mothers and daughters in the Chicano/Chicana community, finally rendering a vision of revolution, led by courageous *vendidas,* as the only recourse to (re)claim the race.

Moraga begins her exploration of the Chicano mother-daughter relationship by focusing on *la familia,* a locus of multiple oppressions, "wounds," that relate to a larger sociopolitical context. She states, "My identity as a Chicana, a lesbiana, a mujer always had to do with the relationship between my deeply personal side and the whole political construct. I had to look at my family, at the contradictions and the mixed messages . . . the good stuff and the negative stuff" (quoted in Lovato, 23). Having been born and reared in a family with an Anglo father and a Chicana mother, Moraga had been encouraged to emphasize her "whiteness." In **"La Güera"** she writes, "It was through my mother's desire to protect her children from poverty and illiteracy that we became 'anglocized'; the more effectively we could pass in the white world, the better guaranteed our future" (*Loving in the War Years,* 50). Passing also meant appropriating the language of the dominant culture; therefore, Moraga spoke English, filtering out her mother's fluent Spanish.

Not only had Moraga attempted to pass as an Anglo, but she also had attempted to pass as a heterosexual, these two disguises becoming equally oppressive. This oppression was not lifted until Moraga heard Ntozake Shange read her poetry and experienced a profound "revelation," in which she realized that she had denied "the brown in me," that she had denied the language that spoke to the "emotions in my poems," and that she had denied "the voice of my own brown mother" (*Loving in the War Years,* 55). At this point she began her quest for a more authentic self and a more authentic poetic voice. In **"A Long Line of Vendidas,"** she asserts, "To be a woman fully necessitated my claiming the race of my mother" (*Loving in the War Years,* 94).

Claiming the race of the mother meant claiming its myths and legends and acknowledging the codes and signs of the dominant ideology, its institutions and institutional practices. According to Nancy Saporta Sternbach, Moraga "draws upon, conjures, reinvents, and reinterprets Mexican myth and pre-Hispanic heritage" (52). In particular, Moraga draws upon the myth of La Malinche.[2] However, while most writers concentrate on Malinche herself, Moraga focuses on Malinche's mother—the mother who sacrificed herself for men and the mother who betrayed the daughter by colluding with the dominant ideology. In one version of the myth, Malinche's mother wanted her son by a second marriage to inherit the estate so she sold her daughter into slavery (Mirandé and Enríquez, 24-25). Moraga explores this legacy of betrayal in her works—not just betrayal by the mother but betrayal by any woman of another. In an interview with Mirtha N. Quintanales, she discusses this theme and links it with her search for the meaning of love: "And for me, the conditions [for love] have always had something to do with the issue of separation—leaving and the consequences of leaving" (12). She admits that she has a "deep racial memory that the Chicana could *not* betray a sister, a daughter, a compañera in the service of the man and his institutions if somewhere in the chain of historical events and generations, she were allowed to love herself as both female and mestiza" (***Loving in the War Years***, 136).

To Moraga, Malinche, because she was a woman, had very little choice in her situation; therefore, her association with the downfall of her people is unjustified. Denigrating her, and by association denigrating all women, is a political act of a patriarchal system. In fact, several extant accounts mention her sensitive and loving nature. According to one chronicler, Malinche showed no vindictiveness when she encountered her mother and half-brother years later; instead, she treated them with mercy and love (Del Castillo, 126). Adelaida R. Del Castillo argues, "No one, not Cortés, not the Catholic Church, not her own husband, not even history itself, not the mestizo nation she gives birth to realize the great injustice they have done her by obscuring her in defamation" (143). By labeling her a traitor, "man is attempting to submerge the female character in negativism and Mexican culture does it through demeaning the character of Doña Marina—La Malinche" (146). Norma Alarcón asserts, "Her almost half century of mythic existence, until recent times mostly in the oral traditions, [has] turned her into a handy reference point not only for controlling, interpreting or visualizing women, but also to wage a domestic battle of stifling proportions" (182).

Moraga's mother also became a Malinche figure, a traitor, because she married an Anglo. Moraga herself, because she refuses to marry and serve any man, becomes the worst traitor or "malinchista" of all (Sternbach, 53). She reasons in **"A Long Line of Vendidas"**:

> My mother then is the modern-day Chicana, Malinche marrying a white man, my father, to produce the bastards my sister, my brother, and I are. Finally, I—a half-breed Chicana—further betray my race by *choosing* my sexuality which excludes all men, and therefore most dangerously, Chicano men.
>
> *I come from a long line of Vendidas.* (***Loving in the War Years***, 117)

Sternbach observes that "her [Moraga's] conclusion brings her back to her people, the people of her mother. . . . although she is obviously giving a new and perhaps reclaimed meaning, if such a thing is possible, to the word *vendida*" (55).

The myth of La Malinche works in various combinations with two other myths: La Virgen de Guadalupe and La Llorona.[3] All are images of motherhood. The Virgin of Guadalupe is the virgin mother, sexless and pure, whereas Malinche is "the violated mother" (Paz, 85), sexual and adulterated. La Llorona, historically linked to Malinche, is the suffering mother: she suffers, according to one legend, because she has deviated from her proper role as "good" wife and mother. Like the Virgin of Guadalupe and La Malinche, La Llorona "reflects a cultural heritage that is relentless in its expectations of feminine roles" (Mirandé and Enríquez, 33).

The two contrasting figures of Malinche of Tenépal and the Virgin of Guadalupe, or the polarities of whore or virgin, linked with La Llorona, the Weeping Woman, have become entrenched in the Mexican and Chicano cultures, providing major stumbling blocks to women in their quests for self-determination. To avoid being labeled *mujer mala*, a woman must adhere to certain prescriptions: she must serve the males, take care of the home, mother the children, and give priority to the sons. Moraga states, "You are a traitor to your race if you do not put the man first" (***Loving in the War Years***, 103). She must give her allegiance not only to the institution of *la familia* but also to the institution of the Catholic Church, for "familial restrictions share close covenant with the Catholic faith" (Feyder, 5). For Moraga, embracing the mother means acknowledging the mother's roles in the society and the effects of those roles on her—and her daughter's—racial/sexual identity.

Somewhat autobiographical, ***Shadow of a Man*** focuses on *la familia*, examining how betrayal works in the context of the family structure. Hortensia, a traditional wife and mother, has allowed the dominant ideology to define her totally; she exists primarily to serve others, especially her husband and son. She is a prime example of the mother who "sells" her daughters into patriarchal slavery. Gloria Anzaldúa asserts, "I abhor some of my culture's ways, how it cripples its women, *como burras*, our strengths used against us, lowly *burras* bearing humility with dignity. The ability to serve, claim the males, is our highest virtue" (21). During the course of the play, Hortensia cooks, serves meals, folds clothes, and dresses and undresses her husband, Manuel. But still she feels that she is invisible to Manuel and demands that he see her: "Yo existo. (Pause.) Manuel, yo existo. Existo yo" (32).

Mainly, Hortensia exists for her children, defining herself primarily as mother. Even her husband is a little boy to her. She tells her youngest daughter, Lupe: "Funny, when a man is asleep, tha's when you really get to know him. You see the child's look on his face, before he wakes up and remembers he's a man again. In his half dream, tiene la voz de un niño." She admits, however, that her children, not her husband, receive her allegiance: "But your husband really isn't your child. He di'nt come from your body. Y no matter cuántas veces le das el pecho, tu marido no es tu hijo. Your blood never mixes. He stays a stranger in his own home" (44).

Her primary allegiance, though, is the one she bestows on her son. Moraga comments on the Chicana mother's preference for sons:

> Ask, for example, any Chicano mother about her children and she is quick to tell you she loves them all the same, but she doesn't. *The boys are different.* Sometimes I sense that she feels this way because she wants to believe that through her mothering, she can develop the kind of man she would have liked to have married, or even have been. That through her son she can get a small taste of male privilege, since without race or class privilege that's all there is to be had. The daughter can never offer the mother such hope, straddled by the same forces that confine the mother. (*Loving in the War Years,* 101-102)

Irene I. Blea concurs: "Even at birth Chicano females and males do not start out the same. Boy babies are still preferred" (127). In a scene that reveals her phallocentric view, Hortensia tells her daughters: "Mira, qué lindo es [the baby's penis] . . . like a little jewel. Mi machito. Tha's one thing, you know, the men can never take from us. The birth of a son." Leticia retorts, "Well, I don't see you getting so much credit." "But the woman knows," explains Hortensia. "Tú no entiendes. Wait until you have your own son" (29).

Having internalized the belief that men are superior to women, Hortensia perpetuates these attitudes in her relations with her two daughters, indoctrinating them into a dualistic behavior system. The son, a fledgling *macho*, may venture from the home to test his wings and to develop a masculine identity (Mirandé and Enríquez, 114), but the daughter may not leave freely. When Leticia wants more freedom—like the males in the culture—Hortensia tells her: "If God had wanted you to be a man, he would of given you something between your legs." Rejecting this assessment of woman as "lack," Leticia responds, "I have something between my legs" (44). However, Hortensia perpetuates the double standard within the culture and defines women as dirty and whorelike if they desire the same privileges as men.

At one point Hortensia defines herself as whorelike, impure and unclean. After being abused and rejected by Manuel, she proclaims, "¡Estoy cochina! ¡Filthy!" She pours vinegar over herself and informs her daughters: "Tu padre thinks I stink, pues now I stink for sure" (34). Unable to feel "clean," she almost murders her daughter Lupe, her child by her husband's friend Conrado. Years before, in a classic "exchange of women among men" personal (and ultimately political) act, Hortensia had been offered to Conrado by Manuel as a sexual partner for one night. Lupe is the product of that liaison. Consumed by guilt, Hortensia symbolically renames herself *la chingada*—the traitor (also "the violated one").

Lupe, the twelve-year-old youngest daughter, internalizes the mother's "teachings" and assumes a caretaker's role. Following her mother's example, she waits upon her father, existing in his "shadow" and literally and symbolically sitting at his feet (69). Betty Garcia-Bahne, in "La Chicana and the Chicano Family," discusses this "modeling" and its effects upon Chicano women. She points out several "myths" that bolster the Chicano family structure and shows how they establish women's dependency and "mitigate against the development and exercise of self-determination" (43). One of these myths is that family members can be assured of well-being if they are under the leadership of a male. Garcia-Bahne argues that this type of hierarchical construct undermines the woman's sense of worth and potential. It also places too much responsibility and pressure on the male (44). By modeling the mother's behavior, Lupe enters into the traditional configuration of the family and, by extension, other umbrella institutions.

One of those institutions is the Catholic Church, which casts a long shadow over the bodies and psyches of the women. Lupe, identifying with her mother, takes on the negativism of Malinche, confusing the family's "secret" with her own secretly budding sexuality. In the first image of the play, Lupe appears wearing a Catholic school uniform and holding a votive candle under her chin. Only her face is seen, staring into a mirror. On the wall the shadow of a crucifix can be seen. She reflects, "I have x-ray eyes. . . . I can see through her [Sister Genevieve's] habit. . . . She has a naked body under there. . . . I think there's something wrong with me" (30). She tries to confess to the priest but is unable to reveal her sexual dilemmas. She realizes: "No matter how many times I make confession, no matter how many times I try to tell the priest what I hold insida me, I know I'm still lying. Sinning. Keeping secrets" (12). Yvonne Yarbro-Bejarano posits that "Catholicism in its institutionalized form . . . inculcates in [women] the need to sublimate the body and its desires, as captured in the image of Lupe's disembodied head illuminated by a candle in the shadow of the cross" ("Cherríe Moraga's *Shadow of a Man,*" 99-100).

Lupe's identity quest in the context of family, culture, and institutional religion is the controlling element of the play (her monologues begin and end the production). At one point, she considers her new confirmation name, vacillating between Cecilia and Magdalena—one burned at the stake, the other considered a prostitute—women who encode the dualities. Finally, eschewing all female saints, she decides on Frances, a masculine name she appropriates in order to align with a rebellious female friend. In the last image of the play, Lupe stares at the mirror, again speaking to her reflection: "I've decided my confirmation name will be Frances 'cuz that's what Frankie Pacheco's name is and I wanna be in her body. When she sits, she doesn't hold her knees together like my mom and the nuns are always telling me to. She jus' lets them fly an' fall wherever they want . . . real natural-like . . . like they was wings instead of knees" (49). With this decision, Lupe begins to rebel against the systems that have constrained and repressed her, represented by the mother and the church.

In the last action of the play, Lupe covers the mirror, a signifier with multiple references, with a rebozo, a black shawl. The family is on the way to the father's funeral, and Aunt Rosario instructs Lupe to cover the mirror because she does not want Lupe's father to come back and try to take them with him. In *Borderlands/La Frontera*, Anzaldúa discusses the multiple symbolism of the mirror in Chicano culture. The mirror is "a door through which the soul may 'pass' to the other side." It is also "an ambivalent symbol, reproducing images but also containing and absorbing them. In addition, it is a path to knowledge, a way of 'seeing through' an experience" (42). In Freudian/Lacanian terms the mirror reflects patriarchal ideology that she cannot enter. By taking on both "masculine" and "feminine" aspects and by taking on a name that blurs the dualities, thereby adding a new sexual dimension, Lupe threatens and challenges the existing power structure, based on male privilege and heterosexuality.

Another daughter who threatens and challenges the existing order is Lupe's older sister, Leticia, called the *política* by her mother. From the outset of the play, Leticia is a radical feminist, fighting oppression, not only for women but also for the *raza*. She has no respect for male-centered power structures, often countering her mother's phallocentric views. When her mother refuses to allow her the freedom she allows her brother Rigo, Leticia, in frustration, declares: "Es hombre. Es hombre. I'm sick of hearing that. It's not fair." Hortensia returns, "Well, you better get use to things not being fair. Whoever said the world was goin' to be fair?" Leticia proclaims, "Well, my world's going to be fair!" (18). When her mother tries to convince her that having sons is a sublime experience, Leticia pronounces, "Who knows? Maybe I won't have kids" (29). Choosing not to have children constitutes a challenge to male-based ideologies that control women through marriage and motherhood—a choice

that is an attempt "to undo the power men everywhere wield over women, power that has become a model for every other form of exploitation and illegitimate control" (Rich, "Compulsory Heterosexuality and Lesbian Existence," 202).

In another act of defiance, Leticia gives away her virginity, taking away the power of the patriarchy to use her as a commodity. When her mother asks her, "Why you give your virginidad away for nothing?" Leticia responds: "I was tired of carrying it around . . . that weight of being a woman with a prize. Walking around with that special secret, that valuable commodity, waiting for some lucky guy to put his name on it. I wanted it to be worthless, Mama. Don't you see? Not for me to be worthless, but to know that my worth had nothing to do with it" (45). By the end of the play both Lupe and Leticia refuse to be sold out by the mother and the race, and both refuse to have their sexuality repressed or exploited.

Giving Up the Ghost, also somewhat autobiographical, focuses on betrayal in the family context but extends the examination into personal relationships. The mother is absent from the text, but her influence is omnipresent. Significantly, the epigraph of the play is a song Moraga's mother sang: "If I had the wings like an angel / over these prison walls / I would fly" (3). One of the "prisons" to which Moraga refers is the prison of rigidly defined sexual roles, set up by patriarchal ideologies to bolster power structures. Adrienne Rich calls this prison "institutional heterosexuality" and points out that it is "a major buttress of male power." In 1979, in *On Lies, Secrets, and Silence*, she called for a close scrutiny of the "indoctrination of women toward heterosexuality" and for "a politics of *asking women's questions,* demanding a world in which the integrity of all women— not a chosen few—shall be honored and validated in every aspect of culture" (17). Moraga takes up this challenge in *Giving Up the Ghost.* In the opening scene, Marisa (Moraga), the daughter, writes in a sketchbook that she is going to consider "the question of prisons/politics/sex" (6). In **"A Long Line of Vendidas,"** Moraga writes: "The one aspect of our identity which has been uniformly ignored by every existing political movement in this country is sexuality, both as a source of oppression and a means of liberation" (*Loving in the War Years,* 109).

One of the main points the play makes is that heterosexual relations are often harmful to the body and spirit and that lesbian relations are often restorative and healing. Historian Linda Gordon writes, "For women . . . heterosexual relations are always intense, frightening, high-risk situations which ought, if a woman has any sense of self-preservation, to be carefully calculated" (quoted in Rich, *On Lies, Secrets, and Silence,* 196). Marisa's goal is to fight institutional heterosexuality. At the beginning of the play, she speaks directly to the audience: "My mother was a heterosexual, I couldn't save her. My failures follow thereafter" (8). In *Giving Up the Ghost,* Marisa also attempts to save Amalia, a mother figure, from institutional heterosexuality. Paradoxically, Amalia feels like a failure, too. Her first words are "I am a failure" (8). But Amalia's lack of self worth stems from patriarchal neglect and abuse. Marisa insightfully recognizes this in her mother and then later in Amalia. Her failure to rescue these women, both the mother and the mother figure, depresses and angers her. Later in the same scene, she states, "I wanna talk about betrayal, about a battle I will never win and never stop fighting. The dick beats me every time" (9). Moraga, in *Loving in the War Years,* proclaims, "I love women to the point of killing for us all" (117). As a result, Mary K. DeShazer calls Moraga a "sister in arms" because of her fight against multiple oppressions, noting that her battle cry is "neither hyperbolic nor malevolent; it reflects instead the historical, ideological, and affective locus from which she speaks" ("Making *Familia,*" 282). It reflects her love and commitment to Chicanas, grounded in her love for her mother.

Marisa's love of Amalia is a transferal from the love of the mother to the love of an older woman.[4] Although heterosexual at the beginning of the play, Amalia connects sexually and spiritually with Marisa as the play progresses. According to Teresa de Lauretis, in "Sexual Indifference and Lesbian Representation," "the play itself [moves] away from any simple opposition of 'lesbian' to 'heterosexual' and into the conceptual and experiential continuum of a female, Chicana subjectivity from where the question of lesbian desire must finally be posed" (175). According to Alarcón, "Moraga puts into play the concepts 'man' and 'woman' (and the parodic 'butch/femme'), with the intuitive knowledge that they operate in our subjectivities, so that it is difficult to analyze them, except in the way she has done" (156).

The use of a split subject, Marisa/Corky, and the blurring of time and sequence contribute to Moraga's quest to dismantle limiting concepts of Chicana identity. The split subject, moving back and forth through time, avoids a unified subject and narrativity. In "The Female Subject in Chicano Theatre: Sexuality, 'Race,' and Class," Yarbro-Bejarano notes, "The juxtaposition of past and present in the text reveals the cultural construction of female identity, specifically through the restricted gender roles of masculine/feminine, active/passive, subject/object, penetrator/penetrated defined in Chicano-specific cultural terms through the myth of *La Malinche* and the *chingón/chingada* polarity" (147). "The chingón," writes Octavio Paz, "is the macho, the male; he rips open the chingada, the female, who is pure passivity, defenseless against the exterior world" (77).

Giving Up the Ghost presents this "defenseless" position of women in the culture. Corky, Marisa's twelve-year-old self, assumes a male-identified persona in order to escape the oppression she witnesses in the culture. Her mother's powerlessness in the face of sexism and racism contributes to her sexual determination. Sue-Ellen Case contends that Corky can only inhabit a subject position in society if she enters as "male-identified" (132).

However, when she is raped, Corky is forced "to confront her internal split between her identification with the subjugating male and her repressed self-knowledge as female" (Yarbro-Bejarano, "Cherríe Moraga's *Giving Up the Ghost,*" 116). For example, the rape episode reveals that Corky has internalized societal attitudes. At one point, she decides: "I knew I musta done somet'ing real wrong / to get myself in this mess" (28). In **"A Long Line of Vendidas,"** Moraga discusses the historical practice of blaming the rape victim and links it to the Malinche myth: "In the very act of intercourse with Cortés, Malinche is seen as having been violated. She is not, however, an innocent victim, but the guilty party—ultimately responsible for her own sexual victimization" (*Loving in the War Years,* 118). Alarcón points out that "because Malintzin aided Cortés in the conquest of the New World, she is seen as concretizing women's sexual weakness and interchangeability, always open to sexual exploitation." She writes, "Indeed, as along as we continue to be seen in that way, we are earmarked to be abusable matter, not just by men of another culture, but all cultures including the one that breeds us" (184). The rape also confirms Corky's "femaleness" because she feels absent, objectified: "I suddenly feel like I'm floating in the air / my thing kina attached to no body / flapping in the wind like a bird a wounded bird" (28). When she is penetrated, Corky cries, "He made me a hole!" (29). This declaration of nothingness and despair is a rite of passage for Corky/Marisa, for she realizes that she is vulnerable in the society. Yarbro-Bejarano maintains that "the rape brings home Corky's sex to her as an inescapable fact, confirming her culture's definition of female as being taken" ("The Female Subject in Chicano Theatre," 147). María Herrera-Sobek, in "The Politics of Rape: Sexual Transgression in Chicana Fiction," posits that Moraga encodes in *Giving Up the Ghost* the construct in the act of raping, of making (i.e., of "engendering"), women: "In this process of engendering, fabricating, that is, making a gender, the end result is a hole and absence: women as invisible, voiceless, worthless, devalued objects." She further notes that women are "silent entities dominated by ingrained patriarchal vectors where the Name of the Father is Law, and years of socialization to obey the Father's Law transforms the female subject into a quavering accomplice in her own rape." Women, then, betray themselves as well as other women: "Women are socialized into being participants in their own [and other women's] oppression" (172-173).

Women in the culture are socialized to betray each other because of the culture's directive to put the male first. This process occurs between mothers and daughters such as

Lupe and Leticia in *Shadow of a Man* and occurs between women friends and/or lovers. Marisa bears the wounds of these betrayals: "The women I have loved the most have always loved the man more than me, even in their hatred of him" (14). Consequently, she fears that Amalia will leave her. Moraga's dramatization of Marisa's jealousy and pain illuminates the complexities of their relationship.

Marisa's decision to battle for women, to save them, begins with the physical and psychical "wounding" she experiences during the rape. Partly, Marisa relates to Amalia because Amalia has also been wounded by men. Marisa believes, "It was not natural or right that she got beat down so damn hard, and that all those crimes had nothing to do with the girl she once was two, three, four decades ago" (35). Also, Marisa relates to Amalia because Amalia's wounds remind her of her mother's. Healing Amalia, then, by extension, means healing the mother. Using her hands as "weapons of war," Marisa attempts to restore Amalia, "making her body remember, it didn't have to be that hurt" (35). Together, the women heal each other. Spiritually, they connect, suggesting "the possibility of mutual salvation" (Yarbro-Bejarano, "Cherríe Moraga's *Giving Up the Ghost*," 118), their love for each other becoming a religious experience. When Amalia tells Marisa, "You make love to me like worship," Marisa wants to say, but does not: "Sí, la mujer es mi religion" (34). Temporarily, the women find salvation not in God but in each other. Yarbro-Bejarano notes that "for Moraga the lesbian couple is the microcosm in which the dynamic of faith works itself out, becoming a metaphor for feminism" ("Cherríe Moraga," 173-174).

Partly, Marisa relates to Amalia as a way to embrace the race of the mother. Ultimately, embracing the mother's race means embracing, or accepting, one's mestiza heritage, one's Indian roots, in particular. The longing to connect with the mother's culture is finally a longing for community. In turn, Amalia, longing for her Indian roots, finds a connection to them in Marisa's mestiza features. Moraga dramatizes the women's connection to the past through the dream sequences, in which the women are Indians, dancing or making tortillas, clapping them together in time to indigenous music. The most significant sequence is the one in which Amalia dreams that they are Indians and have broken some taboo in the village. Amalia is afraid until she realizes that "it is *you* who have gone against the code of our people." She also realizes that she does not fear punishment from "los dioses"; instead, she fears the breaking of the taboo—the fact that "the taboo *could* be broken." She concludes, "And if this law nearly transcribed in blood could go, then what else? What *was* there to hold to? What immutable truths were left?" (33). Amalia represents the culture's fears when laws are broken, laws that provide the glue to hold the society together. Ultimately, she fears the downfall of the entire race. If a lesbian, the worst traitor or "malinchista"

of all, could break the culture's sexual mandate, then the culture itself could be in danger of unraveling. Embedded in this dream vision is Moraga's hope of a new, liberating cultural configuration.

Overall, in *Giving Up the Ghost,* Moraga addresses the continuum of mother-daughter love. She implies that daughters receive a legacy of love from the mother that is nourishing and healing, unlike the legacy from the father that is often demeaning and damaging. To Moraga, women should tap into this source of sustenance in order to heal and save each other. Marisa draws from this source but is unable to convince other women, including Amalia, to eschew heterosexual relationships.

The ending of *Giving Up the Ghost* is somewhat despairing. Marisa states, "I am preparing myself for the worst" (35). However, the beginning is hopeful (the play is not linear in form). In a flashback, Marisa writes that her love for Amalia was a "blessing" that convinced her that she was not "trapped" (7). On a personal level, Marisa finds love that transcends the material. On a political level, she wages a war to redeem women, including her mother, from the "prison" of institutional heterosexuality.

In *Heroes and Saints,* which is "an unusual blend of realism, surrealism, and political theater" (Gelb, 518), Moraga extends the issue of betrayal beyond the somewhat insular family sphere to the more all-encompassing Chicano community. In order to demonstrate this, she draws two different mother figures: one who perpetuates institutional beliefs and practices, the Catholic Church, in particular, and one who challenges them.

Dolores, like Hortensia in *Shadow of a Man,* perpetuates institutional ideologies, her racial/sexual identity having been shaped by an oppressive and relentless socialization process, grounded in traditional Catholicism. "It is a faith," assesses Linda Feyder, "that has placed taboos on female sexuality making the Hispanic woman ashamed of her own body" (5). In the main, Catholicism is the overriding belief system that informs her identity. By colluding with this belief system in the socialization of her own daughters, she betrays them, limiting their potential, sexually and politically. According to Hal Gelb, "The mother is reactionary, a sexually and otherwise repressive, fatalistic figure who must be overthrown" (519).

Dolores, the traditional, self-sacrificing mother, is coded as the mother of La Malinche, who sells her daughter into servitude and submission, and La Llorona, who weeps for her lost children and grieves for her "sins." Motherhood is not only her "work," as she proclaims, but it is also her identity. In the words of Garcia-Bahne, "Women accept this definition of themselves because of some security that comes with the role, but this acceptance lends itself to a subtle but pernicious undermining of women's self-esteem" (39). For example, she loses this identity, this sense of selfhood, when she loses her children: "It doesn't matter," she relates, "how old they get or how far away they go, son tus hijos and they always take a piece of you with them. So you walk around full of holes from all the places they take from you." Also, to Dolores, motherhood is a sacred vocation, one she equates with saintliness: "El Dios es el único que nos llena" (130).

One of her sacred missions is to protect her daughters from the "outside" world. She does this by keeping them voiceless, sexless, and invisible. The house, or the traditional family structure, is another one of Moraga's "prisons" or "cages." Dolores literally imprisons her youngest daughter, Cerezita, inside the house, never allowing her to be seen or heard. Although political and social turmoil is occurring in the community, Dolores does not define herself as a member of a community but as a mother of an insular traditional family unit. Garcia-Bahne postulates, "The Chicano family can thus be seen as a vehicle which incorporates those strengthening qualities that are necessary for social units to survive under exploitive conditions and paradoxically embodies those values which mitigate against the development and exercise of self-determination" (43).

Amparo is the nontraditional mother figure, coded as La Malinche because she challenges institutional beliefs and practices. She is considered a "bad" woman, a deviant, because she has "assertive social skills and self-confidence" (Garcia-Bahne, 41). With this particular character, Moraga offers a new definition of mother and nurturer. Amparo, although married, has no biological children, but she and her husband have "adopted" all of the community's children, "show[ing] the guts to fight para sus niños" (130) and organizing the Mothers and Friends of McLaughlin. Unlike Dolores, who believes the home is a safe, nurturing place, Amparo believes the home has become a "prison"—unsafe and life-denying. Also, unlike Dolores, Amparo rejects traditional Catholicism, informing her: "I don' even go to church no more, ni recibir comunión . . . coz I'm tire of swallowing what they want to shove down my throat" (102). Her rejection of the institutions of the traditional family and church is a movement away from oppressive, closed systems and a movement toward liberating, expanding definitions of *la madre* and *la familia*.

Yolanda, the oldest daughter, represents the unmarried mother, still trapped in the traditional home. Her baby daughter's illness and death from pesticide poisoning marks her transformation from stasis to action. First, she rejects the church, telling her mother: "He's [God's] forgotten you and me and everybody else in this goddamn valley." Secondly, she rejects the veiling and silencing of women, ex-

posing herself to the men in the helicopter and daring them: "Take me!" (131). In despair, she asks her mother: "Don't you see, 'amá? I gotta find her killer. Put a face to him, a name, track him down and make him suffer the way we suffer. I want to kill him, 'amá. I want to kill some . . . goddamn body!" (132). With this declaration, Yolanda aligns with Amparo and joins the protests.

The youngest daughter, Cerezita, born without a "body," is a multiple referent. Because she has been wounded by pesticide poisoning, she is a reference to the children who are sick and dying in the Chicano community. Her severed head designates the separation of body and mind, and the "decapitation" of women or the denial (or "cutting off") of sexual desire by repressive cultures. It also represents her "virgin-like," "saint-like" state, prompting her mother to name her "virgencita" (137). In addition, the privileging of the head is a visual attack on the biologism that ultimately bolsters the privileging of the body. Furthermore, it is an attack on those who attribute lesbianism to biological factors. Significantly, Moraga attributes lesbianism "to social factors and/or luck—certainly not to physiology" (**"Algo secretamente amado,"** 151).

Cerezita's mother, a proxy for institutional heterosexuality, indoctrinates her daughter in several ways. When she removes the anatomy books in order to eliminate worldly temptations, she is mimicking church teachings: "The biggest sins are in the mind" (113). When she prevents her from going outside and from looking out the window, she is attempting to repress her sensuality and to curb her quest for self-determination. In addition, when she attempts to "cut off" her tongue, a multiple signifier of sensuality, sexuality, and language (108-109), silencing her in order to "protect" her, she is molding her to comply with societal norms. This conditioning of Cerezita's mind and the condition of her body demonstrate how the mind and body are controlled by church and state. Rich writes, "This culture of manipulated passivity, nourishing violence at its core, has every stake in opposing women actively laying claim to our own lives" (*On Lies, Secrets, and Silence*, 14).

When Cerezita rejects her mother's socializing methods and aligns with Amparo's social activism, she also rejects the reductive appellation "virgencita" and aligns with the liberating signifier La Virgen of Guadalupe. At the conclusion, she offers herself as a sacrifice, not as a traditional self-sacrificing mother but as a new liberated and liberating mother, "Madre . . . Liberated" (148). When Cerezita appropriates the Virgin's image, clothing herself in the signifier, she gives the political act a spiritual dimension. In **"A Long Line of Vendidas,"** Moraga observes that a movement's effectiveness often depends on "a spiritual imperative. Spirituality which inspires activism and, similarly, politics which move the spirit—which draw from the deep-seated place of our greatest longings for freedom—give meaning to our lives." She maintains that "such a vision can hold and heal us in the worst of times, and is in direct opposition to an apolitical spiritualist view of the world or a totally materialistic perspective" (**Loving in the War Years,** 130).

Moraga's examination of the La Malinche legacy and its effect on the mothers' and daughters' racial/sexual identities is a political act to challenge, and ultimately to dismantle, patriarchal systems, based on institutional heterosexuality. In all three of her plays, she looks closely at the ways mothers (and mother figures) and daughters interact during the socialization process. All of the women are at different stages of self-realization and self-actualization. All are "betrayers," either "selling out" the daughters by preparing them to serve the patriarchy or "selling out" the culture by daring to criticize it. The lesbian is the most daring of the *vendidas* or *chingadas*, for she not only "sells out" the cultural contract, but also blurs the distinctions between the dualities, threatening the very foundations of the power structures. In her last play, **Heroes and Saints,** Moraga takes her characters into the realm of the absurd to magnify the physical and psychical wounds women have borne under repressive institutions and to render a vision of revolution. This revolution, however, not only (re)claims Chicana women but also (re)claims the race.

Overall, Moraga dares, in these dramatic works, to critique the Chicano culture, ironically becoming *la vendida* in the process. But she argues, in **"A Long Line of Vendidas,"** that "to be critical of one's culture is not to betray that culture" (108); in fact, not to critique the culture would be an "act of self betrayal" (112), as well as a betrayal of her mother and, by extension, all Chicanas. To critique the culture, then, is an act of love, an act of reclamation. She writes, "It is the daughters that can be relied upon. Las hijas who remain faithful a la madre, a la madre de la madre" (**Loving in the War Years,** 139).

NOTES

1. In 1986 she received the American Book Award from the Before Columbus Foundation for *This Bridge Called My Back: Writings by Radical Women of Color* (1981), which she co-edited with Gloria Anzaldúa. *Loving in the War Years: Lo que nunca pasó por sus labios,* a compilation of her poems, short stories, and essays, was published in 1983. This book contains two seminal essays that inform Moraga's works: "La Güera" and "A Long Line of Vendidas." Although she calls herself primarily a poet, she has written several plays: *Giving Up the Ghost: A Stage Play in Three Portraits* (first staged reading 1984; first produced 1987); *La extranjera* (1985); *Shadow of a Man* (first staged reading 1989; first produced 1990); and *Heroes and Saints* (first staged reading 1989; first produced 1992). *Shadow of a Man* is a recipient of the Fund for New American Plays Award.

2. According to Adelaida R. Del Castillo, in "Malintzin Tenépal: A Preliminary Look into a New Perspective," Malintzin Tenépal (her Aztec name), also known as La Malinche and Doña Marina, was sold to the Mayans by her mother in tandem with her second husband; she was later given to Hernán Cortés as a gift, along with several other young women. A brilliant woman who could speak several languages, she became invaluable to Cortés as an interpreter and guide. Partly, she assisted him because she believed, as many Aztecs did, that he was the god Quetzalcoatl, whose arrival had been predicted on the very day Cortés and his men came ashore. Because of her strong faith, Malintzin became the first Indian to be baptized as a Christian in her native land. Although she and Cortés had a son, he eventually married her off to another Spaniard, Don Juan Jaramillo. After Malintzin's death at the age of twenty-two (probably from small-pox), Jaramillo tortured and robbed her children of their rightful inheritance.

3. Octavio Paz, in *The Labyrinth of Solitude: Life and Thought in Mexico*, relates that the Virgin appeared in 1531, about ten years after the Spanish conquest, to an Indian, Juan Diego, on the Hill of Tepeyac, where a temple had stood in pre-Hispanic times dedicated to the Aztec goddess of fertility, Tonantzin, known to the Indians as "Our Mother" (84). In "The Virgin of Guadalupe: A Mexican National Symbol," Eric R. Wolf explains that to the Indians, and later to the mestizos, this revelation linked their ancient gods and goddesses to the new order, validating their existence and assuring them salvation. (During the time of the conquest, Spanish officials debated whether the Indians were worthy or capable of being saved. If they were subhuman, then there was justification for oppression and exploitation.) The Virgin of Guadalupe represents on one level maternal warmth, life, hope, and health. She also represents a sexless, yet motherly state, the ideal to which Chicanas should aspire. On another level she represents major political aspirations: "The myth of the Guadalupe thus validates the Indian's right to legal defense, orderly government, to citizenship; to supernatural salvation, but also to salvation from random oppression" (37).

In *La Chicana: The Mexican-American Woman,* Alfredo Mirandé and Evangelina Enríquez offer several versions of the La Llorona myth dating back to pre-Columbian times. All reflect the culture's attitudes toward women. Prior to the arrival of Cortés, her voice was heard, crying for her lost children. Later, she was associated with La Malinche. Legends surrounding her have migrated to the southwestern United States; California and Texas have their own unique versions. In all the interpretations, she is a woman who has transgressed in her proper role as "mother, wife, mistress, lover, or patriot" (31-33).

4. In *Loving in the War Years*, Moraga writes about her profound love for her mother, the source from which her love for other women emanates. In her poem "La Dulce Culpa," she asks,

> What kind of lover have you made me, mother
> *so in love*
> with what is left
> unrequited. (15)

Provocatively, Adrienne Rich states, in "Compulsory Heterosexuality and Lesbian Existence," "If women are the earliest sources of emotional caring and physical nurture for both female and male children, it would seem logical, from a feminist perspective at least, to pose the following questions: whether the search for love and tenderness in both sexes does not originally lead toward *women; why in fact women ever redirect that search* . . ." (182).

5. *Chingón and chingada* have multiple meanings in Spanish, Mexican, and Chicano cultures; basically *chingón* refers to an active, aggressive male; *chingada* to a passive, violated female (Paz, 77).

6. The image of the Virgin carried on banners united farmworkers during strikes and demonstrations in California and Texas (Anzaldúa, 29).

WORKS CITED

Alarcón, Norma. "Chicana's Feminist Literature: A Re-vision through Malintzin/or Malintzin: Putting Flesh Back on the Object." In *This Bridge Called My Back: Writings by Radical Women of Color*, ed. Cherríe Moraga and Gloria Anzaldúa, 182-190. Watertown: Persephone, 1981.

——. "Making *Familia* from Scratch: Split Subjectivities in the Work of Helena María Viramontes and Cherríe Moraga." In *Chicana Creativity and Criticism: Charting New Frontiers in American Literature*, ed. María Herrera-Sobek and Helena María Viramontes, 147-159. Houston: Arte Público, 1988.

Anzaldúa, Gloria. *Borderlands/La Frontera: The New Mestiza*. San Francisco: Spinsters, 1987.

Blea, Irene I. *La Chicana and the Intersection of Race, Class, and Gender*. New York: Praeger, 1992.

Case, Sue-Ellen. "From Split Subject to Split Britches." In *Feminine Focus: The New Women Playwrights*, ed. Enoch Brater, 126-146. New York: Oxford University Press, 1989.

de Lauretis, Teresa. "Sexual Indifference and Lesbian Representation.*" Theatre Journal* 40 (May 1988): 155-177.

Del Castillo, Adelaida R. "Malintzin Tenépal: A Preliminary Look into a New Perspective." In Sánchez and Cruz, 124-149.

DeShazer, Mary K. "'Sisters in Arms': The Warrior Construct in Writings by Contemporary U.S. Woman of Color." In *Writing the Woman Artist: Essays on Poetics, Politics, and Portraiture*, ed. Suzanne W. Jones, 261-286. Philadelphia: University of Pennsylvania Press, 1991.

Feyder, Linda, ed. "Introduction." In *Shattering the Myth: Plays by Hispanic Women*, 5-8. Houston: Arte Público, 1992.

Garcia-Bahne, Betty. "La Chicana and the Chicano Family." In Sánchez and Cruz, 30-47.

Gelb, Hal. "Heroes and Saints." *Nation* (Nov. 2, 1992): 518-520.

Herrera-Sobek, María. "The Politics of Rape: Sexual Transgression in Chicana Fiction." In *Chicana Criticism: Charting New Frontiers in American Literature*, ed. María Herrera-Sobek and Helena María Viramontes, 171-181. Houston: Arte Público, 1988.

Lovato, Roberto. "Yo Existo: The Woman of Color Breaks the Silence." *City* (Nov. 1990): 23-24.

Mirandé, Alfredo, and Evangelina Enríquez. *La Chicana: The Mexican-American Woman*. Chicago: University of Chicago Press, 1979.

Moraga, Cherríe. "Algo secretamente amado." In *The Sexuality of Latinas*, ed. Norma Alarcón, Ana Castillo, and Cherríe Moraga, 151-156. Berkeley: Third Woman, 1993.

——. *Giving Up the Ghost: A Stage Play in Three Portraits*. Albuquerque: West End, 1994 (all references to the play are from this source).

——. *Heroes and Saints*. In *Heroes and Saints and Other Plays: Giving Up the Ghost, Shadow of a Man, Heroes and Saints*, 85-149. Albuquerque: West End, 1994 (all references to the play are from this source).

——. *Loving in the War Years: Lo que nunca pasó por sus labios*. Boston: South End, 1983.

——. *Shadow of a Man*. In *Shattering the Myth: Plays by Hispanic Women*, ed. Linda Feyer, 9-49. Houston: Arte

Público Press, 1992 (all references to the play are from this source).

Paz, Octavio. *The Labyrinth of Solitude: Life and Thought in Mexico.* Trans. Lysander Kemp. New York: Grove, 1961.

Quintanales, Mirtha N. "Loving in the War Years: An Interview with Cherríe Moraga." *off our backs* (Jan. 1985): 12-13.

Rich, Adrienne. "Compulsory Heterosexuality and Lesbian Existence." In *Powers of Desire: The Politics of Sexuality*, ed. Ann Snitow, Christine Stansell, and Sharon Thompson, 177-205. New York: Monthly Review, 1983.

——. *On Lies, Secrets, and Silence: Selected Prose 1966-1978.* New York: W. W. Norton, 1979.

Sánchez, Rosaura, and Rosa Martinez Cruz, eds. *Essays on La Mujer.* Los Angeles: University of California Press, 1977.

Sternbach, Nancy Saporta. "'A Deep Racial Memory of Love': The Chicana Feminism of Cherríe Moraga." In *Breaking Boundaries: Latina Writing and Critical Readings*, ed. Asunción Horno-Delgado et al., 48-61. Amherst: University of Massachusetts Press, 1989.

Wolf, Eric R. "The Virgin of Guadalupe: A Mexican National Symbol." *Journal of American Folklore* 71 (Jan.-Mar. 1958): 34-39.

Yarbro-Bejarano, Yvonne. "Cherríe Moraga." In *Chicano Writers: First Series*, ed. Francisco A. Lomeli and Carl R. Shirley, 165-177. Vol. 82 of *Dictionary of Literary Biography*. Detroit: Gale, 1989.

——. "Cherríe Moraga's *Giving Up the Ghost*: The Representation of Female Desire." *Third Woman* 3 (1986): 113-120.

——. "Cherríe Moraga's 'Shadow of a Man': Touching the Wound in Order to Heal." In *Acting Out: Feminist Performances*, ed. Lynda Hart and Peggy Phelan, 85-104. Ann Arbor: University of Michigan Press, 1993.

——. "The Female Subject in Chicano Theatre: Sexuality, 'Race,' and Class." In *Performing Feminisms: Feminist Critical Theory and Theatre*, ed. Sue-Ellen Case, 131-149. Baltimore: Johns Hopkins University Press, 1990.

Kirkus Reviews (review date 15 November 1997)

SOURCE: Review of *Waiting in the Wings: Portrait of a Queer Motherhood*, in *Kirkus Reviews*, November 15, 1997, p. 1692.

[*In the following review, the critic praises the evocative immediacy of Moraga's motherhood experiences in* Waiting in the Wings: Portrait of a Queer Motherhood.]

[*Waiting in the Wings: Portrait of a Queer Motherhood* is] an honest, introspective memoir of evolving lesbian motherhood.

When Chicana lesbian writer Moraga (coeditor, *This Bridge Called My Back*, not reviewed) was 40, she decided to have a child. She asked her white lover (who is called Ella here, the Spanish word for "she") to help, not so much to be the other mother as to continue to be Moraga's partner and support; inevitably, though, Ella does turn out to be a "co-mother." Moraga asks her much younger Mexican friend Pablo to donate sperm; he too ends up becoming very involved with the baby. Against the odds, Moraga gets pregnant the first time they try. In this memoir, Moraga muses honestly on how she feels about having a boy (at first ambivalent, then pleased). She is also thoughtful on the meaning of blood and family; as a lesbian, she's always created her own "*familia*," yet she is also quite close to her parents and sister, and it was important to her that her baby's father also be Mexican. Both her sister and Ella are present at Rafael's birth, which is premature, and he fights for his life the first few months. Moraga writes well about the struggle and the exhaustion of daily facing this new loved one's death after months of creating his life. When Rafael is well, Moraga battles to find the energy to write. Her relationship with Ella suffers and Ella moves out, though it seems they may stay together. Some of the writing in this memoir is a bit indulgent, having been culled from journals. However, much of it is powerful, and the journal form does give the narrative a sense of immediacy.

A strong, though sometimes scattered, account of a baby's struggle for survival and a mother's struggle to define her own new life.

Catherine Wiley (essay date Spring 1998)

SOURCE: "*Teatro* Chicano and the Seduction of Nostalgia," in *Melus*, Vol. 23, No. 1, Spring 1998, pp. 99-115.

[*In the following essay, Wiley discusses how the notion of nostalgia relates to Moraga's and other Chicano artists drama.*]

In Cherríe Moraga's first published play, *Giving Up the Ghost,* the character Amalia leaves her home in Los Angeles to visit Mexico in an attempt to renew her physical and spiritual energy. She muses:

I thought . . . maybe it was the American influence that causes the blood to be sucked dry from
you so early. Nothing was wrong with me, really.
My bones ached. I needed rest. Nothing Mexico
couldn't cure. (24)

She imagines Mexico, a short bus ride away, as a space of
regeneration and identification that does not exist for her
north of the border. Her effort as a Mexican-born, dark-
skinned woman artist to succeed in a culture that neither
values nor understands her is exhausting. But Amalia returns to the United States upon learning of her Mexican
lover's death, resigns herself to a life as a Mexican-American whose home, conflicted though it may be, is Los Angeles.

Amalia's realization that her home is not necessarily where
her heart is, that she loves Mexico but belongs in the United
States, is a theme common to most *teatro* Chicano. An
American art form, *teatro*—like Chicano culture generally—
depends on Mexico not only for its origins, but for its essential meaning as well. This dependence fosters a dual
nostalgia for and resentment of the homeland as a territory
of desire and impossibility, of exotic *naturaleza* (nature/na-
tionality) and material poverty.[1] Chicanos' ancestors left
Mexican territory for many of the same reasons European
and Asian immigrants left their nations of origin: to provide
a richer life for those to come. But Mexico exerts a different
power for Chicanos than the homeland does for other ethnic minority groups, and it is this difference that finds expression in *teatro*. In the three plays I will discuss
here—Moraga's **Giving Up the Ghost** (staged reading 1984;
published 1986 and 1994), Luis Valdez's *The Shrunken Head
of Pancho Villa* (1968) and El Centro Su Teatro's *La Carpa
Aztlán Presents "I Don't Speak English Only"* (1994)—nostalgia shapes characterization, plot, and theme. Nostalgia
also dictates more subtly the ways in which the plays' mixed
audiences (Chicano and non-Chicano) perceive the realities
of contemporary Chicano culture outside the theater.

Moraga focuses on personal history, Valdez on the history
of a people, and *La Carpa Aztlán* fuses the two concerns
into a debate about cultural history's impact on individuals.
All three plays stage the confrontation of Chicanos with
Mexico as well as the confrontation of Chicanos with assimilated Mexican-Americans, representing these confrontations as a conflict of nostalgia. Nostalgia's temporal aspect,
its relation to history, is as significant here as its spatial aspect. The three plays, representative of the decades in which
they were written and first staged, offer contemporary readers and spectators an historical scope through which to
imagine Chicano life and art. Valdez's work as a playwright
grew out of his collaboration with actors and other artists,
and while *Pancho Villa* was written by Valdez exclusively,
its form and tone reflect the collective tenor of early *teatro*

Chicano, as well as the ethnic pride that inaugurated the
1960s Chicano movement.[2] Nearly twenty years after Valdez,
Moraga writes independently of any particular theater company and her play reflects the challenge to the Chicano
movement mounted by women's and gay rights activists.
And finally, *La Carpa Aztlán*, a collective piece whose authorship is not dominated by an individual, reflects the
sense of retrenchment felt by most nationalist movements
in the 1990s. Public sentiments imposing English Only
laws, anti-immigrant policy, cut-backs in affirmative action and the resurgence of ethnic hostility are the play's
dominant themes. The yearning represented in and by *La
Carpa Aztlán* is as much for the optimism and pride of
the Chicano movement—and the *teatro* so instrumental
in representing that movement—of the 1960s and 1970s
as it is for Mexico.

A powerful aspect of memory, nostalgia tries to recall an old
place in a former time, with its subject either imaginatively—
or, occasionally, really—returning to that place, or by insert-
ing the past into the present. According to Susan Stewart,
"Nostalgia is a sadness without an object, a sadness which
creates a longing that of necessity is inauthentic because it
does not take part in lived experience . . . the past it seeks
has never existed except as narrative" (23). A potentially dangerous fantasy, nostalgia unmediated by historical knowledge threatens to immerse the nostalgic subject in passive
despondency. The word nostalgia combines the Greek words
for a return home and pain (either a painful return or a return to pain); its first definition in the *Oxford English Dictionary* is "a form of melancholia caused by prolonged
absence from one's home or country." It did not come into
English usage until the late eighteenth century, when nostalgia was used to describe the disease of homesickness.
Stewart goes further in her description by calling nostalgia
"the desire for desire" (23); in other words, nostalgia seeks
out a space and time in which the subject finds origin, a
womb-like entity which is irretrievably lost except in memory.
It seduces the desiring subject—i.e., all of us—with a promise of feeling at home only if we let go of the present, if we
court a return to that past-future which is death.

The seduction of nostalgia, with its allusions to home and
the human desire to feel at home, is a useful idea to apply
to immigration. Immigrants for the most part leave or escape
their birthplace because it is unlivable and their lifelong
struggle becomes one of home-making in a strange land,
while looking with longing at what has been left. Nostalgia
is, however, complicated for the Chicano in the Southwest,
who in essence immigrates to a former homeland. Indeed,
the term Aztlán, popular among Chicano nationalists since
the 1960s, is one of nostalgia.[3] Aztlán is an Indian name for
a large area of the Southwest, predating the Spanish conquest of Mexico by centuries, and like all Indian artifacts in
the Americas today carries the weight of authenticity and

loss. Many Chicanos, especially those who have traced their Indian origins, believe that their homes in Texas and Arizona, for example, truly are a piece of Mexico temporarily occupied by foreigners. In Indian culture, nothing originating in the earth is ever completely lost. As Amalia puts it in **Giving Up the Ghost,** *"'Regresaré,' nos promete* [I will return, she—the Earth—promises us]. When they 'discovered' El Templo Mayor beneath the walls of this city, they had not realized that it was She who discovered them. Nothing remains buried forever" (25). The land eulogized by Amalia is in and beneath Mexico City, but she also refers to a more generalized (and not necessarily abstract) spiritual zone that includes the southwestern United States. Amalia's problem is that despite the ancient connection of her present home with the foreign country to which she feels tied, the forces of history have severed irrevocably the once united lands. She and her fellow Mexican-Americans embody this severance and its accompanying emotional complications.

Mexico's presence in Chicano culture is always doubled, as the source of ethnic pride and frustration. The loss of one-third of her territory in the Mexican-American War and the current economic disparity between the two nations place Mexico in a defensive position vis-a-vis the United States. But many Mexican-Americans long for acceptance in Mexico, as Mexicans. As poet Lorna Dee Cervantes puts it in the ironically titled "Heritage:"

> I didn't ask to be brought up tonta!
> My name hangs about me like a loose tooth.
> Old women know the secret,
> "Es la culpa de los antepasados."
> Blame it on the old ones.

Cervantes's persona feels like a fool because her American identity is transparent despite her name: her forefathers and mothers bequeathed a nationality upon her that cannot be discarded at the border. The desire to belong in the homeland, although it may never have been home, is common to most Americans of immigrant background. And even those who do not visit tend to harbor illusions about life there, as a simpler and more honest existence than their current one, unencumbered by the American race for the dollar.

Chicanos, unlike European and Asian immigrants, are literally close to the homeland as well; those living in border towns can see Mexico, what and where they or their ancestors came from, every day. Such proximity can invest Chicano nostalgia with a power it may not have for other immigrants. While Homi K. Bhabha theorizes that all cultures and peoples currently exist on and between borders, such an attractive abstraction ignores the differences among borders and border dwellers. The U.S./Canadian border, for instance, does not resonate with the economic and ethnic tension of Mexico's border with the U.S. It is, however, useful to consider the border maker of history itself as unfixed and porous as a national boundary. In Bhabha's words, we might refigure the past "as a contingent 'in-between' space, that innovates and interrupts the performance of the present. The 'past-present' becomes part of the necessity, not the nostalgia, of living" (7). An incorporation of the past rather than a distanced reverence for it allows for home-making in what was originally an alien land. Historical memory, then, can be a tool immigrants and border dwellers use for mediating the power of nostalgia.

Nostalgia is not the same as remembering, which is necessary for construction and maintenance of personal and cultural identity, a home away from home. Nostalgia literally connects the ideas of return and pain, but conventionally refers to a sentimental clinging to the past, often a glorified past colored by an undistinguished or conflicted present. As Bhabha implies, nostalgia clouds its subject's relationship with his or her own history, by imposing the idealized space and time of "long ago and far away" on the present. I will argue here that the dangers of nostalgia are exemplified in the comedy of *teatro* Chicano, which is an inherently bicultural performance genre. *Teatro* mixes dialects of English, Spanish, and Chicano English, Mexican style vaudeville, melodrama and cinema with American psychological realism. It incorporates Mexican performance tradition into present-day Chicano issues, representing real life in a medium from the past.

Theater is a particularly appropriate medium for coming to terms with nostalgia. Actors, whom the audience recognizes as real people and pretend characters simultaneously, physically inscribe the past's integration into the present. Due to their liminal presence in a space—the stage—that is both real and unreal, actors are essential border dwellers and playwrights exemplify border writers. For D. Emily Hicks, because of their ability to see from and to both sides of the border, "border writers ultimately undermine the distinction between original and alien culture" (xxiii). The border subject is decentered and the object of desire—be it home or self or both—is displaced to the other side of where she or he stands. Theater also decenters both actor and spectator, permitting a critical and imaginative reevaluation of the world it represents.

Hicks uses the coyote as a metaphor for the border subject, as the coyote is someone whose life consists of continuously passing through the border, moving in both directions, pledging allegiance to neither side. Human coyotes, the people who daily move Mexicans through the Mexico/U.S. border, share much with their animal namesake. Coyotes are noted for their ability to scavenge a living on the outskirts of both wild and urban landscapes, making their homes wherever they find themselves. Often considered a pest by

Anglo-Americans, the coyote is also a trickster figure for many American Indians, changing shape and identity—like an actor—whenever necessary to wreak havoc on rigid and supposedly stable institutions.

Hicks also stresses the border writer's ability to mediate cultures rather than replace one with the other. As a bi- or even tri-cultural performance genre, *teatro* mediates Mexican, American, and Chicano cultures. It is both oppositional and parasitic, to and of the United States as well as Mexico. According to Ramón Saldívar, Chicano culture is "potentially liberating when as the contrastive other Chicano culture has produced for Chicanos a consistent and highly articulated set of oppositions to the dominant cultural system surrounding it" (4). Liberation in *teatro*, however, is intrinsically paradoxical because its representation depends upon a remembering and modified recuperation of what Mexico and Mexicans have lost to the United States. Distinct from the two dominant cultures that influence it, *teatro* Chicano balances its identity between, among, and apart from them. The history of loss and recuperation plays a pivotal role in Chicano cultural identity, as it does in *teatro*. I will preface my discussion of the three plays with some historical background to *teatro* itself as an art form in an effort to clarify *teatro*'s ongoing relationship with the larger culture. F. Arturo Rosales argues that the Latino community in the United States supported theater longer than did the dominant Anglo culture, in part because mainstream media influenced this community less. He also argues that, as opposed to acting as a retarding factor in the Latino community's assimilation into the mainstream, theater and the community's attachment to it must be seen as an institutionalized negotiation with the dominant culture (15). Due to the large numbers of Mexican-Americans in the Southwest United States before the massive, industry-fueled immigration of the late nineteenth century, Mexican theater was well established north of the border by that time. As early as the 1840s, that is, before the Mexican-American War, theaters producing exclusively Spanish language plays and extravaganzas existed in Los Angeles and San Francisco, and travelling troupes of Mexican and Spanish performers toured Northern Mexico and California, roving as far as Texas and Arizona. By the 1920s over twenty Spanish-language theaters thrived in Los Angeles and San Antonio, theaters serving as community centers as well as entertaining people from outside the cities (Kanellos "An Overview" 7-10). As Rosales puts it:

> Theatrical performances assisted in local networking, interacting and intertwining with the other barrio institutions to provide cohesion and stability in a way that contemporary mass media, even that which is geared to the Hispanic public, cannot do. (18)

Not only were theaters used as sites for community cohesion, often staging fundraisers for locals with legal or police trouble, but they also encouraged cultural retention.[4] The roles of cohesion and retention remain significant today, especially in the few spaces left in the United States devoted exclusively to *teatro*. Spanish-language theaters staged seasonal Church plays, such as the story of Juan Diego and the Virgin Mary at Christmas (a version of this story, *The Miracle at Tepeyac*, is produced annually in various Catholic churches by El Centro Su Teatro in Denver), Spanish classical drama, as well as the *revistas* (one-act sketches), melodrama, vaudeville, and *zarzuelas* (musical comedy, forerunner to operetta) common to the Mexican travelling shows.

In the 1920s and 1930s, before and during the Great Depression which saw the repatriation, both forced and voluntary, of thousands of Mexicans and Mexican-Americans, nostalgia was a common theme of the *revistas*. Romualdo Tirado, one of the many impresarios working as director, singer, actor and general theater promoter, was also a famous *pelado*. While the *pelado* (literally "the naked one") was a stock character in Mexican theater, serving as the poor but wily Everyman, in Mexican-American theater he became the abused but never vanquished immigrant. Tirado wrote "De Mexico a Los Angeles," [From Mexico to Los Angeles] an immensely popular *revista* in Los Angeles in 1920 and 1921. Part of the play's theme song, so popular that Mexican-Americans sang it on the streets, is as follows:

> Asi pasa a muchos
> Que aqui conozco
> Cuando aprenden un poco
> De Americano
> Y se visten catines
> Y van al baile.
> Y el que niega a su raza
> Ni madre tiene,
> Pues no hay nada en el mundo
> Tan asqueroso
> Como la ruin figura del renegado.

> [Many here whom I know go by like this; when they learn a little American, they think they're something to look out for at the dance. But he who denies his race/homeland no longer has a mother, since there is nothing more despicable in the world than the ugly face of one who renounces (his past)].
> (Kanellos "A History" 63).

This song reflects the tension common to any immigrant culture between a desire for material success and the necessity of remembering one's roots. A Mexican immigrant who "learns a little American" should not elevate himself above others in his community, for if he forgets his past he becomes ugly to other Mexicans. And no matter how much American he learns, he will never be one of them, so in order not to get lost he must stand by his community of origin.

The titles of other *revistas* popular in the 1920s and 1930s reflect this attempt to safeguard memories of the original homeland while succeeding in the new culture: "Regreso a mi tierra" [Return to my Homeland], "Los repatriados" [The Repatriated Ones], "El desterrado" [The Landless One], "El alma de México" [The Soul of Mexico], and "Nuestro Egoismo" [Our Pride], as well as the difficulties of assimilation: "Los Angeles en Piyamas" [The Angels or L.A. in Pajamas], "Los efectos de la crisis" [The Effects of the Crisis], "Esclavos" [Slaves] and "Whiskey, morfina y marihuana." (Kanellos "A History" 66-67). These titles allude to homesickness while also warning of the dangers of losing oneself, figuratively or literally, in an effort to get by. Spectators during this period were themselves sometimes on the verge of repatriation; like contemporary Chicano audiences, even those who have "made it," they understood intimately the intricacies of balancing two often conflicting ways of being.

While Mexican-American theaters suffered a loss of patronage during the Depression and Repatriation due to the exile of many actors in addition to the influx of cinemas, the *carpas* were small enough to survive and, according to Kanellos, never completely died out. Referring to the tents that originally housed them, *carpas* were travelling troupes, often family-based, that easily passed from north to south along the border. *Carpas* performed mostly in small farming towns between harvests and were thus not subject to the vagaries of population shifts in larger cities (Ybarro-Frausto 46). In Kanellos's words, "Their comic routines became a sounding board for the culture conflict that Mexican-Americans felt in language usage, assimilation to American tastes and life-styles, discrimination in the United States, and pocho status in Mexico" ("A History" 100). Chicanos faced discrimination not only in their American home, but in Mexico as well, because they had to americanize themselves enough to survive and were no longer considered proper Mexicans.

Giving Up the Ghost, whose title refers to personal as well as cultural phantoms, opens with an image of the unique complexity of Chicano identity. The play's abstract set and background music evoke the streets of 1980s Los Angeles and the Mexican desert, and the main character Corky/Marisa bears strong Indian features but dresses *cholo* style (pressed khakis and a white undershirt; slicked back hair). Corky represents the teenage Marisa, a girl beginning to understand her outlawed desire for women as she searches for her indigenous and Mexican past. Marisa's first adult love

is Mexican-born painter Amalia, who nurtures the younger woman's ripening artistry and self-knowledge. Amalia says of Marisa, "Her nostalgia for the land she had never seen was everywhere. In her face, her drawings, her love of the hottest sand by the sea" (17). While Moraga does not use the comedy and word-play of conventional *teatro* in *Giving Up the Ghost,* her focus on the characters' nostalgia for Mexico—whether it exists as they imagine it or not—belongs in the *teatro* tradition.

The Shrunken Head of Pancho Villa, a comedy using the satire common to *teatro,* tells the story of a Mexican-American family experiencing the generational clash of Mexican parents and Chicano children. The father is a drunken *sonavaviche,* the mother stalwart but ineffectual, with one son a sellout, the next son a rebellious *pachuco* (streetwise youth, often associated with petty crime), and the daughter a whining teenager who envisions pregnancy as her only life-choice. The eldest son, however, is an enormous head who believes he is Pancho Villa, and his gargantuan appetite provides the focus for the action of the play. As Mingo, the sell-out son, says: "You gotta accept it, Ma. Chorty's head, that's it. . . . All these years we been poor and stinkin, working the fields for what? To stuff his fat belly, which he don't even got!" (190) "Chorty" embodies, as it were, both the seductive face of nostalgia as a source of national honor and its dangerous potential for overwhelming the present.

Set in the near future (the year 2021), *La Carpa Aztlán Presents "I Don't Speak English Only"* shows us a Chicano college student being led back to his Mexican heritage by an underground theater group, whose title, "La Carpa Aztlán," refers to both actual Mexican performance practice—*la carpa*—and to the mythical homeland—Aztlán—to which politicized Chicanos long to return. *La Carpa Aztlán* illustrates the translation of a nineteenth century Mexican performance tradition to contemporary community-based, political theater. All three plays treat nostalgia as a significant ingredient in their characters' lives, as well as a space in which their spectators can identify the characters' stories. Nostalgia for a Mexico and for a past that never was infuses each play, reminding us both to remember history and the homeland and their malleable construction in memory. Each play's audience is shown the inevitable romanticization of Mexico in the collective Chicano memory. While such romanticization is not exclusively negative, it does not replace the accurate historical understanding needed for Mexico to be used effectively as a site of identification and pride for Mexican-Americans. Such an understanding, however, is complicated by Chicanos' inferiority in the eyes of Anglo-American culture, as well as Mexico's perceived inferiority vis-a-vis the United States.

The relative invisibility of Chicano culture compounds this difficulty. Part of contemporary *teatro*'s role is to enlarge and complicate dominant American culture's vision of itself, to *show* us the interdependence of American, Mexican, and Chicano identities, to stage the desire for home that is common to us all. Not only does the American landscape owe a literal debt to Mexican territorial losses, but the traditional American dream of assimilation into the mainstream depends upon Mexican-Americans knowing what aspect of themselves they must negate. Politicized Chicanos, on the other hand, who desire neither assimilation nor repatriation, must show an ability to navigate two distinct cultures along with their own, third, "in-between" culture.

In a still rare nod to *teatro*'s significance, *The Shrunken Head of Pancho Villa* is included, with translations of the Spanish and Chicano phrases, in Jerome Beaty and J. Paul Hunter's 1990 anthology *New Worlds of Literature*. Anthologized elsewhere, it is thus accessible to students in the United States in a way few other *teatro* pieces are, and is bound to be influential in shaping perceptions of this art form, as well as of Chicano culture generally. The play tackles nostalgia "head-on," using a disembodied head as a character representing Mexico's revolutionary past. This head, called Chorty or Belarmino, is so hungry—for justice, as he explains—that he consumes not only his family's food supply, but threatens to eat them as well.

The setting is a shabby but brightly painted house in a generic California barrio in the 1950s. The set becomes shabbier as the play progresses, with red cockroaches dotting and finally covering its walls. Valdez describes the play as a "transcendental expression of the social condition of La Raza in los Estados Unidos," one that "reflect[s] the psychological reality of the barrio" (154). In 1968, Valdez's view of his peoples' social condition appears pessimistic, but this view also calls for a re-evaluation of the realities underlying that condition. Comedy combined with an historical element is an appropriate didactic medium, as it was in early Mexican-American *teatro*. While the father character, Pedro, recites drunken dreams of his imagined participation with Pancho Villa's troops in the Mexican Revolution, the mother, Cruz, tries in vain to keep her family fed. The literally disintegrating home space, while hilarious to look at, (especially when the starving characters begin to furtively eat the cockroaches), points to the difficulty of building a home and maintaining cultural pride in a hostile society.

When the eldest able-bodied son Mingo arrives home a decorated war hero, he announces his intention to move his family out of the barrio and into the American dream. While the playwright allows for the validity of part of this aspiration, he also creates in Mingo a stereotype of the ethnic minority sell-out. Jokes about selling out to Anglo-American culture, or *agringamiento*, have been a staple of Mexican and Mexican-American theater since the nineteenth century. *Carpas* poked subversive fun at assimilated Mexican-Americans' inability to understand Spanish, while also teasing Mexicans from across the border about their ignorance of English. Selling out completely was laughable, but so was the inability to get along in two distinct cultures. As the second son, Joaquin, exclaims to Mingo, picking lice from his own head,: "We're greasy and lousy, but we're your family! . . . You dirty cabrón. I'm proud to be a stinking Mexican" (187, 193).

But according to the play, it is not enough to be proud to be a stinking Mexican. Nor is it enough to remember the heroic exploits of the peasant bandit and military hero Pancho Villa.

Because Pedro is caught in the past, he is unable to guide his family in the painful but necessary adjustment to living as Chicanos rather than as Mexicans. Pedro dreams aloud: "Just imagine, to rescue the general's head from the hands of the gringos, then to take it back to Mexico con honor! In a big train like the old days! Qué caray, maybe even the Revolución break out again! Maybe they give us a rancho en Zacatecas!" (181) Waiting passively for a new revolution may be an acceptable daydream, but it ignores the necessity of solving contemporary problems.

In real history, according to the play, it was not Pedro but his wife, Cruz, who participated in the *Revolución*. She knew Pancho Villa and is thus certain that her disembodied son is indeed hers and not *el general*. Belarmino still serves to politicize Joaquin, who resents Mingo's determination to live well, eating steak and drinking orange juice, while the rest of the family snatches roaches to eat off the walls. As Joaquin tells Belarmino: "It was only a stinking cockroach. Dumb Mexican . . . not you, ese, this stupid cucaracha I squish. They love to be step on" (176). Joaquin understands the realities of discrimination, but lacks a sense of Mexican history that might give him a model of constructive rebellion. Belarmino asks him, "*¿Que no sabes que estamos en territorio enemigo?*" [Don't you know we're in enemy territory?] (178). For Belarmino, who believes himself to be Pancho Villa, north of the border is enemy territory, but Joaquin was born here. If the territory is hostile, which to a *pachuco* or Chicano "punk" like Joaquin, it is, he must change it. Returning "home" is not the option it seems to be for his father, longing for a ranch in Zacatecas. Home for the Chicano is the United States and neither a literal nor a figurative return to Mexico can make this country more homelike.

Valdez's play ends ambiguously, with Mingo assimilating completely to the point of changing his name to "Sunday" and Joaquin returning home from jail without a head. Belarmino is prepared to latch himself onto the available body, joining Mexico's glorious but powerless past to the Chicano's amnesia-prone but still active body. The daughter, however, has given birth to another disembodied head and claims Joaquin's body for her child. Perhaps historical memory will become activated to create a unified Chicano identity; perhaps it will not. Belarmino ends the play with a speech of determination: "So don' worry my people, because one of this [sic] days Pancho Villa will pass among you again. Look to your mountains, your pueblos, your barrios. He will be there" (207). As a metaphor for a nostalgia that simultaneously enriches and impoverishes his family, Belarmino represents the potential for a strong Chicano community, but he is forever incomplete without a body—a people—to define him.

La Carpa Aztlán likewise sends its audience an ambiguous message about the role of Mexico for contemporary Chicanos. Its medium, however, that of Denver's El Centro Su Teatro, is eternally optimistic. One of the longest surviving amateur *teatro* Chicanos in the country, Su Teatro was founded in the early 1970s by a group of college students.[5] Situated in an old Denver barrio, it continues the tradition of activist community theater inspired by Luis Valdez's Teatro Campesino, created during the United Farm Workers' strikes of 1965. This play uses the *carpa* tradition of local humor and a circus-like ambiance to make its plea for historical memory. One example of such humor uses the most conservative and the most liberal cities in Colorado: a *carpero* says, "The day I [joined the *carpa*], I had been having a very rough day. Colorado Springs had just been declared the New Holy City and the Pope was coming down from Boulder for the ceremony" (no page numbers). Denver audiences chuckle at this nod to both Colorado Springs's reputation as a home base for the Christian Right and at Boulder's self-image as an ultra-liberal haven for political correctness. In another scene, three figures on a typical multicultural Denver mural—the Indian, the Spaniard, and the Mestizo—debate their respective cultures, while giving the audience a lesson in the history of conquest.

History, of Mexico and Mexican-Americans, dominates this non-linear play. Its main character personifies an audience ignorant about its own past, but clearly able to learn once the effects of Anglo-American indoctrination have been recognized. Albert, the young student who has lost his way on a class field trip, meets Don Guillermo, who argues with him about the realities of the United States in the year 2021, an apparently post-multicultural nation. According to Albert, "It is common knowledge that everyone has achieved the American Dream. Anyway, disbelief in the American Dream has been illegal since the turn of the century. Where on earth have you been?" Don Guillermo lives in the underworld because he was once arrested by the language police for speaking Spanish and for reading a Spanish newspaper (perhaps Denver's *La Voz* or *El Semanario*). Their meeting uses the verbal slapstick of Abbott and Costello, a staple of the traditional *carpa*, to underline Albert's confusion over

where his home lies. As an assimilated Chicano, he lives between "there and there," and the here in which he finds himself makes him feel lost. He tells Don Guillermo, "Don't you understand, I want to go home, this place is so unfamiliar . . . it's too different." The don responds, "But you came back. Here." It is natural, in other words, for Chicanos in the twenty-first century to feel homeless, but if they can look to the past without being engulfed by it, they may return to a "here" that has always been.

Eventually Albert becomes so distraught that he reverts to a comfortable, infantile past, remembering the *Mama* and *abuela* who raised him, but Spanish is illegal in his present world. Don Guillermo teases Albert (now Alberto) about finding his roots and the boy accuses him of ending every serious argument with a joke. Asked whether joking, too, is illegal in the post-multicultural America, Alberto says, "There is an approved humor. It must not come at the expense of the established social order." In a response to the oxymoronic "approved humor," Don Guillermo switches to physical comedy, forcing Alberto into a juggling match with his hat, mirroring the need to juggle his identity as a Chicano and a citizen of a nation that denies his heritage.

Like the older *carpas*, *La Carpa Aztlán* consists of short vignettes, both comic and melodramatic, songs, mime, clowning, and an audience sing-along. Don Guillermo tells the audience: "Simon mi querido publico, estan watchando la primera carpa in todo Los Estados Unidos. [Yes, my dear public, you are watching the first carpa in the entire United States]. Maybe the only carpa. Kind of like being the only *teatro*." Here he mixes Spanish with Chicanismos such as *simon* and *watchando*, and he jokes about El Centro Su Teatro's precarious position as the only *teatro* in town.

La Carpa Aztlán's setting in the near future renegotiates nostalgia's distortion of the past, allowing spectators to imagine the now of the 1990s as a period in history. The past's malleability is embodied by actors playing characters who live a quarter-century after their performance; thus the future is literally in the spectators' hands. We can, if we learn from the play, change what will happen once the play is over. One of the skits involves Chicano Man and his wife, Chicano Woman, caricatures of 1960s and 1970s activists who describe a fantasy of life after the 1990s. Chicano Man says:

> By the mid-1990s, in order to prove you weren't in a gang, you had to become as nonthreatening as possible. For those who were born with the malignant Chicano Militant [gene] face a daily battle to maintain their secret identities as . . . Chicano Man! . . . I have organized my coworkers so that the bosses all are trembling. Our neighborhood is safe, and the gangs all work at the co-op nursery that I built one night when I

couldn't sleep. I am also a teacher at the Escuela Che Guevara. . . .

But in 2021, Chicano Man and Woman are underground; they had assimilated so well in the 1990s that they disappeared from the mainstream and thus exist only in the imaginary spectacle of the *carpa.*

Naturally, Alberto resists what he considers the indoctrination of the *carperos.* He says of Mexico: "[It's] as dead as my abuela, as dead as my father and mother. All those memories have vanished, just the same as my parents. So don't try to stir up that dead consciousness by playing on some lost emotion." The emotion, of course, is not lost nor is the consciousness dead, and they cannot be ignored once they have been remembered. But at the end of the play, the *carperos* and their magic disappear, leaving Alberto alone and looking for his school group. The play ends with a hopeful song, but the *carperos* have returned to the relative safety of the underground. Alberto, presumably, must work to make a space in which they can perform in the open. But the space, at least in this play, stays within the secure and imaginary confines of the theater: *La Carpa Aztlán* is only a play, after all. *Teatro* has become a repository for positive nostalgia, an enactment of the "past-present" that is now part of the spectators' collective conscious. It is up to us as the living reflections of Alberto to use what we have learned of the past to construct a future for Chicano identity.

Unlike *Pancho Villa* and *La Carpa Aztlán,* **Giving Up the Ghost** uses none of the verbal and physical humor of early *teatro* to evoke and criticize nostalgia. Instead it combines sexual and ethnic politics, focusing on Chicanos' mostly repressed Indian heritage as an echo of women's repressed sexuality. Nostalgia for Mexico proves to be a desire that can be incorporated into an individual's life as a source of strength rather than regret: what is lost, both personally and collectively, can be remembered without being mourned. Personal interaction between the three characters, Corky, Marisa (who are the same person at different ages), and Amalia, dominates; thus the politics of Chicano identity are inferred, unlike in *Pancho Villa* and *La Carpa Aztlán.* In its first publication, Moraga self-consciously calls the piece "*teatro* in two acts" on the title page, while in the 1994 publication it is subtitled "a stage play in three portraits." While *Giving Up the Ghost* resembles traditional *teatro* the least of the three plays in terms of form and style, being poetic and dreamlike rather than comic, its content deals the most directly with nostalgia. The self-identification achieved by Marisa and Amalia corresponds with a larger cultural self-awareness; the Chicana learns she is a woman with an indigenous relation to the earth and neither element of this self need dominate or denigrate the other.

What little plot evolves in this drama concerns Corky's evolution to the mature persona of Marisa, growth nurtured by love for Amalia and for Mexico. The most harrowing monologue of the play is Corky's description of her adolescent rape by a janitor at her school. He made her, she cries, a hole, "with no teeth / with no hate / with no voice / only a hole / a hole!" (29) Like the enormous hole gashed in Mexican territory after 1848, Corky's loss cannot be recuperated. The rape that violates her early adolescence destroys Corky, but she can become Marisa from those ruins. Her desire for Amalia combined with a burgeoning love for Mexico rehabilitates her as a complete human being, and while her loss of innocence is not forgotten, just as Mexico is not forgotten, it defines her life without disabling it.

As a figure of memory for Marisa, Corky embodies a healing figure, similar to the role some American Indian societies granted the homosexual (Allen 2). Marisa's difference, her love for women, finds expression in the recuperation of an indigenous past common to all Chicanos, but understood and accepted by few. In one early scene, Corky is described as "wearing a native bruja mask . . . [dancing] across the stage with rattles in her hand" (19). She is an image in Marisa's mind, of both her own childhood and the early days of the Chicano people. Amalia shares this desire for recuperation, telling Marisa:

> I dreamed we were indias. In our village, some terrible taboo had been broken. There was thunder and lightning. I am crouched down in terror, unable to move when I realize it is *you* who have gone against the code of our people. . . . I did not fear that los dioses [the gods] would enact their wrath against el pueblo [the people] for the breaking of the taboo. It was merely that the taboo *could* be broken. (33)

Exactly which taboo has been violated is not clear: a woman loving a woman, a Mexican-born Chicana loving an American-born Chicana, an artist loving a *pachuca,* or the acceptance that home is no longer Mexico. If all of these taboos are unstable, then other assumptions about cultural and individual identity may be malleable as well.

"Giving up the ghost," then, involves abandoning the nostalgia that keeps us from living in the present. In Moraga's play the ghost is patriarchal and colonial oppression, of women and indigenous people, but it is also more subtly the ghost of the Chicano's loneliness in the United States. While Amalia insists that Mexico describes her own loneliness, the play shows us that her alienation is more than personal; it is collective and can be borne constructively. The loss of the past is irreversible, but the past can be carried into the present and future as a guide and not necessarily a burden. It cannot be used at all, however, until it is known and remembered, incorporated into the body politic as an element of imagination and hope. *Teatro* Chicano provides such an incorporation, staging history for all who would understand Chicano identity today.

I have argued here that *teatro* represents history, both cultural and personal, as a negotiation with nostalgia. Nostalgia for an idealized Mexico seduces the Chicano, on stage and off, as well as the non-Chicano American who wishes to posit Mexico as a quaint space of inexpensive vacations marked almost exclusively by its difference from the United States. When those of us north of the Rio Grande pretend that Mexico today is dominated by glories—either Aztec and Mayan or revolutionary—long past, we blind ourselves to our own mixed culture's debts to the Mexican present. If we take Chicano culture's reconstruction of Aztlán seriously, however, as a simultaneously real (in the past), lived-in (in the present) and hoped-for (in the unoccupied future) location of Mexican-American-Indian identity, we can resist nostalgia. The borders of "Mexico" have shifted in time and they are as attached to history as to geography. Chicanos who believe in Aztlán describe their homeland as an area comprising both the U.S. and Mexico, in between and of them both, but separate. Desire for such an unfixed space, an area whose definitions remain alterable by our action in the present, can become a project of rejuvenation, of tempering nostalgia with hope.

NOTES

[1] Unless noted otherwise, all translations are my own.

[2] See the work of Yolanda Broyles-Gonzáles, both essay and book, for a feminist critique of Teatro Campesino's collective values.

[3] For a full explanation of the term Aztlán, see Gloria Anzaldúa, *Borderlands/La Frontera*, especially 1-13.

[4] A scene near the end of Robert M. Young's 1982 film, *The Ballad of Gregorio Cortez*, illustrates this aspect of teatro. To raise money for his forthcoming appeal, Cortez's supporters enact his exploits escaping the Texas Rangers, set to music, on a makeshift stage before the courthouse where he has been found guilty of murder by an all-white jury.

[5] I use amateur in the best sense of the word here—a lover of—to indicate El Centro Su Teatro's status as a non-equity, non-professional (actors are paid little or nothing for their work), community-based company.

WORKS CITED

Allen, Paula Gunn. *The Sacred Hoop: Recovering the Feminine in American Indian Traditions*. Boston: Beacon, 1986.

Anzaldúa, Gloria. *Borderlands/La Frontera: The New Mestiza*. San Francisco: Spinsters/Aunt Lute, 1987.

Beaty, Jerome, and J. Paul Hunter, eds. *New Worlds of Literature*. New York: Norton, 1989.

Bhabha, Homi K. *The Location of Culture*. New York: Routledge, 1994.

Broyles-González, Yolanda. *El Teatro Campesino: Theater in the Chicano Movement*. Austin: U of Texas P, 1994.

——. "Toward a Re-Vision of Chicano Theatre History: The Women of El Teatro Campesino." *Making a Spectacle: Feminist Essays on Contemporary Women's Theatre*. Ed. Lynda Hart. Ann Arbor: U of Michigan P, 1989: 209-38.

Cervantes, Lorna Dee. "Heritage." *Hispanic American Literature*. Ed. Nicolás Kanellos. New York: HarperCollins, 278.

El Centro Su Teatro. *La Carpa Aztlán Presents "I Don't Speak English Only."* Unpublished, 1994.

Hicks, D. Emily. *Border Writing: The Multidimensional Text*. Minneapolis: U of Minnesota P, 1991.

Kanellos, Nicolás. "An Overview of Hispanic Theatre in the United States." *Hispanic Theatre in the United States*. Ed. Nicolás Kanellos. Houston: Arte Público, 1984, 7-13.

——. *A History of Hispanic Theatre in the United States: Origins to 1940*. Austin: U of Texas P, 1990.

Moraga, Cherríe. "Giving Up the Ghost." *Heroes and Saints and Other Plays*. Albuquerque: West End, 1994, 1-36.

Rosales, F. Arturo. "Spanish-Language Theatre and Early Mexican Immigration." *Hispanic Theatre in the United States*. Ed. Nicolás Kanellos. Houston: Arte Público, 1984, 15-23.

Saldívar, Ramón. *Chicano Narrative: The Dialectics of Difference*. Madison: U of Wisconsin P, 1990.

Stewart, Susan. *On Longing: Narratives of the Miniature, the Gigantic, the Souvenir, the Collection*. Baltimore: Johns Hopkins UP, 1984.

Valdez, Luis. *The Shrunken Head of Pancho Villa*. In Jorge Huerta, ed. *Necessary Theater: Six Plays About the Chicano Experience*. Houston: Art Público, 1989, 142-207.

Ybarra-Frausto, Tomás. "I Can Still Hear the Applause. La

Farandola Chicana: Carpas y Tandas de Variedad." *Hispanic Theatre in the United States*. Ed. Nicolás Kanellos. Houston: Arte Público, 1984, 45-60.

FURTHER READING

Criticism

Adams, Kate. "Northamerican Silences: History, Identity, and Witness in the Poetry of Gloria Anzaldúa, Cherríe Moraga, and Leslie Marmon Silko." In *Listening to Silences: New Essays in Feminist Criticism*, pp. 130-45. Edited by Elaine Hedges and Shelley Fisher Fishkin. New York and Oxford: Oxford University Press, 1994.

Explores the ways in which the poetry of Moraga, along with Anzaldúa and Silko, challenges "the silencing forces of cultural and literary history."

Foster, David William. "Homoerotic Writing and Chicano Authors." In *Sexual Textualities: Essays on Queer/ing Latin American Writing,* pp. 73-86. Austin: University of Texas Press, 1997.

Contains a discussion of Moraga that focuses on "the intersection between Moraga's Chicana lesbianism and the relationship between Spanish and English that is established through bilingual code-switching."

Gaspar de Alba, Alicia. "*Tortillerismo*: Work by Chicana Lesbians." *Signs* 18, No. 4 (Summer 1993): 956-63.

Surveys works published in the United States by and about Chicana lesbians, including Moraga's *This Bridge Called My Back*.

Additional coverage of Moraga's life and career is contained in the following sources published by Gale: *Contemporary Authors,* Vol. 131; *Contemporary Authors New Revision Series,* Vol. 66; *DISCovering Authors: Multicultural Authors Module*; *Dictionary of Literary Biography,* Vol. 82; and *Hispanic Writers.*

Anne Perry
1938-

(Born Juliet Marion Hulme) English mystery writer.

The following entry provides an overview of Perry's career through 1998.

INTRODUCTION

Anne Perry is known for her evocation of Victorian England, which she uses as backdrop in her two mystery series. Her novels are characterized by vivid characters, intricate relationships, and the exploration of moral dilemmas.

Biographical Information

Anne Perry was born Juliet Marion Hulme in London, England. As a child she suffered from various lung illnesses, causing her parents to move the family to New Zealand for the better climate. Perry spent most of her solitary childhood in hospitals. In New Zealand she struck up a fatal friendship with Pauline Parker, who convinced Perry to help her kill Parker's mother. Perry and Parker were both convicted of the 1954 murder and subsequently spent five and a half years in prison. When she was released, she returned to live with her mother in England and took her stepfather's last name Perry. She never finished her formal education and began a series of odd jobs, including flight attendant, assistant buyer for a department store, and a limousine dispatcher. Perry moved from England to the United States and while working as a nanny, she discovered the Mormon religion to which she has remained committed ever since. Perry began writing historical novels in 1972, but had trouble focusing on historical detail. She redirected her efforts to the mystery genre, and sold her first novel, *The Cater Street Hangman,* which was published in 1979. Perry is a prolific, best-selling writer who has published steadily since her first book. There was significant publicity surrounding her previous identity upon the release of the 1994 film *Heavenly Creatures,* which chronicled the infamous New Zealand murder. Rather than hindering her book sales, however, fans remained loyal, and interest in Perry's work by those previously not acquainted with her escalated.

Major Works

Perry sets her detective novels in Victorian England and uses historical detail to create setting and atmosphere. Perry's novels are characterized by observations of morals and values in the Victorian era. She often uses the fear of loss or an ethical conundrum as motives in her narratives. Perry has

two major mystery series. The first focuses on Charlotte and Thomas Pitt. She is an upper-class woman who has chosen to "marry down." He is a middle-class police officer. Perry often plays off the pair's obvious differences. Pitt is familiar with the seedy side of London and the psychology of the criminal mind. Charlotte opens aristocratic doors to Pitt which would normally be forever sealed. Perry uses her novels to uncover moral issues that plagued Victorian England. The Pitts uncover the crime of infanticide in *Callander Square* (1980) and incest and child abuse in *Cardington Crescent* (1987). *Bethlehem Road* (1990), investigates the severity of Victorian property laws, *Highgate Rise* (1991) investigates high society members who are secretly slum lords, and *Ashworth Hall* (1997) tackles the politically controversial "Irish Question." William Monk and his friend Hester Latterly are the protagonists of Perry's other series, which begins with *The Face of a Stranger* (1990). The plot twist here is that Monk suffers from amnesia due to a carriage accident. He is simultaneously constructing his own identity as he moves through criminal investigations, first as a police officer and later as a private investigator. In *A Sudden, Fearful Death* (1993), Perry addresses the questions of women's rights and abortion through Monk's investigation of the rape of a young woman and the earlier murder of a nurse. In *Cain His Brother* (1995), Monk looks into the disappearance of a man whose wife suspects her husband's brother of foul play.

Critical Reception

Reviewers often mention Perry's desire to expose the moral and social problems of Victorian England. Rosemary Herbert stated, "her intent has been to entertain the reader with well-paced action and strong plot lines while uncovering societal woes." Critics compliment Perry on her command and elicitation of the Victorian era in her novels. Emily Melton stated, "Perry is wonderfully adept at depicting the customs, manners, morality, fashions, and speech of Victorian London." Some critics, however, find Perry's Victorian details wholly inaccurate. Anthony Lejeune asserted, "[Perry's novels] have been praised by the upmarket American press for their historical authenticity and atmospheric plausibility but authentic and plausible, to anyone with the slightest knowledge of the period, they are certainly not." Reviewers have also accused Perry of infusing too much melodrama in her novels, thus slowing the usual suspense of the detective story. Yet, Perry has developed a loyal following of readers who are drawn to both her characters and their milieus. Linda DuVal concluded, "Although she's a master storyteller, it's her finely drawn characters and her penchant for dealing with social and moral issues that keep readers coming back."

PRINCIPAL WORKS

The Cater Street Hangman (novel) 1979
Callander Square (novel) 1980
Paragon Walk (novel) 1981
Resurrection Row (novel) 1982
Rutland Place (novel) 1983
Bluegate Fields (novel) 1984
Death in the Devil's Acre (novel) 1985
Cardington Crescent (novel) 1987
Silence in Hanover Close (novel) 1988
Bethlehem Road (novel) 1990
The Face of a Stranger (novel) 1990
A Dangerous Mourning (novel) 1991
Highgate Rise (novel) 1991
Belgrave Square (novel) 1992
Defend and Betray (novel) 1992
Farriers' Lane (novel) 1993
A Sudden, Fearful Death (novel) 1993
The Hyde Park Headsman (novel) 1994
The Sins of the Wolf (novel) 1994
Cain His Brother (novel) 1995
Traitors Gate (novel) 1995

Pentecost Alley (novel) 1996
Weighed in the Balance (novel) 1996
Ashworth Hall (novel) 1997
The Silent Cry (novel) 1997

CRITICISM

Publishers Weekly (review date 5 April 1991)

SOURCE: A review of *Highgate Rise*, in *Publishers Weekly*, Vol. 238, No. 16, April 5, 1991, p. 138.

[*In the following review, the critic concludes, "Rounded out by a host of lively characters, [The Face of a Stranger] is a memorable tale."*]

Having temporarily abandoned Victorian police inspector Thomas Pitt and his highborn wife, Charlotte, in her last, highly acclaimed novel, **The Face of a Stranger,** Perry features the duo once again. She exhibits her customary skill in recreating 19th-century London, but here her well-drawn contrasts of upstairs and downstairs Victorian society have added psychological acuity. And her focus on a social issue—the secret ownership by members of high society of appalling slum housing—lends depth to the mystery surrounding the death of Clemency Shaw, a courageous woman who devoted her life—and may have lost it—to exposing those who built their fortunes on the misery of the poor. Highgate is a posh Victorian neighborhood that becomes the scene of some highly dramatic house fires that consume people dear to Dr. Shaw, Clemency's husband, a free-speaking liberal who is Perry's most dynamic character to date. Just who is the target of these infernos? Thomas and Charlotte seek answers, while Charlotte in particular finds that Clemency's legacy of compassion did not die with her. Rounded out by a host of lively characters, this is a memorable tale.

Anne Perry with Diana Cooper Clark (Fall-Winter 1992)

SOURCE: "Interview with Anne Perry," in *Clues*, vol. 3, no. 2, pp. 52-65.

[*In the following interview, Perry discusses her writing style, her major characters, and the reason she places her detective fiction in the Victorian Era.*]

[*Cooper Clark:*] *You first published* **The Cater Street Hangman** *in 1979. As a novelist who is relatively new to the world of detective fiction, what kinds of problems have* *you encountered? In getting acknowledged? Having your books available? With sales? Advertising?*

In America I have had few problems, although I don't know about advertising of course, not having been there. In Britain unfortunately I have had almost every problem—neither advertising nor reviews, except one in a local paper. I took my book to the paper myself because I happened to know the journalist. But other than that, nothing in Britain. I have been very fortunate with reviews in America which my publisher has sent me, and I have received letters from readers.

In the last three years you've published four detective novels and you have written two more. In addition, you've written two non-mystery novels. How do you account for this prolific output? Are you bursting with things to say?

Yes, I am. I love to work morning, afternoon and evening. I love to describe things, I love history, I love to try and take a reader into the world that I see: to feel it, taste it, smell it, hear it, to feel as the people concerned feel. There's an old proverb that I believe comes from this part of the world: if you could only walk a mile in the other man's moccasins you'd know how he felt. I suppose this is what I'm trying to say. Historically, everybody has something in common with us today. There's an old French proverb, with which I don't entirely agree, which says that "to understand all is to forgive all." I wouldn't go so far as to say we should forgive all, but to understand all is perhaps at least to love if not to forgive, which is not necessarily the same thing. The essence of my writing is the exploration of the nature of self-mastery, courage and compassion.

Your books reflect this. They remind me of Thoreau's admonition to "Be a Columbus of the mind."

I think that's wonderful. I'd love to be a Columbus of the mind and a Marco Polo and a Magellan.

In what sense?

To be somewhere that I have not been before. I would also like to shed new light on the old possibilities. How is that for a compromise?

Why did you choose to write Victorian mysteries? What is it about the period that attracts you? Was it perhaps the dichotomy and schizophrenia of Victorian society—the woman as whore or Madonna, the very rich and the very poor, the moral rectitude and moral decadence, the violence and obscenity lying under the mannered surface, or as you say in your novel **Paragon Walk** *the nasty little secrets that snap through the civilized veneer?*

Exactly. I couldn't have put it as well myself. It is all of that

and I also love the civilized violence of some of their conversation, I love their insults, and I like the sense of wit that's wrapped so neatly but is so barbed. I like the sense of period dress as well; it's wonderfully elegant on the exterior. These dramatic contrasts are most interesting.

You can see that cultural dichotomy even in their dress. The well-dressed Victorian woman went out of her house with ten to thirty pounds of clothing on, yet she maintained the illusion of fragility and delicacy.

It's the contrast between illusion and reality which is very satisfying for a mystery writer because after all the essence of mystery is that you should uncover a little at a time and that things should not be obvious. Therefore, I think that the Victorian period is ideal for a mystery writer because so many things are not what they seem.

Yes. In your novel **Resurrection Row** *Aunt Vespasia says that "society is all to do with what seems, and nothing to do with what is." Is that what you're talking about through the character of Aunt Vespasia?*

Yes, to a certain extent. She goes a bit further than I would, but a great deal of society is what seems rather than what is. The Victorians had a marvellous ability not to see what they didn't wish to see. They carried it to an even greater art than we have today. Of course, they had to. If they were to look at what was really there, it would have been unbearable, wouldn't it? But I think we today still have a great ability not to see what we don't wish to see.

I agree with that. On the subject of historical mysteries, Peter Lovesey has written: "And how productive the nineteenth century was of motives for murder. The need to achieve security by inheritance, or life insurance, or marriage; the risk of losing it when scandal threatened; the equating of sex with sin; the stigma of insanity; the things that went unsaid. Our world of social welfare and easier divorce and psychiatric care has removed many of the bad old reasons for murder. How uninspiring, too, by contrast with times past, are the modern weapons—the gun with telescopic sights, the car bomb and hypodermic syringe. Give me Jack the Ripper's knife or Neill Cream's bag of poisons or Lizzie Borden's axe."

He's said it all there. I think in a good mystery story the reader should identify with the criminal and feel that in those circumstances. "I might well have felt compelled to do the same thing if I was frightened enough and cornered. It's not outside understanding that a person should do this." I don't like motives of just pure greed or just pure malice unless there is a very strong reason. I like to feel that the reader would identify with the criminal, with all the people involved, and with the detective. I always feel that insanity or just pure basic greed are cop-outs. I don't exactly want the reader to feel "there but for the grace of God go I," but at least the reader should understand why it was that this person felt this way. I agree with Peter Lovesey. There were so many more motives in Victorian society. They were far more restricted. Other alternatives were not there.

Do you think that everybody's capable of murder, given the right circumstances?

I should think most people are, yes, if they are frightened enough and they have to act quickly enough either in defence of themselves or in defence of somebody else they care for deeply and the means are at hand. I don't know about absolutely everybody but a great many people. But whether it would be classed as murder or self-defence or whatever, I'm not sure. May we say capable of killing rather than capable of murder?

That's perhaps a better distinction.

Murder presupposes a certain guilt whereas killing can be justifiable homicide. I would think most women were capable of killing to defend a child, probably most men to defend their children or their wives or their homes, especially if they didn't have time to think, to find another way out. Time is a strong element.

Would you be capable of killing?

I don't know. I would think probably, if I felt that it was the only answer. Almost certainly, yes, if I was defending somebody else.

I'm thinking here of your character Dominic, because one of the points that you make in two books is that he doesn't have the passion or imagination to kill. Do you think that somebody with, let's say extreme sensibility and intense emotion within themselves, would be more capable of killing?

Yes, but Dominic might kill if he was cornered and it was a matter of self-defence, but he'd have to be driven very hard.

To change the subject, is your "sleuth," Charlotte, the new emerging woman that Thomas Hardy speaks about in his novels? She's a woman who dares to defy convention by marrying a policeman, Thomas Pitt, a man who is socially beneath her.

Charlotte is just me. If she wants something badly enough she'd do it and think afterwards; she'll do it and pay the price, thinking later, "good heavens, what have I done, what has it cost me." But it's an emotional thing, it's not sitting down and thinking, "should I do this or shall I do that?"

So Charlotte isn't really a feminist?

Not consciously but probably subconsciously. You see, I have never been consciously a feminist unless I see a particular case of injustice. I've always been brought up in a family where I have been treated as an equal with my brother so I've never had to fight for intellectual and social equality. Therefore the idea of having to fight for women's rights has only come to me relatively recently. The character of Charlotte is not written with the brain; she's written with the emotions and the guts. She is a lot of me.

In **The Cater Street Hangman** *Charlotte is not a "sleuth." But in your subsequent novels she is. How do you account for this change?*

It probably never occurred to her that it was possible for her to do it. She really didn't have much of an opportunity until the murder happened in her own immediate area and then, of course, when she married the policeman she discovered that meddling was rather fun.

Peter Lovesey and Jean Stubbs have suggested that the vicarious need for excitement in very dull lives was important in the Victorian upper class.

Oh yes, I think so. Everything that I have read would indicate that that was very strongly so and a lot of their excesses sprang from boredom. Imagine if there was nothing that you needed to do how quickly you would get bored. If you go on holiday, the first day of doing nothing is marvellous, the second day is less marvellous and by the third day it's driving you crazy. If you have life where you are unnecessary really, it breeds not only boredom but a lack of self-worth.

That's important to Charlotte.

Yes it is. It's important to everybody even if they don't realize it. Many of the people who indulged in some of the peculiar Victorian vices and the general wasting of time—gambling, crazy carriage races, wild flirtations and affairs and what have you—behaved this way because it sprang from boredom. Sometimes this behavior springs from a need to convince yourself that you're alive, that you have a purpose, and that you have an identity.

You're right that everyone needs self-worth but the definition of worth for the beautiful ladylike Victorian woman was that she was useless. It was a way of defining yourself as beautiful—the privilege of not having to work. Uselessness was aesthetic.

Yes, that's true. But if society says that, does it necessarily make for happiness?

That's a good point because Charlotte certainly doesn't accept society's definition of her role in life.

And her sister, Emily, increasingly is finding the static upper class life less satisfying; she enjoys a jolly good meddle as well.

Usually detectives are male and either celibate or with a wife firmly in the background. But Charlotte Pitt is not only highly visible and incorporated into the story, she also becomes involved in the detective work. This is unusual in the Victorian mystery story. Of course she is married to a policeman, and she and her sister Emily can infiltrate the world of "Society"; they can hear things Thomas would not. When you were thinking of the character of Charlotte, is this one of the ways in which you thought you could ease her into her role as sleuth?

I started by wanting to show both upstairs and downstairs in a Victorian household and thereby get both sides of the story. I used Charlotte and her husband, Thomas Pitt, to do this. I'm not sure honestly which idea came first, it sort of happened. This was one way to explore the dichotomy you were referring to earlier. One person wouldn't see both sides behaving naturally. If Charlotte had gone downstairs to the kitchen, the servants would have immediately altered their behavior and if Pitt had gone upstairs into the drawing-room the upper class likewise would have altered their behavior. So in order to see both worlds naturally, I had to have two people from different classes.

I'd like to get back to the subject of women. Women were extremely limited in the Victorian period. Charlotte's father would not allow her to read the newspaper because as the narrator writes in **Callander Square,** *newspapers carry "little else but crime and scandal, and such political notions as were undesirable for the consideration of women, as well, of course, as intellectually beyond them." In addition, men did not like a tongue as frank and undisciplined as Charlotte's.*

It's still not so popular for a woman to have intellectual opinions and be quite as frank as Charlotte. I hadn't realized this focus until you asked the question but probably it's a good deal of my own feeling coming through because I've found myself a little less than popular on occasion for being articulate, having opinions and perhaps being less reticent than I might have been about expressing them.

To continue with that, throughout your novels we see that Charlotte has political convictions with regard to Reform Bills in Parliament such as the Poor Laws. Why hasn't her interest (given that she is a woman who is more than aware of the unequal position of women in her society) focused on Women's Property Rights, the Divorce Laws and women's suffrage? Dependence in the Victorian period was a part not only of woman's supposed nature, but also it was incorporated into English law. I wonder why Charlotte has so much compassion and sympathy for the poor when she herself is in a position that is inferior by law and by society.

Give me time, I'll get around to it (laughs). I think it's a very good idea. It's possibly a jolly good motive for another crime. I feel I ought to deal with one thing at a time or it's going to become too confused. But you've given me a good idea, I'll get around to that. We've had quite a number of women suffrage programs on television and I just didn't want to get on the bandwagon. Also women's property rights are now fairly well settled and some of the other things that I've dealt with, in some cases, are still open wounds. You'll have noticed that I've covered child pornography quite a bit; well, you know that's currently on the rise. That is a valid thing to be concerned about because a significant number of children are still abused. Quite a lot of the things I've covered are current whereas women's suffrage is not. We do have the vote and for goodness sake we've got a lady Prime Minister (laughs). We haven't got anything like equal representation in Parliament but there's nothing the law can do about that.

You have a proportionately high number of female murderers in your books. In five novels, you have three female murderers. Why?

Because women were so limited, as we've said before, in their dealing with things. The law didn't give them an opportunity to get out of their difficult situations and when you are as restricted as that you have to take matters into your own hands if you're going to solve the problem to your liking. The more restricted you are by outside circumstances the more inventive and perhaps the more violent you tend to be within those limits. Perhaps it is also because I am a woman that I can think of situations in which a woman might do those things, not that I'm suggesting that it's acceptable or excusable. Possibly the women's motives were stronger because Victorian men had so many other ways out of their particular problems.

Your ratio of female murderers is statistically high but then literature is not sociology.

Also the idea happened to occur to me. When I start to write, the first thing that comes to me before anything else is motive. Now what is a strong motive for a crime? Then I build upon the motives that have occurred to me and it just seems to have been the ones that have been the most appropriate for women.

You said before that Charlotte is yourself, a kind of alter-ego.

A part of me anyway.

I'd like you to clarify those parts and also what about Thomas Pitt? He seems to be a part of you, although perhaps in a lesser way.

Charlotte is physically quite a lot like me or at least when I was her age. I think probably her speech patterns, her thoughts, her instinctive ideas, and much of her behavior is me. But she doesn't have my darker side. I'm more of a fighter than Charlotte. I don't think there is a character that's really as close to me in the detective stories as there is in my historical ones. In my historical novels there are people who are more like me. Also Charlotte has no particular religious conviction, therefore, that whole side of my life which is possibly the most predominant side, is not there. I would like to be as compassionate as Thomas Pitt is, and I would like to have Aunt Vespasia's sense of humor.

Is Charlotte in any way a fantasy for you? Other writers have admitted that their main characters were. The reader is told several times in several novels that Charlotte is Pitt's haven.

Not really. I think if I were going to identify in that sense with either one of them it would be Pitt. Charlotte is far more domestic than I am. I would love to wear the clothes of that period, but that's about as far as the fantasy goes. If I wanted the life of any one of those people it would be Aunt Vespasia's. She has tremendous courage, she's outrageous, she's a fighter, she's compassionate, she's at the top of her tree socially, and there's a streak of ruthlessness in Aunt Vespasia—ruthlessness and courage in fighting for what she wants but yet with great compassion. I don't admire ruthlessness in itself but I admire courage and single-mindedness. If you have power, you have the responsibility to use it well. Power is opportunity; it's opportunity to do well or do badly. If you make a mess of it the penalty is very dreadful but if you do it well what you can achieve is enormous. One of the things that I admire in Aunt Vespasia is that she feels responsible; she has the best qualities of her class, of knowing that every privilege carries a very great responsibility.

She's involved in the Poor Laws.

Yes, she has power, therefore, she knows that she must be responsible for change, for improving things, for seeing that those who do not have the power are cared for. I don't think she would ever walk by on the other side. I hope Charlotte is going to become like her but I can't do it in a hurry be-

cause Charlotte is still only young. You see, Charlotte is quite a bit younger than I am.

P. D. James has said about women who write detective fiction: "I think women like writing about human beings and their reaction to each other, and detective novels ... as well are about human beings and their reaction to extreme stress. I think that we often write about a fairly domestic situation; the contrast between this and the horror of the actual murder is very effective." Do you agree with that?

Very much, she's put it beautifully. I am really less interested in "who did it" than I am in the stress of the investigation afterwards, and all the other little sins you turn up, as well as the major crime. It's the little sins and what people will do to hide them that I find the most interesting and the most enthralling. It is like peeling the layers off an onion.

*We can see this interest in all your novels. In your next novel, **Funeral at Rutland Place,** the narrator says that "the mystery of murder was ephemeral, even paltry: it was the emotions, the fire of pain, and the long wastelands afterwards that were real." In **Callander Square,** we're told that "murder and investigation reveal to us so many things about each other which we would rather not have known." In **Resurrection Row,** Pitt wonders whether Dominic is "afraid of the scandal and all the dark, corroding suspicions, the old sores opened up that investigation always brings." In **The Cater Street Hangman,** nobody can trust anyone else. Charlotte understands that it's "like ripples on a pool, and perhaps the rings would never stop." As recently as 1980, the police urged British women to think carefully about all the men that they knew, including their husbands and fathers, in case one of them was the dreaded Yorkshire Ripper.*

This is exactly what I'm trying to write about—the distress and the suspicion and the fear and the re-examination of everything that you've previously taken for granted. I can remember frequently the radio, television and newspapers advising us to not exclude anybody. I wrote **Cater Street** before this happened but it's just this sort of situation and really I'm only using the crime as a catalyst to peel off the layers of everything else in people's lives and lay bare the truth. Truth has a fascination for me even if it's an unpleasant truth. There is something beautiful even in the most naked, bare or otherwise ugly truth simply because it is truth and in the end you have to return to it. Maybe you can't take it all at once but there isn't anything else to build upon.

Do you read detective fiction?

I've been reading quite a bit since I came here to Toronto and haven't had a television. I've been buying different authors and reading maybe three or four of their works and studying them and I've learned a lot. Before that I've thoroughly enjoyed people like Josephine Tey but really I have done very little reading. I was only writing to my own needs, instincts and obsessions but not to a formula. I do plan my book out before I start because I couldn't possibly just start writing and hope it would end up in the right place. I have to know the end before I write the beginning. Even in the historicals I'm writing toward a conclusion the entire time.

You've written two (as yet unpublished) non-mystery novels. Do you fear that fans will tie you to Charlotte and Thomas Pitt Victorian mysteries? Ruth Rendell's fans clamor for more Wexford novels every time she tries to write a non-Wexford and she'd like to do other things. Or are you still at the stage where you're very happy that people are clamoring for Charlotte and Thomas?

I'm delighted that people like Charlotte and Pitt. I'm aware that there is a difficulty with the historical novels I write because they are not "romantic." I know that there is a difficulty in classifying them but I'm not prepared to alter them. I'll just have to let my agent and such publishers as might be interested worry about what they're going to do. They might have to be published under a man's name because I understand that historical novels written by a woman are automatically slotted into "romance" but when they are written by a man they are slotted into perhaps the more political power struggle. My novels focus on the political power struggle. If readers see a woman's name on the jacket, the ones who want the political focus will not look at it and the ones that want romance will look at it and see that it's not what they wanted and put it down. As a result nobody will buy my book (both laugh).

Do mystery and non-mystery stories satisfy different parts of your literary being and if so in what way?

I suppose they do. I hadn't really thought about that but, yes, they do satisfy different parts of my personality. I enjoy constructing a mystery and then peeling it off bit by bit. The Victorian era is very different from the other historical periods that I have chosen. I think lots of people like a mystery. It is the same as filling in a crossword puzzle or discovering anything little by little. There is in most people something that likes to unwrap layer by layer and spin out the pleasure of discovering a mystery. My historicals deal with fictional people observing very tumultuous and conflicting real events. I just love the drama and the knowledge that this really happened. Human beings like myself experienced these things and were torn apart by these fears, terrors, beliefs and ideals, and writing about it is the next best thing to going back and actually seeing it. In fact, it's even better because you have all the excitement and the internal knowledge without the actual pain or physical danger. I have written a novel about the Spanish Inquisition called *Thou*

With Clean Hands. I think the Spanish Inquisition period for the ethical conflict was one of the most fascinating. Many of the conflicts, particularly over "free agency," are still very apposite today. We don't these days feel passionately about religion but we do about politics and we'll bomb other people to death for their own good (laughs).

That's like the Crusades.

Yes, "better dead than red" or whatever it might happen to be which is the same basic feeling as "better dead than a heretic"—"we must cut out this infection before it spreads any further; you may not realize this, dear, but for your own good, better we should kill part of you than that all of you should fall to whatever it is that we don't like whether it's communism or Lutheranism or Catharism or whatever it might be." One can understand that there was a certain genuine feeling with the Inquisitors, "I'm saving your soul and if it has to be at your body's expense, well, that's dreadful but better your body perish than your soul." I must respect that. I can exalt, preach, teach, love and plead with you but if at the end of that you choose to believe differently that is your right. It's a very difficult conclusion to come to and even now we all try to persuade people who are closest to us of our own way of belief and we feel we are doing them a favor and that we have a responsibility to do so. It's very difficult to allow people you care for to go the way that you believe is a mistake. I have also written a novel about the French Revolution, *Lower Than The Angels.* The more I look at the tragic revolutions that we keep having in the world (how many we've had in the last forty years!) they do almost always seem to follow a very similar pattern. The French Revolution was perhaps in some ways the most dramatic because it had so many larger-than-life figures in it and it's sufficiently distant from us that we can see it more clearly now. Yet it's sufficiently close to us that there's a great deal of record about it down to what people actually said and what they wore and many diaries still extant. I think it is a valid thing to explore because we know a great deal about it and the pattern seems to persist tragically.

*The Victorians hadn't accepted the combination of good and evil in one person. They could not accept ambivalence. Martha Prebble in **The Cater Street Hangman** is a good example of this. There's always a sense of irreconcilable pain and suffering in your novels. This creates tension between the Victorian rigidity and the Victorian disorder.*

I would like to think that I don't tie these important experiences up because life isn't like that. Any crime is going to scar. Crime is a tragedy and it is going to scar a lot of people. It isn't going to be tidied away and the police can't put it in a bag and carry it off and that's the end of it. It's bound to leave wounds behind in almost everybody it touches. I would like to make my novels true to life at least in that respect.

In **Paragon Walk,** *Pitt says that he dislikes hanging although it was "a part of society's mechanics to purge itself of a disease." W. H. Auden has talked about this and so has Julian Symons.*

Characters at one time or another say a lot of things that I don't necessarily agree with. In the most recent novel I've written (which is as yet unpublished), **Bluegate Fields,** I made a fairly strong statement about hanging and that's what I really feel. Until such time as we can be absolutely sure that we are justified, I question hanging as a solution to crime. And even so I like to give people the opportunity to repent because people do change. I believe very, very passionately in the opportunity to repent. I can't afford not to have the opportunity and don't want to refuse it to anybody else. As far as hanging people is concerned, many mistakes have been made through British law. If you put somebody in prison and you discover afterwards that they were not guilty, that is bad enough; you could never give them back those years and the damage you've done them. But if you hang them, there is nothing at all you can do. If God were the judge, all right; He doesn't make mistakes but we do. Therefore, we can't afford to do something irreparable.

Would you feel that way if your mother or father had been the victim of a murder?

I don't know but I hope so. The fact that a person is my mother or father doesn't make them any more valuable than if they were somebody else's mother or father or nobody's mother or father. A wound to me is not more serious than a wound to anybody else.

Don't you think then that revenge is in any way mythically purging or psychologically purging as some people do?

No, it compounds the wound. It may have been Bacon who said, "He who revenges himself upon his enemy is equal, he who forgives him is superior," and I believe that very strongly. "Vengeance is mine sayeth the Lord, I will repay." If you harbor hatred, you may damage somebody else but you certainly damage yourself. So, no, I don't agree that vengeance is purging. I think you've committed a second wrong against yourself.

You've written novels that belong to the tradition of murder as the inexcusable act and justice as the inevitable end. But in some of your novels the murderer escapes society's kind of justice. Nancy Wingate, who wrote a very good article on characters in detective fiction who have escaped society's retribution, believes that the satisfaction of the traditional mystery story comes not *from the reader's certainty of the immanence of justice but from his/her certainty of the immanence of truth. It doesn't matter who does the killing, but only that the reader knows who did the crime. In your next novel,* **Funeral at Rutland Place,** *the reader discovers the murderer, but Charlotte lets the killer go free. Do you agree that detective stories gratify a passion for truth, not a passion for justice?*

Yes, I agree. But while I believe that morality is absolute, it is also complex. I think we are becoming much less rigid in our requirements of detective fiction. We used to be very black and white. Killers were always beyond the pale regardless of how harshly they had been provoked and the law always had to catch up with them or they had to be killed or commit suicide or whatever. We're now getting away from the black and white and nearer to the shades of gray. The public will accept that the killer doesn't necessarily have to either shoot him or herself or get carried away in handcuffs to find a satisfactory end. We're getting much subtler as time goes by. And we're beginning to learn that there are an awful lot of other sins that are not necessarily crimes because it isn't practical in law to have them as such. Nevertheless, there are other things which are almost as unpardonable as killing.

Such as incest or child pornography?

Child pornography, yes, depending upon whether your mind is deranged. Incest, I feel, is a crime of distress and so is pederasty. Usually the people who offend are even more pathetic than the victims.

You are a Mormon with strong beliefs. Harry Kemelman uses the rubric of detective novels to convey the world of Judaism and his beliefs. Father William Kienzle does the same for Roman Catholicism in his detective stories. How do you incorporate your Mormon faith into your novels if you do?

It's there in my philosophy, in my beliefs, but it's never stated. It's coming through subconsciously. It must be in my characters' standards, their values, their beliefs, their sense of responsibility, and the sense that every human being is a son or daughter of God, that there is no separateness from any person regardless of age, sex, color or whatever. Yes, I am my brother's keeper; there is somebody to whom I am answerable. I'm answerable to God not only for what I do but for what I say and what I think. God is my father. To me, a father is somebody who has absolute standards but who will love me even though he doesn't always approve of me and who in the last extreme will do everything he can to save me.

I remember that you talked to me about the pragmatism of

the Mormon faith. And Charlotte and Thomas are very pragmatic. Could you explain what you mean by that because I thought it was beautiful?

There is a great deal of deep doctrine which does touch on things of God, things of Holiness, but, yes, it's a very practical religion. It teaches you everything that you need to know to make your life more satisfactory, to help you realize your fullest potential. Mormonism teaches, "man is, that he might have joy," which, to me, is a wonderful thought. Everything that is, exists so that it might fulfill the measure of its creation, whatever it is. If it's a bird, it exists so that it might be the best possible bird; if it's a human being, it exists so that it might fulfill every good potential within it. I suppose Mormonism is such an ingrained part of my life, and it should be, that it comes through everything without having to be said.

I'm delighted. That's the nicest compliment you could possibly pay me.

Charlotte may be more you, but Thomas, as we said before, has your compassion. Did you choose the Victorian period because the gap between the "haves" and the "have nots" is so starkly and painfully emphasized?

Yes, because they are so closely side by side. I do love the dramatic, I must admit. The Victorian period is marvellously picturesque too, isn't it, it's beautifully visual. And the two extremes really rub shoulders in the street. I mean, the Devils Acres is in the shadow of Westminster. It's because they are so closely positioned side by side that the effect is so dramatic.

One of the things that strikes me about your novels is that Pitt only explores the upper class, the aristocracy. Why never the lower and middle class?

For a start, the aristocracy is more articulate, therefore, it gives me more scope for generally expressing my feelings and for getting a little bit of humor in. I like the scenery of the beautiful clothes and again, if you are entirely with the less well-off people, you don't get the dichotomy between the two totally different classes. Maybe it's a little bit of wish fulfillment but I identify much more easily with the upper class; I can imagine myself in that situation. We have many really excellent writers in Britain who write of the working class background and its people. I don't feel competent to handle it because I know that I don't understand it although my own grandparents and great-grandparents and great-great-grandparents, certainly on one side, were very ordinary people. I didn't know them, I've not been brought up in that background and I really think I'd probably make a hash of it. I can glimpse it, I hope, but I feel far more comfortable with the other people. It is more fun to get these

catty drawing room parties. The upper class people are much more devious whereas the poorer people would be less subtle perhaps; they wouldn't need to mask things, they wouldn't have the leisure with which to develop these abilities and therefore I think it would be less fun to write about.

Also it allows Pitt the opportunity to exercise his psychological perception of people in an age where there was no forensic medicine or other modern tools of investigation.

Added to which, again, the sort of motive I deal with is more likely to crop up in the upper classes where they have something to protect. If you are very poor, your motives for murder are not likely to be those of protecting your situation or reputation.

In **Funeral at Rutland Place,** *Charlotte wonders if people who get murdered have some "flaw in them that invites murder. . . . Like Shakespearean tragic heroes—one fatal deformity of soul that mars all the rest that might have been good." In a way that disturbs me because it means that the victim is responsible for his or her murder.*

I'm not thinking of murder for gain or chance victims; I'm thinking of domestic situations where the person who is the victim and the person who is the offender have known each other for a long time and it's the result of a relationship. I believe that most murders are domestic. There is very often a flaw or something that has provoked the situation because murder is an awfully extreme way out of anything. In any relationship that is unsatisfactory it's very, very seldom contributed to by only one party. Nearly always both parties contribute to it and that was what Charlotte meant.

Victorians called them "bed" murders. What kind of research do you do for your books—newspapers, books on fashion and furniture, history books, books like Kellow Chesney's The Victorian Underworld?

Yes, particularly *The Victorian Underworld*. It's a marvellous book. I've got a whole shelf of books at home right from Kellow Chesney up to the High Society. There is a lovely book called, I think but I'm not sure, *The Party That Lasted a Hundred Days* about the London High Society Season. Also I've got two enormous copies of the illustrated *London News* for a couple of years in the 1880s and I go through those as well for the advertisements. I do use the books more. I've always been afraid of over-researching since I've been criticised for it earlier on and stories should be about people. Your research should only prevent you from making mistakes. There's tremendous temptation when you find research fascinating yourself to cram in every fact you know and kill the story and thereby kill the relationship between people.

Your novels are complete stories in themselves but they are also linked. There's an evolution. When you wrote **The Cater Street Hangman** *did you have a plan for a series or did it just evolve organically?*

It just happened. When I wrote **Cater Street** I only intended to write one novel. I got rather taken with the idea and I thought this is a lot of fun.

What did you think you'd write after **Cater Street?**

I was thinking of going back to historicals again. But when **Cater Street** was accepted that was absolutely marvellous. That was the first book I'd ever had accepted. I think it was my agent who said to me, "Have you thought of doing another one?" Besides I enjoy them.

How did you think of Charlotte and Pitt?

Occasionally, if you are fortunate, you get a character that does more than you expect just as sometimes you get characters you think are going to be great and they die on you. You realize you've written five chapters and you haven't mentioned them again. Pitt, however, sort of charged in and took over. I hadn't particularly intended him to come to life so much but I think I was a little enamored of him myself by the time I had finished.

Many detective novelists such as P. D. James and Friedrich Durrenmatt, believe that the detective and the criminal are mirror images of each other. I don't see that in your books at all.

It isn't there. It's something I've never seen myself. I hadn't even thought of it until I heard other people say so.

Writers like George Bernard Shaw and Colin Wilson have written about the relationship between the artist and the criminal. What do you make of these analogies?

You see, I'm just writing a story; I'm not trying to be as symbolic as that. I'm not being consciously intellectual. Of course, many protagonists have a capacity for evil but one's capacity for evil is pretty much governed by your situation and how tempted you are. Charlotte has a capacity to sometimes be thoughtless as well as all are and her evil is usually unintentional, but then a lot of people's evil is unintentional. It's mixed with fear, confusion and stupidity. Charlotte has hurt people along the way, said and done silly things, which after all is the level of evil that most of us reach. Very often if the evil that you do is greater than that it's because the circumstances have compounded to make your actions result in something much more evil.

In **The Cater Street Hangman** *Charlotte said that when*

Verity was killed she had been abrupt with her, sharp with her, and now she was dead and she couldn't make it up to her. We talked a little before about how you create a plot. I believe you said that motive comes first.

The motive and the crime come first because I believe very strongly, as you probably observed, in making the crime spring from a very strong feeling. I was thinking the other day about the basic motives for crime that I find satisfactory—fear is one of the strongest, not necessarily physical fear but fear of losing something that is desperately important to you such as reputation, prestige or status. Also hatred, if you've been offended against so desperately that you simply cannot bear it. Anger must be a red hot thing or else outrage that somebody is surviving and is going to continue to do something so monstrous and there is no way within the law that you can prevent them. Greed is a motive but there are times when it's a satisfactory one. I don't like the motive that hinges on inheriting money, I would rather it be the capacity to make more money and somebody stands between you and it. I think I've used that once or twice. I don't like cold-blooded motives; I like people to be driven into corners because then you can identify with them. I view crime as a tragedy, not as an intellectual exercise.

What do you mean?

I suppose here you come back to the Mormon philosophy. Mormon philosophy teaches that the whole of life is progress and every good thing you do increases your spiritual growth while every evil thing you do or opportunity for the good lost, sets you back a step. Although you may well offend against others and you may offend against God, the greatest offence is against yourself because you have diminished what you might have been. If you commit an offence of any sort, the person who suffers irreparably is yourself because it is your soul that you have damaged. Therefore, any crime is a tragedy most of all for the person who commits it; of course, it's a tragedy for the person against whom it is committed but that may be reparable if not in this world perhaps in the next. As the offender, you can never be as if you hadn't done it; you may repent, you may learn from it, and you may forgive yourself, and certainly if you repent the Lord will forgive you, but the real damage you've done is to yourself.

Anne, why do you write?

I love to, I have to, it's necessary to me. The other day somebody said to me, "You shouldn't write so much, you are turning out too much," and I spoke to my agent Nancy, and said, "I don't know that I can help it." Her reply: "You can't write less, it's like telling the birds not to sing."

As Carlos Fuentes has said, a story is like something burn-

ing in your hand. You must let it go. You told me that this is the first interview that you've ever done. Some writers like V. S. Naipaul think that interviews are wounding, they take a part of you away. Other writers like the Nobel Prize winner Saul Bellow says that interviews are like a thumbprint on his windpipe, yet the great poet and novelist James Dickey thinks that interviews are a great art form of our time. Do you find interviews both enjoyable and/or useful as both a writer and a reader?

I would have said that an interview by a good interviewer, such as yourself, is a mirror and therefore it is very useful indeed. It will hopefully show you your best side and perhaps some of the flaws because if you don't see the flaws you can't do anything about them. I find it enjoyable and extremely useful as a writer. I enjoy reading good interviews; if the creative process and the thought process and the beliefs of the writers are gone into, it gives an added dimension to their work. If I don't learn from this interview, I'm stupid.

Finally, are you comfortable with physical and/or psychological violence? Why do you think you write physical violence so well?

I find physical violence relatively easy to write even if it distresses me horribly when I read it back. I don't know. It's something I haven't resolved. It's a dark side of me that I don't understand yet.

Emily Melton (review date 15 March 1993)

SOURCE: A review of *Farrier's Lane,* in *Booklist,* March 15, 1993, p. 1300.

[*In the following review, Melton lauds Perry's* Farrier's Lane.]

Perry's Thomas and Charlotte Pitt mysteries, set in Victorian London, are a long-running success on the historical whodunit circuit. In the duo's thirteenth adventure [*Farrier's Lane*], Thomas is investigating the murder of a prominent judge, a crime he feels is linked to the macabre Farrier's Lane murder. A young Jew, Aaron Godman, was hanged for the Farrier's Lane crime some years before, but the murdered judge, who heard Godman's final appeal, seemed to be considering reopening the case. The evidence in both murders is frustratingly difficult to uncover and the witnesses strangely reluctant to talk. The stymied Pitt is under pressure from his superiors to solve the judge's murder quickly and leave the earlier case buried. It's Charlotte to the rescue, proving that a wife's social contacts are as valuable as a copper's badge. Perry is wonderfully adept at depicting the customs, manners, morality, fashions, and speech of Victorian London. Her characters are authentically and appeal-

ingly drawn, and her plot is sinister, gripping, and intense, with a surprising but satisfying ending. Like the earlier entries in the series, this is certain to be popular with fans of historical mysteries.

Thomas Boyle (review date 17 October 1993)

SOURCE: "Strangled by Gaslight," in *New York Times Book Review,* October 17, 1993, p. 47.

[*In the following review, Boyle attributes many of the problems of Perry's* A Sudden, Fearful Death, *to its unfocused protagonist William Monk.*]

Anne Perry has published more than a dozen crime novels set in Victorian England. Her labors have brought her a wide readership and a certain beyond-the-genre literary distinction. *A Sudden, Fearful Death* is the fourth in a series whose nominal hero is William Monk, a police officer who left the London force under an unspecified cloud to set up shop as one of the first private detectives. He is subsidized by Lady Callandra Daviot, an unkempt widow of means and good intentions, whose only requirement is that Monk disclose to her some of the details of his adventures in the demimonde.

In the early pages of the novel, Monk is summoned to investigate the rape of a respectable young woman in her family's backyard. With little legwork or concrete evidence, Monk solves the case summarily. The remainder of the novel concerns the mystery of the fatal strangling of an educated and ambitious nurse who had served with Florence Nightingale in the Crimea (the time of the action is 1857, a year after the end of that war). This investigation is carried out not only by Monk but also by the regular police, with amateur turns provided by Lady Callandra and another Crimea-veteran nurse.

Unfortunately, *A Sudden, Fearful Death* is a miasma of narrative infelicities that makes one yearn for a revival of the *real* Victorian practitioners of unreadable melodrama—Bulwer-Lytton, say, or Mrs. Henry Wood. Much of its difficulty seems centered on the unfocused character of Monk, who, we are told early on, had been in a recent accident "and woken . . . knowing nothing of himself at all, not even his name. Certainly it was the crack to his head which had brought it on, but as fragments of memory had returned, snatches here and there, there was still a black horror which held most of it from him, a dread of learning the unbearable. . . . He still felt a dark fear about things he might yet discover."

A detective with a shattered memory who thinks in overheated, equally shattered prose is a most unpromising guide through a suspense thriller. Moreover, the mystery of

Monk's "dark fear" of his past is never resolved in the book, leaving one to wonder why it is introduced at all. This absence of development is reflected in a larger way in the minimal sense of any movement toward a solution to the central crime, the murder of the nurse, until, *deus ex machina,* an innocent—and apparently extremely stupid—woman remembers in the closing pages that she has in her possession letters that will identify with certainty not only villain but motive and finally bring to an end the interminable investigation and climactic trial.

Nor are such lines and situations anomalies in this novel. Barely a page goes by without another example of grammatical and narrative incoherence, as if the text has been constructed as a kind of mirror image of Monk's identity crisis. Frequently the dialogue and expository passages seem to have been constructed by two different, noncommunicating intelligences. A serious question is posed by a detective, usually "dryly"; the respondent then comes back with a remark accompanied by an inexplicable smile or some other puzzling display of humor—puzzling considering the gravity of the situation, and since none of these facial tics lead to any revelation of character or advancement of the plot. ("Monk smiled with a downturn of the corners of his mouth," an act that, after considerable experimentation, proves physically impossible.)

It would seem that Ms. Perry (and her editors) have set out to satisfy two of the most enduring—and most base—of the undiscriminating reader's desires. These are the provision of speciously significant information, which makes the lazy reader feel educated without requiring him actually to *learn* anything, and, secondly, the illusion of having one's social consciousness raised, giving complacency to couch potatoes.

So, yes, as the plot grinds on we are exposed to patches of the social history of Victorian England, about as much as can be garnered in a half-hour of documentary television. Yes, the streets were cesspools and the hospitals breeding grounds of disease and the methods of the regular police (and forensic science) rudimentary at best.

And, yes, again, the sensitive and *au courant* subjects of women's rights and abortion are raised, indeed are essential to the final explanation of the killing. But anyone looking in these pages for enlightenment will be disappointed. Ms. Perry's ultimate message is as hopelessly muddled as Monk's memory.

Anne Perry with John Darnton (interview date 5 March 1995)

SOURCE: "Writer Perry Faces Up to Dark Secret of Murder," in *Star Tribune,* March 5, 1995, p. 1F.

[*In the following interview, Perry discusses her involvement in a 1954 murder in New Zealand.*]

Interviewing Anne Perry, the detective novelist who harbored the dark secret of her identity as an adolescent murderer, is frustrating. It's like trying to capture the mist that rolls off the mountains in the Scottish Highlands where she makes her home.

It is not that she is reluctant to talk. Far from it. The words come out in compulsive torrents. With little prompting she speaks about her early years, her childhood pneumonia and bronchitis, the "courage and love" of her parents, her deep attachment to her father, a time of trial in prison, her epiphanic conversion to the Mormon church in northern California.

It's that when all the words are added up, she has shed little light on the crime that shocked a nation 40 years ago and half a world away. The motives that caused two young girls to conspire and kill the mother of one in August 1954, after taking afternoon tea in a sunny park in Christchurch, New Zealand, are as elusive as ever.

"Like any other traumatic experience, nature helps you to put it away," she said. "All I can remember was feeling very afraid and very jammed into a corner. I didn't want to do it and I couldn't think of any way of getting out of it."

She cannot, she said, recall anything at all about the crime itself and very few details about the subsequent trial, other than "the sense of helplessness when people tell lies about you and you can't say, 'No, that's not how it was.'"

Perry, 55, was forced to admit her prior identity as 15-year-old Juliet Marion Hulme because of interest in the murder case stirred up by *Heavenly Creatures.* The film, which she refuses to see, opened in the United States in November but did not open in Scotland until mid-February.

To counter what she insists is a grotesque and distorted portrait of herself, she has participated in a publicity campaign to tell the world "who I really am." What began as "damage control" has turned into a single-minded and self-absorbed crusade of revelation, obfuscation, justification and attack.

"I think it's time that possibly we question the acceptability of making a film about people who are still living, because of the damage it can do," she said. "It can ruin lives."

Six months ago Perry was beginning to enjoy the luxuries of a writer on the verge of making it truly big: a 12-room stone cottage with a spectacular view of Dornoch Firth and two Jaguars in the driveway. Her 82-year-old mother lives in a nearby fishing village.

Since 1978, her Victorian-era mysteries featuring police superintendent Pitt and inspector Monk have been building a steady readership, especially in the United States, where 3 million copies are in print: She recently signed a $1 million contract to deliver eight more books over the next three years. Her life, outwardly at least, was something of a Scottish idyll, filled with achievement and modest contentment.

Then, with a phone call from her London agent, the idyll ended. The agent was puzzled by calls from a New Zealand reporter with a curious tale, a simple case of mistaken identity, which should be swiftly refuted.

Perry recalled, "I had to say, 'I'm sorry, but you can't. It is true.' I thought I would lose everything. I really thought it would kill my mother."

And so began the mystery writer's long revelation of her own mystery, beginning with a visit to her mother, who had expected the secret to break someday, and phone calls to friends and business colleagues who had no idea of her past. It was, she said, "one of the worst days I've ever lived through."

The 1954 case was a seminal event for New Zealand. It seared the repressive, conservative, English-aping society like a red-hot poker, the way certain murder cases do.

The prosecutor who won a guilty verdict called it a "coldly, callously planned murder committed by two highly intelligent and sane but precocious and dirty-minded little girls." They were sent to prison for 5 ½ years, and released with new identities on the condition that they never see each other again.

The film tries to explain the crime as an outgrowth of an aberrationally intense friendship with lesbian overtones between Pauline Yvonne Parker, 16, poor and withdrawn, and Juliet Marion Hulme, 15, affluent and English, who suffered from weak lungs that forced her into periods away from her parents.

Based in part on diaries kept by Pauline, the film depicts the two as outcasts in school who spin an elaborate fantasy world of movie idols and imaginary princes and villains. As family relationships deteriorate, they are drawn into a peculiar emotional symbiosis, and the world turns violent.

And when they are about to be separated, because Juliet is being sent to live with a relative in South Africa and Pauline's mother refuses to let her go along, they decide their only recourse is to murder Pauline's mother. Luring her down a pathway in the park, they repeatedly strike her on the head with a brick inside a stocking. They make no attempt to cover up the act or even the incriminating, strangely jocular diary in which the plan for "moidering" Mother was laid out.

Perry tries to refute this version. She is especially upset at any suggestion of psychological deviance or lesbianism. "I find it grossly offensive," she said. "I was so innocent sexually then." Between sentences, she spits out the prosecutor's words with venom: "dirty-minded little girls!"

She insists that even as a child she knew "the difference between fantasy and reality." Aside from "normal childhood imagination," she did not construct elaborate games with clay figures, she says. And she goes so far as to assert that she was not really that close to Pauline. She simply felt a debt of obligation because Pauline had written letters to her when she was confined to a sanitarium.

The details are sketchy, she insists, and perhaps her behavior was affected by a medication she was taking for her lungs that she heard somewhere was later taken off the market because it "warps judgment." She feared that Pauline would die or commit suicide if she did not join in the plot.

"All I can actually remember feeling is: I don't want to do this. How can I get out of it, hysterically, how can I get out of it? I can't. Because if I don't do it, she's going to die and that's going to be even worse. I'm going to be responsible for a death one way or the other. And this one stood by me, that one I didn't even know.

"My father lost his job and my parents were going to be divorced and that all happened within a matter of days, and we were going to leave the country and Pauline was ill. I just knew she was throwing up after every meal."

Bulimia? "I'm not going to put a name to it. I just know that she was throwing up regularly after most meals, and I believed that if I did not do what I did she would take her own life. I'm not putting words in her mouth. All I will say is this is what I believed.

"I mean certainly we were good friends, but it was a debt of honor. It wasn't a great 'I can't live without you' business that these idiotic movie makers are making out of it."

Following her release from prison, she returned to England and eventually obtained a visa to the United States, where she worked as a saleswoman, a limousine dispatcher and a flight attendant. Twenty-six years ago, she converted to the Church of Jesus Christ of Latter-day Saints and is still an active Mormon.

Attempts to distinguish between right and wrong preoccupy her writing. A sense of persecution threads through her conversation, and expressions of remorse are not volunteered. But she said she accepted responsibility for her deed after a few months in prison and "worked through all that." She has not seen or heard from Pauline since the trial ended. "I wish her well," she said, "but I have nothing to say."

Anne Perry with Mary Ann Grossman (interview date 15 March 1995)

SOURCE: "Long Ago Murder Haunts Mystery Writer Author Anne Perry," in *St. Paul Pioneer Press,* March 15, 1995.

[*In the following interview, Grossman talks about her life and how she is dealing with the publicity surrounding her past.*]

When Anne Perry says that "courage, compassion and integrity are the three greatest virtues," there isn't much doubt she's talking about the importance of these qualities in her own life.

Perry is the internationally known author of 20 Victorian mysteries, praised by critics and fans for their historical accuracy, attention to detail and explorations of the nuances of life in England when the sun never set on the Empire. The British-born author has been touring to promote her newest novel featuring Thomas and Charlotte Pitt, *Traitors Gate* and the paperback of the previous Pitt story, *The Hyde Park Headsman.*

But as she travels the country, she's also squarely facing questions about the storm of publicity that broke last fall when a reporter revealed Perry was imprisoned in New Zealand 40 years ago for helping a young girlfriend commit murder.

"I really never thought it would come out," says Perry, a tall and graceful 56-year-old. "I thought that after so long nobody would know or care about a couple of girls on the other side of the world. I was wrong. Now, I want to encourage others who fall flat on their faces to pick themselves up and never give up on themselves or anyone else. So often, young people who make a mistake are written off. There is redemption."

Perry's story, the inspiration for Peter Jackson's film *Heavenly Creatures,* has been in all the major U.S. media. Most of the stories have been sympathetic, but she's feeling bruised over what she describes as a mean-spirited article by John Darnton in the *New York Times.*

"It was an awful piece," she says. "The writer kept harping on the fact I can't remember the crime. Why would I want to remember? When you pay, you put it behind you. Repentance means living life as best you can. He wrote about how there were two Jaguars in my driveway. He didn't say we'd had a good laugh about the fact that those cars are 9 and 16 years old. He made it seem as though I'm living the high life, but out of this whole thing (publicity about the crime) I've only made 100 pounds (about $150). That was paid by a television station who photographed my house during an interview and I gave that money to a woman with young children who needs household help."

In Darnton's piece, Perry comes off as cold and unfeeling. She's not; she's pleasant, warm, interesting.

In the middle of a description of Victorian women's fashions, for instance, she stretches in her chair and says, "everything then was so elegant. I'd like to dress like that for a couple of days and come slowly down a winding staircase wearing a dress very slim down here (gesturing with both hands toward her hips), with a big, big hat."

Perry was born Juliet Hulme in London in 1938, the year Hitler began his assault on Europe. Her father was a physicist and college administrator, her mother a schoolteacher.

"My mother, who lives a mile from me, is a woman of immense courage," Perry says. "During the war she had breast surgery, my little brother was 6 months old and I was not well. With her arm in a sling, she had to say goodbye to my father, who was traveling. We lived near an arsenal and we were bombed during most of the blitz. Almost every night we ran to the shelter in our back yard. I can still smell the damp earth and feel the cold."

When Perry was 8, she developed chest complications and the family moved to the friendlier climate of New Zealand.

It was during her confinement in a sanatorium for tuberculosis that Perry became good friends with schoolmate Pauline Parker. When the Perry's decided to leave the country, they offered to take Pauline with them, but Pauline's mother refused. So, the 15-year-old girls decided to kill the woman. Perry says she was under the influence of a drug, since withdrawn from the market, that impaired her judgment and that she remembers nothing about who hit the woman repeatedly with a brick. She refuses to see the movie, but is especially angry at the film's portrayal of a sexual relationship between her and Pauline, whom she hasn't seen since their sensational trial in 1954.

Perry served 5 ½ years at New Zealand's maximum security prison, incarcerated with women who'd been convicted of everything from performing abortions and prostitution to theft, embezzling and crimes of violence.

She was 21 when she was released and she returned to her family in the Northumberland area of England. In some ways, she felt as though she'd had no childhood because she'd been ill from 13 to 15, and then in prison.

"It was hard to get used to living in the outside world and I was socially awkward," she recalls. "But I was pretty well read and I'd passed university entrance examinations in English, Latin, history and geography."

Taking her stepfather's name, Perry, she held a variety of jobs in retail selling, fashion and as an airline hostess. By 1967, she'd decided the United States held her future and got a job as a nanny.

She was in California when neighbors introduced her to the Church of Jesus Christ of Latter-Day Saints. With the Mormons, the young woman who was "basically raised agnostic" had found her spiritual home.

Free will and personal responsibility are themes that surface often in Perry's conversation and in her novels, and these are qualities that drew her to the Mormon faith.

"Most Christian churches teach that the fall from Eden— the fall from innocence—was a tragedy and we are seeking to get back to that state," she explains. "Mormons believe knowledge between good and evil is a necessity, that the purpose of life is not to get back to innocence but to progress until we know the difference between bitter and sweet and choose the sweet, the good, out of that knowledge."

She links her faith to her own past in a simple way: "Christ is the son of God and redeemer of this world. Because of the life He led, it is possible for us to repent and start over. I did that. I believe you have to understand why what you did was wrong, not do it or anything else like it again, and you have to forgive others."

When Perry left her nanny job, she took all her possessions on a bus to Bakersfield, Calif., where Mormons Edmund and Peggy Welles made her one of their family. She still considers their home her American base.

By 1972, Perry had returned to England, and it was a conversation with her stepfather that finally set her to writing mysteries.

"I'd been writing steadily, mostly historical novels with plots that were in shambles," she says with amusement. "That's why I succeeded with mysteries; they forced me to write a proper plot structure instead of getting sidetracked on research that interested me but didn't interest the reader. My stepfather had a theory about who Jack the Ripper was. I

wasn't interested in that, but I was interested in what happens to people under intense pressure, how they discover all the things they'd rather not know about themselves and others."

Her exploration of how Victorians in a middle-class London neighborhood behave after a series of murders was the basis for her first Pitt mystery, *The Cater Street Hangman*, published in 1978.

Since then, she's written 15 mysteries about Police Inspector Pitt and his smart wife, Charlotte, which explore timeless topics such as spouse and child abuse, backstreet abortion, women's rights and incest.

Perry's other five books, set in the 1850s, center on private investigator William Monk and his friend Hester Latterley, a nurse who served in the Crimea.

Perry's Inspector Monk books, the first of which came out in 1990, are darker than the Pitt stories because Monk suffers from amnesia and his condition allows Perry to explore responsibilities, especially when the person can't remember what happened. Although she doesn't say so, there seems little doubt Inspector Monk is not far removed from Anne Perry, who can't remember bricks descending on a woman's skull years ago.

Although it took Perry 10 books to earn enough money to support herself, she's recently signed a $1 million contract for eight books over three years, alternating Pitt and Monk stories.

She'll write those stories in her stone house, the shell of which was built in 1813, in the village of Portmahomack, Scotland. When she isn't working, she walks her three dogs and in the evenings "I like to put my feet up and knit while I watch TV."

She says her family, and the people in the village, have been wonderfully supportive since the news of her imprisonment came out. When a couple reporters went door to door "trying to dig up dirt" about her, nobody would speak to them.

Perry's labor-of-love is her forthcoming fantasy, centered on a woman in an alternative world who goes on a long and powerful spiritual journey to discover "every human being is a child of God."

Is this Anne Perry's soul story?

"It's a spiritual biography," she replies, a smile lighting her face. "It's the closest I get to writing from the heart."

Barbara Wickens (essay date 27 March 1995)

SOURCE: "Haunted by Homicide," in *Maclean's,* Vol. 108, No. 13, March 27, 1995, p. 61.

[*In the following essay, Wickens discusses the problems that have plagued Ann Perry since the revelation of her involvement in a 1954 homicide in New Zealand.*]

Anne Perry is nothing if not persistent. For years she led the sort of hand-to-mouth lifestyle that has become the stereotype for the struggling artist. She began writing historical fiction when she was in her mid-20s, enduring 13 years of rejection slips before a publisher finally accepted her first novel in 1979. Even after that, she continued to support herself with odd jobs, from limousine dispatcher in Beverly Hills, Calif., to a series of clerical positions in her native Britain. "It was just six years ago that I made enough money from my writing to finally pay income tax," she said while in Toronto earlier this month to promote her 20th murder mystery, *Traitors Gate.* At last Perry, who now lives in the tiny Scottish Highlands village of Portmahomack overlooking the North Sea, has achieved the security that many writers only dream of: she recently signed a $1.4-million contract to write a further eight books in the next four years. But the tranquillity that came with her success evaporated last summer. In August, *The Sunday News* of Auckland, New Zealand, revealed that Perry was one of the two 15-year-old murderers portrayed in the current movie *Heavenly Creatures.* The film had revived interest in the 1954 slaying of Honora Parker by her daughter Pauline and Pauline's close friend, Perry. The two served 5 1/2 years in prison.

That revelation resulted in a maelstrom of publicity for Perry, 56, who until then had been best known for the historical accuracy and domestic detail of her murder mysteries set in Victorian London. The media scrutiny has come in waves coinciding with the release dates of the movie worldwide. And Perry's attempts to discredit the film, which she refuses to see, have contributed to her continuing notoriety. Her description of it as a grotesque and distorted portrait of her life prompted Miramax Films to place a recent advertisement in *The New York Times* promising to arrange a screening for her. "Please see the movie before you judge it or speak out against it," the ad read.

Despite suggestions by some commentators that such publicity is a great promotional tool for her books—more than three million are in print—Perry says it is not only unwanted but has been devastating for her emotionally. Since her release from prison in 1960, only her family, closest friends and members of the Mormon church, which she joined when she lived in California in the late 1960s, have known that she was the once-infamous Juliet Hulme. She left New Zealand, where her family had moved seeking relief for her

various chest ailments, and took the surname of her stepfather, Bill Perry, who was originally from Winnipeg. Anne Perry says that her 83-year-old mother, who lives near her, "has suffered very much." She adds that people in Portmahomack have been remarkably supportive, as have employees at her North American publisher, Ballantine Books, who offered to release her from the current book-promotion tour. "I very nearly stayed home," she said, "but I've got to either stay in hiding for the rest of my life, or go through this and come out the other side."

Perry seems genuinely mystified by the frenzied fascination with her past. "I thought, 'After 40 years, who cares?' The Berlin Wall has come down, Communism has fallen, the whole world has changed since then." She is also bitter about some of the comments made about her, both then and now—particularly the notion that there was a sexual component to her relationship with Pauline Parker. Perry will not discuss details of the murder, saying only that she remembers little because she was on a medication for her lungs that has since been taken off the market because of its judgment-altering side-effects.

Her voice becomes even edgier when she notes that because she was a minor, she was not allowed to testify at the trial. Adding to her frustration is the fact that the prosecution's case (like the movie) was based largely on the diaries of Pauline, who had outlined her plans to kill her mother. "I don't know how you can use one person's diary as evidence of another person's behavior," Perry says, adding that such scribblings are wide open to misinterpretation. For instance, Pauline, whom she says she has not seen or spoken to since the trial, wrote about seeing "George in the night," says Perry. "I believe that in North America the equivalent is 'the john,' but the prosecution tried to make out that she had a lover."

Her greatest scorn, however, is reserved for those who say she shows no remorse. A proper, almost brusque, Englishwoman, she is indeed no meek penitent. But she insists that "the misrepresentation is pretty high—I always expressed remorse." For now, her goal is to get back into the daily rhythm of her life in Portmahomack, where she lives alone— she never married—in a converted stone barn. Perry, who writes in longhand, works six days a week. *Traitors Gate* is the 15th installment of the chronicles of police Supt. Thomas Pitt and his wife, Charlotte, who uses her highborn connections to help her husband solve cases. Perry has also written five books featuring William Monk, a detective in 1850s London. Under the terms of her new contract she will produce one book a year in each mystery series. She will also finally get to publish some of her historical fiction, including a novel set during the French Revolution. It is one of the books publishers have rejected; Perry is now on her fifth rewrite. But now that her past has been widely publicized, it will be especially difficult for her readers to think about Perry without also thinking about murder.

Emily Melton (review date August 1995)

SOURCE: A review of *Cain His Brother*, in *Booklist*, August, 1995, p. 1911.

[*In the following review, Melton praises Perry's* Cain His Brother *for its "superb plotting, fine writing, intriguing characters, and outstanding historical detail."*]

Perry's lingering fame from the murder she committed as an adolescent won't hurt her latest book's popularity, but there's no doubt that her historical mysteries would be critical and popular successes no matter what her background. Victorian detective William Monk returns [in *Cain His Brother*], this time in one of the most challenging cases he's ever faced. Genevieve Stonefield begs Monk to find her missing husband, Angus, whom she fears has been killed by his twin brother, Caleb. Angus, a respected businessman, loyal husband and father, and pillar of the community, has disappeared after a visit to Caleb, who's as different from Angus as it's possible to be; he's a violent thief, ruffian, and blackguard who lives in one of London's most dangerous slums. Genevieve's fears that Angus is dead at Caleb's hand seem well founded; all Monk has to do is find the means, the motive, the opportunity—and the body. But the more he investigates, the more bizarre twists and frustrating dead ends he encounters, until his persistence finally breaks the case wide open in a stunning climax that surprises even the unflappable Monk. This one deserves high marks for superb plotting, fine writing, intriguing characters, and outstanding historical detail. Buy multiple copies.

Publishers Weekly (review date 22 January 1996)

SOURCE: A review of *Pentecost Alley*, in *Publishers Weekly*, January 22, 1996, p. 62.

[*In the following review, the critic praises* Pentecost Alley *stating, "As Perry edges toward her surprise ending, she crafts her tale with elegance, narrative depth and gratifying scope."*]

The 16th Thomas and Charlotte Pitt mystery [*Pentecost Alley*], demonstrates Perry's trademark skill for enhancing well-designed mystery plots with convincing historical settings and cleverly drawn relationships among characters. In this outing, Pitt, last seen in *Traitors Gate*, tackles a case that could cost him his career. As it has been only two years since the unsolved Jack the Ripper murders, the Home Office anxiously anticipates the speedy arrest of the person who has murdered a Whitechapel prostitute with her own stocking. Finlay FitzJames, a young diplomat who is the son of a powerful merchant banker, is the prime suspect, even though the evidence against him is circumstantial: an old Hellfire Club badge, inscribed with Finlay's name, was found under the prostitute in bed, and cufflinks with his initials were discovered in the room. While Pitt grapples with this politically sensitive case, his sister-in-law, Emily Radley, makes friends with Finlay's younger sister, a social butterfly named Tallulah. Thanks to Pitt's diligence (and Emily's and Tallulah's meddling), the case is closed. Or so it seems until another very similar murder occurs. Whitechapel residents are terrified anew. Parliament is filled with grumblings, the Queen conveys her displeasure and newspaper reporters are turning the investigation into a case study in police incompetence and corruption. As Perry edges toward her surprise ending, she crafts her tale with elegance, narrative depth and gratifying scope.

Anthony Lejeune (review date 6 May 1996)

SOURCE: "A Little Knowledge," in *National Review*, May 6, 1996, pp. 54-5.

[*In the following review, Lejeune discusses the effect of knowing Perry's background on our reading of her work.*]

"An incredible three million copies of her books have been sold in America," boast Anne Perry's British publishers. Incredible, no; if they say so, I believe them. A bit puzzling, yes; the reason for such popularity is not altogether clear. But the operative word in that boast is "America." Although Miss Perry is a British writer, living in Britain, her books are much less well known on the eastern side of the Atlantic. And that's not puzzling at all.

Her novels, set in Victorian London, are—like those of Martha Grimes, an American mystery writer who has set nearly all her books in Britain—full of slight solecisms and anomalies liable to set sensitive English teeth on edge. They have been praised by the upmarket American press for their historical authenticity and atmospheric plausibility but authentic and plausible, to anyone with the slightest knowledge of the period, they are certainly not.

Miss Perry's books fall into two, scarcely distinguishable, series, both featuring police detectives who pursue their investigations through foggy streets to the clip-clop of hansom cabs, from the drawing rooms of Mayfair to the stews of Limehouse. In the latest, *Cain His Brother,* ex-Inspector Monk (now an "Agent of Inquiry," long before Sherlock Holmes claimed to be the only "consulting detective" in the world) searches for a missing man in the fever-ridden slums of the East End. His quarry, a saintly character, had an evil twin brother, who may have murdered him: but there is no body, and the villain is quite confident that none will be found. A trial ensues nevertheless, with a melodramatic denouement.

The mood is gloomy throughout, and, squalor being squalor, well-founded in sociologically inclined history books. So far, so plausible—until the narrative moves into the more socially complex regions of the Bar and the professional classes, where it suddenly becomes apparent that the author does not know what she's talking about. London barristers don't have "offices" in a street near Lincoln's Inn Fields: they had, and have, chambers in one of the Inns of Court. They don't "approach the witness stand" like Perry Mason. Nor are English clergymen called "Reverend Wyndham"—or, at least, they weren't before Hollywood's influence.

In all Miss Perry's books, modern prejudices, particularly about class and the position of women, are constantly insinuated and heavily emphasized. Victorians, however radical, simply didn't think in those terms. Gentlemen, she tells us, "only dabbled, they did not actually work"; which would have astonished some very energetic Victorian gentlemen. As for women, they were "the weaker vessel, expected to weep, to lean on others"; which would have amazed many tough-minded Victorian ladies. On the other hand, no respectable Victorian man would ever have said "what the hell" in the presence of a lady. Still less would a respectable woman have used such language herself ("bloody incompetent generals").

The most recent book in Miss Perry's other series, **Traitors Gate** (why no apostrophe?), set in higher social circles, was even more liable to such solecisms. In it Superintendent Pitt, aided by his wife, Charlotte, investigates a murder in a gentlemen's club. The crime involves Important People: it touches on the colonial struggle for Africa and a sinister anti-democratic conspiracy, the Inner Circle.

Miss Perry has conscientiously studied the background details. She knows London's street plan, what songs were sung in the music halls, what fashions the ladies wore: and she makes sure we know she knows. The effect is spoiled by things in some ways less obscure but perhaps not quite so readily swotted up. The club she writes about, crucial to the story, has a "manager" and "stewards," like an American club, not a "secretary" and "waiters"; it has a "foyer" and a quite impossible inner room for senior members only. The club's domestic arrangements are important because they affect the solution, described as "very clever and very efficient" but in fact absurd.

Even that sort of thing might not matter if the Victorian *feel* were right. There are some other curious Americanisms—

"As close to Westminster as we live" (no Englishman, now or then, would insert the first "as"), "French doors" instead of "French windows," and (admittedly not often) some hilariously dreadful dialogue—"Must be damned urgent to seek a fellow out at his club, what?" When a high flyer at the Colonial Office is described as academically outstanding because he graduated from Cambridge at age 23, one can only ask what took him so long. Again we have the word "bloody" used in the presence of, indeed addressed to, a lady.

Has Miss Perry never seen *Pygmalion*? Has she never read Victorian novels—Trollope, Wilkie Collins, *The Dolly Dialogues, The Four Feathers,* or even the Sherlock Holmes stories? Or another, equally famous, Victorian tale which had better not be named for fear of giving away the twist at the end of **Cain His Brother**? The surprising answer is "Possibly not."

A glance at her biography, as given by the publishers, reveals that, although seemingly a conventional middle-class, middle-aged Englishwoman, she grew up in New Zealand, worked for a while in California, and now lives in a remote Scottish village. But that's not all.

While **Traitors Gate** was in preparation a movie called *Heavenly Creatures* was released, about a forty-year-old case, famous in New Zealand still, in which two young girls, for psychologically obscure reasons, battered to death the mother of one of them. A New Zealand reporter somehow got on the trail of Miss Perry. When asked, she immediately admitted that she had been one of those girls, though not the one whose mother was murdered. She had served five and a half years in a women's prison, was released at age 21, returned to England, where she had been born, and changed her name.

She claims to remember little of the murder and to have long ago lost touch with the other girl. She has never denied her identity but, naturally enough, doesn't like talking about it. She has become a devoted Christian. But she did miss out on a good deal of education.

The publicity that followed the revelation has been handled not so much discreetly as carefully, with well-controlled articles and interviews. Everybody on both sides of the Atlantic who is at all interested in her books now knows the facts. Despite her initial unsophisticated fear that her publishers might drop her if they knew, the story has predictably helped, not harmed, her sales.

All credit to her for making a new life and a successful career. However, I cannot help feeling, as she probably does, that it would be better, from a literary as well as a personal point of view, if we didn't know. People reading her books are now bound to ask: "Can you tell?"

The most spectacular parallel instance is that of James Morris, who underwent a highly publicized sex change while writing his (or her) trilogy about the British Empire. Nobody can read those excellent books now without trying to see the join, the point where the sex change happened. But there is no perceptible join. Nothing alters.

This provokes a much broader and deeper question about authors in general. Which is the real person—the one whose apparently intimate acquaintance we make on the page, or the frequently disappointing figure whose hand we may shake or whom we may see blathering on a television talk show? How do we feel about a woman protagonist, perhaps narrating in the first person, created by a male author—or the other way around? Would we feel differently were we unaware of the author's sex?

Are the currently fashionable courtroom thrillers distinctly better for being written by lawyers? Or *romans policiers* for being written by policemen? Erle Stanley Gardner was a lawyer and Dashiell Hammett had been a private eye, but they both learned more from working on *Black Mask* than from experience in the field. Carroll John Daly, the first begetter of the hard-boiled thriller genre, was rather a nervous man who once thought he should carry a pistol to see what it felt like—and was promptly arrested. Mystery fiction need not be realistic; realism is not the point.

The same applies to espionage fiction. Some writers of good spy stories did have experience in intelligence work, but you would never guess it from their unrealistic tales. Yet John le Carré's not very happy time in the British Secret Intelligence Service provided the pungency of his novels. And the Rumpole stories would be much less fun if John Mortimer were not so familiar with lawyers and judges.

So which is the rule and which are the exceptions? Truthfully, there is no rule. Trying to deduce one leads only into what le Carré calls "a wilderness of mirrors." Homer and Shakespeare are enhanced, not diminished, because we know so little about them. Anne Perry's work would lose nothing if we knew less about her.

Publishers Weekly   (review date 2 September 1996)

SOURCE: A review of *Weighed in the Balance*, in *Publishers Weekly*, September 2, 1996, p. 116.

[*In the following review, the critic lauds the courtroom scenes in* Weighed in the Balance.]

The byzantine politics and aristocratic squabbles of a small German principality called Felzburg exasperate and puzzle William Monk in his seventh distinctive appearance (**Cain His Brother**) [**Weighed in the Balance**]. Monk, a Victorian-era "agent of inquiry," is still haunted by a baffling amnesia, and he feels that his associates—the rigidly proper barrister Sir Oliver Rathbone and the uncompromising and outspoken nurse Hester Latterly—have taken on more than they can handle when Sir Oliver decides to defend Countess Zorah Rostova against a slander charge. The patriotic Zorah has accused Princess Gisela of Felzburg of murdering her husband, Prince Friedrich, heir to the throne, who presumably had died as a result of a fall from a horse. Gisela is suing. The issue of slander is almost lost in all the politicking. Gisela and Friedrich had lived in English exile, Gisela having played a sort of Wallis Simpson role to Friedrich's Edward. But Friedrich dreamed of returning triumphant to Felzburg in order to defend the statelet's independence against the unifying tide of Germany. Zorah's defense requires that Monk polish his image, refine his abrasive nature and interview some devious, scheming—and perhaps murderous—aristocrats. Was Friedrich poisoned? Was Gisela the intended target? Who profits? Are personal or political motives dominant? Perry indulges her characters in a bit too much unproductive speculation, but the novel springs to life in the courtroom scenes, where careful investigation and astute teamwork produce some astonishing revelations that presage the end of Victorian propriety and an era's pretense of innocence.

Marietta Dunn   (review date 29 January 1997)

SOURCE: A review of *Weighed in the Balance*, in *Philadelphia Inquirer*, January 29, 1997.

[*In the following review, Dunn asserts that although* Weighed in the Balance *is not Perry's best work, the continuing narrative of William Monk does keep the reader coming back.*]

Since 1979, the prolific Anne Perry has been turning out a stream of Victorian detective novels featuring Inspector Thomas Pitt and his high-born wife, Charlotte, as they uncover social evils in England and unmask the hypocrisy of those in high society.

Several years ago, Perry added a second Victorian series, one with a clever conceit at its core. The series has as its hero the imperious, brooding, sharp-tongued William Monk, an investigator who has lost his memory in a carriage accident.

Weighed in the Balance is the seventh of these William Monk mysteries.

Because of Monk's memory loss, each book is a double mystery—Monk and his allies seek to solve their cases, while Monk, through brief feelings and flashes from the past, painfully learns more about the person he was—and the person he has become.

In this latest novel, Monk must help barrister Oliver Rathbone discover the truth in a slander case. Zorah Rostova, a noblewoman from a Germanic principality, has accused a princess of murdering her prince while the exiled couple were on holiday in England. The princess, in turn, accuses the noblewoman of slander, leading to a trial. To clear Zorah Rostova, Rathbone and Monk must learn more about the political climate that has divided the principality.

In addition to Monk and Rathbone, the series focuses on Hester Latterly, a nurse who served in the Crimea with Florence Nightingale. Hester is all the things Monk dislikes in a woman—she is outspoken, independent, unbending. She rankles him; he rankles her. Neither Monk nor Rathbone can quite admit what they feel for Hester, who frequently puts herself at risk to help them with their cases.

Always in Perry's books there is an element of romance—a sweetness, however fleeting, amid the horror. This leads those who prefer the hard-boiled style of detective fiction to dismiss Perry's work as so much Victorian piffle. And yet—and yet—the social ills that she bluntly chronicles in her books were very much realities of Victorian times—child abuse, suicide, anti-Semitism, financial and political double-dealing, class prejudice and abject poverty.

On the surface, civility reigns among the upper classes, who adhere to a code of proper social behavior. But Perry strips away the veneer to show the ravages of the age.

Perry is a compelling writer, a wonderful scene-setter, presenting detail after detail that evokes life in Victorian England.

Is *Weighed in the Balance* her best William Monk novel? The answer is no. It's the second book in the series, *A Dangerous Mourning,* that really stays in the mind. In fact, Perry's 16 novels in the Thomas Pitt series are, on the whole, more satisfying reads.

Still, there is something about William Monk that keeps the reader coming back. Perhaps it is the mystery of his past; perhaps it is the uncertainty of his feelings for Hester Latterly.

All in all, it is the richness, the urgency, the almost-overripeness of Perry's writing—and her ability to build tension, even when the plot is a bit thin—that impels the reader to go on.

Rich Gotshall (review date 27 April 1997)

SOURCE: A review of *Ashworth Hall,* in *Indianapolis Star,* April 27, 1997, p. D6.

[*In the following review, Gotshall asserts that readers of Perry's Thomas and Charlotte Pitt series will not be disappointed with* Ashworth Hall.]

Anne Perry is a novelist for the '90s.

The 1890s.

Her mysteries take place during the heyday of Victorian England. Her attention to detail and sense of social order make them read like the best of the works written during that period, rather than re-creations a century later.

Ashworth Hall is the 17th novel featuring Superintendent Thomas and Charlotte Pitt. Yet, the work stands alone, both in terms of background and character.

First-time readers are apt to fall in love with the Pitt's and seek out *Pentecost Alley, Traitor's Gate, The Hyde Park Headsman* and the other novels. And readers of those works will enjoy this installment every bit as much.

Representatives from England and Ireland are meeting in Ashworth Hall, a country estate, to find a way to resolve "the Irish problem," as the British government calls it. Their purpose is to forge a peace between the nations, who have been fighting over religion for three decades.

Superintendent Pitt is assigned to security detail for the gathering, since Ashworth belongs to his sister-in-law, but without revealing his role to either side. Despite Pitt's best intentions, a prominent political figure is soon bashed over the head. Even better, the man was killed while taking a bath in what might as well have been a locked room.

Was it a jealous lover? Irish rebels? Members of a British faction who don't want peace? The only sure thing is that the killer is somewhere in Ashworth Hall.

Who dunnit?

Then a dynamite bomb blows up a desk and another of the negotiators with it. Now it clearly appears someone wants the talks derailed, but is it an Irishman or an Englishman?

There is a bit of levity in scenes involving Gracie, the Pitts' ward, who travels to Ashworth as Charlotte's maid, and Tellman, Thomas' police assistant, who must masquerade as a valet.

Tellman has no idea what to do, and the teen-age Gracie tutors him so he won't embarrass the master and mistress.

The novel has a leisurely pace, as befits a Victorian mystery, but it's by no means plodding.

Readers are likely to be struck by the parallels with the strife in Northern Ireland, showing how little things have changed over the course of a century.

Linda DuVal (essay date 30 April 1997)

SOURCE: "Ann Perry Is a Master at Creating Fascinating Characters, Moral Dilemmas," in *Gazette Telegraph,* April 30, 1997.

[*In the following essay, DuVal discusses Perry's writing style and use of characterization in her novels.*]

British mystery writer Anne Perry is a master at creating fascinating characters and dramatic moral dilemmas. It's territory she's explored in her life, as well as her art.

As a teen-ager, Perry helped a friend murder her friend's mother. She served time for it, and doesn't talk about it in her interviews and book tours.

It's hard to believe this poised, compassionate woman was once convicted of a crime. She has said in interviews that she can't remember the extent of her involvement, and the fact is, she has led an exemplary life since.

But it's a tantalizing clue for readers who marvel at how Perry is able to create such realistic situations and characters in her novels. Her characters are taken, bit by bit, from herself and from people she has known. And she must deal with many people in the course of her daily life, whether it's the workmen who are helping remodel her home in Scotland or the hordes of fans who flock to her book signings.

"I like something about almost everyone," she said during a recent stop in Colorado Springs.

Perry, 58, is the prolific author of two dozen Victorian-era mysteries. She writes two series—one featuring a husband-wife team of policeman Thomas Pitt and his well-born wife, Charlotte; the other centered around a darker character, Inspector William Monk.

Although she's a master storyteller, it's her finely drawn characters and her penchant for dealing with social and moral issues that keep readers coming back.

"I think a mystery can be anything you want it to be—a light romp or a serious exploration of issues," Perry says. "I choose the latter." Her books have dealt with rape, child labor, incest, usury, political corruption, censorship, treatment of the disabled and insane, and many more issues that plagued society 100 years ago—and still do.

"I often get my ideas from current events," she says. "We haven't solved most of those problems yet, have we? It would be lovely to think we've gotten past racial bigotry, child abuse and such."

When she takes on those issues in the Victorian setting—a much more secretive time—they become "that much more shocking," she says. "In many ways, it makes it a much better mystery, a better story, set in those times. Today, everyone seems compelled to talk about their darkest secrets on the television."

In her latest novel, **Ashworth Hall,** Perry deals with the question of home rule for Ireland. The story is so balanced it's difficult to tell where Perry's personal allegiance lies. What's obvious is that she can see both sides of the question and, ultimately, abhors the violence that the issue has bred.

Perry says she tries very hard to understand both sides of an issue. "If I think about it long enough, I can almost always see the other person's point of view," she says. "I have a hard time saying, 'this one's right and that one's wrong.' It's hardly ever that clear, is it?"

She also seldom paints a picture of a character as purely good or unremittingly evil.

"Do you know anyone who is? I don't."

She believes there is good in the worst of us, wicked tendencies in the best.

"We all have things we have to be forgiven for," she says with a wry smile. Perry could well be referring to the dark secret of her own past, which became public three years ago. As a teen-ager, Perry helped a friend murder her friend's mother. She served time for it, missing much of her later formal education because of it.

But what she missed in school, she made up by reading on her own. She loves the writings of G. K. Chesterton, and poetry from the late 1800s to the early 1900s.

"I like the discipline, the form and formality of that poetry," she says. "A perfect sonnet is such a gem."

To ensure her own writing meets her standards, Perry often reads what she has written aloud. "It's my ambition to say something in exactly the right words," she says.

Perry, sporting a short, easy-care haircut, is impeccably dressed in a natty navy wool pants suit with cream trim. It fits her trim, 5-foot-7 frame well. She bought it in New York, and says she loves to shop for clothes in America.

"I wear a size 10, right off the rack," she says. "It's wonderful. At home, I have to have everything altered."

She also enjoys the fan base she has built in the United States and meeting her readers on book-signing tours.

"I like people," she says.

"One of the best training grounds for me has been the church," she says. A longtime member of the Mormon Church, she has been very active in it. "You see the same people week after week and you get to know them pretty well."

As Relief Society president for the church, for example, she had to go into homes of church members who were having a difficult time.

"I was responsible for the temporal welfare of other women in the church. I had to bridge the differences in lifestyle and background, and be nonjudgmental, to deal with people on a meaningful level," she says. "It gave me a much wider insight into other people's lives. It enhanced my own spiritual life and made me not only a better person, but a better writer, I think."

Her compassion for others shows in her books. In *Weighed in the Balance,* for example, she reintroduces a young woman from a previous Inspector Monk novel. The young lady was physically damaged by her father in an incestuous relationship, is in constant pain and can never bear children. In this book, she meets a young man who has become a paraplegic as the result of an illness, and a romance blooms.

It's as if Perry couldn't abandon the character after the first book. She had to resolve her situation and give her some happiness.

"It's true, there's a bit of me in each character, and when I write about them, I become them for a short time," she says.

Her characters are complex, intriguing people. Thomas and Charlotte Pitt, for example, come from very different walks of life. "I created them so that I could have permanent characters to give me the masculine and feminine points of view, and the upstairs-downstairs points of view," she says.

It gives her a much broader spectrum from which to explore each mystery, she adds.

"Women notice little things that men don't, and tell things to each other they'd never tell a man," she says. "Men see things women don't, too. This way, it's a much more complete story."

With her Inspector Monk character, she added an unusual twist. Monk lost his memory in a carriage accident, so he's constantly trying to unravel the mystery of his own past as well as the current murder he's working on.

"I wanted someone who would have to explore themselves as someone else saw them," she says. "If you judged yourself as harshly as you judge others, you'd be horrified. Eventually, he'll bring that compassion (he gains in judging himself) to others."

Hester Latterly, a friend of Monk's, is a nurse who served in the Crimean War.

"Hester is what I might have been if I'd lived then—if I'd had the courage," Perry says with a laugh.

Her characters have flaws. They're real. They make mistakes. "We don't do things without a reason," Perry says. "When we do them, it seems like the rational thing to do at the time."

Though she knows it's risky, Perry would like to try her hand at something other than British mysteries. She's currently working on a book that defies categorization, "a fantasy of sorts, a woman's journey of self-discovery. It has a religious, ethical tone—I don't know, I hope it does well."

She also wants to write a mystery set during the French Revolution. But she won't abandon her thoughtful characterization and her examination of moral issues.

Sensing a sympathetic ear, readers tend to tell Perry about their personal travails.

"About the best thing that ever happens to me is when people tell me they were going through a tough time—a bereavement, or an illness—and reading my books helped get them through it," she says.

"I'm always amazed at people's strength. There's a spark of something in us. People have an amazing amount of courage, sometimes."

"It's true, there's a bit of me in each character, and when I write about them, I become them for a short time."

Jane Dickinson (review date 19 October 1997)

SOURCE: A review of *The Silent Cry,* in *Rocky Mountain News,* October 19 1997, p. 4E.

[*In the following excerpt, Dickinson complains of the obvious ending and difficult to believe plot of Perry's* The Silent Cry.*]*

. . . Anne Perry's novels of Victorian England are prominent on the list of historical mysteries, a rapidly growing niche within the genre that some of us find a bit hard to take. Nevertheless, the best of the bunch deserve the attention of all mystery lovers. **The Silent Cry,** alas, is not among the best.

Perry's 1996 novel **Pentecost Alley** was one of the weaker nominees for an Edgar this year. **The Silent Cry,** though less turgid, also suffers from major flaws that only Perry's biggest fans will be willing to overlook.

When the bodies of respected solicitor Leighton Duff and his barely breathing son Rhys are discovered, kicked and beaten, in a slum street, mystery surrounds not only the assaults but why the duo were in Water Lane in the first place. Police detective John Evan does his best to trace their trail, but it's not until William Monk, no longer on the force but working privately, looks into the murders of several prostitutes that the story takes shape.

Meanwhile, the compellingly dark Monk pursues his personal demons, piecing together the life he lost when an accident wiped out his memory.

Despite some forceful characters, the novel demands disbelief when the conscientious inquiries of Evan turn up few clues, while Monk cracks the case by following much the same path and methods. Perry stretches the reader's patience again in casting the villains in the piece. She never convinces us they're nasty enough or wily enough for the double life they've supposedly been leading. Finally, the ending is at least partially obvious as early as the second chapter.

One reviewer has accused Perry of exploiting the past. Perhaps the inherent problem faced by a writer attempting to mine Victorian England is that Dickens already did it, and very well indeed. . . .

Margo Kaufman (review date 23 November 1997)

SOURCE: A review of *The Silent Cry,* in *Los Angeles Times,* November 23, 1997, p. E2.

[*In the following excerpt, Kaufman praises Perry's* The Silent Cry, *stating that "[t]he denouement is shocking, and the characters are so richly drawn that you'll miss them when they're gone."*]

. . . Anne Perry's new Victorian thriller, **The Silent Cry,** featuring surly amnesiac investigator William Monk and feisty nurse Hester Latterly, is the author's best effort in a couple of years.

Leighton Duff, a respected solicitor, is found beaten to death in St. Giles, a festering slum "only a stone's throw from Regent Street in the heart of London." Lying beside him, barely alive, is his brutally beaten son, Rhys. The pair are discovered by John Evan, Monk's only friend on the police force. Were they attacked by local ruffians while out for an evening's whoring? Is the widow involved? While Evan struggles to come up with a motive, he arranges for Hester to care for the wounded Rhys.

Coincidentally, Monk is engaged by Vida Hopgood, the wife of an East End sweatshop owner, to investigate the brutal rapes and beatings of local prostitutes. It's no surprise that Monk discovers a connection between the crimes, but longtime followers will be pleased that he also gains insight into his feud with his former supervisor Runcorn. The action careers between the low- and high-born in Victorian society. The denouement is shocking, and the characters are so richly drawn that you'll miss them when they're gone. . . .

Alex Auswaks (review date 16 January 1998)

SOURCE: A review of *Pentecost Alley,* in *Jerusalem Post,* January 16, 1998, p. 99.

[*In the following excerpt, Auswaks discusses the questions raised in Perry's* Pentecost Alley.]

. . . Two years after the unsolved Ripper murders a young prostitute is found murdered [in **Pentecost Alley**]. The personal effects of Finlay FitzJames (including a Hellfire Club pin), a handsome and spoilt scion of a rich family, are found in her bed. Is he guilty?

His father is rich and powerful. No policeman dares move against such a family. The family refuses to cooperate. The prostitute's pimp is arrested, tried, sentenced and hanged. But then a second prostitute is murdered and the circumstances are in every particular the same as the first. Again everything points to Finlay FitzJames. Riots break out. There is the threat of the breakdown of public order. Have the coppers framed an innocent man for a rich man's son to get away with murder? This time the FitzJames family cooperates.

Then a third. . . .

The book is full of the language and thoughts of prostitutes: "Some geezers get high on garters. Guess fancy ladies don't wear 'em. All whalebone stays and cotton drawers. . . . Some toffs like ter laugh. Makes 'em feel less like they're in the gutter. Feel like it's a real woman. Them as can't laugh wiv their la-di-da wives."

There is much witty conversation, the subtle put-downs by the upper classes. Interesting questions are raised. What does a playboy do if he marries a rich widow, falls in love with her and wishes to impress her? What do you do if your brother is suspected of murder? What if you are a policeman and your wife has been conducting her own investigation so as to endanger yours?

An entertaining historical piece drawing on the fears of Londoners in the aftermath of the Ripper murders. And a very convincing Whitechapel in 1890. . . .

Lori A. Curnin (review date 26 April 1998)

SOURCE: A review of *Brunswick Gardens,* in *St. Louis Post-Dispatch,* April 26, 1998, p. D5.

[*In the following review, Curnin lauds Perry's strong characterization in* Brunswick Gardens.]

The mystery in **Brunswick Gardens** is simple: who pushed Unity Bellwood down the staircase, causing her death? The answer is not as simple as Anne Perry takes us back to a time in the late 1890s London, where intelligent women were forced to the sidelines, it was legal to beat a disobedient wife and Darwin's theory of evolution was just coming to light.

Inspector Thomas Pitt, a recurring Perry character, has the unenviable task of investigating the murder of Bellwood, an employee in the home of the Rev. Ramsay Parmenter. At first it seems clear cut; Miss Bellwood was heard to cry out "No, no, Reverend" before she was found at the foot of the stairs. But no one really believes such a respected man would kill anyone, even if the person hired to help him in his research of ancient languages taunted him with her atheist beliefs.

Thomas Pitt and his wife, Charlotte, are like old friends to fans of Perry's work and her descriptive writing fleshes out each character, so they are more than black ink on white paper. She also throws in a healthy dose of editorializing the meaning of love and justice through the words of her characters. The mystery itself could be wrapped up in a two-hour television movie; but by allowing the characters voices we want to hear, Perry gives the reader a book in which to become immersed.

Margo Kaufman (review date 4 October 1998)

SOURCE: A review of *A Breach of Promise,* in *Los Angeles Times,* October 4, 1998, p. 2.

[*In the following excerpt, Kaufman praises "the long-awaited romantic denouement* [*of Perry's* A Breach of Promise], *which brought tears to my eyes."*]

Usually while reading Anne Perry's Victorian mysteries, I am struck by how little humanity has changed in a hundred years. But her latest William Monk novel, **A Breach of Promise,** knocked me for a loop.

Barrister Oliver Rathbone must defend Killian Melville, a talented young architect being sued for refusing to marry his alleged fiancee, Zillah Lambert, a charming and beautiful heiress. It is inconceivable that a man could face financial, professional and social ruin for changing his mind about a betrothal, but, as Perry explains it, in a society where appearance is everything, if a man breaks off an engagement to marry (or seems to), people will raise questions as to the lady's morals. . . .

When Melville refuses to give Rathbone a reason for his actions, Rathbone appeals to his partners in crime: detective Monk and feisty private-duty nurse Hester Latterly, who is loved by both men. Unfortunately, before they can ferret out the truth, the trial comes to a premature and tragic halt. But not to worry. No one weaves plot and subplots as seamlessly as Perry, and even a closed case has a funny way of refusing to go away.

Refreshingly, the surly and distant Monk appears to have had a personality transplant since the last book, though Hester, ministering to a soldier who was disfigured in the Indian Massacre, is strangely subdued. Though I would have liked to have seen a final confrontation with the villain, most fans will be delighted by the long-awaited romantic denouement, which brought tears to my eyes. . . .

FURTHER READING

Criticism

Batliner, Doris J. Review of *Pentecost Alley,* by Anne Perry. *Courier-Journal* (10 August 1996): p. A9.
　　Asserts that "The plot of [*Pentecost Alley*] is convoluted and surprising, and the solution absolutely satisfying."

Coughlin, Ruth. Review of *Cain His Brother*, by Anne Perry. *People* (13 November 1995): 3.

> Complains of Perry's use of Cockney speech in *Cain His Brother*.

Dickinson, Jane. Review of *A Breach of Promise*, by Anne Perry. *Rocky Mountain News* (20 September 1998): 4E.

> Calls *A Breach of Promise* "satisfyingly complex."

Foyt, Michelle. Review of *Brunswick Gardens*, by Anne Perry. *Library Journal* 123, No. 2 (1 February 1998): 116.

> States that Perry examines modern themes within a Victorian context in *Brunswick Gardens*.

Review of *Ashworth Hall*, by Anne Perry. *Maclean's* (23 June 1997): 54.

> Praises *Ashworth Hall* for its juxtaposition of Victorian society with the "Irish Problem."

Pate, Nancy. Review of *Ashworth Hall*, by Anne Perry. *Orlando Sentinel* (16 March 1997): F7.

> Praises Perry's mastery of the Victorian setting in *Ashworth Hall*.

Review of *Farrier's Lane*, by Anne Perry. *Publishers Weekly* 240, No. 6 (8 February 1993): 79.

> Calls *Farrier's Lane* "a convincing look at the seamy side of Victorian life."

Review of *The Silent Cry*, by Anne Perry. *Publishers Weekly* 244, No. 28 (14 July 1997): 67.

> Complains that "readers may feel they are bearing the weight of [the plot's] contrivance like so much over-packed luggage."

Additional coverage of Perry's life and career is contained in the following sources published by Gale: *Contemporary Authors*, **Vol. 101; and** *Contemporary Authors New Revision Series*, **Vols. 22, and 50.**

Ntozake Shange
1948-

(Born Paulette Williams) American playwright, poet, novelist, and essayist.

The following entry provides an overview of Shange's career through 1994. For further information on her life and works, see *CLC* Volumes 8, 25, 38, and 74.

INTRODUCTION

Ntozake Shange is best known for her first dramatic production, *for colored girls who have considered suicide / when the rainbow is enuf* (1975). In this work, she incorporates poetic monologue into a dramatic performance, a form she has termed the "choreopoem," and which has also been referred to as "staged poetry." Shange is noted for her dramatic representations of the experiences of African-American women in a theatrical style which incorporates poetry, dance, and music into dramatic monologues. Her novels, like her dramatic works, incorporate a variety of forms, such as recipes, dreams, songs, and letters in a pastiche format, rather than in a conventional narrative. Her collections of poetry share the poetic form incorporated into her dramatic writing. Shange has been both praised and criticized for the ways in which she foregrounds the intersection of race and gender oppression in the experiences of African-American women. Her portrayals of relationships between African-American women and men have also received mixed reactions from critics. Her portrayals of African-American men have been criticized as unsympathetic portraits where the men serve as obstacles in the path of African-American women. While Shange focuses on the pain of their experiences, her characters maintain a sense of triumph over their circumstances, often through finding inner strength and celebrating friendship with other women.

Biographical Information

Shange was born Paulette Williams, the eldest child in a professional middle class black family. Her father was a surgeon and her mother a psychiatric social worker. During Shange's youth she was exposed to many of the foremost black intellectuals and musicians of the time through her parents' social interactions with people such as Dizzy Gillespie, Miles Davis, Chuck Berry, and W. E. B. Du Bois. She received a B.A. from Barnard college and an M.A. in American Studies from the University of Southern California. During college, she went through a period of depression after separating from her husband, and attempted suicide several times. During her years in graduate school

she chose the name Ntozake Shange for herself as a way of connecting with her African roots; "Ntozake" means "she who comes with her own things," and "Shange" signifies "she who walks like a lion." Shange has taught playwriting and creative writing at the University of Houston in Texas.

Major Works

For colored girls who have considered suicide / when the rainbow is enuf is Shange's first dramatic production, and the work which defined her career and reputation. It began as a series of poems, which were later incorporated into a single dramatic performance. *For colored girls* is structured as a series of vignettes relayed through the poetic monologues of the seven principal characters, all African-American women. These monologues incorporate music and dance into the poetic form, as each woman conveys painful experiences such as rape, illegal abortion, and discordant relationships. The message of the play is ultimately triumphant, as Shange's characters conclude that African-American women should look to a female God within themselves for strength, and appreciate that the "rainbow" of their own color is sufficient to sustain them. Shange's second dramatic production, *Spell #7* (1979), is similar in form and style to *for colored girls,* but focuses primarily on racial issues. In *Spell #7,* a group of African-American actors congregate at a local bar, and relate painful experiences, in poetic monologue, dealing with racial matters in their lives. While emphasizing the poetic monologue, *Spell #7* has a more conventional narrative than *for colored girls,* in that the characters interact with one another in the context of a semi-developed story line. *Mother Courage and Her Children* (1980) was adapted from the Bertolt Brecht drama. While the original play was set in seventeenth-century Europe, Shange sets her characters in the post-Civil War era in the United States, where African American soldiers were employed to aid in the massacre of Native Americans in the West. Mother Courage supports herself by selling wares to white people, without concern for the moral implications of her actions. Shange's first full-length novel, *Sassafrass, Cypress and Indigo* (1982), was adapted from her novella entitled *Sassafrass* (1976). The story centers on three sisters and their relationships with men and each other. Sassafrass is a weaver who cannot leave Mitch, a musician who abuses drugs and beats her. Cypress, a dancer in feminist productions, struggles against becoming romantically involved. Indigo, the youngest sister, retreats into her imagination, befriending her childhood dolls, seeing only the poetry and magic of the world. The novel is written in a pastiche style, which includes recipes, magic spells, poetry, letters and other written forms to build its narrative. *Betsey Brown* (1985) focuses on a middle-class adolescent girl in St. Louis in the late 1950s, during a time when American schools were first integrated. Betsey, the main character, is bussed to a predominantly white school, where she is confronted for the first time with racial difference. Betsey must learn to reconcile her African-American heritage with her new environment. *Liliane: Resurrection of a Daughter* (1994) continues Shange's pastiche style, as conversations between Liliane and her psychiatrist are interspersed with first person narratives from Liliane's lovers and friends. Shange's various books of poetry, including *Nappy Edges* (1978), *Some Men* (1981), *A Daughter's Geography* (1983) and *Ridin' the Moon in Texas* (1987), share with her dramatic plays and novels a concern with the experiences of African American women and a non-traditional use of language which captures the rhythms of Black English speech patterns.

Critical Reception

Discussion of *for colored girls* has revolved around the play's unique theatrical form of the "choreopoem," its use of Black English, and the politics of race and gender which it expresses. Martin Godfried praises the production for its form, theatricality and linguistic style in representing African-American experience. He writes: "The essence of the

show remains its pure and perfectly captured blackness. Black language, black mannerisms, black tastes and black feelings have never been so completely and artistically presented. . . . [t]his is truth, energy and strength, theater on the highest level, musical and choreographic to its roots." Shange's dramatic piece *Spell #7* has been described by Don Nelsen as "black magic," and "a biting piece of sorcery." He proclaims the play to be " . . . a celebration of blackness, the joy and pride along with the horror of it. It is a shout, a cry, a bitter laugh, a sneer. It is an extremely fine theater piece." In *Mother Courage,* Mel Gussow affirms that Shange "has performed a venturesome feat of reinterpretation." He explains that "scene by scene, almost line by line, she has translated Brecht into a Black idiom, names, places, slang and heroine." *Sassafrass, Cypress and Indigo* is noted by critic Doris Grumbach as a "narrative potpourri," into which Shange "tosses all the graphic elements of southern black life: wonderful recipes . . . spells and potions (how to rid oneself of the scent of evil), prescriptions (how to care for open wounds when they hurt), letters from Mama to her beloved but straying and erring daughters, full of calm reason and uncritical love, always advising accommodation to the hostility and blindness of the white world)." The novel is praised for its skillful use of a variety of voices representing Black English speech patterns. Reviewing *Betsey Brown,* Nancy Willard states that "Shange is a superb storyteller who keeps her eye on what brings her characters together rather than what separates them: courage and love, innocence and the loss of it, home and homelessness." Reviewers laud Shange's novel *Liliane* for its narrative form, citing consistently penetrating language and important intellectual content. A *Publishers Weekly* commentator praises the novel for its portrayal of the special burdens of a generation of young African Americans.

PRINCIPAL WORKS

for colored girls who have considered suicide / when the rainbow is enuf: A Choreopoem (drama) 1975
Sassafrass (novella) 1976
Natural Disasters and Other Festive Occasions (poetry and prose) 1977
A Photograph: A Still Life with Shadows/A Photograph: A Study of Cruelty (drama) 1977; revised as *A Photograph: Lovers-in-Motion,* 1979
Nappy Edges (poetry) 1978
Boogie Woogie Landscapes (drama) 1979
Spell #7 (drama) 1979
Mother Courage & Her Children [adapted; from the drama *Mother Courage and Her Children,* by Bertolt Brecht] (drama) 1980
Some Men (poetry) 1981

CRITICISM

Carolyn Mitchell (essay date 1984)

SOURCE: "'A Laying on of Hands': Transcending the City in Ntozake's Shange's *for colored girls who have considered suicide / when the rainbow is enuf*," in *Women Writers and the City: Essays in Feminist Literary Criticism,* edited by Susan Merrill Squier, University of Tennessee Press, 1984, pp. 230-248.

[*In the following essay, Mitchell discusses Shange's choreopoem in terms of how it portrays an African American woman's perspective of the city.*]

Ntozake Shange's choreopoem, *for colored girls who have considered suicide / when the rainbow is enuf,* presents the paradox of the modern American city as a place where black women experience the trauma of urban life, yet find the strength to transcend the pain.[1] The women depicted by Shange become physically and spiritually whole, thus free, through the psychic/psychological healing power that resides in the ancient, fundamentally religious act called "the laying on of hands." The believer "knows" that touch can heal if the one who touches is empowered by God; thus, touching stabilizes a person physically while freeing the troubled soul to soar spiritually.

Shange uses the physically and morally desolate cityscape as a backdrop before which to reveal her spiritual vision of female strength and survival. In this respect, therefore, *colored girls* differs from the legion of literary works that depict the lives of urban Afro-Americans.[2] She neither denies nor romanticizes urban black experiences: the choreopoem graphically describes the complex ways in which the rape victim is further victimized by the "authorities"; it reveals the loneliness and guilt of the woman who decides to have an abortion; it details the betrayal women continue to experience in their relationships with men.[3]

While none of these problems is uniquely urban, they are exacerbated by the human estrangements that characterize city life. But Ntozake Shange does have a larger vision. One might think of this vision in terms of two concentric circles, with the outer circle temporarily more powerful than the other. The geographical and psychological "settings" represent one circle; the other is a fragile circle promising transcendence. The external circle is clearly discernible from the beginning; the internal is revealed slowly, growing in strength and intensity until *it* is the dominant one at the end. The second circle, at first a figurative one, becomes a visible, magic enclosure of women who, in joining hands, bless and heal one another while naming their own empowering female god.

Though the presence of the women in the cities cited by Shange may be a matter of exigency, the question of how to find and maintain hope in the face of despair is a crucial one. In spite of the dichotomies established between country and city and though much is made of the romance of country life, humankind has relentlessly gravitated to biblical, literary, and historical cities, the problems and pitfalls notwithstanding. To substitute the word "metropolis" for "city" sheds some light on what seems to be the primal search of all people for a centered, balanced existence. This partial explanation is valid because cities are geographically contained or "centered" entities, as opposed to the random "layout" of the country. Thus, two important ideas surface immediately from the notion of the city as a "contained entity." Paul Tillich, the theologian, offers both: the city as a "centralizing and inclusive place" and the city as a place that accepts both the "strange and the familiar."[4]

First, Tillich, in discussing the "centralizing and inclusive" nature of the city which, he says "influences the character of *man's* (emphasis mine) spiritual creativity," suggests that

> we may take our point of departure from the Greek word *metropolis,* signifying the mother or central city. Everything that exists has the power to be only insofar as it is centered. This is especially true of human personalities and social groups. The power of being, often called vitality, increases in proportion to the degree of diversity which is united at a center. Therefore, man has more power of being than any animal, and a spiritual man has greater vitality than a man with an underdeveloped spirituality. . . .
>
> In applying this ontology of the metropolis to the spiritual life of man, we find that the big city has two functions. It serves in a centralizing capacity and also in an including capacity, and each is dependent upon the other.[5]

According to Tillich, a "metropolis . . . is a center city. It is likewise an including city. It includes everything of which it is the center, and encompasses diversity and freedom of individual creativity and competition."[6]

Tillich uses the word "mother" to identify the genesis of the city, but the city he describes, paradoxically, is masculine.[7] It is an idealized, romanticized, theoretical place where men interact, where ideas flow, where creativity flourishes, and where competition works for the good of all. This vision of the city is one which supports equality of aspiration, mobility of action, and freedom of community that women, in fact, have never known. Tillich and Shange are diametrically opposed to one another in their interpretations of the city; I shall discuss later the ways in which Tillich's idealized city is transformed by Ntozake Shange into a more realistic image. Her poem, **"i usedta live in the world,"** is the psychological turning point in the play and is most indicative of her different view.[8]

"i usedta live in the world" is set in Harlem, the black city within New York City, which figures in Afro-American literature as "Mecca," "the City of Refuge," and in current vernacular as the "Big Apple."[9] However, Harlem has not lived up to its promise; thus it is no surprise that one of the most powerful poems in *for colored girls* is located there.

The woman in blue compares the vastness of her former life in the "world" to life in Harlem where her "universe is now six blocks."

> i usedta live in the world
> then i moved to HARLEM
> & my universe is now six blocks
>
> when i walked in the pacific
> i imagined waters ancient from accra/ tunis
> cleansin me/ feedin me
> now my ankles are coated in grey filth
> from the puddle neath the hydrant
>
> my oceans were life
> what waters i have here sit stagnant
> circlin ol men's bodies
> shit & broken lil whiskey bottles
> left to make me bleed. (28)

She juxtaposes the memory of wading in the Pacific and being washed and nurtured to the filthy water running in the city gutter. The "oceans" were life to her, which suggests the religious reading of the ocean as "Source" or God.[10] In contrast, the city water, instead of cleansing, holds suspended whiskey bottles whose jagged edges threaten her life. The stagnant water also symbolically holds suspended the bodies of old men—the winos, the "flotsam and jetsam" of city humanity. These men and the water circling them form part of the gross external circle mentioned above. They are the reasons why the spiritual self/circle is such a fragile entity, for it is impossible at this point to deal with

this self in the face of the threat to basic survival; the broken bottles in the hands of these men are potential murder weapons.

The poem continues, revealing "a tunnel with a train// i can ride any where// remaining a stranger" (29). The image of the tunnel/ train simultaneously suggests two meanings: the momentary enclosure necessary to arrive at a "larger" destiny/destination and the ultimate enclosure of estrangement which is the life of the stranger in the city. The city subways do reach destinations and one can "ride" them "anywhere," but, in fact, the lady in blue "rides" the subway and finds herself trapped by a twelve-year-old boy who makes sexual advances. She responds,

> NO MAN YA CANT GO WIT ME/ I
>   DON'T EVEN
> KNOW YOU/ NO/ I DON'T WANNA
>   KISS YOU/
> YOU AINT BUT 12 YRS OLD/ NO MAN/
>   PLEASE
> PLEASE PLEASE LEAVE ME ALONE/
>   TOMORROW/ YEAH/ (29)

Her hysterical response and the extorted promise of a meeting tomorrow capture the fear women in the city have for their lives. Granted that the boy may not be a fully grown sexual being, but he most likely possesses a gun or a knife, clearly approved extensions of male sexuality and power. The ambiguous words, "NO/ PLEASE/ I CAN'T USE IT," suggest that this neophyte of a man, having been temporarily stalled, attempts to give or sell some trinket to the woman. This offer further belittles and objectifies the woman, who mourns the loss of her freedom metaphorically rendered in her "imagined waters." Commenting on her current life, she says, "i come in at dusk// stay close to the curb," clearly common-sense tactics for survival in the city.

The twelve-year-old on the subway becomes an urban "everyman" whose violence is contained by the "tunnel" image now suggested in the "straight up brick walls" of the city tenements. The "young man fulla his power" emerges in relief against the limp, powerless "women hangin outta windows//like ol silk stockings." The lady in blue continues:[11]

> wdnt be good
>   not good at all
>   to meet a tall short black brown young man
> fulla his power
>   in the dark
>   in my universe of six blocks
>   straight up brick walls
>   women hangin outta windows

like ol silk stockings. (29)

The helter-skelter, impersonally violent life in Harlem is compared to a more gentle existence when:

I usedta live in the world
really be in the world
free & sweet talkin
good morning & thank-you & nice day. (30)

The poem concludes, and the woman, no longer trusting, courteous, outgoing, reveals that her six-block universe is a cruel, hopeless, inhuman dead end, a closed tunnel ending the promise of freedom in the city. Life in Harlem is a cruel hoax:

> i cant be nice to nobody
> nice is such a rip-off
> reglar beauty & a smile in the street
> is just a set-up
>
> i usedta be in the world
> a woman in the world
> i hadda right to the world
> then i moved to harlem
> for the set-up
> a universe
> six blocks of cruelty
> piled up on itself
> a tunnel
> closin (30-31)

The city described by Shange offers none of the characteristics idealized by Tillich. Rather than encompass diversity, it reflects the fear of racial and sexual diversity. "Individual creativity" is perverted into desperate schemes for survival. "Competition" becomes the "dog-eat-dog" syndrome, rather than the mythologized earn-and-share, secular spirituality of the marketplace. Few can discover a spiritual center in this environment. For Shange, the city must be demystified and demythologized so that the price of human survival there can be truly estimated. The paradox is that the women embody the essence of the *metropolis*, even though they (as black women) are doubly absent from the "defining" language.

Paul Tillich's second point is that the metropolis supports both the strange and the familiar:

The anti-provincial experience furnished by the metropolis is typified by encounters with that which is strange. Meeting the strange can have two consequences. It can produce hate against the strange, and usually against the stranger, because its existence threatens the self-certainty of the familiar. Or it can af-

ford the courage to question the familiar. In the metropolis, it is impossible to remove the strange and the stranger, because every neighbor is mostly a stranger. Thus the second alternative of questioning the familiar ordinarily prevails. . . .

Since the strange leads to questions and undermines familiar tradition, it serves to elevate reason to ultimate significance. If all traditions are questionable, nothing but reason is left as the way to new spiritual content. There lies the connection between the metropolis and critical rationality—between the metropolis and the intelligentsia as a social group. The importance of the encounter with the strange for all forms of the spiritual life cannot be overestimated.[12]

For Tillich, the "strange" and the "familiar" are separate forces that collide with one another, providing the change necessary for a dynamic spiritual life. For Ntozake Shange, the strange and the familiar are the double face of a single entity colliding with itself and with its societal counterpart. The strange/stranger is housed within the individual self *and* in the neighbor next door; the "familiar" has an unrecognizable "face." The orderly process by which "the strange leads to questions and undermines familiar tradition" and finally elevates "reason to ultimate significance" is absent, for, as Shange shows, the path to spiritual transcendence for the urban dispossessed is a decidedly irrational one.

The family is the traditional, familiar entity which provides the sanctuary from which the strange is questioned. Contrary to form, Shange's "family" revealed in "a nite with beau willie brown," shows how the strange and the familiar coexist as one. For example, violence is at once "strange" and "familiar," as are the ignorance, poverty, and promiscuity that preclude any possibility of Willie and his "wife," Crystal, belonging to Tillich's "intelligentsia." Willie and Crystal are the "underside," the "sewer" side of the metropolis.

"a nite with beau willie brown" is set geographically in the prototypical ghetto (Harlem is suggested to me) and psychologically in Vietnam, whereas **"i usedta live in the world"** is split between the geographical Harlem and a psychological place on the Pacific Ocean. The mounting tension in the play as a whole climaxes in **"beau willie"** because there are no pleasant mythic memories (as in the "imagined waters" of the Pacific); there are only the nightmare memories of Vietnam. Vietnam, in this context, clearly embodies the strange and the familiar simultaneously: a strange place and people, but familiar violence. The madness at the core of America is reflected in the Vietnam experience and in the fact that Beau Willie is "shell-shocked" long before he reaches Vietnam. He is a young version of the old men in **"i usedta live in the world."** They are static, trapped in stagnant water, and Willie is like

Fred Daniels in Richard Wright's short story, "The Man Who Lived Underground," who is almost swept away by the torrent of sewer water into which he has dropped while running from the police.[13] One knows instinctively that Willie will not live long enough to grow static, for the aftermath of Vietnam finds him speeding to destruction. Beau Willie is the perennial stranger in American life for whom the familiar only provides additional trauma.

Tillich's familiar seems obvious in the family structure represented by Willie, Crystal, and their children Naomi Kenya and Kwame Beau Willie Brown. But Shange creates a monster in Beau Willie. He is hardly the comfortable image of the next-door-neighbor-as-stranger. Willie is ruined by the war experience, which is clearly the last in a series of psychological events that have crippled him. He is the dominant figure in the poem, but he is bound to his woman Crystal. He is a dope addict; he is paranoid. The lady in red speaks for him:

> there was no air/the sheets made ripples under his
> body like crumpled paper napkins in a summer park/
> & lil specks of somethin from tween his toes or the
> biscuits from the day before ran in the sweat that
> tucked the sheet into his limbs like he was an ol frozen bundle of chicken/ & he'd get up to make coffee,
> drink wine, drink water/ he wished one of his friends
> who knew where he waz wd come by with some blow
> or some shit/ anythin/ there was no air/ he'd see the
> spotlights in the alleyways downstairs movin in the air/
> cross his wall over his face/ & get under the covers &
> wait for an all clear or till he cd hear traffic again/ (43-44)

The words "there was no air" suggest that Willie's external and internal environment are closing in on him. Both are hostile elements because he is shell-shocked from his war experience and reacts to his urban world as if he were still under fire, as he clearly is. He is obsessed with Crystal who has been

> his girl since she waz thirteen/ when he caught
>   her
> on the stairway/
>
> he came home crazy as hell/ he tried to get
>   veterans benefits
> to go to school & they kept right on puttin him in
> remedial classes/ he cdnt read wortha damn/
>   so beau
> cused the teachers of holdin him back & got
>   himself
> a gypsy cab to drive/ but his cab kept breakin
> down/ & the cops was always messin with
>   him/ plus not

getting much bread/

> & crystal went & got pregnant again/ beau
>   most beat
> her to death when she tol him/ (44)

Like Richard Wright's Fred Daniels, Willie is harassed by the police. His attempt to make a living driving a cab backfires. He has no money. As I mentioned above, he is the perennial stranger; his city is the cruel, demeaning world of social ignorance, illiteracy, promiscuity, and unemployment.

Beau Willie's madness increases as the poem progresses. His "war" is complicated and Crystal is the object of his anger and hostility because her ambivalence about marrying him calls his manhood into question. For Beau, Crystal is clearly crazy because

>   . . . he just wanted
>   to marry her/ that's what/ he wanted to marry
>   her/ &
>   have a family/ but the bitch was crazy/ beau
>   willie
>   waz sittin in this hotel in his drawers drinkin
>   coffee & wine in the heat of the day spillin shit all
>   over hisself/ laughin/ bout how he was gonna
>   get crystal
>   to take him back/ & let him be a man in the
>   house/ & she
>   wdnt even have to go to work no more /he got
>   dressed
>   all up in his ivory shirt & checkered pants to go see
>   crystal & get this mess all cleared up/
>   he knocked on the door to crystal's rooms/ & she
>   didn't answer/ he beat on the door & crystal & naomi
>   started cryin/ beau gotta shoutin again how he wanted
>   to marry her/ & waz she always gonna be a whore/ or
>   did she wanna a husband/ (46)

The poem comes to a monstrous end as Beau breaks down the door and pleads with Crystal for another chance, coaxing her to let him hold the children. Using them as hostages and holding them out of the fifth story window, Beau extorts the promise of marriage from Crystal. He urges her to "say to alla the neighbors// you gonna marry me/" (48), but she is too stunned to speak above a whisper:[14]

> i stood by beau in the window/ with naomi reachin
> for me/ kwame screaming mommy mommy from the
>   fifth
> story/ but i cd only whisper/ & he dropped em (48)

Though Willie is the focus of the poem, the story is, in fact, Crystal's story. Shange uses the portrait of male violence to comment on the ways in which women are robbed of life. Willie's monstrous act strips Crystal of her identity as a woman and a mother. Just as Willie is an extension of the twelve-year-old boy, she is truly the sister of the woman who tells her story in **"i usedta live in the world."** She is also the symbolic sister of all the women who speak in and identify with the play. The extremity of her life mirrors the worst that can happen to a woman's dreams and aspirations. Through Crystal's story Shange reveals the inner circle mentioned above. Having broken down the city and its female inhabitants to their most elemental level, and, having redefined the conventional interpretations of the strange and the familiar offered by Tillich, Shange re-creates a picture more faithful to the irrational forces that have traditionally shaped female lives and female spirituality.

The name Crystal is interesting, for Willie is truly addicted to her as if she were indeed heroin. He cannot live with or without her and what should be the sanctuary of a love relationship instead "inspires" him to brutality. On the other hand, Crystal's name suggests the clarity and purity of the vision of the city of God:

> Then he showed me the river of the water of
> life, sparkling like crystal, flowing from the throne of
> God and of the Lamb down the middle of the city's
> streets.[15]

To understand the dual role that Crystal plays is to understand the quantum leap from **"a nite with beau willie brown"** to the last poem, **"a layin on of hands,"** for her reality is grounded both in the gross world of Willie and the ghetto and in the spiritual vision of the women she represents. Her tragedy insures the transcendence of the women for her tears are like the waters of the biblical river.

The fragile inner circle that represents the spiritual is first apparent in the title and is alluded to throughout the choreopoem. The promise of transition from despair to hope is revealed in the words of lady in brown, "& this is for colored girls who have considered suicide// but moved to the ends of their own rainbows" (3). The first "community" mentioned in the play is one composed of "colored girls who have considered suicide." Suicide, whether physical, psychological, or spiritual, is a dominant factor in modern life; therefore, it is significant that this is the point around which the "new" community is rebuilt, for gathering together to deny suicide is a life-affirming, spiritual act. Shange says, "One day I was driving home after a class, and I saw a huge rainbow over Oakland. I realized that women could survive if we decide that we have as much right and as much purpose for being here as the air and mountains do."[16] Preparation for the "layin on of hands" and the discovery of God at the end of the play begins here. Women should have the freedom to live and must claim it. The rain-

bow suggests the mythic covenant between God and Noah, symbolizing hope and life; it foreshadows the end when the declaration, "i found god in myself," explains why the "rainbow is enuf."

To claim the right "to be" is to confront antilife forces. This self-affirmation is the first step toward spiritual affirmation. The rainbow represents the promise of a whole life, and Shange reveals her unique vision, for she draws a new covenant when she alters the gender of God, finding "her" in self, and declaring love for "her." This "mother" god will certainly heal her battered daughters. For this reason, too, Crystal's loss of her children is significant; the rules of patriarchy which allow mother and children to be held hostage must be rewritten.[17]

The sisterhood revealed at the conclusion of the play is foreshadowed in several poems about stunted male/female relationships. The poem, **"pyramid,"** discusses the competitiveness of dating in which women are pitted against one another—primarily because men are in short supply. The man in **"pyramid"** "plays the field," thereby compromising the friendships of three women, but the poem ends on a positive note as the women console one another:

> she held her head on her lap
> the laps of her sisters soakin up tears
> each understandin how much love stood
>   between them
> how much love between them
> love between them
> love like sisters (33)

Here the women affirm the power of touch ("she held her head on her lap") and the power of sisterly love. The ambiguous use of the pronoun "her" in the first line addresses the merger of the individual woman into collective "woman," whose psyche cannot be divided by competition.

The lady in orange turns her love song into a "requiem" for her old self because she can no longer avoid her own face; she needs to "die" to be "reborn" into spiritual life and to claim her own identity:

> so this is a requium for myself/ cuz i
> have died in a real way/ not wid aqua coffins &
>   du-wop cadillacs/
> i used to joke abt when i waz messin round/
>   but a real dead
> lovin is here for you now/ cuz i don't know
>   anymore/ how
> to avoid my own face wet with my tears/ cuz i
>   had convinced
> myself colored girls had no right to sorrow/ & i
>   lived

& loved that way & kept sorrow on the curb/
   allegedly
for you/ but i did it for myself/
i cdnt stand it
i cdnt stand being sorry & colored at the same
   time
it's so redundant in the modern world (34)

In **"no more love poems #3,"** the lady in blue deals with the accusation that black women are too emotional:

we deal wit emotion too much
so why don't we go on ahead & be white then/
   . . .

I'll find a way to make myself
come without you/ no fingers or other objects
   just thot
which isnt spiritual evolution cuz its empty &
   godliness
is plenty ripe & fertile/ (35)

The definition of godliness as "plenty ripe & fertile" is a crucial turning point in female consciousness. Shange here addresses the central contradiction in Tillich's identification of the *metropolis* as "mother or central city," but defining its primary function as the repository of reason, when reason is the one attribute women are accused of lacking. The fecundity of women's emotions with their life-giving and life-sustaining properties is juxtaposed to "thot (thought)// which isn't spiritual evolution cuz its empty." The words "plenty ripe & fertile" echo at the end of the play, for the bonding of the women suggests the female fertility cults of old.

In **"no more love poems #4,"** the lady in yellow makes the essential link between worldly and spiritual love:

but bein alive & bein a woman & bein colored
   is a metaphysical
dilemma/ i havent conquered yet/ do you see
   the point
my spirit is too ancient to understand the
   separation of
soul & gender/ my love is too delicate to have
   thrown
back on my face (36)

At the end of these poems, the ladies celebrate the beauty and energy of their love, lifting it above romantic trivialization. To disavow the "separation of// soul & gender" prefigures the female god, both as human woman claiming her place and as "god the mother." Of the many lines the women sing to describe the significance of their love, the most telling is chanted by the lady in purple: "my love is too sanctified to have thrown back on my face" (36), which places absolute value on human love and prefigures the sanctified holy love implicit in the laying on of hands.

Crystal, then, is the woman whose specific tragedy is an adumbration of all female tragedy. She is the victim who is overwhelmed, at least momentarily, by the fury of the madman. Through Crystal, each woman discovers the hope in herself, with "all the gods comin into me// laying me open to myself" (49). Each woman now understands what the lady in red means when she says "i waz missin somethin" (49). The lady in blue declares that what is missing is "not a man" (50). And the lady in purple is clear that it is neither her mother, nor motherhood that is missing:

not my mama/ holdin me tight/ sayin
I'm always gonna be her girl
not a layin on of bosom & womb
a layin on of hands
the holiness of myself released (50)

The lady in red considers suicide:

I sat up one night walkin a boardin house
screaming/ cryin/ the ghost of another woman
who waz missin what i was missin
i wanted to jump outta my bones
& be done wit myself
leave me alone
& go on in the wind
it was too much (50)

She is split into two beings, but this confrontation with self (strange and the familiar) is the point at which healing and renewal begins:

i fell into a numbness
til the only tree i cd see
took me up in her branches
held me in the breeze
made me dawn dew
that chill at daybreak
the sun wrapped me up swingin rose light
   everywhere
the sky laid over me like a million men
i waz cold/ i waz burnin up/ a child
& endlessly weavin garments for the moon
wit my tears (50)

The concrete landscape of the city with its occasional tree—unremarkable, lone, bare, struggling for survival in an environment indifferent or hostile to it—unfolds here. The lady in red "fell into a numbness" that, paradoxically, is relieved through the life-giving properties of the tree.

Adrienne Rich suggests that the tree "is a female symbol," and is sacred.[18] Shange's tree is the sacred "mother," and her branches loving, cradling arms. The tree connects symbolically with Crystal as the final arbiter for the women, an idea that is enhanced by these words from Revelation, "On either side of the river stood a tree of life. . . , the leaves of the tree[s] serve for the healing of nations" (22:2).

The sun embraces the lady in red and "the sky laid over [her] like a million men." Shange alludes to the classical notion of the sky as male principle and the break with "earthly" men makes realignment with nature's balance possible. Through the images of hot and cold, she re-creates the fever associated with childhood, and prepares the way for rebirth. Female affinity and empathy with the moon are suggested in the image of one "endlessly weavin garments for the moon// with my tears." All the cosmic forces come together here as a unifying and healing whole.

The lines from the end of **"no more love poems #4"** provide a context for the discovery of God. The lady in yellow says:

> do you see the point
> my spirit is too ancient to understand the
> separation of
> soul & gender/ (36)

These lines suggest that body (gender) and soul cannot be separated; thus the woman knows wholeness. The final words of the lady in red contain the triumph of all the women, for she is finally and fully centered as she says, "i found god in myself/ & i loved her fiercely." The identification of God as female is one of the most problematic points in the play, for it redefines the image of God. But Shange truly understands what it means to be created in the image of God, for discovery of self is discovery of God. This is a declaration of freedom from a patriarchial god who supports the men from whom the women have split.

The poem, **"a layin on of hands,"** suggests a specially formed community which has grown from the brokenness of life in the city. Crystal reminds me of Revelation, but the connection between her transcendence and that found in *colored girls* is that Shange's triumphant city is not the product of an apocalyptic vision, but is the result of new sight, for the physical metropolis remains unchanged. As Denise Levertov in her poem, "City Psalm," says,

> Nothing was changed, all was revealed
> otherwise;
> not that horror was not, not that the killings did
> not continue,
> not that I thought there was to be no more
> despair,

> but that as if transparent all disclosed
> an otherness that was blessèd, that was bliss.
> *I saw Paradise in the dust of the street.*[19]

Levertov's image of the "transparent all" echoes the moment of crystal purity, which is the moment of revelation that "disclosed/ an otherness." "It is "in the dust of the street" that Shange's women suffer and grow in knowledge of the "strangeness of the familiar." It is their immersion in this paradoxical reality which forces them to confront themselves and which prepares them to have a dynamic spiritual vision. The women simply could not have been reborn had they not been cleansed and bound together by these unique experiences. They are not ghouls, children of horror, the joke, animals, or crazy people. They no longer need "somebody/anybody" to sing their song. They are no longer scattered half-notes.[20] But they differ radically from the idealized city beings hypothesized by Tillich. Through the life-enhancing hope of the rainbow, they form a covenant with a woman-God. They are "new" and now sing their own "righteous gospel." The laying on of hands is validated in the "holiness of myself released" (50). The women enter into a tightly wrought circle, symbolic of their spiritual vision and their earthly solidarity. This is the second, "inner" circle mentioned above, which is in tension throughout the play with the external circle. Here, the power and meaning of the inner circle are fully revealed. And the lady in brown dedicates the moment:

> this is for colored girls who have considered
> suicide/ but are movin to the ends of their own
> rainbows (51)

Notes

1. Ntozake Shange, *for colored girls who have considered suicide/ when the rainbow is enuf* (New York: Macmillan, 1977). All citations are from this edition and are given in the text parenthetically. Shange does not use punctuation in a conventional way. Thus, the double slash (//) is used in my text to indicate the end of line of poetry since Shange uses the single (/) throughout the choreopoem as a poetic device.

The term "choreopoem" is used in my text as a synonym for the word "play." This is Shange's word and is found on the title page of her book. It reflects Shange's intent that the play be understood as a choral recitation of poems upon which limited dramatic form has been imposed.

2. The cities have been repositories of promise for blacks migrating from rural to urban America. They have sought economic and political freedom, psychological and cultural autonomy. During the first two decades of the twentieth-

century southern black people, seeking to escape white violence and economic disaster, migrated to the North. The traditional myth of opportunity in the North was enhanced by national preparations for World War I and the hope for employment in the emerging defense industries. The promise of safety and a better economic life is usually seized upon by analysts as the sole interest of the emigrating black masses, but Alain Locke, editor of the anthology *The New Negro* (New York: Atheneum, 1970), 6, suggests in the title essay that the black peasant was inspired by a newly emerging and more complex vision:

> The tide of Negro migration, northward and cityward, is not to be fully explained as a blind flood started by the demands of war industry coupled with the shutting off of foreign migration, or by the pressure of poor crops coupled with increased social terrorism in certain sections of the South and Southwest. Neither labor demand, the boll-weevil nor the Ku Klux Klan is a basic factor, however contributory any or all of them may have been. The wash and rush of this human tide on the beach line of the northern city centers is to be explained primarily in terms of a new vision of opportunity, of social and economic freedom, of a spirit to seize, even in the face of an extortionate and heavy toll, a chance for the improvement of conditions. With each successive wave of it, the movement of the Negro becomes more and more a mass movement toward the larger and more democratic chance—in the Negro's case a deliberate flight not only from countryside to city, but from medieval America to modern.

These migration patterns continued until the 1970s, when many black people, inspired by the gains of the civil rights movement, retraced the steps of their ancestors back to the South. However, since the original migrations were to the North, life in northern cities is the focus of many 20th-century Afro-American writers. Authors such as James Weldon Johnson, Rudolph Fisher, Wallace Thurman, Jessie Fauset, to name a few early writers of the decade, and more modern, perhaps better-known writers such as Langston Hughes, Richard Wright, James Baldwin, Ann Petry, Ralph Ellison, Gwendolyn Brooks depict the Afro-American urban experience.

3. The first two poems mentioned here are "latent rapists' [sic] (12-16), "abortion cycle #1" (16-17). Most of the poems in *for colored girls* deal in some way with betrayal, but this is the specific theme of "no assistance" (10), and "somebody almost walked off wid alla my stuff" (39-41).

4. Paul J. Tillich, "The Metropolis: Centralizing and Inclusive," and "The Strange and the Familiar in the Metropolis," in *The Metropolis in Modern Life*, ed. Robert Moore Fisher (New York: Doubleday, 1955), 346-47. Shange identifies the "familiar" cities, but establishes the women as "strangers." For example, the characters in the play do not have "proper names," except in poems where she creates a story within a story; the women are "named" by the colors they wear, suggesting anonymity. They are placed *outside* the cities: the lady in red, "I'm outside baltimore"; the lady in blue, "I'm outside manhattan," etc.

5. Ibid., 346.

6. Ibid., 346-47.

7. Tillich's language is exclusively masculine. His central image is power; his primary example of power is the pope and the Roman Catholic Church.

8. The preceding poems interweave fascinating pictures of city landscape with the emerging consciousness of the women as they grow from late adolescence in, for example, "graduation nite" (4-7), to adult complexity in the poem entitled "one" (24-28), in which a lonely urban woman takes a stranger home to bed, but must finally face the fact that the chance encounter is not satisfying and that she is lonelier than ever at its conclusion.

9. A mentor to many of the young black artists flocking to Harlem in the twenties, described it as "one of the most beautiful and healthful sections of the city." He ended his commentary on Harlem with the following words:

> I believe that the Negro's advantages and opportunities are greater in Harlem than in any other place in the country, and that Harlem will become the intellectual, the cultural, and the financial center for Negroes of the United States, and will exert a vital influence upon all Negro people.

James Weldon Johnson, "Harlem: The Culture Capital," in *The New Negro*, ed. Alain Locke (New York: Atheneum, 1970), 311. Johnson's words proved not to be prophetic. The promise of Harlem in the 1920s as a place where the urban dream of American blacks would come true failed and Harlem's prominence has eroded in the last two decades. It is interesting that Johnson's ideas are a secular echo of Tillich's and ironic that the diversity of the city described by Tillich is not fully realized as whites flee from areas into which black people move thereby compromising the vitality of place and creating ghettoes. Johnson's dream, therefore, cannot be realized because "the intellectual, the cultural, and the financial" are defined and controlled by white people, who remove these elements when they leave.

10. I am thinking, here, of the connection made by Jonathan Edwards, in his meditation number 77 on "Rivers" from

Images or Shadows of Divine Things, "There is a wonderful analogy between what is seen in rivers, their gathering from innumerable small branches beginning at a great distance one from another in different regions . . . yet all gathering more and more together the nearer they come to their common end and ultimate issue, and all at length discharging themselves at one mouth into the same ocean. Here is livelily represented how all things tend to one, even to God, the boundless ocean" (*The Norton Anthology of American Literature*, I, ed. Gottesman, Holland, Kalstone, et al., [New York: Norton, 1979], 261).

11. In the stage directions, the other women silently enter here; their presence is a symbolic commentary on the universality of the problem.

12. Tillich, 347.

13. Richard Wright, "The Man Who Lived Underground," in *Black Voices*, ed. Abraham Chapman (New York: New American Library, 1968), 114-60. Shange's image of old men suspended in stagnant water is reminiscent of Wright's character who finds—literally and figuratively—all of life's potential amenities rotted or dead floating by in the sewer water. Just as I suggested that Willie and Crystal are the "sewer" side of the metropolis, so Fred Daniels's world is that of the sewer, a metaphorical commentary on the quality of Afro-American life in the city.

14. The starkness of Beau Willie's infanticide has led critics to accuse Ntozake Shange of hating men. It is my opinion that she graphically, but compassionately, depicts the inhumanity of a system that in its racist, biased indifference to life, stunts a man's aspirations, makes him a murderer, and reduces him to insanity. His time in Vietnam is the most important factor to consider in his treatment of Crystal and the children. This point is endorsed by one of the most powerful dramatic productions of the postwar Vietnam veteran's life. This play is Emily Mann's *Still Life*, in which Mark, the veteran, in talking of his projection of violence, identifies his wife, Cheryl, as the war casualty.

15. Revelation 22:1, *New English Bible* (New York: Cambridge Univ. Press, 1971). Crystal's name also suggests the paradox of experience for the Afro-American mother that is captured in Langston Hughes's poem, "Mother to Son," in *Black Writers of America: A Comprehensive Anthology*, ed. Kinnamon and Barksdale (New York: Macmillan, 1972), 518.

> Well, son, I'll tell you:
> Life for me ain't been no crystal stair.
> It's had tacks in it,
> And splinters,
> And boards torn up,

> And places with no carpet on the floor—
> Bare.
> But all the time
> I'se been a-climbin' on,
> And reachin' landin's,
> And turnin' corners,
> And sometimes goin' in the dark
> Where there ain't been no light.
> So boy, don't you turn back.
> Don't you set down on the steps
> 'Cause you finds it's kinder hard.
> Don't you fall now—
> For I'se still goin', honey,
> I'se still climbin',
> And life for me ain't been no crystal stair.

16. Carol P. Christ, *Diving Deep and Surfacing: Women Writers on Spiritual Quest* (Boston: Beacon, 1980), 99, as quoted from Ntozake Shange, *for colored girls Who Have Considered Suicide/ When the Rainbow Is Enuf* (original Broadway cast recording) (New York: Buddha Records, 1976), jacket notes. One of the most sensitive, cogent, and pertinent discussions of the choreopoem appears in Carol Christ's essay, "'i found god in myself . . . & i loved her fiercely': Ntozake Shange." Christ's analysis of *for colored girls* stresses the processes of self-discovery, self-healing, and spiritual transcendence. In Christ's interpretation, the truth of the "*colored girls*'" growth into personhood and faith overshadows the bitter commentary and misinterpretation that characterize most criticism, which is that the play "trashes" black men, and reveals things about black people that would be better left unsaid or certainly not said in public. Christ, however, does not deal with the significance of the city in the play.

17. The basis for my thoughts on patriarchy comes from Adrienne Rich, "The Kingdom of the Fathers," in *Of Women Born: Motherhood as Experience and Institution* (New York: Norton, 1976), 56-83.

18. Ibid., 100.

19. Denise Levertov, "City Psalm," *The Sorrow Dance* (New York: New Directions, 1966), 72.

> The Killings continue, each second
> pain and misfortune extend themselves
> in the genetic chain, injustice is done know
>   ingly, and the air
> bears the dust of decayed hopes,
> yet breathing those fumes, walking the
>   thronged
> pavements among crippled lives, jackhammers
> raging, a parking lot painfully agleam
> in the May sun, I have seen

not behind but within, within the
dull grief, blown grit, hideous
concrete facades, another grief, a gleam
    as of dew, an abode of mercy,
have heard not behind but within noise
a humming that drifted into a quiet smile.
Nothing was changed, all was revealed
        otherwise;
not that horror was not, not that the killings did
        not continue,
not that I thought there was to be no more
        despair,
but that as if transparent all disclosed
an otherness that was blesséd, that was bliss.
    I saw Paradise in the dust of the street.

20. The images in these three sentences are taken from the first poem in **for colored girls** entitled, "dark phases" (1-2).

Carole Woddis (review date June 1985)

SOURCE: A review of *Spell No. 7*, in *Plays and Players*, No. 381, June, 1985, pp. 28-9.

[*Woddis critiques a production of Ntozake Shange's play* Spell No. 7 *performed by the Women's Playhouse Trust.*]

Ntozake Shange is nothing if not controversial. It's not so much what she is talking about, although that in itself crashes through boundaries, but the way in which she does it. Possibly not since Dylan Thomas's 'Under Milk Wood' can I remember a dramatic piece that played with language with such exuberance, and structure with such daring. **'Spell No. 7'** takes risks not just because it is confronting racism and black identity in a culture dominated by the white face but because it does so through a loosely knit structure that breaks conventional rules and is reliant on the monologue for its major impact. Several voices at the interval the night I was there could be heard saying 'but it's not really "a play", is it?'

Insofar as it eschews narrative, **'Spell No. 7'** does not fit easily into that particular pigeon-hole. What it does do is weave a textural pattern of racial histories, memories, anecdotes, testaments, sometimes through interrelating dialogue, predominantly through personal account, creating a rich socio/cultural picture of what it means to be black—and especially female—in America—with Shange's shimmering words as the driving force.

Reading some of the script before its opening, it seemed to me that the Women's Playhouse Trust and in particular,

director Sue Parrish, had bitten off more, this time, than they could chew. How could a white English director and black English cast take on the style and nuance of Shange's Americo-centric milieu. The answer is that, but for one or two weak passages, she and they have done themselves proud. These are stories that need to be told, and they tell them with conviction and vitality. Set mostly in a downtown New York bar where a group of actors and actresses are gathered, the atmosphere is set by the entrance of Erick Ray Evans (Lou), a sleek, white-suited MC, magician figure; with bitter irony, he sings of the spell that cannot be weaved—turning black skin into white—quickly joined by a black tie and tail chorus which, with equal speed, neatly subverts the comfortable white image of the jolly, black hoofer, and entertainer.

Bitterness is a theme that runs violently throughout many of the episodes later recounted—in the humiliations and indignities encountered in the segregated South; in the stereotypical images of casting limiting black actresses either to subservient maids or sassy whores, or even, most ironically as one actress (Amanda Symons) vivaciously recalls, not being cast as a black because her skin is too light. Women, Shange is saying, are doubly penalised—first by racism, twice over by sexism from black men ('oh baby, you're so pr-ee-tty'), epitomised in a wickedly funny send-up on The Platters, sung by the cast's male actors to the actresses. It is this self-mockery which saves **'Spell No. 7'** from being just a catalogue of bitterness—that, the evocatory power of Shange's language and the celebratory impulse of being black to counter-balance the pain. Above all, there are performances which dig deep into the white conscience. It will be a long time before I forget Claudette Williams (a dazzling new discovery) painting a biting portrait of contempt mixed with envy conveyed in the single gesture of a young white woman 'flinging her hair'. **'Spell No. 7'** does not always make comfortable viewing; its first half does indeed drag but the power of its emotional truth carries its own momentum and weaves a black magic entirely on its own.

Evelyn C. White (review date November 1985)

SOURCE: "Growing Up Black," in *Women's Review of Books*, Vol. 3, No. 2, November, 1985, p. 11.

[*In the following book review, White praises both Jamaica Kincaid's novel* Annie John *and Shange's novel* Betsey Brown *for their representations of young African American women.*]

So complementary are their titles and tan jacket covers that a precious childlike innocence seems to grace the bookshelf when Jamaica Kincaid's *Annie John* and Ntozake Shange's **Betsey Brown** sit next to each other. But these novels are not likely to spend much time on dusty shelves or in attic cartons.

With poignancy and a kind of bashful simplicity, the authors portray the growing pains of two young black girls. Kincaid, a staff writer for *The New Yorker*, crafts equally fetching moments of joy and sorrow for her seemingly autobiographical protagonist, Annie John. The quick prose and distinctive detail that are the hallmarks of successful short stories are often difficult to achieve in longer works. Characters and images that breathed fully on twelve pages can be found huffing and puffing at a hundred. Sometimes the only recourse is to perform a type of literary euthanasia. That Kincaid, in her first novel, does not produce one clause that tempts one to "pull the plug," is a testament both to the rich texture of her West Indian childhood and her extraordinary skill as a writer.

Banana fritters, ripe guavas and pumpkin soup color Annie's world on the lush island of Antigua. Like the blue-green tropical land-scapes of Gauguin, Kincaid's pages are brushed with images that glisten like swaying palm trees in the sunlight.

> Her face was big and round and red, like a moon a red moon. She had big, broad, flat feet, and they were naked to the bare ground; her dress was dirty, the skirt and blouse tearing away from each other at one side; the red hair that I had first seen standing up on her head was matted and tangled; her hands were big and fat, and her fingernails held at least ten anthills of dirt under them. And on top of that, she had such an unbelievable wonderful smell as if she had never taken a bath in her whole life.

Although characters like the Red Girl and Gwen, a beloved classmate, earn Annie's adoration, the singular force in her life is her mother. Their relationship is a bittersweet one that Kincaid depicts in a way that any daughter who has ever felt at odds with her mother can understand.

For example: blissful days spent in the protection of a mother graced with "such a beautiful mouth I could have looked at it forever if I had to and not mind" come to an abrupt and cataclysmic end for Annie John at age twelve, when on a shopping trip her mother tells her that they can no longer wear dresses made from the same cloth. "To say I felt the earth swept away from under me would not be going too far." This sudden and, in Annie's eyes, drastic change in the intimate bond with her mother is an episode Kincaid uses to symbolize the painful words and actions that can separate mother and daughter during the turbulent pubescent years. Annie stands among the bright bolts of cloth

that had for years adorned the two of them as her mother says, "You just cannot go around the rest of your life looking like a little me." The sense of loss and abandonment is profound. From that moment on, Annie's feelings about her mother and her own identity are fraught with the confusion and rebellion that make adolescence a time few wish to relive.

The day she begins to menstruate, Annie expresses a sentiment whose accuracy makes one revel—and then despair.

> I walked to school with Gwen feeling as I supposed a dog must feel when it has done something wrong and is ashamed of itself and trying to get somewhere quick, where it can lie low. The cloth between my legs grew heavier and heavier with every step I took ... For the first time in my life, I fainted ... Nurse said it was the fright of all the unexpected pain ... but I knew that I'd fainted after I brought to my mind a clear picture of myself sitting at my desk in my own blood. (p. 52)

The "my mother/myself" currents of Annie's life reach full force when she turns fifteen. Feeling "more unhappy than I had ever imagined anyone could be," she must nonetheless go to school, go to church, and worst of all, continue to live with a mother who has "suddenly turned into a crocodile." Instead of raised voices or angrily slammed doors, Kincaid uses simple whispers to create the emotional strain of the parental relationship all adolescents (and adults too) struggle with. "When I started to walk down the road, my steps were quick and light, and as I walked these words would go around in my head: 'My mother would kill me if she got the chance. I would kill my mother if I had the courage.'"

The courage of the youthful spirit, even when it is broken or tormented, bursts like a ripe mango in *Annie John*. Although Kincaid touches upon the inharmonious consequences of colonization in the West Indies (Annie is punished for "defacing" a picture of Christopher Columbus), political polemics are an aside to the personal passage of a young girl.

Perhaps Kincaid's writing has less of the charged racial intensity that is often found in the works by blacks born in America because she grew up on an island filled with the culture and traditions of her ancestors. The British may well have ruled the physical earth of Antigua, but they were not masters of the heart or spirit of a people who knew that the country pulsed with their lives, deaths, history and dreams.

The black American experience is steeped in different racial configurations. Whether with her sassiness, her tenderness or her self-described "combat breath," Ntozake Shange writes about our experiences in a voice few have surpassed in recent years.

Since her debut in 1974 with the Broadway production of her magnificent choreopoem, *for colored girls who have considered suicide/when the rainbow is enuf*, she has proven that she can portray black life with a depth and rhythmic cadence that make readers see, hear, smell and feel every word she writes.

Like *Annie John*, **Betsey Brown** appears to be an autobiographical work. There is much in this humorous and melodic novel that parallels Ntozake Shange's own upbringing in a prominent black family during the 1950s. Shange starts living up to her spirited literary reputation promptly. Betsey's father, a St. Louis doctor, quizzes his children each morning in a colorful ritual that includes dancing to the beat of a Conga drum. "When Jane entered the kitchen, the line of children melted into hugs and kisses good-bye to Grandma and thanks to Daddy for the extra nickel for correctly answered questions at morning drill ... Betsey's word had been 'psychopath' one time and she answered, 'Mama's patients, niggahs what ain't got no sense.'"

Jane, Betsey's mother, has to deal with the demands of four children, a frolicsome husband and her own identity as a social worker. Her life is a multi-threaded fabric that, all by itself, affirms the diversity among black women. Shange's message, as I read it, is that it is as important to write about black women who set their tables with crystal as it is to support those who scrape daily for basic necessities. Through Jane, Shange claims and skillfully portrays a black female experience that has been shaped by more privileges than sacrifices. Still, the comfort of Jane's physical world does not protect her from the emotional turmoil all black women face. In Jane, Shange has drawn a full-fleshed black woman whose "chandeliers of every shape and size" do not make her personal burdens any less real.

In the midst of the crystal chandeliers and the mahogany staircase, Betsey and her siblings live the rough-and-tumble life of most children. They tease each other, fight, jump double-dutch, break dishes and get a thrill out of striking matches. But Betsey, at the cross-roads of childhood and adolescence, soon finds herself with another concern—integration. Court-ordered desegregation forces her to leave her neighborhood school and enroll in a white one. Her adolescent self-consciousness and confusion are compounded by her daily expeditions into "another country" where there are "no Twandas, Veejays and Charlotte Anns ... not even any dill pickles wrapped in brown paper or candies like Mr. Robinson's."

The lengthy bus rides to and from the white school separate Betsey physically, emotionally and culturally from all that has been familiar. After missing an outing with her neighborhood friends because of a late bus, Betsey takes out her frustrations on the sidewalk.

> The street was vacant. Like a big old movie set. Nothing. Nobody to do a thing with. What could she do alone that could exclude the white folks, who were nowhere to be seen except in her wounds and aches of memories. Betsey decided to play hop-scotch, but she laid the hop-scotch pattern out with enough room to write 'For Colored Only,' 'Crackers and Dogs Not Allowed,' 'Peckerwoods Got No Welcome Here,' 'Guineas Go Home.' Betsey's hop-scotch was something to behold. Chalk never seemed so powerful as when it messed with white folks.   (p. 112)

Although Shange writes candidly about racial and class conflicts, **Betsey Brown** is about the human emotions that unify people as well as the political forces that divide. It is a book about love, loss, fear, courage, about learning how to live in a world where certain people just might not like dill pickles.

After major successes in their "adult" voices, Ntozake Shange and Jamaica Kincaid have chosen to express themselves through the eyes and hearts of young black girls. These novels will do much to enrich and provide counterpoint to an already sumptuous body of black women's literature. After all, once upon a time Sula, Shug Avery and the women of Brewster Place were all little black girls happily chanting "Little Sally Walker, sitting in a saucer."

"Innocent" and "fragile" are words that are used all too rarely to describe black women. Now, perhaps, because of *Annie John* and **Betsey Brown**, those words too will be used whenever there is mention of "the strong black woman"—as well they should be.

Ntozake Shange with Brenda Lyons (interview date Winter 1987)

SOURCE: "Interview with Ntozake Shange," in *Massachusetts Review*, Vol. XXVIII, No. 4, Winter, 1987, pp. 687-696.
[*In the following interview, Lyons questions Shange about the various criticisms of her work that have been launched by feminists, and about her own perspective on the role of gender in her writing.*]

[*Lyons:*] **colored girls** *raised a furor in the 70s. In addition to much acclaim and many awards, you were attacked as a traitor to your race and put down as a writer and a black woman. Reflecting on that reaction now, ten years later, how do you feel about having been positioned as an angry young black feminist?*

[Ntozake Shange:] I think it's O.K. to have been what I was. I'm not sure that I'm still not.

Has it affected your writing?

I think on a couple of things I got very pointedly satirical about people, for example in **"Just Like a Man,"** at about that time. There are some things in *Sassafras* that are about that, too, where I can make fun of sexism, misogynists . . . . It's like creating a world of women that's woman-centered, so aberrant male forms really look aberrant.

Some women have criticized **Sassafras, Cypress & Indigo** *as homophobic.*

I'm not absolutely certain, but I'm pretty sure that's not true. There used to be a phalanx of feminists who were as difficult to deal with as some misogynists. I used to think twice about whether I was going to see a man. I lost a job because I was heterosexual. It wasn't that I lost it; I wasn't ever given it, and that was the primary reason. So I wanted to point out that when you're seeking love and companionship, you can't just say, well, this is a sexist society and men are the enemy, therefore I'm gonna seek women. Because that's not going to save you. I think I was trying to be honest about the gay community. There are a lot of people who are not honest in their relationships with people. I think the relationship between Idrina and her girlfriend is perfectly fine. They don't have a problem. I figured that was gonna happen and I didn't really care because I was saying what I had to say. It's the same as black people who didn't want to hear about things that didn't look absolutely perfect. The characters in *Sassafras* did say awful things and trash one another, but there are people who do. In the time of the *Sassafras* narrative certain women's collectives existed that were very dramatic and people had a lot of lovers. We didn't even call it promiscuity. It was very different from the environment today. People today sit down and think about how they really want to be monogamous. It was not anybody's goal fifteen years ago.

Is there a link between the title **Colored Girls** *and the change in language to "people of color"?*

I know that fifteen years ago when I said "colored girls" I meant "people of color." The first group I worked with was black, white, Asian, and native American. And in San Francisco that's what we meant. It was our own little tongue-in-cheek thing. When I moved back East, they couldn't deal with that. It was too difficult. "Color" meant "black people," so that's what it became, but syntactically and in terms of what's in the piece itself that's not true. I think now when you say "people of color" that's another way of saying "*colored girls*" but getting away from the trap I fell into. I don't think we did anything to stir it on, but I think that's what we meant.

Between **colored girls** *and* **Betsey Brown** *I read a movement away from radical feminist politics—although I don't like the word "feminist"—toward what seems a return to family-centered values.*

Well, I don't know how to get outta there. I have to create a world that a feminist can come from. You see, I didn't have any books I could read where I could see a child who was actually trying to come in from—a book of different women's perspectives of the world AND different politics—so I thought it was important to create a person who could do that and say, yes, these things are possible. Feminists don't start up at twenty-one and know the correct way. It's something that all of us can reach toward, and it's something that's available to any little girl or little boy. It's something you have to come to, and you have to come from someplace to get it. That's one of the problems I have with family. You're right. When I was writing **Betsey Brown** I thought I was gonna go crazy, because I had to see the world from a thirteen-year-old girl's point of view. It was absolutely crazy. I thought it was horrible. And it was just so good and clean and asexual, I couldn't stand it. Several months after I finished it I started the next novel, which is incredibly sexual. I guess Liliane, the protagonist, is an existential feminist. I don't know, she's one of these full-sided ones, like what I was talkin' about—the feminist who sprung up at twenty-one from Zeus's head, from her father's head. I had to have a change from Betsey. A friend said, "You finally got tired of all that menarche," and I said, "You're right, I couldn't stand it." So yeah, it's almost—I was reading some of it the other day and I said, "Oh, my god, you must have been terribly, terribly horny," because it's not quite explicitly sexual, but it's loose and wild, that's for sure. So I am coming back to what I feel more comfortable in. But **Betsey Brown** was something I just had to do, because it was too pretty a story to let go . . . . Liliane is, yes, related to the *Bible* and to Minerva.

What's the relationship between Betsey and Indigo from **Sassafras**?

I've thought about that, because the only other time I wrote about children I wrote about Indigo. Indigo has a history and spiritual forces that support her and that she's in touch with without having to be told she has the right. Except for her contact with Uncle John and the women from the church, she doesn't really have a whole lot of conflict going on in her immediate family the way Betsey does. So they're different in that sense. Indigo has a knowing sense of what's possible and who she can be. We discover with Betsey what her possibilities are, which is different, I think, from Indigo giving us permission to share what she already knows.

Indigo seems more magical.

Yeah, that's what I mean. I didn't want to use that word, because I didn't want to make her like an other-worldly person. But she is in contact with spiritual forces that have been disrupted in Betsey's life. For instance, Indigo thinks she hears and sees the slaves in the bottom of the cock-fighting place, and Betsey has to be told about these things. She only hears the drums in something that's very abstract, very different from coming in contact with ghost slaves.

Do you think of your audience as you write?

I think I always see a young child or an adolescent of color, but not necessarily right this minute. I started writing because there's an absence of things I was familiar with or that I dreamed about. One of my senses of anger is related to this vacancy—a yearning I had as a teenager. I hate that word. But as an adolescent—to have done something that I didn't have and I didn't know what it was 'cause I had never heard about it. I knew some of the Harlem Renaissance people, and Ralph Ellison and Richard Wright and Leroi Jones and Margaret Walker, and that was about it. And I thought there was a searching and yearning going on in me, as a teenager, and when I get ready to write I think I'm trying to fill that and I can't quite give you a name and place and date of birth of this child I'm writing to. There was a collection of poetry to do with refugee children called *Children of the Sun* a decade or so ago or longer. A lot of those children will never get a chance to tell how our life was. And I want to have something here for the next batch of kids who come along. I don't want them to come into a world unannounced, with no past, with nothing to hold onto. I can't stand children's books. I want something ready for when they hit eighteen or twenty or when they're forty-five and they still haven't ever heard about themselves. I want to recreate and save what our being alive has been so their being will stay alive, won't be such a surprise.

Does sexism operate differently in the black and white literary communities?

Yeah, I think so. I think unless black women are writing the pieces, we're being left out the same way we used to be left out of literature. We don't appear in things unless we write them ourselves. In the white male literary establishment women attain what looks like positions of power or influence or economic stability, but they're structured in such a way that they become unthreatening.

Do you know the piece by Calvin Hernton called "The Sexual Mountain and Black Women Writers"?

No. I know Calvin.

Well, in this article he identifies a black feminist perspective in contemporary Afro-American literature, and consistent with that perspective, an aesthetic. As he puts it, "form, language, syntax, sequence, and metaphoric rendering of experience that's different and expansive compared to male-authored literature." Do you agree?

Yeah, I do.

What does that mean in terms of your literary work?

As far as we know, in my fiction the plot is not going forward. It undulates, I hope. And I hope it has more to do with the flow of rivers and streams and tides and lakes, because I relate to life more completely in that way and it feels more real to me. If I'm dealing with somebody who is having daydreams or whose life takes place in sequences that are arranged in terms of importance to her, she recreates history only insofar as she tells us what she experienced, given where she was and who she was at that time, to the best of her ability, and that makes her life valid to me. So I think there are certain risks that I've been taking in terms of the way I choose to present and develop my pieces. If they're juxtaposed to traditional expectations of novels . . . . I keep telling people that the meaning of the word "novel" is "new," but for some reason people still seem to think that they should know how to read this or they should feel at ease immediately with this. That's crazy, because when you meet new people you can't do that. You can't just fall into somebody's life and be done with them in a few days or three hours of reading. It just doesn't make sense. Because you can't learn somebody's personal imagery and their personal iconography that quickly. I think Calvin is probably right. If I was gonna give a physical metaphor, I think that women's novels for me are more like breathing and men's novels are more like running.

Do you think black women's writing is different?

I've been reading a lot of books by women this year. Not all novels so much, but a lot of J. California Cooper and June Jordan and Toni Morrison and others. J. is a storyteller and short story writer and playwright in Oakland; June is a political poet from Stonybrook, and she wrote an incredible essay that's been the spark of life to me. I find ours to be more colloquial and rooted in folklore and embedded in the politics of the family in a way almost as mythology, a more readily approachable mythology than white feminist books are to me. I don't know if it's because our lives are incredible and when we see it on paper we're astonished and so raise the characters themselves to a mythological level, or if it's in the writing. I have a feeling it's a little of both. Because a lot of white feminists—I hate that word, too—are from working-class backgrounds and their novels seem to take on the whole town and the company. In most black novels—I don't know if it's because we're left out of the industrial, technological process or because it's the way we choose to see the world—our personalities and our interpersonal reactions and relationships and our relations as solitary figures with the universe seem paramount to me in a way they don't seem when I read novels by people who are not of color.

You've produced work in several, and sometimes overlapping, genres—dramatic performance pieces, poetry, short stories, and the novel. Do you feel closest to or strongest in any one of them?

It really has a lot to do with my own psychological path. Each piece has tended to give me what I emotionally needed at that point in time in terms of how I was going to deal with my work and what my work would give back to me. When I need to be by myself and not talk to a lot of other people about what I'm doing, I write novels. I left here [Houston] to write novels on purpose because I simply could not stand talkin' to other people. I could not stand it—and then—writing novels is terribly terribly lonely–and so I had to go back—so I could be interacting with other people. I used to think that theater—by which I mean institutionalized theater, not performance pieces—was terribly alien to me. It was something that fell upon me as opposed to me falling upon it ... because I had been quite happy with my pieces when they were on East 3rd Street, and having to deal with people who were looking to go The Great White Way had never occurred to me. But it HAD occurred to me to write novels and poems. So I have created a distance between myself as a theatrical writer and myself as a poet.

I just read and really like "Aw baby you so pretty" ...

Yeah, I liked that one, too, and I like being in the pieces that I like. I like being on stage, so that's why this year I'm doing a lot more acting in other people's work than I have before. This year I'm gonna do *Cat on a Hot Tin Roof* in New Orleans and I'm gonna do a piece of my own in San Francisco, a stage version of a short story I wrote called **"Melissa & Smith."**

I'd been trying to find "Melissa & Smith" ...

It was a chapbook from Bookslinger Press in Minneapo-

lis. It was really pretty—all handmade paper. Those are the things I wanted when I dreamed about being a writer. I wanted beautiful chapbooks. I just wanted books. I never ever thought about anything but having books, and so I think I'm much more, well, now it's changed a little because I get fuller gratification from actual performance. I did that as a poet, too. But I'm getting it from being an actress now. I really feel a great sense of accomplishment and pride and satisfaction after a piece in a show, which I didn't used to have.

Can you talk about what you're working on now? Plans for forthcoming writing?

Yeah, I'm working on the novel about Liliane, and she's very exciting to me because she IS a grown woman and she's worldly and politically committed and she's very sensually alive and she encounters people and events who make history. For that reason she's very, very sacred in a different way, say, that's for me not depressive. 'Cause Sassafras in a sense IS history and Liliane is in a process of making it, but in a very unselfconscious way. I hope. Because she's so vitally committed to experiencing herself and having those experiences impact on the world around her that she doesn't really leave us thinking that she is wanting for too much or that she's unable to fend for herself. She's a real challenge to write about and, on the other hand, real gratifying, because more often than not she gets what she wants. And if it's not what she wants she figures out in some kinda way that that was enough. [Laughter] And she moves on to the next thing. She's a person who uses the information she has within her power as a woman to make her life and the lives of those people around her better. But she's not a holy roller, and she's not Mother Teresa. She's a very worldly, sophisticated person.

To what extent are your characters autobiographical? That's an age-old question, and not a very popular one now either, but. ...

Six o' one, half a dozen o' the other. Some people, some characters just come out of the clear blue sky—the unknown, the unconscious—the other six are modeled on people I've known in life. There are some things that are facsimiles of reality—either hearsay or direct experience that has been reformed—in the psyches of my characters. And then there's some information that just comes out of the clear blue sky. A lot of it is what I call "terror thinking"—which would be transcription of nightmares or daydreams that are fiendish—and/or "wish thinking," which would be a transcription of events that I wish would happen instead of what did happen. And so I make it real for myself by writing. But when I write it I know it's not for me; it's for this character in there. So that distances it, and it becomes non-autobiographical for me. Once I've adjusted something so that it fits a character it's no longer autobiographical, because its ... hell, because if it's autobiographical, I couldn't have fixed it [laughing].

Do you have childhood memories of Miles or Dizzy or DuBois or ... ?

Yeah, I do. I remember when Dizzy Gillespie came to our house in St. Louis. He used to come visit us a lot, whenever he came through town. And at that point in time, St. Louis and Nashville and Chicago had a real strong rhythm and blues and jazz circuit. He gave me my first horn—my first cornet that was designed like his. I'll never forget that. And one time my father took us to see where Miles Davis was staying. It was in a black hotel in town, and I saw him in the lobby and I heard him whisper that horny whisper....

Very sexy. ...

Yeah, really ... and DuBois, I remember. I was too young to remember Paul Robeson coming to dinner, except that he had this incredible sense of humor about him. I remember this big brown man that looked sort of like my dad, who was with us in the dining room at dinner time. Vague things like that. I remember when Walter White came and they had a cocktail party. I used to sit up on the stairway in the front of the house and watch the people come in and I could listen to the talk going on in the back. I remember the night Walter White came because the people from the NAACP had a raffle. He was one of the very important civil rights leaders of the 40s and early 50s, and he was very, very light-skinned, so he could get into tense situations with the Klan or where there were riots going on or where there was discrimination, and see for himself and the NAACP exactly what was going on.

When passing was a necessity. ...

Uh huh. He was a very, very brilliant man and a lot of his articles are in *The Crisis* magazine.

What about DuBois?

I remember him because my mother used to talk to me about him all the time. And he apparently was a very crotchety man. Really. He didn't like children. That's what my mother said. He didn't like children. And for some reason he liked me. The way the story goes, Dr. DuBois took me upstairs and put me to sleep one night, which everybody thought was amazing, because he wasn't supposed to like babies. So I heard about him forever after that. And then, of course, Cesar Chavez used to be at our house. My father—we used to raise money for the grape strike. And Muhammad Ali and Sugar Ray Robinson. ...

How did your father know all these people?

My father was a ring physician and rodeo physician or any other kind of sports physician. He also worked in a huge public hospital. If there were fights or knifings in night clubs—black night clubs—the black people got sent to the black hospitals. And so when anybody got shot or knifed, whether they were famous or not, they would go to this black hospital, and that's where he was doing his residency. So we met a lot of people that way.

Do you remember Robeson's voice?

Yeah, I remember his laugh. What I remember is conversation at dinner that seemed to be very vital, and a big ... just an incredible presence.

Is there anything you'd like to tell your contemporary readers?

Oh, I know. One of the things that's been bothering me most is the homogenizing of language. Of contemporary English. And I've been feeling that the power of the language that black and Latin and women writers, who are exploring and unleashing in the last decade, is being encroached upon in a very serious way. For instance, on the news last night there was a fire and eight people died and one pregnant woman. But instead of saying "one pregnant woman" the newscaster said "one pregnant woman and one unborn child." That's a very dangerous use of language. And an obsessive use of language. It's something that we are exposed to in a steady, innocuous drone and it then will become part of someone's psyche in a way that multiplies in terrifying leaps and bounds. Another thing, for instance, is that every major soap opera right now, in *Dallas* and *Dynasty*—as soon as the word "abortion" is mentioned the female characters spend weeks having guilt and terror about having an abortion. See, this gives the wrong idea that you can take weeks to do this. And you can't. Also, we don't have to spend weeks being terrorized about it. Those are two things. And the other is this murder that went on at Howard Beach when the crowd of white people went running around. What happened is—in one newscast they said that white *youths* of sixteen and seventeen did something. Right. And the following local news report about a local 7-11 robbery—a black *man* of sixteen did something. So I think we not only have to begin to take very seriously what's presented to us, but we have to take very seriously how our written language—the word on the page—has alerted the powers that be that these ideas—that these people have been suggesting—must be stopped. Therefore, we will not discuss it the way they discuss it.

Do you have any advice for aspiring writers?

That no matter what—and I have to give this to myself, too, every once in a while I have real problems, a really severe writer's block—that no matter what happens, never think it's not worth-while. And never be afraid, whatever it is, that it's too beautiful or too terrible to tell.

Deborah R. Geis (essay date 1989)

SOURCE: "Distraught at Laughter: Monologue in Shange's Theatre Pieces," in *Feminine Focus: New Women Playwrights*, Oxford University Press, 1989, pp. 210-225.

[*In the following essay, Geis discusses Shange's use of language as an expression of African American women's experience in her performance pieces.*]

> . . . bein alive & bein a woman & bein colored is a
> metaphysical dilemma/ i havent conquered yet/ do you
> see the point my spirit is too ancient to understand the
> separation of soul & gender/ my love is too delicate
> to have thrown back on my face
>
> —Ntoazke Shange, *for colored girls who have considered*
> *suicide / when the rainbow is enuf*

Ntozake Shange's works defy generic classifications: just as her poems (published in *Nappy Edges* and *A Daughter's Geography*) are also performance pieces, her works for the theater defy the boundaries of drama and merge into the region of poetry. Her most famous work, *for colored girls who have considered suicide/ when the rainbow is enuf,* is subtitled "a choreopoem." Similarly, she has written *Betsey Brown* as a novel and then again (with Emily Mann) in play form, and her first work of fiction, *Sassafrass, Cypress & Indigo,* is as free with its narrative modes—including recipes, spells, letters—as Joyce was in *Ulysses.* Perhaps more so than any other practicing playwright, Shange has created a poetic voice that is uniquely her own—a voice which is deeply rooted in her experience of being female and black, but also one which, again, refuses and transcends categorization. Her works articulate the connection between the doubly "marginalized" social position of the black woman and the need to invent and appropriate a language with which to articulate a self.

In their revelation of such a language, Shange's theatrical narratives move subtly and forcefully between the comic and the tragic. A brief passage from *for colored girls* underscores the precarious path between laughter and pain which Shange's characters discover they are forced to tread:

> distraught laughter fallin

> over a black girl's shoulder
> it's funny/it's hysterical
> the melody-less-ness of her dance
> don't tell nobody, don't tell a soul
> she's dancin on beer cans & shingles[1]

The images associated with the word *hysterical* in this passage show the multilayered and interdependent qualities of the "black girl's" experience: *hysterical* connotes a laughter which has gone out of control, a madness historically—if not accurately—connected with femaleness. Moreover, the admonition "don't tell nobody, don't tell a soul" suggests the call to silence, the fear that to speak of her pain will be to violate a law of submission. The onlooker will aestheticize the dance or call attention to its comic qualities rather than realize the extent to which the dance and the laughter are a reaction against—and are even motivated by—the uncovering of pain.

The key here is the complexity, for Shange, of the performative experience. In her plays, especially *for colored girls* and *spell #7,* Shange develops her narration primarily through monologues because monologic speech inevitably places the narrative weight of a play upon its spoken language and upon the performances of the individual actors. But she does not use this device to develop "character" in the same fashion as Maria Irene Fornes and other Method-inspired playwrights who turn toward monologic language in order more expressively to define and "embody" their characters both as women and as individuals. Rather, Shange draws upon the uniquely "performative" qualities of monologue to allow her actors to take on *multiple* roles and therefore to emphasize the centrality of *storytelling* to her work. This emphasis is crucial to Shange's articulation of a black feminist aesthetic (and to the call to humanity to accept that "black women are inherently valuable")[2] on two counts. First, the incorporation of role-playing reflects the ways that blacks (as "minstrels," "servants," "athletes," etc.) and women (as "maids," "whores," "mothers," etc.) are expected to fulfill such roles on a constant basis in Western society.[3] Second, the space between our enjoyment of the "spectacle" of Shange's theater pieces (through the recitation of the monologues and through the dancing and singing which often accompany them), and our awareness of the urgency of her call for blacks/women to be allowed "selves" free of stereotypes, serves as a "rupturing" of the performance moment; it is the uncomfortableness of that space, that rupture, which moves and disturbs us.

In **"takin a solo/ a poetic possibility/ a poetic imperative,"** the opening poem of *Nappy Edges*, Shange argues that just as the great jazz musicians each have a recognizable sound and musical style, so too should the public develop a sensitivity to the rhythms and nuances of black writers and that the writers themselves should cultivate "sounds" which distinguish them as individuals. She writes:

> as we demand to be heard/ we want you to
> hear us, we come to you the way leroi jenkins comes
> or cecil taylor/ or b.b. king, we come to you alone/ in
> the theater/ in the story/ & the poem, like with billie
> holiday or betty carter/ we shd give you a moment
> that cnnot be recreated/ a specificity that cannot be
> confused, our language shd let you know who's
> talkin, what we're talkin abt & how we cant stop
> sayin this to you, some urgency accompanies the text,
> something important is going on, we are speakin,
> reachin for yr person/ we cannot hold it/ we don't
> wanna sell it/ we give you ourselves/ if you listen.[4]

Although Shange's remarks were intended to address the larger issue of Afro-American writing, her words hold true for the speakers of monologue in her plays as well, for the monologue is another way of "takin a solo." For Shange's actors/characters (it is sometimes difficult to draw the distinction between the two, as the actors frequently portray actors who in turn portray multiple characters), monologues issue forth with the same sense that "some urgency accompanies the text" and that, in delivering the speeches, they are "reachin for yr person." In this respect the characters seem to aspire toward a specificity which would make them stand as if independent of their author. But the hallmark of the very "imperative" which Shange has announced in the first place is the unmistakable sense that all of the speakers' voices are ultimately parts of one voice: that of Shange, their creator and the play's primary monologist or storyteller.

All of Shange's theatrical pieces, even *a photograph: lovers in motion* and *boogie woogie landscapes,* unfold before the audience as collections of stories rather than as traditionally linear narratives; the events are generated less from actual interactions as they unfold in the "present" of the play (except perhaps in *a photograph*) than from the internal storytellers' *recreations* of individual dramas. The implied privilege of the storyteller to create alternate worlds, as well as the fluidity of the stories themselves and the characters in them, relies heavily upon the immense power that African and Afro-American tradition have assigned to the spoken word. According to James Hatch, Africans traditionally believe that "words and the art of using them are a special power that can summon and control spirit."[5] Furthermore, as Geneviève Fabre explains in *Drumbeats Masks and Metaphor*:

> The oral tradition holds a prominent place in Afro-American culture. For slaves (who were often forbidden to learn to write) it was the safest means of communication. It provided basic contact with Africa

as a homeland and a source of folklore, a contract also between ethnic groups unified under a common symbolic heritage, between generations, and finally, between the speaker and his audience. . . . Because the oral tradition has long remained a living practice in Afro-American culture, the dramatic artist has been tempted to emulate not only the art and techniques of the storyteller, but also his prestigious social function— that of recording and reformulating experience, of shaping and transmitting values, opinions, and attitudes, and of expressing a certain collective wisdom.[6]

Shange takes the notion of exchange and collectivity among storytellers even further in her use of the space in which her pieces are performed. Monologue creates "narrative space"; Shange depends upon the power and magic of the stories within her plays to create the scenes without the use of backdrops and other "theatrical" effects. *for colored girls* is the most "open" of the plays in this sense, as it calls for no stage set, only lights of different colors and specific places for the characters to enter and exit. *boogie woogie landscapes* conjures up the mental images of the title within the confines of Layla's bedroom: "there is what furniture a bedroom might accommodate, though not too much of it, the most important thing is that a bedroom is suggested."[7] Although the sets of both *spell #7* and *a photograph* are fairly specific (a huge minstrel mask as a backdrop and, later, a bar in lower Manhattan for the former; a photographer's apartment for the latter), they still call for this space to be reborn in different imaginary ways as the characters come forth and tell their stories.

for colored girls, Shange's first major theater piece, evolved from a series of poems modeled on Judy Grahn's *Common Woman*. The play received its first performances in coffeehouses in San Francisco and on the Lower East Side of Manhattan; eventually, it attracted critical and public attention and moved to the New Federal Theater, the Public Theater, and then to Broadway in 1976. *for colored girls* draws its power from the performances—in voice, dance, and song—of its actors, as well as from the ways it articulates a realm of experience which heretofore had been suppressed in the theater; the "lady in brown" speaks to the release of this suppression when she says near the beginning of the piece:

> sing a black girl's song
> bring her out
> to know her self
> . . . she's been dead so long
> closed in silence so long
> she doesn't know the sound
> of her own voice
> her infinite beauty
> (pp. 2-3)

The instruments for releasing and expressing the "infinite beauty" of the "black girl's song" become the characters, who do not have names and specific identities of their own (except through their physical presences), but rather take on multiple identities and characters as the "lady in brown," "lady in red," "lady in yellow," etc. These "ladies" put on the metaphorical masks of various characters in order to enact the "ceremony" of the play, which gathers them together in a stylized, ritualistic fashion. The ritual is a religious one to the extent that the participants turn to the "spirit" which might be best described as the black female collective unconscious; it is a celebratory one in that their immersion in it is ultimately a source of joy and strength. In this sense the ritual is a festival that depends as much upon the bonds of the group as it does upon individual expression; Fabre makes this connection explicit when she says that "the group . . . takes possession of space and enlarges it to express communion."[8]

As the characters assume their different "masks," we see them enact a complex series of microdramas, some joyful and others painful. So it is that the "lady in purple" narrates the tale of Sechita, who "kicked viciously thru the nite/ catchin' stars tween her toes" (p. 26), while the lady in green "plays" Sechita and dances out the role. Both of these characters "are" Sechita, for the identity of this character within a character merges in the spoken narration and the accompanying movement. Yet it also becomes clear in the course of the play that these actors/ characters are *not* simply assuming masks or roles for the sake of a dramatic production; they must enact the "dramas" and wear the "masks" of black women every day of their lives. Shange has taken on the difficult task, then, of universalizing her characters in the play without allowing them to fall into roles that are essentially stereotypes. She discusses the need for this balance between the "idiosyncratic" and the "representative" in an interview with Claudia Tate:

I feel that as an artist my job is to appreciate the differences among my women characters. We're usually just thrown together, like "tits and ass," or a good cook, or how we can really "f——" [*sic*]. Our personalities and distinctions are lost. What I appreciate about the women whom I write about, the women whom I know, is how idiosyncratic they are. I take delight in the very peculiar or particular things that fascinate or terrify them. Also, I discovered that by putting them all together, there are some things they all are repelled by, and there are some things they are all attracted to. I only discovered this by having them have their special relationships to their dreams and their unconscious.[9]

At times the storytellers within *for colored girls* seem to be putting on "masks" of humor which they wear, as part of the assumption of a role or character, in order to create a way of channeling the fear and anger they experience into the mode of performance. For instance, in one monologue the lady in red expresses the pain of a rejected love with a sardonic "itemization" of what she has been through:

> without any assistance or guidance from you
> i have loved you assiduously for 8 months 2
>   wks & a day
> i have been stood up four times
> I've left 7 packages on yr doorstep
>   forty poems 2 plants & 3 handmade notecards
>   i left
> town so i cd send to you have been no help to
>   me
> on my job
>   you call at 3:00 in the mornin on weekdays
> so i cd drive 27 ½ miles cross the bay before i
>   go to work
> charmin charmin
> but you are of no assistance
> (p. 13)

The disruptive power of this and other "comic" narratives in the play comes from the realization that what we are laughing at, though merely amusing and exaggerated on the surface, has an underside of bitterness and even torment. Often the shift from humor to pathos is so sudden that the effect is as if we have been slapped, which is precisely the way Shange describes the transition to the story on "latent rapist bravado" ("we cd even have em over for dinner/ & get raped in our own houses/ by invitation/ a friend" [p. 21]). Helene Keyssar points out in *The Curtain and the Veil* that the spectator is likely to overlook the pain in favor of the humor in the play's earliest vignettes, but as the work moves into such searing narratives as the lady in blue's story of an abortion, we begin to feel increasingly uncomfortable with our own laughter. The candor of the speakers combined with the persistent irony, says Keyssar, "prevents the display of emotion from becoming melodramatic and allows the spectators a vulnerability to their own feelings that can renew their ability to act with others in the world outside the theater."[10] But there is also another way to view this generation of "vulnerability": as a result of the disjunction between the guise of humor and the realization that such moments in the play are actually imbued with pain and anger, the spectator experiences the feeling of having entered an uncomfortable "space" between the two strategies of performance. Like Brecht, Shange seems to believe that inhabiting such a "space" causes the audience to question its own values and beliefs; unlike Brecht, though, she engages the emotions directly in this process. She says in her interview with Tate, "I write to get at the part of people's emotional lives that they don't have control over, the part that can and will respond."[11]

The most emotionally difficult (and most controversial)

monologue in the play in terms of this vulnerability is the **"Beau Willie Brown"** sequence, the only story with a male protagonist. It concerns Beau Willie, a Vietnam veteran who beats up Crystal, the mother of their two children, so many times that she gets a court order restraining him from coming near them. When Beau Willie forces his way into Crystal's apartment and insists that she marry him, she refuses, and he takes the children away from her and holds them out on the window ledge. In the devastating final moments of the story, the lady in red, who has been telling the story, suddenly shifts from referring to Crystal in the third person to using "I":

> i stood by beau in the window/ with naomi
> reachin for me/ & kwame screaming mommy mommy
> from the fifth story/ but i cd only whisper/ & he
> dropped em   (p. 63)

It is as if, in this wrenching moment, the lady in red has abandoned the sense that she is "acting out" a story; she "becomes" the character she has been narrating. As she closes the space between her role as narrator and the character of Crystal, this moment of the story itself brings to an end the distancing effect created by Shange's use of spectacle up to this point: the piece is no longer an "entertainment" but a ritualized release of pure feeling which is experienced rather than "performed."

Because of the resonance of the **"Beau Willie Brown"** story, *for colored girls* seems on the brink of despair; instead, though, the intensity and raw emotion of the lady in red's/Crystal's narrative serves to bring the women together and to acknowledge the strength they derive from each other. They characterize this final affirmation in religious terms, but it is a piety derived from within rather than from an outward deity:

> a layin' on of hands
> the holiness of myself released
> . . . i found god in myself.
> & i loved her/ i loved her fiercely
> (pp. 66-67)

Janet Brown justly indicates the need for a movement toward such a resolution when she says that the "successful resolution to the search for autonomy is attributable first to the communal nature of the struggle."[12] However, these last two sequences of the play have come under fire by some critics because they feel that Shange had ultimately failed to translate the personal into the political. Andrea Benton Rushing criticizes Shange's isolation in *for colored girls* "from salient aspects of black literary and political history," the "shockingly ahistorical" way it seems to ignore "white responsibility for our pain," and its final "rejection of political solutions."[13] Similarly, Erskine Peters

is appalled by the apparent manipulativeness of the **"Beau Willie Brown"** monologue:

> This climax is the author's blatantly melodramatic attempt to turn the work into tragedy without fulfilling her obligations to explore or implicate the historical and deeper tragic circumstances. There is a very heated attempt to rush the play toward an evocation of pity, horror, and suffering. The application of such a cheap device at this critical thematic and structural point is an inhumane gesture to the Black community[14]

Rushing and Peters raise a valid issue when they say that *for colored girls* is not a direct and forceful indictment of white supremacist politics, at least not in as immediate a sense as *spell #7*. But Peters' accusation that Crystal's story constitutes a "cheap device" which turns the play into a pseudotragedy seems unfounded, for such an argument ignores the declaration of community which comes at the end of the play in response to the individual pain which reached its peak in the **"Beau Willie Brown"** narrative. Indeed, one might argue that the placement of this story before the play's closing ritual is Shange's attempt to avoid having the spectator convert the final moments into cathartic ones—for as Augusto Boal argues so convincingly in *Theater of the Oppressed*, catharsis can have the "repressive" or "coercive" effect of lulling the spectator into complacency.[15] Or, as Michael W. Kaufman says of the black revolutionary theater of Baraka, Reed, and others, "The very notion of catharsis, an emotional purgation of the audience's collective energies, means that theatre becomes society's buffer sponging up all the moral indignities that if translated into action could effect substantial change."[16]

If the ending of the play is dissatisfying because it seems to be administering a palliative to the audience, that is precisely the point: Shange is suggesting the sources of possible strength and redemption by having the characters *perform* the play's closing "ritual." But since the **"Beau Willie Brown"** story has closed the gulf between narrator and narrative, this final "performance" *cannot* be only a "show." Just as the "ladies" are no longer playing "roles," the spectacle of their concluding ritual automatically conveys a sense of urgency which—coupled with the sheer emotional impact of the **"Beau Willie Brown"** sequence—prevents the audience from experiencing the ending as cathartic.

Kimberly Benston discusses black American theater's movement away from European-American structures and toward African-rooted ones in terms of the shift from *mimesis*/drama to *methexis*/ritual. Not only, she claims, does the ritual create a sense of community, as we have discussed in *for colored girls,* but it also breaks down the barriers that have traditionally existed between the performers and the spectators.[17] This is perhaps why, in the opening of Shange's *spell #7* (1979), there is a "huge blackface mask" visible on the stage even while the audience is still coming into the theater. Shange says that "in a way the show has already begun, for the members of the audience must integrate this grotesque, larger than life misrepresentation of life into their pre-show chatter."[18] We might say that she thus attempts to erase distinctions between "play" and "audience": not only does the performance address the spectators, but in this case the spectators are also forced to "address" the performance. At the beginning of the play, the performers parade in minstrel masks identical to the huge one which looms overhead; they eventually shed their masks and pose instead as "actors" (or actors playing actors who, in turn, play at being actors), but the image of the minstrel mask is a sign that even modern black actors are still often conceived of as little more than minstrels. As the actor/character Bettina complains, "if that director asks me to play it any blacker/ I'm gonna have to do it in a mammy dress" (p. 14).

Shange, then, makes the minstrel-masking into a ceremony of sorts in the opening scene of *spell #7,* and the resemblance of the giant minstrel face above the stage to an African voodoo mask is wholly intentional. At the same time, though, the blackface masks that the actors wear at the beginning of the play also invoke the *travesty* of a ceremony, for the masks represent the "parts" each must play (in the Western tradition) in order to get a job. Shange connects this to her feelings about her own "masking" in an interview with Tate:

> It was risky for us to do the minstrel dance in *spell #7,* but I insisted upon it because I thought the actors in my play were coming from pieces they didn't want to be in but pieces that helped them pay their bills. Black characters are always being closed up in a "point." They decided, for instance, that *spell #7* by Zaki Shange is a feminist piece and therefore not poetry. Well, that's a lie. That's giving me a minstrel mask . . . . We're not free of our paint yet! The biggest money-makers—*The Wiz, Bubblin' Brown Sugar, Ain't Misbehavin'*—are all minstrel shows.[19]

In the course of the play, though, the actors/characters also use "masking" in a different way; they try on various "masks" or roles, as in *for colored girls*, to perform the monologues and group pieces that provide both mirrors and alternatives for the various "selves" they create under pressure from a society governed by white values and images. So, for instance, one of the nameless and faceless performers behind a minstrel mask at the beginning of the play becomes the actor Natalie in the next scene, who in turn "becomes" Sue-Jean, a young woman who desperately wants a baby, as she and Alec (another of the "minstrels"

revealed as actor/character) alternate in narrating her story while she mimes it out.

Unlike *for colored girls, spell #7* makes use of a central storyteller figure, Lou, who "directs" the monologues which are performed in the course of the play. It is appropriate that Lou is a magician, for even the title of *spell #7* (the subtitle of which is "geechee jibara quik magic trance manual for technologically stressed third world people") refers to magic making. In his opening speech, though, Lou warns of the power (and danger) of "colored" magic:

> my daddy retired from magic & took
> up another trade cuz this friend a mine
> from the 3rd grade/ asked to be made white
> on the spot
>
> what cd any self-respectin colored american
>   magician
> do wit such an outlandish request/ cept
> put all them razzamatazz hocus pocus zippity-
>   doo-dah
> thingamajigs away cuz
> colored chirren believin in magic
> waz becomin politically dangerous for the race
>   . . .
>
> all things are possible
> but ain't no colored magician in his right mind
> gonna make you   white
> i mean
>   this is blk magic
> you lookin at
> & I'm fixin you up good/ fixin you up good &
>   colored
>
> (pp. 7-8)

The image of the narrator as "magician" implies that the storytellers themselves will be under the control of a certain "author"; yet as the actors perform their pieces, the stories seem at times to slip away from a guiding narratorial force and to become deeply personal. In a sense, the performers threaten to overpower the narrator in the same way that the third grader's request to be made white is beyond the power of Lou's magician father: the stories take on a kind of magic which is independent of their "director," and yet to enter this realm may be painful and perilous, Lou, then, is like a surrogate author who is responsible for the content of the play, but who also cannot fully control what happens to it once the performers begin to take part.

Lou's position in relation to the performers is most fully evident when, after Lily becomes wholly absorbed in her monologue about the network of dreams she has built around her image of her hair, he stands up and points to her.

Shange indicates in the stage directions that Lou "reminds us that it is only thru him that we are able to know these people without the 'masks'/ the lies/ & he cautions that all their thoughts are not benign, they are not safe from what they remember or imagine" (p. 27). He says, partly to Lily and partly to the audience:

> you have t come with me/ to this place where
>   magic is/
> to hear my song/ some times i forget & leave
>   my tune
> in the corner of the closet under all the dirty
>   clothes/
> in this place/ magic asks me where I've been/
>   how I've
> been singin/ lately i leave my self in all the
>   wrong hands/
> in this place where magic is involved in undoin
>   our masks/ i
> am able to smile & answer that.
> in this place where magic always asks for me
> i discovered a lot of other people who talk
>   without mouths
> who listen to what you say/ by watchin yr
>   jewelry dance
> & in this place where magic stays
> you can let yrself in or out
> but when you leave yrself at home/ burglars &
>   daylight thieves
> pounce on you & sell your skin/ at cut-rate on
>   tenth avenue
>
>   (p. 27)

The "place where magic is" means, within the most literal context of the play, the bar where the actors meet and feel free to try on various roles. But it is also the theater, and the implication is that, as such, it is both a safe place and an unsafe place: certain inhibitions are lifted and certain feelings can be portrayed, but one risks vulnerability in exposing one's memories and emotions. Finally, "this place where magic is" marks the space in which the actor/writer/ artist allows creativity to happen. The impulse to safeguard it—"lately i leave my self in all the wrong hands"—echoes the fear of loss which Shange turns into a similar set of metaphors in the "somebody almost walked off wid alla my stuff" poem in *for colored girls*. But something interesting occurs as the result of Lou's delivery of this speech: although he designs it to reinforce his power as the play's magician/narrator, its effect is to establish *him* as being in a position not altogether different from that of the other characters, for the speech reveals his vulnerability, his disguises and defenses, and his need to inhabit a "safe" place in which to create.

If Lou is indeed addressing the audience as well as Lily, the implication is that he is inviting the spectator to become similarly vulnerable. Not surprisingly, then, the play's two "centerpiece" monologues attempt—as in *for colored girls*—to take hold of the spectator in the gap that the performers create between the "safe" region of spectacle/ entertainment and the "unsafe" region of pain and emotional assailability. In the first of the two monologues, Alec tells of his wish for all of the white people all over the world to kneel down for three minutes of silence in formal apology for the pain that they have given to black people:

> i just want to find out why no one has even
> been able to sound a gong & all the reporters recite
> that the gong is ringin/ while we watch all the white
> people/ immigrants & invaders/ conquistadors &
> relatives of london debtors from georgia/ kneel &
> apologize to us/ just for three or four minutes. now/
> this is not impossible.
>
>   (p. 46)

Of course, the image is an absurd one, and Lou calls attention to this when he responds to Alec, "what are you gonna do with white folks kneeling all over the country anyway/ man" (p. 47). The humor in Alec's rather extreme proposal is undercut, however, by the suffering which stands behind such a request. Perhaps the most savage example of anger transferred to the realm of the comic, though, and one which cannot fail to disturb the audience, is Natalie's "today I'm gonna be a white girl" monologue. She takes on the voice of the vacuous and hypocritical "white girl" who flings her hair, waters her plants, and takes twenty Valiums a day:

> . . . I'm still waiting for my cleaning lady & the
> lady who takes care of my children & the lady who
> caters my parties & the lady who accepts quarters at
> the bathroom in sardi's, those poor creatures shd be
> sterilized/ no one shd have to live such a life. cd you
> hand me a towel/ thank-you caroline. I've left all of
> maxime's last winter clothes in a pile for you by the
> back door, they have to be cleaned but i hope yr girls
> can make gd use of them.   (p. 49)

Freud says in *Jokes and Their Relation to the Unconscious* that the ability to laugh at something is interfered with when the "joke" material also produces a strong affect and so another emotion "blocks" one's capacity to generate laughter;[20] for this reason, it is not surprising that the "white girls" in the audience at whom this monologue is aimed may feel too angry at Natalie's speech to consider it funny. Or they may laugh because they distance themselves from the reality of her words. Similarly, the very intensity of Natalie's emotions as she speaks this piece shows both the amount of pain which gradually interferes with her ability to sustain the joking tone of her own speech at the end and the intensified need for release through humor which her bitterness engenders. As Freud indicates,

> precisely in cases where there is a release of affect one can observe a particularly strong difference in expenditure bring about the automatism of release. When Colonel Butler answers Octavio's warnings be exclaiming 'with a bitter laugh': '*Thanks* from the House of Austria!' his embitterment does not prevent his laughing. The laugh applies to his memory of the disappointment he believes he has suffered; and on the other hand the magnitude of the disappointment cannot be portrayed more impressively by the dramatist than by his showing it capable of forcing a laugh in the midst of the storm of feelings that have been released.[21]

It is also striking that the play's final monologue, spoken by Maxine, comes forth because she is "compelled to speak by natalie's pain" (i.e., after Natalie delivers the "white girl" monologue [p. 49]). As in *for colored girls*, the play's penultimate sequence seems to be different in tone from the earlier monologues—and again, the effect is a closure of the "gaps" we have discussed. Here Maxine speaks of the way her world was shattered when she realized as a child that blacks were not exempt from the diseases, crimes, and so on, that white people experienced. She closes with a description of her decision to appropriate gold chains, bracelets, and necklaces as a symbol of "anything hard to get & beautiful./ anything lasting/ wrought from pain," followed by the shattering remark that "no one understands that surviving the impossible is sposed to accentuate the positive aspects of a people" (p. 51). Lou, as "director" of the action, freezes the players before they can fully respond to Maxine's words, and he repeats the closing portion of his opening speech: "And you gonna be colored all yr life/ & you gonna love it/ bein colored/ all yr life." As the minstrel mask reappears above them, he leads the actors in the chant "colored & love it/ love it bein colored" (p. 52). Shange notes in the stage directions that the chant is a "serious celebration, like church/ like home" (p. 52). Her words are entirely appropriate to the dual nature of the ending: it is true that the characters are celebrating themselves, but the resonance of the preceding monologue, which was fraught with pain—as well as the overwhelming presence of the minstrel mask—recalls the anger and frustration which also underlie their chant. The characters, then, are imprisoned in the stereotypes and social position which the world has assigned to them, but like the women in *for colored girls* they call for unity as a source of strength. Their chant of "colored & love it/ love it bein colored" suggests that they intend to escape from their prison by redefining it so that it is no longer a prison. But the possibility remains that for the time being the escape may be only a partial one. As Shange writes in **"unrecovered losses/ black theater traditions,"** the minstrel face which de-

scends, is "laughing at all of us for having been so game/ we believed we cd escape his powers."[22]

Spell #7's ultimate vision may be more cynical than that of *for colored girls*, but its call for redefinitions is one which echoes throughout Shange's theater pieces. She invites a reconsideration of role-playing which suggests that in the process of acting out the various "masks" that blacks/ women are *expected* to assume, one undergoes an experience of interior drama. Liberated through monologic language and by dance, song, etc., which release different, richer, more complex characters and experiences, the very nature of role-playing has been appropriated as a tool for "performing a self." She sees role-playing as a way simultaneously to give her characters an archetypal fluidity and to confront role-oriented stereotypes. On some level Shange's characters are always aware that they are speaking to an audience; perhaps this emphasis is an acknowledgment of the sense that women—as John Berger discusses in *Ways of Seeing*—are always the objects of vision and so are constantly watching themselves being watched.[23] Rather than decentering the position of authorship in her plays by providing a sense that the characters are as if "self-created," though, Shange appears to share Michelene Wandor's view that deliberate attention to the author's role as "storyteller" provides a backbone, a controlling structure, for the play.[24] Interwoven with this is a revision of spectacle as a vehicle for amusement; Shange's interpretation of "spectacle" insists upon questioning both the *mode* of performance which lures the audience's attention (as in the minstrel show at the beginning of *spell #7*) and the *subtext* of the spectacle itself. The monologue, then, is both an object for transformation and a means by which transformations can occur. Above all, Shange feels passionately that "we must move our theater into the drama of our lives."[25] Her works attempt to speak, in the way that she says Layla's unconscious does in *boogie woogie landscapes*, of "unspeakable realities/ for no self-respecting afro-american girl wd reveal so much of herself of her own will/ there is too much anger to handle assuredly/ too much pain to keep on truckin/ less ya bury it."[26]

Notes

1. Ntozake Shange, *for colored girls who have considered suicide/ when the rainbow is enuf* (1977; reprint New York: Bantam, 1981), pp. 1-2. Subsequent references to the play are to this edition and will be indicated in the text. N.B.: Shange's spelling, punctuation, and diction make up her unique style and have been reproduced as printed in the texts of her works.

2. Combahee River Collective, "A Black Feminist Statement," in *But Some of Us Are Brave: Black Women's Stud-*

ies, ed. Gloria Hull, Patricia Bell, and Barbara Smith (New York: Feminist Press, 1982), p. 15.

3. Cf. Alice Walker, "In Search of Our Mothers' Gardens," in *In Search of Our Mothers' Gardens* (New York and San Diego: Harcourt Brace Jovanovich, 1983), p. 237.

4. Ntozake Shange, *Nappy Edges* (London: Methuen, 1987), p. 11.

5. James Hatch, "Some African Influences on the Afro-American Theatre," in *The Theater of Black Americans*, ed. Errol Hill (Englewood Cliffs, N.J.: Prentice-Hall, 1980), vol. 1, p. 25.

6. Geneviève Fabre, *Drumbeats Masks and Metaphor: Contemporary Afro-American Theatre*, trans. Melvin Dixon (Cambridge, Mass.: Harvard University Press, 1983), p. 219.

7. Ntozake Shange, *boogie woogie landscapes*, in *Three Pieces* (New York: St. Martin's Press, 1981), p. 113.

8. Fabre, *Drumbeats Masks and Metaphor*, p. 226.

9. Claudia Tate, ed., *Black Women Writers at Work* (New York: Continuum, 1983), p. 153.

10. Helene Keyssar, *The Curtain and the Veil: Strategies in Black Drama* (New York: Burt Franklin, 1981), pp. 213-15.

11. Tate, *Black Women Writers*, p. 156.

12. Janet Brown, *Feminist Drama* (Metuchen, N.J.: Scarecrow Press, 1979), p. 129.

13. Andrea Benton Rushing, "*for colored girls*, Suicide or Struggle," *Massachusetts Review* 22 (Autumn 1981), 544, 546, 550. Certainly, it would be difficult for Rushing to make the same accusations of *spell #7*.

14. Erskine Peters, "Some Tragic Propensities of Ourselves: The Occasion of Ntozake Shange's '*for colored girls who have considered suicide/ when the rainbow is enuf*,'" *Journal of Ethnic Studies* 6, no. 1 (Spring 1978), 82.

15. August Boal, *Theater of the Oppressed*, trans. Charles A. McBride and Maria-Odilia Leal McBride (New York: Urizen, 1979), p. 25.

16. Michael W. Kaufman, "The Delicate World of Reprobation: A Note on the Black Revolutionary Theatre," in *The Theater of Black Americans*, ed. Erroll Hill (Englewood Cliffs, N.J.: Prentice-Hall, 1980), vol. 1, pp. 206-7.

17. Kimberly W. Benston, "The Aesthetic of Modern Black Drama," in *The Theater of Black Americans*, ed. Erroll Hill (Englewood Cliffs, N.J.: Prentice-Hall, 1980), vol. 1, pp. 62-63.

18. Ntozake Shange, *spell #7*, in *Three Pieces* (New York: St. Martin's Press, 1981), p. 7. Subsequent references to the play are to this edition and will be indicated in the text.

19. Tate, *Black Women Writers*, p. 173.

20. Sigmund Freud, *Jokes and Their Relation to the Unconscious*, trans. James Strachey (New York: Norton, 1960), pp. 220-21.

21. *Ibid.*

22. Ntozake Shange, "unrecovered losses/ black theater traditions," in *Three Pieces* (New York: St. Martin's Press, 1981), p. xiii.

23. John Berger, *Ways of Seeing* (Middlesex: Penguin/ BBC, 1972), pp. 446-47.

24. Michelene Wandor, *Carry On, Understudies: Theater and Sexual Politics*, rev. ed. (London: Routledge & Kegan Paul, 1986), p. 128.

25. Shange, "unrecovered losses," p. ix.

26. *Ibid.*, p. xiv.

Barbara Frey Waxman (essay date Fall 1994)

SOURCE: "Dancing Out of Form, Dancing into Self: Genre and Metaphor in Marshall, Shange, and Walker," in *Melus*, Vol. 19, No. 3, Fall, 1994, p. 91-107.

[*In the following essay, Waxman discusses the novels of Paule Marshall, Alice Walker, and Ntozake Shange in terms of the ways in which they incorporate dance forms and metaphors into their representations of African American women.*]

Western culture has typically seen dance as an empowering activity, offering a forum for individual self-expression, or acting like a religious ritual that binds the community and spiritually renews the individual. In literature, the dance for centuries has been a conventional celebratory ending, all of Shakespeare's comedies, for example, conclude with a wedding dance. Northrop Frye has noted dance's presence in the masque, during which audience participation with the actors was encouraged (288); he also emphasizes the "participation mystique" of dance, comparing it to religious lyrics and "poems of community" (295-96). In modern American popular culture, dance has been associated with opportunities for individual self-expression. For example, in American musical plays such as *My Fair Lady*, Eliza Doolittle's linguistic triumph at the ball is noted in "I Could Have Danced All Night." The Jets and Sharks of West Side Story sing, strut, and leap their masculine prowess, while Maria whirls in space, singing her love and female self-appreciation in "I Feel Pretty." And more recently, the heroine of the film *Dirty Dancing* has danced her way into independence and sexual maturity. For our culture, inherent in the act of dancing are, in varying degrees, self-affirmation, eroticism, spiritual renewal, and communal bonding, suggesting dance's ability to heal the mind/body split.

This split, which especially afflicts women transculturally, is identified by Adrienne Rich, Jane Gallop, and others as a major force perpetuating patriarchal culture for American women. Leslie Gotfrit has argued that not only dancing but also writing about dance (and reading about it, I would add) helps to heal this mind/body division: "Dancing precipitates an incredible longing. To recover the pleasure—in the imagining and re-membering,' the connecting again with my limbs, my breath, my body—is to ignite desire. These are rare moments of realizing my body and mind as not distinct, and of feeling the power of creativity when embodied. This is my history and investment in dance, always in the shadow of the writing" (176). This reintegration of body with mind is central to women's empowerment and to any political agenda that they may pursue (Gotfrit 184). Gotfrit explains how the physicality of the music and pleasure in the movement liberate women's normally controlled sexual feelings, a control society expects of women: in dance, "letting go of the tight rein women often keep on their sexuality is possible . . . dancing permits and frees the body to experience sensuality and desire, [and] sexuality (frequently and area of silence and pain in women's lives) is allowed expression", a dancing woman thus experiences pleasure from contacting her own sexuality and also feels in control of herself (178-79). Because she is in control, a woman can resist attempts to turn her body into a sexual object. Eroticism, resistance to sexual oppression, and self-proclamation, as well as communal unification and spiritual rejuvenation, then, are some of the pleasures of dance sought by Western women.

African cultures also recognize dance's affective and spiritual powers, giving dance a central place in their communal events, both secular and religious. As John S. Mbiti

indicates in his book, *Introduction to African Religion,* music, singing, and dance together are used "in all activities of African life: in cultivating the fields, fishing, herding, performing ceremonies, praising rulers and warriors, hushing babies to sleep . . . " (8). Mbiti describes the function of music and dance during communal worship as a way of dissolving barriers between each person's mind, body, and spirit: "Through music, singing, and dancing, people are able to participate emotionally and physically in the act of worship. The music and dancing penetrate into the very being of the worshipping individuals" (61). Dance celebrations also dissolve barriers between individuals: "The dancing and rejoicing strengthen community solidarity and emphasize the corporateness of the whole group" (Mbiti, African Religion and Philosophy 182). In praising warriors and rulers through dance, Africans also recognize the individuality affirming aspect of dance. Borderlands between the human world and the spirit world also merge in the dancing or religious mediums—often women—who communicate with spirits or are possessed by them (Mbiti, Introduction 157). While Mbiti's generalizing about all African cultures does not attend to specific tribes's practices concerning dance, his observations about the individually affirming and communal elements of dance for participants and spectators alike are still applicable to many tribes.

Inheritors of both African and American cultural practices and attitudes, many African American writers, particularly women who are finding their own voices as writers, have turned to dance as a thematic or metaphoric motif for empowerment and self-proclamation, as well as for literary sisterhood. From a feminist perspective, it is not surprising that African American women writers, three of whom I will focus on in this essay, are attracted to dance. Although Gotfrit writes about women disco dancing with other women at Toronto dance clubs as feminist resistance to traditional couples's dancing, the writers discussed in this essay imagine a new space for women's dancing far beyond "imperatives like coupled heterosexuality and politely restrained dancing" (191), and Gotfrit's conception of the sexual politics of dancing applies to these texts. Thus, an African American woman writer may be drawn to dance for its ideological implication, while also being attracted to the religious fervor and renewal associated with dance in African contexts.

These African American women authors not only use themes and metaphors of dance, but also adopt literally the African belief (as presented by Mbiti) in dance's power to dissolve boundaries: they write texts which dissolve literary borders, generic boundaries. Moreover, they nudge readers to relinquish distinctions between the personal essay and lyric poetry, between poetry and performative drama, between analytical and affective writing, and between literature and music/choreography. This is not to say that African, American, and African American cultures as represented in these texts are always knowable, coherent, and unchanging over time and place, that all African American women writers write about dance in consistently predictable ways, or that African American women when writing always take up themes of self-empowerment, convey these themes through dance metaphors, and challenge generic conventions, I agree with William J. Spurlin's assertion that text-centered readings of black texts and discussions of such "black" literary tropes of African American discourse as signifying, are essentializing: "It becomes theoretically difficult to speak of the black text or of a notion of a social and cultural African-American whole without inevitably reducing the multiplicities within each to a homogenized essence that excludes the similarities to Western forms [and also African forms] of discourse which African American texts both inscribe and in which they are always already inscribed" (735). To avoid essentializing, this essay considers simply how some African American women writers seek new ways of expressing the multiplicity and complexity of black womanhood through innovative texts that transcend traditional genres. This essay offers readings of three "hybrid-generic" texts written, respectively, by Ntozake Shange, Paule Marshall, and Alice Walker: ***For Colored Girls Who Have Considered Suicide When the Rainbow Is Enuf***, *Praisesong for the Widow*, and "Beauty: When the Other Dancer Is the Self."

In these texts, the female protagonists are in quest of themselves, endeavoring to understand and express their multiple selves by tracing where they came from and how experiences have changed them. This quest for identity and self-expression and the results of this quest, including spiritual renewal, self-acceptance, and newly defined identities, are described through dance. Marshall's Avey Johnson is purged of her middle-class New York values and inhibitors during a trip to the Caribbean. There she makes contact with her African ancestry and embraces its ideals and values by participating in an island ceremony; with the African rhythms pulsing in her blood, she "dances her nation." Similarly, a group of women characters in Shange's text poetically celebrate their kinship and support of each other as they dance the blues of race and gender. They chant in choral poems and dance, solo and ensemble, their personal encounters with racism and sexism, as well as the loves and triumphs that define their individual identities as black women. Finally, Walker's autobiographical essay presents Walker's persona as a woman who comes to value the physical imperfection of her eye, out of which she has developed a strong, wise, and sympathetic personality. Walker's text choronologically traces incidents in her persona's life in which her damaged and disfigured eye played a role, up to the point at which she can accept her

eye's role in determining who Alice Walker is. This acceptance is symbolized in the persona's dance-embrace with another part of herself in a dream.

When the protagonists of Paule Marshall, Ntozake Shange, and Alice Walker dance, these authors are using dance as a metaphor to signify their character's self-discoveries, self-expression, and self-endorsement. While dance events within the narrative free the protagonists to redefine and be themselves, dance rhythms often pervade these author's prose, freeing the texts from traditional language, structures, and genres. As Barbara Christian observes, "In every society where there is the denigrated Other . . . , the Other struggles to declare the truth and therefore create the truth in forms that exist for her or him" ("Creating" 160). If the forms do not exist, writers who are Others depicting marginality must create new forms. These new structures or genres in themselves perform "formal signifying" (Gates 294), structurally parodic commentary on or protest against earlier texts and styles, especially those of white patriarchal literary tradition, but also those of earlier African American writers. Creating these new structures or genres is an act of "rhetorical self-definition" (Gates 290) for Marshall, Shange, and Walker. Furthermore, the new genres encourage readers to find new ways to make meanings about race and gender, to read these texts with greater flexibility.

Marshall had been attracted to dance as a thematic metaphor for self-expression and self-development in 1959 in her first novel, *Brown Girl, Brownstones*. In that novel, the heroine, Selina Boyce, dances the life-cycle of the self near the end of the book with an all-white dance group. This experience, including its aftermath, where she has a confrontation with the mother of one of the dancers, teaches her the role that racism must play in the life-cycle of an African American woman. However, this text, in its structure and narrative perspective, is a conventional, though powerful, representation of the novel as genre. In contrast, *Praisesong for the Window* (1983) uses dance metaphors and offers some innovations on the novel as genre.

In *Praisesong*, Avey Johnson is introduced as an assimilated, middle-class black woman from North White Plains, New York—readers will note the play on "White." Recently widowed, Avey experiences a sense of dislocation from herself while on a Caribbean cruise; she feels a mind/body split: her "mind in a way wasn't even in her body" (10). Her mind/body split is also apparent in her loss of contact with the ethnicity of her newlywed days, when she danced with her husband Jay while listening to the gospel and blues music on the radio on Sunday mornings. Marshall names the praisesongs and blues melodies as well as the singers and the lyrics, vividly depicting the couple's private dancing, its sensuality and ethnicity. Avey has also lost touch with those summer days of her childhood spent on the South Carolina seacoast island of Tatem, where her Aunt Cuney tried to teach her racial reverence, a form of African ancestral worship, by recounting myths of the island's Landing and early African inhabitants, the Ibos. Aunt Cuney herself had danced as a way of worshipping and contacting her African ancestors: she had done a "forbidden" (anti-Christian) dance before the Christian church in Tatem, "crossing her feet' in a Ring Shout"—a step that at once repudiated the Western, white Christian values adopted by Tatem's church-going citizens and celebrated the spirits of Africa (33). Avey, however, has neglected her racial past, the values and traditions of Africa. That she has consequently lost contact with aspects of her own identity is clear as she peers into mirrors and observes a well-dressed, acceptable-looking (to white society) black woman, whom she does not recognize, but upon whom she smugly remarks: "She would never be sent to eat in the kitchen when company came" (48-49). Upon second glance, she realizes this stranger in the mirror is herself. Readers feel almost as distant from Avey as she is from herself in this early stage of the novel, put off by her "Marian Anderson reserve," her "white" propriety.

Marshall then traces Avey's journey back to herself and her Caribbean and African ancestry. Guided by an island native, Lebert Joseph, Avey takes the Carriacou Excursion, a ritual of renewal through reinforcement of kinship undertaken annually by the outislanders of Grenada; they return to their home island of Carriacou to give the Old Parents, the Long-Time People, their remembrance and their reverence, through singing, dancing and ceremonial. On Carriacou, Avey participates in the Big Drum ceremony, hears the Beg Pardon song—begging pardon for her lapses of racial memory—and joins "the endless procession of dancers over the years" (235) as she performs the Carriacou tramp of the Aradas, her ancestral tribe in Africa. She also becomes reconnected to the other Carriacou islanders, the people on Tatem, and her earliest New York community. Marshall's narrator describes Avey's dancing in this way: "Just as her feet of their own accord had discovered the old steps, her hips under the linen shirtdress slowly began to weave from side to side on their own, stiffly at first and then in a smooth wide arc as her body responded more deeply to the music. . . . All of her moving suddenly with a vigor and passion she hadn't felt in years" (249). As a reader, I was also swept into the dance movements by Marshall's rhythmic prose descriptions of Avey's experience. Avey's body and her memory move her into a mystical, reverential state. She dances her ancestry uninhibitedly, in bodily expression of the psychic process of remembering. In the act of dancing, she finds and names herself, reclaiming her ancestral name of Avatara and re-experiencing African religious ritual. Avatara dances herself into contact with a rich heritage and self-pride that spiritually recharges her.

Barbara Christian notes a connection between the spiritual process that Avery undergoes and the four-part structure or Marshall's novel. The novel's four sections, titled "Runagate," "Sleeper's Wake," "Lave Tete," and "The Beg Pardon," trace the gradual purging, cleansing, and immersion of Avey in African rituals and also reflect "a change in Avey Johnson's character and context" (151). In the first section she escapes her bondage to her white middle-class ethos as she leaves the cruise ship and heads for Grenada. In the second section, she is like a sleeper awakening spiritually as she reassesses her past, especially her marriage to Jay. She finally mourns the transformation of the ethnic, erotic, fun-loving Jay into the "sanitized," dour, ambitious Jerome. The third section marks Avey's ritual cleansing and purging in preparation for her excursion to Carriacou. As Christian notes, this section is associated with a cleansing Haitian voodoo ceremony (154); Avey, now having become a clean slate, is prepared, with the help of Lebert Joseph, to recreate her history and to write her history anew. Her actual boat trip to Carriacou provides the ultimate purgation: the terrible seasickness that Marshall describes unsparingly suggests Avey is dislodging and expelling the sick values of her North White Plains existence. Afterwards, she is bathed as if she were a baby, ritually cleansed by Lebert's daughter, Rosalie Parvay. Finally, in the fourth section, after all this psychic and physical preparation, Avey is able to undergo the ritualistic music and dance ceremony that links her securely to her ancestry.

While readers will be aware of this neat narrative structure of the novel because of the page divisions and breaks in the chronology of Avey's story, Marshall at the same time ruffles the neatness and white Western reader's expectations, both by connecting this structure to African and Haitian rituals and by bringing together elements of fiction, history, music, and dance to form a new, differently energized novelistic genre. The atmosphere of this new genre enables readers to empathize more with Avey's story. We might call the genre a mythopoetic, fictionalized history of African Americans. This genre broadcasts its African and Caribbean elements not only through structure, but also through the increasing presence of the lilting English rhythm and inverted syntax of the Caribbean islander and through the lively Caribbean patois, as spoken by Joseph (" . . . when you see me down on my knees at the Big Drum is not just for me one . . . Oh, no! Is for tout moun'" [236]), by his daughter Rosalie ("Come, oui, . . . is time now to have your skin bathe. And this time I gon' give you a proper washdown'" [217]), by another islander Milda ("The nation dances starting up . . . Is only the old people dances them'" [238]) and even, in the fourth section, by Avey herself. When Avey speaks like an islander, readers recognize how far she has moved toward her origins: "Tel pere tel file. She was unmistakably the old man's daughter" (216), and "Over by the tree Avey Johnson slowly lifted her head. And for an instant as she raised up it almost seemed to be her great aunt standing there beside her in the guise of the big-boned maid. Pa'done mwe. What next was to come?" (237). The inverted syntax of the final sentence gives it an especially strong Caribbean flavor. In addition, pa'done mwe, the Caribbean patios phrase for "pardon me," present here in Avey's thoughts, is repeated by other islanders, ritualistically chanted throughout the fourth section, echoing the Beg Pardon Ceremony and the central theme of rapprochement between an individual and her ancestors.

In the fourth section, moreover, the dance and song threads introduced individually in the earlier sections now are interwoven, like themes of a fugue or dance composition; praisesongs, Ring Shouts, Beg Pardons, Big Drums converge, representing the richly woven fabric of African American culture. As Christian points out, the final ceremony "combines rituals from several black societies: the Ring Dances of Tatem, the Bojangles of New York, the voodoo drums of Haiti, the rhythms of the various African peoples . . . also specifically the embodiment of the history and culture of New World blacks . . . [in the notes that distinguish] Afro-American blues, spirituals and jazz, Afro-Caribbean Calypso and Reggae, Brazilian music" (157). Avey is especially moved by one "dark, plangent note" of music at the Big Drum, a note that comes from "the bruised still-bleeding innermost chamber of the collective heart" (244-45). She relearns the history of her people through such music, then expresses and extends that history through her dancing.

Dancing enables Avey thus to think through her body (Jane Gallop's term), to grasp mentally and viscerally her collective and individual history. Her active embrace of her collective and individual ethnic history will change her own life after this journey, inspiring her to the role of extending to other Americans these African and African American cultural myths (McCluskey 333), teaching her children, grandchildren, and her wider New York community about the richness of their heritage.

As she does the Carriacou tramp, Avey carefully follows the rule of not letting her feet lose contact with the ground, a rule which metaphorically implies the principle of maintaining contact with her ancestral soil, her people, and their traditions. That is why Marshall calls this dance "the shuffle designed to stay the course of history" (250)—designed to subvert the drift of historical events that have prevented African American and Afro-Caribbeans from maintaining contact with their African cultures. Similarly, Marshall's novel, with its Caribbean linguistic play, its blend of mythopoesis and fictionalized African American history, and its synthesis of literary, musical, and dance elements, creates a hybrid genre that arrests the course of American—including African American—literary history and expands the perimeters of the "universal" themes and forms present in canonical twentieth-century American fiction.

The colorfully dressed women in Ntozake Shange's *For Colored Girls Who Have Considered Suicide When the Rainbow is Enuf* assertively take control of the stage and create a blended poetry-dance-theatrical experience, a staged "choreopoem" that surely alters the course of dramatic and dance history in America. Gotfrit's observation about women dancing in the Toronto dance club is equally applicable to Shange's performative text: "The appropriating of space [through dancing] exclusively for women's pleasure, control, and solidarity is radical" (186). Reading Shange's innovative text is also a radicalizing experience. Hearing it read or performed is even more radicalizing. This hybrid genre is both choreographed poetry and Greek choral drama (although we note with amusement Shange's revision of Greek drama in the text's demand for only women, while Greek choral dramas featured only men). Individual actor-dancers recite their poems as they gesture and move to the meanings and the feelings of their words—thinking through the body—while the rest of the ensemble is immobile and silent; or the ensemble chants and moves together in response to the individual's solo plaint, physically and verbally supporting her in travail. This travail usually involves the woman's search for identity, mistreatment by a man, the problems of poverty, or racial prejudice. Even when the other women of the ensemble are apart from the dancer/speaker who is in the spotlight, their attentive listening to her recitation creates a unifying and supportive energy, which also elicits the support of the reader/audience.

Unity and support are apparent, for example, in the poignant **"no more love poems #4,"** where the lady in yellow, solo, through speech and gestures discloses her surprise at her persistent vulnerability to pain and disappointment in a love relationship: "i shd be immune/if i'm still alive" (47). She then confesses that she is not immune, that in her future she will still need to love and be loved even though she will probably be hurt again. She survives "on intimacy and tomorrow" (48). The slang diction ("the music waz like smack" [48]), unconventional spelling, and non-capitalization of the words signal to readers the vernacular quality of the language and the ordinary, candid, human cast of this woman's words. Through these linguistic devices, we feel as if she is conversing with us (she asks us, "do you see the point?" [48]). We sense an urgency in the woman's communication and feel an intimacy with the communicant. Then the woman distills the essence of being black and female in these words: "bein alive & bein a woman & bein colored is a metaphysical dilemma/I haven't conquered yet/ . . . my spirit is too ancient to understand the separation of soul and gender/my love is too delicate to have thrown back in my face" (48). The lady in yellow attempts to re-solve her metaphysical dilemma by declaring her commit-ment to love, by refusing to endure men's abuse of this love, and by proclaiming the humanity of her soul. She re-fuses to be dehumanized as a sex object.

The lady in yellow's words strike a responsive chord in her listening sisters, who have just reentered onstage and are frozen statues in the background. The lady in yellow looks at them and repeats her final line about refusing to let her too delicate love be thrown back in her face. Then that line resonates in each of the other differently colored ladies, each actor in quick succession modulating the line, mak-ing it her own by substituting for "too delicate," "too beau-tiful" (lady in brown), "too sanctified" (lady in purple), "too magic" (lady in blue), "too Saturday nite" (lady in orange), "too complicated" (lady in red), "too music" (lady in green). Next, representing a rainbow of the varied experi-ences of colored women, they all join together physically and linguistically to dance and describe some shared quali-ties of colored women's lives. Dancing and chanting, they build to a fevered pitch that mesmerizes readers, using the same word order of the individual chants, but now reciting together the words "music," "beautiful," "sanctified," "magic," "Saturday nite," and "complicated." Their unified chant increases to orgasmic intensity as they urge one another's right to love an be loved with dignity. Shange's stage directions indicate the physical, linguistic, and psy-chological movement of the scene: "The dance reaches a climax and all of the ladies fall out tried but full of life and togetherness" (52).

Thus, dance motifs that alternate immobility with energetic motion and apartness with unity, together with dramatic staging, colorful costumes, choral interpretations of poetry, and the quickening tempo of chanting all convey the cen-trality and intensity of love and sisterhood in these women of color's lives. Generic innovations that merge dance, choral recitative, poetry, and drama implement Shange's feminist commitment to rethink conventional genres's de-pictions of women, iterating her desire to depict and clarify individual women's lives, "unearthing the mislaid, forgot-ten, &/or misunderstood, women writers, painters, others, cowgirls, & union leaders of our pasts" (xiv-xv). Charles Johnson has perceptively written that Shange's play both fits in with the tradition of avant-garde black theatre estab-lished by Baraka and also "transcends the imperialism of male gender that dominated many earlier plays in the his-tory of black drama" (99).

As Shange's women express through verse and dance their individual stories of pain and triumph, they explain what prompts them to dance: "to keep from cryin, to keep from dyin, . . . come to share our worlds witchu/we come here to be dancin" (15-16). Dance is both an individually

inspiriting, self-affirming medium and a means of spiritual bonding with a community for Shange's characters, as it is for Avey Johnson. Almost like a cathartic religious ritual, dance helps the women shake off despair and isolation by enabling them to communicate more effectively with each other, with audiences, and with their private selves. Danc-ing, moreover, frees them to express physically a reverence for their own ethnicity and femaleness. In the preface to her choreopoem, Shange says of her own dancing: "With dance I discovered my body more intimately that I had imagined possible. With the acceptance of the ethnicity of my thighs & backside, came a clearer understanding of my voice as a woman & as a poet. The freedom to move in space, to demand of my own sweat a perfection that could continually be approached, though never known, waz poem to me, my body & mind ellipsing, probably for the first time in my life" (xv).

Besides creating in her choreopoem the freedom for her actor-poets to move imaginatively in space, Shange also "dances" innovatively in her use of language. She seizes the freedom to write what Gates calls a "speakerly" language "that privilege[s] the representation of the speaking black voice" (296), language that her women can recite unaffect-edly, passionately. As mentioned earlier, the unorthodox orthography, diction, and syntax of this language create an intimacy between the women and the reader. These linguis-tic devices also reflect the women's African American ethnicity, their Otherness resisting the American "standard English" of the politically empowered. The language is, moreover, astringently funny, as when, for example, one of the ladies, exasperated by a lover who has taken for granted her willingness to debase herself for the sake of his love, finally decides to end their one-sided affair and keep her dignity. She writes him this note, which she reads to the audience: "i am endin this affair/this note is attached to a plant/i've been waterin since the day i met you/you may water it/yr damn self" (14). As Charles Johnson has ob-served, the humor in these women's speakerly language tempers the pain revealed in their stories (98-99); it also subverts the power of the male oppressors, exposing one of their "womanish" strategies for surviving the hardships in their lives.

These linguistic and generic innovations of Shange, then, resist the "anxiety of influence" of white/male and even black/male literary texts, enabling her to write of black women's experiences freshly and empathically. Claudia Tate, in an interview with Shange, reports that as an aspect of her artistic credo Shange assumes the responsibility to discover the causes of the pain of women and all black people, to respect their suffering, and to communicate it with honesty (150-56). She does these things very well in the language, dance metaphors and movements, and form of this choreopoem *for colored girls.*

Alice Walker also uses a dance metaphor to chart the development of a central character, her persona, in her autobiographical essay, "Beauty: When the Other Dancer Is the Self," from her collection of essays In Search of Our Mothers' Gardens: Womanist Prose. In this essay, moreover, Walker dances over conventional generic categories. She begins with the personal essay or memoir, which typically contains self-revelations, self-analysis, and conscious, selective shaping of chronological events into a narrative history. Then she extends this form by merging it with a lyrical poem and with another beautifully orchestrated dance-poem of the unconscious mind, which acts as the coda to the essay.

Walker's essay traces the development of the author's self-image through her life, as shaped by several keenly remembered, emotionally charged events from childhood, adolescence, and adulthood. The events are carefully selected and arranged, beginning with her memories of being a pretty, admired little girl, loved and favored especially by her father, whom she adored. Walker flashes back to herself at two-and-half and describes the scene in the present tense, a sign to readers that the event is as clearly recalled as if it had happened yesterday, so vividly does the Wordsworthian "picture of the mind" revive. The beribboned Alice is being readied by her parents for the county fair. Then she moves to her six-year-old self, again describing in the present tense the beautifully attired pretty girl confidently delivering her speech on Easter Sunday, 1950.

The mood of the essay shifts as Walker's persona next chronicles the traumatic event that undermines her self-approval, withdraws from her the approval of the world, especially Daddy, and turns her world upside down: an injury to her eye that blinds and disfigures her when she is eight years old. Almost dispassionately, as if she is keeping tight rein on a flood of emotion inside her, she describes the loss of vision in her right eye resulting from a BB pellet shot from her brother's gun: "There is a tree growing from underneath the porch that climbs past the railing to the roof. It is the last thing my right eye sees I watch as its trunk, its branches, and then its leaves are blotted out by the rising blood" (387). With a little more emotion, she describes the real impact of this accident on her. "But it is really how I look that bothers me most. Where the BB pellet struck there is a glob of whitish scar tissue, a hideous cataract . . . . Now when I stare at people . . . they will stare back. Not at the cute' little girl, but at her scar. For six years I do not stare at anyone, because I do not raise my head" (387). In this way Walker marks her withdrawal from the world, her fear of people's disgust, her anticipation of taunts, of being called a "one-eyed bitch" (388). She remembers with particular pain her father on that fateful day: "I consider that day the last time my father . . . chose me, and that I suf-

fered and raged inside because of this" (391). Tersely she sums up her feeling about her eye at age twelve: "I do not pray for sight. I pray for beauty" (389).

The essay also records her sister and mother's ignorance of this accident's impact on her psyche. Years later Walker asks them whether she changed after the accident, and their answer, "You did not change,'" becomes a haunting refrain in the essay, repeated after she records each event that reveals how much the accident damaged her emotionally. Each repetition of this sentence underscores for readers the insensitivity of others to the emotional effects of Walker's disfigurement and Walker's pain at their insensitivity. With the help of her brother Bill, not the brother who injured her eye but the only family member who understands her "feelings of shame and ugliness" (389), Walker has surgery to remove the white blob, which transforms her at age fourteen into an outgoing, attractive, successful high school student again.

Then Walker's narrative jumps ahead to the recent past of Walker the successful writer, revealing persistent self-consciousness about her eye as she is about to be photographed for the cover of a magazine and her anxiety about how her three-year-old daughter will react to her eye. So far, Walker's piece sounds like a conventionally structured autobiographical essay; this is not to minimize its power and interest, which derive from its painfully personal tone, so personal that I almost felt like a voyeur when I read it. Yet I think its interest and power increase as Walker goes on to stretch the confines of the autobiographical essay. Sandwiched between the recollections of the photo session and her daughter's view of her eye, creating a bridge between them, is a lyrical passage where Walker finally moves beyond the accident and her appearance to the accident and her eyesight. The passage celebrates vision and expresses her immense gratitude for the capacity of her good eye to reward her with the breathtaking view of the desert. A poem "On Sight" is placed in this lyrical passage, blurring the essay's generic lines, to mark her transformation from anger and shame into thankfulness and joy: "I am so thankful I have seen/ The Desert/ And the creatures in the desert/ And the desert itself./ The desert has its own moon/Which I have seen/With my own eye" (391). A religious reverence for vision is conveyed in this psalm-like poem of joy.

The journey into joy of Walker's persona is completed as she moves from self-rejection to self-acceptance and integration of that part of herself that is an injured eye. She describes this movement in her final recollection through the medium of a dramatic dialogue, or rather, a partial dialogue and partial interior analysis of her response to Rebecca's words. Walker shares with readers her daughter's awed response to her eye: "Mommy, there's a world in your eye . . . . Mommy, where did you get that world in your eye?"' (393). Rebecca's words enable Walker to see the world which her eye has given her, an internal and external world of profound proportions: "There was a world in my eye. And I saw that it was possible to love it: that in fact, for all it had taught me of shame and anger and inner vision, I did love it" (393). In analyzing her response to Rebecca's word, Walker finally realizes that who she is is inseparable from her eye, and that her eye has made her who she is: this eye is "deeply suitable to my personality and even characteristic of me" (393). By accepting her scarred eye as part of herself, she heals the emotional scars of thirty years. Walker's personal essay could end conventionally here with this analysis of her response to her daughter's words and her assessment of the change in her attitude toward herself.

However, Walker decides instead to add a lyrical coda to her essay, in which she celebrates both the exhilaration of her self-acceptance—describing it as a physical embrace through music and dance metaphors—and also the exhilaration of literary freedom from rigid generic categories. In the coda, she orchestrates a dance scene within her unconscious, a dream filled with psychically resonant symbols that demand interpretation, as a poem would: "That night I dream I am dancing to Stevie Wonder's song Always' . . . .As I dance, whirling and joyous, happier than I've ever been in my life, another bright-faced dancer joins me. We dance and kiss each other . . . The other dancer has obviously come through all right, as I have done. She is beautiful, whole and free. And she is also me" (293). The love song that energizes the scene, sung by a popular, blind, black, male musician, suggests Walker's newly achieved self-acceptance—sexually, racially and visually. The title of the song (as she hears it) indicates the permanence of her loving relationship with her dance partner, that persona formed after her accident, and it also suggests their enduring loyalty to each other. As the two dance, they marvel at the "wonder" (Stevie's and theirs) of their having "come through all right." They are strong, proud survivors, and their dance expresses almost a religious awe and gratitude at their survival. The embrace of the two in their whirling dance is also the celebration of Walker's newly achieved integrity. As John Clifford points out, we can read Walker's coda as depicting either her former "personal and racial schizophrenic behavior," or "the submerged pain of alienation," or her final "self acceptance [and the] joy of feeling integrated" (57). In fact, all three interpretations can stand, if we see recognition of the first two as the prelude to the third.

In the process of interpreting the coda, readers relinquish conventional distinctions between fiction and fact in autobiography; that is, they understand the "facts" of Walker's life as a consciously selected, arranged, and described artifice of her "life" (Clifford 56). They also relinquish distinctions between the personal essay and lyrical poetry, between analytical and affective writing, and between literature and music/choreography. Walker's dance metaphor cuts a swath across the dream-vision of her coda while her coda is helping to dismantle traditional generic considerations.

The trope of dance within the narratives of Marshall, Shange, and Walker thus liberates African American female protagonists and inspires their creators at the same time to dance their way into new literary forms to portray their heroines. These contemporary writers take their place among other African American writers who use dance scenes metaphorically. Nella Larsen, for example, creates a dance scene in Quicksand (1928) to describe Helga Crane's celebration of the negritude within herself; Helga dances to "a thumping of unseen tomtoms . . . the savage strains of [jungle]music" in Harlem(59). Themes of racial pride and spiritual contact with African ancestors are evident in Larsen's use of dance metaphor, even though her text's genre and narrative structure remain conventional, perhaps because she was writing in an early era of African American literary history.

Sixty years later, in *Beloved* (1987), Toni Morrison is able to use dance metaphor and experiment with form, galvanized by such writers as Marshall, Shange, and Walker. In *Beloved*, Baby Suggs "abandons referential discourse for the affective language of music and dance" (Cummings 568-69) when she dances in the Clearing. There she creates a semiotic language of maternal love for her race and exorcizes the effects of racial prejudice on them, wooing her brethren to dance together their self-love, communal love, and racial pride (88-89). Their dance becomes a religious ritual, a communal celebration of each individual's lovableness. As daringly as the unconventional Baby Suggs, Morrison ventures beyond conventional narrative forms such as Larsen's shaping an innovative, historicized, psychological narrative that is a linguistic *tour de force*. The narrative's piecemeal reconstructions of a central act of matricide and stream-of-consciousness passages reinterpret from a gendered perspective the history of slavery and its impact on male slaves, slave mothers, and motherless slave children. For many postmodern African American women writers like Morrison, such innovative literary forms seem to go hand in hand with celebration of the racial and gendered self, and with rejection of old standards, old attitudes, old constricting ways.

The feminist critic—black or white, male or female—can extend this creative liberation by doing what Deborah E. McDowell urges black feminist critics to do: studying and celebrating "the ways Black women writers employ literary devices in a distinct way" and comparing "the ways Black women writers create their own mythic structures"

(196). This essay has studied, compared, and celebrated ways in which works by Paule Marshall, Ntozake Shange, and Alice Walker articulate truths about the multiple selves of African American women by creating new mythopoetic genres and tropes that mediate synergistically between the word and the dance.

Works Cited

Christian, Barbara. *Black Feminist Criticism: Perspectives on Black Women Writers.* New York: Pergamon P, 1985. 159-63.

Clifford, John. "A Response Pedagogy for Noncanonical Literature." *Reader* 15 (spring 1986): 48-61.

Cummings, Katherine. "Reclaiming the Mother('s) Tongue: Beloved, Ceremony, Mothers and Shadows." *College English* 52 (September 1990): 552-69.

Frye, Northrop. *Anatomy of Criticism.* Princeton, NJ: Princeton UP, 1957.

Gates, Henry Louis, Jr. "The Blackness of Blackness: A Critique of the Sign and the Signifying Monkey." *Black Literature and Literary Theory.* Ed. Gates. New York and London: Methuen, 1984. 285-321.

Gotfrit, Leslie. "Women Dancing Back: Disruption and the Politics of Pleasure." *Postmodernism, Feminism, and Cultural Politics.* Ed. Henry A. Giroux. Albany: State U of New York P, 1991. 174-95.

Johnson, Charles. *Being & Race.* Bloomington: Indiana U P, 1988.

Larsen, Nella. *Quicksand and Passing.* Ed. Deborah E. McDowell. New Brunswick, NJ.: Rutgers U P, 1986.

Marshall, Paule. *Praisesong for the Widow.* New York: Dutton, 1983.

—. *Brown Girl, Brownstones.* 1959. Old Westbury, NY: Feminist P, 1981.

Mbiti, John S. *African Religions and Philosophy.* Garden City, NJ: Anchor/Doubleday, 1970.

—. Introduction to African Religion. London: Heinemann, 1975.

McCluskey, John, Jr. "And Called Every Generation Blessed: Theme, Setting, and Ritual in the Works of Paule Marshall." *Black Women Writers 1950-1980.* Ed. Mari Evans. Garden City, NJ: Anchor/Doubleday, 1984. 316-34.

McDowell, Deborah E. "New Directions for Black Feminist Criticism." *The New Feminist Criticism: Essays on Women, Literature and Theory.* Ed. Elaine Showalter. New York: Pantheon, 1985. 186-99.

Morrison, Toni. Beloved. New York: Knopf, 1987.

Shange, Ntozake. *For Colored Girls Who Have Considered Suicide When the Rainbow Is Enuf.* New York: Bantam, 1975.

Spurlin, William J. "Theorizing Signifyin(g) and the Role of the Reader: Possible Directions for African American Literary Criticism." *College English* 52 (November 1990): 732-42.

Tate, Claudia. "Ntozake Shange." *Black Women Writers at Work.* Ed. Claudia Tate. New York: Crossroad/Continuum, 1983. 149-74.

Walker, Alice. *In Search of Our Mothers' Gardens: Womanist Prose.* New York: Harcourt Brace Jovanovich, 1983.

Publishers Weekly (review date 14 November 1994)

SOURCE: A review of "I Live in Music," in *Publishers Weekly,* November 14, 1994, p. 65.

[*In the following review of* "I Live in Music," *the reviewer emphasizes the musical elements of the poems and makes note of the "mixed-media art" by Bearden which complements the poems.*]

This galvanic fusion of poetry and mixed-media art in **"I Live in Music"** leads readers on a dreamy stroll though a jazz-and-blues-drenched universe, from an urban setting to a bayou. Novelist/playwright Shange provides the synaesthetic text, imagining music through all the senses: "sound / falls round me like rain on other folks / . . . / i cd even smell it / wear sound on my fingers." Visually melodious collages by Bearden (1912-1988) offer a lyrical counterpart to Shange's verse. A biography at book's end quotes the artist as saying that as a painter, "You must become a blues singer—only you sing on the canvas"; his dynamic compositions, listed by title on the final page, effectively echo the music, alternately somber and lively. Golden watercolor tones illuminate areas of lush green in the collage and watercolor *Theresa*; in patchwork assemblages, scraps of bright paper resemble aging advertisements peeling off a building's facade. A portrait of a trumpet player, *Solo Interval*, seems literally to smoulder—the mute resembles a chunk of glowing ash. Phrases from Shange's poem insinuate their own meaning into Bearden's visions for an un-usually rewarding experience.

Laurel Elkind (review date December 1994)

SOURCE: "Liliane: Resurrection of the Daughter," in *Boston Review*, Vol. 19, December, 1994, p. 38.

[*In the following review of Shange's novel* Liliane, *Elkind praises the way in which Shange, through her central character, "fleshes out . . . the complexities that Black women face in America, the divergent demands of feminism and the traditional roles of women in the Black community."*]

Ntozake Shange has given us a powerful portrait of Liliane, the central character in her new novel [*Liliane*], Liliane is introduced immediately as a sensual, self-possessed lover and a brazen artist—"a woman who [sees] the most pristine forms, dazzling color in anythin' [and feels] the texture for stuff: rice, skin, water. . . ." She enters into fast intimacy, speaks with brutal honesty. It's a compelling picture, all the more so because Liliane's powerful sensuality and poignant aestheticism are so hard won, forged in the midst of the complex and conflicting demands on a woman born Black, born rich, growing up in the muddied world of Mississippi during the last stages of desegregation.

Like Shange (*Betsey Brown, Sassafras, Cypress & Indigo*), Liliane is born into an upper middle class family, living in the shadow of Jim Crow and the Ku Klux Klan. Liliane and the other "young well-to-do Midwestern and Southeastern children of the Talented Tenth" grow up under a heavy burden of expectations: to be no less than the future leaders of their race. As Liliane says: "The issue was this issue: that we should crossbreed or intrafertilize and become the Beyond Belief Brood (offspring) of the Talented Tenth." Reproduction is politicized and Liliane's generation–educated, attractive–are, to their elite parents, an investment and a promise. That's a heavy weight to bear, and Liliane is a subtle and fascinating portrait of its consequences.

Recognizing the value—political and monetary—of his daughter's virginity, Liliane's father monitors her closely in an attempt to preserve it. We see her "sprawled and hugged up with Danny Stuyvesant," while her father approaches the house to rescue her. But rescue her from what? Liliane's experience with Danny is nothing less than loving, and what her father fears isn't taking place here—it already has, with the very men he esteems as potential husbands, "in a college frivolity known as gang banging."

Despite her father's chaperoning, Liliane wrestles principally with her mother, Sunday Bliss, over the conflicting pulls of sexual liberty and her responsibility to uphold "the race." Then, in an unforgivable act, Sunday Bliss abandons her family for a White man. Liliane's father arranges a false funeral to pronounce his wife dead—a decision Liliane later rationalizes in therapy:

> The white people made my father kill off my mother, take my mother away from me. It was such an affront to his 'manhood,' his 'dignity,' that he couldn't allow my mother to live in the house with a white man in her heart.

And here, really, is the problem that haunts *Liliane*: Bliss's decision to leave her husband opens the door on a world of conflicting pulls. True, Bliss warns her daughter that "you girls have to realize the freedom you wage your most serious battle for is your own mind. No white man on this earth has the power or the right . . . to control a single inch of your brain." But the oppression is only intellectually the White man's: in Liliane's emotional experience—as well as her mother's—the enemy appears more immediately as her Black father, despite her love for him. And so Shange fleshes out the complexities with which Liliane lives; the complexities that Black women face in America, the divergent demands of feminism and the traditional roles of women in the Black community.

It is satisfying to see Liliane transcend these clashing conceptions of her identity. She will not be torn apart with the world around her; her art and her sensuality define her. Despite the pressures to capitalize on her birthright in Black society, then, Liliane holds on to her passionate, aesthetic vision of life.

Shange's portrait of Liliane brings into play all of her celebrated narrative tools—poetry, plays, musically syncopated language, song quotes, and dreams. She uses a variety of narrative viewpoints and voices, interweaves monologues and fragments from Liliane's friends. Like Zora Neale Hurston, Alice Walker, and Toni Morrison, Shange is after a radical depiction of the full complexity of life for Black American women; her use of traditional forms of storytelling and a spectrum of voices aims to articulate the difficulty of a life lived between two loyalties—to one's race, to one's sex.

For the most part she succeeds, and even when she fails—as in her use of transcriptions from Liliane's psychoanalytic sessions—that failure is an endorsement of the power of the book's other, richer narrative tools. We're meant, through Liliane's sessions with her analyst, to experience her epiphanies as she has them. But these interludes lack the depth of the other chapters: when we listen in on

Liliane's analysis, her "otherness" as a black woman disappears. She's raw, fully exposed, but, ironically, the rich dramatic insight of the other voices disappears and the intimacy we've come to feel is thwarted. It's as if we're eavesdropping rather than experiencing, and we feel estranged.

But even this narrative technique comes to life when Liliane talks of men. And there are a lot of them in the novel, an expanded African Diaspora: a French pianist from Guadeloupe, a bad boy from a prestigious Creole family, a Puerto Rican from the Lower East Side. Here, Liliane's affection is so simple, so natural, that it seems impossible that it could provide a setting for sexual politicking. But it does, and without any feeling of a roman d'idées. That's the triumph of Shange's writing: the language is so consistently penetrating and the intellectual content so dramatically important that the two become inseparable in Shange's portrait of Liliane.

Adapted to stage, the voices of this complex, beautiful novel would look like so many frozen figures waiting for the spotlight to bring them to life. The continuity relies on strands of stories that are passed from one character to the next—now a past lover, now a friend, now the probing psychoanalyst. Triumphantly, **Liliane** emerges whole from the cast of demanding characters and discordant voices.

Valerie Sayers (review date 1 January 1995)

SOURCE: "A Life in Collage," in *New York Times*, Vol. CXLIV, No. 49, 928, January 1, 1995, p. 6.

[*In the following review of* Liliane, *Sayers praises the collage structure of the narrative which combines conversations between Liliane and her psychotherapist with a first-person narrative by Liliane, her friends, and her lovers.*]

Liliane Lincoln, "anybody's colored child, anybody's daughter," is raised among her mother's orchids, and her story is told in hothouse prose: Ntozake Shange's new novel, **"Liliane: Resurrection of the Daughter,"** is warm, damp and bright. The portrait of a post-modern artist whose works are political and conceptual, the novel is driven by an esthetic that seems more firmly rooted in modernism: its lush metaphors are akin to Jean Toomer's; its puckish delight in sexual imagery has a Man Ray feel.

As it happens, I'm big on Jean Toomer and Man Ray, and as a reviewer I suppose I should admit to my other prejudices. In fiction, I generally prefer the spare to the lush, the implicit to the explicit. I'm in favor of maximalism, not

minimalism, but I like my emotions expressed in action, and get nervous when the narrative frets too much. That said, much of **"Liliane"**—which is certainly maximalist, lush, explicit and emotional—is moving and evocative. Ms. Shange, a playwright and poet, is best known for her 1976 hit play, **"For Colored Girls Who Have Considered Suicide / When the Rainbow Is Enuf." "Liliane"** is her third and most formally playful novel. It is constructed as a psychoanalytic puzzle: Liliane's conversations with her analyst, punctuated by silences, alternate with first-person accounts from her childhood friends, lovers and Liliane herself. The collage form is particularly well suited to the story; we get the picture, piece by piece.

In the course of the narrative, Liliane makes art, travels, takes lovers, casts lovers aside, sustains her girlhood friends, mourns some of their deaths and celebrates. She grew up in the last days of segregation, when a little girl could think that if she went to church she "could be so much blood-soaked cloud and dust, scraggly blackened wood beam smoldering in my glowing flesh, so many colored buds, colored blossoms, to be picked at by coroners." Her father was a judge; she sprang from that social class whose decision whether to send a child to Princeton or Tennessee A & T "depended on how one's parents felt about uplifting the race." She was a colored girl—equal emphasis on each word—and her sense of self was shattered again and again by those who found that identity threatening.

Like any "black colored Negro person" in America, Liliane has seen too much violence and has lost too many loved ones. As a little girl visiting Mississippi, she witnessed a (strangely abbreviated) Klan attack, and as a teen-ager she was set upon by Italian-Americans in Queens. (A friend says, "If you black in the 'burg you outta bounds.") Sawyer, the boy she had seen in her childhood as her "destiny," was shot four times in the head by "somebody from East St. Louis," and Liliane says that he "died just like the little hoodlum boys I grew up with who lost all they sense or all they bones in Vietnam or Oakland. Sawyer wasn't all he coulda been, maybe. But like Papa used to say, he was definitely one of us."

The identification "one of us" is a central concern as Liliane struggles to construct a vision of self. The phrase is apt: she is one, wholly herself, and she is part of her race, part of her sex. Her choice of a white lover turns out to be of tremendous significance.

The plot hinges on revelations made in her psychoanalytic sessions concerning her mother's death. I admire Ms. Shange's decision to make the events and the cause of their revelation large enough for tragedy; if anything, the frenetic drama of the session in which we learn of her mother's disappearance could have been slowed down. The pacing here, and in the traumatizing racial attacks, is intentionally abrupt; the artistic reason for the speed is clear, but the reader is disoriented.

Ms. Shange takes pains to bring the novel to true resolution in the novel's most engaging character, one of Liliane's lovers, a photographer named Victor-Jesus Maria, who tells his part of the story in a voice that is emphatically male, Spanglish and empathetic. What a pleasure it is to hear Ntozake Shange singing in so many different keys, so many different tempos. Her "Liliane" is a dense, ambitious, worthy song.

Deirdre Neilen (review date Summer 1995)

SOURCE: A review of *Liliane,* in *World Literature Today,* Vol. 69, Summer, 1995, p. 584.

[*In the following review of* Liliane, *Neilen praises the structure of the novel, which interweaves the main character's therapy sessions with the perspectives of her friends and lovers. She emphasizes that Liliane, although subject to racism and sexism, "emerges triumphant, able to forgive and forge a future that encompasses both art and love."*]

Liliane, the eponymous heroine of Ntozake Shange's third novel [*Liliane*], is a painter who finds her colors more often in her lovers and friends than in a paintbox. And what a rich and varied canvas they provide: Jean-Rene, Victor-Jesus, Sawyer, Rorie, Lollie, Bernadette, Hyacinthe are characters who slip in and out of the narrative as easily as Liliane plays approach-avoidance with her therapist. By juxtaposing reminiscence and psychoanalytic dialogue, the novel deepens the portrait of the troubled Liliane as she is shaped by the tumultuous canvas of her times. Liliane is a survivor of racism, sexism, and secrets kept by her father, but in Shange's sure hands she emerges triumphant, able to forgive and forge a future that encompasses both art and love. Women are not usually so fortunate.

The novel is structurally compelling as well. Therapy sessions pull us along with Liliane, who baits, flirts with, curses, and opens up to the appealingly calm and humane doctor who interprets her dreams and never condescends. These weekly encounters are framed by scenes from Liliane's childhood and recent history. In those, Shange allows different characters to take over the narrative. Liliane then is seen not only in her own voice but through the eyes of those who loved her. The men's limitations appear as each seeks to hold the artist in a picture of his own making. Like her father, Judge Parnell Lincoln, the men love her deeply, but they have rules which a woman breaks at

great risk. This is ironic, of course, since the men are subject to the white world's rules, and yet (as Shange's works always remind) sexism transcends race. Nevertheless, this novel is about healing; Liliane is able to understand her father's actions toward her mother and not to fear her own love.

Liliane's heroine is sexy and funny, yet her story contains much pain and suffering. Ku Klux Klansmen, vicious Southern crackers, and hypocritical Northern liberals make appearances in her life, take away the innocence of youth, kill friends and lovers. How people preserve not only sanity but also decency and dignity in the midst of these givens is another of the book's triumphs. As Liliane reminds one of her friends, however, "There's so much more to life than what white folks have to do with."

The black and Hispanic characters are fully drawn; they are artists, musicians, lawyers, orchid growers, dancers—people who enrich their world with their many talents and gifts. Shange deftly demonstrates how much the country is losing by its schizophrenic attitudes and treatment of these citizens. Not a polemic, the novel nevertheless is political as well as poetic. *Liliane* joyfully celebrates the complexity of sexual relationships, the dynamics of family and friendship, and the emerging multicultural ethos that is America.

FURTHER READING

Criticism

Murray, Timothy. "Screening the Camera's Eye: Black and White Confrontations of Technological Representations." *Modern Drama* XXVIII, No. 1 (March, 1985): 110-124.
    Essay in which Murray applies postmodern theory and film theory to discuss visual texts in terms of their representation of race. Special focus on Shange's play *A Photograph.*

Interviews

Lester, Neal A. "At the Heart of Shange's Feminism: An Interview." *Black American Literature Forum* 24, No. 4 (Winter 1990): 717-30.
    Interview in which Shange speaks about her ideas on feminism in her life and works.

————."An Interview with Ntozake Shange." *Studies in American Drama* 5 (1990): 42-66.
    Interview in which Shange discusses her form of the "choreopoem," her use of language in terms of gender, and her writing process.

Additional coverage of Shange's life and career is contained in the following sources published by Gale: *Authors and Artists for Young Adults,* Vol. 9; *Black Literature Criticism,* Vol. 3; *Black Writers,* Vol. 2; *Contemporary Authors,* Vol. 85, 88; *Contemporary Authors New Revision Series,* Vol. 27, 48; *Dictionary of Literary Biography,* Vol. 38; *Drama Criticism,* Vol. 3; *Major Twentieth-Century Writers,* Vol. 1, 2.

Yevgeny Yevtushenko
1933-

Russian poet, novelist, essayist, dramatist, screenwriter, autobiographer, and editor.

The following entry presents an overview of Yevtushenko's career through 1997. For further information on his life and works, see *CLC*, Volumes 1, 3, 13, 26, and 51.

INTRODUCTION

A remarkably prolific and charismatic writer, Yevtushenko has enjoyed an unprecedented degree of artistic and personal freedom throughout his career as the former Soviet Union's most famous and best-publicized contemporary poet. Foremost among the first post-Stalin generation of Russian poets, Yevtushenko has attracted a large audience and acquired an international reputation with dramatic readings of his own poetry. His poetry articulates both civic and personal themes in a politically-charged style reminiscent of the poetic forms and passionate language of an earlier period in Soviet history. Dozens of Yevtushenko's poems also have been made into popular Russian songs. Yevtushenko's writing inspired Soviet classical composer Dmitri Shostakovich to base his *Symphony No. 13* on "Babi Yar," (1960) one cf Yevtushenko's best-known poems. Despite strict Soviet artistic standards imposed from the late 1960s through the mid-1980s, Yevtushenko has maintained his personal convictions and artistic integrity. With the advent of glasnost in the late 1980s, Yevtushenko became a leading activist in the struggle to reform Soviet society. As a briefly elected member of the Soviet Congress, Yevtushenko is credited with originating the governmental policy of perestroika and continues to speak out against political abuses of power in Russia. Although critical and popular reception of Yevtushenko's work has mostly hinged on the Soviet political climate, critics have generally praised the multicultural quality of his writings and regard Yevtushenko as Russia's premier but unofficial cultural emissary to the world.

Biographical Information

Yevtushenko is a fourth-generation descendant of Ukrainians who were exiled to Siberia. He was born in Zima, a small town on the Trans-Siberian railway featured in his first important narrative poem, *Stantsiya Zima* (1956; *Winter Station*). As a teenager, Yevtushenko joined his father on geological expeditions in Kazakhstan and later studied world literature at the prestigious Gorky Literary Institute in Moscow, where he published his first book of poems,

Razvedchiki gryaduschego (1952). As subsequent volumes appeared throughout the late 1950s and early 1960s, Yevtushenko emerged as the voice of Soviet youth and as a leading proponent of the Cold War "thaw" in diplomatic and cultural relations between the Soviet Union and the United States. In 1960 Soviet authorities permitted Yevtushenko to read his poems in Russia, the United States, and Europe. The result initiated a modest cultural exchange between East and West, making Yevtushenko an international celebrity. Soon afterward, he published and recited some of his best-known political poetry, including "Babi Yar" and *The Heirs of Stalin* (1962), which generated controversy and publicity in Russia and abroad. Yevtushenko independently published *A Precocious Autobiography* in English in 1963. After the publication of *A Precocious Autobiography*, Soviet officials revoked his privileges. But following the publication of *Bratskaya GES* (1965; *New Works: The Bratsk Station*)—considered by many critics to be his finest poetic work—Soviet officials relented.

During the 1970s, when cultural stagnation and political repression prevailed under Leonid Brezhnev, Yevtushenko began to experiment with literary forms other than poetry, including films and audio recordings. His first novel, *Yagodnyye mesta* (1981; *Wild Berries*), was a finalist for the Ritz Paris Hemingway Prize, and another novel, *Ne umira prezhde smerti* (1993; *Don't Die before You're Dead)*, hit the Russian bestseller list in 1995. Meanwhile, Yevtushenko continued to write poetry, including *Invisible Threads* (1982) and *Almost at the End* (1987). In 1989, Yevtushenko was elected to the Soviet Congress of People's Deputies, where he led the democratic reform movement and bolstered its momentum by issuing both *The Collected Poems, 1952-1990,* and *Fatal Half Measures* in 1991. During the failed coup attempt in 1991, Yevtushenko remained to defend the Parliament building as tanks circled. During the ordeal, Yevtushenko composed a poem that he later read to Western television journalists. In 1996, Yevtushenko joined the faculty at Queens College.

Major Works

As represented in *The Collected Poems,* Yevtushenko's poetry comprises a wide range of forms and themes that reflect his changing literary style and illumine the strong bond between political and poetic expression in Russian culture. Generally personal or declamatory in tone, Yevtushenko's poems blend political and social concerns of contemporary Soviet society with issues of personal morality. His poems also contrast Western values against the legacy of Stalin's regime, while still showing a deep loyalty to Russia. Yevtushenko's first critical success, *Winter Station,* for instance, lyrically describes the poet's return to his birthplace as he struggles with personal doubts regarding Stalin's social programs. *The Heirs of Stalin,* published at the height of the Cuban missile crisis, unsparingly attacks the former Russian ruler and his followers, warning against a resurgence of Stalinism. "Babi Yar," a poem lamenting the Nazi slaughter of tens of thousands of Ukrainian Jews in a ravine near Kiev during World War II, implies that the Soviet regime and Russian people generally sanction anti-Semitic sentiment. Yevtushenko's most ambitious cycle of poems, *Bratskaya GES,* draws parallels between modern Russian experiences and historical antecedents. The poems contrast the symbol of a Siberian power plant bringing light to Russia with the symbol of Siberia as a prison throughout Russian history. The title poem compares Russian workers responsible for building the power plant with slaves who built Egyptian pyramids. As the Soviet regime increased restrictions on artistic expression, Yevtushenko's poems began to exhibit a more somber tone to conform to official styles and themes. Although *Stolen Apples* (1971) addresses themes such as love, travel, and history, *The Face behind the Face* (1979) asserts the social relevance of poets and poetry in the Soviet Union. Another work of this period includes *Pod kozhey Statui Svobody* (1972; *Under the Skin of the Statue of Liberty*),

a series of dramatic sketches set in the United States that denounce American violence but extol the idealism of its youth. Among his later poetry collections, *Invisible Threads* (1982) focuses on the need for international unity and is alternately optimistic and pessimistic — a theme common to most of Yevtushenko's work. *Almost at the End* (1987) gathers poetry and prose written in the Gorbachev era and examines differences between the East and West, along with effects of restricted personal freedom and censorship. Notable in this work is "Fuku," a long poem that deconstructs various Western historical figures. Yevtushenko's contribution to literature also includes the novel *Wild Berries,* which ostensibly celebrates Russian philosophy and existence but resembles an American-style thriller with action, sex, and exotic locales. Yevtushenko's *Don't Die before You're Dead* is a fast-paced, quasi-fictional account of the 1991 coup attempt and its psychological consequences for ordinary citizens. *Fatal Half Measures* is a collection of Yevtushenko's speeches and essays on themes advocating glasnost and Soviet democratic reform.

Critical Reception

Despite implicit criticism of contemporary Soviet society and his tendency to occasionally test the literary standards of socialist realism, Yevtushenko has drawn enthusiastic response from young muscovites, as well as official approval from the Soviet regime. Later critics have speculated about Yevtushenko's literary merits since he generally has conformed to Soviet censors in his writing. Maura Reynolds attributes Yevtushenko's fluctuating reputation "as much to politics as poetry," noting that his knack "for ducking and riding political waves . . . has earned him both praise and derision, at different times, from many of the same people." Many commentators believe Yevtushenko has stood behind his early reputation for outspokenness, and that since the mid-1960s he has taken fewer risks, both politically and artistically. Skeptical about his exuberant personality abroad and suspicious about his intentions at home, some critics have found his poetry crude and artificial. However, Yevtushenko's writings have retained a broad, popular audience. Most critics have recognized Yevtushenko's efforts to relate the diverse cultures of a modernized, multinational Soviet Union with the literary cultures of the contemporary West. Other critics point to the vitality and authenticity of Yevtushenko's personal poems as evidence of his literary significance. Patricia Pollock Brodsky calls Yevtushenko an "engaged and engaging poet, one of the important, questioning voices of our age."

PRINCIPAL WORKS

Razvedchiki gryaduschego (poetry) 1952

Tretii sneg: Kniga liriki (poetry) 1955

Shosse entusiastov (poetry) 1956

Stantsiya Zima [*Winter Station*] (poetry) 1956; originally published in journal *Oktiabr*

Obeschanie (poetry) 1957

Luk i lira: Stikhi o Gruzii (poetry) 1959

"Babi Yar" (poetry) 1960; originally published in journal *Literaturnaya gazeta*

Yabloko (poetry) 1960

Nezhnost: Novyii Stikhi (poetry) 1962

Posie Stalina (poetry) 1962

Selected Poems (poetry) 1962

Vzmakh ruki (poetry) 1962

Zamlung (poetry) 1962

I Am Cuba [with Enrique Pineda Barnet] (screenplay) 1963

A Precocious Autobiography (autobiography) 1963

Selected Poetry (poetry) 1963

The Poetry of Yevgeny Yevtushenko, 1953-1965 (poetry) 1964

Bratskaya GES (poetry) 1965; also published as *New Works: The Bratsk Station* and *Bratsk Station and Other New Poems*

The City of Yes and the City of No and Other Poems (poetry) 1966

Flowers and Bullets & Freedom to Kill (poetry) 1970

Stolen Apples (poetry) 1971

Pod kozhey Statui Svobody [*Under the Skin of the Statue of Liberty*] (verse drama) 1972

The Face behind the Face (poetry) 1979

Ivan the Terrible and Ivan the Fool (poetry) 1979

Yagodnyye mesta [*Wild Berries*] (novel) 1981

A Dove in Santiago: A Novella in Verse (poetry) 1982

Invisible Threads (poetry) 1982

Ardabiola (novella) 1984

Almost at the End (prose and poetry) 1987

Divided Twins: Alaska and Siberia (essays) 1988

Early Poems (poetry) 1989

Fatal Half Measures: The Culture of Democracy in the Soviet Union (essays, speeches, lectures) 1991

The Collected Poems (poetry) 1993

Ne umira prezhde smerti: Russka, skzka [*Don't Die before You're Dead*] (novel) 1993

Net let (poetry) 1993

Twentieth Century Russian Poetry: Silver and Steel, an Anthology [compiler and author of introduction] (poetry) 1993

CRITICISM

The Economist (essay date 30 January 1988)

SOURCE: "Past, Implacable," in *The Economist*, Vol. 306, No. 7535, January 30, 1988, pp. 75-6.

[*In the following essay, the critic draws parallels between Yevtushenko's poetic themes and glasnost, concentrating on "Bukharin's Widow" and "Monuments Not Yet Erected."*]

Yevgeny Yevtushenko, the modern Russian poet the West knows best, is not only delighted about glasnost; he takes some personal credit for it. Those now trying to push through reforms, he thinks, are probably the same people who went to his poetry readings in the late 1950s and early 1960s in clubs and factories and theatres round the country; the new openness is "an echo of our poetry." And it is poetry, in Mr Yevtushenko's eyes, that will have to drive glasnost on.

He is playing his part with his usual fierceness. Last June, after a meeting with the widow of Nikolai Bukharin, a Bolshevik leader executed by Stalin in 1938, he wrote **"Bukharin's Widow"**, a poem intended to push forward the campaign to rehabilitate Bukharin and demolish Stalin; later last year, in **"Monuments not yet Erected"**, he called for a public memorial to the victims of Stalins's purges. Both poems have just reached the West. When **"Monuments"** was published in Moscow, in November, it inspired furious letters to *Izvestia*; one suggested that Mr Yevtushenko should be sent "in good Stalinist fashion" to Siberia—from which he comes, and which has been the subject of much of his most lyrical poetry.

"Bukharin's Widow" has caused an even greater uproar. Although it was submitted to a magazine, *Ogonyek*, last summer on the understanding that it would appear at once, it has not yet been published. Mr Yevtushenko read it aloud at the end of October at a meeting organised by *Ogonyek* with the editor on the platform; the editor implied then that he would publish it if Bukharin turned out to have official approval. In November Mr Mikhail Gorbachev mentioned Bukharin in a speech, and there have been several long articles about Bukharin since; but because he is not yet wholly rehabilitated, **"Bukharin's Widow"** has not yet appeared. This makes Mr Yevtushenko bitter. He was bold enough to write about Bukharin before the others, without any official nod, and he is now in danger of looking like a camp follower.

Neither **"Bukharin's Widow"** nor **"Monuments"** are new themes for him. His most famous poem of protest, **"Babiy Yar"** (1961), described, as **"Monuments"** does, the shamefulness of victims buried in mass graves with no memorial; in **"Babiy Yar"**, the victims were Jews. (For Mr Yevtushenko, the son of a geologist, the strongest image is often that of digging down through the earth and forcing bodies, like unpleasant facts, to the surface.) Another theme is anonymity: the official namelessness to which people may be subjected, after death, in the hope that they will go unremembered. For Mr Yevtushenko, the present cannot be addressed until the past has been faced honestly. In **"Bukharin's Widow"** it is Bukharin himself, the non-person, who must be faced:

> I saw that picture not in our country, but
>   abroad:
> a Norodnik-type beard, a driver's cap on
>   his brow,
> the black prophetically funereal sheen of
> his Bolshevik leather coat,
> and the gaze, used to surveillance . . .

It is not that Mr Yevtushenko distrusts Mr Gorbachev; but he does not know quite how devoted an anti-Stalinist he is, and he is worried about the inertia he has to deal with. He wants to nudge him on a bit. Mr Yevtushenko is quite shrewd about choosing his moments to push. This is how he has survived, "skilfully and professionally evading the toro's horns", as he puts it, while other poets such as Mr Joseph Brodsky—who won the Nobel Prize for literature last year—are gored and go into exile. There have been moments when Mr Yevtushenko has appeared, probably unfairly, to be a lapdog, and when his work has looked subservient. He is now struggling to consolidate his role within glasnost. As the bold scout ahead of the pack, he suddenly finds himself being overtaken by other writers eager to be noticed.

Mr Yevtushenko's claim that poetry has given birth to glasnost is not universally shared, however, even among writers. Poets and novelists have often played the role of holy fools in Russia; being half-mad, they are allowed to be at least half-honest. But Mr Mikhail Shatrov, the principal political playwright in the Soviet Union, thinks that "blows from literature" are not enough. Only facts, he says, will convince the powers that be (if they can be convinced at all) to change their attitude. Mr Shatrov writes his plays as historical dissertations, using actual documents and minutes from party meetings. His latest, *Onward, Onward, Onward!*, has just been published in a literary monthly and is about to go into production in Moscow and Leningrad. It contends that Stalin was a murderer, a traitor to the Revolution and not Lenin's heir. Mr Shatrov tries to say, as an historian (and thus, in Russia, as near the establishment as a writer can get), precisely what Mr Yevtushenko is shouting on the other side of the street.

Both men have lived too long in Russia, under regimes of varying tolerance and callousness, to be over-optimistic about the future. They doubt whether Stalin's ghost can ever be successfully exorcised. At the end of *Onward* comes a poignant stage direction: "Everybody wants Stalin to leave . . . but he remains on the stage." As for free expression, that fragile hope, it still seems not much nearer than the nightingale in Mr Yevtushenko's **"Zima Junction"**:

> Unbroken forest round,
> no way to him at all
> not walking and not riding,
> not walking and not riding,
> and not flying,
> and not flying.

Thomas D'Evelyn (review date 8 March 1991)

SOURCE: "A Soviet Whitman," in *The Christian Science Monitor*, March 8, 1991, p. 10.

[*In the following review, D'Evelyn emphasizes the public and social aspects of Yevtushenko's poetic practices evident in* The Complete Poems.]

For about 30 years now, Yevgeny Yevtushenko has lit up the international scene with his unique fireworks, a blend of chutzpah, charm, and sheer gall. His most recent coup—a teaching stint at the University of Pennsylvania—brings the career of this Soviet poet to a pinnacle of success. Now the publication of his complete poems in English [*The Complete Poems*] will provide opportunities for a long look at the basis of his career, a large body of poems of diverse kinds that is at once accessible and beguilingly obscure.

Yevtushenko was 20 when Stalin died. He rode the anti-Stalin wave to prominence, reading in front of thousands and selling tens of thousands of his books of poetry. Even when the inevitable swerve came and Khrushchev attacked modern art, Yevtushenko kept baiting dogmatic bureaucrats and those he would call "comradwhatifers" in a poem. He also spoke in solidarity with Jews. In 1963, the great hammer fell. Yevtushenko was forced to confess his irreparable error. While others, like Solzhenitsyn, chose silence, Yevtushenko got a second wind and was praised by party organs for his civic-mindedness.

This patriot, who has achieved extraordinary freedom of movement, uses the word "international" as a term of highest praise. In one of his earliest and most publicized poems, **"Babii Yar,"** he addresses his audience: "O my Russian people! / I know / you / are international to the core." While this cannot be taken literally, it does confirm usage elsewhere. For Yevtushenko, patriotism and internationalism do not conflict.

Yet the springs of Yevtushenko's art appear to well up from the same source that fed the great Russian novelists of the

19th century. In his introduction to *The Collected Poems, 1952-1990,* Albert C. Todd says, "Confession, grappling with self-understanding, is the impetus behind most of the poems that are mistakenly understood to be merely social or political. His sharpest attacks on moral cowardice begin with a struggle within his own conscience."

Yevtushenko wrote in 1965: "The first presentiment of a poem / in a true poet / is the feeling of sin / committed somewhere, sometime." His experience in the '60s gave him many opportunities for his brand of poetry. In 1964 he published the big patriotic poem "**Bratsk Hydroelectric Station.**" Although he's silent about the cruel slave labor used to erect the station, in a section entitled "Monologue of the Egyptian Pyramid," he does mention the whip under which the Egyptian slaves labored. The comparison seems obvious and intentional.

Yevtushenko often uses the monologue to speak indirectly about himself. In "**Monologue of an Actress,**" he speaks as an actress from Broadway who can't find a suitable role. "Without some sort of role, life / is simply slow rot," she says.

This throws light on the public nature of Yevtushenko's calling as a poet, as well as on his passivity toward events. Despite the confessional nature of much of his poetry, he needs public events—including his own feelings, which he makes public—to become inspired.

In "**Monologue of a Loser**" (1978), he voices the moral ambiguity of one who has played the game of moral dice, the game into which every poet in a closed society must buy if he wishes a big public. "My modest loss was this: / dozens of tons of verses, / the whole globe, / my country, / my friends, / my wife,/ I myself— / but on that account, however, / I'm not very upset. / Such trifles / as honor / I forgot to consider."

Other poems put his difficulties more objectively.

In "**My Handwriting,**" he symbolizes the Soviet ship of state as a "pugnacious coastal freighter." The lurch and list of the freighter makes it difficult for the poet to write neatly. Besides that, it's very cold. "Here— / fingers simply grew numb. / Here— / the swell slyly tormented. / Here— / the pen jerked with uncertainty / away from some mean shoal." Nevertheless, sometimes "an idea breaks through the way a freighter on the Lena / breaks through to the arctic shore—." Most poets wouldn't shift the metaphor this way, using it first as a narrative idea, then using it to point to a specific experience.

Todd suggests in the introduction that "ultimately Yevtushenko will be judged as a poet, a popular people's poet in the tradition of Walt Whitman." But Yevtushenko himself uses the uncompromising standards of art to illuminate his moral life. In "**Verbosity,**" he confesses, "I am verbose both in my daily life / and in my verse—that's your bad luck— / but I am cunning: I realize / that there's no lack of will / behind this endless drivel, / rather my strong ill will!" In the end, though, he admits that "Eternal verities rest on the precise; / precision, though, consists in sacrifice. / Not for nothing does the bard get scared— / the price of brevity is blood. / Like fear of prophecies contained in dreams, / the fear of writing down eternal words / is the real reason for verbosity." Writing this clearly about the moral intersection of poetry and precision is no mean achievement.

It helps to read Yevtushenko literally. Doubtless Yevtushenko felt he was speaking for thousands like him. In "**The Art of Ingratiating,**" he seems to speak for the whole country. "Who among us has not become a stutterer, / when, like someone dying of hunger / begging from ladies on the porch steps, / we mealymouth: / 'I want to call long-distance . . . ' / How petty authorities / propagate themselves! / How they embody / the supreme insolence!" Then he reports a prophetic dream: "By breeding / bulldogs / from mutts, / we ourselves / have fostered / our own boors. / I have a nightmare / that in the Volga / our groveling / has begotten / a crocodile." The well wisher who now contemplates the self-destruction of perestroika may well hear in Yevtushenko's words the feelings of Gorbachev himself. Bulldogs and crocodiles indeed!

On the other hand, it's tempting to simply say of Yevtushenko's collected poems, "how they embody the supreme insolence!" For all his clarity, Yevtushenko does not seem to anticipate certain cruel ironies. He writes "**To Incomprehensible Poets,**" and confesses, "My guilt is in my simplicity. / My crime is my clarity. / I am the most comprehensible of worms," he may not hear his audiences silently agreeing. When he says to the incomprehensible poets (he has in mind some of the main lines of modern Russian poetry), "No restraint frightens you. / No one has bridled you with clear ideas." But he may not realize that the kinds of "restraint" he accepts as a public poet are child's play compared with the restraints accepted by Pasternak and Joseph Brodsky, restraints that originate in the subtlety of their analysis and the purity of their taste. Finally, when he says, "All the same it is frightening / to be understood like me / in the wrong way, / all of my life / to write comprehensibly / and depart / so hopelessly uncomprehended," one cannot be too sympathetic.

Long ago he stuck up for the Jews and recited his poem "**Babii Yar**" one too many times. Khrushchev exploded at him. This was the turning point of his career and his life.

He knew what mattered most to him. He wanted a role in society; he wanted to be accepted as a poet.

In his own eyes, on his own terms, Yevtushenko has been highly successful. If he does not go down as a great Russian poet, it's because choosing to be what he has become meant he could not travel the higher road of art.

Rushworth M. Kidder (essay date 8 March 1991)

SOURCE: "Perestroika Redefines the Poet's Role," in *The Christian Science Monitor,* March 8, 1991, p. 11.

[*In the following essay, Kidder expresses Yevtushenko's concerns about the state of Russian politics, poetry, and attitudes toward indigenous cultural traditions in the era of perestroika.*]

Yevgeny Yevtushenko is a man at a crossroads. Still one of the Soviet Union's best-known poets, he treats each conversation almost like a performance—arms flying to emphasize his points, metaphors abounding in a rush of language, political opinions jostling with personal probings. To talk with him is to see poetry being made while you watch.

But in the past few years, something odd has been happening. The traditional elements of his brand of Russian poetry—the high oratory, detailed allegory, vivid metaphor, and direct syntax of verse forms meant to be heard as much as read—are still there. What has changed is the context. Under Mikhail Gorbachev's policy of glasnost, the political oppression and literary censorship that made Soviet poetry such a furtive, powerful, and necessary part of the mental landscape has begun to drain away.

"I just finished writing a long article, **'Censorship as the Best Reader,'**" he says during an hour-long interview in Washington. "It's a bitter irony. I am talking how I am longing for censorship—because nobody better than censors understood all the subtle nuances of poetry. Nobody appreciated us so highly."

These days, he notes, the censors have all but disappeared—and with them the need for those "subtle nuances of poetry."

That change in the political landscape has touched Russian poetry in ways difficult for Westerners to appreciate. In 600 years of pre-Gorbachev Russian history, Mr. Yevtushenko can add up no more than a total of 12 months without the kind of censorship imposed first by Tartar despots, then by the Czars, and finally by the Communists.

In that context, he says, the poet became "a voice of all the voiceless." The importance of poetry arose, he explains, because "it was only possible for the conscience of the people to be expressed in a metaphorical way. That's why poetry was a kind of spiritual newspaper of the people. Sometimes we published our unpublished poetry in the pages of the open air, with our own voices. Published poetry was a great spiritual power. Being oppressed, being sometimes not published, a poet in Russia is a little bit like a holy man—they are always martyrs in the understanding of people."

How has that changed today? He points to the use of what he calls "anecdote." The Russians, he says, "were very great in the art of anecdote. Now there is no art of anecdote anymore, because all our magazines, all our newspapers, are officially publishing jokes, anecdotes, and caricatures of government figures."

This new freedom of public criticism has brought "an incredible development of newspapers," which are "very beautiful, very bold, very well written—very high professionalism." But as a result, he says, "poetry is in a completely different situation. It's very difficult for me to be adapted to it." Now it must be "more and more concentrated on the intimate problems, on the abysses of psychology."

Such changes, he thinks, are also affecting the next generation of Russian poets. "We were idealists—we were people of the '60s," he says. "But many of our ideals were broken, and we had a very bitter experience afterward."

He worries that today's young poets, while "full of energy," have not got "even little drops of idealism in their soul. In our country, they are full of skepticism, full of irony. And I think that's destructive. Naive idealism is destructive, of course. But lack of idealism is also destructive. Their irony is their shield against corruption, against the potential deception of idealism. But their psychology becomes too shielded, too defended, too protected. They are protected from assaults of life, but also they are criminally protected from sentimental human feelings."

Will rock music replace poetry as the dominant cultural form for the young? That, he says, is already happening. "I'm not against rock music. I am against having rock music or any kind of music forbidden in the Soviet Union. But at the same time, we have a very dangerous sign: For the first time in many years, you can easily get tickets for symphony concerts in the Soviet Union."

Yevtushenko, who grew up knowing the symphonic music of the great Russian composers, finds the change especially troubling. He also worries that the younger generation is not very well read—neither in such Russian writers as Dostoyevsky and Tolstoy, nor in such "American classics" as Hemingway, Faulkner, and Stephen Crane.

"This generation is more audio than we were. They imitate the superficial features of Western mass culture, and they think that is culture. They wear black-leather jackets and metal chains, and they feel themselves citizens of the world. They idolize America as a country with mountains made from blue jeans and rivers of Coca-Cola.

"If you chew American chewing gum," he adds, "probably ignorance is chewing you at the same time."

As his country moves rapidly to embrace Western mass culture, he notes what he sees as a "frightening sign": the resurgence of the "hard-liners" who "want to resurrect censorship." Does he worry that Mr. Gorbachev's current hard line on separatist movements in the Baltic republics could herald the end of glasnost?

"We are very divided on these questions," he says. "I represent people who began perestroika before perestroika, when Mr. Gorbachev was just a student."

But with the reforms of the last several years, he observes, there is no longer a "silent majority" in the Soviet Union. "The majority screams, shouts in the streets. And sometimes it shouts very good things, and sometimes very wrong things—because they are desperate, because our economical life is very difficult, our daily life is getting more and more hellish."

Under the pressure of those screams, and responding to the situations in the Baltics, he feels that Gorbachev has retreated much too far to the right. "In my opinion, we must give the Baltic peoples their right to separate, to leave the Soviet Union." At the same time, he says, the rights of the Russian minorities living in the Baltics must be preserved.

Does the current situation spell the end for Gorbachev?

"I don't know any politician who doesn't make mistakes," says Yevtushenko, who was elected to the Soviet Parliament in 1989. But Gorbachev, he says, has "begun to make mistakes too often. I think he relies mostly now on right-wing advisors, the yes-men advisors. I think that's his weakness. He now, himself, is [farther to the right] than the majority of the Russian population. He must find again where the center is."

Carol Rumens (review date 15 March 1991)

SOURCE: "Half Free," in *New Statesman & Society,* March 15, 1991, p. 37.

[*In the following review, Rumens evaluates the themes and styles of* The Collected Poems *with respect to Yevtushenko's emerging poetic identity.*]

"Who the hell is this damned Y Y?" asks Yevtushenko in the forward to **Stolen Apples** (1973), ironically parroting his various critics: "An unofficial diplomat performing secret missions for the Kremlin? . . . A Soviet Beatle? . . . An export item, perhaps, like vodka or black caviar? . . . When is Yevtushenko sincere? When he is writing about Vietnam or Babii Yar?"

Perhaps he has had to be many different people. Yet the **Collected Poems,** for all its variety, is a consistent narrative, dominated by the haunted figure of a Russian poet, as deeply rooted as any of his breed, sent by success and the mid-20th-century publicity machine into dizzy orbit between the two arch-enemies of the cold war, beaming messages first to one, then the other, and emotionally involved in both. A complex character, living in highly complex times, Yevtushenko often likes to picture himself as a skinny, wily Siberian street urchin, living off his wits. Maybe this figure is the clue to the "real" man, who unites the rebel and the opportunist, the cheerleader and the dissident, the people's poet and the tormented soul-searcher under one skin.

He was born in 1933 in Zima, a largish town on the Trans-Siberian railway, the grandson of a Ukrainian revolutionary exiled to Irkutsk. His first book was published in 1952, but it was the long poem of 1955, **Zima Station** (mistranslated here, as usual, as **Zima Junction**) that first excited attention. A sentimental but fresh, earthy and heartfelt narrative, it gave the young poet the accreditation to set out on more risky projects such as **"Babii Yar"** and **Stalin's Heirs.** By the time these poems were published, in the early sixties, the leadership was also beginning to ask questions about Stalinism. Yevtushenko's was the right voice at the right time.

Just as quick to catalogue the sins of the bourgeois imperialists, he was able to please the conformists at home and the radicals abroad, and to keep his integrity. At least, unlike some of the more single-minded dissidents, he was not blind to the flaws in our so-called western democracies. If the tone of his righteous anger sometimes jars, it's because he tends to use the big, conscience words as a form of emotional shorthand. He can colonise My Lai or El Salvador in a moral gesture that still leaves us a million miles from the hurt and shock of those epicentres.

Imaginative detail (which we will never get from politicians or newscasters) is what's required, even when it's of the more inventive kind—as when he takes off on a startling metaphorical flight inspired by what could have been a too-easy Yevtushenkan subject, the neutron bomb: "Pillows will start looting / Neanderthal skulls from museums. / Shirts / all alone / will pull themselves on statues and skeletons / . . . A mass hanging of neckties from trees / will take place."

Yevtushenko is a vividly colloquial writer working for the most part in traditional rhyme and metre (in Russian, writing formally does not mean strutting in period costume). His American translators provide him with a looser garment, but convey the breezy energy and the sometimes *macho* swagger of his tone ("And like a slugger's hook / across the chops of the ages, / a line!").

The mood of many later poems (1986-90) is somewhat darker, the swagger has gone and, whether contemplating himself or his society, the poet sees doom and exhaustion: rust, ghosts, chasms, things smashed. But the energy of the language flows back, bringing a wealth of tender domestic detail, when he writes about his native region, as in **"Siberian Wooing"**.

And in the sombre, flat statements of **"Half Measure"**, the poet shows he is still game for questioning the system: "With every half-effective / half measure / half the people / remain half pleased. / The half sated /are half hungry. / The half free / are half enslaved."

Tomas Venclova　(review date 6 May 1991)

SOURCE: "Making It," in *The New Republic,* May 6, 1991, pp. 33-7.

[*In the following review, Venclova traces the evolution of Yevtushenko's "accommodating" tone, themes, and style in both his poetry and prose and his changing relevance to Russian politics and literature.*]

An interesting article by Yevgeny Yevtushenko, part essay, part memoir, recently appeared in *Literaturnaya Gazeta* in Moscow, in which the poet dwells at length on his skirmishes with Soviet reactionaries. The title of the article is **"Fencing with a Pile of Dung,"** which is meant to be a bold metaphor. Among other tales, Yevtushenko tells the story of his visit to the pre-perestroika Kremlin, where he was to be honored with the Order of the Red Banner:

> The Order was presented by a vice-chairman of the Presidium of the Supreme Soviet, an Azerbaijani whose last name I cannot, for the life of me, recall. Pin-

ning the order to the lapel of my jacket and inviting me to a hunting party in Azerbaijan, he awkwardly pierced my jacket, my shirt, and even pricked me. It was rather painful. The Kremlin people hurt me often enough. They hurt others, too.

The next story deals with the presentation of a State Prize to Yevtushenko in 1984 for his long poem **"Momma and the Neutron Bomb."** "The censorship office attempted to ban the poem," he writes, "but it did not succeed." Yevtushenko took his medal and his certificate (and his money). According to the requirements of Soviet protocol, he was expected to express his gratitude to the Party at the ceremony. His wrath was so impossible to contain, however, that he neglected etiquette and returned to his seat without breaking his proud silence. His bravery, he tells us, inspired several other recipients of the prize, who also refused to say thanks.

Now, there is something fundamentally wrong about this picture. You are pampered by a totalitarian government, or you are persecuted by it. You are given honors and awards by party functionaries, or you are not. You are invited to their hunting parties, or you are their open enemy. But both cannot happen to you at the same time. Andrei Sakharov received perks similar to Yevtushenko's while he was busy with the Soviet nuclear program; but later his moral rectitude led him to the camp of the dissidents, and the world knows what followed. You see, you cannot fence with a pile of dung. You either sink into it or you leave it. To pretend otherwise requires extraordinary cynicism, extraordinary naïveté, or both. When Yevtushenko implicitly compares the pain caused by that pricking pin to the sufferings of Sakharov, Pasternak, and many, many others, he goes beyond the limits of naïveté, and even of cynicism. He approaches the obscene.

The case of Yevtushenko is one of the most unusual cases of our times. (Stanislaw Baranczak recently listed it, in *Newsday,* among the top ten hoaxes of the twentieth century.) Two large books by Yevtushenko, which just appeared in English, provide an opportunity to study it more closely. The first is a volume of verse [***The Collected Poems***] put into English by many translators, including some of the masters of the language. The second is a collection of political speeches, essays, travelogues, and divagations on Russian writers [***Fatal Half Measures***]. Both books are provided with rapturous introductions and blurbs: the author is "the legendary Russian literary leader," "a people's poet in the tradition of Walt Whitman," "a seeker of Truth like all great writers," and so on. It seems that many members in good standing of the American literary establishment consider these descriptions to be true, or at least partly true. Unfortunately, they are false.

One thing has to be admitted: Yevtushenko is an incredibly prolific writer who is endowed with a buoyant personality. He is not only a versifier and an essayist, but also a scriptwriter, a film director, an actor, a photographer, a novelist, a political figure, and a world traveler—a Soviet cultural emissary in virtually all parts of the globe, which is a function that he inherited from Vladimir Mayakovsky and Ilya Erenburg, who played the same role on a less extensive scale. In his tender years, Yevtushenko was also a goalkeeper and a folk dancer of repute.

The amount of energy, the sheer labor, devoted to all these enterprises cannot fail to impress. Yevtushenko says about himself, without false modesty but not without reason: "my fate is supernatural, / my destiny astonishing." Sixty-four countries visited by 1976 (by now the number is larger) and forty-six books of original poetry so far—this certainly is supernatural, if we recall that permission to travel abroad once or twice was the sweetest dream of almost any Soviet writer before the Gorbachev era, and that many good poets of the USSR considered themselves lucky if they managed to publish a slim and heavily blue-penciled volume once in a decade. On top of all that, we learn (from his editor Antonina W. Bouis) that Yevtushenko "has been banned, threatened, censored, and punished," though he has not been imprisoned.

The tales of Yevtushenko's tribulations are not totally unfounded. In the beginning, he did not fit snugly into the Procrustean bed of Stalinist literature, and he was attacked by some of the worst hacks of the period, not least by the anti-Semites. (Yevtushenko has no Jewish background, but his Latvian father's last name, Gangnus, looked suspicious.) Yet the controversy about Yevtushenko was always a quarrel *within* the Soviet literary framework. Yevtushenko never displayed the slightest inclination to work outside it.

A fight within the Soviet establishment, even if it is conducted for a liberal cause, is bound to degenerate into a fight for the benevolence of the authorities. In this regard, Yevtushenko happened to be more skillful, and incomparably more successful, than his dull opponents. And so they never forgave him. Yevtushenko is still denounced by the lunatic fringe, by the Pamyat people and their supporters. (Pamyat has done him a great favor: its opposition has been adduced as proof of his credentials as a humanist and a fighter for freedom.) Much less publicized is the fact that democratic and dissident Soviet critics exposed Yevtushenko's literary weaknesses and moral vacillations long ago and mercilessly. Today hardly anyone in that literary community considers his work worthy of serious study.

He started out, in 1949, at the age of 16, as an average if precocious maker of Soviet-style poems. His first book appeared at the very nadir of Stalinism, in 1952, and suited the time rather nicely: it was optimistic, full of clichés, and boring. But after coming from his native Siberia to the Moscow Literary Institute, Yevtushenko felt the first timid stirrings of the post-Stalin mood and expressed them, too, in his verses. This stage of his poetry is amply represented in the new English collection. In the era of glasnost, it looks antediluvian. Still, there is something attractive in it: youthful sentimentality, straightforward intonation, impetuous imagery.

Yevtushenko was among the first writers of the period to introduce into his work a slice of real Soviet life—of the so-called *byt,* the daily grind of tedium, hardship, and deprivation. Here and there he mentioned queues, dirty staircases, bedbugs, fences with obscene inscriptions, and so on. (Later even such taboo subjects as condoms and drinking eau de cologne appeared in his lyrics.) He also wrote about love and its betrayals; and though they are essentially Victorian, those poems provoked attacks on Yevtushenko as an advocate of promiscuity.

His early verses can be read as an anthology of modes and fads of the bygone days. Some of his heroes (including the narrator) were *stilyagas,* the scornful name for a member of the Soviet "golden youth" who were fond of Western clothes, dances, and so on—a sort of mixture of hippie and yuppie; and the message of Yevtushenko's poetry was that they were good Soviet people who would bravely fight for their socialist fatherland. Yevtushenko played up his Siberian heritage, moreover, and employed all the trivial mythology of Siberia—not the land of the Gulag, but the magnificent wilderness inhabited by rough and honest men. And he emphasized his manifestly difficult childhood ("I started out as a lonely wolf cub"). All these traits were at their most obvious in the long poem **"Zima Junction,"** which appeared in 1955. It made Yevtushenko's reputation.

"Zima Junction," a narrative poem about Yevtushenko's visit to his native Siberia, very cautiously touched the political sensitivities of its era: the so-called Doctors' Plot, Stalin's death, the fall of Beria. On the whole, it was full of the usual stuff—decent Chekists, naive but nice Red cavalrymen, upright but flawed Russian peasants, and the author himself, a young lad in search of a way to serve his country. It was attacked by literary conservatives, but it was also instrumental in generating strong support for Yevtushenko in some circles of the Party, among people whose background and experience were similar to his own. There is a persistent rumor that Mikhail Gorbachev was one of them.

Today Yevtushenko states that "in 1953 it seemed I was all the dissidents rolled up into one." And "the early poetry of my generation is the cradle of glasnost." Such revelations are less than modest. In addition, they are untrue. There were many thousands of dissidents in 1953. Most of them were in prison camps or in internal exile. Some of them, like Pasternak, Akhmatova, and Nadezhda Mandelshtam, were still at large, but they were totally cut off from their readers and from the general public. Glasnost—to be more precise, the revolution taking place in the Soviet Union today—was the fruit of their untold suffering, and their incredibly stubborn efforts to maintain moral and cultural standards during that era of contempt. Yevtushenko and his ilk, in other words, took the place that rightfully belonged to others. They promoted literature and ideology that was adapted to their totalitarian milieu, into which they introduced a measure of half truth and half decency.

Many Western critics are fond of uncovering the influences of Mayakovsky, Yesenin, Pasternak, and Blok in Yevtushenko's poetry, thereby suggesting that he is a rightful heir to the giants. The poet himself never tires of invoking their shades, although he does not transcend the level of schoolboyish clichés when he talks about their heritage. His real mentors, however, were second-rate, incurably Soviet, and largely obscure poets such as Stepan Shchipachev, Mikhail Svetlov, Aleksandr Mezhirov, and Konstantin Vanshenkin. (Numerous dedications to them can be found throughout *The Collected Poems.*)

For a time their heir Yevtushenko surpassed them, since he became genuinely popular. His popularity might have been owed in part to his great histrionic gifts. As Andrei Sinyavsky has observed, Yevtushenko managed to revive the theatrical concept of a poet's destiny (rejected by Pasternak, but characteristic of Mayakovsky and Tsvetaeva), according to which a poet's biography had to become an integral part, even the principal part, of his or her work. Readers and audiences had to be well acquainted with a poet's personal life, with his or her everyday dramas. For Mayakovsky and Tsvetaeva, the theatrics were genuinely tragic. For Yevtushenko, in accordance with the worn Marxist dictum, they tended to be farcical.

He succeeded in creating an image of a nice guy, an old chap, a macho simpleton who matter-of-factly recounts his family problems, his sexual exploits, his daily chores and daily doubts. Yevtushenko's audience of Soviet youths, immature and disoriented after several decades of Stalinist isolation, longing for a touch of sincerity, hungrily gulped down anything "Western" and "modern," and adopted Yevtushenko (together with Voznesensky and several others) as their idol. This did not last too long; the more sophisticated part of the audience found real, previously suppressed Russian poetry, and the other and larger part became rather apathetic to all poetry, including Yevtushenko's.

I should acknowledge that two early poems by Yevtushenko made history. Politically, if not poetically, they have a lasting place in the annals of Soviet liberalism. **"Babii Yar"** (1961) treated anti-Semitic tendencies in Russian life, and provoked a rabid reaction in fascist and fascistoid circles. It was a noble public act, perhaps the high point of Yevtushenko's personal and political career. And it differs favorably from Voznesensky's poems on the same topic; it is more measured, discreet, and restrained, and it avoids formal experimentation and the homespun surrealism that is decidedly out of place when one speaks about the Holocaust. Still, it is poetically feeble, and full of sentimental clichés ("Anne Frank / transparent as a branch in April"). But perhaps these weaknesses may be overlooked.

The other famous poem is *The Heirs of Stalin* (1962). In its case, the situation is different. Most likely **"Babii Yar"** was a spontaneous outpouring. *The Heirs of Stalin* was a calculated gamble, a move in the intra-Party game of old fashioned Stalinists and Khrushchevian liberals. It did not avoid dubious statements, like "prison camps are empty." (In 1962 they were not.) *The Heirs of Stalin* impressed Khrushchev and was printed in *Pravda*. Yevtushenko had managed to place his bet on the winning horse. In his memoirs of the time, the poet portrays himself as a virtual outcast, but the scene that follows in his telling leaves the reader a bit doubtful about the depth of his predicament. At a reception in Havana, presumably in Castro's residence, where Mikoyan also is present, Yevtushenko picks up the issue of *Pravda* with his provocative poem. "[Mikoyan] handed Castro the newspaper. Mikoyan apparently thought that I knew all about it and was rather shocked to see me practically tear the newspaper out of Castro's hands." Hardly an episode in the life of a freedom fighter.

Of course the world traveler did not confine himself to Cuba. Travelogues in verse and prose, including long and not terribly interesting poems on Chile, Japan, the United States, and other places, make up a very considerable part of his creative output. The Western establishment, eager for reassuring signs of moral and cultural revival in Russia, was encouraged by the sight of an audacious person who seemed enlightened and tractable compared with the typical Soviet *nyet* people. And the advertising tricks usually reserved for movie stars were trotted out on the poet's behalf, which increased his already appreciable vanity. (Yevtushenko proudly recounts instances when a Western cultural figure called him "Mayakovsky's son.")

Some misunderstandings with the authorities ensued. Some credit must be given to Yevtushenko, since he behaved with dignity even when he was assaulted by Khrushchev himself. (At his famous meeting with the intelligentsia, Khrushchev delivered himself of the Russian proverb that "hunchbacks are corrected by the grave," at which Yevtushenko retorted:

"The time when people were corrected by the grave has passed.") Still, it was as clear as the noon sun that he remained totally loyal to the Party, even if he was a bit heterodox in secondary matters. Thus the campaign against him fizzled. In 1964 he expiated his sins by writing the long poem **"Bratsk Hydroelectric Station."** The poem, long selections of which are included in the English volume, marked a new stage in Yevtushenko's development: an era of resourceful compromises, cheating moves, and clever adaptations to existing conditions (which became more and more stifling after Khrushchev's removal in October 1964). The poet himself pictured his rushing about as a wise stratagem serving the liberal cause. But not many Russian and non-Russian intellectuals agreed with him; the dissident movement virtually discarded Yevtushenko as an ally. And that was irreversible.

"Bratsk Hydroelectric Station" is a paean to one of the typical Soviet industrial projects in Siberia. (Today such projects, usually unprofitable and fraught with ecological disasters, are repudiated by public opinion, and even by the government itself.) The central part of the poem consists of an argument between an Egyptian pyramid and the Siberian powerhouse: the former symbolizes all the conservative and enslaving tendencies of history (Stalinism supposedly included), while the latter defends the cause of idealist faith and human emancipation. Yevtushenko overlooked the fact that the opposition is far from perfect: slave labor or near-slave labor played an approximately identical part in building both monuments. And the forces of freedom are represented in the poem by rather dubious figures. One of them is Stenka Razin, leader of a savage peasant revolt in the seventeenth century, whose confessions sound chilling ("No, it is not in this I have sinned, my people, / for hanging boyars from the towers. / I have sinned in my own eyes in this, / that I hanged too few of them"). There is also a scene where young Lenin (never named but perfectly recognizable) guides a drunken woman (supposedly Mother Russia) by the elbow, and she blesses him as her true son. This transformation of Lenin into a Christ-like figure insulted equally the followers of Lenin and the followers of Christ.

Virtually the same applies to many of Yevtushenko's later poetic works. The long poem **"Kazan University"** (1970) described czarist Russia with some wit and verve. Reactionary tendencies of the nineteenth century brought to mind Brezhnevian stagnation, and the liberal scholar Lesgaft, harassed by the authorities, might be easily interpreted as a forebear of Sakharov. But the university of Kazan was also the breeding ground for Lenin, who, according to the author (and to the Soviet textbooks), was the crown prince of Russian democracy. Never mind that Lenin was the very opposite of democracy—and that he never attempted to conceal it. Transforming him into a prophet of human rights,

of brotherhood and justice, into a Gandhi or a Sakharov *avant la lettre,* is nauseating. (It is also un-Marxist.)

Many of Yevtushenko's poems on Western topics are characterized by the same doublethink. Harangues against the "doltish regime" of Salazar, against the Chilean murderers or American bureaucrats (**"Under the Skin of the Statue of Liberty,"** 1968) can be construed as transparent allegories: in fact, the poet is attacking native Soviet deficiencies. But at the same time the attacks perfectly conform to the general tenor of the Party's propaganda; Salazar, Pinochet, the FBI, and the Pentagon always were convenient bugaboos, and in that capacity helped the Party to keep the people silent and loyal. Moreover, the general picture of the West in these poems is usually touristy and superficial. Fascinated by material standards and the ever changing fashions of the First World, Yevtushenko nevertheless mythologizes his role as "the ambassador of all the oppressed" and a Russian (and Soviet) patriot. There are also endless exhortations for peaceful coexistence and friendship of peoples ("Russia and America, / Swim closer!"), essentially noble, but less than irreproachable in the era of détente.

The poet's editors and promoters tend to emphasize his heroic gestures during the crisis periods in the USSR. It is true that he sent a telegram to Brezhnev protesting the Czech invasion. It is also said that he phoned Andropov to express his intention to die on the barricades if Solzhenitsyn was imprisoned. But his protests were incomparably more cautious, and much less resonant, than the protests of real dissenters, who paid with their freedom. And the telegram to Brezhnev has the air of an intimate exchange of views between allies: Yevtushenko speaks in it about "our action," which is a damaging mistake, "a great gift to all the reactionary forces in the world." The poem **"Russian Tanks in Prague,"** moreover, was circulated secretly and reached a very limited circle, so as to avoid doing any harm to the poet's career.

A poet's dubious moral and political stance does not always preclude good poetry. In Yevtushenko's case, though, it does. His verses, as a rule, do not belong to the realm of poetry at all. They are made up of middlebrow journalism and an interminable flow of didactic chatter; they have virtually nothing in common with the true problems of modern (or any) poetics. For all his declarations of ardor and fervor, Yevtushenko is hackneyed, kitschy, and lukewarm. On almost every page you stumble on something like "eyelashes laden / with tears and storms," or "eyes half-shut with ecstasy and pain." Melodramatic effusions ("My love is a demolished church / above the turbid river of memories") alternate with revelations worthy of a sex manual ("When we love, / nothing is base or tasteless. / When we love, / nothing is shameful.").

I am trying not to be unfair. There are some concessions I must make in Yevtushenko's favor. He is usually free of Voznesensky's pretentiousness. You can find in his books good similes, successful vignettes of daily life, touching characters, and hair-raising stories that may, alas, be true. And his weaknesses become more obvious in translation. I would be inclined to praise such poems as **"Handrolled Cigarettes"** or **"The Ballad of the Big Stamp"** (the latter is hilarious, though it suffers in translation since it lacks a factual commentary about Russian religious sects). And of course Yevtushenko is a figure to reckon with because of his inexhaustible energy. But all these attractive traits are deeply tainted by his taste for comfort and accommodation, by his eagerness to play humiliating games with the censors, by the mixture of self-admiration, self-pity, and coquettish self-deprecation that have become his indelible mark.

Today Yevtushenko is a member—by no means the leader—of the liberal wing of the perestroika establishment. His book of journalistic prose, *Fatal Half Measures,* from which I have quoted extensively, traces his political career between 1962, when *A Precocious Autobiography,* published in the West, caused a passing commotion, and 1990, when his speeches resounded, rather hollowly, in several public forums. The book is preceded by a poem in which Yevtushenko seems to be admonishing Gorbachev: "Don't half recoil, / lost in broad daylight, / half rebel, / half suppressor / of the half insurrection / you gave birth to!"

But the book's title perfectly applies to the poet's own style of action. Fatal half measures, indeed. Yevtushenko lags desperately behind events. The gap between his wordy, complacent prose and the Soviet public mood became unbridgeable long ago. In the book, Yevtushenko launches crusades against nuclear war, against the monopoly of the Party, against Russian chauvinism, against cruelty to animals, and lots of other unsavory phenomena. Most of his thoughts on these topics are with the angels. But they are still wrapped in the old Soviet discourse, and that discourse is finally as dead as nails. He strives to improve his fatherland without rejecting the main part of the ideology that makes such a project hopeless. He is what he always was, a man of fatal half-truths, of fatal half measures. In this way, he is the counterpart of his presumably avid reader Gorbachev. Both attempt to promote something like totalitarianism with a human face. It never worked. It never will.

James Finn Cotter (review date Summer 1991)

SOURCE: "The Truth of Poetry," in *The Hudson Review,* Vol. XLIV, No. 2, Summer, 1991, pp. 343-45.

[*In the following excerpt, Cotter outlines the principal themes of Yevtushenko's poetry in* The Collected Poems.]

I once reviewed a sequence of poems about a marriage and divorce. The story was detailed, painful, funny, and fully involving. I later learned that the poet had made up the whole thing. I was delighted. I had been taken in by the author's voice and the entire situation he had imagined. The truth of poetry is not in reciting facts but in creating veracity. I ask a poem to be true to itself, to convince me and to capture my attention with its thought, emotion, imagery, and language. Do not preach or put on airs, I tell the poem. Tell the truth, and I'll believe you. What more can a reader ask?

"I'm no good . . . I have a weak link with life," Yevgeny Yevtushenko complains in **"I don't understand,"** a poem from his newly collected poetry [*The Collected Poems*]. He qualifies his disarming admission, however, with an ingenuous self-defense: "But if I connect with so many things, / I must, apparently, stand for something." Yevtushenko has stood for many good causes in the past thirty years: poetry as a voice that rallies public consciousness, freedom to speak out in protest against human rights violations, a world view that transcends nationalist boundaries, and the power of the individual against bureaucracy and oppression. Yevtushenko has also represented poetry turned to publicity and performance, for propaganda or self-aggrandizement. What is the truth?

The answer is not simple. Even the 684-page *Collected Poems,* as we learn from translator Albert Todd's informative and defensive introduction, is a selection from the three-volume Russian edition. Yevtushenko has been a prolific poet, making his travels, domestic crises, politics, reading, and life grist for his mill. He is a chameleon, writing in a variety of styles, the satiric epic of Pushkin, the nationalistic narrative of Blok, the pastoral lyrics of Pasternak, and the personal confessions of Lowell and Akhmadulina. In **"Poetry is a great power,"** he writes:

> Poetry is a kingdom
> in which the truth rules in every city,
> where one is judged both for poverty and riches,
> where the ruler is whoever becomes its slave.

The capital of this country is Pushkin, Lermontov is a city, Yesmin a village, and Pasternak "the eternal suburb." Yevtushenko obviously wants to be the whole globe.

Yevtushenko gets around: from his youth in remote Siberia, to Europe, America, South America, Africa, and Japan; he protests in Moscow, New York City, Ulster, South Africa; he is in Chile when Allende is murdered and in **"A Dove in Santiago: A Novella in Verse"** relates that death to a young man's suicide. The poet's power to narrate seems as inexhaustible as his passion to be everywhere at once. His eye for detail and ear for conversation are matched by his need to generalize about what he sees and hears. On the deeper, or higher, level of thought he often disappoints. He has both too much and too little to say.

Even when he is shallow, Yevtushenko can be engaging. In his blast at modern writers, **"The Incomprehensible Poets,"** he admits: "My guilt is my simplicity. / My crime is my clarity." He declares in **"I Would Like"**: "I would like to belong to all times, / shock all history so much / that it would be amazed / what a smart aleck I was." From stealing his grandmother's ring for a soccer ticket to envying an eight-year-old poet who shares the platform with him, Yevtushenko shows himself as a vain, suspicious, gregarious, trusting and untrustworthy human being. He says in **"Verbosity"**:

> I am verbose both in my daily life
> and in my verse—that's your bad luck—
> but I am cunning: I realize
> that there's no lack of will
> behind this endless drivel,
> rather my strong ill will!

For fear of being eternal, the poet is eager to run on in time.

In the fine autobiographical poem **"Zima Junction: A Poem,"** Yevtushenko describes returning to his birthplace at nineteen, meeting again his aunts and uncles in the open spaces and rich country life of Siberia. Beneath the surface, however, he discovers a loss of purpose and disillusioned lives; the two uncles he admires turn out to be a drunkard and a womanizer. He confesses his despair to an old schoolmate friend who asks: "Do you think it's only you?" The poet's success has been to tap the discontent not just in the Soviet system but in modern life. He preaches and poses, he overexplains, he exasperates with clichés ("freedom is calling") and moralizing ("Let's be equal to it"), but bumbling, boasting, bemusing, Yevtushenko is our latter-day Whitman, the kosmos we have come to be, glasnost and all.

The poems that will live on may not be the public ones like **"Babii Yar"** and **"Russian Tanks in Prague"** but personal accounts like **"On a Bicycle"** and **"Flowers for Grandmother."** **"Blue Fox"** combines concern for animals with an allegory of the collective state; **"Monologue of an Actress"** is a witty complaint by an aging actress that no worthwhile roles are left to play. Many of the New York poems, ably translated by John Updike, have a resonance of time and place that ring true. Stanley Kunitz, Ted Hughes, James Dickey, Richard Wilbur, and editor Albert Todd are among the poets who have rendered Yevtushenko into clear, readable English.

Patricia Pollock Brodsky (review date Winter 1992)

SOURCE: A review of *The Collected Poems 1952-1990*, in *World Literature Today*, Winter, 1992, pp. 156-57.

[In the following review, Brodsky provides a thematic and stylistic overview of the contents of The Collected Poems.*]*

The new *Collected Poems 1952-1990* reflects Yevgeny Yevtushenko's poetic career in microcosm: vast and uneven, sometimes irritating, often appealing, and ever astonishing in its variety. The title is somewhat misleading, since the volume offers only a selection from Yevtushenko's extensive oeuvre, and in addition, several long poems are represented in excerpts only. Yevtushenko's allusiveness can be a problem for Western readers; a few names and terms are explained in footnotes, but this practice could profitably have been expanded. A helpful feature is the chronological list of poems with their Russian titles, date and place of first publication, and location, if any, in the 1983 *Sobranie sochinenii* (see *WLT* 59:4).

Like the poems themselves, the translations by twenty-five translators vary in quality. A few are revisions of earlier versions. Most of Yevtushenko's poems use slant rhyme relying heavily on assonance, a practice so closely associated with him as to be called "Yevtushenkean rhyme" (*evtushenkovskaia rifma*). Russian's rich phonetic structure allows almost limitless use of this kind of rhyme; a master of the form and clearly one of Yevtushenko's teachers was the poet Marina Tsvetaeva. Wisely, few attempts are made to retain this feature in the English translations, or indeed to use rhyme at all.

From the beginning of his prolific career in the early 1950s, Yevtushenko's poetry has been characterized by strong stances on political issues. He praises Allende and Che Guevara, condemns the Vietnam War, and deplores the situation in Northern Ireland. His criticism is not limited to the West, however. A popular and privileged poet whose readings at one time filled football stadiums and who was given unprecedented freedom to travel abroad, he nevertheless warned against abuses at home, castigating militarists, dishonest bureaucrats, and toadies of all kinds. These critical poems range from *The Heirs of Stalin* and **"Babi Yar"** in the early 1960s to **"Momma and the Neutron Bomb"** and poems about the dissident Andrei Sakharov and the Afghanistan war in the 1980s. The roots of his ferocious morality are to be found in his love for Russia, and in his stubborn belief in the ideals of the revolution.

Even the semiofficial poet was not immune from censorship, however. Included in the new collection are a number of poems that were written during the sixties but for political reasons could not be published until many years later. Among them are verses to fellow poets Tsvetaeva (1967/1987) and Esenin (1965/1988), **"Russian Tanks in Prague"** (1968/1990), and **"The Ballad of the Big Stamp,"** a bawdy tale about castration for the good of the party (1966/1989).

Yevtushenko is at his best when he is specific and detailed, and this happens most frequently in poems dealing with his native Siberia, its nature and history, its sailors, whalers, berry pickers. These include the long poem **"Zima Junction"** (1955) and a series written in 1964 about life on the northern frontier. Yevtushenko has a strong visual sense (he is an accomplished photographer), and color often plays an important role in his works. In the fairy-tale-like **"Snow in Tokyo: A Japanese Poem"** (1974), for example, a proper and repressed Japanese matron discovers the wonders of painting and finds the courage to rebel against her stultifying life through the world of color.

A thread running through Yevtushenko's work is the importance of poetry and the responsibility of the poet to mankind. He constantly questions his own talent and mission, thus continuing the Russian tradition of meta-poetry. Likewise very Russian is the dialogue between writers living and dead that Yevtushenko carries on, in poems addressed to or evoking Pushkin, Pasternak, Neruda, and Jack London, along with numerous others.

Finally, Yevtushenko's poetry is a kind of personal diary which details his extensive travels and especially his many love affairs and marriages. Remarkable love poems follow the poet from first love, to the birth of his sons, to the sadness of falling out of love again. The poems contain a rich fabric of quarrels, memories, farewells, even a conversation with his dog, who shares the poet's grief that his woman has gone. Perhaps the most attractive thing about Yevtushenko is his human breadth, his willingness to lay himself open to our reactions. *The Collected Poems* provides the reader with numerous opportunities to become acquainted with this engaged and engaging poet, one of the important, questioning voices of our age.

Lee B. Croft (review date Winter 1992)

SOURCE: A review of *Fatal Half Measures,* in *World Literature Today,* Winter, 1992, p. 159.

[*In the following review, Croft vaunts the rich detail and informed perspective of Soviet society in* Fatal Half Measures.]

Yevgeny Yevtushenko has been particularly blessed by the *glasnost* era in Soviet politics. Now he is able to shed every vestige of compromise and live his own legend. He has become a truly uncompromising man, and he has decided to use his fame as a poet and his powers of persuasion for political effect. This is a switch, to be sure. Soviet poets have long attempted, albeit futilely, to remain apart from politics. However, Yevtushenko was elected to the Soviet Congress of People's Deputies in 1989, and he has by now clearly become one of the leaders of the Soviet democratic movement. During the attempted coup of August 1991, he was among those who opposed a return to totalitarian methods. He was, in fact, in the Russian Parliament Building while it was still surrounded by tanks, composing a poem to honor Boris Yeltsin's leadership. Who can forget him reading his own English translation of it to Western reporters as the coup's demise became apparent?

In *Fatal Half Measures,* a collection of speeches, essays, and reminiscences, Yevtushenko seems to be urging Soviet society on toward democracy as one would goad a stalled mule. "On the brink of precipices," he writes, "we can't jump halfway across." In powerful speeches he reminds his countrymen of past woe, the Stalinist terror: "Half memory leads to half conscience. . . . Children on the banks of the Kolyma River to this day will bring you blueberries in human skulls they find and smile in innocent absence of memory." He ridicules those who resist trying the new freedoms: "Instead of Vasilii Belov's vigilant thesis that can be reduced to 'Every Xerox under surveillance,' I propose the thesis: 'A personal Xerox for every Soviet citizen.' Perhaps a Xerox would help him with his writing." As ever, he compares the different lots of Soviet and Western counterparts who remain as oblivious of each other as "Gina Lollobrigida and Red Square."

Although the issue of Soviet democracy is paramount, Yevtushenko provides a wide range of recollections from his long history of international travels and from his knowledge of Russian literary figures. In the section called "Beyond Borders" we visit France, Brazil, China, and a host of other countries. We read of Doris Day and Pablo Picasso and meet the Eskimo poet Zoya Nenlyumkina. In the section titled "Russian Geniuses" Yevtushenko comments on Russian poets from Pushkin, Baratynsky, and Tiutchev to Mayakovsky, Tsvetaeva, and Pasternak. He examines the character of prose writers like Leo Tolstoy (starting with an anecdote about Jacqueline Kennedy), Dostoevsky, Chekhov, Gorky, Alexei Tolstoy (a "pen of genius," lacking only "pangs of conscience"), and Andrei Platonov (a comparison of one of his characters with the late Armand Hammer concludes with the title notion **"The Proletariat Does Not Need Psychosis"**). He includes here as well the composer Dmitri Shostakovich (a talent "Pushkinesque in scope" whom he talked out of signing an official letter against the Prague Spring in 1968).

Yevtushenko has been almost everywhere. He knows almost everybody. He remembers it all and he writes wonderfully. This is what makes *Fatal Half Measures* such a feast. For anyone interested in Soviet society and especially those of a literary bent, it is truly a delight. Antonina Bouis deserves much credit too, not only for her able selection and translation but also for her explanatory notes and her inclusion of a useful index.

Jonathan Z. Ludwig (review date Spring 1992)

SOURCE: A review of *Fatal Half Measures,* in *Slavic and East European Journal,* Vol. 36, No. 1, Spring, 1992, pp. 120-22.

[*In the following review, Ludwig outlines the principal themes of* Fatal Half Measures, *revealing their significance to Yevtushenko's poetic works.*]

Until the publication of this book [*Fatal Half Measures*], the title of which comes from the 1989 poem which precedes the introduction, Yevgeny Yevtushenko was known in the English speaking world primarily through translations of his poetry. In her introduction, however, Antonina Bouis, borrowing the opening line of Yevtushenko's **"Bratsk Hydroelectric Station,"** notes "A POET in Russia is more than a poet." To understand any Russian poet, especially Yevtushenko who has been a political player for almost thirty years, one must look beyond poetry. Therefore, with the help of the author, she has collected and translated this series of political essays, speeches, travelogues, and works of literary criticism, the majority of which were composed in the 1980s, to show that there is more to Yevtushenko than poetry. As she states, her hope is to show "the range and scope of his concerns."

The book is divided into a prologue plus six sections, each containing essays which center around a specific theme. The prologue consists of Yevtushenko's first "nonpoetic political protest," his telegram to Brezhnev after the invasion of Czechoslovakia, and his June 1989 speech before the First Congress of People's Deputies. These are entirely political in nature as is the first section, "The Memorial Society," a series of treatises and speeches designed to raise money for the memorial to the victims of Stalinism and to support their rehabilitation. As political treatises, these selections are of little literary value. Nevertheless, they should not be brushed aside, for they do further reveal Yevtushenko's political beliefs, a desire for freedom and justice, which is an inherent part of his poetry.

More interesting is the second section, "Glasnost and

Perestroika," in which politics and literature are intertwined. In the first essay, **"Cradle of Glasnost,"** Yevtushenko declares, "The early poetry of my generation is the cradle of Glasnost," for it was "the first truth-seeking poetry after so many years of official lies." This statement sets the tenor for the remainder of this section. In the same essay he calls **"Babi Yar"** and *The Heirs of Stalin* the first truth poems. He continues this discussion in the second essay, **"Censorship Is the Best Reader,"** recalling an argument with a censor over his poem **"Bratsk Hydroelectric Station"** and in the fourth essay, **"Pass to a Trial,"** in which he gives his impressions of the 1966 Daniel-Sinyavsky trial. In both of these, Yevtushenko writes in a style that allows the reader to picture events lucidly as he reveals them. After returning to strictly political themes for several essays, the section concludes with two very literary philosophical essays, **"Politics Is Everyone's Privilege,"** in which he evokes Pasternak, Wilde, and Dostoevsky, and **"Every Person Is a Superpower,"** in which he quotes numerous philosophers from Plato and Seneca to Nietzsche and Thoreau, attempting to awaken the human spirit.

The third section, "Soviet Life," returns to the political sphere, revealing Yevtushenko's feelings toward several contemporary Soviet issues including party membership and women in the Soviet Union. Nevertheless, this section is not without certain literary merit, seen most clearly in the second essay, **"Wooden Moscow,"** in which Yevtushenko romantically intertwines his life and the history of Moscow from his youth under Stalinism to the present in an almost fairy-tale atmosphere. Also interesting in this section are the philosophical treatise **"Religion As Part of Culture"** in which he discusses his concept of morality and **"Who's Stronger in This Painting,"** a piece of artistic criticism centering around Oleg Celkov's painting *Birthday Party with Rembrandt.*

The fourth section, "Brief Excerpts from Selected Prose," contains portions of the previously published *Ardabiola, Wild Berries,* and *A Precocious Autobiography* as well as excerpts from a 1987 interview with Ogonëk and the screenplay *The End of the Musketeers.* The majority of these selections, however, are simply excerpts "from various articles" which focus on the issue of "the poet's role in society," the subtitle of this section. Since these vignettes are, at times, enlightening, it is unfortunate that no indication of their original source is given, thus making it extremely difficult to locate them in their entirety.

The fifth section, "Beyond Borders," is a collection of travelogues in which Yevtushenko tells of journeys to Brazil, Alaska, Asia, France to visit Picasso, and Bulgaria. These essays are free from all but the subtlest political overtones, instead relating impressions of the places visited and meetings with people there, set against an historical backdrop. Throughout, the reader again feels in step with Yevtushenko, readily visualizing what he is describing. The most impressive of these is the second essay, **"Divided Twins,"** which is a cunning intermingling of fiction and non-fiction, for in the midst of revealing the common histories and contemporary similarities of Siberia and Alaska, he tells the story of a Siberian sable who hops from ice floe to ice floe, avoiding hunters, to meet his Alaskan mate. The true value of this section, however, is the new perspective several of these essays give to the series of "travel poems" Yevtushenko wrote in the late 1960s after visiting these places for the first time, poems such as **"Love Is Always in Danger"** about Japan and **"Cemetery of Whales"** and **"Monologue of a Polar Fox on an Alaskan Fur Farm"** about Alaska and Siberia. Here, in essays written after later visits, the images and inspiration behind these poems are still clear.

The final section, "Russian Geniuses," is a collection of literary criticism that begins with a series of paragraph length impressions of fourteen writers, including Pushkin, Dostoevsky, Gorky, Bulgakov, and Solzhenitsyn. The remainder is a series of six essays on Tolstoy and *Anna Karenina*, Mayakovsky, Shostakovich, Cvetaeva, Platonov, and Pasternak. These are wonderfully fluid and poignant essays written from a comparativist point of view. Tolstoy is juxtaposed, in one instance, with Flaubert. Mayakovsky is compared with Pushkin, as is Cvetaeva, and Lermontov. Platonov, at one point, is mentioned in the same breath as Dostoevsky. Only Shostakovich is not compared to any other artist. Most fascinating, however, is the essay on Pasternak, for this essay not only gives Yevtushenko's impressions of him, but also Pasternak's reactions to the poetry of the young Yevtushenko. What stands out most clearly in this essay, though, as in the others, is the uncovering of what Yevtushenko himself looks for in literature: the same quest for the spiritual and yearning for freedom that is found in much of his own poetry.

This book is well translated and wide-ranging. For the reader not overly familiar with Russian and Soviet history and politics, Antonina Bouis has provided an introduction to several of the essays, explaining the contemporary and historical context behind them. She has also generously added footnotes throughout to explain names, dates, and other historical references made by Yevtushenko. The only serious drawback to this collection is that no indication is given as to the original place of publication of each of these essays, making it difficult to track down the Russian originals. It would also be good to know whether a further collection of Yevtushenko's essays, those written in the 1960s and 1970s, will be forthcoming. Regardless of these shortcomings, this collection is a fine place to start if one wishes to begin to understand what stands behind and provides inspiration for Yevtushenko's poetry.

Maura Reynolds (essay date 6 May 1993)

SOURCE: "Russian Poet Still Pleases, Provokes," in *The San Diego Union-Tribune,* May 6, 1993, p. F1.

[*In the following essay, Reynolds discusses Yevtushenko's reputation in relation to his politics.*]

If it is hard for a poet to become a legend in his time, surely remaining a legend is still harder.

Yet for the last three decades, through shifting regimes and ideologies, Yevgeny Yevtushenko has managed to remain the most famous of Russia's living poets.

From **"Babi Yar,"** the 1961 poem that forced the Soviet Union to confront its anti-Semitism, to a forthcoming novel about the August 1991 coup that eventually launched Boris Yeltsin to the Russian presidency, Yevtushenko has somehow managed to have a hand in most of the political upheavals that have wracked his motherland in the last 30 years.

Many praise his courage to probe the social and political wounds of Soviet history, from anti-Semitism to neo-fascism.

"Mr. Yevtushenko told the truth in the Soviet Union when it was a dangerous thing to do, and he is still telling the truth," said Watson Branch, chairman of the English department at the Bishop's School in La Jolla, who introduced the poet's first reading at SDSU's Don Powell Theater Tuesday night.

But others, especially émigrés, deride this same ability, seeing Yevtushenko as more political opportunist than artist.

"He has a consummate grasp of the obvious," one Russian literature professor scoffed privately by phone this week.

At readings and receptions during a three-day visit here, his first to San Diego, it is clear that even as he approaches 60, for whatever reason, Yevtushenko's power to please and provoke is far from ebbing. In fact, the poet retains a beguiling charm, even when admitting his own vanity.

"Modesty," Yevtushenko says candidly, "has never been one of my biggest flaws."

As he takes the stage, Yevtushenko looks less a poet than a

schoolteacher, gazing over lowered bifocals at his audience, eyebrows deeply furrowed.

But when he recites verse, Yevtushenko springs around the stage, hopping and skipping like he did as a boy, performing folk dances at war weddings in Siberia. His dramatic gestures, too, have a confidence that is equally youthful, even naive.

At the reading, a translator reads his poems in English, and Yevtushenko follows with a reading in Russian.

"I would like to be born in every country, have passports for them all," he bellows, stretching his arms out wing-like. "I would like to dive into the water of Siberian Lake Baikal and surface, snorting, somewhere. Why not . . . ," he whispers, "the Mississippi?" The audience laughs.

"He pulls you in, even if you don't understand Russian," said spectator Peggy Caetano, leaving the theater after the two-hour reading. "He has incredible charisma."

By any analysis—including his own—Yevtushenko's fame has always had as much to do with politics as poetry. Indeed, it is his very talent for ducking and riding political waves that has earned him both praise and derision, at different times, from many of the same people.

But Quincy Troupe, the award-winning poet and UCSD literature professor, sees Yevtushenko's politics as a strength, not a weakness. The fact that Yevtushenko writes about topical issues makes his poetry more accessible to ordinary people, both Russian and Western, Troupe says.

"The academics have looked on him with a certain amount of disdain, but no one comes to hear them read," Troupe says. In fact, Troupe credits Yevtushenko with helping revive the oral tradition in poetry, comparing him to American poets like Allen Ginsberg and Amiri Baraka. Yevtushenko's stage power comes from both the accessibility of his verse and his energetic antics in delivering it.

In *The City of Yes and the City of No,* the 6-foot-tall Yevtushenko plunges brazenly into the audience, kissing hands and peering intently into faces as he recites the litany of *da*'s and *nyet*'s that lace the poem. His blue eyes flash with pleasure as his targets blush and giggle.

Yevtushenko became a sensation in 1952 at 19 when he published his first volume of poetry and was inducted into the Soviet Writer's Union as its youngest member. He drew international attention in 1961 with **"Babi Yar,"** which, for the first time, described the World War II massacre of 40,000 Jews near Kiev and the Soviet anti-Semitism that left the mass grave unmarked for two decades. A few years later he began to tour the West, packing concert halls, including New York's Carnegie Hall.

Under Brezhnev, many Russian were disappointed that Yevtushenko failed to adequately defend dissidents like Andrei Sakharov, and too readily accepted Kremlin medals and praise. But in December 1985, Yevtushenko resurrected his flagging stature by delivering a speech to the Soviet Writer's Union, signaling that Gorbachev would extend his new policy of glasnost to the arts.

In August 1991, he wound up behind the barricades with Yeltsin during the hard-line coup.

"Many Russian writers are stuck in the past right now, writing about concentration camps, the gulag," Yevtushenko says as an ocean breeze dishevels the thin, gray hair on his forehead. "But I have written a truly contemporary novel. It is called **Don't Die Before your Death.**" The book, published last month in Russian in Jerusalem, is due out in English this summer.

For Yevtushenko, staying contemporary may be the key to longevity. "It is a novel I wrote for everybody, of course, but is also a gift to myself, a gift for my 60th birthday," he says.

As for his critics, Yevtushenko is happy, at least, for the attention.

"I'm now full of beans," he insists, giving a little skip to prove the point.

Boyd Tonkin (review date 8 October 1993)

SOURCE: A review of *Twentieth Century Russian Poetry,* in *New Statesman & Society,* Vol. 6, No. 273, October 8, 1993, p. 42.

[*In the following review, Tonkin commends the selections of* Twentieth Century Russian Poetry.]

"The history of the Russian and Soviet peoples in the 20th century is a bizarre, fantastic fable that could not have been invented by the wildest imagination." As I read that, the heroic defender of Russian liberty in August 1991 turned his tanks on the parliament. In Moscow's tragic pantomime of role-reversal, each new turn upstages the army of journalists who try to fix in print the chaos of post-communism.

While punditry fades in the light of tomorrow's headlines, poetry keeps its bloom. This year's most enticing book about Russia will be Yevgeny Yevtushenko's magnificent anthology of *Twentieth Century Russian Poetry* (edited by Albert C Todd and Max Hayward). Its 1,000-plus pages close with a poem by Ilya Krichevsky, killed at the White House in 1991: "Still yet a long, long way to go / still yet many who will lie in ditches . . ."

In a country where slim volumes of verse can sell out editions of 200,000 in a couple of days, poetry has never lost its direct line to the people's imagination. This epic compilation—830 poems and 253 authors—amounts to a history of the nation's inner life as well as a guided trek across schools, movements and ideologies. Yevtushenko's anti-Soviet foes often saw him as a beanie-capped Kremlin stooge in dissident's clothing, but he also stood between the tanks and the parliament in 1991. He claims to have banished political bias from the selection, "because civil war in literature, like civil war itself, is fratricidal".

The normal roster of star names appears; from Blok, Akhmatova and Pasternak through to Brodsky and Akhmadulina. Even more rewarding is the chance to discover writers without western renown, such as the "absurdist" Daniil Kharms or the hugely popular bard Bulat Okudzhava. Reds and Whites, backwoods patriots and cosmopolitan émigrés; all nestle side-by-side in unusual harmony. And the works chosen prove that many of the greatest figures belonged only to the party of ambivalence.

In this, of all weeks, it's impossible to overlook the melancholy repetition of protests against bloodshed and autocracy. As another "Kremlin mountaineer" makes law from the barrels of tanks, we can turn to Osip Mandelstam's famous satire on Stalin, which hastened his arrest: "Like horseshoes he forges decree after decree— / Some get it in the forehead, some in the brow / some in the groin and some in the eye".

From the twilight of the Romanovs to the implosion of Bolshevism, the poet's voice rises above the growl of violence and fear. This superb compendium gives hope that Russia's true opposition can survive even its new Tsar. As Nina Grachova (born 1971) writes: "It is not the whips' and cannons' power I revere, / but the anguish of the land."

ies are the most exciting movies, rediscoveries from by-gone years are providing some of this season's most interesting fare.

At the head of the list comes *I Am Cuba,* a remarkable 1964 picture that literally defies description.

Belatedly brought to theaters by Martin Scorsese and Francis Ford Coppola, who have admirable records of digging out overlooked cinematic gems, the movie has an episodic plot about freedom fighters, urban rebels, sugar-cane harvesters, and other figures from Cuban society just before Fidel Castro's revolution ousted the old capitalist regime.

The film meanders from one storyline to another, sometimes pausing long enough to build effective suspense, sometimes moving on before anything of consequence has happened. If its forced nostalgia for Cuban socialism were all it had to offer, it would be little more than a historical curiosity, even if it does boast a loquacious screenplay by Yevgeny Yevtushenko, the legendary Russian poet, and Enrique Pineda Barnet, his respected Cuban counterpart. What ranks *I Am Cuba* among the most thrilling films in recent memory is neither its subject nor its soundtrack, but the astounding cinematic style of Russian director Mikhail Kalatozov, whose pyrotechnics are more imaginative than 95 percent of the stuff Hollywood cranks out with special-effects resources never dreamed of by this comparatively low-tech artist. His camera flies, dives, swoops, and soars, enveloping the viewer in a dazzling cascade of almost hallucinatory visions.

While the content of the shots is often little more than public-relations flack for Cuban-Soviet solidarity, the imagery is so visually transcendent that it lifts the picture far above its literal level, just as a superb musical setting may render the words of a song largely irrelevant.

Open your eyes to *I Am Cuba,* and it may be a long time before you see movies in the same way again. A big vote of thanks is due to Milestone Films for teaming with Scorsese and Coppola to bring this hidden masterpiece to light.

David Sterritt (review date 10 March 1995)

SOURCE: "Rediscovered Gems Play Again," in *The Christian Science Monitor,* March 10, 1995, p. 13.

[*In the following review, Sterritt praises the cinematic style of* I Am Cuba.]

Confounding the conventional view that the newest mov-

Vancouver Sun (essay date 6 May 1995)

SOURCE: "Yevtushenko–Poet of Love and Politics," in *Vancouver Sun,* May 6, 1995, p. D2.

[*In the following essay, the critic profiles Yevtushenko's life and career with respect to the poet's politics and literary themes.*]

Nikita Khrushchev called him ungovernable—but left him alone (more or less) to write the scathing poetic outbursts of moral indignation against Communist oppression that made him the voice of his generation.

Envious writer colleagues, watching his rise to fame in Russia and (more importantly) abroad, called him a licensed dissenter—one who sold out to the authorities as a tame tiger in exchange for privilege and foreign travel.

Yevgeny Yevtushenko calls himself an independent-minded loyalist.

He stood on the Moscow barricades alongside the defenders of Russia's precarious democracy during the attempted White House coup by military hard-liners in 1991 and versified eloquently about it from the balcony.

Yet his moral anger at the slaughter in Chechnya was so great that when Yeltsin offered him a decoration last November for his part in defeating the coup, he turned it down.

He shrugs when you suggest this was a brave man's act.

"It wasn't political gesture for me," he says. "I didn't want to make any kind of political capital. But it was a moral impossibility for me—I couldn't imagine myself receiving this order when so many innocent people were dying. It was a moral impossibility. That's all."

He is in Vancouver on the second stop on a cross-Canada reading tour to publicize his new novel, ***Don't Die Before You're Dead,*** and to give a reading . . . as part of the Vancouver International Writers Festival's author series.

He's 62 now, and spends as much time in the West (he teaches film in Tulsa, Oklahoma) as Moscow. He has the successful Russian intellectual's waywardness of dress.

The color of his thin, expensive jacket is an electric magenta spattered with black. His open shirt exposes his hairless chest as far as his sternum, above which a cross-bearing pendant hangs from a gold chain. He has a jaunty flat cap in a pale orange tartan.

When ***Don't Die Before You're Dead*** was published in Russia last year, it sold out its 100,000 print run at the rate of 2,000 copies a day, and it's not hard to see why.

He calls the book a Russian fairy tale. In fact, it's a thinly disguised view of the state of the Russian nation at the time of the 1991 coup—ripely entertaining and richly satirical in the finest Russian classic tradition.

"Whether it is a good or bad book is not for me to decide," he writes in an introduction. "But in opening it, you open the soul of today's Russia."

He remains, still, a potent voice of that soul, though the range has changed. The poetry that made his name couched his personal protest in writing that was rhetorical, conversational, accessible—all the things that made it so popular he could fill soccer stadiums for readings.

The new novel, on the other hand, is a sprawling true fable covering a vivid tapestry of character (only one of them himself).

"I always wanted to be the writer of those who don't write," he says. "I didn't fulfil what I wanted, but I'm on the way. I haven't left poetry; I wrote 35 poems this year, but now I am concentrating on prose. When I began to publish poetry, when I was 15, my poetry was overtaking my knowledge of life. Now my knowledge of life is overtaking my writing."

He is currently juggling four novels ("like a crazy chessplayer") and he has five film scripts (he's also a film director) waiting for funding.

As we talk he gestures, slouches, pulls up a chair to rest his feet, leans back on his folded arms. As ideas animate him he squints and squeezes his ice-blue eyes, thumps the table, rubs his head. His thin, fair hair, so carefully casual at the start of our talk, becomes rumpled and disheveled.

For all the tales of diminished powers, his ability to captivate an audience seems undimmed. The night before our talk, he was in Calgary for a signing. The place was packed—one woman brought all 18 books he has published in English.

"There were 300 people . . . I signed probably 500 books. I never expected such a crowd." One woman asked him to sign a ticket she had saved since 1962 from his historic first reading in Kiev of his famous protest over the Jewish pogrom, "Babi Yar."

He was struck by the fact that many people at the Calgary gathering were from what he calls the technical intelligentsia—engineers, electricians, oil people. That's common in Russia, he says—"the technical intelligentsia is the backbone of our intelligentsia"—but not so in North America.

That reminds him of a cowboy poets' gathering ("real cowboys, not operetta cowboys") he recently attended in Colorado: 10 days, a 1,600-seat theatre, $12 a ticket—sold out from noon to night. He was the only non-cowboy.

"I discovered so many great readers of literature: we'd sit round talking about Dostoyevsky . . . it was unbelievable. Sometimes we don't know who our readers are."

He's the son of a Siberian peasant mother and a Latvian intellectual father, and the duality shows in his writing—an internationalist of enduring Russian loyalties (a "sentimental internationalist," as he puts it in the new book), a simple sophisticate with a sharp intelligence, a keen sense of irony and an ability to pitch his work to a broad-based audience.

In terms of breadth and enthusiasm of readership, some observers have drawn parallels between Yevtushenko and Pushkin (1799-1838), perhaps the best loved (certainly in Russia) of all Russia's great writers.

In his first novel, *Wild Berries,* Yevtushenko wrote that if God would give him the right to resurrect one man, he would resurrect Pushkin, and while he is quick to disclaim any kind of equality—"there's great gap between us, I'm just a modest disciple"—he agrees that similarities exist.

According to Yevtushenko, a man who has been married four times, Pushkin, who died in a duel defending his wife's honor, "was a great lover, faithful friend, not an extremist. You could laugh and cry with his writing. He was a Renaissance man, and this I admire."

In particular, Pushkin "was a poet of love and politics. And I am a poet of love and politics." Some days, in fact, he writes poems on both these topics—because "it is very harmful to write only about politics. It dries you out.

"When you fight for months, as politicians do, your skin becomes your shield. But your shield that saves you from poisoned daggers becomes hard, and then you cannot feel the touch of someone who tries to caress you. It happens with professional politicians. All the wives of professional politicians are unhappy."

It is the responsibility of every poet to maintain that soft skin, that vulnerability. "If I didn't, I would cease to be a poet." That's why he turned down the suggestion that he should become Russia's minister of culture.

"I knew it would be my death as a writer—when I spent three years as a deputy [in the Russian Parliament] it was my worst three years as a writer. And then, how could I criticize government and be part of government? Impossible."

Certainly, he has always been willing to criticize government—though he will also give praise where he thinks praise is due. For instance, he admonished Gorbachev, in a poem, not to be half-hearted in what he had to do:

Half measures can kill when on the brink of precipices,
Chafing in terror at the bit,
We strain and sweat and foam because we cannot
Jump just halfway across.

Yet he defends Gorbachev still. "I think the Russian people were criminally ungrateful to him. Many people now mock him." In his last year, maybe he was less than the ideal leader—"but he abolished the danger of nuclear war between two superpowers: for that one thing we should be grateful. He stopped war in Afghanistan. He abolished censorship. They should be grateful to him for ever."

As we have been talking, some sheets of paper—background material, my notes for the interview—have strayed across the table, partially obscuring his new book. He brushes them gently, absently aside and contemplates its cover as he talks.

"One of Russia's most adventurous writers," the cover proclaims. It's a quote from Henry Miller. Probably no one would disagree. Except, perhaps, Yevtushenko himself.

For all the famous bombast, for all the noisy criticism, he balks at the suggestion that he remains the Russian incarnation of the angry young man.

"I just don't hide what I think. I don't want to lie and pretend to be a man of great courage. Each time I made some dangerous action I was scared.

"But to me it's sometimes a moral impossibility not to do it—or to do what the authorities suggest. I just would like to sleep calmly. And I have no insomnia."

So he is at ease with his conscience?

"Oh, I couldn't say that. No no no no no no no. I could say I didn't betray anyone except myself—but I am also part of humanity. If you betray yourself, you also betray humanity."

In what way did he betray himself?

"By being lazy, for instance . . . there are many things: loving my own wife and sometimes looking around, so many reasons not to have your conscience completely calm."

At the end of **"Zima Junction,"** the poem that brought him his first taste of fame in the late 1950s, the little Siberian town in which he was born tells him to "hold out, meditate, listen. Explore. Travel the world over."

And "love people." After a lifetime of holding out, meditating, listening, exploring the world over, does he still love people?

"What's the reason to live if you don't love people?" he says. "You could hate, despise some bastards—but I've been in 94 countries, and I think the majority of humanity is wonderful."

He pauses.

"Unfortunately," he says, "the minority is much better organized."

Anthony Wilson-Smith (review date 12 June 1995)

SOURCE: "Russian Roue," in *Maclean's*, June 12, 1995, pp. 60-62.

[*In the following review, Wilson-Smith assesses the literary merits of* Don't Die before You're Dead, *concentrating on characterization and thematic emotion.*]

If Yevgeny Yevtushenko did not exist, another author might have invented him as the central character in one of those sweeping epics that Russian writers adore. The problem would be that, as a work of fiction, Yevtushenko's real life strains credulity. A literary superstar in Russia since his teens, he attracts stadium crowds of up to 30,000 for his poetry readings. He moonlights as an actor, director, screenwriter and political activist. And his passion for life includes filling significant parts of it in the company of women and good wine. Appropriately for someone whose achievements seem larger than life, he is, at six feet, three inches, larger than most people around him, dresses in an eclectic, electric manner that would do the lead singer of a rock band proud, and, with his famous piercing blue eyes undimmed at age 61, has just as much stage presence. As befits someone who has spent close to half a century being acclaimed, Yevtushenko has an ego in keeping with his achievements. "I am the spiritual grandchild of Pushkin," he says, cheerfully likening himself to the man generally regarded as Russia's greatest writer.

Sometimes, although not always, the quality of Yevtushenko's writing approaches the level of such a claim. As a poet, his work has ranged from the sublime, such as his 1961 epic **"Babi Yar"**–dealing with Russian and German anti-Semitism during the war—to the incomprehensible, including much of the work he did in the 1970s. Yevtushenko himself once cheerfully declared that his poetry is 70-per-cent "garbage" and 30-per-cent "OK." His new book, ***Don't Die Before You're Dead,*** marks a turn to prose. It also lives up to another of Yevtushenko's asser-

tions–that he reflects Russia's troubled soul. "People may like this book, or they may not," he said in the course of a recent two-hour interview in Toronto. "Either way, they should accept that it represents Russia the way it is."

On one level, its title reflects Yevtushenko's concern that Russians, inured to a life of constant fear and deprivation during the worst years of the old Soviet Union, often die a spiritual death before their physical one. It is also the advice that "Boat," the book's most vivid character, gives to her sometime lover, a former soccer star named Prokhor (Lyza) Zalyzin. Sprawling, bombastic, occasionally overwrought, and filled with black humor, ***Don't Die Before You're Dead*** sweeps through daily life in the former Soviet Union from the Second World War until the early 1990s. In the process, Yevtushenko evokes a dizzying and often brilliant panoply of emotions and characters. All are instantly recognizable to anyone familiar with the alternately challenging and deadening qualities of everyday existence in Russia.

The central event of the book is the brief real-life coup of August, 1991, by a group of hard-line Communists disenchanted with the reform policies of then-President Mikhail Gorbachev. Their object was to restore the Soviet Union to its former status as a world power: in fact, more than anyone else, they hastened its dissolution.

But Yevtushenko spends little time investigating the event's historical importance. Rather, it serves as a backdrop and catalyst for the manner in which ordinary people confront an extraordinary event. The record is mixed: those who joined current Russian President Boris Yeltsin in resisting the *putsch* ranged from Yevtushenko himself and other favored figures in the old Soviet regime to smugglers, black market operators and those motivated by little more than a keen eye for the main chance. At the time of the coup, Yevtushenko writes, the country was, in the balance, "divided into three countries. One was frightened and wanted to return to yesterday. The second did not yet know what tomorrow would be like, but did not want to return to yesterday. The third was waiting."

Much of the public discussion of the book so far has centred on Yevtushenko's portraits of such figures as Gorbachev, former Soviet Foreign Affairs Minister Eduard Shevardnadze and President Boris Yeltsin. They are written in a breezy manner that combines some psycho-babble, such as speculation on the forces that affected Gorbachev early in life, with an easy mix of anecdote and insight that reflects the intimate access Yevtushenko had to top levels of the Soviet leadership. Yevtushenko remains, overall, a fan of all three men, despite the fact that he declined a medal from Yeltsin last year as a protest against Russian army behavior in Chechnya. "Yeltsin," he says, "is a good axe, but we need a jewel, not an axe, now." Yevtushenko also confesses regret over the breakup of the Soviet Union, "not for what it was, but for the brotherhood of different groups that it could have been."

Yevtushenko's closeness with former Soviet leaders also serves as a reminder of the suspicions that some Russians still harbor towards him. That resentment is based on the fact that he lived a privileged life in the former regime even while presenting himself as one of its most ardent internal critics. Of that, Yevtushenko says wearily, "people should look at my record. They cannot say I only pretended to criticize when the record shows so clearly that I spoke against bad policies very publicly many times."

The real charm of *Don't Die Before You're Dead,* and Yevtushenko's strength as a writer, lies in the skill with which he reflects the contradictory elements that vie for control of the Russian soul. The book's most enduring and endearing figures are both fictional: the middle-aged, disillusioned and alcoholic Zalyzin, and Boat, an earthy and physically imposing woman whose determination and strength of character only emphasize Zalyzin's weaknesses, and the paradox of her devotion to him. Her nickname derives from her promise to be "the boat that is always waiting for you." Still, their relationship is ultimately doomed: in less skillful hands than Yevtushenko's, their story would be soppy. But the author knows his characters too well to allow that, and their relationship is all the more compelling for the fact that he emphasizes their flaws. Yevtushenko, who has been married for nine years to his fourth wife, Masha, a physician (they have two children), says that Zalyzin "is really me." And Boat "is a woman who loved me madly, and who I did not have the good sense to love back until it was too late."

Other fictional characters include Stepan Palchikov, a Moscow police officer who joins the side of the coup resisters. He is a classic figure in detective fiction: the weary cop who buries himself in his job to hide from a disintegrating marriage. Yevtushenko himself also appears, in first person, recalling his role in the events. Few other authors would have the cheek to include themselves not once, but in two different characters, in the same book.

With his fondness for epic tragedy and layered prose, and his eagerness to mine the depths of the Russian soul, Yevtushenko is an obvious heir to a literary tradition of mega-page gloom and doom that extends back to such figures as Dostoyevsky and Pushkin. But Yevtushenko is a highly contradictory man. Despite the despair that suffuses some of his writing, he maintains a huge appetite for life. His angry impatience with the swift passing of time is coupled with concern over how much is left him. "I hate death as a monster which swallows us," he says. "I pray and pray every day that I will get at least 25 more years of life. With that, I could direct 10 more films, write five more novels."

He now spends half of each year teaching Russian studies at the University of Tulsa in Oklahoma, describing himself as "the ultimate citizen of the world." Considering that he speaks fluent English, French and Spanish as well as Russian, and that his work has been translated into more than 70 different languages, that may be true. And he delights in recounting the fact that American author John Steinbeck, shortly before his death, predicted to Yevtushenko, then known only as a poet, that he would one day become known as "a great writer of prose." "You see?" says Yevtushenko, after a great swallow from a glass of Burgundy wine, "I must have more time, to fulfil my destiny, and Steinbeck's prediction." He says that his sequel to this book, which he has already started writing, will be called *Don't Die After You're Dead.* And Yevtushenko hopes to take that advice personally.

Alessandra Stanley (review date 12 November 1995)

SOURCE: "Yevtushenko's Revolution," in *The New York Times Book Review,* November 12, 1995, p. 53.

[*In the following review, Stanley situates* Don't Die Before You're Dead *in a contemporary Russian literary and social context, addressing the relevance of Yevtushenko's literary art.*]

It can take a while, but success and fame in Russia are always punished eventually. Throughout the 1960's, 70's and 80's and even up until the moment the statues of Lenin came tumbling down, Yevgeny Yevtushenko was the Russian "superpoet," worshiped by millions. They packed soccer stadiums to hear him recite his ringing, defiant verse, and in the West he was lionized for his talent and extravagant charm. Mr. Yevtushenko's stature was so inviolable it daunted even the KGB, which skittered between intimidation and clumsy attempts to flatter and co-opt him.

These days an iron curtain of indifference surrounds the 62-year-old Mr. Yevtushenko in his own country. He still has fans, particularly in the provinces, but the editors, artists and politicians who used to fawn on him and celebrate his every word have stonily turned away. He no longer fills soccer stadiums. His latest novel was barely reviewed at home.

Don't Die Before You're Dead, Mr. Yevtushenko's account of the August 1991 coup, well translated by Antonia W. Bouis, is nominally about the redemption of those Russians who shook off their fear and passivity and flocked to the barricades to defend democracy against Communist hard-liners. But at its core the novel represents Mr. Yevtushenko's stubborn struggle to keep his career alive in a society that wants to bury him quietly in the past tense.

To recapture those fleeing readers, Mr. Yevtushenko has abandoned the form that made him famous, perhaps because poetry, once venerated, has slipped out of fashion; he has nimbly made the transition to prose, producing writing dipped both in magic realism and the kind of social satire perfected by Gogol.

Readers familiar with the writer's unstinting self-regard will not be disappointed. The "author's note" in the English edition of the novel includes a compliment he received from John Steinbeck after his *Precocious Autobiography* was published in 1963: "You know, perhaps in some future encyclopedia they will write about you as a prose writer who began as a celebrated poet." A more fainthearted writer would have persuaded a friend to write the introduction.

Don't Die Before Dying is a semi-autobiographical tale, blending historical fact and fiction, and meshing the lives of fictional ordinary people—a soccer has-been, an eccentric female Siberian rock climber, a police detective, a plumber—with some of the best-known personalities of the coup: Boris N. Yeltsin and Mikhail S. Gorbachev, some of the plotters of the coup and a great poet—himself.

Mr. Yevtushenko refers to himself and his fictional characters by name, but perhaps too whimsically devises transparent pseudonyms for the real ones: the Human Cello for Mstislav Rostropovich, the Global Georgian for Eduard Shevardnadze, the former Soviet Foreign Minister, now the leader of Georgia. His proletarian fictional characters are weird and beguiling. The personal lives of the public figures are strangely familiar, and described in repetitive fashion. All are emotionally torn, secretly haunted by past sins and acts of omission that cloud their ability to act.

The KGB general who at the last minute orders his elite Alpha troops to disobey orders to fire on Boris Yeltsin's White House is prompted to do so by guilty memories of his role in Afghanistan. Tiptoeing into Mikhail Gorbachev's innermost thoughts while he is under house arrest in Crimea, Mr. Yevtushenko discovers dueling Gorbachevs: the "Peasant Son," a closet rebel who can't forget or forgive the arrest of his grandfathers during collectivization, at war with the "Occupied Kid" who has become the "Rising *Apparatchik*" and closes his eyes to brutality in his quest for power.

Even the hero of the coup, Mr. Yeltsin, is haunted by his decision to obey Kremlin orders when he was the party boss in Sverdlovsk (formerly and now Yekaterinburg) in 1977

by razing the Ipatyev House, where the Czar and his family had been murdered in 1918, and which had over the years become a shrine for intellectuals, religious believers and opponents of the Communist regime. As he sits in his dacha, preparing to return to Moscow and stare down the tanks, Mr. Yeltsin is visited by the ghost of the slain Grand Duchess Olga, who whispers her last poems into his ear.

Perhaps because even to American readers these men's personalities are well known, their inner children exhaustively drawn out for us by the likes of Gail Sheehy and Barbara Walters, they are less intriguing than the troubled men and women Mr. Yevtushenko has invented.

The one famous figure who is free of any remorse or self-blame is Mr. Yevtushenko. During the Soviet period, he did not step over the line from defiance to resistance, and was able to secure a measure of official sanction—and privilege—that more daring dissidents came to resent. Mr. Yevtushenko does not examine the ambiguities of his almost unique position.

Tossed into his warm, rushing narrative are thin, icy bursts of righteous indignation about the envy and ingratitude of fellow writers. "I tried not to think badly of him and I'm still trying now," he writes of a younger poet he calls Akhmatova's Favorite, who bad-mouthed him in New York and who resembles Joseph Brodsky. "But he could never forgive me for the jacket I offered him out of simple kindness."

But the strongest emotion painted by Mr. Yevtushenko is sorrow. Poets helped tear down the Soviet state, yet one of the most bitter consequences of the collapse of the Soviet Union is that while Communism still thrives in Russia, poetry is in a deep decline. Russia has tired of heroes, but Mr. Yevtushenko was one of his generation's most soaring voices. As a young man, he had the courage to denounce anti-Semitism in the famous poem **"Babi Yar"** and the Soviet system in *The Heirs of Stalin*; he craftily defied the regime when so many of his peers meekly played along. *Don't Die Before You're Dead* does not have the reach or power of his earlier works, but these are not passionate times. Mr. Yevtushenko still has much to say. Perhaps American readers will listen more generously to him than his fellow countrymen do.

Lesley Chamberlain (review date 17 November 1995)

SOURCE: A review of *Don't Die Before You're Dead*, in *Times Literary Supplement*, November 17, 1995, p. 27.

[*In the following review, Chamberlain appreciates the vi-*

tality and balance of the account of the 1991 Russian putsch in Don't Die Before You're Dead.]

Yevgeny Yevtushenko is a household name in Russia, where his poetry has entered the language. His ability to survive in a position of privilege through four decades of Soviet life has, however, so damaged his moral reputation that a few years ago his enemies burnt him in effigy. It is a mark of his professionalism as a writer that this novel [***Don't Die before You're Dead***], in which he appears as a character, does not reduce to an apologia. It is a vast, emotionally satisfying tableau of Russian lives rooted in fear.

In August 1991, the world held its breath for three days when Gorbachev was under house arrest in the Crimea and Yeltsin stood on a tank outside the Moscow White House, defending democracy. This is an account of what it felt like to be on the scene, fighting and hoping. The vivid characters include a python and a clockwork toy. Even the python drags her history with her, an image of a typical dialectic of freedom and imprisonment, trust and terror. A drink-sodden ex-football star and the woman he should have married twenty-five years before represent the resilience of human nature. A policeman and some key players in the *putsch* are caught, less happily, in the embrace of politics. Then there is "Yevtushenko" himself, happy, famous, a poet, yet viewed with suspicion and hostility. By the weaving of fact and fiction, all these characters meet together, either on the balcony of the White House or in the surging crowd below.

Poetry is also a character. A Russian lady from Paris, a White poet who fled the Revolution and happens to be visiting Moscow at this new historic hour, offers a short, anti-Hegelian philosophy of history: "History is a living creature and susceptible to influences. Don't instill in history a fear of itself, the feeling of being doomed to blood and crime. So many writers have done that. The hell with them!" Yevtushenko's prose is bright and unselfconscious. His novel is strikingly even-handed. The re-creations of those, like Gorbachev, whom many Russians now hold to be arch-villains, are rounded and humane. Nor is there any mumbo-jumbo about Mother Russia.

Lawrence Hansen (review date 11 January 1996)

SOURCE: A review of the *Babi Yar Symphony*, in *American Record Guide*, January 11, 1996, pp. 174-5.

[*In the following review, Hansen highlights the musical significance of literary allusions to* Babi Yar *in an audio recording of Shostakovich's symphonic version of the poem.*]

Can there be a body of music more suited than Shostakovich's to sum up the 20th Century? This music is angry, violent, bitter, biting, depressive, ugly, coarse, brutal, sardonic, haunted, enigmatic, gloomy, desperate, terrified, sentimental, brooding, ironic, and always fiercely emotional under the bleak surface. So how can it be that I am willing to suggest that he is our century's greatest symphonist, when I have often in these pages ground the ax that the primary purpose of music is to create beauty and take us to a level of consciousness beyond the ordinary world? Can it be that beauty is a rather difficult commodity to create from thin air in a century whose main contribution to history is the perfection of the technology to commit atrocities on a scale only dreamt of in nightmares by previous ages? In the controversial set of memoirs compiled by Solomon Volkov that may or may not be from Shostakovich's mouth, Shostakovich is supposed to have stated on one occasion that each of his works is a tombstone, a monument to some unhappy soul forcibly torn from this life too soon and often in the most unspeakable manner. If we keep that in mind, we can look at Shostakovich's symphonies as a series of lamentations for what has been lost, an extended threnody for a world shorn of beauty, love, compassion, kindness, and fundamental humanity. After Hitler and Stalin, the Bomb and MAD, Bosnia and O.J., a belief in the perfectibility of mankind is pretty untenable if not outright absurd. The human race is not inexorably evolving to a greater state of perfection. It has just as easily devolved into forms of barbarism that no other species of the animal kingdom has ever remotely approximated. Could that be Heaven around the next corner . . . or some new Hell?

I've been immersing myself in *Babi Yar* for some weeks now, and I suppose it shows. One doesn't walk away from this symphony or its successor in an upbeat frame of mind. I wouldn't recommend listening to it after a bad day at work. In the process, I've made a survey of just about all of the readily available CD recordings—Masur (Teldec), Kamu (Chandos), Rostropovich (Erato), Haitink (Philips)—and I can say that the work is very well represented on discs. Despite the stiff competition, the Solti recording is a welcome addition. Perhaps taking its cue from Masur—whose concert recording includes an over-the-top reading by Yevtushenko himself of the opening poem, **"Babi Yar,"** followed by a newly written, post-Soviet poem called **"The Loss"**—London has had the good sense to engage actor Anthony Hopkins to recite the poems, much in the same way RCA added a reciter to Previn's old recording of the Vaughan Williams *Sea Symphony*. It works very well, but I wonder why the poems for the last three movements are read as a clump after II (fear of upsetting the musical flow?). But you can program it otherwise.

Even more than in the average vocal symphony, the text of

"Babi Yar" is the key to the whole work. The opening poem, about the Nazi slaughter of hundreds of thousands of Soviet Jews outside of Kiev in 1941, is really the jumping-off point for an extended criticism of the Soviet system. The composer uses the Babi Yar tragedy as an introductory analogy for the Stalinist reign of terror over all Russians, Jewish or otherwise. This was rather daring stuff even in the early 1960s, and the poems, let alone the symphony, could not have been performed in public 10 or even 5 years before. IV, called "Fears", given Shostakovich's characteristic Largo marking, is the heart of the work, reaching a devastating climax at 9:20 in a performance that carries terrifying weight and oppressive force in Solti's hands. The poem is called **"Fears"**:

> Fears are dying out in Russia . . . I remember when they were powerful and mighty at the court of the lie triumphant . . . All this seems remote today. It is even strange to remember now. The secret fear of an anonymous denunciation, the secret fear of a knock at the door. Yes, and the fear of speaking to foreigners? Foreigners? . . . even to your own wife! I see new fears dawning: the fear of being untrue to one's country, the fear of dishonestly debasing ideas which are self-evident truths: the fear of boasting oneself into a stupor . . . And while I am writing these lines, at times unintentionally hurrying, I write haunted by the single fear of not writing with all my strength.

It is as if the composer and poet say with a sad ironic half-smile, "This is the way it used to be, but of course now it doesn't happen anymore". The audience at the premiere must have ruefully savored the bitter irony. Yevtushenko's texts are not all dark and oppressive—there is sardonic humor, defiance, even outright silliness in places—and Shostakovich's music reflects and magnifies the impact of the words. The work is a universal masterpiece, because it speaks not only to those who suffered in Stalinist Russia but to anybody who recognizes the pervasive evil of oppression and tyranny and its many forms, even in a "free" society like our own.

Solti, the Chicago Symphony, and the superb chorus are an ideal combination for this work. The brutal, vicious parts have a magnificent wild energy, and the sullen rebellion lurking under the surface of the slow movements never conceals the powerful emotion fueling it all. Yet they are still able to convey the lighter, almost frivolous quality of portions of the finale. Close comparisons with the recent Masur are unavoidable, but Solti and the CSO edge out the Teldec issue in just about every major category. The CSO's brass have the truly sepulchral, guttural, Russian sound so vital to this symphony. For comparison, listen to the tavern episode in I. Solti gives us focused, biting, malevolent energy and whip-crack precision where Masur is rather

soggy and weak. Or the climax of the movement at "Nyet! Eta ledokhod!" with its stentorian, ponderous brass bellowings rising over shrieking, terrified strings and woodwinds and a fusillade of thunderous percussion. Solti makes the episode shattering, where Masur merely indicates for the listener that there is some sort of important dramatic event in progress. Masur's soloist, Sergei Leiferkus, is no mean vocalist, but his voice is too lightweight for the music. Aleksashkin, on the other hand, has the rich, sonorous, dark chocolate roar reminiscent of a Christoff or Ghiaurov in their prime.

One continues to be impressed and gratified by what borders on an artistic rebirth in the Indian Summer of Solti's career. For most of the 1980s he seemed to settle into the late-career revisiting of a handful of favorite works typical of many great conductors. But he is too restless, too exploratory a conductor to settle for that. He needs new music and new challenges for his remarkable energy, and Shostakovich has supplied that kind of stimulus. In the album notes, Sir George commented on his belated discovery of this work and Shostakovich's music as a whole: "I didn't know much about his life . . . I didn't trust what I heard, and everything that was Stalinism was suspect: so I didn't want to touch it. Until I heard the *Fifth Symphony* and that made a strong impression on me. I thought 'That must be genuine, because there is so much oppression in the piece, such a real, hopeless, Moussorgskian oppression. That cannot be a political fake, it is real'. I felt I had to do this symphony now. I will do all that I can to show what a musical masterpiece it is, and what a glorious partnership there is between Shostakovich and Yevtushenko . . . I feel it's my duty to do it. And of course duty is not enough . . . It should be as good as possible. That's the duty." Sir George, don't worry: you've fulfilled your duty and then some.

Phoebe-Lou Adams (review date February 1996)

SOURCE: A review of *Don't Die before You're Dead*, in *The Atlantic Monthly*, Vol. 277, No. 2, February 1996, pp. 113-14.

[*In the following review, Adams comments on the vivid narrative techniques of* Don't Die before You're Dead.]

Mr. Yevtushenko's exciting novel [**Don't Die before You're Dead**] about the 1991 attempt to overthrow Mikhail Gorbachev's government puts the reader right on the barricades along with the author. It throws together personal observation, real and imaginary characters, actual and fictional events, satire and tragedy, past and present, prose and poetry. The fictional characters include an honest, and therefore disaffected, policeman, an émigré poet returned from Paris, and a former soccer star fallen into drunken decay. The real characters, with the exception of Gorbachev, Boris Yeltsin, and the author, are given generic names such as 'the Crystal-Clear Communist' and 'the Great Degustator.' The fictional characters permit the author to portray aspects of Soviet society such as the expatriate literary colony in Paris and the future of superannuated athletes. The soccer player provides some superb comedy—a ludicrous teenage drinking party and a tournament in which a team of creaky but wily veterans tries to lose at least one game to its generous but inept local hosts. The dazzling variety of effects in Mr. Yevtushenko's semi-history winds down with a wistful poem, **'Goodbye Our Red Flag,'** and a postscript denouncing the war in Chechnya: 'Now Russia is nowhere—between the past and the future. Nevertheless that is better than ending up behind the barbed wire of the past. Maturity is measured by the number of lost illusions.'

Mary Wade Burnside (essay date 28 March 1996)

SOURCE: "Well Versed," in *Charleston (West Virginia) Gazette,* March 28, 1996, p. 1D.

[*In the following essay, Burnside provides an overview of Yevtushenko's literary career in comparison to contemporary and past writers and themes.*]

When a friend took Yevgeny Yevtushenko to Babi Yar, the site near Kiev where the Nazis massacred more than 30,000 Jews in two days, he felt enraged. Not only at the thought of what the Nazis had done, but also at how the site stood barren, as if nothing had ever happened there.

Moved by what he saw as a "dumpy ravine" holding "so many bones of innocent people," the Soviet poet picked up a pen and wrote his own monument [**"Babi Yar"**], a response to an act that led him to both reproach anti-Semites and declare his Russian ancestry.

"It's a miracle how quickly I wrote it," he said during a telephone interview from Queens College in Forest Hills, N.Y, where he has been teaching poetry. "As many poems are, it was already written by someone, and I just used my hand to write it."

In 1961, the Siberian native, who grew up both in his own homeland as well as in Moscow published the poem **"Babi Yar"** to much acclaim. He even appeared on the cover of *Time* magazine in 1962. Already allowed to travel abroad,

the events secured his reputation and turned Yevtushenko into a chic literary figure during the turbulent '60s.

More than 30 years later Yevtushenko will appear in Charleston, where he will read **"Babi Yar"** in his typically vivid and stirring manner to a limited audience . . . at the University of Charleston. Later . . . , he will lecture and give dramatic readings before . . . [a] reception during an event titled "From Russia With Love."

The evening also features a show of sketches by a friend of Yevtushenko's, author Kurt Vonnegut. William Plumley, a professor of English, will play a taped interview with Vonnegut during the event.

Yevtushenko's dramatic recitations come naturally to someone who learned poetry at the knee of his father, a man who emphasized not only the written word but also the way someone speaks it. "My father gave me a wonderful example," the poet said.

It should come as no surprise that Yevtushenko has a flair for performance considering his other endeavors: he wrote the screenplay of the artistically acclaimed 1964 film *I Am Cuba,* and he has directed two movies.

As an internationally known poet, Yevtushenko came to know author Vonnegut. The two developed rapport as they hosted one another in their respective countries.

"We met very often in beloved flea markets in New York. It's a place of my childhood when I was singing in flea markets during the Second World War as a child," Yevtushenko said.

That conflict also had an immense impact on Vonnegut, who fought in the war and was captured by German troops during the Battle of the Bulge.

Vonnegut's time as a prisoner in Dresden, during the American bombing of the city known for the manufacture of china and as a center for arts, affected him immensely and served as the subject for one of his most famous novels, *Slaughterhouse Five,* which Yevtushenko cites as his favorite book by his friend.

In a telephone interview from his New York City apartment, Vonnegut said he had never discussed the war with Yevtushenko. "But it comes through in his poems," Vonnegut said. "He is as American as I am."

In fact, Yevtushenko's loyalties have always been in question. While Alexandr Solzehnitsyn retreated to the hills of Vermont and physicist Andrei Sakharov lived in internal exile, Yevtushenko traveled freely, supporting a kinder brand of Communism and trying to establish a link between the U.S. and the U.S.S.R.

In the 1960s, Yevtushenko held court with both Robert F. Kennedy and Fidel Castro, the latter of whom he admired greatly until the poet decided power had changed him. "It is very disappointing what happened," Yevtushenko said.

He also tells a story of how Kennedy once asked him to step into a bathroom and turned on the shower in order to hold a private conversation. The senator told the poet how the U.S. government surreptitiously had turned in two double agents to the Kremlin, an event that resulted in a controversial public trial.

When Yevtushenko asked the senator why the government would do such a thing, the poet recalls Kennedy's reply: "Because our people wanted to take advantage of the situation, and your people took the bait. Because of Vietnam, our standing has begun to diminish both at home and abroad. We needed a propaganda counterweight."

Yevtushenko has spent his life fighting for more of a balance between the two superpowers and trying to prove that his country was not always treated fairly. Right up to the collapse of the Soviet Union, as Hollywood continued to release *Rambo* movies and *Red Dawn* Red Threat films, Yevtushenko issued press statements calling for a boycott on such "warnography."

"I'm not an enemy of hamburgers, but if we will learn the best from the West, and refuse the worst of the West, that could be the best way," he said. "The West could learn a lot from Russia too. For instance, our love of poetry."

In Russia, Yevtushenko notes, he appears on a weekly, half-hour television show reading poetry. On the other hand, he notes how only in America has he been allowed to work as a professor because he was expelled from school in his homeland.

"Here, officials permit me to teach, but, paradoxically, in Russia, because Russian bureaucracy is very strong and I have no diploma, I couldn't teach."

All during Yevtushenko's reign as a leading poet, he has battled rumors on both sides—that he was too supportive of Communism, that he was becoming too chummy with his Western friends.

In 1972, during a public reading in St. Paul, Minn., Ukrainian natives attacked him—either because of the anger fostered by **"Babi Yar,"** or because they resented the hard-line Communism being waged back home, depending on which account one reads.

"Paradoxically, what they didn't know was that months before, I pulled a Ukrainian nationalist from prison," he said. "It was not easy to continue this fight."

When asked about rumors of his comfortable apartment he kept in Moscow during the height of housing shortages in the U.S.S.R., plus the dacha he visited out in the country, the generally affable Yevtushenko turns agitated as well as a bit melodramatic.

"I'm asked so much about it in the West," he said. "Sometimes I have the impression you all would be very comfortable if I lived in a puddle of my own blood."

Although he does not compare his work to that of the great Russian poet Alexander Pushkin, he considers their plights similar:

"He was accused to be too much of a free thinker by the government, and by extremist liberals he was accused not to be enough provocative in his poetry and not to be enough challenging," Yevtushenko said.

"But Pushkin understood that if poetry sometimes provokes riots that each riot against injustice could be transformed into new bloodshed and injustice."

Yevtushenko sympathizes with his artistic countryman Dimitri Shostakovich, who also earned the disapproval of the Stalin-led government. Apparently, the feeling was mutual. One day in 1962, the composer called Yevtushenko and asked if he could set **"Babi Yar"** to music.

"I said, 'Why do you ask me? Of course you have my permission to compose music.' And he replied, 'Thank you for your kindness. Could you come over? The music is ready.' We became friends."

Yevtushenko has read **"Babi Yar"** during several performances of Shostakovich's piece, *Symphony No. 13*, which the poet calls "the best monument to Babi Yar."

Before Yevtushenko and Vonnegut ever met, the American author's stepson had a chance encounter with the poet in South America.

Vonnegut will recount the story via a taped interview about how his stepson served a stint in the Peace Corps in Peru and decided to "go home the hard way" on a boat, down the Rio Negro River; which connects with the Amazon.

One night, he and his friends had a party. A man saw the boat flying an American flag and stopped to chat. As Vonnegut's son prepared to leave, the man announced, "I am the poet Yevtushenko. Have you heard of me?"

"And my son said, 'Yes, of course,' because he was a world figure by then," Vonnegut recalled. "And Yevtushenko said, 'I will give you a name for your boat—you should call it *The Huckleberry Finn.*"

The story offers a few ironies. Mark Twain serves as a link to both Vonnegut and Yevtushenko. Vonnegut has been compared to him. And Yevtushenko often pays Twain a literary debt, along with Walt Whitman, to whom he often has been compared and whose sense of a yearning for an ideal society the poet admires.

"I have very deep peasant roots, and because I was in a village, I figure if I could be something like a strange mixture of Walt Whitman and Robert Frost—that's what I'm trying to do," said the poet.

He uses his fondness for Whitman to illustrate the line he walks between the two countries where he makes his homes.

"I didn't like socialism in our version, but I don't think capitalism in today's version is ideal. I'm trying to put the seeds in my poetry for another kind of society. I don't know the name of this society, but this society would not repeat the crime and mistakes of both these systems. I think Walt Whitman is close to this philosophy."

These days, Yevtushenko shuttles between Russia and the United States, teaching and giving poetry readings. He has a house in Tulsa, Okla., where he settled his wife and two young sons because he likes the place.

"I admire this little city," he said. "Many Americans say 'How can you like this boring, Bible Belt city?' But I didn't find it boring. I feel the people are very warm here."

As someone who wants to change society with his poetry, he looks for how the written word can act as a link. He recalls seeing two black women on the subway reading graffiti, which happened to be in the form of a poem by Anna Akhanotova, "one of our great poets."

"One of them asked me, 'Do you know who she is?' and I said, 'Of course I know. I am Russian,' and she said, 'Are you kidding?'"

Yevtushenko remembers the poem in Russian but has trouble translating the words to English. "It is about the power of compassion and about how easy it·is to suffer and how difficult it is to share somebody's suffering."

The poet also recalls spending time in Colorado at a cowboy poetry gathering, which he calls "the best poetry festival in America."

"We think about cowboys in cliche, like John Wayne-style of cowboy, but I never supposed I could sit down at the table and sip beer and talk with professional American cowboys about Tolstoy, Chekov, and Dostoevsky."

As for the momentous changes in the land of his birth, Yevtushenko supported the reforms made by former Communist leader Mikhail Gorbachev as well as his eventual political demise. Now he notes wryly instead of an Iron Curtain, his compatriots face what he calls a "green curtain," or a lack of money.

But, always optimistic, he looks for the plight of his country to improve, not regress. This, in spite of a looming presidential election in June, in which incumbent Boris Yeltsin will be challenged by both Communists and by ultranationalist Vladimir Zhirinovsky, the Pat Buchanan of Russia.

"You know one thing—Russia will not come back into Stalin's past," he said. "I do not want to play the dubious role of a fortuneteller; but this is what I believe. I'm not happy to imitate any other kind of capitalist society. We are a different country and we have to find our own way."

Ewa M. Thompson　(review date 6 July 1996)

SOURCE: A review of *Don't Die before You're Dead*, in *America*, Vol. 175, No. 1, July 6, 1996, pp. 34-5.

[*In the following review, Thompson pans* Don't Die before You're Dead, *charging Yevtushenko with obfuscating historical realities.*]

Between the cold-blooded planners of Soviet strategy, on the one hand, and those who adamantly refused to participate in the Soviet enterprise, on the other, there has always been enough crawl space to accommodate people like Yevgeny Yevtushenko, a Russian poet and court dissident during the Krushchev and Brezhnev years. His first novel [*Don't Die before You're Dead*] depicts the ups and downs of Gorbachev's perestroika and its aftermath, the Yeltsin years. It is written in a style reminiscent of John Dos Passos, and its "newsreel" chapters are replete with flash-blacks and split personalities. Borrowings from Russian writers likewise abound. The plot unfolds over a period of three days, recalling a similar schedule in Dostoevsky's *The Brothers Karamazov.* The author's effort to portray representatives of all social classes recalls Doctor Zhivago's chaotic panorama of Russian life. Gorbachev's internal monologue imitates the musings of Stalin in Solzhenitsyn's *The First Circle.* In a characteristic detail showing Yevtushenko's proclivity to edit history, Gorbachev is nowhere called "First Secretary" but rather "Mr. President." This is reminiscent of the Soviet habit of removing from history books inconvenient facts and faces. The book piles up bits of dialogue and internal monologue, usually too articulate for the character in question, like a huge salad of questionable freshness.

Chapter One of **Don't Die Before You're Dead** begins with the adventures of a certain Palchikov who is so devoted to his KGB tasks that his wife, complaining of neglect, leaves him. They are happily reunited in the end. A raucous Moscow youth vomits all over his aunt's apartment but eventually becomes a famous soccer player. His youthful love, a girl from Siberia nicknamed Boat, a mountain climber by profession, meets her death while climbing a chimney during the 1991 putsch. Her goal is to save Gorbachev, and her beloved Lyza (the soccer player) joins her in that effort. Yevtushenko himself is present, piping over his good fortune and pointing out that he has often brushed shoulders with the almighty, indeed has almost become Gorbachev's personal friend.

Assorted generals, artists, prime ministers and leaders also make their appearance. Hardly anyone among the Russians is depicted as evil; at worst, they are just confused. In a remarkable passage, Yevtushenko assures us that Russian generals "are not evil men . . . and they do not intend to kill anyone." (Tell that to the Chechens.)

The Russian political players of recent years are not mentioned by name but by nicknames assigned to them by the author. In addition to the generals and other party members, some of whom evolved into democrats, there appear Rostropovich ("the Human Cello"), Solzhenitsyn ("the Great Camp Inmate"), and Shevardnadze ("the Global Georgian"). But Yevtushenko's portrayal of Zviad Gamsakhurdia, who was elected President of Georgia in 1991, is objectionable. Gamsakhurdia (referred to in the novel as "son of a writer") declared his country independent and then had to flee Russian-inspired insurgents. Significantly, though a Christian, he found shelter among the Muslim Chechens who have likewise been victims of Russian colonialism. Yevtushenko maligns this man by suggesting that "nationalism," "hatred of Russia" and personal vanity were the motivating forces in Gamsakhurdia's rise. Gamsakhurdia died in unexplained circumstances, a pawn in the conflicts so skillfully stirred up by Russians in the Caucasus region to implement the divide *et impera* rule of colonial empires. To speak ill of this victim of Russian Real-politik is grossly tactless.

The colonialist aspect of the Russian enterprise escapes Yevtushenko's attention. The drafting of Tadjik men to settle Russia's internal disputes and forcing them to serve under Russian generals (I am referring to historical events men-

tioned in the novel) are bits of colonial lore that Yevtushenko seems unable to comprehend. It is in episodes like these, rather than in the sophomoric plot or the tired witticisms with which the author sprinkles his narrative, that the book becomes engaging as a document of the latest jingoist stage of Russian nationalist consciousness. In an unselfconscious manner, the author portrays characters from Central Asia and the Caucasus as marginal appendices to Russian history; he speaks of the lands of the Russian Federation as Russian property, even though they include such ethically and territorially distinct entities as Tatarstan, Bashkortostan, Sakha, Tuva and Chechnya.

Thus Yevtushenko's descriptions of historical characters are reminiscent of Stalin's prose style in works such as *Marxism and Problems of Linguistics* (1950), where Stalin's clumsy phrases conveyed to the faithful the absolute knowledge of how language should be understood. Similarly, Yevtushenko's pronouncements — each sentence a separate paragraph — ponderously declare what people are or are not, how they feel and how they behave.

But it is hard to make a drama out of a palace coup. Yevtushenko fails to show that the changes in Russian politics amounted to little more than a reshuffle at the top. While there have been a few genuine attempts to remake Russia into a normal nation-state, very little in recent history indicates that they have borne fruit. Yevtushenko himself remarks that the crowd surrounding the building of the Supreme Soviet in 1991 was exceedingly small, and that the people "remained speechless," to borrow a phrase from Pushkin's *Boris Godunov*. The bitter truth is that in a city of 10 million, only a few thousand showed up to support Yeltsin and his then-democratic program. In view of that, Palchikov's transformation into a democrat and Lyza Zalyzin's and Boat's heroics on behalf of the parliamentary system sound rather exceptional. Unlike the Central Europeans, the Russians did not demonstrate that they craved freedom and were willing to offer freedom to their minorities. Yevtushenko is at pains to obscure that fact.

The narrative reflects the author's belief that Russian belching and sneezing are of interest to Americans just because they are Russian. He may be right. If this tome had been written by a Bulgarian, no American publisher would have touched it. The exaggerated appetite for things Russian that developed during the cold war still allows many Russians to make careers in this country for no good reason.

Allen Linkowski (review date 19 September 1996)

SOURCE: A review of an audio recording of *Babi Yar Sym-*

phony, in *American Record Guide,* September 19, 1996, pp. 202-3.

[*In the following review, Linkowski praises an audio recording of Shostakovich's* Babi Yar Symphony, *detailing its origins in Yevtushenko's poem and its premier performance in 1962.*]

Russian Anti-Semitism is not a well-guarded secret. The Czars had their pogroms and the commissars their purges. Even those who were accomplished in the Arts and Sciences were not free from the ever-present shadow of discrimination. When the doors of the prison finally opened, thousands of Jews fled to new lives in the West. This unthinking racism was not solely the province of the illiterate *mujik,* but also of the intelligencia. Dostoyevsky was a noted hater of Jews. But so then were such composers of beautiful, soulful, romantic music as Balakirev, Moussorgsky, and Tchaikovsky. Even Stravinsky engaged in the fashionable Western European anti-Semitism of his time.

Rimsky-Korsakoff was an exception, and so was Shostakovich, who spoke out against such mindless discrimination. He grew up and worked in the Stalinist period where everyone was a potential victim of a paranoid tyrant. It has recently come out that Stalin had his own "Final Solution" in mind and planned to make his own domain *Judenrein.*

Another artist who was appalled by rampant Russian anti-Semitism was the poet Yevgeny Yevtushenko; and in 1961, barely eight years after Stalin's death, in the clear air of the so-called thaw of the Khrushchev years, wrote a poem **"Babi Yar,"** using the horrible 1941 Nazi massacre of some 34,000 (some have placed the number as high as 100,000) Jewish men, women, and children at the site of a ravine on the outskirts of Kiev as a vehicle to cry out against Russian anti-Semitism.

Shostakovich immediately wanted to set it to music. To make a symphony he added settings of four more Yevtushenko poems: **"Humor,"** a grotesque scherzo praising the immortality of the political joke; **"In the Store,"** illustrating the dreariness of daily Soviet life; **"Fears"** (written by the poet expressly for the symphony), depicting the terror that infiltrated every aspect of existence in the Soviet Union; and **"Careers,"** in praise of those who were true to themselves, often at great financial and personal sacrifice.

Even though **"Babi Yar"** appeared in print without making many waves, the idea of a Shostakovich symphony based on the poem was too much for the authorities to swallow. Mravinsky, scheduled for the premiere, withdrew, allegedly because of government pressure. Yet, as a purported anti-Semite, the great conductor most likely wanted no part of the affair. Kyril Kondrashin, Van Cliburn's favorite Russian conductor, who himself was to emigrate Westward, led the first performance December 18, 1962. The unhappy authorities not only forbade the printing of the text in the concert's program but also cordoned off the entire square in front of the Moscow Conservatory. Though the hall was filled, the official box was empty. The audience response was overwhelming. *Pravda* made a one-line mention of the event, and the government forced Yevtushenko to amend the text of the title poem to memorialize the Russians and Ukrainians who also perished at the site.

Any new recording of this masterpiece is an event, especially one emanating from the former Soviet Union. Saulius Sendeckis, without striving for effect, offers a natural, unforced reading and has a trump card in his soloist. Sergei Baikov sounds as though he is living every word Yevtushenko's poems. I found his performance riveting.

The engineering is very good, but there are no texts or translations. Just a summary of each poem is offered. Outrageous! The meaning of every word is important! My first choice is Kondrashin, recorded in decent stereo at the 1962 premiere (Russian Disc). Of the more recent Western recordings Haitink (London) gets closest to this work and is superbly recorded. Solti's Chicago reading is most effective in the work's more extroverted moments but is spoiled by the interspersed readings of the poems by Anthony Hopkins. Masur disappoints because Sergei Leiferkus lacks the vocal weight this music demands.

Mark Swed (review date 9 November 1996)

SOURCE: "A Concert Stage Too Small for Morality and Art," in *Los Angeles Times,* November 9, 1996, p. 1.

[*In the following review, Swed assesses the viability of composer Shostakovich's symphonic rendition of* Babi Yar, *focusing on the musical presentation of the poem's themes and tones.*]

Shostakovich's *Symphony No. 13* is courageous, moral music. As much a cantata as a symphony, its five movements each set — for bass soloist, male choir and orchestra — a poem by Yevgeny Yevtushenko. The first movement is Shostakovich's somber intoning of **"Babi Yar,"** the dissident poet's famous evocation of Soviet anti-Semitism at a time, 1962, when such topics were possible but still dangerous to express publicly.

The poem **"Babi Yar"** concerns the slaughter of thousands

of Jews by Nazis in 1941 outside Kiev. It and the symphony, which has also come to be known as *Babi Yar,* has meant a great deal to dissident Russians. Yet when Shostakovich's work finally got a hearing in Los Angeles Thursday night for the first time, there was a steady trickle of patrons leaving the Dorothy Chandler Pavilion during the performance. It was well played by the Los Angeles Philharmonic and competently led by Estonian conductor Eri Klas, so that surely was not cause for dissatisfaction.

Nor is it thinkable that the defectors were neo-Nazis or unreformed, '50s-style Soviet agents offended by the symphony's political convictions—civilized society endorses the basic issues of good and evil that are unambiguously spelled out in the score. No, most likely concertgoers were turned off by Shostakovich's preachy tone.

Music is not often successful when it tries to become a moral art. It is music's nasty little truism that something like Wagner's "Die Meistersinger" will always be loved, even though it has elements of blatant anti-Semitism scattered among its outpourings of humanity, while audiences will probably always walk out on Shostakovich's 13th, vitamin-good though it be for us.

The fact is that Wagner's opera is a great work and Shostakovich's symphony is not, and morality cannot compete (it never could) with great art. Shostakovich lays it on with a shovel in the gloomy first movement, but he gets worse as he goes along. The second movement, "Humor," contains the kind of irony in which every sarcasm is underlined, italicized and boldfaced. The last three movements are slow enough so that one is sure to feel the pain of never-ending suffering, but it soon enough feels like whining, although the composer pulls out of it at the end with some very beautiful solo string writing.

Klas led an absolutely firm performance. He is a conductor who values exact playing, a solid exposition of the music's form. His dramatic gestures are big but without exaggeration. He might have been helped, however, by a more dramatic bass than Mikhail Kit, flown in from the Kirov Opera on short notice to replace an indisposed Aage Haugland. Kit is an understated singer, and he seemed uncomfortably swamped by the orchestra and the ringing National Male Choir of Estonia, but in the subdued music at the end he was eloquent.

That choir was the evening's highlight in the first half of the program as it offered six examples of nationalist Estonian music by Mihkel Ludig, Eduard Tubin, Rudolf Tobias, Rudolf Tobias, Tuudur Vettik and Villem Kapp. Only Tubin has become known in the West, but all these composers—whose music ranged from late last century well into our

own—had a certain distinctive quality. They favored unusual sound combinations and offbeat folk-derived harmonies and texts (Tubin's "Two Islanders" concerns a headless hero).

The performances of these works were enthusiastic and winning. But, nice touch as they were, the two halves of the evening felt at odds. How much better it might have been to take the **"Babi Yar"** theme further and pair it with the ferocious orchestral piece of that name by Steve Martland, the uppity and controversial young British composer.

The Philharmonic made the Shostakovich further alienating by inviting actor Michael Laskin to read Yevtushenko's poems before the movements of the symphony. Though an effective presence, Laskin missed the point by adopting a lofty, rabbinical tone. Yevtushenko, who read the poems himself recently before a New York Philharmonic performance of the symphony, was so much more effective in his Russian manner, since **"Babi Yar,"** in particular, is meant to convey the reaction of non-Jews to the plight of Jews as a symbol for a more universal persecution. And Shostakovich's symphony needs all the right kind of help it can get on its rare outings.

Sidney C. Schaer (essay date 4 April 1997)

SOURCE: "In His Own Words," in *Newsday,* April 4, 1997, p. A6.

[In the following essay, Schaer reports his impressions of Yevtushenko's public reading of his poetry during a visit to Long Island, New York, providing an overview of the poet's career.]

Yevgeny Yevtushenko sat in the library director's office fidgeting with a pile of his poems, and the words he was murmuring were anything but lyrical: "too much, too much . . . I have to cut it down."

Russia's most famous living poet had come to the Connetquot Public Library in Bohemia, and minutes before he was to appear in the library's community room, he was hastily winnowing out poems from his program and concluding his rehearsal with his translator. "Is there a crowd out there?" he asked.

At 63, Yevtushenko is a poet with a long history, who in his own country could fill a Moscow soccer stadium with poetry lovers. But on Wednesday, he was wondering how he would play in a medium-sized community library that draws on 40,000 residents who live in Ronkonkoma, Oakdale and Bohemia, an area of diverse population but not crammed with people who could be expected to understand a poet reading his words in Russian.

But when he strode onto the tiny stage, accompanied by his former student John O'Donnell, who would provide English translations, Yevtushenko found a filled room.

"You never know where you are going to find good readers," he said. He is widely regarded as Russia's most popular post-Stalinist poet, with an international reputation earned more than 30 years ago with the publication of his 1961 **"Babii Yar,"** an angry condemnation of anti-Semitism in the Soviet Union that recalled the horrors of thousands of Jews being slaughtered in a ravine near Kiev.

Born in Siberia at a small lumber station made famous in his early poem **"Zima Junction,"** Yevtushenko spent his youth mostly in Moscow. His first book of poetry was published in 1952, but eventually his poetry would begin questioning the Stalinist era and challenging socialist doctrine. He was an early dissident, attacking the Soviet Union's invasion of Czechoslovakia in 1968 and helping promote former President Mikhail Gorbachev's effort to promote openness known as glasnost. He is, along with being a poet, a novelist and filmmaker, but while sitting and sipping tea in the library's small kitchen, he attacked intellectual snobbery.

"You will find sophisticated readers in unexpected places, such as the cowboy who came with his family to one of my readings in Elko, Nevada, and brought all eighteen editions of my poetry," he said.

Yevtushenko, a tenured professor on leave from Queens College, is dividing his time between Russia and the United States. He spends summers in Moscow and the rest of the year in Oklahoma, where he is a visiting professor at the University of Tulsa, teaching classes in poetry and cinema.

Yevtushenko, fairly fluent in English, seemed much more comfortable reciting in Russian.

And when the library's adult-program director, Inez Horwitz, saw one of his performances last year at an East End synagogue, she immediately thought he might be a candidate to recite his poems at her library.

"He didn't think it was a strange idea," she said, after having tracked him down in Tulsa. When they agreed on a fee, he happily came east for a long weekend with his wife, Maria.

"I was amazed he would appear at a little library in Suffolk," said Maria Beitch, a student teacher at Sayville High School who grew up in Moscow.

Wednesday would turn out to be a long day. He arrived at LaGuardia [airport] a little past 1 p.m., and before coming to the library, he fulfilled a lifelong dream of visiting the birthplace of Walt Whitman, one of his poet heroes.

"We are both children of great spaces," he told a small gathering at the poet's birthplace in West Hills, "and we are all from Whitman's womb." He ended up buying a first-edition facsimile of *Leaves of Grass,* while trying to find out how many books Whitman sold in his lifetime.

Eventually, he got to Connetquot, and by 7:30 p.m., all 250 seats were filled in a room decorated with wall-sized murals of children's fairy tales such as Snow White and the Wizard of Oz. In the audience were teachers, lawyers, the curious, and a dozen members of the Sayville High School Russian club, who came en masse and afterward waited for him to personalize their volumes of his poetry, including a new edition the library allowed him to sell that evening.

Yevtushenko, for his part, may have decided what poems would play in Bohemia, but when he scanned the audience, he discovered an old friend, Vera S. Dunham, of Port Jefferson, one of his translators.

And so halfway through, he added a poem she has translated into English, the 1966 **"Dwarf Birches,"** which metaphorically talks about the courage of dissident poetry and the struggle to stay alive in such in an inhospitable world "like splinters, under the nails of frosts."

Yevtushenko recited his poetry with a flamboyance of an actor given a fabulous part to play, and when it was over, he had danced across the stage and into the audience for nearly 90 minutes.

Describing himself as a "old poet, but a young novelist," he opened the program reading from a work-in-progress novella about his childhood in war-torn Russia in 1941, followed by 10 poems, old and new, including the classic **"Babii Yar,"** with the lines: " . . . Here all things scream silently, and baring my head, slowly I feel myself turning gray. And I myself am one massive, soundless scream above the thousand thousand buried here."

But it was his presentation of a new poem, **"New York Taxis,"** that seemed to resonate with the audience.

"What is astounding about Zhenia [a diminutive for Yevgeny] is his ability to communicate," Dunham said. "He is a great performer, but he seems capable of crossing all cultures, and with all that, he also has depth and courage, and people feel that."

FURTHER READING

Biography

Van Blema, David. "Yevgeny Yevtushenko." *People Weekly* (31 March 1986): 70-7, 75-7.

Incorporates Yevtushenko's commentary during a visit to New York City, providing an overview of his life and career.

Criticism

Bayley, John. "Poet of the Appropriate." *Times Literary Supplement* (14 June 1991): 3.

Discusses the public nature of Yevtushenko's poetry and essays in *The Collected Poems* and *Fatal Half Measures.*

Brown, Clarence F. "Ashes and Crumbs." *Times Literary Supplement* (7 January 1994): 8.

Reviews the selection and organization of *Twentieth Century Russian Poetry,* disputing factual information and calling the anthology "a mess."

Lloyd, John. "Perestroika and Its Discontents." *London Review of Books* (11 July 1991): 12.

Questions the sincerity of Yevtushenko's political motives as represented in *Fatal Half Measures.*

Mano, D. Keith. "Yevtushenko." *National Review* (17 July 1987): 53-5.

Outlines the literary and cultural significance of Yevtushenko's career.

Yevtushenko, Yevgeny. "A Poet's View of *Glasnost.*" *Time* (9 February 1987): 32-3.

Offers Yevtushenko's views of the social and political changes under Gorbachev's rule.

Interview

Vanden Heuvel, Katrina. "Yevtushenko Feels a Fresh Wind Blowing." *Progressive* (24 April 1987): 24-31.

Addresses Yevtushenko's views on Russian politics, poetry's public service, glasnost, and relations with the West.

Additional coverage of Yevtushenko's life and career is contained in the following sources published by Gale: *Contemporary Authors,* Vols. 81-84; *Contemporary Authors New Revision Series,* Vols. 33, 54; *DISCovering Authors: Poets Module*; *Major Twentieth-Century Writers,* Vol. 1.

☐ Contemporary Literary Criticism

Indexes

**Literary Criticism Series
Cumulative Author Index
Cumulative Topic Index
Cumulative Nationality Index
Title Index, Volume 126**

How to Use This Index

The main references

Camus, Albert
    1913-1960 . . . . . . .CLC 1, 2, 4, 9, 11,
    14, 32, 69; DA; DAB; DAC; DAM
    DRAM, MST, NOV; DC2; SSC 9;
    WLC

list all author entries in the following Gale Literary Criticism series:

BLC = *Black Literature Criticism*
BLCS = *Black Literature Criticism Supplement*
CLC = *Contemporary Literary Criticism*
CLR = *Children's Literature Review*
CMLC = *Classical and Medieval Literature Criticism*
DA = *DISCovering Authors*
DAB = *DISCovering Authors: British*
DAC = *DISCovering Authors: Canadian*
DAM = *DISCovering Authors Modules*
  DRAM = *dramatists;* *MST* = *most-studied*
  authors; *MULT* = *multicultural authors;* *NOV* =
  novelists; *POET* = *poets;* *POP* = *popular/genre*
  writers; *DC* = *Drama Criticism*
HLC = *Hispanic Literature Criticism*
LC = *Literature Criticism from 1400 to 1800*
NCLC = *Nineteenth-Century Literature Criticism*
PC = *Poetry Criticism*
SSC = *Short Story Criticism*
TCLC = *Twentieth-Century Literary Criticism*
WLC = *World Literature Criticism, 1500 to the Present*
WLCS = *World Literature Criticism Supplement*

The cross-references

See also CA 89-92; DLB 72; MTCW

list all author entries in the following Gale biographical and literary sources:

AAYA = *Authors & Artists for Young Adults*
AITN = *Authors in the News*
BEST = *Bestsellers*
BW = *Black Writers*
CA = *Contemporary Authors*
CAAS = *Contemporary Authors Autobiography Series*
CABS = *Contemporary Authors Bibliographical Series*
CANR = *Contemporary Authors New Revision Series*
CAP = *Contemporary Authors Permanent Series*
CDALB = *Concise Dictionary of American Literary Biography*
CDBLB = *Concise Dictionary of British Literary Biography*

DLB = *Dictionary of Literary Biography*
DLBD = *Dictionary of Literary Biography Documentary Series*
DLBY = *Dictionary of Literary Biography Yearbook*
HW = *Hispanic Writers*
JRDA = *Junior DISCovering Authors*
MAICYA = *Major Authors and Illustrators for Children and Young Adults*
MTCW = *Major 20th-Century Writers*
NNAL = *Native North American Literature*
SAAS = *Something about the Author Autobiography Series*
SATA = *Something about the Author*
YABC = *Yesterday's Authors of Books for Children*

SSC 1; WLC
See also AAYA 30; CA 104; 121; CANR 61;
CDALB 1917-1929; DA3; DLB 4, 9, 86;
DLBD 1; MTCW 1, 2

Andier, Pierre
See Desnos, Robert

Andouard
See Giraudoux, (Hippolyte) Jean

Andrade, Carlos Drummond de   **CLC 18**
See also Drummond de Andrade, Carlos

Andrade, Mario de 1893-1945   **TCLC 43**

Andreae, Johann V(alentin) 1586-1654 **LC 32**
See also DLB 164

Andreas-Salome, Lou 1861-1937   **TCLC 56**
See also CA 178; DLB 66

Andress, Lesley
See Sanders, Lawrence

Andrewes, Lancelot 1555-1626   **LC 5**
See also DLB 151, 172

Andrews, Cicily Fairfield
See West, Rebecca

Andrews, Elton V.
See Pohl, Frederik

Andreyev, Leonid (Nikolaevich) 1871-1919
TCLC 3
See also CA 104

Andric, Ivo 1892-1975   **CLC 8; SSC 36**
See also CA 81-84; 57-60; CANR 43, 60; DLB
147; MTCW 1

Androvar
See Prado (Calvo), Pedro

Angelique, Pierre
See Bataille, Georges

Angell, Roger 1920-   **CLC 26**
See also CA 57-60; CANR 13, 44, 70; DLB 171,
185

Angelou, Maya 1928- **CLC 12, 35, 64, 77; BLC
1; DA; DAB; DAC; DAM MST, MULT,
POET, POP; WLCS**
See also AAYA 7, 20; BW 2, 3; CA 65-68;
CANR 19, 42, 65; CDALBS; CLR 53; DA3;
DLB 38; MTCW 1, 2; SATA 49

Anna Comnena 1083-1153   **CMLC 25**

Annensky, Innokenty (Fyodorovich) 1856-1909
TCLC 14
See also CA 110; 155

Annunzio, Gabriele d'
See D'Annunzio, Gabriele

Anodos
See Coleridge, Mary E(lizabeth)

Anon, Charles Robert
See Pessoa, Fernando (Antonio Nogueira)

Anouilh, Jean (Marie Lucien Pierre) 1910-1987
CLC 1, 3, 8, 13, 40, 50; DAM DRAM; DC 8
See also CA 17-20R; 123; CANR 32; MTCW
1, 2

Anthony, Florence
See Ai

Anthony, John
See Ciardi, John (Anthony)

Anthony, Peter
See Shaffer, Anthony (Joshua); Shaffer, Peter
(Levin)

Anthony, Piers 1934-   **CLC 35; DAM POP**
See also AAYA 11; CA 21-24R; CANR 28, 56,
73; DLB 8; MTCW 1, 2; SAAS 22; SATA 84

Anthony, Susan B(rownell) 1916-1991 **TCLC 84**
See also CA 89-92; 134

Antoine, Marc
See Proust, (Valentin-Louis-George-Eugene-)
Marcel

Antoninus, Brother
See Everson, William (Oliver)

Antonioni, Michelangelo 1912-   **CLC 20**
See also CA 73-76; CANR 45, 77

Antschel, Paul 1920-1970
See Celan, Paul
See also CA 85-88; CANR 33, 61; MTCW 1

Anwar, Chairil 1922-1949   **TCLC 22**
See also CA 121

Anzaldua, Gloria 1942-
See also CA 175; DLB 122; HLCS 1

Apess, William 1798-1839(?) **NCLC 73; DAM
MULT**
See also DLB 175; NNAL

Apollinaire, Guillaume 1880-1918 **TCLC 3, 8,
51; DAM POET; PC 7**
See also Kostrowitzki, Wilhelm Apollinaris de
See also CA 152; MTCW 1

Appelfeld, Aharon 1932-   **CLC 23, 47**
See also CA 112; 133; CANR 86

Apple, Max (Isaac) 1941-   **CLC 9, 33**
See also CA 81-84; CANR 19, 54; DLB 130

Appleman, Philip (Dean) 1926-   **CLC 51**
See also CA 13-16R; CAAS 18; CANR 6, 29,
56

Appleton, Lawrence
See Lovecraft, H(oward) P(hillips)

Apteryx
See Eliot, T(homas) S(tearns)

Apuleius, (Lucius Madaurensis) 125(?)-175(?)
CMLC 1
See also DLB 211

Aquin, Hubert 1929-1977   **CLC 15**
See also CA 105; DLB 53

Aquinas, Thomas 1224(?)-1274   **CMLC 33**
See also DLB 115

Aragon, Louis 1897-1982 **CLC 3, 22; DAM
NOV, POET**
See also CA 69-72; 108; CANR 28, 71; DLB
72; MTCW 1, 2

Arany, Janos 1817-1882   **NCLC 34**

Aranyos, Kakay
See Mikszath, Kalman

Arbuthnot, John 1667-1735   **LC 1**
See also DLB 101

Archer, Herbert Winslow
See Mencken, H(enry) L(ouis)

Archer, Jeffrey (Howard) 1940-   **CLC 28;
DAM POP**
See also AAYA 16; BEST 89:3; CA 77-80;
CANR 22, 52; DA3; INT CANR-22

Archer, Jules 1915-   **CLC 12**
See also CA 9-12R; CANR 6, 69; SAAS 5;
SATA 4, 85

Archer, Lee
See Ellison, Harlan (Jay)

Arden, John 1930- **CLC 6, 13, 15; DAM DRAM**
See also CA 13-16R; CAAS 4; CANR 31, 65,
67; DLB 13; MTCW 1

Arenas, Reinaldo 1943-1990 **CLC 41; DAM
MULT; HLC 1**
See also CA 124; 128; 133; CANR 73; DLB
145; HW 1; MTCW 1

Arendt, Hannah 1906-1975   **CLC 66, 98**
See also CA 17-20R; 61-64; CANR 26, 60;
MTCW 1, 2

Aretino, Pietro 1492-1556   **LC 12**

Arghezi, Tudor 1880-1967   **CLC 80**
See also Theodorescu, Ion N.
See also CA 167

Arguedas, Jose Maria 1911-1969 **CLC 10, 18;
HLCS 1**
See also CA 89-92; CANR 73; DLB 113; HW 1

Argueta, Manlio 1936-   **CLC 31**
See also CA 131; CANR 73; DLB 145; HW 1

Arias, Ron(ald Francis) 1941-
See also CA 131; CANR 81; DAM MULT; DLB
82; HLC 1; HW 1, 2; MTCW 2

Ariosto, Ludovico 1474-1533   **LC 6**

Aristides
See Epstein, Joseph

Aristophanes 450B.C.-385B.C. **CMLC 4; DA;
DAB; DAC; DAM DRAM, MST; DC 2;
WLCS**
See also DA3; DLB 176

Aristotle 384B.C.-322B.C.   **CMLC 31; DA;
DAB; DAC; DAM MST; WLCS**
See also DA3; DLB 176

Arlt, Roberto (Godofredo Christophersen)
1900-1942 **TCLC 29; DAM MULT; HLC 1**
See also CA 123; 131; CANR 67; HW 1, 2

Armah, Ayi Kwei 1939- **CLC 5, 33; BLC 1;
DAM MULT, POET**
See also BW 1; CA 61-64; CANR 21, 64; DLB
117; MTCW 1

Armatrading, Joan 1950-   **CLC 17**
See also CA 114

Arnette, Robert
See Silverberg, Robert

**Arnim, Achim von (Ludwig Joachim von
Arnim)** 1781-1831   **NCLC 5; SSC 29**
See also DLB 90

Arnim, Bettina von 1785-1859   **NCLC 38**
See also DLB 90

Arnold, Matthew 1822-1888 **NCLC 6, 29; DA;
DAB; DAC; DAM MST, POET; PC 5;
WLC**
See also CDBLB 1832-1890; DLB 32, 57

Arnold, Thomas 1795-1842   **NCLC 18**
See also DLB 55

Arnow, Harriette (Louisa) Simpson 1908-1986
CLC 2, 7, 18
See also CA 9-12R; 118; CANR 14; DLB 6;
MTCW 1, 2; SATA 42; SATA-Obit 47

Arouet, Francois-Marie
See Voltaire

Arp, Hans
See Arp, Jean

Arp, Jean 1887-1966   **CLC 5**
See also CA 81-84; 25-28R; CANR 42, 77

Arrabal
See Arrabal, Fernando

Arrabal, Fernando 1932-   **CLC 2, 9, 18, 58**
See also CA 9-12R; CANR 15

Arreola, Juan Jose 1918-
See also CA 113; 131; CANR 81; DAM MULT;
DLB 113; HLC 1; HW 1, 2

Arrick, Fran   **CLC 30**
See also Gaberman, Judie Angell

Artaud, Antonin (Marie Joseph) 1896-1948
TCLC 3, 36; DAM DRAM
See also CA 104; 149; DA3; MTCW 1

Arthur, Ruth M(abel) 1905-1979   **CLC 12**
See also CA 9-12R; 85-88; CANR 4; SATA 7,
26

Artsybashev, Mikhail (Petrovich) 1878-1927
TCLC 31
See also CA 170

Arundel, Honor (Morfydd) 1919-1973 **CLC 17**
See also CA 21-22; 41-44R; CAP 2; CLR 35;
SATA 4; SATA-Obit 24

Arzner, Dorothy 1897-1979   **CLC 98**

Asch, Sholem 1880-1957   **TCLC 3**
See also CA 105

Ash, Shalom
See Asch, Sholem

Ashbery, John (Lawrence) 1927- **CLC 2, 3, 4,
6, 9, 13, 15, 25, 41, 77, 125; DAM POET;**

PC 26
See also CA 5-8R; CANR 9, 37, 66; DA3; DLB 5, 165; DLBY 81; INT CANR-9; MTCW 1, 2

Ashdown, Clifford
See Freeman, R(ichard) Austin

Ashe, Gordon
See Creasey, John

Ashton-Warner, Sylvia (Constance) 1908-1984 **CLC 19**
See also CA 69-72; 112; CANR 29; MTCW 1, 2

Asimov, Isaac 1920-1992 **CLC 1, 3, 9, 19, 26, 76, 92; DAM POP**
See also AAYA 13; BEST 90:2; CA 1-4R; 137; CANR 2, 19, 36, 60; CLR 12; DA3; DLB 8; DLBY 92; INT CANR-19; JRDA; MAICYA; MTCW 1, 2; SATA 1, 26, 74

Assis, Joaquim Maria Machado de
See Machado de Assis, Joaquim Maria

Astley, Thea (Beatrice May) 1925- **CLC 41**
See also CA 65-68; CANR 11, 43, 78

Aston, James
See White, T(erence) H(anbury)

Asturias, Miguel Angel 1899-1974 **CLC 3, 8, 13; DAM MULT, NOV; HLC 1**
See also CA 25-28; 49-52; CANR 32; CAP 2; DA3; DLB 113; HW 1; MTCW 1, 2

Atares, Carlos Saura
See Saura (Atares), Carlos

Atheling, William
See Pound, Ezra (Weston Loomis)

Atheling, William, Jr.
See Blish, James (Benjamin)

Atherton, Gertrude (Franklin Horn) 1857-1948 **TCLC 2**
See also CA 104; 155; DLB 9, 78, 186

Atherton, Lucius
See Masters, Edgar Lee

Atkins, Jack
See Harris, Mark

Atkinson, Kate **CLC 99**
See also CA 166

Attaway, William (Alexander) 1911-1986 **CLC 92; BLC 1; DAM MULT**
See also BW 2, 3; CA 143; CANR 82; DLB 76

Atticus
See Fleming, Ian (Lancaster); Wilson, (Thomas) Woodrow

Atwood, Margaret (Eleanor) 1939- **CLC 2, 3, 4, 8, 13, 15, 25, 44, 84; DA; DAB; DAC; DAM MST, NOV, POET; PC 8; SSC 2; WLC**
See also AAYA 12; BEST 89:2; CA 49-52; CANR 3, 24, 33, 59; DA3; DLB 53; INT CANR-24; MTCW 1, 2; SATA 50

Aubigny, Pierre d'
See Mencken, H(enry) L(ouis)

Aubin, Penelope 1685-1731(?) **LC 9**
See also DLB 39

Auchincloss, Louis (Stanton) 1917- **CLC 4, 6, 9, 18, 45; DAM NOV; SSC 22**
See also CA 1-4R; CANR 6, 29, 55; DLB 2; DLBY 80; INT CANR-29; MTCW 1

Auden, W(ystan) H(ugh) 1907-1973 **CLC 1, 2, 3, 4, 6, 9, 11, 14, 43; DA; DAB; DAC; DAM DRAM, MST, POET; PC 1; WLC**
See also AAYA 18; CA 9-12R; 45-48; CANR 5, 61; CDBLB 1914-1945; DA3; DLB 10, 20; MTCW 1, 2

Audiberti, Jacques 1900-1965 **CLC 38; DAM DRAM**
See also CA 25-28R

Audubon, John James 1785-1851 **NCLC 47**

Auel, Jean M(arie) 1936- **CLC 31, 107; DAM POP**
See also AAYA 7; BEST 90:4; CA 103; CANR 21, 64; DA3; INT CANR-21; SATA 91

Auerbach, Erich 1892-1957 **TCLC 43**
See also CA 118; 155

Augier, Emile 1820-1889 **NCLC 31**
See also DLB 192

August, John
See De Voto, Bernard (Augustine)

Augustine 354-430 **CMLC 6; DA; DAB; DAC; DAM MST; WLCS**
See also DA3; DLB 115

Aurelius
See Bourne, Randolph S(illiman)

Aurobindo, Sri
See Ghose, Aurabinda

Austen, Jane 1775-1817 **NCLC 1, 13, 19, 33, 51, 81; DA; DAB; DAC; DAM MST, NOV; WLC**
See also AAYA 19; CDBLB 1789-1832; DA3; DLB 116

Auster, Paul 1947- **CLC 47**
See also CA 69-72; CANR 23, 52, 75; DA3; MTCW 1

Austin, Frank
See Faust, Frederick (Schiller)

Austin, Mary (Hunter) 1868-1934 **TCLC 25**
See also CA 109; 178; DLB 9, 78, 206

Averroes 1126-1198 **CMLC 7**
See also DLB 115

Avicenna 980-1037 **CMLC 16**
See also DLB 115

Avison, Margaret 1918- **CLC 2, 4, 97; DAC; DAM POET**
See also CA 17-20R; DLB 53; MTCW 1

Axton, David
See Koontz, Dean R(ay)

Ayckbourn, Alan 1939- **CLC 5, 8, 18, 33, 74; DAB; DAM DRAM**
See also CA 21-24R; CANR 31, 59; DLB 13; MTCW 1, 2

Aydy, Catherine
See Tennant, Emma (Christina)

Ayme, Marcel (Andre) 1902-1967 **CLC 11**
See also CA 89-92; CANR 67; CLR 25; DLB 72; SATA 91

Ayrton, Michael 1921-1975 **CLC 7**
See also CA 5-8R; 61-64; CANR 9, 21

Azorin **CLC 11**
See also Martinez Ruiz, Jose

Azuela, Mariano 1873-1952 **TCLC 3; DAM MULT; HLC 1**
See also CA 104; 131; CANR 81; HW 1, 2; MTCW 1, 2

Baastad, Babbis Friis
See Friis-Baastad, Babbis Ellinor

Bab
See Gilbert, W(illiam) S(chwenck)

Babbis, Eleanor
See Friis-Baastad, Babbis Ellinor

Babel, Isaac
See Babel, Isaak (Emmanuilovich)

Babel, Isaak (Emmanuilovich) 1894-1941(?) **TCLC 2, 13; SSC 16**
See also CA 104; 155; MTCW 1

Babits, Mihaly 1883-1941 **TCLC 14**
See also CA 114

Babur 1483-1530 **LC 18**

Baca, Jimmy Santiago 1952-
See also CA 131; CANR 81; DAM MULT; DLB 122; HLC 1; HW 1, 2

Bacchelli, Riccardo 1891-1985 **CLC 19**
See also CA 29-32R; 117

Bach, Richard (David) 1936- **CLC 14; DAM NOV, POP**
See also AITN 1; BEST 89:2; CA 9-12R; CANR 18; MTCW 1; SATA 13

Bachman, Richard
See King, Stephen (Edwin)

Bachmann, Ingeborg 1926-1973 **CLC 69**
See also CA 93-96; 45-48; CANR 69; DLB 85

Bacon, Francis 1561-1626 **LC 18, 32**
See also CDBLB Before 1660; DLB 151

Bacon, Roger 1214(?)-1292 **CMLC 14**
See also DLB 115

Bacovia, George **TCLC 24**
See also Vasiliu, Gheorghe
See also DLB 220

Badanes, Jerome 1937- **CLC 59**

Bagehot, Walter 1826-1877 **NCLC 10**
See also DLB 55

Bagnold, Enid 1889-1981 **CLC 25; DAM DRAM**
See also CA 5-8R; 103; CANR 5, 40; DLB 13, 160, 191; MAICYA; SATA 1, 25

Bagritsky, Eduard 1895-1934 **TCLC 60**

Bagrjana, Elisaveta
See Belcheva, Elisaveta

Bagryana, Elisaveta 1893-1991 **CLC 10**
See also Belcheva, Elisaveta
See also CA 178; DLB 147

Bailey, Paul 1937- **CLC 45**
See also CA 21-24R; CANR 16, 62; DLB 14

Baillie, Joanna 1762-1851 **NCLC 71**
See also DLB 93

Bainbridge, Beryl (Margaret) 1933- **CLC 4, 5, 8, 10, 14, 18, 22, 62; DAM NOV**
See also CA 21-24R; CANR 24, 55, 75; DLB 14; MTCW 1, 2

Baker, Elliott 1922- **CLC 8**
See also CA 45-48; CANR 2, 63

Baker, Jean H. **TCLC 3, 10**
See also Russell, George William

Baker, Nicholson 1957- **CLC 61; DAM POP**
See also CA 135; CANR 63; DA3

Baker, Ray Stannard 1870-1946 **TCLC 47**
See also CA 118

Baker, Russell (Wayne) 1925- **CLC 31**
See also BEST 89:4; CA 57-60; CANR 11, 41, 59; MTCW 1, 2

Bakhtin, M.
See Bakhtin, Mikhail Mikhailovich

Bakhtin, M. M.
See Bakhtin, Mikhail Mikhailovich

Bakhtin, Mikhail
See Bakhtin, Mikhail Mikhailovich

Bakhtin, Mikhail Mikhailovich 1895-1975 **CLC 83**
See also CA 128; 113

Bakshi, Ralph 1938(?)- **CLC 26**
See also CA 112; 138

Bakunin, Mikhail (Alexandrovich) 1814-1876 **NCLC 25, 58**

Baldwin, James (Arthur) 1924-1987 **CLC 1, 2, 3, 4, 5, 8, 13, 15, 17, 42, 50, 67, 90; BLC 1; DA; DAB; DAC; DAM MST, MULT, NOV, POP; DC 1; SSC 10, 33; WLC**
See also AAYA 4; BW 1; CA 1-4R; 124; CABS 1; CANR 3, 24; CDALB 1941-1968; DA3; DLB 2, 7, 33; DLBY 87; MTCW 1, 2; SATA 9; SATA-Obit 54

Ballard, J(ames) G(raham) 1930- **CLC 3, 6, 14, 36; DAM NOV, POP; SSC 1**
See also AAYA 3; CA 5-8R; CANR 15, 39, 65;

DA3; DLB 14, 207; MTCW 1, 2; SATA 93

Balmont, Konstantin (Dmitriyevich) 1867-1943
TCLC 11
See also CA 109; 155

Baltausis, Vincas
See Mikszath, Kalman

Balzac, Honore de 1799-1850 **NCLC 5, 35, 53;
DA; DAB; DAC; DAM MST, NOV; SSC
5; WLC**
See also DA3; DLB 119

Bambara, Toni Cade 1939-1995 **CLC 19, 88;
BLC 1; DA; DAC; DAM MST, MULT;
SSC 35; WLCS**
See also AAYA 5; BW 2, 3; CA 29-32R; 150;
CANR 24, 49, 81; CDALBS; DA3; DLB 38;
MTCW 1, 2

Bamdad, A.
See Shamlu, Ahmad

Banat, D. R.
See Bradbury, Ray (Douglas)

Bancroft, Laura
See Baum, L(yman) Frank

Banim, John 1798-1842 **NCLC 13**
See also DLB 116, 158, 159

Banim, Michael 1796-1874 **NCLC 13**
See also DLB 158, 159

Banjo, The
See Paterson, A(ndrew) B(arton)

Banks, Iain
See Banks, Iain M(enzies)

Banks, Iain M(enzies) 1954- **CLC 34**
See also CA 123; 128; CANR 61; DLB 194;
INT 128

Banks, Lynne Reid **CLC 23**
See also Reid Banks, Lynne
See also AAYA 6

Banks, Russell 1940- **CLC 37, 72**
See also CA 65-68; CAAS 15; CANR 19, 52,
73; DLB 130

Banville, John 1945- **CLC 46, 118**
See also CA 117; 128; DLB 14; INT 128

Banville, Theodore (Faullain) de 1832-1891
NCLC 9

Baraka, Amiri 1934- **CLC 1, 2, 3, 5, 10, 14, 33,
115; BLC 1; DA; DAC; DAM MST, MULT,
POET, POP; DC 6; PC 4; WLCS**
See also Jones, LeRoi
See also BW 2, 3; CA 21-24R; CABS 3; CANR
27, 38, 61; CDALB 1941-1968; DA3; DLB
5, 7, 16, 38; DLBD 8; MTCW 1, 2

Barbauld, Anna Laetitia 1743-1825 **NCLC 50**
See also DLB 107, 109, 142, 158

Barbellion, W. N. P. **TCLC 24**
See also Cummings, Bruce F(rederick)

Barbera, Jack (Vincent) 1945- **CLC 44**
See also CA 110; CANR 45

Barbey d'Aurevilly, Jules Amedee 1808-1889
NCLC 1; SSC 17
See also DLB 119

Barbour, John c. 1316-1395 **CMLC 33**
See also DLB 146

Barbusse, Henri 1873-1935 **TCLC 5**
See also CA 105; 154; DLB 65

Barclay, Bill
See Moorcock, Michael (John)

Barclay, William Ewert
See Moorcock, Michael (John)

Barea, Arturo 1897-1957 **TCLC 14**
See also CA 111

Barfoot, Joan 1946- **CLC 18**
See also CA 105

Barham, Richard Harris 1788-1845 **NCLC 77**
See also DLB 159

Baring, Maurice 1874-1945 **TCLC 8**
See also CA 105; 168; DLB 34

Baring-Gould, Sabine 1834-1924 **TCLC 88**
See also DLB 156, 190

Barker, Clive 1952- **CLC 52; DAM POP**
See also AAYA 10; BEST 90:3; CA 121; 129;
CANR 71; DA3; INT 129; MTCW 1, 2

Barker, George Granville 1913-1991 **CLC 8,
48; DAM POET**
See also CA 9-12R; 135; CANR 7, 38; DLB
20; MTCW 1

Barker, Harley Granville
See Granville-Barker, Harley
See also DLB 10

Barker, Howard 1946- **CLC 37**
See also CA 102; DLB 13

Barker, Jane 1652-1732 **LC 42**

Barker, Pat(ricia) 1943- **CLC 32, 94**
See also CA 117; 122; CANR 50; INT 122

Barlach, Ernst (Heinrich) 1870-1938 **TCLC 84**
See also CA 178; DLB 56, 118

Barlow, Joel 1754-1812 **NCLC 23**
See also DLB 37

Barnard, Mary (Ethel) 1909- **CLC 48**
See also CA 21-22; CAP 2

Barnes, Djuna 1892-1982 **CLC 3, 4, 8, 11, 29;
SSC 3**
See also CA 9-12R; 107; CANR 16, 55; DLB
4, 9, 45; MTCW 1, 2

Barnes, Julian (Patrick) 1946- **CLC 42; DAB**
See also CA 102; CANR 19, 54; DLB 194;
DLBY 93; MTCW 1

Barnes, Peter 1931- **CLC 5, 56**
See also CA 65-68; CAAS 12; CANR 33, 34,
64; DLB 13; MTCW 1

Barnes, William 1801-1886 **NCLC 75**
See also DLB 32

Baroja (y Nessi), Pio 1872-1956 **TCLC 8; HLC
1**
See also CA 104

Baron, David
See Pinter, Harold

Baron Corvo
See Rolfe, Frederick (William Serafino Austin
Lewis Mary)

Barondess, Sue K(aufman) 1926-1977 **CLC 8**
See also Kaufman, Sue
See also CA 1-4R; 69-72; CANR 1

Baron de Teive
See Pessoa, Fernando (Antonio Nogueira)

Baroness Von S.
See Zangwill, Israel

Barres, (Auguste-) Maurice 1862-1923 **TCLC
47**
See also CA 164; DLB 123

Barreto, Afonso Henrique de Lima
See Lima Barreto, Afonso Henrique de

Barrett, (Roger) Syd 1946- **CLC 35**

Barrett, William (Christopher) 1913-1992
CLC 27
See also CA 13-16R; 139; CANR 11, 67; INT
CANR-11

Barrie, J(ames) M(atthew) 1860-1937 **TCLC
2; DAB; DAM DRAM**
See also CA 104; 136; CANR 77; CDBLB 1890-
1914; CLR 16; DA3; DLB 10, 141, 156;
MAICYA; MTCW 1; SATA 100; YABC 1

Barrington, Michael
See Moorcock, Michael (John)

Barrol, Grady
See Bograd, Larry

Barry, Mike
See Malzberg, Barry N(athaniel)

Barry, Philip 1896-1949 **TCLC 11**
See also CA 109; DLB 7

Bart, Andre Schwarz
See Schwarz-Bart, Andre

Barth, John (Simmons) 1930- **CLC 1, 2, 3, 5, 7,
9, 10, 14, 27, 51, 89; DAM NOV; SSC 10**
See also AITN 1, 2; CA 1-4R; CABS 1; CANR
5, 23, 49, 64; DLB 2; MTCW 1

Barthelme, Donald 1931-1989 **CLC 1, 2, 3, 5, 6,
8, 13, 23, 46, 59, 115; DAM NOV; SSC 2**
See also CA 21-24R; 129; CANR 20, 58; DA3;
DLB 2; DLBY 80, 89; MTCW 1, 2; SATA 7;
SATA-Obit 62

Barthelme, Frederick 1943- **CLC 36, 117**
See also CA 114; 122; CANR 77; DLBY 85;
INT 122

Barthes, Roland (Gerard) 1915-1980 **CLC 24,
83**
See also CA 130; 97-100; CANR 66; MTCW
1, 2

Barzun, Jacques (Martin) 1907- **CLC 51**
See also CA 61-64; CANR 22

Bashevis, Isaac
See Singer, Isaac Bashevis

Bashkirtseff, Marie 1859-1884 **NCLC 27**

Basho
See Matsuo Basho

Basil of Caesaria c. 330-379 **CMLC 35**

Bass, Kingsley B., Jr.
See Bullins, Ed

Bass, Rick 1958- **CLC 79**
See also CA 126; CANR 53; DLB 212

Bassani, Giorgio 1916- **CLC 9**
See also CA 65-68; CANR 33; DLB 128, 177;
MTCW 1

Bastos, Augusto (Antonio) Roa
See Roa Bastos, Augusto (Antonio)

Bataille, Georges 1897-1962 **CLC 29**
See also CA 101; 89-92

Bates, H(erbert) E(rnest) 1905-1974 **CLC 46;
DAB; DAM POP; SSC 10**
See also CA 93-96; 45-48; CANR 34; DA3;
DLB 162, 191; MTCW 1, 2

Bauchart
See Camus, Albert

Baudelaire, Charles 1821-1867 **NCLC 6, 29,
55; DA; DAB; DAC; DAM MST, POET;
PC 1; SSC 18; WLC**
See also DA3

Baudrillard, Jean 1929- **CLC 60**

Baum, L(yman) Frank 1856-1919 **TCLC 7**
See also CA 108; 133; CLR 15; DLB 22; JRDA;
MAICYA; MTCW 1, 2; SATA 18, 100

Baum, Louis F.
See Baum, L(yman) Frank

Baumbach, Jonathan 1933- **CLC 6, 23**
See also CA 13-16R; CAAS 5; CANR 12, 66;
DLBY 80; INT CANR-12; MTCW 1

Bausch, Richard (Carl) 1945- **CLC 51**
See also CA 101; CAAS 14; CANR 43, 61; DLB
130

Baxter, Charles (Morley) 1947- **CLC 45, 78;
DAM POP**
See also CA 57-60; CANR 40, 64; DLB 130;
MTCW 2

Baxter, George Owen
See Faust, Frederick (Schiller)

Baxter, James K(eir) 1926-1972 **CLC 14**
See also CA 77-80

Baxter, John
See Hunt, E(verette) Howard, (Jr.)

Bayer, Sylvia
See Glassco, John

See also BW 2, 3; CA 151; DLB 117
Benson, E(dward) F(rederic) 1867-1940
    TCLC 27
    See also CA 114; 157; DLB 135, 153
Benson, Jackson J. 1930-   **CLC 34**
    See also CA 25-28R; DLB 111
Benson, Sally 1900-1972   **CLC 17**
    See also CA 19-20; 37-40R; CAP 1; SATA 1,
    35; SATA-Obit 27
Benson, Stella 1892-1933   **TCLC 17**
    See also CA 117; 155; DLB 36, 162
Bentham, Jeremy 1748-1832   **NCLC 38**
    See also DLB 107, 158
Bentley, E(dmund) C(lerihew) 1875-1956
    TCLC 12
    See also CA 108; DLB 70
Bentley, Eric (Russell) 1916-   **CLC 24**
    See also CA 5-8R; CANR 6, 67; INT CANR-6
Beranger, Pierre Jean de 1780-1857 **NCLC 34**
Berdyaev, Nicolas
    See Berdyaev, Nikolai (Aleksandrovich)
Berdyaev, Nikolai (Aleksandrovich) 1874-1948
    TCLC 67
    See also CA 120; 157
Berdyayev, Nikolai (Aleksandrovich)
    See Berdyaev, Nikolai (Aleksandrovich)
Berendt, John (Lawrence) 1939-   **CLC 86**
    See also CA 146; CANR 75; DA3; MTCW 1
Beresford, J(ohn) D(avys) 1873-1947 **TCLC 81**
    See also CA 112; 155; DLB 162, 178, 197
Bergelson, David 1884-1952   **TCLC 81**
Berger, Colonel
    See Malraux, (Georges-)Andre
Berger, John (Peter) 1926-   **CLC 2, 19**
    See also CA 81-84; CANR 51, 78; DLB 14, 207
Berger, Melvin H. 1927-   **CLC 12**
    See also CA 5-8R; CANR 4; CLR 32; SAAS 2;
    SATA 5, 88
Berger, Thomas (Louis) 1924-**CLC 3, 5, 8, 11,**
    18, 38; DAM NOV
    See also CA 1-4R; CANR 5, 28, 51; DLB 2;
    DLBY 80; INT CANR-28; MTCW 1, 2
Bergman, (Ernst) Ingmar 1918- **CLC 16, 72**
    See also CA 81-84; CANR 33, 70; MTCW 2
Bergson, Henri(-Louis) 1859-1941 **TCLC 32**
    See also CA 164
Bergstein, Eleanor 1938-   **CLC 4**
    See also CA 53-56; CANR 5
Berkoff, Steven 1937-   **CLC 56**
    See also CA 104; CANR 72
Bermant, Chaim (Icyk) 1929-   **CLC 40**
    See also CA 57-60; CANR 6, 31, 57
Bern, Victoria
    See Fisher, M(ary) F(rances) K(ennedy)
Bernanos, (Paul Louis) Georges 1888-1948
    TCLC 3
    See also CA 104; 130; DLB 72
Bernard, April 1956-   **CLC 59**
    See also CA 131
Berne, Victoria
    See Fisher, M(ary) F(rances) K(ennedy)
Bernhard, Thomas 1931-1989 **CLC 3, 32, 61**
    See also CA 85-88; 127; CANR 32, 57; DLB
    85, 124; MTCW 1
Bernhardt, Sarah (Henriette Rosine) 1844-1923
    TCLC 75
    See also CA 157
Berriault, Gina 1926- **CLC 54, 109; SSC 30**
    See also CA 116; 129; CANR 66; DLB 130
Berrigan, Daniel 1921-   **CLC 4**
    See also CA 33-36R; CAAS 1; CANR 11, 43,
    78; DLB 5

Berrigan, Edmund Joseph Michael, Jr. 1934-
    1983
    See Berrigan, Ted
    See also CA 61-64; 110; CANR 14
Berrigan, Ted   **CLC 37**
    See also Berrigan, Edmund Joseph Michael, Jr.
    See also DLB 5, 169
Berry, Charles Edward Anderson 1931-
    See Berry, Chuck
    See also CA 115
Berry, Chuck   **CLC 17**
    See also Berry, Charles Edward Anderson
Berry, Jonas
    See Ashbery, John (Lawrence)
Berry, Wendell (Erdman) 1934- **CLC 4, 6, 8,**
    27, 46; DAM POET; PC 28
    See also AITN 1; CA 73-76; CANR 50, 73; DLB
    5, 6; MTCW 1
Berryman, John 1914-1972**CLC 1, 2, 3, 4, 6, 8,**
    10, 13, 25, 62; DAM POET
    See also CA 13-16; 33-36R; CABS 2; CANR
    35; CAP 1; CDALB 1941-1968; DLB 48;
    MTCW 1, 2
Bertolucci, Bernardo 1940-   **CLC 16**
    See also CA 106
Berton, Pierre (Francis Demarigny) 1920-
    CLC 104
    See also CA 1-4R; CANR 2, 56; DLB 68; SATA
    99
Bertrand, Aloysius 1807-1841   **NCLC 31**
Bertran de Born c. 1140-1215   **CMLC 5**
Besant, Annie (Wood) 1847-1933   **TCLC 9**
    See also CA 105
Bessie, Alvah 1904-1985   **CLC 23**
    See also CA 5-8R; 116; CANR 2, 80; DLB 26
Bethlen, T. D.
    See Silverberg, Robert
Beti, Mongo **CLC 27; BLC 1; DAM MULT**
    See also Biyidi, Alexandre
    See also CANR 79
Betjeman, John 1906-1984 **CLC 2, 6, 10, 34,**
    43; DAB; DAM MST, POET
    See also CA 9-12R; 112; CANR 33, 56; CDBLB
    1945-1960; DA3; DLB 20; DLBY 84;
    MTCW 1, 2
Bettelheim, Bruno 1903-1990   **CLC 79**
    See also CA 81-84; 131; CANR 23, 61; DA3;
    MTCW 1, 2
Betti, Ugo 1892-1953   **TCLC 5**
    See also CA 104; 155
Betts, Doris (Waugh) 1932- **CLC 3, 6, 28**
    See also CA 13-16R; CANR 9, 66, 77; DLBY
    82; INT CANR-9
Bevan, Alistair
    See Roberts, Keith (John Kingston)
Bey, Pilaff
    See Douglas, (George) Norman
Bialik, Chaim Nachman 1873-1934 **TCLC 25**
    See also CA 170
Bickerstaff, Isaac
    See Swift, Jonathan
Bidart, Frank 1939-   **CLC 33**
    See also CA 140
Bienek, Horst 1930-   **CLC 7, 11**
    See also CA 73-76; DLB 75
Bierce, Ambrose (Gwinett) 1842-1914(?)
    TCLC 1, 7, 44; DA; DAC; DAM MST; SSC
    9; WLC
    See also CA 104; 139; CANR 78; CDALB
    1865-1917; DA3; DLB 11, 12, 23, 71, 74,
    186
Biggers, Earl Derr 1884-1933   **TCLC 65**
    See also CA 108; 153

Billings, Josh
    See Shaw, Henry Wheeler
Billington, (Lady) Rachel (Mary) 1942- **CLC**
    43
    See also AITN 2; CA 33-36R; CANR 44
Binyon, T(imothy) J(ohn) 1936-   **CLC 34**
    See also CA 111; CANR 28
Bioy Casares, Adolfo 1914-1999**CLC 4, 8, 13,**
    88; DAM MULT; HLC 1; SSC 17
    See also CA 29-32R; 177; CANR 19, 43, 66;
    DLB 113; HW 1, 2; MTCW 1, 2
Bird, Cordwainer
    See Ellison, Harlan (Jay)
Bird, Robert Montgomery 1806-1854**NCLC 1**
    See also DLB 202
Birkerts, Sven 1951-   **CLC 116**
    See also CA 128; 133; 176; CAAE 176; CAAS
    29; INT 133
Birney, (Alfred) Earle 1904-1995**CLC 1, 4, 6,**
    11; DAC; DAM MST, POET
    See also CA 1-4R; CANR 5, 20; DLB 88;
    MTCW 1
Biruni, al 973-1048(?)   **CMLC 28**
Bishop, Elizabeth 1911-1979 **CLC 1, 4, 9, 13,**
    15, 32; DA; DAC; DAM MST, POET; PC
    3
    See also CA 5-8R; 89-92; CABS 2; CANR 26,
    61; CDALB 1968-1988; DA3; DLB 5, 169;
    MTCW 1, 2; SATA-Obit 24
Bishop, John 1935-   **CLC 10**
    See also CA 105
Bissett, Bill 1939-   **CLC 18; PC 14**
    See also CA 69-72; CAAS 19; CANR 15; DLB
    53; MTCW 1
Bissoondath, Neil (Devindra) 1955-**CLC 120;**
    DAC
    See also CA 136
Bitov, Andrei (Georgievich) 1937-   **CLC 57**
    See also CA 142
Biyidi, Alexandre 1932-
    See Beti, Mongo
    See also BW 1, 3; CA 114; 124; CANR 81;
    DA3; MTCW 1, 2
Bjarme, Brynjolf
    See Ibsen, Henrik (Johan)
Bjoernson, Bjoernstjerne (Martinius) 1832-
    1910   **TCLC 7, 37**
    See also CA 104
Black, Robert
    See Holdstock, Robert P.
Blackburn, Paul 1926-1971   **CLC 9, 43**
    See also CA 81-84; 33-36R; CANR 34; DLB
    16; DLBY 81
Black Elk 1863-1950 **TCLC 33; DAM MULT**
    See also CA 144; MTCW 1; NNAL
Black Hobart
    See Sanders, (James) Ed(ward)
Blacklin, Malcolm
    See Chambers, Aidan
Blackmore, R(ichard) D(oddridge) 1825-1900
    TCLC 27
    See also CA 120; DLB 18
Blackmur, R(ichard) P(almer) 1904-1965
    CLC 2, 24
    See also CA 11-12; 25-28R; CANR 71; CAP 1;
    DLB 63
Black Tarantula
    See Acker, Kathy
Blackwood, Algernon (Henry) 1869-1951
    TCLC 5
    See also CA 105; 150; DLB 153, 156, 178
Blackwood, Caroline 1931-1996**CLC 6, 9, 100**
    See also CA 85-88; 151; CANR 32, 61, 65; DLB

14, 207; MTCW 1

Blade, Alexander
See Hamilton, Edmond; Silverberg, Robert

Blaga, Lucian 1895-1961 **CLC 75**
See also CA 157

Blair, Eric (Arthur) 1903-1950
See Orwell, George
See also CA 104; 132; DA; DAB; DAC; DAM MST, NOV; DA3; MTCW 1, 2; SATA 29

Blair, Hugh 1718-1800 **NCLC 75**

Blais, Marie-Claire 1939-**CLC 2, 4, 6, 13, 22; DAC; DAM MST**
See also CA 21-24R; CAAS 4; CANR 38, 75; DLB 53; MTCW 1, 2

Blaise, Clark 1940- **CLC 29**
See also AITN 2; CA 53-56; CAAS 3; CANR 5, 66; DLB 53

Blake, Fairley
See De Voto, Bernard (Augustine)

Blake, Nicholas
See Day Lewis, C(ecil)
See also DLB 77

Blake, William 1757-1827 **NCLC 13, 37, 57; DA; DAB; DAC; DAM MST, POET; PC 12; WLC**
See also CDBLB 1789-1832; CLR 52; DA3; DLB 93, 163; MAICYA; SATA 30

Blasco Ibanez, Vicente 1867-1928 **TCLC 12; DAM NOV**
See also CA 110; 131; CANR 81; DA3; HW 1, 2; MTCW 1

Blatty, William Peter 1928-**CLC 2; DAM POP**
See also CA 5-8R; CANR 9

Bleeck, Oliver
See Thomas, Ross (Elmore)

Blessing, Lee 1949- **CLC 54**

Blish, James (Benjamin) 1921-1975 **CLC 14**
See also CA 1-4R; 57-60; CANR 3; DLB 8; MTCW 1; SATA 66

Bliss, Reginald
See Wells, H(erbert) G(eorge)

Blixen, Karen (Christentze Dinesen) 1885-1962
See Dinesen, Isak
See also CA 25-28; CANR 22, 50; CAP 2; DA3; MTCW 1, 2; SATA 44

Bloch, Robert (Albert) 1917-1994 **CLC 33**
See also AAYA 29; CA 5-8R, 179; 146; CAAE 179; CAAS 20; CANR 5, 78; DA3; DLB 44; INT CANR-5; MTCW 1; SATA 12; SATA-Obit 82

Blok, Alexander (Alexandrovich) 1880-1921 **TCLC 5; PC 21**
See also CA 104

Blom, Jan
See Breytenbach, Breyten

Bloom, Harold 1930- **CLC 24, 103**
See also CA 13-16R; CANR 39, 75; DLB 67; MTCW 1

Bloomfield, Aurelius
See Bourne, Randolph S(illiman)

Blount, Roy (Alton), Jr. 1941- **CLC 38**
See also CA 53-56; CANR 10, 28, 61; INT CANR-28; MTCW 1, 2

Bloy, Leon 1846-1917 **TCLC 22**
See also CA 121; DLB 123

Blume, Judy (Sussman) 1938- **CLC 12, 30; DAM NOV, POP**
See also AAYA 3, 26; CA 29-32R; CANR 13, 37, 66; CLR 2, 15; DA3; DLB 52; JRDA; MAICYA; MTCW 1, 2; SATA 2, 31, 79

Blunden, Edmund (Charles) 1896-1974 **C L C 2, 56**
See also CA 17-18; 45-48; CANR 54; CAP 2;

DLB 20, 100, 155; MTCW 1

Bly, Robert (Elwood) 1926-**CLC 1, 2, 5, 10, 15, 38; DAM POET**
See also CA 5-8R; CANR 41, 73; DA3; DLB 5; MTCW 1, 2

Boas, Franz 1858-1942 **TCLC 56**
See also CA 115; 181

Bobette
See Simenon, Georges (Jacques Christian)

Boccaccio, Giovanni 1313-1375 **CMLC 13; SSC 10**

Bochco, Steven 1943- **CLC 35**
See also AAYA 11; CA 124; 138

Bodel, Jean 1167(?)-1210 **CMLC 28**

Bodenheim, Maxwell 1892-1954 **TCLC 44**
See also CA 110; DLB 9, 45

Bodker, Cecil 1927- **CLC 21**
See also CA 73-76; CANR 13, 44; CLR 23; MAICYA; SATA 14

Boell, Heinrich (Theodor) 1917-1985 **CLC 2, 3, 6, 9, 11, 15, 27, 32, 72; DA; DAB; DAC; DAM MST, NOV; SSC 23; WLC**
See also CA 21-24R; 116; CANR 24; DA3; DLB 69; DLBY 85; MTCW 1, 2

Boerne, Alfred
See Doeblin, Alfred

Boethius 480(?)-524(?) **CMLC 15**
See also DLB 115

Boff, Leonardo (Genezio Darci) 1938-
See also CA 150; DAM MULT; HLC 1; HW 2

Bogan, Louise 1897-1970 **CLC 4, 39, 46, 93; DAM POET; PC 12**
See also CA 73-76; 25-28R; CANR 33, 82; DLB 45, 169; MTCW 1, 2

Bogarde, Dirk 1921-1999 **CLC 19**
See also Van Den Bogarde, Derek Jules Gaspard Ulric Niven
See also CA 179; DLB 14

Bogosian, Eric 1953- **CLC 45**
See also CA 138

Bograd, Larry 1953- **CLC 35**
See also CA 93-96; CANR 57; SAAS 21; SATA 33, 89

Boiardo, Matteo Maria 1441-1494 **LC 6**

Boileau-Despreaux, Nicolas 1636-1711 **LC 3**

Bojer, Johan 1872-1959 **TCLC 64**

Boland, Eavan (Aisling) 1944- **CLC 40, 67, 113; DAM POET**
See also CA 143; CANR 61; DLB 40; MTCW 2

Boll, Heinrich
See Boell, Heinrich (Theodor)

Bolt, Lee
See Faust, Frederick (Schiller)

Bolt, Robert (Oxton) 1924-1995**CLC 14; DAM DRAM**
See also CA 17-20R; 147; CANR 35, 67; DLB 13; MTCW 1

Bombal, Maria Luisa 1910-1980 **SSC 37; HLCS 1**
See also CA 127; CANR 72; HW 1

Bombet, Louis-Alexandre-Cesar
See Stendhal

Bomkauf
See Kaufman, Bob (Garnell)

Bonaventura **NCLC 35**
See also DLB 90

Bond, Edward 1934- **CLC 4, 6, 13, 23; DAM DRAM**
See also CA 25-28R; CANR 38, 67; DLB 13; MTCW 1

Bonham, Frank 1914-1989 **CLC 12**
See also AAYA 1; CA 9-12R; CANR 4, 36;

JRDA; MAICYA; SAAS 3; SATA 1, 49; SATA-Obit 62

Bonnefoy, Yves 1923- **CLC 9, 15, 58; DAM MST, POET**
See also CA 85-88; CANR 33, 75; MTCW 1, 2

Bontemps, Arna(ud Wendell) 1902-1973**C L C 1, 18; BLC 1; DAM MULT, NOV, POET**
See also BW 1; CA 1-4R; 41-44R; CANR 4, 35; CLR 6; DA3; DLB 48, 51; JRDA; MAICYA; MTCW 1, 2; SATA 2, 44; SATA-Obit 24

Booth, Martin 1944- **CLC 13**
See also CA 93-96; CAAS 2

Booth, Philip 1925- **CLC 23**
See also CA 5-8R; CANR 5; DLBY 82

Booth, Wayne C(layson) 1921- **CLC 24**
See also CA 1-4R; CAAS 5; CANR 3, 43; DLB 67

Borchert, Wolfgang 1921-1947 **TCLC 5**
See also CA 104; DLB 69, 124

Borel, Petrus 1809-1859 **NCLC 41**

Borges, Jorge Luis 1899-1986**CLC 1, 2, 3, 4, 6, 8, 9, 10, 13, 19, 44, 48, 83; DA; DAB; DAC; DAM MST, MULT; HLC 1; PC 22; SSC 4; WLC**
See also AAYA 26; CA 21-24R; CANR 19, 33, 75; DA3; DLB 113; DLBY 86; HW 1, 2; MTCW 1, 2

Borowski, Tadeusz 1922-1951 **TCLC 9**
See also CA 106; 154

Borrow, George (Henry) 1803-1881 **NCLC 9**
See also DLB 21, 55, 166

Bosch (Gavino), Juan 1909-
See also CA 151; DAM MST, MULT; DLB 145; HLCS 1; HW 1, 2

Bosman, Herman Charles 1905-1951 **T C L C 49**
See also Malan, Herman
See also CA 160

Bosschere, Jean de 1878(?)-1953 **TCLC 19**
See also CA 115

Boswell, James 1740-1795**LC 4, 50; DA; DAB; DAC; DAM MST; WLC**
See also CDBLB 1660-1789; DLB 104, 142

Bottoms, David 1949- **CLC 53**
See also CA 105; CANR 22; DLB 120; DLBY 83

Boucicault, Dion 1820-1890 **NCLC 41**

Boucolon, Maryse 1937(?)-
See Conde, Maryse
See also BW 3; CA 110; CANR 30, 53, 76

Bourget, Paul (Charles Joseph) 1852-1935 **TCLC 12**
See also CA 107; DLB 123

Bourjaily, Vance (Nye) 1922- **CLC 8, 62**
See also CA 1-4R; CAAS 1; CANR 2, 72; DLB 2, 143

Bourne, Randolph S(illiman) 1886-1918 **TCLC 16**
See also CA 117; 155; DLB 63

Bova, Ben(jamin William) 1932- **CLC 45**
See also AAYA 16; CA 5-8R; CAAS 18; CANR 11, 56; CLR 3; DLBY 81; INT CANR-11; MAICYA; MTCW 1; SATA 6, 68

Bowen, Elizabeth (Dorothea Cole) 1899-1973 **CLC 1, 3, 6, 11, 15, 22, 118; DAM NOV; SSC 3, 28**
See also CA 17-18; 41-44R; CANR 35; CAP 2; CDBLB 1945-1960; DA3; DLB 15, 162; MTCW 1, 2

Bowering, George 1935- **CLC 15, 47**
See also CA 21-24R; CAAS 16; CANR 10; DLB 53

Bowering, Marilyn R(uthe) 1949- **CLC 32**
See also CA 101; CANR 49

Bowers, Edgar 1924- **CLC 9**
See also CA 5-8R; CANR 24; DLB 5

Bowie, David **CLC 17**
See also Jones, David Robert

Bowles, Jane (Sydney) 1917-1973 **CLC 3, 68**
See also CA 19-20; 41-44R; CAP 2

Bowles, Paul (Frederick) 1910- **CLC 1, 2, 19, 53; SSC 3**
See also CA 1-4R; CAAS 1; CANR 1, 19, 50, 75; DA3; DLB 5, 6; MTCW 1, 2

Box, Edgar
See Vidal, Gore

Boyd, Nancy
See Millay, Edna St. Vincent

Boyd, William 1952- **CLC 28, 53, 70**
See also CA 114; 120; CANR 51, 71

Boyle, Kay 1902-1992 **CLC 1, 5, 19, 58, 121; SSC 5**
See also CA 13-16R; 140; CAAS 1; CANR 29, 61; DLB 4, 9, 48, 86; DLBY 93; MTCW 1, 2

Boyle, Mark
See Kienzle, William X(avier)

Boyle, Patrick 1905-1982 **CLC 19**
See also CA 127

Boyle, T. C. 1948-
See Boyle, T(homas) Coraghessan

Boyle, T(homas) Coraghessan 1948- **CLC 36, 55, 90; DAM POP; SSC 16**
See also BEST 90:4; CA 120; CANR 44, 76; DA3; DLBY 86; MTCW 2

Boz
See Dickens, Charles (John Huffam)

Brackenridge, Hugh Henry 1748-1816 **NCLC 7**
See also DLB 11, 37

Bradbury, Edward P.
See Moorcock, Michael (John)
See also MTCW 2

Bradbury, Malcolm (Stanley) 1932- **CLC 32, 61; DAM NOV**
See also CA 1-4R; CANR 1, 33; DA3; DLB 14, 207; MTCW 1, 2

Bradbury, Ray (Douglas) 1920- **CLC 1, 3, 10, 15, 42, 98; DA; DAB; DAC; DAM MST, NOV, POP; SSC 29; WLC**
See also AAYA 15; AITN 1, 2; CA 1-4R; CANR 2, 30, 75; CDALB 1968-1988; DA3; DLB 2, 8; MTCW 1, 2; SATA 11, 64

Bradford, Gamaliel 1863-1932 **TCLC 36**
See also CA 160; DLB 17

Bradley, David (Henry), Jr. 1950- **CLC 23, 118; BLC 1; DAM MULT**
See also BW 1, 3; CA 104; CANR 26, 81; DLB 33

Bradley, John Ed(mund, Jr.) 1958- **CLC 55**
See also CA 139

Bradley, Marion Zimmer 1930- **CLC 30; DAM POP**
See also AAYA 9; CA 57-60; CAAS 10; CANR 7, 31, 51, 75; DA3; DLB 8; MTCW 1, 2; SATA 90

Bradstreet, Anne 1612(?)-1672 **LC 4, 30; DA; DAC; DAM MST, POET; PC 10**
See also CDALB 1640-1865; DA3; DLB 24

Brady, Joan 1939- **CLC 86**
See also CA 141

Bragg, Melvyn 1939- **CLC 10**
See also BEST 89:3; CA 57-60; CANR 10, 48; DLB 14

Brahe, Tycho 1546-1601 **LC 45**

Braine, John (Gerard) 1922-1986 **CLC 1, 3, 41**
See also CA 1-4R; 120; CANR 1, 33; CDBLB 1945-1960; DLB 15; DLBY 86; MTCW 1

Bramah, Ernest 1868-1942 **TCLC 72**
See also CA 156; DLB 70

Brammer, William 1930(?)-1978 **CLC 31**
See also CA 77-80

Brancati, Vitaliano 1907-1954 **TCLC 12**
See also CA 109

Brancato, Robin F(idler) 1936- **CLC 35**
See also AAYA 9; CA 69-72; CANR 11, 45; CLR 32; JRDA; SAAS 9; SATA 97

Brand, Max
See Faust, Frederick (Schiller)

Brand, Millen 1906-1980 **CLC 7**
See also CA 21-24R; 97-100; CANR 72

Branden, Barbara **CLC 44**
See also CA 148

Brandes, Georg (Morris Cohen) 1842-1927 **TCLC 10**
See also CA 105

Brandys, Kazimierz 1916- **CLC 62**

Branley, Franklyn M(ansfield) 1915- **CLC 21**
See also CA 33-36R; CANR 14, 39; CLR 13; MAICYA; SAAS 16; SATA 4, 68

Brathwaite, Edward (Kamau) 1930- **CLC 11; BLCS; DAM POET**
See also BW 2, 3; CA 25-28R; CANR 11, 26, 47; DLB 125

Brautigan, Richard (Gary) 1935-1984 **CLC 1, 3, 5, 9, 12, 34, 42; DAM NOV**
See also CA 53-56; 113; CANR 34; DA3; DLB 2, 5, 206; DLBY 80, 84; MTCW 1; SATA 56

Brave Bird, Mary 1953-
See Crow Dog, Mary (Ellen)
See also NNAL

Braverman, Kate 1950- **CLC 67**
See also CA 89-92

Brecht, (Eugen) Bertolt (Friedrich) 1898-1956 **TCLC 1, 6, 13, 35; DA; DAB; DAC; DAM DRAM, MST; DC 3; WLC**
See also CA 104; 133; CANR 62; DA3; DLB 56, 124; MTCW 1, 2

Brecht, Eugen Berthold Friedrich
See Brecht, (Eugen) Bertolt (Friedrich)

Bremer, Fredrika 1801-1865 **NCLC 11**

Brennan, Christopher John 1870-1932 **TCLC 17**
See also CA 117

Brennan, Maeve 1917-1993 **CLC 5**
See also CA 81-84; CANR 72

Brent, Linda
See Jacobs, Harriet A(nn)

Brentano, Clemens (Maria) 1778-1842 **NCLC 1**
See also DLB 90

Brent of Bin Bin
See Franklin, (Stella Maria Sarah) Miles (Lampe)

Brenton, Howard 1942- **CLC 31**
See also CA 69-72; CANR 33, 67; DLB 13; MTCW 1

Breslin, James 1930-1996
See Breslin, Jimmy
See also CA 73-76; CANR 31, 75; DAM NOV; MTCW 1, 2

Breslin, Jimmy **CLC 4, 43**
See also Breslin, James
See also AITN 1; DLB 185; MTCW 2

Bresson, Robert 1901- **CLC 16**
See also CA 110; CANR 49

Breton, Andre 1896-1966 **CLC 2, 9, 15, 54; PC 15**
See also CA 19-20; 25-28R; CANR 40, 60; CAP 2; DLB 65; MTCW 1, 2

Breytenbach, Breyten 1939(?)- **CLC 23, 37, 126; DAM POET**
See also CA 113; 129; CANR 61

Bridgers, Sue Ellen 1942- **CLC 26**
See also AAYA 8; CA 65-68; CANR 11, 36; CLR 18; DLB 52; JRDA; MAICYA; SAAS 1; SATA 22, 90; SATA-Essay 109

Bridges, Robert (Seymour) 1844-1930 **TCLC 1; DAM POET; PC 28**
See also CA 104; 152; CDBLB 1890-1914; DLB 19, 98

Bridie, James **TCLC 3**
See also Mavor, Osborne Henry
See also DLB 10

Brin, David 1950- **CLC 34**
See also AAYA 21; CA 102; CANR 24, 70; INT CANR-24; SATA 65

Brink, Andre (Philippus) 1935- **CLC 18, 36, 106**
See also CA 104; CANR 39, 62; INT 103; MTCW 1, 2

Brinsmead, H(esba) F(ay) 1922- **CLC 21**
See also CA 21-24R; CANR 10; CLR 47; MAICYA; SAAS 5; SATA 18, 78

Brittain, Vera (Mary) 1893(?)-1970 **CLC 23**
See also CA 13-16; 25-28R; CANR 58; CAP 1; DLB 191; MTCW 1, 2

Broch, Hermann 1886-1951 **TCLC 20**
See also CA 117; DLB 85, 124

Brock, Rose
See Hansen, Joseph

Brodkey, Harold (Roy) 1930-1996 **CLC 56**
See also CA 111; 151; CANR 71; DLB 130

Brodskii, Iosif
See Brodsky, Joseph

Brodsky, Iosif Alexandrovich 1940-1996
See Brodsky, Joseph
See also AITN 1; CA 41-44R; 151; CANR 37; DAM POET; DA3; MTCW 1, 2

Brodsky, Joseph 1940-1996 **CLC 4, 6, 13, 36, 100; PC 9**
See also Brodskii, Iosif; Brodsky, Iosif Alexandrovich
See also MTCW 1

Brodsky, Michael (Mark) 1948- **CLC 19**
See also CA 102; CANR 18, 41, 58

Bromell, Henry 1947- **CLC 5**
See also CA 53-56; CANR 9

Bromfield, Louis (Brucker) 1896-1956 **TCLC 11**
See also CA 107; 155; DLB 4, 9, 86

Broner, E(sther) M(asserman) 1930- **CLC 19**
See also CA 17-20R; CANR 8, 25, 72; DLB 28

Bronk, William (M.) 1918-1999 **CLC 10**
See also CA 89-92; 177; CANR 23; DLB 165

Bronstein, Lev Davidovich
See Trotsky, Leon

Bronte, Anne 1820-1849 **NCLC 71**
See also DA3; DLB 21, 199

Bronte, Charlotte 1816-1855 **NCLC 3, 8, 33, 58; DA; DAB; DAC; DAM MST, NOV; WLC**
See also AAYA 17; CDBLB 1832-1890; DA3; DLB 21, 159, 199

Bronte, Emily (Jane) 1818-1848 **NCLC 16, 35; DA; DAB; DAC; DAM MST, NOV, POET; PC 8; WLC**
See also AAYA 17; CDBLB 1832-1890; DA3; DLB 21, 32, 199

Brooke, Frances 1724-1789 **LC 6, 48**
See also DLB 39, 99

Brooke, Henry 1703(?)-1783 **LC 1**
See also DLB 39

Brooke, Rupert (Chawner) 1887-1915 **TCLC 2, 7; DA; DAB; DAC; DAM MST, POET; PC 24; WLC**
See also CA 104; 132; CANR 61; CDBLB 1914-1945; DLB 19; MTCW 1, 2

Brooke-Haven, P.
See Wodehouse, P(elham) G(renville)

Brooke-Rose, Christine 1926(?)- **CLC 40**
See also CA 13-16R; CANR 58; DLB 14

Brookner, Anita 1928- **CLC 32, 34, 51; DAB; DAM POP**
See also CA 114; 120; CANR 37, 56; DA3; DLB 194; DLBY 87; MTCW 1, 2

Brooks, Cleanth 1906-1994 **CLC 24, 86, 110**
See also CA 17-20R; 145; CANR 33, 35; DLB 63; DLBY 94; INT CANR-35; MTCW 1, 2

Brooks, George
See Baum, L(yman) Frank

Brooks, Gwendolyn 1917- **CLC 1, 2, 4, 5, 15, 49, 125; BLC 1; DA; DAC; DAM MST, MULT, POET; PC 7; WLC**
See also AAYA 20; AITN 1; BW 2, 3; CA 1-4R; CANR 1, 27, 52, 75; CDALB 1941-1968; CLR 27; DA3; DLB 5, 76, 165; MTCW 1, 2; SATA 6

Brooks, Mel **CLC 12**
See also Kaminsky, Melvin
See also AAYA 13; DLB 26

Brooks, Peter 1938- **CLC 34**
See also CA 45-48; CANR 1

Brooks, Van Wyck 1886-1963 **CLC 29**
See also CA 1-4R; CANR 6; DLB 45, 63, 103

Brophy, Brigid (Antonia) 1929-1995 **CLC 6, 11, 29, 105**
See also CA 5-8R; 149; CAAS 4; CANR 25, 53; DA3; DLB 14; MTCW 1, 2

Brosman, Catharine Savage 1934- **CLC 9**
See also CA 61-64; CANR 21, 46

Brossard, Nicole 1943- **CLC 115**
See also CA 122; CAAS 16; DLB 53

Brother Antoninus
See Everson, William (Oliver)

The Brothers Quay
See Quay, Stephen; Quay, Timothy

Broughton, T(homas) Alan 1936- **CLC 19**
See also CA 45-48; CANR 2, 23, 48

Broumas, Olga 1949- **CLC 10, 73**
See also CA 85-88; CANR 20, 69

Brown, Alan 1950- **CLC 99**
See also CA 156

Brown, Charles Brockden 1771-1810 **NCLC 22, 74**
See also CDALB 1640-1865; DLB 37, 59, 73

Brown, Christy 1932-1981 **CLC 63**
See also CA 105; 104; CANR 72; DLB 14

Brown, Claude 1937- **CLC 30; BLC 1; DAM MULT**
See also AAYA 7; BW 1, 3; CA 73-76; CANR 81

Brown, Dee (Alexander) 1908- **CLC 18, 47; DAM POP**
See also AAYA 30; CA 13-16R; CAAS 6; CANR 11, 45, 60; DA3; DLBY 80; MTCW 1, 2; SATA 5, 110

Brown, George
See Wertmueller, Lina

Brown, George Douglas 1869-1902 **TCLC 28**
See also CA 162

Brown, George Mackay 1921-1996 **CLC 5, 48, 100**
See also CA 21-24R; 151; CAAS 6; CANR 12, 37, 67; DLB 14, 27, 139; MTCW 1; SATA 35

Brown, (William) Larry 1951- **CLC 73**

See also CA 130; 134; INT 133

Brown, Moses
See Barrett, William (Christopher)

Brown, Rita Mae 1944- **CLC 18, 43, 79; DAM NOV, POP**
See also CA 45-48; CANR 2, 11, 35, 62; DA3; INT CANR-11; MTCW 1, 2

Brown, Roderick (Langmere) Haig-
See Haig-Brown, Roderick (Langmere)

Brown, Rosellen 1939- **CLC 32**
See also CA 77-80; CAAS 10; CANR 14, 44

Brown, Sterling Allen 1901-1989 **CLC 1, 23, 59; BLC 1; DAM MULT, POET**
See also BW 1, 3; CA 85-88; 127; CANR 26; DA3; DLB 48, 51, 63; MTCW 1, 2

Brown, Will
See Ainsworth, William Harrison

Brown, William Wells 1813-1884 **NCLC 2; BLC 1; DAM MULT; DC 1**
See also DLB 3, 50

Browne, (Clyde) Jackson 1948(?)- **CLC 21**
See also CA 120

Browning, Elizabeth Barrett 1806-1861 **NCLC 1, 16, 61, 66; DA; DAB; DAC; DAM MST, POET; PC 6; WLC**
See also CDBLB 1832-1890; DA3; DLB 32, 199

Browning, Robert 1812-1889 **NCLC 19, 79; DA; DAB; DAC; DAM MST, POET; PC 2; WLCS**
See also CDBLB 1832-1890; DA3; DLB 32, 163; YABC 1

Browning, Tod 1882-1962 **CLC 16**
See also CA 141; 117

Brownson, Orestes Augustus 1803-1876 **NCLC 50**
See also DLB 1, 59, 73

Bruccoli, Matthew J(oseph) 1931- **CLC 34**
See also CA 9-12R; CANR 7; DLB 103

Bruce, Lenny **CLC 21**
See also Schneider, Leonard Alfred

Bruin, John
See Brutus, Dennis

Brulard, Henri
See Stendhal

Brulls, Christian
See Simenon, Georges (Jacques Christian)

Brunner, John (Kilian Houston) 1934-1995 **CLC 8, 10; DAM POP**
See also CA 1-4R; 149; CAAS 8; CANR 2, 37; MTCW 1, 2

Bruno, Giordano 1548-1600 **LC 27**

Brutus, Dennis 1924- **CLC 43; BLC 1; DAM MULT, POET; PC 24**
See also BW 2, 3; CA 49-52; CAAS 14; CANR 2, 27, 42, 81; DLB 117

Bryan, C(ourtlandt) D(ixon) B(arnes) 1936- **CLC 29**
See also CA 73-76; CANR 13, 68; DLB 185; INT CANR-13

Bryan, Michael
See Moore, Brian

Bryan, William Jennings 1860-1925 **TCLC 99**

Bryant, William Cullen 1794-1878 **NCLC 6, 46; DA; DAB; DAC; DAM MST, POET; PC 20**
See also CDALB 1640-1865; DLB 3, 43, 59, 189

Bryusov, Valery Yakovlevich 1873-1924 **TCLC 10**
See also CA 107; 155

Buchan, John 1875-1940 **TCLC 41; DAB; DAM POP**

See also CA 108; 145; DLB 34, 70, 156; MTCW 1; YABC 2

Buchanan, George 1506-1582 **LC 4**
See also DLB 152

Buchheim, Lothar-Guenther 1918- **CLC 6**
See also CA 85-88

Buchner, (Karl) Georg 1813-1837 **NCLC 26**

Buchwald, Art(hur) 1925- **CLC 33**
See also AITN 1; CA 5-8R; CANR 21, 67; MTCW 1, 2; SATA 10

Buck, Pearl S(ydenstricker) 1892-1973 **CLC 7, 11, 18; DA; DAB; DAC; DAM MST, NOV**
See also AITN 1; CA 1-4R; 41-44R; CANR 1, 34; CDALBS; DA3; DLB 9, 102; MTCW 1, 2; SATA 1, 25

Buckler, Ernest 1908-1984 **CLC 13; DAC; DAM MST**
See also CA 11-12; 114; CAP 1; DLB 68; SATA 47

Buckley, Vincent (Thomas) 1925-1988 **CLC 57**
See also CA 101

Buckley, William F(rank), Jr. 1925- **CLC 7, 18, 37; DAM POP**
See also AITN 1; CA 1-4R; CANR 1, 24, 53; DA3; DLB 137; DLBY 80; INT CANR-24; MTCW 1, 2

Buechner, (Carl) Frederick 1926- **CLC 2, 4, 6, 9; DAM NOV**
See also CA 13-16R; CANR 11, 39, 64; DLBY 80; INT CANR-11; MTCW 1, 2

Buell, John (Edward) 1927- **CLC 10**
See also CA 1-4R; CANR 71; DLB 53

Buero Vallejo, Antonio 1916- **CLC 15, 46**
See also CA 106; CANR 24, 49, 75; HW 1; MTCW 1, 2

Bufalino, Gesualdo 1920(?)- **CLC 74**
See also DLB 196

Bugayev, Boris Nikolayevich 1880-1934 **TCLC 7; PC 11**
See also Bely, Andrey
See also CA 104; 165; MTCW 1

Bukowski, Charles 1920-1994 **CLC 2, 5, 9, 41, 82, 108; DAM NOV, POET; PC 18**
See also CA 17-20R; 144; CANR 40, 62; DA3; DLB 5, 130, 169; MTCW 1, 2

Bulgakov, Mikhail (Afanas'evich) 1891-1940 **TCLC 2, 16; DAM DRAM, NOV; SSC 18**
See also CA 105; 152

Bulgya, Alexander Alexandrovich 1901-1956 **TCLC 53**
See also Fadeyev, Alexander
See also CA 117; 181

Bullins, Ed 1935- **CLC 1, 5, 7; BLC 1; DAM DRAM, MULT; DC 6**
See also BW 2, 3; CA 49-52; CAAS 16; CANR 24, 46, 73; DLB 7, 38; MTCW 1, 2

Bulwer-Lytton, Edward (George Earle Lytton) 1803-1873 **NCLC 1, 45**
See also DLB 21

Bunin, Ivan Alexeyevich 1870-1953 **TCLC 6; SSC 5**
See also CA 104

Bunting, Basil 1900-1985 **CLC 10, 39, 47; DAM POET**
See also CA 53-56; 115; CANR 7; DLB 20

Bunuel, Luis 1900-1983 **CLC 16, 80; DAM MULT; HLC 1**
See also CA 101; 110; CANR 32, 77; HW 1

Bunyan, John 1628-1688 **LC 4; DA; DAB; DAC; DAM MST; WLC**
See also CDBLB 1660-1789; DLB 39

Burckhardt, Jacob (Christoph) 1818-1897 **NCLC 49**

Burford, Eleanor
See Hibbert, Eleanor Alice Burford
Burgess, Anthony CLC 1, 2, 4, 5, 8, 10, 13, 15, 22, 40, 62, 81, 94; DAB
See also Wilson, John (Anthony) Burgess
See also AAYA 25; AITN 1; CDBLB 1960 to Present; DLB 14, 194; DLBY 98; MTCW 1
Burke, Edmund 1729(?)-1797 LC 7, 36; DA; DAB; DAC; DAM MST; WLC
See also DA3; DLB 104
Burke, Kenneth (Duva) 1897-1993 CLC 2, 24
See also CA 5-8R; 143; CANR 39, 74; DLB 45, 63; MTCW 1, 2
Burke, Leda
See Garnett, David
Burke, Ralph
See Silverberg, Robert
Burke, Thomas 1886-1945 TCLC 63
See also CA 113; 155; DLB 197
Burney, Fanny 1752-1840 NCLC 12, 54, 81
See also DLB 39
Burns, Robert 1759-1796 LC 3, 29, 40; DA; DAB; DAC; DAM MST, POET; PC 6; WLC
See also CDBLB 1789-1832; DA3; DLB 109
Burns, Tex
See L'Amour, Louis (Dearborn)
Burnshaw, Stanley 1906- CLC 3, 13, 44
See also CA 9-12R; DLB 48; DLBY 97
Burr, Anne 1937- CLC 6
See also CA 25-28R
Burroughs, Edgar Rice 1875-1950 TCLC 2, 32; DAM NOV
See also AAYA 11; CA 104; 132; DA3; DLB 8; MTCW 1, 2; SATA 41
Burroughs, William S(eward) 1914-1997 CLC 1, 2, 5, 15, 22, 42, 75, 109; DA; DAB; DAC; DAM MST, NOV, POP; WLC
See also AITN 2; CA 9-12R; 160; CANR 20, 52; DA3; DLB 2, 8, 16, 152; DLBY 81, 97; MTCW 1, 2
Burton, Sir Richard F(rancis) 1821-1890 NCLC 42
See also DLB 55, 166, 184
Busch, Frederick 1941- CLC 7, 10, 18, 47
See also CA 33-36R; CAAS 1; CANR 45, 73; DLB 6
Bush, Ronald 1946- CLC 34
See also CA 136
Bustos, F(rancisco)
See Borges, Jorge Luis
Bustos Domecq, H(onorio)
See Bioy Casares, Adolfo; Borges, Jorge Luis
Butler, Octavia E(stelle) 1947- CLC 38, 121; BLCS; DAM MULT, POP
See also AAYA 18; BW 2, 3; CA 73-76; CANR 12, 24, 38, 73; DA3; DLB 33; MTCW 1, 2; SATA 84
Butler, Robert Olen (Jr.) 1945- CLC 81; DAM POP
See also CA 112; CANR 66; DLB 173; INT 112; MTCW 1
Butler, Samuel 1612-1680 LC 16, 43
See also DLB 101, 126
Butler, Samuel 1835-1902 TCLC 1, 33; DA; DAB; DAC; DAM MST, NOV; WLC
See also CA 143; CDBLB 1890-1914; DA3; DLB 18, 57, 174
Butler, Walter C.
See Faust, Frederick (Schiller)
Butor, Michel (Marie Francois) 1926- CLC 1, 3, 8, 11, 15
See also CA 9-12R; CANR 33, 66; DLB 83;

MTCW 1, 2
Butts, Mary 1892(?)-1937 TCLC 77
See also CA 148
Buzo, Alexander (John) 1944- CLC 61
See also CA 97-100; CANR 17, 39, 69
Buzzati, Dino 1906-1972 CLC 36
See also CA 160; 33-36R; DLB 177
Byars, Betsy (Cromer) 1928- CLC 35
See also AAYA 19; CA 33-36R; CANR 18, 36, 57; CLR 1, 16; DLB 52; INT CANR-18; JRDA; MAICYA; MTCW 1; SAAS 1; SATA 4, 46, 80; SATA-Essay 108
Byatt, A(ntonia) S(usan Drabble) 1936- CLC 19, 65; DAM NOV, POP
See also CA 13-16R; CANR 13, 33, 50, 75; DA3; DLB 14, 194; MTCW 1, 2
Byrne, David 1952- CLC 26
See also CA 127
Byrne, John Keyes 1926-
See Leonard, Hugh
See also CA 102; CANR 78; INT 102
Byron, George Gordon (Noel) 1788-1824 NCLC 2, 12; DA; DAB; DAC; DAM MST, POET; PC 16; WLC
See also CDBLB 1789-1832; DA3; DLB 96, 110
Byron, Robert 1905-1941 TCLC 67
See also CA 160; DLB 195
C. 3. 3.
See Wilde, Oscar
Caballero, Fernan 1796-1877 NCLC 10
Cabell, Branch
See Cabell, James Branch
Cabell, James Branch 1879-1958 TCLC 6
See also CA 105; 152; DLB 9, 78; MTCW 1
Cable, George Washington 1844-1925 TCLC 4; SSC 4
See also CA 104; 155; DLB 12, 74; DLBD 13
Cabral de Melo Neto, Joao 1920- CLC 76; DAM MULT
See also CA 151
Cabrera Infante, G(uillermo) 1929- CLC 5, 25, 45, 120; DAM MULT; HLC 1
See also CA 85-88; CANR 29, 65; DA3; DLB 113; HW 1, 2; MTCW 1, 2
Cade, Toni
See Bambara, Toni Cade
Cadmus and Harmonia
See Buchan, John
Caedmon fl. 658-680 CMLC 7
See also DLB 146
Caeiro, Alberto
See Pessoa, Fernando (Antonio Nogueira)
Cage, John (Milton, Jr.) 1912-1992 CLC 41
See also CA 13-16R; 169; CANR 9, 78; DLB 193; INT CANR-9
Cahan, Abraham 1860-1951 TCLC 71
See also CA 108; 154; DLB 9, 25, 28
Cain, G.
See Cabrera Infante, G(uillermo)
Cain, Guillermo
See Cabrera Infante, G(uillermo)
Cain, James M(allahan) 1892-1977 CLC 3, 11, 28
See also AITN 1; CA 17-20R; 73-76; CANR 8, 34, 61; MTCW 1
Caine, Hall 1853-1931 TCLC 99
Caine, Mark
See Raphael, Frederic (Michael)
Calasso, Roberto 1941- CLC 81
See also CA 143
Calderon de la Barca, Pedro 1600-1681 LC 23; DC 3; HLCS 1

Caldwell, Erskine (Preston) 1903-1987 CLC 1, 8, 14, 50, 60; DAM NOV; SSC 19
See also AITN 1; CA 1-4R; 121; CAAS 1; CANR 2, 33; DA3; DLB 9, 86; MTCW 1, 2
Caldwell, (Janet Miriam) Taylor (Holland) 1900-1985 CLC 2, 28, 39; DAM NOV, POP
See also CA 5-8R; 116; CANR 5; DA3; DLBD 17
Calhoun, John Caldwell 1782-1850 NCLC 15
See also DLB 3
Calisher, Hortense 1911- CLC 2, 4, 8, 38; DAM NOV; SSC 15
See also CA 1-4R; CANR 1, 22, 67; DA3; DLB 2; INT CANR-22; MTCW 1, 2
Callaghan, Morley Edward 1903-1990 CLC 3, 14, 41, 65; DAC; DAM MST
See also CA 9-12R; 132; CANR 33, 73; DLB 68; MTCW 1, 2
Callimachus c. 305B.C.-c. 240B.C. CMLC 18
See also DLB 176
Calvin, John 1509-1564 LC 37
Calvino, Italo 1923-1985 CLC 5, 8, 11, 22, 33, 39, 73; DAM NOV; SSC 3
See also CA 85-88; 116; CANR 23, 61; DLB 196; MTCW 1, 2
Cameron, Carey 1952- CLC 59
See also CA 135
Cameron, Peter 1959- CLC 44
See also CA 125; CANR 50
Camoens, Luis Vaz de 1524(?)-1580
See also HLCS 1
Camoes, Luis de 1524(?)-1580
See also HLCS 1
Campana, Dino 1885-1932 TCLC 20
See also CA 117; DLB 114
Campanella, Tommaso 1568-1639 LC 32
Campbell, John W(ood, Jr.) 1910-1971 CLC 32
See also CA 21-22; 29-32R; CANR 34; CAP 2; DLB 8; MTCW 1
Campbell, Joseph 1904-1987 CLC 69
See also AAYA 3; BEST 89:2; CA 1-4R; 124; CANR 3, 28, 61; DA3; MTCW 1, 2
Campbell, Maria 1940- CLC 85; DAC
See also CA 102; CANR 54; NNAL
Campbell, (John) Ramsey 1946- CLC 42; SSC 19
See also CA 57-60; CANR 7; INT CANR-7
Campbell, (Ignatius) Roy (Dunnachie) 1901-1957 TCLC 5
See also CA 104; 155; DLB 20; MTCW 2
Campbell, Thomas 1777-1844 NCLC 19
See also DLB 93; 144
Campbell, Wilfred TCLC 9
See also Campbell, William
Campbell, William 1858(?)-1918
See Campbell, Wilfred
See also CA 106; DLB 92
Campion, Jane CLC 95
See also CA 138
Campos, Alvaro de
See Pessoa, Fernando (Antonio Nogueira)
Camus, Albert 1913-1960 CLC 1, 2, 4, 9, 11, 14, 32, 63, 69, 124; DA; DAB; DAC; DAM DRAM, MST, NOV; DC 2; SSC 9; WLC
See also CA 89-92; DA3; DLB 72; MTCW 1, 2
Canby, Vincent 1924- CLC 13
See also CA 81-84
Cancale
See Desnos, Robert
Canetti, Elias 1905-1994 CLC 3, 14, 25, 75, 86
See also CA 21-24R; 146; CANR 23, 61, 79; DA3; DLB 85, 124; MTCW 1, 2
Canfield, Dorothea F.
See Fisher, Dorothy (Frances) Canfield

Canfield, Dorothea Frances
  See Fisher, Dorothy (Frances) Canfield
Canfield, Dorothy
  See Fisher, Dorothy (Frances) Canfield
Canin, Ethan 1960- **CLC 55**
  See also CA 131; 135
Cannon, Curt
  See Hunter, Evan
Cao, Lan 1961- **CLC 109**
  See also CA 165
Cape, Judith
  See Page, P(atricia) K(athleen)
Capek, Karel 1890-1938 **TCLC 6, 37; DA;**
  DAB; DAC; DAM DRAM, MST, NOV; DC
  1; SSC 36; WLC
  See also CA 104; 140; DA3; MTCW 1
Capote, Truman 1924-1984CLC 1, 3, 8, 13, 19,
  34, 38, 58; DA; DAB; DAC; DAM MST,
  NOV, POP; SSC 2; WLC
  See also CA 5-8R; 113; CANR 18, 62; CDALB
  1941-1968; DA3; DLB 2, 185; DLBY 80,
  84; MTCW 1, 2; SATA 91
Capra, Frank 1897-1991 **CLC 16**
  See also CA 61-64; 135
Caputo, Philip 1941- **CLC 32**
  See also CA 73-76; CANR 40
Caragiale, Ion Luca 1852-1912 **TCLC 76**
  See also CA 157
Card, Orson Scott 1951-CLC 44, 47, 50; DAM
  POP
  See also AAYA 11; CA 102; CANR 27, 47, 73;
  DA3; INT CANR-27; MTCW 1, 2; SATA 83
Cardenal, Ernesto 1925- **CLC 31; DAM**
  MULT, POET; HLC 1; PC 22
  See also CA 49-52; CANR 2, 32, 66; HW 1, 2;
  MTCW 1, 2
Cardozo, Benjamin N(athan) 1870-1938
  TCLC 65
  See also CA 117; 164
Carducci, Giosue (Alessandro Giuseppe) 1835-
  1907 **TCLC 32**
  See also CA 163
Carew, Thomas 1595(?)-1640 **LC 13**
  See also DLB 126
Carey, Ernestine Gilbreth 1908- **CLC 17**
  See also CA 5-8R; CANR 71; SATA 2
Carey, Peter 1943- **CLC 40, 55, 96**
  See also CA 123; 127; CANR 53, 76; INT 127;
  MTCW 1, 2; SATA 94
Carleton, William 1794-1869 **NCLC 3**
  See also DLB 159
Carlisle, Henry (Coffin) 1926- **CLC 33**
  See also CA 13-16R; CANR 15, 85
Carlsen, Chris
  See Holdstock, Robert P.
Carlson, Ron(ald F.) 1947- **CLC 54**
  See also CA 105; CANR 27
Carlyle, Thomas 1795-1881 **NCLC 70; DA;**
  DAB; DAC; DAM MST
  See also CDBLB 1789-1832; DLB 55; 144
Carman, (William) Bliss 1861-1929 TCLC 7;
  DAC
  See also CA 104; 152; DLB 92
Carnegie, Dale 1888-1955 **TCLC 53**
Carossa, Hans 1878-1956 **TCLC 48**
  See also CA 170; DLB 66
Carpenter, Don(ald Richard) 1931-1995CLC 41
  See also CA 45-48; 149; CANR 1, 71
Carpenter, Edward 1844-1929 **TCLC 88**
  See also CA 163
Carpentier (y Valmont), Alejo 1904-1980 C L C
  8, 11, 38, 110; DAM MULT; HLC 1; SSC 35
  See also CA 65-68; 97-100; CANR 11, 70; DLB

113; HW 1, 2
Carr, Caleb 1955(?)- **CLC 86**
  See also CA 147; CANR 73; DA3
Carr, Emily 1871-1945 **TCLC 32**
  See also CA 159; DLB 68
Carr, John Dickson 1906-1977 **CLC 3**
  See also Fairbairn, Roger
  See also CA 49-52; 69-72; CANR 3, 33, 60;
  MTCW 1, 2
Carr, Philippa
  See Hibbert, Eleanor Alice Burford
Carr, Virginia Spencer 1929- **CLC 34**
  See also CA 61-64; DLB 111
Carrere, Emmanuel 1957- **CLC 89**
Carrier, Roch 1937-CLC 13, 78; DAC; DAM
  MST
  See also CA 130; CANR 61; DLB 53; SATA
  105
Carroll, James P. 1943(?)- **CLC 38**
  See also CA 81-84; CANR 73; MTCW 1
Carroll, Jim 1951- **CLC 35**
  See also AAYA 17; CA 45-48; CANR 42
Carroll, Lewis **NCLC 2, 53; PC 18; WLC**
  See also Dodgson, Charles Lutwidge
  See also CDBLB 1832-1890; CLR 2, 18; DLB
  18, 163, 178; DLBY 98; JRDA
Carroll, Paul Vincent 1900-1968 **CLC 10**
  See also CA 9-12R; 25-28R; DLB 10
Carruth, Hayden 1921- CLC 4, 7, 10, 18, 84;
  PC 10
  See also CA 9-12R; CANR 4, 38, 59; DLB 5,
  165; INT CANR-4; MTCW 1, 2; SATA 47
Carson, Rachel Louise 1907-1964 **CLC 71;**
  DAM POP
  See also CA 77-80; CANR 35; DA3; MTCW 1,
  2; SATA 23
Carter, Angela (Olive) 1940-1992 CLC 5, 41,
  76; SSC 13
  See also CA 53-56; 136; CANR 12, 36, 61;
  DA3; DLB 14, 207; MTCW 1, 2; SATA 66;
  SATA-Obit 70
Carter, Nick
  See Smith, Martin Cruz
Carver, Raymond 1938-1988 CLC 22, 36, 53,
  55, 126; DAM NOV; SSC 8
  See also CA 33-36R; 126; CANR 17, 34, 61;
  DA3; DLB 130; DLBY 84, 88; MTCW 1, 2
Cary, Elizabeth, Lady Falkland 1585-1639
  LC 30
Cary, (Arthur) Joyce (Lunel) 1888-1957
  TCLC 1, 29
  See also CA 104; 164; CDBLB 1914-1945;
  DLB 15, 100; MTCW 2
Casanova de Seingalt, Giovanni Jacopo 1725-
  1798 **LC 13**
Casares, Adolfo Bioy
  See Bioy Casares, Adolfo
Casely-Hayford, J(oseph) E(phraim) 1866-1930
  TCLC 24; BLC 1; DAM MULT
  See also BW 2; CA 123; 152
Casey, John (Dudley) 1939- **CLC 59**
  See also BEST 90:2; CA 69-72; CANR 23
Casey, Michael 1947- **CLC 2**
  See also CA 65-68; DLB 5
Casey, Patrick
  See Thurman, Wallace (Henry)
Casey, Warren (Peter) 1935-1988 **CLC 12**
  See also CA 101; 127; INT 101
Casona, Alejandro **CLC 49**
  See also Alvarez, Alejandro Rodriguez
Cassavetes, John 1929-1989 **CLC 20**
  See also CA 85-88; 127; CANR 82
Cassian, Nina 1924- **PC 17**

Cassill, R(onald) V(erlin) 1919- **CLC 4, 23**
  See also CA 9-12R; CAAS 1; CANR 7, 45;
  DLB 6
Cassirer, Ernst 1874-1945 **TCLC 61**
  See also CA 157
Cassity, (Allen) Turner 1929- **CLC 6, 42**
  See also CA 17-20R; CAAS 8; CANR 11; DLB
  105
Castaneda, Carlos (Cesar Aranha) 1931(?)-
  1998 **CLC 12, 119**
  See also CA 25-28R; CANR 32, 66; HW 1;
  MTCW 1
Castedo, Elena 1937- **CLC 65**
  See also CA 132
Castedo-Ellerman, Elena
  See Castedo, Elena
Castellanos, Rosario 1925-1974CLC 66; DAM
  MULT; HLC 1
  See also CA 131; 53-56; CANR 58; DLB 113;
  HW 1; MTCW 1
Castelvetro, Lodovico 1505-1571 **LC 12**
Castiglione, Baldassare 1478-1529 **LC 12**
Castle, Robert
  See Hamilton, Edmond
Castro (Ruz), Fidel 1926(?)-
  See also CA 110; 129; CANR 81; DAM MULT;
  HLC 1; HW 2
Castro, Guillen de 1569-1631 **LC 19**
Castro, Rosalia de 1837-1885 **NCLC 3, 78;**
  DAM MULT
Cather, Willa
  See Cather, Willa Sibert
Cather, Willa Sibert 1873-1947 TCLC 1, 11,
  31, 99; DA; DAB; DAC; DAM MST, NOV;
  SSC 2; WLC
  See also AAYA 24; CA 104; 128; CDALB 1865-
  1917; DA3; DLB 9, 54, 78; DLBD 1; MTCW
  1, 2; SATA 30
Catherine, Saint 1347-1380 **CMLC 27**
Cato, Marcus Porcius 234B.C.-149B.C.
  CMLC 21
  See also DLB 211
Catton, (Charles) Bruce 1899-1978 **CLC 35**
  See also AITN 1; CA 5-8R; 81-84; CANR 7,
  74; DLB 17; SATA 2; SATA-Obit 24
Catullus c. 84B.C.-c. 54B.C. **CMLC 18**
  See also DLB 211
Cauldwell, Frank
  See King, Francis (Henry)
Caunitz, William J. 1933-1996 **CLC 34**
  See also BEST 89:3; CA 125; 130; 152; CANR
  73; INT 130
Causley, Charles (Stanley) 1917- **CLC 7**
  See also CA 9-12R; CANR 5, 35; CLR 30; DLB
  27; MTCW 1; SATA 3, 66
Caute, (John) David 1936- **CLC 29; DAM**
  NOV
  See also CA 1-4R; CAAS 4; CANR 1, 33, 64;
  DLB 14
Cavafy, C(onstantine) P(eter) 1863-1933
  TCLC 2, 7; DAM POET
  See also Kavafis, Konstantinos Petrou
  See also CA 148; DA3; MTCW 1
Cavallo, Evelyn
  See Spark, Muriel (Sarah)
Cavanna, Betty **CLC 12**
  See also Harrison, Elizabeth Cavanna
  See also JRDA; MAICYA; SAAS 4; SATA
  1, 30
Cavendish, Margaret Lucas 1623-1673LC 30
  See also DLB 131
Caxton, William 1421(?)-1491(?) **LC 17**
  See also DLB 170

Cayer, D. M.
See Duffy, Maureen
Cayrol, Jean 1911-   **CLC 11**
See also CA 89-92; DLB 83
Cela, Camilo Jose 1916- **CLC 4, 13, 59, 122;**
    DAM MULT; HLC 1
See also BEST 90:2; CA 21-24R; CAAS 10;
    CANR 21, 32, 76; DLBY 89; HW 1; MTCW
    1, 2
Celan, Paul   **CLC 10, 19, 53, 82; PC 10**
See also Antschel, Paul
See also DLB 69
Celine, Louis-Ferdinand CLC 1, 3, 4, 7, 9, 15,
    47, 124
See also Destouches, Louis-Ferdinand
See also DLB 72
Cellini, Benvenuto 1500-1571   **LC 7**
Cendrars, Blaise 1887-1961   **CLC 18, 106**
See also Sauser-Hall, Frederic
Cernuda (y Bidon), Luis 1902-1963 **CLC 54;**
    DAM POET
See also CA 131; 89-92; DLB 134; HW 1
Cervantes, Lorna Dee 1954-
See also CA 131; CANR 80; DLB 82; HLCS 1;
    HW 1
Cervantes (Saavedra), Miguel de 1547-1616
    LC 6, 23; DA; DAB; DAC; DAM MST,
    NOV; SSC 12; WLC
Cesaire, Aime (Fernand) 1913- **CLC 19, 32,**
    112; BLC 1; DAM MULT, POET; PC 25
See also BW 2, 3; CA 65-68; CANR 24, 43,
    81; DA3; MTCW 1, 2
Chabon, Michael 1963-   **CLC 55**
See also CA 139; CANR 57
Chabrol, Claude 1930-   **CLC 16**
See also CA 110
Challans, Mary 1905-1983
See Renault, Mary
See also CA 81-84; 111; CANR 74; DA3;
    MTCW 2; SATA 23; SATA-Obit 36
Challis, George
See Faust, Frederick (Schiller)
Chambers, Aidan 1934-   **CLC 35**
See also AAYA 27; CA 25-28R; CANR 12, 31,
    58; JRDA; MAICYA; SAAS 12; SATA 1,
    69, 108
Chambers, James 1948-
See Cliff, Jimmy
See also CA 124
Chambers, Jessie
See Lawrence, D(avid) H(erbert Richards)
Chambers, Robert W(illiam) 1865-1933
    TCLC 41
See also CA 165; DLB 202; SATA 107
Chamisso, Adelbert von 1781-1838 **NCLC 82**
See also DLB 90
Chandler, Raymond (Thornton) 1888-1959
    TCLC 1, 7; SSC 23
See also AAYA 25; CA 104; 129; CANR 60;
    CDALB 1929-1941; DA3; DLBD 6; MTCW
    1, 2
Chang, Eileen 1920-1995   **SSC 28**
See also CA 166
Chang, Jung 1952-   **CLC 71**
See also CA 142
Chang Ai-Ling
See Chang, Eileen
Channing, William Ellery 1780-1842**NCLC 17**
See also DLB 1, 59
Chao, Patricia 1955-   **CLC 119**
See also CA 163
Chaplin, Charles Spencer 1889-1977 **CLC 16**
See also Chaplin, Charlie

Chaplin, Charlie
See Chaplin, Charles Spencer
See also DLB 44
Chapman, George 1559(?)-1634**LC 22; DAM**
    DRAM
See also DLB 62, 121
Chapman, Graham 1941-1989   **CLC 21**
See also Monty Python
See also CA 116; 129; CANR 35
Chapman, John Jay 1862-1933   **TCLC 7**
See also CA 104
Chapman, Lee
See Bradley, Marion Zimmer
Chapman, Walker
See Silverberg, Robert
Chappell, Fred (Davis) 1936-   **CLC 40, 78**
See also CA 5-8R; CAAS 4; CANR 8, 33, 67;
    DLB 6, 105
Char, Rene(-Emile) 1907-1988**CLC 9, 11, 14,**
    55; DAM POET
See also CA 13-16R; 124; CANR 32; MTCW
    1, 2
Charby, Jay
See Ellison, Harlan (Jay)
Chardin, Pierre Teilhard de
See Teilhard de Chardin, (Marie Joseph) Pierre
Charles I 1600-1649   **LC 13**
Charriere, Isabelle de 1740-1805   **NCLC 66**
Charyn, Jerome 1937-   **CLC 5, 8, 18**
See also CA 5-8R; CAAS 1; CANR 7, 61;
    DLBY 83; MTCW 1
Chase, Mary (Coyle) 1907-1981   **DC 1**
See also CA 77-80; 105; SATA 17; SATA-Obit 29
Chase, Mary Ellen 1887-1973   **CLC 2**
See also CA 13-16; 41-44R; CAP 1; SATA 10
Chase, Nicholas
See Hyde, Anthony
Chateaubriand, Francois Rene de 1768-1848
    NCLC 3
See also DLB 119
Chatterje, Sarat Chandra 1876-1936(?)
See Chatterji, Saratchandra
See also CA 109
Chatterji, Bankim Chandra 1838-1894
    NCLC 19
Chatterji, Saratchandra   **TCLC 13**
See also Chatterje, Sarat Chandra
Chatterton, Thomas 1752-1770   **LC 3, 54;**
    DAM POET
See also DLB 109
Chatwin, (Charles) Bruce 1940-1989**CLC 28,**
    57, 59; DAM POP
See also AAYA 4; BEST 90:1; CA 85-88; 127;
    DLB 194, 204
Chaucer, Daniel
See Ford, Ford Madox
Chaucer, Geoffrey 1340(?)-1400 **LC 17; DA;**
    DAB; DAC; DAM MST, POET; PC 19;
    WLCS
See also CDBLB Before 1660; DA3; DLB 146
Chavez, Denise (Elia) 1948-
See also CA 131; CANR 56, 81; DAM MULT;
    DLB 122; HLC 1; HW 1, 2; MTCW 2
Chaviaras, Strates 1935-
See Haviaras, Stratis
See also CA 105
Chayefsky, Paddy   **CLC 23**
See also Chayefsky, Sidney
See also DLB 7, 44; DLBY 81
Chayefsky, Sidney 1923-1981
See Chayefsky, Paddy
See also CA 9-12R; 104; CANR 18; DAM DRAM

Chedid, Andree 1920-   **CLC 47**
See also CA 145
Cheever, John 1912-1982 **CLC 3, 7, 8, 11, 15,**
    25, 64; DA; DAB; DAC; DAM MST, NOV,
    POP; SSC 1; WLC
See also CA 5-8R; 106; CABS 1; CANR 5, 27,
    76; CDALB 1941-1968; DA3; DLB 2, 102;
    DLBY 80, 82; INT CANR-5; MTCW 1, 2
Cheever, Susan 1943-   **CLC 18, 48**
See also CA 103; CANR 27, 51; DLBY 82; INT
    CANR-27
Chekhonte, Antosha
See Chekhov, Anton (Pavlovich)
Chekhov, Anton (Pavlovich) 1860-1904**TCLC**
    3, 10, 31, 55, 96; DA; DAB; DAC; DAM
    DRAM, MST; DC 9; SSC 2, 28; WLC
See also CA 104; 124; DA3; SATA 90
Chernyshevsky, Nikolay Gavrilovich 1828-1889
    NCLC 1
Cherry, Carolyn Janice 1942-
See Cherryh, C. J.
See also CA 65-68; CANR 10
Cherryh, C. J.   **CLC 35**
See also Cherry, Carolyn Janice
See also AAYA 24; DLBY 80; SATA 93
Chesnutt, Charles W(addell) 1858-1932
    TCLC 5, 39; BLC 1; DAM MULT; SSC 7
See also BW 1, 3; CA 106; 125; CANR 76; DLB
    12, 50, 78; MTCW 1, 2
Chester, Alfred 1929(?)-1971   **CLC 49**
See also CA 33-36R; DLB 130
Chesterton, G(ilbert) K(eith) 1874-1936
    TCLC 1, 6, 64; DAM NOV, POET; PC 28;
    SSC 1
See also CA 104; 132; CANR 73; CDBLB
    1914-1945; DLB 10, 19, 34, 70, 98, 149,
    178; MTCW 1, 2; SATA 27
Chiang, Pin-chin 1904-1986
See Ding Ling
See also CA 118
Ch'ien Chung-shu 1910-   **CLC 22**
See also CA 130; CANR 73; MTCW 1, 2
Child, L. Maria
See Child, Lydia Maria
Child, Lydia Maria 1802-1880   **NCLC 6, 73**
See also DLB 1, 74; SATA 67
Child, Mrs.
See Child, Lydia Maria
Child, Philip 1898-1978   **CLC 19, 68**
See also CA 13-14; CAP 1; SATA 47
Childers, (Robert) Erskine 1870-1922
    TCLC 65
See also CA 113; 153; DLB 70
Childress, Alice 1920-1994**CLC 12, 15, 86, 96;**
    BLC 1; DAM DRAM, MULT, NOV; DC 4
See also AAYA 8; BW 2, 3; CA 45-48; 146;
    CANR 3, 27, 50, 74; CLR 14; DA3; DLB 7,
    38; JRDA; MAICYA; MTCW 1, 2; SATA 7,
    48, 81
Chin, Frank (Chew, Jr.) 1940-   **DC 7**
See also CA 33-36R; CANR 71; DAM MULT;
    DLB 206
Chislett, (Margaret) Anne 1943-   **CLC 34**
See also CA 151
Chitty, Thomas Willes 1926-   **CLC 11**
See also Hinde, Thomas
See also CA 5-8R
Chivers, Thomas Holley 1809-1858**NCLC 49**
See also DLB 3
Choi, Susan   **CLC 119**
Chomette, Rene Lucien 1898-1981
See Clair, Rene
See also CA 103

See also CA 17-20R; CANR 8, 22, 74; DLB 14; INT CANR-22; MTCW 1

Coleman, Emmett
See Reed, Ishmael

Coleridge, M. E.
See Coleridge, Mary E(lizabeth)

Coleridge, Mary E(lizabeth) 1861-1907**TCLC 73**
See also CA 116; 166; DLB 19, 98

Coleridge, Samuel Taylor 1772-1834**NCLC 9, 54; DA; DAB; DAC; DAM MST, POET; PC 11; WLC**
See also CDBLB 1789-1832; DA3; DLB 93, 107

Coleridge, Sara 1802-1852   **NCLC 31**
See also DLB 199

Coles, Don 1928-   **CLC 46**
See also CA 115; CANR 38

Coles, Robert (Martin) 1929-   **CLC 108**
See also CA 45-48; CANR 3, 32, 66, 70; INT CANR-32; SATA 23

Colette, (Sidonie-Gabrielle) 1873-1954**TCLC 1, 5, 16; DAM NOV; SSC 10**
See also CA 104; 131; DA3; DLB 65; MTCW 1, 2

Collett, (Jacobine) Camilla (Wergeland) 1813-1895   **NCLC 22**

Collier, Christopher 1930-   **CLC 30**
See also AAYA 13; CA 33-36R; CANR 13, 33; JRDA; MAICYA; SATA 16, 70

Collier, James L(incoln) 1928-**CLC 30; DAM POP**
See also AAYA 13; CA 9-12R; CANR 4, 33, 60; CLR 3; JRDA; MAICYA; SAAS 21; SATA 8, 70

Collier, Jeremy 1650-1726   **LC 6**

Collier, John 1901-1980   **SSC 19**
See also CA 65-68; 97-100; CANR 10; DLB 77

Collingwood, R(obin) G(eorge) 1889(?)-1943 **TCLC 67**
See also CA 117; 155

Collins, Hunt
See Hunter, Evan

Collins, Linda 1931-   **CLC 44**
See also CA 125

Collins, (William) Wilkie 1824-1889**NCLC 1, 18**
See also CDBLB 1832-1890; DLB 18, 70, 159

Collins, William 1721-1759 **LC 4, 40; DAM POET**
See also DLB 109

Collodi, Carlo 1826-1890   **NCLC 54**
See also Lorenzini, Carlo
See also CLR 5

Colman, George 1732-1794
See Glassco, John

Colt, Winchester Remington
See Hubbard, L(afayette) Ron(ald)

Colter, Cyrus 1910-   **CLC 58**
See also BW 1; CA 65-68; CANR 10, 66; DLB 33

Colton, James
See Hansen, Joseph

Colum, Padraic 1881-1972   **CLC 28**
See also CA 73-76; 33-36R; CANR 35; CLR 36; MAICYA; MTCW 1; SATA 15

Colvin, James
See Moorcock, Michael (John)

Colwin, Laurie (E.) 1944-1992**CLC 5, 13, 23, 84**
See also CA 89-92; 139; CANR 20, 46; DLBY 80; MTCW 1

Comfort, Alex(ander) 1920-**CLC 7; DAM POP**
See also CA 1-4R; CANR 1, 45; MTCW 1

Comfort, Montgomery
See Campbell, (John) Ramsey

Compton-Burnett, I(vy) 1884(?)-1969**CLC 1, 3, 10, 15, 34; DAM NOV**
See also CA 1-4R; 25-28R; CANR 4; DLB 36; MTCW 1

Comstock, Anthony 1844-1915   **TCLC 13**
See also CA 110; 169

Comte, Auguste 1798-1857   **NCLC 54**

Conan Doyle, Arthur
See Doyle, Arthur Conan

Conde (Abellan), Carmen 1901-
See also CA 177; DLB 108; HLCS 1; HW 2

Conde, Maryse 1937-   **CLC 52, 92; BLCS; DAM MULT**
See also Boucolon, Maryse
See also BW 2; MTCW 1

Condillac, Etienne Bonnot de 1714-1780 **LC 26**

Condon, Richard (Thomas) 1915-1996**CLC 4, 6, 8, 10, 45, 100; DAM NOV**
See also BEST 90:3; CA 1-4R; 151; CAAS 1; CANR 2, 23; INT CANR-23; MTCW 1, 2

Confucius 551B.C.-479B.C.   **CMLC 19; DA; DAB; DAC; DAM MST; WLCS**
See also DA3

Congreve, William 1670-1729 **LC 5, 21; DA; DAB; DAC; DAM DRAM, MST, POET; DC 2; WLC**
See also CDBLB 1660-1789; DLB 39, 84

Connell, Evan S(helby), Jr. 1924-**CLC 4, 6, 45; DAM NOV**
See also AAYA 7; CA 1-4R; CAAS 2; CANR 2, 39, 76; DLB 2; DLBY 81; MTCW 1, 2

Connelly, Marc(us Cook) 1890-1980   **CLC 7**
See also CA 85-88; 102; CANR 30; DLB 7; DLBY 80; SATA-Obit 25

Connor, Ralph   **TCLC 31**
See also Gordon, Charles William
See also DLB 92

Conrad, Joseph 1857-1924**TCLC 1, 6, 13, 25, 43, 57; DA; DAB; DAC; DAM MST, NOV; SSC 9; WLC**
See also AAYA 26; CA 104; 131; CANR 60; CDBLB 1890-1914; DA3; DLB 10, 34, 98, 156; MTCW 1, 2; SATA 27

Conrad, Robert Arnold
See Hart, Moss

Conroy, Pat
See Conroy, (Donald) Pat(rick)
See also MTCW 2

Conroy, (Donald) Pat(rick) 1945-**CLC 30, 74; DAM NOV, POP**
See also Conroy, Pat
See also AAYA 8; AITN 1; CA 85-88; CANR 24, 53; DA3; DLB 6; MTCW 1

Constant (de Rebecque), (Henri) Benjamin 1767-1830   **NCLC 6**
See also DLB 119

Conybeare, Charles Augustus
See Eliot, T(homas) S(tearns)

Cook, Michael 1933-   **CLC 58**
See also CA 93-96; CANR 68; DLB 53

Cook, Robin 1940-   **CLC 14; DAM POP**
See also AAYA 32; BEST 90:2; CA 108; 111; CANR 41; DA3; INT 111

Cook, Roy
See Silverberg, Robert

Cooke, Elizabeth 1948-   **CLC 55**
See also CA 129

Cooke, John Esten 1830-1886   **NCLC 5**
See also DLB 3

Cooke, John Estes

See Baum, L(yman) Frank

Cooke, M. E.
See Creasey, John

Cooke, Margaret
See Creasey, John

Cook-Lynn, Elizabeth 1930-   **CLC 93; DAM MULT**
See also CA 133; DLB 175; NNAL

Cooney, Ray   **CLC 62**

Cooper, Douglas 1960-   **CLC 86**

Cooper, Henry St. John
See Creasey, John

Cooper, J(oan) California (?)-**CLC 56; DAM MULT**
See also AAYA 12; BW 1; CA 125; CANR 55; DLB 212

Cooper, James Fenimore 1789-1851**NCLC 1, 27, 54**
See also AAYA 22; CDALB 1640-1865; DA3; DLB 3; SATA 19

Coover, Robert (Lowell) 1932- **CLC 3, 7, 15, 32, 46, 87; DAM NOV; SSC 15**
See also CA 45-48; CANR 3, 37, 58; DLB 2; DLBY 81; MTCW 1, 2

Copeland, Stewart (Armstrong) 1952-**CLC 26**

Copernicus, Nicolaus 1473-1543   **LC 45**

Coppard, A(lfred) E(dgar) 1878-1957 **TCLC 5; SSC 21**
See also CA 114; 167; DLB 162; YABC 1

Coppee, Francois 1842-1908   **TCLC 25**
See also CA 170

Coppola, Francis Ford 1939-   **CLC 16, 126**
See also CA 77-80; CANR 40, 78; DLB 44

Corbiere, Tristan 1845-1875   **NCLC 43**

Corcoran, Barbara 1911-   **CLC 17**
See also AAYA 14; CA 21-24R; CAAS 2; CANR 11, 28, 48; CLR 50; DLB 52; JRDA; SAAS 20; SATA 3, 77

Cordelier, Maurice
See Giraudoux, (Hippolyte) Jean

Corelli, Marie 1855-1924   **TCLC 51**
See also Mackay, Mary
See also DLB 34, 156

Corman, Cid 1924-   **CLC 9**
See also Corman, Sidney
See also CAAS 2; DLB 5, 193

Corman, Sidney 1924-
See Corman, Cid
See also CA 85-88; CANR 44; DAM POET

Cormier, Robert (Edmund) 1925-**CLC 12, 30; DA; DAB; DAC; DAM MST, NOV**
See also AAYA 3, 19; CA 1-4R; CANR 5, 23, 76; CDALB 1968-1988; CLR 12, 55; DLB 52; INT CANR-23; JRDA; MAICYA; MTCW 1, 2; SATA 10, 45, 83

Corn, Alfred (DeWitt III) 1943-   **CLC 33**
See also CA 179; CAAE 179; CAAS 25; CANR 44; DLB 120; DLBY 80

Corneille, Pierre 1606-1684   **LC 28; DAB; DAM MST**

Cornwell, David (John Moore) 1931- **CLC 9, 15; DAM POP**
See also le Carre, John
See also CA 5-8R; CANR 13, 33, 59; DA3; MTCW 1, 2

Corso, (Nunzio) Gregory 1930-   **CLC 1, 11**
See also CA 5-8R; CANR 41, 76; DA3; DLB 5, 16; MTCW 1, 2

Cortazar, Julio 1914-1984**CLC 2, 3, 5, 10, 13, 15, 33, 34, 92; DAM MULT, NOV; HLC 1; SSC 7**
See also CA 21-24R; CANR 12, 32, 81; DA3; DLB 113; HW 1, 2; MTCW 1, 2

Corties, Hernan 1484-1547   LC 31
Corvinus, Jakob
    See Raabe, Wilhelm (Karl)
Corwin, Cecil
    See Kornbluth, C(yril) M.
Cosic, Dobrica 1921-   CLC 14
    See also CA 122; 138; DLB 181
Costain, Thomas B(ertram) 1885-1965CLC 30
    See also CA 5-8R; 25-28R; DLB 9
Costantini, Humberto 1924(?)-1987   CLC 49
    See also CA 131; 122; HW 1
Costello, Elvis 1955-   CLC 21
Costenoble, Philostene
    See Ghelderode, Michel de
Cotes, Cecil V.
    See Duncan, Sara Jeannette
Cotter, Joseph Seamon Sr. 1861-1949 T C L C
    28; BLC 1; DAM MULT
    See also BW 1; CA 124; DLB 50
Couch, Arthur Thomas Quiller
    See Quiller-Couch, SirArthur (Thomas)
Coulton, James
    See Hansen, Joseph
Couperus, Louis (Marie Anne) 1863-1923
    TCLC 15
    See also CA 115
Coupland, Douglas 1961-   CLC 85; DAC;
    DAM POP
    See also CA 142; CANR 57
Court, Wesli
    See Turco, Lewis (Putnam)
Courtenay, Bryce 1933-   CLC 59
    See also CA 138
Courtney, Robert
    See Ellison, Harlan (Jay)
Cousteau, Jacques-Yves 1910-1997 CLC 30
    See also CA 65-68; 159; CANR 15, 67; MTCW
    1; SATA 38, 98
Coventry, Francis 1725-1754   LC 46
Cowan, Peter (Walkinshaw) 1914-   SSC 28
    See also CA 21-24R; CANR 9, 25, 50, 83
Coward, Noel (Peirce) 1899-1973CLC 1, 9, 29,
    51; DAM DRAM
    See also AITN 1; CA 17-18; 41-44R; CANR
    35; CAP 2; CDBLB 1914-1945; DA3; DLB
    10; MTCW 1, 2
Cowley, Abraham 1618-1667   LC 43
    See also DLB 131, 151
Cowley, Malcolm 1898-1989   CLC 39
    See also CA 5-8R; 128; CANR 3, 55; DLB 4,
    48; DLBY 81, 89; MTCW 1, 2
Cowper, William 1731-1800 NCLC 8; DAM
    POET
    See also DA3; DLB 104, 109
Cox, William Trevor 1928-   CLC 9, 14, 71;
    DAM NOV
    See Trevor, William
    See also CA 9-12R; CANR 4, 37, 55, 76; DLB
    14; INT CANR-37; MTCW 1, 2
Coyne, P. J.
    See Masters, Hilary
Cozzens, James Gould 1903-1978 CLC 1, 4,
    11, 92
    See also CA 9-12R; 81-84; CANR 19; CDALB
    1941-1968; DLB 9; DLBD 2; DLBY 84, 97;
    MTCW 1, 2
Crabbe, George 1754-1832   NCLC 26
    See also DLB 93
Craddock, Charles Egbert
    See Murfree, Mary Noailles
Craig, A. A.
    See Anderson, Poul (William)
Craik, Dinah Maria (Mulock) 1826-1887

NCLC 38
    See also DLB 35, 163; MAICYA; SATA 34
Cram, Ralph Adams 1863-1942   TCLC 45
    See also CA 160
Crane, (Harold) Hart 1899-1932 TCLC 2, 5,
    80; DA; DAB; DAC; DAM MST, POET;
    PC 3; WLC
    See also CA 104; 127; CDALB 1917-1929;
    DA3; DLB 4, 48; MTCW 1, 2
Crane, R(onald) S(almon) 1886-1967CLC 27
    See also CA 85-88; DLB 63
Crane, Stephen (Townley) 1871-1900 T C L C
    11, 17, 32; DA; DAB; DAC; DAM MST,
    NOV, POET; SSC 7; WLC
    See also AAYA 21; CA 109; 140; CANR 84;
    CDALB 1865-1917; DA3; DLB 12, 54, 78;
    YABC 2
Cranshaw, Stanley
    See Fisher, Dorothy (Frances) Canfield
Crase, Douglas 1944-   CLC 58
    See also CA 106
Crashaw, Richard 1612(?)-1649   LC 24
    See also DLB 126
Craven, Margaret 1901-1980 CLC 17; DAC
    See also CA 103
Crawford, F(rancis) Marion 1854-1909
    TCLC 10
    See also CA 107; 168; DLB 71
Crawford, Isabella Valancy 1850-1887
    NCLC 12
    See also DLB 92
Crayon, Geoffrey
    See Irving, Washington
Creasey, John 1908-1973   CLC 11
    See also CA 5-8R; 41-44R; CANR 8, 59; DLB
    77; MTCW 1
Crebillon, Claude Prosper Jolyot de (fils) 1707-
    1777   LC 1, 28
Credo
    See Creasey, John
Credo, Alvaro J. de
    See Prado (Calvo), Pedro
Creeley, Robert (White) 1926-CLC 1, 2, 4, 8,
    11, 15, 36, 78; DAM POET
    See also CA 1-4R; CAAS 10; CANR 23, 43; DA3;
    DLB 5, 16, 169; DLBD 17; MTCW 1, 2
Crews, Harry (Eugene) 1935- CLC 6, 23, 49
    See also AITN 1; CA 25-28R; CANR 20, 57;
    DA3; DLB 6, 143, 185; MTCW 1, 2
Crichton, (John) Michael 1942-CLC 2, 6, 54,
    90; DAM NOV, POP
    See also AAYA 10; AITN 2; CA 25-28R; CANR
    13, 40, 54, 76; DA3; DLBY 81; INT CANR-
    13; JRDA; MTCW 1, 2; SATA 9, 88
Crispin, Edmund   CLC 22
    See also Montgomery, (Robert) Bruce
    See also DLB 87
Cristofer, Michael 1945(?)-   CLC 28; DAM
    DRAM
    See also CA 110; 152; DLB 7
Croce, Benedetto 1866-1952   TCLC 37
    See also CA 120; 155
Crockett, David 1786-1836   NCLC 8
    See also DLB 3, 11
Crockett, Davy
    See Crockett, David
Crofts, Freeman Wills 1879-1957   TCLC 55
    See also CA 115; DLB 77
Croker, John Wilson 1780-1857   NCLC 10
    See also DLB 110
Crommelynck, Fernand 1885-1970   CLC 75
    See also CA 89-92
Cromwell, Oliver 1599-1658   LC 43

Cronin, A(rchibald) J(oseph) 1896-1981
    CLC 32
    See also CA 1-4R; 102; CANR 5; DLB 191;
    SATA 47; SATA-Obit 25
Cross, Amanda
    See Heilbrun, Carolyn G(old)
Crothers, Rachel 1878(?)-1958   TCLC 19
    See also CA 113; DLB 7
Croves, Hal
    See Traven, B.
Crow Dog, Mary (Ellen) (?)-   CLC 93
    See also Brave Bird, Mary
    See also CA 154
Crowfield, Christopher
    See Stowe, Harriet (Elizabeth) Beecher
Crowley, Aleister   TCLC 7
    See also Crowley, Edward Alexander
Crowley, Edward Alexander 1875-1947
    See Crowley, Aleister
    See also CA 104
Crowley, John 1942-   CLC 57
    See also CA 61-64; CANR 43; DLBY 82;
    SATA 65
Crud
    See Crumb, R(obert)
Crumarums
    See Crumb, R(obert)
Crumb, R(obert) 1943-   CLC 17
    See also CA 106
Crumbum
    See Crumb, R(obert)
Crumski
    See Crumb, R(obert)
Crum the Bum
    See Crumb, R(obert)
Crunk
    See Crumb, R(obert)
Crustt
    See Crumb, R(obert)
Cruz, Victor Hernandez 1949-
    See also BW 2; CA 65-68; CAAS 17; CANR
    14, 32, 74; DAM MULT, POET; DLB 41;
    HLC 1; HW 1, 2; MTCW 1
Cryer, Gretchen (Kiger) 1935-   CLC 21
    See also CA 114; 123
Csath, Geza 1887-1919   TCLC 13
    See also CA 111
Cudlip, David R(ockwell) 1933-   CLC 34
    See also CA 177
Cullen, Countee 1903-1946TCLC 4, 37; BLC
    1; DA; DAC; DAM MST, MULT, POET;
    PC 20; WLCS
    See also BW 1; CA 108; 124; CDALB 1917-
    1929; DA3; DLB 4, 48, 51; MTCW 1, 2;
    SATA 18
Cum, R.
    See Crumb, R(obert)
Cummings, Bruce F(rederick) 1889-1919
    See Barbellion, W. N. P.
    See also CA 123
Cummings, E(dward) E(stlin) 1894-1962CLC
    1, 3, 8, 12, 15, 68; DA; DAB; DAC; DAM
    MST, POET; PC 5; WLC
    See also CA 73-76; CANR 31; CDALB 1929-
    1941; DA3; DLB 4, 48; MTCW 1, 2
Cunha, Euclides (Rodrigues Pimenta) da 1866-
    1909   TCLC 24
    See also CA 123
Cunningham, E. V.
    See Fast, Howard (Melvin)
Cunningham, J(ames) V(incent) 1911-1985
    CLC 3, 31
    See also CA 1-4R; 115; CANR 1, 72; DLB 5

Cunningham, Julia (Woolfolk) 1916- **CLC 12**
See also CA 9-12R; CANR 4, 19, 36; JRDA;
MAICYA; SAAS 2; SATA 1, 26
Cunningham, Michael 1952- **CLC 34**
See also CA 136
Cunninghame Graham, R(obert) B(ontine)
1852-1936 **TCLC 19**
See also Graham, R(obert) B(ontine)
Cunninghame
See also CA 119; DLB 98
Currie, Ellen 19(?)- **CLC 44**
Curtin, Philip
See Lowndes, Marie Adelaide (Belloc)
Curtis, Price
See Ellison, Harlan (Jay)
Cutrate, Joe
See Spiegelman, Art
Cynewulf c. 770-c. 840 **CMLC 23**
Czaczkes, Shmuel Yosef
See Agnon, S(hmuel) Y(osef Halevi)
Dabrowska, Maria (Szumska) 1889-1965
CLC 15
See also CA 106
Dabydeen, David 1955- **CLC 34**
See also BW 1; CA 125; CANR 56
Dacey, Philip 1939- **CLC 51**
See also CA 37-40R; CAAS 17; CANR 14, 32,
64; DLB 105
Dagerman, Stig (Halvard) 1923-1954
TCLC 17
See also CA 117; 155
Dahl, Roald 1916-1990 **CLC 1, 6, 18, 79; DAB;**
DAC; DAM MST, NOV, POP
See also AAYA 15; CA 1-4R; 133; CANR 6,
32, 37, 62; CLR 1, 7, 41; DA3; DLB 139;
JRDA; MAICYA; MTCW 1, 2; SATA 1, 26,
73; SATA-Obit 65
Dahlberg, Edward 1900-1977 **CLC 1, 7, 14**
See also CA 9-12R; 69-72; CANR 31, 62; DLB
48; MTCW 1
Daitch, Susan 1954- **CLC 103**
See also CA 161
Dale, Colin **TCLC 18**
See also Lawrence, T(homas) E(dward)
Dale, George E.
See Asimov, Isaac
Dalton, Roque 1935-1975
See also HLCS 1; HW 2
Daly, Elizabeth 1878-1967 **CLC 52**
See also CA 23-24; 25-28R; CANR 60; CAP 2
Daly, Maureen 1921- **CLC 17**
See also AAYA 5; CANR 37, 83; JRDA;
MAICYA; SAAS 1; SATA 2
Damas, Leon-Gontran 1912-1978 **CLC 84**
See also BW 1; CA 125; 73-76
Dana, Richard Henry Sr. 1787-1879 **NCLC 53**
Daniel, Samuel 1562(?)-1619 **LC 24**
See also DLB 62
Daniels, Brett
See Adler, Renata
Dannay, Frederic 1905-1982 **CLC 11; DAM**
POP
See also Queen, Ellery
See also CA 1-4R; 107; CANR 1, 39; DLB 137;
MTCW 1
D'Annunzio, Gabriele 1863-1938 **TCLC 6, 40**
See also CA 104; 155
Danois, N. le
See Gourmont, Remy (-Marie-Charles) de
Dante 1265-1321 **CMLC 3, 18; DA; DAB;**
DAC; DAM MST, POET; PC 21; WLCS
See also DA3
d'Antibes, Germain

See Simenon, Georges (Jacques Christian)
Danticat, Edwidge 1969- **CLC 94**
See also AAYA 29; CA 152; CANR 73;
MTCW 1
Danvers, Dennis 1947- **CLC 70**
Danziger, Paula 1944- **CLC 21**
See also AAYA 4; CA 112; 115; CANR 37; CLR
20; JRDA; MAICYA; SATA 36, 63, 102;
SATA-Brief 30
Da Ponte, Lorenzo 1749-1838 **NCLC 50**
Dario, Ruben 1867-1916 **TCLC 4; DAM**
MULT; HLC 1; PC 15
See also CA 131; CANR 81; HW 1, 2; MTCW
1, 2
Darley, George 1795-1846 **NCLC 2**
See also DLB 96
Darrow, Clarence (Seward) 1857-1938
TCLC 81
See also CA 164
Darwin, Charles 1809-1882 **NCLC 57**
See also DLB 57, 166
Daryush, Elizabeth 1887-1977 **CLC 6, 19**
See also CA 49-52; CANR 3, 81; DLB 20
Dasgupta, Surendranath 1887-1952 **TCLC 81**
See also CA 157
Dashwood, Edmee Elizabeth Monica de la Pas-
ture 1890-1943
See Delafield, E. M.
See also CA 119; 154
Daudet, (Louis Marie) Alphonse 1840-1897
NCLC 1
See also DLB 123
Daumal, Rene 1908-1944 **TCLC 14**
See also CA 114
Davenant, William 1606-1668 **LC 13**
See also DLB 58, 126
Davenport, Guy (Mattison, Jr.) 1927- **CLC 6,**
14, 38; SSC 16
See also CA 33-36R; CANR 23, 73; DLB 130
Davidson, Avram (James) 1923-1993
See Queen, Ellery
See also CA 101; 171; CANR 26; DLB 8
Davidson, Donald (Grady) 1893-1968 **CLC 2,**
13, 19
See also CA 5-8R; 25-28R; CANR 4, 84;
DLB 45
Davidson, Hugh
See Hamilton, Edmond
Davidson, John 1857-1909 **TCLC 24**
See also CA 118; DLB 19
Davidson, Sara 1943- **CLC 9**
See also CA 81-84; CANR 44, 68; DLB 185
Davie, Donald (Alfred) 1922-1995 **CLC 5, 8,**
10, 31
See also CA 1-4R; 149; CAAS 3; CANR 1, 44;
DLB 27; MTCW 1
Davies, Ray(mond Douglas) 1944- **CLC 21**
See also CA 116; 146
Davies, Rhys 1901-1978 **CLC 23**
See also CA 9-12R; 81-84; CANR 4; DLB
139, 191
Davies, (William) Robertson 1913-1995 **C L C**
2, 7, 13, 25, 42, 75, 91; DA; DAB; DAC;
DAM MST, NOV, POP; WLC
See also BEST 89:2; CA 33-36R; 150; CANR
17, 42; DA3; DLB 68; INT CANR-17;
MTCW 1, 2
Davies, Walter C.
See Kornbluth, C(yril) M.
Davies, William Henry 1871-1940 **TCLC 5**
See also CA 104; 179; DLB 19, 174
Davis, Angela (Yvonne) 1944- **CLC 77;**
DAM MULT

See also BW 2, 3; CA 57-60; CANR 10, 81; DA3
Davis, B. Lynch
See Bioy Casares, Adolfo; Borges, Jorge Luis
Davis, B. Lynch
See Bioy Casares, Adolfo
Davis, H(arold) L(enoir) 1894-1960 **CLC 49**
See also CA 178; 89-92; DLB 9, 206
Davis, Rebecca (Blaine) Harding 1831-1910
TCLC 6
See also CA 104; 179; DLB 74
Davis, Richard Harding 1864-1916 **TCLC 24**
See also CA 114; 179; DLB 12, 23, 78, 79, 189;
DLBD 13
Davison, Frank Dalby 1893-1970 **CLC 15**
See also CA 116
Davison, Lawrence H.
See Lawrence, D(avid) H(erbert Richards)
Davison, Peter (Hubert) 1928- **CLC 28**
See also CA 9-12R; CAAS 4; CANR 3, 43, 84;
DLB 5
Davys, Mary 1674-1732 **LC 1, 46**
See also DLB 39
Dawson, Fielding 1930- **CLC 6**
See also CA 85-88; DLB 130
Dawson, Peter
See Faust, Frederick (Schiller)
Day, Clarence (Shepard, Jr.) 1874-1935
TCLC 25
See also CA 108; DLB 11
Day, Thomas 1748-1789 **LC 1**
See also DLB 39; YABC 1
Day Lewis, C(ecil) 1904-1972 **CLC 1, 6, 10;**
DAM POET; PC 11
See also Blake, Nicholas
See also CA 13-16; 33-36R; CANR 34; CAP 1;
DLB 15, 20; MTCW 1, 2
Dazai Osamu 1909-1948 **TCLC 11**
See also Tsushima, Shuji
See also CA 164; DLB 182
de Andrade, Carlos Drummond 1892-1945
See Drummond de Andrade, Carlos
Deane, Norman
See Creasey, John
Deane, Seamus (Francis) 1940- **CLC 122**
See also CA 118; CANR 42
de Beauvoir, Simone (Lucie Ernestine Marie
Bertrand)
See Beauvoir, Simone (Lucie Ernestine Marie
Bertrand) de
de Beer, P.
See Bosman, Herman Charles
de Brissac, Malcolm
See Dickinson, Peter (Malcolm)
de Chardin, Pierre Teilhard
See Teilhard de Chardin, (Marie Joseph) Pierre
Dee, John 1527-1608 **LC 20**
Deer, Sandra 1940- **CLC 45**
De Ferrari, Gabriella 1941- **CLC 65**
See also CA 146
Defoe, Daniel 1660(?)-1731 **LC 1, 42; DA;**
DAB; DAC; DAM MST, NOV; WLC
See also AAYA 27; CDBLB 1660-1789; CLR
61; DA3; DLB 39, 95, 101; JRDA; MAICYA;
SATA 22
de Gourmont, Remy(-Marie-Charles)
See Gourmont, Remy (-Marie-Charles) de
de Hartog, Jan 1914- **CLC 19**
See also CA 1-4R; CANR 1
de Hostos, E. M.
See Hostos (y Bonilla), Eugenio Maria de
de Hostos, Eugenio M.
See Hostos (y Bonilla), Eugenio Maria de
Deighton, Len **CLC 4, 7, 22, 46**

See also Deighton, Leonard Cyril
See also AAYA 6; BEST 89:2; CDBLB 1960 to Present; DLB 87

Deighton, Leonard Cyril 1929-
See Deighton, Len
See also CA 9-12R; CANR 19, 33, 68; DAM NOV, POP; DA3; MTCW 1, 2

Dekker, Thomas 1572(?)-1632   **LC 22; DAM DRAM**
See also CDBLB Before 1660; DLB 62, 172

Delafield, E. M. 1890-1943   **TCLC 61**
See also Dashwood, Edmee Elizabeth Monica de la Pasture
See also DLB 34

de la Mare, Walter (John) 1873-1956**TCLC 4, 53; DAB; DAC; DAM MST, POET; SSC 14; WLC**
See also CA 163; CDBLB 1914-1945; CLR 23; DA3; DLB 162; MTCW 1; SATA 16

Delaney, Franey
See O'Hara, John (Henry)

Delaney, Shelagh 1939-**CLC 29; DAM DRAM**
See also CA 17-20R; CANR 30, 67; CDBLB 1960 to Present; DLB 13; MTCW 1

Delany, Mary (Granville Pendarves) 1700-1788   **LC 12**

Delany, Samuel R(ay, Jr.) 1942-**CLC 8, 14, 38; BLC 1; DAM MULT**
See also AAYA 24; BW 2, 3; CA 81-84; CANR 27, 43; DLB 8, 33; MTCW 1, 2

De La Ramee, (Marie) Louise 1839-1908
See Ouida
See also SATA 20

de la Roche, Mazo 1879-1961   **CLC 14**
See also CA 85-88; CANR 30; DLB 68; SATA 64

De La Salle, Innocent
See Hartmann, Sadakichi

Delbanco, Nicholas (Franklin) 1942- **C L C 6, 13**
See also CA 17-20R; CAAS 2; CANR 29, 55; DLB 6

del Castillo, Michel 1933-   **CLC 38**
See also CA 109; CANR 77

Deledda, Grazia (Cosima) 1875(?)-1936   **TCLC 23**
See also CA 123

Delgado, Abelardo B(arrientos) 1931-
See also CA 131; CAAS 15; DAM MST, MULT; DLB 82; HLC 1; HW 1, 2

Delibes, Miguel   **CLC 8, 18**
See also Delibes Setien, Miguel

Delibes Setien, Miguel 1920-
See Delibes, Miguel
See also CA 45-48; CANR 1, 32; HW 1; MTCW 1

DeLillo, Don 1936- **CLC 8, 10, 13, 27, 39, 54, 76; DAM NOV, POP**
See also BEST 89:1; CA 81-84; CANR 21, 76; DA3; DLB 6, 173; MTCW 1, 2

de Lisser, H. G.
See De Lisser, H(erbert) G(eorge)
See also DLB 117

De Lisser, H(erbert) G(eorge) 1878-1944   **TCLC 12**
See also de Lisser, H. G.
See also BW 2; CA 109; 152

Deloney, Thomas 1560(?)-1600   **LC 41**
See also DLB 167

Deloria, Vine (Victor), Jr. 1933-**CLC 21, 122; DAM MULT**
See also CA 53-56; CANR 5, 20, 48; DLB 175; MTCW 1; NNAL; SATA 21

Del Vecchio, John M(ichael) 1947-   **CLC 29**
See also CA 110; DLBD 9

de Man, Paul (Adolph Michel) 1919-1983   **CLC 55**
See also CA 128; 111; CANR 61; DLB 67; MTCW 1, 2

De Marinis, Rick 1934-   **CLC 54**
See also CA 57-60; CAAS 24; CANR 9, 25, 50

Dembry, R. Emmet
See Murfree, Mary Noailles

Demby, William 1922-**CLC 53; BLC 1; DAM MULT**
See also BW 1, 3; CA 81-84; CANR 81; DLB 33

de Menton, Francisco
See Chin, Frank (Chew, Jr.)

Demetrius of Phalerum c. 307B.C.-**CMLC 34**

Demijohn, Thom
See Disch, Thomas M(ichael)

de Molina, Tirso 1580-1648
See also HLCS 2

de Montherlant, Henry (Milon)
See Montherlant, Henry (Milon) de

Demosthenes 384B.C.-322B.C.   **CMLC 13**
See also DLB 176

de Natale, Francine
See Malzberg, Barry N(athaniel)

Denby, Edwin (Orr) 1903-1983   **CLC 48**
See also CA 138; 110

Denis, Julio
See Cortazar, Julio

Denmark, Harrison
See Zelazny, Roger (Joseph)

Dennis, John 1658-1734   **LC 11**
See also DLB 101

Dennis, Nigel (Forbes) 1912-1989   **CLC 8**
See also CA 25-28R; 129; DLB 13, 15; MTCW 1

Dent, Lester 1904(?)-1959   **TCLC 72**
See also CA 112; 161

De Palma, Brian (Russell) 1940-   **CLC 20**
See also CA 109

De Quincey, Thomas 1785-1859   **NCLC 4**
See also CDBLB 1789-1832; DLB 110; 144

Deren, Eleanora 1908(?)-1961
See Deren, Maya
See also CA 111

Deren, Maya 1917-1961   **CLC 16, 102**
See also Deren, Eleanora

Derleth, August (William) 1909-1971**CLC 31**
See also CA 1-4R; 29-32R; CANR 4; DLB 9; DLBD 17; SATA 5

Der Nister 1884-1950   **TCLC 56**

de Routisie, Albert
See Aragon, Louis

Derrida, Jacques 1930-   **CLC 24, 87**
See also CA 124; 127; CANR 76; MTCW 1

Derry Down Derry
See Lear, Edward

Dersonnes, Jacques
See Simenon, Georges (Jacques Christian)

Desai, Anita 1937-**CLC 19, 37, 97; DAB; DAM NOV**
See also CA 81-84; CANR 33, 53; DA3; MTCW 1, 2; SATA 63

Desai, Kiran 1971-   **CLC 119**
See also CA 171

de Saint-Luc, Jean
See Glassco, John

de Saint Roman, Arnaud
See Aragon, Louis

Descartes, Rene 1596-1650   **LC 20, 35**

De Sica, Vittorio 1901(?)-1974   **CLC 20**
See also CA 117

Desnos, Robert 1900-1945   **TCLC 22**
See also CA 121; 151

Destouches, Louis-Ferdinand 1894-1961**C L C 9, 15**
See also Celine, Louis-Ferdinand
See also CA 85-88; CANR 28; MTCW 1

de Tolignac, Gaston
See Griffith, D(avid Lewelyn) W(ark)

Deutsch, Babette 1895-1982   **CLC 18**
See also CA 1-4R; 108; CANR 4, 79; DLB 45; SATA 1; SATA-Obit 33

Devenant, William 1606-1649   **LC 13**

Devkota, Laxmiprasad 1909-1959 **TCLC 23**
See also CA 123

De Voto, Bernard (Augustine) 1897-1955   **TCLC 29**
See also CA 113; 160; DLB 9

De Vries, Peter 1910-1993 **CLC 1, 2, 3, 7, 10, 28, 46; DAM NOV**
See also CA 17-20R; 142; CANR 41; DLB 6; DLBY 82; MTCW 1, 2

Dewey, John 1859-1952   **TCLC 95**
See also CA 114; 170

Dexter, John
See Bradley, Marion Zimmer

Dexter, Martin
See Faust, Frederick (Schiller)

Dexter, Pete 1943-   **CLC 34, 55; DAM POP**
See also BEST 89:2; CA 127; 131; INT 131; MTCW 1

Diamano, Silmang
See Senghor, Leopold Sedar

Diamond, Neil 1941-   **CLC 30**
See also CA 108

Diaz del Castillo, Bernal 1496-1584   **LC 31; HLCS 1**

di Bassetto, Corno
See Shaw, George Bernard

Dick, Philip K(indred) 1928-1982**CLC 10, 30, 72; DAM NOV, POP**
See also AAYA 24; CA 49-52; 106; CANR 2, 16; DA3; DLB 8; MTCW 1, 2

Dickens, Charles (John Huffam) 1812-1870   **NCLC 3, 8, 18, 26, 37, 50; DA; DAB; DAC; DAM MST, NOV; SSC 17; WLC**
See also AAYA 23; CDBLB 1832-1890; DA3; DLB 21, 55, 70, 159, 166; JRDA; MAICYA; SATA 15

Dickey, James (Lafayette) 1923-1997 **CLC 1, 2, 4, 7, 10, 15, 47, 109; DAM NOV, POET, POP**
See also AITN 1, 2; CA 9-12R; 156; CABS 2; CANR 10, 48, 61; CDALB 1968-1988; DA3; DLB 5, 193; DLBD 7; DLBY 82, 93, 96, 97, 98; INT CANR-10; MTCW 1, 2

Dickey, William 1928-1994   **CLC 3, 28**
See also CA 9-12R; 145; CANR 24, 79; DLB 5

Dickinson, Charles 1951-   **CLC 49**
See also CA 128

Dickinson, Emily (Elizabeth) 1830-1886   **NCLC 21, 77; DA; DAB; DAC; DAM MST, POET; PC 1; WLC**
See also AAYA 22; CDALB 1865-1917; DA3; DLB 1; SATA 29

Dickinson, Peter (Malcolm) 1927-**CLC 12, 35**
See also AAYA 9; CA 41-44R; CANR 31, 58; CLR 29; DLB 87, 161; JRDA; MAICYA; SATA 5, 62, 95

Dickson, Carr
See Carr, John Dickson

Dickson, Carter
See Carr, John Dickson

Diderot, Denis 1713-1784   **LC 26**

Didion, Joan 1934- **CLC 1, 3, 8, 14, 32; DAM NOV**
See also AITN 1; CA 5-8R; CANR 14, 52, 76; CDALB 1968-1988; DA3; DLB 2, 173, 185; DLBY 81, 86; MTCW 1, 2

Dietrich, Robert
See Hunt, E(verette) Howard, (Jr.)

Difusa, Pati
See Almodovar, Pedro

Dillard, Annie 1945- **CLC 9, 60, 115; DAM NOV**
See also AAYA 6; CA 49-52; CANR 3, 43, 62; DA3; DLBY 80; MTCW 1, 2; SATA 10

Dillard, R(ichard) H(enry) W(ilde) 1937-
CLC 5
See also CA 21-24R; CAAS 7; CANR 10; DLB 5

Dillon, Eilis 1920-1994 **CLC 17**
See also CA 9-12R, 182; 147; CAAE 182; CAAS 3; CANR 4, 38, 78; CLR 26; MAICYA; SATA 2, 74; SATA-Essay 105; SATA-Obit 83

Dimont, Penelope
See Mortimer, Penelope (Ruth)

Dinesen, Isak **CLC 10, 29, 95; SSC 7**
See also Blixen, Karen (Christentze Dinesen)
See also MTCW 1

Ding Ling **CLC 68**
See also Chiang, Pin-chin

Diphusa, Patty
See Almodovar, Pedro

Disch, Thomas M(ichael) 1940- **CLC 7, 36**
See also AAYA 17; CA 21-24R; CAAS 4; CANR 17, 36, 54; CLR 18; DA3; DLB 8; MAICYA; MTCW 1, 2; SAAS 15; SATA 92

Disch, Tom
See Disch, Thomas M(ichael)

d'Isly, Georges
See Simenon, Georges (Jacques Christian)

Disraeli, Benjamin 1804-1881 **NCLC 2, 39, 79**
See also DLB 21, 55

Ditcum, Steve
See Crumb, R(obert)

Dixon, Paige
See Corcoran, Barbara

Dixon, Stephen 1936- **CLC 52; SSC 16**
See also CA 89-92; CANR 17, 40, 54; DLB 130

Doak, Annie
See Dillard, Annie

Dobell, Sydney Thompson 1824-1874
NCLC 43
See also DLB 32

Doblin, Alfred **TCLC 13**
See also Doeblin, Alfred

Dobrolyubov, Nikolai Alexandrovich 1836-1861
NCLC 5

Dobson, Austin 1840-1921 **TCLC 79**
See also DLB 35; 144

Dobyns, Stephen 1941- **CLC 37**
See also CA 45-48; CANR 2, 18

Doctorow, E(dgar) L(aurence) 1931- **CLC 6, 11, 15, 18, 37, 44, 65, 113; DAM NOV, POP**
See also AAYA 22; AITN 2; BEST 89:3; CA 45-48; CANR 2, 33, 51, 76; CDALB 1968-1988; DA3; DLB 2, 28, 173; DLBY 80; MTCW 1, 2

Dodgson, Charles Lutwidge 1832-1898
See Carroll, Lewis
See also CLR 2; DA; DAB; DAC; DAM MST, NOV, POET; DA3; MAICYA; SATA 100; YABC 2

Dodson, Owen (Vincent) 1914-1983 **CLC 79; BLC 1; DAM MULT**

See also BW 1; CA 65-68; 110; CANR 24; DLB 76

Doeblin, Alfred 1878-1957 **TCLC 13**
See also Doblin, Alfred
See also CA 110; 141; DLB 66

Doerr, Harriet 1910- **CLC 34**
See also CA 117; 122; CANR 47; INT 122

Domecq, H(onorio Bustos)
See Bioy Casares, Adolfo

Domecq, H(onorio) Bustos
See Bioy Casares, Adolfo; Borges, Jorge Luis

Domini, Rey
See Lorde, Audre (Geraldine)

Dominique
See Proust, (Valentin-Louis-George-Eugene-) Marcel

Don, A
See Stephen, Sir Leslie

Donaldson, Stephen R. 1947- **CLC 46; DAM POP**
See also CA 89-92; CANR 13, 55; INT CANR-13

Donleavy, J(ames) P(atrick) 1926- **CLC 1, 4, 6, 10, 45**
See also AITN 2; CA 9-12R; CANR 24, 49, 62, 80; DLB 6, 173; INT CANR-24; MTCW 1, 2

Donne, John 1572-1631 **LC 10, 24; DA; DAB; DAC; DAM MST, POET; PC 1; WLC**
See also CDBLB Before 1660; DLB 121, 151

Donnell, David 1939(?)- **CLC 34**

Donoghue, P. S.
See Hunt, E(verette) Howard, (Jr.)

Donoso (Yanez), Jose 1924-1996 **CLC 4, 8, 11, 32, 99; DAM MULT; HLC 1; SSC 34**
See also CA 81-84; 155; CANR 32, 73; DLB 113; HW 1, 2; MTCW 1, 2

Donovan, John 1928-1992 **CLC 35**
See also AAYA 20; CA 97-100; 137; CLR 3; MAICYA; SATA 72; SATA-Brief 29

Don Roberto
See Cunninghame Graham, R(obert) B(ontine)

Doolittle, Hilda 1886-1961 **CLC 3, 8, 14, 31, 34, 73; DA; DAC; DAM MST, POET; PC 5; WLC**
See H. D.
See also CA 97-100; CANR 35; DLB 4, 45; MTCW 1, 2

Dorfman, Ariel 1942- **CLC 48, 77; DAM MULT; HLC 1**
See also CA 124; 130; CANR 67, 70; HW 1, 2; INT 130

Dorn, Edward (Merton) 1929- **CLC 10, 18**
See also CA 93-96; CANR 42, 79; DLB 5; INT 93-96

Dorris, Michael (Anthony) 1945-1997 **C L C 109; DAM MULT, NOV**
See also AAYA 20; BEST 90:1; CA 102; 157; CANR 19, 46, 75; CLR 58; DA3; DLB 175; MTCW 2; NNAL; SATA 75; SATA-Obit 94

Dorris, Michael A.
See Dorris, Michael (Anthony)

Dorsan, Luc
See Simenon, Georges (Jacques Christian)

Dorsange, Jean
See Simenon, Georges (Jacques Christian)

Dos Passos, John (Roderigo) 1896-1970 **C L C 1, 4, 8, 11, 15, 25, 34, 82; DA; DAB; DAC; DAM MST, NOV; WLC**
See also CA 1-4R; 29-32R; CANR 3; CDALB 1929-1941; DA3; DLB 4, 9; DLBD 1, 15; DLBY 96; MTCW 1, 2

Dossage, Jean
See Simenon, Georges (Jacques Christian)

Dostoevsky, Fedor Mikhailovich 1821-1881
NCLC 2, 7, 21, 33, 43; DA; DAB; DAC; DAM MST, NOV; SSC 2, 33; WLC
See also DA3

Doughty, Charles M(ontagu) 1843-1926
TCLC 27
See also CA 115; 178; DLB 19, 57, 174

Douglas, Ellen **CLC 73**
See also Haxton, Josephine Ayres; Williamson, Ellen Douglas

Douglas, Gavin 1475(?)-1522 **LC 20**
See also DLB 132

Douglas, George
See Brown, George Douglas

Douglas, Keith (Castellain) 1920-1944
TCLC 40
See also CA 160; DLB 27

Douglas, Leonard
See Bradbury, Ray (Douglas)

Douglas, Michael
See Crichton, (John) Michael

Douglas, (George) Norman 1868-1952
TCLC 68
See also CA 119; 157; DLB 34, 195

Douglas, William
See Brown, George Douglas

Douglass, Frederick 1817(?)-1895 **NCLC 7, 55; BLC 1; DA; DAC; DAM MST, MULT; WLC**
See also CDALB 1640-1865; DA3; DLB 1, 43, 50, 79; SATA 29

Dourado, (Waldomiro Freitas) Autran 1926-
CLC 23, 60
See also CA 25-28R; 179; CANR 34, 81; DLB 145; HW 2

Dourado, Waldomiro Autran 1926-
See Dourado, (Waldomiro Freitas) Autran
See also CA 179

Dove, Rita (Frances) 1952- **CLC 50, 81; BLCS; DAM MULT, POET; PC 6**
See also BW 2; CA 109; CAAS 19; CANR 27, 42, 68, 76; CDALBS; DA3; DLB 120; MTCW 1

Doveglion
See Villa, Jose Garcia

Dowell, Coleman 1925-1985 **CLC 60**
See also CA 25-28R; 117; CANR 10; DLB 130

Dowson, Ernest (Christopher) 1867-1900
TCLC 4
See also CA 105; 150; DLB 19, 135

Doyle, A. Conan
See Doyle, Arthur Conan

Doyle, Arthur Conan 1859-1930 **TCLC 7; DA; DAB; DAC; DAM MST, NOV; SSC 12; WLC**
See also AAYA 14; CA 104; 122; CDBLB 1890-1914; DA3; DLB 18, 70, 156, 178; MTCW 1, 2; SATA 24

Doyle, Conan
See Doyle, Arthur Conan

Doyle, John
See Graves, Robert (von Ranke)

Doyle, Roddy 1958(?)- **CLC 81**
See also AAYA 14; CA 143; CANR 73; DA3; DLB 194

Doyle, Sir A. Conan
See Doyle, Arthur Conan

Doyle, Sir Arthur Conan
See Doyle, Arthur Conan

Dr. A
See Asimov, Isaac; Silverstein, Alvin

Echeverria, (Jose) Esteban (Antonino) 1805-1851 **NCLC 18**

Echo
See Proust, (Valentin-Louis-George-Eugene-) Marcel

Eckert, Allan W. 1931- **CLC 17**
See also AAYA 18; CA 13-16R; CANR 14, 45; INT CANR-14; SAAS 21; SATA 29, 91; SATA-Brief 27

Eckhart, Meister 1260(?)-1328(?) **CMLC 9**
See also DLB 115

Eckmar, F. R.
See de Hartog, Jan

Eco, Umberto 1932- **CLC 28, 60; DAM NOV, POP**
See also BEST 90:1; CA 77-80; CANR 12, 33, 55; DA3; DLB 196; MTCW 1, 2

Eddison, E(ric) R(ucker) 1882-1945 **TCLC 15**
See also CA 109; 156

Eddy, Mary (Ann Morse) Baker 1821-1910 **TCLC 71**
See also CA 113; 174

Edel, (Joseph) Leon 1907-1997 **CLC 29, 34**
See also CA 1-4R; 161; CANR 1, 22; DLB 103; INT CANR-22

Eden, Emily 1797-1869 **NCLC 10**

Edgar, David 1948- **CLC 42; DAM DRAM**
See also CA 57-60; CANR 12, 61; DLB 13; MTCW 1

Edgerton, Clyde (Carlyle) 1944- **CLC 39**
See also AAYA 17; CA 118; 134; CANR 64; INT 134

Edgeworth, Maria 1768-1849 **NCLC 1, 51**
See also DLB 116, 159, 163; SATA 21

Edison, Thomas 1847-1931 **TCLC 96**

Edmonds, Paul
See Kuttner, Henry

Edmonds, Walter D(umaux) 1903-1998 **CLC 35**
See also CA 5-8R; CANR 2; DLB 9; MAICYA; SAAS 4; SATA 1, 27; SATA-Obit 99

Edmondson, Wallace
See Ellison, Harlan (Jay)

Edson, Russell **CLC 13**
See also CA 33-36R

Edwards, Bronwen Elizabeth
See Rose, Wendy

Edwards, G(erald) B(asil) 1899-1976 **CLC 25**
See also CA 110

Edwards, Gus 1939- **CLC 43**
See also CA 108; INT 108

Edwards, Jonathan 1703-1758 **LC 7, 54; DA; DAC; DAM MST**
See also DLB 24

Efron, Marina Ivanovna Tsvetaeva
See Tsvetaeva (Efron), Marina (Ivanovna)

Ehle, John (Marsden, Jr.) 1925- **CLC 27**
See also CA 9-12R

Ehrenbourg, Ilya (Grigoryevich)
See Ehrenburg, Ilya (Grigoryevich)

Ehrenburg, Ilya (Grigoryevich) 1891-1967 **CLC 18, 34, 62**
See also CA 102; 25-28R

Ehrenburg, Ilyo (Grigoryevich)
See Ehrenburg, Ilya (Grigoryevich)

Ehrenreich, Barbara 1941- **CLC 110**
See also BEST 90:4; CA 73-76; CANR 16, 37, 62; MTCW 1, 2

Eich, Guenter 1907-1972 **CLC 15**
See also CA 111; 93-96; DLB 69, 124

Eichendorff, Joseph Freiherr von 1788-1857 **NCLC 8**
See also DLB 90

Eigner, Larry **CLC 9**
See also Eigner, Laurence (Joel)
See also CAAS 23; DLB 5

Eigner, Laurence (Joel) 1927-1996
See Eigner, Larry
See also CA 9-12R; 151; CANR 6, 84; DLB 193

Einstein, Albert 1879-1955 **TCLC 65**
See also CA 121; 133; MTCW 1, 2

Eiseley, Loren Corey 1907-1977 **CLC 7**
See also AAYA 5; CA 1-4R; 73-76; CANR 6; DLBD 17

Eisenstadt, Jill 1963- **CLC 50**
See also CA 140

Eisenstein, Sergei (Mikhailovich) 1898-1948 **TCLC 57**
See also CA 114; 149

Eisner, Simon
See Kornbluth, C(yril) M.

Ekeloef, (Bengt) Gunnar 1907-1968 **CLC 27; DAM POET; PC 23**
See also CA 123; 25-28R

Ekelof, (Bengt) Gunnar
See Ekeloef, (Bengt) Gunnar

Ekelund, Vilhelm 1880-1949 **TCLC 75**

Ekwensi, C. O. D.
See Ekwensi, Cyprian (Odiatu Duaka)

Ekwensi, Cyprian (Odiatu Duaka) 1921- **CLC 4; BLC 1; DAM MULT**
See also BW 2, 3; CA 29-32R; CANR 18, 42, 74; DLB 117; MTCW 1, 2; SATA 66

Elaine **TCLC 18**
See also Leverson, Ada

El Crummo
See Crumb, R(obert)

Elder, Lonne III 1931-1996 **DC 8**
See also BLC 1; BW 1, 3; CA 81-84; 152; CANR 25; DAM MULT; DLB 7, 38, 44

Elia
See Lamb, Charles

Eliade, Mircea 1907-1986 **CLC 19**
See also CA 65-68; 119; CANR 30, 62; MTCW 1

Eliot, A. D.
See Jewett, (Theodora) Sarah Orne

Eliot, Alice
See Jewett, (Theodora) Sarah Orne

Eliot, Dan
See Silverberg, Robert

Eliot, George 1819-1880 **NCLC 4, 13, 23, 41, 49; DA; DAB; DAC; DAM MST, NOV; PC 20; WLC**
See also CDBLB 1832-1890; DA3; DLB 21, 35, 55

Eliot, John 1604-1690 **LC 5**
See also DLB 24

Eliot, T(homas) S(tearns) 1888-1965 **CLC 1, 2, 3, 6, 9, 10, 13, 15, 24, 34, 41, 55, 57, 113; DA; DAB; DAC; DAM DRAM, MST, POET; PC 5; WLC**
See also AAYA 28; CA 5-8R; 25-28R; CANR 41; CDALB 1929-1941; DA3; DLB 7, 10, 45, 63; DLBY 88; MTCW 1, 2

Elizabeth 1866-1941 **TCLC 41**

Elkin, Stanley L(awrence) 1930-1995 **CLC 4, 6, 9, 14, 27, 51, 91; DAM NOV, POP; SSC 12**
See also CA 9-12R; 148; CANR 8, 46; DLB 2, 28; DLBY 80; INT CANR-8; MTCW 1, 2

Elledge, Scott **CLC 34**

Elliot, Don
See Silverberg, Robert

Elliott, Don
See Silverberg, Robert

Elliott, George P(aul) 1918-1980 **CLC 2**
See also CA 1-4R; 97-100; CANR 2

Elliott, Janice 1931- **CLC 47**
See also CA 13-16R; CANR 8, 29, 84; DLB 14

Elliott, Sumner Locke 1917-1991 **CLC 38**
See also CA 5-8R; 134; CANR 2, 21

Elliott, William
See Bradbury, Ray (Douglas)

Ellis, A. E. **CLC 7**

Ellis, Alice Thomas **CLC 40**
See also Haycraft, Anna
See also DLB 194; MTCW 1

Ellis, Bret Easton 1964- **CLC 39, 71, 117; DAM POP**
See also AAYA 2; CA 118; 123; CANR 51, 74; DA3; INT 123; MTCW 1

Ellis, (Henry) Havelock 1859-1939 **TCLC 14**
See also CA 109; 169; DLB 190

Ellis, Landon
See Ellison, Harlan (Jay)

Ellis, Trey 1962- **CLC 55**
See also CA 146

Ellison, Harlan (Jay) 1934- **CLC 1, 13, 42; DAM POP; SSC 14**
See also AAYA 29; CA 5-8R; CANR 5, 46; DLB 8; INT CANR-5; MTCW 1, 2

Ellison, Ralph (Waldo) 1914-1994 **CLC 1, 3, 11, 54, 86, 114; BLC 1; DA; DAB; DAC; DAM MST, MULT, NOV; SSC 26; WLC**
See also AAYA 19; BW 1, 3; CA 9-12R; 145; CANR 24, 53; CDALB 1941-1968; DA3; DLB 2, 76; DLBY 94; MTCW 1, 2

Ellmann, Lucy (Elizabeth) 1956- **CLC 61**
See also CA 128

Ellmann, Richard (David) 1918-1987 **CLC 50**
See also BEST 89:2; CA 1-4R; 122; CANR 2, 28, 61; DLB 103; DLBY 87; MTCW 1, 2

Elman, Richard (Martin) 1934-1997 **CLC 19**
See also CA 17-20R; 163; CAAS 3; CANR 47

Elron
See Hubbard, L(afayette) Ron(ald)

Eluard, Paul **TCLC 7, 41**
See also Grindel, Eugene

Elyot, Sir Thomas 1490(?)-1546 **LC 11**

Elytis, Odysseus 1911-1996 **CLC 15, 49, 100; DAM POET; PC 21**
See also CA 102; 151; MTCW 1, 2

Emecheta, (Florence Onye) Buchi 1944- **CLC 14, 48; BLC 2; DAM MULT**
See also BW 2, 3; CA 81-84; CANR 27, 81; DA3; DLB 117; MTCW 1, 2; SATA 66

Emerson, Mary Moody 1774-1863 **NCLC 66**

Emerson, Ralph Waldo 1803-1882 **NCLC 1, 38; DA; DAB; DAC; DAM MST, POET; PC 18; WLC**
See also CDALB 1640-1865; DA3; DLB 1, 59, 73

Eminescu, Mihail 1850-1889 **NCLC 33**

Empson, William 1906-1984 **CLC 3, 8, 19, 33, 34**
See also CA 17-20R; 112; CANR 31, 61; DLB 20; MTCW 1, 2

Enchi, Fumiko (Ueda) 1905-1986 **CLC 31**
See also CA 129; 121; DLB 182

Ende, Michael (Andreas Helmuth) 1929-1995 **CLC 31**
See also CA 118; 124; 149; CANR 36; CLR 14; DLB 75; MAICYA; SATA 61; SATA-Brief 42; SATA-Obit 86

Endo, Shusaku 1923-1996 **CLC 7, 14, 19, 54, 99; DAM NOV**
See also CA 29-32R; 153; CANR 21, 54; DA3; DLB 182; MTCW 1, 2

Fecamps, Elise
See Creasey, John

Federman, Raymond 1928- **CLC 6, 47**
See also CA 17-20R; CAAS 8; CANR 10, 43, 83; DLB 80

Federspiel, J(uerg) F. 1931- **CLC 42**
See also CA 146

Feiffer, Jules (Ralph) 1929- **CLC 2, 8, 64; DAM DRAM**
See also AAYA 3; CA 17-20R; CANR 30, 59; DLB 7, 44; INT CANR-30; MTCW 1; SATA 8, 61, 111

Feige, Hermann Albert Otto Maximilian
See Traven, B.

Feinberg, David B. 1956-1994 **CLC 59**
See also CA 135; 147

Feinstein, Elaine 1930- **CLC 36**
See also CA 69-72; CAAS 1; CANR 31, 68; DLB 14, 40; MTCW 1

Feldman, Irving (Mordecai) 1928- **CLC 7**
See also CA 1-4R; CANR 1; DLB 169

Felix-Tchicaya, Gerald
See Tchicaya, Gerald Felix

Fellini, Federico 1920-1993 **CLC 16, 85**
See also CA 65-68; 143; CANR 33

Felsen, Henry Gregor 1916-1995 **CLC 17**
See also CA 1-4R; 180; CANR 1; SAAS 2; SATA 1

Fenno, Jack
See Calisher, Hortense

Fenollosa, Ernest (Francisco) 1853-1908
TCLC 91

Fenton, James Martin 1949- **CLC 32**
See also CA 102; DLB 40

Ferber, Edna 1887-1968 **CLC 18, 93**
See also AITN 1; CA 5-8R; 25-28R; CANR 68; DLB 9, 28, 86; MTCW 1, 2; SATA 7

Ferguson, Helen
See Kavan, Anna

Ferguson, Samuel 1810-1886 **NCLC 33**
See also DLB 32

Fergusson, Robert 1750-1774 **LC 29**
See also DLB 109

Ferling, Lawrence
See Ferlinghetti, Lawrence (Monsanto)

Ferlinghetti, Lawrence (Monsanto) 1919(?)- **CLC 2, 6, 10, 27, 111; DAM POET; PC 1**
See also CA 5-8R; CANR 3, 41, 73; CDALB 1941-1968; DA3; DLB 5, 16; MTCW 1, 2

Fernandez, Vicente Garcia Huidobro
See Huidobro Fernandez, Vicente Garcia

Ferre, Rosario 1942- **SSC 36; HLCS 1**
See also CA 131; CANR 55, 81; DLB 145; HW 1, 2; MTCW 1

Ferrer, Gabriel (Francisco Victor) Miro
See Miro (Ferrer), Gabriel (Francisco Victor)

Ferrier, Susan (Edmonstone) 1782-1854
NCLC 8
See also DLB 116

Ferrigno, Robert 1948(?)- **CLC 65**
See also CA 140

Ferron, Jacques 1921-1985 **CLC 94; DAC**
See also CA 117; 129; DLB 60

Feuchtwanger, Lion 1884-1958 **TCLC 3**
See also CA 104; DLB 66

Feuillet, Octave 1821-1890 **NCLC 45**
See also DLB 192

Feydeau, Georges (Leon Jules Marie) 1862-1921 **TCLC 22; DAM DRAM**
See also CA 113; 152; CANR 84; DLB 192

Fichte, Johann Gottlieb 1762-1814 **NCLC 62**
See also DLB 90

Ficino, Marsilio 1433-1499 **LC 12**

Fiedeler, Hans
See Doeblin, Alfred

Fiedler, Leslie A(aron) 1917- **CLC 4, 13, 24**
See also CA 9-12R; CANR 7, 63; DLB 28, 67; MTCW 1, 2

Field, Andrew 1938- **CLC 44**
See also CA 97-100; CANR 25

Field, Eugene 1850-1895 **NCLC 3**
See also DLB 23, 42, 140; DLBD 13; MAICYA; SATA 16

Field, Gans T.
See Wellman, Manly Wade

Field, Michael 1915-1971 **TCLC 43**
See also CA 29-32R

Field, Peter
See Hobson, Laura Z(ametkin)

Fielding, Henry 1707-1754 **LC 1, 46; DA; DAB; DAC; DAM DRAM, MST, NOV; WLC**
See also CDBLB 1660-1789; DA3; DLB 39, 84, 101

Fielding, Sarah 1710-1768 **LC 1, 44**
See also DLB 39

Fields, W. C. 1880-1946 **TCLC 80**
See also DLB 44

Fierstein, Harvey (Forbes) 1954- **CLC 33; DAM DRAM, POP**
See also CA 123; 129; DA3

Figes, Eva 1932- **CLC 31**
See also CA 53-56; CANR 4, 44, 83; DLB 14

Finch, Anne 1661-1720 **LC 3; PC 21**
See also DLB 95

Finch, Robert (Duer Claydon) 1900- **CLC 18**
See also CA 57-60; CANR 9, 24, 49; DLB 88

Findley, Timothy 1930- **CLC 27, 102; DAC; DAM MST**
See also CA 25-28R; CANR 12, 42, 69; DLB 53

Fink, William
See Mencken, H(enry) L(ouis)

Firbank, Louis 1942-
See Reed, Lou
See also CA 117

Firbank, (Arthur Annesley) Ronald 1886-1926
TCLC 1
See also CA 104; 177; DLB 36

Fisher, Dorothy (Frances) Canfield 1879-1958
TCLC 87
See also CA 114; 136; CANR 80; DLB 9, 102; MAICYA; YABC 1

Fisher, M(ary) F(rances) K(ennedy) 1908-1992
CLC 76, 87
See also CA 77-80; 138; CANR 44; MTCW 1

Fisher, Roy 1930- **CLC 25**
See also CA 81-84; CAAS 10; CANR 16; DLB 40

Fisher, Rudolph 1897-1934 **TCLC 11; BLC 2; DAM MULT; SSC 25**
See also BW 1, 3; CA 107; 124; CANR 80; DLB 51, 102

Fisher, Vardis (Alvero) 1895-1968 **CLC 7**
See also CA 5-8R; 25-28R; CANR 68; DLB 9, 206

Fiske, Tarleton
See Bloch, Robert (Albert)

Fitch, Clarke
See Sinclair, Upton (Beall)

Fitch, John IV
See Cormier, Robert (Edmund)

Fitzgerald, Captain Hugh
See Baum, L(yman) Frank

FitzGerald, Edward 1809-1883 **NCLC 9**
See also DLB 32

Fitzgerald, F(rancis) Scott (Key) 1896-1940
TCLC 1, 6, 14, 28, 55; DA; DAB; DAC; DAM MST, NOV; SSC 6, 31; WLC
See also AAYA 24; AITN 1; CA 110; 123; CDALB 1917-1929; DA3; DLB 4, 9, 86; DLBD 1, 15, 16; DLBY 81, 96; MTCW 1, 2

Fitzgerald, Penelope 1916- **CLC 19, 51, 61**
See also CA 85-88; CAAS 10; CANR 56, 86; DLB 14, 194; MTCW 2

Fitzgerald, Robert (Stuart) 1910-1985 **CLC 39**
See also CA 1-4R; 114; CANR 1; DLBY 80

FitzGerald, Robert D(avid) 1902-1987 **CLC 19**
See also CA 17-20R

Fitzgerald, Zelda (Sayre) 1900-1948 **TCLC 52**
See also CA 117; 126; DLBY 84

Flanagan, Thomas (James Bonner) 1923-
CLC 25, 52
See also CA 108; CANR 55; DLBY 80; INT 108; MTCW 1

Flaubert, Gustave 1821-1880 **NCLC 2, 10, 19, 62, 66; DA; DAB; DAC; DAM MST, NOV; SSC 11; WLC**
See also DA3; DLB 119

Flecker, Herman Elroy
See Flecker, (Herman) James Elroy

Flecker, (Herman) James Elroy 1884-1915
TCLC 43
See also CA 109; 150; DLB 10, 19

Fleming, Ian (Lancaster) 1908-1964 **CLC 3, 30; DAM POP**
See also AAYA 26; CA 5-8R; CANR 59; CDBLB 1945-1960; DA3; DLB 87, 201; MTCW 1, 2; SATA 9

Fleming, Thomas (James) 1927- **CLC 37**
See also CA 5-8R; CANR 10; INT CANR-10; SATA 8

Fletcher, John 1579-1625 **LC 33; DC 6**
See also CDBLB Before 1660; DLB 58

Fletcher, John Gould 1886-1950 **TCLC 35**
See also CA 107; 167; DLB 4, 45

Fleur, Paul
See Pohl, Frederik

Flooglebuckle, Al
See Spiegelman, Art

Flying Officer X
See Bates, H(erbert) E(rnest)

Fo, Dario 1926- **CLC 32, 109; DAM DRAM; DC 10**
See also CA 116; 128; CANR 68; DA3; DLBY 97; MTCW 1, 2

Fogarty, Jonathan Titulescu Esq.
See Farrell, James T(homas)

Follett, Ken(neth Martin) 1949- **CLC 18; DAM NOV, POP**
See also AAYA 6; BEST 89:4; CA 81-84; CANR 13, 33, 54; DA3; DLB 87; DLBY 81; INT CANR-33; MTCW 1

Fontane, Theodor 1819-1898 **NCLC 26**
See also DLB 129

Foote, Horton 1916- **CLC 51, 91; DAM DRAM**
See also CA 73-76; CANR 34, 51; DA3; DLB 26; INT CANR-34

Foote, Shelby 1916- **CLC 75; DAM NOV, POP**
See also CA 5-8R; CANR 3, 45, 74; DA3; DLB 2, 17; MTCW 2

Forbes, Esther 1891-1967 **CLC 12**
See also AAYA 17; CA 13-14; 25-28R; CAP 1; CLR 27; DLB 22; JRDA; MAICYA; SATA 2, 100

Forche, Carolyn (Louise) 1950- **CLC 25, 83, 86; DAM POET; PC 10**
See also CA 109; 117; CANR 50, 74; DA3; DLB 5, 193; INT 117; MTCW 1

Ford, Elbur
See Hibbert, Eleanor Alice Burford

Ford, Ford Madox 1873-1939**TCLC 1, 15, 39, 57; DAM NOV**
See also CA 104; 132; CANR 74; CDBLB 1914-1945; DA3; DLB 162; MTCW 1, 2

Ford, Henry 1863-1947   **TCLC 73**
See also CA 115; 148

Ford, John 1586-(?)   **DC 8**
See also CDBLB Before 1660; DAM DRAM; DA3; DLB 58

Ford, John 1895-1973   **CLC 16**
See also CA 45-48

Ford, Richard 1944-   **CLC 46, 99**
See also CA 69-72; CANR 11, 47, 86; MTCW 1

Ford, Webster
See Masters, Edgar Lee

Foreman, Richard 1937-   **CLC 50**
See also CA 65-68; CANR 32, 63

Forester, C(ecil) S(cott) 1899-1966   **CLC 35**
See also CA 73-76; 25-28R; CANR 83; DLB 191; SATA 13

Forez
See Mauriac, Francois (Charles)

Forman, James Douglas 1932-   **CLC 21**
See also AAYA 17; CA 9-12R; CANR 4, 19, 42; JRDA; MAICYA; SATA 8, 70

Fornes, Maria Irene 1930-**CLC 39, 61; DC 10; HLCS 1**
See also CA 25-28R; CANR 28, 81; DLB 7; HW 1, 2; INT CANR-28; MTCW 1

Forrest, Leon (Richard) 1937-1997   **CLC 4; BLCS**
See also BW 2; CA 89-92; 162; CAAS 7; CANR 25, 52; DLB 33

Forster, E(dward) M(organ) 1879-1970 **C L C 1, 2, 3, 4, 9, 10, 13, 15, 22, 45, 77; DA; DAB; DAC; DAM MST, NOV; SSC 27; WLC**
See also AAYA 2; CA 13-14; 25-28R; CANR 45; CAP 1; CDBLB 1914-1945; DA3; DLB 34, 98, 162, 178, 195; DLBD 10; MTCW 1, 2; SATA 57

Forster, John 1812-1876   **NCLC 11**
See also DLB 144, 184

Forsyth, Frederick 1938- **CLC 2, 5, 36; DAM NOV, POP**
See also BEST 89:4; CA 85-88; CANR 38, 62; DLB 87; MTCW 1, 2

Forten, Charlotte L.   **TCLC 16; BLC 2**
See also Grimke, Charlotte L(ottie) Forten
See also DLB 50

Foscolo, Ugo 1778-1827   **NCLC 8**

Fosse, Bob   **CLC 20**
See also Fosse, Robert Louis

Fosse, Robert Louis 1927-1987
See Fosse, Bob
See also CA 110; 123

Foster, Stephen Collins 1826-1864 **NCLC 26**

Foucault, Michel 1926-1984   **CLC 31, 34, 69**
See also CA 105; 113; CANR 34; MTCW 1, 2

Fouque, Friedrich (Heinrich Karl) de la Motte 1777-1843   **NCLC 2**
See also DLB 90

Fourier, Charles 1772-1837   **NCLC 51**

Fournier, Pierre 1916-   **CLC 11**
See also Gascar, Pierre
See also CA 89-92; CANR 16, 40

Fowles, John (Philip) 1926- **CLC 1, 2, 3, 4, 6, 9, 10, 15, 33, 87; DAB; DAC; DAM MST; SSC 33**
See also CA 5-8R; CANR 25, 71; CDBLB 1960 to Present; DA3; DLB 14, 139, 207; MTCW

1, 2; SATA 22

Fox, Paula 1923-   **CLC 2, 8, 121**
See also AAYA 3; CA 73-76; CANR 20, 36, 62; CLR 1, 44; DLB 52; JRDA; MAICYA; MTCW 1; SATA 17, 60

Fox, William Price (Jr.) 1926-   **CLC 22**
See also CA 17-20R; CAAS 19; CANR 11; DLB 2; DLBY 81

Foxe, John 1516(?)-1587   **LC 14**
See also DLB 132

Frame, Janet 1924- **CLC 2, 3, 6, 22, 66, 96; SSC 29**
See also Clutha, Janet Paterson Frame

France, Anatole   **TCLC 9**
See also Thibault, Jacques Anatole Francois
See also DLB 123; MTCW 1

Francis, Claude 19(?)-   **CLC 50**

Francis, Dick 1920-**CLC 2, 22, 42, 102; DAM POP**
See also AAYA 5, 21; BEST 89:3; CA 5-8R; CANR 9, 42, 68; CDBLB 1960 to Present; DA3; DLB 87; INT CANR-9; MTCW 1, 2

Francis, Robert (Churchill) 1901-1987
CLC 15
See also CA 1-4R; 123; CANR 1

Frank, Anne(lies Marie) 1929-1945**TCLC 17; DA; DAB; DAC; DAM MST; WLC**
See also AAYA 12; CA 113; 133; CANR 68; DA3; MTCW 1, 2; SATA 87; SATA-Brief 42

Frank, Bruno 1887-1945   **TCLC 81**
See also DLB 118

Frank, Elizabeth 1945-   **CLC 39**
See also CA 121; 126; CANR 78; INT 126

Frankl, Viktor E(mil) 1905-1997   **CLC 93**
See also CA 65-68; 161

Franklin, Benjamin
See Hasek, Jaroslav (Matej Frantisek)

Franklin, Benjamin 1706-1790 **LC 25; DA; DAB; DAC; DAM MST; WLCS**
See also CDALB 1640-1865; DA3; DLB 24, 43, 73

Franklin, (Stella Maria Sarah) Miles (Lampe) 1879-1954   **TCLC 7**
See also CA 104; 164

Fraser, (Lady) Antonia (Pakenham) 1932-
CLC 32, 107
See also CA 85-88; CANR 44, 65; MTCW 1, 2; SATA-Brief 32

Fraser, George MacDonald 1925-   **CLC 7**
See also CA 45-48, 180; CAAE 180; CANR 2, 48, 74; MTCW 1

Fraser, Sylvia 1935-   **CLC 64**
See also CA 45-48; CANR 1, 16, 60

Frayn, Michael 1933-**CLC 3, 7, 31, 47; DAM DRAM, NOV**
See also CA 5-8R; CANR 30, 69; DLB 13, 14, 194; MTCW 1, 2

Fraze, Candida (Merrill) 1945-   **CLC 50**
See also CA 126

Frazer, J(ames) G(eorge) 1854-1941**TCLC 32**
See also CA 118

Frazer, Robert Caine
See Creasey, John

Frazer, Sir James George
See Frazer, J(ames) G(eorge)

Frazier, Charles 1950-   **CLC 109**
See also CA 161

Frazier, Ian 1951-   **CLC 46**
See also CA 130; CANR 54

Frederic, Harold 1856-1898   **NCLC 10**
See also DLB 12, 23; DLBD 13

Frederick, John
See Faust, Frederick (Schiller)

Frederick the Great 1712-1786   **LC 14**

Fredro, Aleksander 1793-1876   **NCLC 8**

Freeling, Nicolas 1927-   **CLC 38**
See also CA 49-52; CAAS 12; CANR 1, 17, 50, 84; DLB 87

Freeman, Douglas Southall 1886-1953
TCLC 11
See also CA 109; DLB 17; DLBD 17

Freeman, Judith 1946-   **CLC 55**
See also CA 148

Freeman, Mary E(leanor) Wilkins 1852-1930
TCLC 9; SSC 1
See also CA 106; 177; DLB 12, 78

Freeman, R(ichard) Austin 1862-1943
TCLC 21
See also CA 113; CANR 84; DLB 70

French, Albert 1943-   **CLC 86**
See also BW 3; CA 167

French, Marilyn 1929-**CLC 10, 18, 60; DAM DRAM, NOV, POP**
See also CA 69-72; CANR 3, 31; INT CANR-31; MTCW 1, 2

French, Paul
See Asimov, Isaac

Freneau, Philip Morin 1752-1832   **NCLC 1**
See also DLB 37, 43

Freud, Sigmund 1856-1939   **TCLC 52**
See also CA 115; 133; CANR 69; MTCW 1, 2

Friedan, Betty (Naomi) 1921-   **CLC 74**
See also CA 65-68; CANR 18, 45, 74; MTCW 1, 2

Friedlander, Saul 1932-   **CLC 90**
See also CA 117; 130; CANR 72

Friedman, B(ernard) H(arper) 1926- **CLC 7**
See also CA 1-4R; CANR 3, 48

Friedman, Bruce Jay 1930-   **CLC 3, 5, 56**
See also CA 9-12R; CANR 25, 52; DLB 2, 28; INT CANR-25

Friel, Brian 1929- **CLC 5, 42, 59, 115; DC 8**
See also CA 21-24R; CANR 33, 69; DLB 13; MTCW 1

Friis-Baastad, Babbis Ellinor 1921-1970
CLC 12
See also CA 17-20R; 134; SATA 7

Frisch, Max (Rudolf) 1911-1991**CLC 3, 9, 14, 18, 32, 44; DAM DRAM, NOV**
See also CA 85-88; 134; CANR 32, 74; DLB 69, 124; MTCW 1, 2

Fromentin, Eugene (Samuel Auguste) 1820-1876   **NCLC 10**
See also DLB 123

Frost, Frederick
See Faust, Frederick (Schiller)

Frost, Robert (Lee) 1874-1963**CLC 1, 3, 4, 9, 10, 13, 15, 26, 34, 44; DA; DAB; DAC; DAM MST, POET; PC 1; WLC**
See also AAYA 21; CA 89-92; CANR 33; CDALB 1917-1929; DA3; DLB 54; DLBD 7; MTCW 1, 2; SATA 14

Froude, James Anthony 1818-1894 **NCLC 43**
See also DLB 18, 57, 144

Froy, Herald
See Waterhouse, Keith (Spencer)

Fry, Christopher 1907- **CLC 2, 10, 14; DAM DRAM**
See also CA 17-20R; CAAS 23; CANR 9, 30, 74; DLB 13; MTCW 1, 2; SATA 66

Frye, (Herman) Northrop 1912-1991   **C L C 24, 70**
See also CA 5-8R; 133; CANR 8, 37; DLB 67, 68; MTCW 1, 2

Fuchs, Daniel 1909-1993   **CLC 8, 22**
See also CA 81-84; 142; CAAS 5; CANR 40;

DLB 9, 26, 28; DLBY 93

Fuchs, Daniel 1934-   **CLC 34**
See also CA 37-40R; CANR 14, 48

Fuentes, Carlos 1928-CLC 3, 8, 10, 13, 22, 41,
    60, 113; DA; DAB; DAC; DAM MST,
    MULT, NOV; HLC 1; SSC 24; WLC
See also AAYA 4; AITN 2; CA 69-72; CANR
    10, 32, 68; DA3; DLB 113; HW 1, 2; MTCW
    1, 2

Fuentes, Gregorio Lopez y
See Lopez y Fuentes, Gregorio

Fuertes, Gloria 1918-   **PC 27**
See also CA 178, 180; DLB 108; HW 2

Fugard, (Harold) Athol 1932-CLC 5, 9, 14, 25,
    40, 80; DAM DRAM; DC 3
See also AAYA 17; CA 85-88; CANR 32, 54;
    MTCW 1

Fugard, Sheila 1932-   **CLC 48**
See also CA 125

Fuller, Charles (H., Jr.) 1939-CLC 25; BLC 2;
    DAM DRAM, MULT; DC 1
See also BW 2; CA 108; 112; DLB 38; INT 112;
    MTCW 1

Fuller, John (Leopold) 1937-   **CLC 62**
See also CA 21-24R; CANR 9, 44; DLB 40

Fuller, Margaret   **NCLC 5, 50**
See also Fuller, Sarah Margaret

Fuller, Roy (Broadbent) 1912-1991CLC 4, 28
See also CA 5-8R; 135; CAAS 10; CANR 53,
    83; DLB 15, 20; SATA 87

Fuller, Sarah Margaret 1810-1850
See Fuller, Margaret
See also CDALB 1640-1865; DLB 1, 59, 73, 83

Fulton, Alice 1952-   **CLC 52**
See also CA 116; CANR 57; DLB 193

Furphy, Joseph 1843-1912   **TCLC 25**
See also CA 163

Fussell, Paul 1924-   **CLC 74**
See also BEST 90:1; CA 17-20R; CANR 8, 21,
    35, 69; INT CANR-21; MTCW 1, 2

Futabatei, Shimei 1864-1909   **TCLC 44**
See also CA 162; DLB 180

Futrelle, Jacques 1875-1912   **TCLC 19**
See also CA 113; 155

Gaboriau, Emile 1835-1873   **NCLC 14**

Gadda, Carlo Emilio 1893-1973   **CLC 11**
See also CA 89-92; DLB 177

Gaddis, William 1922-1998CLC 1, 3, 6, 8, 10,
    19, 43, 86
See also CA 17-20R; 172; CANR 21, 48; DLB
    2; MTCW 1, 2

Gage, Walter
See Inge, William (Motter)

Gaines, Ernest J(ames) 1933- **CLC 3, 11, 18,
    86; BLC 2; DAM MULT**
See also AAYA 18; AITN 1; BW 2, 3; CA 9-
    12R; CANR 6, 24, 42, 75; CDALB 1968-
    1988; DA3; DLB 2, 33, 152; DLBY 80;
    MTCW 1, 2; SATA 86

Gaitskill, Mary 1954-   **CLC 69**
See also CA 128; CANR 61

Galdos, Benito Perez
See Perez Galdos, Benito

Gale, Zona 1874-1938TCLC 7; DAM DRAM
See also CA 105; 153; CANR 84; DLB 9, 78

Galeano, Eduardo (Hughes) 1940- **CLC 72;
    HLCS 1**
See also CA 29-32R; CANR 13, 32; HW 1

Galiano, Juan Valera y Alcala
See Valera y Alcala-Galiano, Juan

Galilei, Galileo 1546-1642   **LC 45**

Gallagher, Tess 1943-   **CLC 18, 63; DAM
    POET; PC 9**

See also CA 106; DLB 212

Gallant, Mavis 1922-   **CLC 7, 18, 38; DAC;
    DAM MST; SSC 5**
See also CA 69-72; CANR 29, 69; DLB 53;
    MTCW 1, 2

Gallant, Roy A(rthur) 1924-   **CLC 17**
See also CA 5-8R; CANR 4, 29, 54; CLR 30;
    MAICYA; SATA 4, 68, 110

Gallico, Paul (William) 1897-1976   **CLC 2**
See also AITN 1; CA 5-8R; 69-72; CANR 23;
    DLB 9, 171; MAICYA; SATA 13

Gallo, Max Louis 1932-   **CLC 95**
See also CA 85-88

Gallois, Lucien
See Desnos, Robert

Gallup, Ralph
See Whitemore, Hugh (John)

Galsworthy, John 1867-1933TCLC 1, 45; DA;
    DAB; DAC; DAM DRAM, MST, NOV;
    SSC 22; WLC
See also CA 104; 141; CANR 75; CDBLB
    1890-1914; DA3; DLB 10, 34, 98, 162;
    DLBD 16; MTCW 1

Galt, John 1779-1839   **NCLC 1**
See also DLB 99, 116, 159

Galvin, James 1951-   **CLC 38**
See also CA 108; CANR 26

Gamboa, Federico 1864-1939   **TCLC 36**
See also CA 167; HW 2

Gandhi, M. K.
See Gandhi, Mohandas Karamchand

Gandhi, Mahatma
See Gandhi, Mohandas Karamchand

Gandhi, Mohandas Karamchand 1869-1948
    TCLC 59; DAM MULT
See also CA 121; 132; DA3; MTCW 1, 2

Gann, Ernest Kellogg 1910-1991   **CLC 23**
See also AITN 1; CA 1-4R; 136; CANR 1, 83

Garcia, Cristina 1958-   **CLC 76**
See also CA 141; CANR 73; HW 2

Garcia Lorca, Federico 1898-1936TCLC 1, 7,
    49; DA; DAB; DAC; DAM DRAM, MST,
    MULT, POET; DC 2; HLC 2; PC 3; WLC
See also CA 104; 131; CANR 81; DA3; DLB
    108; HW 1, 2; MTCW 1, 2

Garcia Marquez, Gabriel (Jose) 1928-CLC 2,
    3, 8, 10, 15, 27, 47, 55, 68; DA; DAB; DAC;
    DAM MST, MULT, NOV, POP; HLC 1;
    SSC 8; WLC
See also AAYA 3; BEST 89:1, 90:4; CA 33-
    36R; CANR 10, 28, 50, 75, 82; DA3; DLB
    113; HW 1, 2; MTCW 1, 2

Garcilaso de la Vega, El Inca 1503-1536
See also HLCS 1

Gard, Janice
See Latham, Jean Lee

Gard, Roger Martin du
See Martin du Gard, Roger

Gardam, Jane 1928-   **CLC 43**
See also CA 49-52; CANR 2, 18, 33, 54; CLR
    12; DLB 14, 161; MAICYA; MTCW 1;
    SAAS 9; SATA 39, 76; SATA-Brief 28

Gardner, Herb(ert) 1934-   **CLC 44**
See also CA 149

Gardner, John (Champlin), Jr. 1933-1982
    CLC 2, 3, 5, 7, 8, 10, 18, 28, 34; DAM NOV,
    POP; SSC 7
See also AITN 1; CA 65-68; 107; CANR 33,
    73; CDALBS; DA3; DLB 2; DLBY 82;
    MTCW 1; SATA 40; SATA-Obit 31

Gardner, John (Edmund) 1926-CLC 30; DAM
    POP
See also CA 103; CANR 15, 69; MTCW 1

Gardner, Miriam
See Bradley, Marion Zimmer

Gardner, Noel
See Kuttner, Henry

Gardons, S. S.
See Snodgrass, W(illiam) D(e Witt)

Garfield, Leon 1921-1996   **CLC 12**
See also AAYA 8; CA 17-20R; 152; CANR 38,
    41, 78; CLR 21; DLB 161; JRDA; MAICYA;
    SATA 1, 32, 76; SATA-Obit 90

Garland, (Hannibal) Hamlin 1860-1940
    TCLC 3; SSC 18
See also CA 104; DLB 12, 71, 78, 186

Garneau, (Hector de) Saint-Denys 1912-1943
    TCLC 13
See also CA 111; DLB 88

Garner, Alan 1934-CLC 17; DAB; DAM POP
See also AAYA 18; CA 73-76, 178; CAAE 178;
    CANR 15, 64; CLR 20; DLB 161; MAICYA;
    MTCW 1, 2; SATA 18, 69; SATA-Essay 108

Garner, Hugh 1913-1979   **CLC 13**
See also CA 69-72; CANR 31; DLB 68

Garnett, David 1892-1981   **CLC 3**
See also CA 5-8R; 103; CANR 17, 79; DLB
    34; MTCW 2

Garos, Stephanie
See Katz, Steve

Garrett, George (Palmer) 1929-CLC 3, 11, 51;
    SSC 30
See also CA 1-4R; CAAS 5; CANR 1, 42, 67;
    DLB 2, 5, 130, 152; DLBY 83

Garrick, David 1717-1779   **LC 15; DAM
    DRAM**
See also DLB 84

Garrigue, Jean 1914-1972   **CLC 2, 8**
See also CA 5-8R; 37-40R; CANR 20

Garrison, Frederick
See Sinclair, Upton (Beall)

Garro, Elena 1920(?)-1998
See also CA 131; 169; DLB 145; HLCS 1;
    HW 1

Garth, Will
See Hamilton, Edmond; Kuttner, Henry

Garvey, Marcus (Moziah, Jr.) 1887-1940
    TCLC 41; BLC 2; DAM MULT
See also BW 1; CA 120; 124; CANR 79

Gary, Romain   **CLC 25**
See also Kacew, Romain
See also DLB 83

Gascar, Pierre   **CLC 11**
See also Fournier, Pierre

Gascoyne, David (Emery) 1916-   **CLC 45**
See also CA 65-68; CANR 10, 28, 54; DLB 20;
    MTCW 1

Gaskell, Elizabeth Cleghorn 1810-1865NCLC
    70; DAB; DAM MST; SSC 25
See also CDBLB 1832-1890; DLB 21, 144, 159

Gass, William H(oward) 1924-CLC 1, 2, 8, 11,
    15, 39; SSC 12
See also CA 17-20R; CANR 30, 71; DLB 2;
    MTCW 1, 2

Gassendi, Pierre 1592-1655   **LC 54**

Gasset, Jose Ortega y
See Ortega y Gasset, Jose

Gates, Henry Louis, Jr. 1950-CLC 65; BLCS;
    DAM MULT
See also BW 2, 3; CA 109; CANR 25, 53, 75;
    DA3; DLB 67; MTCW 1

Gautier, Theophile 1811-1872   **NCLC 1, 59;
    DAM POET; PC 18; SSC 20**
See also DLB 119

Gawsworth, John
See Bates, H(erbert) E(rnest)

See also AITN 1; BW 1, 3; CA 13-16R; 128; CANR 12, 25, 76

Gunnars, Kristjana 1948- **CLC 69**
See also CA 113; DLB 60

Gurdjieff, G(eorgei) I(vanovich) 1877(?)-1949 **TCLC 71**
See also CA 157

Gurganus, Allan 1947- **CLC 70; DAM POP**
See also BEST 90:1; CA 135

Gurney, A(lbert) R(amsdell), Jr. 1930- **C L C 32, 50, 54; DAM DRAM**
See also CA 77-80; CANR 32, 64

Gurney, Ivor (Bertie) 1890-1937 **TCLC 33**
See also CA 167

Gurney, Peter
See Gurney, A(lbert) R(amsdell), Jr.

Guro, Elena 1877-1913 **TCLC 56**

Gustafson, James M(oody) 1925- **CLC 100**
See also CA 25-28R; CANR 37

Gustafson, Ralph (Barker) 1909- **CLC 36**
See also CA 21-24R; CANR 8, 45, 84; DLB 88

Gut, Gom
See Simenon, Georges (Jacques Christian)

Guterson, David 1956- **CLC 91**
See also CA 132; CANR 73; MTCW 2

Guthrie, A(lfred) B(ertram), Jr. 1901-1991 **CLC 23**
See also CA 57-60; 134; CANR 24; DLB 212; SATA 62; SATA-Obit 67

Guthrie, Isobel
See Grieve, C(hristopher) M(urray)

Guthrie, Woodrow Wilson 1912-1967
See Guthrie, Woody
See also CA 113; 93-96

Guthrie, Woody **CLC 35**
See also Guthrie, Woodrow Wilson

Gutierrez Najera, Manuel 1859-1895
See also HLCS 2

Guy, Rosa (Cuthbert) 1928- **CLC 26**
See also AAYA 4; BW 2; CA 17-20R; CANR 14, 34, 83; CLR 13; DLB 33; JRDA; MAICYA; SATA 14, 62

Gwendolyn
See Bennett, (Enoch) Arnold

H. D. **CLC 3, 8, 14, 31, 34, 73; PC 5**
See also Doolittle, Hilda

H. de V.
See Buchan, John

Haavikko, Paavo Juhani 1931- **CLC 18, 34**
See also CA 106

Habbema, Koos
See Heijermans, Herman

Habermas, Juergen 1929- **CLC 104**
See also CA 109; CANR 85

Habermas, Jurgen
See Habermas, Juergen

Hacker, Marilyn 1942- **CLC 5, 9, 23, 72, 91; DAM POET**
See also CA 77-80; CANR 68; DLB 120

Haeckel, Ernst Heinrich (Philipp August) 1834-1919 **TCLC 83**
See also CA 157

Hafiz c. 1326-1389 **CMLC 34**

Hafiz c. 1326-1389(?) **CMLC 34**

Haggard, H(enry) Rider 1856-1925 **TCLC 11**
See also CA 108; 148; DLB 70, 156, 174, 178; MTCW 2; SATA 16

Hagiosy, L.
See Larbaud, Valery (Nicolas)

Hagiwara Sakutaro 1886-1942 **TCLC 60; PC 18**

Haig, Fenil
See Ford, Ford Madox

Haig-Brown, Roderick (Langmere) 1908-1976 **CLC 21**
See also CA 5-8R; 69-72; CANR 4, 38, 83; CLR 31; DLB 88; MAICYA; SATA 12

Hailey, Arthur 1920- **CLC 5; DAM NOV, POP**
See also AITN 2; BEST 90:3; CA 1-4R; CANR 2, 36, 75; DLB 88; DLBY 82; MTCW 1, 2

Hailey, Elizabeth Forsythe 1938- **CLC 40**
See also CA 93-96; CAAS 1; CANR 15, 48; INT CANR-15

Haines, John (Meade) 1924- **CLC 58**
See also CA 17-20R; CANR 13, 34; DLB 212

Hakluyt, Richard 1552-1616 **LC 31**

Haldeman, Joe (William) 1943- **CLC 61**
See also Graham, Robert
See also CA 53-56, 179; CAAE 179; CAAS 25; CANR 6, 70, 72; DLB 8; INT CANR-6

Hale, Sarah Josepha (Buell) 1788-1879 **NCLC 75**
See also DLB 1, 42, 73

Haley, Alex(ander Murray Palmer) 1921-1992 **CLC 8, 12, 76; BLC 2; DA; DAB; DAC; DAM MST, MULT, POP**
See also AAYA 26; BW 2, 3; CA 77-80; 136; CANR 61; CDALBS; DA3; DLB 38; MTCW 1, 2

Haliburton, Thomas Chandler 1796-1865 **NCLC 15**
See also DLB 11, 99

Hall, Donald (Andrew, Jr.) 1928- **CLC 1, 13, 37, 59; DAM POET**
See also CA 5-8R; CAAS 7; CANR 2, 44, 64; DLB 5; MTCW 1; SATA 23, 97

Hall, Frederic Sauser
See Sauser-Hall, Frederic

Hall, James
See Kuttner, Henry

Hall, James Norman 1887-1951 **TCLC 23**
See also CA 123; 173; SATA 21

Hall, Radclyffe
See Hall, (Marguerite) Radclyffe
See also MTCW 2

Hall, (Marguerite) Radclyffe 1886-1943 **TCLC 12**
See also CA 110; 150; CANR 83; DLB 191

Hall, Rodney 1935- **CLC 51**
See also CA 109; CANR 69

Halleck, Fitz-Greene 1790-1867 **NCLC 47**
See also DLB 3

Halliday, Michael
See Creasey, John

Halpern, Daniel 1945- **CLC 14**
See also CA 33-36R

Hamburger, Michael (Peter Leopold) 1924- **CLC 5, 14**
See also CA 5-8R; CAAS 4; CANR 2, 47; DLB 27

Hamill, Pete 1935- **CLC 10**
See also CA 25-28R; CANR 18, 71

Hamilton, Alexander 1755(?)-1804 **NCLC 49**
See also DLB 37

Hamilton, Clive
See Lewis, C(live) S(taples)

Hamilton, Edmond 1904-1977 **CLC 1**
See also CA 1-4R; CANR 3, 84; DLB 8

Hamilton, Eugene (Jacob) Lee
See Lee-Hamilton, Eugene (Jacob)

Hamilton, Franklin
See Silverberg, Robert

Hamilton, Gail
See Corcoran, Barbara

Hamilton, Mollie
See Kaye, M(ary) M(argaret)

Hamilton, (Anthony Walter) Patrick 1904-1962 **CLC 51**
See also CA 176; 113; DLB 191

Hamilton, Virginia 1936- **CLC 26; DAM MULT**
See also AAYA 2, 21; BW 2, 3; CA 25-28R; CANR 20, 37, 73; CLR 1, 11, 40; DLB 33, 52; INT CANR-20; JRDA; MAICYA; MTCW 1, 2; SATA 4, 56, 79

Hammett, (Samuel) Dashiell 1894-1961 **C L C 3, 5, 10, 19, 47; SSC 17**
See also AITN 1; CA 81-84; CANR 42; CDALB 1929-1941; DA3; DLBD 6; DLBY 96; MTCW 1, 2

Hammon, Jupiter 1711(?)-1800(?) **NCLC 5; BLC 2; DAM MULT, POET; PC 16**
See also DLB 31, 50

Hammond, Keith
See Kuttner, Henry

Hamner, Earl (Henry), Jr. 1923- **CLC 12**
See also AITN 2; CA 73-76; DLB 6

Hampton, Christopher (James) 1946- **CLC 4**
See also CA 25-28R; DLB 13; MTCW 1

Hamsun, Knut **TCLC 2, 14, 49**
See also Pedersen, Knut

Handke, Peter 1942- **CLC 5, 8, 10, 15, 38; DAM DRAM, NOV**
See also CA 77-80; CANR 33, 75; DLB 85, 124; MTCW 1, 2

Handy, W(illiam) C(hristopher) 1873-1958 **TCLC 97**
See also BW 3; CA 121; 167

Hanley, James 1901-1985 **CLC 3, 5, 8, 13**
See also CA 73-76; 117; CANR 36; DLB 191; MTCW 1

Hannah, Barry 1942- **CLC 23, 38, 90**
See also CA 108; 110; CANR 43, 68; DLB 6; INT 110; MTCW 1

Hannon, Ezra
See Hunter, Evan

Hansberry, Lorraine (Vivian) 1930-1965 **CLC 17, 62; BLC 2; DA; DAB; DAC; DAM DRAM, MST, MULT; DC 2**
See also AAYA 25; BW 1, 3; CA 109; 25-28R; CABS 3; CANR 58; CDALB 1941-1968; DA3; DLB 7, 38; MTCW 1, 2

Hansen, Joseph 1923- **CLC 38**
See also CA 29-32R; CAAS 17; CANR 16, 44, 66; INT CANR-16

Hansen, Martin A(lfred) 1909-1955 **TCLC 32**
See also CA 167

Hanson, Kenneth O(stlin) 1922- **CLC 13**
See also CA 53-56; CANR 7

Hardwick, Elizabeth (Bruce) 1916- **CLC 13; DAM NOV**
See also CA 5-8R; CANR 3, 32, 70; DA3; DLB 6; MTCW 1, 2

Hardy, Thomas 1840-1928 **TCLC 4, 10, 18, 32, 48, 53, 72; DA; DAB; DAC; DAM MST, NOV, POET; PC 8; SSC 2; WLC**
See also CA 104; 123; CDBLB 1890-1914; DA3; DLB 18, 19, 135; MTCW 1, 2

Hare, David 1947- **CLC 29, 58**
See also CA 97-100; CANR 39; DLB 13; MTCW 1

Harewood, John
See Van Druten, John (William)

Harford, Henry
See Hudson, W(illiam) H(enry)

Hargrave, Leonie
See Disch, Thomas M(ichael)

Harjo, Joy 1951- **CLC 83; DAM MULT; PC 27**
See also CA 114; CANR 35, 67; DLB 120, 175;

MTCW 2; NNAL

Harlan, Louis R(udolph) 1922-   **CLC 34**
See also CA 21-24R; CANR 25, 55, 80;

Harling, Robert 1951(?)-   **CLC 53**
See also CA 147

Harmon, William (Ruth) 1938-   **CLC 38**
See also CA 33-36R; CANR 14, 32, 35;
SATA 65

Harper, F. E. W.
See Harper, Frances Ellen Watkins

Harper, Frances E. W.
See Harper, Frances Ellen Watkins

Harper, Frances E. Watkins
See Harper, Frances Ellen Watkins

Harper, Frances Ellen
See Harper, Frances Ellen Watkins

Harper, Frances Ellen Watkins 1825-1911
    **TCLC 14; BLC 2; DAM MULT, POET;
PC 21**
See also BW 1, 3; CA 111; 125; CANR 79;
DLB 50

Harper, Michael S(teven) 1938-   **CLC 7, 22**
See also BW 1; CA 33-36R; CANR 24; DLB 41

Harper, Mrs. F. E. W.
See Harper, Frances Ellen Watkins

Harris, Christie (Lucy) Irwin 1907- **CLC 12**
See also CA 5-8R; CANR 6, 83; CLR 47; DLB
88; JRDA; MAICYA; SAAS 10; SATA 6, 74

Harris, Frank 1856-1931   **TCLC 24**
See also CA 109; 150; CANR 80; DLB 156,
197

Harris, George Washington 1814-1869
    NCLC 23
See also DLB 3, 11

Harris, Joel Chandler 1848-1908   **TCLC 2;
SSC 19**
See also CA 104; 137; CANR 80; CLR 49; DLB
11, 23, 42, 78, 91; MAICYA; SATA 100;
YABC 1

Harris, John (Wyndham Parkes Lucas) Beynon
1903-1969
See Wyndham, John
See also CA 102; 89-92; CANR 84

Harris, MacDonald   **CLC 9**
See also Heiney, Donald (William)

Harris, Mark 1922-   **CLC 19**
See also CA 5-8R; CAAS 3; CANR 2, 55, 83;
DLB 2; DLBY 80

Harris, (Theodore) Wilson 1921-   **CLC 25**
See also BW 2, 3; CA 65-68; CAAS 16; CANR
11, 27, 69; DLB 117; MTCW 1

Harrison, Elizabeth Cavanna 1909-
See Cavanna, Betty
See also CA 9-12R; CANR 6, 27, 85

Harrison, Harry (Max) 1925-   **CLC 42**
See also CA 1-4R; CANR 5, 21, 84; DLB 8;
SATA 4

Harrison, James (Thomas) 1937- **CLC 6, 14,
33, 66; SSC 19**
See also CA 13-16R; CANR 8, 51, 79; DLBY
82; INT CANR-8

Harrison, Jim
See Harrison, James (Thomas)

Harrison, Kathryn 1961-   **CLC 70**
See also CA 144; CANR 68

Harrison, Tony 1937-   **CLC 43**
See also CA 65-68; CANR 44; DLB 40;
MTCW 1

Harriss, Will(ard Irvin) 1922-   **CLC 34**
See also CA 111

Harson, Sley
See Ellison, Harlan (Jay)

Hart, Ellis

See Ellison, Harlan (Jay)

Hart, Josephine 1942(?)- **CLC 70; DAM POP**
See also CA 138; CANR 70

Hart, Moss 1904-1961 **CLC 66; DAM DRAM**
See also CA 109; 89-92; CANR 84; DLB 7

Harte, (Francis) Bret(t) 1836(?)-1902 **TCLC 1,
25; DA; DAC; DAM MST; SSC 8; WLC**
See also CA 104; 140; CANR 80; CDALB
1865-1917; DA3; DLB 12, 64, 74, 79, 186;
SATA 26

Hartley, L(eslie) P(oles) 1895-1972 **CLC 2, 22**
See also CA 45-48; 37-40R; CANR 33; DLB
15, 139; MTCW 1, 2

Hartman, Geoffrey H. 1929-   **CLC 27**
See also CA 117; 125; CANR 79; DLB 67

Hartmann, Eduard von 1842-1906 **TCLC 97**

Hartmann, Sadakichi 1867-1944   **TCLC 73**
See also CA 157; DLB 54

Hartmann von Aue c. 1160-c. 1205 **CMLC 15**
See also DLB 138

Hartmann von Aue 1170-1210   **CMLC 15**

Haruf, Kent 1943-   **CLC 34**
See also CA 149

Harwood, Ronald 1934-   **CLC 32; DAM
DRAM, MST**
See also CA 1-4R; CANR 4, 55; DLB 13

Hasegawa Tatsunosuke
See Futabatei, Shimei

Hasek, Jaroslav (Matej Frantisek) 1883-1923
    TCLC 4
See also CA 104; 129; MTCW 1, 2

Hass, Robert 1941-   **CLC 18, 39, 99; PC 16**
See also CA 111; CANR 30, 50, 71; DLB 105,
206; SATA 94

Hastings, Hudson
See Kuttner, Henry

Hastings, Selina   **CLC 44**

Hathorne, John 1641-1717   **LC 38**

Hatteras, Amelia
See Mencken, H(enry) L(ouis)

Hatteras, Owen   **TCLC 18**
See also Mencken, H(enry) L(ouis); Nathan,
George Jean

Hauptmann, Gerhart (Johann Robert) 1862-
1946   **TCLC 4; DAM DRAM; SSC 37**
See also CA 104; 153; DLB 66, 118

Havel, Vaclav 1936-   **CLC 25, 58, 65; DAM
DRAM; DC 6**
See also CA 104; CANR 36, 63; DA3; MTCW
1, 2

Haviaras, Stratis   **CLC 33**
See also Chaviaras, Strates

Hawes, Stephen 1475(?)-1523(?)   **LC 17**
See also DLB 132

Hawkes, John (Clendennin Burne, Jr.) 1925-
1998   **CLC 1, 2, 3, 4, 7, 9, 14, 15, 27, 49**
See also CA 1-4R; 167; CANR 2, 47, 64; DLB
2, 7; DLBY 80, 98; MTCW 1, 2

Hawking, S. W.
See Hawking, Stephen W(illiam)

Hawking, Stephen W(illiam) 1942- **CLC 63,
105**
See also AAYA 13; BEST 89:1; CA 126; 129;
CANR 48; DA3; MTCW 2

Hawkins, Anthony Hope
See Hope, Anthony

Hawthorne, Julian 1846-1934   **TCLC 25**
See also CA 165

Hawthorne, Nathaniel 1804-1864 **NCLC 39;
DA; DAB; DAC; DAM MST, NOV; SSC
3, 29; WLC**
See also AAYA 18; CDALB 1640-1865; DA3;
DLB 1, 74; YABC 2

Haxton, Josephine Ayres 1921-
See Douglas, Ellen
See also CA 115; CANR 41, 83

Hayaseca y Eizaguirre, Jorge
See Echegaray (y Eizaguirre), Jose (Maria
Waldo)

Hayashi, Fumiko 1904-1951   **TCLC 27**
See also CA 161; DLB 180

Haycraft, Anna 1932-
See Ellis, Alice Thomas
See also CA 122; CANR 85; MTCW 2

Hayden, Robert E(arl) 1913-1980   **CLC 5, 9,
14, 37; BLC 2; DA; DAC; DAM MST,
MULT, POET; PC 6**
See also BW 1, 3; CA 69-72; 97-100; CABS 2;
CANR 24, 75, 82; CDALB 1941-1968; DLB
5, 76; MTCW 1, 2; SATA 19; SATA-Obit 26

Hayford, J(oseph) E(phraim) Casely
See Casely-Hayford, J(oseph) E(phraim)

Hayman, Ronald 1932-   **CLC 44**
See also CA 25-28R; CANR 18, 50; DLB 155

Haywood, Eliza (Fowler) 1693(?)-1756 **LC
1, 44**
See also DLB 39

Hazlitt, William 1778-1830   **NCLC 29, 82**
See also DLB 110, 158

Hazzard, Shirley 1931-   **CLC 18**
See also CA 9-12R; CANR 4, 70; DLBY 82;
MTCW 1

Head, Bessie 1937-1986 **CLC 25, 67; BLC 2;
DAM MULT**
See also BW 2, 3; CA 29-32R; 119; CANR 25,
82; DA3; DLB 117; MTCW 1, 2

Headon, (Nicky) Topper 1956(?)-   **CLC 30**

Heaney, Seamus (Justin) 1939- **CLC 5, 7, 14,
25, 37, 74, 91; DAB; DAM POET; PC 18;
WLCS**
See also CA 85-88; CANR 25, 48, 75; CDBLB
1960 to Present; DA3; DLB 40; DLBY 95;
MTCW 1, 2

Hearn, (Patricio) Lafcadio (Tessima Carlos)
1850-1904   **TCLC 9**
See also CA 105; 166; DLB 12, 78, 189

Hearne, Vicki 1946-   **CLC 56**
See also CA 139

Hearon, Shelby 1931-   **CLC 63**
See also AITN 2; CA 25-28R; CANR 18, 48

Heat-Moon, William Least   **CLC 29**
See also Trogdon, William (Lewis)
See also AAYA 9

Hebbel, Friedrich 1813-1863 **NCLC 43; DAM
DRAM**
See also DLB 129

Hebert, Anne 1916- **CLC 4, 13, 29; DAC; DAM
MST, POET**
See also CA 85-88; CANR 69; DA3; DLB 68;
MTCW 1, 2

Hecht, Anthony (Evan) 1923- **CLC 8, 13, 19;
DAM POET**
See also CA 9-12R; CANR 6; DLB 5, 169

Hecht, Ben 1894-1964   **CLC 8**
See also CA 85-88; DLB 7, 9, 25, 26, 28, 86

Hedayat, Sadeq 1903-1951   **TCLC 21**
See also CA 120

Hegel, Georg Wilhelm Friedrich 1770-1831
    NCLC 46
See also DLB 90

Heidegger, Martin 1889-1976   **CLC 24**
See also CA 81-84; 65-68; CANR 34; MTCW
1, 2

Heidenstam, (Carl Gustaf) Verner von 1859-
1940   **TCLC 5**
See also CA 104

Heifner, Jack 1946-   **CLC 11**
See also CA 105; CANR 47

Heijermans, Herman 1864-1924   **TCLC 24**
See also CA 123

Heilbrun, Carolyn G(old) 1926-   **CLC 25**
See also CA 45-48; CANR 1, 28, 58

Heine, Heinrich 1797-1856 **NCLC 4, 54; PC 25**
See also DLB 90

Heinemann, Larry (Curtiss) 1944-   **CLC 50**
See also CA 110; CAAS 21; CANR 31, 81;
DLBD 9; INT CANR-31

Heiney, Donald (William) 1921-1993
See Harris, MacDonald
See also CA 1-4R; 142; CANR 3, 58

Heinlein, Robert A(nson) 1907-1988 **CLC 1, 3,
8, 14, 26, 55; DAM POP**
See also AAYA 17; CA 1-4R; 125; CANR 1,
20, 53; DA3; DLB 8; JRDA; MAICYA;
MTCW 1, 2; SATA 9, 69; SATA-Obit 56

Helforth, John
See Doolittle, Hilda

Hellenhofferu, Vojtech Kapristian z
See Hasek, Jaroslav (Matej Frantisek)

Heller, Joseph 1923- **CLC 1, 3, 5, 8, 11, 36, 63;
DA; DAB; DAC; DAM MST, NOV, POP;
WLC**
See also AAYA 24; AITN 1; CA 5-8R; CABS
1; CANR 8, 42, 66; DA3; DLB 2, 28; DLBY
80; INT CANR-8; MTCW 1, 2

Hellman, Lillian (Florence) 1906-1984 **CLC 2,
4, 8, 14, 18, 34, 44, 52; DAM DRAM; DC 1**
See also AITN 1, 2; CA 13-16R; 112; CANR
33; DLB 7; DLBY 84; MTCW 1, 2

Helprin, Mark 1947- **CLC 7, 10, 22, 32; DAM
NOV, POP**
See also CA 81-84; CANR 47, 64; CDALBS;
DA3; DLBY 85; MTCW 1, 2

Helvetius, Claude-Adrien 1715-1771 **LC 26**

Helyar, Jane Penelope Josephine 1933-
See Poole, Josephine
See also CA 21-24R; CANR 10, 26; SATA 82

Hemans, Felicia 1793-1835   **NCLC 71**
See also DLB 96

Hemingway, Ernest (Miller) 1899-1961 **C L C
1, 3, 6, 8, 10, 13, 19, 30, 34, 39, 41, 44, 50,
61, 80; DA; DAB; DAC; DAM MST, NOV;
SSC 1, 25, 36; WLC**
See also AAYA 19; CA 77-80; CANR 34;
CDALB 1917-1929; DA3; DLB 4, 9, 102,
210; DLBD 1, 15, 16; DLBY 81, 87, 96, 98;
MTCW 1, 2

Hempel, Amy 1951-   **CLC 39**
See also CA 118; 137; CANR 70; DA3;
MTCW 2

Henderson, F. C.
See Mencken, H(enry) L(ouis)

Henderson, Sylvia
See Ashton-Warner, Sylvia (Constance)

Henderson, Zenna (Chlarson) 1917-1983
SSC 29
See also CA 1-4R; 133; CANR 1, 84; DLB 8;
SATA 5

Henkin, Joshua   **CLC 119**
See also CA 161

Henley, Beth   **CLC 23; DC 6**
See also Henley, Elizabeth Becker
See also CABS 3; DLBY 86

Henley, Elizabeth Becker 1952-
See Henley, Beth
See also CA 107; CANR 32, 73; DAM DRAM,
MST; DA3; MTCW 1, 2

Henley, William Ernest 1849-1903   **TCLC 8**
See also CA 105; DLB 19

Hennissart, Martha
See Lathen, Emma
See also CA 85-88; CANR 64

Henry, O.   **TCLC 1, 19; SSC 5; WLC**
See also Porter, William Sydney

Henry, Patrick 1736-1799   **LC 25**

Henryson, Robert 1430(?)-1506(?)   **LC 20**
See also DLB 146

Henry VIII 1491-1547   **LC 10**
See also DLB 132

Henschke, Alfred
See Klabund

Hentoff, Nat(han Irving) 1925-   **CLC 26**
See also AAYA 4; CA 1-4R; CAAS 6; CANR
5, 25, 77; CLR 1, 52; INT CANR-25; JRDA;
MAICYA; SATA 42, 69; SATA-Brief 27

Heppenstall, (John) Rayner 1911-1981
CLC 10
See also CA 1-4R; 103; CANR 29

Heraclitus c. 540B.C.-c. 450B.C.   **CMLC 22**
See also DLB 176

Herbert, Frank (Patrick) 1920-1986 **CLC 12,
23, 35, 44, 85; DAM POP**
See also AAYA 21; CA 53-56; 118; CANR 5,
43; CDALBS; DLB 8; INT CANR-5; MTCW
1, 2; SATA 9, 37; SATA-Obit 47

Herbert, George 1593-1633   **LC 24; DAB;
DAM POET; PC 4**
See also CDBLB Before 1660; DLB 126

Herbert, Zbigniew 1924-1998   **CLC 9, 43;
DAM POET**
See also CA 89-92; 169; CANR 36, 74;
MTCW 1

Herbst, Josephine (Frey) 1897-1969 **CLC 34**
See also CA 5-8R; 25-28R; DLB 9

Heredia, Jose Maria 1803-1839
See also HLCS 2

Hergesheimer, Joseph 1880-1954   **TCLC 11**
See also CA 109; DLB 102, 9

Herlihy, James Leo 1927-1993   **CLC 6**
See also CA 1-4R; 143; CANR 2

Hermogenes fl. c. 175-   **CMLC 6**

Hernandez, Jose 1834-1886   **NCLC 17**

Herodotus c. 484B.C.-429B.C.   **CMLC 17**
See also DLB 176

Herrick, Robert 1591-1674 **LC 13; DA; DAB;
DAC; DAM MST, POP; PC 9**
See also DLB 126

Herring, Guilles
See Somerville, Edith

Herriot, James 1916-1995 **CLC 12; DAM POP**
See also Wight, James Alfred
See also AAYA 1; CA 148; CANR 40; MTCW
2; SATA 86

Herrmann, Dorothy 1941-   **CLC 44**
See also CA 107

Herrmann, Taffy
See Herrmann, Dorothy

Hersey, John (Richard) 1914-1993 **CLC 1, 2, 7,
9, 40, 81, 97; DAM POP**
See also CA 17-20R; 140; CANR
33; CDALBS; DLB 6, 185; MTCW 1, 2;
SATA 25; SATA-Obit 76

Herzen, Aleksandr Ivanovich 1812-1870
NCLC 10, 61

Herzl, Theodor 1860-1904   **TCLC 36**
See also CA 168

Herzog, Werner 1942-   **CLC 16**
See also CA 89-92

Hesiod c. 8th cent. B.C.-   **CMLC 5**
See also DLB 176

Hesse, Hermann 1877-1962 **CLC 1, 2, 3, 6, 11,
17, 25, 69; DA; DAB; DAC; DAM MST,**

NOV; SSC 9; WLC
See also CA 17-18; CAP 2; DA3; DLB 66;
MTCW 1, 2; SATA 50

Hewes, Cady
See De Voto, Bernard (Augustine)

Heyen, William 1940-   **CLC 13, 18**
See also CA 33-36R; CAAS 9; DLB 5

Heyerdahl, Thor 1914-   **CLC 26**
See also CA 5-8R; CANR 5, 22, 66, 73; MTCW
1, 2; SATA 2, 52

Heym, Georg (Theodor Franz Arthur) 1887-
1912   **TCLC 9**
See also CA 106; 181

Heym, Stefan 1913-   **CLC 41**
See also CA 9-12R; CANR 4; DLB 69

Heyse, Paul (Johann Ludwig von) 1830-1914
TCLC 8
See also CA 104; DLB 129

Heyward, (Edwin) DuBose 1885-1940
TCLC 59
See also CA 108; 157; DLB 7, 9, 45; SATA 21

Hibbert, Eleanor Alice Burford 1906-1993
CLC 7; DAM POP
See also BEST 90:4; CA 17-20R; 140; CANR
9, 28, 59; MTCW 2; SATA 2; SATA-Obit 74

Hichens, Robert (Smythe) 1864-1950 **TCLC 64**
See also CA 162; DLB 153

Higgins, George V(incent) 1939- **CLC 4, 7,
10, 18**
See also CA 77-80; CAAS 5; CANR 17, 51;
DLB 2; DLBY 81, 98; INT CANR-17;
MTCW 1

Higginson, Thomas Wentworth 1823-1911
TCLC 36
See also CA 162; DLB 1, 64

Highet, Helen
See MacInnes, Helen (Clark)

Highsmith, (Mary) Patricia 1921-1995 **CLC 2,
4, 14, 42, 102; DAM NOV, POP**
See also CA 1-4R; 147; CANR 1, 20, 48, 62;
DA3; MTCW 1, 2

Highwater, Jamake (Mamake) 1942(?)- **CLC
12**
See also AAYA 7; CA 65-68; CAAS 7; CANR
10, 34, 84; CLR 17; DLB 52; DLBY 85;
JRDA; MAICYA; SATA 32, 69; SATA-Brief
30

Highway, Tomson 1951- **CLC 92; DAC; DAM
MULT**
See also CA 151; CANR 75; MTCW 2; NNAL

Higuchi, Ichiyo 1872-1896   **NCLC 49**

Hijuelos, Oscar 1951- **CLC 65; DAM MULT,
POP; HLC 1**
See also AAYA 25; BEST 90:1; CA 123; CANR
50, 75; DA3; DLB 145; HW 1, 2; MTCW 2

Hikmet, Nazim 1902(?)-1963   **CLC 40**
See also CA 141; 93-96

Hildegard von Bingen 1098-1179   **CMLC 20**
See also DLB 148

Hildesheimer, Wolfgang 1916-1991   **CLC 49**
See also CA 101; 135; DLB 69, 124

Hill, Geoffrey (William) 1932- **CLC 5, 8, 18,
45; DAM POET**
See also CA 81-84; CANR 21; CDBLB 1960
to Present; DLB 40; MTCW 1

Hill, George Roy 1921-   **CLC 26**
See also CA 110; 122

Hill, John
See Koontz, Dean R(ay)

Hill, Susan (Elizabeth) 1942-   **CLC 4, 113;
DAB; DAM MST, NOV**
See also CA 33-36R; CANR 29, 69; DLB 14,
139; MTCW 1

See also CA 114; 165

Hornung, E(rnest) W(illiam) 1866-1921
TCLC 59
See also CA 108; 160; DLB 70

Horovitz, Israel (Arthur) 1939-CLC 56; DAM
DRAM
See also CA 33-36R; CANR 46, 59; DLB 7

Horvath, Odon von
See Horvath, Oedoen von
See also DLB 85, 124

Horvath, Oedoen von 1901-1938   TCLC 45
See also Horvath, Odon von
See also CA 118

Horwitz, Julius 1920-1986   CLC 14
See also CA 9-12R; 119; CANR 12

Hospital, Janette Turner 1942-   CLC 42
See also CA 108; CANR 48

Hostos, E. M. de
See Hostos (y Bonilla), Eugenio Maria de

Hostos, Eugenio M. de
See Hostos (y Bonilla), Eugenio Maria de

Hostos, Eugenio Maria
See Hostos (y Bonilla), Eugenio Maria de

Hostos (y Bonilla), Eugenio Maria de 1839-1903
TCLC 24
See also CA 123; 131; HW 1

Houdini
See Lovecraft, H(oward) P(hillips)

Hougan, Carolyn 1943-   CLC 34
See also CA 139

Household, Geoffrey (Edward West) 1900-1988
CLC 11
See also CA 77-80; 126; CANR 58; DLB 87;
SATA 14; SATA-Obit 59

Housman, A(lfred) E(dward) 1859-1936
TCLC 1, 10; DA; DAB; DAC; DAM MST,
POET; PC 2; WLCS
See also CA 104; 125; DA3; DLB 19; MTCW
1, 2

Housman, Laurence 1865-1959   TCLC 7
See also CA 106; 155; DLB 10; SATA 25

Howard, Elizabeth Jane 1923-   CLC 7, 29
See also CA 5-8R; CANR 8, 62

Howard, Maureen 1930-   CLC 5, 14, 46
See also CA 53-56; CANR 31, 75; DLBY 83;
INT CANR-31; MTCW 1, 2

Howard, Richard 1929-   CLC 7, 10, 47
See also AITN 1; CA 85-88; CANR 25, 80; DLB
5; INT CANR-25

Howard, Robert E(rvin) 1906-1936   TCLC 8
See also CA 105; 157

Howard, Warren F.
See Pohl, Frederik

Howe, Fanny (Quincy) 1940-   CLC 47
See also CA 117; CAAS 27; CANR 70; SATA-
Brief 52

Howe, Irving 1920-1993   CLC 85
See also CA 9-12R; 141; CANR 21, 50; DLB
67; MTCW 1, 2

Howe, Julia Ward 1819-1910   TCLC 21
See also CA 117; DLB 1, 189

Howe, Susan 1937-   CLC 72
See also CA 160; DLB 120

Howe, Tina 1937-   CLC 48
See also CA 109

Howell, James 1594(?)-1666   LC 13
See also DLB 151

Howells, W. D.
See Howells, William Dean

Howells, William D.
See Howells, William Dean

Howells, William Dean 1837-1920 TCLC 7,
17, 41; SSC 36

See also CA 104; 134; CDALB 1865-1917;
DLB 12, 64, 74, 79, 189; MTCW 2

Howes, Barbara 1914-1996   CLC 15
See also CA 9-12R; 151; CAAS 3; CANR 53;
SATA 5

Hrabal, Bohumil 1914-1997   CLC 13, 67
See also CA 106; 156; CAAS 12; CANR 57

Hroswitha of Gandersheim c. 935-c. 1002
CMLC 29
See also DLB 148

Hsun, Lu
See Lu Hsun

Hubbard, L(afayette) Ron(ald) 1911-1986
CLC 43; DAM POP
See also CA 77-80; 118; CANR 52; DA3;
MTCW 2

Huch, Ricarda (Octavia) 1864-1947TCLC 13
See also CA 111; DLB 66

Huddle, David 1942-   CLC 49
See also CA 57-60; CAAS 20; DLB 130

Hudson, Jeffrey
See Crichton, (John) Michael

Hudson, W(illiam) H(enry) 1841-1922 T C L C
29
See also CA 115; DLB 98, 153, 174; SATA 35

Hueffer, Ford Madox
See Ford, Ford Madox

Hughart, Barry 1934-   CLC 39
See also CA 137

Hughes, Colin
See Creasey, John

Hughes, David (John) 1930-   CLC 48
See also CA 116; 129; DLB 14

Hughes, Edward James
See Hughes, Ted
See also DAM MST, POET; DA3

Hughes, (James) Langston 1902-1967CLC 1,
5, 10, 15, 35, 44, 108; BLC 2; DA; DAB;
DAC; DAM DRAM, MST, MULT, POET;
DC 3; PC 1; SSC 6; WLC
See also AAYA 12; BW 1, 3; CA 1-4R; 25-28R;
CANR 1, 34, 82; CDALB 1929-1941; CLR
17; DA3; DLB 4, 7, 48, 51, 86; JRDA;
MAICYA; MTCW 1, 2; SATA 4, 33

Hughes, Richard (Arthur Warren) 1900-1976
CLC 1, 11; DAM NOV
See also CA 5-8R; 65-68; CANR 4; DLB 15,
161; MTCW 1; SATA 8; SATA-Obit 25

Hughes, Ted 1930-1998   CLC 2, 4, 9, 14, 37,
119; DAB; DAC; PC 7
See also Hughes, Edward James
See also CA 1-4R; 171; CANR 1, 33, 66; CLR
3; DLB 40, 161; MAICYA; MTCW 1, 2;
SATA 49; SATA-Brief 27; SATA-Obit 107

Hugo, Richard F(ranklin) 1923-1982 CLC 6,
18, 32; DAM POET
See also CA 49-52; 108; CANR 3; DLB 5, 206

Hugo, Victor (Marie) 1802-1885NCLC 3, 10,
21; DA; DAB; DAC; DAM DRAM, MST,
NOV, POET; PC 17; WLC
See also AAYA 28; DA3; DLB 119, 192; SATA
47

Huidobro, Vicente
See Huidobro Fernandez, Vicente Garcia

Huidobro Fernandez, Vicente Garcia 1893-
1948   TCLC 31
See also CA 131; HW 1

Hulme, Keri 1947-   CLC 39
See also CA 125; CANR 69; INT 125

Hulme, T(homas) E(rnest) 1883-1917 T C L C
21
See also CA 117; DLB 19

Hume, David 1711-1776   LC 7

See also DLB 104

Humphrey, William 1924-1997   CLC 45
See also CA 77-80; 160; CANR 68; DLB 212

Humphreys, Emyr Owen 1919-   CLC 47
See also CA 5-8R; CANR 3, 24; DLB 15

Humphreys, Josephine 1945-   CLC 34, 57
See also CA 121; 127; INT 127

Huneker, James Gibbons 1857-1921TCLC 65
See also DLB 71

Hungerford, Pixie
See Brinsmead, H(esba) F(ay)

Hunt, E(verette) Howard, (Jr.) 1918- CLC 3
See also AITN 1; CA 45-48; CANR 2, 47

Hunt, Francesca
See Holland, Isabelle

Hunt, Kyle
See Creasey, John

Hunt, (James Henry) Leigh 1784-1859N C L C
1, 70; DAM POET
See also DLB 96, 110, 144

Hunt, Marsha 1946-   CLC 70
See also BW 2, 3; CA 143; CANR 79

Hunt, Violet 1866(?)-1942   TCLC 53
See also DLB 162, 197

Hunter, E. Waldo
See Sturgeon, Theodore (Hamilton)

Hunter, Evan 1926- CLC 11, 31; DAM POP
See also CA 5-8R; CANR 5, 38, 62; DLBY 82;
INT CANR-5; MTCW 1; SATA 25

Hunter, Kristin (Eggleston) 1931-   CLC 35
See also AITN 1; BW 1; CA 13-16R; CANR
13; CLR 3; DLB 33; INT CANR-13;
MAICYA; SAAS 10; SATA 12

Hunter, Mary
See Austin, Mary (Hunter)

Hunter, Mollie 1922-   CLC 21
See also McIlwraith, Maureen Mollie Hunter
See also AAYA 13; CANR 37, 78; CLR 25; DLB
161; JRDA; MAICYA; SAAS 7; SATA 54,
106

Hunter, Robert (?)-1734   LC 7

Hurston, Zora Neale 1903-1960CLC 7, 30, 61;
BLC 2; DA; DAC; DAM MST, MULT,
NOV; SSC 4; WLCS
See also AAYA 15; BW 1, 3; CA 85-88; CANR
61; CDALBS; DA3; DLB 51, 86; MTCW 1,
2

Huston, John (Marcellus) 1906-1987 CLC 20
See also CA 73-76; 123; CANR 34; DLB 26

Hustvedt, Siri 1955-   CLC 76
See also CA 137

Hutten, Ulrich von 1488-1523   LC 16
See also DLB 179

Huxley, Aldous (Leonard) 1894-1963 CLC 1,
3, 4, 5, 8, 11, 18, 35, 79; DA; DAB; DAC;
DAM MST, NOV; WLC
See also AAYA 11; CA 85-88; CANR 44;
CDBLB 1914-1945; DA3; DLB 36, 100,
162, 195; MTCW 1, 2; SATA 63

Huxley, T(homas) H(enry) 1825-1895 N C L C
67
See also DLB 57

Huysmans, Joris-Karl 1848-1907TCLC 7, 69
See also CA 104; 165; DLB 123

Hwang, David Henry 1957- CLC 55; DAM
DRAM; DC 4
See also CA 127; 132; CANR 76; DA3; DLB
212; INT 132; MTCW 2

Hyde, Anthony 1946-   CLC 42
See also CA 136

Hyde, Margaret O(ldroyd) 1917-   CLC 21
See also CA 1-4R; CANR 1, 36; CLR 23; JRDA;
MAICYA; SAAS 8; SATA 1, 42, 76

Author Index

Jeffers, (John) Robinson 1887-1962 **CLC 2, 3, 11, 15, 54; DA; DAC; DAM MST, POET; PC 17; WLC**
See also CA 85-88; CANR 35; CDALB 1917-1929; DLB 45, 212; MTCW 1, 2

Jefferson, Janet
See Mencken, H(enry) L(ouis)

Jefferson, Thomas 1743-1826　　**NCLC 11**
See also CDALB 1640-1865; DA3; DLB 31

Jeffrey, Francis 1773-1850　　**NCLC 33**
See also DLB 107

Jelakowitch, Ivan
See Heijermans, Herman

Jellicoe, (Patricia) Ann 1927-　　**CLC 27**
See also CA 85-88; DLB 13

Jen, Gish　　**CLC 70**
See also Jen, Lillian

Jen, Lillian 1956(?)-
See Jen, Gish
See also CA 135

Jenkins, (John) Robin 1912-　　**CLC 52**
See also CA 1-4R; CANR 1; DLB 14

Jennings, Elizabeth (Joan) 1926-　**CLC 5, 14**
See also CA 61-64; CAAS 5; CANR 8, 39, 66; DLB 27; MTCW 1; SATA 66

Jennings, Waylon 1937-　　**CLC 21**

Jensen, Johannes V. 1873-1950　　**TCLC 41**
See also CA 170

Jensen, Laura (Linnea) 1948-　　**CLC 37**
See also CA 103

Jerome, Jerome K(lapka) 1859-1927 **TCLC 23**
See also CA 119; 177; DLB 10, 34, 135

Jerrold, Douglas William 1803-1857 **NCLC 2**
See also DLB 158, 159

Jewett, (Theodora) Sarah Orne 1849-1909
TCLC 1, 22; SSC 6
See also CA 108; 127; CANR 71; DLB 12, 74; SATA 15

Jewsbury, Geraldine (Endsor) 1812-1880
NCLC 22
See also DLB 21

Jhabvala, Ruth Prawer 1927- **CLC 4, 8, 29, 94; DAB; DAM NOV**
See also CA 1-4R; CANR 2, 29, 51, 74; DLB 139, 194; INT CANR-29; MTCW 1, 2

Jibran, Kahlil
See Gibran, Kahlil

Jibran, Khalil
See Gibran, Kahlil

Jiles, Paulette 1943-　　**CLC 13, 58**
See also CA 101; CANR 70

Jimenez (Mantecon), Juan Ramon 1881-1958
TCLC 4; DAM MULT, POET; HLC 1; PC 7
See also CA 104; 131; CANR 74; DLB 134; HW 1; MTCW 1, 2

Jimenez, Ramon
See Jimenez (Mantecon), Juan Ramon

Jimenez Mantecon, Juan
See Jimenez (Mantecon), Juan Ramon

Jin, Ha 1956-　　**CLC 109**
See also CA 152

Joel, Billy　　**CLC 26**
See also Joel, William Martin

Joel, William Martin 1949-
See Joel, Billy
See also CA 108

John, Saint 7th cent.　　**CMLC 27**

John of the Cross, St. 1542-1591　　**LC 18**

Johnson, B(ryan) S(tanley William) 1933-1973
CLC 6, 9
See also CA 9-12R; 53-56; CANR 9; DLB 14, 40

Johnson, Benj. F. of Boo

See Riley, James Whitcomb

Johnson, Benjamin F. of Boo
See Riley, James Whitcomb

Johnson, Charles (Richard) 1948- **CLC 7, 51, 65; BLC 2; DAM MULT**
See also BW 2, 3; CA 116; CAAS 18; CANR 42, 66, 82; DLB 33; MTCW 2

Johnson, Denis 1949-　　　　**CLC 52**
See also CA 117; 121; CANR 71; DLB 120

Johnson, Diane 1934-　　**CLC 5, 13, 48**
See also CA 41-44R; CANR 17, 40, 62; DLBY 80; INT CANR-17; MTCW 1

Johnson, Eyvind (Olof Verner) 1900-1976
CLC 14
See also CA 73-76; 69-72; CANR 34

Johnson, J. R.
See James, C(yril) L(ionel) R(obert)

Johnson, James Weldon 1871-1938 **TCLC 3, 19; BLC 2; DAM MULT, POET; PC 24**
See also BW 1, 3; CA 104; 125; CANR 82; CDALB 1917-1929; CLR 32; DA3; DLB 51; MTCW 1, 2; SATA 31

Johnson, Joyce 1935-　　　　**CLC 58**
See also CA 125; 129

Johnson, Judith (Emlyn) 1936-　　**CLC 7, 15**
See also Sherwin, Judith Johnson
See also CA 25-28R; 153; CANR 34

Johnson, Lionel (Pigot) 1867-1902 **TCLC 19**
See also CA 117; DLB 19

Johnson, Marguerite (Annie)
See Angelou, Maya

Johnson, Mel
See Malzberg, Barry N(athaniel)

Johnson, Pamela Hansford 1912-1981 **CLC 1, 7, 27**
See also CA 1-4R; 104; CANR 2, 28; DLB 15; MTCW 1, 2

Johnson, Robert 1911(?)-1938　　**TCLC 69**
See also BW 3; CA 174

Johnson, Samuel 1709-1784　　**LC 15, 52; DA; DAB; DAC; DAM MST; WLC**
See also CDBLB 1660-1789; DLB 39, 95, 104, 142

Johnson, Uwe 1934-1984　　**CLC 5, 10, 15, 40**
See also CA 1-4R; 112; CANR 1, 39; DLB 75; MTCW 1

Johnston, George (Benson) 1913-　　**CLC 51**
See also CA 1-4R; CANR 5, 20; DLB 88

Johnston, Jennifer 1930-　　　　**CLC 7**
See also CA 85-88; DLB 14

Jolley, (Monica) Elizabeth 1923- **CLC 46; SSC 19**
See also CA 127; CAAS 13; CANR 59

Jones, Arthur Llewellyn 1863-1947
See Machen, Arthur
See also CA 104; 179

Jones, D(ouglas) G(ordon) 1929-　　**CLC 10**
See also CA 29-32R; CANR 13; DLB 53

Jones, David (Michael) 1895-1974 **CLC 2, 4, 7, 13, 42**
See also CA 9-12R; 53-56; CANR 28; CDBLB 1945-1960; DLB 20, 100; MTCW 1

Jones, David Robert 1947-
See Bowie, David
See also CA 103

Jones, Diana Wynne 1934-　　　　**CLC 26**
See also AAYA 12; CA 49-52; CANR 4, 26, 56; CLR 23; DLB 161; JRDA; MAICYA; SAAS 7; SATA 9, 70, 108

Jones, Edward P. 1950-　　　　**CLC 76**
See also BW 2, 3; CA 142; CANR 79

Jones, Gayl 1949-　　**CLC 6, 9; BLC 2; DAM MULT**

See also BW 2, 3; CA 77-80; CANR 27, 66; DA3; DLB 33; MTCW 1, 2

Jones, James 1921-1977　　**CLC 1, 3, 10, 39**
See also AITN 1, 2; CA 1-4R; 69-72; CANR 6; DLB 2, 143; DLBD 17; DLBY 98; MTCW 1

Jones, John J.
See Lovecraft, H(oward) P(hillips)

Jones, LeRoi　　**CLC 1, 2, 3, 5, 10, 14**
See also Baraka, Amiri
See also MTCW 2

Jones, Louis B. 1953-　　　　**CLC 65**
See also CA 141; CANR 73

Jones, Madison (Percy, Jr.) 1925-　　**CLC 4**
See also CA 13-16R; CAAS 11; CANR 7, 54, 83; DLB 152

Jones, Mervyn 1922-　　　　**CLC 10, 52**
See also CA 45-48; CAAS 5; CANR 1; MTCW 1

Jones, Mick 1956(?)-　　　　**CLC 30**

Jones, Nettie (Pearl) 1941-　　　　**CLC 34**
See also BW 2; CA 137; CAAS 20

Jones, Preston 1936-1979　　　　**CLC 10**
See also CA 73-76; 89-92; DLB 7

Jones, Robert F(rancis) 1934-　　　　**CLC 7**
See also CA 49-52; CANR 2, 61

Jones, Rod 1953-　　　　**CLC 50**
See also CA 128

Jones, Terence Graham Parry 1942- **CLC 21**
See also Jones, Terry; Monty Python
See also CA 112; 116; CANR 35; INT 116

Jones, Terry
See Jones, Terence Graham Parry
See also SATA 67; SATA-Brief 51

Jones, Thom 1945(?)-　　　　**CLC 81**
See also CA 157

Jong, Erica 1942- **CLC 4, 6, 8, 18, 83; DAM NOV, POP**
See also AITN 1; BEST 90:2; CA 73-76; CANR 26, 52, 75; DA3; DLB 2, 5, 28, 152; INT CANR-26; MTCW 1, 2

Jonson, Ben(jamin) 1572(?)-1637　　**LC 6, 33; DA; DAB; DAC; DAM DRAM, MST, POET; DC 4; PC 17; WLC**
See also CDBLB Before 1660; DLB 62, 121

Jordan, June 1936- **CLC 5, 11, 23, 114; BLCS; DAM MULT, POET**
See also AAYA 2; BW 2, 3; CA 33-36R; CANR 25, 70; CLR 10; DLB 38; MAICYA; MTCW 1; SATA 4

Jordan, Neil (Patrick) 1950-　　　　**CLC 110**
See also CA 124; 130; CANR 54; INT 130

Jordan, Pat(rick M.) 1941-　　　　**CLC 37**
See also CA 33-36R

Jorgensen, Ivar
See Ellison, Harlan (Jay)

Jorgenson, Ivar
See Silverberg, Robert

Josephus, Flavius c. 37-100　　　　**CMLC 13**

Josipovici, Gabriel 1940-　　　　**CLC 6, 43**
See also CA 37-40R; CAAS 8; CANR 47, 84; DLB 14

Joubert, Joseph 1754-1824　　　　**NCLC 9**

Jouve, Pierre Jean 1887-1976　　　　**CLC 47**
See also CA 65-68

Jovine, Francesco 1902-1950　　　　**TCLC 79**

Joyce, James (Augustine Aloysius) 1882-1941
TCLC 3, 8, 16, 35, 52; DA; DAB; DAC; DAM MST, NOV, POET; PC 22; SSC 3, 26; WLC
See also CA 104; 126; CDBLB 1914-1945; DA3; DLB 10, 19, 36, 162; MTCW 1, 2

Jozsef, Attila 1905-1937　　　　**TCLC 22**
See also CA 116

DLB 41; MTCW 2

Knight, Sarah Kemble 1666-1727   **LC 7**
    See also DLB 24, 200

Knister, Raymond 1899-1932   **TCLC 56**
    See also DLB 68

Knowles, John 1926-   **CLC 1, 4, 10, 26; DA;**
    DAC; DAM MST, NOV
    See also AAYA 10; CA 17-20R; CANR 40, 74,
    76; CDALB 1968-1988; DLB 6; MTCW 1,
    2; SATA 8, 89

Knox, Calvin M.
    See Silverberg, Robert

Knox, John c. 1505-1572   **LC 37**
    See also DLB 132

Knye, Cassandra
    See Disch, Thomas M(ichael)

Koch, C(hristopher) J(ohn) 1932-   **CLC 42**
    See also CA 127; CANR 84

Koch, Christopher
    See Koch, C(hristopher) J(ohn)

Koch, Kenneth 1925-   **CLC 5, 8, 44; DAM**
    POET
    See also CA 1-4R; CANR 6, 36, 57; DLB 5;
    INT CANR-36; MTCW 2; SATA 65

Kochanowski, Jan 1530-1584   **LC 10**

Kock, Charles Paul de 1794-1871   **NCLC 16**

Koda Shigeyuki 1867-1947
    See Rohan, Koda
    See also CA 121

Koestler, Arthur 1905-1983 **CLC 1, 3, 6, 8, 15,**
    33
    See also CA 1-4R; 109; CANR 1, 33; CDBLB
    1945-1960; DLBY 83; MTCW 1, 2

Kogawa, Joy Nozomi 1935-   **CLC 78; DAC;**
    DAM MST, MULT
    See also CA 101; CANR 19, 62; MTCW 2;
    SATA 99

Kohout, Pavel 1928-   **CLC 13**
    See also CA 45-48; CANR 3

Koizumi, Yakumo
    See Hearn, (Patricio) Lafcadio (Tessima Carlos)

Kolmar, Gertrud 1894-1943   **TCLC 40**
    See also CA 167

Komunyakaa, Yusef 1947- **CLC 86, 94; BLCS**
    See also CA 147; CANR 83; DLB 120

Konrad, George
    See Konrad, Gyoergy

Konrad, Gyoergy 1933-   **CLC 4, 10, 73**
    See also CA 85-88

Konwicki, Tadeusz 1926-   **CLC 8, 28, 54, 117**
    See also CA 101; CAAS 9; CANR 39, 59;
    MTCW 1

Koontz, Dean R(ay) 1945-   **CLC 78; DAM**
    NOV, POP
    See also AAYA 9, 31; BEST 89:3, 90:2; CA 108;
    CANR 19, 36, 52; DA3; MTCW 1; SATA 92

Kopernik, Mikolaj
    See Copernicus, Nicolaus

Kopit, Arthur (Lee) 1937- **CLC 1, 18, 33; DAM**
    DRAM
    See also AITN 1; CA 81-84; CABS 3; DLB 7;
    MTCW 1

Kops, Bernard 1926-   **CLC 4**
    See also CA 5-8R; CANR 84; DLB 13

Kornbluth, C(yril) M. 1923-1958   **TCLC 8**
    See also CA 105; 160; DLB 8

Korolenko, V. G.
    See Korolenko, Vladimir Galaktionovich

Korolenko, Vladimir
    See Korolenko, Vladimir Galaktionovich

Korolenko, Vladimir G.
    See Korolenko, Vladimir Galaktionovich

Korolenko, Vladimir Galaktionovich 1853-

1921   **TCLC 22**
    See also CA 121

Korzybski, Alfred (Habdank Skarbek) 1879-
    1950   **TCLC 61**
    See also CA 123; 160

Kosinski, Jerzy (Nikodem) 1933-1991 **CLC 1,**
    2, 3, 6, 10, 15, 53, 70; DAM NOV
    See also CA 17-20R; 134; CANR 9, 46; DA3;
    DLB 2; DLBY 82; MTCW 1, 2

Kostelanetz, Richard (Cory) 1940-   **CLC 28**
    See also CA 13-16R; CAAS 8; CANR 38, 77

Kostrowitzki, Wilhelm Apollinaris de 1880-
    1918
    See Apollinaire, Guillaume
    See also CA 104

Kotlowitz, Robert 1924-   **CLC 4**
    See also CA 33-36R; CANR 36

Kotzebue, August (Friedrich Ferdinand) von
    1761-1819   **NCLC 25**
    See also DLB 94

Kotzwinkle, William 1938-   **CLC 5, 14, 35**
    See also CA 45-48; CANR 3, 44, 84; CLR 6;
    DLB 173; MAICYA; SATA 24, 70

Kowna, Stancy
    See Szymborska, Wislawa

Kozol, Jonathan 1936-   **CLC 17**
    See also CA 61-64; CANR 16, 45

Kozoll, Michael 1940(?)-   **CLC 35**

Kramer, Kathryn 19(?)-   **CLC 34**

Kramer, Larry 1935- **CLC 42; DAM POP; DC**
    8
    See also CA 124; 126; CANR 60

Krasicki, Ignacy 1735-1801   **NCLC 8**

Krasinski, Zygmunt 1812-1859   **NCLC 4**

Kraus, Karl 1874-1936   **TCLC 5**
    See also CA 104; DLB 118

Kreve (Mickevicius), Vincas 1882-1954 **TCLC**
    27
    See also CA 170

Kristeva, Julia 1941-   **CLC 77**
    See also CA 154

Kristofferson, Kris 1936-   **CLC 26**
    See also CA 104

Krizanc, John 1956-   **CLC 57**

Krleza, Miroslav 1893-1981   **CLC 8, 114**
    See also CA 97-100; 105; CANR 50; DLB 147

Kroetsch, Robert 1927- **CLC 5, 23, 57; DAC;**
    DAM POET
    See also CA 17-20R; CANR 8, 38; DLB 53;
    MTCW 1

Kroetz, Franz
    See Kroetz, Franz Xaver

Kroetz, Franz Xaver 1946-   **CLC 41**
    See also CA 130

Kroker, Arthur (W.) 1945-   **CLC 77**
    See also CA 161

Kropotkin, Peter (Aleksieevich) 1842-1921
    TCLC 36
    See also CA 119

Krotkov, Yuri 1917-   **CLC 19**
    See also CA 102

Krumb
    See Crumb, R(obert)

Krumgold, Joseph (Quincy) 1908-1980   **CLC**
    12
    See also CA 9-12R; 101; CANR 7; MAICYA;
    SATA 1, 48; SATA-Obit 23

Krumwitz
    See Crumb, R(obert)

Krutch, Joseph Wood 1893-1970   **CLC 24**
    See also CA 1-4R; 25-28R; CANR 4; DLB 63,
    206

Krutzch, Gus

    See Eliot, T(homas) S(tearns)

Krylov, Ivan Andreevich 1768(?)-1844 **N C L C**
    1
    See also DLB 150

Kubin, Alfred (Leopold Isidor) 1877-1959
    TCLC 23
    See also CA 112; 149; DLB 81

Kubrick, Stanley 1928-1999   **CLC 16**
    See also AAYA 30; CA 81-84; 177; CANR 33;
    DLB 26

Kumin, Maxine (Winokur) 1925- **CLC 5, 13,**
    28; DAM POET; PC 15
    See also AITN 2; CA 1-4R; CAAS 8; CANR 1,
    21, 69; DA3; DLB 5; MTCW 1, 2; SATA 12

Kundera, Milan 1929-   **CLC 4, 9, 19, 32, 68,**
    115; DAM NOV; SSC 24
    See also AAYA 2; CA 85-88; CANR 19, 52,
    74; DA3; MTCW 1, 2

Kunene, Mazisi (Raymond) 1930-   **CLC 85**
    See also BW 1, 3; CA 125; CANR 81; DLB
    117

Kunitz, Stanley (Jasspon) 1905- **CLC 6, 11, 14;**
    PC 19
    See also CA 41-44R; CANR 26, 57; DA3; DLB
    48; INT CANR-26; MTCW 1, 2

Kunze, Reiner 1933-   **CLC 10**
    See also CA 93-96; DLB 75

Kuprin, Aleksandr Ivanovich 1870-1938
    TCLC 5
    See also CA 104; 182

Kureishi, Hanif 1954(?)-   **CLC 64**
    See also CA 139; DLB 194

Kurosawa, Akira 1910-1998   **CLC 16, 119;**
    DAM MULT
    See also AAYA 11; CA 101; 170; CANR 46

Kushner, Tony 1957(?)- **CLC 81; DAM DRAM;**
    DC 10
    See also CA 144; CANR 74; DA3; MTCW 2

Kuttner, Henry 1915-1958   **TCLC 10**
    See Vance, Jack
    See also CA 107; 157; DLB 8

Kuzma, Greg 1944-   **CLC 7**
    See also CA 33-36R; CANR 70

Kuzmin, Mikhail 1872(?)-1936   **TCLC 40**
    See also CA 170

Kyd, Thomas 1558-1594 **LC 22; DAM DRAM;**
    DC 3
    See also DLB 62

Kyprlanos, Iossif
    See Samarakis, Antonis

La Bruyere, Jean de 1645-1696   **LC 17**

Lacan, Jacques (Marie Emile) 1901-1981
    CLC 75
    See also CA 121; 104

Laclos, Pierre Ambroise Francois Choderlos de
    1741-1803   **NCLC 4**

La Colere, Francois
    See Aragon, Louis

Lacolere, Francois
    See Aragon, Louis

La Deshabilleuse
    See Simenon, Georges (Jacques Christian)

Lady Gregory
    See Gregory, Isabella Augusta (Persse)

Lady of Quality, A
    See Bagnold, Enid

La Fayette, Marie (Madelaine Pioche de la
    Vergne Comtes 1634-1693   **LC 2**

Lafayette, Rene
    See Hubbard, L(afayette) Ron(ald)

La Fontaine, Jean de 1621-1695   **LC 50**
    See also MAICYA; SATA 18

Laforgue, Jules 1860-1887 **NCLC 5, 53; PC 14;**

SSC 20
Lagerkvist, Paer (Fabian) 1891-1974 **CLC 7,
10, 13, 54; DAM DRAM, NOV**
See also Lagerkvist, Par
See also CA 85-88; 49-52; DA3; MTCW 1, 2
Lagerkvist, Par   **SSC 12**
See also Lagerkvist, Paer (Fabian)
See also MTCW 2
Lagerloef, Selma (Ottiliana Lovisa) 1858-1940
TCLC 4, 36
See also Lagerlof, Selma (Ottiliana Lovisa)
See also CA 108; MTCW 2; SATA 15
Lagerlof, Selma (Ottiliana Lovisa)
See Lagerloef, Selma (Ottiliana Lovisa)
See also CLR 7; SATA 15
La Guma, (Justin) Alex(ander) 1925-1985
CLC 19; BLCS; DAM NOV
See also BW 1, 3; CA 49-52; 118; CANR 25,
81; DLB 117; MTCW 1, 2
Laidlaw, A. K.
See Grieve, C(hristopher) M(urray)
Lainez, Manuel Mujica
See Mujica Lainez, Manuel
See also HW 1
Laing, R(onald) D(avid) 1927-1989 **CLC 95**
See also CA 107; 129; CANR 34; MTCW 1
Lamartine, Alphonse (Marie Louis Prat) de
1790-1869NCLC 11; DAM POET; PC 16
Lamb, Charles 1775-1834   **NCLC 10; DA;
DAB; DAC; DAM MST; WLC**
See also CDBLB 1789-1832; DLB 93, 107, 163;
SATA 17
Lamb, Lady Caroline 1785-1828   **NCLC 38**
See also DLB 116
Lamming, George (William) 1927- **CLC 2, 4,
66; BLC 2; DAM MULT**
See also BW 2, 3; CA 85-88; CANR 26, 76;
DLB 125; MTCW 1, 2
L'Amour, Louis (Dearborn) 1908-1988 **C L C
25, 55; DAM NOV, POP**
See, also AAYA 16; AITN 2; BEST 89:2; CA 1-
4R; 125; CANR 3, 25, 40; DA3; DLB 206;
DLBY 80; MTCW 1, 2
Lampedusa, Giuseppe (Tomasi) di 1896-1957
TCLC 13
See also Tomasi di Lampedusa, Giuseppe
See also CA 164; DLB 177; MTCW 2
Lampman, Archibald 1861-1899   **NCLC 25**
See also DLB 92
Lancaster, Bruce 1896-1963   **CLC 36**
See also CA 9-10; CANR 70; CAP 1; SATA 9
Lanchester, John   **CLC 99**
Landau, Mark Alexandrovich
See Aldanov, Mark (Alexandrovich)
Landau-Aldanov, Mark Alexandrovich
See Aldanov, Mark (Alexandrovich)
Landis, Jerry
See Simon, Paul (Frederick)
Landis, John 1950-   **CLC 26**
See also CA 112; 122
Landolfi, Tommaso 1908-1979   **CLC 11, 49**
See also CA 127; 117; DLB 177
Landon, Letitia Elizabeth 1802-1838 **N C L C
15**
See also DLB 96
Landor, Walter Savage 1775-1864 **NCLC 14**
See also DLB 93, 107
Landwirth, Heinz 1927-
See Lind, Jakov
See also CA 9-12R; CANR 7
Lane, Patrick 1939-   **CLC 25; DAM POET**
See also CA 97-100; CANR 54; DLB 53; INT
97-100

Lang, Andrew 1844-1912   **TCLC 16**
See also CA 114; 137; CANR 85; DLB 98, 141,
184; MAICYA; SATA 16
Lang, Fritz 1890-1976   **CLC 20, 103**
See also CA 77-80; 69-72; CANR 30
Lange, John
See Crichton, (John) Michael
Langer, Elinor 1939-   **CLC 34**
See also CA 121
Langland, William 1330(?)-1400(?)   **LC 19;
DA; DAB; DAC; DAM MST, POET**
See also DLB 146
Langstaff, Launcelot
See Irving, Washington
Lanier, Sidney 1842-1881   **NCLC 6; DAM
POET**
See also DLB 64; DLBD 13; MAICYA; SATA
18
Lanyer, Aemilia 1569-1645   **LC 10, 30**
See also DLB 121
Lao-Tzu
See Lao Tzu
Lao Tzu fl. 6th cent. B.C.-   **CMLC 7**
Lapine, James (Elliot) 1949-   **CLC 39**
See also CA 123; 130; CANR 54; INT 130
Larbaud, Valery (Nicolas) 1881-1957TCLC 9
See also CA 106; 152
Lardner, Ring
See Lardner, Ring(gold) W(ilmer)
Lardner, Ring W., Jr.
See Lardner, Ring(gold) W(ilmer)
Lardner, Ring(gold) W(ilmer) 1885-1933
TCLC 2, 14; SSC 32
See also CA 104; 131; CDALB 1917-1929;
DLB 11, 25, 86; DLBD 16; MTCW 1, 2
Laredo, Betty
See Codrescu, Andrei
Larkin, Maia
See Wojciechowska, Maia (Teresa)
Larkin, Philip (Arthur) 1922-1985CLC 3, 5, 8,
9, 13, 18, 33, 39, 64; DAB; DAM MST,
POET; PC 21
See also CA 5-8R; 117; CANR 24, 62; CDBLB
1960 to Present; DA3; DLB 27; MTCW 1, 2
Larra (y Sanchez de Castro), Mariano Jose de
1809-1837   **NCLC 17**
Larsen, Eric 1941-   **CLC 55**
See also CA 132
Larsen, Nella 1891-1964   **CLC 37; BLC 2;
DAM MULT**
See also BW 1; CA 125; CANR 83; DLB 51
Larson, Charles R(aymond) 1938-   **CLC 31**
See also CA 53-56; CANR 4
Larson, Jonathan 1961-1996   **CLC 99**
See also AAYA 28; CA 156
Las Casas, Bartolome de 1474-1566   **LC 31**
Lasch, Christopher 1932-1994   **CLC 102**
See also CA 73-76; 144; CANR 25; MTCW 1,
2
Lasker-Schueler, Else 1869-1945   **TCLC 57**
See also DLB 66, 124
Laski, Harold 1893-1950   **TCLC 79**
Latham, Jean Lee 1902-1995   **CLC 12**
See also AITN 1; CA 5-8R; CANR 7, 84; CLR
50; MAICYA; SATA 2, 68
Latham, Mavis
See Clark, Mavis Thorpe
Lathen, Emma   **CLC 2**
See also Hennissart, Martha; Latsis, Mary J(ane)
Lathrop, Francis
See Leiber, Fritz (Reuter, Jr.)
Latsis, Mary J(ane) 1927(?)-1997
See Lathen, Emma

See also CA 85-88; 162
Lattimore, Richmond (Alexander) 1906-1984
CLC 3
See also CA 1-4R; 112; CANR 1
Laughlin, James 1914-1997   **CLC 49**
See also CA 21-24R; 162; CAAS 22; CANR 9,
47; DLB 48; DLBY 96, 97
Laurence, (Jean) Margaret (Wemyss) 1926-
1987   **CLC 3, 6, 13, 50, 62; DAC; DAM
MST; SSC 7**
See also CA 5-8R; 121; CANR 33; DLB 53;
MTCW 1, 2; SATA-Obit 50
Laurent, Antoine 1952-   **CLC 50**
Lauscher, Hermann
See Hesse, Hermann
Lautreamont, Comte de 1846-1870NCLC 12;
SSC 14
Laverty, Donald
See Blish, James (Benjamin)
Lavin, Mary 1912-1996CLC 4, 18, 99; SSC 4
See also CA 9-12R; 151; CANR 33; DLB 15;
MTCW 1
Lavond, Paul Dennis
See Kornbluth, C(yril) M.; Pohl, Frederik
Lawler, Raymond Evenor 1922-   **CLC 58**
See also CA 103
Lawrence, D(avid) H(erbert Richards) 1885-
1930 **TCLC 2, 9, 16, 33, 48, 61, 93; DA;
DAB; DAC; DAM MST, NOV, POET; SSC
4, 19; WLC**
See also CA 104; 121; CDBLB 1914-1945;
DA3; DLB 10, 19, 36, 98, 162, 195; MTCW
1, 2
Lawrence, T(homas) E(dward) 1888-1935
TCLC 18
See also Dale, Colin
See also CA 115; 167; DLB 195
Lawrence of Arabia
See Lawrence, T(homas) E(dward)
Lawson, Henry (Archibald Hertzberg) 1867-
1922   **TCLC 27; SSC 18**
See also CA 120; 181
Lawton, Dennis
See Faust, Frederick (Schiller)
Laxness, Halldor   **CLC 25**
See also Gudjonsson, Halldor Kiljan
Layamon fl. c. 1200-   **CMLC 10**
See also DLB 146
Laye, Camara 1928-1980 **CLC 4, 38; BLC 2;
DAM MULT**
See also BW 1; CA 85-88; 97-100; CANR 25;
MTCW 1, 2
Layton, Irving (Peter) 1912-**CLC 2, 15; DAC;
DAM MST, POET**
See also CA 1-4R; CANR 2, 33, 43, 66; DLB
88; MTCW 1, 2
Lazarus, Emma 1849-1887   **NCLC 8**
Lazarus, Felix
See Cable, George Washington
Lazarus, Henry
See Slavitt, David R(ytman)
Lea, Joan
See Neufeld, John (Arthur)
Leacock, Stephen (Butler) 1869-1944TCLC 2;
DAC; DAM MST
See also CA 104; 141; CANR 80; DLB 92;
MTCW 2
Lear, Edward 1812-1888   **NCLC 3**
See also CLR 1; DLB 32, 163, 166; MAICYA;
SATA 18, 100
Lear, Norman (Milton) 1922-   **CLC 12**
See also CA 73-76
Leautaud, Paul 1872-1956   **TCLC 83**

MTCW 1, 2; SATA 66

Levin, Meyer 1905-1981 **CLC 7; DAM POP**
See also AITN 1; CA 9-12R; 104; CANR 15; DLB 9, 28; DLBY 81; SATA 21; SATA-Obit 27

Levine, Norman 1924- **CLC 54**
See also CA 73-76; CAAS 23; CANR 14, 70; DLB 88

Levine, Philip 1928-**CLC 2, 4, 5, 9, 14, 33, 118; DAM POET; PC 22**
See also CA 9-12R; CANR 9, 37, 52; DLB 5

Levinson, Deirdre 1931- **CLC 49**
See also CA 73-76; CANR 70

Levi-Strauss, Claude 1908- **CLC 38**
See also CA 1-4R; CANR 6, 32, 57; MTCW 1, 2

Levitin, Sonia (Wolff) 1934- **CLC 17**
See also AAYA 13; CA 29-32R; CANR 14, 32, 79; CLR 53; JRDA; MAICYA; SAAS 2; SATA 4, 68

Levon, O. U.
See Kesey, Ken (Elton)

Levy, Amy 1861-1889 **NCLC 59**
See also DLB 156

Lewes, George Henry 1817-1878 **NCLC 25**
See also DLB 55, 144

Lewis, Alun 1915-1944 **TCLC 3**
See also CA 104; DLB 20, 162

Lewis, C. Day
See Day Lewis, C(ecil)

Lewis, C(live) S(taples) 1898-1963**CLC 1, 3, 6, 14, 27, 124; DA; DAB; DAC; DAM MST, NOV, POP; WLC**
See also AAYA 3; CA 81-84; CANR 33, 71; CDBLB 1945-1960; CLR 3, 27; DA3; DLB 15, 100, 160; JRDA; MAICYA; MTCW 1, 2; SATA 13, 100

Lewis, Janet 1899-1998 **CLC 41**
See also Winters, Janet Lewis
See also CA 9-12R; 172; CANR 29, 63; CAP 1; DLBY 87

Lewis, Matthew Gregory 1775-1818**NCLC 11, 62**
See also DLB 39, 158, 178

Lewis, (Harry) Sinclair 1885-1951 **TCLC 4, 13, 23, 39; DA; DAB; DAC; DAM MST, NOV; WLC**
See also CA 104; 133; CDALB 1917-1929; DA3; DLB 9, 102; DLBD 1; MTCW 1, 2

Lewis, (Percy) Wyndham 1882(?)-1957**TCLC 2, 9; SSC 34**
See also CA 104; 157; DLB 15; MTCW 2

Lewisohn, Ludwig 1883-1955 **TCLC 19**
See also CA 107; DLB 4, 9, 28, 102

Lewton, Val 1904-1951 **TCLC 76**

Leyner, Mark 1956- **CLC 92**
See also CA 110; CANR 28, 53; DA3; MTCW 2

Lezama Lima, Jose 1910-1976**CLC 4, 10, 101; DAM MULT; HLCS 2**
See also CA 77-80; CANR 71; DLB 113; HW 1, 2

L'Heureux, John (Clarke) 1934- **CLC 52**
See also CA 13-16R; CANR 23, 45

Liddell, C. H.
See Kuttner, Henry

Lie, Jonas (Lauritz Idemil) 1833-1908(?) **TCLC 5**
See also CA 115

Lieber, Joel 1937-1971 **CLC 6**
See also CA 73-76; 29-32R

Lieber, Stanley Martin
See Lee, Stan

Lieberman, Laurence (James) 1935- **CLC 4, 36**
See also CA 17-20R; CANR 8, 36

Lieh Tzu fl. 7th cent. B.C.-5th cent. B.C. **CMLC 27**

Lieksman, Anders
See Haavikko, Paavo Juhani

Li Fei-kan 1904-
See Pa Chin
See also CA 105

Lifton, Robert Jay 1926- **CLC 67**
See also CA 17-20R; CANR 27, 78; INT CANR-27; SATA 66

Lightfoot, Gordon 1938- **CLC 26**
See also CA 109

Lightman, Alan P(aige) 1948- **CLC 81**
See also CA 141; CANR 63

Ligotti, Thomas (Robert) 1953-**CLC 44; SSC 16**
See also CA 123; CANR 49

Li Ho 791-817 **PC 13**

Liliencron, (Friedrich Adolf Axel) Detlev von 1844-1909 **TCLC 18**
See also CA 117

Lilly, William 1602-1681 **LC 27**

Lima, Jose Lezama
See Lezama Lima, Jose

Lima Barreto, Afonso Henrique de 1881-1922 **TCLC 23**
See also CA 117; 181

Limonov, Edward 1944- **CLC 67**
See also CA 137

Lin, Frank
See Atherton, Gertrude (Franklin Horn)

Lincoln, Abraham 1809-1865 **NCLC 18**

Lind, Jakov **CLC 1, 2, 4, 27, 82**
See also Landwirth, Heinz
See also CAAS 4

Lindbergh, Anne (Spencer) Morrow 1906- **CLC 82; DAM NOV**
See also CA 17-20R; CANR 16, 73; MTCW 1, 2; SATA 33

Lindsay, David 1878-1945 **TCLC 15**
See also CA 113

Lindsay, (Nicholas) Vachel 1879-1931 **TCLC 17; DA; DAC; DAM MST, POET; PC 23; WLC**
See also CA 114; 135; CANR 79; CDALB 1865-1917; DA3; DLB 54; SATA 40

Linke-Poot
See Doeblin, Alfred

Linney, Romulus 1930- **CLC 51**
See also CA 1-4R; CANR 40, 44, 79

Linton, Eliza Lynn 1822-1898 **NCLC 41**
See also DLB 18

Li Po 701-763 **CMLC 2**

Lipsius, Justus 1547-1606 **LC 16**

Lipsyte, Robert (Michael) 1938-**CLC 21; DA; DAC; DAM MST, NOV**
See also AAYA 7; CA 17-20R; CANR 8, 57; CLR 23; JRDA; MAICYA; SATA 5, 68

Lish, Gordon (Jay) 1934- **CLC 45; SSC 18**
See also CA 113; 117; CANR 79; DLB 130; INT 117

Lispector, Clarice 1925(?)-1977 **CLC 43; HLCS 2; SSC 34**
See also CA 139; 116; CANR 71; DLB 113; HW 2

Littell, Robert 1935(?)- **CLC 42**
See also CA 109; 112; CANR 64

Little, Malcolm 1925-1965
See Malcolm X
See also BW 1, 3; CA 125; 111; CANR 82; DA;

DAB; DAC; DAM MST, MULT; DA3; MTCW 1, 2

Littlewit, Humphrey Gent.
See Lovecraft, H(oward) P(hillips)

Litwos
See Sienkiewicz, Henryk (Adam Alexander Pius)

Liu, E 1857-1909 **TCLC 15**
See also CA 115

Lively, Penelope (Margaret) 1933- **CLC 32, 50; DAM NOV**
See also CA 41-44R; CANR 29, 67, 79; CLR 7; DLB 14, 161, 207; JRDA; MAICYA; MTCW 1, 2; SATA 7, 60, 101

Livesay, Dorothy (Kathleen) 1909-**CLC 4, 15, 79; DAC; DAM MST, POET**
See also AITN 2; CA 25-28R; CAAS 8; CANR 36, 67; DLB 68; MTCW 1

Livy c. 59B.C.-c. 17 **CMLC 11**
See also DLB 211

Lizardi, Jose Joaquin Fernandez de 1776-1827 **NCLC 30**

Llewellyn, Richard
See Llewellyn Lloyd, Richard Dafydd Vivian
See also DLB 15

Llewellyn Lloyd, Richard Dafydd Vivian 1906-1983 **CLC 7, 80**
See also Llewellyn, Richard
See also CA 53-56; 111; CANR 7, 71; SATA 11; SATA-Obit 37

Llosa, (Jorge) Mario (Pedro) Vargas
See Vargas Llosa, (Jorge) Mario (Pedro)

Lloyd, Manda
See Mander, (Mary) Jane

Lloyd Webber, Andrew 1948-
See Webber, Andrew Lloyd
See also AAYA 1; CA 116; 149; DAM DRAM; SATA 56

Llull, Ramon c. 1235-c. 1316 **CMLC 12**

Lobb, Ebenezer
See Upward, Allen

Locke, Alain (Le Roy) 1886-1954 **TCLC 43; BLCS**
See also BW 1, 3; CA 106; 124; CANR 79; DLB 51

Locke, John 1632-1704 **LC 7, 35**
See also DLB 101

Locke-Elliott, Sumner
See Elliott, Sumner Locke

Lockhart, John Gibson 1794-1854 **NCLC 6**
See also DLB 110, 116, 144

Lodge, David (John) 1935-**CLC 36; DAM POP**
See also BEST 90:1; CA 17-20R; CANR 19, 53; DLB 14, 194; INT CANR-19; MTCW 1, 2

Lodge, Thomas 1558-1625 **LC 41**
See also DLB 172

Loennbohm, Armas Eino Leopold 1878-1926
See Leino, Eino
See also CA 123

Loewinsohn, Ron(ald William) 1937-**CLC 52**
See also CA 25-28R; CANR 71

Logan, Jake
See Smith, Martin Cruz

Logan, John (Burton) 1923-1987 **CLC 5**
See also CA 77-80; 124; CANR 45; DLB 5

Lo Kuan-chung 1330(?)-1400(?) **LC 12**

Lombard, Nap
See Johnson, Pamela Hansford

London, Jack **TCLC 9, 15, 39; SSC 4; WLC**
See also London, John Griffith
See also AAYA 13; AITN 2; CDALB 1865-1917; DLB 8, 12, 78, 212; SATA 18

London, John Griffith 1876-1916

1, 2

Mannheim, Karl 1893-1947　　　**TCLC 65**
Manning, David
　　See Faust, Frederick (Schiller)
Manning, Frederic 1887(?)-1935　　**TCLC 25**
　　See also CA 124
Manning, Olivia 1915-1980　　**CLC 5, 19**
　　See also CA 5-8R; 101; CANR 29; MTCW 1
Mano, D. Keith 1942-　　　　**CLC 2, 10**
　　See also CA 25-28R; CAAS 6; CANR 26, 57;
　　DLB 6
Mansfield, KatherineTCLC 2, 8, 39; DAB; SSC
　　9, 23; WLC
　　See also Beauchamp, Kathleen Mansfield
　　See also DLB 162
Manso, Peter 1940-　　　　　　**CLC 39**
　　See also CA 29-32R; CANR 44
Mantecon, Juan Jimenez
　　See Jimenez (Mantecon), Juan Ramon
Manton, Peter
　　See Creasey, John
Man Without a Spleen, A
　　See Chekhov, Anton (Pavlovich)
Manzoni, Alessandro 1785-1873　　**NCLC 29**
Map, Walter 1140-1209　　　　**CMLC 32**
Mapu, Abraham (ben Jekutiel) 1808-1867
　　NCLC 18
Mara, Sally
　　See Queneau, Raymond
Marat, Jean Paul 1743-1793　　　**LC 10**
Marcel, Gabriel Honore 1889-1973　**CLC 15**
　　See also CA 102; 45-48; MTCW 1, 2
March, William 1893-1954　　　**TCLC 96**
Marchbanks, Samuel
　　See Davies, (William) Robertson
Marchi, Giacomo
　　See Bassani, Giorgio
Margulies, Donald　　　　　　**CLC 76**
Marie de France c. 12th cent. -　**CMLC 8; PC**
　　22
　　See also DLB 208
Marie de l'Incarnation 1599-1672　　**LC 10**
Marier, Captain Victor
　　See Griffith, D(avid Lewelyn) W(ark)
Mariner, Scott
　　See Pohl, Frederik
Marinetti, Filippo Tommaso 1876-1944TCLC
　　10
　　See also CA 107; DLB 114
Marivaux, Pierre Carlet de Chamblain de 1688-
　　1763　　　　　　　　　**LC 4; DC 7**
Markandaya, Kamala　　　　**CLC 8, 38**
　　See also Taylor, Kamala (Purnaiya)
Markfield, Wallace 1926-　　　　**CLC 8**
　　See also CA 69-72; CAAS 3; DLB 2, 28
Markham, Edwin 1852-1940　　　**TCLC 47**
　　See also CA 160; DLB 54, 186
Markham, Robert
　　See Amis, Kingsley (William)
Marks, J
　　See Highwater, Jamake (Mamake)
Marks-Highwater, J
　　See Highwater, Jamake (Mamake)
Markson, David M(errill) 1927-　　**CLC 67**
　　See also CA 49-52; CANR 1
Marley, Bob　　　　　　　　**CLC 17**
　　See also Marley, Robert Nesta
Marley, Robert Nesta 1945-1981
　　See Marley, Bob
　　See also CA 107; 103
Marlowe, Christopher 1564-1593 **LC 22, 47;**
　　DA; DAB; DAC; DAM DRAM, MST; DC
　　1; WLC

See also CDBLB Before 1660; DA3; DLB 62
Marlowe, Stephen 1928-
　　See Queen, Ellery
　　See also CA 13-16R; CANR 6, 55
Marmontel, Jean-Francois 1723-1799　**LC 2**
Marquand, John P(hillips) 1893-1960CLC 2, 10
　　See also CA 85-88; CANR 73; DLB 9, 102;
　　MTCW 2
Marques, Rene 1919-1979　　**CLC 96; DAM**
　　MULT; HLC 2
　　See also CA 97-100; 85-88; CANR 78; DLB
　　113; HW 1, 2
Marquez, Gabriel (Jose) Garcia
　　See Garcia Marquez, Gabriel (Jose)
Marquis, Don(ald Robert Perry) 1878-1937
　　TCLC 7
　　See also CA 104; 166; DLB 11, 25
Marric, J. J.
　　See Creasey, John
Marryat, Frederick 1792-1848　　　**NCLC 3**
　　See also DLB 21, 163
Marsden, James
　　See Creasey, John
Marsh, Edward 1872-1953　　　**TCLC 99**
Marsh, (Edith) Ngaio 1899-1982 **CLC 7, 53;**
　　DAM POP
　　See also CA 9-12R; CANR 6, 58; DLB 77;
　　MTCW 1, 2
Marshall, Garry 1934-　　　　　**CLC 17**
　　See also AAYA 3; CA 111; SATA 60
Marshall, Paule 1929-　**CLC 27, 72; BLC 3;**
　　DAM MULT; SSC 3
　　See also BW 2, 3; CA 77-80; CANR 25, 73;
　　DA3; DLB 157; MTCW 1, 2
Marshallik
　　See Zangwill, Israel
Marsten, Richard
　　See Hunter, Evan
Marston, John 1576-1634LC 33; DAM DRAM
　　See also DLB 58, 172
Martha, Henry
　　See Harris, Mark
Marti (y Perez), Jose (Julian) 1853-1895
　　NCLC 63; DAM MULT; HLC 2
　　See also HW 2
Martial c. 40-c. 104　　　　**CMLC 35; PC 10**
　　See also DLB 211
Martin, Ken
　　See Hubbard, L(afayette) Ron(ald)
Martin, Richard
　　See Creasey, John
Martin, Steve 1945-　　　　　　**CLC 30**
　　See also CA 97-100; CANR 30; MTCW 1
Martin, Valerie 1948-　　　　　**CLC 89**
　　See also BEST 90:2; CA 85-88; CANR 49
Martin, Violet Florence 1862-1915 **TCLC 51**
Martin, Webber
　　See Silverberg, Robert
Martindale, Patrick Victor
　　See White, Patrick (Victor Martindale)
Martin du Gard, Roger 1881-1958 **TCLC 24**
　　See also CA 118; DLB 65
Martineau, Harriet 1802-1876　　**NCLC 26**
　　See also DLB 21, 55, 159, 163, 166, 190; YABC
　　2
Martines, Julia
　　See O'Faolain, Julia
Martinez, Enrique Gonzalez
　　See Gonzalez Martinez, Enrique
Martinez, Jacinto Benavente y
　　See Benavente (y Martinez), Jacinto
Martinez Ruiz, Jose 1873-1967
　　See Azorin; Ruiz, Jose Martinez

See also CA 93-96; HW 1
Martinez Sierra, Gregorio 1881-1947TCLC 6
　　See also CA 115
Martinez Sierra, Maria (de la O'LeJarraga)
　　1874-1974　　　　　　　　**TCLC 6**
　　See also CA 115
Martinsen, Martin
　　See Follett, Ken(neth Martin)
Martinson, Harry (Edmund) 1904-1978 C L C
　　14
　　See also CA 77-80; CANR 34
Marut, Ret
　　See Traven, B.
Marut, Robert
　　See Traven, B.
Marvell, Andrew 1621-1678　　**LC 4, 43; DA;**
　　DAB; DAC; DAM MST, POET; PC 10;
　　WLC
　　See also CDBLB 1660-1789; DLB 131
Marx, Karl (Heinrich) 1818-1883　**NCLC 17**
　　See also DLB 129
Masaoka Shiki　　　　　　　**TCLC 18**
　　See also Masaoka Tsunenori
Masaoka Tsunenori 1867-1902
　　See Masaoka Shiki
　　See also CA 117
Masefield, John (Edward) 1878-1967CLC 11,
　　47; DAM POET
　　See also CA 19-20; 25-28R; CANR 33; CAP 2;
　　CDBLB 1890-1914; DLB 10, 19, 153, 160;
　　MTCW 1, 2; SATA 19
Maso, Carole 19(?)-　　　　　　**CLC 44**
　　See also CA 170
Mason, Bobbie Ann 1940-CLC 28, 43, 82; SSC
　　4
　　See also AAYA 5; CA 53-56; CANR 11, 31,
　　58, 83; CDALBS; DA3; DLB 173; DLBY
　　87; INT CANR-31; MTCW 1, 2
Mason, Ernst
　　See Pohl, Frederik
Mason, Lee W.
　　See Malzberg, Barry N(athaniel)
Mason, Nick 1945-　　　　　　**CLC 35**
Mason, Tally
　　See Derleth, August (William)
Mass, William
　　See Gibson, William
Master Lao
　　See Lao Tzu
Masters, Edgar Lee 1868-1950　**TCLC 2, 25;**
　　DA; DAC; DAM MST, POET; PC 1;
　　WLCS
　　See also CA 104; 133; CDALB 1865-1917;
　　DLB 54; MTCW 1, 2
Masters, Hilary 1928-　　　　　**CLC 48**
　　See also CA 25-28R; CANR 13, 47
Mastrosimone, William 19(?)-　　**CLC 36**
Mathe, Albert
　　See Camus, Albert
Mather, Cotton 1663-1728　　　　**LC 38**
　　See also CDALB 1640-1865; DLB 24, 30, 140
Mather, Increase 1639-1723　　　**LC 38**
　　See also DLB 24
Matheson, Richard Burton 1926-　**CLC 37**
　　See also AAYA 31; CA 97-100; DLB 8, 44; INT
　　97-100
Mathews, Harry 1930-　　　　**CLC 6, 52**
　　See also CA 21-24R; CAAS 6; CANR 18, 40
Mathews, John Joseph 1894-1979　**CLC 84;**
　　DAM MULT
　　See also CA 19-20; 142; CANR 45; CAP 2;
　　DLB 175; NNAL
Mathias, Roland (Glyn) 1915-　　**CLC 45**

See also CA 97-100; CANR 19, 41; DLB 27

Matsuo Basho 1644-1694 **PC 3**
See also DAM POET

Mattheson, Rodney
See Creasey, John

Matthews, Brander 1852-1929 **TCLC 95**
See also DLB 71, 78; DLBD 13

Matthews, Greg 1949- **CLC 45**
See also CA 135

Matthews, William (Procter, III) 1942-1997 **CLC 40**
See also CA 29-32R; 162; CAAS 18; CANR 12, 57; DLB 5

Matthias, John (Edward) 1941- **CLC 9**
See also CA 33-36R; CANR 56

Matthiessen, Peter 1927-**CLC 5, 7, 11, 32, 64; DAM NOV**
See also AAYA 6; BEST 90:4; CA 9-12R; CANR 21, 50, 73; DA3; DLB 6, 173; MTCW 1, 2; SATA 27

Maturin, Charles Robert 1780(?)-1824**NCLC 6**
See also DLB 178

Matute (Ausejo), Ana Maria 1925- **CLC 11**
See also CA 89-92; MTCW 1

Maugham, W. S.
See Maugham, W(illiam) Somerset

Maugham, W(illiam) Somerset 1874-1965 **CLC 1, 11, 15, 67, 93; DA; DAB; DAC; DAM DRAM, MST, NOV; SSC 8; WLC**
See also CA 5-8R; 25-28R; CANR 40; CDBLB 1914-1945; DA3; DLB 10, 36, 77, 100, 162, 195; MTCW 1, 2; SATA 54

Maugham, William Somerset
See Maugham, W(illiam) Somerset

Maupassant, (Henri Rene Albert) Guy de 1850-1893**NCLC 1, 42; DA; DAB; DAC; DAM MST; SSC 1; WLC**
See also DA3; DLB 123

Maupin, Armistead 1944-**CLC 95; DAM POP**
See also CA 125; 130; CANR 58; DA3; INT 130; MTCW 2

Maurhut, Richard
See Traven, B.

Mauriac, Claude 1914-1996 **CLC 9**
See also CA 89-92; 152; DLB 83

Mauriac, Francois (Charles) 1885-1970 **CLC 4, 9, 56; SSC 24**
See also CA 25-28; CAP 2; DLB 65; MTCW 1, 2

Mavor, Osborne Henry 1888-1951
See Bridie, James
See also CA 104

Maxwell, William (Keepers, Jr.) 1908-**CLC 19**
See also CA 93-96; CANR 54; DLBY 80; INT 93-96

May, Elaine 1932- **CLC 16**
See also CA 124; 142; DLB 44

Mayakovski, Vladimir (Vladimirovich) 1893-1930 **TCLC 4, 18**
See also CA 104; 158; MTCW 2

Mayhew, Henry 1812-1887 **NCLC 31**
See also DLB 18, 55, 190

Mayle, Peter 1939(?)- **CLC 89**
See also CA 139; CANR 64

Maynard, Joyce 1953- **CLC 23**
See also CA 111; 129; CANR 64

Mayne, William (James Carter) 1928-**CLC 12**
See also AAYA 20; CA 9-12R; CANR 37, 80; CLR 25; JRDA; MAICYA; SAAS 11; SATA 6, 68

Mayo, Jim
See L'Amour, Louis (Dearborn)

Maysles, Albert 1926- **CLC 16**
See also CA 29-32R

Maysles, David 1932- **CLC 16**

Mazer, Norma Fox 1931- **CLC 26**
See also AAYA 5; CA 69-72; CANR 12, 32, 66; CLR 23; JRDA; MAICYA; SAAS 1; SATA 24, 67, 105

Mazzini, Guiseppe 1805-1872 **NCLC 34**

McAlmon, Robert (Menzies) 1895-1956**TCLC 97**
See also CA 107; 168; DLB 4, 45; DLBD 15

McAuley, James Phillip 1917-1976 **CLC 45**
See also CA 97-100

McBain, Ed
See Hunter, Evan

McBrien, William Augustine 1930- **CLC 44**
See also CA 107

McCaffrey, Anne (Inez) 1926-**CLC 17; DAM NOV, POP**
See also AAYA 6; AITN 2; BEST 89:2; CA 25-28R; CANR 15, 35, 55; CLR 49; DA3; DLB 8; JRDA; MAICYA; MTCW 1, 2; SAAS 11; SATA 8, 70

McCall, Nathan 1955(?)- **CLC 86**
See also BW 3; CA 146

McCann, Arthur
See Campbell, John W(ood, Jr.)

McCann, Edson
See Pohl, Frederik

McCarthy, Charles, Jr. 1933-
See McCarthy, Cormac
See also CANR 42, 69; DAM POP; DA3; MTCW 2

McCarthy, Cormac 1933- **CLC 4, 57, 59, 101**
See also McCarthy, Charles, Jr.
See also DLB 6, 143; MTCW 2

McCarthy, Mary (Therese) 1912-1989**CLC 1, 3, 5, 14, 24, 39, 59; SSC 24**
See also CA 5-8R; 129; CANR 16, 50, 64; DA3; DLB 2; DLBY 81; INT CANR-16; MTCW 1, 2

McCartney, (James) Paul 1942- **CLC 12, 35**
See also CA 146

McCauley, Stephen (D.) 1955- **CLC 50**
See also CA 141

McClure, Michael (Thomas) 1932-**CLC 6, 10**
See also CA 21-24R; CANR 17, 46, 77; DLB 16

McCorkle, Jill (Collins) 1958- **CLC 51**
See also CA 121; DLBY 87

McCourt, Frank 1930- **CLC 109**
See also CA 157

McCourt, James 1941- **CLC 5**
See also CA 57-60

McCourt, Malachy 1932- **CLC 119**

McCoy, Horace (Stanley) 1897-1955**TCLC 28**
See also CA 108; 155; DLB 9

McCrae, John 1872-1918 **TCLC 12**
See also CA 109; DLB 92

McCreigh, James
See Pohl, Frederik

McCullers, (Lula) Carson (Smith) 1917-1967 **CLC 1, 4, 10, 12, 48, 100; DA; DAB; DAC; DAM MST, NOV; SSC 9, 24; WLC**
See also AAYA 21; CA 5-8R; 25-28R; CABS 1, 3; CANR 18; CDALB 1941-1968; DA3; DLB 2, 7, 173; MTCW 1, 2; SATA 27

McCulloch, John Tyler
See Burroughs, Edgar Rice

McCullough, Colleen 1938(?)- **CLC 27, 107; DAM NOV, POP**
See also CA 81-84; CANR 17, 46, 67; DA3; MTCW 1, 2

McDermott, Alice 1953- **CLC 90**
See also CA 109; CANR 40

McElroy, Joseph 1930- **CLC 5, 47**
See also CA 17-20R

McEwan, Ian (Russell) 1948- **CLC 13, 66; DAM NOV**
See also BEST 90:4; CA 61-64; CANR 14, 41, 69; DLB 14, 194; MTCW 1, 2

McFadden, David 1940- **CLC 48**
See also CA 104; DLB 60; INT 104

McFarland, Dennis 1950- **CLC 65**
See also CA 165

McGahern, John 1934-**CLC 5, 9, 48; SSC 17**
See also CA 17-20R; CANR 29, 68; DLB 14; MTCW 1

McGinley, Patrick (Anthony) 1937- **CLC 41**
See also CA 120; 127; CANR 56; INT 127

McGinley, Phyllis 1905-1978 **CLC 14**
See also CA 9-12R; 77-80; CANR 19; DLB 11, 48; SATA 2, 44; SATA-Obit 24

McGinniss, Joe 1942- **CLC 32**
See also AITN 2; BEST 89:2; CA 25-28R; CANR 26, 70; DLB 185; INT CANR-26

McGivern, Maureen Daly
See Daly, Maureen

McGrath, Patrick 1950- **CLC 55**
See also CA 136; CANR 65

McGrath, Thomas (Matthew) 1916-1990**CLC 28, 59; DAM POET**
See also CA 9-12R; 132; CANR 6, 33; MTCW 1; SATA 41; SATA-Obit 66

McGuane, Thomas (Francis III) 1939-**CLC 3, 7, 18, 45**
See also AITN 2; CA 49-52; CANR 5, 24, 49; DLB 2, 212; DLBY 80; INT CANR-24; MTCW 1

McGuckian, Medbh 1950- **CLC 48; DAM POET; PC 27**
See also CA 143; DLB 40

McHale, Tom 1942(?)-1982 **CLC 3, 5**
See also AITN 1; CA 77-80; 106

McIlvanney, William 1936- **CLC 42**
See also CA 25-28R; CANR 61; DLB 14, 207

McIlwraith, Maureen Mollie Hunter
See Hunter, Mollie
See also SATA 2

McInerney, Jay 1955-**CLC 34, 112; DAM POP**
See also AAYA 18; CA 116; 123; CANR 45, 68; DA3; INT 123; MTCW 2

McIntyre, Vonda N(eel) 1948- **CLC 18**
See also CA 81-84; CANR 17, 34, 69; MTCW 1

McKay, Claude **TCLC 7, 41; BLC 3; DAB; PC 2**
See also McKay, Festus Claudius
See also DLB 4, 45, 51, 117

McKay, Festus Claudius 1889-1948
See McKay, Claude
See also BW 1, 3; CA 104; 124; CANR 73; DA; DAC; DAM MST, MULT, NOV, POET; MTCW 1, 2; WLC

McKuen, Rod 1933- **CLC 1, 3**
See also AITN 1; CA 41-44R; CANR 40

McLoughlin, R. B.
See Mencken, H(enry) L(ouis)

McLuhan, (Herbert) Marshall 1911-1980 **CLC 37, 83**
See also CA 9-12R; 102; CANR 12, 34, 61; DLB 88; INT CANR-12; MTCW 1, 2

McMillan, Terry (L.) 1951- **CLC 50, 61, 112; BLCS; DAM MULT, NOV, POP**
See also AAYA 21; BW 2, 3; CA 140; CANR 60; DA3; MTCW 2

McMurtry, Larry (Jeff) 1936-**CLC 2, 3, 7, 11, 27, 44; DAM NOV, POP**
See also AAYA 15; AITN 2; BEST 89:2; CA 5-8R; CANR 19, 43, 64; CDALB 1968-1988; DA3; DLB 2, 143; DLBY 80, 87; MTCW 1, 2
McNally, T. M. 1961- **CLC 82**
McNally, Terrence 1939- **CLC 4, 7, 41, 91; DAM DRAM**
See also CA 45-48; CANR 2, 56; DA3; DLB 7; MTCW 2
McNamer, Deirdre 1950- **CLC 70**
McNeal, Tom **CLC 119**
McNeile, Herman Cyril 1888-1937
See Sapper
See also DLB 77
McNickle, (William) D'Arcy 1904-1977 **CLC 89; DAM MULT**
See also CA 9-12R; 85-88; CANR 5, 45; DLB 175, 212; NNAL; SATA-Obit 22
McPhee, John (Angus) 1931- **CLC 36**
See also BEST 90:1; CA 65-68; CANR 20, 46, 64, 69; DLB 185; MTCW 1, 2
McPherson, James Alan 1943- **CLC 19, 77; BLCS**
See also BW 1, 3; CA 25-28R; CAAS 17; CANR 24, 74; DLB 38; MTCW 1, 2
McPherson, William (Alexander) 1933- **CLC 34**
See also CA 69-72; CANR 28; INT CANR-28
Mead, George Herbert 1873-1958 **TCLC 89**
Mead, Margaret 1901-1978 **CLC 37**
See also AITN 1; CA 1-4R; 81-84; CANR 4; DA3; MTCW 1, 2; SATA-Obit 20
Meaker, Marijane (Agnes) 1927-
See Kerr, M. E.
See also CA 107; CANR 37, 63; INT 107; JRDA; MAICYA; MTCW 1; SATA 20, 61, 99; SATA-Essay 111
Medoff, Mark (Howard) 1940- **CLC 6, 23; DAM DRAM**
See also AITN 1; CA 53-56; CANR 5; DLB 7; INT CANR-5
Medvedev, P. N.
See Bakhtin, Mikhail Mikhailovich
Meged, Aharon
See Megged, Aharon
Meged, Aron
See Megged, Aharon
Megged, Aharon 1920- **CLC 9**
See also CA 49-52; CAAS 13; CANR 1
Mehta, Ved (Parkash) 1934- **CLC 37**
See also CA 1-4R; CANR 2, 23, 69; MTCW 1
Melanter
See Blackmore, R(ichard) D(oddridge)
Melies, Georges 1861-1938 **TCLC 81**
Melikow, Loris
See Hofmannsthal, Hugo von
Melmoth, Sebastian
See Wilde, Oscar
Meltzer, Milton 1915- **CLC 26**
See also AAYA 8; CA 13-16R; CANR 38; CLR 13; DLB 61; JRDA; MAICYA; SAAS 1; SATA 1, 50, 80
Melville, Herman 1819-1891 **NCLC 3, 12, 29, 45, 49; DA; DAB; DAC; DAM MST, NOV; SSC 1, 17; WLC**
See also AAYA 25; CDALB 1640-1865; DA3; DLB 3, 74; SATA 59
Menander c. 342B.C.-c. 292B.C. **CMLC 9; DAM DRAM; DC 3**
See also DLB 176
Menchu, Rigoberta 1959-
See also HLCS 2

Menchu, Rigoberta 1959-
See also CA 175; HLCS 2
Mencken, H(enry) L(ouis) 1880-1956 **TCLC 13**
See also CA 105; 125; CDALB 1917-1929; DLB 11, 29, 63, 137; MTCW 1, 2
Mendelsohn, Jane 1965(?)- **CLC 99**
See also CA 154
Mercer, David 1928-1980**CLC 5; DAM DRAM**
See also CA 9-12R; 102; CANR 23; DLB 13; MTCW 1
Merchant, Paul
See Ellison, Harlan (Jay)
Meredith, George 1828-1909 **TCLC 17, 43; DAM POET**
See also CA 117; 153; CANR 80; CDBLB 1832-1890; DLB 18, 35, 57, 159
Meredith, William (Morris) 1919-**CLC 4, 13, 22, 55; DAM POET; PC 28**
See also CA 9-12R; CAAS 14; CANR 6, 40; DLB 5
Merezhkovsky, Dmitry Sergeyevich 1865-1941 **TCLC 29**
See also CA 169
Merimee, Prosper 1803-1870**NCLC 6, 65; SSC 7**
See also DLB 119, 192
Merkin, Daphne 1954- **CLC 44**
See also CA 123
Merlin, Arthur
See Blish, James (Benjamin)
Merrill, James (Ingram) 1926-1995**CLC 2, 3, 6, 8, 13, 18, 34, 91; DAM POET; PC 28**
See also CA 13-16R; 147; CANR 10, 49, 63; DA3; DLB 5, 165; DLBY 85; INT CANR-10; MTCW 1, 2
Merriman, Alex
See Silverberg, Robert
Merriman, Brian 1747-1805 **NCLC 70**
Merritt, E. B.
See Waddington, Miriam
Merton, Thomas 1915-1968 **CLC 1, 3, 11, 34, 83; PC 10**
See also CA 5-8R; 25-28R; CANR 22, 53; DA3; DLB 48; DLBY 81; MTCW 1, 2
Merwin, W(illiam) S(tanley) 1927- **CLC 1, 2, 3, 5, 8, 13, 18, 45, 88; DAM POET**
See also CA 13-16R; CANR 15, 51; DA3; DLB 5, 169; INT CANR-15; MTCW 1, 2
Metcalf, John 1938- **CLC 37**
See also CA 113; DLB 60
Metcalf, Suzanne
See Baum, L(yman) Frank
Mew, Charlotte (Mary) 1870-1928 **TCLC 8**
See also CA 105; DLB 19, 135
Mewshaw, Michael 1943- **CLC 9**
See also CA 53-56; CANR 7, 47; DLBY 80
Meyer, Conrad Ferdinand 1825-1905 **NCLC 81**
See also DLB 129
Meyer, June
See Jordan, June
Meyer, Lynn
See Slavitt, David R(ytman)
Meyer-Meyrink, Gustav 1868-1932
See Meyrink, Gustav
See also CA 117
Meyers, Jeffrey 1939- **CLC 39**
See also CA 73-76, 181; CAAE 181; CANR 54; DLB 111
Meynell, Alice (Christina Gertrude Thompson) 1847-1922 **TCLC 6**
See also CA 104; 177; DLB 19, 98

Meyrink, Gustav **TCLC 21**
See also Meyer-Meyrink, Gustav
See also DLB 81
Michaels, Leonard 1933- **CLC 6, 25; SSC 16**
See also CA 61-64; CANR 21, 62; DLB 130; MTCW 1
Michaux, Henri 1899-1984 **CLC 8, 19**
See also CA 85-88; 114
Micheaux, Oscar (Devereaux) 1884-1951 **TCLC 76**
See also BW 3; CA 174; DLB 50
Michelangelo 1475-1564 **LC 12**
Michelet, Jules 1798-1874 **NCLC 31**
Michels, Robert 1876-1936 **TCLC 88**
Michener, James A(lbert) 1907(?)-1997 **CLC 1, 5, 11, 29, 60, 109; DAM NOV, POP**
See also AAYA 27; AITN 1; BEST 90:1; CA 5-8R; 161; CANR 21, 45, 68; DA3; DLB 6; MTCW 1, 2
Mickiewicz, Adam 1798-1855 **NCLC 3**
Middleton, Christopher 1926- **CLC 13**
See also CA 13-16R; CANR 29, 54; DLB 40
Middleton, Richard (Barham) 1882-1911 **TCLC 56**
See also DLB 156
Middleton, Stanley 1919- **CLC 7, 38**
See also CA 25-28R; CAAS 23; CANR 21, 46, 81; DLB 14
Middleton, Thomas 1580-1627 **LC 33; DAM DRAM, MST; DC 5**
See also DLB 58
Migueis, Jose Rodrigues 1901- **CLC 10**
Mikszath, Kalman 1847-1910 **TCLC 31**
See also CA 170
Miles, Jack **CLC 100**
Miles, Josephine (Louise) 1911-1985**CLC 1, 2, 14, 34, 39; DAM POET**
See also CA 1-4R; 116; CANR 2, 55; DLB 48
Militant
See Sandburg, Carl (August)
Mill, John Stuart 1806-1873 **NCLC 11, 58**
See also CDBLB 1832-1890; DLB 55, 190
Millar, Kenneth 1915-1983 **CLC 14; DAM POP**
See also Macdonald, Ross
See also CA 9-12R; 110; CANR 16, 63; DA3; DLB 2; DLBD 6; DLBY 83; MTCW 1, 2
Millay, E. Vincent
See Millay, Edna St. Vincent
Millay, Edna St. Vincent 1892-1950 **TCLC 4, 49; DA; DAB; DAC; DAM MST, POET; PC 6; WLCS**
See also CA 104; 130; CDALB 1917-1929; DA3; DLB 45; MTCW 1, 2
Miller, Arthur 1915-**CLC 1, 2, 6, 10, 15, 26, 47, 78; DA; DAB; DAC; DAM DRAM, MST; DC 1; WLC**
See also AAYA 15; AITN 1; CA 1-4R; CABS 3; CANR 2, 30, 54, 76; CDALB 1941-1968; DA3; DLB 7; MTCW 1, 2
Miller, Henry (Valentine) 1891-1980**CLC 1, 2, 4, 9, 14, 43, 84; DA; DAB; DAC; DAM MST, NOV; WLC**
See also CA 9-12R; 97-100; CANR 33, 64; CDALB 1929-1941; DA3; DLB 4, 9; DLBY 80; MTCW 1, 2
Miller, Jason 1939(?)- **CLC 2**
See also AITN 1; CA 73-76; DLB 7
Miller, Sue 1943- **CLC 44; DAM POP**
See also BEST 90:3; CA 139; CANR 59; DA3; DLB 143
Miller, Walter M(ichael, Jr.) 1923-**CLC 4, 30**
See also CA 85-88; DLB 8

Millett, Kate 1934- **CLC 67**
See also AITN 1; CA 73-76; CANR 32, 53, 76; DA3; MTCW 1, 2

Millhauser, Steven (Lewis) 1943-**CLC 21, 54, 109**
See also CA 110; 111; CANR 63; DA3; DLB 2; INT 111; MTCW 2

Millin, Sarah Gertrude 1889-1968 **CLC 49**
See also CA 102; 93-96

Milne, A(lan) A(lexander) 1882-1956**TCLC 6, 88; DAB; DAC; DAM MST**
See also CA 104; 133; CLR 1, 26; DA3; DLB 10, 77, 100, 160; MAICYA; MTCW 1, 2; SATA 100; YABC 1

Milner, Ron(ald) 1938-**CLC 56; BLC 3; DAM MULT**
See also AITN 1; BW 1; CA 73-76; CANR 24, 81; DLB 38; MTCW 1

Milnes, Richard Monckton 1809-1885 **NCLC 61**
See also DLB 32, 184

Milosz, Czeslaw 1911- **CLC 5, 11, 22, 31, 56, 82; DAM MST, POET; PC 8; WLCS**
See also CA 81-84; CANR 23, 51; DA3; MTCW 1, 2

Milton, John 1608-1674 **LC 9, 43; DA; DAB; DAC; DAM MST, POET; PC 19; WLC**
See also CDBLB 1660-1789; DA3; DLB 131, 151

Min, Anchee 1957- **CLC 86**
See also CA 146

Minehaha, Cornelius
See Wedekind, (Benjamin) Frank(lin)

Miner, Valerie 1947- **CLC 40**
See also CA 97-100; CANR 59

Minimo, Duca
See D'Annunzio, Gabriele

Minot, Susan 1956- **CLC 44**
See also CA 134

Minus, Ed 1938- **CLC 39**

Miranda, Javier
See Bioy Casares, Adolfo

Mirbeau, Octave 1848-1917 **TCLC 55**
See also DLB 123, 192

Miro (Ferrer), Gabriel (Francisco Victor) 1879-1930 **TCLC 5**
See also CA 104

Mishima, Yukio 1925-1970**CLC 2, 4, 6, 9, 27; DC 1; SSC 4**
See also Hiraoka, Kimitake
See also DLB 182; MTCW 2

Mistral, Frederic 1830-1914 **TCLC 51**
See also CA 122

Mistral, Gabriela **TCLC 2; HLC 2**
See also Godoy Alcayaga, Lucila
See also MTCW 2

Mistry, Rohinton 1952- **CLC 71; DAC**
See also CA 141; CANR 86

Mitchell, Clyde
See Ellison, Harlan (Jay); Silverberg, Robert

Mitchell, James Leslie 1901-1935
See Gibbon, Lewis Grassic
See also CA 104; DLB 15

Mitchell, Joni 1943- **CLC 12**
See also CA 112

Mitchell, Joseph (Quincy) 1908-1996**CLC 98**
See also CA 77-80; 152; CANR 69; DLB 185; DLBY 96

Mitchell, Margaret (Munnerlyn) 1900-1949 **TCLC 11; DAM NOV, POP**
See also AAYA 23; CA 109; 125; CANR 55; CDALBS; DA3; DLB 9; MTCW 1, 2

Mitchell, Peggy
See Mitchell, Margaret (Munnerlyn)

Mitchell, S(ilas) Weir 1829-1914 **TCLC 36**
See also CA 165; DLB 202

Mitchell, W(illiam) O(rmond) 1914-1998**CLC 25; DAC; DAM MST**
See also CA 77-80; 165; CANR 15, 43; DLB 88

Mitchell, William 1879-1936 **TCLC 81**

Mitford, Mary Russell 1787-1855 **NCLC 4**
See also DLB 110, 116

Mitford, Nancy 1904-1973 **CLC 44**
See also CA 9-12R; DLB 191

Miyamoto, (Chujo) Yuriko 1899-1951 **TCLC 37**
See also CA 170, 174; DLB 180

Miyazawa, Kenji 1896-1933 **TCLC 76**
See also CA 157

Mizoguchi, Kenji 1898-1956 **TCLC 72**
See also CA 167

Mo, Timothy (Peter) 1950(?)- **CLC 46**
See also CA 117; DLB 194; MTCW 1

Modarressi, Taghi (M.) 1931- **CLC 44**
See also CA 121; 134; INT 134

Modiano, Patrick (Jean) 1945- **CLC 18**
See also CA 85-88; CANR 17, 40; DLB 83

Moerck, Paal
See Roelvaag, O(le) E(dvart)

Mofolo, Thomas (Mokopu) 1875(?)-1948 **TCLC 22; BLC 3; DAM MULT**
See also CA 121; 153; CANR 83; MTCW 2

Mohr, Nicholasa 1938-**CLC 12; DAM MULT; HLC 2**
See also AAYA 8; CA 49-52; CANR 1, 32, 64; CLR 22; DLB 145; HW 1, 2; JRDA; SAAS 8; SATA 8, 97

Mojtabai, A(nn) G(race) 1938- **CLC 5, 9, 15, 29**
See also CA 85-88

Moliere 1622-1673**LC 10, 28; DA; DAB; DAC; DAM DRAM, MST; WLC**
See also DA3

Molin, Charles
See Mayne, William (James Carter)

Molnar, Ferenc 1878-1952 **TCLC 20; DAM DRAM**
See also CA 109; 153; CANR 83

Momaday, N(avarre) Scott 1934- **CLC 2, 19, 85, 95; DA; DAB; DAC; DAM MST, MULT, NOV, POP; PC 25; WLCS**
See also AAYA 11; CA 25-28R; CANR 14, 34, 68; CDALBS; DA3; DLB 143, 175; INT CANR-14; MTCW 1, 2; NNAL; SATA 48; SATA-Brief 30

Monette, Paul 1945-1995 **CLC 82**
See also CA 139; 147

Monroe, Harriet 1860-1936 **TCLC 12**
See also CA 109; DLB 54, 91

Monroe, Lyle
See Heinlein, Robert A(nson)

Montagu, Elizabeth 1720-1800 **NCLC 7**

Montagu, Mary (Pierrepont) Wortley 1689-1762 **LC 9; PC 16**
See also DLB 95, 101

Montagu, W. H.
See Coleridge, Samuel Taylor

Montague, John (Patrick) 1929- **CLC 13, 46**
See also CA 9-12R; CANR 9, 69; DLB 40; MTCW 1

Montaigne, Michel (Eyquem) de 1533-1592 **LC 8; DA; DAB; DAC; DAM MST; WLC**

Montale, Eugenio 1896-1981**CLC 7, 9, 18; PC 13**
See also CA 17-20R; 104; CANR 30; DLB 114; MTCW 1

Montesquieu, Charles-Louis de Secondat 1689-1755 **LC 7**

Montgomery, (Robert) Bruce 1921(?)-1978
See Crispin, Edmund
See also CA 179; 104

Montgomery, L(ucy) M(aud) 1874-1942 **TCLC 51; DAC; DAM MST**
See also AAYA 12; CA 108; 137; CLR 8; DA3; DLB 92; DLBD 14; JRDA; MAICYA; MTCW 2; SATA 100; YABC 1

Montgomery, Marion H., Jr. 1925- **CLC 7**
See also AITN 1; CA 1-4R; CANR 3, 48; DLB 6

Montgomery, Max
See Davenport, Guy (Mattison, Jr.)

Montherlant, Henry (Milon) de 1896-1972 **CLC 8, 19; DAM DRAM**
See also CA 85-88; 37-40R; DLB 72; MTCW 1

Monty Python
See Chapman, Graham; Cleese, John (Marwood); Gilliam, Terry (Vance); Idle, Eric; Jones, Terence Graham Parry; Palin, Michael (Edward)
See also AAYA 7

Moodie, Susanna (Strickland) 1803-1885 **NCLC 14**
See also DLB 99

Mooney, Edward 1951-
See Mooney, Ted
See also CA 130

Mooney, Ted **CLC 25**
See also Mooney, Edward

Moorcock, Michael (John) 1939-**CLC 5, 27, 58**
See also Bradbury, Edward P.
See also AAYA 26; CA 45-48; CAAS 5; CANR 2, 17, 38, 64; DLB 14; MTCW 1, 2; SATA 93

Moore, Brian 1921-1999**CLC 1, 3, 5, 7, 8, 19, 32, 90; DAB; DAC; DAM MST**
See also CA 1-4R; 174; CANR 1, 25, 42, 63; MTCW 1, 2

Moore, Edward
See Muir, Edwin

Moore, G. E. 1873-1958 **TCLC 89**

Moore, George Augustus 1852-1933**TCLC 7; SSC 19**
See also CA 104; 177; DLB 10, 18, 57, 135

Moore, Lorrie **CLC 39, 45, 68**
See also Moore, Marie Lorena

Moore, Marianne (Craig) 1887-1972**CLC 1, 2, 4, 8, 10, 13, 19, 47; DA; DAB; DAC; DAM MST, POET; PC 4; WLCS**
See also CA 1-4R; 33-36R; CANR 3, 61; CDALB 1929-1941; DA3; DLB 45; DLBD 7; MTCW 1, 2; SATA 20

Moore, Marie Lorena 1957-
See Moore, Lorrie
See also CA 116; CANR 39, 83

Moore, Thomas 1779-1852 **NCLC 6**
See also DLB 96, 144

Mora, Pat(ricia) 1942-
See also CA 129; CANR 57, 81; CLR 58; DAM MULT; DLB 209; HLC 2; HW 1, 2; SATA 92

Moraga, Cherrie 1952-**CLC 126; DAM MULT**
See also CA 131; CANR 66; DLB 82; HW 1, 2

Morand, Paul 1888-1976 **CLC 41; SSC 22**
See also CA 69-72; DLB 65

Morante, Elsa 1918-1985 **CLC 8, 47**
See also CA 85-88; 117; CANR 35; DLB 177; MTCW 1, 2

Norris, Frank 1870-1902   SSC 28
  See also Norris, (Benjamin) Frank(lin, Jr.)
  See also CDALB 1865-1917; DLB 12, 71, 186
Norris, (Benjamin) Frank(lin, Jr.) 1870-1902
    TCLC 24
  See also Norris, Frank
  See also CA 110; 160
Norris, Leslie 1921-   CLC 14
  See also CA 11-12; CANR 14; CAP 1; DLB 27
North, Andrew
  See Norton, Andre
North, Anthony
  See Koontz, Dean R(ay)
North, Captain George
  See Stevenson, Robert Louis (Balfour)
North, Milou
  See Erdrich, Louise
Northrup, B. A.
  See Hubbard, L(afayette) Ron(ald)
North Staffs
  See Hulme, T(homas) E(rnest)
Norton, Alice Mary
  See Norton, Andre
  See also MAICYA; SATA 1, 43
Norton, Andre 1912-   CLC 12
  See also Norton, Alice Mary
  See also AAYA 14; CA 1-4R; CANR 68; CLR
    50; DLB 8, 52; JRDA; MTCW 1; SATA 91
Norton, Caroline 1808-1877   NCLC 47
  See also DLB 21, 159, 199
Norway, Nevil Shute 1899-1960
  See Shute, Nevil
  See also CA 102; 93-96; CANR 85; MTCW 2
Norwid, Cyprian Kamil 1821-1883 NCLC 17
Nosille, Nabrah
  See Ellison, Harlan (Jay)
Nossack, Hans Erich 1901-1978   CLC 6
  See also CA 93-96; 85-88; DLB 69
Nostradamus 1503-1566   LC 27
Nosu, Chuji
  See Ozu, Yasujiro
Notenburg, Eleanora (Genrikhovna) von
  See Guro, Elena
Nova, Craig 1945-   CLC 7, 31
  See also CA 45-48; CANR 2, 53
Novak, Joseph
  See Kosinski, Jerzy (Nikodem)
Novalis 1772-1801   NCLC 13
  See also DLB 90
Novis, Emile
  See Weil, Simone (Adolphine)
Nowlan, Alden (Albert) 1933-1983   CLC 15;
    DAC; DAM MST
  See also CA 9-12R; CANR 5; DLB 53
Noyes, Alfred 1880-1958   TCLC 7; PC 27
  See also CA 104; DLB 20
Nunn, Kem   CLC 34
  See also CA 159
Nye, Robert 1939-   CLC 13, 42; DAM NOV
  See also CA 33-36R; CANR 29, 67; DLB 14;
    MTCW 1; SATA 6
Nyro, Laura 1947-   CLC 17
Oates, Joyce Carol 1938-CLC 1, 2, 3, 6, 9, 11,
    15, 19, 33, 52, 108; DA; DAB; DAC; DAM
    MST, NOV, POP; SSC 6; WLC
  See also AAYA 15; AITN 1; BEST 89:2; CA 5-
    8R; CANR 25, 45, 74; CDALB 1968-1988;
    DA3; DLB 2, 5, 130; DLBY 81; INT CANR-
    25; MTCW 1, 2
O'Brien, Darcy 1939-1998   CLC 11
  See also CA 21-24R; 167; CANR 8, 59
O'Brien, E. G.
  See Clarke, Arthur C(harles)

O'Brien, Edna 1936- CLC 3, 5, 8, 13, 36, 65,
    116; DAM NOV; SSC 10
  See also CA 1-4R; CANR 6, 41, 65; CDBLB
    1960 to Present; DA3; DLB 14; MTCW 1, 2
O'Brien, Fitz-James 1828-1862   NCLC 21
  See also DLB 74
O'Brien, Flann   CLC 1, 4, 5, 7, 10, 47
  See also O Nuallain, Brian
O'Brien, Richard 1942-   CLC 17
  See also CA 124
O'Brien, (William) Tim(othy) 1946- CLC 7,
    19, 40, 103; DAM POP
  See also AAYA 16; CA 85-88; CANR 40, 58;
    CDALBS; DA3; DLB 152; DLBD 9; DLBY
    80; MTCW 2
Obstfelder, Sigbjoern 1866-1900   TCLC 23
  See also CA 123
O'Casey, Sean 1880-1964CLC 1, 5, 9, 11, 15,
    88; DAB; DAC; DAM DRAM, MST;
    WLCS
  See also CA 89-92; CANR 62; CDBLB 1914-
    1945; DA3; DLB 10; MTCW 1, 2
O'Cathasaigh, Sean
  See O'Casey, Sean
Ochs, Phil 1940-1976   CLC 17
  See also CA 65-68
O'Connor, Edwin (Greene) 1918-1968CLC 14
  See also CA 93-96; 25-28R
O'Connor, (Mary) Flannery 1925-1964 C L C
    1, 2, 3, 6, 10, 13, 15, 21, 66, 104; DA; DAB;
    DAC; DAM MST, NOV; SSC 1, 23; WLC
  See also AAYA 7; CA 1-4R; CANR 3, 41;
    CDALB 1941-1968; DA3; DLB 2, 152;
    DLBD 12; DLBY 80; MTCW 1, 2
O'Connor, Frank   CLC 23; SSC 5
  See also O'Donovan, Michael John
  See also DLB 162
O'Dell, Scott 1898-1989   CLC 30
  See also AAYA 3; CA 61-64; 129; CANR 12,
    30; CLR 1, 16; DLB 52; JRDA; MAICYA;
    SATA 12, 60
Odets, Clifford 1906-1963CLC 2, 28, 98; DAM
    DRAM; DC 6
  See also CA 85-88; CANR 62; DLB 7, 26;
    MTCW 1, 2
O'Doherty, Brian 1934-   CLC 76
  See also CA 105
O'Donnell, K. M.
  See Malzberg, Barry N(athaniel)
O'Donnell, Lawrence
  See Kuttner, Henry
O'Donovan, Michael John 1903-1966CLC 14
  See also O'Connor, Frank
  See also CA 93-96; CANR 84
Oe, Kenzaburo 1935- CLC 10, 36, 86; DAM
    NOV; SSC 20
  See also CA 97-100; CANR 36, 50, 74; DA3;
    DLB 182; DLBY 94; MTCW 1, 2
O'Faolain, Julia 1932-   CLC 6, 19, 47, 108
  See also CA 81-84; CAAS 2; CANR 12, 61;
    DLB 14; MTCW 1
O'Faolain, Sean 1900-1991 CLC 1, 7, 14, 32,
    70; SSC 13
  See also CA 61-64; 134; CANR 12, 66; DLB
    15, 162; MTCW 1, 2
O'Flaherty, Liam 1896-1984CLC 5, 34; SSC 6
  See also CA 101; 113; CANR 35; DLB 36, 162;
    DLBY 84; MTCW 1, 2
Ogilvy, Gavin
  See Barrie, J(ames) M(atthew)
O'Grady, Standish (James) 1846-1928 T C L C
    5
  See also CA 104; 157

O'Grady, Timothy 1951-   CLC 59
  See also CA 138
O'Hara, Frank 1926-1966 CLC 2, 5, 13, 78;
    DAM POET
  See also CA 9-12R; 25-28R; CANR 33; DA3;
    DLB 5, 16, 193; MTCW 1, 2
O'Hara, John (Henry) 1905-1970CLC 1, 2, 3,
    6, 11, 42; DAM NOV; SSC 15
  See also CA 5-8R; 25-28R; CANR 31, 60;
    CDALB 1929-1941; DLB 9, 86; DLBD 2;
    MTCW 1, 2
O Hehir, Diana 1922-   CLC 41
  See also CA 93-96
Ohiyesa
  See Eastman, Charles A(lexander)
Okigbo, Christopher (Ifenayichukwu) 1932-
    1967 CLC 25, 84; BLC 3; DAM MULT,
    POET; PC 7
  See also BW 1, 3; CA 77-80; CANR 74; DLB
    125; MTCW 1, 2
Okri, Ben 1959-   CLC 87
  See also BW 2, 3; CA 130; 138; CANR 65; DLB
    157; INT 138; MTCW 2
Olds, Sharon 1942-   CLC 32, 39, 85; DAM
    POET; PC 22
  See also CA 101; CANR 18, 41, 66; DLB 120;
    MTCW 2
Oldstyle, Jonathan
  See Irving, Washington
Olesha, Yuri (Karlovich) 1899-1960   CLC 8
  See also CA 85-88
Oliphant, Laurence 1829(?)-1888   NCLC 47
  See also DLB 18, 166
Oliphant, Margaret (Oliphant Wilson) 1828-
    1897   NCLC 11, 61; SSC 25
  See also DLB 18, 159, 190
Oliver, Mary 1935-   CLC 19, 34, 98
  See also CA 21-24R; CANR 9, 43, 84; DLB 5,
    193
Olivier, Laurence (Kerr) 1907-1989 CLC 20
  See also CA 111; 150; 129
Olsen, Tillie 1912-CLC 4, 13, 114; DA; DAB;
    DAC; DAM MST; SSC 11
  See also CA 1-4R; CANR 1, 43, 74; CDALBS;
    DA3; DLB 28, 206; DLBY 80; MTCW 1, 2
Olson, Charles (John) 1910-1970CLC 1, 2, 5,
    6, 9, 11, 29; DAM POET; PC 19
  See also CA 13-16; 25-28R; CABS 2; CANR
    35, 61; CAP 1; DLB 5, 16, 193; MTCW 1, 2
Olson, Toby 1937-   CLC 28
  See also CA 65-68; CANR 9, 31, 84
Olyesha, Yuri
  See Olesha, Yuri (Karlovich)
Ondaatje, (Philip) Michael 1943-CLC 14, 29,
    51, 76; DAB; DAC; DAM MST; PC 28
  See also CA 77-80; CANR 42, 74; DA3; DLB
    60; MTCW 2
Oneal, Elizabeth 1934-
  See Oneal, Zibby
  See also CA 106; CANR 28, 84; MAICYA;
    SATA 30, 82
Oneal, Zibby   CLC 30
  See also Oneal, Elizabeth
  See also AAYA 5; CLR 13; JRDA
O'Neill, Eugene (Gladstone) 1888-1953TCLC
    1, 6, 27, 49; DA; DAB; DAC; DAM DRAM,
    MST; WLC
  See also AITN 1; CA 110; 132; CDALB 1929-
    1941; DA3; DLB 7; MTCW 1, 2
Onetti, Juan Carlos 1909-1994   CLC 7, 10;
    DAM MULT, NOV; HLCS 2; SSC 23
  See also CA 85-88; 145; CANR 32, 63; DLB
    113; HW 1, 2; MTCW 1, 2

O Nuallain, Brian 1911-1966
See O'Brien, Flann
See also CA 21-22; 25-28R; CAP 2

Ophuls, Max 1902-1957　　　　　**TCLC 79**
See also CA 113

Opie, Amelia 1769-1853　　　　　**NCLC 65**
See also DLB 116, 159

Oppen, George 1908-1984　　**CLC 7, 13, 34**
See also CA 13-16R; 113; CANR 8, 82; DLB 5, 165

Oppenheim, E(dward) Phillips 1866-1946
　TCLC 45
See also CA 111; DLB 70

Opuls, Max
See Ophuls, Max

Origen c. 185-c. 254　　　　　**CMLC 19**

Orlovitz, Gil 1918-1973　　　　　**CLC 22**
See also CA 77-80; 45-48; DLB 2, 5

Orris
See Ingelow, Jean

Ortega y Gasset, Jose 1883-1955　　**TCLC 9;**
DAM MULT; HLC 2
See also CA 106; 130; HW 1, 2; MTCW 1, 2

Ortese, Anna Maria 1914-　　　　**CLC 89**
See also DLB 177

Ortiz, Simon J(oseph) 1941-　**CLC 45; DAM**
MULT, POET; PC 17
See also CA 134; CANR 69; DLB 120, 175;
NNAL

Orton, Joe　　　　**CLC 4, 13, 43; DC 3**
See also Orton, John Kingsley
See also CDBLB 1960 to Present; DLB 13;
MTCW 2

Orton, John Kingsley 1933-1967
See Orton, Joe
See also CA 85-88; CANR 35, 66; DAM
DRAM; MTCW 1, 2

Orwell, George　**TCLC 2, 6, 15, 31, 51; DAB;**
WLC
See also Blair, Eric (Arthur)
See also CDBLB 1945-1960; DLB 15, 98, 195

Osborne, David
See Silverberg, Robert

Osborne, George
See Silverberg, Robert

Osborne, John (James) 1929-1994**CLC 1, 2, 5,**
11, 45; DA; DAB; DAC; DAM DRAM,
MST; WLC
See also CA 13-16R; 147; CANR 21, 56;
CDBLB 1945-1960; DLB 13; MTCW 1, 2

Osborne, Lawrence 1958-　　　　**CLC 50**

Osbourne, Lloyd 1868-1947　　　**TCLC 93**

Oshima, Nagisa 1932-　　　　　**CLC 20**
See also CA 116; 121; CANR 78

Oskison, John Milton 1874-1947　**TCLC 35;**
DAM MULT
See also CA 144; CANR 84; DLB 175; NNAL

Ossian c. 3rd cent. -　　　　　**CMLC 28**
See also Macpherson, James

Ostrovsky, Alexander 1823-1886**NCLC 30, 57**

Otero, Blas de 1916-1979　　　　**CLC 11**
See also CA 89-92; DLB 134

Otto, Rudolf 1869-1937　　　　　**TCLC 85**

Otto, Whitney 1955-　　　　　**CLC 70**
See also CA 140

Ouida　　　　　　　　　　　**TCLC 43**
See also De La Ramee, (Marie) Louise
See also DLB 18, 156

Ousmane, Sembene 1923-　　**CLC 66; BLC 3**
See also BW 1, 3; CA 117; 125; CANR 81;
MTCW 1

Ovid 43B.C.-17 **CMLC 7; DAM POET; PC 2**
See also DA3; DLB 211

Owen, Hugh
See Faust, Frederick (Schiller)

Owen, Wilfred (Edward Salter) 1893-1918
　TCLC 5, 27; DA; DAB; DAC; DAM MST,
POET; PC 19; WLC
See also CA 104; 141; CDBLB 1914-1945;
DLB 20; MTCW 2

Owens, Rochelle 1936-　　　　　**CLC 8**
See also CA 17-20R; CAAS 2; CANR 39

Oz, Amos 1939-**CLC 5, 8, 11, 27, 33, 54; DAM**
NOV
See also CA 53-56; CANR 27, 47, 65; MTCW
1, 2

Ozick, Cynthia 1928- **CLC 3, 7, 28, 62; DAM**
NOV, POP; SSC 15
See also BEST 90:1; CA 17-20R; CANR 23,
58; DA3; DLB 28, 152; DLBY 82; INT
CANR-23; MTCW 1, 2

Ozu, Yasujiro 1903-1963　　　　**CLC 16**
See also CA 112

Pacheco, C.
See Pessoa, Fernando (Antonio Nogueira)

Pacheco, Jose Emilio 1939-
See also CA 111; 131; CANR 65; DAM MULT;
HLC 2; HW 1, 2

Pa Chin　　　　　　　　　　**CLC 18**
See also Li Fei-kan

Pack, Robert 1929-　　　　　　**CLC 13**
See also CA 1-4R; CANR 3, 44, 82; DLB 5

Padgett, Lewis
See Kuttner, Henry

Padilla (Lorenzo), Heberto 1932-　　**CLC 38**
See also AITN 1; CA 123; 131; HW 1

Page, Jimmy 1944-　　　　　　**CLC 12**

Page, Louise 1955-　　　　　　**CLC 40**
See also CA 140; CANR 76

Page, P(atricia) K(athleen) 1916- **CLC 7, 18;**
DAC; DAM MST; PC 12
See also CA 53-56; CANR 4, 22, 65; DLB 68;
MTCW 1

Page, Thomas Nelson 1853-1922　　**SSC 23**
See also CA 118; 177; DLB 12, 78; DLBD 13

Pagels, Elaine Hiesey 1943-　　　**CLC 104**
See also CA 45-48; CANR 2, 24, 51

Paget, Violet 1856-1935
See Lee, Vernon
See also CA 104; 166

Paget-Lowe, Henry
See Lovecraft, H(oward) P(hillips)

Paglia, Camille (Anna) 1947-　　　**CLC 68**
See also CA 140; CANR 72; MTCW 2

Paige, Richard
See Koontz, Dean R(ay)

Paine, Thomas 1737-1809　　　　**NCLC 62**
See also CDALB 1640-1865; DLB 31, 43, 73,
158

Pakenham, Antonia
See Fraser, (Lady) Antonia (Pakenham)

Palamas, Kostes 1859-1943　　　　**TCLC 5**
See also CA 105

Palazzeschi, Aldo 1885-1974　　　**CLC 11**
See also CA 89-92; 53-56; DLB 114

Pales Matos, Luis 1898-1959
See also HLCS 2; HW 1

Paley, Grace 1922- **CLC 4, 6, 37; DAM POP;**
SSC 8
See also CA 25-28R; CANR 13, 46, 74; DA3;
DLB 28; INT CANR-13; MTCW 1, 2

Palin, Michael (Edward) 1943-　　**CLC 21**
See also Monty Python
See also CA 107; CANR 35; SATA 67

Palliser, Charles 1947-　　　　　**CLC 65**
See also CA 136; CANR 76

Palma, Ricardo 1833-1919　　　　**TCLC 29**
See also CA 168

Pancake, Breece Dexter 1952-1979
See Pancake, Breece D'J
See also CA 123; 109

Pancake, Breece D'J　　　　　　**CLC 29**
See also Pancake, Breece Dexter
See also DLB 130

Panko, Rudy
See Gogol, Nikolai (Vasilyevich)

Papadiamantis, Alexandros 1851-1911**T C L C**
29
See also CA 168

Papadiamantopoulos, Johannes 1856-1910
See Moreas, Jean
See also CA 117

Papini, Giovanni 1881-1956　　　**TCLC 22**
See also CA 121; 180

Paracelsus 1493-1541　　　　　　**LC 14**
See also DLB 179

Parasol, Peter
See Stevens, Wallace

Pardo Bazan, Emilia 1851-1921　　**SSC 30**

Pareto, Vilfredo 1848-1923　　　　**TCLC 69**
See also CA 175

Parfenie, Maria
See Codrescu, Andrei

Parini, Jay (Lee) 1948-　　　　　**CLC 54**
See also CA 97-100; CAAS 16; CANR 32

Park, Jordan
See Kornbluth, C(yril) M.; Pohl, Frederik

Park, Robert E(zra) 1864-1944　　**TCLC 73**
See also CA 122; 165

Parker, Bert
See Ellison, Harlan (Jay)

Parker, Dorothy (Rothschild) 1893-1967**C L C**
15, 68; DAM POET; PC 28; SSC 2
See also CA 19-20; 25-28R; CAP 2; DA3; DLB
11, 45, 86; MTCW 1, 2

Parker, Robert B(rown) 1932-**CLC 27; DAM**
NOV, POP
See also AAYA 28; BEST 89:4; CA 49-52;
CANR 1, 26, 52; INT CANR-26; MTCW 1

Parkin, Frank 1940-　　　　　　**CLC 43**
See also CA 147

Parkman, Francis Jr., Jr. 1823-1893**NCLC 12**
See also DLB 1, 30, 186

Parks, Gordon (Alexander Buchanan) 1912-
　CLC 1, 16; BLC 3; DAM MULT
See also AITN 2; BW 2, 3; CA 41-44R; CANR
26, 66; DA3; DLB 33; MTCW 2; SATA 8,
108

Parmenides c. 515B.C.-c. 450B.C. **CMLC 22**
See also DLB 176

Parnell, Thomas 1679-1718　　　　**LC 3**
See also DLB 94

Parra, Nicanor 1914-　　**CLC 2, 102; DAM**
MULT; HLC 2
See also CA 85-88; CANR 32; HW 1; MTCW
1

Parra Sanojo, Ana Teresa de la 1890-1936
See also HLCS 2

Parrish, Mary Frances
See Fisher, M(ary) F(rances) K(ennedy)

Parson
See Coleridge, Samuel Taylor

Parson Lot
See Kingsley, Charles

Partridge, Anthony
See Oppenheim, E(dward) Phillips

Pascal, Blaise 1623-1662　　　　　**LC 35**

Pascoli, Giovanni 1855-1912　　　**TCLC 45**
See also CA 170

Pasolini, Pier Paolo 1922-1975 **CLC 20, 37, 106; PC 17**
See also CA 93-96; 61-64; CANR 63; DLB 128, 177; MTCW 1

Pasquini
See Silone, Ignazio

Pastan, Linda (Olenik) 1932- **CLC 27; DAM POET**
See also CA 61-64; CANR 18, 40, 61; DLB 5

Pasternak, Boris (Leonidovich) 1890-1960 **CLC 7, 10, 18, 63; DA; DAB; DAC; DAM MST, NOV, POET; PC 6; SSC 31; WLC**
See also CA 127; 116; DA3; MTCW 1, 2

Patchen, Kenneth 1911-1972 **CLC 1, 2, 18; DAM POET**
See also CA 1-4R; 33-36R; CANR 3, 35; DLB 16, 48; MTCW 1

Pater, Walter (Horatio) 1839-1894 **NCLC 7**
See also CDBLB 1832-1890; DLB 57, 156

Paterson, A(ndrew) B(arton) 1864-1941 **TCLC 32**
See also CA 155; SATA 97

Paterson, Katherine (Womeldorf) 1932-**C L C 12, 30**
See also AAYA 1, 31; CA 21-24R; CANR 28, 59; CLR 7, 50; DLB 52; JRDA; MAICYA; MTCW 1; SATA 13, 53, 92

Patmore, Coventry Kersey Dighton 1823-1896 **NCLC 9**
See also DLB 35, 98

Paton, Alan (Stewart) 1903-1988 **CLC 4, 10, 25, 55, 106; DA; DAB; DAC; DAM MST, NOV; WLC**
See also AAYA 26; CA 13-16; 125; CANR 22; CAP 1; DA3; DLBD 17; MTCW 1, 2; SATA 11; SATA-Obit 56

Paton Walsh, Gillian 1937-
See Walsh, Jill Paton
See also CANR 38, 83; JRDA; MAICYA; SAAS 3; SATA 4, 72, 109

Patton, George S. 1885-1945 **TCLC 79**

Paulding, James Kirke 1778-1860 **NCLC 2**
See also DLB 3, 59, 74

Paulin, Thomas Neilson 1949-
See Paulin, Tom
See also CA 123; 128

Paulin, Tom **CLC 37**
See also Paulin, Thomas Neilson
See also DLB 40

Pausanias c. 1st cent. - **CMLC 36**

Paustovsky, Konstantin (Georgievich) 1892-1968 **CLC 40**
See also CA 93-96; 25-28R

Pavese, Cesare 1908-1950 **TCLC 3; PC 13; SSC 19**
See also CA 104; 169; DLB 128, 177

Pavic, Milorad 1929- **CLC 60**
See also CA 136; DLB 181

Pavlov, Ivan Petrovich 1849-1936 **TCLC 91**
See also CA 118; 180

Payne, Alan
See Jakes, John (William)

Paz, Gil
See Lugones, Leopoldo

Paz, Octavio 1914-1998**CLC 3, 4, 6, 10, 19, 51, 65, 119; DA; DAB; DAC; DAM MST, MULT, POET; HLC 2; PC 1; WLC**
See also CA 73-76; 165; CANR 32, 65; DA3; DLBY 90, 98; HW 1, 2; MTCW 1, 2

p'Bitek, Okot 1931-1982 **CLC 96; BLC 3; DAM MULT**
See also BW 2, 3; CA 124; 107; CANR 82; DLB 125; MTCW 1, 2

Peacock, Molly 1947- **CLC 60**
See also CA 103; CAAS 21; CANR 52, 84; DLB 120

Peacock, Thomas Love 1785-1866 **NCLC 22**
See also DLB 96, 116

Peake, Mervyn 1911-1968 **CLC 7, 54**
See also CA 5-8R; 25-28R; CANR 3; DLB 15, 160; MTCW 1; SATA 23

Pearce, Philippa **CLC 21**
See also Christie, (Ann) Philippa
See also CLR 9; DLB 161; MAICYA; SATA 1, 67

Pearl, Eric
See Elman, Richard (Martin)

Pearson, T(homas) R(eid) 1956- **CLC 39**
See also CA 120; 130; INT 130

Peck, Dale 1967- **CLC 81**
See also CA 146; CANR 72

Peck, John 1941- **CLC 3**
See also CA 49-52; CANR 3

Peck, Richard (Wayne) 1934- **CLC 21**
See also AAYA 1, 24; CA 85-88; CANR 19, 38; CLR 15; INT CANR-19; JRDA; MAICYA; SAAS 2; SATA 18, 55, 97; SATA-Essay 110

Peck, Robert Newton 1928- **CLC 17; DA; DAC; DAM MST**
See also AAYA 3; CA 81-84, 182; CAAE 182; CANR 31, 63; CLR 45; JRDA; MAICYA; SAAS 1; SATA 21, 62, 111; SATA-Essay 108

Peckinpah, (David) Sam(uel) 1925-1984**C L C 20**
See also CA 109; 114; CANR 82

Pedersen, Knut 1859-1952
See Hamsun, Knut
See also CA 104; 119; CANR 63; MTCW 1, 2

Peeslake, Gaffer
See Durrell, Lawrence (George)

Peguy, Charles Pierre 1873-1914 **TCLC 10**
See also CA 107

Peirce, Charles Sanders 1839-1914 **TCLC 81**

Pellicer, Carlos 1900(?)-1977
See also CA 153; 69-72; HLCS 2; HW 1

Pena, Ramon del Valle y
See Valle-Inclan, Ramon (Maria) del

Pendennis, Arthur Esquir
See Thackeray, William Makepeace

Penn, William 1644-1718 **LC 25**
See also DLB 24

PEPECE
See Prado (Calvo), Pedro

Pepys, Samuel 1633-1703 **LC 11; DA; DAB; DAC; DAM MST; WLC**
See also CDBLB 1660-1789; DA3; DLB 101

Percy, Walker 1916-1990**CLC 2, 3, 6, 8, 14, 18, 47, 65; DAM NOV, POP**
See also CA 1-4R; 131; CANR 1, 23, 64; DA3; DLB 2; DLBY 80, 90; MTCW 1, 2

Percy, William Alexander 1885-1942**TCLC 84**
See also CA 163; MTCW 2

Perec, Georges 1936-1982 **CLC 56, 116**
See also CA 141; DLB 83

Pereda (y Sanchez de Porrua), Jose Maria de 1833-1906 **TCLC 16**
See also CA 117

Pereda y Porrua, Jose Maria de
See Pereda (y Sanchez de Porrua), Jose Maria de

Peregoy, George Weems
See Mencken, H(enry) L(ouis)

Perelman, S(idney) J(oseph) 1904-1979 **C L C 3, 5, 9, 15, 23, 44, 49; DAM DRAM; SSC 32**

See also AITN 1, 2; CA 73-76; 89-92; CANR 18; DLB 11, 44; MTCW 1, 2

Peret, Benjamin 1899-1959 **TCLC 20**
See also CA 117

Peretz, Isaac Loeb 1851(?)-1915 **TCLC 16; SSC 26**
See also CA 109

Peretz, Yitzkhok Leibush
See Peretz, Isaac Loeb

Perez Galdos, Benito 1843-1920 **TCLC 27; HLCS 2**
See also CA 125; 153; HW 1

Peri Rossi, Cristina 1941-
See also CA 131; CANR 59, 81; DLB 145; HLCS 2; HW 1, 2

Perrault, Charles 1628-1703 **LC 3, 52**
See also MAICYA; SATA 25

Perry, Anne 1938- **CLC 126**
See also CA 101; CANR 22, 50, 84

Perry, Brighton
See Sherwood, Robert E(mmet)

Perse, St.-John
See Leger, (Marie-Rene Auguste) Alexis Saint-Leger

Perutz, Leo(pold) 1882-1957 **TCLC 60**
See also CA 147; DLB 81

Peseenz, Tulio F.
See Lopez y Fuentes, Gregorio

Pesetsky, Bette 1932- **CLC 28**
See also CA 133; DLB 130

Peshkov, Alexei Maximovich 1868-1936
See Gorky, Maxim
See also CA 105; 141; CANR 83; DA; DAC; DAM DRAM, MST, NOV; MTCW 2

Pessoa, Fernando (Antonio Nogueira) 1888-1935**TCLC 27; DAM MULT; HLC 2; PC 20**
See also CA 125

Peterkin, Julia Mood 1880-1961 **CLC 31**
See also CA 102; DLB 9

Peters, Joan K(aren) 1945- **CLC 39**
See also CA 158

Peters, Robert L(ouis) 1924- **CLC 7**
See also CA 13-16R; CAAS 8; DLB 105

Petofi, Sandor 1823-1849 **NCLC 21**

Petrakis, Harry Mark 1923- **CLC 3**
See also CA 9-12R; CANR 4, 30, 85

Petrarch 1304-1374 **CMLC 20; DAM POET; PC 8**
See also DA3

Petronius c. 20-66 **CMLC 34**
See also DLB 211

Petrov, Evgeny **TCLC 21**
See also Kataev, Evgeny Petrovich

Petry, Ann (Lane) 1908-1997 **CLC 1, 7, 18**
See also BW 1, 3; CA 5-8R; 157; CAAS 6; CANR 4, 46; CLR 12; DLB 76; JRDA; MAICYA; MTCW 1; SATA 5; SATA-Obit 94

Petursson, Halligrimur 1614-1674 **LC 8**

Peychinovich
See Vazov, Ivan (Minchov)

Phaedrus c. 18B.C.-c. 50 **CMLC 25**
See also DLB 211

Philips, Katherine 1632-1664 **LC 30**
See also DLB 131

Philipson, Morris H. 1926- **CLC 53**
See also CA 1-4R; CANR 4

Phillips, Caryl 1958- **CLC 96; BLCS; DAM MULT**
See also BW 2; CA 141; CANR 63; DA3; DLB 157; MTCW 2

Phillips, David Graham 1867-1911 **TCLC 44**
See also CA 108; 176; DLB 9, 12

Phillips, Jack
See Sandburg, Carl (August)
Phillips, Jayne Anne 1952-CLC 15, 33; SSC 16
See also CA 101; CANR 24, 50; DLBY 80; INT
CANR-24; MTCW 1, 2
Phillips, Richard
See Dick, Philip K(indred)
Phillips, Robert (Schaeffer) 1938- CLC 28
See also CA 17-20R; CAAS 13; CANR 8; DLB
105
Phillips, Ward
See Lovecraft, H(oward) P(hillips)
Piccolo, Lucio 1901-1969 CLC 13
See also CA 97-100; DLB 114
Pickthall, Marjorie L(owry) C(hristie) 1883-
1922 TCLC 21
See also CA 107; DLB 92
Pico della Mirandola, Giovanni 1463-1494 LC
15
Piercy, Marge 1936- CLC 3, 6, 14, 18, 27, 62
See also CA 21-24R; CAAS 1; CANR 13, 43,
66; DLB 120; MTCW 1, 2
Piers, Robert
See Anthony, Piers
Pieyre de Mandiargues, Andre 1909-1991
See Mandiargues, Andre Pieyre de
See also CA 103; 136; CANR 22, 82
Pilnyak, Boris TCLC 23
See also Vogau, Boris Andreyevich
Pincherle, Alberto 1907-1990 CLC 11, 18;
DAM NOV
See also Moravia, Alberto
See also CA 25-28R; 132; CANR 33, 63;
MTCW 1
Pinckney, Darryl 1953- CLC 76
See also BW 2, 3; CA 143; CANR 79
Pindar 518B.C.-446B.C. CMLC 12; PC 19
See also DLB 176
Pineda, Cecile 1942- CLC 39
See also CA 118
Pinero, Arthur Wing 1855-1934 TCLC 32;
DAM DRAM
See also CA 110; 153; DLB 10
Pinero, Miguel (Antonio Gomez) 1946-1988
CLC 4, 55
See also CA 61-64; 125; CANR 29; HW 1
Pinget, Robert 1919-1997 CLC 7, 13, 37
See also CA 85-88; 160; DLB 83
Pink Floyd
See Barrett, (Roger) Syd; Gilmour, David; Ma-
son, Nick; Waters, Roger; Wright, Rick
Pinkney, Edward 1802-1828 NCLC 31
Pinkwater, Daniel Manus 1941- CLC 35
See also Pinkwater, Manus
See also AAYA 1; CA 29-32R; CANR 12, 38;
CLR 4; JRDA; MAICYA; SAAS 3; SATA 46,
76
Pinkwater, Manus
See Pinkwater, Daniel Manus
See also SATA 8
Pinsky, Robert 1940- CLC 9, 19, 38, 94, 121;
DAM POET; PC 27
See also CA 29-32R; CAAS 4; CANR 58; DA3;
DLBY 82, 98; MTCW 2
Pinta, Harold
See Pinter, Harold
Pinter, Harold 1930-CLC 1, 3, 6, 9, 11, 15, 27,
58, 73; DA; DAB; DAC; DAM DRAM,
MST; WLC
See also CA 5-8R; CANR 33, 65; CDBLB 1960
to Present; DA3; DLB 13; MTCW 1, 2
Piozzi, Hester Lynch (Thrale) 1741-1821
NCLC 57

See also DLB 104, 142
Pirandello, Luigi 1867-1936 TCLC 4, 29; DA;
DAB; DAC; DAM DRAM, MST; DC 5;
SSC 22; WLC
See also CA 104; 153; DA3; MTCW 2
Pirsig, Robert M(aynard) 1928-CLC 4, 6, 73;
DAM POP
See also CA 53-56; CANR 42, 74; DA3; MTCW
1, 2; SATA 39
Pisarev, Dmitry Ivanovich 1840-1868 NCLC
25
Pix, Mary (Griffith) 1666-1709 LC 8
See also DLB 80
Pixerecourt, (Rene Charles) Guilbert de 1773-
1844 NCLC 39
See also DLB 192
Plaatje, Sol(omon) T(shekisho) 1876-1932
TCLC 73; BLCS
See also BW 2, 3; CA 141; CANR 79
Plaidy, Jean
See Hibbert, Eleanor Alice Burford
Planche, James Robinson 1796-1880 NCLC 42
Plant, Robert 1948- CLC 12
Plante, David (Robert) 1940- CLC 7, 23, 38;
DAM NOV
See also CA 37-40R; CANR 12, 36, 58, 82;
DLBY 83; INT CANR-12; MTCW 1
Plath, Sylvia 1932-1963 CLC 1, 2, 3, 5, 9, 11,
14, 17, 50, 51, 62, 111; DA; DAB; DAC;
DAM MST, POET; PC 1; WLC
See also AAYA 13; CA 19-20; CANR 34; CAP
2; CDALB 1941-1968; DA3; DLB 5, 6, 152;
MTCW 1, 2; SATA 96
Plato 428(?)B.C.-348(?)B.C. CMLC 8; DA;
DAB; DAC; DAM MST; WLCS
See also DA3; DLB 176
Platonov, Andrei TCLC 14
See also Klimentov, Andrei Platonovich
Platt, Kin 1911- CLC 26
See also AAYA 11; CA 17-20R; CANR 11;
JRDA; SAAS 17; SATA 21, 86
Plautus c. 251B.C.-184B.C. CMLC 24; DC 6
See also DLB 211
Plick et Plock
See Simenon, Georges (Jacques Christian)
Plimpton, George (Ames) 1927- CLC 36
See also AITN 1; CA 21-24R; CANR 32, 70;
DLB 185; MTCW 1, 2; SATA 10
Pliny the Elder c. 23-79 CMLC 23
See also DLB 211
Plomer, William Charles Franklin 1903-1973
CLC 4, 8
See also CA 21-22; CANR 34; CAP 2; DLB
20, 162, 191; MTCW 1; SATA 24
Plowman, Piers
See Kavanagh, Patrick (Joseph)
Plum, J.
See Wodehouse, P(elham) G(renville)
Plumly, Stanley (Ross) 1939- CLC 33
See also CA 108; 110; DLB 5, 193; INT 110
Plumpe, Friedrich Wilhelm 1888-1931 TCLC
53
See also CA 112
Po Chu-i 772-846 CMLC 24
Poe, Edgar Allan 1809-1849 NCLC 1, 16, 55,
78; DA; DAB; DAC; DAM MST, POET;
PC 1; SSC 34; WLC
See also AAYA 14; CDALB 1640-1865; DA3;
DLB 3, 59, 73, 74; SATA 23
Poet of Titchfield Street, The
See Pound, Ezra (Weston Loomis)
Pohl, Frederik 1919- CLC 18; SSC 25
See also AAYA 24; CA 61-64; CAAS 1; CANR

11, 37, 81; DLB 8; INT CANR-11; MTCW
1, 2; SATA 24
Poirier, Louis 1910-
See Gracq, Julien
See also CA 122; 126
Poitier, Sidney 1927- CLC 26
See also BW 1; CA 117
Polanski, Roman 1933- CLC 16
See also CA 77-80
Poliakoff, Stephen 1952- CLC 38
See also CA 106; DLB 13
Police, The
See Copeland, Stewart (Armstrong); Summers,
Andrew James; Sumner, Gordon Matthew
Polidori, John William 1795-1821 NCLC 51
See also DLB 116
Pollitt, Katha 1949- CLC 28, 122
See also CA 120; 122; CANR 66; MTCW 1, 2
Pollock, (Mary) Sharon 1936-CLC 50; DAC;
DAM DRAM, MST
See also CA 141; DLB 60
Polo, Marco 1254-1324 CMLC 15
Polonsky, Abraham (Lincoln) 1910- CLC 92
See also CA 104; DLB 26; INT 104
Polybius c. 200B.C.-c. 118B.C. CMLC 17
See also DLB 176
Pomerance, Bernard 1940- CLC 13; DAM
DRAM
See also CA 101; CANR 49
Ponge, Francis (Jean Gaston Alfred) 1899-1988
CLC 6, 18; DAM POET
See also CA 85-88; 126; CANR 40, 86
Poniatowska, Elena 1933-
See also CA 101; CANR 32, 66; DAM MULT;
DLB 113; HLC 2; HW 1, 2
Pontoppidan, Henrik 1857-1943 TCLC 29
See also CA 170
Poole, Josephine CLC 17
See also Helyar, Jane Penelope Josephine
See also SAAS 2; SATA 5
Popa, Vasko 1922-1991 CLC 19
See also CA 112; 148; DLB 181
Pope, Alexander 1688-1744 LC 3; DA; DAB;
DAC; DAM MST, POET; PC 26; WLC
See also CDBLB 1660-1789; DA3; DLB 95,
101
Porter, Connie (Rose) 1959(?)- CLC 70
See also BW 2, 3; CA 142; SATA 81
Porter, Gene(va Grace) Stratton 1863(?)-1924
TCLC 21
See also CA 112
Porter, Katherine Anne 1890-1980CLC 1, 3, 7,
10, 13, 15, 27, 101; DA; DAB; DAC; DAM
MST, NOV; SSC 4, 31
See also AITN 2; CA 1-4R; 101; CANR 1, 65;
CDALBS; DA3; DLB 4, 9, 102; DLBD 12;
DLBY 80; MTCW 1, 2; SATA 39; SATA-
Obit 23
Porter, Peter (Neville Frederick) 1929-CLC 5,
13, 33
See also CA 85-88; DLB 40
Porter, William Sydney 1862-1910
See Henry, O.
See also CA 104; 131; CDALB 1865-1917; DA;
DAB; DAC; DAM MST; DA3; DLB 12, 78,
79; MTCW 1, 2; YABC 2
Portillo (y Pacheco), Jose Lopez
See Lopez Portillo (y Pacheco), Jose
Portillo Trambley, Estela 1927-1998
See also CANR 32; DAM MULT; DLB 209;
HLC 2; HW 1
Post, Melville Davisson 1869-1930 TCLC 39
See also CA 110

Potok, Chaim 1929- **CLC 2, 7, 14, 26, 112; DAM NOV**
See also AAYA 15; AITN 1, 2; CA 17-20R; CANR 19, 35, 64; DA3; DLB 28, 152; INT CANR-19; MTCW 1, 2; SATA 33, 106

Potter, Dennis (Christopher George) 1935-1994 **CLC 58, 86**
See also CA 107; 145; CANR 33, 61; MTCW 1

Pound, Ezra (Weston Loomis) 1885-1972 **CLC 1, 2, 3, 4, 5, 7, 10, 13, 18, 34, 48, 50, 112; DA; DAB; DAC; DAM MST, POET; PC 4; WLC**
See also CA 5-8R; 37-40R; CANR 40; CDALB 1917-1929; DA3; DLB 4, 45, 63; DLBD 15; MTCW 1, 2

Povod, Reinaldo 1959-1994 **CLC 44**
See also CA 136; 146; CANR 83

Powell, Adam Clayton, Jr. 1908-1972 **CLC 89; BLC 3; DAM MULT**
See also BW 1, 3; CA 102; 33-36R; CANR 86

Powell, Anthony (Dymoke) 1905- **CLC 1, 3, 7, 9, 10, 31**
See also CA 1-4R; CANR 1, 32, 62; CDBLB 1945-1960; DLB 15; MTCW 1, 2

Powell, Dawn 1897-1965 **CLC 66**
See also CA 5-8R; DLBY 97

Powell, Padgett 1952- **CLC 34**
See also CA 126; CANR 63

Power, Susan 1961- **CLC 91**

Powers, J(ames) F(arl) 1917-1999 **CLC 1, 4, 8, 57; SSC 4**
See also CA 1-4R; 181; CANR 2, 61; DLB 130; MTCW 1

Powers, John J(ames) 1945-
See Powers, John R.
See also CA 69-72

Powers, John R. **CLC 66**
See also Powers, John J(ames)

Powers, Richard (S.) 1957- **CLC 93**
See also CA 148; CANR 80

Pownall, David 1938- **CLC 10**
See also CA 89-92; 180; CAAS 18; CANR 49; DLB 14

Powys, John Cowper 1872-1963 **CLC 7, 9, 15, 46, 125**
See also CA 85-88; DLB 15; MTCW 1, 2

Powys, T(heodore) F(rancis) 1875-1953 **TCLC 9**
See also CA 106; DLB 36, 162

Prado (Calvo), Pedro 1886-1952 **TCLC 75**
See also CA 131; HW 1

Prager, Emily 1952- **CLC 56**

Pratt, E(dwin) J(ohn) 1883(?)-1964 **CLC 19; DAC; DAM POET**
See also CA 141; 93-96; CANR 77; DLB 92

Premchand **TCLC 21**
See also Srivastava, Dhanpat Rai

Preussler, Otfried 1923- **CLC 17**
See also CA 77-80; SATA 24

Prevert, Jacques (Henri Marie) 1900-1977 **CLC 15**
See also CA 77-80; 69-72; CANR 29, 61; MTCW 1; SATA-Obit 30

Prevost, Abbe (Antoine Francois) 1697-1763 **LC 1**

Price, (Edward) Reynolds 1933- **CLC 3, 6, 13, 43, 50, 63; DAM NOV; SSC 22**
See also CA 1-4R; CANR 1, 37, 57; DLB 2; INT CANR-37

Price, Richard 1949- **CLC 6, 12**
See also CA 49-52; CANR 3; DLBY 81

Prichard, Katharine Susannah 1883-1969 **CLC 46**

See also CA 11-12; CANR 33; CAP 1; MTCW 1; SATA 66

Priestley, J(ohn) B(oynton) 1894-1984 **CLC 2, 5, 9, 34; DAM DRAM, NOV**
See also CA 9-12R; 113; CANR 33; CDBLB 1914-1945; DA3; DLB 10, 34, 77, 100, 139; DLBY 84; MTCW 1, 2

Prince 1958(?)- **CLC 35**

Prince, F(rank) T(empleton) 1912- **CLC 22**
See also CA 101; CANR 43, 79; DLB 20

Prince Kropotkin
See Kropotkin, Peter (Aleksieevich)

Prior, Matthew 1664-1721 **LC 4**
See also DLB 95

Prishvin, Mikhail 1873-1954 **TCLC 75**

Pritchard, William H(arrison) 1932- **CLC 34**
See also CA 65-68; CANR 23; DLB 111

Pritchett, V(ictor) S(awdon) 1900-1997 **CLC 5, 13, 15, 41; DAM NOV; SSC 14**
See also CA 61-64; 157; CANR 31, 63; DA3; DLB 15, 139; MTCW 1, 2

Private 19022
See Manning, Frederic

Probst, Mark 1925- **CLC 59**
See also CA 130

Prokosch, Frederic 1908-1989 **CLC 4, 48**
See also CA 73-76; 128; CANR 82; DLB 48; MTCW 2

Propertius, Sextus c. 50B.C.-c. 16B.C. **CMLC 32**
See also DLB 211

Prophet, The
See Dreiser, Theodore (Herman Albert)

Prose, Francine 1947- **CLC 45**
See also CA 109; 112; CANR 46; SATA 101

Proudhon
See Cunha, Euclides (Rodrigues Pimenta) da

Proulx, Annie
See Proulx, E(dna) Annie

Proulx, E(dna) Annie 1935- **CLC 81; DAM POP**
See also CA 145; CANR 65; DA3; MTCW 2

Proust, (Valentin-Louis-George-Eugene-) Marcel 1871-1922 **TCLC 7, 13, 33; DA; DAB; DAC; DAM MST, NOV; WLC**
See also CA 104; 120; DA3; DLB 65; MTCW 1, 2

Prowler, Harley
See Masters, Edgar Lee

Prus, Boleslaw 1845-1912 **TCLC 48**

Pryor, Richard (Franklin Lenox Thomas) 1940- **CLC 26**
See also CA 122; 152

Przybyszewski, Stanislaw 1868-1927 **TCLC 36**
See also CA 160; DLB 66

Pteleon
See Grieve, C(hristopher) M(urray)
See also DAM POET

Puckett, Lute
See Masters, Edgar Lee

Puig, Manuel 1932-1990 **CLC 3, 5, 10, 28, 65; DAM MULT; HLC 2**
See also CA 45-48; CANR 2, 32, 63; DA3; DLB 113; HW 1, 2; MTCW 1, 2

Pulitzer, Joseph 1847-1911 **TCLC 76**
See also CA 114; DLB 23

Purdy, A(lfred) W(ellington) 1918- **CLC 3, 6, 14, 50; DAC; DAM MST, POET**
See also CA 81-84; CAAS 17; CANR 42, 66; DLB 88

Purdy, James (Amos) 1923- **CLC 2, 4, 10, 28, 52**
See also CA 33-36R; CAAS 1; CANR 19, 51;

DLB 2; INT CANR-19; MTCW 1

Pure, Simon
See Swinnerton, Frank Arthur

Pushkin, Alexander (Sergeyevich) 1799-1837 **NCLC 3, 27; DA; DAB; DAC; DAM DRAM, MST, POET; PC 10; SSC 27; WLC**
See also DA3; DLB 205; SATA 61

P'u Sung-ling 1640-1715 **LC 49; SSC 31**

Putnam, Arthur Lee
See Alger, Horatio Jr., Jr.

Puzo, Mario 1920-1999 **CLC 1, 2, 6, 36, 107; DAM NOV, POP**
See also CA 65-68; CANR 4, 42, 65; DA3; DLB 6; MTCW 1, 2

Pygge, Edward
See Barnes, Julian (Patrick)

Pyle, Ernest Taylor 1900-1945
See Pyle, Ernie
See also CA 115; 160

Pyle, Ernie 1900-1945 **TCLC 75**
See also Pyle, Ernest Taylor
See also DLB 29; MTCW 2

Pyle, Howard 1853-1911 **TCLC 81**
See also CA 109; 137; CLR 22; DLB 42, 188; DLBD 13; MAICYA; SATA 16, 100

Pym, Barbara (Mary Crampton) 1913-1980 **CLC 13, 19, 37, 111**
See also CA 13-14; 97-100; CANR 13, 34; CAP 1; DLB 14, 207; DLBY 87; MTCW 1, 2

Pynchon, Thomas (Ruggles, Jr.) 1937- **CLC 2, 3, 6, 9, 11, 18, 33, 62, 72; DA; DAB; DAC; DAM MST, NOV, POP; SSC 14; WLC**
See also BEST 90:2; CA 17-20R; CANR 22, 46, 73; DA3; DLB 2, 173; MTCW 1, 2

Pythagoras c. 570B.C.-c. 500B.C. **CMLC 22**
See also DLB 176

Q
See Quiller-Couch, Sir Arthur (Thomas)

Qian Zhongshu
See Ch'ien Chung-shu

Qroll
See Dagerman, Stig (Halvard)

Quarrington, Paul (Lewis) 1953- **CLC 65**
See also CA 129; CANR 62

Quasimodo, Salvatore 1901-1968 **CLC 10**
See also CA 13-16; 25-28R; CAP 1; DLB 114; MTCW 1

Quay, Stephen 1947- **CLC 95**

Quay, Timothy 1947- **CLC 95**

Queen, Ellery **CLC 3, 11**
See also Dannay, Frederic; Davidson, Avram (James); Lee, Manfred B(ennington); Marlowe, Stephen; Sturgeon, Theodore (Hamilton); Vance, John Holbrook

Queen, Ellery, Jr.
See Dannay, Frederic; Lee, Manfred B(ennington)

Queneau, Raymond 1903-1976 **CLC 2, 5, 10, 42**
See also CA 77-80; 69-72; CANR 32; DLB 72; MTCW 1, 2

Quevedo, Francisco de 1580-1645 **LC 23**

Quiller-Couch, Sir Arthur (Thomas) 1863-1944 **TCLC 53**
See also CA 118; 166; DLB 135, 153, 190

Quin, Ann (Marie) 1936-1973 **CLC 6**
See also CA 9-12R; 45-48; DLB 14

Quinn, Martin
See Smith, Martin Cruz

Quinn, Peter 1947- **CLC 91**

Quinn, Simon
See Smith, Martin Cruz

Quintana, Leroy V. 1944-
See also CA 131; CANR 65; DAM MULT; DLB 82; HLC 2; HW 1, 2
Quiroga, Horacio (Sylvestre) 1878-1937 **TCLC 20; DAM MULT; HLC 2**
See also CA 117; 131; HW 1; MTCW 1
Quoirez, Francoise 1935-   **CLC 9**
See also Sagan, Francoise
See also CA 49-52; CANR 6, 39, 73; MTCW 1, 2
Raabe, Wilhelm (Karl) 1831-1910 **TCLC 45**
See also CA 167; DLB 129
Rabe, David (William) 1940-   **CLC 4, 8, 33; DAM DRAM**
See also CA 85-88; CABS 3; CANR 59; DLB 7
Rabelais, Francois 1483-1553 **LC 5; DA; DAB; DAC; DAM MST; WLC**
Rabinovitch, Sholem 1859-1916
See Aleichem, Sholom
See also CA 104
Rabinyan, Dorit 1972-   **CLC 119**
See also CA 170
Rachilde 1860-1953   **TCLC 67**
See also DLB 123, 192
Racine, Jean 1639-1699 **LC 28; DAB; DAM MST**
See also DA3
Radcliffe, Ann (Ward) 1764-1823 **NCLC 6, 55**
See also DLB 39, 178
Radiguet, Raymond 1903-1923   **TCLC 29**
See also CA 162; DLB 65
Radnoti, Miklos 1909-1944   **TCLC 16**
See also CA 118
Rado, James 1939-   **CLC 17**
See also CA 105
Radvanyi, Netty 1900-1983
See Seghers, Anna
See also CA 85-88; 110; CANR 82
Rae, Ben
See Griffiths, Trevor
Raeburn, John (Hay) 1941-   **CLC 34**
See also CA 57-60
Ragni, Gerome 1942-1991   **CLC 17**
See also CA 105; 134
Rahv, Philip 1908-1973   **CLC 24**
See also Greenberg, Ivan
See also DLB 137
Raimund, Ferdinand Jakob 1790-1836 **NCLC 69**
See also DLB 90
Raine, Craig 1944-   **CLC 32, 103**
See also CA 108; CANR 29, 51; DLB 40
Raine, Kathleen (Jessie) 1908-   **CLC 7, 45**
See also CA 85-88; CANR 46; DLB 20; MTCW 1
Rainis, Janis 1865-1929   **TCLC 29**
See also CA 170
Rakosi, Carl 1903-   **CLC 47**
See also Rawley, Callman
See also CAAS 5; DLB 193
Raleigh, Richard
See Lovecraft, H(oward) P(hillips)
Raleigh, Sir Walter 1554(?)-1618   **LC 31, 39**
See also CDBLB Before 1660; DLB 172
Rallentando, H. P.
See Sayers, Dorothy L(eigh)
Ramal, Walter
See de la Mare, Walter (John)
Ramana Maharshi 1879-1950   **TCLC 84**
Ramoacn y Cajal, Santiago 1852-1934 **TCLC 93**
Ramon, Juan
See Jimenez (Mantecon), Juan Ramon

Ramos, Graciliano 1892-1953   **TCLC 32**
See also CA 167; HW 2
Rampersad, Arnold 1941-   **CLC 44**
See also BW 2, 3; CA 127; 133; CANR 81; DLB 111; INT 133
Rampling, Anne
See Rice, Anne
Ramsay, Allan 1684(?)-1758   **LC 29**
See also DLB 95
Ramuz, Charles-Ferdinand 1878-1947 **TCLC 33**
See also CA 165
Rand, Ayn 1905-1982 **CLC 3, 30, 44, 79; DA; DAC; DAM MST, NOV, POP; WLC**
See also AAYA 10; CA 13-16R; 105; CANR 27, 73; CDALBS; DA3; MTCW 1, 2
Randall, Dudley (Felker) 1914- **CLC 1; BLC 3; DAM MULT**
See also BW 1, 3; CA 25-28R; CANR 23, 82; DLB 41
Randall, Robert
See Silverberg, Robert
Ranger, Ken
See Creasey, John
Ransom, John Crowe 1888-1974 **CLC 2, 4, 5, 11, 24; DAM POET**
See also CA 5-8R; 49-52; CANR 6, 34; CDALBS; DA3; DLB 45, 63; MTCW 1, 2
Rao, Raja 1909-   **CLC 25, 56; DAM NOV**
See also CA 73-76; CANR 51; MTCW 1, 2
Raphael, Frederic (Michael) 1931- **CLC 2, 14**
See also CA 1-4R; CANR 1, 86; DLB 14
Ratcliffe, James P.
See Mencken, H(enry) L(ouis)
Rathbone, Julian 1935-   **CLC 41**
See also CA 101; CANR 34, 73
Rattigan, Terence (Mervyn) 1911-1977 **CLC 7; DAM DRAM**
See also CA 85-88; 73-76; CDBLB 1945-1960; DLB 13; MTCW 1, 2
Ratushinskaya, Irina 1954-   **CLC 54**
See also CA 129; CANR 68
Raven, Simon (Arthur Noel) 1927-   **CLC 14**
See also CA 81-84; CANR 86
Ravenna, Michael
See Welty, Eudora
Rawley, Callman 1903-
See Rakosi, Carl
See also CA 21-24R; CANR 12, 32
Rawlings, Marjorie Kinnan 1896-1953 **TCLC 4**
See also AAYA 20; CA 104; 137; CANR 74; DLB 9, 22, 102; DLBD 17; JRDA; MAICYA; MTCW 2; SATA 100; YABC 1
Ray, Satyajit 1921-1992   **CLC 16, 76; DAM MULT**
See also CA 114; 137
Read, Herbert Edward 1893-1968   **CLC 4**
See also CA 85-88; 25-28R; DLB 20, 149
Read, Piers Paul 1941-   **CLC 4, 10, 25**
See also CA 21-24R; CANR 38, 86; DLB 14; SATA 21
Reade, Charles 1814-1884   **NCLC 2, 74**
See also DLB 21
Reade, Hamish
See Gray, Simon (James Holliday)
Reading, Peter 1946-   **CLC 47**
See also CA 103; CANR 46; DLB 40
Reaney, James 1926-   **CLC 13; DAC; DAM MST**
See also CA 41-44R; CAAS 15; CANR 42; DLB 68; SATA 43
Rebreanu, Liviu 1885-1944   **TCLC 28**

See also CA 165
Rechy, John (Francisco) 1934- **CLC 1, 7, 14, 18, 107; DAM MULT; HLC 2**
See also CA 5-8R; CAAS 4; CANR 6, 32, 64; DLB 122; DLBY 82; HW 1, 2; INT CANR-6
Redcam, Tom 1870-1933   **TCLC 25**
Reddin, Keith   **CLC 67**
Redgrove, Peter (William) 1932- **CLC 6, 41**
See also CA 1-4R; CANR 3, 39, 77; DLB 40
Redmon, Anne   **CLC 22**
See also Nightingale, Anne Redmon
See also DLBY 86
Reed, Eliot
See Ambler, Eric
Reed, Ishmael 1938- **CLC 2, 3, 5, 6, 13, 32, 60; BLC 3; DAM MULT**
See also BW 2, 3; CA 21-24R; CANR 25, 48, 74; DA3; DLB 2, 5, 33, 169; DLBD 8; MTCW 1, 2
Reed, John (Silas) 1887-1920   **TCLC 9**
See also CA 106
Reed, Lou   **CLC 21**
See also Firbank, Louis
Reeve, Clara 1729-1807   **NCLC 19**
See also DLB 39
Reich, Wilhelm 1897-1957   **TCLC 57**
Reid, Christopher (John) 1949-   **CLC 33**
See also CA 140; DLB 40
Reid, Desmond
See Moorcock, Michael (John)
Reid Banks, Lynne 1929-
See Banks, Lynne Reid
See also CA 1-4R; CANR 6, 22, 38; CLR 24; JRDA; MAICYA; SATA 22, 75, 111
Reilly, William K.
See Creasey, John
Reiner, Max
See Caldwell, (Janet Miriam) Taylor (Holland)
Reis, Ricardo
See Pessoa, Fernando (Antonio Nogueira)
Remarque, Erich Maria 1898-1970 **CLC 21; DA; DAB; DAC; DAM MST, NOV**
See also AAYA 27; CA 77-80; 29-32R; DA3; DLB 56; MTCW 1, 2
Remington, Frederic 1861-1909   **TCLC 89**
See also CA 108; 169; DLB 12, 186, 188; SATA 41
Remizov, A.
See Remizov, Aleksei (Mikhailovich)
Remizov, A. M.
See Remizov, Aleksei (Mikhailovich)
Remizov, Aleksei (Mikhailovich) 1877-1957 **TCLC 27**
See also CA 125; 133
Renan, Joseph Ernest 1823-1892   **NCLC 26**
Renard, Jules 1864-1910   **TCLC 17**
See also CA 117
Renault, Mary   **CLC 3, 11, 17**
See also Challans, Mary
See also DLBY 83; MTCW 2
Rendell, Ruth (Barbara) 1930-   **CLC 28, 48; DAM POP**
See also Vine, Barbara
See also CA 109; CANR 32, 52, 74; DLB 87; INT CANR-32; MTCW 1, 2
Renoir, Jean 1894-1979   **CLC 20**
See also CA 129; 85-88
Resnais, Alain 1922-   **CLC 16**
Reverdy, Pierre 1889-1960   **CLC 53**
See also CA 97-100; 89-92
Rexroth, Kenneth 1905-1982 **CLC 1, 2, 6, 11, 22, 49, 112; DAM POET; PC 20**

See also CA 5-8R; 107; CANR 14, 34, 63; CDALB 1941-1968; DLB 16, 48, 165, 212; DLBY 82; INT CANR-14; MTCW 1, 2

Reyes, Alfonso 1889-1959 **TCLC 33; HLCS 2**
See also CA 131; HW 1

Reyes y Basoalto, Ricardo Eliecer Neftali
See Neruda, Pablo

Reymont, Wladyslaw (Stanislaw) 1868(?)-1925 **TCLC 5**
See also CA 104

Reynolds, Jonathan 1942- **CLC 6, 38**
See also CA 65-68; CANR 28

Reynolds, Joshua 1723-1792 **LC 15**
See also DLB 104

Reynolds, Michael Shane 1937- **CLC 44**
See also CA 65-68; CANR 9

Reznikoff, Charles 1894-1976 **CLC 9**
See also CA 33-36; 61-64; CAP 2; DLB 28, 45

Rezzori (d'Arezzo), Gregor von 1914-1998 **CLC 25**
See also CA 122; 136; 167

Rhine, Richard
See Silverstein, Alvin

Rhodes, Eugene Manlove 1869-1934 **TCLC 53**

Rhodius, Apollonius c. 3rd cent. B.C.- **CMLC 28**
See also DLB 176

R'hoone
See Balzac, Honore de

Rhys, Jean 1890(?)-1979 **CLC 2, 4, 6, 14, 19, 51, 124; DAM NOV; SSC 21**
See also CA 25-28R; 85-88; CANR 35, 62; CDBLB 1945-1960; DA3; DLB 36, 117, 162; MTCW 1, 2

Ribeiro, Darcy 1922-1997 **CLC 34**
See also CA 33-36R; 156

Ribeiro, Joao Ubaldo (Osorio Pimentel) 1941- **CLC 10, 67**
See also CA 81-84

Ribman, Ronald (Burt) 1932- **CLC 7**
See also CA 21-24R; CANR 46, 80

Ricci, Nino 1959- **CLC 70**
See also CA 137

Rice, Anne 1941- **CLC 41; DAM POP**
See also AAYA 9; BEST 89:2; CA 65-68; CANR 12, 36, 53, 74; DA3; MTCW 2

Rice, Elmer (Leopold) 1892-1967 **CLC 7, 49; DAM DRAM**
See also CA 21-22; 25-28R; CAP 2; DLB 4, 7; MTCW 1, 2

Rice, Tim(othy Miles Bindon) 1944- **CLC 21**
See also CA 103; CANR 46

Rich, Adrienne (Cecile) 1929- **CLC 3, 6, 7, 11, 18, 36, 73, 76, 125; DAM POET; PC 5**
See also CA 9-12R; CANR 20, 53, 74; CDALBS; DA3; DLB 5, 67; MTCW 1, 2

Rich, Barbara
See Graves, Robert (von Ranke)

Rich, Robert
See Trumbo, Dalton

Richard, Keith **CLC 17**
See also Richards, Keith

Richards, David Adams 1950- **CLC 59; DAC**
See also CA 93-96; CANR 60; DLB 53

Richards, I(vor) A(rmstrong) 1893-1979 **CLC 14, 24**
See also CA 41-44R; 89-92; CANR 34, 74; DLB 27; MTCW 2

Richards, Keith 1943-
See Richard, Keith
See also CA 107; CANR 77

Richardson, Anne
See Roiphe, Anne (Richardson)

Richardson, Dorothy Miller 1873-1957 **TCLC 3**
See also CA 104; DLB 36

Richardson, Ethel Florence (Lindesay) 1870-1946
See Richardson, Henry Handel
See also CA 105

Richardson, Henry Handel **TCLC 4**
See Richardson, Ethel Florence (Lindesay)
See also DLB 197

Richardson, John 1796-1852 **NCLC 55; DAC**
See also DLB 99

Richardson, Samuel 1689-1761 **LC 1, 44; DA; DAB; DAC; DAM MST, NOV; WLC**
See also CDBLB 1660-1789; DLB 39

Richler, Mordecai 1931- **CLC 3, 5, 9, 13, 18, 46, 70; DAC; DAM MST, NOV**
See also AITN 1; CA 65-68; CANR 31, 62; CLR 17; DLB 53; MAICYA; MTCW 1, 2; SATA 44, 98; SATA-Brief 27

Richter, Conrad (Michael) 1890-1968 **CLC 30**
See also AAYA 21; CA 5-8R; 25-28R; CANR 23; DLB 9, 212; MTCW 1, 2; SATA 3

Ricostranza, Tom
See Ellis, Trey

Riddell, Charlotte 1832-1906 **TCLC 40**
See also CA 165; DLB 156

Ridge, John Rollin 1827-1867 **NCLC 82; DAM MULT**
See also CA 144; DLB 175; NNAL

Ridgway, Keith 1965- **CLC 119**
See also CA 172

Riding, Laura **CLC 3, 7**
See also Jackson, Laura (Riding)

Riefenstahl, Berta Helene Amalia 1902-
See Riefenstahl, Leni
See also CA 108

Riefenstahl, Leni **CLC 16**
See also Riefenstahl, Berta Helene Amalia

Riffe, Ernest
See Bergman, (Ernst) Ingmar

Riggs, (Rolla) Lynn 1899-1954 **TCLC 56; DAM MULT**
See also CA 144; DLB 175; NNAL

Riis, Jacob A(ugust) 1849-1914 **TCLC 80**
See also CA 113; 168; DLB 23

Riley, James Whitcomb 1849-1916 **TCLC 51; DAM POET**
See also CA 118; 137; MAICYA; SATA 17

Riley, Tex
See Creasey, John

Rilke, Rainer Maria 1875-1926 **TCLC 1, 6, 19; DAM POET; PC 2**
See also CA 104; 132; CANR 62; DA3; DLB 81; MTCW 1, 2

Rimbaud, (Jean Nicolas) Arthur 1854-1891 **NCLC 4, 35, 82; DA; DAB; DAC; DAM MST, POET; PC 3; WLC**
See also DA3

Rinehart, Mary Roberts 1876-1958 **TCLC 52**
See also CA 108; 166

Ringmaster, The
See Mencken, H(enry) L(ouis)

Ringwood, Gwen(dolyn Margaret) Pharis 1910-1984 **CLC 48**
See also CA 148; 112; DLB 88

Rio, Michel 19(?)- **CLC 43**

Ritsos, Giannes
See Ritsos, Yannis

Ritsos, Yannis 1909-1990 **CLC 6, 13, 31**
See also CA 77-80; 133; CANR 39, 61; MTCW 1

Ritter, Erika 1948(?)- **CLC 52**

Rivera, Jose Eustasio 1889-1928 **TCLC 35**
See also CA 162; HW 1, 2

Rivera, Tomas 1935-1984
See also CA 49-52; CANR 32; DLB 82; HLCS 2; HW 1

Rivers, Conrad Kent 1933-1968 **CLC 1**
See also BW 1; CA 85-88; DLB 41

Rivers, Elfrida
See Bradley, Marion Zimmer

Riverside, John
See Heinlein, Robert A(nson)

Rizal, Jose 1861-1896 **NCLC 27**

Roa Bastos, Augusto (Antonio) 1917- **CLC 45; DAM MULT; HLC 2**
See also CA 131; DLB 113; HW 1

Robbe-Grillet, Alain 1922- **CLC 1, 2, 4, 6, 8, 10, 14, 43**
See also CA 9-12R; CANR 33, 65; DLB 83; MTCW 1, 2

Robbins, Harold 1916-1997 **CLC 5; DAM NOV**
See also CA 73-76; 162; CANR 26, 54; DA3; MTCW 1, 2

Robbins, Thomas Eugene 1936-
See Robbins, Tom
See also CA 81-84; CANR 29, 59; DAM NOV, POP; DA3; MTCW 1, 2

Robbins, Tom **CLC 9, 32, 64**
See also Robbins, Thomas Eugene
See also AAYA 32; BEST 90:3; DLBY 80; MTCW 2

Robbins, Trina 1938- **CLC 21**
See also CA 128

Roberts, Charles G(eorge) D(ouglas) 1860-1943 **TCLC 8**
See also CA 105; CLR 33; DLB 92; SATA 88; SATA-Brief 29

Roberts, Elizabeth Madox 1886-1941 **TCLC 68**
See also CA 111; 166; DLB 9, 54, 102; SATA 33; SATA-Brief 27

Roberts, Kate 1891-1985 **CLC 15**
See also CA 107; 116

Roberts, Keith (John Kingston) 1935- **CLC 14**
See also CA 25-28R; CANR 46

Roberts, Kenneth (Lewis) 1885-1957 **TCLC 23**
See also CA 109; DLB 9

Roberts, Michele (B.) 1949- **CLC 48**
See also CA 115; CANR 58

Robertson, Ellis
See Ellison, Harlan (Jay); Silverberg, Robert

Robertson, Thomas William 1829-1871 **NCLC 35; DAM DRAM**

Robeson, Kenneth
See Dent, Lester

Robinson, Edwin Arlington 1869-1935 **TCLC 5; DA; DAC; DAM MST, POET; PC 1**
See also CA 104; 133; CDALB 1865-1917; DLB 54; MTCW 1, 2

Robinson, Henry Crabb 1775-1867 **NCLC 15**
See also DLB 107

Robinson, Jill 1936- **CLC 10**
See also CA 102; INT 102

Robinson, Kim Stanley 1952- **CLC 34**
See also AAYA 26; CA 126; SATA 109

Robinson, Lloyd
See Silverberg, Robert

Robinson, Marilynne 1944- **CLC 25**
See also CA 116; CANR 80; DLB 206

Robinson, Smokey **CLC 21**
See also Robinson, William, Jr.

Robinson, William, Jr. 1940-
See Robinson, Smokey

See also CA 116

Robison, Mary 1949-   **CLC 42, 98**
See also CA 113; 116; DLB 130; INT 116

Rod, Edouard 1857-1910   **TCLC 52**

Roddenberry, Eugene Wesley 1921-1991
See Roddenberry, Gene
See also CA 110; 135; CANR 37; SATA 45;
SATA-Obit 69

Roddenberry, Gene   **CLC 17**
See also Roddenberry, Eugene Wesley
See also AAYA 5; SATA-Obit 69

Rodgers, Mary 1931-   **CLC 12**
See also CA 49-52; CANR 8, 55; CLR 20; INT
CANR-8; JRDA; MAICYA; SATA 8

Rodgers, W(illiam) R(obert) 1909-1969**CLC 7**
See also CA 85-88; DLB 20

Rodman, Eric
See Silverberg, Robert

Rodman, Howard 1920(?)-1985   **CLC 65**
See also CA 118

Rodman, Maia
See Wojciechowska, Maia (Teresa)

Rodo, Jose Enrique 1872(?)-1917
See also CA 178; HLCS 2; HW 2

Rodriguez, Claudio 1934-   **CLC 10**
See also DLB 134

Rodriguez, Richard 1944-
See also CA 110; CANR 66; DAM MULT; DLB
82; HLC 2; HW 1, 2

Roelvaag, O(le) E(dvart) 1876-1931**TCLC 17**
See also CA 117; 171; DLB 9

Roethke, Theodore (Huebner) 1908-1963**CLC
1, 3, 8, 11, 19, 46, 101; DAM POET; PC 15**
See also CA 81-84; CABS 2; CDALB 1941-
1968; DA3; DLB 5, 206; MTCW 1, 2

Rogers, Samuel 1763-1855   **NCLC 69**
See also DLB 93

Rogers, Thomas Hunton 1927-   **CLC 57**
See also CA 89-92; INT 89-92

Rogers, Will(iam Penn Adair) 1879-1935
TCLC 8, 71; DAM MULT
See also CA 105; 144; DA3; DLB 11; MTCW
2; NNAL

Rogin, Gilbert 1929-   **CLC 18**
See also CA 65-68; CANR 15

Rohan, Koda   **TCLC 22**
See also Koda Shigeyuki

Rohlfs, Anna Katharine Green
See Green, Anna Katharine

Rohmer, Eric   **CLC 16**
See also Scherer, Jean-Marie Maurice

Rohmer, Sax   **TCLC 28**
See also Ward, Arthur Henry Sarsfield
See also DLB 70

Roiphe, Anne (Richardson) 1935-   **CLC 3, 9**
See also CA 89-92; CANR 45, 73; DLBY 80;
INT 89-92

Rojas, Fernando de 1465-1541**LC 23; HLCS 1**

Rojas, Gonzalo 1917-
See also HLCS 2; HW 2

Rojas, Gonzalo 1917-
See also CA 178; HLCS 2

**Rolfe, Frederick (William Serafino Austin
Lewis Mary)** 1860-1913   **TCLC 12**
See also CA 107; DLB 34, 156

Rolland, Romain 1866-1944   **TCLC 23**
See also CA 118; DLB 65

Rolle, Richard c. 1300-c. 1349   **CMLC 21**
See also DLB 146

Rolvaag, O(le) E(dvart)
See Roelvaag, O(le) E(dvart)

Romain Arnaud, Saint
See Aragon, Louis

Romains, Jules 1885-1972   **CLC 7**
See also CA 85-88; CANR 34; DLB 65;
MTCW 1

Romero, Jose Ruben 1890-1952   **TCLC 14**
See also CA 114; 131; HW 1

Ronsard, Pierre de 1524-1585**LC 6, 54; PC 11**

Rooke, Leon 1934-   **CLC 25, 34; DAM POP**
See also CA 25-28R; CANR 23, 53

Roosevelt, Franklin Delano 1882-1945**TCLC
93**
See also CA 116; 173

Roosevelt, Theodore 1858-1919   **TCLC 69**
See also CA 115; 170; DLB 47, 186

Roper, William 1498-1578   **LC 10**

Roquelaure, A. N.
See Rice, Anne

Rosa, Joao Guimaraes 1908-1967   **CLC 23;
HLCS 1**
See also CA 89-92; DLB 113

Rose, Wendy 1948-**CLC 85; DAM MULT; PC
13**
See also CA 53-56; CANR 5, 51; DLB 175;
NNAL; SATA 12

Rosen, R. D.
See Rosen, Richard (Dean)

Rosen, Richard (Dean) 1949-   **CLC 39**
See also CA 77-80; CANR 62; INT CANR-30

Rosenberg, Isaac 1890-1918   **TCLC 12**
See also CA 107; DLB 20

Rosenblatt, Joe   **CLC 15**
See also Rosenblatt, Joseph

Rosenblatt, Joseph 1933-
See Rosenblatt, Joe
See also CA 89-92; INT 89-92

Rosenfeld, Samuel
See Tzara, Tristan

Rosenstock, Sami
See Tzara, Tristan

Rosenstock, Samuel
See Tzara, Tristan

Rosenthal, M(acha) L(ouis) 1917-1996   **CLC
28**
See also CA 1-4R; 152; CAAS 6; CANR 4, 51;
DLB 5; SATA 59

Ross, Barnaby
See Dannay, Frederic

Ross, Bernard L.
See Follett, Ken(neth Martin)

Ross, J. H.
See Lawrence, T(homas) E(dward)

Ross, John Hume
See Lawrence, T(homas) E(dward)

Ross, Martin
See Martin, Violet Florence
See also DLB 135

Ross, (James) Sinclair 1908-1996   **CLC 13;
DAC; DAM MST; SSC 24**
See also CA 73-76; CANR 81; DLB 88

Rossetti, Christina (Georgina) 1830-1894
**NCLC 2, 50, 66; DA; DAB; DAC; DAM
MST, POET; PC 7; WLC**
See also DA3; DLB 35, 163; MAICYA; SATA
20

Rossetti, Dante Gabriel 1828-1882 **NCLC 4,
77; DA; DAB; DAC; DAM MST, POET;
WLC**
See also CDBLB 1832-1890; DLB 35

Rossner, Judith (Perelman) 1935-**CLC 6, 9, 29**
See also AITN 2; BEST 90:3; CA 17-20R;
CANR 18, 51, 73; DLB 6; INT CANR-18;
MTCW 1, 2

Rostand, Edmond (Eugene Alexis) 1868-1918
**TCLC 6, 37; DA; DAB; DAC; DAM
DRAM, MST; DC 10**
See also CA 104; 126; DA3; DLB 192; MTCW 1

Roth, Henry 1906-1995   **CLC 2, 6, 11, 104**
See also CA 11-12; 149; CANR 38, 63; CAP 1;
DA3; DLB 28; MTCW 1, 2

Roth, Philip (Milton) 1933-**CLC 1, 2, 3, 4, 6, 9,
15, 22, 31, 47, 66, 86, 119; DA; DAB; DAC;
DAM MST, NOV, POP; SSC 26; WLC**
See also BEST 90:3; CA 1-4R; CANR 1, 22,
36, 55; CDALB 1968-1988; DA3; DLB 2,
28, 173; DLBY 82; MTCW 1, 2

Rothenberg, Jerome 1931-   **CLC 6, 57**
See also CA 45-48; CANR 1; DLB 5, 193

Roumain, Jacques (Jean Baptiste) 1907-1944
TCLC 19; BLC 3; DAM MULT
See also BW 1; CA 117; 125

Rourke, Constance (Mayfield) 1885-1941
TCLC 12
See also CA 107; YABC 1

Rousseau, Jean-Baptiste 1671-1741   **LC 9**

Rousseau, Jean-Jacques 1712-1778**LC 14, 36;
DA; DAB; DAC; DAM MST; WLC**
See also DA3

Roussel, Raymond 1877-1933   **TCLC 20**
See also CA 117

Rovit, Earl (Herbert) 1927-   **CLC 7**
See also CA 5-8R; CANR 12

Rowe, Elizabeth Singer 1674-1737   **LC 44**
See also DLB 39, 95

Rowe, Nicholas 1674-1718   **LC 8**
See also DLB 84

Rowley, Ames Dorrance
See Lovecraft, H(oward) P(hillips)

Rowson, Susanna Haswell 1762(?)-1824
NCLC 5, 69
See also DLB 37, 200

Roy, Arundhati 1960(?)-   **CLC 109**
See also CA 163; DLBY 97

Roy, Gabrielle 1909-1983 **CLC 10, 14; DAB;
DAC; DAM MST**
See also CA 53-56; 110; CANR 5, 61; DLB 68;
MTCW 1; SATA 104

Royko, Mike 1932-1997   **CLC 109**
See also CA 89-92; 157; CANR 26

Rozewicz, Tadeusz 1921-   **CLC 9, 23; DAM
POET**
See also CA 108; CANR 36, 66; DA3; MTCW
1, 2

Ruark, Gibbons 1941-   **CLC 3**
See also CA 33-36R; CAAS 23; CANR 14, 31,
57; DLB 120

Rubens, Bernice (Ruth) 1923-   **CLC 19, 31**
See also CA 25-28R; CANR 33, 65; DLB 14,
207; MTCW 1

Rubin, Harold
See Robbins, Harold

Rudkin, (James) David 1936-   **CLC 14**
See also CA 89-92; DLB 13

Rudnik, Raphael 1933-   **CLC 7**
See also CA 29-32R

Ruffian, M.
See Hasek, Jaroslav (Matej Frantisek)

Ruiz, Jose Martinez   **CLC 11**
See also Martinez Ruiz, Jose

Rukeyser, Muriel 1913-1980**CLC 6, 10, 15, 27;
DAM POET; PC 12**
See also CA 5-8R; 93-96; CANR 26, 60; DA3;
DLB 48; MTCW 1, 2; SATA-Obit 22

Rule, Jane (Vance) 1931-   **CLC 27**
See also CA 25-28R; CAAS 18; CANR 12; DLB
60

Rulfo, Juan 1918-1986   **CLC 8, 80; DAM
MULT; HLC 2; SSC 25**

See Crumb, R(obert)
Seabrook, John
    See Hubbard, L(afayette) Ron(ald)
Sealy, I. Allan 1951-   **CLC 55**
Search, Alexander
    See Pessoa, Fernando (Antonio Nogueira)
Sebastian, Lee
    See Silverberg, Robert
Sebastian Owl
    See Thompson, Hunter S(tockton)
Sebestyen, Ouida 1924-   **CLC 30**
    See also AAYA 8; CA 107; CANR 40; CLR 17;
        JRDA; MAICYA; SAAS 10; SATA 39
Secundus, H. Scriblerus
    See Fielding, Henry
Sedges, John
    See Buck, Pearl S(ydenstricker)
Sedgwick, Catharine Maria 1789-1867 **N C L C
    19**
    See also DLB 1, 74
Seelye, John (Douglas) 1931-   **CLC 7**
    See also CA 97-100; CANR 70; INT 97-100
Seferiades, Giorgos Stylianou 1900-1971
    See Seferis, George
    See also CA 5-8R; 33-36R; CANR 5, 36;
        MTCW 1
Seferis, George   **CLC 5, 11**
    See also Seferiades, Giorgos Stylianou
Segal, Erich (Wolf) 1937-   **CLC 3, 10; DAM
    POP**
    See also BEST 89:1; CA 25-28R; CANR 20,
        36, 65; DLBY 86; INT CANR-20; MTCW 1
Seger, Bob 1945-   **CLC 35**
Seghers, Anna   **CLC 7**
    See also Radvanyi, Netty
    See also DLB 69
Seidel, Frederick (Lewis) 1936-   **CLC 18**
    See also CA 13-16R; CANR 8; DLBY 84
Seifert, Jaroslav 1901-1986   **CLC 34, 44, 93**
    See also CA 127; MTCW 1, 2
Sei Shonagon c. 966-1017(?)   **CMLC 6**
Séjour, Victor 1817-1874   **DC 10**
    See also DLB 50
Sejour Marcou et Ferrand, Juan Victor
    See Séjour, Victor
Selby, Hubert, Jr. 1928- **CLC 1, 2, 4, 8; SSC 20**
    See also CA 13-16R; CANR 33, 85; DLB 2
Selzer, Richard 1928-   **CLC 74**
    See also CA 65-68; CANR 14
Sembene, Ousmane
    See Ousmane, Sembene
Senancour, Etienne Pivert de 1770-1846
    NCLC 16
    See also DLB 119
Sender, Ramon (Jose) 1902-1982 **CLC 8; DAM
    MULT; HLC 2**
    See also CA 5-8R; 105; CANR 8; HW 1;
        MTCW 1
Seneca, Lucius Annaeus c. 1-c. 65 **CMLC 6;
    DAM DRAM; DC 5**
    See also DLB 211
Senghor, Leopold Sedar 1906- **CLC 54; BLC
    3; DAM MULT, POET; PC 25**
    See also BW 2; CA 116; 125; CANR 47, 74;
        MTCW 1, 2
Senna, Danzy 1970-   **CLC 119**
    See also CA 169
Serling, (Edward) Rod(man) 1924-1975 **C L C
    30**
    See also AAYA 14; AITN 1; CA 162; 57-60;
        DLB 26
Serna, Ramon Gomez de la
    See Gomez de la Serna, Ramon

Serpieres
    See Guillevic, (Eugene)
Service, Robert
    See Service, Robert W(illiam)
    See also DAB; DLB 92
Service, Robert W(illiam) 1874(?)-1958**TCLC
    15; DA; DAC; DAM MST, POET; WLC**
    See also Service, Robert
    See also CA 115; 140; CANR 84; SATA 20
Seth, Vikram 1952-**CLC 43, 90; DAM MULT**
    See also CA 121; 127; CANR 50, 74; DA3; DLB
        120; INT 127; MTCW 2
Seton, Cynthia Propper 1926-1982   **CLC 27**
    See also CA 5-8R; 108; CANR 7
Seton, Ernest (Evan) Thompson 1860-1946
    TCLC 31
    See also CA 109; CLR 59; DLB 92; DLBD 13;
        JRDA; SATA 18
Seton-Thompson, Ernest
    See Seton, Ernest (Evan) Thompson
Settle, Mary Lee 1918-   **CLC 19, 61**
    See also CA 89-92; CAAS 1; CANR 44; DLB
        6; INT 89-92
Seuphor, Michel
    See Arp, Jean
**Sevigne, Marie (de Rabutin-Chantal) Marquise
    de** 1626-1696   **LC 11**
Sewall, Samuel 1652-1730   **LC 38**
    See also DLB 24
Sexton, Anne (Harvey) 1928-1974**CLC 2, 4, 6,
    8, 10, 15, 53; DA; DAB; DAC; DAM MST,
    POET; PC 2; WLC**
    See also CA 1-4R; 53-56; CABS 2; CANR 3,
        36; CDALB 1941-1968; DA3; DLB 5, 169;
        MTCW 1, 2; SATA 10
Shaara, Jeff 1952-   **CLC 119**
    See also CA 163
Shaara, Michael (Joseph, Jr.) 1929-1988**C L C
    15; DAM POP**
    See also AITN 1; CA 102; 125; CANR 52, 85;
        DLBY 83
Shackleton, C. C.
    See Aldiss, Brian W(ilson)
Shacochis, Bob   **CLC 39**
    See also Shacochis, Robert G.
Shacochis, Robert G. 1951-
    See Shacochis, Bob
    See also CA 119; 124; INT 124
Shaffer, Anthony (Joshua) 1926-   **CLC 19;
    DAM DRAM**
    See also CA 110; 116; DLB 13
Shaffer, Peter (Levin) 1926-**CLC 5, 14, 18, 37,
    60; DAB; DAM DRAM, MST; DC 7**
    See also CA 25-28R; CANR 25, 47, 74; CDBLB
        1960 to Present; DA3; DLB 13; MTCW 1, 2
Shakey, Bernard
    See Young, Neil
Shalamov, Varlam (Tikhonovich) 1907(?)-1982
    CLC 18
    See also CA 129; 105
Shamlu, Ahmad 1925-   **CLC 10**
Shammas, Anton 1951-   **CLC 55**
Shange, Ntozake 1948-**CLC 8, 25, 38, 74, 126;
    BLC 3; DAM DRAM, MULT; DC 3**
    See also AAYA 9; BW 2; CA 85-88; CABS 3;
        CANR 27, 48, 74; DA3; DLB 38; MTCW 1,
        2
Shanley, John Patrick 1950-   **CLC 75**
    See also CA 128; 133; CANR 83
Shapcott, Thomas W(illiam) 1935-   **CLC 38**
    See also CA 69-72; CANR 49, 83
Shapiro, Jane   **CLC 76**
Shapiro, Karl (Jay) 1913- **CLC 4, 8, 15, 53;**

    PC 25
    See also CA 1-4R; CAAS 6; CANR 1, 36, 66;
        DLB 48; MTCW 1, 2
Sharp, William 1855-1905   **TCLC 39**
    See also CA 160; DLB 156
Sharpe, Thomas Ridley 1928-
    See Sharpe, Tom
    See also CA 114; 122; CANR 85; INT 122
Sharpe, Tom   **CLC 36**
    See also Sharpe, Thomas Ridley
    See also DLB 14
Shaw, Bernard   **TCLC 45**
    See also Shaw, George Bernard
    See also BW 1; MTCW 2
Shaw, G. Bernard
    See Shaw, George Bernard
Shaw, George Bernard 1856-1950**TCLC 3, 9,
    21; DA; DAB; DAC; DAM DRAM, MST;
    WLC**
    See also Shaw, Bernard
    See also CA 104; 128; CDBLB 1914-1945;
        DA3; DLB 10, 57, 190; MTCW 1, 2
Shaw, Henry Wheeler 1818-1885   **NCLC 15**
    See also DLB 11
Shaw, Irwin 1913-1984 **CLC 7, 23, 34; DAM
    DRAM, POP**
    See also AITN 1; CA 13-16R; 112; CANR 21;
        CDALB 1941-1968; DLB 6, 102; DLBY 84;
        MTCW 1, 21
Shaw, Robert 1927-1978   **CLC 5**
    See also AITN 1; CA 1-4R; 81-84; CANR 4;
        DLB 13, 14
Shaw, T. E.
    See Lawrence, T(homas) E(dward)
Shawn, Wallace 1943-   **CLC 41**
    See also CA 112
Shea, Lisa 1953-   **CLC 86**
    See also CA 147
Sheed, Wilfrid (John Joseph) 1930-**CLC 2, 4,
    10, 53**
    See also CA 65-68; CANR 30, 66; DLB 6;
        MTCW 1, 2
Sheldon, Alice Hastings Bradley 1915(?)-1987
    See Tiptree, James, Jr.
    See also CA 108; 122; CANR 34; INT 108;
        MTCW 1
Sheldon, John
    See Bloch, Robert (Albert)
Shelley, Mary Wollstonecraft (Godwin) 1797-
    1851**NCLC 14, 59; DA; DAB; DAC; DAM
    MST, NOV; WLC**
    See also AAYA 20; CDBLB 1789-1832; DA3;
        DLB 110, 116, 159, 178; SATA 29
Shelley, Percy Bysshe 1792-1822   **NCLC 18;
    DA; DAB; DAC; DAM MST, POET; PC
    14; WLC**
    See also CDBLB 1789-1832; DA3; DLB 96,
        110, 158
Shepard, Jim 1956-   **CLC 36**
    See also CA 137; CANR 59; SATA 90
Shepard, Lucius 1947-   **CLC 34**
    See also CA 128; 141; CANR 81
Shepard, Sam 1943- **CLC 4, 6, 17, 34, 41, 44;
    DAM DRAM; DC 5**
    See also AAYA 1; CA 69-72; CABS 3; CANR
        22; DA3; DLB 7, 212; MTCW 1, 2
Shepherd, Michael
    See Ludlum, Robert
Sherburne, Zoa (Lillian Morin) 1912-1995
    CLC 30
    See also AAYA 13; CA 1-4R; 176; CANR 3,
        37; MAICYA; SAAS 18; SATA 3
Sheridan, Frances 1724-1766   **LC 7**

See also DLB 39, 84

Sheridan, Richard Brinsley 1751-1816 N C L C
5; DA; DAB; DAC; DAM DRAM, MST;
DC 1; WLC
See also CDBLB 1660-1789; DLB 89

Sherman, Jonathan Marc   **CLC 55**

Sherman, Martin 1941(?)-   **CLC 19**
See also CA 116; 123; CANR 86

Sherwin, Judith Johnson 1936-
See Johnson, Judith (Emlyn)
See also CANR 85

Sherwood, Frances 1940-   **CLC 81**
See also CA 146

Sherwood, Robert E(mmet) 1896-1955 T C L C
3; DAM DRAM
See also CA 104; 153; CANR 86; DLB 7, 26

Shestov, Lev 1866-1938   **TCLC 56**

Shevchenko, Taras 1814-1861   **NCLC 54**

Shiel, M(atthew) P(hipps) 1865-1947 TCLC 8
See also Holmes, Gordon
See also CA 106; 160; DLB 153; MTCW 2

Shields, Carol 1935-   **CLC 91, 113; DAC**
See also CA 81-84; CANR 51, 74; DA3; MTCW
2

Shields, David 1956-   **CLC 97**
See also CA 124; CANR 48

Shiga, Naoya 1883-1971   **CLC 33; SSC 23**
See also CA 101; 33-36R; DLB 180

Shikibu, Murasaki c. 978-c. 1014   **CMLC 1**

Shilts, Randy 1951-1994   **CLC 85**
See also AAYA 19; CA 115; 127; 144; CANR
45; DA3; INT 127; MTCW 2

Shimazaki, Haruki 1872-1943
See Shimazaki Toson
See also CA 105; 134; CANR 84

Shimazaki Toson 1872-1943   **TCLC 5**
See also Shimazaki, Haruki
See also DLB 180

Sholokhov, Mikhail (Aleksandrovich) 1905-
1984   **CLC 7, 15**
See also CA 101; 112; MTCW 1, 2; SATA-Obit
36

Shone, Patric
See Hanley, James

Shreve, Susan Richards 1939-   **CLC 23**
See also CA 49-52; CAAS 5; CANR 5, 38, 69;
MAICYA; SATA 46, 95; SATA-Brief 41

Shue, Larry 1946-1985 CLC 52; DAM DRAM
See also CA 145; 117

Shu-Jen, Chou 1881-1936
See Lu Hsun
See also CA 104

Shulman, Alix Kates 1932-   **CLC 2, 10**
See also CA 29-32R; CANR 43; SATA 7

Shuster, Joe 1914-   **CLC 21**

Shute, Nevil   **CLC 30**
See also Norway, Nevil Shute
See also MTCW 2

Shuttle, Penelope (Diane) 1947-   **CLC 7**
See also CA 93-96; CANR 39, 84; DLB 14, 40

Sidney, Mary 1561-1621   **LC 19, 39**

Sidney, Sir Philip 1554-1586 LC 19, 39; DA;
DAB; DAC; DAM MST, POET
See also CDBLB Before 1660; DA3; DLB 167

Siegel, Jerome 1914-1996   **CLC 21**
See also CA 116; 169; 151

Siegel, Jerry
See Siegel, Jerome

Sienkiewicz, Henryk (Adam Alexander Pius)
1846-1916   **TCLC 3**
See also CA 104; 134; CANR 84

Sierra, Gregorio Martinez
See Martinez Sierra, Gregorio

Sierra, Maria (de la O'LeJarraga) Martinez
See Martinez Sierra, Maria (de la O'LeJarraga)

Sigal, Clancy 1926-   **CLC 7**
See also CA 1-4R; CANR 85

Sigourney, Lydia Howard (Huntley) 1791-1865
NCLC 21
See also DLB 1, 42, 73

Siguenza y Gongora, Carlos de 1645-1700 L C
8; HLCS 2

Sigurjonsson, Johann 1880-1919   **TCLC 27**
See also CA 170

Sikelianos, Angelos 1884-1951   **TCLC 39**

Silkin, Jon 1930-   **CLC 2, 6, 43**
See also CA 5-8R; CAAS 5; DLB 27

Silko, Leslie (Marmon) 1948-CLC 23, 74, 114;
DA; DAC; DAM MST, MULT, POP; SSC
37; WLCS
See also AAYA 14; CA 115; 122; CANR 45,
65; DA3; DLB 143, 175; MTCW 2; NNAL

Sillanpaa, Frans Eemil 1888-1964   **CLC 19**
See also CA 129; 93-96; MTCW 1

Sillitoe, Alan 1928-   CLC 1, 3, 6, 10, 19, 57
See also AITN 1; CA 9-12R; CAAS 2; CANR
8, 26, 55; CDBLB 1960 to Present; DLB 14,
139; MTCW 1, 2; SATA 61

Silone, Ignazio 1900-1978   **CLC 4**
See also CA 25-28; 81-84; CANR 34; CAP 2;
MTCW 1

Silver, Joan Micklin 1935-   **CLC 20**
See also CA 114; 121; INT 121

Silver, Nicholas
See Faust, Frederick (Schiller)

Silverberg, Robert 1935- CLC 7; DAM POP
See also AAYA 24; CA 1-4R; CAAS 3; CANR
1, 20, 36, 85; CLR 59; DLB 8; INT CANR-
20; MAICYA; MTCW 1, 2; SATA 13, 91;
SATA-Essay 104

Silverstein, Alvin 1933-   **CLC 17**
See also CA 49-52; CANR 2; CLR 25; JRDA;
MAICYA; SATA 8, 69

Silverstein, Virginia B(arbara Opshelor) 1937-
CLC 17
See also CA 49-52; CANR 2; CLR 25; JRDA;
MAICYA; SATA 8, 69

Sim, Georges
See Simenon, Georges (Jacques Christian)

Simak, Clifford D(onald) 1904-1988CLC 1, 55
See also CA 1-4R; 125; CANR 1, 35; DLB 8;
MTCW 1; SATA-Obit 56

Simenon, Georges (Jacques Christian) 1903-
1989   CLC 1, 2, 3, 8, 18, 47; DAM POP
See also CA 85-88; 129; CANR 35; DA3; DLB
72; DLBY 89; MTCW 1, 2

Simic, Charles 1938-   CLC 6, 9, 22, 49, 68;
DAM POET
See also CA 29-32R; CAAS 4; CANR 12, 33,
52, 61; DA3; DLB 105; MTCW 2

Simmel, Georg 1858-1918   **TCLC 64**
See also CA 157

Simmons, Charles (Paul) 1924-   **CLC 57**
See also CA 89-92; INT 89-92

Simmons, Dan 1948-   CLC 44; DAM POP
See also AAYA 16; CA 138; CANR 53, 81

Simmons, James (Stewart Alexander) 1933-
CLC 43
See also CA 105; CAAS 21; DLB 40

Simms, William Gilmore 1806-1870   **NCLC 3**
See also DLB 3, 30, 59, 73

Simon, Carly 1945-   **CLC 26**
See also CA 105

Simon, Claude 1913-1984   CLC 4, 9, 15, 39;
DAM NOV
See also CA 89-92; CANR 33; DLB 83;

MTCW 1

Simon, (Marvin) Neil 1927-CLC 6, 11, 31, 39,
70; DAM DRAM
See also AAYA 32; AITN 1; CA 21-24R; CANR
26, 54; DA3; DLB 7; MTCW 1, 2

Simon, Paul (Frederick) 1941(?)-   **CLC 17**
See also CA 116; 153

Simonon, Paul 1956(?)-   **CLC 30**

Simpson, Harriette
See Arnow, Harriette (Louisa) Simpson

Simpson, Louis (Aston Marantz) 1923-CLC 4,
7, 9, 32; DAM POET
See also CA 1-4R; CAAS 4; CANR 1, 61; DLB
5; MTCW 1, 2

Simpson, Mona (Elizabeth) 1957-   **CLC 44**
See also CA 122; 135; CANR 68

Simpson, N(orman) F(rederick) 1919-CLC 29
See also CA 13-16R; DLB 13

Sinclair, Andrew (Annandale) 1935-   CLC 2,
14
See also CA 9-12R; CAAS 5; CANR 14, 38;
DLB 14; MTCW 1

Sinclair, Emil
See Hesse, Hermann

Sinclair, Iain 1943-   **CLC 76**
See also CA 132; CANR 81

Sinclair, Iain MacGregor
See Sinclair, Iain

Sinclair, Irene
See Griffith, D(avid Lewelyn) W(ark)

Sinclair, Mary Amelia St. Clair 1865(?)-1946
See Sinclair, May
See also CA 104

Sinclair, May 1863-1946   **TCLC 3, 11**
See also Sinclair, Mary Amelia St. Clair
See also CA 166; DLB 36, 135

Sinclair, Roy
See Griffith, D(avid Lewelyn) W(ark)

Sinclair, Upton (Beall) 1878-1968 CLC 1, 11,
15, 63; DA; DAB; DAC; DAM MST, NOV;
WLC
See also CA 5-8R; 25-28R; CANR 7; CDALB
1929-1941; DA3; DLB 9; INT CANR-7;
MTCW 1, 2; SATA 9

Singer, Isaac
See Singer, Isaac Bashevis

Singer, Isaac Bashevis 1904-1991CLC 1, 3, 6,
9, 11, 15, 23, 38, 69, 111; DA; DAB; DAC;
DAM MST, NOV; SSC 3; WLC
See also AAYA 32; AITN 1, 2; CA 1-4R; 134;
CANR 1, 39; CDALB 1941-1968; CLR 1;
DA3; DLB 6, 28, 52; DLBY 91; JRDA;
MAICYA; MTCW 1, 2; SATA 3, 27; SATA-
Obit 68

Singer, Israel Joshua 1893-1944   **TCLC 33**
See also CA 169

Singh, Khushwant 1915-   **CLC 11**
See also CA 9-12R; CAAS 9; CANR 6, 84

Singleton, Ann
See Benedict, Ruth (Fulton)

Sinjohn, John
See Galsworthy, John

Sinyavsky, Andrei (Donatevich) 1925-1997
CLC 8
See also CA 85-88; 159

Sirin, V.
See Nabokov, Vladimir (Vladimirovich)

Sissman, L(ouis) E(dward) 1928-1976CLC 9,
18
See also CA 21-24R; 65-68; CANR 13; DLB 5

Sisson, C(harles) H(ubert) 1914-   **CLC 8**
See also CA 1-4R; CAAS 3; CANR 3, 48,
84; DLB 27

Trimball, W. H.
   See Mencken, H(enry) L(ouis)
Tristan
   See Gomez de la Serna, Ramon
Tristram
   See Housman, A(lfred) E(dward)
Trogdon, William (Lewis) 1939-
   See Heat-Moon, William Least
   See also CA 115; 119; CANR 47; INT 119
Trollope, Anthony 1815-1882 NCLC 6, 33; DA;
   DAB; DAC; DAM MST, NOV; SSC 28;
   WLC
   See also CDBLB 1832-1890; DA3; DLB 21,
   57, 159; SATA 22
Trollope, Frances 1779-1863   NCLC 30
   See also DLB 21, 166
Trotsky, Leon 1879-1940   TCLC 22
   See also CA 118; 167
Trotter (Cockburn), Catharine 1679-1749 L C
   8
   See also DLB 84
Trotter, Wilfred 1872-1939   TCLC 99
Trout, Kilgore
   See Farmer, Philip Jose
Trow, George W. S. 1943-   CLC 52
   See also CA 126
Troyat, Henri 1911-   CLC 23
   See also CA 45-48; CANR 2, 33, 67; MTCW 1
Trudeau, G(arretson) B(eekman) 1948-
   See Trudeau, Garry B.
   See also CA 81-84; CANR 31; SATA 35
Trudeau, Garry B.   CLC 12
   See also Trudeau, G(arretson) B(eekman)
   See also AAYA 10; AITN 2
Truffaut, Francois 1932-1984   CLC 20, 101
   See also CA 81-84; 113; CANR 34
Trumbo, Dalton 1905-1976   CLC 19
   See also CA 21-24R; 69-72; CANR 10; DLB
   26
Trumbull, John 1750-1831   NCLC 30
   See also DLB 31
Trundlett, Helen B.
   See Eliot, T(homas) S(tearns)
Tryon, Thomas 1926-1991 CLC 3, 11; DAM
   POP
   See also AITN 1; CA 29-32R; 135; CANR 32,
   77; DA3; MTCW 1
Tryon, Tom
   See Tryon, Thomas
Ts'ao Hsueh-ch'in 1715(?)-1763   LC 1
Tsushima, Shuji 1909-1948
   See Dazai Osamu
   See also CA 107
Tsvetaeva (Efron), Marina (Ivanovna) 1892-
   1941   TCLC 7, 35; PC 14
   See also CA 104; 128; CANR 73; MTCW 1, 2
Tuck, Lily 1938-   CLC 70
   See also CA 139
Tu Fu 712-770   PC 9
   See also DAM MULT
Tunis, John R(oberts) 1889-1975   CLC 12
   See also CA 61-64; CANR 62; DLB 22, 171;
   JRDA; MAICYA; SATA 37; SATA-Brief 30
Tuohy, Frank   CLC 37
   See also Tuohy, John Francis
   See also DLB 14, 139
Tuohy, John Francis 1925-1999
   See Tuohy, Frank
   See also CA 5-8R; 178; CANR 3, 47
Turco, Lewis (Putnam) 1934-   CLC 11, 63
   See also CA 13-16R; CAAS 22; CANR 24, 51;
   DLBY 84
Turgenev, Ivan 1818-1883   NCLC 21; DA;

DAB; DAC; DAM MST, NOV; DC 7; SSC
7; WLC
Turgot, Anne-Robert-Jacques 1727-1781 L C
   26
Turner, Frederick 1943-   CLC 48
   See also CA 73-76; CAAS 10; CANR 12, 30,
   56; DLB 40
Tutu, Desmond M(pilo) 1931- CLC 80; BLC 3;
   DAM MULT
   See also BW 1, 3; CA 125; CANR 67, 81
Tutuola, Amos 1920-1997 CLC 5, 14, 29; BLC
   3; DAM MULT
   See also BW 2, 3; CA 9-12R; 159; CANR 27,
   66; DA3; DLB 125; MTCW 1, 2
Twain, Mark TCLC 6, 12, 19, 36, 48, 59; SSC
   34; WLC
   See also Clemens, Samuel Langhorne
   See also AAYA 20; CLR 58, 60; DLB 11, 12,
   23, 64, 74
Tyler, Anne 1941- CLC 7, 11, 18, 28, 44, 59,
   103; DAM NOV, POP
   See also AAYA 18; BEST 89:1; CA 9-12R;
   CANR 11, 33, 53; CDALBS; DLB 6, 143;
   DLBY 82; MTCW 1, 2; SATA 7, 90
Tyler, Royall 1757-1826   NCLC 3
   See also DLB 37
Tynan, Katharine 1861-1931   TCLC 3
   See also CA 104; 167; DLB 153
Tyutchev, Fyodor 1803-1873   NCLC 34
Tzara, Tristan 1896-1963   CLC 47; DAM
   POET; PC 27
   See also CA 153; 89-92; MTCW 2
Uhry, Alfred 1936-   CLC 55; DAM DRAM,
   POP
   See also CA 127; 133; DA3; INT 133
Ulf, Haerved
   See Strindberg, (Johan) August
Ulf, Harved
   See Strindberg, (Johan) August
Ulibarri, Sabine R(eyes) 1919- CLC 83; DAM
   MULT; HLCS 2
   See also CA 131; CANR 81; DLB 82; HW 1, 2
Unamuno (y Jugo), Miguel de 1864-1936
   TCLC 2, 9; DAM MULT, NOV; HLC 2;
   SSC 11
   See also CA 104; 131; CANR 81; DLB 108;
   HW 1, 2; MTCW 1, 2
Uncliffe, Errol
   See Campbell, (John) Ramsey
Underwood, Miles
   See Glassco, John
Undset, Sigrid 1882-1949 TCLC 3; DA; DAB;
   DAC; DAM MST, NOV; WLC
   See also CA 104; 129; DA3; MTCW 1, 2
Ungaretti, Giuseppe 1888-1970 CLC 7, 11, 15
   See also CA 19-20; 25-28R; CAP 2; DLB 114
Unger, Douglas 1952-   CLC 34
   See also CA 130
Unsworth, Barry (Forster) 1930-   CLC 76
   See also CA 25-28R; CANR 30, 54; DLB 194
Updike, John (Hoyer) 1932- CLC 1, 2, 3, 5, 7,
   9, 13, 15, 23, 34, 43, 70; DA; DAB; DAC;
   DAM MST, NOV, POET, POP; SSC 13, 27;
   WLC
   See also CA 1-4R; CABS 1; CANR 4, 33, 51;
   CDALB 1968-1988; DA3; DLB 2, 5, 143;
   DLBD 3; DLBY 80, 82, 97; MTCW 1, 2
Upshaw, Margaret Mitchell
   See Mitchell, Margaret (Munnerlyn)
Upton, Mark
   See Sanders, Lawrence
Upward, Allen 1863-1926   TCLC 85
   See also CA 117; DLB 36

Urdang, Constance (Henriette) 1922- CLC 47
   See also CA 21-24R; CANR 9, 24
Uriel, Henry
   See Faust, Frederick (Schiller)
Uris, Leon (Marcus) 1924- CLC 7, 32; DAM
   NOV, POP
   See also AITN 1, 2; BEST 89:2; CA 1-4R;
   CANR 1, 40, 65; DA3; MTCW 1, 2; SATA
   49
Urista, Alberto H. 1947-
   See Alurista
   See also CA 45-48, 182; CANR 2, 32; HLCS 1;
   HW 1
Urmuz
   See Codrescu, Andrei
Urquhart, Guy
   See McAlmon, Robert (Menzies)
Urquhart, Jane 1949-   CLC 90; DAC
   See also CA 113; CANR 32, 68
Usigli, Rodolfo 1905-1979
   See also CA 131; HLCS 1; HW 1
Ustinov, Peter (Alexander) 1921-   CLC 1
   See also AITN 1; CA 13-16R; CANR 25, 51;
   DLB 13; MTCW 2
U Tam'si, Gerald Felix Tchicaya
   See Tchicaya, Gerald Felix
U Tam'si, Tchicaya
   See Tchicaya, Gerald Felix
Vachss, Andrew (Henry) 1942-   CLC 106
   See also CA 118; CANR 44
Vachss, Andrew H.
   See Vachss, Andrew (Henry)
Vaculik, Ludvik 1926-   CLC 7
   See also CA 53-56; CANR 72
Vaihinger, Hans 1852-1933   TCLC 71
   See also CA 116; 166
Valdez, Luis (Miguel) 1940- CLC 84; DAM
   MULT; DC 10; HLC 2
   See also CA 101; CANR 32, 81; DLB 122; HW
   1
Valenzuela, Luisa 1938- CLC 31, 104; DAM
   MULT; HLCS 2; SSC 14
   See also CA 101; CANR 32, 65; DLB 113; HW
   1, 2
Valera y Alcala-Galiano, Juan 1824-1905
   TCLC 10
   See also CA 106
Valery, (Ambroise) Paul (Toussaint Jules) 1871-
   1945   TCLC 4, 15; DAM POET; PC 9
   See also CA 104; 122; DA3; MTCW 1, 2
Valle-Inclan, Ramon (Maria) del 1866-1936
   TCLC 5; DAM MULT; HLC 2
   See also CA 106; 153; CANR 80; DLB 134;
   HW 2
Vallejo, Antonio Buero
   See Buero Vallejo, Antonio
Vallejo, Cesar (Abraham) 1892-1938 TCLC 3,
   56; DAM MULT; HLC 2
   See also CA 105; 153; HW 1
Valles, Jules 1832-1885   NCLC 71
   See also DLB 123
Vallette, Marguerite Eymery
   See Rachilde
Valle Y Pena, Ramon del
   See Valle-Inclan, Ramon (Maria) del
Van Ash, Cay 1918-   CLC 34
Vanbrugh, Sir John 1664-1726 LC 21; DAM
   DRAM
   See also DLB 80
Van Campen, Karl
   See Campbell, John W(ood, Jr.)
Vance, Gerald
   See Silverberg, Robert

See also CA 5-8R; 139; CANR 10, 43; DLB 2; DLBY 81, 92; INT CANR-10

Yeats, W. B.
See Yeats, William Butler

Yeats, William Butler 1865-1939**TCLC 1, 11, 18, 31, 93; DA; DAB; DAC; DAM DRAM, MST, POET; PC 20; WLC**
See also CA 104; 127; CANR 45; CDBLB 1890-1914; DA3; DLB 10, 19, 98, 156; MTCW 1, 2

Yehoshua, A(braham) B. 1936-   **CLC 13, 31**
See also CA 33-36R; CANR 43

Yellow Bird
See Ridge, John Rollin

Yep, Laurence Michael 1948-   **CLC 35**
See also AAYA 5, 31; CA 49-52; CANR 1, 46; CLR 3, 17, 54; DLB 52; JRDA; MAICYA; SATA 7, 69

Yerby, Frank G(arvin) 1916-1991   **CLC 1, 7, 22; BLC 3; DAM MULT**
See also BW 1, 3; CA 9-12R; 136; CANR 16, 52; DLB 76; INT CANR-16; MTCW 1

Yesenin, Sergei Alexandrovich
See Esenin, Sergei (Alexandrovich)

Yevtushenko, Yevgeny (Alexandrovich) 1933-**CLC 1, 3, 13, 26, 51, 126; DAM POET**
See also CA 81-84; CANR 33, 54; MTCW 1

Yezierska, Anzia 1885(?)-1970   **CLC 46**
See also CA 126; 89-92; DLB 28; MTCW 1

Yglesias, Helen 1915-   **CLC 7, 22**
See also CA 37-40R; CAAS 20; CANR 15, 65; INT CANR-15; MTCW 1

Yokomitsu Riichi 1898-1947   **TCLC 47**
See also CA 170

Yonge, Charlotte (Mary) 1823-1901**TCLC 48**
See also CA 109; 163; DLB 18, 163; SATA 17

York, Jeremy
See Creasey, John

York, Simon
See Heinlein, Robert A(nson)

Yorke, Henry Vincent 1905-1974   **CLC 13**
See also Green, Henry
See also CA 85-88; 49-52

Yosano Akiko 1878-1942   **TCLC 59; PC 11**
See also CA 161

Yoshimoto, Banana   **CLC 84**
See also Yoshimoto, Mahoko

Yoshimoto, Mahoko 1964-
See Yoshimoto, Banana

See also CA 144

Young, Al(bert James) 1939-   **CLC 19; BLC 3; DAM MULT**
See also BW 2, 3; CA 29-32R; CANR 26, 65; DLB 33

Young, Andrew (John) 1885-1971   **CLC 5**
See also CA 5-8R; CANR 7, 29

Young, Collier
See Bloch, Robert (Albert)

Young, Edward 1683-1765   **LC 3, 40**
See also DLB 95

Young, Marguerite (Vivian) 1909-1995 **CLC 82**
See also CA 13-16; 150; CAP 1

Young, Neil 1945-   **CLC 17**
See also CA 110

Young Bear, Ray A. 1950-   **CLC 94; DAM MULT**
See also CA 146; DLB 175; NNAL

Yourcenar, Marguerite 1903-1987**CLC 19, 38, 50, 87; DAM NOV**
See also CA 69-72; CANR 23, 60; DLB 72; DLBY 88; MTCW 1, 2

Yuan, Chu 340(?)B.C.-278(?)B.C.   **CMLC 36**

Yurick, Sol 1925-   **CLC 6**
See also CA 13-16R; CANR 25

Zabolotsky, Nikolai Alekseevich 1903-1958
TCLC 52
See also CA 116; 164

Zagajewski, Adam   **PC 27**

Zamiatin, Yevgenii
See Zamyatin, Evgeny Ivanovich

Zamora, Bernice (B. Ortiz) 1938-   **CLC 89; DAM MULT; HLC 2**
See also CA 151; CANR 80; DLB 82; HW 1, 2

Zamyatin, Evgeny Ivanovich 1884-1937**TCLC 8, 37**
See also CA 105; 166

Zangwill, Israel 1864-1926   **TCLC 16**
See also CA 109; 167; DLB 10, 135, 197

Zappa, Francis Vincent, Jr. 1940-1993
See Zappa, Frank
See also CA 108; 143; CANR 57

Zappa, Frank   **CLC 17**
See also Zappa, Francis Vincent, Jr.

Zaturenska, Marya 1902-1982   **CLC 6, 11**
See also CA 13-16R; 105; CANR 22

Zeami 1363-1443   **DC 7**

Zelazny, Roger (Joseph) 1937-1995 **CLC 21**
See also AAYA 7; CA 21-24R; 148; CANR 26, 60;

DLB 8; MTCW 1, 2; SATA 57; SATA-Brief 39

Zhdanov, Andrei Alexandrovich 1896-1948**TCLC 18**
See also CA 117; 167

Zhukovsky, Vasily (Andreevich) 1783-1852**NCLC 35**
See also DLB 205

Ziegenhagen, Eric   **CLC 55**

Zimmer, Jill Schary
See Robinson, Jill

Zimmerman, Robert
See Dylan, Bob

Zindel, Paul 1936-**CLC 6, 26; DA; DAB; DAC; DAM DRAM, MST, NOV; DC 5**
See also AAYA 2; CA 73-76; CANR 31, 65; CDALBS; CLR 3, 45; DA3; DLB 7, 52; JRDA; MAICYA; MTCW 1, 2; SATA 16, 58, 102

Zinov'Ev, A. A.
See Zinoviev, Alexander (Aleksandrovich)

Zinoviev, Alexander (Aleksandrovich) 1922-
CLC 19
See also CA 116; 133; CAAS 10

Zoilus
See Lovecraft, H(oward) P(hillips)

Zola, Emile (Edouard Charles Antoine) 1840-1902**TCLC 1, 6, 21, 41; DA; DAB; DAC; DAM MST, NOV; WLC**
See also CA 104; 138; DA3; DLB 123

Zoline, Pamela 1941-   **CLC 62**
See also CA 161

Zorrilla y Moral, Jose 1817-1893   **NCLC 6**

Zoshchenko, Mikhail (Mikhailovich) 1895-1958
TCLC 15; SSC 15
See also CA 115; 160

Zuckmayer, Carl 1896-1977   **CLC 18**
See also CA 69-72; DLB 56, 124

Zuk, Georges
See Skelton, Robin

Zukofsky, Louis 1904-1978**CLC 1, 2, 4, 7, 11, 18; DAM POET; PC 11**
See also CA 9-12R; 77-80; CANR 39; DLB 5, 165; MTCW 1

Zweig, Paul 1935-1984   **CLC 34, 42**
See also CA 85-88; 113

Zweig, Stefan 1881-1942   **TCLC 17**
See also CA 112; 170; DLB 81, 118

Zwingli, Huldreich 1484-1531   **LC 37**
See also DLB 179

Literary Criticism Series
Cumulative Topic Index

This index lists all topic entries in Gale's *Classical and Medieval Literature Criticism, Contemporary Literary Criticism, Literature Criticism from 1400 to 1800, Nineteenth-Century Literature Criticism,* and *Twentieth-Century Literary Criticism.*

Topic Index

Topic Index

Topic Index

Symbolist Movement, French NCLC 20:
169-249
  background and characteristics, 170-86
  principles, 186-91
  attacked and defended, 191-7
  influences and predecessors, 197-211
  and Decadence, 211-6
  theater, 216-26
  prose, 226-33
  decline and influence, 233-47

Television and Literature TCLC 78: 283-
426
  television and literacy, 283-98
  reading vs. watching, 298-341
  adaptations, 341-62
  literary genres and television, 362-90
  television genres and literature, 390-410
  children's literature/children's television,
    410-25

Theater of the Absurd TCLC 38: 339-415
  "The Theater of the Absurd," 340-7
  major plays and playwrights, 347-58
  and the concept of the absurd, 358-86
  theatrical techniques, 386-94
  predecessors of, 394-402
  influence of, 402-13

Tin Pan Alley
See **American Popular Song, Golden Age
of**

Transcendentalism, American NCLC 24:
1-99
  overviews, 3-23
  contemporary documents, 23-41
  theological aspects of, 42-52
  and social issues, 52-74
  literature of, 74-96

Travel Writing in the Nineteenth Century
NCLC 44: 274-392
  the European grand tour, 275-303
  the Orient, 303-47
  North America, 347-91

Travel Writing in the Twentieth Century
TCLC 30: 407-56
  conventions and traditions, 407-27
  and fiction writing, 427-43
  comparative essays on travel writers,
    443-54

True-Crime Literature CLC 99: 333-433
  history and analysis, 334-407
  reviews of true-crime publications, 407-
    23
  writing instruction, 424-29
  author profiles, 429-33

Ulysses **and the Process of Textual
Reconstruction** TCLC 26: 386-416
  evaluations of the new *Ulysses,* 386-94
  editorial principles and procedures, 394-
    401
  theoretical issues, 401-16

Utopian Literature, Nineteenth-Century
NCLC 24: 353-473
  definitions, 354-74
  overviews, 374-88
  theory, 388-408
  communities, 409-26
  fiction, 426-53
  women and fiction, 454-71

Utopian Literature, Renaissance LC-32:
1-63
  overviews, 2-25
  classical background, 25-33
  utopia and the social contract, 33-9
  origins in mythology, 39-48
  utopia and the Renaissance country
    house, 48-52
  influence of millenarianism, 52-62

Vampire in Literature TCLC 46: 391-454
  origins and evolution, 392-412
  social and psychological perspectives,
    413-44
  vampire fiction and science fiction, 445-
    53

Victorian Autobiography NCLC 40: 277-
363
  development and major characteristics,
    278-88
  themes and techniques, 289-313
  the autobiographical tendency in Victorian
    prose and poetry, 313-47
  Victorian women's autobiographies, 347-
    62

Victorian Fantasy Literature NCLC 60:
246-384
  overviews, 247-91
  major figures, 292-366
  women in Victorian fantasy literature,
    366-83

Victorian Hellenism NCLC 68: 251-376
  overviews, 252-78
  the meanings of Hellenism, 278-335
  the literary influence, 335-75

Victorian Novel NCLC 32: 288-454
  development and major characteristics,
    290-310
  themes and techniques, 310-58
  social criticism in the Victorian novel,
359-97
  urban and rural life in the Victorian novel,
    397-406
  women in the Victorian novel, 406-25
  Mudie's Circulating Library, 425-34
  the late-Victorian novel, 434-51

Vietnam War in Literature and Film CLC
91: 383-437
  overview, 384-8
  prose, 388-412
  film and drama, 412-24
  poetry, 424-35

Vorticism TCLC 62: 330-426
  Wyndham Lewis and Vorticism, 330-8
  characteristics and principles of
    Vorticism, 338-65
  Lewis and Pound, 365-82
  Vorticist writing, 382-416
  Vorticist painting, 416-26

Well-Made Play, The NCLC 80: 331-370
  overviews, 332-45
  Scribe's style, 345-56
  the influence of the well-made play, 356-
    69

**Women's Autobiography, Nineteenth
Century** NCLC 76: 285-368
  overviews, 287-300
  autobiographies concerned with religious
    and political issues, 300-15
  autobiographies by women of color, 315-
    38
  autobiographies by women pioneers, 338-
    51
  autobiographies by women of letters, 351-
    68

Women's Diaries, Nineteenth-Century
NCLC 48: 308-54
  overview, 308-13
  diary as history, 314-25
  sociology of diaries, 325-34
  diaries as psychological scholarship, 334-
    43
  diary as autobiography, 343-8
  diary as literature, 348-53

Women Writers, Seventeenth-Century
LC 30: 2-58
  overview, 2-15
  women and education, 15-9
  women and autobiography, 19-31
  women's diaries, 31-9

Contemporary Literary Criticism
Cumulative Nationality Index

CONTEMPORARY LITERARY CRITICISM

Nationality Index

CLC-126 Title Index

Title Index

ISBN 0-7876-3201-5

90000